Women Filmmakers
& Their Films

Women Filmmakers
& Their Films

With Introductory Essays by
Gwendolyn Audrey Foster
Katrien Jacobs

Editor
Amy L. Unterburger

ST. JAMES PRESS

AN IMPRINT OF GALE

DETROIT • NEW YORK • LONDON

Amy L. Unterburger, *Editor*
David E. Salamie, *Contributing Editor*

Nicolet V. Elert
Project Coordinator

Laura Standley Berger, Joann Cerrito, Dave Collins, Miranda Ferrara,
Kristin Hart, Margaret Mazurkiewicz, Michael J. Tyrkus,
St. James Press Staff

Peter M. Gareffa, *Managing Editor, St. James Press*

Mary Beth Trimper, *Production Director*
Shanna Heilveil, *Production Assistant*

Cynthia Baldwin, *Product Design Manager*
Pamela A. E. Galbreath, *Art Director*
Pamela A. Reed, *Photography Coordinator*
Randy Bassett, *Image Database Supervisor*
Robert Duncan, Mike Logusz, *Imaging Specialists*

Women filmmakers & their films / with introductory essays by Gwendolyn
Audrey Foster, Katrien Jacobs ; editor, Amy L. Unterburger.
   p. cm.
  Includes filmographies, bibliographical references, and indexes.
  ISBN 1-55862-357-4 (alk. paper)
  1. Women motion picture producers and directors--Biography-
-Dictionaries. 2. Women in the motion picture industry-
-Dictionaries. I. Foster, Gwendolyn Audrey. II. Jacobs, Katrien.
III. Unterburger, Amy L.
PN1998.2.W66 1998
791.43'082--dc21
  [B]   98-6817
                                         CIP

Printed in the United States of America

Cover photograph: Dorothy Arzner, courtesy The Kobal Collection.

St. James Press is an imprint of Gale
10 9 8 7 6 5 4 3 2

CONTENTS

EDITOR'S NOTE   *page* vii

CHRONOLOGY OF WOMEN FILMMAKERS   ix

"THE EVOLUTION OF THE WOMAN FILMMAKER" BY GWENDOLYN AUDREY FOSTER   xv

"THE STATUS OF CONTEMPORARY WOMEN FILMMAKERS" BY KATRIEN JACOBS   xix

ADVISERS AND CONTRIBUTORS   xxvii

LIST OF ENTRANTS AND FILMS   xxxi

WOMEN FILMMAKERS & THEIR FILMS   1

NATIONALITY INDEX   469

OCCUPATION INDEX   475

AWARDS INDEX   481

FILM TITLE INDEX   493

SELECTED LIST OF DISTRIBUTORS OF FILMS BY WOMEN FILMMAKERS   561

PICTURE ACKNOWLEDGEMENTS   565

NOTES ON ADVISERS AND CONTRIBUTORS   569

EDITOR'S NOTE

This first edition of *Women Filmmakers & Their Films* comprises more than 250 entries. More than 190 of the entries are on women filmmakers, a category that encompasses not only directors but also women in many important behind-the-camera vocations, including producers, animators, art directors, editors, writers, and costume designers. Each of these entries consists of a brief biography, a complete filmography, a selected bibliography of works on and by the entrant, and an expository essay by a specialist in the field. The remaining entries are on films in which women filmmakers have had a major role; each film entry contains production information, lists of cast and crew, a selected bibliography of works about the film, and an essay by a specialist in the field. As film is primarily a visual medium, many of the entries are illustrated, either by a portrait or a still.

The selection of films and filmmakers to include is a difficult process and is based on the recommendations of the advisers listed on page xxvii. The book is intended to represent the wide range of interests within North American and European film scholarship and criticism. The entries selected were deemed to be both interesting and of lasting interest, including both popular filmmakers and films, as well as those that are critically acclaimed. The eclecticism in both the list of entries and the critical stances of the different writers emphasizes the multifarious notions of the cinema.

Thanks are due to the following: the staff of St. James Press, especially the indefatigable Nicolet Elert; David Salamie of InfoWorks Development Group, for all his assistance and research; and all the advisers and contributors for their gracious participation.

A NOTE ON THE ENTRIES

Filmmakers

Boldface rubrics in the biographical section make the various types of information (e.g., birth date, awards, agent's address) easier to locate. Non-English-language film titles are ordinarily given in the original language or a transliteration of it. Alternate release titles in the original language(s) are found in italic within parentheses, followed by release titles in English (American then British if there is a difference) and translations. The date of a film is understood to refer to its year of release in its country of origin unless stated otherwise.

In the list of films in each entry, a name in parentheses following a film title is that of the director(s). Information within the parentheses following the director's name, modifies, if necessary, then adds to the subject's principal function(s). A film title in boldface indicates that an entry on that film has also been included in this volume.

Films

In the top portion of the entries, titles are generally given in the language of the country in which the film was released, followed by alternate release titles and translation in parentheses. The country or countries where the film originated is provided along with the year it was registered and the director(s).

The section of production information includes such details as production company, film stock, format, running time, sound type, length, date and location of release, dates and location of filming, and cost. The list of crew members has rubrics for ease in identifying specific people. The cast list is followed by a separate section of awards garnered by the film.

Abbreviations

The most common abbreviations used are:

anim	animator or animation
assoc	associate
asst	assistant
d	director
des	designer
ed	editor
exec pr	executive producer
mus	music
ph	cinematographer or director of photography
pr	producer
ro	role
sc	scenarist or scriptwriter
st	story

"Co-" preceding a function indicates collaboration with one or more persons. Other abbreviations that may be used to clarify the nature of an individual film are "doc"—documentary, and "ep"—episode.

CHRONOLOGY OF WOMEN FILMMAKERS

Note: Also featured in this chronology are seminal film history events of a general nature, which are included for the sake of context.

1893

Thomas Alva Edison (1847-1931) shoots *Fred Ott's Sneeze,* which in 1894 becomes the first whole film on record at the Library of Congress. Edison's early films are shot using the Kinetograph, his motion-picture camera, and are viewed through the Kinetoscope, his peephole viewer.

1895

The Lumière brothers of France—Louis (1864-1948) and Auguste (1862-1954)—shoot their first film, *La Sortie des Usines Lumière* (*Workers Leaving the Lumière Factory*), which then becomes the first film to be projected in a theater. Their early films utilize their Cinématographe, a combination camera-projector.

The first movie theater opens in Paris on 28 December.

1896

French producer-director Alice Guy (1873-1968), the world's first woman filmmaker, exhibits her film *La Fée aux choux* (*The Cabbage Fairy*) at the International Exhibition in Paris. Some historians contend this was the first fictional film.

1906

Elvira Notari (1875-1946), Italy's first—and most prolific—female filmmaker, begins directing, co-producing, and writing films. By 1930, she will have worked on about 60 feature films and more than 100 documentaries and shorts.

1913

Olga Wohlbrück becomes the first German woman filmmaker with the release of *Ein Mädchen zu Verschenken* (*A Girl for Giving Away*), the only film she directs.

1915

American director Julia Crawford Ivers becomes the first woman general manager of a Hollywood studio, Bosworth, Inc.

American Viola Lawrence (d. 1973), considered the first female film editor, begins her career. She will later work with such noted Hollywood directors as John Ford, Howard Hawks, and Orson Welles.

Lois Weber (1882-1939), the first consistently successful American woman filmmaker, is hired by Universal Studios at the then-astounding salary of $5,000 per week. She is the highest-paid director at Universal and the highest-paid woman director of the silent era.

1916

American screenwriter Anita Loos (1888-1981) writes subtitles for D. W. Griffith's *Intolerance.* Loos is considered the first to use only "talking titles" (titles that convey dialogue) in silent films.

Canadian-born actress Mary Pickford (1893-1979) creates the Mary Pickford Film Corporation in Hollywood, becoming the first movie star to form and own a film company.

Russian filmmaker Olga Preobrazhenskaya (1881-1971), considered Russia's first female director, is co-director of *Baryshnia krestianka* (*The Lady Peasant*), her directorial debut.

American filmmaker Lois Weber (1882-1939) directs two important films: *Where Are My Children?,* a groundbreaking movie about birth control, which costs $12,000 to make and reportedly earns $500,000; and the major historical drama, *The Dumb Girl of Portici,* which introduces the Russian ballerina Anna Pavlova to the screen.

1917

The Technicolor Corporation is founded in the United States and begins experimenting with color film.

American actress Marion E. Wong is the first president of the Mandarin Film Company of Oakland, California. This organization, the first film production company to be staffed entirely by Chinese Americans, had its own studio and starred Wong and her sister in its first movie, *The Curse of Quon Qwan,* released in 1917.

1918

French director-actress-writer Musidora (1889-1957) forms her own production company, La Société des Films Musidora.

1919

American film editor Anne Bauchens (1882-1967) becomes the first film editor to be written into a director's contract, that of Cecil B. DeMille. She edits all of DeMille's films from this year forward.

Australian director-actress Lottie Lyell (1890-1925) is the screenwriter, art director, editor, and production assistant (and uncredited co-director or director) of her masterpiece, *The Sentimental Bloke,* in which she also stars. The film brings in more money than any previous Australian film and earns enormous praise.

Actress-director-producer Mary Pickford (1893-1979) co-founds United Artists with D. W. Griffith, Charlie Chaplin, and Douglas Fairbanks, Sr.

1920

American actress Lillian Gish (1896-1993) makes her only foray into directing with *Remodeling Her Husband.* In an "all-woman" production, Gish co-writes the screenplay with her sister Dorothy, who also stars, and recruits the American writer Dorothy Parker to write the intertitles.

1922

American writer Jane Murfin (1893-1955) is the first person to write a film script starring a dog. Starting in 1922, five pictures were made for First National that were written by Murfin and starred Strongheart, a German shepherd who had formerly served in a Red Cross unit in the army.

1926

Working as a production team, the McDonagh sisters—Isobel (1899-1982), Paulette (1901-78), and Phyllis (1900-78)—are the first women in Australia to produce a feature film, with their debut, *Those Who Love.*

German-born British filmmaker Lotte Reiniger (1899-1981) creates the first full-length animated film *Die Geschichte des Prinzen Achmed* (*The Adventures of Prince Achmed*), working in Germany and using silhouette figures made out of cardboard, tin, and paper.

1927

The Academy of Motion Picture Arts and Sciences is founded on 4 May.

The sound era begins when *The Jazz Singer* opens on 6 October featuring a synchronized soundtrack on its musical numbers.

British writer Bryher (1894-1983) founds *Close-Up,* the first serious film journal, in Vevey, Switzerland.

French filmmaker Germaine Dulac (1882-1942) is the first person to make a surrealist film, *La Coquille et le clergyman* (*The Seashell and the Clergyman*).

Soviet Ukrainian filmmaker Esther Shub (1894-1959), a pioneer of the Soviet compilation film, creates two of her best-known works, *Padenye dinastii romanovykh* (*The Fall of the Romanov Dynasty*) and *Veliky put'* (*The Great Road*), both compiled for the tenth anniversary of the Russian Revolution.

German writer Thea von Harbou (1888-1954) writes the screenplay for *Metropolis,* which is directed by her then-husband, Fritz Lang.

1928

The first all-talking film, *The Lights of New York,* is released.

1929

American director Dorothy Arzner (1900-79) is the first woman to direct a sound film, with *The Wild Party.* In the process, she creates the first overhead microphone by attaching a mike to a fishing pole.

1931

The first Academy Awards are presented two years later on 16 May.

American writer-director Frances Marion (1890-1973), who earned the moniker "Dean of Hollywood Screenwriters" in the 1920s and 1930s, wins an Academy Award for *The Big House* (1930). She wins again in 1932 for *The Champ.*

Austrian filmmaker Leontine Sagan (1899-1974) directs *Mädchen in Uniform,* notable for its all-woman cast, its antifascist stance, and its groundbreaking treatment of lesbian themes. Made in Germany, it is the first German film directed by a woman and the first German film whose profits are shared cooperatively. The film is later banned by German Minister for Propaganda Joseph Goebbels.

American film animator Claire Parker (1906-81) co-invents (with Russian filmmaker Alexander Alexeieff) the "pinboard" animation technique, a process analogous to using halftones in black-and-white photography. Parker and Alexeieff first use this technique in *Une Nuit sur le Mont Chauve* (*Night on Bald Mountain*), released in 1933.

1935

German documentary filmmaker Leni Riefenstahl (1902-) directs *Triumph des Willens* (*Triumph of the Will*).

1937

Walt Disney (1901-66) produces *Snow White and the Seven Dwarfs,* the first feature-length animated cartoon in color.

1938

American costume designer Edith Head (1897-1981) becomes the first woman to head a studio design department, when she attains the post of chief designer at Paramount Studio. Over the course of her long career, Head is nominated for 35 Academy Awards, and wins the award eight times, garnering her more Oscars than any other designer in history.

Olympia, Leni Riefenstahl's documentary about the 1936 Olympic Games in Berlin, makes its premiere on Adolf Hitler's birthday.

1939

The first Cannes International Film Festival is held in the resort town of Cannes, France, with opening night on 1 September.

American film editor Margaret Booth (1898-)—having edited a number of noted MGM films, including *The Barretts of Wimpole Street, Romeo and Juliet,* and *Camille*—is appointed head of editing at MGM and will supervise the editing of MGM films for the next three decades. She is awarded an honorary Academy Award in 1977 "for 62 years of exceptionally distinguished service to the motion picture industry as a film editor."

American film editor Dorothy Spencer (1909-) is nominated for an Academy Award for her work on *Stagecoach.* Over a 50-year career, she is nominated for three more Oscars—never winning—and edits numerous noted films, including *To Be or Not to Be* (1942), *My Darling Clementine* (1946), *Decision before Dawn* (1952), *Cleopatra* (1963), and *Earthquake* (1974).

1940

British animator Joy Batchelor (1914-91) co-founds Halas & Batchelor Cartoon Films in England with her husband, the Hungarian animator John Halas. Over the next five decades, this company, an innovator in the production of animated film, produces and directs hundreds of cartoons for cinema, television, and commercials as well as for promotional, scientific, and instructional films.

American Anne Bauchens (1882-1967)—the editor of every one of Cecil B. DeMille's films from *We Can't Have Everything* in 1918 to his last in 1956—becomes the first woman to receive an Academy Award for film editing for her work on *Northwest Mounted Police.*

1942

American costume designer Irene (1901-62) becomes chief designer at MGM, a position she will hold through 1950, during which time she will design costumes for dozens of films.

1945

American writer and producer Virginia Van Upp (1902-70) is made executive producer for Columbia Pictures, second-in-command to studio boss Harry Cohn.

1946

British writer-director Muriel Box (1905-91) shares an Academy Award for original screenplay with her husband Sydney for *The Seventh Veil.*

Russian-born American Maya Deren (1917-61), the first woman to succeed as an independent filmmaker, is awarded a Guggenheim Fellowship for work in creative film. Deren, whose seminal work is the 1943 film *Meshes of the Afternoon,* is the first person to receive an award from the John Simon Guggenheim Memorial Foundation.

Danish filmmaker Astrid Henning-Jensen (1914-) serves as assistant director to husband Bjarne on their breakthrough film, *Ditte Menneskebarn (Ditte: Child of Man).*

1947

Polish filmmaker Wanda Jakubowska (1907-), co-founder in 1930 of the radical Society of the Devotees of the Artistic Film (START), directs *Ostatni etap (The Last Stop),* one of the first films about the Nazi concentration camps, basing it on her own experiences.

1949

French filmmaker Jacqueline Audry (1908-77) directs *Gigi,* the first of several films she will make based on the writings of Colette.

1951

The first Berlin International Film Festival is held.

Irene Sharaff (1910-93), American costume designer, handles the costume design for *An American in Paris,* for which she is awarded an Academy Award, her first of five Oscars.

1953

First film produced in CinemaScope, *The Robe,* is released.

American director-actress Ida Lupino (1918-95) directs and co-writes *The Hitch-Hiker,* her most successful film, both critically and commercially.

Japanese director-actress Kinuyo Tanaka (1910-77) directs *Koibumi (Love Letters),* becoming the first Japanese female director.

1954

Agnès Varda (1928-)—the Belgian filmmaker known as the "grandmother of the New Wave" of French filmmaking—writes, produces, and directs what some consider the first film of the French New Wave, *La Pointe courte,* which juxtaposes twin story lines, one fictional, one real.

1959

French director-writer Marguerite Duras (1914-96) writes the screenplay for the acclaimed *Hiroshima mon amour.*

1961

Belgian filmmaker Agnès Varda (1928-) writes and directs *Cléo de cinq à sept (Cleo from 5 to 7),* noteworthy for its groundbreaking use of physical time, with events happening at the same tempo as they would in real life.

1962

Vera Chytilová (1929-), perhaps the most important woman director of the Czech cinema, makes her directorial debut with *Strop (The Ceiling),* for which she also wrote the screenplay.

American filmmaker Shirley Clarke (1925-97) co-founds, with Jonas Mekas, the New York Film-makers Cooperative, a nonprofit distribution company for independent films.

French film editor Agnès Guillemot (1931-), who edited all of Jean-Luc Godard's films from 1961 to 1969, edits Godard's *Vivre sa vie (My Life to Live).*

1963

Shirley Clarke (1919-97), an American filmmaker, directs *The Cool World,* the first commercial film to be shot on location in Harlem.

American writer Ruth Prawer Jhabvala (1927-) is the screenwriter for *The Householder,* the first of her numerous collaborations with Merchant Ivory Productions.

1967

In recognition of her skill and creativity in editing *Bonnie and Clyde,* American film editor Dede Allen (1925-) is the first person in her field to receive a solo credit among the screen titles. For the same film, Theadora Van Runkle (c. 1940-) made her debut as a costume designer, garnering an Academy Award nomination in the process.

American filmmaker Carolee Schneemann (1939-) directs *Fuses,* generally considered her best film and a key film of the 1960s avant-garde film movement.

1971

Actress Barbara Loden (1934-80) becomes the first American feminist film director with her direction of *Wanda,* winner of the International Critics Prize, Venice.

1972

The First International Festival of Women's Film is held in New York City.

French filmmaker Sarah Maldoror (1929-), of Guadeloupian descent, directs *Sambizanga,* a film about a female revolutionary in Angola and a prizewinner at several international film festivals.

1973

Pamela Douglas becomes the first black woman producer at a major motion-picture studio, namely Universal Pictures.

British/American cinematographer-director Brianne Murphy (1937-) becomes the first woman member of the American Society of Cinematographers.

1974

Julia Miller Phillips (1944-) is the first woman to win an Academy Award as a producer, for *The Sting,* which wins the Oscar for best picture.

1975

Belgian filmmaker Chantal Akerman (1950-), who was the first to work with an all-female staff of technicians, directs the acclaimed *Jeanne Dielman, 23 Quai du Commerce, 1080 Bruxelles.*

American director Dorothy Arzner (1900-79) is honored for her career by the Directors Guild of America, becoming the first woman member of the Directors Guild.

Award-winning Mexican director-writer Marcela Fernández Violante (1941-) becomes the first woman to join the Mexican film director's union.

American Verna Fields (1918-82) is the editor on the blockbuster *Jaws,* for which she is awarded an Academy Award. The following year, Universal Pictures promotes her to vice president of feature productions, a post she holds for the remainder of her life.

1976
American documentary filmmaker Barbara Kopple (1946-) directs and produces *Harlan County, U.S.A.,* the first feature-length documentary about a labor dispute. Among several other honors, the film is awarded the Academy Award for Best Feature Documentary.

Italian director Lina Wertmüller (1928-) is nominated for an Academy Award for *Pasqualino settebellezze* (*Seven Beauties*), becoming the first woman ever nominated in the category of best director.

1979
The first International Women's Film Festival is held in Sceaux, France, with a total audience of 3,000 moviegoers. In later years, this showcase for women filmmakers the world over is held in Créteil, France, and by the 1990s attendance surpasses 35,000.

Australian filmmaker Gillian Armstrong (1950-) directs her first feature film, the acclaimed *My Brilliant Career.* The film is reportedly the first commercial feature film directed by an Australian woman in 46 years.

1980
American film editor Thelma Schoonmaker (1940-) edits Martin Scorsese's *Raging Bull,* for which she receives an Academy Award. She will edit all of Scorsese's films from this date forward.

1982
Spanish director Pilar Miró (1940-97), an award-winning and commercially successful filmmaker, is appointed Culture Ministry director general of cinematography for the Spanish government, a post she will hold until 1985. While in office, the "Miró Law" is passed, which provides generous subsidies to Spanish filmmakers, including such notables as Pedro Almodóvar and Fernando Trueba.

Filmmaker Susan Seidelman (1952-) is the first American to direct an independent film (*Smithereens*) shown in competition at the Cannes International Film Festival in France. Three years later, she directs the surprise box-office hit *Desperately Seeking Susan.*

1983
Euzhan Palcy (1957-), French West Indian director-writer-producer, writes and directs the internationally acclaimed *La Rue cases nègres* (*Sugar Cane Alley*), her feature-film debut.

Barbra Streisand (1942-) is the first woman to produce, direct, co-write, star in, and sing in a major motion picture, performing multiple roles in her film, *Yentl.*

1985
The first Sundance Film Festival is held in Sundance, Utah, bringing attention to the world of independent filmmakers.

Polish filmmaker Agnieszka Holland (1948-) gains major international acclaim with her direction of *Bittere ernte* (*Angry Harvest*), which is nominated for Best Foreign-Language Film.

1986
American filmmaker Donna Deitch (1945-) directs *Desert Hearts,* the first lesbian love story to obtain mainstream distribution.

1987
American movie executive Dawn Steel (1946-97) is named president of Columbia Pictures, a post she holds until 1991.

1988
Christine Choy (1952-) co-directs the Academy Award-nominated *Who Killed Vincent Chin?* Choy, an American filmmaker born in China to a Korean father and a Chinese mother, is the first Asian-American woman to achieve a successful career in documentary filmmaking.

American filmmaker Penny Marshall (1942-) directs the box-office smash *Big.*

Mira Nair (1957-), Indian filmmaker, directs her breakthrough film, *Salaam Bombay!,* about street children of Bombay. The film is nominated for an Academy Award for Best Foreign-Language Film, is awarded several prizes at international film festivals, and enjoys considerable box-office success in India and the West.

1989
Russian/Ukrainian director Kira Muratova (1934-), whose pre-glasnost films were consistently banned, creates her most highly regarded film, *Astenicheskii Sindrom* (*The Asthenic Syndrome*). Despite glasnost, this film too is banned, but only for a brief time.

With the release of her *A Dry White Season,* French West Indian director-writer-producer Euzhan Palcy (1957-) is the first black woman to direct a feature-length Hollywood film.

1990
Dutch filmmaker Annette Apon (1949-) directs her best-known film, the quirky comedy *Krokodillen in Amsterdam* (*Crocodiles in Amsterdam*).

1992
Leslie Harris (1959-) writes, produces, and directs *Just Another Girl on the I.R.T.,* making her the first African-American woman to release her own feature film.

1993
New Zealand director Jane Campion's (1954-) film *The Piano* wins the Palme d'Or at the Cannes International Film Festival.

Canada-based Native American documentary filmmaker Alanis Obomsawin (1932-) directs *Kanehsatake: 270 Years of Resistance,* winner of 18 awards and international acclaim for its coverage of the 1990 standoff between Mohawks and the government in Quebec.

1995
Dutch director-writer Marleen Gorris's (1948-) *Antonia* (*Antonia's Line*) earns international renown, and garners the Best Foreign-Language Film Academy Award.

1996
Australian-based Chinese filmmaker Clara Law (1957-) directs the first Australian feature film that is not mostly in English, *Floating Life,* which wins the Silver Leopard at the Locarno International Film Festival.

1997
El perro del hortelano (*The Dog in the Manger*), directed by Spaniard Pilar Miró (1940-97) in 1995, wins seven prizes at the 1997 Goya Awards, including Best Director.

INTRODUCTION

The Evolution of the Woman Filmmaker

The history of women filmmakers is a rich and fertile body of knowledge that has been largely ignored, until recently, by mainstream film historians. Nevertheless, women were very much involved in the creation of the visual art form known as motion pictures from its beginnings until the present. In fact, women were at one time far more prominent in film production circles than they are now. In the early days of film, women such as Alice Guy, Gene Gauntier, Hanna Henning, Ida May Park, Olga Preobrazhenskaya, Nell Shipman, Ruth Stonehouse, Lucille McVey Drew, Elvira Notari, Lois Weber, Dorothy Arzner, Germaine Dulac, Marie Epstein, Grace Cunard, and many others were involved in creating the new visual format. Unfortunately, when the first surveys of film history were written, and when the first pantheons of directors and major players were drawn up, most of the accomplishments of women directors, producers, and scenarists were overlooked. Even feminists tended to believe that there simply were no women involved in the production end of early films; women were viewed as objects of a voyeuristic "male gaze," in films that were supposedly all directed and created by men.

Women were written out of history as active participants in the production and creation of film, film movements, special effects, the star system, the studio system, independent and experimental forms, and genres. It seems as if historians were primarily interested in women in front of the camera as actors and sex objects. Creative women, however, were very much participants in the history of filmmaking. For example, Alice Guy, a French women director is generally credited as having directed the first "narrative" film. Her film, *La Fée aux choux,* is in many ways a film like that of her male contemporaries; it tells the story of a fairy tale in which a woman who cannot bear children creates them in a cabbage patch. Guy was instrumental in the development of such early pioneering techniques as special effects (masking, superimposition, and other in-camera effects). She was also very much a pioneer of the very first genre vehicles, yet Alice Guy is rarely cited as the originator of these genres. The hundreds of films she directed include everything from melodramas to gangster films, horror films, fairy tales, and even short music films featuring famous opera singers—forerunners to today's music videos.

Claiming a Place in History

It is hard to underestimate the talented contributions of this pioneering woman director who worked in early primitive color techniques such as hand-painting and stamping and also created some of the first examples of sound films, recorded on wax cylinders. And Alice Guy was not by any means the only woman producer/writer/director to contribute to the development of the film form. Internationally, many other women, most of whom are barely remembered today, were also prominent in silent-film production. For example, in Australia, the McDonagh sisters (Paulette, Phyllis, and Isobel) taught themselves filmmaking from the vantage point of being actresses. Their early films were only recently "rediscovered" and written back into Australian film history. Hanna Henning, a German woman director who made many silent films awaits rediscovery as does Ida May Park, an American woman director who made scores of films in the silent-film period. The years have been a bit kinder to Lois Weber, Cleo Madison, Dorothy Davenport Reid, and Dorothy Arzner, all of whom have had their films survive and who have been rediscovered and celebrated in film festivals and archival retrospectives such as those at the Museum of Modern Art in New York and the American Museum of the Moving Picture in Astoria.

Women directors thrived in a short period in the beginning of filmmaking production, especially in the teens and early 1920s. In this period, before film directing was seen as primarily a "masculine" occupation, women directors were numerous and busy. This period is well covered by Anthony Slide in his book, *Early Women Directors.* So many women were active in film production: Julia Crawford Ivers, Nell Shipman, Ruth Stonehouse, Lottie Lyell, Musidora, Margery Wilson, and many others. Many women were employed at the Universal Studios, where Carl Laemmle was not averse to hiring women as directors. Women were also highly active in this period as screenwriters.

Many women directors of color worked outside the studio system as independent producer/directors. African-American women directors such as Eloice Gist and Zora Neale Hurston developed and introduced the independent personal film director. Gist was a preacher who wrote, produced, directed, and self-distributed her own films; she lectured with them as she went from town to town, speaking with films such as her *Hellbound Train,* which depicted the narratives of figures bound for hell because of various moral trespasses. Zora Neale Hurston, as many now know, pioneered the ethnographic film that featured the insider informant. Hurston's films were ahead of their time in that she understood the value of herself as an insider informant in the stories she told about the African-American community.

Beyond the United States, women were instrumental in pioneering schools of film. Women such as French filmmakers Germaine Dulac and Marie Epstein were groundbreakers in the experimentation with film. Dulac is now finally hailed as one of the champions of the experimental French film. She was loosely associated with the Surrealists, the Impressionists, and the poetic realists. Her films are currently championed and lionized as part of a canon of important experimental films that challenged the borders of poetic filmic expression. Epstein is also being reconfigured into the landscape of film history. Her pioneering and mastery of poetic realism, combined with her narrative techniques are finally being included in film history. Agnès Varda, the Belgian woman director who helped pioneer the New Wave is also being finally credited for her contribution to the development of the new school of filmmaking previously only attributed to directors such as François Truffaut, Jean-Luc Godard, and other male directors. In Italy, as Giuliana Bruno uncovered, the early silent filmmaker Elvira Notari was already beginning to embrace the artistic precepts behind Neorealism, a school of film that arose in Italy many years after her death.

By the 1930s there were fewer and fewer women directors. Film was beginning to be viewed as an art form and as a powerful medium in the marketplace. Many women directors left the field when it was clear that society no longer approved of women working in such a high-profile job that clearly indicated power in the public sphere. Among the exceptions were German director Leni Riefenstahl, who is universally credited with pioneering the documentary form and the technique of propaganda. Dorothy Arzner, a lesbian filmmaker, was one of the few prominent women directors in the thirties. Mary Field is credited with pioneering the British nature film at about this time. Mary Ellen Bute was one of the pioneers of the experimental film in the United States. Her use of oscillated light in the formation of lighting patterns choreographed to music were far ahead of their time.

The 1940s was a fertile time for experimental women filmmakers. In this era, Maya Deren and Marie Menken are credited with introducing many of the ideas and forms of experimental avant-garde cinema. In Britain, Joy Batchelor created animated films. In France, Jacqueline Audry directed glossy studio-produced films. In the Soviet Union, Wanda Jakubowska pioneered many of the Soviet ideals of the social document film. In Mexico, Matilde Landeta fought to direct her own productions after having served as an assistant director for many, many years. She managed to direct a few of her own projects despite the sexism of the industry.

In the 1950s Ida Lupino claimed that she did her work simply because there was no one else available, but the passion of her efforts belies such modesty. She tackled controversial subject matter and invented many of the techniques and themes associated with film noir. In the 1960s many women directed personal experimental films. Mai Zetterling, for example, began as an actress, but soon tired of working within the confines of a male-dominated system, and created her own visions of the world. Sara Aldrege was another important innovator in experimental film. One of the greatest of the experimental directors of the sixties, Carolee Schneemann deals with issues of sexuality, power, and gender, as does Barbara Hammer, who began working as a director in the early seventies. The multiplicity of visions among women directors is startling; it forces us to look at ourselves as women, and as members of society, in a series of entirely new and enlightening ways.

In the 1970s, 1980s, and the 1990s, there has been an international rise in the number of women filmmakers, both independent and studio directors. Women have been prominent as filmmakers in both developed and developing countries. Despite the rise in the number of women filmmakers, the auteur film director continues to be thought of as male. Despite women's contributions to the development of the art form and many of its pivotal movements (from Surrealism to New Wave to documentary and the personal film), women filmmakers continue to be marginalized in dominant discourse. Women filmmakers, through their exclusion from history books, have been denied a sisterhood. Each generation of women filmmakers stands from its earlier predecessors. Remedying the paucity of scholarship on women directors is compounded by an unavailability of many of the films made by women in the early days of cinema, many of which have been lost, neglected, or destroyed. Film scholars have produced a remarkably persuasive body of film criticism that begins the belated recognition process of women film directors and their achievements.

Sowing the Seeds of the Future

Despite a clear lineage, women filmmakers have managed to be influenced by one another, even if they have been marginalized or excluded from film scholarship. Barbara Hammer and several women directors credit, for example, the work of Maya Deren, whose experimental films were profoundly personal and expressed a female camera-eye. Diana Barrie claims she was most influenced by Deren's *Meshes of the Afternoon*. Alice Guy was a mentor and influence on Lois Weber, who followed in her footsteps to produce, write, and direct her own material. Weber, in turn, had a profound effect upon the career of Dorothy Arzner, who had a successful directorial career within the confines of the studio system of Hollywood in the thirties.

Dorothy Arzner however, admitted she stifled her criticism of other filmmaker's studio projects. As the only woman director in the studio system, she felt she "ought not complain," and yet she carefully maintained that no obstacles were put in her way by men in the business. Elinor Glyn, the famous author and early filmmaker, seemingly did not recognize the clearly sexist critical lambasting she received for her adroit and sharply observed comedy, *Knowing Men*. Ida May Park, another woman among many who directed in the 1920s, refused her first job directing, thinking it an unfeminine job. Even contemporary women directors find the notion of a feminist approach to filmmaking incompatible with their need for acceptance in the industry. The recently deceased Shirley Clarke refused invitations to women's film festivals, even if she agreed that women directors should be recognized. French filmmaker Diane Kurys finds the idea of women's cinema "negative, dangerous, and reductive," at the same time claiming, "I am a feminist because I am a woman, I can't help it."

Other women directors make absolutely no excuses for their feminism. Carolee Schneemann, Yvonne Rainer, and Barbara Hammer, for example, make films that deal directly and uncompromisingly with issues of sexuality, power, and gender. Donna Deitch was primarily motivated to make *Desert Hearts* because she saw a lack of films—especially commercial films—that center around a lesbian relationship. Hammer was drawn to experimental formalist filmmaking precisely because it did not seem to be (yet) the exclusive domain of men.

Some women directors wish to make films that employ newly defined heroines or that reverse gender expectations. Sally Potter's *The Gold Diggers* is a case in point. Michelle Citron's *Daughter Rite* consists of a narrative about two sisters and their mother and ignores the trappings of heroism. Doris Dörrie's film *Men...* is an attempt to see men as comic gender reversals of the mythic Marilyn Monroe type. Social concerns are also prevalent in the films and voices of women directors. Barbara Kopple's *American Dream* covers union battles. Marguerite Duras, a French critic and writer, and Trinh T. Minh-ha, a Vietnamese deconstructionist critic and documentarian, are centrally concerned with depriviliging the screen from its power to distort social reality. Trinh T. Minh-ha questions the ability of the image itself as a historicist account of truth. Clearly then, women directors are often compelled to redefine the boundaries of cinema.

Women directors not only face lack of support as a result of their gender, but also because they have a remarkable tendency to choose "controversial" or "difficult" subject matter. Shirley Clarke had enormous difficulties funding *The Cool World*, an early 1960s experimental film (shot in 35mm) about racism and drug dependency. British feature director Muriel Box faced similar difficulties proving herself in a male-dominated industry. Jodie Foster and Penny Marshall stand as proof that some women manage to find funding and support from Hollywood executives, but both have had to use their acting as leverage in the decision-making process.

Racism in Hollywood is a problem only compounded by sexism against women of color. The new African-American "wave" of feature filmmaking is predominated by men such as Spike Lee and John Singleton. African-American women directors such as Julie Dash, Kathleen Collins, Alile Sharon Larkin, and Barbara McCullough have so far not been offered lucrative package deals by industry executives. Similarly, Asian-American women directors have had major difficulties finding funding and distribution. Christine Choy faced enormous interference and lack of support in the production of her film *Who Killed Vincent Chin?*, a film about violence and racism directed against Asian Americans. Kathleen Collins spent more than a year trying to fund her film *Women, Sisters, and Friends*.

Julie Dash continues to have to search aggressively for funding, even after the critical success of her Afrocentric *Daughters of the Dust*. Claire Denis was forced to face humiliation and scorn when attempting to finance her independent feature *Chocolat*, a film that directly attacks African colonization. Similarly, Ann Hui's *Boat People*, a critically successful film that documents the harsh realities of Vietnamese refugees, clearly deserves wider distribution. Distribution and finance remain as formidable barriers that independent filmmakers find themselves up against. An unbelievable amount of hardship seems to have been suffered by women directors, yet an unrivaled degree of perseverance seems to be a common factor in many of their experiences. Early pioneering film director Dorothy Davenport Reid faced the resentment of her male colleagues, as she struggled to create her own cinematic visions of the woman's plight in American society. Yet Reid went on to make a series of intensely personal films that argued against drug addiction, prostitution, and sexism. Yvonne Rainer recently managed to fund a film about menopause, *Privilege,* despite its supposedly taboo subject matter, because of an incredibly loyal following and a fierce determination to make the film. For all of these women, the need to make films is a fierce desire they must simply obey, no matter what the cost.

Whether working in the industry, or making films with the aid of grants and personal financial subsidies, women filmmakers have helped to shape the world of film as we know it today. Some women film practitioners see themselves as harbingers of change, instructional forces, barometers of social reintegration; other women see themselves as workers within a tradition that they attempt to subvert from within. The immense contribution made by these women is a legacy that is rich in personal insight, hard work, careful study, and often sacrifice to achieve the aims they held for their creative endeavors.

Gwendolyn Audrey Foster
University of Nebraska, Lincoln

Bibliography

Bruno, Giuliana, *Streetwalking on a Ruined Map: Cultural Theory and the City Films of Elvira Notari,* Princeton, New Jersey, 1993.

Cook, Pam, and Philip Dodd, editors, *Women and Film: A Sight and Sound Reader,* Philadelphia, 1993.

Flitterman-Lewis, Sandy, *To Desire Differently: Feminism and the French Cinema,* Urbana, Illinois, 1990.

Foster, Gwendolyn Audrey, *Women Film Directors: An International Bio-Critical Dictionary,* Westport, Connecticut, 1995.

Foster, Gwendolyn Audrey, *Women Filmmakers of the African and Asian Diaspora,* Carbondale, Illinois, 1997.

Guy, Alice, *Autobiographie d'une pionnière du cinéma 1873-1968,* Paris, 1976; published as *The Memoirs of Alice Guy-Blaché,* translated by Roberta and Simone Blaché, edited by Anthony Slide, Metuchen, New Jersey, 1986.

Heck-Rabi, Louise, *Women Filmmakers: A Critical Reception,* Metuchen, New Jersey, 1984.

Kuhn, Annette, and Susannah Radstone, editors, *Women in Film: An International Guide,* London, 1990.

Mayne, Judith, *The Woman at the Keyhole: Feminism and Women's Cinema,* Bloomington, Indiana, 1990.

Quart, Barbara Koenig, *Women Directors: The Emergence of a New Cinema,* New York, 1988.

Slide, Anthony, *Early Women Directors,* South Brunswick, New Jersey, 1977; rev. ed. as *The Silent Feminists: America's First Women Directors,* Lanham, Maryland, 1996.

INTRODUCTION

The Status of Contemporary Women Filmmakers

Apocalypse 2000: Women Filmmakers and Budgets

As we are slowly starting to unfold the contributions of women filmmakers throughout the 20th century, it is perhaps time to ask ourselves how much their "status" and collective spirit will resonate beyond the year 2000? After talking to filmmakers, distributors, and researchers internationally, I noticed that there is a pervasive feeling that women's film cultures in the next century will be totally transformed, and that they will be most likely sustained by economic rationalist ideologies rather than state-funded attempts to promote feminism. When I interviewed German filmmaker Monika Treut about the transformation of women's film cultures in the next century, her answer was blunt: "The 1970s until the mid-1980s was a time in Germany when women's films had a [small] audience and received funding. Those times are over. Now 'women's films' is a 'dirty' word in Germany."[1] Treut further explained that she regrets the current "trend towards the destruction of cinema culture," in particular the fact that movie theaters all over the world have stopped showing the format of 16mm film and that most small art houses are caught up in a struggle for survival. Treut's major feature films portraying women's sexual encounters, *Seduction: The Cruel Woman* (1985) and *The Virgin Machine* (1988), were still funded by regional German grants and television corporations, but she has recently become more alerted to the fact that the "post-cinema" era is pushing her work underground. Treut feels that she will survive the new era and she professes that a new vital movement of underground cinema will rise out of the ashes of the nationally funded independent cinema of the 1960s and 1970s. New movements in women's filmmaking, as this essay argues, will include a proliferation of portraits of the female body, indigenous and cross-cultural filmmakers, collaborations between feminist film theory and practice, and the circulation of women's films within and through new technologies.

Following the film industry's global trend toward privatization, corporate ideologies, and populist aesthetics, women filmmakers today mostly have to strive towards the production of "big-budget films" suitable for international audiences and the demands of the free market. In order to estimate the "status" they receive once engaged in this endeavor, however, we should consider not only their (often painful and frustrating) advances in the film industry, but also their participation in a larger phenomenon called "film culture." Film culture includes the industry's production, distribution, and exhibition mechanisms as well as the more diffuse and contradictory critical, educational, promotional, and activist discourses and commentaries that surround films. Film culture includes practitioners and thinkers who criticize the increasing corporatization of the arts, and women filmmakers have been at the forefront of this enterprise. Whereas national film boards in countries such as Canada, Australia, and the United States have become more market driven and have severely cut down on the funding of independent filmmakers and feminist film organizations, women's activism, academic research, and alternative practices are still a solid foundation for a vibrant film culture in the next century.

Sasha Waters, a young American filmmaker who is about to finish a master of fine arts degree at Temple University, believes that periods of consolidation in the mainstream media often provoke the most interesting and exciting work from the margins. For instance, the growth of the cable market in the 1980s and the more recent wave of multimedia producers on the World Wide Web revived a flagging interest in the possibilities of documentary production and distribution.[2] Waters sees an obvious distinction between women filmmakers who work at the intersection of feminism and other political issues such as race (Tracey Moffatt, Coco Fusco), sexuality and gender (Julie Gustafson, Su Friedrich), and class-consciousness (Martha Rosler); and women who have established themselves within the dominant film industry, such as Barbara Kopple. Waters wishes that those women who now have an unprecedented degree of editorial control in the commercial industry, would "push the envelope a bit further."[3]

Women working in the commercial film industry can take a variety of ideological and pragmatic feminist positions, and independent filmmakers have to create new alliances with private corporations. Treut's short film *The Taboo Parlor* (1994), an erotica film documenting the adventures of a luscious pair of lipstick lesbians, was co-produced by a small Hollywood studio, Group I Films. *The Taboo Parlor* is part of a 90-minute production, *Erotique* (1994), which includes two other works by major women filmmakers, Lizzie Borden and Clara Law. *Erotique* targets an existing erotica sales market, yet also appeals to other audiences by blending aspects of Hollywood-style entertainment, art-house cinema, documentary, and avant-garde, into one. *Erotique* was released in major film festivals in Germany, Hong Kong, Brazil, and the United States. It played in Los Angeles movie theaters for six months and is now out on video. Treut testifies that it is unclear whether *Erotique* became a commercial success. What was obvious to her throughout the production process was the tension between the producers and directors. In her own words, "It was quite a nasty experience for the directors and the talent since the producers wanted to control everything."[4] As a feminist film about female sexuality and sex workers, *Erotique* shows complexities in the characters that the commercial erotica industry tends to flatten out, and thus the film reconstructs the average erotica viewer.

In the essay "*Female Misbehavior*: The Cinema of Monika Treut," Julia Knight writes that Treut's feature films were often negatively received by mainstream audiences. After the opening of *The Virgin Machine* in Berlin, Helmut Schoedel, critic for *Die Zeit,* pronounced that films such as Treut's were destroying the cinema.[5] *The Virgin Machine* disrespects the generic conventions of the feature film. It alternates a stylized art-house presentation of the protagonist's sexual awakening with humorous documentary sequences, which feature the mundane advice of sex workers such as Susie Bright and Annie Sprinkle. According to Knight, Treut's negative reception is due to the fact that most critical writing on the New German Cinema has focused on the contributions of male auteurs such as Fassbinder, Wenders, and Herzog. Although these directors use a radical film aesthetics and controversial content, Treut's films are more counter-cinematic and border on taboo because they portray female protagonists who enjoy their sexual identities without fear of punishment or the need for containment within marriage.[6]

Women's Films and the Sexual Body

Although topics of sexuality abound in the mass media, little progress has been made in the film and television industry's acceptance of women's and feminist perspectives on sexuality. Sasha Waters complains that the American television corporation HBO refuses to consider her documentary *Whipped* (1996), another complex portrait of sadomasochist sex workers, because it has to compete with the more sensationalized *Fetishes* (1996), made by Nick Broomfield.[7] Waters explains that *Whipped* is in many ways a response to a media environment that promotes images of women as Other: "My impression is that women who choose to work in the sex industry—especially educated, middle-class women who could certainly have made more traditional career choices—is extremely threatening to people because it challenges the misconception of such women as marginalized 'freaks' with whom 'normal' people have nothing in common."[8] Waters intends to casts a new light on sadomasochist "submissives" and "dominatrixes," showing the psychological and material conditions of their private and public lives. For example, *Whipped* shows in detail how mistress Carrie combines marriage and pregnancy with daily sessions and club life in her dungeon. Broomfield's documentary *Fetishes* ignores the motivated choices of independent women and sex workers and zooms in on the sensational aspects of their sadomasochistic rituals.

Another case of neglect and censorship of women's sexuality portraits is narrated by Debra Zimmerman, executive director of Women Make Movies, Inc. (WMM), based in New York City. Zimmerman explains in an interview that in 1997, members of Congress and the American Family Association started a campaign against WMM for its promotion of "offensive" and "pornographic" films. The campaign was part of a larger attempt to defund the National Endowment for the Arts (NEA), which was one of WMM's sponsors. The result of the 1997 reauthorization hearing was that the NEA did get funded again by Congress, but WMM lost their NEA grant. This development was not entirely new to Zimmerman, who entered the company 15 years ago when WMM was falling apart, having just been defunded by Congress in the Reagan era. Zimmerman then decided that WMM should survive independently of government funding, as a noncommercial, nonprofit organization. WMM now operates with a million dollar budget, primarily established through the successful rental and selling of tapes, and only a small percentage of the budget comes from state funding. Zimmerman explains that the company is economically sound, yet she does regret that there is a right-wing backlash as WMM becomes more visible through their bulky and illustrated catalogue.

One of the sexually explicit images in the WMM catalogue was under severe attack during the NEA hearings. It was a promotion picture for the short *Unbound* (1994) showing a woman touching her breasts. *Unbound* is a docudrama made by Claudia Morgado Escanilla, in which 16 women of different nationalities, ethnicities, and ideologies free themselves from societal definitions, stereotypes, and the prison of the bra. In the act of unbinding, they speak directly to the camera with humor and insight about the significance of their breasts in their lives and diverse cultures. According to Zimmerman, the picture caused a stir because it shows a woman in control of her own body, and it would have gone unnoticed if the hands on the breasts were male hands.

Zimmerman concludes that women's films on the body and sexuality have not received due support from the American government. She also explains that documentary has been a very important place of intersection for feminism and filmmaking. Since the 1960s, the feminist movement has met with women who want to create images that are different from images created by the mass media. Feminist documentaries have had a tendency to deconstruct the filmmaking apparatus in order to personalize and politicize the film text, yet women filmmakers have not always received due credit for this contribution to documentary film.[9]

Women's Films and Popular Culture

Canadian film scholar Kay Armatage explains the transformation of a national women's cinema in Canada. During the first decades after World War II, films made by Canadian women such as Laura Boulton, Jane Marsh, and Margaret Perry became part of the Canadian collective unconscious.[10] Their films were distributed for free by the National Film Board of Canada and there were outlets in every town in the country as well as through the school boards. Although Canada had the largest number of women working in film compared with any other country, they were largely concentrated in "gynocentric" areas such as independent documentary, avant-garde (what Armatage calls "the short-film ghetto"), and children's television programming.[11] Asked in an interview if women's film cultures still pervade the national unconscious today, Armatage explains that the formation of the Canadian unconscious is now mainly constituted through American pop culture, rather than any type of national feminism.

In her essay "Skirting the Issues: Popular Culture and Canadian Women's Cinema," Armatage outlines how the 1988 Free Trade Agreement between Canada and the United States destroyed a vibrant national film culture of the 1970s, which included the National Film Board's Studio D or "the women's studio," "The affirmation of Canadian national culture of the 1970s had by the late 1980s reached the zenith."[12] Armatage sees a parallel development in feminist film theory and criticism, which is now turning to commercial cinema and broadcast television as its principal objects of study. Although Armatage bemoans the overall Americanization of Canadian film cultures, she also believes that the reconstitution of national borders through the global economy has made Canadians more sensitive to cultural diversity, and to the fact that Canada consists of different ethnic cultures with competing sets of values and ideologies.

Cross-Cultural Filmmaking

It is important to recognize a new movement of indigenous filmmakers and cross-cultural women filmmakers whose work often contains a critique of the nation-state as a coherent ideological unit. Gina Marchetti, visiting senior fellow at Nanyang Technological University in Singapore, mentions the significance of Asian-American women filmmakers such as Helen Lee, Pam Tom, Shu Lea Chang, Janice Tanaka, and Rea Tahjiri, who now are at the forefront of independent filmmaking in the United States. The cross-cultural or migrant wave of filmmakers provide us with feminisms that linger between non-Western and Western cultures. Clara Law for instance, is an acclaimed filmmaker from Hong Kong who now lives and works in Melbourne, Australia. Her first Australian feature film, *Floating Life* (1996), presents a portrait of suburban life in Australia from the Asian minority's point of view. Upon arrival in a sterile Sydney suburb, the family is as much bothered by the discomfort of flimsy walls and poor public transportation, as the more mythic Australian dangers of sunburn, spiders, and wasps. Critics have noted in *Floating Life* a striking contrast in lighting and cinematography between the Hong Kong and Sydney scenes. Chris Berry writes, "In Australia, everything is bleached out in a brilliant rendering of the mix of light blue, light green, and white in a flat, endless landscape that is so striking to the new migrant.[13] Berry admires the contemplative and melancholic tone of the movie, knowing that most Australian directors are currently being pushed towards more mainstream art-house formulas such as melodrama and quirky comedy. Finally, Berry views Law's treatment of migration as a timely contribution to Australia's overly white screens which are "still populated by blond, blue-eyed surfers and beer-swilling ockers. So far, no one has been able to break that mould and find audience acceptance."[14]

A good promotion and distribution venue for upcoming cross-cultural filmmakers would be nonprofit organizations such as Women Make Movies. Debra Zimmerman believes that the disappearance and/or commercialization of state-funded mechanisms such as Studio D in Canada and Channel Four in Great Britain, has caused a crisis in the American feminist film community, yet more and more work is being produced—including works by ethnic minorities. On the one hand, fewer films are produced by established American avant-garde filmmakers such as Su Friedrich and Yvonne Rainer, who were previously funded by such state institutions as the National Endowment for the Arts, the New York State Council for the Arts, and private foundations. On the other hand, Women Make Movies receives increasingly more submissions from diverse young filmmakers who work at the edges of existing film industries.

Zimmerman describes the plight of contemporary women filmmakers as a mountain to be climbed, where plenty of energy and diversity constitutes the early stages, yet the journey is harder to sustain in the higher regions. A good indication of how difficult this journey would be, is the fact that few women directors are programming women's films in major film festivals around the world.[15] And yet, as Zimmerman explains in a postscript to our interview, as women are underrepresented in major festivals in the West, there is an exciting new development towards women's film festivals in non-Western regions such as Djakarta, Seoul, and Taipei.[16]

This note of optimism is shared by Gina Marchetti, whom I asked to comment on the status of Asian women filmmakers as compared to the situation in the west. Her reply was simple and forthcoming, "They have done much better all around." Marchetti also describes a vibrant tradition of women filmmakers in Hong Kong and mainland China, and adds that the average Western spectator might not be aware of this culture because Western distributors have undervalued those films, or focused mostly on work by men. Marchetti mentions a number of impressive Chinese films that deal with women's memories of the cultural revolution (1966-76) such as *Sacrified Youth* (1985) by Zhang Nuanxin. *Sacrified Youth* documents differences between the sexual lives of Thai and Chinese cultures in a small Chinese bordertown. The female protagonist Li Chun reexamines her rigid Han upbringing and adopts spontaneous Dai ways of living while working among minority peasants. In the essay "Is China the End of Hermeneutics," Esther Yau explains that mainland-Chinese films sought the magical power of minority cultures in the process of recovering from the trauma of the Cultural Revolution. Li Chun's entrance into the realm of the "minority other" makes possible an internal renewal.[17] Marchetti does not omit to say that China's rich heritage of women filmmakers and "women's films" within the genre of melodrama has undergone a crisis after the Tiananmen Square events of 1989. There are more government restrictions on film content, and the government has a colder attitude towards the arts as it hopes to privatize the film industry.

The Feminine as Film Text

In writing a history of women's film cultures in the late 20th century and highlighting the works of great filmmakers such as Marleen Gorris, Lizzie Borden, Sasha Waters, Kira Muratova, Clara Law, Zhang Nuanxin, Monika Treut, and many others, how can we look beyond their circulation in diverse national and international film cultures? Despite the enormous cultural and material differences between filmmakers, women's films have been able to live a full epoch of aesthetic and ideological symbiosis with academic theory and feminist activism, and thus we can see some instances of fruitful interaction between film theory and practice. Filmmakers today are apt to experiment with an "aesthethics of femininity," formulated by early French theorists such as Helene Cixous and Luce Irigaray, and later successfully applied to film analysis by theorists such as Annette Kuhn, Laura Mulvey, and Constance Penley.

In her study, *Women's Pictures: Feminism and Cinema,* Kuhn defines the "feminine film text" as one highly conscious and/or disrespective of illusionistic viewing strategies and gendered pleasures embedded in the dominant cinema.[18] Even if the feminine text as a theoretical model never materialized into a mass cultural practice, it did become in some instances a powerful counter-culture. It became a powerful tool in deconstructing the nation-state as a masculine construct in countries undergoing radical political change.

Filmmakers such as Sasha Waters and Monika Treut are indebted to feminist filmmakers of the sixties and seventies who used a wide variety of visual and performance strategies to attack systems of representation of the film and theater establishments. In this respect it is of utmost importance to mention the significance of the film and video work of Carolee Schneemann, whose carnal erotic rituals were guided by bodily "interior knowledge" as well as theoretical formulations of feminine textuality. Although Schneemann is mostly known for 1960s and 1970s performance-art pieces such as *Meat Joy, Interior Scroll,* and *Up to and Including Her Limits,* she also produced the famous experimental film *Fuses* (1967). With a camera installed in the bedroom, this film documents her sex life, yet she uses the actual film print to modify the imagery by means of scratching, coloring, double exposure, and repetitive montage sequencing. The raw bodily energy is transferred onto film, yet the tactility of the film strip is manipulated to redefine commercial porn images and the restrictive viewing strategies that they impose on the audience.

Another example of feminine text as counter-cinema would be the work of the Russian/Ukrainian filmmaker Kira Muratova. Most of Muratova's work was banned until 1987 and came to represent the Soviet Union's attempt at unshelving censored materials, or what Horton and Brashinsky call "shelf-knowledge."[19] Muratova's use of profanity and male frontal nudity in the glasnost film *The Asthenic Syndrome* (1989) were the official reasons for state censorship, yet one can also easily detect in this film a critique of state institutions, which are associated with male weakness. In *The Zero Hour: Glasnost and Soviet Cinema in Transition,* Horton and Brashinsky emphasize Muratova's steady camera which casts complex women characters in such way that it "allows us the opportunity to study a woman in conflict in much more detail than traditional (male-directed) narrative films."[20] Approaching the film from the perspective of gender, Horton and Brashinskly see it as a strong emotional tale that shows a female doctor, Natasha, on the verge of a nervous breakdown caused initially by the death of her husband. They note the contrast between the strong emotional world of Natasha, which comes to represent the spiritual turmoil of a disintegrating Soviet Union, and the sleeping universe of the male protagonist, Nikolai. The blurring of fiction and nonfiction, the choking of cause-effect relationships in the narrative development, the refusal to subscribe to a sense of closure, these devices can be seen as instances of a feminist aesthetics, as defined by Kuhn and others.

Muratova's cinematography supports the pain and confusion of the female character, as well as the open tide of glasnost: "Such a state of 'unfinalizedness' is hopeful for future Soviet films by and about women. Whether they admit it or not, Soviet filmmakers are beginning to share a feminist viewpoint."[21] Natasha's sufferings after her husband's death and her fits of anger towards public strangers, the entire feminine interior experience is carefully staged in slow and repetitive movements and dysfunctional monologue/dialogue sequences.

A typical scene that illustrates feminist cinematography would be Natasha's return to the hospital, where she walks around and taps the floor loudly and nervously. Natasha's walk imitates and critiques the female professional on the verge of a nervous breakdown. Her alienation from this particular role is also emphasized by the non-diegetic soundtrack, which alternates her tapping heels with silences and a bombastic symphony reminiscent of marching bands and national parades. A proliferation of Russian dialects in the dialogue sequences adds to the polyphonous character of the film. After the stylized black-and-white sequence surrounding the protagonist's breakdown, the film shows a color documentary sequence of a public presentation of the film and the actress in front of a disgruntled audience. The film then moves to show disturbing shots of crowded metro stations and people trampling on each other in an attempt to buy food. *The Asthenic Syndrome* takes the audience into a variety of dispersed genres and scenes, and illicits a wide range of responses in the viewer to the protagonist's and the country's state of collapse.

A more peaceful epic film that incorporates feminist aesthetics is Marleen Gorris's widely acclaimed film, *Antonia's Line* (1996), which received the Academy Award for Best Foreign-Language Film in 1996. *Antonia's Line* is a heartwarming epic tale of female heroism, featuring mother Antonia, the lesbian daughter and artist Danielle, the genius philosophy and musician granddaughter Therese, and the tomboy great-granddaughter Sarah. The film thrives on a romantic-nostalgic cinematography and a grand narrative of women's liberation which casts small-town reproduction in terms of female—rather than male—sexual practices and attitudes. Although *Antonia's Line* has a definite Dutch-Flemish flavor to it, as is apparent in the beautifully delivered voice-over and pastoral cinematography, it is a film suitable for international audiences which will have a positive effect on mainstream perceptions of the "feminist film."

Antonia's genetic makeup or reproductive "line" plays a crucial role in the narrative development of the film, yet the film also demonstrates inventive models of nonreproductive sexuality and eroticism in same sex and postmenopausal relationships. This is probably the reason why the film was still denounced by a considerable number of male critics as being too blatantly "feminist," containing "ditch-the-dudes hostility" or "too many direct attacks on men's crotches."[22] Such hostile reactions to a mainstream and feel-good feminist film show that *Antonia's Line* is still a tour de force for the Hollywood imagination. The film should be praised as a subtle artistic product which retains its feminist values and innovative cinematography, yet manages to penetrate the distribution lines of the global market and film industry.

Conclusion: Women and New Technologies

Despite changes in the global economy and the film industry, new venues are being established that enable the exchange of women's tapes. Recent efforts have been made by distributors to promote and sell videos through the Internet and home video distribution. Some of the major distributors of women's works such as Cinemien (Amsterdam), Video Out (Vancouver), Canadian Filmmakers Distribution Centre (Toronto), PopcornQ/TLA Video (Philadelphia), and Frameline (San Francisco)[23], have made catalogues available on the Internet and enable institutions and private individuals to rent and/or purchase tapes. This new virtual channel of distribution and exchange might eventually contribute to the disappearance of small art-house and collective feminist film cultures, yet it allows individual consumers and institutions to become immersed in a variety of productions, as well as discussion groups and virtual communities. Internet distribution and communication offers a valid alternative to an older established notion of film culture. The critical reception of women's films has been enriched by a refreshing new wave of communication in academic and nonacademic Internet circles.

Scholarship on women filmmakers is increasingly carried out in audiovisual formats such as video, CD-ROM, and websites.[24] Women Make Movies distributes a special collection of recent documentaries about women filmmakers such as *The Lost Garden* by Marquise Lepage will also be distributed as part of a 13-part television series and university program, "Women in Power," including documentaries about internationally renowned women such as Virginia Woolf, Ruth Berlau, and Marilyn Waring.[26] In 1988 Canadian filmmakers Janis Cole and Holly Dale produced the feature-length documentary *Calling the Shots,* featuring major contemporary women filmmakers such as Mira Nair, Lizzie Borden, and Julie Dash, and calling special attention to women's position towards documentary and the feature film.

Audiovisual types of scholarship allow the integration of film sequences into the film text. Avant-garde filmmakers such as Joyce Wieland tend to work in a variety of artistic mediums, hence film can be used to document and enhance the process of assemblage and integration. Audiovisual research also allows the co-existence of several film directors (the documentary maker and the subject) in one work of art, presenting the collaborative effort to larger media-literate audiences and helping the understanding of the unique sensibility and of the film texts.

Even if the theory and practice of women's cinema will be transformed in the next century, women's entry into the rapidly changing world of technology, and their critical position toward technology as a "masculine" ethos, will cause a new wave of remarkable mainstream and underground productions.

Dr. Katrien Jacobs
Edith Cowan University

Special thanks to those who participated in the e-mail and phone interviewing sessions: Kay Armatage, Monika Treut, Holly Dale and Janis Cole, Gina Marchetti, Debra Zimmerman, Sasha Waters, and John Fuegi. For their support and contributions, I would also like to thank Laura McGough, Gillian Hatt, Ned Rossiter, Jo Law, Kate Kirtz, Nina Danko and Grisha Dogopolov, Laura Hudson, Jeff Crawford, and Maija Martin.

Notes

1. From an e-mail interview with the author, 5 February 1998.
2. From an e-mail interview with the author, 9 February 1998.
3. From an e-mail interview with the author, 9 February 1998.
4. From an e-mail interview with the author, 8 February 1998.
5. Knight, Julia, "*Female Misbehavior*: The Cinema of Monika Treut," in *Women and Film: A Sight and Sound Reader,* edited by Pam Cook and Philip Dodd, Philadelphia, 1993, p. 180.
6. Ibid., p. 185.
7. *Fetishes* was directed by Nick Broomfield for HBO. Sasha Waters and Iana Porter co-directed and co-produced *Whipped*; the film was edited by Nancy Roach.
8. From an e-mail interview with the author, 9 February 1998.
9. From a phone interview with the author, 13 February 1998. For information on *Unbound,* see *Women Make Movies, 1998 Film and Video Catalogue,* p. 22.
10. Kuhn, Annette, and Susannah Radstone, editors, *The Women's Companion to International Film,* London, 1990, p. 62.
11. From an e-mail interview with the author, 5 February 1998.
12. Armatage, Kay, "Skirting the Issues: Popular Culture and Canadian Women's Cinema," unpublished manuscript, p. 3.

13. Berry, Chris, *"Floating Life,"* in *Cinemaya* (New Delhi), July/September 1996, p. 36.
14. Ibid., p. 36.
15. An exception being Kay Armatage who programs women's films at the annual Toronto Film Festival.
16. From a phone interview with the author, 11 February 1998.
17. Yau, Esther, "Is China the End of Hermeneutics. Or, Political and Cultural Usage of Non-Han Women in Mainland Chinese Films," in *Multiple Voices in Feminist Film Criticism,* edited by Diane Carson, Linda Dittmar, and Janice Welsch, Minneapolis, 1994, p. 56.
18. Kuhn, Annette, *Women's Pictures: Feminism and Cinema,* London, 1982, pp. 156-77.
19. Horton, Andrew, and Michael Brashinsky, *The Zero Hour: Glasnost and Soviet Cinema in Transition,* Princeton, New Jersey, 1992, p. 35.
20. Ibid., p. 105.
21. Ibid., pp. 106-7, 124.
22. Guthrie, Edward, "Antonia's Tangled Line," in *San Francisco Chronicle,* 14 February 1996.
23. See the following websites http://www.planetout.com/shop/pqvideo (PopcornQ lesbian and gay video shop); http://www.cinemien.nl (Cinemien Homescreen); http://www.frameline.org (Frameline gay and lesbian distribution); http://www.cfmdc.org (The Canadian Filmmakers Distribution Center Database); http://www.video-in.com/distribution/videoout.html (Video Out Distribution).
24. An example of new popular CD-ROM on women filmmakers is *Reel Women: The Untold Story.* This CD-ROM contains rare video footage and photographs and is narrated by Jodie Foster. The CD-ROM consists of "Reel Stories, Profiles" (filmographies and biographies), "Perspectives" (interviews), and "Quick Takes" (a trivia game to test your knowledge about women filmmakers). For information see http://www.ijumpstart.com.
25. The documentary *Artist on Fire* about Joyce Wieland, a pioneer of the feminist avant-garde, was made by Kay Armatage. In *Artist on Fire,* Armatage combines a complex interweaving of multiple unscripted voices which are edited and embedded in an evocative soundtrack of effects and music with an illuminating juxtaposition of "Wieland" images.
26. The "Women in Power" series is produced by John Fuegi and Jo Francis ot *Flare Productions.*

ADVISERS

Jeanine Basinger
Jane Ehrlich
Ilene S. Goldman
Gina Marchetti
Blazena Urgošíková

CONTRIBUTORS

Cynthia Baron
Charles Barr
Doreen Bartoni
Jeanine Basinger
Charles Ramírez Berg
Ronald Bowers
Stephen Brophy
Virginia M. Clark
Samantha Cook
Pamala S. Deane
Denise Delorey
Charles Derry
Maria DiBattista
Wheeler Winston Dixon
Robert Dunbar
Raymond Durgnat
Rob Edelman
Jean Edmunds
Jane Ehrlich
Gretchen Elsner-Sommer
Patricia Erens
Greg S. Faller
Mario Falsetto
Rodney Farnsworth
Cynthia Felando
Leslie Felperin
Particia Ferrara
Lilie Ferrari
Peter Flynn
Alexa L. Foreman
Frances K. Gateward
Verina Glaessner
Ilene S. Goldman
Douglas Gomery
Louise Heck-Rabi
Judy Hoffman
Chris Holmlund
Mark Johnson
Philip Kemp
Judson Knight
Susan Knobloch
Barbara Kosta

Audrey E. Kupferberg
Edith C. Lee
Richard Lippe
Ana M. López
Janet Lorenz
Jon Lupo
Roger Manvell
Donald W. McCaffrey
John McCarty
Caroline Merz
Joseph Milicia
John E. Mitchell
Ib Monty
James Morrison
John Mraz
Cynthia Ning
R. Barton Palmer
Robert Pardi
Sylvia Paskin
Julian Petley
A. Pillai
Susan Perez Prichard
Ken Provencher
Lauren Rabinovitz
Bérénice Reynaud
Allen Grant Richards
Arthur G. Robson
David E. Salamie
Lillian Schiff
P. Adams Sitney
Josef Skvorecký
Anthony Slide
Cecile Starr
Frank Thompson
Doug Tomlinson
Blazena Urgošíková
Fiona Valentine
Ravi Vasudevan
M. B. White
Jessica Wolff
Joanne L. Yeck
Emily Zants
Carole Zucker

Women Filmmakers & Their Films

LIST OF ENTRANTS AND FILMS

Gilda de Abreu
Marianne Ahrne
Chantal Akerman
Zoë Akins
Dede Allen
Jay Presson Allen
Suzana Amaral
Allison Anders
Maya Angelou
Annette Apon
Gillian Armstrong
Dorothy Arzner
Jacqueline Audry

Beth B
The Ballad of Little Jo
Rakhshan Bani-Etemad
Joy Batchelor
Anne Bauchens
María Luisa Bemberg
Big
Kathryn Bigelow
Antonia Bird
Die Bleierne Zeit
Bonnie and Clyde
Margaret Booth
Lizzie Borden
Born in Flames
Betty E. Box
Muriel Box
Leigh Brackett
Anja Breien
Jutta Brückner
Mary Ellen Bute

Camila
Jane Campion
Corinne Cantrill
Ana Carolina
Liliana Cavani
Suso Cecchi d'Amico
Ayoka Chenzira
Abigail Child
Chocolat
Joyce Chopra
Christine Choy
Christopher Strong
Vera Chytilová
Michelle Citron
Shirley Clarke
Cléo de cinq à sept
Lenore J. Coffee
Janis Cole and Holly Dale
Colette
Betty Comden
Martha Coolidge

La Coquille et le clergyman
Jill Craigie

Dance, Girl, Dance
Julie Dash
Zeinabu irene Davis
De cierta manera
The Decline of Western Civilization
Storm De Hirsch
Donna Deitch
Claire Denis
Maya Deren
Desperately Seeking Susan
Deutschland, bleiche Mutter
Diabolo menthe
Carmen Dillon
Doris Dörrie
Germaine Dulac
Marguerite Duras

Judit Elek
Nora Ephron
Marie Epstein
Valie Export

Safi Faye
Marcela Fernández Violante
Verna Fields
Film d'amore e d'anarchia
Jodie Foster
Su Friedrich
Fuses

Gently down the Stream
Girlfriends
Lillian Gish
Elinor Glyn
Jill Godmilow
Sara Gómez
Frances Goodrich
Bette Gordon
Marleen Gorris
Helen Grayson
Maggie Greenwald
Agnès Guillemot
Alice Guy

Barbara Hammer
Marion Hänsel
Harlan County, U.S.A.
Leslie Harris
Joan Harrison
Edith Head
Amy Heckerling
Birgit Hein
Astrid Henning-Jensen

Hester Street
The Hitch-Hiker
Agnieszka Holland
Faith Elliott Hubley
Ann Hui
Danièle Huillet
Hungerjahre

India Song
Irene

Wanda Jakubowska
Jaws
Dorothy Jeakins
*Jeanne Dielman, 23 Quai du Commerce,
   1080 Bruxelles*
Ruth Prawer Jhabvala

Nelly Kaplan
Beeban Kidron
Barbara Kopple
Krokodillen en Amsterdam
Ester Krumbachová
Diane Kurys

Matilde Soto Landeta
Alile Sharon Larkin
Clara Law
Caroline Leaf
Isobel Lennart
Sonya Levien
Carol Littleton
Jennie Livingston
Anita Loos
Ida Lupino
Lottie Lyell

Alison Maclean
Jeanie Macpherson
Madame X—eine absolute Herrscherin
Mädchen in Uniform
Cleo Madison
Sarah Maldoror
Marilú Mallet
Manner...
Frances Marion
Penny Marshall
La Maternelle
June Mathis
Elaine May
McDonagh sisters (Isobel, Phyllis,
   Paulette)
Jeanine Meerapfel
Deepa Mehta
Marie Menken
Bess Meredyth
Meshes of the Afternoon
Márta Mészáros
Pilar Miró
Kira Muratova

Jane Murfin
Brianne Murphy
Musidora
My Brilliant Career

Mira Nair
Napló gyermekeimnek
Near Dark
Gunvor Nelson
Elvira Notari
María Novaro
Une Nuit sur le Mont Chauve
Nüren de Gushi

Alanis Obomsawin
Olympia
Yoko Ono
Ulrike Ottinger

Euzhan Palcy
Paris Is Burning
Claire Parker
Pratibha Parmar
Christine Pascal
Peng Xiaolian
Eleanor Perry
The Piano
Mary Pickford
Anne-Claire Poirier
Léa Pool
Sally Potter
Olga Preobrazhenskaya

Qingchunji

Raging Bull
Yvonne Rainer
Rambling Rose
Lotte Reiniger
Alma Reville
Leni Riefenstahl
Helen Rose
La Rue cases-nègres
Shirley Russell

Leontine Sagan
Salaam Bombay!
Sambizanga
Helke Sander
Helma Sanders-Brahms
Valeria Sarmiento
Nancy Savoca
Greta Schiller
Carolee Schneemann
Thelma Schoonmaker
Susan Seidelman
Coline Serreau
Irene Sharaff
Larissa Shepitko
Nell Shipman

Esther Shub
Joan Micklin Silver
Vera Šimková-Plívová
Sleepless in Seattle
Yulia Solntseva
Dorothy Spencer
Penelope Spheeris
Barbra Streisand
Surname Viet, Given Name Nam

Kinuyo Tanaka
The Thin Line
T'ou-Pen Nu-Hai
Wendy Toye
Monika Treut
Trinh T. Minh-Ha
Nadine Trintignant
Triumph des Willens
Trois hommes et un couffin
Two Small Bodies

Liv Ullmann

Helen van Dongen
Theadora Van Runkle

Virginia Van Upp
Agnès Varda
Die Verlorene Ehre der Katharina Blum
La Vie du Christ
Vital Signs
Vivre sa vie
Patrizia von Brandenstein
Thea von Harbou
Margarethe von Trotta

Wanda
Lois Weber
Claudia Weill
Lina Wertmüller
Mae West
Where Are My Children?
Who Killed Vincent Chin?
Joyce Wieland
Working Girls

Tizuka Yamasaki

Mai Zetterling
Zhang Nuanxin

ABREU, Gilda de

Brazilian director, writer, actress

Born: 1905. **Family:** Married Vicente Celestino. **Career:** With her husband, staged light operas with their own production company; she also performed as a singer and actress in theater, radio, and the cinema; 1946—directed her first film, *The Drunkard,* which became a box-office success; 1951—formed film production company, Pro-Arte. **Died:** June 1979.

Films as Director

1946 *O Ébrio (The Drunkard)*
1949 *Pinguinho de Gente (Tiny Tot)* (+ sc)
1951 *Coração Materno (A Mother's Heart)* (+ ro, sc, pr)
1977 *Cançao de Amor (Song of Love)* (short)

Films as Writer

1955 *Chico Viola Não Morreu (Chico Viola Didn't Die)* (Vinoly Barreto)
1974 *Mestiça, a Escrava Indomavel* (Perroy)

Publication by Abreu

Book

Bonequinha de sêda, Rio de Janeiro, 1967(?).

Publications on Abreu

Books

Pick, Zuzana M., editor, *Latin American Film Makers and the Third Cinema,* Ottawa, 1978.
Foster, Gwendolyn Audrey, *Women Film Directors: An International Bio-Critical Dictionary,* Westport, Connecticut, 1995.

Articles

Paranagua, P. A., "Pioneers: Women Film-makers in Latin American," in *Framework* (Norwich, England), no. 37, 1989.
Torrents, Nissa, in *The Women's Companion to International Film,* edited by Annette Kuhn and Susannah Radstone, London, 1990.
Munerato, Elice, and María Helena Darcy de Oliveira, "When Women Film," in *Brazilian Cinema,* edited by Randal Johnson and Robert Stam, New York, expanded ed., 1995.

* * *

A standard introduction to Brazilian cinema cannot begin without mentioning the important role that women have played in the industry, not only as actresses, but as writers, directors, and producers. Gilda de Abreu's contributions include producing, writing, directing, screenwriting, acting, songwriting, and singing.

A multitalented performer, Abreu acted and sang in radio, theater, and film. She wrote novels, plays, and songs in addition to adapting other authors' novels and plays for the stage and screen. With her husband Vicente Celestino, Abreu staged light operas in Rio de Janeiro through the couple's production company.

Abreu's directorial film debut, *O Ébrio* seemed to position her for instant stardom within the industry. An adaptation of a play by Celestino, *O Ébrio,* a musical melodrama and biopic, was wildly popular in Brazil and a record five hundred prints were struck in order to meet theatrical exhibition demand for the film.

The 1940s, however, were a difficult time to be a woman producing and directing films in Brazil. The famed Brazilian "machismo" made it difficult for Abreu to gain the respect of her crew, largely male, who had a hard time taking orders from a woman. Abreu wore pants on the set of *O Ébrio,* reportedly to minimize her female appearance in an effort to gain her crew's confidence. Despite the success of *O Ébrio,* Abreu was hindered by this gender divide and found it nearly impossible to round up a crew and financing for her second feature. This film, *Pinguinho de Gente,* was not nearly as well-received as her first. Consequently, Abreu's problems as a woman in the film industry continued.

Abreu took matters into her own hands by producing herself a third feature, *A Mother's Heart.* In addition to producing, writing, and directing the film, Abreu acted in it, proving once again her versatility.

A combination of factors, including *machista* attitudes and Brazil's economic situation, caused Abreu to quit filmmaking after *A Mother's Heart.* She was persuaded in 1955 to write the script for *Chico Viola Didn't Die* and later, in 1973, Lenita Perroy talked her into adapting one of her own stage plays for the screen.

The incredible box-office success of *O Ébrio* and the relative success of her third feature and her screenwriting efforts leave the aficionado of Brazilian cinema wondering how much more she might have contributed to the evolution of a national art form had she not been thwarted because of her sex. As late as 1979, just before her death, Abreu continued writing novels and plays, proving that her diverse talents remained vital even though she was out of the public eye.

—Ilene S. Goldman

AHRNE, Marianne

Swedish director

Born: Lund, Sweden, 1940. **Education:** Attended University of Lund, foreign languages, B.A. 1966; entered the Stockholm Film

School, 1967. **Career:** Late 1960s—actress at the Student Theater at the University of Lund, in France at Théâtre des Carmes
(Avignon), and in Denmark at the experimental theater Odinteatret;
early 1970s—launched directing career making documentaries for
Swedish and Italian TV, producing a number of them in France;
1976—directed first full-length feature film, *Near and Far Away*;
1991—directed TV series *Rosenholm,* parts 1-17. **Awards:** Swedish Gold Bug for Best Director, Swedish Film Institute, for *Near
and Far Away,* 1976.

Films as Director

1970   *Balladen om Therese (The Ballad of Therese); Illusionernas
        Natt (Palace of Illusions); Ferai*
1971   *Få mig att skratta (Make Me Laugh); Abortproblem i
        Frankrike (Abortion Problems in France)* (doc);
        Skilsmässoproblem i italien (Divorce Problems in Italy)
        (doc)
1972   *Den sista riddarvampyren (The Last Knight Vampire)*
        (short); *Storstadsvampyrer (Big-City Vampires)*;
        *Camargue, det forlorade landet (Camargue—The Lost
        Country)*
1973   *Fem dagar i Falköping (Five Days in Falköping)* (+ co-sc,
        ed) (released in 1975 as half of *Två kvinnor [Two Women]*,
        a double feature packaged as one film)
1974   *Drakar, drümmar och en flicka från verkligheten (Drag-
        ons, Dreams—and a Girl from Reality); Promenad i de
        gamlas land (Promenade in the Land of the Aged)* (doc
        for TV)
1976   *Långt borta och nära (Near and Far Away)* (+ co-sc, ed)
1978   *Frihetens murar (Roots of Grief, The Walls of Freedom)* (+
        co-sc, ed)
1981   *Svenska färger* (for TV)
1986   *På liv och död (A Matter of Life and Death)* (+ co-sc, ed)
1989   *Maskrosbarn (Dandelion Child)* (for TV) (+ sc)
1995   *Gott om pojkar—ont om män? (Plenty of Boys, Shortage of
        Men?)* (+ ro, sc, ed)
1997   *Flickor, kvinnor och en och annan drake (Girls, Women—
        and Once in a While a Dragon)*

Other Films

1968   *Fanny Hill (The Swedish Fanny Hill)* (Ahlberg) (ro)
1990   *Jag skall bli Sveriges Rembrandt eller dö!* (Grunér) (ro as
        Madame Dupuis)

Publications by Ahrne

Books

Äppelblom och ruiner (novel), Stockholm, 1980.
With Barbara Vodakova, *Den tredje lyckan: efter ett orginalmanus för
    TV,* Stockholm, 1983.
Katarina Horowitz drömmar (fiction), Stockholm, 1990.
Äventyr, vingslag (travel book), Stockholm, 1992.
Och tänk den fagra prinsessan [And imagine the fair princess]
    (novel), Stockholm, 1994.
With others, *Hur jag blev författare* [How I became a writer],
    Stockholm, 1996.

Articles

"Varför falla i farstun?," in *Chaplin* (Stockholm), no. 120, 1973.
"Åska över slätterna," in *Chaplin* (Stockholm), no. 133, 1974.
"Jorden är människans hem," interview with N.-H. Geber, in *Chaplin*
    (Stockholm), no. 5, 1974.
"Nadaskottet," in *Chaplin* (Stockholm), no. 148, 1977.
Interview with E. Eszeki, in *Filmkultura* (Budapest), March/April
    1982.

Publications on Ahrne

Books

McIlroy, Brian, *World Cinema 2: Sweden,* London, 1986.
Kuhn, Annette, and Susannah Radstone, editors, *The Women's Com-
    panion to International Film,* London, 1990.
Foster, Gwendolyn Audrey, *Women Film Directors: An International
    Bio-Critical Dictionary,* Westport, Connecticut, 1995.

*   *   *

Swedish filmmaker Marianne Ahrne—who is also an accomplished
novelist and journalist—began her film career as an actress at the
Student Theater at the University of Lund, following that with stints
at the Théâtre des Carmes in Avignon, France, and the experimental
theater Odinteatret in Denmark. She entered the Stockholm Film
School in 1967 to study acting, but by 1970 she had begun directing,
initially making documentaries for Swedish and Italian television.
Although Ahrne dislikes being considered a "woman filmmaker"
with its limiting connotations, her films have often focused on
"women's" or feminist issues, as evidenced by her early documentaries *Abortion Problems in France* and *Divorce Problems in Italy,* as
well as by 1974's *Promenade in the Land of the Aged,* her collaboration with Simon de Beauvoir, and a film considered one of her most
important. The latter was one of many early documentaries that she
made in France.

Several of Ahrne's initial forays into fictional film were fantasies:
The Last Knight Vampire and *Big-City Vampires* from 1972 and
Dragons, Dreams—and a Girl from Reality from 1974 (she would
return to this genre in 1997 with *Girls, Women—and Once in a
While a Dragon*). In 1973 Ahrne directed *Five Days in Falköping,*
which depicts a 29-year-old film actress's five-day-long return to the
town where she grew up. This 45-minute-long film was released—
at least in the United States—in an odd 1975 double-feature package
as the second part of *Two Women* (the first part being Stig Bjorkman's
The White Wall).

Ahrne made her first full-length feature film in 1976, *Near and
Far Away,* for which she won a Gold Bug award for best director
from the Swedish Film Institute. In it, a female student (Mania,
played by Finland's Lilga Kovanko) helping at a mental institution
befriends a mute young man on her ward, eventually encouraging
him to speak (he is played by Britain's Robert Farrant). In addition to
depicting the developing relationship between these two misfits, the
film also functions as a very effective attack on psychiatrists—his
muteness is not a result of illness but rather a matter of choice.
Reviewed rather harshly in the United States, *Near and Far Away*
was received much more warmly in Europe.

In Ahrne's next feature, 1978's *Roots of Grief,* she tells the story
of a young Argentinean immigrant (Sergio, played by Italian Renzo
Casali, who also co-wrote the screenplay with Ahrne), who—hav-

ing fled from political oppression—finds his new home of Stockholm to be rather cold in more ways than one. Sergio does befriend his elderly translator-landlady, a younger switchboard operator cum jazz singer, and the singer's nine-year-old daughter, but each of the female characters becomes jealous of the attention Sergio pays to the others, and eventually he decides to leave Sweden for warmer climes closer to his Argentinean roots. Although critical of the film's clichés, a *Variety* reviewer said, "[Ahrne's] people and her action comes alive in both a humorous and truly affecting way by the leading actresses and by rotund Renzo Casali."

Ahrne has increasingly spent time writing novels and other books in the 1980s and 1990s, but has continued to make motion pictures as well (in addition to her work for television). In 1986 she directed the semiautobiographical *A Matter of Life and Death,* which details a woman's long relationship with a married man. Both this film and *Roots of Grief* are particularly evocative of Ahrne's disdain for "women's films," since she treats her male characters with particular sensitivity. For *A Matter of Life and Death,* she has said that a main theme of the film is the difficulty that many men have in "speaking about their private emotions"— that, unlike relationship-centered women, men often believe that "if they had this emotional quality ... it would be considered a weakness."

Given her string of varied cinematic achievements—not to mention her ability to effectively handle both male and female characters—one can only hope that Ahrne's fascinatingly diverse oeuvre will eventually receive the attention that it deserves in the United States.

—David E. Salamie

AKERMAN, Chantal
Belgian director

Born: Brussels, 6 June 1950. **Education:** Attended INSAS film school, Brussels, 1967-68; studied at Université Internationale du Théâtre, Paris, 1968-69. **Career:** 1971—*Blow up My Town* entered in Oberhausen festival; 1972—lived in New York; 1973—returned to France; 1997—instructor at Harvard University. **Address:** c/o National Tourist Office, 61 Rue de Marche Aux Herbes, Brussels, B1000, Belgium.

Films as Director

1968 *Saute ma ville (Blow up My Town)* (short) (+ ro)
1971 *L'Enfant aimé (The Beloved Child)* (short)
1972 *Hotel Monterey* (short); *La Chambre 1; La Chambre 2*
1973 *Le 15/8* (co-d); *Hanging out—Yonkers* (unfinished)
1974 *Je, tu, il, elle* (+ sc, ro as Julie)
1975 ***Jeanne Dielman, 23 Quai du Commerce, 1080 Bruxelles*** (+ sc, ro as voice of neighbor)
1977 *News from Home* (+ sc, ro as voice)
1978 *Les Rendez-vous d'Anna* (+ sc)
1980 *Dis-moi (Tell Me)* (for TV)
1982 *Toute une nuit (All Night Long)* (+ sc)
1983 *Les Années 80 (The Eighties)* (co-sc); *Un Jour Pina m'a demandé (One Day Pina Asked Me)* (for TV)
1984 *L'Homme à la valise (The Man with the Suitcase)* (for TV); "J'ai faim, j'ai froid" ("I'm Hungry, I'm Cold") ep. of *Paris vu par...20 ans après; Family Business* (short—for TV); *New York, New York Bis* (short); *Lettre d'un cineaste (Letter from a Filmmaker)* (short—for TV)
1986 *Le Marteau (The Hammer)* (short); *La Paresse (Sloth)* (short); *Window Shopping (The Golden Eighties)*
1987 *Seven Women, Seven Sins* (co-d)
1989 *Les Trois dernières sonatas de Franz Shubert (Franz Schubert's Last Three Sonatas)* (short); *Trois strophes sur le nom de Sacher (Three Stanzas on the Name Sacher)* (short); *Histoires d'Amérique: Food, Family and Philosophy (American Stories)*
1991 *Nuit et jour (Night and Day)* (+ co-sc); *Contre l'oubli (Against Oblivion)* (co)
1993 *D'est* (+ sc); *Moving In (Le Déménagement)* (for TV)
1994 *Portrait d'une jeune fille de la fin des années 60 à Bruxelles (Portrait of a Young Girl at the End of the 1960s in Brussels)* (+ sc)
1996 *Un Divan à New York (A Couch in New York)* (+ co-sc)

Other Film

1985 *Elle à passe tant d'heures sous les sunlights* (Garrel) (ro)

Publications by Akerman

Book

Les Rendez-vous d'Anna, Paris, 1978.

Articles

Interview with C. Alemann and H. Hurst, in *Frauen und Film* (Berlin), March 1976.
Interview with Danièle Dubroux and others, in *Cahiers du Cinéma* (Paris), July 1977.
Interview with P. Carcassone and L. Cugny, in *Cinématographe* (Paris), November 1978.
Interview in *Stills* (London), December 1984/January 1985.
Interview in *Interview* (New York), February 1985.
Interview in *Cinéma* (Paris), 25 June 1986.
Interview in *Nouvel Observateur* (Paris), 28 September 1989.
Interview in *Filmihullu,* no. 4, 1991.

Publications on Akerman

Books

Acker, Ally, *Reel Women: Pioneers of the Cinema, 1896 to the Present,* New York, 1991.
Foster, Gwendolyn Audrey, *Women Film Directors: An International Bio-Critical Dictionary,* Westport, Connecticut, 1995.
Margulies, Ivone, *Nothing Happens: Chantal Akerman's Hyperrealist Everyday,* Durham, North Carolina, 1996.

Articles

Bertolina, G., "Chantal Akerman: il cinema puro," in *Filmcritica* (Rome), March 1976.

Creveling, C., "Women Working," in *Camera Obscura* (Berkeley), Fall 1976.

Mairesse, E., "A propos des films de Chantal Akerman: Un temps atmosphere," in *Cahiers du Cinéma* (Paris), October 1977.

Bergstrom, Janet, in *Camera Obscura* (Berkeley), Fall 1978.

Martin, Angela, "Chantal Akerman's Films," in *Feminist Review,* no. 3, 1979.

Seni, N., in *Frauen und Film* (Berlin), September 1979.

Perlmutter, Ruth, "Visible Narrative, Visible Woman," in *Millennium* (New York), Spring 1980.

Delavaud, G., "Les chemins de Chantal Akerman," in *Cahiers du Cinéma* (Paris), April 1981.

Philippon, A., "Fragments bruxellois/Nuit torride," in *Cahiers du Cinéma* (Paris), November 1982.

Barrowclough, S., "Chantal Akerman: Adventures in Perception," in *Monthly Film Bulletin* (London), April 1984.

Squire, C., "Toute une heure," in *Screen* (London), November/December 1984.

Dossier on Akerman, in *Versus* (Nijmegen), no. 1, 1985.

Castiel, E., in *24 Images* (Montreal), nos. 34/35, 1987.

Paskin, Sylvia, "Waiting for the Next Shot," in *Monthly Film Bulletin* (London), March 1990.

Williams, B., "Splintered Perspectives: Counterpoint and Subjectivity in the Modernist Film Narrative," in *Film Criticism* (Meadville, Pennsylvania), no. 2, 1991.

Bahg, P. von, "Keskusteluvourossa: Chantal Akerman," in *Filmihullu,* no. 4, 1991.

Roberti, B., "Tradire l'immagine," *Filmcritica* (Rome), September/October 1991.

Klerk, N. de, "Chantal Akerman," in *Skrien* (Amsterdam), June/July 1992.

McRobbie, A., "Passionate Uncertainty," in *Sight and Sound* (London), September 1992.

Chang, Chris, "Ruined," in *Film Comment* (New York), November/December 1993.

Hoberman, J., "Have Camera, Will Travel," in *Premiere* (New York), July 1994.

* * *

At the age of 15 Chantal Akerman saw Godard's *Pierrot le fou* and realized that filmmaking could be experimental and personal. She dropped in and out of film school and has since created short and feature films for viewers who appreciate the opportunity her works provide to think about sounds and images. Her films are often shot in real time, and in space that is part of the characters' identity.

During a self-administered apprenticeship in New York (1972-73) shooting short films on very low budgets, Akerman notes that she learned much from the work of innovators Michael Snow and Stan Brakhage. She was encouraged to explore organic techniques for her personal subject matter. In her deliberately paced films there are long takes, scenes shot with stationary camera, and a play of light in relation to subjects and their space. (In *Jeanne Dielman, 23 Quai du Commerce, 1080 Bruxelles,* as Jeanne rides up or down in the elevator, diagonals of light from each floor cut across her face in a regular rhythm.) Her films feature vistas down long corridors, acting with characters' backs to the camera, and scenes concluded with several seconds of darkness. In Akerman films there are hotels and journeys, little conversation. Windows are opened and sounds let in, doors opened and closed; we hear a doorbell, a radio, voices on the telephone answering machine, footsteps, city noises. Each frame is carefully composed, each gesture the precise result of Akerman's directions. A frequent collaborator is her sensitive cameraperson, Babette Mangolte, who has worked with Akerman on such works as *Jeanne Dielman, News from Home,* and *Toute une nuit.* Mangolte has also worked with avant-gardists Yvonne Rainer, Marcel Hanoun, and Michael Snow.

Plotting is minimal or nonexistent in Akerman films. Old welfare clients come and go amid the impressive architecture of a once-splendid hotel on New York's Upper West Side in *Hotel Monterey.* New York City plays its busy, noisy self for the camera as Akerman's voice on the soundtrack reads concerned letters from her mother in Belgium in *News from Home.* A young filmmaker travels to Germany to appear at a screening of her latest film, meets people who distress her, and her mother who delights her, and returns home in *Les Rendez-vous d'Anna.* Jeanne Dielman, super-efficient housewife, earns money as a prostitute to support herself and her son. Her routine breaks down by chance, and she murders one of her customers.

The films (some of which are semiautobiographical) are not dramatic in the conventional sense, nor are they glamorized or eroticized; the excitement is inside the characters. In a film which Akerman has called a love letter to her mother, Jeanne Dielman is seen facing the steady camera as members of a cooking class might see her, and she prepares a meat loaf—in real time. Later she gives herself a thorough scrubbing in the bathtub; only her head and the motion of her arms are visible. Her straightening and arranging and smoothing are seen as a child would see and remember them.

In *Toute une nuit* Akerman displays her precision and control as she stages the separate, audience-involving adventures of a huge cast of all ages that wanders out into Brussels byways on a hot, stormy night. In this film, reminiscent of Wim Wenders and his wanderers and Marguerite Duras's inventive soundtracks, choreography, and sense of place, Akerman continues to explore her medium using no conventional plot, few spoken words, many sounds, people who leave the frame to a lingering camera, and appealing images. A little girl asks a man to dance with her, and he does. The filmmaker's feeling for the child and the child's independence cannot be mistaken.

Akerman's *Moving In,* meanwhile, centers on a monologue delivered by a man who has just moved into a modern apartment. A film of "memory and loss," according to *Film Comment,* he has left behind "a melancholy space of relations, relations dominated by his former neighbors, a trio of female 'social science students.'"

—Lillian Schiff

AKINS, Zoë
American writer

Born: Humansville, Missouri, 30 October 1886. **Family:** Married Hugo Rumbold, 1932 (died 1932). **Career:** Playwright: plays produced from 1915, with much critical attention after success of *Déclassée,* 1919; 1930—first solo screenplay, *Sarah and Son;* 1930-31—contract as writer with Paramount, and with MGM, 1934-38. **Awards:** Pulitzer Prize (for drama) for *The Old Maid,* 1936. **Died:** In Los Angeles, California, 20 October 1958.

Films as Writer (often in collaboration)

1925   *Eve's Secret* (Badger); *Déclassée* (*The Social Exile*) (Vignola)
        (play)
1929   *Her Private Life* (A. Korda) (play)
1930   *Anybody's Woman* (Arzner); *The Right to Love* (Wallace);
        Sarah and Son (Arzner); *Ladies Love Brutes* (R. V. Lee)
        (st); *The Furies* (st)
1931   *Women Love Once* (Goodman); *Once a Lady* (McClintic);
        Working Girls (Arzner); *Girls about Town* (Cukor) (st)
1932   *The Greeks Had a Word for Them* (*Three Broadway Girls*)
        (L. Sherman) (play)
1933   **Christopher Strong** (Arzner); *Morning Glory* (L. Sherman)
        (play)
1934   *Outcast Lady* (Leonard)
1936   *Accused* (Freeland); *Lady of Secrets* (Gering)
1937   *Camille* (Cukor)
1938   *The Toy Wife* (Thorpe); *Zaza* (Cukor)
1939   *The Old Maid* (E. Goulding)
1947   *Desire Me* (Cukor and LeRoy)
1953   *How to Marry a Millionaire* (Negulesco) (co-play)
1958   *Stage Struck* (Lumet) (play)

Publications by Akins

Plays

Interpretations (verse), New York, 1912.
Cake upon the Waters, New York, 1919.
Papa, New York, 1919.
Déclassée, Daddy's Gone A-Hunting, and *Greatness*, New York,
    1923.
Such a Charming Young Man, New York, 1924.
The Old Maid, New York, 1935.
The Little Miracle, New York, 1936.
The Hills Grow Smaller, New York, 1937.
Forever Young, New York, 1941.
Mrs. January and Mr. Ex, New York, 1948.
The Swallow's Nest, New York, 1950.

Publications on Akins

Book

*In the Shadow of Parnassus: Zoë Akins's Essays on American Po-
    etry,* edited by Catherine N. Parke, Selinsgrove, Pennsylvania,
    1994.

Articles

Slide, Anthony, in *American Screenwriters,* edited by Robert E.
    Morsberger, Stephen O. Lesser, and Randall Clark, Detroit, 1984.
Obituary in *New York Times,* 30 October 1958.

* * *

Zoë Akins is best known as the winner of the Pulitzer Prize for
drama for *The Old Maid* and as a playwright of light comedies and
social dramas. Unfortunately she has not been recognized as a screenwriter excelling in adapting plays and novels—her own and several

from French and Hungarian sources—to film form. Her woman-
centered scripts portrayed feminine consciousness in American and
Continental settings with shocking candor and worldly wit. She
deftly chronicled her characters' conflicts with shifting social standards within the complete spectrum of comedy, from slapstick farce
to sentimental romance to urbane satire. Many of her stage plays,
among them *Déclassée, Her Private Life,* and *The Furies,* were
adapted to the screen by others. Two of her plays, relatively unsuccessful in the United States, were produced abroad: *Papa* (1919) in
Germany and *The Human Element* (1939) in Hungary. Akins's ability for dramatic adaptation was the key to her success as a screenwriter.

Her first plays, *Papa* and *The Magical City,* were produced by the
Washington Square Players in 1919. Akins's first hit play, *Déclassée,*
portrayed marital infidelity and the consequences of divorce for the
wife. It was one of Ethel Barrymore's most popular vehicles, "the
richest and most interesting play that has fallen to her in all her years
upon the stage" (*The New York Times*). The screen version was titled
Her Private Life.

Throughout Akins's twin careers, her works consistently received
mixed reviews, with the exceptions of her hit plays, *Déclassée, The
Greeks Had a Word for Them, The Old Maid* and its film version,
and the film *Camille.* George Jean Nathan attributed to her plays
"grace and humor and droll insight."

Subsequent to her Broadway productions of the 1920s—*Moon-
flower, Daddy's Gone A-Hunting, First Love, The Furies,* and *The
Love Duel*—Akins earned her first screenwriting credit, with G.
Morris and Doris Anderson, for *Anybody's Woman.* Next she captured the antics and anxieties of three young models searching for
wealthy husbands in *The Greeks Had a Word for Them.* This very
funny and popular comedy also pleased audiences of the film version, which was adapted by Sidney Howard. (The 1953 film *How to
Marry a Millionaire* was based both on the Akins play and *Loco,* by
Dale Eunson and Katharine Albert.) Akins then wrote the screenplay
for *Women Love Once,* based on her play *Daddy's Gone A-Hunting,*
which was a moderate success. Her next assignment was the adaptation of Gilbert Frankau's novel *Christopher Strong.* It starred
Katharine Hepburn as an aviatrix facing a career/marriage choice.
Critics at the time disliked it, and the film failed. *Variety* stated, "The
story is a weak vehicle for a new star ... so overloaded with play
wright device that it is just that and nothing more.... The people are
merely glamorous puppets."

When Akins's most successful play, *The Old Maid,* based on the
Edith Wharton novel chronicling the woes of an unmarried mother
and her daughter, won the Pulitzer Prize, many protests were voiced.
Enraged New York drama critics formed their own group, the Drama
Critics Circle, to give their own awards. Judith Anderson and Helen
Menken starred in the play; Bette Davis and Miriam Hopkins in the
film that Akins scripted. Critics rated the film pictorially perfect, the
acting superb, and the production nearly flawless.

Writing with Frances Marion and James Hilton, Akins scripted
the critically and commercially successful *Camille,* starring Greta
Garbo and Robert Taylor. According to *Time* the film kept "intact the
story's inherent emotional vitality." *The Toy Wife* and *Zaza* were
rated mediocre successes. Critics faulted *Desire Me,* written with
Marguerite Roberts, for a labored story line that was a variant of the
Enoch Arden tale, and for miscast actors.

Akins differed from her Pulitzer Prize-winning dramatist peers
Zona Gale and Susan Glaspell in two ways. Unlike them, she was
essentially a comedic writer; and she wrote for stage and screen
simultaneously for two decades. She was considered the best-known

woman playwright of her time, achieving the record of 16 plays on Broadway in 16 years. Her reputation rests primarily upon her prolific and lengthy career as a playwright and secondarily upon her success as a screenwriter skilled in adapting literary works to film.

—Louise Heck-Rabi

ALLEN, Dede
American editor

Born: Dorothea Carothers Allen in Cincinnati, Ohio, 1925. **Family:** Married the director Stephen Fleischman, one son and one daughter. **Career:** 1943—worked as messenger, then in sound laboratory and as assistant editor for Columbia; editor on commercial and industrial films before becoming feature-film editor; 1981—received Academy Award nomination for editing of *Reds*. **Awards:** British Academy of Film and Television Arts Award, for *Dog Day Afternoon,* 1975. **Address:** c/o United Talent, 9560 Wilshire Boulevard, Suite 500, Beverly Hills, CA 90212, U.S.A.

Films as Editor

1948   *Story of Life (Because of Eve)* (Bretherton)
1957   *Endowing Your Future* (Engel—short)
1958   *Terror from the Year 5000 (Cage of Doom)* (Gurney)
1959   *Odds against Tomorrow* (Wise)
1961   *The Hustler* (Rossen)
1964   *America, America (The Anatolian Smile)* (Kazan)
1965   *It's Always Now* (Wilmot—short)
1967   ***Bonnie and Clyde*** (A. Penn)
1968   *Rachel, Rachel* (P. Newman)
1970   *Alice's Restaurant* (A. Penn); *Little Big Man* (A. Penn)
1972   *Slaughterhouse-Five* (G. R. Hill)
1973   *Serpico* (Lumet) (co); *Visions of Eight* (A. Penn) (co)
1975   *Night Moves* (A. Penn); *Dog Day Afternoon* (Lumet)
1976   *The Missouri Breaks* (A. Penn) (co)
1977   *Slap Shot* (G. R. Hill)
1978   *The Wiz* (Lumet)
1981   *Reds* (Beatty) (co, + co-exec pr)
1984   *Harry & Son* (P. Newman); *Mike's Murder* (Bridges) (co)
1985   *The Breakfast Club* (Hughes)
1986   *Off Beat* (Dinner) (co)
1988   *The Milagro Beanfield War* (Redford) (co)
1989   *Let It Ride* (Pytka) (co)
1990   *Henry and June* (Kaufman) (co)
1991   *The Addams Family* (Sonnenfeld) (co)

Film as Production Assistant

1969   *Storia di una donna (Story of a Woman)* (Bercovici)

Publications by Allen

Articles

Show (New York), May 1970.

Wide Angle (Athens, Ohio), vol. 2, no. 1, 1977.
American Film (Washington, D.C.), November 1985.

Publications on Allen

Book

Acker, Ally, *Reel Women: Pioneers of the Cinema, 1896 to the Present,* New York, 1991.

Articles

Film Comment (New York), March/April 1977.
American Film (Washington, D.C.), December 1985.
Interview with Vincent LoBrutto in *Selected Takes,* 1991.

* * *

Between 1961 and 1981, Dede Allen reigned as American cinema's most celebrated editor. This period championed the auteur director and Allen emerged as an auteur editor, working with many of Hollywood's best auteurs (Arthur Penn, Sidney Lumet, Robert Wise, Robert Rossen, Elia Kazan, and George Roy Hill) and developing her own editorial signature.

Her first important feature film (after 16 years in the industry) was *Odds against Tomorrow.* Urged by Robert Wise to experiment, Allen developed one of her major techniques: the audio shift. Instead of stopping both a shot and its accompanying audio at the same time (the common practice), she would overlap sound from the beginning of the next shot into the end of the previous shot (or vice versa). The overall effect increased the pace of the film—something always happened, visually or aurally, in a staccato-like tempo.

When she started work on her next feature, *The Hustler,* the French Nouvelle Vague and the British "angry young men" films hit America. The realism of the British school and the radical editing of the French school made strong impressions on Allen. She credits Tony Gibbs's editing on *Look Back in Anger* (1959) as very influential. *The Hustler* employs a similar style: lengthy two-shots, unexpected shot/reverse-shot patterns, and strategically placed "jump cuts." "Jump cutting" helped launch the Nouvelle Vague, and before Allen began editing, Robert Rossen asked her to watch Jean-Luc Godard's *A bout de souffle,* one of the seminal films of the French movement. Although she felt the jump cuts were only partially successful, she incorporated the basic principle into *The Hustler* by using a straight cut instead of a dissolve or an invisible continuity edit. The combination of these two schools and the focus on character over a seamless narrative flow gives *The Hustler* its unique quality of realism and modernism.

With *Bonnie and Clyde* (the first of six films with Arthur Penn), Allen further developed the principle of the jump cut by marrying it to classical Hollywood editing and television commercial editing. Instead of using the jump cut as a modernist reflexive device or a stylistic flourish, Allen combined its spatial and temporal discontinuity with a clear narrative and strong character identification (from Hollywood) and nontraditional shot combinations and short duration shots (from television commercials). Allen's synthesis of the Nouvelle Vague, the angry young men, Hollywood, and television defined her other major editing technique, what Andrew Sarris called "shock cutting ... wild contrasts from one shot to the next, which give the film a jagged, menacing quality and create a sort of syncopated rhythm." Bonnie's sexual frustration and ennui at the start of

Bonnie and Clyde find perfect expression in a series of jump/shock cuts. The chaos of the gun fights and the immeasurably influential ending (which also shows Allen's debt to Eisenstein's montage) pushed screen violence to a new, visually stunning level.

In short, Allen must be credited with bringing modernist editing to Hollywood. Whether labeled American New Wave or Postclassical Hollywood, *The Hustler* and *Bonnie and Clyde* stand as benchmark films in the history of editing. And like *A bout de souffle*, *The Hustler* and *Bonnie and Clyde* deviated enough from the norm to be originally perceived as "badly edited," a perception fully inverted today.

Allen's "shock cutting" in *Bonnie and Clyde* produced two long-lasting effects: 1) the American public began to recognize and openly discuss editing as an art form; and 2) the standard was set for rapid editing in every subsequent action film. From Sam Peckinpah to John Woo, editorial pacing continually moved toward shorter and flashier sequences. Her influence also manifests itself in other visual media; television commercials, music videos, animation, and children's television compress many images into very short sequences. Almost every music video owes its rapid, nontraditional editing constructs to Dede Allen. In retrospect, Allen expresses concern about her contribution to increased editing tempo—"I wonder if we're raising enough people in a generation who are able to sit and look at a scene play out without getting bored if it doesn't change every two seconds. We talk an awful lot about cutting; we talk very little about not lousing something up by cutting just to make it move faster. I'm afraid that's the very thing I helped promulgate.... It may come to haunt us, because attention spans are short."

Allen continued to refine her editorial signature (audio shifts, shock cutting, and montage) through her subsequent films, especially the temporal and spatial jumps of *Slaughterhouse-Five* and *Dog Day Afternoon* (her first Academy Award nomination). In *Dog Day Afternoon*, after a slow, tension-building opening, the protagonist's discovery of the SWAT team unleashes a brief moment of chaos which Allen augments into ten, breathless seconds of screen time by overlapping audio, intercutting multiple interior and exterior locations, and employing jarring shot combinations and temporal ellipses. Since Sidney Lumet used a double camera setup on Al Pacino and Chris Sarandon during their phone conversations, Allen used various takes of each, which produced jump cuts and violated screen direction, but intensified their performances. In *Reds*, Allen combined documentary editing and her signature narrative techniques to weave a historical and biographical tapestry of refined complexity. This documentary/narrative blend won her an Academy Award.

Since *Reds*, Allen's work remains consistently professional, especially in the usually overlooked dialogue scenes, but fails to convey the innovation of the sixties and seventies. This is not her fault. In the 1980s, not only did Hollywood become more an industry and less a developer of film artists, but Allen's techniques became fully integrated into everyday film and television editing. What once appeared radical became commonplace. When asked to edit *The Addams Family*, Allen needed to balance special effects, a greater emphasis on spectacle and set design, the demands of stars, shorter viewer attention span, a more cost-conscious Hollywood, and a script based on a 1960s television show. These constraints resulted in a polished film, but one with little of her signature, except for the loony glee of the vault slide and the intercutting of Gomez's train sequence. When working on independent projects, more of her creativity emerges. The curious jumble of edgy character interaction in *The Breakfast Club* and *Let It Ride* depends on the pacing her editing provides. In *Henry and June*, she experimented with fades and partial fades to blur time and point of view.

Allen has co-edited most of her films since *Reds* with younger editors, providing invaluable training for them. Her mentoring of others has produced a new generation of top-rank editors. After nearly 40 years in Hollywood, Allen's style, technical skill, groundbreaking films, and teaching secure her status as a legend of American editing.

—Greg S. Faller

ALLEN, Jay Presson
American writer

Born: Jacqueline Presson in San Angelo, Texas, 3 March 1922. **Family:** Married the producer Lewis Maitland Allen (second marriage), 1955, one daughter: Brooke. **Career:** Author—first novel published in 1948; 1963—film version of her play *Wives and Lovers* produced by Paramount; 1964—first film script, *Marnie*; 1969—play adaptation of the novel *The Prime of Miss Jean Brodie* published; also wrote screen version; 1976-80—creator and script consultant, TV series *Family*; 1980—produced first film, *Just Tell Me What You Want*, first of several films with Sidney Lumet; 1995—appeared on camera and provided commentary in the documentary *The Celluloid Closet*. **Agent:** ICM Agency, 40 West 57th Street, New York, NY 10019, U.S.A.

Films as Writer

1964   *Marnie* (Hitchcock)
1969   *The Prime of Miss Jean Brodie* (Neame)
1972   *Cabaret* (Fosse); *Travels with My Aunt* (Cukor) (co)
1973   *The Borrowers* (Miller)
1975   *Funny Lady* (Ross) (co)
1980   *Just Tell Me What You Want* (Lumet) (+ co-pr)
1981   *Prince of the City* (Lumet) (co, + pr)
1982   *Deathtrap* (Lumet) (+ exec pr)
1986   *The Morning After* (Lumet) (co)
1990   *Lord of the Flies* (Hook); *Year of the Gun* (Frankenheimer) (co)
1995   *Copycat* (Amiel) (co)

Other Films

1980   *It's My Turn* (Weill) (pr)
1988   *Hothouse* (*The Center*) (Gyllenhaal) (pr)
1995   *The Celluloid Closet* (Epstein and Friedman—doc) (interviewee)

Publications by Allen

Books

Spring Riot (novel), New York, 1948.
Forty Carats (play), New York, 1969.
The Prime of Miss Jean Brodie (play), New York, 1969.
Just Tell Me What You Want (novel), New York, 1975.
A Little Family Business (play adapted from *Potiche* by Pierre Barillet), New York, 1983.

Jay Presson Allen

Articles

Los Angeles Times, 11 May 1975.
"Writer by Default," interview with Pat McGilligan, in *Backstory 3: Interviews with Screenwriters of the 1960s,* Berkeley, 1997.

Publications on Allen

Book

Acker, Ally, *Reel Women: Pioneers of the Cinema, 1896 to the Present,* New York, 1991.

Articles

Roddick, Nick, in *American Screenwriters,* edited by Robert E. Morsberger, Stephen O. Lesser, and Randall Clark, Detroit, 1984.

Francke, Lizzie, in *Script Girls: Women Screenwriters in Hollywood,* London, 1994.

*   *   *

Jay Presson Allen is a curiously overlooked screenwriter whose work has never received the attention it deserves. This may be in part because of a debut film which seemed inauspicious at the time, but which has grown in critical estimation: her screenplay for Alfred Hitchcock's *Marnie.* Although criticized at the time for what was regarded as facile psychoanalyzing, the screenplay is actually a finely constructed work, presenting with great subtlety, voyeurism, and yet sympathy, an emotionally disturbed woman who can hold her own with those female creations of Bergman and Antonioni of the same period, but who, perhaps typical of her American context, is able to overcome her problems. Providing Hitchcock with the screenplay for this, one of his two or three greatest films, is certainly a notable achievement, even more apparent if one is familiar with the original novel by Winston Graham and knows how well (and radically) Allen adapted the material. Her power to adapt brilliantly is present also in her screenplay for *The Prime of Miss Jean Brodie,* based on the novel by Muriel Spark, which once again presented sympathetically a three-dimensional, deeply disturbed woman.

Allen's greatest critical acclaim came for her adaptation for Bob Fosse of *Cabaret,* which not only threw out most of the sentimental trappings of the Broadway musical, but also had the courage to go back to the original Christopher Isherwood stories and to make explicit in the film itself the central homosexuality of the character generally patterned on Isherwood. By providing Fosse with a screenplay which allowed him to express his characteristic cynicism in great displays of technical razzle-dazzle, Allen made an inestimable contribution to the institution of the American musical; in its portrait of Nazism and German society, *Cabaret* claimed definitively for the musical a kind of laudable pretension and seriousness, as well as providing for Liza Minnelli one of the American cinema's great roles—yet another of Allen's portraits of neurotic women.

Allen's most underrated screenplay is the surprising *Just Tell Me What You Want,* directed by Sidney Lumet, which offered an excellent Hollywood story and provided Ali McGraw the chance to turn in her most accomplished performance. Allen expanded the scope of her career somewhat by writing the screenplay for Sidney Lumet's *Prince of the City,* with its largely masculine milieu and adapting (again for Lumet) the thriller *Deathtrap,* perhaps her least interesting or successful project. Like many of her screenwriting colleagues, Allen became a sometime hyphenate, taking increased control of her work by functioning as her own producer as well. She also expanded into television and theater work.

Tru, a one-man show based on the life of Truman Capote which she wrote and directed, had great success on Broadway. Allen's theatrical follow-up was *The Big Love,* adapted from a novella by Florence Aadland. Co-written with Allen's daughter, Brooke Allen, the play was produced by Allen's husband, Lewis Allen, and Home Box Office, and later appeared on the cable network. In 1994 Allen returned to film, discussing her work on *Cabaret* in *The Celluloid Closet,* a documentary on gay representations in Hollywood films. Allen also co-wrote the script for *Copycat,* a thriller featuring Sigourney Weaver as an agoraphobic psychologist. The apologetic mother (Tracey Ullman) in *The Big Love* and *Copycat*'s distraught detective (Holly Hunter) and paranoid psychologist are further examples of Allen's effective portraits of neurosis.

—Charles Derry/Mark Johnson

AMARAL, Suzana
Brazilian director

Born: São Paolo, Brazil, 1933. **Education:** Attended film schools at the University of São Paolo and New York University; attended acting and directing classes at New York's Actors Studio. **Family:** Married to a physician and divorced, nine children. **Career:** Decided she wanted to pursue a career after 12 years of marriage and motherhood; early 1970s—worked as a public television station news reporter; mid-1970s—began working on television documentaries, eventually making 50 one-hour films examining various social issues; 1980s—worked in television after living in New York for three years; 1985—directed her first feature, *The Hour of the

Star. **Awards:** Best Film, Havana Film Festival, Best Film, Brasilia Film Festival, Best Director, International Woman's Film Festival, for *The Hour of the Star,* 1985. **Address:** Concine/National Cinema Council, Rua Mayrink Velga 28, Rio de Janeiro, Brazil.

Films as Director

1971   *Semana de 22 (The Week of 1922)*
1972   *Coleçao de marfil (Ivory Collection)*
1980   *Projeto pensamiento e linguajen (A Project for Thought and
          Speech)* (short)
1981   *São Paolo de todos nos (Our São Paolo)*
1985   *A Hora da Estrêla (The Hour of the Star)* (+ co-sc)

Other Film

1996   *O Regresso do Homem Que Não Gostava de Sair de Casa
          (Costa e Silva)* (ro)

Publications by Amaral

Articles

Interview with Dennis West, in *Cineaste* (New York), vol. 15, no. 4, 1987.
"Listening to the Silence," in *Monthly Film Bulletin* (London), May 1987.

Publications on Amaral

Books

Foster, Gwendolyn Audrey, *Women Film Directors: An International Bio-Critical Dictionary,* Westport, Connecticut, 1995.
Stone, Judy, *Eye on the World: Conversations with International Filmmakers,* Los Angeles, 1997.

Articles

Rothstein, M., "Suzana Amaral: Her 'Hour' Has Come," in *New York Times,* 18 January 1987.
Arcos, M., "Cuba te espera," in *London Magazine,* June 1987.
Aufderheide, Pat, "*La hora da Estrêla,*" in *Formato 16* (Panama), October 1987.

*   *   *

The cliché "better late than never" perfectly describes the career of Suzana Amaral. She had been married to a physician for 12 years and had eight of her nine children when she decided that she also wanted an education, and a vocation. She enrolled at the University of São Paolo along with her eldest son; the pair even shared some of the same classes. Eventually, she worked as a public-television news reporter, and made 50 hour-long documentaries. By the time Amaral directed *The Hour of the Star,* she was 50-plus, and a divorcee with seven grandchildren.

The Hour of the Star not only is Amaral's first feature, but it is her lone feature to date. Notwithstanding, it is one of the top Brazilian films of the 1980s: a neorealist slice-of-life, set in São Paolo, which records the plight and fate of Macabea, a thoroughly ordinary, virginal 19 year old. Macabea is employed as a typist, even though she barely can type and is oblivious to her inadequacies. She is an orphan who is all alone in the world and new to the city; she is a *baiano,* a northeastern Brazilian who migrates south.

Macabea is plain-looking and slow-witted, unhygienic and uncouth. She always is apologizing, even when there is nothing for which to be sorry. At one point, she declares, "I'm not much of a person." Her favorite off-hours activity is riding the São Paolo subway, which she describes as "nice." In her own way, she is as disconnected from the world around her as Travis Bickle, Martin Scorsese's *Taxi Driver.*

Macabea may have romantic fantasies (which involve her staring longingly at a wedding dress-garbed mannequin in a store window and dreaming of becoming a movie star) and sexual longings (which she fulfills via masturbation), but she is socially and sexually inept. She only can envy a bitchy, voluptuous co-worker, who brags about all her boyfriends and abortions. At one point, Macabea thinks two men are admiring her. The first is a transit cop, who tells her that she is standing beyond a subway station safety line. The second reveals himself to be blind.

For a good portion of *The Hour of the Star,* Macabea dates the pretentious and self-involved Olimpico, who sports his own delusions of grandeur. It remains a mystery why he agrees to see her beyond their first meeting, and their relationship (which is devoid of romance or sex) consists of her asking him the meanings of words and spouting factoids she has heard on the radio. When he finally breaks off with her, he does so by pronouncing, "You're a hair in my soup." At the finale, a fortune-teller reports to Macabea that her life will change. Her now ex-boyfriend will want to marry her. Her boss will not fire her. A wealthy foreigner, a "gringo," will give her lots of money, as well as love her and marry her. The scenario segues into fantasy as Macabea purchases a sunny blue-and-white polka-dot dress. But the "gringo" hits her with his car, leaving her a bloody corpse. He gets out of the car, and runs toward her. Then, magically, she comes alive, and runs toward him....

Amaral paints a fully developed portrait of Macabea, whose thickheadedness ordinarily might make her easy to dismiss. Yet as her hopes and fantasies are visualized, Macabea becomes a three-dimensional character whose shallowness makes her sympathetic. *The Hour of the Star* works as a chronicle of the manner in which lack of money and knowledge may cause a person to feel (and, in many ways, be) less-than-human, and a reminder that even those who are unattractive and none-too-bright are individuals, with their very own feelings and longings. And in more political terms, it is a vivid depiction of disenfranchisement on the part of the poor in a modern industrial society.

The Hour of the Star was an impressive first film for Amaral. Unfortunately, it apparently will be her lone directorial credit. Given her age, and the time that has passed since its release, it is highly unlikely that she will be adding additional credits to her filmography.

—Rob Edelman

ANDERS, Allison
American director

Born: Ashland, Kentucky, 16 November 1954; daughter of the actress Luana Anders. **Education:** Attended junior college and was graduated from the University of Southern California at Los Angeles, School of Theater, Film and Television. **Family:** Two daughters. **Career:** Early 1980s—became acquainted with Wim Wenders; 1983—kept a journal while on the set of Wenders's *Paris, Texas*; 1988—co-directed first feature, *Border Radio*; 1992—earned international acclaim for second feature, *Gas Food Lodging.* **Awards:** Nicholl Fellowship, Academy of Motion Picture Arts and Sciences; Samuel Goldwyn Award, for screenplay *Lost Highway;* Best New Director, New York Film Critics Circle, for *Gas Food Lodging,* 1992. **Address:** Cineville, Inc., Skywalker Studios, 1861 South Bundy Drive, Los Angeles, CA 90025, U.S.A.

Films as Director and Writer

1988   *Border Radio* (co-d with Lent, co-sc)
1992   *Gas Food Lodging*
1993   *Mi Vida Loca* (*My Crazy Life*)
1995   "The Missing Ingredient" ep. of *Four Rooms*
1996   *Grace of My Heart*

Publications by Anders

Book

Four Friends: Four Friends Telling Four Stories Making One Film, New York, 1995.

Articles

"*Gas Food Lodging,*" interview with D. E. Williams, in *Film Threat* (Beverly Hills), October 1992.
"Girl Gangs Get Their Colors," interview with Sheila Benson, in *Interview* (New York), June 1994.
"Four x Four," interview with Peter Biskind, in *Premiere* (New York), November 1995.
Interview with Graham Fuller, in *Interview* (New York), September 1996.
"Cut to the *Grace,*" in *Premiere* (New York), October 1996.

Publications on Anders

Book

Foster, Gwendolyn Audrey, *Women Film Directors: An International Bio-Critical Dictionary,* Westport, Connecticut, 1995.

Articles

Benenson, L. H., "A Director's Life Fuels Her Film," in *New York Times,* 26 July 1992.
Connelly, C., "Allison Anders," in *Premiere* (New York), August 1992.
Dargis, M., "Giving Direction," in *Village Voice* (New York), 18 August 1992.
Kort, Michele, "Filmmaker Allison Anders: Her Crazy Life," in *Ms. Magazine* (New York), May/June 1994.
McDonagh, Maitland, "Sad Girls," in *Film Comment* (New York), September/October 1994.

* * *

Allison Anders directing *Grace of My Heart.*

Allison Anders's most consequential film to date is *Gas Food Lodging,* a sharply observed character study which is most effective as a refreshingly realistic look at the travails of motherhood without fatherhood. Set within a family whose members are all women, it is a story of motherly love and concern, daughterly yearnings for freedom and independence, the realities of romantic love, and the characters' vulnerabilities and cravings for compassion and understanding.

Anders tells the story of Nora Evans (Brooke Adams), a truck-stop waitress in the dusty town of Laramie, New Mexico. Nora is attempting to rear her two teenaged daughters, whose father "walked off" when they were very young. The eldest, 17-year-old Trudi (Ione Skye), is as rebellious and promiscuous as she is pretty. She has accumulated one too many unexcused absences from school; among her peers, she has earned a reputation for being "easy." Nora and Trudi constantly squabble, most particularly over Trudi's arrival home at ungodly hours after hot-and-heavy dates with men who promise her the love and affection she covets. Nora is distressed because she does not want Trudi to be victimized by suitors who will promise commitments they have no intention of keeping.

Trudi's kid sister, Shade (Fairuza Balk), is a sweetly innocent romantic who has not yet discovered the pitfalls of sexuality. Her concept of love has been gained from watching corny Spanish-language movies at the local theater. Shade longs for the traditional nuclear family, and is intent upon instigating a relationship between

her mom and a man—just about any male who might make an appropriate mate for Nora and stepdad for her and Trudi. Will such a situation ever be possible? Or will there always be roadblocks that will prevent Shade's dream from becoming real (or, more to the point, from reflecting the outcomes of the movies to which she is addicted)?

The latter is certain to be the case, because Anders's characters exist within a world that is more reflective of reality. Unlike more traditional celluloid portraits of women on their own, none of the characters ends up being saved by a man. There are no handsome hunks on white horses to whisk them away from the drudgery of their lives. *Gas Food Lodging* is the polar opposite of a Hollywood assembly-line product such as *Pretty Woman,* a Cinderella story whose spunky, squeaky-clean heroine just so happens to be a Hollywood Boulevard whore. She may love old movies just as passionately as Shade, do dental floss rather than crack, and be played by Julia Roberts; her savior may be a profiteer, but he is cute, doesn't drink, says no to drugs, and is transformed by love into a constructive citizen. *Pretty Woman* is a sugary entertainment package which, in its own perverse way, serves as a recruiting poster for a career as a hooker. It is also the type of film which, one safely assumes, would disgust Allison Anders.

Furthermore, in *Gas Food Lodging* Anders depicts characters you rarely see in Hollywood films: blue-collar workers who live ordinary lives and struggle for survival in unglamorous environments. Nora's plight as a single mother may be common in today's society, but it is one that rarely is acknowledged with any thought or depth in mainstream movies. Yet the lives of such characters are rich in dramatic possibility. At the core of *Gas Food Lodging* is an intelligent, nonsensationalistic story featuring women's points-of-view regarding men, sex, love, and dreams. Additionally, the film is highly autobiographical. While trying to jump-start her career, Anders herself worked as a waitress—and she is the single mother of two daughters (born in 1974 and 1977). The filmmaker has claimed, however, that she modeled the character of Nora Evans after her own mother.

The films Anders made before and after *Gas Food Lodging* have been much less spectacular. *Border Radio,* set amid the Los Angeles punk scene, was barely noticed. *Mi Vida Loca (My Crazy Life)* is a well-intentioned chronicle of the plights of Latina gang members in East Los Angeles. Unlike most "teen-gang" movies, which focus on the personalities of males—with their female counterparts appearing as either decorations or prizes to be won in rumbles—*Mi Vida Loca* offers portraits of adolescent girls. Their evocative nicknames—Sad Girl, Mousie, Whisper—tell you all you need to know about them. And here, too, Anders is mostly interested in the manner in which the characters share camaraderie and form identities apart from the men. Unfortunately, the result is dramatically vague, a series of pasted-together episodes that do not add up to a cohesive whole.

Anders's attempt at a full-bodied portrayal of Latino girls in *Mi Vida Loca* may be linked to a secondary plot line in *Gas Food Lodging.* At one point, Trudi callously dismisses a young Mexican-American busboy as a wetback; later on, a friend of Shade whispers that the same character is a *cholo,* a gangster and dope dealer who robs pizza deliverymen and steals car radios to support his illegitimate children. The lad, of course, proves to be something else altogether, an entirely sympathetic character.

Anders's segment in *Four Rooms,* a four-part feature co-directed with Alexandre Rockwell, Robert Rodríguez, and Quentin Tarantino, is equally run-of-the-mill. Titled "The Missing Ingredient" it is the senseless story of a coven of witches who go about trying to raise their goddess from the dead.

Anders's career is at a crossroads. Will she be able to come up with a commendable follow-up to *Gas Food Lodging,* or will history prove her a one-shot artist, a footnote among women filmmakers?

—Rob Edelman

ANGELOU, Maya
American writer and producer

Born: Marguerite Annie Johnson in St. Louis, Missouri, 4 April 1928. **Education:** Attended George Washington High School, San Francisco; studied dance with Pearl Primus, New York City; studied acting with Frank Silvera; numerous honorary degrees. **Family:** Married (1) Tosh Angelos (divorced); (2) Vusumzi Make (divorced 1963); (3) Paul DuFeu, 1973; son: Guy Johnson. **Career:** Taught modern dance; 1960s—northern co-ordinator Southern Christian Leadership Conference; 1963-65—writer for the Ghanaian Broadcasting Corporation; 1969—published first novel, the critically acclaimed best-seller *I Know Why the Caged Bird Sings;* 1970—writer-in-residence University of Kansas-Lawrence; 1972—wrote the script and score for *Georgia, Georgia;* 1977—appeared in TV miniseries *Roots;* since 1981—Reynolds Professor of American Studies at Wake Forest University; 1993—delivered her poem

"On the Pulse of Morning" at Presidential inauguration; 1998—directed first feature film, *Down in the Delta.* **Address:** Reynolds Professor, Wake Forest University, Box 7314, Winston-Salem, NC 27109. **Agent:** Dave La Camera, Lordly & Dame, Inc., 51 Church Street, Boston, MA 02116-5493, U.S.A.

Films as Writer

1972 *Georgia, Georgia* (Bjorkman) (+ score)
1979 *I Know Why the Caged Bird Sings* (Cook—for TV) (co-sc)
1982 *Sister, Sister* (Berry—for TV, produced 1980) (+ co-pr)
1996 *America's Dream* (Barclay, Duke, and Sullivan) (sc based on story "The Reunion")

Other Films

1957 *Calypso Heat Wave* (Sears) (ro as herself)
1993 *Poetic Justice* (Singleton) (poetry, + ro as Aunt June); *There Are No Children Here* (Addison) (ro as grandmother)
1995 *How to Make an American Quilt* (Moorhouse) (ro as Anna)
1998 *Down in the Delta* (d)

Publications by Angelou

Books

I Know Why the Caged Bird Sings, New York, 1969.
Just Give Me a Cool Drink of Water 'Fore I Diiie, New York, 1971.
Gather Together in My Name, New York, 1974.
Oh Pray My Wings Are Gonna Fit Me Well, New York, 1975.
Singin' and Swingin' and Gettin' Merry Like Christmas, New York, 1976.
And Still I Rise, New York, 1978.
The Heart of a Woman, New York, 1981.
Shaker, Why Don't You Sing?, New York, 1983.
All God's Children Need Traveling Shoes, New York, 1986.
Now Sheba Sings the Song, New York, 1987.
I Shall Not Be Moved, New York, 1990.
Lessons in Living, New York, 1993.
Life Doesn't Frighten Me (children's), New York, 1993.
Wouldn't Take Nothing for My Journey Now, New York, 1993.
My Painted House, My Friendly Chicken, and Me (children's), New York, 1994.
Phenomenal Woman, New York, 1994.
A Brave and Startling Truth, New York, 1995.
Kofi and His Magic (children's), New York, 1996.
Even the Stars Look Lonesome, New York, 1997.

Articles

"Women in Film: Maya Angelou," interview with Gordon R. Watkins, in *Millimeter* (New York), July/August 1974.
"Oprah Winfrey," in *Ms.* (New York), January/February 1989.

Publications on Angelou

Books

McPherson, Dolly A., *Order Out of Chaos: The Autobiographical Works of Maya Angelou,* New York, 1990.

Acker, Ally, *Reel Women: Pioneers of the Cinema, 1896 to the Present,* New York, 1991.

Articles

Cooper, Arthur, "Caged Bird," in *Newsweek* (New York), 3 April 1972.
"Maya Angelou Has Joined AFI Greystone Faculty," in *Boxoffice* (Kansas City, Missouri), 6 March 1978.
Taylor, Howard, "She Wants to Change TV's Image of Blacks," in *New York Times,* 22 April 1979.
O'Connor, John J., *"Caged Bird Sings,* and Tales of Girlhood," in *New York Times,* 27 April 1979.
Safran, Don, "Finding Directing Assignments Tough," in *Hollywood Reporter* (Los Angeles), 6 November 1979.
Current Biography, New York, 1994.

* * *

Truly a renaissance woman, Maya Angelou has had an enchantingly colorful career. Nicknamed "Maya" by her beloved older brother Bailey, she has worked as a dancer, composer, poet, historian, author, actress, playwright, civil-rights activist, in addition to film producer, screenwriter, and director. She was even the first black and female streetcar fare collector in San Francisco. In the realm of motion pictures, she has been nothing less than a pioneer for women of color; and, like most pioneers, she faced enormous challenges in her early efforts to bring more varied, realistic, and nuanced portrayals of African Americans to film and television screens.

Angelou was the first African-American woman to write the script and musical score for a feature film, *Georgia, Georgia.* Adapted from one of her stories, it is about a beautiful, sharp-tongued black woman, played by Diana Sands, from an impoverished Southern background who has gained international fame as a pop singer. On tour in Sweden, she responds flippantly when reporters ask her about a number of "Black issues," and later, supposedly caught in the throes of the so-called "white fever," she has a relationship with a handsome, white photographer. But the heroine's attraction to white culture creates a conflict with her black companion, a grandmotherly woman who hates whites as much as Georgia loves them. Angelou was thoroughly dissatisfied with the completed film because she disagreed with the approach of the director, Stig Bjorkman. She considered that as a Swedish man, Bjorkman had no understanding of African Americans and had failed to bring the essence of her work, especially its romance, to the screen. While in Sweden, Angelou assiduously studied the craft of cinematography, as she explained, learning everything from "breaking down a script and putting it on a 'day chart' to breaking down a camera." Consequently, she was prompted to pursue work as a director in order to attempt to more effectively convey the multifaceted "rhythms" of African-American life on-screen. Subsequently, producer David Wolper cast her in the monumental television miniseries *Roots,* with the understanding that she would later be a given a project of her own to direct; however, her chance was lost when Wolper sold his production company.

In 1972 Angelou optioned her autobiography, *I Know Why the Caged Bird Sings,* with a film producer who agreed to let her direct her own project, but he later reneged. So, she bought her script back and proclaimed that she would write and direct any film she made in the future. Nevertheless, in 1978, she reluctantly signed a contract with CBS Television that limited her involvement in the production of *I Know Why the Caged Bird Sings* to co-writing the script. She later confessed to a *New York Times* interviewer that she made the

deal with CBS because she felt compelled to abandon her long-held conviction that black films should be produced by black filmmakers, though she maintained that it behooved white filmmakers to actively endeavor to learn about and to respect black sensibilities. The resulting film was acclaimed for offering a poignant account of Angelou's childhood during the Great Depression in the segregated South, especially her close relationships with her brother Bailey and with her grandparents who raised the two after their parents divorced, as well as of the rape that rendered her mute for several years after her rapist was killed by outraged friends. Critics likewise boasted that the film represented one of television's infrequent efforts to examine racism and the African-American family in more contemporary terms, outside the context of slavery. Although Angelou herself was pleased with the results, she lamented that, in general, there were considerable strains for an author working in television where, as she put it, "everyone and his dog has a chance to pick at a writer's work."

Seeking a more advantageous relationship with Hollywood, Angelou signed a writer-producer contract with 20th Century-Fox in 1978 that made her the first African-American woman to sign such a deal with a major production company. As a result, she made a television movie for NBC entitled *Sister, Sister,* which she wrote and co-produced with a one-and-a-half million dollar budget. Dubbed Angelou's "black-Americanization of Chekhov" by an NBC executive, the network was notably reticent about releasing it: it was four years before the film was screened. In addition, Angelou was informed that in order to procure the director the executive producer wanted, she would have to agree to share her co-producer credit. She agreed, but the producer later insisted that he wanted sole producer credit or he would file a complaint with the Writers Guild in order to acquire half of the writing credit.

Angelou has had several stage and screen acting parts over the years and she has made hundreds of guest appearances on television. Furthermore, she has directed plays for public television, and has written, directed, and produced television documentaries, including *Black! Blues! Black!* for the National Education Television network. In the 1970s Angelou had vehemently objected to Hollywood's depictions of blacks and singled out the "blaxploitation" film genre, in particular, for what she claimed were their demeaning, distorted, and stereotypical conceptions. Further, she advocated the notion of black investment in black film projects in order to counter prevailing stereotypes. But, she questioned whether the ideal situation was for black filmmakers to make films about black people, or to produce films that have nothing to do with being black. Notably, since that time, and with Angelou's considerable assistance, her dream has become a reality on both counts as increasing numbers of black directors, screenwriters, and producers have recently made many successful feature films, thus inspiring some critics to declare the 1990s a period of "black renaissance" in Hollywood.

—Cynthia Felando

APON, Annette
Dutch director

Born: The Netherlands, 1949. **Education:** Graduated from the Netherlands Film Academy, Amsterdam, 1972. **Career:** 1973—made first film, *Eigen Haard is Goud Waard*; 1973 to about 1980—made documentaries with the Amsterdam City Newsreel collective; 1982—gained recognition for her first full-length feature film, *Golven*;

1990—released best-known film, *Krokodillen in Amsterdam*. **Address:** c/o *Skrien*: Vondepark 3, 1071 AA, Amsterdam, Netherlands.

Films as Director

1973 *Eigen Haard is Goud Waard* (short)
1974 *Overloop is Sloop* (short)
1975 *Van Brood Alleen Kan een Mens Niet Leven* (short)
1976 *Een Schijntje Vrijheid* (short)
1978 *Het Bosplan* (short)
1979 *Politiewerk* (short)
1980 *Kakafonische Notities* (short)
1982 *Golven* (*The Waves*) (+ sc)
1983 *Giovanni* (+ sc)
1984 *Projekties*
1985 *Ornithopter*
1988 *Reis Zonder Einde*
1990 **Krokodillen in Amsterdam** (*Crocodiles in Amsterdam*) (+ co-sc)
1993 *Naarden Vesting*
1994 *Een Winter in Zuiderwoude* (*A Winter in Zuiderwoude*) (doc, short) (+ sc, ed); *Wakers en Dromers* (*Wakers and Dreamers*) (doc) (+ sc, ed)
1996 *Het is de Schraapzucht, Gentlemen* (for TV) (+ sc)

Other Film

1995 *Laagland* (Entius—for TV) (scenario adviser)

Publications by Apon

Articles

With G. Verhage, "Cinestud 1973: Een Korte Kritiek," in *Skrien* (Amsterdam), January/February 1974.
"L'Affiche Rouge," in *Skrien* (Amsterdam), March 1977.
"Padre Padrone," in *Skrien* (Amsterdam), November 1977.
"Pesaro," in *Skrien* (Amsterdam), November 1977.
"Resnais: Gesprek Over een Zoekend Kunstenaar," in *Skrien* (Amsterdam), December 1977.
"Marguerite Duras," in *Skrien* (Amsterdam), February 1978.
"Kiezen Tussen Avant-Garde en Conventie: Johan v.d. Keuken," in *Skrien* (Amsterdam), May 1978.
With H. Alofs, "'(Tien Duizend) 10.00 Megawatt': Een Voortgezette Discussie," in *Skrien* (Amsterdam), September 1978.
"*Camping*: de Filmische Uitstraling van het Werkteater," in *Skrien* (Amsterdam), September 1978.
"Film Marathon," in *Skrien* (Amsterdam), October 1978.
"Brecht in *Skrien*: de Nederlandse Film en de Markt," in *Skrien* (Amsterdam), Winter 1978-79.
"Onderweg Naar de Autonome Vrouw: Chantal Akerman: *Les Rendez-vous d'Anna*," in *Skrien* (Amsterdam), February 1979.
With T. de Graaff, "Jean-Luc Godard: het Gevaar van het Isolement," in *Skrien* (Amsterdam), March 1979.
"Camera Esthetiek en Techniek [Interview with Theo van de Sande]," in *Skrien* (Amsterdam), September 1979.
"Esthetiek en Techniek [Interview with Erik Langhout]," in *Skrien* (Amsterdam), November 1979.
"Cahiers," in *Skrien* (Amsterdam), February 1980.

"Film International: *De Meester en de Reus*," in *Skrien* (Amsterdam), February 1980.
With T. de Graaff, "Esthetiek en Techniek: Louis Andriessen," in *Skrien* (Amsterdam), March 1980.
"Russen in Pesaro: Alsof de Wereld Stillstatt," in *Skrien* (Amsterdam), September 1980.
"*Aurelia Steiner*," in *Skrien* (Amsterdam), February 1981.
"La Reprise du Travail Chez Wonder," in *Skrien* (Amsterdam), April/May 1989.
"Conversione con Annette Apon," interview with F. Bono, in *Cineforum* (Bergamo, Italy), October 1990.

Publications on Apon

Book

Foster, Gwendolyn Audrey, *Women Film Directors: An International Bio-Critical Dictionary,* Westport, Connecticut, 1995.

Articles

Verbong, B., and others, "Fassbinder: Van Anti-Theater naar Melodrama," in *Skrien* (Amsterdam), January 1978.
de Graaff, T., "*Golven*: Zes Personages op Zoek naar een Rol," in *Skrien* (Amsterdam), February 1982.
Kroon, H., "Een Film Biedt Weerstand," in *Skrien* (Amsterdam), May/June 1982.
de Boer, L., "Annette Apon en *Giovanni*: 'Er Moet Wel een Soort Duidelijkheid Over de Werkelijkheid in Blijven'," in *Skoop* (Amsterdam), October 1983.
Koole, C., "Annette Apon en *Ornithopter*: het Eeuwige Dilemma om Ergens Bij te Willen Horen en ook Weer Niet," in *Skoop* (Amsterdam), June/July 1985.
Waal, F. de, "Annette Apon en de Pers: *Ornithopter* en de Gatlikkers," in *Skoop* (Amsterdam), August 1985.

* * *

Filmmaker Annette Apon is well known in the Netherlands, though her work is generally unknown in the United States. She has directed several low-budget, long and short films—both fiction and documentary, but is known primarily for her documentary work. In addition, she has written extensively on the subject of film and is a co-founder of the serious film journal *Skrien,* as well as a co-founder of the Amsterdam City Newsreel collective. In general, her films feature clever styles and structures that refuse familiar narrative conventions in favor of more personal, experimental approaches that combine realism and antirealism.

After spending seven years making documentaries with the Amsterdam City Newsreel collective, Apon garnered critical praise for her first full-length feature film, *Golven,* in which she returned to the experimental forms of her earlier short films. Adapted from Virginia Woolf's novel *The Waves,* it was praised by critics who predicted that it heralded a promising career for Apon. Set in the 1920s, *Golven* is a decidedly low-key, yet fascinating, exploration of the thoughts and feelings of six people, on the verge of adulthood, as they prepare for and attend a farewell dinner party for the mysterious Percival, an important figure in each of their lives. Their varied personalities, lost hopes, insecurities, mixed emotions, and ambitions are conveyed via their thoughts, which are related in offscreen and on-screen monologues set in the present. The film's performances are especially interesting, inasmuch as the acting is mostly confined to facial expression.

The central element of Apon's absorbing second full-length feature film, *Giovanni* (funded in part by the Netherlands's Film Fund), is a Rome hotel room, in which a fashion photographer is staying for work and to look for a man she once knew—Giovanni. The film's clever conceit is that the camera remains trained on the hotel room even when the photographer is gone, thus revealing a motley assortment of events—from the room's changing light and sounds, to the maid and valet who go through her things, and a trysting couple who briefly spend time there. Eventually, even Giovanni visits, but the photographer is destined to miss the note he leaves, as a man with a gun wound climbs into and out of her room, thus making the police suspicious about her and her untidy room. The film ends compellingly anticlimactically, with the photographer's departure after less than 48 hours as the maid prepares the room for the next guests.

In the United States, *Crocodiles in Amsterdam* is Apon's best-known feature film, in which she wittily crafts a distinctly fantastic world where it seems that crocodiles could indeed roam through Amsterdam. Critics were generally enthusiastic, appreciating in particular its wacky sense of fun and humor, as well as its crafty re-working of the conventions of the buddy movie so as to feature lesbians. One critic characterized the film as a "whimsical allegory of lesbian desire." It is indeed a quirky comedy, which follows an unlikely couple on a series of wild adventures. Politically committed Nina wants to attack a bomb factory but her plans are thwarted by Gino's impetuous ideas. Consequently, their shaky relationship seems on the verge of an explosive dissolution.

Another noteworthy Apon film is *A Winter in Zuiderwoude,* a short black-and-white documentary that has been characterized as a study of the Dutch winter in variations of white, black, and gray. Entirely without interviews, voice-over narration, or dialogue, the film provides a fascinating portrait of a Dutch landscape throughout several cold winter months. Filmed with a static camera that shows a changing exterior of snow and freezing weather, as well as a collection of cows in their snug sheds waiting impatiently for spring.

Wakers and Dreamers is another documentary that focuses on the Dutch landscape, in this case, to explore the way that the Netherlands's many dikes shape the landscape and enrich the Dutch language. The function of dikes to control water by keeping it in or keeping it out, serves as a metaphor for society's unrelenting urge to likewise channel and regulate. Thus, people craft a set of fish stairs to accommodate fish that are unable to swim upstream, but they erect barriers against the "flood" of foreign immigrants into the Netherlands. Indeed, as Apon's film suggests, both protest and contradiction are essential parts of the urge to create.

Despite that her films are not as well-known as those of her contemporary, Marleen Gorris, Apon's films have been screened internationally on the film festival circuit, including Berlin; Films de Femmes in Créteil, France; Montreal Women's Film Festival; and New York and San Francisco's International Lesbian and Gay film festivals.

—Cynthia Felando

ARMSTRONG, Gillian
Australian director

Born: Melbourne, 18 December 1950. **Education:** Attended Swinburne College, studied filmmaking in Melbourne and at Australian Film and Television School, Sydney. **Family:** Married the editor John Pfeffer, two daughters. **Career:** Worked as production assistant, editor, art director, and assistant designer, and directed several short films; 1979—directed first feature, *My Brilliant Career*; 1984—directed first American film, *Mrs. Soffel*; 1987—returned to Australia to direct *High Tide*; has since made films both in Australia and the United States; also director of documentaries and commercials. **Awards**: Best Short Fiction Film, Sydney Festival, for *The Singer and the Dancer,* 1976; British Critics' Award, and Best Film and Best Director, Australian Film Institute Awards, for *My Brilliant Career,* 1979. **Agent:** Judy Scott-Fox, William Morris Agency, 151 El Camino Drive, Beverly Hills, CA 90212, U.S.A.

Films as Director

1970 *Old Man and Dog* (short)
1971 *Roof Needs Mowing* (short)
1973 *Gretel; Satdee Night; One Hundred a Day* (short)
1975 *Smokes and Lollies* (doc)
1976 *The Singer and the Dancer* (+ pr, sc)
1979 ***My Brilliant Career***
1980 *Fourteen's Good, Eighteen's Better* (doc) (+ pr); *Touch Wood* (doc)
1982 *Starstruck*
1983 *Having a Go* (doc); *Not Just a Pretty Face*
1984 *Mrs. Soffel*
1986 *Hard to Handle: Bob Dylan with Tom Petty and the Heartbreakers*
1987 *High Tide*
1988 *Bingo, Bridesmaids and Braces* (doc) (+ pr)
1991 *Fires Within*
1992 *The Last Days of Chez Nous*
1994 *Little Women*
1996 *Not Fourteen Again* (doc) (+ sc, co-pr)
1997 *Oscar & Lucinda*

Publications by Armstrong

Articles

Interviews in *Cinema Papers* (Melbourne), January 1974, March/April 1979, October 1992.
Films in Review (New York), June/July 1983.
Interview in *Encore* (Manly, New South Wales), 31 January 1985.
"Gillian Armstrong Returns to Eden," interview with A. Grieve, in *Cinema Papers* (Melbourne), May 1987.
Interview in *Encore* (Manly, New South Wales), 29 September 1988.
"Women's Director," interview with Sheila Benson, in *Variety* (New York), 1 May 1995.

Publications on Armstrong

Books

Tulloch, John, *Australian Cinema: Industry, Narrative, and Meaning,* Sydney and London, 1982.

McFarlane, Brian, *Words and Images: Australian Novels into Films,* Richmond, Victoria, 1983.

Mathews, Sue, *35mm Dreams: Conversations with Five Australian Directors,* Ringwood, Victoria, 1984.

Hall, Sandra, *Critical Business: The New Australian Cinema in Review,* Adelaide, 1985.

Moran, Albert, and Tom O'Regan, editors, *An Australian Film Reader,* Sydney, 1985.

McFarlane, Brian, *Australian Cinema 1970-85,* London, 1987.

Acker, Ally, *Reel Women: Pioneers of the Cinema, 1896 to the Present,* New York, 1991.

Foster, Gwendolyn Audrey, *Women Film Directors: An International Bio-Critical Dictionary,* Westport, Connecticut, 1995.

Articles

"Profile," in *Time Out* (London), 24 January 1980.

Rickey, C., "Where the Girls Are," in *American Film* (Washington, D.C.), January/February 1985.

Enker, D., "Coming in from the Cold," in *Cinema Papers* (Melbourne), July 1985.

Grieve, A., "Gillian Armstrong Returns to Eden," in *Cinema Papers* (Melbourne), May 1987.

Forsberg, M., "Partnership Swells *High Tide,*" in *New York Times,* 6 March 1988.

Harker, P., "Gillian Armstrong and Three Times Three," in *Cinema Papers* (Melbourne), November 1988.

Graham, N., "Directors' Pet Projects," in *Premiere* (New York), December 1988.

Mordue, Mark, "Homeward Bound: A Profile of Gillian Armstrong," in *Sight and Sound* (London), Autumn 1989.

Urban, A. L. *"The Last Days of Chez Nous,"* in *Cinema Papers* (Melbourne), May 1991.

Cohen, Jessica, "Gillian Armstrong: Showing Women's Strength," in *Interview* (New York), March 1993.

Dargis, Manohla, "Her Brilliant Career," in *Village Voice* (New York), 2 March 1993.

Haskell, Molly, "Wildflowers," in *Film Comment* (New York), March/April 1993.

Dougherty, Margot, "Look Homeward, Aussie," in *Premiere* (New York), May 1993.

Current Biography 1995, New York, 1995.

*   *   *

While women directors in film industries around the world are still seen as anomalous (if mainstream) or marginalized as avant-garde, the Antipodes have been home to an impressive cadre of female filmmakers who negotiate and transcend such notions.

Before the promising debuts of Ann Turner (*Celia*) and Jane Campion (*Sweetie*), Gillian Armstrong blazed a trail with *My Brilliant Career,* launching a brilliant career of her own as an international director. Like Turner and Campion, Armstrong makes films that resist easy categorization as either "women's films" or Australian ones. Her films mix and intermingle genres in ways which undermine and illuminate afresh, if not openly subvert, filmic conventions—as much as the films of her male compatriots, such as Peter Weir, Bruce Beresford, or Paul Cox. Formally, however, the pleasures of her films are traditional ones, such as sensitive and delicate cinematography (often by Russell Boyd), fluid editing, an evocative feel for setting and costume, and most importantly, a commitment to solid character development and acting. All in all, her work reminds one of the best of classical Hollywood cinema, and the question of whether her aim is parody or homage is often left pleasingly ambiguous.

Although Armstrong has often spoken in interviews about her discomfort at being confined to the category of woman filmmaker of women's films, and has articulated her desire to reach an audience of both genders and all nationalities, her work continually addresses sexual politics and family tensions. Escape from and struggle with traditional sex roles and the pitfalls and triumphs therein are themes frequently addressed in her films—from *One Hundred a Day,* her final-year project at the Australian Film and Television School, through *My Brilliant Career,* her first and best-known feature, to *High Tide.* Even one of her earliest films at Swinburne College, the short *Roof Needs Mowing,* obliquely tackled this theme, using a typical student filmmaker's pastiche of advertising and surrealism. Like most maturing filmmakers with an eye on wider distribution, Armstrong dropped the "sur" from surrealism in her later work, so that by *One Hundred a Day*—an adaptation of an Alan Marshall story about a shoe-factory employee getting a back-street abortion in the 1930s—she developed a more naturalistic handling of material, while her use of soundtrack and fast editing remained highly stylized and effective.

Made on a tiny budget and heavily subsidized by the Australian Film Commission, the award-winning *The Singer and the Dancer* was a precocious study of the toll men take on women's lives that marked the onset of Armstrong's mature style. On the strength of this and *One Hundred a Day,* producer Margaret Fink offered Armstrong the direction of *My Brilliant Career.* Daunted at first by the scale of the project and a lack of confidence in her own abilities, she accepted because she "thought it could be bungled by a lot of men."

While *The Singer and the Dancer* had been chastised by feminist critics for its downbeat ending, in which the heroine returns to her philandering lover after a halfhearted escape attempt, *My Brilliant Career* was widely celebrated for its feminist fairy-tale story as well as its employment of women crew members. Adapted from Miles Franklin's semiautobiographical novel, *My Brilliant Career,* with its turn-of-the-century setting in the Australian outback, works like *Jane Eyre* in reverse (she does not marry him), while retaining the romantic allure of such a story and all the glossy production values of a period setting that Australian cinema had been known for up until then. Distinguished by an astonishing central performance by the then-unknown Judy Davis (fresh from playing Juliet to Mel Gibson's Romeo on the drama-school stage), the film managed to present a positive model of feminine independence without belying the time in which it was set. Like Armstrong's later *Mrs. Soffel, My Brilliant Career* potently evokes smothered sensuality and conveys sexual tension by small, telling details, as in the boating scene.

Sadly, few of Armstrong's later films have been awarded commensurate critical praise or been as widely successful, possibly because of her refusal to conform to expectations and churn out more upbeat costume dramas. Her next feature. *Starstruck,* although it too features a spunky, ambitious heroine, was a rock musical set in the present and displaying a veritable rattle bag of influences—including Judy Garland-Mickey Rooney "let's-put-on-a-show" films, Richard Lester editing techniques, new-wave pop videos, and even Sternberg's *Blond Venus,* when the heroine sheds her kangaroo suit to sing her "torch song" à la Marlene Dietrich. Despite a witty script and fine bit characters, the music is somewhat monotonous, and the film was only mildly successful.

Armstrong's first film to be financed and filmed in America was *Mrs. Soffel.* Based on a true story and set at the turn of the century, it

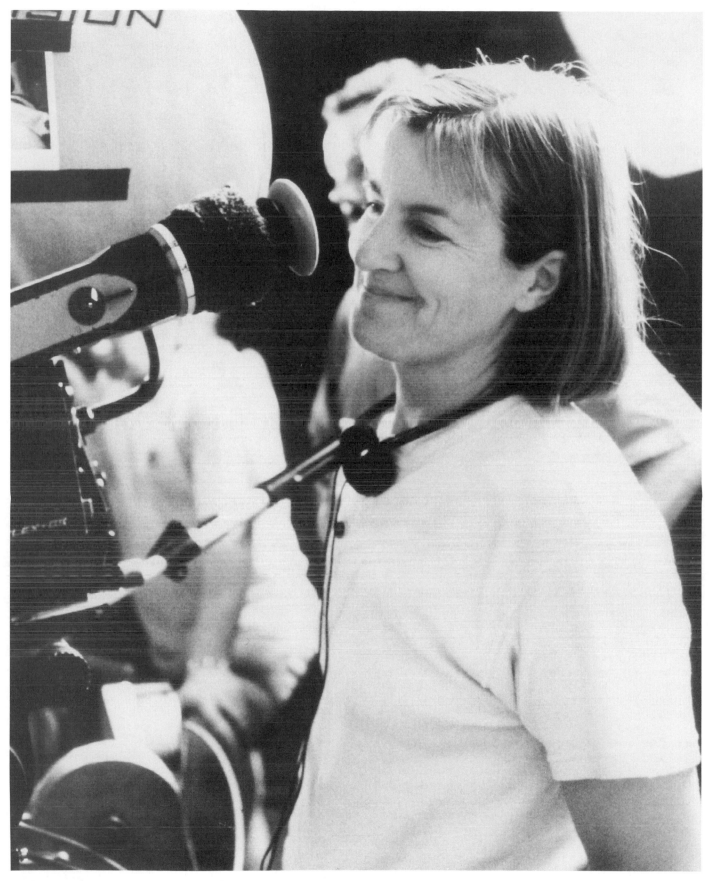

Gillian Armstrong on the set of *Little Women*.

delineated the tragic story of a prison warden's wife who falls in love with a convict, helps him escape, and finally runs off with him. The bleak, monochrome cinematography is powerfully atmospheric but was not to all reviewers' tastes, especially in America. For Armstrong, the restricted palette was quite deliberate, so that the penultimate images of blood on snow would be all the more striking and effective. A sadly underrated film, it features some unexpectedly fine performances from Diane Keaton in the title role, Mel Gibson as her paramour (a fair impersonation of young Henry Fonda), and the young Matthew Modine as his kid brother. At its best, it recalls, if not *McCabe and Mrs. Miller,* then at least *Bonnie and Clyde.*

High Tide returns to Australia for its setting in a coastal caravan park, and comes up trumps as an unabashedly sentimental weepie, and none the worse for it. It features three generations of women: Lilli (Judy Davis again), backup singer to an Elvis impersonator and drifter; Ally (Claudia Karvan), the pubescent daughter she left behind; and mother-in-law Bet (Jan Adele), who vies with Lilli for Ally's affections. In terms of camera work, it is Armstrong's most restless film, utilizing nervous zip pans, fast tracking, and boomshots, and then resting for quiet, intense close-ups on surfboards, legs being shaved, and shower nozzles, all highly motivated by the characters' perspectives. Like *Mrs. Soffel, High Tide* uses colors symbolically to contrast the gentle tones of the seaside's natural landscape with the garish buildings of the town called Eden.

Armstrong wears her feminist credentials lightly, never on her sleeve. Nevertheless, her fiction films—like her documentaries, which have followed three women from the ages of 14 to 25—can be seen as charting over the years the trajectory of the women's movement: *My Brilliant Career* in the 1970s celebrated women's independence, as Sybylla rejects the roles of wife and mother; *Mrs. Soffel* in the mid-1980s reopens negotiations with men (with tragic results); and finally *High Tide* returns to the rejected motherhood role, with all its attendant joys and anxieties.

Fires Within is a well-meaning but insipid tale of a Cuban political prisoner and his encounter with his family in Miami. A fiasco, Armstrong lost control of the project during post-production. The filmmaker bounced back strongly, however, with two impressive films centering on the relationships between female siblings.

The Last Days of Chez Nous, which Armstrong directed back in Australia, is a thoughtful, well-acted drama focusing on the emotional plight of a pair of sisters. One (Lisa Harrow) is a bossy, fortysomething writer, and the other (Kerry Fox) has just emerged from an unhappy love affair. The scenario centers on events that take place after the latter becomes romantically involved with the former's husband (Bruno Ganz). The film's major strength is the depth and richness of its female characters. Its theme, consistent with Armstrong's best previous work, is the utter necessity of women's self-sufficiency.

Little Women, based on Louisa May Alcott's venerable 1868 novel of four devoted sisters coming of age in Concord, Massachusetts, during the Civil War, was Armstrong's first successful American-made film. It may be linked to *My Brilliant Career* as a story of feminine independence set in a previous era. Alcott's book had been filmed a number of times before: a silent version, made in 1918; most enjoyably by George Cukor, with Katharine Hepburn, in 1933; far less successfully, with a young Elizabeth Taylor (among others), in 1949; and in a made-for-television movie in 1978. Armstrong's version is every bit as fine as the Cukor-Hepburn classic. Her cast is just about perfect, with Winona Ryder deservedly earning an Academy Award nomination as the headstrong Jo March. Ryder is ably supported by Trini Alvarado, Claire Danes, Samantha Mathis, and

Kirsten Dunst, and Susan Sarandon offers her usual solid performance as Marmee, the March girls' mother. If the film has one fault, it is the contemporary-sounding feminist rhetoric that Marmee spouts: the dialogue is completely out of sync with the spirit and reality of the times. But this is just a quibble. This new *Little Women* is a fine film, at once literate and extremely enjoyable.

—Leslie Felperin/Rob Edelman

ARZNER, Dorothy
American director

Born: San Francisco, 3 January 1900. **Education:** Studied medicine at University of Southern California. **Military Service:** Ambulance driver in World War I, 1917-18. **Career:** 1919—typist for William C. de Mille, at Famous Players-Lasky (Paramount); 1922—editor for "Realart," a subsidiary of Paramount; 1926—wrote and edited *Old Ironsides*; 1929—directed Paramount's first sound film, *The Wild Party*; 1943—retired from directing. **Awards:** Honored at First International Festival of Women's Films, New York, 1972, and by Director's Guild of America, 1975. **Died:** In La Quinta, California, 1 October 1979.

Films as Director

1927 *Fashions for Women*; *Get Your Man*; *10 Modern Commandments*
1928 *Manhattan Cocktail*
1929 *The Wild Party* (+ ro)
1930 "The Gallows Song—Nichavo" sequence in *Paramount on Parade*; *Anybody's Woman*; *Sarah and Son*; *Behind the Makeup* (co-d); *Charming Sinners* (co-d, uncredited)
1931 *Honor among Lovers*; *Working Girls*
1932 *Merrily We Go to Hell*
1933 **Christopher Strong**
1934 *Nana* (*Lady of the Boulevards*)
1936 *Craig's Wife*
1937 *The Bride Wore Red*; *The Last of Mrs. Cheyney* (co-d, uncredited)
1940 **Dance, Girl, Dance**
1943 *First Comes Courage*

Other Films

1922 *Blood and Sand* (Niblo) (ed)
1923 *The Covered Wagon* (Cruze) (ed)
1924 *Inez from Hollywood* (A. E. Green) (ed, sc); *The Bread of the Border* (sc); *The No-Gun Man* (sc)
1925 *Red Kimono* (W. Lang) (sc); *When Husbands Flirt* (Wellman) (sc)
1926 *Old Ironsides* (Cruze) (ed, sc)
1936 *Theodora Goes Wild* (Boleslawski) (pr)

Publications by Arzner

Article

Interview with Gerald Peary, in *Cinema* (Beverly Hills), no. 34, 1974.

Dorothy Arzner

Publications on Arzner

Books

Brownlow, Kevin, *The Parade's Gone By,* New York, 1968.

Johnston, Claire, *Notes on Women's Cinema,* London, 1973.

Pratt, George, *Spellbound in Darkness: A History of Silent Film,* Greenwich, Connecticut, 1973.

Rosen, Marjorie, *Popcorn Venus: Women, Movies, and the American Dream,* New York, 1973.

Haskell, Molly, *From Reverence to Rape: The Treatment of Women in the Movies,* New York, 1974.

Johnston, Claire, editor, *The Work of Dorothy Arzner: Towards a Feminist Cinema,* London, 1975.

Smith, Sharon, *Women Who Make Movies,* New York, 1975.

Slide, Anthony, *Early Women Directors,* South Brunswick, New Jersey, 1977.

Heck-Rabi, Louise, *Women Filmmakers: A Critical Reception,* Metuchen, New Jersey, 1984.

Penley, Constance, editor, *Feminism and Film Theory,* London, 1988.

Acker, Ally, *Reel Women: Pioneers of the Cinema, 1896 to the Present,* New York, 1991.

Mayne, Judith, *Directed by Dorothy Arzner,* Bloomington, Indiana, 1994.

Foster, Gwendolyn Audrey, *Women Film Directors: An International Bio-Critical Dictionary,* Westport, Connecticut, 1995.

Articles

"Hollywood Notes," in *Close-Up* (London), April 1928.

Cruikshank, H., "Sketch," in *Motion Picture Classic* (Brooklyn), September 1929.

Potamkin, H. A., "The Woman as Film Director," in *American Cinematographer* (Los Angeles), January 1932.

St. John, Adela Rogers, "Get Me Dorothy Arzner," in *Silver Screen* (New York), December 1933.

"They Stand Out from the Crowd," in *Literary Digest* (New York), 3 November 1934.

Feldman, J. and H., "Women Directors," in *Films in Review* (New York), November 1950.

Pyros, J., "Notes on Women Directors," in *Take One* (Montreal), November/December 1970.

Henshaw, Richard, "Women Directors," in *Film Comment* (New York), November 1972.

Parker, F., "Approaching the Art of Arzner," in *Action* (Los Angeles), July/August 1973.

Slide, Anthony, "Forgotten Early Women Directors," in *Films in Review* (New York), March 1974.

Castle, W., "Tribute to Dorothy Arzner," in *Action* (Los Angeles), March/April 1975.

Kaplan, E. Ann, "Aspects of British Feminist Film Theory," in *Jump Cut* (Berkeley), no. 12-13, 1976.

Johnston, Claire, in *Jump Cut* (Berkeley), 30 December 1976.

Bergstrom, J., "Rereading the Work of Claire Johnston," in *Camera Obscura* (Berkeley), Summer 1979.

Obituary, in *New York Times,* 12 October 1979.

Houston, Beverle, "Missing in Action: Notes on Dorothy Arzner," in *Wide Angle* (Athens, Ohio), vol. 6, no. 3, 1984.

Forster, A., "*Dance, Girl, Dance,*" in *Skrien* (Amsterdam), September/October 1984.

*   *   *

Dorothy Arzner's career as a commercial Hollywood director covered little more than a decade, but she had prepared for it by extensive editing and script-writing work. Ill health forced her to abandon a career that might eventually have led to the recognition she deserved from her contemporaries. One of only a handful of women operating within the structure of Hollywood's post-silent boom, Arzner has been the subject of feminist critical attention, with film retrospectives of her work both in the United States and United Kingdom in the 1970s, when her work was "rediscovered."

Most feminists would recognize that the mere reinsertion of women into a dominant version of film history is a dubious activity, even while asserting that women's contributions to cinema have been excluded from most historical accounts. Recognition of the work of a "popular" director such as Arzner and an evaluation of her contribution to Hollywood cinema must be set against an awareness of her place in the dominant patriarchal ideology of classic Hollywood cinema. Arzner's work is particularly interesting in that it was produced *within* the Hollywood system with all its inherent constraints (time, budget, traditional content requirements of particular genres, etc.).

While Arzner directed "women's pictures"—classic Hollywood fare—she differed from other directors of the genre in that, in place of a narrative seen simply from a female point of view, she actually succeeded in challenging the orthodoxy of Hollywood from within, offering perspectives that questioned the dominant order.

The films often depict women seeking independence through career—a burlesque queen and an aspiring ballerina (*Dance, Girl, Dance*), a world-champion aviatrix (*Christopher Strong*). Alternatively, the escape route can be through exit from accepted female positions in the hierarchy—a rich daughter "escaping" into marriage with a poverty-stricken drunk (*Merrily We Go to Hell*). Even excess can be a way of asserting independence, as with the obsessive housekeeper rejecting family relationships in favor of a passion for domesticity and the home (*Craig's Wife*).

The films frequently play with notions of female stereotyping (most notably in *Dance, Girl, Dance,* with its two central female types of Nice Girl and Vamp). Arzner's "nice girls" are likely to have desires that conflict with male desires, while narrative requirements will demand that they still please the male. While these tensions are not always resolved, Arzner's strategies in underlining these opposing desires are almost gleeful at times.

In addition, Arzner's films offer contradictions that disturb the spectator's accepted relationship with what is on screen—most notably in *Dance, Girl, Dance,* when dancer Judy O'Brien turns on her burlesque (male) audience and berates them for their voyeurism. This scene has been the focus for much debate about the role of the spectator in relation to the woman as spectacle (notably in the work of Laura Mulvey).

Although the conventions of plot and development are present in Arzner's films, Claire Johnston sees these elements as subverted by a "women's discourse": the films may offer us the kinds of narrative closure we expect from the classic Hollywood text—the "happy" or the "tragic" ending—but Arzner's insistence on this female discourse gives the films an exciting and unsettling quality. In Arzner's work, Johnston argues, it is the male universe which invites scrutiny and which is "rendered strange."

Dorothy Arzner's position inside the studio system has made her a unique subject for debate. As the women's movement set about reassessing the role of women in history, so feminist film theorists began not only to reexamine the role of women as a creative force in cinema, but also to consider the implications behind the notion of women as spectacle. The work of Dorothy Arzner has proved a rich area for investigation into both these questions.

—Lilie Ferrari

AUDRY, Jacqueline
French director

Born: Orange, France, 25 September 1908. **Family:** Married the writer Pierre Laroche. **Career:** 1933—entered the French film industry as a script girl; 1930s—became an assistant director, working with G. W. Pabst, Max Ophüls, Jean Delannoy, and others; 1943—directed her first short, *Les Chevaux du Vercors*; 1945—directed her first feature, *Les Malheurs de Sophie*. **Died:** Poissy, France, 1977.

Films as Director

1943   *Les Chevaux du Vercors* (short)
1945   *Les Malheurs du Sophie*
1948   *Sombre dimanche*
1949   *Gigi*
1950   *Minne, l'Ingénue libertine* (*Minne, the Innocent Libertine*)
1951   *Olivia* (*Pit of Loneliness*)
1953   *La Caraque blonde* (*The Blonde Gypsy*)
1954   *Huis clos* (*No Exit*)
1956   *Mitsou*
1957   *La Garçonne*; *C'est la faute d'Adam*
1958   *L'École des cocottes* (*School for Coquettes*)
1960   *Le Secret du Chevalier d'Éon*
1961   *Les Petits matins*; *Cadavres en Vacances*
1966   *Fruits amers* (*Bitter Fruit*; *Soledad*) (+ co-sc)
1971   *Le Lis de mer*
1972   *Un grand amour de Balzac*

Publications on Audry

Book

Foster, Gwendolyn Audrey, *Women Film Directors: An International Bio-Critical Dictionary*, Westport, Connecticut, 1995.

Articles

Oukrate, F., "À Jacqueline Audry, presque une fable," in *Revue du Cinéma* (Paris), April 1974.
Obituary in *Variety* (New York), 6 July 1977.
Passek, J., obituary in *Cinéma* (Paris), October 1977.

*   *   *

Jacqueline Audry's career is significant not only because she was one of the rare female directors working in a motion-picture industry dominated by men, but because she created a body of work that consistently featured strong-willed and independent-minded female characters. Audry often depicted her heroines in psychological terms, with more than a few of her films touching on open sexuality or lesbianism. Yet while behaving in ways that were anything but conventional, her characters never were viewed as oddities or aberrations who needed to be roped in and tamed by good, strong males—unlike the propaganda found in countless postwar Hollywood films featuring self-reliant female characters who by the finale had to be taught that true happiness only came with subservience to men.

Audry's heroines generally are perceptively and sensitively realized, with their alternative lifestyles becoming models of liberation. While she directed with a sure hand, however, her films on occasion are visually unimaginative; they lack the originality and flair that was to characterize the French New Wave that practically all of her films predated.

Most of Audry's films are literary adaptations based on the work of both male and female writers, and were scripted by her husband, Pierre Laroche. Three of the more notable—each starring Danièle Delorme—are from the writings of Colette (who worked closely with Audry and Laroche in developing the scripts). The first, *Gigi*, the story of a girl who is trained by her aunt to be a high-class courtesan but who rebelliously opts for love and marriage, was released nine years before the Academy Award-winning Hollywood musical version. While the title character chooses a traditional lifestyle, the point is that it is her option; she is active rather than passive as she goes against the teachings of her aunt and, in the process, reforms the playboy whom she weds. *Minne, l'Ingenue libertine* tells of a disaffected married woman who distances herself sexually from her husband and drifts into a pair of extramarital relationships as she searches for love. Because of its theme, and the depiction of its heroine, *Minne, l'Ingenue libertine* became the initial film to earn an "X" certificate in Great Britain. In a *New York Times* review, it was noted that the film "has been somewhat abridged, for reasons of moral discretion, from its original length." Finally, *Mitsou* chronicles the predicament of a young, uncultivated chorus girl who seeks the help of an older and more experienced paramour in order to improve herself. Here, too, the female character does not remain submissive but chooses to take action to alter her life.

Easily Audry's most notorious—and, arguably, best-known—film is *Olivia*, a landmark of lesbian cinema if only because it was produced during an era in which even hints of same-sex relationships were practically absent from the screen. *Olivia* (which was retitled *Pit of Loneliness* for its American release) is set in the late 19th century, and is based on an autobiographical novel by Lytton Strachey's sister, Dorothy Bussy (which originally was published under a pseudonym). It is thematically reminiscent of *Mädchen in Uniform* in that it depicts the stirrings of a romantic relationship that develops between the title character, a new student at an all-girls' boarding school, and one of her headmistresses. Not surprisingly, the film was heavily censored; 11 minutes were snipped from it prior to its release in England. Another important Audry credit is her version of *No Exit*, based on Jean-Paul Sartre's existential play about three individuals who have died, and who find themselves trapped in a hotel room where they are fated to remain together for eternity.

Additional Audry heroines include a blond gypsy who has become a celebrated dancer (in *La Caraque blonde*); a young woman who exerts her independence upon discovering her fiancé is cheating on her (*La Garçonne*); a flirt who becomes celebrated throughout Paris after having an affair with a pianist (*L'École des cocottes*); and a young hitchhiker who attracts many men while traveling from Belgium to the Riviera (*Les Petits matins*). The characters in each are placed in romantic or sexual situations. They may evolve in a Pygmalion-like manner, fall in love and are cheated on, have many sexual liaisons, or choose to forgo sex altogether until they find love. But again, their ultimate courses of action are theirs. And in her latter films Audry expanded her gallery of women, depicting them as revolutionaries (*Fruits amers*) and as being forced to pose as boys to win inheritances (*Le Secret du Chevalier d'Éon*).

As with so many other proficient but lesser-known film makers of both sexes, little has been written about Audry in the standard film references. Most certainly, her career is ripe for a further, deeper analysis.

—Rob Edelman

B, Beth
American director

Born: New York, 14 April 1955. **Education:** Attended San Diego State University and the University of California, Irvine; graduated from the School of Visual Arts. **Family:** Married the filmmaker Scott B (divorced). **Career:** Late 1970s-early 1980s—with her then-husband, Scott B, emerged as a prominent figure in the New York independent/underground/No-Wave film scene; 1980—co-directed (with Scott B) her first feature, *The Offenders*; 1984-86—directed the music videos *Dominatrix, Joan Jett: I Need Someone,* and *Taka Boom*; 1987—directed her first feature on her own, *Salvation!*; 1980s-90s—created multimedia environments, art exhibits/installations and photographic series, which have been exhibited around the world; 1995—a retrospective of her work presented at New York's Anthology Film Archive. **Awards:** New York Film Festival Award, for *Vortex*, 1983. **Address:** B Movies Inc., 45 Crosby Street, New York, NY 10012, U.S.A.

Films as Director

1978   *G-Man* (co-d with Scott B—short); *Black Box* (co-d with Scott B—short)
1979   *Letters to Dad* (co-d with Scott B—short)
1980   *The Offenders* (co-d with Scott B, + co-sc, co-ph, co-music)
1981   *The Trap Door* (co-d with Scott B, + co-sc, co-pr, co-ph, co-music)
1983   *Vortex* (co-d with Scott B, + co-sc, co-ed, co-music)
1987   *Salvation!* (*Salvation! Have You Said Your Prayers Today?*; *Benefactors*) (+ co-sc, co-pr, music)
1989   *Belladonna* (co-d with Applebroog—short) (+ ro)
1991   *Thanatopsis* (short); *Stigmata* (short); *Shut Up and Suffer* (short)
1992   *Amnesia* (short)
1993   *Two Small Bodies* (+ sc, co-pr); *Under Lock and Key* (short)
1994   *High Heel Nights* (short)
1995   *Out of Sight/Out of Mind* (short)
1996   *Visiting Desire* (doc) (+ ph, pr, sound)

Publications by Beth B

Articles

"An Interview with Beth and Scott B," interview with Gina Marchetti and Keith Tishkin, in *Millennium* (New York), Fall/Winter, 1981-82.

"*Vortex*: An Interview with Beth and Scott B," interview with S. MacDonald, in *Framework* (Norwich, England), no. 20, 1983.

"Interview with Beth and Scott B," interview with S. MacDonald, in *October* (Cambridge, Massachusetts), Spring 1983.

Publications on Beth B

Book

Foster, Gwendolyn Audrey, *Women Film Directors: An International Bio-Critical Dictionary,* Westport, Connecticut, 1995.

Articles

Hoberman, J., "Voice Arts: No Wavelength: The Para-Punk Underground," in *Village Voice* (New York), 21 May 1979.
MacDonald, S., "8mm/super-8: Some Thoughts on Six Filmmakers," in *Cinemanews* (Larkspur, California), no. 2, 1981.
Sterritt, David, "New B Movies," in *Christian Science Monitor* (Boston), 5 November 1981.
Reynaud, Bérénice, "Petit dictionnaire du cinéma independent new-yorkais," in *Cahiers du Cinéma* (Paris), September 1982.
Gallagher, J., "Close-ups: Scott B and Beth B," in *Millimeter* (New York), May 1983.
Rickey, Carrie, "Where the Girls Are," in *American Film* (Washington, D.C.), January/February 1984.
Schaefer, S., "The Right and Mr. Right," in *Film Comment* (New York), December 1986.
Field, S., "The State of Things," in *Monthly Film Bulletin* (London), January 1987.
Field, S., "*The Offenders*: Beth B and Scott B," in *Monthly Film Bulletin* (London), July 1987.
Heartney, Eleanor, "Ida Applebroog and Beth B at Feldman," in *Art in America* (New York), January 1990.
Reynaud, Bérénice, "German Co-Production: A Mixed Blessing for Sara Driver and Beth B," in *Independent Film and Video Monthly* (New York), December 1993.
Biskind, Peter, "Killer B," in *Premiere* (New York), January 1994.
Skov, B., and L. Ingemann, "New York New York," in *Kosmorama* (Copenhagen), Spring 1994.
Williams, D. E., "Not So Small," in *Film Threat* (Beverly Hills), June 1994.
Taubin, Amy, "Beth B—A Retrospective," in *Village Voice* (New York), 28 November 1995.
Hess, Elizabeth, "Major Medical," in *Village Voice* (New York), 19 December 1995.
Heartney, Eleanor, "Beth B at P.P.O.W. and The Crosby Street Project," in *Art in America* (New York), February 1996.
"Art Short List," in *Village Voice* (New York), 25 February 1997.
Frankel, David, "Beth B," in *Artforum* (New York), March 1996.
"Art Short List," in *Village Voice* (New York), 25 February 1997.

*   *   *

During the late 1970s early 1980s, Beth and Scott B were among the most significant proponents of the No-Wave, no-budget style of underground punk filmmaking. Working out of New York's East Village in conjunction with performance artists and musicians and in the Super-8mm format, they created a series of noisy, scruffy, deeply personal short films in which they combine violent themes and darkly sinister images to explore the manner in which the individual is constrained by society.

These films are at once contemplative and confrontational, penetrating and politically loaded. In *G-Man,* Beth and Scott B attack society's power structures as they depict a cop who feels compelled to employ a dominatrix. In *Letters to Dad,* various people read letters to the camera (and the viewer, who takes on the role of "dad"). At the finale, it is disclosed that the letters were written by followers of notorious cult leader Jim Jones immediately prior to their mass suicide. The result is that the viewer has unknowingly assumed the part of Jones. *Black Box* is the name of a torture contraption that was devised in the United States and utilized in foreign nations. In the film, a man is imprisoned in one such box, where he is tortured—and the viewer endures his suffering.

The brief length of these films allows them to effectively assault the viewer in a hit-and-run, belt-in-the-gut manner. But when Beth and Scott B ventured into the realm of feature-length filmmaking, they were unable to attain a similar effect. *The Offenders,* also shot in Super-8mm, is a poorly photographed, acted, and directed punk melodrama about a kidnapping; it originally was presented as a serial that was screened at New York's Max's Kansas City. *The Trap Door,* their final Super-8mm production, is the muddled account of the plight of an unemployed and directionless man. *Vortex,* shot in 16mm, is a monotonous, film noirish drama featuring frequent Beth B collaborator Lydia Lunch as a detective who becomes immersed in corporate chicanery and the exploitation of politicians by companies soliciting defense contracts.

After *Vortex,* Beth and Scott B ended their partnership. The feature films Beth B has since made on her own are ambitious in content. Her most consistent themes, which are extensions of her earlier work, are sexual repression and violence, the boundaries of sexual desire, and the manner in which authority figures act out their own neuroses while trying to control others. Unfortunately, these films have too often fallen short in execution. *Salvation!* is her first major solo credit, a black comedy about a hypocritical television evangelist who preaches hellfire-and-brimstone sermons while becoming involved in a sex scandal. Despite some genuinely funny moments, this potentially explosive material mostly is squandered. The film has the look of a music video, which disrupts the narrative flow, and the characters are cliched and underdeveloped. *Visiting Desire* is a structural throwback to her earliest work. Its premise is intriguing: Strangers come together to act out their sexual fantasies in the presence of each other, and the camera. The encounters are titled Aggression, Innocence, Trust, Loss of Innocence, Control, Vulnerability.... Unfortunately, the result is boring and pretentious.

Two Small Bodies may be linked to *Visiting Desire* as an exploration of eroticism and fantasy. And it is Beth B's most effective feature to date, a bizarre but compelling two-character psychodrama in which a distrustful cop investigates the disappearance of the two children of a divorcee who works as a cocktail waitress in a strip joint, and who appears to be curiously unmoved by her predicament. The cop is at once attracted to and disturbed by the woman's unconventional behavior. Meanwhile, she psychologically toys with him, resulting in a sexual power struggle which is fascinating yet depressing, given that both characters are thoroughly wretched individuals.

Easily Beth B's best later works are her short films. *Thanatopsis,* performed and written by Lydia Lunch, is a pointed meditation on the absurdity and inevitability of war in a male-dominated society. *Stigmata* poignantly charts the disturbing stories of six drug addicts. Especially noteworthy is *Belladonna,* co-directed by Beth B and her mother, installation artist/painter Ida Applebroog, which was screened as part of one of Applebroog's exhibitions. It consists of rapidly intercut close-ups of talking heads reading statements from a Sigmund Freud case history; affidavits attesting to the atrocities of Dr. Josef Mengele, the Nazi war criminal; and journals from the trial of New Yorker Joel Steinberg, accused of killing his adopted daughter. "What emerges here," wrote Eleanor Heartney, reviewing the film in *Art in America,* "is a picture of a chain of abuse in which victims become victimizers and disturbed individuals hold together their fragile egos by compartmentalizing their darker urges even as they act upon them.... This film offers a degree of understanding, but no comfort. Violence breeds violence, the child who suffers becomes the adult who inflicts suffering. Human cruelty here is a closed circuit which feeds off its own energy."

Early in her career, Beth B's films were purposefully noncommercial. They were meant to be screened in lofts, clubs, and alternative spaces, rather than cinemas. Indeed, they might be described as anti-cinema and, like the punk rock movement which they parallel, they are nihilistic. Ironically, her more recent features, while maintaining their individual edges, are more commercially structured. "No matter how modest the distribution deal, a theatrical release is why I continue to make films," she wrote in a "filmmaker diary" at the 1996 Independent Feature Film Market, which she attended to pitch a new project, titled *The Naked Bride.*

—Rob Edelman

THE BALLAD OF LITTLE JO
USA, 1993
Director: Maggie Greenwald

Production: PolyGram Filmed Entertainment, a Joco production; 35mm, Technicolor, Panavision, Dolby sound; 121 minutes; 10,902 feet; filmed in Red Lodge and Carson County, Montana.

Producers: Fred Berner and Brenda Goodman; **executive producers:** Ira Deutchman and John Sloss; **associate producer:** Anne Dillon; **production coordinator:** Livia Perez-Borrero; **production manager:** Alysse Bezahler; **screenplay:** Maggie Greenwald; **assistant directors:** Lisa Zimble, Cas Donovan, and Amy Schmidt; **photography:** Declan Quinn; **second unit director of photography:** Mitchell Amundsen; **editor:** Keith Reamer; **supervising sound editor:** Wendy Hedin; **sound editor:** Stuart Emmanuel; **sound mixer:** Felipe Borrero; **re-recording mixer:** Rick Dior; **special effects:** J. C. Brotherhood; **production designer:** Mark Friedberg; **set decorator:** Stephanie Carroll; **art director:** Ginger Tougas; **music:** David Mansfield, song "Ballad for Little Jo" written by David Mansfield, sung by Nan O'Byrne; **music editor:** James Flatto; **costume designer:** Claudia Brown; **makeup:** Lori Hicks; **stunt coordinators:** Buddy Joe Hooker and Jeffrey Dashnaw; **choreography/movement coach:** Joann Fregalette Jansen.

Cast: Suzy Amis (*Little Jo Monaghan*); Bo Hopkins (*Frank Badger*); Ian McKellen (*Percy Corcoran*); David Chung (*Tinman Wong*); Heather Graham (*Mary Addie*); René Auberjonois (*Streight Hollander*); Carrie Snodgress (*Ruth Badger*); Anthony Heald (*Henry Grey*); Melissa Leo (*Mrs. Grey*); Sam Robards (*Jasper Hill*); Olinda Turturro (*Elvira*); Ruth Maleczech (*Shopkeeper*); Tom Bower (*Lyle*); Jeffrey Andrews (*Sam*); Cathy Haase (*Mrs. Addie*); Peadair S. Addie Sr. (*Mr. Addie*); Irina Pasmur (*Russian Mother*); Michael Ruud (*Russian Father*); Sasha Pasmur (*Nick at 14*); David Ruben Plowman (*Nick at 9*); Rusty Pegar (*Duke Billy*); Troy A. Smith (*Soldier #1*); Keith Kamppinen (*Soldier #2*); Jenny Lynch (*Helen Monaghan*); Vince O'Neil (*Amos Monaghan*); Dennis McNiven (*Mortician*); Barbara Jean Marsh (*Laundress*); Robert Erickson (*Wilkins*); Sean Murphy (*Young Henry Grey*); Renee Tafoya (*Photographer*); Richard Osterman (*Traveling Judge*); Karen Johnson (*Farm Wife*); Jaime Crabtree (*Jo's Baby*); Tracy Mayfield (*John*); Julianne Kirst (*Nora Monaghan*); Deborah J. Richard (*Mabel*); Netha Goodrich (*Lucy*); Becca Busch (*Little Sue*); Jim Dunkin (*Mr. Brown*); Homer Simon (*Fiddler*); Eryn L. Bent (*Russian Girl*); Peter Plowman (*Russian Boy—Young*); Joe Freed (*Russian Boy—Older*); Anne Plowman (*Russian Girl—Young*); Melissa Ladvala (*Russian Girl—Older*); Yeugeuiy Yasyriu (*Russian Father*); Duane Ebel (*Nick at 40*).

Publications

Articles

Backstein, Karen, "*The Ballad of Little Jo,*" in *Cineaste* (New York), Spring 1993.

Lee, Linda, "When Men Were Men (and So Were Women)," in *New York Times,* 15 August 1993.

Travers, Peter, "*The Ballad of Little Jo,*" in *Rolling Stone* (New York), 19 August 1993.

Levy, Emanuel, "*The Ballad of Little Jo,*" in *Variety* (New York), 30 August 1993.

Bellafante, Ginia, "Little Sex Change on the Prairie," in *Time* (New York), 30 August 1993.

Baldassarre, Angela, "Frontier Women. Maggie Greenwald Puts the Boots to the Old West," in *eye WEEKLY* (Toronto), 14 October 1993.

Rich, B. Ruby, "At Home on the Range," in *Sight and Sound* (London), November 1993.

Monk, Claire, "*The Ballad of Little Jo,*" in *Sight and Sound* (London), April 1994.

Greenwald, Maggie, "Cowgirls," in *Sight and Sound* (London), October 1994.

Deloria, Philip J., "*The Ballad of Little Jo,*" in *American Historical Review* (Washington, D.C.), October 1995.

Modleski, Tania, "Our Heroes Have Sometimes Been Cowgirls: An Interview with Maggie Greenwald," in *Film Quarterly* (Berkeley), Winter 1995.

Chen, Chiung Hwang, "Feminization of Asian (American) Men in the U.S. Mass Media: An Analysis of *The Ballad of Little Jo,*" in *Journal of Communication Inquiry* (Iowa City, Iowa), Fall 1996.

Modleski, Tania, "A Woman's Gotta Do...What A Man's Gotta Do? Cross-Dressing in the Western," in *Signs* (Chicago), Spring 1997.

* * *

The Ballad of Little Jo's title character is a woman passing as a man, and its director a woman working with traditionally male forms. Maggie Greenwald's third feature solidified her reputation as a leading feminist in 1990s American independent film. Greenwald, like contemporary male independents, takes not only financing and distribution from mainstream Hollywood but also plots and iconography. Greenwald herself notes, however, that her revisions of established Hollywood forms are distinguished by her belief that male-dominated productions tell women's (and men's) stories in voices alien to women. Greenwald works from an explicit desire to fill the resultant blanks, by fathoming Hollywood genres strongly associated with male authors and audiences for what she perceives as feminine undercurrents, and by claiming a novelly central place for female characters.

Ballad begins with a woman (Suzy Amis), well-dressed in late 1800s style, incongruously walking a dirt road. A peddler offers her a ride, and she repays him by persuading a wavering female customer to buy. He gives her a commission—the first money she says she has ever made—but that night, while she is reading aloud a passage from *The Scarlet Letter* (unattributed), up ride two soldiers to whom he has sold her. Already the film has established three of its major themes: human two-facedness and its dangers, female economic initiative and its benefits, and the sexual double standard and its injustices.

Greenwald's style of storytelling is also already clear: each moment is self-contained and understated but loaded. Greenwald discussed with the feminist theorist Tania Modleski how Jo's situation mirrors that of a female viewer working to fit herself into the shoes of a traditional, male Western hero. Greenwald's elliptical, laconic style asks viewers to piece together much about the story, and the characters' conceivable feelings, for themselves.

Thus only the briefest flashbacks show the heroine's wealthy East Coast parents disowning her after her premarital motherhood; she has left her son with her married sister. Now escaping the soldiers, she decides on the spur of the moment to outfit herself as a man. Josephine becomes Little Jo, and proceeds to a mining camp where the men haze her by calling her a (male) homosexual. Taking her for an adolescent boy, Percy, a wifeless local, befriends Jo, but when Percy disfigures a female prostitute for refusing him oral sex, Jo leaves town for the winter to work as a shepherd. Over the years—superimposed titles marking their passing—Jo earns enough to build her own homestead, where she eventually takes as servant and then secret mate a Chinese man, whom she has rescued when her friend and former boss Frank Badger is about to lynch him. Her lover, Tinman, falls sick. Rapacious Eastern cattlemen come to the area and kill a neighbor family. Jo's heartbreak prompts her to agree to sell them her land, a decision that she rescinds only after she meets the cattle king's family, just when Tinman rises from his sickbed. In a shoot-out, Frank kills one cattleman and Jo two. A final segment reveals Jo dying alone, her womanhood only revealed to the town postmortem.

There are several features in *Ballad* that seem particularly to emphasize Greenwald's intention to infuse traditional Western images and actions with femaleness. One extended shot of the underbelly of Jo's horse emphasizes that it is a mare. Philosophically speaking, violence is not easy for Jo, whether against animals or men (several reviewers deplore her becoming a "man killer," not a human-killer). After she has shot a cattleman off his horse, in a long shot that is exciting in a traditional action-adventure way, the camera moves from behind her to the side of her face, revealing the tear that runs down her cheek.

The Ballad of Little Jo

The scope of the film's social concerns is huge. In her writing about *Ballad,* Modleski extensively traces out the crossroads of gender, sexuality, race, and class at which the film stands. *Ballad* suggests that its hero's outsider status, combined with her "female" capacity to express and maybe feel emotions more strongly than men do, allows her to stand as the champion for all conceivable outsiders. Some critics have argued that Jo the white, straight woman simply takes over as hero from her male counterpart, still leaving people of color and homosexuals of both genders with no voice except through her.

One of the film's most subtle revisions concerns its elaboration of some novel, female-specific reasons for Jo's decision to stand against the cattlemen. When the cattle baron Grey rides up to Jo's homestead with his young son, Mrs. Grey is the embodiment of the rich, Eastern wife and mother whom Jo could have been. The film might oppose the two women starkly. Speaking to Jo, however, Mrs. Grey runs her fingers over her left cheek. This is the same cheek that Jo has scarred in order to complete her male disguise, a point made clear in the boy's immediate question to Jo about the scar. Though Mrs. Grey scolds the child, her gesture has linked her body to Jo's, and her perceptions to her son's. The three share a complicated kind of identification typical of that between many of *Ballad*'s characters, an interconnection built of both sympathy and rage, unity and distance.

After Jo goes inside with Grey, her sudden refusal to sign his contract coincides with a number of shots from Jo's point of view: one of Tinman

reemerging from his sick room, but also several of Mrs. Grey and the boy. Greenwald shoots them through a window whose glass is rough. It is as if the realistic materials out of which Greenwald builds her West serve here to materialize Jo's lingering vision of the son and the conventional womanhood she left behind, blurry as it may be. Rejecting Grey, Jo asks him if his wife knows how many people he has had killed. It seems that Jo, in part, is striking a blow for the future of women like Mrs. Grey and boys like both their sons, by causing at least some trouble for predatory patriarchal and capitalist power. The film's hope for a female-influenced future comes out further in the final shots of the town: as Frank rolls in with Jo's body, "respectable" women in twos and threes walk down the street. For all of its highly politicized innovations within Western traditions, perhaps *Ballad*'s biggest message is that more films with its impulses are crying to be made.

—Susan Knobloch

BANI-ETEMAD, Rakhshan
Iranian director

Born: Tehran, 1954. **Education:** Attended Tehran's College of Dramatic Arts, 1975–79, graduating with a degree in film directing.

Family: Married (second) to the film producer Jahan gir Kousari, 1983; son: Tandis Ghahremani, and daughter: Baran. **Career:** 1979-83—"script girl" and reporter for National Iranian Radio and Television (NIRT); 1980—assistant director on Mehdi Sabaghzadeh's *Aftab Nechinha*; 1983-87—directed four documentaries for NIRT; 1988—directed her first feature, *Off the Limits,* a comedy that became a box-office hit. **Awards:** Crystal Simorgh for Best Director, Fajr International Film Festival, Tehran, and Best Film of the Year, Iranian Film Critics, for *Nargess,* 1992; Crystal Simorgh for Best Script, Fajr International Film Festival, Tehran, Bronze Leopard, Locarno International Film Festival, and Silver Award, Iranian Society of Filmmakers, for *The Blue-Veiled,* 1995. **Agent:** Farabi Cinema Foundation, 55 Sie-Tir Avenue, IR Tehran 11358, Iran.

Films as Director

1984 *Farahang-e-Massraffi* (*Consumer Culture*) (doc—for TV)
1985 *Mohojereen Roustai* (*Employment of the Rural Migrants in Town*) (doc—for TV)
1986 *Ta 'dabir Eghtessadi-y-Janghi* (*Economic Measures at the Time of War*) (doc—for TV)
1987 *Tamarkoze* (*Centralization*) (doc—for TV)
1988 *Kharejaz Mahdoudeh* (*Off the Limits*)
1989 *Zard-e Ghanari* (*Canary Yellow*) (+ co-sc)
1990 *Poul-e Khareji* (*Foreign Currency*)
1992 *Nargess* (+ co-sc)
1992-94 *Report of 1993* (doc, video); *Spring to Spring* (doc, video); *To Whom Are You Showing These Films?* (doc, video)
1995 *Rusariye Abi* (*The Blue-Veiled*) (+ sc)
1996 *The Last Visit to Ms. Iran Daftari* (doc, video)
1997 *Under the Skin of the City* (doc, video)
1998 *The May Lady*

Other Films

1980 *Aftab Nechinha* (Sabaghzadeh) (asst d)
1983 *Golhayeh Davoodi* (Sadr Ameli) (planning manager)
1984 *Tanoureh Deev* (Ayari) (planning manager)
1985 *Tohfehha* (Vahidzadeh) (planning manager)

Publications by Bani-Etemad

Articles

Interview in *Film International,* vol. 2, no. 3.
"Face to Face with Rakhshan Bani-Etemad," interview in *Cinema '96* (Los Angeles), June/July 1996.

Publications on Bani-Etemad

Books

Kuhn, Annette, and Susannah Radstone, editors, *The Women's Companion to International Film,* London, 1990.
Catalogue, 48 Festival internazionale del film Locarno, 1995.
Foster, Gwendolyn Audrey, *Women Film Directors: An International Bio-Critical Dictionary,* Westport, Connecticut, 1995.

Article

Guérin, Marie-Anne, "En Iran les femmes sont amoureuses," in *Cahiers du Cinéma,* October 1995.

* * *

One of the nine women currently working as feature-film directors in Iran, Rakhshan Bani-Etemad has imposed herself both at home and abroad by a rigorous filmic *écriture* and a powerful mise en scène. Having started her career as a documentarist for television, she combines an acute, sometimes ironical, sense of observation with a compassionate gaze and the construction of characters firmly rooted in reality. Even after she started directing features, she never stopped getting involved with documentary issues, and, in the early 1990s, she used video to continue exploring the topics she was interested in while waiting for the green light for her next feature.

Her early documentaries, dealing with peasant migration to the cities, war efforts, or postrevolutionary consumerism, were controversial, but her first feature, *Off the Limits,* a satire of bureaucratic mix-ups, struck an immediate chord with local Iranian audiences. It was followed by two pungent comedies, one, *Canary Yellow,* plunging into darker waters in which economic survival and personal integrity overlap, while *Foreign Currency* takes an affectionate poke at the mores and foibles of the Iranian bourgeoisie. With *Nargess,* her first international success, Bani-Etemad staged two powerful figures of women from the most disenfranchised classes. Before writing the script, she interviewed women jailed for theft and prostitution: "I do not do research to find a story," she says, "but to get closer to people." While bringing her father to the hospital, Nargess, a poor, but sweet and delicate young woman, meets the attractive Adel, unaware that he is in fact hiding from the police after a botched burglary. For Adel, Nargess represents an impossible dream of salvation, and he persuades his "mother," Afagh, to propose marriage. Once abandoned in the streets, Adel was raised as a thief by Afagh who later became his lover. Afagh, a complex, tormented character, accepts the arrangement, and the marriage takes place. Love and ignorance blind Nargess to the abjection her new husband is struggling to escape, till reality catches up. As Adel gradually becomes a pitiful character, Bani-Etemad depicts the relationship between the two women with master strokes. Afagh shows surprising resilience in her passion for Adel, and even the "innocent" Nargess proves a tiger ready to fight for what she believes.

In *The Blue-Veiled,* Bani-Etemad switches the action from the lower depths of Tehran to the countryside. Rashul, a good-natured widower and the wealthy owner of a large tomato plantation, adored by his married daughters, seems content with his lot. Yet, a newly hired young peasant, Nobar, slowly tears apart the shroud of his fake happiness. After resisting their mutual feelings of attraction, Nobar and Rashul eventually start living together "on the sly," until societal pressure, in the guise of Rashul's "well-meaning" but class-conscious daughters, brings trouble in paradise. "In *Nargess* and *The Blue-Veiled,* I show women who don't have childhood, don't have youth, who become older too soon; they don't have anybody to support them, and because they have to stand on their own feet, they bear a lot of hardship," says Bani-Etemad. "I would like for people to pay attention to them, but I also want to show their hidden roles, their hidden loves, and their hidden goals."

Bani-Etemad, who refuses to be considered a "female director," but a director who happens to be a woman, nevertheless takes pride in her portrayal of strong, believable, complex female characters.

Her latest film, *The May Lady,* just released in Iran, shows the plight of a professional woman through a combination of documentary and fiction. As the director herself is the first to admit, under the chador a woman can virtually go anywhere in Iran, even in places where men can not, and bring to the silver screen stories and characters that their male colleagues might have passed by.

—Bérénice Reynaud

BATCHELOR, Joy
British animator

Born: Watford, Hertfordshire, England, 12 May 1914. **Family:** Married the Hungarian animator John Halas in late 1930s, two children. **Career:** 1935—began working in films as artist; 1937—hired as designer and animator to work on *The Music Man*; 1940—with John Halas, co-founder of Halas & Batchelor Cartoon Films; 1940-45—made numerous information and propaganda films for British government; 1951-54—produced only feature-length British cartoon, *Animal Farm,* based on George Orwell novel; 1968—Halas & Batchelor bought by Trident Television; Batchelor and Halas concentrated on individual projects working through their other company, Educational Film Centre; from 1968 to 1972 not responsible for films produced by Halas & Batchelor production company; 1974—Halas & Batchelor sold back to Halas after losing money for corporation; 1973—Batchelor retired but continued to act as adviser to animation students at International Film School, London. **Died:** In London, 14 May 1991.

Films as Co-Director with John Halas

1940   *Train Trouble* (+ co-pr, anim); *Carnival in the Clothes Cupboard* (+ co-pr, co-des, co-anim)
1941   *Filling the Gap* (+ co-pr, co-sc, co-anim); *Dustbin Parade* (+ co-pr, co-sc, co-des, co-anim); *The Pocket Cartoon* (+ co-sc, co-anim) (may not have been released); *The Brave Tin Soldier* (+ co-sc, co-anim) (may not have been released)
1942   *Digging for Victory* (+ co-pr, co-sc, co-anim, des)
1943   *Jungle Warfare* (+ co-pr, co-des, co-anim)
1944   *Cold Comfort* (+ co-pr, co-sc, co-anim); *From Rags to Stitches* (+ co-pr, co-sc, co-anim); *Blitz on Bugs* (+ co-pr, co-sc, co-anim); *Mrs. Sew and Sew* (+ co-pr, co-sc, co-anim); *Christmas Wishes* (+ co-pr, co-sc, co-anim)
1945   *Tommy's Double Trouble* (+ co-pr, co-anim); *Six Little Jungle Boys* (+ co-anim)
1946   *Modern Guide to Health* (+ co-pr, co-des; sc); *Old Wives' Tales* (+ co-pr, co-des; sc); *Road Safety* (+ co-pr, co-anim); *Britain Must Export* (+ co-pr, co-anim); *Export or Die* (+ co-pr, co-anim); *Export! Export! Export!* (+ co-pr, co-anim); *The Keys of Heaven* (+ co-pr, co-anim); *Good King Wenceslas* (+ co-pr, co-anim)
1947   *First Line of Defence* (+ co-pr, co-sc); *This Is the Air Force* (+ co-pr, co-sc); *What's Cooking?* (+ co-pr, co-des, sc); *Dolly Put the Kettle On* (+ co-pr, co-des, sc)
1948   *Oxo Parade* (+ co-pr, co-des, sc); *Heave Away My Johnny* (+ co-pr, co-sc)

1949   *The Shoemaker and the Hatter* (+ co-pr, co-sc, co-des); *Submarine Control* (co-d with Privett and Crick); *Fly about the House* (+ co-pr, co-des, sc); *A Well Kept Machine* (+ co-pr); *A Little Forethought* (+ co-pr); *A Better Spirit* (+ co-pr); *Start with What Is under Your Nose* (+ co-pr)
1950   *The British Army at Your Service* (+ co-pr)
1951   *The Flu-ing Squad* (+ co-pr)
1952   *Linear Accelerator*
1953   *The Figurehead*
1954   *Animal Farm* (feature, begun 1951) (+ co-pr, co-sc, co-des)
1956   *The Candlemaker* (+ co-sc)
1958   *Dam the Delta* (+ sc)
1959   *All Lit Up* (+ co-pr, sc); *Piping Hot* (+ co-pr, sc); *For Better for Worse* (+ co-pr, sc)
1973   *Contact* (+ co-sc)

Abu Series—

1943-44   *Abu's Dungeon*; *Abu's Poisoned Well*; *Abu's Harvest*; *Abu Builds a Dam* (+ co-pr, co-anim)

Charley Series—

1946-49   *Charley in the New Towns*; *Charley in the New Schools*; *Charley in "Your Very Good Health"*; *Charley in the New Mines*; *Charley Junior's Schooldays*; *Charley's March of Time* (+ co-pr, co-sc, co-des); *Robinson Charley* (+ co-pr, co-des); *Farmer Charley* (+ co-pr, co-sc); *Charley's Black Magic* (+ co-pr, co-sc)

Other Films

1938   *The Music Man* (Halas) (co-anim)
1944-45   *Handling Ships* (Halas and Privett—feature) (co-pr)
1948   *Magic Canvas* (Halas) (co-pr); *Water for Firefighting* (feature) (Halas and Crick) (co-pr)
1950   *As Old as the Hills* (Privett) (co-pr); *Fowl Play* (Dyer and Kirley) (co-pr)
1951   *Moving Spirit* (co-d: Halas) (co-sc)
1952   *We've Come a Long Way* (co-sc); *Service: Garage Handling* (Crick and Privett) (co-pr, co-sc); *The Owl and the Pussycat* (Halas and Borthwick) (co-pr)
1953   *Power to Fly* (co-sc); *The Figurehead* (Crick) (co-pr); *Coastal Navigation and Pilotage* (Dahl) (co-pr)
1954   *Down a Long Way* (Privett) (co-sc)
1955   *Animal Vegetable Mineral* (co-sc); *The World That Nature Forgot* (co-pr); *Basic Fleetwork* (co-pr); *Refinery at Work* (co-pr)
1956   *To Your Health* (co-sc); *The World of Little Ig* (Halas) (sc, co-pr); *Think of the Future* (co-pr); *Invisible Exchange* (co-pr)
1957   *Midsummer Nightmare* (Halas) (co-pr, co-sc); *Queen of Hearts* (co-anim); *History of the Cinema* (Halas) (co-pr)
1958   *Speed the Plough* (Privett) (co-sc); *The First Ninety-Nine* (d, co-pr, co-sc); *The Christmas Visitor* (co-pr, co-sc); *Best Seller* (Potterton) (co-pr, co-sc)
1959   *How to Be a Hostess* (live action) (sc); *Energy Picture* (sc, co-pr)
1960   *The Wonder of Wool* (Halas) (co-pr)

1961   *The Monster of Highgate Pond* (sc); *Hamilton the Musical Elephant* (Halas) (co-pr); *Hamilton in the Musical Festival* (Halas) (co-pr)

1962   *Barnaby—Father Dear Father* (Halas) (co-pr); *Barnaby—Overdue Dues Blues* (Halas) (co-pr)

1963   *Automania 2000* (Halas) (co-pr, co-sc); *Pulmonary Function* (Halas) (co-pr)

1964   *Paying Bay* (co-sc, co-pr); *Follow that Car* (co-sc, co-pr); *Ruddigore* (feature) (d, co-pr, sc)

1966   *Dying for a Smoke* (Halas) (co-sc)

1967   *The Colombo Plan* (d, co-pr, sc); *The Commonwealth* (d, co-pr, sc)

1968   *Bolly* (d, co-pr, sc)

1970   *Short Tall Story* (Halas) (co-pr); *The Five* (d, co-pr, sc); *Wot Dot* (d, co-pr, sc); *Flurina* (Halas) (co-pr); *Sputum* (Borthwick) (pr); *This Love Thing* (Dunbar) (co-pr)

1971   *Children and Cars* (Halas) (co-pr, co-sc)

1973   *Children Making Cartoons* (P. Halas) (co-pr, co-sc)

1974   *The Ass and the Stick* (d, co-sc); *Christmas Feast* (Halas) (co-sc); *Carry on Milkmaids* (d, sc)

1977   *How the Motor Car Works: The Carburettor* (Seager) (co-anim)

1979   "No. 10" ep. of *Ten for Survival* (*Together for Children: Principle 10*) (Halas) (sc)

Poet and Painter Series—

1951   Programme 1: *Two Corbies*; *Spring and Winter*; Programme 2: *Winter Garden*; *Sailor's Consolation*; *Check to Song*; Programme 3: *In Time of Pestilence*; *The Pythoness*; Programme 4: *John Gilpin* (Halas) (co-pr)

Foo-Foo Series—

1960   *The Scapegoat*; *The Gardener*; *The Birthday Treat*; *A Denture Adventure*; *A Misguided Tour*; *The Caddies*; *Burglar Catcher*; *The Art Lovers*; *The Three Mountaineers*; *Foo-Foo's New Hat*; *The Big Race*; *The Treasure Hunt*; *The Magician*; *The Spy Train*; *Insured for Life*; *Automation Blues*; *The Beggar's Uproar*; *Sleeping Beauty*; *The Reward*; *The Dinner Date*; *Beauty Treatment*; *The Ski Resort*; *Lucky Street*; *The Stowaway*; *A Hunting We Will Go*; *The Pearl Divers*; *Foo-Foo's Sleepless Night*; *The Salesman*; *Art for Art's Sake*; *The Dog Pound*; *The Hypnotist*; *Low Finance* (co-pr)

Snip and Snap Series—

1960   *Bagpipes*; *Treasure of Ice Cake Island*; *Spring Song*; *Snakes and Ladders*; *In the Jungle*; *Lone World Sail*; *Thin Ice*; *Magic Book*; *Circus Star*; *Moonstruck*; *Snap and the Beanstalk*; *Goodwill to All Dogs*; *In the Cellar*; *The Grand Concert*; *The Beggar's Uproar*; *The Birthday Cake*; *Snap Goes East*; *The Hungry Dog*; *Tog Dogs* (co-d: Halas) (co-pr)

Classic Fairy Tales Series—

1966   6 films (d, sc, co-pr)

Publications by Batchelor (with John Halas)

Articles

"The Film Cartoonist," in *Working for the Films,* London, 1947.

"The Animated Film," in *Art and Industry* (London), July 1947.

"From Script to Screen," in *Art and Industry* (London), August 1947.

"Cartoon Films in Commerce," in *Art and Industry* (London), November 1947.

"The Approach to Cartoon Film Scriptwriting," in *This Film Business,* London, 1948.

"Introducing Hamilton...and Some of the People Who Gave Him Birth," in *Films and Filming* (London), June 1962.

"Talking with Halas and Batchelor," in *1000 Eyes* (New York), February 1976.

"The Way Forward," in *Film* (London), March 1979.

Plateau, vol. 5, no. 3, 1984.

Animatrix, no. 1, December 1984.

Animatrix, no. 2, November 1985.

Publications on Batchelor

Books

Manvell, Roger, *Art and Animation,* London, 1980.

Foster, Gwendolyn Audrey, *Women Film Directors: An International Bio-Critical Dictionary,* Westport, Connecticut, 1995.

Articles

"Halas and Batchelor: Profile of a Partnership," in *Film* (London), March 1955.

"Halas and Batchelor," in *International Film Guide,* London, 1965.

"Halas and Batchelor," in *Film* (London), Spring 1966.

Cineforum (Bergamo, Italy), December 1983.

Plateau, vol. 5, no. 2, 1984.

New Orleans Review, vol. 18, no. 4, 1991.

Obituary, in *Times* (London), 16 May 1991.

Obituary, in *Variety* (New York), 27 May 1991.

Obituary in *Animator,* October 1991.

*   *   *

Joy Batchelor is one of the rare pioneer female animators, working in a discipline historically dominated by men. She began her career as a commercial artist and, in the late 1930s, met Hungarian-born animator John Halas, whom she was to join in a full professional partnership. Batchelor and Halas, who later were married, maintained control of their work by establishing, in 1940, their own production company, Halas & Batchelor Cartoon Films. Over the next five decades it was to become one of the most active animation houses in Europe, with Batchelor and Halas producing an extraordinary array of films: informational and propaganda pieces for the British government; scientific, educational, industrial, and promotional films; television entertainment programs and commercials; animated short subjects on more artistic topics; and, most significantly, a version of George Orwell's *Animal Farm,* the first-ever British feature-length animated film. Their studio even became a haven in which other animators from Europe and America could work and thrive.

The first film Batchelor and Halas made at their studio was *Train Trouble,* a celluloid commercial for Kellogg's Cornflakes. During World War II, they produced more than 70 original and cleverly animated government films: how-to instructionals, which were meant to educate the public on ways to help contribute to victory against the Axis, and more technical-oriented training films. One of the latter, *Handling Ships,* an instructional film financed by the British Admiralty, was the first-ever British cartoon in Technicolor.

After the war, Batchelor and Halas turned to more aesthetic subjects. Working in collaboration with Henry Moore, Ronald Searle, and others, they created a *Poet and Painter* series of animated shorts. They worked experimentally with stereoscopy, the prototypical three-projection form of Cinerama, and sophisticated forms of film puppetry. They created the initial animated version of a Gilbert and Sullivan operetta, *Ruddigore,* and won an Academy Award nomination for *Automania 2000,* an animated vision of a future dominated by cars. Among their more commercial projects were the *Foo-Foo* and *Snip and Snap* cartoon series, produced for television, with the latter introducing paper-sculpture animals.

Batchelor and Halas's best-known work is *Animal Farm,* released in 1954 after three years in production. The film is of further note for its portrayal of animated animal characters who are seriously dramatic, rather than the sweet and lovable inhabitants of escapist children's fantasies. In Batchelor's *Variety* obituary, it was noted that *Animal Farm* was the film that "put Britain on the world animation map."

The scenario follows what happens when a group of animals assume operation of a farm upon successfully revolting against their brutal overseer. It is a sobering and distinctly political allegory, with a point of view that those who lead democratic uprisings against oppressors may become just as despotic once they gain power. Batchelor and Halas chose to caricature the heavies of the story—most especially the pigs who lead the revolt—while realistically representing the other animals.

In a bow to commercial considerations, Batchelor and Halas altered and brightened the story's original ending, going against Orwell's pessimistic view regarding the future of democratic movements. Nonetheless, their *Animal Farm* does put forth a jarringly unsentimental world view, one that differs markedly not just from other animated features but from most other 1950s' cinematic fare. This is most fully illustrated by the fate of Boxer, a courageous horse who ends up not emerging triumphant but being carted off to the glue factory.

In no way was Joy Batchelor the passive partner in her relationship with John Halas. She is most deserving of her place, alongside her husband and the likes of J. Stuart Blackton, Winsor McCay, Emile Cohl, Chuck Jones, Ub Iwerks, Dave and Max Fleischer, Walt Disney, and all the rest, as an innovative and influential animator.

—Rob Edelman

BAUCHENS, Anne
American editor

Born: St. Louis, Missouri, 2 February 1882 (some sources say 1881). **Education:** Studied drama with actor-director Hugh Ford; later studied dancing and gymnastics. **Career:** Worked as a tele-phone operator at the *St. Louis Post-Dispatch*; moved to New York City with the intention of becoming a Broadway actress; worked as a secretary in a real-estate company; 1912—hired as a secretary to William C. de Mille; 1915—accompanied de Mille to Hollywood; 1918—worked as an assistant and script supervisor to Cecil B. DeMille and began editing DeMille-directed films; 1934—first of four Academy Award nominations for best film editing, for *Cleopatra*; worked for DeMille until his death, at which point she retired in 1959. **Awards:** Academy Award, Best Film Editing, for *Northwest Mounted Police,* 1940; ACE (Achievement Award of the American Cinema Editors), for *The Greatest Show on Earth,* 1952. **Died:** In Woodland Hills, California, 7 May 1967.

Films as Editor

1918   *We Can't Have Everything* (C. B. DeMille) (co-d); *Till I Come Back to You* (C. B. DeMille); *The Squaw Man* (C. B. DeMille)

1919   *Male and Female* (C. B. DeMille); *For Better, for Worse* (C. B. DeMille); *Don't Change Your Husband* (C. B. DeMille)

1920   *Why Change Your Wife?* (C. B. DeMille); *Something to Think About* (C. B. DeMille)

1921   *Forbidden Fruit* (C. B. DeMille); *Fool's Paradise* (C. B. DeMille); *The Affairs of Anatol* (C. B. DeMille)

1922   *Saturday Night* (C. B. DeMille); *Manslaughter* (C. B. DeMille)

1923   *The Ten Commandments* (C. B. DeMille); *Adam's Rib* (C. B. DeMille)

1924   *Triumph* (C. B. DeMille); *Feet of Clay* (C. B. DeMille)

1925   *The Road to Yesterday* (C. B. DeMille); *The Golden Bed* (C. B. DeMille)

1926   *The Volga Boatman* (C. B. DeMille)

1927   *The King of Kings* (C. B. DeMille) (co); *Chicago* (Urson)

1928   *Ned McCobb's Daughter* (Cowan); *Craig's Wife* (W. C. de Mille)

1929   *Noisy Neighbors* (Reisner); *The Godless Girl* (C. B. DeMille); *Dynamite* (C. B. DeMille)

1930   *Lord Byron of Broadway* (Nigh and Beaumont); *This Mad World* (W. C. de Mille) (co); *Madam Satan* (*Madame Satan*) (C. B. DeMille)

1931   *The Squaw Man* (*The White Man*) (C. B. DeMille); *Guilty Hands* (Van Dyke); *The Great Meadow* (Brabin) (co)

1932   *The Sign of the Cross* (C. B. DeMille); *The Beast of the City* (*City Sentinel*) (Brabin); *The Wet Parade* (Fleming)

1933   *Tonight Is Ours* (Walker); *Cradle Song* (Leisen); *This Day and Age* (C. B. DeMille)

1934   *Four Frightened People* (C. B. DeMille); *Cleopatra* (C. B. DeMille); *Menace* (Murphy); *Mrs. Wiggs of the Cabbage Patch* (Taurog); *One Hour Late* (Murphy)

1935   *The Crusades* (C. B. DeMille)

1936   *The Plainsman* (C. B. DeMille)

1937   *This Way Please* (Florey)

1938   *Bulldog Drummond in Africa* (L. King); *Hunted Men* (*Crime Gives Orders*) (L. King); *Sons of the Legion* (Hogan); *The Buccaneer* (C. B. DeMille)

1939   *Television Spy* (Dmytryk); *Union Pacific* (C. B. DeMille)

1940   *Women without Names* (Florey); *Northwest Mounted Police* (C. B. DeMille)

1941   *Land of Liberty*

1942   *Reap the Wild Wind* (C. B. DeMille); *Mrs. Wiggs of the Cabbage Patch* (Murphy)

1943   *The Commandos Strike at Dawn* (Farrow)

1944   *The Story of Dr. Wassell* (C. B. DeMille); *Tomorrow the World* (Fenton)

1945   *Love Letters* (Dieterle)

1947   *Unconquered* (C. B. DeMille)

1949   *Samson and Delilah* (C. B. DeMille)

1952   *The Greatest Show on Earth* (C. B. DeMille)

1956   *The Ten Commandments* (C. B. DeMille)

Publication by Bauchens

Article

"Cutting the Film," essay in *We Make the Movies,* edited by Nancy Naumburg, New York, 1937.

Publications on Bauchens

Articles

Khoury, Phil, "A Very Handy Lady with the Shears," in *New York Times* (New York), 6 April 1947.

Waller, William, "She 'Cuts' Those Super Movies," in *St. Louis Globe-Democrat,* 3 May 1947.

Sammis, Constance Sharp, "Film Editor Indefatigable," in *Christian Science Monitor* (New York), 11 February 1957.

Arthur, Art, "A Tribute to Anne Bauchens," in *Cinema Editors Magazine,* February 1961.

Obituary in *Los Angeles Times,* 9 May 1967.

Obituary in *New York Times,* 9 May 1967.

Sharples, Win Jr., and Elias Savada, "Prime Cut: The Work of the Film Editor," in *Film Comment* (New York), March/April 1977.

* * *

"Some hundreds of millions of people, at least, have seen Anne Bauchens' name on the screen as film editor," wrote Cecil B. DeMille in his autobiography. "It has meant nothing to them—except to the few who know that gracious white-haired lady or who know, as we in the business know, how much a film's success or failure is due to the way it is edited."

While it was fitting for DeMille to cite Bauchens and praise her profession in his book (which was published posthumously in 1959), the fact remains that the status of film editors was considered lowly for decades. It was deemed not so much a profession as a craft—and this was one reason why women were allowed to become editors. The insignificance of editors is reflected by the listings in the section headed "Personnel of Studios—U.S. & Canada," published in the 1928 *Film Daily Year Book.* Cited under the heading Pathé-DeMille Studio are employees from President (Cecil B. DeMille) down through Technical Director (Ted Dickson, Julia Heron), Chief of Props (William House), Chief Electrician (William Whistler), Still Cameraman (Fred Archer) and Paymaster (I. F. Dawson). There is no listing for Editor, and no mention of Bauchens.

Nevertheless, Bauchens (whom DeMille called "Annie B.") is as much a movie industry pioneer as the man who steadily employed her for just under four decades. She had worked as secretary to DeMille's brother William C. de Mille, a director-playwright-screenwriter, before becoming C.B.'s assistant, script supervisor, and finally editor (or cutter, as they were called when she earned her first screen credit). DeMille's decision to train Bauchens resulted in her becoming one of the industry's first script supervisors and female editors. (Many sources credit Bauchens as the very first female editor; however, Viola Lawrence [also known as Viola Mallory], for one, predated her by two years.) She developed into a solid and strong-willed craftswoman, and a pivotal member of DeMille's moviemaking team. Her various Academy Award nominations, and her Oscar for editing *Northwest Mounted Police,* attest to her editing acumen.

On occasion, Bauchens worked on the films of other directors (including William Dieterle, John Farrow, Victor Fleming, and Mitchell Leisen). But she was almost exclusively employed by DeMille, editing every one of his films from *We Can't Have Everything* in 1918 all the way to his last, 1956's *The Ten Commandments,* made when she was in her mid-seventies. On *The Ten Commandments,* Bauchens was entrusted to retain the story's thrust and dramatic power while editing down to 12,000 feet the 100,000-plus feet of film shot by DeMille.

When a film was in its editing stage, Bauchens was known to work 16-plus hour days. And she was no shrinking violet who would acquiesce without comment to DeMille's demands; she would offer creative input, and even argue with her boss if she felt strongly about her point of view.

Later in his career, whenever DeMille signed a contract to direct a film, he claimed to have insisted on the inclusion of a clause stipulating that Bauchens would be hired as editor. "This is not sentiment, or at least not only sentiment," DeMille explained in his autobiography. "She is still the best film editor I know."

—Rob Edelman and Audrey E. Kupferberg

BEMBERG, María Luisa
Argentinean director and writer

Born: Buenos Aires, 14 April 1922. **Family:** Divorced, four children. **Career:** Established Argentina's Teatro del Globo theater company, 1950s; wrote her first screenplay, *Chronicle of a Woman,* 1971; moved to New York and attended the Strasberg Institute, late 1970s; returned to Argentina and directed her first feature, *Momentos,* 1981. **Died:** 7 May 1995.

Films as Director and Writer

1981   *Momentos (Moments)*

1982   *Señora de Nadie (Nobody's Woman)*

1984   **Camila**

1987   *Miss Mary*

1990   *Yo, la peor de todas (I, the Worst of Them All)*

1993   *De eso no se habla (I Don't Want to Talk about It)* (co-sc)

Films as Writer Only

1971   *Cronica de una Señora (Chronicle of a Woman)* (de la Torre)

1972   *El Mundo de la Mujer* (short)

1975   *Triangulo de Cuatro* (Ayala)

1978   *Juguetes* (short)

Publications by Bemberg

Articles

"María Luisa Bemberg: El rescate de la mujer en el cine Argentino,"
     interview with J. C. Huayhuaca and others, in *Hablemos de Cine*
     (Lima), March 1984.
Interview with K. Jaehne and G. Crowdus, in *Cineaste* (New York),
     vol. 14, no. 3, 1986.
Interview with Sheila Whitaker, in *Monthly Film Bulletin* (London),
     October 1987.
Interview with E. M. Abbe, in *Angles* (Milwaukee), vol. 2, no. 3,
     1994.
"María Luisa Bemberg Tells the World," interview with Caleb Bach,
     in *Americas* (Washington, D.C.), March/April 1994.
"Bemberg's Late-Blooming Career Thrives with Mastroianni Starrer,"
     interview in *Film Journal* (New York), September 1994.

Publications on Bemberg

Books

King, John, and Nissa Torrents, *The Garden of Forking Paths: Ar-
     gentine Cinema,* London, 1988.
Fontana, Clara, *María Luisa Bemberg,* Buenos Aires, 1993.
Foster, Gwendolyn Audrey, *Women Film Directors: An International
     Bio-Critical Dictionary,* Westport, Connecticut, 1995.

Articles

Maeckley, Monika, "Machismo Takes a Knock," in *Guardian* (Lon-
     don), 10 December 1982.
Rich, B. Ruby, "After the Revolutions: The Second Coming of Latin
     American Cinema," in *Village Voice* (New York), 10 February 1987.
Jackson, Lynne, and Karen Jaehne, "Eavesdropping on Female
     Voices: A Who's Who of Contemporary Women Filmmakers," in
     Cineaste (New York), vol. 16, no. 1/2, 1987-88.
Obituary, in *Times* (London), 19 May 1995.
Obituary, in *Time* (New York), 22 May 1995.

* * *

María Luisa Bemberg entered the filmmaking world only after
leading an "asphyxiating and uneventful" life (her own words). Born
into one of the wealthiest families in Buenos Aires, she entered the
film industry at age 46, after her children had grown and she had
obtained a divorce. Despite her belated entry into the profession,
Bemberg was one of the most subversive and popular Argentinean
directors. In addition, she was acclaimed in Europe and the States.

Bemberg's first (semiautobiographical) screenplay, *Chronicle of a
Woman,* gained acclaim as a contemporary domestic drama, focusing on a regressive political system as it affected the female protagonist. Wishing to exert more control over her screenplays, but with no
formal training, she spent three months as an actress at the Lee
Strasberg Institute in New York and returned to Argentina to direct.
In 1982 she caused a stir with *Nobody's Woman,* which featured a
friendship between a gay man and a separated woman, challenging
in one swoop the sacred notions of marriage, family, and the Church.
Released on the day that Argentina invaded the Malvinas (Falklands),
the film's impact was overshadowed somewhat by political events,
but the crumbling state of the military regime (which had exerted so

much censorship and control over the country's film industry that by
the late 1970s only 12 films were being produced per year) ultimately helped the film succeed. Hugely popular with female audiences, it made a powerful and overtly feminist intervention into a
culture crippled by its own repression and machismo.

After the overthrow of the military regime, and the humiliation of
defeat in the Falklands War, Bemberg still saw much to come to
terms with and much to struggle against in her national identity. She
felt that her role as a filmmaker, and as a woman in a fiercely patriarchal society, was to explore political oppression as a backdrop and
context for intense personal conflict. Her films dwell anxiously on
Argentina's troubled past, and suggest that only by coming to terms
with it can the nation—and the individual—put it to rest.

In 1984 Bemberg directed *Camila,* the first Argentinean film ever
to break into the American market. Recipient of an Oscar nomination for best foreign-language film, it is all the more remarkable in that
many other directors who wanted to film this true story of illicit love
between a priest and a young woman in 1847 had previously been
prevented from doing so by the government. By casting the priest as
a beautiful object of desire and Camila (historically portrayed as the
innocent victim) as the temptress, Bemberg created a passionate
melodrama in which she consciously moved away from her earlier,
hard-bitten domestic dramas into a more emotional, lyrical sphere.
The historical basis of *Camila* offers a mythical arena in which to
explore her very real contemporary political concerns.

Miss Mary continues to focus on these concerns, exploring English influence over the Argentinean upper class in the years before
World War II through the crucial figure of the nanny. Politics and
history are expressed through family structures, sexuality, and human behavior. Female characters, even the repressed and unsympa-
thetic nanny (played by Julie Christie), are portrayed with understanding—although Miss Mary is a reactionary agent of oppression,
the film works to explore *why* she is so—in an attempt to study the
forces that could create her and the sick family for which she works.

Bemberg's strong sense of the melancholy is an integral part of
her work, causing an uneasy tension in all her films: while all her
works indict the reactionary political system, they are also impreg-
nated with a tragic sensibility that presents events as somehow out of
the protagonists' control. The bleak endings (in which transgressors
are punished and traditional structures remain apparently intact) of
Bemberg's films might seem pessimistic. But the very expression of
transgression in the films—along with the tentative exploration of
the disruptions that inevitably threaten an apparently monolithic system—by an individual who could so easily be a victim of that system
(female, bourgeois, divorced), is not merely laudable, but remarkable.

Camila and *Miss Mary* remain exceptional films, the former a
passionate and profound examination of a doomed romance and the
latter a sumptuous, evocative account of a repressed woman. If both
films are not overtly autobiographical, they do deal in very personal
ways with Bemberg's own identity as a woman existing in a male-
dominated society. A third, most impressive, feature from Bemberg
is *I, the Worst of Them All,* set in Mexico during the 17th century.
Her heroine is a nun possessed of a deep thirst for knowledge who
becomes a writer. She also is destined to becomes the antagonist of
her country's misogynist archbishop. Bemberg followed that up
with *I Don't Want to Talk about It,* a fitfully interesting drama about
two women—one a dwarf and the other her physically appealing but
obnoxiously controlling mother—who become involved with an aging but still-suave bachelor (impeccably played by Marcello
Mastroianni).

The unfortunate aspect of Bemberg's career is that it began so late in her life, thus robbing her of time to write and direct other films. Still, she was able to transcend the repressive political forces at work in her country and the constraints placed upon her because of her sex. Moreover, her films show her ability to discerningly philosophize about these aspects of existence in her country.

—Samantha Cook/Rob Edelman

BIG
USA, 1988
Director: Penny Marshall

Production: 20th Century-Fox/Gracie Films; DuArt/Deluxe color, 35mm; running time: 104 minutes. Dolby sound. Released June 1988.

Producers: James L. Brooks and Robert Greenhut; **associate producers:** Gary Ross and Anne Spielberg; **screenplay:** Gary Ross and Anne Spielberg; **first assistant director:** Thomas Reilly; **second assistant director:** Ken Ornstein; **photography:** Barry Sonnenfeld; **editor:** Barry Malkin; **sound:** Les Lazarowitz; **production designer:** Santo Loquasto; **set designers:** Susan Bode and George DeTitta Jr.; **art directors:** Speed Hopkins and Tom Warren; **music:** Howard Shore; **costumes:** Judianna Makovsky; **makeup:** Mickey Scott; **title design:** Saul Bass and Elaine Bass.

Cast: Tom Hanks (*Josh*); Elizabeth Perkins (*Susan*); Robert Loggia (*MacMillan*); John Heard (*Paul*); Jared Rushton (*Billy*); David Moscow (*Young Josh*); Jon Lovitz (*Scotty Brennan*); Mercedes Ruehl (*Mrs. Baskin*); Josh Clark (*Mr. Baskin*); Kimberlee M. Davis (*Cynthia Benson*); with: Oliver Block; Erika Katz; Allan Wasserman; Mark Ballou; Gary Howard Klar; Alec von Sommer; Chris Dowden; Rockets Redglare.

Awards: Golden Globe for Best Actor—musical/comedy (Hanks).

Publications

Books

Kael, Pauline, *Hooked,* New York, 1989.
Acker, Ally, *Reel Women: Pioneers of the Cinema, 1896 to the Present,* New York, 1991.

Articles

Kremski, P., "*Big* von Penny Marshall," in *Filmbulletin* (Zurich), vol. 30, no. 5, 1988.
Geller, L., "The Key to Scoring *Big*," in *Premiere* (New York), June 1988.
Yakir, D., in *Film Journal* (New York), June 1988.
Galbraith, J., in *Variety* (New York), 1 June 1988.
Ebert, Roger, in *New York Post,* 3 June 1988.
Gelmis, Joseph, in *Newsday,* 3 June 1988.
Hinson, Hal, in *Washington Post,* 3 June 1988.
Maslin, Janet, in *New York Times,* 3 June 1988.

Thomas, Kevin, in *Los Angeles Times,* 3 June 1988.
Ansen, David, "The Arts: Movies: Man-Child in the Corporate Land," in *Newsweek* (New York), 6 June 1988.
Clarke, G., "Cinema: Little Boy Lost and Found," in *Time* (New York), 6 June 1988.
Hoberman, J., "Film: The Body that Failed," in *Village Voice* (New York), 7 June 1988.
Denby, David, "Movies: Boy's Town," in *New York Magazine,* 13 June 1988.
Harmetz, A., "Hanks Bashes Stallone at Movie Box Offices," in *New York Times,* 15 June 1988.
Kauffmann, Stanley, in *New Republic* (New York), 4 July 1988.
O'Brien, T., "Screen: Women and Children First," in *Commonweal,* 15 July 1988.
Simon, J., in *National Review,* 22 July 1988.
Groves, D. and J. Robbins, "Chill Between Fox, Odeon Circuit over *Big* Booking in Rival Site," in *Variety* (New York), 27 July 1988.
Matthews, T., in *Boxoffice* (Hollywood, California), August 1988.
Painchaud, J., in *24 Images* (Montreal), Fall 1988.
Benjamin, D., in *Séquences* (Montreal), September 1988.
Rosenbaum, J., "L'été Americain," in *Cahiers du Cinéma* (Paris), September 1988.
Cine-Tele-Revue (Brussels, Belgium), 1 September 1988.
Brauerhoch, A., in *EPD Film* (Frankfurt), October 1988.
Fiorillo, C. M., "Big Films," in *Revu* (New York), October 1988.
Floyd, Nigel, in *Monthly Film Bulletin* (London), October 1988.
Arthur, P., "The Reel World: A Cold Look at Hot-Weather Films," in *USA Today* (Arlington, Virginia), November 1988.
Ferguson, K., "Tom Hanks Hitting It *Big*," in *Photoplay Movies & Video* (London), November 1988.
Frank, A., in *Photoplay Movies & Video* (London), November 1988.
Noel, P., in *Grand Angle* (Mariembourg, Belgium), November 1988.
Abbott, Denise, "Actress/Director Penny Marshall: A Big Success in Post-Production," in *American Cinemeditor* (Los Angeles), vol. 39, no. 1, 1989.
Kinder, Marsha, "Back to the Future in the 80s with Fathers & Sons, Supermen & PeeWees, Gorillas & Toons," in *Film Quarterly* (Berkeley), vol. 42, no. 4, 1989.
Giacovelli, E., in *Cinema Sud* (Avellino, Italy), March/April 1989.
Modleski, Tania, "The Incredible Shrinking He(r)man: Male Regression, the Male Body, and Film," in *Differences,* vol. 2, no. 2, 1990.

*   *   *

The extraordinarily successful Hollywood director Penny Marshall is known for making big-budget movies with big-budget stars. Starting with the feature film, *Big,* she has been enormously successful in the Hollywood studio system and has gained a formidable position of power. Her films are characterized by unabashed nostalgia and simple, formulaic stories with predictable themes, including the innocence of childhood that is depicted in *Big,* and the camaraderie of women during the politically conservative 1940s in the baseball hit, *A League of Their Own.* Likewise, she is comfortable with sappy emotions and feminist critics have complained that her work betrays a lack of feminist awareness. But, film critics in general have praised her unobtrusive, tactful directorial skills—especially her skill with actors.

Marshall's hugely popular second feature film was the comic fantasy *Big.* Co-scripted by Anne Spielberg, sister of Steven Spielberg, it was originally meant to be directed by Steven who had intended to cast Harrison Ford in the lead role. A scheduling conflict prevented

Big

him from helming the picture, which provided a key opportunity for Marshall who had been replaced for lack of experience on *Peggy Sue Got Married.* In addition, her first film, 1986's *Jumpin' Jack Flash,* had been received less than enthusiastically by critics and audiences.

Big's hero is Josh Baskin, a suburban kid on the verge of puberty who is filled with dreams of being a grown-up. Understandably too, since at school he is surrounded by girls his own age who tower over and completely overlook him in favor of the big boys. For Josh, life seems to be a series of traumas related to his diminutive size, as when a pretty blond girl he wants to impress watches as he is refused admission at an amusement park ride—for being too short. Mortified, he finds an ancient fortune-telling machine where he makes a simple yet momentous request of the genie inside, "I wish I was big." The next morning, he discovers that his wish has been granted when he does not recognize the 30-year-old face that greets him in the mirror. Next, despite his explanations, his mother mistakes him for a burglar and orders him from the house. With his easier-to-convince best friend Billy, Josh makes his way to the playground of New York City where he rooms at a scary Times Square flophouse and finds work as a computer specialist at a toy company. Soon, however, he is discovered at the legendary FAO Schwarz by the toy company's top executive, who is charmed by his boyish enthusiasm and gives him a job as a toy tester. His success attracts the attention

of Susan, a sexy, executive ladder-climber who throws over her co-executive boyfriend when it appears that Josh is on a faster track to the top. Ultimately, Josh must make a decision about whether to remain an adult or to return to childhood.

Big has a predictable story and a not-very progressive view of gender relations, but Marshall directed it with great comic assurance; indeed, this is a genuinely funny, charming movie. In general, Marshall's skills are her technical proficiency, though she has not been known for breaking new directorial ground; instead, her strengths are providing brilliantly cast and strong performers with the room to shine. Moreover, her affinity for actors is certainly due to her own early career as a television sitcom actress. In *Big,* Hanks's engaging and witty interpretation of Josh makes it easy to suspend disbelief and to accept him as a young teen who is alternately guileless, filled with bravado, and with longing for home. His eager innocence contrasts sharply with the jaded opportunistic adults around him, whose motivations are entirely indiscernible to Josh. But many of the film's best comic moments are based on Josh's ignorance of the social codes of adults; and Hanks succeeds in making Josh's hesitant bluffing seem like improvisation. Thus, when one of his computer colleagues tells him that an attractive co-worker "will wrap her legs around you until you beg for mercy," Josh replies naively, "Well, I'll be sure to stay away from her." Also indicative of

Marshall's skills are the exchanges between Josh and his best friend that suggest the special intimacy of children.

As noted above, the film's gender politics are hardly feminist. Most noteworthy is Marshall's acceptance of the premise that Josh can provide precisely the moral and human awakening that Susan needs. Initially, she is a brazen opportunist who has apparently slept her way to the executive suites. But Marshall treats her transformation from a neurotic overachiever to a romantic who falls in love with Josh's playful sweetness, entirely without irony. The suggestion that what every successful woman wants—or, worse, needs—is a boy-man who will enable her to be a girl is the film's weakness. Accordingly, the film's satire is not about the misogyny of the corporate realm or about Hollywood's stereotypical corporate femme fatales, but instead it is about the idiocy of corporate games and ethics, and more importantly, about adults who have forgotten the finer points of childish naïveté. Not surprisingly, the toy company's top executive is the character most immediately able to relate to and appreciate Josh's innocent honesty. According to her production notes, Marshall wanted to convey "how a child's innocence can touch people and make them realize certain things about themselves that, getting caught up in the rat race of life, they forget."

Critics praised *Big* as the best of the body-switching movies that were then proliferating in Hollywood, such as *Vice Versa* (1988), *Like Father, Like Son* (1987), and *18 Again* (1988). And, *Big* was the most profitable of the bunch. Critics likewise praised Marshall's refusal to indulge the sexual innuendo possible in the attraction between Josh and Susan. The film earned more than $100 million at the box office, thus ensuring that Hollywood would continue to recruit Marshall to direct major studio films. Consequently, her next project was *Awakenings,* a sentimental hospital drama that starred Robert De Niro and Robin Williams.

—Cynthia Felando

BIGELOW, Kathryn
American director and writer

Born: San Francisco, 1953. **Education:** After high school, studied art at the San Francisco Art Institute, graduated in 1972; won scholarship to the Whitney Museum in New York, in 1972, where she switched to film studies; moved to Columbia Graduate Film School, studied under Milos Forman, graduated in 1979. **Family:** Married the director James Cameron, 1989 (divorced 1991). **Career:** Worked with radical NY British art collective, Art and Language; photographed by Robert Mapplethorpe; 1978—directed short graduation film, *The Set-Up*; 1982—co-directed debut feature, *The Loveless*; 1983—lectured in film at California Institute of the Arts; 1993—co-directed TV miniseries, *Wild Palms.* **Agent:** Creative Artists Agency, 9830 Wilshire Boulevard, Beverly Hills, CA 90212, U.S.A.

Films as Director

1978   *The Set-Up* (short)
1982   *The Loveless* (*Breakdown*) (co-d with M. Montgomery, + co-sc)
1987   **Near Dark** (+ co-sc)
1990   *Blue Steel* (+ co-sc)

1991   *Point Break*
1995   *Strange Days*
1997   *Ohio*

Other Films

1980   *Union City* (Reichert) (script supervisor)
1983   **Born in Flames** (Borden) (ro as newspaper editor)
1995   *Undertow* (Red) (sc)

Publications by Bigelow

Articles

"Dark by Design," interview with Victoria Hamburg and Firooz Zahedi, in *Interview* (New York), August 1989.

Interview with Elvis Mitchell, in *Interview* (New York), March 1990.

"James Cameron and Kathryn Bigelow," interview in *American Film* (Hollywood), July 1991.

Interview with Ana Maria Bahiana, in *Cinema Papers* (Melbourne), January 1992.

"Momentum and Design," interview with Gavin Smith, in *Film Comment* (New York), September/October 1995.

"Big Bad Bigelow," interview with Graham Fuller, in *Interview* (New York), November 1995.

"Reality Bytes," interview with Andrew Hultkrans, in *Artforum* (New York), November 1995.

"Vicarious Thrills," interview with Sheila Johnston, in *Index on Censorship* (London), November/December 1995.

"Happy New Millennium," interview with Roald Rynning, in *Film Review* (London), April 1996.

"No Retreat, No Surrender," interview with Ian Nathan, in *Empire* (London), April 1996.

Publications on Bigelow

Books

Hillier, Jim, *The New Hollywood,* London, 1993.

Foster, Gwendolyn Audrey, *Women Film Directors: An International Bio-Critical Dictionary,* Westport, Connecticut, 1995.

Articles

Travers, Peter, "Women on the Verge: Four Women Attempt to Infiltrate a Male Stronghold: The Director's Chair," in *Rolling Stone* (New York), 21 September 1989.

Taubin, Amy, "Genre Bender," in *Village Voice* (New York), 22 November 1989.

Hoban, Phoebe, "Happiness Is a Warm Gun," in *Premiere* (New York), April 1990.

Cook, Pam, "Walk on the Wild Side," in *Monthly Film Bulletin* (London), November 1990.

James, Nick, "From Style to Steel," in *City Limits* (London), 29 November 1990.

Powell, Anna, "Blood on the Borders—*Near Dark* and *Blue Steel,*" in *Screen* (London), Summer 1994.

Murphy, Kathleen, "Black Arts," in *Film Comment* (New York), September/October 1995.

Kathryn Bigelow on the set of *Blue Steel*.

Charity, Tom, "Extra Sensory Projection," in *Time Out* (London), 25 October 1995.

Francke, Lizzie, "Virtual Fears," in *Sight and Sound* (London), December 1995.

Raphael, Amy, "American Bigelow," in *New Musical Express* (London), 2 March 1996.

Keane, Colleen, "Director as 'Adrenaline Junkie'," in *Metro* (Melbourne), 1997.

*   *   *

If nothing else, Kathryn Bigelow has lastingly scotched the assumption that the terms "woman director" and "action movie" are somehow incompatible. She herself has grown understandably weary of questioning along these lines, responding tersely that she does not see directing as "a gender-related job." But it is undeniable that no other female director has shown herself so adept at handling the intricate, kinetic ballets of stylized violence indispensable to the current Hollywood action genre. At the same time, Bigelow has never been content simply to adopt the language of the genre to produce routine, competent roller-coaster exercises; instead, she transforms it, through her own preoccupations and distinctive vision, into something wholly individual.

Not content with simply colonizing genre material, Bigelow bends and blends it into fertile new mutations. Her co-directed first feature, *The Loveless,* put a dreamy Sirkian spin on the standard biker movie. *Near Dark* is a vampire Western, *Blue Steel* laces a cop drama with horror film conventions, and *Point Break* crosses a surfing movie with a heist thriller. For *Strange Days* Bigelow mixed an even richer cocktail: science fiction plus love story plus political satire plus murder mystery. All, though vigorously paced and tinged with ironic humor, are shot through with Bigelow's dark romanticism; and all of them, by delving deeper into formal, psychological, and thematic patterns than mainstream Hollywood generally cares to, lift their material some way towards the condition of art-house fare.

The complexity of Bigelow's moral and aesthetic concerns has meant that, though her films are avowedly aimed at a wide audience ("I see film as an extraordinary social tool that could reach tremendous numbers of people"), as a filmmaker she remains a slightly marginal figure. It is a stance reflected in her choice of protagonists: for her, as two decades earlier for Arthur Penn, "a society has its mirror in its outcasts." The black-leather bikers of *The Loveless,* the nomadic vampire clan of *Near Dark,* the surfing bank robbers of *Point Break* are all seemingly defined by their opposition to conventional mores, yet they represent an alternative dark-side structure, respectable society's hidden needs and appetites made manifest. A local citizen, gazing fascinated at the bikers' remote otherness, fantasizes about being "them for a day or two"; while Bodhi, leader of the surfboard criminals, even claims their heist exploits are aimed at inspiring the downtrodden masses. "We show them that the human spirit is still alive!" he exults.

Bigelow's artistic training—prior to becoming a filmmaker, she worked, in her own words, as "a conceptual artist and poststructuralist theoretician"—shows in the stylized and highly textured look of her films. Her images are tactile, often sensual to the point of fetishism: in the opening shot of *Blue Steel,* light caresses the curves of a handgun in extreme close-up, transforming it into an abstract study of curves and shadows. This close-grained visual intensity becomes another means of subverting and reappropriating generic material, turning it to her own ends—just as her dark, at times nihilistic plots serve as prelude to soft-edged, sentimental denouements in which love conquers all. Not least of the contradictions that fuel her work is that, while not shying away from graphic incidents of violence against women—the rape scene in *Strange Days* sparked widespread outrage—her films generally feature women as the strongest, most focused characters, acting as mentors and protectors to the self-doubting males.

In her first three solo films Bigelow played these various tensions off against each other, deftly maintaining a balance between mainstream and "serious" audience appeal. With *Strange Days* the strategy came unstuck. Bigelow herself describes the film as "the ultimate Rorschach," an artifact lending itself to as many interpretations as it has viewers. Drawing its inspiration from an eclectic multiplicity of sources—Hawks, Hitchcock, and Ridley Scott; cyberpunk fiction; and Michael Powell's *Peeping Tom*—the film torments and probes us, forcing us to question not only what we are seeing but our own motives in wanting to watch it. In creating such an intricate, demanding collage, inviting simultaneous engagement on any number of levels, Bigelow may have outpaced her public. *Strange Days,* though raved over by many if not all reviewers, stalled badly at the box office and dented its director's career, setting back her long-cherished Joan of Arc project, *Company of Angels.* Only temporarily, it is to be hoped. Few current directors are better placed than Bigelow to give us a fresh take on the woman who most famously trespassed on sacrosanct male territory.

—Philip Kemp

BIRD, Antonia
British director

Born: 1959. **Career:** 1974-76—ran away from home at age 16 to pursue a career as an actress, and worked for two years in a repertory theater; 1970s-80s—switched to directing, helming mostly new plays by Hanif Kureishi, Jim Cartwright, and Trevor Griffiths, and became Resident Director of the Royal Court Theatre in London, a post she held for six years; began directing television dramas, series, and miniseries, with her credits including *Submariners,* 1983, *TECX,* 1990, *The Men's Room,* 1990, *Inspector Morse,* 1991, and *A Masculine Ending,* 1992; 1993—directed her first television feature, *Safe;* 1994—directed her first theatrical feature, *Priest.* **Awards:** Named best TV film, British Academy of Film and Television Arts, Charles Chaplin Prize for Best First Feature, Edinburgh International Film Festival, and Special Jury Prize (Silver Hitchcock), Dinard Film Festival, for *Safe,* 1993; People's Choice Award, Toronto International Film Festival, and Michael Powell Award, Best British Feature, Edinburgh International Film Festival, FIPRESCI International

Critics Prize, Berlin International Film Festival, Alexander Korda Award, Best British Feature Film, for *Priest,* 1994.

Films as Director

1993   *Safe* (for TV)
1994   *Priest*
1995   *Mad Love*
1997   *Face*
1998   *Without Apparent Motive*

Publication by Bird

Article

Interview with Judy Stone, in *Sacramento Bee,* 19 April 1995.

Publications on Bird

Articles

Ahlund, J., "Antonia Bird siktar hugt," in *Chaplin* (Stockholm), no. 2, 1995.
Shacter, S., "Sundance: Antonia Bird & Danny Boyle," in *BOMB* (New York), Spring 1995.
Thompson, Anne, with Cynthia Littleton, "A Holy War over *Priest,*" in *Entertainment Weekly* (New York), 31 March 1995.
Kelleher, E., "British Filmmaker Antonia Bird Serves up *Priest* and *Mad Love,*" in *Film Journal* (New York), April 1995.
Calderale, M., "Filmografie," in *Segnocinema* (Vicenza, Italy), May/June 1995.

*   *   *

If women filmmakers are supposed to be preoccupied with making the kinds of movies that it is assumed women only want to see—touchy feely dramas, for example, or romantic soapers, female bonding stories and explorations of budding female sexuality—then Antonia Bird is one woman filmmaker who has little interest in making "women's films." She is fully capable of directing action scenes, and one can see her helming a special effects-laden, megabudget epic. Only that film would not focus solely on explosions and glitz. Amid the mayhem would be complex characters whose deep conflicts are explored within the framework of the scenario, and an unyielding point-of-view regarding human relations and the manner in which society attempts to control its unruly outsiders and nonconformists.

To date, Bird's best films have been jarring, hit-'em-in-the gut dramas featuring characters who are deeply troubled, or on-the-edge. After establishing herself as a director of British television action/detective dramas and miniseries, she won acclaim for *Safe,* a based-on-fact feature made for the BBC. *Safe* is an uncompromisingly (but necessarily) grim portrait of homelessness and hopelessness in contemporary London, centering on 48 hours in the lives of two young street people. Next came her debut theatrical release, the thoughtful—and controversial—*Priest.* The media hype surrounding the film was that it chronicled the predicament of a pastor who just so happens to be gay. In this regard, *Priest* is a powder keg of a movie. But the film is about so much more than a cleric who is a sexually active homosexual. It is a riveting drama that opens up for discussion a wealth of moral, ethical, and religious issues.

The scenario centers around the conflict of a young Catholic priest, Father Greg Pilkington (Linus Roache), who is assigned to a working-class parish in urban England. At first, Father Greg is presented as a holier-than-thou prig who preaches conventionally meaningless rhetoric at his parishioners without having any understanding of the realities of their lives. He declares that it is up to each person to make moral choices not to sin, as if the daily pressures one experiences have no bearing on individual thought or action. This generic "just say no" approach is frowned upon by Father Greg's outspoken fellow priest, Father Matthew. In turn, Father Greg chastises the liberal Father Matthew for sermonizing about social responsibility, not to mention breaking his vow of chastity by having a relationship with a woman. "We're not bloody social workers," Father Greg exclaims. He is convinced that a priest's sole responsibility begins and ends with offering his parishioners "moral guidance."

What qualifies a priest to offer moral guidance? What if that priest is himself in dire need of instruction and direction regarding his own conduct? These are but a few of the questions posed in *Priest.*

Furthermore, in the course of the story, a 14-year-old girl tells Father Greg at the confessional that she is being sexually abused by her father. The terrified child refuses to inform her mother, or any other adult. If he intercedes on her behalf, Father Greg will be breaking the confidentiality of the confessional. If he does not, the child's suffering will continue unabated.

While all this is transpiring, Father Greg himself is harboring a secret. One evening, he removes his collar, shows up in a gay bar and promptly hooks up with another man for a night of sex. He does not want to quit the priesthood, because he firmly believes that "God wanted me to be a priest." Here, another question arises, How can Father Greg reconcile his own actions with the content of his sermons, let alone the teachings of the church that homosexuality is a sin and a priest's celibacy is "a gift from God?"

The point of the film is that men of the cloth are human beings, with human needs. But Bird and her scriptwriter, Jimmy McGovern, stretch this view to the furthest degree. They put forth the premise that it is unnatural to sublimate those needs even if they entail a physical attraction to a person of the same sex. Herein lies the controversy surrounding the film.

Priest is an intricate film that astutely examines what it means to be truly religious, and how one goes about practicing that religion. Other concerns are the priestly relationship with Christ, and clergy who care more about the trappings of power than the teachings of Christ. *Priest* may be a film about ideas and issues, but it never, ever becomes pedantic or boring. Beyond the points it tackles, it works as a highly entertaining drama sprinkled with clever touches of dark humor.

The same may be said of *Face,* which deals with an entirely different set of characters. At its core, *Face* is a combination taut crime drama/allegory about political idealism gone awry in post-Thatcherite London. It tells the story of Ray (Robert Carlyle), a streetwise, working class antihero who once was a political activist but has since channeled his outside-the-system rage into a career as an armed robber.

On one level, *Face* is a conventional genre film as Ray and his mates plot out and pull off a major heist. Only their take is less than expected, and the scenario goes on to chart their subsequent violent falling-out. Nevertheless, unlike action dramas that spotlight in-your-face theatrics at the expense of relationships and emotion, Bird adds deep humanity to all the characters. Ray is the primary one, and he is a classic antihero: a lawbreaker who is sympathetically presented. He is a kindhearted soul who exists in a world in which all that

counts is the size of the wad of cash in a man's pocket. Good and evil have become irrelevant, as are cops and robbers, politics, friendship, and even sex. Ray has come to believe that the world never will be changed by political activism. So he lives aimlessly, steals for a living and at one point tellingly declares, "I'm just chasin' money like everybody else."

By abandoning his ideals and becoming a thief, Ray has lost his soul. His most meaningful human connections are destroyed by greed, and the violence that results from an "I want it all" world view. He is a casualty of the British class system, just as Father Greg is a casualty of religious dogma.

Bird's direction of *Face* is seamless. The film is visually dazzling, with its loud and busy soundtrack paralleling the camera movement and editing. On strictly genre terms, *Face* is a first-rate thriller. Like *Priest,* however, it is radical in theme. Its intention is to make you think as well as entertain you. This becomes clear when Bird intersperses scenes of a gun battle between the thieves and the cops with shots of the police violently breaking up a political demonstration.

In between *Priest* and *Face,* Bird slumped with her American debut, *Mad Love,* a superficial teen-lovers-against-the-world road movie but with a twist: the heroine is "clinically depressed," and a typical Bird character in that she is an outsider who is misunderstood by her strict, controlling father. Despite this misstep, one can look toward to Bird's future film projects with anticipation—just so long as she remains on her home turf, and is not further lured by Hollywood. If they are anything like her best earlier work, they will be made with intelligence and compassion.

—Rob Edelman

DIE BLEIERNE ZEIT
(The German Sisters; Marianne and Juliane; Leaden Times)
Germany, 1981
Director: Margarethe von Trotta

Production: Bioskop Film; Fujicolor, 35mm; running time: 107 minutes.

Producer: Eberhard Junkersdorf; **screenplay:** Margarethe von Trotta; **assistant director:** Helenka Hummel; **photography:** Franz Rath; **editor:** Dagmar Hirtz; **sound:** Vladimir Vizner and Hans Dieter Schwartz; **art directors:** George von Kieseritzky and Barbara Kloth; **music:** Nicolas Economou; **costumes:** Monica Hasse and Jorge Jara.

Cast: Jutta Lampe (*Juliane*); Barbara Sukowa (*Marianne*); Rüdiger Volger (*Wolfgang*); Doris Schade (*Mother*); Verena Rudolph (*Sabine*); Luc Bondy (*Werner*); Franz Rudnick (*Father*); Julia Biedermann (*Marianne, Age 16*); Ina Robinski (*Juliane, Age 17*); Patrick Estrada-Pox (*Jan*).

Awards: Golden Lion, Venice.

Publications

Script

von Trotta, Margarethe, *Die Bleierne Zeit,* Frankfurt, 1981.

Books

Kaplan, E. Ann, *Women and Film: Both Sides of the Camera,* Methuen, 1983.

Todd, Janet, *Women and Film,* New York, 1988.

Frieden, Sandra, *Gender and German Cinema: Feminist Interventions—Volume II: German Film History/German History on Film,* Oxford, 1993.

Articles

Variety (New York), 16 September 1981.

Nave, B., "Les années de plomb: Margarethe von Trotta ou le refus de l'oubli," in *Jeune Cinéma* (Paris), November 1981.

Pellizzari, L., and others, "Speciale anni di piombo," in *Cineforum* (Bergamo, Italy), March 1982.

Celemenski, M., and others, "Margarethe von Trotta," in *Cinématographe* (Paris), April 1982.

Amiel, M., *Cinéma* (Paris), May 1982.

Sauvaget, D., *Image et Son* (Paris), May 1982.

Milne, Tom, *Monthly Film Bulletin* (London), June 1982.

Johnston, S., *Films and Filming* (London), July 1982.

Rabinowicz, L., "Dark Times," in *Cinema Papers* (Melbourne), August 1982.

Sklar, R., and A. Harris, *Cineaste* (New York), Vol. XII, no. 3, 1983.

Alemanno, R., "La prassi delle conoscenza in 'Anni di piombo,'" in *Cinema Nuovo* (Bari), August/October 1983.

DiCaprio, L., "Baader-Meinhof Fictionalized," in *Jump Cut* (Chicago), February 1984.

Delorme, C., "On the Film *Marianne and Juliane* by Margarethe von Trotta," in *Journal of Film & Video* (Boston), Spring 1985.

Seiter, Ellen, "The Political Is Personal: Margarethe von Trotta's *Marianne and Juliane,*" in *Journal of Film & Video* (Boston), Spring 1985.

Kaplan, E. Ann, "Discourses in Terrorism, Feminism, and the Family in von Trotta's *Marianne and Juliane,*" in *Persistence of Vision* (Maspeth, New York), Fall 1985.

Donougho, M., "Margarethe von Trotta: Gynemagogucry and the Dilemmas of a Filmmaker," in *Literature Film Quarterly* (Salisbury, Maryland), July 1989.

* * *

The German Sisters is based in part on the life of Gudrun Ensslin, one of the best-known members of the Baader-Meinhof Group (or Rote Armee Fraktion) which carried out a campaign of terrorism in Germany in the late 1960s and into the 1970s. She was arrested in 1972 and sentenced to life imprisonment. In 1977 she and two other group members were found dead in their cells at Stammheim prison. The authorities claimed they had committed suicide, but this explanation has never been accepted by many, including Gudrun's sister Christiane, to whom this film is dedicated.

In *The German Sisters* Gudrun becomes Marianne and Christiane becomes Juliane, the daughters of a pastor in the German Lutheran Church. As we see through a number of flashbacks, both grow up in an atmosphere which is at the same time both patriarchal and also socially liberal and concerned. It is also strongly antifascist. In childhood, Marianne is dutiful and well-behaved, and Juliane is the rebel. But in the film's present, Marianne has become a terrorist, whilst Juliane has decided to try to change society peacefully by embarking on what was known at the time as "the long march through the institutions" and becoming a journalist on a liberal women's magazine.

As the flashback structure suggests, *The German Sisters* concerns the weight of the past on the present. Its original German title translates as "Leaden Times," which could be taken as referring either to the Nazi past (which has shaped, in quite different ways, Marianne's and Juliane's oppositional attitudes to the German present), or to the dreariness of the 1950s in which they had their childhood and in which they were shaped by rather more personal forces, such as sibling rivalry and patriarchal authority. The film shows us two ways of relating to these pasts—violent rejection, or reformist feminism—and is, as Ellen Seiter has claimed, "an effective dramatization of the feminist slogan 'the personal is political,' locating as it does the characters in their experience in the nuclear family within a specific historical, national and cultural instance."

This is where the problems begin, however, since the film—dedicated to the real-life Christiane, and told very much from the fictional Juliane's point of view—does undoubtedly privilege reformism over terrorism. (Of course, had it done the opposite it would not have been made in the first place.) Especially problematic is the fact that, since all but one of the flashbacks concern the sisters' childhoods, we have no idea why Marianne joined Baader-Meinhof in the first place, nor do we learn anything about the group's ideology and its reasons for choosing the terrorist strategy. Given this lacuna, one is almost bound to look for the explanation for Marianne's actions in the carefully delineated family circumstances in which she grew up, and to fall back on the psychoanalytic suggestion that "Marianne's blind devotion to her father, as against Juliane's resistance and identification with her mother, has made her susceptible to a new form of fanaticism." But, taken in association with Juliane's accusation that "a generation ago and you would have become a member of the Bund Deutscher Mädchen" (a Nazi version of the Girl Guides), this simply suggests that certain family structures produce members who are attracted to terrorist organizations and that there is thus no real fundamental difference between left- and right-wing terrorist groups (see for example Gillian Becker's *Hitler's Children,* and Helm Stierlin's *Family Terrorism and Public Terrorism*). Radical politics, left or right, are reduced to rebellion against the authoritarian father, Juliane is a model of responsible, social-democratic oppositional politics, and Marianne epitomizes fanatical, pathological rejectionism.

While there is some truth in these charges, they do not entirely do the film justice. It is true that, while she is alive, Marianne frequently comes across as unpleasant. But this impression is mitigated by the flashback scenes, especially those in which she watches film of the concentration camps or of American atrocities in Vietnam, in which we begin to understand what might lead a socially conscious young woman down the path from protest to terrorism. Furthermore, there is a sense in which, as Ann Kaplan has suggested, "it is tempting to read Marianne as some kind of 'double' for Juliane—the repressed self that Juliane wanted to be." This is most evident in the *Persona*-like scene in prison in which, thanks to the glass screen between them and the way the scene is filmed, Juliane and Marianne seem to fuse together. But it is also there throughout the latter part of the film in which, suspecting murder, Juliane absorbs herself totally in reenacting Marianne's death. She also thereby comes up against the real brutality of the German state, and gets an inkling of what confirmed Marianne in her hatred of and total opposition to it.

At the end of the film, Juliane takes in Marianne's son Jan, who had been fostered when she was on the run and then in prison. The fact that he has been badly burned by children who found out that he was a terrorist's son suggests a cyclical pattern, with parents' deeds being endlessly revisited on their children. On the other hand the fact that he asks to be told everything about his mother, having earlier ripped up her photograph, suggests that Jan will not reject his parents like Marianne rejected hers. Nevertheless, as Kaplan notes: "The act locates what is important firmly in the realm of the interpersonal. The vision is bleak in terms of bringing about change in the public realm." In this she is echoing von Trotta herself: "Hope arises from the realisation that you have to find the way back to yourself. This is less of a rallying call than a pessimistic statement. Personally I see very few chances of exploding the power complex established by the alliance between economics and science and, above all, I see no movement on the present political horizon capable of achieving this."

—Julian Petley

BONNIE AND CLYDE

USA, 1967
Director: Arthur Penn
Editor: Dede Allen
Costume designer: Theadora Van Runkle

Production: Tatira-Hiller; Technicolor, 35mm; running time: 111 minutes. Released August 1967. Filmed during 1967 on location in Texas.

Producer: Warren Beatty; **production manager:** Russell Saunders; **screenplay:** David Newman and Robert Benton; **editor:** Dede Allen; **photography:** Burnett Guffey; **assistant director:** Jack N. Reddish; **sound:** Francis E. Stahl; **art director:** Dean Tavoularis; **set decoration:** Raymond Paul; **special effects:** Danny Lee; **music:** Charles Strouse, theme "Foggy Mountain Breakdown" by Lester Flatt and Earl Scruggs; **costumes:** Theadora Van Runkle; **makeup:** Robert Jiras; **consultant:** Robert Towne.

Cast: Warren Beatty (*Clyde Barrow*); Faye Dunaway (*Bonnie Parker*); Gene Hackman (*Buck Barrow*); Estelle Parsons (*Blanche*); Michael J. Pollard (*C. W. Moss*); Dub Taylor (*Ivan Moss*); Denver Pyle (*Frank Hamer*); Evans Evans (*Velma Davis*); Gene Wilder (*Eugene Grizzard*); Martha Adcock (*Bank Customer*); Harry Appling (*Bonnie's Uncle*); Mabel Cavitt (*Bonnie's Mother*); Frances Fisher (*Bonnie's Aunt*); Sadie French (*Bank Customer*); Garry Goodgion (*Billy*); Clyde Howdy (*Deputy*); Russ Marker (*Bank Guard*); Ken Mayer (*Sheriff Smoot*); Ann Palmer (*Bonnie's Sister*); James Stiver (*Grocery Store Owner*); Ada Waugh (*Bonnie's Aunt*).

Awards: Academy Awards for Best Supporting Actress (Parsons) and Best Cinematography; New York Film Critics Award, Best Screenwriting; National Society of Film Critics Awards for Best Supporting Actor (Hackman) and Best Screenplay; Writers Guild of America, Best-Written American Drama and Best Original Screenplay.

Publications

Script

Newman, David, and Robert Benton, *Bonnie and Clyde,* in *The Bonnie and Clyde Book,* edited by Sandra Wake and Nicola Hayden, New York, 1972.

Books

Gelman, B., and R. Lackman, *The Bonnie and Clyde Scrapbook,* New York, 1967.

Wood, Robin, *Arthur Penn,* New York, 1969.

Rubin, Martin, and Eric Sherman, *The Director's Event,* New York, 1970.

Pechter, William S., *24 Times a Second,* New York, 1971.

Cawelti, John G., editor, *Focus on* Bonnie and Clyde, Englewood Cliffs, New Jersey, 1973.

Shadoin, Jack, *Dreams and Dead Ends: The American Gangster/Crime Film,* Cambridge, Massachusetts, 1977.

Murray, Edward, *10 Film Classics,* New York, 1978.

Kolker, Robert Phillip, *A Cinema of Loneliness: Penn, Kubrick, Coppola, Scorsese, Altman,* Oxford, 1980; rev. ed., 1988.

Zuker, Joel A., *Arthur Penn: A Guide to References and Resources,* Boston, 1980.

Giannetti, Louis, *Masters of the American Cinema,* Englewood Cliffs, New Jersey, 1981.

Cagin, Seth, and Philip Dray, *Hollywood Films of the 1970s: Sex, Drugs, Violence, Rock 'n' Roll, and Politics,* New York, 1984.

Haustrate, Gaston, *Arthur Penn,* Paris, 1986.

Thomson, David, *Warren Beatty: A Life and a Story,* London, 1987.

Articles

Lightman, Herb, "Raw Cinematic Realism in the Photography of *Bonnie and Clyde,*" in *American Cinematographer* (Los Angeles), April 1967.

Alpert, Hollis, in *Saturday Review* (New York), 5 August 1967.

Crowther, Bosley, in *New York Times,* 14 August 1967.

Sarris, Andrew, in *Village Voice* (New York), 24 August 1967.

Gulshanok, Paul, in *Cineaste* (New York), Fall 1967.

Rhode, Eric, "A Middle Western," in *Listener* (London), 14 September 1967.

Kael, Pauline, in *Saturday Review* (New York), 21 October 1967.

Ciment, Michel, "Montréal 1967, le règne de l'image," in *Positif* (Paris), November 1967.

Penn, Arthur, in *Positif* (Paris), November 1967.

Geduld, Carolyn, "*Bonnie and Clyde:* Society vs. the Clan," in *Film Heritage* (Dayton, Ohio), Winter 1967-68.

Johnson, Albert, in *Film Quarterly* (Berkeley), Winter 1967-68.

Macklin, Anthony, "*Bonnie and Clyde:* Beyond Violence to Tragedy," in *Film Heritage* (Dayton, Ohio), Winter 1967-68.

Kauffmann, Stanley, in *New American Review* (Cranford, New Jersey), January 1968.

Samuels, Charles T., in *Hudson Review* (Nutley, New Jersey), Spring 1968.

Benayoun, Robert, in *Positif* (Paris), March 1968.

Laura, Ernesto G., in *Bianco e Nero* (Rome), March/April 1968.

Chevalier, Jacques, in *Image et Son* (Paris), April 1968.

Comolli, Jean-Louis, and André S. Labarthe, "*Bonnie and Clyde:* An Interview with Arthur Penn," in *Evergreen Review* (New York), June 1968.

Brode, Douglas, "Reflections on the Tradition of the Western," in *Cineaste* (New York), Fall 1968.

Farber, Stephen, in *Sight and Sound* (London), Autumn 1968.

Comuzio, Ermanno, "Gangster Story," in *Cineforum* (Bergamo), September 1968.

Penn, Arthur, in *Cineforum* (Bergamo), September 1968.

Free, William J., "Aesthetic and Moral Value in *Bonnie and Clyde,*" in *Quarterly Journal of Speech* (Falls Church, Virginia), October 1968.

Bonnie and Clyde

Lawson, John Howard, "Our Film and Theirs: *Grapes of Wrath* and *Bonnie and Clyde*," in *American Dialogue* (New York), Winter 1968-69.

Cook, Jim, in *Screen* (London), July/August 1969.

Gould Boyum, Joy, and Adrienne Scott, in *Films as Film: Critical Responses to Film Art,* Boston, 1971.

Kinder, Marsha, and Beverle Houston, in *Close-up: A Critical Perspective on Film,* New York, 1972.

Cawelti, John, "*Bonnie and Clyde* Revisited," in *Focus!* (Chicago), Spring 1972 and Autumn 1972.

Childs, James, "Closet Outlaws," in *Film Comment* (New York), March/April 1973.

Corliss, Richard, in *Talking Pictures: Screenwriters in the American Cinema,* New York, 1975.

Yacowar, Maurice, "Dick, Jane, Rocky and T. S. Eliot," in *Journal of Popular Film and Television* (Bowling Green, Ohio), Winter 1977.

Corliss, Richard, "The Hollywood Screenwriter, Take 2," in *Film Comment* (New York), July/August 1978.

Eorsi, I., "Veszelyes egyensuly: Penn: *Bonnie and Clyde,*" in *Filmkultura* (Budapest), March/April 1979.

Leroux, A., interview with Arthur Penn, in *24 Images* (Montreal), June 1983.

Combs, Richard, in *Listener* (London), 18 July 1985.

Pym, J., "Black Hat Yellow Hat," in *Sight and Sound* (London), no. 4, 1990.

Wilmington, Michael, "Road Warriors: Outlaw Lovers on the Run," in *Chicago Tribune,* 28 August 1994.

* * *

Bonnie and Clyde is one of the defining films of its era, a union of visual stylistics and graphic violence joined to a romanticized portrayal of its antihero title characters: the duo of Bonnie Parker and Clyde Barrow, real-life Depression-era miscreants who are depicted as strangers in a strange land, outsiders/antiestablishment rebels who are alienated by an apathetic, workaday American mainstream. These fictionalizations allowed Bonnie and Clyde to become idealized role models for coming-of-age baby boomer moviegoers during the tumultuous late 1960s.

Dede Allen's editing style backs up the film's intention to show Bonnie and Clyde as characters who are isolated from the rest of their society and sometimes even cut off from each other. Allen accomplishes this by presenting the two in relatively brief shots, often with only one character appearing in the frame. The shots are linked so that there is a disjointed breakup in space, rather than a flow of shots from one angle alone. The result is a character isolated in a finite space, linked to another character seemingly imprisoned in another finite space. An example of this editing style appears in the sequence that begins when Clyde tells Bonnie that now that he has murdered a man, she may be better off going out on her own, perhaps returning to her mother. The scene starts with a series of head shots of Clyde, then a head shot of Bonnie, a full shot of Bonnie, a full shot of Clyde, then Bonnie, then Clyde. The sequence builds to a series of short close-up shots where finally the two heads appear together in the frame. The editing in this scene is apropos of the subject matter: two people who exist in their individual spaces join together as a couple (as Bonnie and Clyde come to the decision that they will remain together, even in the face of tremendous risk-taking). Furthermore, the sequence serves as a lead-in to a sex scene, again a joining of two into one accomplished symbolically by the placement of individual shots in a certain well-planned succession.

A further example of the editing serving to show the isolation of the characters within their world comes during the portion of the film in which Bonnie and Clyde have a reunion of sorts with Bonnie's mother and others in her family. The gathering is presented in a series of many brief shots, each disconnected from the next. The result is a rapid succession of vignettes which makes the point that these people have come together but that communication among them is limited, a string of many brief gestures and nothing more.

One of the key components in *Bonnie and Clyde* is the manner in which the violence in the scenario is visually represented. Until the release of such films as *Bonnie and Clyde* and *The Wild Bunch,* bloodletting on-screen was practically bloodless. Characters who were killed in war films or Westerns or crime dramas simply fell over and died, with no mess and little fuss. But with the advent of the Vietnam War, in which the grim reality of combat was endlessly broadcast into American homes on the nightly news, the movies cried out for more honest and realistic depictions of what happens to flesh when it is ripped apart by speeding bullets. If today graphic bloodletting is utilized by filmmakers more for exploitation purposes and viewers have become desensitized to violent images, *Bonnie and Clyde* added an oddly welcome dose of in-your-face realism to motion pictures.

Allen's manner of editing the violent robberies and shoot-outs was so effective that it became the basic cinematic language of future crime films. The sequences are developed from a conventional establishing shot or two to frenetic disconnected shots, many of which last only a few frames and most of which capture the essence of some violent motion. The viewer has no time to contemplate the face of a dying man or the slow oozing of blood from a wound. It happens slapdash: now you see it, now you do not. And not one extra frame is included. To heighten the effect, loud jarring noise blares on the soundtrack in the form of nervous banjo music or an uninterrupted spray of bullets. The ear is bombarded with upsetting sounds as the eye is accosted with a spray of images. Examples of this style of editing are the first bank robbery accomplished by the Barrow Gang and the celebrated final ambush of Bonnie and Clyde. That finale, controversial for the extent of its violence, is composed of split-second close-ups. A loud spray of bullets on the soundtrack accompanies one violent image after another, spewed out as a Gatling gun would do. In a daring sequence of three quick shots at slow-motion speed, Allen has Clyde—now in one movement flowing

through space—fall to the ground riddled with bullet holes. This form, or formalism, of editing was then unheard of in Hollywood filmmaking. Indeed, its most notable usage is the series of several shots of a woman rising in Sergei Eisenstein's Odessa Steps sequence in *Battleship Potemkin.* The effect of presenting one movement in three separate shots is that the movement is made somehow grand, larger-than-life. Therefore, the fall of Clyde is shown to be a fall of heroic proportion.

Theodora Van Runkle's period costumes (along with the cars, music, and other furnishings) evocatively replicate the 1930s. Although Bonnie's hairdo and makeup ring more true of the 1960s than the thirties, the duo's fashion-conscious clothing recalls the flashy costumes of Warner Bros. pre-Production Code gangster features and the gold-diggers' films (a sequence of which appears within *Bonnie and Clyde*). The public was quick to copy the fashions worn by these attractive criminals. Men began wearing closed white-collared shirts with vests, and no tie. Also they wore double-breasted pinstriped suits. Some even sported fedoras. Women adopted Bonnie's sleek mid-calf A-line skirts with long fitted cardigans or fitted suit jackets often belted at the waist. Her berets were particularly popular. And both sexes enjoyed wearing the casual woolen newsboy caps that sidekick C. W. Moss sported throughout the film.

The willingness of the American public to ape the dress of two ambitious but uneducated outlaws proves that Bonnie Parker and Clyde Barrow—at least as their myth is portrayed in this film—were not of their frayed-collar, sharecropping social class, nor of their robbing and murdering livelihood. Their existence purely is in a stylized fictional world, a world carefully presented as sequestered from the truth by stylized editing and flattering costume design.

—Audrey E. Kupferberg

BOOTH, Margaret
American editor

Born: Los Angeles, 1898; sister of the actor Elmer Booth. **Career:** Entered films as "joiner" for D. W. Griffith; then worked in Paramount Laboratories; 1921—assistant editor for Mayer (later MGM); 1939-68—supervising film editor, MGM. **Awards:** Special Academy Award, 1977.

Films as Editor

1924   *Why Men Leave Home* (Stahl) (co); *Husbands and Lovers* (Stahl) (co)
1925   *Fine Clothes* (Stahl) (co)
1926   *Memory Lane* (Stahl); *The Gay Deceiver* (Stahl)
1927   *The Enemy* (Niblo); *Bringing Up Father* (Conway); *Lovers?* (Stahl); *In Old Kentucky* (Stahl) (co)
1928   *Telling the World* (Wood) (co); *The Mysterious Lady* (Niblo); *A Lady of Chance* (Leonard)
1929   *The Bridge of San Luis Rey* (Brabin); *Wise Girls* (*Kempy*) (E. M. Hopper)
1930   *The Rogue Song* (L. Barrymore); *Redemption* (Niblo); *Strictly Unconventional* (Burton); *The Lady of Scandal* (*The High Road*) (Franklin); *A Lady's Morals* (*The Soul Kiss*; *Jenny Lind*) (Franklin)

1931   *New Moon* (Conway); *The Southerner* (*The Prodigal*) (Pol-
        lard); *It's a Wise Child* (Leonard); *The Cuban Love Song*
        (Van Dyke); *Five and Ten* (*Daughter of Luxury*) (Leonard);
        Susan Lenox, Her Fall and Rise (*The Rise of Helga*) (Leonard)
1932   *Lovers Courageous* (Leonard); *Smilin' Through* (Franklin);
        Strange Interlude (*Strange Interval*) (Leonard); *The Son-
        Daughter* (C. Brown)
1933   *White Sister* (Fleming); *Peg o' My Heart* (Leonard); *Storm at
        Daybreak* (Boleslavsky); *Bombshell* (Fleming); *Dancing
        Lady* (Leonard)
1934   *Riptide* (E. Goulding); *The Barretts of Wimpole Street*
        (Franklin)
1935   *Reckless* (Fleming); *Mutiny on the Bounty* (Lloyd)
1936   *Romeo and Juliet* (Cukor)
1937   *Camille* (Cukor)

Films as Editorial Supervisor

1937   *A Yank at Oxford* (Conway)
1970   *The Owl and the Pussycat* (Ross)
1972   *Fat City* (J. Huston)
1973   *The Way We Were* (Pollack)
1975   *The Sunshine Boys* (Ross); *The Black Bird* (Giler) (uncred-
        ited); *Funny Lady* (Ross)
1976   *Murder by Death* (Moore)
1977   *The Goodbye Girl* (Ross)
1978   *California Suite* (Ross)
1979   *Chapter Two* (Moore) (+ assoc pr)
1980   *Seems Like Old Times* (J. Sandrich) (+ assoc pr)
1982   *Annie* (J. Huston)

Other Films

1963   *The V.I.P.s* (Asquith) (prod adviser)
1978   *The Cheap Detective* (Moore) (assoc pr)
1982   *The Toy* (R. Donner) (assoc pr)
1985   *The Slugger's Wife* (Ashby) (exec pr)

Publications by Booth

Articles

Film Weekly (London), 9 October 1937.
"The Cutter," in *Behind the Screen,* edited by Stephen Watts, London, 1938.
Focus on Film (London), Summer/Autumn 1976.

Publications on Booth

Book

Acker, Ally, *Reel Women: Pioneers of the Cinema, 1896 to the
    Present,* New York, 1991.

Articles

Film Comment (New York), March/April 1977.
American Cinemeditor (Los Angeles), Spring/Summer 1977.
American Film (Washington, D.C.), October 1979.

* * *

Margaret Booth was one of the great film editors in Hollywood history. She started out as a patcher (film joiner) for D. W. Griffith and ended her career some 60 years later as one of the true insiders at MGM. The classic Hollywood film is surely defined by its characteristics of editing. Booth was one of the innovators who shepherded the classic Hollywood editing style through the coming of sound, color, and wide-screen.

Like many of her contemporaries, Booth joined the American film industry without any formal training. She took her first job with D. W. Griffith's company right out of high school. She then moved to Famous Players and the Mayer studios. By the early 1930s she ranked as one of the top editors at MGM. In 1939 she was appointed MGM's supervising film editor, a position she held until the studio collapsed in 1968.

Booth was, if anything, a survivor. Once she left MGM, she began to work as a freelance editor on such 1970s blockbusters as *The Way We Were, The Sunshine Boys,* and *Murder by Death.* She was one of those rare individuals whose career encompassed the history of Hollywood from its beginnings through the studio years into the age of television.

There have been few opportunities for women behind the camera in Hollywood. "Film editing," noted the *New York Times* in 1936, "is one of the few important functions in a studio in which women play a substantial part." And at MGM Booth was able to advance in the ranks so that she held a position of substantial creative power in the 1930s and 1940s. Her patron was Louis B. Mayer himself, for Booth had worked as a secretary with the old Mayer studio before it ever merged into MGM.

Booth's career neatly divides into two parts. During the first, up through her appointment as head of editing at MGM, she cut many a noted film. These include a number of MGM classics: *The Barretts of Wimpole Street, Romeo and Juliet,* and *Camille.* Somewhat surprisingly for one with so much industry power and influence, Booth received only one Academy Award nomination for film editing. This was for the 1935 version of *Mutiny on the Bounty.* She did not win the award. Nevertheless, it should be noted that Booth did get an honorary Oscar in 1977 to denote "62 years of exceptionally distinguished service to the motion picture industry as film editor."

In the second half of her career Margaret Booth worked strictly as an editing supervisor. According to her, she did no actual editing for 30 years. But she assigned those who did, and approved their work and performance. As such she held immense power and continued the tradition of a style of classic editing for which Hollywood films of the studio years have now become famous. All filmmakers from the late 1930s through the late 1960s who worked at MGM had, in the end, to go through Booth to have the final editing of sound and image approved. Thus for three decades she represented one of the truly important but relatively unknown powers in the history of Hollywood filmmaking.

—Douglas Gomery

BORDEN, Lizzie
American director

Born: Linda Elizabeth Borden in Detroit, Michigan, 3 February 1950. **Education:** Studied painting at Wellesley College, Massachusetts, received degree in fine arts. **Career:** 1976—made first film

Lizzie Borden

Regrouping; formed production company, Alternate Current; 1983—directed widely discussed feature film *Born in Flames*; 1986—second feature film *Working Girls*; from 1992—director of Hollywood feature films and TV anthologies.

Films as Director

1976   *Regrouping*
1983   **Born in Flames** (+ sc, ph)
1986   **Working Girls** (+ pr, sc, ed)
1992   *Inside Out* (for TV); *Love Crimes* (+ co-pr)
1994   "Let's Talk about Sex" ep. of *Erotique* (for TV) (+ co-sc)
1995   "Juarez" ep. of *Red Shoe Diaries* (for TV)

Publications by Borden

Articles

Interview with Anne Friedberg, in *Women and Performance* (New York), Winter 1984.
"Goodbye to All That," interview with S. Jenkins, in *Monthly Film Bulletin* (London), February 1984.
"The World According to Lynch," in *Village Voice* (New York), 23 September 1986.
Interview with Coco Fusco, in *Afterimage* (London), December 1986.

"Labor Relations," interview with Lynne Jackson, in *Cineaste* (New York), vol. 15, no. 3, 1987.
"Lizzie Borden: Adventures in the Skin Trade," interview with K. Dieckmann, in *Village Voice* (New York), 10 March 1987.
Interview with M. Judge and L. Spring, in *CineAction!* (Toronto), Spring 1987.

Publications on Borden

Books

Todd, Janet, *Women and Film,* New York, 1988.
Erens, Patricia, editor, *Issues in Feminist Film Criticism,* Bloomington, Indiana, 1990.
Mayne, Judith, *The Woman at the Keyhole: Feminism and Women's Cinema,* Bloomington, Indiana, 1990.
Mellencamp, Patricia, *Avant-Garde Film, Video, & Feminism,* Bloomington, Indiana, 1990.
Cole, Janis, and Holly Dale, *Calling the Shots: Profiles of Women Filmmakers,* Kingston, Ontario, 1993.
Creed, Barbara, *The Monstrous Feminine: Film, Feminism, Psycho-analysis,* London, 1993.
Gibson, Pamela Church, and Roma Gibson, editors, *Dirty Looks: Women, Pornography and Power,* London, 1993.

Articles

Pally, Marcia, "Is Their Revolution after the Revolution?" in *Village Voice* (New York), 15 November 1983.
Hulser, Kathleen, "Les Guérillères," in *Afterimage* (London), January 1984.
de Lauretis, Teresa, "Rethinking Women's Cinema: Aesthetics and Feminist Theory," in *Technologies of Gender: Essays on Theory, Film, and Fiction,* Bloomington, Indiana, 1987.
Field, S., "The State of Things," in *Monthly Film Bulletin* (London), January 1987.
Baron, S., "Independent Means: United States," in *Stills* (London), February 1987.
Lucia, Cynthia, "Redefining Female Sexuality in the Cinema," in *Cineaste* (New York), vol. 19, no. 2/3, 1992.
Cook, Pam, "Border Crossings, Women and Film in Context," in *Women and Film: A Sight and Sound Reader,* edited by Pam Cook and Philip Dodd, Philadelphia, 1993.
Laden, T., and J. Painter, "Dirty Dames," in *Film Threat* (Beverly Hills), June 1994.

*   *   *

Lizzie Borden emerged on the film scene as part of the new generation of American independent women filmmakers in the 1970s and early 1980s, when she earned a reputation for making feminist films that offer unflinching examinations of a range of women's issues.

After writing art criticism for *Artforum* which she did after graduation from university, Borden decided she wanted to pursue a career as a filmmaker. She determined to teach herself filmmaking and editing. In 1976 she made a film titled *Regrouping,* and then founded her own production company, Alternate Current. Subsequently, she started planning her first feature film, the radical science-fiction masterpiece *Born in Flames,* which exploded on the feminist film scene in 1983. Widely praised by critics, it garnered Borden considerable publicity despite a low budget—about $30,000. The film was much discussed in feminist circles and was much appreciated given the increasing political conservatism of the early Reagan era.

Set in a postapocalyptic near-future in a place much like lower Manhattan, *Born in Flames* is a radical feminist allegory about sexism, racism, classism, and the media's complicity in maintaining them. Likewise, it disputes the utopian notion that a single sweeping social revolution will entirely eliminate oppression. It portrays the process by which a seemingly successful cultural revolution only ten years old begins to unravel and return to the old patterns of male dominance and the marginalization of women and their issues. In response, several apparently disparate groups of women who refuse to "grin and bear" it—including blacks, Latinas, lesbians, intellectuals, activists, and punks, among others—build a coalition by acknowledging rather than ignoring the differences, in order to battle the forces that aim to keep them divided. The film has a distinctively feminist perspective, but Borden does not conceive of her audience as homogeneous, so *Born in Flames* provides a range of possible identifications. In part, the film reflects upon the invisibility of black women and lesbians in films produced by white women, and in feminism in general. Borden developed the script in close collaboration with the performers who played the main characters, so the script ultimately combined her original plan with the actors' ideas. The film has a challenging, unconventional form that is characterized by a fragmented narrative, quick editing, a documentary look with a science-fiction sensibility, a fast-paced music track, and an incoherence between soundtrack and screen. Borden also refused to visually objectify women, thus asking her viewers to question the more familiar cinematic representations of women. Her purported aim was to question the characteristics of narrative in general, as well as those of race and class. Since its release, *Born in Flames* has become a part of the feminist independent film canon; however, some feminists have objected to its utopian suggestion that women can work together despite disparate racial and class positions.

Borden's next independent feature film, *Working Girls*, attracted even more attention for its distinctly feminist perspective, and because its simpler narrative treated a more familiar subject—prostitution. It offers a fascinating and occasionally amusing account of a day in the lives of ten prostitutes who work in a nondescript, middle-class Manhattan brothel that serves a procession of male clients. Borden's best-known film, it offers a trenchant portrayal of the prostitutes' motivations for working, the details of their workaday routine, as well as telling glimpses of the johns. Along with its striking look at a much-mythologized world—especially by Hollywood—it refreshingly demystifies prostitution and denies the male fantasy of mutual ecstasy. Inspired by her association with COYOTE, the coalition of feminist prostitutes working to legalize prostitution, Borden depicts prostitution as a viable economic alternative for women who are marginalized in the labor market. Prior to making *Working Girls*, Borden eschewed traditional narrative filmmaking. Yet, although this film has a more conventional organization, it retains her commitment to feminism and a willingness to treat controversial women's issues.

Throughout her film career, sparse though it has been, Borden has retained a commitment to making films that are entertaining, even if the larger purpose seems to be audience edification or the confrontation of passive viewers, as in her early career. Yet feminist critics who praised her choice to avoid objectifying women's bodies in her first two features, chastised her for featuring them in *Love Crimes*, and accused her of losing her personal vision to work in mainstream Hollywood. An erotic thriller, it tells the story of a female district

attorney who is enticed into sadomasochistic sex games with a photographer-murderer who "enlightens" her about her sexual desires. The film's abrupt ending is due to the studio's refusal to use Borden's original ending, and their substitution of a new one. Since then, she has been directing episodes of soft-core series for cable television.

—Cynthia Felando

BORN IN FLAMES
USA, 1983
Director: Lizzie Borden

Production: Alternate Current; color; 35mm; running time: 90 minutes. Released November 1983.

Producer: Lizzie Borden; **screenplay:** Lizzie Borden; **photography:** Ed Bowes and Al Santana; **editor:** Lizzie Borden; **music:** The Bloods, Ibis, and The Red Crayola; **special effects:** Hisa Tayo.

Cast: Jeanne Satterfield (*Adelaide Norris*); Honey (*Honey "Phoenix Radio"*); Adele Bertei (*Isabel "Radio Regazza"*); Flo Kennedy (*Zellie Wylie*); with: Pat Murphy; Kathryn Bigelow; Becky Johnston; Ron Vawter; John Coplans; Hillary Hurst; Sheila McLaughlin; Marty Pottenger; John Rudolph; Valerie Smaldone; Warner Schreiner.

Publications

Articles

Maslin, Janet, "Film: *Born in Flames,* Radical Feminist Ideas," in *New York Times,* 10 November 1983.

Pally, Marcia, "Is Their Revolution after the Revolution?," in *Village Voice* (New York), 15 November 1983.

Taubin, Amy, in *Village Voice* (New York), 15 November 1983.

Hulser, Kathleen, "Les Guérillères," in *Afterimage* (London), January 1984.

Barrowclough, Susan, in *Monthly Film Bulletin* (London), February 1984.

Jenkins, S., "Goodbye to All That," in *Monthly Film Bulletin* (London), February 1984.

Coleman, John, "Films: De Palma Ham," in *New Statesman* (London), 3 February 1984.

Gross, Linda, in *Los Angeles Times,* 7 March 1984.

Jaehne, Karen, in *Film Quarterly* (Berkeley), Summer 1984.

Molloy, "*Born in Flames,*" in *Film* (London), April/May 1985.

de Lauretis, Teresa, "Rethinking Women's Cinema: Aesthetics and Feminist Theory," in *Technologies of Gender: Essays on Theory, Film, and Fiction,* Bloomington, Indiana, 1987.

*   *   *

Born in Flames was produced and directed by the extraordinarily gutsy independent feminist filmmaker Lizzie Borden. An exceedingly low-budget science-fiction film, it was her first feature and it remains her filmic masterpiece. In addition, when it was released it successfully incited a critical buzz that was testimony to the radical possibilities it posed. That is, mainstream film critics generally praised it for its wit and imagination, while scoffing at its revolutionary intentions, and feminists energetically discussed the myriad questions it raised.

Set in a postapocalyptic near-future in New York City, *Born in Flames* offers a radical feminist allegory about sexism, racism, classism, and the media's complicity in maintaining them. Ten years after a peaceful "Social-Democratic War of Liberation," it is all too clear to many discontented women that the old patterns of male dominance are still pervasive, including rape, misogyny, homophobia, and a dismal lack of child-care facilities. The film focuses on four groups of women struggling for change: a militant and racially diverse lesbian Women's Army that is committed to day care and self defense, including a bicycling crew of women that patrols the streets to prevent or intervene in rapes; Phoenix Radio, an underground station that features the wisdom of Honey, a striking black woman; Radio Ragazza, another underground station on which Isabel performs; and, finally, the group of white, privileged intellectual women who represent an older generation of feminism because they are quite satisfied to work within the larger social system for gradual change. After the Women's Army leader Adelaide Norris is arrested and then found dead in her cell, her death prompts the four groups of women to unite in a revolutionary struggle. The women ultimately resort to terrorist actions, including taking over a television station to broadcast their beliefs on the evening news—though, ironically, they interrupt the president's announcement that he finally is proposing a program to pay wages to housewives.

The women, including an assortment of blacks, Latinas, lesbians, intellectuals, activists, and punks among others, determinedly build a strong coalition by acknowledging rather than ignoring their differences, in order to more effectively battle the forces that aim to keep them divided and powerless. Among the topics the women discuss during their planning sessions are the reasons for using weapons and the wisdom of using a photograph of their martyred leader in order to inflame support for their cause, since such a use might serve to fetishize her dead body. Notably, the multifaceted points of view the women express reveal the variety of contemporaneous feminist positions. Also, despite the seriousness of their arguments and positions, Borden finds considerable humor to exploit; in addition, their wide-ranging discussions allude to the repression of such topics in the contemporary media and political dialogues.

Part of Borden's project in *Born in Flames* was to dispute the simplistic utopian notion that a single sweeping revolution can entirely prevail over social oppression. She successfully demonstrates how feminist dialogue and strategizing may produce conflicts and exclusivity among feminists. In addition, although the film has a distinctly feminist perspective, Borden refuses the notion that feminist audiences are homogeneous, and *Born in Flames* provides a range of possible identifications. Another of Borden's professed intentions was to explore the characteristics of film narrative in general, as well as those of race and class. Thus, in part, the film counters the invisibility of black women and lesbians in the films produced by white feminists. Notably, Borden developed the script in collaboration with the performers who played the main characters, so the final script was a combination of her original plan and the actresses' ideas.

Born in Flames had a remarkably low budget—between $30 and $40 thousand—and it took four years, on-and-on, to complete. Nonetheless, it boasts a challenging, inventive form that is characterized by a fragmented narrative, frenetic editing, a combination of film styles, a fast-paced music track, and an occasional incoherence between soundtrack and screen. Further, its arguments are laced with humor, while the profound moments resonate with intensity. Unlike most Hollywood features of the time, whether or not they focused on female heroines, Borden carefully avoided visually objectifying the actresses in order to challenge viewers to question those more familiar cinematic representations of women.

Born in Flames continues to hold a place in the feminist independent film canon, though some feminists have objected to its optimistic suggestion that women can work together despite their disparate racial and class positions, although others claimed that Borden was too cynical—both about feminism and the possibilities of revolution. Still other critics complained that it was diffuse and superficial in its refusal to advocate specific solutions and for its gentle mocking of the female characters' determination to craft a concrete definition of feminism. Yet, one of the film's key points is the acknowledgment and celebration of the differences among women, as well as the endorsement of a feminism that includes a wide range of women who work across the lines of class, race, ethnicity, and sexual preference. Interestingly, unlike many of the 1970s feminist political films that eschewed the pleasures of movie-watching, Borden's film is a fast, fun representation of feminist warriors. Furthermore, for many it was a breath of fresh air given the increasingly conservative political tenor of the early Reagan era.

—Cynthia Felando

BOX, Betty E.
British producer

Born: Beckenham, Kent, 25 September 1920; sister of the writer/producer Sydney Box. **Family:** Married second husband, producer Peter Rogers, 1949. **Career:** Trained as a commercial artist; began as tea girl at Gainsborough Studios, worked at Verity Films, and moved back to Gainsborough as successful producer. **Awards:** British Women in Films Achievement Award, 1992. Commander, Order of the British Empire, 1958. **Address:** c/o Pinewood Studios, Iver Heath, Buckinghamshire, SL0 0HN, England.

Films as Producer

1945 *The Seventh Veil* (Bennett) (assoc)
1946 *The Years Between* (Bennett) (assoc)
1947 *Dear Murderer* (Crabtree); *When the Bough Breaks* (Huntington)
1948 *Miranda* (Annakin); *The Blind Goddess* (French); *Vote for Huggett* (Annakin); *Here Come the Huggetts* (Annakin)
1949 *Don't Ever Leave Me* (Crabtree); *The Huggetts Abroad* (Annakin); *Marry Me!* (Fisher); *It's Not Cricket* (Roome and Rich)
1950 *So Long at the Fair* (Fisher and Darnborough); *The Clouded Yellow* (Thomas)
1951 *Appointment with Venus* (*Island Rescue*) (Thomas)
1952 *The Venetian Bird* (*The Assassin*) (Thomas)
1953 *A Day to Remember* (Thomas)
1954 *Doctor in the House* (Thomas); *Mad about Men* (Thomas)
1955 *Doctor at Sea* (Thomas)
1956 *Checkpoint* (Thomas); *Iron Petticoat* (Thomas)
1957 *Doctor at Large* (Thomas)

Betty E. Box

1958   Campbell's Kingdom (Thomas); A Tale of Two Cities (Thomas); The Wind Cannot Read (Thomas)
1959   The 39 Steps (Thomas); Upstairs and Downstairs (Thomas)
1960   Conspiracy of Hearts (Thomas); Doctor in Love (Thomas)
1961   No Love for Johnnie (Thomas); No, My Darling Daughter (Thomas); A Pair of Briefs (Thomas)
1962   The Wild and the Willing (Young and Willing) (Thomas)
1963   Doctor in Distress (Thomas)
1964   Hot Enough for June (Agent 8¾) (Thomas)
1965   The High Bright Sun (McGuire, Go Home!) (Thomas)
1966   Deadlier than the Male (Thomas); Doctor in Clover (Carnaby, M.D.) (Thomas)
1968   Nobody Runs Forever (The High Commissioner) (Thomas)
1969   Some Girls Do (Thomas)
1970   Doctor in Trouble (Thomas); Percy (Thomas)
1972   The Love Ban (It's a 2' 6" above the Ground World) (Thomas)
1974   It's Not the Size that Counts (Percy's Progress) (Thomas)

Publications by Box

Article

Cinema Today (London), 26 January 1974.

Publications on Box

Articles

Picturegoer, vol. 15, no. 673, 7 December 1946.
Cinema Studio, vol. 6, no. 124, August 1951.

*   *   *

Betty Box and her work are at the center of a dynastic structure in British postwar cinema that is as complex as anything in the Hollywood system. Sister of Sydney Box, and sister-in-law of Muriel Box, she gained her first experience of film production working for Sydney's companies in the 1940s; she then embarked on a collaboration with director Ralph Thomas which lasted more than 20 years, while her husband, Peter Rogers, formed an equally prolific producer/director association with Ralph's brother, Gerald. In contrast to the relentless homogeneity of the Rogers/Thomas output (some low-budget action films, and then the Carry On series), the work of Box/Thomas is striking in its generic variety, moving easily between comedy, thriller, and melodrama. The films are, however, consistent in the level of their aim—the middlebrow popular domestic audience—and in the correspondingly unadventurous cinematic strategies they adopt.

Box and Thomas operated as a production team within the Rank Organisation, and their films, more than anyone else's, typify the style of Rank's product from the early 1950s onward. At the end of World War II, Rank had expanded boldly, confident of finding a place in the American market for high-quality British films, but the industry's postwar financial crisis forced a change in policy. Ambitious independents such as Powell and Pressburger, David Lean, and Launder and Gilliat went to work elsewhere, and more pragmatic operators such as Box and Thomas moved in. Their first big success was Doctor in the House in 1954, a comedy about medical trainees which led to several sequels and established a pattern of casting which served them well in other films too: its stars, Dirk Bogarde and Kenneth More, were supported by a multitude of British character actors each doing their economical, predictable bit. Bogarde and More belonged to the last generation of actors to get the old-fashioned star buildup in the British market, and Box and Thomas assiduously built many films around them and contemporaries such as Michael Craig: More starred in their lightweight remake of The 39 Steps, and Bogarde alternated the Doctor sequels with roles as adventurer (Campbell's Kingdom) and romantic hero (The Wind Cannot Read).

In their prolific 1950s output, Box and Thomas played the domestic market with energy and expertise; when that market changed in the 1960s they adapted by putting more sex in the comedies and more violence in the adventure films, and also attempting some New Wave subjects such as politics (No Love for Johnnie) and youth (The Wild and the Willing), but the days of their kind of British cinema, based on a modest continuity of production, were clearly numbered. They did, however, have a late one-off commercial success with Percy, the story of a penis transplant.

Throughout the long and evidently harmonious partnership with Ralph Thomas, Betty Box received at least equal attention in the press—Miss Box Office was a label that stuck. This was partly due to the novelty value of a high-profile woman filmmaker operating in a male-dominated industry, but it also reflected her creative role as producer. It would be hard to do much with an auteurist study of Ralph Thomas, in terms of directorial signature, nor (one feels) would he have been interested in such an approach. These are producer's films, packages created by careful planning, casting, budgeting, scheduling, and marketing. Box brought to her work for Rank the knowledge of all sides of the business, and the rigorous financial discipline that she had learned in working for her brother Sydney, latterly at Gainsborough; such productions as *The Seventh Veil* (1945) had also enhanced her understanding of how to reach the female audience. Her Rank films, typically of the decade, were lacking in strong female stars (though she was proud of introducing a youthful Bardot in *Doctor at Sea*) but they appealed consistently to women through their artful presentation of heroes in need of motherly attention: Dirk Bogarde's romantic image and box-office status were built up largely through these films. Along with Michael Balcon at Ealing, Betty Box can be called the dominant British feature producer of the early postwar years.

—Charles Barr

BOX, Muriel
British writer and director

Born: Violette Muriel Baker in Tolworth, Surrey, 22 September 1905. **Family:** Married 1) the writer/producer Sydney Box, 1935 (divorced 1969); 2) Lord Gardiner, 1970. **Career:** 1920s-30s—typist, continuity girl, and script editor at British Instructional Films, and at Elstree with Michael Powell, and at Gaumont; directed shorts and documentaries for Sydney Box's production company, Verity Films; 1946—became head of Script Department at Gainsborough Studios, collaborated with Sydney Box writing and directing numerous films; 1952—directed first solo feature, *The Happy Family*; mid-1960s—retired from filmmaking and set up publishing house, Femina Books, with the novelist Vera Brittain. **Awards:** Academy Award, for *The Seventh Veil*, 1945. **Died:** In London, 18 May 1991.

Films as Writer with Sydney Box

1935   *Alibi Inn* (Tennyson)
1945   *The Seventh Veil* (Bennett); *29 Acacia Avenue* (*Facts of Love*)
            (Cass)
1946   *The Years Between* (Bennett); *The Girl in a Million* (Searle)
1947   *The Brothers* (Macdonald); *Daybreak* (Bennett); *Dear Murderer* (Crabtree) (+ pr); *Holiday Camp* (Annakin); *The Man Within* (*The Smugglers*) (Knowles) (+ pr); *When the Bough Breaks* (Huntington)
1948   *The Blind Goddess* (French); *Easy Money* (Knowles); *Portrait from Life* (*The Girl in the Painting*) (Fisher); *Here Come the Huggetts* (Annakin)
1949   *Christopher Columbus* (D. Macdonald)
1950   *So Long at the Fair* (Fisher and Darnborough); *The Astonished Heart* (Fisher and Darnborough) (sole writer); *Good Time Girl* (D. Macdonald)

Films as Writer and Director

1949   *The Lost People* (*Cockpit*) (Knowles) (additional scenes only)
1952   *The Happy Family* (*Mr. Lord Says No!*)

1953   *Street Corner* (*Both Sides of the Law*; *The Gentle Arm*; *The Policewoman*)
1957   *The Passionate Stranger* (*A Novel Affair*)
1958   *The Truth about Women* (+ pr)

Films as Director

1953   *A Prince for Cynthia*
1955   *The Beachcomber*
1956   *To Dorothy a Son* (*Cash on Delivery*); *Simon and Laura*; *Eyewitness*
1959   *This Other Eden* (+ co-pr); *Subway in the Sky*
1960   *Too Young to Love*; *The Piper's Tune*
1964   *Rattle of a Simple Man*

Publications by Box

Books

The Big Switch (novel), London, 1964.
(Editor) *The Trial of Marie Stopes* (autobiography), London, 1967.
Odd Woman Out (autobiography), London, 1974.
Rebel Advocate: A Biography of Gerald Gardiner, London, 1983.

Publications on Box

Book

Foster, Gwendolyn Audrey, *Women Film Directors: An International Bio-Critical Dictionary,* Westport, Connecticut, 1995.

Articles

Sight and Sound (London), vol. 27, no. 6, Autumn 1958.
Heck-Rabi, Louise, in *Women Filmmakers: A Critical Reception,* London, 1984.
National Film Theatre Booklet (London), September 1984.
Aude, F., "Creteil 1990," in *Positif* (Paris), January 1991.
Obituary, in *Times* (London), 22 May 1991.
Merz, Caroline, "The Tension of Genre: Wendy Toye and Muriel Box," in *Film Criticism* (Meadville, Pennsylvania), Fall/Winter 1991-92.

*   *   *

Muriel Box was a true craftswoman of the cinema, as director as well as screenwriter. Her prolific output in both roles spanned more than 30 years: the three decades that saw the rise and fall of British cinema production through the documentary movement of the 1930s, the boom years of war and its aftermath, the precarious continuity of the 1950s, then decline in the 1960s.

Box's apprenticeship as a writer was served as a playwright. Always a popular storyteller rather than an "artist," she aimed her plays mainly at repertory groups and amateur dramatic societies. She became a sought-after writer of plays for all-women casts—many are still performed today—which strikingly anticipated her future work (in partnership with her first husband, Sydney Box) for Gainsborough Studios, with its dominant roles for women stars and its strong appeal to female audiences.

Although she had worked in the film industry for many years, it was the outbreak of war in 1939 which offered Muriel (like many

Muriel Box with Thomas Mitchell

other women) the chance to progress. It was for Verity Films—the production company Sydney had formed—that Muriel had her first solo credits both as a writer (the road safety film *A Ride with Uncle Joe,* commissioned by the Ministry of Information), and as a director (the short documentary on *The English Inn,* commissioned by the British Council).

In the boom conditions of postwar cinema the Box partnership moved into independent feature production and almost immediately had a huge popular and critical success with *The Seventh Veil,* for which they won a joint screenwriting Oscar. Gainsborough Studios signed them up, Sydney as head of production and Muriel as script editor.

Gainsborough had become a household name during World War II for their vigorous melodramas, especially popular with women, who could identify with their romantic often transgressive heroines, motivated by romantic and sexual desire. Muriel supervised, and often herself wrote, a series of woman-centered postwar melodramas both historical/costume (such as *Jassy*) and contemporary (for example, *Good Time Girl*), films which contrast starkly with the

more tasteful middle-class products of, for example, Ealing Studios under Michael Balcon.

Significantly, it was Balcon who had turned her down as a director, declaring that a woman "didn't have the strength" to handle a film unit. During the 1950s and early 1960s she was to prove him spectacularly wrong, directing 14 features across a wide range of mainstream genres. Many of these she also wrote herself (including the typically unpretentious but carefully crafted drama *Street Corner* about female police officers) or adapted from short stories and plays; one example of the latter, *Simon and Laura,* a comedy about live television production, has a wit and sharpness not since rivaled by films on similar themes.

It was another adaptation, *Rattle of a Simple Man,* which effectively ended Box's career as a director in 1964. Perceived at the time as a "sex comedy" and poorly received, this story of an encounter between prostitute and client can be seen today as a rather audacious film, ahead of its time in its treatment of the ideology of the male group and its crude sexism. Indeed the same kind of rereading can be applied to many of Box's films, as a new generation of feminist critics has enthusiastically discovered.

Along with many other filmmakers of her generation, Muriel Box's career in cinema ended in the 1960s. Her activities as a writer and a feminist, however, continued undiminished. She began to write novels; the first to be published was *The Big Switch,* which had a strong feminist theme. In 1966 she co-founded Britain's first feminist press, Femina Books, and edited the first book to be published under its imprint—*The Trial of Marie Stopes.*

—Caroline Merz

BRACKETT, Leigh

American writer

Born: Leigh Douglass Brackett in Los Angeles, 7 December 1915. **Family:** Married the writer Edmond Hamilton, 1946 (died 1977). **Career:** Freelance writer; first novel published, *No Good from a Corpse,* 1944; 1945—first film as writer, *The Vampire's Ghost*; 1946—first of several films for Howard Hawks, *The Big Sleep*; also worked for TV series *Checkmate, Suspense,* and *Alfred Hitchcock Presents.* **Died:** In Lancaster, California, 18 March 1978.

Films as Writer

1945   *The Vampire's Ghost* (Selander)
1946   *The Big Sleep* (Hawks) (co); *Crime Doctor's Man Hunt* (Castle)
1959   *Rio Bravo* (Hawks)
1961   *Gold of the Seven Saints* (G. Douglas)
1962   *Hatari!* (Hawks); *13 West Street* (*The Tiger among Us*) (Leacock) (st only)
1967   *El Dorado* (Hawks)
1970   *Rio Lobo* (Hawks)
1973   *The Long Goodbye* (Altman)
1980   *The Empire Strikes Back* (Kershner) (co)

Publications by Brackett

Fiction

No Good from a Corpse, New York, 1944.
Stranger at Home (ghost-written for George Sanders), New York, 1946.
Shadow over Mars, New York, 1951, as *The Nemesis from Terra,* New York, 1961.
The Starman, New York, 1952, as *The Galactic Breed,* New York, 1955, as *The Starman of Llyrdis,* New York, 1976.
The Sword of Rhiannon, New York, 1953.
The Big Jump, New York, 1955.
The Long Tomorrow, New York, 1955.
An Eye for an Eye, New York, 1957.
The Tiger among Us, New York, 1957, as *Fear No Evil,* London, 1960, as *13 West Street,* New York, 1962.
Rio Bravo (novelization of screenplay), New York, 1959.
Alpha Centauri—or Die!, New York, 1963.
Follow the Free Wind, New York, 1963.
People of the Talisman, the Secret of Sinharat, New York, 1964.

The Coming of the Terrans (stories), New York, 1967.
Silent Partner, New York, 1969.
The Halflings and Other Stories, New York, 1973.
The Ginger Star, New York, 1974.
The Best of Leigh Brackett (stories), New York, 1977.
Eric John Stark, Outlaw of Mars, New York, 1982.

Other Books

With William Faulkner and Jules Furthman, *The Big Sleep* (screenplay), in *Film Scripts One,* edited by George P. Garrett, O. B. Harrison Jr., and Jane Gelfmann, 1971.
(Editor) *The Best of Planet Stories 1,* New York, 1975.
(Editor) *Strange Adventures in Other Worlds,* New York, 1975.
The Book of Skaith (includes *The Hound of Skaith* and *The Reavers of Skaith*), New York, 1976.
(Editor) *The Best of Edmond Hamilton,* New York, 1977.
With Lawrence Kasdan, *The Empire Strikes Back* (screenplay), in *The Empire Strikes Back Notebook,* edited by Diane Attias and Lindsay Smith, New York, 1980.

Articles

Take One (Montreal), September/October 1972.
Films in Review (New York), August/September 1976.

Publications on Brackett

Books

Arbur, Rosemarie, *Leigh Brackett, Marion Zimmer Bradley, Anne McCaffrey: A Primary and Secondary Bibliography,* Boston, 1982.
Carr, John L., *Leigh Brackett: American Writer,* Polk City, Iowa, 1986.
Acker, Ally, *Reel Women: Pioneers of the Cinema, 1896 to the Present,* New York, 1991.

Articles

Biografären, October 1966.
Film Comment (New York), Winter 1970-71.
Cinéma (Paris), July 1977.
Obituary, in *New York Times,* 26 March 1978.
Obituary, in *Variety* (New York), 29 March 1978.
Obituary, in *Take One* (Montreal), November 1978.
Monthly Film Bulletin (London), July 1980.
Silver, Alain, and Elizabeth Ward, in *American Screenwriters,* edited by Robert M. Morsberger, Stephen O. Lesser, and Randall Clark, Detroit, 1984.

*   *   *

Upon being asked about Leigh Brackett's work on *El Dorado* in the book *Hawks on Hawks,* director Howard Hawks replied: "She wrote that like a man. She writes good." Therein lies not only Hawks's opinion of Brackett but also his screen heroes' reaction to a person who comes through in a tight spot. "You were good back there" (*The Big Sleep*), "You were good in there tonight" (*Rio Bravo*), were the best compliments that a Hawks character could pay. And Brackett did come through for Hawks, writing screenplays for five of his films, beginning with *The Big Sleep.*

By the time that Brackett began working with Hawks, the director already had a definite style. The "Hawksian woman" as she is now known—a strong-willed character who gambles, drinks, can use a gun, and still remains feminine—had made appearances in previous films. Hawks normally shaped his action around two or more men and their reaction to pressure and to the Hawksian woman. Brackett's contribution as one of Hawks's screenwriters was to hone the male-female relationships, and to connect scenes and action that Hawks gave her. Hawks preferred his writers to be present on the set, and there was constant rewriting as dialogue was changed and then changed again. During their period together, Brackett and Hawks produced ensemble films in which the hero is helped by a group of oddball characters who surround him and aid him in a life or death situation. In four of the five films they did together (*Rio Bravo, Hatari!, El Dorado, Rio Lobo*), John Wayne was that hero.

Brackett believed, as Hawks did, that the usual Hollywood leading ladies were not very strong or interesting, and the Hawksian woman was a necessary character in their films. The screenwriter and the director also agreed that you had to depend on yourself because others can fail you in any situation—especially love. And while the characters of their films reject help in a tight situation, they receive it from unexpected places. On the subject of love, the characters usually have an unlucky past record with someone who left them, and they are wary of new relationships. Both the hero and the heroine tentatively approach a possible relationship by sarcastic bantering back and forth, testing the waters, aware that it might not last. Even the first kiss is a test: "I'm glad we tried it a second time. It's better when two people do it," Feathers tells Chance in *Rio Bravo*. But once started, the relationship is strong.

Without Hawks, Brackett wrote the script for *The Long Goodbye*, directed by Robert Altman and, like *The Big Sleep*, based on a Raymond Chandler story. This script, however, was more brutal than anything that Brackett wrote for Hawks, and it portrayed a modern-day Marlowe who, like the 1940s detective, has definite values of honor and trust and plays down danger with a flippant attitude. This Marlowe reacts to events with "O.K. with me," but, unlike his 1940s counterpart, he is truly alone. He is betrayed by everyone, including his cat, and in the end he shoots a friend, Terry, who has deceived him. Brackett admitted that she changed the ending of the Chandler story because she felt Marlowe could not walk away from such a betrayal. Later, in *Take One*, she explained, in typically graphic terms, "It seemed that the only satisfactory ending was for the cruelly diddled Marlowe to blow Terry's guts out ... something the old Marlowe would never have done."

Shortly before she died Brackett wrote a draft for *The Empire Strikes Back*. Concerned for the most part with Luke Skywalker's battle against evil (in others and in himself), the film has Brackett touches—most obviously the strong sarcastic Leia, the daring Han Solo, and their relationship. When Solo attempts to kiss her, Leia says, "Being held by you isn't quite enough to get me excited." But the attraction was there, and like Vivian and Marlowe, and Feathers and Chance, it is only a matter of time.

—Alexa L. Foreman

BREIEN, Anja
Norwegian director

Born: Oslo, 12 July 1940. **Education:** Studied filmmaking in Paris at the IDHEC film school. **Career:** 1966—worked as a script girl and assistant to Henning Carlsen; 1967—began making short films and documentaries; 1971—directed her first feature, *Rape—The Anders Case*; 1972—directed the Norwegian television documentaries *Herbergisterne,* about alcoholism, and *Mine soskend Goddad,* 1973, about artist Arne Bendik Sjur; 1975—won international success with *Hustruer*; has also directed for the Norwegian stage. **Awards:** Best Short Film, Oberhausen Film Festival, for *17 May, a Film about Rituals,* 1969; Special Mention, Cannes Film Festival, for *Next of Kin,* 1979; Special Mention, Venice Film Festival, for *The Witch Hunt,* 1981; Amanda (Norwegian Academy Award), Best Film, for *Wives: 10 Years After,* 1985. **Address:** Mellbydalen 8, 0287 Oslo, Norway.

Films as Director

1967   *Jostedalsrypa* (short)
1969   *Anskiter (Faces)* (short); *17, maj—en film om ritualer* (*17 May, a Film about Rituals*) (short)
1971   *Voldtekt-Tilfellet Anders (Rape—The Anders Case)*
1975   *Hustruer (Wives)* (+ sc)
1977   *Den Allvarsamma leken (The Serious Game; Games of Love and Loneliness)* (+ co-sc)
1979   *Arven (Next of Kin; L'Heritage)* (+ co-sc)
1981   *Forfølgelsen (The Witch Hunt)* (+ sc)
1985   *Papirfuglen (Pappersdraken; Paper Bird)* (+ sc); *Hustruer—10 år etter (Wives: 10 Years After)* (+ co-sc)
1990   *Smykketyven (Twice upon a Time)* (+ co-sc)
1996   *Hustruer III (Wives III)* (+ co-sc)

Other Films

1966   *Sult (Hunger; Svält)* (Carlsen) (continuity girl)
1994   *Trollsyn (Second Sight)* (Solum) (sc)

Publications by Breien

Book

Forfølgelsen, Oslo, 1981.

Script

Trollysyn: filmmanus, Oslo, 1994.

Publications on Breien

Book

Foster, Gwendolyn Audrey, *Women Film Directors: An International Bio-Critical Dictionary,* Westport, Connecticut, 1995.

Articles

Grelier, R., "Entretien avec Anja Breien," in *Revue du Cinéma* (Paris), June/July 1977.
Grelier, R., "Bilderstuermur und Realisten," in *Film und Fernsehen* (Berlin), no. 3, 1982.
Lerche, A., "Aamotstatuetten til Anja Breien," in *Film & Kino* (Oslo), no. 5, 1982.

Anja Breien

Hoass, Solrun, "Anja Breien: Film Director," in *Cinema Papers* (Melbourne), August 1982.

Hoass, Solrun, "Norwegian Cinema: A Gentler Wave," in *Cinema Papers* (Melbourne), August 1982.

"Director Carps re: State Funding; Norsk Film Chief Says Yes, But...," in *Variety* (New York), 13 October 1982.

Jarto, G., "Anja Breien: Vi er ikke representative, men morsomme," in *Film & Kino* (Oslo), no. 8, 1983.

Gautneb, H., "Rimini: Norsk film i Fellinis fotspor," in *Film & Kino* (Oslo), no. 8, 1985.

Fonn, H., "Kvinner i norsk film 1970-1986," in *Film & Kino* (Oslo), no. 4, 1987.

Kindem, Gorham A., "Norway's New Generation of Women Directors: Anja Breien, Vibeke Lokkeberg and Laila Mikkelson," in *Journal of Film and Video,* Fall 1987.

Lochen, K., "I grenselandet mellom galskap og kgaerlighet," in *Film & Kino* (Oslo), no. 5, 1990.

Iverson, G., "Og Gud skapte mannen," in *Film & Kino* (Oslo), no. 6, 1990.

Gjerde, E., "Uavklark smykketyveri," in *Z Filmtidsskrift* (Oslo), no. 35, 1991.

Wiese, I., "Den norske filmmen," in *Z Filmtidsskrift* (Oslo), no. 43, 1993.

* * *

In England over the course of three decades, Michael Apted produced a series of sociological documentaries, titled *7 Up, 14 Up, 21 Up, 28 Up,* and *35 Up,* in which he filmed a group of individuals, from all British classes, beginning in 1963 and starting at age seven. Then he reappeared every seven years to find out how they had matured, and if their youthful aspirations had been met as they reached adulthood.

In Norway, Anja Breien created an equally unique and absorbing series with her fictional *Wives* trilogy: three films, the first directed in 1975 with each follow-up coming a decade later, which chronicle the lives of a trio of women played by the same actresses: Anne Marie Ottersen (cast as Mie); Katja Medboe (playing Kaja); and Froydis Armand (in the role of Heidrun). While Breien is credited as the screenwriter or co-screenwriter of each film, she worked in conjunction with the actresses to create characterizations and dialogue. The result is a revealing look at the evolution of contemporary middle-class women and their enduring friendship.

The first installment is titled, simply, *Wives.* Its scenario is inspired by *Husbands,* the 1970 John Cassavetes feature which charts the response of three middle-aged suburbanites to the sudden death of their best friend; *Wives* also predates John Sayles's *The Return of the Secaucus Seven,* Lawrence Kasdan's *The Big Chill* and Anne-Claire Poirier's *Over Forty* as a generational reunion movie. The women once were close friends, but had not seen each other in years. Now, all are married, with two already mothers and the third pregnant. They come together after a school reunion and spend three days in each other's company where they recollect old times and, as they are picked up by a pair of men, explore the choice of marital fidelity versus infidelity.

More to the point, the women collectively rekindle a girlish spirit and sense of freedom they had not experienced in ages. They do express some desperation over and disappointment with the course of their present lives; still, *Wives* primarily is a vigorous, clever, and quick-witted story of female friendship, and the bond that exists across the years among friends both male and female, if that friendship is predicated on emotional honesty.

In *Wives: 10 Years After,* the same three characters first meet on Christmas Eve, and then spend several days sharing their company and updating each other (and the audience) on the progress of their lives—especially the children they are raising, and the men to whom they are married (contrasted to those they really want to be with). In this installment, the characters must deal with the reality that time is passing. They are becoming even further separated from their girlish pasts as they are fast approaching 40—and middle age.

In *Wives III,* the women reunite for Kaja's surprise birthday party, an event that symbolizes the further passage of time. Here, the characters are well-ensconced in middle age, but their fantasies and dreams are just as distinctly portrayed. Their lives may be disparate, but the feelings, thoughts, tears, and smiles they share attest to the substance of their lifelong bond. Indeed, the camaraderie between Mie, Kaja and Heidrun is extra-special, and transcends their individual relationships with their husbands.

In countless movies, an earlier photograph of an actor may be placed on a wall or desk to add authenticity to a setting. But because of the unique structure of the *Wives* trilogy, and the fact that the same actresses are cast in each film, Breien is able to include flashbacks, made up of footage from the previous films. Thus, the audience sees the characters literally age before their eyes—the same feature which makes Apted's documentaries so riveting.

Beyond the *Wives* trilogy, Breien has worked successfully in a variety of genres. Her debut feature, *Rape—The Anders Case,* is a jarring black-and-white chronicle of a rape case told from the point of view of the accused. *The Serious Game,* a project Breien took over when its original director, Per Blom, became ill, is the story of a newspaperman whose rigidity prevents him from marrying his true love. *Next of Kin* is a comedy about the manner in which various family members react upon inheriting immense wealth. *The Witch Hunt,* set in the 17th century, chronicles the plight of a woman whose independent spirit and open sexuality results in her being prosecuted (and eventually beheaded) as a witch. *Paper Bird* may be a thriller about a woman who attempts to solve the mystery surrounding the death of her father, but it primarily explores the personality of the protagonist. *Twice upon a Time* is the story of a middle-aged Casanova who has lost his touch with women; its point of view is that relations between the sexes must be predicated on emotional commitment, rather than sexual conquest.

The films of Anja Breien are collectively ambitious and provocative, as well as intensely personal—particularly when they spotlight the intimate connections between individuals, and the absolute need for (as well as benefits of) integrity in interpersonal relationships.

—Rob Edelman

BRÜCKNER, Jutta

German director

Born: Düsseldorf, Germany, 25 June 1941. **Education:** Studied political science, philosophy, and history in Berlin, Paris, and Munich, granted a Ph.D. in 1973. **Career:** 1976—wrote film scripts, *Coup de grâce,* with Margarethe von Trotta, directed by Volker Schlöndorff, and *A Woman with Responsibility* for TV, directed by Ula Stöckl, 1977; has also written essays in film theory, film reviews, and radio plays; has been a professor at the *Hochschule der Künste,* in Berlin. **Address:** Brückner Filmproduktion, Goltzstrasse 13A, 10781 Berlin, Germany.

Films as Director

1975 *Tue recht und scheue niemand* (*Do Right and Fear No-one*)
1977 *Ein ganz und gar verwahrlostes Mädchen* (*A Thoroughly Demoralized Girl: A Day in the Life of Rita Rischak*)
1979 **Hungerjahre** (*Years of Hunger*)
1980 *Laufen lernen* (*Learning to Run*)
1982 "Luftwurzeln" ep. of *Die Erbtöchter* (*The Daughter's Inheritance* (six-part omnibus co-d with Stöckl and Sanders-Brahms)
1984 *Kolossale Liebe* (*Colossal Love*)
1986 *Ein Blick—und die Liebe bricht aus* (*One Glance, and Love Breaks Out*)

Films as Writer

1976 *Der Fangschuss* (*Coup de grâce*) (Schlöndorff) (co)
1977 *Eine Frau mit Verantwortung* (*A Woman with Responsibility*) (Stöckl—forTV)

Publications by Brückner

Book

Cinema, Regard, Violence, Brussels, 1982.

Articles

"Jutta Brückner: le feminisme de Berlin," interview with Roland Schneider, in *CinémAction* (Conde-sur-Noireau), vol. 28.
Interview with Patricia Harbord, in *Screen Education* (London), Autumn/Winter 1981-82.
"Women behind the Camera," in *Feminist Aesthetics,* edited by Gisela Ecker, translated by Harriet Anderson, Boston, 1986.
"Women's Films Are Searches for Traces," in *West German Filmmakers on Film,* edited by Eric Rentschler, New York, 1988.
"Recognizing Collective Gestures," interview with Marc Silberman, in *Gender and German Cinema: Feminist Interventions,* Volume 2, *German Film History/German History on Film,* edited by Sandra Frieden, Richard W. McCormick, Vibeke R. Petersen, and Laurie Melissa Vogelsang, Oxford, 1993.

Publications on Brückner

Books

Sandford, John, *The New German Cinema,* London, 1980.
Knight, Julia, *Women and the New German Cinema,* London, 1992.
Multiple Voices in Feminist Film Criticism, edited by Diane Carson, Linda Dittmar, and Janice Welsch, Minneapolis, 1994.
Foster, Gwendolyn Audrey, *Women Film Directors: An International Bio-Critical Dictionary,* Westport, Connecticut, 1995.

Articles

Dormann, G., and others, "Le *Coup de grâce* Issue," of *Avant-Scène du Cinéma* (Paris), 1 February 1977.
"*Hungerjahre,*" in *Variety* (New York), 5 March 1980.
"Filmpolitik," Special Issue of *Frauen und Film* (Frankfurt).
Mayne, Judith, Helen Fehervary, and Claudia Lensson, "From Hitler to Hepburn: A Discussion of Women's Film Production and Reception," in *New German Critique,* Fall/Winter 1981-82.
"Female Narration, Women's Cinema," in *New German Critique,* Fall/Winter 1981-82.
Raynaert, P., and G. Payez, "De Brooks à Brückner," in *Visions,* November 1982.
Aude, F., "Les Cahiers du grif Special Jutta Brückner: Cinema Regard Violence," in *Positif* (Paris), January 1983.
Holloway, R., "One Glance and Love Breaks Out," in *Kino* (Warsaw), vol. 24/25, 1986-87.
Elsaesser, T., "Public Bodies and Divided Selves: German Women Filmmakers in the 80's," in *Monthly Film Bulletin* (London), December 1987.
"Women Filmmakers in West Germany: A Catalogue," in *Camera Obscura* (Bloomington, Indiana), Fall 1990.
Kosta, Barbara, "Representing Female Sexuality: Jutta Brückner's Film *Years of Hunger,*" in *Gender and German Cinema: Feminist Interventions,* Volume 2, *German Film History/German History on Film,* edited by Sandra Frieden, Richard W. McCormick, Vibeke R. Petersen, and Laurie Melissa Vogelsang, Oxford, 1993.

* * *

Jutta Brückner's career as a filmmaker coincided with the strongest historical moments of feminism in West Germany. Feminism flourished in West Germany starting in the mid-1970s, provoked by a variety of historical factors—the failure of the student movement to enact change, the rise of terrorism, and the general collapse of collectivity and consensus among the German left. These factors—coupled with the rise of international feminism—stimulated women to strike out on their own; they were bound by their rejection of violent solutions to political problems, as well as their disapproval of dogmatic, hard-line Marxism. The other major crucible for Brückner was her adolescence in postwar Germany, as part of a generation of *trümmerkinden,* raised amidst the ruins left by Allied bombings. Brückner witnessed a Germany rebuilt according to the status quo. A galvanic force for women growing up in the postwar period was the immediate reinstatement of the ruinous authoritarian patriarchal order, and the unquestioning submission of their mothers to the restoration of this destructive state of affairs.

Unlike other women filmmakers of her generation, Brückner has a strong academic background (a doctorate in political science and philosophy), and did not study at a film school, nor undergo a variety of apprenticeships before making her first film. She wrote several screenplays for other directors (Volker Schlöndorff and Ula Stöckl) before sending a synopsis of a script to a section of West German television (DGZ) that encouraged experimental work—*das kleine Fernschispiel* [The little television play]—and was a boon to emerging women filmmakers. Much to her surprise, they agreed to produce the film.

Brückner's first film, *Do Right and Fear No-one,* was prompted by a series of mysterious illnesses, which the director felt were connected to repressed material from her childhood, and which she needed to express through her filmmaking. *Do Right,* like most of Brückner's films, is highly autobiographical; it is a portrait of her mother. The director assembled a montage of still photos from family albums and history books, intermingled with photographs by August Sander. Brückner was interested in exploring not only the life of her mother, but the impact of class and history on the individual. Her mother, not given to self-reflection, at first refused to participate in the project, but finally became intensely involved, ultimately supplying the voice-over ruminations that mark the film's narrative. When the film was shown, Brückner's mother forced her dying husband to watch the film when it was televised, saying, "in it are all the things you don't know about me."

Brückner is greatly concerned with the investigation of private life, using her personal experience as a springboard to larger issues, and the recognition of what she calls "collective gestures," among women. She claims, in her theoretical writings, that women's perception of time and space is different from men's, that the oppression of women by the patriarchy has resulted not only in a distortion of their sexuality, but also of their very physical being and perceptual abilities. She believes that film empowers women to display this psychic and physical disintegration, a capacity that literature does not have. Brückner sees film as nothing less than a recovery for women of the ability to look, to perceive.

The director's next work was also commissioned for German television, and is called *A Thoroughly Demoralized Girl: A Day in the Life of Rita Rischak.* The film is a melange of docudrama-style scenes accompanied by the voice-over of the protagonist's interior thoughts, mixed with Rita being interviewed. It is the story of an office worker, longing for different forms of fulfillment, but with only the most chaotic ideas of how to achieve her desires. The film details her problematic relations with her parents, child, lovers, and work. Again, Rita's personal problems and self-destructive tendencies are tied to the social structure in which she is mired.

The film for which Brückner is justifiably most well known, *Hunger Years,* followed, and was screened at the Berlin Film Festival. The film was universally well-received, except in France, where the director's audacious shot of a bloody sanitary napkin was considered tasteless. *Hunger Years* takes place between 1953 and 1956, the years of the West German "economic miracle." It details the upsurge of material prosperity, the increasing grip of cold war politics and the rehabilitation of numerous Nazis. The repression, denial, and soullessness of the sociopolitical milieu is mirrored by the adolescent Ursula's family life, particularly in the disavowal by the girl's mother of her daughter's developing body and sexuality. The mother's disgust with her own body—she says at one point, "We should be able to tear out our ovaries," is communicated all too clearly to Ursula, who comes to despise who and what she is. Psychologically and physically, Ursula desperately attempts to obliterate her feelings of self-alienation, and fill her emptiness with secret eating binges, which not only exacerbate her negative self-image, but also further isolate her from the social world. The young girl sinks further into self-mutilation, silence, and finally, a suicide attempt.

Brückner says, "this film is an attempt at a psychoanalytic cinematic form." The films interest lies not only in the complexity with which she treats the subject matter, but also in formal play with narrative voice, documentary footage intercut with the fiction, inner monologues, poems, nursery rhymes, and fantasies that serve to reveal the inner life of the protagonist. The bloody sanitary napkin is an emblem of all those things in women's lives that cannot be shown. As Brückner says, "Film can integrate and release women's collective neuroses and maimings ..., because film creates a public space for experience."

The director's remaining films, *Learning to Run,* about a woman whose breast cancer scare causes her to rethink her life, *The Daughter's Inheritance,* an omnibus film made with other women directors, and *One Glance, and Love Breaks Out,* a series of performance pieces revolving around sadomasochistic fantasies have received little critical attention. Jutta Brückner appears to have stopped making films, and taken a position in academia.

—Carole Zucker

BUTE, Mary Ellen
American abstract filmmaker and animator

Born: Houston, Texas, 1904. **Education:** Attended Yale School of Drama, graduated 1925. **Family:** Married the cinematographer Ted Nemeth, 1940, two sons: Theodore Jr. and James. **Career:** 1925—drama director for "floating university," on a cruise around the world; worked with Thomas Wilford designing Clavilux light organ; joined studio of Leon Theremin; directed visual department of Gerard Warburg Studio, headed by Joseph Schillinger; 1932—provided abstract drawings for *Synchronization,* an unfinished work by Schillinger and filmmaker, later film historian, Lewis Jacobs; 1934-59—worked with Ted Nemeth and others on short abstract animated films, first in black and white then in color after *Parabola,* 1937, set to musical works in the mainstream classical repertory; 1936—began self-distribution of films to Radio City Music Hall and similar venues; 1950—began working with Dr. Ralph Potter of Bell Telephone Laboratories to develop circuit to use oscilloscope as controlled source of light for drawing, first used for *Abstronic,* 1952; 1956—produced live-action short film, *The Boy Who Saw Through,* directed by George Stoney; 1965—directed live-action feature film based on James Joyce novel, *Finnegans Wake.* The Mary Ellen Bute papers are stored at Yale University. **Awards:** Best Short Film, Brussels International Experimental Film Festival, for *Mood Contrasts,* 1953. **Died:** In New York, 17 October 1983.

Abstract Films (in collaboration with Ted Nemeth, 1934-59)

1932   *Synchromy No. 1 (Synchronization)* (unfinished; collaborators: Joseph Schillinger and Lewis Jacobs)
1934   *Rhythm in Light* (collaborators: Melville Webber and Ted Nemeth)
1935   *Synchromy No. 2*
1936   *Dada (Universal Clip); Anitra's Dance*
1937   *Parabola* (collaborators: Rutherford Boyd, Ted Nemeth, and Bill Nemeth); *Escape (Synchromy No. 4)* (collaborators: Ted Nemeth and Bill Nemeth); *Evening Star*
1939   *Spook Sport* (collaborators: Norman McLaren and Ted Nemeth)
1940   *Tarantella (Synchromy No. 9); Toccata and Fugue*
1947   *Polka Graph (Fun with Music), Mood Lyric*
1948   *Color Rhapsodie*
1950   *Pastorale* (collaborators: Ted Nemeth and Hillary Harris)
1952   *Abstronic*
1953   *Mood Contrasts*
1958   *Imaginations*
1959   *RCA: New Sensations in Sound*
1964   *The Skin of Our Teeth*

Live-Action Films

1956   *The Boy Who Saw Through* (Stoney) (pr)
1965   *Finnegans Wake (Passages from James Joyce's Finnegans Wake)* (d, pr)

Publications by Bute

Articles

Collaborated with Leon Theremin on his thesis, "The Perimeters of Light and Sound and Their Possible Synchronization," 1932.

"Light*Form*Movement*Sound," in *Design 42*, April 1941.
"Abstronics," in *Films in Review* (New York), June/July 1954.
"Mary Ellen Bute—Reaching for Kinetic Art (1976)," in *Field of Vision*, published by the Art Institute of Chicago, Spring 1985.

Publications on Bute

Books

Acker, Ally, *Reel Women: Pioneers of the Cinema, 1896 to the Present*, New York, 1991.
Rabinovitz, Lauren, *Points of Resistance: Women, Power and Politics in the New York Avant-Garde Cinema, 1943-1971*, Urbana and Chicago, 1991.
Pilling, Jayne, editor, *Women & Animation: A Compendium*, London, 1993.
Foster, Gwendolyn Audrey, *Women Film Directors: An International Bio-Critical Dictionary*, Westport, Connecticut, 1995.

Articles

Jacobs, Lewis, "Avant-Garde Production in America," in Roger Manvell's *Experiments in the Film*.
Weinberg, Herman G., "A Forward Glance at the Abstract Film," in *Design 42*, February 1941.
Jacobs, Lewis, "Experimental Cinema in America, Part 1," in *Hollywood Quarterly 3*, no. 2, Winter 1947-48.
Thompson, Howard, "Random News on Pictures and People," in *New York Times*, 13 April 1952.
Starr, Cecile, "Animation: Abstract & Concrete," in *Saturday Review*, 13 December 1952.
Starr, Cecile, "Mary Ellen Bute," in *Experimental Animation: Origins of a New Art*, edited by Robert Russett and Cecile Starr, New York, 1976.
Mekas, Jonas, "Movie Journal," in *Soho Weekly News*, 23 September 1976.
Obituary, in *New York Times*, 19 October 1983.
Obituary, in *Variety* (New York), 2 November 1983.
Schiff, Lillian, "The Education of Mary Ellen Bute," in *Film Library Quarterly* (New York), vol. 17, nos. 2-4, 1984.
Rabinovitz, Lauren, "Mary Ellen Bute," in *Lovers of Cinema: The First American Film Avant-Garde, 1919-1945*, edited by Jan-Christopher Horak, Madison, Wisconsin, 1995.

* * *

Mary Ellen Bute grew up in Texas, painting pictures of cows and horses à la Rosa Bonheur. Her interest in the depiction of motion took her to the Pennsylvania Academy of Fine Arts, where she studied with Henry McCarter. There, like contemporary European artists such as Hans Richter and Viking Eggeling, she rapidly became disenchanted with the limitations of painting and switched her artistic concerns to multimedia creations. This led her to study stage lighting and design at the Yale School of Drama, from which she was graduated in 1925.

Bute was fascinated by the possibilities of various technologies for the creation of works which could express movement and controlled rhythms, to achieve as she put it, "a time element in abstract forms." Since music generated the strongest creative impulses in her, she began to explore the new light organs developed by such scientists as Thomas Wilford and Leon Theremin. In 1932 she delivered a collaborative paper on the synchronization of light and sound before the New York Musicological Society, while Theremin provided an electronic demonstration.

Through her association with Theremin she was introduced to Joseph Schillinger, a composer and mathematician with whom she went to work at the Gerard Warburg Studio. It was there that she learned a valuable lesson. Bute explained:

> Visual composition is a counterpart of the sound composition, and ... I began to seek for a medium for combining these two and found it in films. I was determined to express this feeling for movement in visual terms, which I had not been able to achieve in painting, and I was determined to paint in film, and that is why I actually started.

After working with Schillinger and filmmaker Lewis Jacobs on an unfinished animation project, Bute set out on her own to make films. In 1934 she used a personal bank loan to pay for a five-minute black-and-white film called *Rhythm in Light*, accompanied by music from Edvard Grieg's *Peer Gynt Suite*. She recruited cinematographer Ted Nemeth for this project, which led to a close collaboration over the next two decades. Bute married Nemeth in 1940; all of her films through *Pastorale* in 1950 were produced by Ted Nemeth Studios. In the 1950s, at least a decade before Nam June Paik, she began using an oscilloscope, her "pencil of light," to generate images that could move without the need for animation techniques.

Bute's films were designed to accompany mostly familiar classical music selections by composers such as Bach, Wagner, Grieg, Saint-Saëns, Liszt, Rimsky-Korsakov, and Shostakovich. This, combined with her aggressive theatrical promotion of her films, made them more popularly available than other similar works. As early as 1935 her *Rhythm in Light* was run as an accompaniment to a feature film in New York's Radio City Music Hall. Her films played there and at other commercial movie theaters around the country well into the 1950s.

Because her unusual marketing of her films set her at odds with the prevailing anticommercial stance of the avant-garde and modernist art communities, Bute eventually fell into an undeserved obscurity. Her work and reputation began to be revived in the 1980s, as part of the feminist project of reclamation of marginalized work by women in film and other arts. Bute is now recognized, along with Oskar Fischinger, as one of the most important avant-garde filmmakers to work in the United States before World War II.

—Stephen Brophy

CAMILA

Argentina-Spain, 1984
Director: María Luisa Bemberg

Production: Gea Cinematográfica S.R.L. (Buenos Aires) and Impala S.A. (Madrid); color; 35 mm; running time: 105 minutes. Released 1984.

Producers: Angel Baldo, Héctor Gallardo, Edecio Imbert, and Osvaldo Cerrutti; **executive producer:** Lita Stantic; **screenplay:** María Luisa Bemberg, Beda Docampo Feijoo, and Juan Bautista Stagnaro; **assistant director:** Alberto Lecchi; **photography:** Fernando Arribas; **editor:** Luis Cesar D'Angiolillo; **sound:** Jorge Stavropulos; **art director:** Miguel Rodríguez; **costumes:** Graciela Galan; **makeup:** Oscar Mulet; **period consulting and set dressing:** Esmeralda Almonacid; **music:** Luis María Serra.

Cast: Susú Pecoraro (*Camila O'Gorman*); Imanol Arias (*Father Ladislao Gutiérrez*); Héctor Alterio (*Adolfo O'Gorman*); Elena Tasisto (*Dona Joaquina O'Gorman*); Carlos Muñoz (*Monsignor Elortondo*); Héctor Pellegrini (*Commandant Soto*); Claudio Gallardou (*Brother Eduardo O'Gorman*); Boris Rubaja (*Ignacio*); Mona Maris (*La Perichona*); with: Juan Leyrado; Cecilio Madanes; Alberto Busaid; Lidia Catalano; Zelmar Guenol; Jorge Hacker; Carlos Marchí.

Awards: Best Actress, Festival of New Latin American Cinema (Pecoraro)

Publications

Articles

Review in *Variety* (New York), 13 June 1984.
Gillett, John, in *Sight and Sound* (London), no. 1, 1984-85.
Torres, M., in *Cine Cubano* (Havana), no. 113, 1985.
Canby, Vincent, "Dark Comedy," in *New York Times,* 15 March 1985.
Harvey, Stephen, "Off Screen: A Passion for Her Work," in *Village Voice* (New York), 26 March 1985.
Hoberman, J., "Film: True Confessions," in *Village Voice* (New York), 26 March 1985.
Rickey, Carrie, "*Camila*: Argentina's Forbidden Story," in *New York Times,* 7 April 1985.
Kauffmann, Stanley, "Spring Cleaning," in *New Republic* (Washington, D.C.), 15 April 1985.
Simon, John, "Film: Near Misses," in *National Review* (New York), 17 May 1985.
Lieb, R. A., in *Film Journal* (New York), June 1985.
Weiss, A., "To See or Not to See," in *Ms.* (New York), August 1985.
Karp, A., in *Boxoffice* (Hollywood), August 1985.

Bemrose, John, in *Maclean's* (Toronto), 19 August 1985.
Cook, P., in *Monthly Film Bulletin* (London), September 1985.
Elley, Derek, in *Films and Filming* (London), September 1985.
Gray, M., in *Photoplay Movies & Video* (London), September 1985.
Coleman, J., "Films: Pursuit of Love," in *New Statesman,* 27 September 1985.
Jaehne, Karen, "Love as a Revolutionary Act: An Interview with María Luisa Bemberg," in *Cineaste* (New York), vol. 14, no. 3, 1986.
Crowdus, Gary, "*Camila*: An Interview with Susu Pecoraro," in *Cineaste* (New York), vol. 14, no. 3, 1986.
Fourlanty, E., in *Séquences* (Montreal), January 1986.

* * *

María Luisa Bemberg's *Camila* is the based-on-fact story of the eternal love between Camila O'Gorman, a highborn young woman, and Ladislao Gutiérrez, a Jesuit priest, who were executed for committing sacrilege in mid-19th-century Argentina. On superficial terms, it is a glossy and lurid soap opera, played to the hilt, whose scenario depicts a forbidden passion and its repercussions. In the hands of Bemberg, however, it becomes a highly politicized drama that reflects the manner in which a woman was required to act in a pre-feminist society, and the way in which she might expect to be dealt with—by the church, by governments, even by her father—if she in any way rebels.

Camila opens with the title character, a little girl, witnessing the arrival of her grandmother at the estate in which she lives. The woman is under house arrest. The particulars of her crime are unspecified, but the implication is that she is being punished for exerting her independence. The disposition of her son (and Camila's father) Adolfo is established as he coldly tells her that she should be thankful that she is not in jail.

Camila (played as an adult by Susú Pecoraro) grows up to be a pampered and protected young princess in a society in which powerful men are expected to think and rule while the sole concerns of their female counterparts are marrying and bearing children. These roles are defined at the outset. In one brief scene, Adolfo (Héctor Alterio) peruses a newspaper and comments on politics as he is bathed by a servant. Cut to two young women who girlishly splash each other as they share a bath. One asks the other, "Is it true that the governor bathes every day?" This query is meant to reflect a woman's utmost intellectual or political concerns. These women know nothing of developing ideas and value systems, or falling in love, or responding to their feelings. They are content to marry a man solely because he possesses money and power.

Nonetheless, in spite of Camila's rebelliousness in the face of such conventions, Bemberg does not de-romanticize her. The first time Camila appears on screen as an adult, she is bathed in light. The white dress she wears practically glows as it is hit by the sunlight streaming through a window into her room. This is an appropriate visual choice inasmuch as Camila's actions throughout the story are predicated on romantic feelings.

Camila's dissatisfaction is evident as she admits during confession that she has yet again argued with her father and sometimes wishes him dead, and that she has dreamt of a man and woman naked. The latter "mewed like a cat," she explains, adding that "the woman was me." Camila is pursued by wealthy Ignacio, the man whom convention tells her she must wed. Ignacio is presented as an extension of Adolfo. His role is to tell Camila what to read and not read, think and not think, do and not do.

Obviously, Ignacio is not the man for Camila. She is distanced from her contemporaries because she is an independent-minded romantic who asks questions and forms opinions, despite her forever unsmiling father's brusk admonition to her to "obey and hurry up." Camila is so bold as to offer an opinion during a family meal, at which point everyone at the table literally freezes in shock over her sacrilegious act. "Sometimes I believe I'll never marry," she confides to a servant, "because the man I imagine is a dream." That dream is realized, in the form of Father Ladislao Gutiérrez (Imanol Arias), her town's new priest.

At their first meeting, Camila stares at Ladislao from afar. And he gazes back at her, watching her as she sings and laughs. Momentarily, these two fall passionately in love. Furthermore, as they do so, the traditional male-female relationship is switched. True to the manner in which she has been characterized to this point, Camila (who is historically portrayed as an innocent victim) is depicted by Bemberg as the aggressor in the relationship, with Ladislao the object of her passion. Additionally, in her involvement with Ladislao, she is opposing the three domains of her society—the church, the state and the family—which are controlled by men.

Ladislao and Camila are humanists, and kindred spirits. In a society in which representatives of the church are expected to keep silent and support the prevailing powers-that-be, Ladislao speaks out against the murder and beheading of a bookseller who had been handling "foreign" publications. Despite his monsignor's declaration to Ladislao that "a woman can be a devil's tool," and the prevailing view that he never can exit the priesthood because his "marriage to God is forever," Ladislao does not disregard his feelings toward Camila. In fact, because of his romantic desires, he comes to realize that he is unable to be a good priest. So, in what for him is an act of courage, he decides to leave the church.

Still, he and Camila both know that, given the boundaries of their society, their relationship only can result in anguish. But they also are aware that their passion is all-encompassing, and cannot be ignored. Otherwise, they will be destined to live lives of silent regret. So they run off together, taking on new names and identities. As they ride away in a carriage, their fate is foretold in the sequence that follows: Adolfo oversees the dismemberment of a slaughtered cow.

The lovers' act is viewed as a scandal, with dire religious and political ramifications. Camila and Ladislao are victims of a church that is obsessed with propriety, politicians who are concerned with maintaining the status quo and summarily keeping their power, and Adolfo—who does nothing to intercede on his daughter's behalf upon her capture—who is interested solely in his name and patriarchal status. "A daughter who betrays her father," he pronounces, "does not deserve forgiveness."

These "miserable unfortunate fugitives" enjoy only a temporary bliss. They eventually are caught, and executed without benefit of a trial. But any feelings Camila has that God is somehow expressing anger at them for their actions are negated when she learns, just before her death, that she is pregnant. Her and Ladislao's love is pure

and beautiful, and will transcend their earthly lives. This is represented by having Camila's and Ladislao's voices speak to each other as their freshly shot corpses lie side-by-side.

Camila is lushly photographed throughout, which helps to establish the mood and the swelling passion between Camila and Ladislao that dominates the story. In a manner similar to her initial adult appearance on screen, Camila and Ladislao's first extended kiss is bathed in sunlight. The noises on the soundtrack add to the mood. One example: during the extended sequence near the finale, in which Camila and Ladislao languish in jail awaiting their predestined executions, the sound of a cold howling wind is heard in the background. And after both are shot, there is dead silence—except for the sound of that wind.

But the strength of the film is that Camila and Ladislao are far from stock figures. Their actions may be predictable but their characters are slowly and purposefully delineated, resulting in a complex, multidimensional display of emotions and feelings and a poignant commentary on life in a patriarchal, pre-feminist society.

—Rob Edelman

CAMPION, Jane
New Zealander director

Born: Wellington, New Zealand, 30 April 1954; daughter of the opera/theater director Richard Campion and the actress/writer Edith Campion; sister of the director Anna Campion. **Education:** Attended Victoria University, Wellington, B.A. in structural arts; Chelsea School of Arts, London, diploma in fine arts (completed at Sydney College of the Arts); Australian Film and Television School, diploma in direction. **Family:** Married the television producer/director Colin Englert. **Career:** Late 1970s—became interested in filmmaking and began making short films; 1981—short film, *Tissues,* led to acceptance into the Australian Film and Television School; 1984—took job with Australia's Women's Film Unit; 1986—directed an episode of the television drama *Dancing Daze*; 1989-90—short films *Peel, Passionless Moments,* and *Girl's Own Story* released theatrically in the United States. **Awards:** Palme d'Or, Best Short Film, Cannes Film Festival, for *Peel,* 1982; Best Experimental Film, Australian Film Institute Awards, for *Passionless Moments,* 1984; Best Direction and Screenplay, Australian Film Institute Awards, for *Girl's Own Story,* 1984; Best Director and Best TV Film, Australian Film Institute Awards, for *2 Friends,* 1985; Academy Award, Best Original Screenplay, and Best Director and Screenplay, Australian Film Institute Awards, for *The Piano,* 1993. **Agent:** Hilary Linstead & Associates, Level 18, Plaza II, 500 Oxford Street, Bondi Junction, NSW 2022, Australia.

Films as Director

1981   *Tissues* (short)
1982   *Peel* (short) (+ sc)
1984   *Mishaps of Seduction and Conquest* (video short) (+ sc); *Passionless Moments* (short) (co-d, + co-sc); *Girl's Own Story* (short) (+ sc); *After Hours* (short) (+ sc)
1985   *2 Friends* (for TV)
1989   *Sweetie* (+ co-sc)

Jane Campion directing *The Portrait of a Lady*.

1990   *An Angel at My Table* (for TV; edited version released theatrically)
1993   **The Piano** (+ sc)
1996   *The Portrait of a Lady*

Publications by Campion

Books

With Gerard Lee, *Sweetie, the Screenplay,* St. Lucia, Queensland, 1991.
The Piano, New York, 1993.
The Piano: The Novel, with Kate Pullinger, New York, 1994.

Articles

Interview with Carla Hall, in *Washington Post,* 4 March 1990.
Interview with Donna Yuzwalk, in *Guardian* (London), 2 May 1990.
Interview with Maitland McDonagh, in *New York Times,* 19 May 1991.
Interview with Elizabeth Drucker, in *American Film* (Los Angeles), July 1991.
Interview with Katharine Dieckmann, in *Interview* (New York), January 1992.
"Jane Campion's Lunatic Women," interview with Mary Cantwell, in *New York Times Magazine,* 19 September 1993.
"Merchant of the Ivories," interview with Anne Thompson, in *Entertainment Weekly* (New York), 19 November 1993.
"Portrait of the Director," interview with Kennedy Fraser, in *Vogue* (New York), January 1997.

Publications on Campion

Book

Foster, Gwendolyn Audrey, *Women Film Directors: An International Bio-Critical Dictionary,* Westport, Connecticut, 1995.

Articles

Quart, Barbara, "The Short Films of Jane Campion," in *Cineaste* (New York), vol. 19, no. 1, 1992.
Ansen, David, and Charles Fleming, "Passion for *Piano,*" in *Newsweek* (New York), 31 May 1993.
Travers, Peter, "Sex and *The Piano,*" in *Rolling Stone* (New York), 9 December 1993.
Current Biography 1994, New York, 1994.
Murphy, Kathleen, "Jane Campion's Shining Moment: Portrait of a Director," in *Film Comment* (New York), November/December 1996.
Feinstein, Howard, "Heroine Chic," in *Vanity Fair* (New York), December 1996.

*   *   *

Whatever their quality, all of Jane Campion's feature films have remained consistent in theme. They depict the lives of girls and women who are in one way or another separate from the mainstream, because of physical appearance (if not outright physical disability) or personality quirk, and she spotlights the manner in which they relate to and function within their respective societies.

Campion began directing features after making several highly acclaimed, award-winning short films which were extensively screened on the international film festival circuit. Her first two features are alike in that they focus on the relationships between two young women, and how they are affected by the adults who control their world. Her debut, *2 Friends,* was made for Australian television in 1985 and did not have its American theatrical premiere until 1996. It is a depiction of the connection between a pair of adolescents, focusing on the changes in their friendship and how they are influenced by adult authority figures. The narrative is told in reverse time: at the outset, the girls are a bit older, and their developing personalities have separated them; as the film continues, they become younger and closer.

Sweetie, Campion's initial theatrical feature, is a pitch-black comedy about a young woman who is overweight, overemotional, and even downright crazy, with the scenario charting the manner in which she relates to her parents and her skinny, shy, easily manipulated sister. The film was controversial in that critics and viewers either raved about it or were turned off by its quirky nature. While not without inspired moments, both *Sweetie* and *2 Friends* lack the assurance of Campion's later work.

The filmmaker's unequivocal breakthrough as a world-class talent came in 1990 with *An Angel at My Table.* The theatrical version of the film is 158 minutes long and is taken from a three-part miniseries made for New Zealand television. *An Angel at My Table* did not benefit from the media hype surrounding *The Piano,* Campion's 1993 international art-house hit, but it is as equally fine a work. It is an uncommonly literate portrait of Janet Frame, a plump, repressed child who was destined to become one of New Zealand's most renowned writers. Prior to her fame, however, she was falsely diagnosed as a schizophrenic, passed eight years in a mental hospital, and received more than 200 electric shock treatments.

Campion evocatively depicts the different stages of Frame's life; the filmmaker elicits a dynamic performance from Kerry Fox as the adult Janet and, in visual terms, she perfectly captures the essence of the writer's inner being. At the same time, Campion bitingly satirizes the manner in which society patronizes those who sincerely dedicate their lives to the creation of art. She depicts pseudo-artists who would not know a poem from a Harlequin Romance, and publishers who think that for Frame to truly be a success she must have a best-seller and ride around in a Rolls-Royce.

If *An Angel at My Table* spotlights the evolution of a woman as an intellectual being, Campion's next work, *The Piano,* depicts a woman's development on a sexual and erotic level. *The Piano,* like *The Crying Game* before it and *Pulp Fiction* later on, became the cinematic cause celebre of its year. It is a deceptively simple story, beautifully told, of Ada (Holly Hunter, in an Academy Award-winning performance), a mute Scottish woman who arrives with her nine-year-old daughter (Anna Paquin, who also won an Oscar) in remote New Zealand during the 1850s. Ada is to be the bride in an arranged marriage with a stern, hesitant farmer (Sam Neill). But she becomes sexually and romantically involved with Baines (Harvey Keitel), her illiterate, vulnerable neighbor to whom she gives piano lessons: an arrangement described by Campion as an "erotic pact."

Campion succeeds in creating a story about the development of love, from the initial eroticism between the two characters to something deeper and more romantic. Ada has a symbolic relationship with the piano, which is both her refuge and mode of self-expression. *The Piano* is an intensely haunting tale of exploding passion and deep, raw emotion, and it put its maker at the forefront of contemporary, world-class cinema. Campion's most recent project is *The Portrait of a Lady,* based on the Henry James novel.

—Rob Edelman

CANTRILL, Corinne
Australian director

Born: Corinne Mozelle Joseph, in Sydney, 6 November 1928. **Education:** Studied botany at Sydney University; studied music in Paris with Nadia Boulanger. **Family:** Married the filmmaker and her collaborator, Arthur Cantrill, 1960, two children. **Career:** 1960-63—made documentaries, experimental shorts, and a series of children's art and craft films for the Australian Broadcasting Service; 1969-70—spent a highly productive period of personal/experimental filmmaking, which was enabled by Arthur's Fellowship in the Creative Arts at the Australian National University in Canberra; 1971—began editing and publishing the independent film journal, *Cantrill's Filmnotes;* 1974—made her film, *At Eltham;* 1982-84—made her masterpiece, *In This Life's Body.* **Awards:** Silver Award, Australian Film Institute, for *Earth Message,* 1970; Second Prize, St. Kilda Film Festival, for *In This Life's Body,* 1984. **Address:** Box 1295 L, GPO, Melbourne, Victoria 3001, Australia.

Films as Co-Director with Arthur Cantrill (unless otherwise noted)

1963   *Mud; Galaxy; Nebulae; Kinegraffiti*
1964-65 *Robert Klippel Sculpture Studies* (5 films)
1965   *Robert Klippel Drawings, 1947-1963*
1966   *The Incised Image; Dream; Adventure Playground*
1968   *Henri Gaudier-Brzeska; Red Stone Dancer*
1969   *Rehearsal at the Arts Laboratory; Imprints; Fud 69; Home Movie—A Day in the Bush; Eikon; White-Orange-Green*
1970   *Bouddi; 4000 Frames, an Eye-Opener Film; Earth Message; Harry Hooton*
1971   *New Movements Generate New Thoughts; The Boiling Electric Jug Film; Blast; Meditations; Nine Image Film; Milky Way Special; Zap; Video Self-Portrait; Gold Fugue; Pink Metronome; Room; The City; Fragments; Island Fuse*
1973   *Skin of Your Eye*
1974   *At Eltham; Reflections on Three Images by Baldwin Spencer, 1901; Negative/Positive on Three Images by Baldwin Spencer, 1901;*
1975   *Studies in Image (De)Generation* (Nos. 1, 2, and 3)
1976   *Three Colour Separation Studies—Landscapes; Three Colour Separation Studies—Still Lifes; Simple Observations of a Solar Eclipse*
1977   *Touching the Earth Series: Ocean at Point Lookout, near Coober Pedy, at Uluru, Katatjuta*
1978   *Moving Picture Postcards; Heat Shimmer; Hillside at Chauritchi; Near Wilmington; Meteor Crater, Gosse Bluff; Ocean; Interior/Exterior*
1979   *Angophora and Sandstone; Coast at Pearl Beach; Notes on the Passage of Time*
1980   *Grain of the Voice Series: Rock Wallaby and Blackbird; Two Women; Seven Sisters; Unthurqua; Warrah; Experiments in Three-Colour Separation; Two-Colour Separation Studies; Pan/Colour Separations*
1981   *The Second Journey (To Uluru); Wilpena; Time/Colour Separations; Floterian—Hand Printings from a Film History*
1983   *Corporeal; Passage*
1984   *At Black Range; Waterfall; In This Life's Body*
1986   *Notes on Berlin, the Divided City*
1987   *Walking Track; The Berlin Apartment*
1988   *Projected Light*
1989   *Myself When Fourteen* (with Ivor Cantrill)
1990   *Bali Film*
1990-97 *The Bemused Tourist*
1991   *Agung Gives Ivor a Haircut*
1992   *View from the Balcony of the Marco Polo Hotel* (revised 1993); *Rendra's Place, Depok*
1993   *Walking to Yeh Pelu; The Pause between Frames; In the Shadow of Gunung Batur; Ming-Wei to Singaraja*
1994   *Ivor's Tiger Xmas Card*
1995   *Ivor's Exhibition; Ramayana/Legong; Jalan Raya, Ubud; Early Morning at Borobudur; Ivor Paints*

Publications by Cantrill

Book

With Arthur Cantrill, *Index to Cantrill's Filmnotes: Issues 1 to 51/52 (1971-1986),* Melbourne, 1987.

Articles

"*At Eltham, a Metaphor on Death,* Corinne Cantrill Writes about Her Film," in *Cantrill's Filmnotes,* December 1974.
With P. Wells, "Trans-Tasman Connections," in *Cantrill's Filmnotes* (Melbourne), November 1982.
"Notes on *In This Life's Body,*" in *Cantrill's Filmnotes* (Melbourne), October 1984.
"The Refracting Glasses," in *Cantrill's Filmnotes* (Melbourne), March 1993.
"The Centenary of Cinema," in *Cantrill's Filmnotes* (Melbourne), November 1994.
"A Journey within Manila, the City of Cities," in *Cantrill's Filmnotes* (Melbourne), November 1994.

Articles (with Arthur Cantrill)

"Film and Video in Auckland," in *Cantrill's Filmnotes* (Melbourne), July 1976.
"Liz England," in *Cantrill's Filmnotes* (Melbourne), July 1976.
"Philip Dadson," in *Cantrill's Filmnotes* (Melbourne), July 1976.
"(Three) Color Separation—Rediscovering an Early Colour Process," in *Cantrill's Filmnotes* (Melbourne), May 1977.
"'Edges of Meaning': A Piece for Primitive Cinema and Voices by Arthur and Corinne Cantrill at La Mama, Melbourne, November 1977," in *Cantrill's Filmnotes* (Melbourne), March 1978.
"'Fields of Vision,'" in *Cantrill's Filmnotes* (Melbourne), February 1979.
"*Grain of the Voice,*" in *Cantrill's Filmnotes* (Melbourne), August 1980.
Interview with T. McCullough, in *Cantrill's Filmnotes* (Melbourne), August 1980.

Corinne Cantrill in her film *In This Life's Body.*

"The 1901 Cinematography of Walter Baldwin Spencer," in *Cantrill's Filmnotes* (Melbourne), April 1982.

"The Baldwin Spencer Film Material—Conflict of Interests," in *Cantrill's Filmnotes* (Melbourne), April 1982.

"*Floterian—Hand Printings from a Film History,*" in *Cantrill's Filmnotes* (Melbourne), November 1982.

"An Interview with Philip Hoffman on His Film, *Passing Through/Torn Formations,*" in *Cantrill's Filmnotes* (Melbourne), September 1989.

"The Prestonia Films: *Projected Light* and *Autumn Light,*" in *Cantrill's Filmnotes* (Melbourne), September 1989.

"Dirk de Bruyn's *Conversations with My Mother,*" in *Cantrill's Filmnotes* (Melbourne), December 1990.

"Interview with Chris Welsby," in *Cantrill's Filmnotes* (Melbourne), December 1990.

"Interview with Gotot Prakosa," in *Cantrill's Filmnotes* (Melbourne), December 1990.

Publications on Cantrill

Books

Reade, Eric, *The Australian Screen,* Melbourne, 1975.

Thoms, A., *Polemics for a New Cinema,* Sydney, 1978.

Cantrill, Arthur, *Midstream: A Survey Exhibition of the Filmwork by Arthur and Corinne Cantrill, 1963-1979,* Parkville, Victoria, Australia, 1979.

Murray, Scott, editor, *The New Australian Cinema,* Melbourne, 1980.

Paroissian, Leon, editor, *Australian Art Review,* 1982.

Treole, V., *Australian Independent Film,* Sydney, 1982.

Blonski, Annette, Barbara Creed, and Freda Freiberg, editors, *Don't Shoot Darling! Women's Independent Filmmaking in Australia,* Richmond, Victoria, Australia, 1987.

Jones, Liz, *La Mama,* Melbourne, 1988.

Bertrand, Ina, editor, *Cinema in Australia, A Documentary History,* Sydney, 1989.

Moran, Albert, and Tom O'Regan, editors, *The Australian Screen,* Melbourne, 1989.

Shirley, Graham, *Australian Cinema,* Sydney, 1989.

Foster, Gwendolyn Audrey, *Women Film Directors: An International Bio-Critical Dictionary,* Westport, Connecticut, 1995.

Articles

Thomas, Kevin, "Showcase for the Unusual," in *Los Angeles Times,* 14 February 1973.

Rohdie, Sam, "Other Cinema," in *Cinema Papers* (Melbourne), April/June 1978.

Rohdie, Sam, "Arthur and Corinne Cantrill," in *Cinema Papers* (Melbourne), May/June 1979.

Bishop, Rod, "The Second Journey to Uluru," in *Cinema Papers* (Melbourne), November/December 1981.

"Arthur et Corinne Cantrill," in *Revue du Cinéma* (Paris), October 1983.

Hemensley, Kris, "*In This Life's Body* by Corinne and Arthur Cantrill," in *Cantrill's Filmnotes* (Melbourne), October 1984.

Tast, B., "Oeffentlich Selbst," in *Medium* (Frankfurt), July 1985.

Kapkc, Barry, "Cinema of the Senses: Selected Films of Arthur and Corinne Cantrill," in *Cinematograph* (San Francisco), vol. 3, 1988.

Cox, David, "The Light on the Hill," in *Filmnews* (Sydney), vol. 19, no. 1, 1989.

Harden, Fred, "Losing the Light," in *Cinema Papers* (Melbourne), January 1989.

Perry, D., "Filmmaking as Personal, as Craft, as Critical ...," in *Filmnews* (Sydney), vol. 21, no. 2, 1991.

Harden, Fred, "(Film) Notes on Technology," in *Cinema Papers* (Melbourne), March 1991.

* * *

Corinne Cantrill is one of Australia's preeminent experimental filmmakers, whose long-term collaboration with her husband Arthur has proved to be both prolific and influential. Before embarking on her film career, Corinne spent time in Europe where she studied music in Paris, sang in a choir in Denmark, and taught English in Italy. After she married Arthur Cantrill, she began making films with him in 1960. Since then, the Cantrills have made more than 150 films, including seven feature-length films.

In the early years of their film career, the Cantrills made a series of documentaries about children and art, and the occasional experimental short. Moreover, they used the money they made selling their films to the Australian Broadcasting Service to purchase a camera and other equipment. Consequently, throughout their productive careers, they have worked at home using their own equipment, without resorting to the more typical film industry mode of hiring facilities and crews.

In 1965 the Cantrills moved to London to seek treatment for their autistic son, and while in Europe they attended an experimental film festival that inspired their full-time commitment to avant-garde cinema. In 1969 they returned to Australia where Arthur accepted a university fellowship, which was instrumental in terms of enabling them to be enormously productive as filmmakers. Since then, they have worked exclusively in the field of personal and experimental film. Over the years, their work has explored numerous aspects of film, including multi-screen projections and film performance, single-frame structuring of film, landscape films that relate film forms to land forms, and works that have addressed the history of film and film technologies. On all of the films, they have worked closely together as equals, though some, such as *At Eltham* and *In This Life's Body* were mainly Corinne's projects. She has explained that she is drawn to experimental filmmaking strategies in particular for the ability they provide to "open up new areas of the film experience."

The Cantrills' extensive body of work ranges from the two-minute *Zap* to the 148-minute *In This Life's Body*. A significant part of their work displays their intense fascination with the landscape, an interest that began with their 1962 film series, *The Native Trees of Stradbroke Island*. Subsequent landscape films include *Bouddi*—filmed on the coast, *Earth Message*—with views of Canberra and its flora, and *Island Fuse*—also made at Stradbroke Island. The films convey a sense of awe for the landscape, and a respect for nature that is almost religious. In addition, the Cantrills have pursued their interest in the materiality and formal properties of film and image analysis, as in *Island Fuse,* in which they reworked existing film footage by refilming it and coloring it with filters frame by frame. Indeed, their formalist films have employed a variety of means to refer to and acknowledge the elements and basic properties of filmmaking, such as how the camera registers and records images, the mutability of celluloid, and projection properties, as well as the larger issues of how a film can structure space, time, and perception. Thus, the Cantrills have explored the properties of film stock, speed, and three-color separation (i.e., by using black-and-white film with red, green, and blue filters), as in their *Three Colour Separation Studies—Landscapes, Still Lifes,* and *Waterfall.* In the latter film, the Cantrills both create and discover many chance happenings and transformations in the natural setting. Also, they have interrogated the history of film form; thus, they have discovered in the anthropological films of Walter Baldwin Spencer a notable intersection between early silent cinema and the materialist concerns of later avant-garde filmmakers. Furthermore, they have explored personal experience and history, as in *In This Life's Body* in which Corinne used a collection of photographs to construct her autobiography. Similarly, Corinne has noted that their affinity for returning to the sites of earlier films is a theme that runs through their body of work, as in 1983's *Corporeal,* which was filmed at the site of their 1979 film, *Angophora and Sandstone* and 1980's *Warrah.*

Corinne's film *At Eltham* continued her fascination with the Australian landscape and it developed her ideas about "playing" the camera's functions like a musical instrument. It depicts the quintessential Australian landscape of eucalyptus-covered hills and the Yarra river seen through the trees. The soundtrack consists of a recording of the natural sounds at Eltham's birds and the river. In one of her essays, Corinne subtitled the film "A Metaphor on Death," thus referring to the Cantrills' despair, at the time, about their future as filmmakers in Australia and their decision to leave the country temporarily to pursue their dreams.

In This Life's Body is undoubtedly Corinne's career masterpiece. A personal and deeply contemplative documentary-autobiography, it provides a simple account of her life and work. She was prompted to make the film after a bout of illness when she became committed to preparing for the "inevitability of death," and had resolved to review and search for meaning in her life. Constructed almost totally with a collection of hundreds of still photographs—snapshots, studio portraits, and self portraits of Corinne alone and with her family and friends—along with bits of her movies, the film has a remarkable additive effect. Specifically, sequences of photographs are accompanied by Corinne's spoken narration, which at one point explains that she is using the photographs to re-create "her own history, her own story." The film's title refers to Corinne's "undogmatic" belief in reincarnation and to the possibility of changing one's life and of creating different stories about one's life. Critics consider it among the most powerful of such personal films.

The Cantrills' work has been screened internationally at film festivals, film museums, and art galleries. Together they have been instrumental in lecturing and writing about Australia's avant-garde film scene and history. And, since 1971, they have published and edited the film journal *Cantrill's Filmnotes,* a bi-annual review of innovative independent film and video that emphasizes experimental film, animation, video art, digital media and works of performance, sound and installation art from Australia and around the world, and that has made a significant contribution to the field of experimental film in Australia.

—Cynthia Felando

CAROLINA, Ana
Brazilian director and writer

Pseudonym: Full name, Ana Carolina Teixeira Soares. **Born:** São Paulo, Brazil, 1943. **Education:** Studied journalism and photography at the Universidade da São Paulo. **Career:** 1967-74—made short and medium length films; 1974—first feature film, the documentary *Getúlio Vargas.*

Films as Director

1968   *A Feira* (short); *Lavrador* (short) (co-d)
1969   *Indústria* (short); *Articulações* (short)
1970   *Tres Desenhos* (short); *Monteiro Lobato* (short) (co-d with Sarno); *As Fiandeiras* (short)
1972   *Guerra do Paraguai* (*War of Paraguay*) (doc, short)
1973   *Pantanal* (doc, short); *O Sonho Acabou* (short)
1974   *Getúlio Vargas* (doc)
1977   *Mar de Rosas* (*Sea of Roses*) (+ sc)
1979   *Nelson Pereira Dos Santos* (doc); *Anatomía do Espectador* (short—16mm)
1982   *Das Tripas Coração* (*Hearts and Guts*) (+ sc)
1987   *Sonho de Valsa* (*The Lady in Shining Armor*) (+ sc)

Publications by Carolina

Articles

Interview with Simon Hartog, in *Framework* (Norwich, England), no. 28, 1985.
Interview in *Cine y Mujer en América Latina: Directoras de Largometrajes de ficción,* edited by Luis Trelles Plazaola, Rio Piedras, Puerto Rico, 1991.

Publications on Carolina

Books

Foster, Gwendolyn Audrey, *Women Film Directors: An International Bio-Critical Dictionary,* Westport, Connecticut, 1995.
Barnard, Timothy, and Peter Rist, editors, *South American Cinema: A Critical Filmography, 1915-1994,* New York, 1996.

Articles

Mosier, John, "The New Brazilian Cinema: Ana Carolina," in *Américas* (Washington, D.C.), May/June 1983.
"*Mar de Rosas*: Critical Dossier," in *Framework* (Norwich, England), no. 28, 1985.

*   *   *

Brazilian Ana Carolina arrived at filmmaking after first pursuing a career in medicine and then in journalism and photography. Her ultimate career choice did not reflect a childhood of moviegoing, in fact her family rarely went to the movies. A medical student in the turbulent sixties, Carolina found herself more attracted to the university's cultural activities and academics than to her medical courses. She fell in love with a film student and began to make films with him. He wanted to make documentaries and that led Carolina first to the production of documentary films. As Carolina commented to Luis Trelles Plazaola in a 1989 interview, "I had no ideology, neither as a cinephile nor in any way." From this rather odd beginning, Carolina quickly progressed to writing, producing, and directing her own films.

In the late 1960s, Brazilian life was ruled by a repressive dictatorship. Brazilian filmmakers concentrated on politicized projects, striving to use film to engage the audience and to incite change. Carolina entered the scene making social, cultural, poetic, and political documentaries, films for which she was imprisoned twice. Made in 1974, her first feature film, *Getúlio Vargas,* documented the political life of Vargas, who ruled Brazil as president from 1930 to 1945 and again from 1951 to 1954, his rule ending with his suicide. With this film, Carolina learned about the commercial aspects of filmmaking, working with producers, restructuring her approach to cinematic time to suit the rhythm of a feature-length film, and anticipating a more commercial audience.

In a 1985 interview, Carolina commented that it was the experience of making *Getúlio Vargas* that made her see the possibility of making feature films. Not only were documentaries not commercially viable, but it was very difficult to express political views in such a "real" way given Brazil's repressed political culture. So, she went inside herself and followed *Getúlio Vargas* with a trilogy of films centered around female protagonists confronting and sometimes subverting their roles within a patriarchal society. It is difficult to classify neatly *Sea of Roses, Hearts and Guts,* or *The Lady in Shining Armor* as any one genre. Here we defer to Carolina who describes the films as "dramatic comedy," lacking any more well-defined category for them.

In *Sea of Roses,* Carolina's best-known film, two generations are contrasted: The mother is pushed around by the macho husband and, even though she attempts to flee with her daughter, she ultimately has no way out. Her daughter, however, might escape the controlling patriarchal family structure. With its nonsensical, even hysterical dialogue, the film might at first seem absurd. Yet, the tension between man and woman and between generations is very real and quite poignant. Called "modern and inventive" by one critic, "at once iconoclastic and malicious" by another, and "schizophrenic" by a third, *Sea of Roses* offers characters informed by Carolina's own experiences, as both the daughter in a patriarchally ordered family and a daughter of Brazil.

Tereza, the protagonist of *The Lady in Shining Armor,* is a single 30-something woman who lives with and seems to have strangely close relationships with her father and brother. The film examines her near-hysterical search for a man, literally a "Prince Charming" who will love her unconditionally for the rest of her life, and her continual disappointment. This plot summary, however, is misleading because it omits the central elements of the film—Tereza's fantasies or nightmares, filled with religious imagery that are at once both humorous and scandalous. Another child of Brazil's recent repressive regime, Tereza's quest for love belies her search for herself—as she says herself early in the film, she has no identity.

Set in a girls' boarding school, *Hearts and Guts* explores the hypocrisy and educational atmosphere that control the students' behavior. The 16- and 17-year-old girls are rebellious and curious. Confused about their identities, especially their sexual identities, these girls go on hysterical (both pathologically and humoristically) romps through the school, obsessing about each other and their teachers.

It is fitting that Carolina's first feature examined Vargas's life, as her subsequent films are peopled by the generation most affected by his rule, and the generation perhaps most responsible for the pushing Brazil toward a representative democracy in the 1960s. Carolina speaks often of "power" and believes that her generation never had any sense of their own power, as individuals or as a group, because of Vargas's paternalistic, repressive regime. Her characters struggle with this, and amuse their audiences with their attempts at rebellion.

—Ilene S. Goldman

CAVANI, Liliana
Italian director and writer

Born: Emilia, Italy, 12 January 1937. **Education:** Attended University of Bologna, B.A. in classic literature; graduated from Rome's film school, Centro Sperimentale di Cinematografia. **Career:** Early 1960s—directed documentaries and dramas for RAI (Italian television); 1966—made her first feature film, *Francesco d'Assisi*; 1974—made her most famous feature film, *The Night Porter.* **Awards:** Ciak

d'Oro, Migliore Allievo al Centro Sperimentale di Cinematografia. **Address:** via Filangeri 4, Rome, Italy.

Films as Director

1961   *Incontro notturno*
1962   *L'evento*
1962-63   *Storia del terzo Reich (Story of the Third Reich)* (doc for TV)
1963   *L'eta' di Stalin (The Age of Stalin)* (doc for TV)
1964   *La Casa in Italia (The House in Italy)* (doc for TV)
1965   *Philippe Pétain: Processo a Vichy (Philippe Petain: Trial at Vichy)* (doc for TV); *La Donna Nella Resistenza (Women of the Resistance)* (doc for TV); *Gesu' mio Fratello (Jesus, My Brother)* (doc for TV); *Il Giorno Della Pace (The Day of Peace)* (doc for TV)
1966   *Francesco d'Assisi* (+ co-sc)
1968   *Galileo* (+ co-sc, co-st)
1969   *I Cannibali (The Cannibals)* (+ co-sc, st)
1971   *L'Ospite (The Hospital; The Guest)* (+ co-sc, st)
1973   *Milarepa* (+ co-sc, st)
1974   *Il Portiere di notte (The Night Porter)* (+ co-sc, st)
1977   *Al di là del bene e del male (Beyond Good and Evil; Oltre il Bene e il Male)* (+ co-sc, st)
1981   *La Pelle (The Skin)* (+ co-sc)
1983   *Beyond the Door (Oltre la Porta)* (+ co-sc, co-st)
1986   *Interno Berlinese (The Berlin Affair; Affair in Berlin)* (+ co-sc)
1988   *Francesco (St. Francis of Assisi)* (+ co-sc, st)
1993   *Dove siete? Io sono qui (Where Are You? I'm Here)* (for TV) (+ co-sc, co-st)

Publications by Cavani

Scripts

Milarepa, Bologna, 1974
Il Portiere di notte, Torino, 1975.
Al di là del bene e del male, Torino, 1977.
Oltre la Porta, Torino, 1982.

Books

Francesco d'Assisi, Torino, 1967.
Lettere dall'interno: Racconto per un film su Simone Weil, Torino, 1974.
Francesco, Milan, 1989.
Dove siete? Io sono qui, Venice, 1993.

Articles

"Liliana Cavani: le mythe, le sexe, et la revolte," interview with Claire Clouzot, in *Ecran* (Paris), June 1974.
Interview with D. Maillet, in *Cinématographe* (Paris), June/July 1974.
"In Liliana Cavani's Love Story, Love Means Always Having to Say Ouch," interview with G. Lichtenstein, in *New York Times,* 13 October 1974.
"Consciousness and Conscience," interview with A. Stuart, in *Films and Filming* (London), February 1975.

Interview with G. Braucourt, in *Ecran* (Paris), 15 March 1977.

Interview with Claire Clouzot, in *Ecran* (Paris), 15 November 1977.

"Jeg lager ikke film for a hjelpe noen," interview with G. Jarto, in *Film & Kino* (Oslo), no. 1, 1982.

Interview with S. Adler, in *Cinema Papers* (North Melbourne), December 1982.

"Nochnoi Port'e," script excerpt, in *Iskusstvo Kino* (Moscow), no. 6, 1991.

"Un antisistema di valori," in *Rivista del Cinematografo* (Rome), July/August 1992.

Publications on Cavani

Books

Smith, Sharon, *Women Who Make Movies*, New York, 1975.

Tiso, Ciriaco, *Cavani: Liliana Cavani*, Florence, 1975.

García del Vall, Arnoldo, *Liliana Cavani*, Madrid, 1980.

de Lauretis, Teresa, *Technologies of Gender: Essays on Theory, Film, and Fiction*, Bloomington, Indiana, 1987.

Bruno, Giuliana, and Maria Nadotti, editors, *Offscreen: Women and Film in Italy*, London, 1988.

Silverman, Kaja, *The Acoustic Mirror*, Bloomington, Indiana, 1988.

Acker, Ally, *Reel Women: Pioneers of the Cinema, 1896 to the Present*, New York, 1991.

Foster, Gwendolyn Audrey, *Women Film Directors: An International Bio-Critical Dictionary*, Westport, Connecticut, 1995.

Busciemi, Francesco, *Invito al cinema die Liliana Cavani*, Milan, 1996.

Marrone, Gaetana, *The Cinema of Liliana Cavani: The Gaze and the Labyrinth*, forthcoming.

Articles

"*The Night Porter*," in *Films and Filming* (London), September 1973.

"Biofilmographie: Liliana Cavani," in *Avant-Scene du Cinèma* (Paris), May 1974.

Meyer, F., "Cavani in N.Y., Crix Pan *Porter* Wow in Europe; Next for Levine," in *Variety* (New York), 9 October 1974.

Salmi, M., in *Film Dope* (Hertfordshire, England), November 1974.

Haskell, Molly, "Are Women Directors Different?," in *Village Voice* (New York), 3 February 1975.

Lennard, E., and N. L. Bernheim, "A Portfolio of European Directors," in *Ms.* (New York), January 1977.

Magny, J., "Le Cas Cavani," in *Telecine* (Paris), December 1977.

Weemaes, G., "Liliana Cavani," in *Film en Televisie* (Brussels), March 1978.

Gasperi, A. de, "Liliana Cavani, par qui le scandale arrive," in *Cine Revue* (Brussels), 8 May 1986.

Helman, A., "Dwie twarze Liliany Cavani," in *Kino* (Warsaw), October 1989.

Marrone, Gaetana, "Narratività e storia in *Interno Berlinese* di Liliana Cavani," in *Romance Languages Annual 1989*, edited by Ben Lawton and Anthony Julian Tamburri, West Lafayette, Indiana, 1990.

Marrone, Gaetana, "L'attualità di *Francesco*: Incontro con Liliana Cavani," in *L'anello che non tiene*, Fall 1990.

Piersanti, A., "Al di la del rumore," in *Rivista del Cinematografo* (Rome), April 1992.

Marrone, Gaetana, "The Staging of Cavani's *Galileo*: The Historiographer's Art," in *Etica cristiana e scrittori del Novecento*, edited by Florinda Iannace, *Forum Italicum*, Library no. 5, 1993.

Filmography, in *Segnocinema* (Vicenza, Italy), November/December 1993.

de Lauretis, Teresa, "Rethinking Women's Cinema," in *Multiple Voices in Feminist Film Criticism*, edited by Diane Carson, Linda Dittmar, and Janice Welsch, Minneapolis, 1994.

Comuzio, E., "Primo Goldoni: Il Cinema di Liliana Cavani," in *Cineforum* (Bergamo, Italy), January/February 1994.

Marrone, Gaetana, "Ideologia, creatività e iconografia nella Chiara di Liliana Cavani," in *Italian Women Mystics*, edited by Dino Cergingi, *Annali d'italianistica*, vol. 13, 1995.

* * *

Since the 1960s, Italian director Liliana Cavani has been a prolific filmmaker. Her film career began when she directed a series of documentary histories and dramas for RAI—Italian television. RAI eventually produced her first feature film, and since then Cavani has focused on making commercial fiction films.

In general, Cavani's films are known for their emphasis on the pleasure and danger of power and politics. Her early work provided compelling new perspectives on historical and mythological figures, including *Francesco d'Assisi*, *Galileo*, *The Cannibals*, and *Milarepa*. Her first fiction feature, for example, was *The Cannibals*, which revisits the myth of Antigone in relation to contemporary political revolts against state repression in Italy. In addition, Cavani has been drawn to German culture themes, as in *Beyond Good and Evil*, about Nietzsche and Lou Andreas Salomé; *The Night Porter*, which looks at Nazism from the perspective of sexual politics; and *The Berlin Affair*, about a Japanese-German lesbian couple—from a Japanese novel that she set in Germany. Cavani's films may be characterized as critiques of political hierarchies, though, interestingly, it is the male characters who embody the critique and speak for change. Her primary interest in male characters and performers is revealed in her strange claim that "each of my [male] actors looks a bit like me." Although most of her films have central male characters, *The Berlin Affair* is about a lesbian relationship; similarly, *Women of the Resistance* is about the struggle of women who fought against fascism. Like her contemporary, Lina Wertmüller, to whom she is often compared, Cavani's films do not typically focus on female protagonists; it is male characters who occupy the privileged positions, in terms of both image and story. Additional exceptions are the female figures of Antigone in *The Cannibals*, and the psychoanalyst Lou Andreas Salomé in *Beyond Good and Evil*.

In the United States, Cavani's best-known work is *The Night Porter*, a difficult and challenging film that tells the dark, melancholy story of a sadomasochistic love affair between an ex-Nazi officer and the concentration camp inmate (Lucia) he raped 15 years earlier. The man, Max, is part of a group of Nazis who have avoided conviction for their crimes when key evidence is destroyed and crucial witnesses are murdered. As a result, Max and Lucia meet again accidentally, in 1957, when he is working as the night porter at a Vienna hotel; soon they resume their relationship. As depicted by Cavani, their "love affair" is a twisted psychological game that allegorically alludes to the unequal yet mutually dependent relationship between oppressor countries and the weaker countries over which they exert their wicked dominance. Critics in the United States panned the film, especially for its "kinky" fascist imagery, but it proved to be financially successful and garnered considerable attention for Cavani.

Liliana Cavani

Cavani has consistently rejected the notion that she brings a different, gender-based perspective to her work; nevertheless, feminist film critics have found ways to read feminist empowerment into her films, inasmuch as they offer unconventional representations of sexuality and they question knowledge and its relation to power. Similarly, her films usually focus on social and political issues; in addition to treating themes of violence and sex. Feminist film scholar Kaja Silverman has argued that Cavani should be considered a true auteur because, in addition to featuring a coherence of themes, her work is unique in relation to both mainstream and experimental cinemas. In addition, she contends that Cavani's films are "neither classically 'feminine' nor overtly feminist." Silverman readily notes the difficulties that feminist viewers have had with her work, since not one of her many features explicitly treats the subject of sexual oppression or depicts active feminist resistance to it. Certainly, Cavani's work is not about women specifically, as are the films of Laura Mulvey, Michelle Citron, and Lizzie Borden, for example; so, her female characters seem to have little to offer feminist analyses. But, Silverman contends that Cavani's films holds the possibility of feminist readings because they demonstrate the "fatal lure of masochism" for their male characters, and they work to elide the boundaries between male and female identity (as when *The Night Porter*'s Max and Lucia trade roles in their sadomasochistic scenarios). Indeed, Silverman suggests that Antigone's male cohort in *The Canni-*

buts, *The Night Porter*'s Max, and Paul in *Beyond Good and Evil* all occupy "feminine" positions that demand passivity, suffering, and sacrifice. Likewise, in her earlier film, *Francesco d'Assisi*, Francesco continually gives away his material possessions—clothing, money, and furniture—thus implying his increasing cultural alienation. That is, his acts are a means by which to refuse power and privilege and to thereby assert the equality between himself and the people around him. Interestingly, Cavani revisited this character in 1988 with *Francesco*, which likewise traces the spiritual awakening of the decadent son of a rich merchant, who experiences a religious call and subsequently abandons his past to help the poor and needy in his community.

In recent years, Cavani has been spending more time directing stage productions and seems to have moved away from film.

—Cynthia Felando

CECCHI D'AMICO, Suso
Italian writer

Born: Giovanna Cecchi in Rome, 21 July 1914; daughter of the writer Emilio Cecchi. **Education:** Studied in Rome and Cambridge.

Family: Married the music critic Fedele D'Amico. **Career:** Journalist; translator of English-language plays; 1946—first film as writer, *Mio figlio professore*; 1977—co-writer for TV miniseries *Gesù di Nazareth* (*Jesus of Nazareth*); writer for TV, *Una moglie,* 1987, *Quattro storie di donne,* 1990. **Awards:** Best script award, Sindicato Nazionale Giornalisti Cinematografici Italiani, for *Let's Hope It's a Girl,* 1986. **Address:** via Paisiello 27, 00198 Rome, Italy.

Films as Writer

1946 *Mio figlio professore* (*Professor My Son*) (Castellani); *Vivere in pace* (*To Live in Peace*) (Zampa); *Roma città libera* (Pagliero)

1947 *Il delitto di Giovanni Episcopo* (*Flesh Will Surrender*) (Lattuada); *L'onorevole Angelina* (*Angelina*) (Zampa)

1948 *Fabiola* (Blasetti); *Ladri di biciclette* (*The Bicycle Thief*) (De Sica) (co); *Patto col diavolo* (Chiarini); *Cielo sulla palude* (*Heaven over the Marshes*) (Genina)

1949 *Le mura di Malapaga* (*The Walls of Malapaga*) (Clément) (co-sc Italian version); *Prohibito rubare* (*Guaglio*) (Comencini)

1950 *Miracolo a Milano* (*Miracle in Milan*) (De Sica) (co); *E primavera* (*It's Forever Springtime*) (Castellani); *E più facile che un cammello* (Zampa); *Romazo d'amore* (Toselli) (Coletti)

1951 *Due mogli sono troppe* (*Honeymoon Deferred*) (Camerini); *Bellissima* (Visconti)

1952 "Primo amore" ep. of *Altri tempi* (*Times Gone By*) (Blasetti); *Processo alla città* (*A Town on Trial*) (Zampa); *Buon Giorno, elefante!* (*Hello, Elephant!*; *Pardon My Trunk*) (Franciolini); *I vinti* (*I nostri figli*) (Antonioni); *Il mondo le condanna* (*His Last Twelve Hours*) (Franciolini)

1953 *Siamo donne* (*We the Women*) (Visconti); "Il pupo" ep. of *Tempi nostri* (*Anatomy of Love*) (Blassetti); *Febbre di vivere* (Gora); *La signora senza camelie* (*Camille without Camellias*; *The Lady without Camellias*) (Antonioni); *Cento anni d'amore* (de Felice)

1954 *Graziella* (Bianchi); *Senso* (*The Wanton Contessa*) (Visconti); *L'allegro squadrone* (Moffa); *Peccato che sia una canaglia* (*Too Bad She's Bad*) (Blasetti); *Proibito* (Monicelli)

1955 *Le amiche* (*The Girlfriends*) (Antonioni)

1956 *La fortuna di essere donna* (*Lucky to Be a Woman*) (Blasetti); *La finestra sul Luna Park* (Comencini); *Kean* (Gassman); *Difendo il mio amore* (Sherman) (co)

1957 *Le notti bianche* (*White Nights*) (Visconti); *Mariti in città* (Comencini)

1958 *Nella città l'inferno* (*And the Wild, Wild Women*) (Castellani); *La sfida* (*The Challenge*) (Rosi); *I soliti ignoti* (*Big Deal on Madonna Street*) (Monicelli)

1959 *Estate violenta* (*Violent Summer*) (Zurlini); *I magliari* (Rosi)

1960 *La contessa azzurra* (Gora); *Rocco e i suoi fratelli* (*Rocco and His Brothers*) (Visconti) (co); *Risate di gioia* (*The Passionate Thief*) (Monicelli); *It Started in Naples* (Shavelson)

1961 *Salvatore Giuiliano* (Rosi); *Il relitto* (*The Wastrel*) (Cacoyannis); *I due nemici* (*The Best of Enemies*) (Hamilton)

1962 "Il lavoro" ("The Job") and "Renzo e Luciana" ("Renzo and Luciana") eps. of *Boccaccio '70* (Visconti and Monicelli);

"Le Lièvre et la tortue" ("The Tortoise and the Hare") ep. of *Les Quatre Vérités* (*Three Fables of Love*) (Blasetti)

1963 *Il gattopardo* (*The Leopard*) (Visconti) (co); *Gli indifferenti* (*Time of Indifference*) (Maselli)

1965 *Casanova '70* (Monicelli); *Vaghe stelle dell'orsa* (*Sandra*) (Visconti)

1966 *Io, io, io ... e gli altri* (Blasetti); "Queen Armenia" ep. of *Le fate* (*The Queens*) (Monicelli); *Spara forte, più forte ... non capisco* (*Shout Loud, Louder ... I Don't Understand*) (De Filippo); *The Taming of the Shrew* (Zeffirelli)

1967 *Lo straniero* (*The Stranger*) (Visconti); *L'uomo, l'orgoglio, la vendetta* (*Man, Pride and Vengeance*) (Bazzoni)

1969 *Metello* (Bolognini); *Infanzia, vocazione, e prime esperienze di Giacomo Casanova, Veneziano* (Comencini); *Senza sapere nulla di lei* (Comencini)

1971 *La mortadella* (*Lady Liberty*) (Monicelli)

1972 *Pinocchio* (Comencini—for TV); *Fratello sole, sorella luna* (*Brother Sun, Sister Moon*) (Zeffirelli); *Il diavolo nel cervello* (Sollima); *I figli chiedono perche* (Zanchin)

1973 *Ludwig* (Visconti); *Amore e ginnastica* (L. F. d'Amico)

1974 *Gruppo di famiglia in un interno* (*Conversation Piece*; *Violence et Passion*) (Visconti); *Prete, fai un miracolo* (Chiari); *Amore amaro* (Vancini) (co)

1976 *L'innocente* (*The Innocent*) (Visconti); *Caro Michele* (Monicelli); *Dimmi che fai tutto per mei* (Festa Campanile)

1980 *La velia* (Ferrero)

1983 *Lighea* (Tuzii) (co); *Les Mots pour le dire* (Pinheiro) (co)

1984 *Cuore* (Comencini—for TV); *Uno scandale per bene* (Festa Campanile); *Bertoldo, Bertoldino e Cacasenno* (Monicelli) (co)

1985 *Le due vite di Mattia Pascal* (*The Two Lives of Mattia Pascal*) (Monicelli) (co)

1986 *I soliti ignoti vent'anni dopo* (*Big Deal on Madonna Street...20 Years Later*) (Todini) (co); *Speriamo che sia femmina* (*Let's Hope It's a Girl*) (Monicelli) (co); *La storia* (*History*) (Comencini) (co)

1987 *L'inchiesta* (Damiani) (co); *Oci ciornie* (*Dark Eyes*) (Mikhalkov) (co); *I picari* (Monicelli)

1988 *Ti presento un'amica* (Massaro)

1989 *Stradivari* (Battiato) (co)

1990 *Il male oscuro* (Monicelli); *Rossini, Rossini* (Monicelli)

1992 *Parenti serpenti* (Monicelli) (co)

1993 *La fine e nota* (Cristina Comencini); *Cari fottutissimi amici* (Monicelli) (co)

1995 *Facciamo paradiso* (Monicelli)

1996 *Bruno aspetta in macchna* (Camerina) (co-st only)

Publications by Cecchi d'Amico

Books

(Translator with Emilio Cecchi) *Otello* in *Teatro,* by Shakespeare, vol. 3, Florence, 1961.

With others, *Bicycle Thieves* (script), London, 1968, as *The Bicycle Thief,* New York, 1968.

With others, *Miracle in Milan* (script), New York, 1968.

With Luchino Visconti, *Senso* and *La terra trema* (scripts), in *Two Screenplays,* New York, 1970.

With others, *The Job, Rocco and His Brothers,* and *White Nights* (scripts), in *Three Screenplays,* New York, 1970.

Articles

Positif (Paris), September 1985.
Revista del Cinematografo, vol. 62, September 1992.
Revista del Cinematografo, vol. 63, 1993.

Publications on Cecchi d'Amico

Book

Hochkofler, Matilde, and Orio Caldiron, *Suso Cecchi d'Amico, scriveri du cinema,* Bari, 1988.

Articles

Sight and Sound (London), Winter 1986-87.
Filmihullu, no. 2, 1989.

*   *   *

Suso Cecchi d'Amico is undoubtedly best known as Visconti's regular scriptwriter, however her work, either alone or in collaboration, with a large number of other directors is at the core of a long list of films which embodies the development of postwar Italian cinema from Blasetti to De Sica, from Rosi to Zeffirelli and Antonioni. It is undoubtedly a tribute to her work that her scripts achieve a certain "transparency," becoming all-but-inextricable from the finished film itself.

She has all too modestly described her work as akin to that of the artisan. This emphasizes her professionalism, the literate well-craftedness of her scripts, and her endless adaptability to the contrasting needs of filmmakers working within competing stylistic conventions. It glosses over the acuteness of her appraisal of particular projects and particular directors. Luigi Comencini may be no great stylist, as she has remarked, his films stand or fall by their overall effect. *Cuore* is a tender and ironic melodrama but anchored cogently to moments in Italian history. Zampa may be a minor talent but with *To Live in Peace* Cecchi d'Amico wrote to the project's integrity and antiheroic pacifism. Her script gives Genina's strange melodrama about a peasant girl's rape and subsequent sanctification, *Heaven over the Marshes,* a much-needed steely quality.

Writing for De Sica made other demands. Cecchi d'Amico has spoken of his need "to borrow from and reproduce" reality, a need that predated any theorization of neorealism. The moral catch-22 behind *The Bicycle Thief* lends De Sica's slice-of-life a bitter edge. Her collaboration with Francesco Rosi has been equally rewarding. A trial transcript provided the source for Salvatore Giuliano's script, the framework for a film of epic dimension honed from events both sordid and sadly routine. But where she worked with a director whose own drive was towards honing away excesses and revealing a structure, the results were less happy. Where Antonioni saw his films as the bare rendition of reality, Cecchi d'Amico saw contemporary fables.

It was the opportunity posed by working for Visconti with his concern for the firm location of characters within a specific time, place, and history that drew from her her best work. She has said that his clarity of vision and sureness made him an easy person to work for, and there is an obvious complementarity between her spareness and Visconti's rhetorical visual style. Initial efforts for him required copious pruning to adapt them to his particular "cinematic rhythm." So completely did Visconti make his projects his own that they escape the category of "literary adaptation," and are rewritten and reformed to his own vision. Where a subject interested him but a suitable text could not be found, Cecchi d'Amico has spoken of the preparation of a script only after a considerable amount of research had been done. Even a contemporary subject might have a literary analogue. Thus Dostoyevsky was a touchstone for *Rocco and His Brothers.*

Rocco, an original story, knits its moral conundrum into a precisely located mise-en-scène, as it follows the attempts of a Southern peasant family to adjust to a new life in the North, and in doing so charts the stresses attendant upon Italy's own path to industrialization.

The script's major coup is the withholding of an explicit statement of the immigrant's code of morality until the final section, where it acquires an especially revelatory force, marking a passage from the certainties of an agrarian society, to notions of compromise embodied in a trade-off between rights and duties. The concern for issues of morality, betrayal, and personal and national history that are present here also underlie many of her other projects for Visconti, including *The Innocent, Senso, Ludwig,* and *Conversation Piece.*

The same concerns give her extraordinary gallery of female characters a memorable distinctiveness. Often transgressive they are always true to their time and place and never airbrushed into stereotype. Another consistent thread has been her collaborations with Monicelli, a director known for his humorously ironic tales of bourgeois life. The 1990 *Il male oscuro* was scripted with Tonino Guerra from a prize-winning 1960s novel (translated as *Incubus* in the United States) by Giuseppe Berto. It studies the relationships between a mediocre writer undergoing analysis, his younger wife, and his obsessive, ambivalent relationship with his father. The family theme is continued with *Parenti serpenti,* an examination of the tensions that arise as three generations of an extended family attempt Christmas together. Humor and irony also underlie her contributions to the script for Mikhalkov's *Dark Eyes.*

Her experience of writing a supposedly "Ben Hecht" script for Wyler's *Roman Holiday* (she took the job out of admiration for the director), which involved stringing together a series of banal generic elements, merely confirmed her observations of the wholly pernicious effect of Hollywood's postwar incursion into Italian filmmaking. (The Italian industry was, in her opinion, to be destroyed and the country opened up as a market for U.S. product.) Occasionally there were other international co-productions, including the Taylor-Burton *The Taming of the Shrew* for which her early experience as a translator of English literature into Italian might in part have prepared her, and on which she worked with Paul Dehn. But her preoccupations lay elsewhere. Cecchi d'Amico has always believed in the necessity of developing a national cinema that would "tell its own stories." It has been an unstinting dedication to this principle which underlies her work.

—Verina Glaessner

CHENZIRA, Ayoka
American producer, director, animator, and writer

Born: Philadelphia, 1956. **Education:** Attended New York University, B.F.A. 1975; Columbia University/Teachers College, M.A. **Family:** Married the choreographer Thomas Osha Pinnock, daugh-

Ayoka Chenzira. Photograph by André Harris.

ter: Haj. **Career:** 1981-84—program director of the Black Filmmakers Foundation; 1984—one of seven writer/directors selected for the Sundance Institute; mid-1980s—formed Red Carnelian, a production and distribution company in New York; founding board member, Production Partners, New York; professor and chair, department of communications, film, and video, City College of New York; 1993—producer/director of a series of animated shorts for the Children's Television Workshop; 1996—consultant to M-Net Television, South Africa. **Awards:** Brooklyn Cultural Crossroads Achievement Award, 1981; Paul Robeson Award, 1984; First Place/Cultural Affairs, National Black Programming Consortium, 1984; Mayor's Award—New York, Outstanding Contributions to the Field, 1987; Mayor's Award—Detroit, Contributions to the Field, 1987; First Place for Animation, Black Filmmakers Hall of Fame, for *Zajota and the Boogie Spirit,* 1990; Best Producer, National Black Programming Consortium, 1990; Silver Apple, National Educational Film and Video Festival, 1990; First Place, Sony Innovator Award in Media, 1991; First Place, John Hanks Award, 1991; First Place, Dance Screen, 1992; Best Overall, Best Drama, and Community Choice Award, Black Filmmakers Hall of Fame, for *MOTV,* 1993. **Address:** Red Carnelian, 1380 Dean Street, Brooklyn, NY 11216, U.S.A.

Films as Director

1979   *Syvilla: They Dance to Her Drum* (doc, short) (+ pr, sc)
1982   *Flamboyant Ladies Speak Out* (short)
1984   *Hair Piece: A Film for Nappyheaded People* (animated short) (+ pr, sc, co-ed, art work, animation)
1985   *Secret Sounds Screaming* (doc, short) (+ pr, mus)
1986   *Five Out of Five* (mus video) (+ ed)
1988   *Boa Morte* (doc, short) (+ co-pr)
1989   *The Lure and the Lore* (short) (+ pr, ed)
1990   *Zajota and the Boogie Spirit* (short) (+ pr, sc, ed, animation)
1992   *Pull Your Head to the Moon* (short—for TV); *Williamswood* (short—for TV) (+ ed)
1993   *Love Potion* (short) (+ pr); *Alma's Rainbow* (+ co-pr, sc); *MOTV (My Own TV)* (+ pr)
1994   *Snowfire* (short) (+ pr, sc, mus, ph)
1995   *Sentry at the Gate: The Comedy of Jane Galvin-Lewis* (+ co-pr, ph)
1997   *In the Rivers of Mercy Angst* (short) (+ pr, sc, ph)

Other Film

1986   *On Becoming a Woman* (Chisolm) (animation)

Publication by Chenzira

Article

"The Joys and Pitfalls of Self Distribution," in *Next Step, the Media Project* (Oregon), Spring 1989.

Publications on Chenzira

Books

Reid, Mark, *Redefining Black Film,* Berkeley, 1993.
Foster, Gwendolyn Audrey, *Women Film Directors: An International Bio-Critical Dictionary,* Westport, Connecticut, 1995.
Foster, Gwendolyn Audrey, *Women Filmmakers of the African Diaspora,* Carbondale, Illinois, 1997.
Moon, Spencer, *Reel Black Talk: A Sourcebook of 50 American Filmmakers,* Westport, Connecticut, 1997.

Articles

Campbell, Loretta, "Reinventing Our Image, Eleven Black Women Filmmakers," in *Heresies,* vol. 16, 1983.
Boseman, Keith, "Ayoka Chenzira: Sharing the Empowerment of Women," in *Black Film Review* (Washington, D.C.), Summer 1986.
Kafi-Akua, Afua, "Ayoka Chenzira, Filmmaker," in *SAGE: A Scholarly Journal on Black Women,* Spring 1987.
Smith, Valerie, "Reconstituting the Image," in *Callaloo: A Journal of Afro-American and African Arts and Letters,* Fall 1988.
Gibson-Hudson, Gloria, "Through Women's Eyes: The Films of Women in Africa and the African Diaspora," in *Western Journal of Black Studies,* vol. 15, no. 2, 1991.
Tate, Greg, "Cinematic Sisterhood," in *Village Voice* (New York), Special Film Issue, June 1991.
Gibson-Hudson, Gloria, "African American Literary Criticism as a Model for the Analysis of Films by African American Women," in *Wide Angle* (Baltimore, Maryland), July/October 1991.
Welbon, Yvonne, "Calling the Shots: Black Women Filmmakers Take the Helm," in *Independent* (New York), March 1992.
Bambara, Toni Cade, "Reading the Signs, Empowering the Eye: *Daughters of the Dust* and the Black Independent Cinema Movement," in *Black American Cinema,* edited by Manthia Diawara, New York, 1993.
Gibson-Hudson, Gloria, "Aspects of Black Feminist Cultural Ideology in Films by Black American Women Independent Artists," in *Multiple Voices in Feminist Film Criticism,* edited by Diane Carson, Linda Dittmar, and Janice R. Welsch, Minneapolis, 1994.
Hall, Amiee, "Ayoka Chenzira: One Step at a Time," in *Black Camera: The Newsletter of the Black Film Center/Archive* (Bloomington, Indiana), vol. 12, no. 1, 1997.

* * *

Ayoka Chenzira, considered one of the first African-American women animators, is an independent film and video artist who has received international renown in the areas of dramatic narrative, experimental, documentary, animation, and cross-genre productions. She brings to her work a diverse background in the arts, including photography, theater, music, and dance. Like many other African-American media artists, Chenzira can also be considered a media activist because her work challenges the exclusionary practices of mainstream media and frees African Americans from the confines of one-dimensional stereotypes. But she can also be considered a media activist in a stricter sense because of her efforts as an educator and her efforts on behalf of other film and video artists. Chenzira's most well-known works are *Hair Piece: A Film for Nappyheaded People* (1984), *Secret Sounds Screaming* (1985), and *Alma's Rainbow* (1993), three very different films, with differing subjects and styles—demonstrating Chenzira's varied talents as a film and video artist.

Hair Piece is a satirical animated short film about the cultural politics of African-American hairstyles. Chenzira uses humor to comment on a very serious and rarely discussed subject—the internalization of European standards of beauty by African Americans and its negative effects. Like "colorism," the preference for lighter-skin tones over darker, the delineation of "good hair" from "bad hair" has had severe consequences for the African-American community, affecting familial relationships, employment, education, and self-esteem. By affirming the natural beauty of natural hair styles over processed, *Hair Piece,* as Gloria Gibson-Hudson states, "dramatizes that exploration and affirmation of self can bring a keener sense of one's personal and cultural identity."

Chenzira was one of the first media producers to address the widespread problem of sexual child abuse with her documentary *Secret Sounds Screaming.* Rather than approaching the subject as one consisting of isolated cases, Chenzira places the abuse of children within a social and cultural context. It is a unique documentary, as it allows individuals from different aspects of the problem to directly address the audience: survivors of sexual child abuse, parents of abused children, and social-service professionals.

Alma's Rainbow, Chenzira's first feature-length film, is a contemporary drama set in Brooklyn, New York. As a coming-of-age film it is uncommon, because it is centered on the experiences of an African-American girl and her relationship with two other female characters: her aunt and her mother.

In addition to her work as a media artist, Chenzira is also a professor of communications, film, and video at City College of New York, Chenzira has been an important force in the lives of the students, department, and institution. In addition to her contributions in the classroom, her tenure at the college has included service as the director of the B.F.A. program in production, development of special workshops and seminars, and facilitating the participation of media professionals such as director Julie Dash, cinematographer Robert Shepard, and editor Lillian Benson, the first African-American woman accepted into the American Cinema Editors union.

In the mid-1980s Chenzira formed Red Carnelian, a New York-based production and distribution company that focuses on media production depicting the life and culture of African Americans. In addition to its successful distribution division, Black Indie Classics, Red Carnelian also provides instruction in film and video making. By providing such a service at a minimal cost to participants, Chenzira is helping to make the field of media production more inclusive, providing access to communities and individuals normally without access and without voice.

She also works as an arts administrator and lobbyist for independent cinema, distributing and exhibiting hundreds of films by African-American artists internationally. As a founding board member of Production Partners, a New York-based nonprofit organization developed for the purpose of increasing the visibility of African-American and Latino films, she was instrumental in providing support for such films as Charles Lane's award-winning feature *Sidewalk Stories.* Chenzira has also served as a media panelist for the Jerome Foundation, the National Endowment for the Arts, and the New

York State Council on the Arts. As a panelist for the Minority Task Force on Public Television, her work, along with 14 other panelists, resulted in the establishment of the first Multi-cultural Public Television Fund.

—Frances K. Gateward

CHILD, Abigail
American director

Born: 1948. **Career:** Lecturer, filmmaker; mid-1970s—began working in cinema in San Francisco on documentary films before shifting to experimental film; 1980—moved to New York.

Films as Director

1970 *Except the People*
1972 *Game*
1975 *Tar People*
1977 *Some Exterior Presence*; *Peripeteia I*
1978 *Daylight Test Section*; *Peripeteia II*
1979 *Pacific Far East Line*; *Ornamentals*

Is This What You Were Born For? collection—

1981 *Prefaces* (Part 1)
1983 *Mutiny* (Part 3)
1984 *Covert Action* (Part 4)
1986 *Perils* (Part 5)
1987 *Mayhem* (Part 6)
1988 *Both* (Part 2)
1989 *Mercy* (Part 7)

Publications by Child

Book

A Motif for Mayhem, Hartford, Connecticut, 1989.

Articles

"Before Agreement," in *Millennium* (New York), Winter/Spring 1989-90.
Interview with Madeline Leskin, in *Motion Picture* (New York), vol. 3, no. 1-2, 1989-90.
"Program Notes: *Is This What You Were Born For?*," San Francisco Cinemateque, 1990.
"Truth Serum," in *Cinematograph* (San Francisco), no. 4, 1991.

Publications on Child

Books

Canyon Cinema Catalogue, San Francisco, 1982.
de Lauretis, Teresa, *Technologies of Gender,* Bloomington, Indiana, 1987.
Film-Makers' Cooperative Catalogue No. 7, New York, 1989.
Butler, Judith, *Gender Trouble,* New York, 1990.
Fuss, Diana, editor, *Inside/Out: Lesbian Theories, Gay Theories,* New York, 1991.

Rabinovitz, Lauren, *Points of Resistance: Women, Power, and Politics in the New York Avant-Garde Cinema, 1943-71,* Urbana, Illinois, 1991.
Gever, Martha, John Greyson, and Pratibha Parmar, editors, *Queer Looks: Perspectives on Lesbian and Gay Film and Video,* New York, 1993.
Gibson, Roma, and Pamela Church, *Dirty Looks: Women, Power, Pornography,* London, 1993.
Foster, Gwendolyn Audrey, *Women Film Directors: An International Bio-Critical Dictionary,* Westport, Connecticut, 1995.

Articles

Turim, Maureen, "Childhood Memories and Household Events in the Feminist Avant-Garde," in *Journal of Film and Video* (Atlanta), Summer/Fall 1986.
Schwendenwien, Jude, "New Erotic Video," in *High Performance,* Fall 1988.
Barone, Dennis, "Abigail Child," in *Arts Magazine,* September 1990.
Tamblyn, Christine, "No More Nice Girls: Recent Transgressive Feminist Art," in *Art Journal,* Summer 1991.

* * *

New York-based filmmaker Abigail Child is primarily known for a seven-part series of films entitled *Is This What You Were Born For?* This intellectually challenging group of films explores genre, issues of representation, sexual identity, and body politics. The films are also significant explorations into film form, including the aesthetic possibilities of sound in cinema. As Lotz claims "Child's short, dense, and highly poetic films work to de-stabilize familiar images, sequences, and tableaux, insistently exploring the artifices which structure narrative, and probing them for moments of rupture and excess." Child's films use radical editing patterns, repetitions, image and sound fragments, and found footage to create their highly stylized, rigorous forms. Her films explicitly reference narrative genres such as film noir and melodrama in their interrogation of narrative codes and theories of representation. Child is representative of those avant-garde filmmakers in the late 1970s and early 1980s who combined the severe structuralist preoccupations of the early 1970s with more explicit ideological explorations. Child's films differ from other theory films of the period in that their ideological inquiry does not overwhelm the formal experimentation and visual poetry in the films. Her work is also intensely musical, and has as much connection to certain kinds of language poetry and experimental music of the 1980s as to other avant-garde films. *Perils,* one of the films from this series, features music by John Zorn on the soundtrack.

Child's most significant and best-known film is the 1987 *Mayhem,* which is specifically concerned with sexual politics and how narrative codes position the viewer ideologically. A difficult work that ends with a sequence from a Japanese pornographic film from the 1920s, *Mayhem* is infused with references to the rhetoric of film noir and melodrama, and creates an elaborate structure to explore the cinematic representation of male and female bodies. Child has stated that this film is her attempt "to create a film in which sound is the character, and to do so focusing on sexuality and the erotic" (Child, "Program Notes," 1990). *Mayhem* includes many shots that employ single-source lighting common to film noir of the 1940s to create highly expressionist images. Characters are dressed in 1940s attire and are frequently framed in ritualized poses. The images constantly intercut between characters looking and being looked at, and individuals engaged in continuous pursuit. Child takes the rhetoric of the 1940s detective genre, a genre associated with danger, desire, violence, narrative entanglement, and obsessive behavior, and omits the narrative context for this rhetoric. *Mayhem* has no story because a story would be irrelevant to the film's project. The film is more interested in examining the language of film and how we position ourselves as viewers.

The most radical aspects of *Mayhem* are its montage, which constantly cuts off shots and scenes before we can make sense of them, and the film's sound construction, which also relies on fragmentation and repetition for its effectiveness. The formal severity of image and sound strategies make it an extremely abstract work despite its reliance on representational imagery. The film undoubtedly invokes the Russian Formalist precept of "laying bare" the workings of art by making the viewer aware of its construction. The rhetoric of discontinuity is paramount in *Mayhem* just as continuity is the primary mode in Hollywood classical cinema. Child's feminist project in *Mayhem* also includes portraying the film's male figures as sex objects. The film's nonlinear, fragmentary style and use of negative imagery creates a kind of dream logic to the proceedings. *Mayhem* ends with a now notorious sequence of two Japanese women engaged in a sex act being observed by a male thief, who is then captured by the women and forced to engage in sex with them. The sound that has been added to this sequence is a jaunty musical tune overlaid with voices of women. In fact, the human voice is a key articulating device throughout the film.

The notion of musicality also enters into *Mercy*, a film that functions all together differently than *Mayhem*. It includes much found footage and is constructed in a collage style with many images referencing the organic and the body. The human figure is presented in a variety of contexts and in radically different film forms. Child includes footage from Hollywood movies, nonfiction films, and her own footage as well. The film also intermingles black-and-white stock with color footage. *Mercy* is a vibrant exploration of the rhythmical principle in cinema, and is much less concerned with sexual politics and feminist ideology than *Mayhem*. It is reminiscent of the films of Bruce Conner and Arthur Lipsett, filmmakers known for their collage stylistics, image and sound interaction, and use of found footage. Once again, sound plays a key role in *Mercy* as it does in most of Child's other work.

Abigail Child is one of the most intriguing filmmakers to emerge in the last 15 years, and her films explore the more complex possibilities of formal experimentation in both image and sound. Her work is aesthetically groundbreaking and deserves thoughtful in-depth analysis, something it has rarely received since much of the critical comment around her films has tended to place her within the narrow context of sexual politics and lesbian filmmaking. Her artwork is much more than that.

—Mario Falsetto

CHOCOLAT

(Chocolate)
France-Germany-Cameroon, 1988
Director: Claire Denis

Production: Wim Wenders Produktions/Le F.O.D.I.C. Cameroun/ Caroline Productions/Cerito Films/Cinémanuel/La Sept Cinéma/MK2 Productions/TF1 Films Productions; color, 35mm; running time: 105 minutes. Released March 1989. Filmed in Cameroon.

Producers: Alain Belmondo and Gérard Crosnier; **associate producers:** Samuel Mabom and Pierre Ilouga Mabout; **screenplay:** Claire Denis and Jean-Pôl Fargeau; **assistant directors:** Bassek Ba Kobhio and Luc Goldenberg; **photography:** Robert Alazraki; **editor:** Claudine Merlin; **sound:** Jean-Louis Ughetto and Dominique Hennequin; **production design:** Thierry Flamand; **music:** Abdullah Ibrahim; **costumes:** Christian Gasc.

Cast: Isaach de Bankolé (*Protée*); Giulia Boschi (*Aimée*); François Cluzet (*Marc*); Jean-Claude Adelin (*Luc*); Mireille Perrier (*France as an adult*); Cécile Ducasse (*France as a girl*); Laurent Arnal (*Machinard*); Kenneth Cranham (*Boothby*); Jacques Denis (*Delpich*); Didier Flamand (*Vedrine*); with: Emmanuelle Chaulet; Emmet Judson Williamson; Jean Bedièbe; Jean Quentin Chatelain; Clementine Essono; Essindi Mindja; Donatus Ngala; Edwige Nto Ngon A Zock; Philemon Blake Ondoua.

Publications

Book

Petrie, Duncan, editor, *Screening Europe: Image and Identity in Contemporary European Cinema*, London, 1992.

Articles

Jousse, T., "Jeux Africains," in *Cahiers du Cinéma* (Paris), May 1988.
Borger, L., in *Variety* (New York), 18 May 1988.
Merat, G., and V. Lacombe, "Echoes from Africa," in *Cinéma* (Paris), 18-24 May 1988.
Bassan, R., in *Revue du Cinéma* (Paris), June 1988.
Marsolais, G., in *24 Images* (Montreal), Fall 1988.
Degoudenne, L., and Joël Noël, in *Grand Angle* (Mariembourg, Belgium), October 1988.
Berthelius, M., "Objektiva Bilder," in *Chaplin* (Stockholm), vol. 31, no. 1, 1989.
Bates, Peter, in *Cineaste* (New York), vol. 17, no. 2, 1989.
Ellero, R., in *Segno*, January 1989.
Beaupre, S., in *Séquences* (Montreal), March 1989.
Chutkow, Paul, "This *Chocolat* Is Bittersweet," in *New York Times*, 5 March 1989.
Canby, Vincent, "Being Caught, Yet Not Really Caught, in Cameroon," in *New York Times*, 10 March 1989.
Stein, E., "Country Matters," in *Village Voice* (New York), 14 March 1989.
Bourdain, G. S., "New Face: Isaach de Bankolé: An Actor's Road Taken to Cameroon of *Chocolat*," in *New York Times*, 24 March 1989.
Denby, David, "Bores of New York," in *New York*, 27 March 1989.
Kroll, Jack, "Out of Africa—in the French Style," in *Newsweek*, 27 March 1989.
Bartholomew, D., in *Film Journal* (Hollins College, Virginia), April 1989.
Forbes, J., in *Monthly Film Bulletin* (London), April 1989.
Mercorio, G., in *Films and Filming* (London), April 1989.
Sante, Luc, "French Colonial," in *Interview* (New York), May 1989.
Sawahata, L., in *Boxoffice* (Hollywood), June 1989.

Blake, R. A., in *America* (New York), 26 August/2 September 1989.

Lueken, V., in *EPD Film* (Frankfurt), September 1989.

Cardullo, B., "Black and White, in Color," in *Hudson Review,* vol. 42, no. 4, 1990.

Mortimer, L., "Colonised Human Relations," in *Filmnews* (Paddington, New South Wales, Australia), vol. 20, no. 9, 1990.

Strauss, Frederic, "Feminin Colonial," in *Cahiers du Cinéma* (Paris), July/August 1990.

Craven, M., in *Cinema Papers* (Melbourne), December 1990.

Stiller, Nikki, in *Film Quarterly* (Berkeley), Winter 1990.

Murphy, Kathleen, "The Color of Home," in *Film Comment* (New York), September/October 1992.

Philibert, Celine, "Memory Process and Feminine Desire in Claire Denis's *Chocolate* and Brigitte Rouan's *Outremer,*" in *Journal of Third World Studies,* Fall 1996.

*   *   *

Chocolat is the remarkable debut feature from the influential French director Claire Denis. It is also her most famous film; in the United States it garnered critical praise as one of 1988's best films and it enjoyed considerable success as an art-house hit. A subtle sophisticated film, it features the aptly named character, "France," a French woman who returns as an adult to her childhood home in West Africa's postcolonial Cameroon, where her father had been a district officer in the late 1950s—during the last years of French colonialism. France's story and growing racial consciousness are revealed via a long flashback to her life as an eight-year-old girl. Interestingly, it was while working as an assistant director on Wim Wenders's *Paris, Texas* in 1984 that Denis had the idea for *Chocolat.* The southwestern landscape prompted her memories of Africa, and the result was a fictional rendering of her own experience as a privileged, white female in colonial West Africa and of the emotional conflicts generated by colonialism.

The film opens with France accepting a ride with an African-American driver and his son, whom she watched on the beach earlier. As she watches the countryside go by, she recalls her early childhood—especially her relationship with her family's African servant Protée. Indeed, it is their close relationship that is central to the film's insights and mood. The two communicate nearly wordlessly, except for the riddles Protée tells her and the lessons he teaches her about Africa. But, France's ordered life is disrupted when an airplane breaks down near her house and forces the stranded passengers to stay with her family for several weeks. The passengers are a motley crew of "typical" colonialists, including an arrogant, racist white plantation owner and his black concubine whom he treats sadistically, and a pair of newlyweds on their way to another post in West Africa. Eventually, the group is joined by a former seminarian who viciously disrupts the rigid lines of protocol that govern the precarious relationships between the colonialists and the colonized.

Denis is known for her outstanding visual and cinematic range of expression, and *Chocolat* is indeed a visually beautiful film, testimony to her familiarity with and affinity for Africa. *Chocolat*'s camera traces breathtakingly rich landscapes that strike emotional chords, and the film's style evokes poetic and musical rhythms. The pace is languid, yet nuanced, and its ambience is quietly evocative—though imbued with repression and frustration. Significantly, Denis includes several reminders that the "balance" the colonialists have created in Africa is precarious. As France's father puts it, when he explains the concept of the horizon line, "you see the line, but it doesn't exist." In addition, throughout the film Denis uses subtle metaphors; for ex-

ample, a cemetery of dead German colonials, who preceded the French, and the rumor that they were killed by the Africans; a gang of vultures on the horizon; and a collection of ants that invade a crisp, white tablecloth. Among Denis's exquisite strengths are her assured yet subtle allusions to the multilayered implications of colonialism and its links to sexuality. The character of Protée is beautiful, polite, and thoughtful, with a handsome face and powerful, glistening body, which are complemented by his proud, self-determined demeanor. There is a palpable yet ambivalent sexual charge between Protée and France's pretty mother, Aimée, that only intensifies when her husband leaves for business trips. But Protée sees everything quite clearly, including Aimée's attraction to him, though he aims to maintain their currently proscribed social roles. Denis effectively complicates the links between power and sexuality, as when Aimée summons Protée to stand guard over her bed while she and France sleep, and when she orders him to help lace her dress and then cannot hold his accusatory gaze. Later, when she tries unsuccessfully to seduce him, Aimée takes her revenge by arranging to have him transferred to a position outside the house. But, Protée exacts his own moment of revenge—combined with self-punishment—when he tricks the young France into burning her hand on a generator's pipe, thus producing a scar that follows her into adulthood.

Interestingly, via the links Denis draws between the adult France and her African-American driver, she effectively problematizes the issue of "native" African identity. That is, both France and the driver have traveled to Africa expecting to find "home," but both discover tenuous ties at best. Indeed, to Africa, they are no more than strangers. The effect is underscored at the end of the film with a deeply poetic scene in which the adult France has returned to the airport, where she watches unseen while the black airport workers load silly, cumbersome tourist items onto a plane, and then chat comfortably as they take shelter from a sudden storm. With the upbeat music that accompanies the scene, Denis suggests a celebration of postcolonial independence.

Denis sought funding for several years before she finally persuaded Wim Wenders to produce her screenplay. When she began writing *Chocolat,* she intended to chronicle the final years of colonialism in Cameroon as seen from the perspective of a black male servant. But, eventually she decided to present the story from a child's perspective, and used her own experiences to shape the film. Thus, the story emphasizes the young white girl's point of view as she witnesses the colonialism, racism, and sexism that characterized her family's house. Interestingly, Denis has explained that although French women typically identify quite easily with *Chocolat,* French men tend to be uncomfortable with and critical of it—which only confirms her commitment to telling the tales of colonialism, despite the discomforts they might cause.

—Cynthia Felando

CHOPRA, Joyce
American director

Born: 1938. **Education:** Studied comparative literature at Brandeis University, graduated; studied acting at the Neighborhood Playhouse in New York City. **Family:** Married the screenwriter Tom Cole, one daughter. **Career:** 1960s—started Club 47, a coffeehouse for folksingers; 1972—co-directed renowned feminist short for PBS,

Joyce at 34; 1985—directed critically well-received first feature film *Smooth Talk*; 1990s—works as television movie director. **Awards:** Bronze Award, Venice International Film Festival, for *A Happy Mother's Day,* 1963; Grand Jury Prize, Sundance Film Festival, for *Smooth Talk,* 1985. **Agent:** Paul Allan Smith, Broder Kurland Webb Uffner, 9242 Beverly Boulevard, Los Angeles, CA 90210, U.S.A.

Films as Director

1963   *A Happy Mother's Day* (doc—co-d with Leacock)
1972   *Joyce at 34* (co-d with Weill—doc short)
1975   *Girls at 12* (doc); *David Wheeler: Theater Company of Boston* (doc)
1976   *Clorae & Albie*
1978   *That Our Children Will Not Die* (doc)
1980   *Martha Clarke Light and Dark: A Dancer's Journal* (co-d, + ed, pr)
1985   *Smooth Talk*
1989   *The Lemon Sisters*
1992   *Baby Snatcher* (for TV); *The Danger of Love* (for TV); *Murder in New Hampshire: The Pamela Wojas Smart Story* (for TV)
1993   *The Disappearance of Nora* (for TV)
1994   *The Corpse Had a Familiar Face* (for TV)
1995   *Deadline for Murder: From the Files of Edna Buchanan* (for TV)
1997   *L.A. Johns* (*Confessions*) (for TV); *Convictions* (for TV)

Publications on Chopra

Books

Kaplan, E. Ann, *Women & Film: Both Sides of the Camera,* New York, 1983.
Brundson, Charlotte, editor, *Films for Women,* London, 1986.
Quart, Barbara Koenig, *Women Directors: The Emergence of a New Cinema,* New York, 1988.
Acker, Ally, *Reel Women: Pioneers of the Cinema, 1896 to the Present,* New York, 1991.
Foster, Gwendolyn Audrey, *Women Film Directors: An International Bio-Critical Dictionary,* Westport, Connecticut, 1995.

Articles

Haskell, Molly, "Unifying the Motley Threads," in *Village Voice* (New York), 22 February 1973.
Maslin, Janet, "At the Movies: Filmmaker Tries Fiction," in *New York Times,* 28 February 1986.
Chase, Donald, "Close-ups: Joyce Chopra," in *Millimeter* (New York), March 1986.
Roberts, J., "Good Girl, Bad Girl," in *New York Magazine,* 17 March 1986.
Rich, B. Ruby, "Good Girls, Bad Girls," in *Village Voice* (New York), 15 April 1986.
"Bridges Called in to Replace Chopra on *Bright Lights,*" in *Variety* (New York), 13 May 1987.
James, C., "*Bright Lights, Big City*—Big Trouble," in *New York Times,* 10 January 1988.

Solway, D., "1989 Previews from 36 Creative Artists," in *New York Times,* 1 January 1989.

* * *

Joyce Chopra gained renown in the early 1970s, especially among feminists, as the co-director and star of *Joyce at 34,* a feminist independent documentary short. She continued to make documentaries until 1986, when she garnered attention for her well-regarded first fiction feature *Smooth Talk.*

Joyce at 34 was one of the earliest and most respected feminist documentaries, like Kate Millett's *Three Lives* and Donna Deitch's *Woman to Woman,* which used simple formats to depict the ordinary details of real women's lives, along with the constraints and successes attached to their endeavors to move into traditionally male realms of work and power. In the case of *Joyce,* the real woman is Chopra herself; she speaks directly to an intended female audience about her life, in particular about the possibilities that marriage, family, and career can be harmoniously combined, and also about the conflicts between her pregnancy and filmmaking aspirations. The film scholar E. Ann Kaplan, however, criticized the film for assuming a position of absolute knowledge, so that viewers are forced into the position of passive consumers. Nevertheless, it has long held a firm position in the feminist film canon.

Chopra was considered by many critics to be a "new" director in 1985 when she made *Smooth Talk,* despite more than ten years of filmmaking experience; yet, the film marked a breakthrough in her career. It focuses on the emergent sexuality of an adolescent young woman who radiates a palpable sensuality, but seems unaware of its power.

Originally intended as a one-hour film for PBS's *American Playhouse,* it developed into a feature film at the script-writing stage. The producer obtained additional funding with the stipulation that the film would screen on PBS 18 months after the theatrical release. The extremely low-budget feature was shot in 32 days entirely on location, and cast and crew all worked for scale. Adapted by her screenwriter-husband Tom Coles from the well-known Joyce Carol Oates short story "Where Are You Going, Where Have You Been?," it minimized the metaphysical elements of Oates's story to focus instead upon the realistic intimations of a young woman's sexual coming-of-age. Notably, it depicts the complexities of both youth and femininity, rather than the mall, fast food, and often insipid, masculine milieu of Hollywood's more typical teenpics. Laura Dern convincingly plays the young heroine who clashes with her family, while finding a giddy camaraderie with her teenage girlfriends, until she is seduced and then raped by a menacing man. As a result, according to some feminist critics, the film seemed to fly in the face of traditional feminism.

That is, mainstream critics praised the film, but many feminist critics disparaged it, especially the formidable B. Ruby Rich who chastised Chopra for depicting a regressive puritanical sexual double standard that seems to punish its young heroine for her sexuality. Rich complained that Chopra's message was intended to stifle youthful feminine sexuality because to express it would ensure that "a grownup bogeyman Arnold Friend will come and get you." She further determined that Chopra was motivated by the fact that she herself had been the mother of a teenage daughter when she made the film. But the film can be interpreted rather differently, in terms of its depiction of the pleasure as well as the dangers of feminine sexual initiation. Further, while the rape of the young heroine is problematic, it nevertheless adheres to Oates's story. Indeed, other feminist critics praised

Chopra for the film's refreshing balance between the characters of the mother and the daughter. Chopra manages to convey the engagingly exuberant yet disturbingly naive sexuality of the daughter as well as her indifference to the adults around her. On the other hand, the mother's poignantly conveyed love, anger, and worry for her daughter, and her regret that they are no longer close is equally important to the film. Certainly, Chopra goes far beyond the usual teenpics with their absent or unjustifiably shrill mothers to give this teen heroine's mother a voice.

Chopra claimed that her primary goal in *Smooth Talk* was to portray the teenagers as "full humans" who speak with individual voices in order to counter the stereotypical teenage voices that predominated in other films. Accordingly, she cited her documentary about 12-year-old girls in Waltham, Massachusetts, as a source for much of *Smooth Talk,* including a moving scene she re-created in which Dern's character sits alone stringing beads in her bedroom. In addition, Chopra's 14-year-old daughter reportedly provided snippets of conversations she had heard at school to add subtlety to the characterizations. Thus, Chopra succeeded in offering a nuanced, realistic depiction of a young woman, who is played with a poignant charm by Dern, during her ambivalent coming-of-age—which is highlighted by her wary sexual attraction to the macho stranger, played with a sinister appeal by Treat Williams.

Following the release of *Smooth Talk,* Chopra was deluged with scripts to direct more typical teenpics. She eventually agreed to direct the film adaptation of Jay McInerney's best-seller, *Bright Lights, Big City,* but three weeks into the production she was replaced by James Bridges (known for directing *The China Syndrome, Urban Cowboy,* and *Perfect*), apparently because the studio considered her feminist perspective problematic. Her second feature film, *The Lemon Sisters,* was produced by Diane Keaton who also starred with Carol Kane. It tells the touching story of an enduring friendship between three girlfriends, from childhood to middle age, who as youngsters growing up in a more-innocent Atlantic City jauntily dubbed themselves the "Lemon Sisters." Despite their relationships with men, both alive and dead, the characters' most important relationships are with each other. The story was loosely inspired by the real-life friendship of the three lead actresses and their shared nostalgia for Atlantic City. A more recent directorial assignment for Chopra was the well-realized television movie, *Murder in New Hampshire,* about the notorious young high-school teacher, Pamela Smart, who was convicted of murder for persuading her teenage lover to kill her husband.

In general, Chopra's work treats the themes of sexuality and sensuality of women; further, her films often focus on the transitional periods in women's lives—puberty in *Smooth Talk,* pregnancy in *Joyce at 34,* as well as the new boyfriends, new lifestyles, and new business ventures that are depicted in *The Lemon Sisters.* In addition, she typically employs fairly conventional filmmaking strategies, including the cinema verité of *Joyce* and the traditional narrative of *Smooth Talk, The Lemon Sisters,* and *Murder in New Hampshire.* Currently, Chopra works as a director of television series and movies.

—Cynthia Felando

CHOY, Christine
American director and cinematographer

Born: Chai Ming Huei, in the People's Republic of China, 1952, to a Chinese mother and Korean father. **Education:** Studied architecture at New York's Manhattanville College of the Sacred Heart; Columbia University, master's degree in urban planning. **Career:** 1960s—became interested in film while living in Korea; 1966—came to the United States by herself; 1971—became involved with Newsreel; 1971—began working in documentary film as an editor and animator; 1972—directed her first documentary, *Teach Our Children*; mid-1970s—became executive director of Third World Newsreel; became associate professor at (and, later, chairperson of) the graduate film/TV department of New York University's Tisch School of the Arts; 1988—received Academy Award nomination for Best Documentary as co-director of *Who Killed Vincent Chin?*; 1991—"Christine Choy: A Retrospective" presented at the Queens (New York) Museum of Art. **Awards:** First Prize, International Black Film Festival, for *Teach Our Children,* 1972; Best Subject Matter, Ann Arbor Film Festival, for *To Love, Honor, and Obey,* 1980; Alfred DuPont Columbia University Award, George Foster Peabody Award, Outstanding Film, London International Film Festival, Best Documentary, Hawaii International Film Festival, and Award Winner at U.S. Film Festival, for *Who Killed Vincent Chin?,* 1988; Ace Award for Best Documentary Special, and First Place, Mannheim International Film Festival, for *Best Hotel on Skid Row,* 1989; Juror's Citation, Black Maria Film Festival, for *Yellow Tale Blues,* 1991; Golden Gate Award, San Francisco Film Festival, *Homes Apart: Korea,* 1991; Achievement Award, Hong Kong International Film Festival, for *Mississippi Triangle,* 1992; Cinematography Award, Sundance Film Festival, for *My America,* 1996. **Address:** Graduate Film Department, Tisch School of the Arts, New York University, 721 Broadway, New York, NY 10003, U.S.A.

Films as Director

1972   *Teach Our Children* (co-d, + ph, ed)
1975   *Fresh Seeds in a Big Apple* (co-d, + ed, sound); *Generation of the Railroad Builder* (+ ed)
1976   *From Spikes to Spindles* (+ pr)
1977   *History of the Chinese Patriot Movement in the U.S.* (+ ed); *North Country Tour* (+ sound rec)
1978   *Inside Women Inside* (co-d, + exec pr, ph); *Loose Pages Bound* (+ pr)
1980   *To Love, Honor, and Obey* (co-d, + ph)
1981   *Bittersweet Survival* (co-d, + pr, 2nd camera); *White Flower Passing*
1982   *Go Between* (+ pr)
1983   *Mississippi Triangle (Mississippi Mah Jong Blues)* (co-d with Long and Siegel, + pr, ph, researcher); *Fei Tien, Goddess in Flight*
1984   *Namibia, Independence Now* (co-d)
1985   *Monkey King Looks West* (+ ph)
1986   *Permanent Wave* (co-d)
1988   *Shanghai Lil's* (+ pr); **Who Killed Vincent Chin?** (co-d with Tajima, + ph)
1989   *China Today* (+ pr); *Best Hotel on Skid Row* (co-d, + co-pr, ph); *Fortune Cookies: The Myth of the Model Minority* (+ pr)
1991   *Yellow Tale Blues: Two American Families* (co-d with Tajima); *Homes Apart: Korea (Homes Apart: The Two Koreas)* (co-d, + pr, ph, interviewer)
1993   *SA-I-GU* (co-d with Kim-Gibson, + pr, ph)
1995   *In the Name of the Emperor* (co-d with Tong, + ph); *Not a Simple Story; Out in Silence*

1997   *The Shot Heard 'Round the World* (co-d with Lampros, + pr)

Other Films

1971   *The Dead Earth* (ed, anim)
1973   *Nigeria, Nigeria One* (ed)
1975   *In the Event That Anyone Disappears* (ed)
1978   *A Dream Is What You Wake Up From* (exec pr)
1979   *People's Firehouse Number 1* (exec pr); *Percussion, Impression & Reality* (exec pr)
1981   *The American Writer's Congress* (unit d); *Boy and Tarzan Appear in a Clearing* (unit d, camera)
1984   *Chronicle of Hope: Nicaragua* (pr)
1987   *Audre Lord Story* (pr, ph); *Haitian Corner* (pr); *Making of the Sun City* (unit d)
1995   *Litany for Survival: The Life and Work of Audre Lord* (co-ph)
1996   *My America ... or Honk if You Love Buddha* (ph)

Publication by Choy

Article

Interview with Bianca Jagger, in *Interview* (New York), January 1991.

Publications on Choy

Books

Acker, Ally, *Reel Women: Pioneers of the Cinema, 1896 to the Present,* New York, 1991.
Foster, Gwendolyn Audrey, *Women Film Directors: An International Bio-Critical Dictionary,* Westport, Connecticut, 1995.

Articles

Millner, S., "Third World Newsreel: Ten Years of Left Film," in *Jump Cut* (Berkeley), July 1982.
Taubin, Amy, "Daughters of Chaos: Feminist and Avant-Garde Filmmakers," in *Village Voice* (New York), 30 November 1982.
Dittus, Erick, "Mississippi Triangle: An Interview with Christine Choy, Worth Long and Allan Siegel," in *Cineaste* (New York), vol. 14, no. 2, 1985.
Goldman, Debra, "*Who Killed Vincent Chin?,*" in *American Film* (New York), May 1988.
Hanson, Peter, "NYU Professor's Journey into Film," in *Washington Square News* (New York), 29 March 1989.
Kaplan, David A., "Film about a Beating Examines a Community," in *New York Times,* 16 July 1989.
Reynaud, Bérénice, "Christine Choy et Renee Tajima," in *Cahiers du Cinéma* (Paris), June 1990.
Leab, D. J., "*In the Name of the Emperor:* War Guilt and the Medium of Film," in *Historical Journal of Film, Radio and Television* (Abingdon, Oxon), no. 3, 1995.
MacKinnon, S., "Remembering the Nanjing Massacre: *In the Name of the Emperor,*" in *Historical Journal of Film, Radio and Television* (Abingdon, Oxon), no. 3, 1995.
Chen, Yung-pei, "Profile—Christine Choy," in *realizASIAN* (New York), October 1996.
Edwards, Sharon, "Shooting for the Stars: Women Cinematographers," in *MovieMaker* (Pasadena, California), July/August 1997.

*   *   *

Christine Choy uses film as a political/humanist tool. Most specifically, she is concerned with injustice as it is perpetrated on individuals or entire peoples. Her films work as oral and visual histories and records of events, with one of her major concerns being the manner in which people of color are represented on screen.

Choy is most involved with issues relating to Asia and Asian Americans, and this is a direct reflection of her own heritage. By exploring the life of an individual or the sides of an issue, Choy wishes to educate and enlighten—and help sustain political and social change. Those of her films that focus on contemporary problems effectively bring these problems to the forefront. Those that spotlight incidents out of history serve as indispensable documents of that history, and become visual records that help ensure that the events chronicled will not be lost in the pages of time. The best-case scenario is that these incidents now will be well remembered and, if they involve injustice, that injustice will not be repeated in the future.

In the early 1970s Choy worked as a film cleaner/cataloguer/sometime editor at Newsreel (later known as Third World Newsreel), an alternative media arts organization that describes itself as being "committed to the creation and appreciation of independent and social issue media by and about people of color, and the peoples of developing countries around the world." Choy recalls: "When the inmates of Attica prison rebelled in 1971, I submitted a proposal to Newsreel. I argued that it was fine for white, upper-middle-class males to document the struggles of the Third World communities, but it was about time that the Third World people have an opportunity to express themselves. I raised some funds and with two other black women I produced my first documentary on Attica, called *Teach Your Children*"—thus beginning a prolific and multi-award-winning directorial career.

A number of Choy's films are portraits of Asian-American individuals, families, and communities. Here, she emphasizes the manner in which individuals live within communities, co-exist with their neighbors, and respond to the world around them. *Mississippi Triangle,* co-directed with Worth Long and Allan Siegel, is a portrait of life on the Mississippi Delta, where Chinese, African Americans, and whites coexist. The history of the area's various communities is placed within the framework of daily life and culture, class and gender, racial friction, and the civil rights movement. *SA-I-GU,* co-directed with Daisil Kim-Gibson, is a look at the citizens of Los Angeles's Koreatown after the Rodney King verdict, with a focus on the effect of the subsequent riots on Korean-American women. Perhaps her most personal film is *Yellow Tale Blues: Two American Families,* co-directed with Renee Tajima, a portrait of the filmmakers' contrasting families—Choy's is immigrant and working class while Tajima's is fourth generation and middle class—and the manner in which their members have assimilated into the American melting pot. The emphasis in *Monkey King Looks West* is the maintenance of cultural tradition. Here, Choy charts the attempts by classically trained Chinese opera performers to pass on their heritage and their art form to young Chinese Americans as they struggle to survive economically in New York's Chinatown. And *Not a Simple Story* and *Out in Silence* are portraits of two Asian Americans living under the specter of AIDS, and who have become AIDS activists: Vince, a gay man, and Robin, a widow who contracted the disease from her husband.

A number of Choy's films deal directly with racism and violence. *Who Killed Vincent Chin?*, also co-directed with Tajima, is arguably Choy's best-known film. She and Tajima investigate the economic and political factors that led to the death of Chin, a 27-year-old Chinese American celebrating his upcoming marriage, in a Detroit bar in 1982. He got into an argument with Ron Ebens, an unemployed auto worker, and Ebens—who thought Chin was Japanese—eventually beat Chin to death with a baseball bat. Similarly, *The Shot Heard 'Round the World,* co-directed with Spiro Lampros, explores the events surrounding the killing of Yoshi Hattori, a Japanese high-school exchange student, who was shot to death in a Baton Rouge suburb in 1992 while attempting to ask directions to a party. These films emphasize the manner in which the fear of individuals who look or speak differently may result not only in miscommunication and racism but violence, and the negligence of the American judicial system with regard to the issue of equal justice for all.

Additionally, Choy is concerned with events out of the past as they relate to her mother continent. *In the Name of the Emperor,* co-directed with Nancy Tong, documents what has come to be known as the "Rape of Nanjing": the massacre of more than 300,000 Chinese civilians by the Japanese during a six-week-long period in 1937, all "in the name of Emperor Hirohito." The film works as a clear-minded record of an event that is little known in the West, that Japan would much rather ignore, and that is in danger of being forgotten forever. Its point, soberingly made, is that the Nazi extermination of the Jews was not the lone Holocaust of the 1930s-40s.

When examining the films of Christine Choy, a question arises: Is it important to evaluate the impact of her work in fostering racial, political, and social enlightenment? After all, Vincent Chin was killed in 1982. Ten years later, Yoshi Hattori lost his life in an act of violence that was just as equally random and racist. In a perfect world, every hatemonger would view *Who Killed Vincent Chin?* and *The Shot Heard 'Round the World* and come away with an aroused conscience while summarily counting him or herself an ex-racist.

Ultimately, the point is not how effective her films have been in perpetuating social change, but that they have been made and seen in the first place—and the result is the potential to impact positively on even one viewer, and compel even one individual to reevaluate his or her world view. It remains essential that dedicated and fair-minded political filmmakers such as Choy—whose concerns are not altered by what is currently in fashion—persist in producing films that are politically savvy, and that seek to expose the bitter truths of their subject matter.

Finally and happily, in her position as an educator at New York University's Tisch School of the Arts, Choy is in the position to positively influence the upcoming generation of documentary filmmakers.

—Rob Edelman

CHRISTOPHER STRONG
USA, 1933
Director: Dorothy Arzner

Production: RKO Radio Pictures Inc.; black and white, 35mm; running time: 77 minutes. Released 1933. Film's working title was *The Great Desire.*

Producers: David O. Selznick, with Pandro S. Berman; **screen-play:** Zoë Akins, from the novel by Gilbert Frankau; **photography:**

Bert Glennon; **uncredited photography:** Sid Hickox; **editor:** Arthur Roberts; **uncredited editor:** Jane Lorring; **sound recordist:** Hugh McDowell Jr.; **production designers:** Van Nest Polglase and Charles Kirk; **music score:** Max Steiner; **special effects:** Vernon Walker; **transitions:** Slavko Vorkapich; **costume designer:** Howard Greer, **uncredited costume designer:** Walter Plunkett; **technical adviser:** Sir Gerald Grove.

Cast: Katharine Hepburn (*Lady Cynthia Darrington*); Colin Clive (*Sir Christopher Strong*); Billie Burke (*Lady Strong*); Helen Chandler (*Monica Strong*); Jack LaRue (*Carlo*); Desmond Roberts (*Bryce Mercer*); Gwendolyn Logan (*Bradford, the maid*); Agostino Borgato (*Fortune teller*); Margaret Lindsey (*Girl at party*); Donald Stewart (*Mechanic*); Zena Savina (*Second maid*).

Publications

Books

Dickens, Homer, *The Films of Katharine Hepburn,* New York, 1971.
Johnson, Claire, *Notes on Women's Cinema,* London, 1973.
Marill, Alvin H., *Katharine Hepburn,* New York, 1973.
Rosen, Marjorie, *Popcorn Venus: Women, Movies and the American Dream,* New York, 1973.
Haskell, Molly, *From Reverence to Rape,* New York, 1974.
Higham, Charles, *Kate: The Life of Katharine Hepburn,* New York, 1975.
Johnston, Claire, editor, *The Work of Dorothy Arzner: Towards a Feminist Cinema,* London, 1975.
Slide, Anthony, *Early Women Directors,* South Brunswick, New Jersey, 1977; rev. ed. as *The Silent Feminists: America's First Women Directors,* Lanham, Maryland, 1996.
Carey, Gary, *Katharine Hepburn: A Biography,* London, 1983.
Britton, Andrew, *Katharine Hepburn: The Thirties and After,* Newcastle-upon-Tyne, 1984.
Freedland, Michael, *Katharine Hepburn,* London, 1984.
Heck-Rabi, Louise, *Women Filmmakers: A Critical Reception,* Metuchen, New Jersey, 1984.
Morley, Sheridan, *Katharine Hepburn: A Celebration,* London, 1984.
Edwards, Anne, *Katharine Hepburn: A Biography,* London, 1986.
Penley, Constance, editor, *Feminism and Film Theory,* London, 1988.

Articles

Variety (New York), 4 March 1933.
New York Times, 10 March 1933.
Tozzi, Romano V., "Katharine Hepburn," in *Films in Review* (New York), December 1957.
Parker, F., "Approaching the Art of Arzner," in *Action* (Los Angeles), July/August 1973.
Peary, G., interview with Dorothy Arzner, in *Cinema* (Beverly Hills), no. 34, 1974.
Bergstrom, J., "Re-reading the Work of Claire Johnston," in *Camera Obscura* (Berkeley), Summer 1979.
Suter, J., "Feminine Discourse in *Christopher Strong,*" in *Camera Obscura* (Berkeley), Summer 1979.
Auty, M., in *Monthly Film Bulletin* (London), August 1980.

* * *

Christopher Strong

There is little doubt that Dorothy Arzner's *Christopher Strong* is more highly regarded now than it was upon its release in 1933. What seemed to contemporary audiences and critics to be a competent, fairly effective but otherwise unexceptional melodrama, now seems an important and articulate step toward the formation of a feminist perspective in the male-oriented, mainstream of Hollywood. There is a freshness to *Christopher Strong* that stems directly from its unique point of view. While a great many movies of the 1930s and 1940s were known as "women's pictures," *Christopher Strong* really is one. Directed, written, and edited by women, the film resonates a certain integrity and honesty towards the female character that few other films, then or now, can boast.

There is something slightly subversive about *Christopher Strong* in the way it so openly uses the soap-opera form as a base. Consequently, it works quite well as a standard "weepie" even as the filmmakers mold, transform, and, ultimately, transcend the genre. Gilbert Frankau's novel, on which the film was based, was about a man torn between two women, his wife of many years and a young, daring aviatrix; the film is about the two women and how they face

their love for the same man. It is, on the face of it, a minor shift in perspective, but Arzner and screenwriter Zoë Akins use it to examine the limited options open to women who submit their own wills and abilities to those of their husbands and lovers.

Interestingly, Dorothy Arzner never admitted to having much interest in feminist philosophy, though she certainly owes the recent reevaluation of her career to it. Of *Christopher Strong* she said, "I was more interested in Christopher Strong, played by Colin Clive, than in any of the women characters. He was a 'man on a cross.' He loved his wife and he fell in love with the aviatrix. He was a man on a rack. I was really more sympathetic with him, but no one seemed to pick that up."

Such a statement does not hold up as one views the film. The women of *Christopher Strong* are vital, adventurous, complex, and emotional while the men are rarely more than stodgy and dull. This is due in part to the demands of the script, but is reinforced by the performances. Lady Cynthia Darrington, the aviatrix, was Katharine Hepburn's first starring role, and her command of the part fluctuates wildly. There is, though, enough of Hepburn in the part to make it intelligent, perceptive, and electric. Billie Burke, as Strong's neglected wife, gives the prime performance of her career, and Helen Chandler, as their daughter, gives a rather winsome role with some unexpectedly dark shadings. Colin Clive, on the other hand, is stiff and ultimately uninteresting; naming the film after this character seems perversely ironic.

Despite Arzner's claim to the contrary, it is Cynthia Darrington who is "on the cross," torn between her great bravery and achievements and her desire for love and a normal life. She finds the resolution to her dilemma only in death, yet *Christopher Strong* is an important step toward a more reasonable presentation of men and women in film.

—Frank Thompson

CHYTILOVÁ, Vera
Czech director

Born: Ostrava, 2 February 1929. **Education:** Studied architecture at Charles University; Film Academy (FAMU), Prague, 1957-62. **Family:** Married the cinematographer Jaroslav Kucera. **Career:** 1956—assistant director on *3 Men Missing*; 1962—directed first film, *The Ceiling*; 1969-76—forbidden to direct or work for foreign producers. **Address:** c/o Barrandov Studios, Prague, Czech Republic.

Films as Director

1962   *Strop (The Ceiling)* (+ sc); *Pytel blech (A Bag of Fleas)* (+ sc)
1963   *O necem jiném (Something Different; Something Else; Another Way of Life)* (+ sc)
1965   "Automat Svet" ("The World Cafe") ep. of *Perlicky na dne (Pearls of the Deep)* (+ co-sc)
1966   *Sedmikrásky (Daisies)* (+ co-sc)
1969   *Ovoce stromu rajských jíme (The Fruit of Paradise; We Eat the Fruit of the Trees of Paradise)* (+ co-sc)
1977   *Hra o jablko (The Apple Game)* (+ sc)
1978   *Cas je neúprosný (Inexorable Time)* (short)
1979   *Panelstory (Prefab Story)* (+ co-sc)
1980   *Kalamita (Calamity)* (+ co-sc)
1981   *Chytilová versus Forman*
1983   *Faunovo prilis pozdni odpoledne (The Very Late Afternoon of a Faun)* (+ co-sc)
1985   *Praha, neklidne srace Europy (Prague, the Restless Heart of Europe)* (short)
1986   *Vlci bouda (Wolf's Hole)* (+ co-sc)
1987   *Sasek a kralovna (The Jester and the Queen)*; *Kopytem Sem, Kopytem Tam (Tainted Horseplay)* (+ sc)
1991   *Mi Prazane me Rozùmeji (My Praguers Understand Me)*
1990   *T.G.M.—Osvoboditel (Tomas G. Masaryk—The Liberator)* (+ sc)
1992   *Dedictví aneb Kurvahošigutntag (The Legacy; The Inheritance or Fuckoffguysgoodbye)*
1993   *Kam Parenky* (+ sc)

Other Films

1956   *Ztracenci (3 Men Missing)* (asst d)

1958   *Konec jasnovidce (End of a Clairvoyant)* (ro as girl in bikini)
1991   *Face of Hope* (sc)

Publications by Chytilová

Articles

"Neznám opravdový cin, který by nebyl riskantní" [I Don't Know Any Action That Would Not Be Risky], interview with Galina Kopanevová, in *Film a doba* (Prague), no. 1, 1963.
"Rezijní explikace k filmu *O nec em jiném*" [The Director's Comments on *Something Different*], in *Film a Doba* (Prague), no. 1, 1964.
"*Sedmikrásky*: rezijní explikace" [*Daisies*: The Directress Comments], in *Film a Doba* (Prague), no. 4, 1966.
Interview in *New York Times,* 12 March 1978.
"A Film Should Be a Little Flashlight," interview with H. Polt, in *Take One* (Montreal), November 1978.
Interview with H. Heberle and others, in *Frauen und Film* (Berlin), December 1978.
Interview with B. Eriksson-Vodakova, in *Chaplin* (Stockholm), vol. 27, no. 6, 1985.

Publications on Chytilová

Books

Bocek, Jaroslav, *Modern Czechoslovak Film 1945-1965,* Prague, 1965.
Janoušek, Jiri, *3 Î,* Prague, 1965.
Dewey, Langdon, *Outline of Czechoslovakian Cinema,* London, 1971.
Skvorecký, Josef, *All the Bright Young Men and Women,* Toronto, 1971.
Liehm, Antonin, *Closely Watched Films,* White Plains, New York, 1974.
Liehm, Mira and Antonin, *The Most Important Art: East European Film after 1945,* Berkeley, 1977.
Habova, Milada, and Jitka Vysekalova, editors, *Czechoslovak Cinema,* Prague, 1982.
Hames, Peter, *The Czechoslovak New Wave,* Berkeley, 1985.
Quart, Barbara, *Women Directors: The Emergence of a New Cinema,* New York, 1988.
Foster, Gwendolyn Audrey, *Women Film Directors: An International Bio-Critical Dictionary,* Westport, Connecticut, 1995.

Articles

Bocek, Jaroslav, "Podobenství Very Chytilové" [The Parable of Vera Chytilová], in *Film a Doba* (Prague), no. 11, 1966.
Hames, Peter, "The Return of Vera Chytilová," in *Sight and Sound* (London), no. 3, 1979.
Martinek, Karel, "Filmový svet Very Chytilové" [The Film World of Vera Chytilová], in *Film a Doba* (Prague), no. 3, 1982.
Zuna, Miroslav, and Vladimir Solecký, in *Film a Doba* (Prague), no. 5, 1982.
Benoit, O., "Dans la grisaille tcheque: Vera Chytilová," in *Cinéma* (Paris), May 1984.
Waller, E., in *Skrien* (Amsterdam), September/October 1984.
Manceau, Jean-Louis, "Vera Chytilová à Creteil," in *Cinéma* (Paris), 18 March 1987.

Young, Deborah, "Czechoslovakia Dragging Its Feet on Perestroika for Filmmakers," in *Variety* (New York), 19 October 1988.
Quart, Barbara, "Three Central European Women Directors Revisited," in *Cineaste* (New York), vol. 19, no. 4, 1993.

* * *

So far the only important woman director of the Czech cinema is Vera Chytilová, its most innovative and probably most controversial personality. She is the only contemporary Czech filmmaker to work in the Eisensteinian tradition. She combines didacticism with often daring experimentation, based in essence on montage. Disregarding chronology and illustrative realism, she stresses the symbolic nature of images as well as visual and conceptual shock. Influenced to some extent also by cinema verité, particularly by its female representatives, and militantly feminist in her attitudes, she nevertheless made excellent use of the art of her husband, the cameraman Jaroslav Kucera, in her boldest venture to date, *Daisies*. This film, Chytilová's best known, is a dazzling display of montage, tinting, visual deformation, film trickery, color processing, etc.—a multifaceted tour de force which, among other things, is also a tribute to the classics of the cinema, from the Lumière brothers to Chaplin and Abel Gance. It contains shots, scenes, and sequences that utilize the most character-istic techniques and motives of the masters. *Daisies* is Chytilová at her most formalist. In her later films, there is a noticeable shift towards realism. All the principles mentioned above, however, still dominate the more narrative approach, and a combination of unusual camera angles, shots, etc., together with a bitterly sarcastic vision, lead to hardly less provocative shock effects.

The didactical content of these highly sophisticated and subtly formalist works of filmic art, as in Eisenstein, is naive and crude: young women should prefer "useful" vocations to "useless" ones (*The Ceiling*); extremes of being active and being inactive both result in frustration (*Something Different*); irresponsibility and reckless-ness lead to a bad end (*Daisies*); a sexual relationship is something serious, not just irresponsible amusement (*The Apple Game*); people should help each other (*Prefab Story, Calamity*). Given the fact that Chytilová has worked mostly under the conditions of an enforced and harshly repressive establishment, a natural explanation of this seeming incongruity offers itself: the "moral messages" of her films are simply libations that enable her, and her friends among the crit-ics, to defend the unashamedly formalist films and the harshly satiri-cal presentation of social reality they contain. This is corroborated by Chytilová's many clashes with the political authorities in Czechoslo-vakia: from an interpellation in the Parliament calling for a ban of *Daisies* because so much food—"the fruit of the work of our toiling

Vera Chytilová

farmers"—is destroyed in the film, to her being fired from the Barrandov studios after the Soviet invasion in 1968, and on to her open letter to President Husák printed in Western newspapers. In each instance she won her case by a combination of publicly stated kosher ideological arguments, stressing the alleged "messages" of her works, and of backstage manipulation, not excluding the use of her considerable feminine charm. Consequently, she is the only one of the new wave of directors from the 1960s who, for a long time, had been able to continue making films in Czechoslovakia without compromising her aesthetic creed and her vision of society, as so many others had to do in order to remain in business (including Jaromil Jireš, Hynek Bocan, Jaroslav Papoušek, and to some extent Jirí Menzel).

Prefab Story and *Calamity* earned her hateful attacks from establishment critics and intrigues from her second-rate colleagues, who thrived on the absence of competition from such exiled or banned directors as Miloš Forman, Ivan Passer, Jan Ne mec, Evald Schorm, and Vojtech Jasný. The two films were practically withdrawn from circulation and can be occasionally seen only in suburban theaters. In 1982 *Film a doba*, Czechoslovakia's only critical film periodical, published a series of three articles which, in veiled terms and using what playwright Václav Havel calls "dialectical metaphysics" ("on the one hand it is bad, but on the other hand it is also good"), defended the director and her right to remain herself. In her integrity, artistic boldness, and originality, and in her ability to survive the most destructive social and political catastrophes, Chytilová was a unique phenomenon in post-invasion Czech cinema. Unfortunately, during the last years of Communist rule in Czechoslovakia, she seems to have lost something of her touch, and her latest films— such as *The Very Late Afternoon of a Faun* or *The Jester and the Queen*—are clearly not on the level of *Daisies* or *Prefab Story*.

However, since the "velvet revolution" she has maintained her independence as idiosyncratically as ever. Refusing to take up any comfortably accommodating position, she has been accused of nostalgia for the Communist years. This would be to misrepresent her position. A fierce campaigner for a state subsidy for the Czech film industry, she cannot but lament the extent to which the implementation of the ideology of the "free market" has been allowed to accomplish what the Soviet regime never quite could—the extinguishing of Czech film culture.

She has made a number of documentary films for television as well as a 1992 comedy about the deleterious effects of sudden wealth, which was publicly well-received but met with critical opprobrium. She has so far failed to find funding for a long-cherished project, *Face of Hope*, about the 19th-century humanist writer Bozena Nemcova. The continuing relevance of *Daisies*, and its depiction of philistinism in several registers, is surely the strongest argument in support of Chytilová's position. It is a film which shines with the sheer craftsmanship Czech cinema achieved in those years.

—Josef Skvorecký/Verina Glaessner

CITRON, Michelle
American director

Born: 1948. **Education:** Studied psychology and film production at University of Wisconsin—Madison; earned Ph.D. in cognitive psychology. **Career:** 1974—taught film and television at Temple University; 1975-78—taught film at William James College in Grand Rapids, Michigan; 1978—first feature film, *Daughter Rite*; 1979 to present—professor of film production at Northwestern University. **Address:** Radio, TV, Video and Film Department, 1905 Sheridan Road, Northwestern University, Evanston, IL 60208, U.S.A.

Films as Director

1973   *Self-Defense*; *April 3, 1973*
1974   *Integration*
1975   *Parthenogenesis*
1978   *Daughter Rite*
1983   *What You Take for Granted* (+ sc, pr, ed); *Mother Right*

Publications by Citron

Articles

With others, "'Milestones': White Punks on Revolution," in *Jump Cut* (Berkeley), Summer 1976.
"*Carrie* Meets *Marathon Man*," in *Jump Cut* (Berkeley), no. 4, 1977.
With others, "The Audience Strikes Back," in *Jump Cut* (Berkeley), May 1980.
"Films of Jan Oxenberg: Comic Critique," in *Jump Cut* (Berkeley), March 1981.
With Ellen Seiter, "Teaching: The Woman with the Movie Camera," in *Jump Cut* (Berkeley), December 1981.
"National Women's Studies Conference," in *Quarterly Review of Film Studies* (Pleasantville, New York) vol. 9, no. 2, 1984.
"Exploring What We Take for Granted," interview with M. White, in *Afterimage* (Rochester, New York), December 1984.
"Concerning *Daughter Rite*," in *Journal of University Film and Video Association* (Carbondale, Illinois), vol. 38, no. 3/4, 1986.
"Women's Film Production: Going Mainstream," in *Female Spectators: Looking at Film and Television*, edited by E. Deidre Pribram, London, 1988.

Publications on Citron

Books

Kuhn, Annette, *Women's Pictures: Feminism and Cinema*, London, 1982.
Kaplan, E. Ann, *Women & Film: Both Sides of the Camera*, New York, 1983.
Miller, Lynn Fieldman, *The Hand That Holds the Camera*, New York, 1988.
Rabinovitz, Lauren, *Points of Resistance: Women, Power & Politics in the New York Avant-Garde, 1943-71*, Urbana, Illinois, 1991.
Mayne, Judith, *Cinema and Spectatorship*, New York, 1993.
Women Make Movies Catalogue, New York, 1994.
Foster, Gwendolyn Audrey, *Women Film Directors: An International Bio-Critical Dictionary*, Westport, Connecticut, 1995.

Articles

Becker, E., and others, "The Last Word: WNET Censorship," in *Jump Cut* (Berkeley), May 1980.

Williams, Linda, and B. Ruby Rich, "The Right of Re-vision: Michelle Citron's *Daughter Rite*," in *Film Quarterly* (Berkeley), vol. 35, no. 1, 1981.

Becker, E., and others, "Lesbians and Film: Introduction," in *Jump Cut* (Berkeley), March 1981.

Elam, JoAnn, "*What You Take for Granted*: Work in a White Man's World," in *Jump Cut* (Berkeley), February 1984.

Feuer, Jane, "*Daughter Rite*: Living with Our Pain and Love," in *Films for Women,* edited by Charlotte Brunsdon, London, 1987.

Welsch, Janice R., "Feminist Film Theory/Criticism in the United States," in *Multiple Voices in Feminist Film Criticism,* edited by Diane Carson, Linda Dittmar, and Janice R. Welsch, Minneapolis, 1994.

* * *

Michelle Citron is well-known as a feminist independent filmmaker. Her best-known films are *Daughter Rite* and *What You Take for Granted,* both of which explore the concepts of realism, modernism, and manipulation of film form. She started as an avant-garde filmmaker and over the years she has gradually moved towards narrative filmmaking.

Unlike many filmmakers who have backgrounds in some area of the arts, Citron was inspired to become a filmmaker during the course of her doctoral studies in cognitive psychology, when she began taking film courses to enhance her dissertation project. In part, she was lured to film as a result of her commitment to political activism—she wanted to make films with which the scores of women involved in feminist "consciousness raising" could identify. In addition, she wanted to make films that challenged passive viewing habits and addressed feminist issues to advantage by using purely formal cinematic methods. Accordingly she experimented with blending documentary filmmaking's more familiar conventions with those of melodrama. In this way, she believed, women would be engaged by their recognition of certain genre characteristics and would perhaps be moved to question the "reality" of cinematic representations of women.

Citron's distinctive and overtly feminist films come from real experiences. For example, *Parthenogenesis* is a study of her sister's concert violin studies with a female instructor. In addition, the stories for *Daughter Rite* and *What You Take for Granted* were developed from her many interviews with women, which she conducted on the model of the feminist consciousness-raising group. From the interviews, Citron identified certain common experiences as the themes of the films. As she puts it, "There needs to be a synthesis between the world and my imagination." Thus her characters are composites of the many women she interviewed.

The experimental film *Daughter Rite* combined fictional, documentary, and experimental elements and proved to be a touchstone in the emerging realm of feminist independent filmmaking. Inspired, in part, by male avant-garde filmmaking, it bridges the gap between narrative and documentary films and uses a mock cinema-verité style to tell the story of two fictional sisters exploring their childhood together—as sisters and as daughters. American cinema verité purported to present objective looks at "reality," without imposing a viewpoint on that which was filmed. *Daughter Rite*'s "documentary" scenes, in which the sisters discuss their mother, employ the visual conventions of cinema-verité (e.g., shots of long duration, zooms in for closer shots, awkward unsteady camera, and on-screen focusing) and are quite convincing and easily confused with "reality." In one compelling scene, the sisters riffle through and comment upon their dead mother's personal belongings for clues about her personality and the details of her life. Further, the documentary-style scenes are intercut with home movies of two little girls with their mother that are slowed to a crawl and looped to run repeatedly; they are accompanied by a woman's voice-over reading journal entries in a thoughtful, flat tone. And, unlike traditional documentaries that use the "voice of god"-style of narration to lend a tone of authority, in *Daughter Rite* the voice-over is ambivalent and fails to provide easy answers or precise meanings; indeed, the voice-over occasionally does not seem to relate to the accompanying images at all. Based on her preliminary interviews, Citron discovered that there were some women who tried to carefully analyze their relationships with their mothers, while others told stories that displayed little self-awareness. The two types are represented in the film: one by the narrator and the other by the two sisters in the "documentary." Interestingly, Citron was surprised that audiences are so attuned to documentary film conventions that they typically believe the pseudo-documentary sequences are real. Indeed, that the film is mostly fictional becomes clear only as the end credits start to roll.

Citron's next film, *What You Take for Granted,* is about both professional and working-class women who work in a variety of jobs traditionally held by men. It suggests that the social and political realities of women doing "men's work" resonate in their personal lives, and that such work comes with heavy challenges, including the hostility of men and isolation. Also a pseudo-documentary, she developed six fictional women based on her preliminary interviews who describe their jobs and how and why they are doing them. Notably, the characters are identified in the film not by name, but by occupation—doctor, sculptor, philosophy professor, carpenter, cable-splicer, and truck driver—in order to generalize their commentary to the larger community of working women. Further, their "interviews" are edited so as to illuminate the similarities and differences of their varied experiences. These sequences alternate with narrative sequences that depict a friendship developing between the doctor and truck driver.

Daughter Rite and *What You Take for Granted* can be understood in the context of the 1970's call for a feminist cinematic language that would effectively "deconstruct" patriarchal film conventions and representations of women, but without providing easy answers. Both films, therefore, suggest that although documentaries pose as more truthful than fiction films, they cannot provide a privileged view of reality and actually may be more deceptive.

Citron is currently working on a feature film entitled *Heartland,* and finishing a book entitled *Home Movies, Autobiography, and Other Necessary Fictions,* about autobiographical film. She is also a professor of film production in the Radio, Television, Video, and Film Department at Northwestern University.

—Cynthia Felando

CLARKE, Shirley
American director

Born: Shirley Brimberg in New York City, 2 October 1919. **Education:** Attended Stephens College, Johns Hopkins University, Bennington College, and University of North Carolina. **Family:** Married the lithographer Bert Clarke, 1943; one daughter, Wendy. **Career:** 1946-53—dancer with Martha Graham and Doris

Humphrey, also chairwoman, National Dance Foundation; 1954—made first film, *A Dance in the Sun;* 1962—co-founder, with Jonas Mekas, Film-Makers Cooperative; late 1960s—worked with Public Broadcast Lab (fired 1969); 1975-85—professor of film and video at University of California, Los Angeles. **Awards:** Maya Deren Award, American Film Institute, 1989. **Died:** In Boston, 23 September 1997.

Films as Director

1954   *A Dance in the Sun* (+ pr, ph, ed, co-choreo); *In Paris Parks* (+ pr, ph, ed, co-choreo)
1955   *Bullfight* (+ pr, co-ph, ed, co-choreo)
1957   *A Moment in Love* (+ pr, co-ph, ed, co-choreo)
1958   *The Skyscraper* (co-d, pr); *Brussels "Loops"* (12 film loops made for Brussels Exposition, destroyed) (+ pr, co-ph, ed)
1959   *Bridges-Go-Round* (+ pr, co-ph, ed)
1960   *A Scary Time* (+ co-sc, ph)
1961   *The Connection* (+ co-pr, ed)
1963   *The Cool World* (+ co-sc, ed); *Robert Frost: A Lover's Quarrel with the World* (co-d)
1967   *Portrait of Jason* (+ pr, ed, voice); *Man in Polar Regions* (11-screen film for Expo '67)
1978   *Trans; One Two Three; Mysterium; Initiation* (all video)
1981   *Savage/Love* (video)
1982   *Tongues* (video/theater collaboration with Sam Shepard)
1985   *Ornette, Made in America*

Other Films

1959   *Opening in Moscow* (Pennebaker) (co-ed)
1969   *Lions Love* (Varda) (ro as herself)
1977   *March on Paris 1914—Of General Obrest Alexander von Kluck—and His Memory of Jessie Holladay* (Gutman) (co-ed)

Publications by Clarke

Articles

"The Expensive Art," in *Film Quarterly* (Berkeley), Summer 1960.
"*The Cool World,*" in *Films and Filming* (London), December 1963.
Interview with Harriet Polt, in *Film Comment* (New York), no. 2, 1964.
Interview with Axel Madsen, in *Cahiers du Cinéma* (Paris), March 1964.
Interview with James Blue, in *Objectif* (Paris), February/March 1965.
Interview with Gretchen Berg, in *Film Culture* (New York), Spring 1967.
"A Statement on Dance and Film," in *Dance Perspectives* (New York), Summer 1967.
"A Conversation—Shirley Clarke and Storm de Hirsch," in *Film Culture* (New York), Autumn 1967 and October 1968.
"Entretiens—Le Depart pour Mars," interview with Michel Delahaye, in *Cahiers du Cinéma* (Paris), October 1968.
"Shirley Clarke: Image and Ideas," interview with Susan Rice, in *Take One* (Montreal), February 1972.
"What Directors Are Saying," in *Action* (Los Angeles), March/April 1975.

Publications on Clarke

Books

Hanhardt, John, and others, editors, *A History of the American Avant-Garde Cinema,* New York, 1976.
Kowalski, Rosemary A. R., *A Vision of One's Own: Four Women Film Directors,* Ann Arbor, Michigan, 1980.
Heck-Rabi, Louise, *Women Filmmakers: A Critical Reception,* Metuchen, New Jersey, 1984.
Acker, Ally, *Reel Women: Pioneers of the Cinema, 1896 to the Present,* New York, 1991.
Rabinovitz, Lauren, *Points of Resistance: Women, Power and Politics in the New York Avant-Garde Cinema, 1943-1971,* Urbana, Illinois, 1991.
Foster, Gwendolyn Audrey, *Women Film Directors: An International Bio-Critical Dictionary,* Westport, Connecticut, 1995.

Articles

Breitrose, Henry, "Films of Shirley Clarke," in *Film Quarterly* (Berkeley), Summer 1960.
Archer, Eugene, "Woman Director Makes the Scene," in *New York Times Magazine,* 26 August 1962.
Pyros, J., "Notes on Woman Directors," in *Take One* (Montreal), November/December 1970.
Mekas, Jonas, in *Village Voice* (New York), 20 May 1971.
Cooper, Karen, "Shirley Clarke," in *Filmmakers Newsletter* (Ward Hill, Massachusetts), June 1972.
Bebb, Bruce, "The Many Media of Shirley Clarke," in *Journal of University Film Association* (Carbondale, Illinois), Spring 1982.
American Film (Washington, D.C.), June 1982.

*   *   *

Shirley Clarke was a leader and major filmmaker in the New York film community in the 1950s and 1960s. Her films, which exemplify the artistic directions of the independent movement, are classic examples of the best work of American independent filmmaking. Clarke began her professional career as a dancer. She participated in the late 1940s in the avant-garde dance community centered around New York City's Young Men's-Young Women's Hebrew Association's (YM-YWHA) performance stage and Hanya Holm's classes for young choreographers. In 1953 Clarke adapted dancer-choreographer Daniel Nagrin's *Dance in the Sun* to film. In her first dance film, Clarke relied on editing concepts to choreograph a new cinematic space and rhythm. She then applied her cinematic choreography to a nondance subject in *In Paris Parks,* and further explored the cinematic possibilities for formal choreography in her dance films, *Bullfight* and *A Moment in Love.*

During this period, Clarke studied filmmaking with Hans Richter at the City College of New York and participated in informal filmmaking classes with director and cinematographer Peter Glushanok. In 1955 she became an active member of the Independent Filmmakers of America (IFA), a short-lived New York organization that tried to improve promotion and distribution for independent films. Through the IFA, Clarke became part of the Greenwich Village artistic circle that included avant-garde filmmakers Maya Deren, Stan Brakhage, and Jonas Mekas. It also introduced her to the importance of an economic structure for the growth of avant-garde film, a cause she championed throughout the 1960s.

Shirley Clarke

Clarke worked with filmmakers Willard Van Dyke, Donn Alan Pennebaker, Ricky Leacock, and Wheaton Galentine on a series of film loops on American life for the U.S. Pavilion at the 1958 World's Fair in Brussels. With the leftover footage of New York City bridges, she then made her experimental film masterpiece, *Bridges-Go-Round,* utilizing editing strategies, camera choreography, and color tints to turn naturalistic objects into a poem of dancing abstract elements. It is one of the best and most widely seen examples of cinematic abstract expressionism in the 1950s.

Clarke made the documentary film *The Skyscraper* in 1958 with Van Dyke, Pennebaker, Leacock, and Galentine, followed by *A Scary Time* (1960), a film commissioned by the United Nations International Children's Emergency Fund (UNICEF). Clarke also began work on a public television film on Robert Frost, *A Lover's Quarrel with the World,* but due to artistic disagreements and other commitments she left the project before the film's completion while retaining a credit as co-director.

Influenced by the developing cinema-verité style in the documentary films of Leacock and Pennebaker, Clarke adapted cinema verité to two feature-length dramatic films, *The Connection* and *The Cool World. The Connection* was a landmark for the emergence of a New York independent feature-film movement. It heralded a new style that employed greater cinematic realism and addressed relevant social issues in black-and-white low-budget films. It was also important because Clarke made the film the first test case in a successful fight to abolish New York State's censorship rules. Her next feature film, *The Cool World,* was the first movie to dramatize a story on black street gangs without relying upon Hollywood-style moralizing, and it was the first commercial film to be shot on location in Harlem. In 1967 Clarke directed a 90-minute cinema-verité interview with a black homosexual. *Portrait of Jason* is an insightful exploration of one person's character while it simultaneously addresses the range and limitations of cinema-verité style. Although Clarke's features had only moderate commercial runs and nominal success in the United States, they have won film festival awards and critical praise in Europe, making Clarke one of the most highly regarded American independent filmmakers among European film audiences.

In the 1960s Clarke also worked for the advancement of the New York independent film movement. She was one of the 24 filmmakers and producers who wrote and signed the 1961 manifesto, "Statement for a New American Cinema," which called for an economic, artistic, and political alternative to Hollywood moviemaking. With Jonas Mekas in 1962, she co-founded Film-Makers Cooperative, a nonprofit distribution company for independent films. Later, Clarke, Mekas, and filmmaker Louis Brigante co-founded Film-Makers Distribution Center, a company for distributing independent features to commercial movie theaters. Throughout the 1960s, Clarke lectured on independent film in universities and museums in the United States and Europe, and in 1969 she turned to video as her major medium in which to work.

—Lauren Rabinovitz

CLÉO DE CINQ À SEPT

(Cleo from 5 to 7)
France-Italy, 1962
Director: Agnès Varda

Production: Rome-Paris Films; black and white and Eastmancolor, 35mm; running time: 90 minutes. Released April 1962, Paris. Filmed in Paris.

Producers: Georges de Beauregard and Carlo Ponti; **associate producer:** Bruno Drigo; **screenplay:** Agnès Varda; **photography:** Jean Rabier; **editor:** Janine Verneau; **sound engineers:** Jean Labussière and Julien Coutellier; **sound editor:** Jacques Maumont; **art director:** Bernard Evein; **music:** Michel Legrand; **lyrics:** Agnès Varda; **costume designer:** Bernard Evein.

Cast: Corinne Marchand (*Cléo*); Antoine Bourseiller (*Antoine*); Dorothée Black (*Dorothée*); Michel Legrand (*Bob, the Pianist*); Dominique Davray (*Angèle*); José-Luis de Villalonga (*Cléo's Lover*); with: Jean-Luc Godard; Anna Karina; Eddie Constantine; Sami Frey; Danièle Delorme; Jean-Claude Brialy; Yves Robert; Alan Scott; Robert Postec; Lucienne Marchand.

Publications

Script

Varda, Agnès, "*Cléo de cinq à sept,*" Paris, 1962; extract as "*Cleo from 5 to 7*" in *Films and Filming* (London), December 1962.

Books

Armes, Roy, *French Cinema since 1946. Volume 2: The Personal Style,* New York, 1966.
Betancourt, Jeanne, *Women in Focus,* Dayton, Ohio, 1974.
Barascq, Leon, *Caligari's Cabinet and Other Grand Illusions; A History of Film Design,* New York, 1976.

Articles

Tailleur, Roger, "Cléo d'ici a l'éternité," in *Positif* (Paris), March 1962.
Avant-Scène du Cinéma (Paris), 15 May 1962.
Roud, Richard, in *Sight and Sound* (London), Summer 1962.
Shivas, M., "*Cléo de cinq à sept* and Agnès Varda," in *Movie* (London), October 1962.
Manvell, Roger, in *Films and Filming* (London), December 1962.
Roud, Richard, "The Left Bank," in *Sight and Sound* (London), Winter 1962-63.
"Pasolini-Varda-Allio-Sarris-Michelson," in *Film Culture* (New York), Fall 1966.
"Agnès Varda," in *Current Biography 1970,* New York, 1970.
Gow, Gordon, interview with Agnès Varda, in *Films and Filming* (London), March 1970.
Confino, Barbara, interview with Agnès Varda, in *Saturday Review* (New York), 12 August 1972.
Levitin, J., "Mother of the New Wave," in *Women and Film* (Santa Monica, California), volume 1, nos. 5-6, 1974.
Mulvey, Laura, "Visual Pleasure and Narrative Cinema," in *Women and Film: A Critical Anthology,* edited by Karyn Kay and Gerald Peary, New York, 1977.
Flitterman, Sandy, "From 'déesse' to 'idée': Agnès Varda's *Cleo from 5 to 7,*" in *Enclitic* (Minneapolis), Fall 1983.
Revault d'Allonnes, Fabrice, *Cinéma* (Paris), 8 January 1986.
Forbes, Jill, "Agnès Varda: The Gaze of the Medusa?," in *Sight and Sound* (London), Spring 1989.

* * *

Agnès Varda's second feature is amongst the most rigorous and delicate films of the French New Wave. While awaiting the results of a cancer test, a pop singer—stage-name Cléo Victoire, a beautiful, dreamy, artificial creature—comes to terms with her newfound fear of death.

First, Cléo's fortune-teller predicts "a transformation"; then her confidante, Angèle, is dismissive; the purchase of a hat only trivially lifts her morale. She dares not share her troubles with her suave lover, José (Villalonga). She is briefly reassured by rehearsals with her pianist, Bob (Michel Legrand, who also wrote the background music), until he misreads her nerviness as mere caprice. Shop-windows reflect her beauty, but also display grotesque masks and sculptures. On the jukebox of a fashionable café, her latest record serves as mere background to chatter. She is warmed by the earthy, natural nudity of her friend Dorothée, a sculptor's model, and responds to a burlesque film (featuring Godard, Karina, Eddie Constantine), with

Cléo de cinq à sept

tions, with their exact time, and the name of a character whose personality at that moment keys the section's style. Only the prologue is in color. Thereafter Cléo's name "christens" sections I (solo on a staircase), III (from hat shop to taxi), V (José), and VII (discovering the street). Angèle's name christens II (the first café) and IV (from taxi into Cléo's apartment). Bob keys VI (the rehearsal); "Some others" VIII (La Dôme to sculpture studio); Dorothée IX (journey to Raoul, the projectionist); Raoul X (the cinema). The park sequence is divided between Cléo (XI), Antoine (XII) and "Cléo et Antoine" (XIII). Bob's extrovert cheerfulness inspires "swinging" camera-movements; Angèle's style is factual and strict; Cléo progresses from an ornamental, self-centered, style (sinuous camera-calligraphy, narrow-lens close-ups of herself) to a simpler style (direct point-of-view/reaction cuts); the last section, bearing two names, suggests a *meeting* of minds, both at one with the landscape, not just "in" them. The cinematic styles evoke de Sica, Ophüls and, of course, Démy, Varda's husband; the settings range from raw reality to a beautifully mannered rococo.

Varda describes *Cléo* as a converse to her second, uncompleted, feature, *La Mélangite,* planned as a maze of stream-of-consciousness shots. It also echoes her short *Opéra-Mouffe,* which depicted the world through the mind of a pregnant woman, though usually off screen. Like that film, *Cléo* involves much direct cinema, and in that sense, "objectivity." If details resonant to Cléo's moods abound, it is as appropriate to mental selectivity generally. The film's reconciliation of objective-casual appearances with "expressionism" (Varda's term; one might prefer "impressionism") is virtuoso work; she perfects a certain French tradition, a blending of "camera-eye" objectivity and Bergsonian subjectivity, which runs from Vigo to Franju, and becomes fully self-interrogating amongst the "Left Bank" documentarists of the New Wave (Varda acknowledges affinities with Resnais and Chris Marker). Some critics felt that *Cléo*'s sensitive surface somehow lacked soul, but Varda's highly articulate interviews confirm the lucidity behind a film whose intricate symbolism, or rather, poetic suggestion (angels/Angèle/flesh/wigs) repays endless analysis, the most sensitive being Roger Tailleur's in *Positif*

—Raymond Durgnat

COFFEE, Lenore J.
American writer

Born: San Francisco, California, c. 1896. **Education:** Attended Dominican College, San Rafael, California. **Family:** Married the director William J. Cowen, one son and one daugher. **Career:** 1919—first film as writer, *The Better Wife;* then writer for Metro, First National, Paramount, MGM in the 1930s, and Warner Bros.; retired to England, but then returned to the Motion Picture Home in California. **Died:** In Woodland Hills, California, 2 July 1984.

Films as Writer

1919   *The Better Wife*
1920   *The Forbidden Woman* (Garson); *For the Soul of Rafael* (Garson) (uncredited); *The Fighting Shepherdess* (*Vindication*) (Jose) (uncredited)
1921   *Ladyfingers* (*Alias Ladyfingers*) (Veiller); *Hush* (Garson) (uncredited)

fast-motion funerals and dark-tinted spectacles. She removes her elaborate wig, and begins to notice the poignant and grotesque details of a certain street-life. In a quiet park, she meets Antoine, a gentle conscript destined for the Algerian war; he accompanies her to the hospital; and she agrees to see him off that evening. The doctor confirms her anxieties, but not her worst fears, and she feels part of life, of "others," at last.

The film's running-time matches the real (or rather, possible, albeit pat) space-and-duration of Cléo's journey round Paris, between 1700 and 1830 hrs on 21 June 1961, and using the radio news for that day (described as a Tuesday, though actually a Wednesday). Cléo's journey can be exactly mapped, and the camera leaves her only twice, and very briefly. Thus the film adapts the classical theater's unities (time, space, action) to a properly fluid film equivalent. Though approximating Cléo's perceptions, Varda avoids restricting herself to first person point-of-view shots, which would overly eliminate Cléo's presence, and therefore her reactions and feelings, from the screen. This near-subjectivism culminates in actual "stream-of-consciousness," a volley of memory-images of earlier moments (*not* flashbacks as they include changes due to mental processes).

This "subjectivism" is countered by a formalism inducing, not "alienation" exactly, but a film-form "concretism." On-screen titles announce a prologue (the fortune-teller sequence), and then 13 sec-

1922 *The Face Between* (Veiller); *The Light That Failed* (Veiller); *Sherlock Brown* (Veiller); *The Dangerous Age* (Stahl) (uncredited)

1923 *Temptation* (Le Saint); *Wandering Daughters* (J. Young); *The Age of Desire* (Borzage); *Daytime Wives* (Chautard); *Thundering Dawn* (Garson); *Strangers of the Night* (Niblo) (uncredited); *The Six Fifty* (N. Ross)

1924 *Fool's Highway* (Cummings); *Bread* (Schertzinger); *The Rose of Paris* (Cummings); *The Great Divide* (Barker) (uncredited)

1925 *Hell's Highroad* (Julian); *East Lynne* (Flynn); *The Swan* (Buchowetzki) (uncredited); *Graustark* (Buchowetzki) (uncredited)

1926 *The Volga Boatman* (C. B. DeMille); *For Alimony Only* (W. de Mille); *The Winning of Barbara Worth* (H. King) (uncredited)

1927 *The Night of Love* (Fitzmaurice); *Lonesome Ladies* (Henabery); *Chicago* (Urson); *The Angel of Broadway* (L. Weber); *The Love of Sunya* (Albert Parker) (uncredited)

1928 *Ned McCobb's Daughter* (Cowan) (uncredited)

1929 *Desert Nights* (Nigh)

1930 *Street of Chance* (Cromwell); *The Bishop Murder Case* (Grinde and Burton); *Mother's Cry* (Henley)

1931 *Possessed* (C. Brown); *The Squaw Man* (*The White Man*) (C. B. DeMille); *The Honor of the Family* (L. Bacon)

1932 *Arsène Lupin* (Conway); *Night Court* (*Justice for Sale*) (Van Dyke); *Downstairs* (Bell); *Rasputin and the Empress* (Boleslawski) (uncredited)

1933 *Torch Singer* (Hall and Somnes)

1934 *Evelyn Prentice* (W. K. Howard); *Four Frightened People* (C. B. DeMille); *Such Women Are Dangerous* (Flood); *All Men Are Enemies* (Fitzmaurice)

1935 *Age of Indiscretion* (Ludwig); *Vanessa: Her Love Story* (W. K. Howard); *David Copperfield* (Cukor) (uncredited)

1936 *Suzy* (Fitzmaurice)

1937 *Parnell* (Shahl) (uncredited)

1938 *Four Daughters* (Curtiz) (co); *White Banners* (E. Goulding)

1939 *Good Girls Go to Paris* (Hall)

1940 *My Son, My Son!* (C. Vidor); *The Way of All Flesh* (L. King)

1941 *The Great Lie* (E. Goulding)

1942 *The Gay Sisters* (Rapper); *We Were Dancing* (Leonard) (uncredited)

1943 *Old Acquaintance* (V. Sherman)

1944 *Till We Meet Again* (Borzage); *Marriage Is a Private Affair* (Leonard)

1946 *Tomorrow Is Forever* (Pichel)

1947 *The Guilt of Janet Ames* (Levin); *Escape Me Never* (Godfrey) (uncredited)

1949 *Beyond the Forest* (K. Vidor)

1951 *Lightning Strikes Twice* (K. Vidor)

1952 *Sudden Fear* (D. Miller)

1955 *Young at Heart* (G. Douglas); *The End of the Affair* (Dmytryk); *Footsteps in the Fog* (Lubin)

1958 *Another Time, Another Place* (L. Allen) (st only)

1960 *Cash McCall* (Pevney)

Publications by Coffee

Books

With William J. Cowen, *Family Portrait* (play), New York, 1939.

Weep No More (novel), London, 1955, as *Another Time, Another Place,* New York, 1956.

The Face of Love (novel), New York, 1959.

A Million Menus for Dining and Entertaining at Home, London, 1964.

The Eye of Memory (novel), Aylesbury, Buckinghamshire, 1973.

Storyline: Recollections of a Hollywood Screenwriter, London, 1973.

Article

In *Backstory: Interviews with Screenwriters of Hollywood's Golden Age,* edited by Pat McGilligan, Berkeley, 1986.

Publications on Coffee

Book

Acker, Ally, *Reel Women: Pioneers of the Cinema, 1896 to the Present,* New York, 1991.

Articles

Obituary, in *Variety* (New York), 11 July 1984.

Slater, Thomas, in *American Screenwriters,* 2nd series, edited by Randall Clark, Detroit, 1986.

* * *

Lenore J. Coffee's own success story is almost as incredible as one of her most romantic screenplays. Born in San Francisco at the turn of the century, Coffee was an avid moviegoer, often unimpressed by the caliber of screenplays she saw. When she read in *The Motion Picture Exhibitor's Herald* that the silent star Clara Kimball Young was looking for a good story, she wrote one. Coffee sent "The Better Wife" to The Garson Studio, they bought it for $100, and less than six months later the aspiring writer was on her way to Hollywood with a one-year contract.

Beginning with that first original story in 1919, Lenore Coffee wrote steadily for motion pictures for 35 years, earning her last credit in 1960. Throughout the 1920s she wrote scenarios as well as title cards for silent films. She worked at various studios—Metro, First National, and DeMille Pictures—writing mostly romances and melodramas.

Her first important picture was *The Volga Boatman,* directed by Cecil B. DeMille. By the end of the decade, Coffee was writing for Hollywood's biggest stars. *The Night of Love* teamed one of the silent screen's most popular couples, Ronald Colman and Vilma Banky. And *Desert Nights* was especially tailored for John Gilbert. To protect the actor as long as possible from the feared transition to sound, Coffee's script had accompanying music and effects, but no dialogue.

During the 1930s Coffee settled in at MGM and continued to specialize in romantic dramas—so-called women's pictures—and mystery-thrillers, establishing her competence in two distinctly different Hollywood genres. While such films as *The Bishop Murder Case, Street of Chance,* and *Arsène Lupin* required fast pacing, intricate plotting, and rapid dialogue, her women's pictures, *Evelyn Prentice, Torch Singer,* and *Vanessa: Her Love Story,* focused on relationships and feelings rather than action. Coffee's script for *Possessed,* starring Joan Crawford and Clark Gable, stands out as one of the most inventive of Crawford's many Cinderella stories at MGM.

In 1938 Coffee left Metro, co-wrote *Four Daughters* with Julius Epstein for Warner Bros., and was nominated for an Academy Award. The story capitalized on her abilities to sensitively portray family conflict and established her, along with Casey Robinson, as the studio's resident women's film expert.

Over the next few years, she wrote some of the romantic genre's best pictures—particularly *The Great Lie, The Gay Sisters,* and *Old Acquaintance.* Coffee brought plausibility, freshness, and even, on occasion, depth of character to these overworked stories. She was able to temper the often maudlin characteristics of the pieces with humor, but never lost sight of the fact that the genre's fundamental appeal lay in the suffering and sacrifice of the leading ladies.

Her later women's films were less successful. *Tomorrow Is Forever,* a reworking of *Ethan Frome*'s plot, was formulaic and tired, and *Beyond the Forest,* despite its eventual cult popularity, was a critical and box-office failure when it was released. In director King Vidor's hands, it became a cynical perversion of the women's film and marked the end of Bette Davis's long career at Warner Bros. Coffee's suspense melodramas of the late 1940s and early 1950s met with mixed reception. The best known are the Joan Crawford vehicle, *Sudden Fear,* and the adaptation of Graham Greene's novel, *The End of the Affair.* Surprisingly, her last screen credit was a comedy, *Cash McCall,* based on a Cameron Hawley novel.

—Joanne L. Yeck

COLE, Janis, and Holly DALE
Canadian directors, producers, writers, and editors

COLE. Born: Canada, 1954. **Education:** Attended Sheridan College, Toronto. **Awards:** Best Short Film, Toronto Festival of Festivals, for *Shaggie,* 1990; Top Ten Award, Writers Guild of Canada, and Bronze Plaque, Columbus Festival, for *Dangerous Offender,* 1996.

DALE. Born: Toronto, 1953. **Education:** Attended Sheridan College, Toronto; the Centre for Advanced Film Studies, 1988. **Awards:** Bessie Award, for commercial directing. **Career:** 1996—directed episode of TV series *Traders,* and TV commercials.

In 1976—completed first film together, as students, *Cream Soda*; 1977—completed critically acclaimed and best-known film, *The Thin Line*; 1990s—co-operators of Spectrum Films. **Awards:** Best Theatrical Documentary, Genie Award, Red Ribbon, American Film Festival, and Grand Prize-Best Human Condition Category and Best Cinematography, York Film & Video Festival, for *P4W,* 1982; Gold Medal, Chicago Film Festival, for *Hookers on Davie,* 1984; Theatrical Producers Achievement Award, Canadian Film and Television Association, 1988; Lillian Gish Award, Los Angeles Women in Film Festival, for *Calling the Shots,* 1988; Toronto Arts Award in Media, 1994. **Address:** Canadian Filmmakers Distribution Centre, 37 Hanna Avenue, Suite 220, Toronto, Ontario M6K 1W8, Canada.

Films as Co-Directors

1976   *Cream Soda* (+ pr, ed); *Minimum Charge No Cover* (+ pr, ed)

1977   *Nowhere to Run* (+ pr, ed); **The Thin Line** (*The Thin Blue Line*) (+ pr, ed)
1982   *P4W* (*Prison for Women*) (+ pr, ed)
1984   *Hookers on Davie* (+ pr, ed)
1985   *Quiet on the Set: Filming Agnes of God* (*The Making of Agnes of God*) (+ pr, ed)
1988   *Calling the Shots* (+ pr, ed)

Other Films

1977   *Starship Invasions* (*Alien Encounter*) (E. Hunt) (Dale: asst pr)
1990   *Shaggie* (Cole: d)
1995   *Blood & Donuts* (Dale: d)
1996   *Dangerous Offender* (for TV) (Dale: d; Cole: sc)

Publications by Cole and Dale

Book

Calling the Shots: Profiles of Women Filmmakers, Kingston, Ontario, 1993.

Articles

"Street People," interview with G. C. Koller, in *Cinema Canada* (Montreal), September/October 1978.
"Nightworld: An Interview with Janis Cole and Holly Dale," in *Cinema Canada* (Quebec), June 1984.

Publications on Cole and Dale

Books

Tregebov, Rhea, editor, *Work in Progress: Building Feminist Culture,* Toronto, 1987.
Foster, Gwendolyn Audrey, *Women Film Directors: An International Bio-Critical Dictionary,* Westport, Connecticut, 1995.

Articles

Delaney, Marshall, "Brutal Art from Mean Streets," in *Saturday Night* (Toronto), June 1978.
Neher, Jack, "Social Concerns," in *Film News* (New York), Summer 1979.
Armitage, Kay, in *The Women's Companion to International Film,* edited by Annette Kuhn and Susannah Radstone, London, 1990.
Baldassarre, A., "Holly Dale Serves up *Blood and Donuts,*" in *Take One* (Toronto), Fall 1994.

*   *   *

"We want to make films so that people can see what they normally are not exposed to and have some kind of understanding." Such are the noble intentions of Janis Cole and Holly Dale, the highly esteemed independent documentary filmmakers from Canada, whose fruitful collaborations have involved sharing the duties of director, producer, and editor. Their films have been widely screened at film festivals around the world, including Berlin, Sydney, Paris, London, Créteil, Los Angeles, and Lyon. Associated with Canada's film boom

Janis Cole (right) and Holly Dale. Photograph by John Walker.

of the 1970s, their work has been praised for tackling marginal, daring, offbeat subjects, including prostitutes, cross-dressers, criminally insane men, and female prisoners, albeit with unusual sensitivity and commitment. Early in their career, they earned a reputation for focusing on those members of society who endure class, gender, and other institutional oppressions—including women film directors. Thus, one critic commented upon their remarkable courage and determination, "Like the best young filmmakers, they don't know that it's impossible to make films, so they go ahead and make them."

Cole and Dale started collaborating as college students when they were 20 years old. Their student film *Cream Soda* provides an unflinching cinema-verité look at massage parlors in downtown Toronto, including footage of the women workers as they chat in their dressing room, and of the customers as they furtively come and go. *Minimum Charge No Cover* is about prostitution, homosexuals, transsexuals, and female impersonators. Interestingly, the film begins without revealing the identity of its subjects, because Cole and Dale wanted to encourage the audience to identify with them as "ordinary people." Critics often have been intrigued about the team's success in getting willing participants to reveal themselves to their cameras; but, as Dale casually explained to an interviewer, "Well, they're all friends of ours." Indeed, at the age of 20, Dale had worked

as an assistant manager at the French Connection, a Toronto massage parlor.

The Thin Line was their first widely seen film, and like their previous work, it explores a usually hidden aspect of society: the therapeutic treatment of criminally insane inmates at a maximum-security prison in Ontario. Cole and Dale use interviews and therapy sessions with patients to reveal the deep capacity for understanding among the men who have committed some of society's most horrible crimes—including rape, assault, and murder—and thereby to humanize them.

Cole and Dale's feature-length films are *P4W* and *Hookers on Davie,* both of which performed well at the box office. *P4W* provides a compelling look at the love and isolation among women in prison—the result of a four-year struggle to gain access to the facility. They collected interviews, monologues, and cinema-verité sequences that poignantly demonstrate the will to survive among a tightly knit community of female prisoners. *Hookers on Davie* provides an excursion into the realm of Vancouver sex workers. Its setting is the Davie strip, Canada's capital of prostitution and its only significant pimp-free zone, where the prostitutes are in charge of their own business. The film is surprising, amusing, and sad; moreover, like all of Cole and Dale's work, it belies expectations about the world of prostitution by refusing conventional morality and presenting the perspectives of the prostitutes themselves. In addition, it celebrates the strength, solidarity, and defiance of the prostitutes who formed the Alliance for the Safety of Prostitutes and distributed "bad trick sheets" to warn colleagues about dangerous customers.

Cole and Dale turned their attention to the world of filmmaking with *Quiet on the Set: Filming Agnes of God,* a behind-the-scenes account of the production of Norman Jewison's 1985 film. Then, a few years later, in *Calling the Shots,* they illuminated the vast contribution of women filmmakers to the world of cinema, as well as the remarkable diversity of their personalities and films. It features interviews with a variety of well- and lesser-known women film workers from around the world about the constraints and successes of their careers in the 1970s and 1980s, including producers, scriptwriters, studio executives, and directors, such as Agnès Varda, Amy Heckerling, Joan Micklin Silver, Martha Coolidge, Lizzie Borden, Susan Seidelman, Ann Hui, Penelope Spheeris, Lee Grant, Joyce Chopra, and Jeanne Moreau. The women tell horror stories as well as amusing and dramatic anecdotes about what drew them to filmmaking and about the subject matter of their work. Notably, the film includes brief segments of women on-the-job: at production meetings and directing scenes. Interestingly, the filmmakers excluded in *Calling the Shots* are Cole and Dale themselves.

Recently, Cole and Dale have each pursued individual projects; perhaps not surprisingly, they chose to tackle subjects and themes that live on the margins of society. In 1990 Cole directed the film short *Shaggie,* about Marlene Moore who was sent to a juvenile detention center when she was 13 and was incarcerated for the next 20 years, until 1988, when she committed suicide in Kingston's Prison for Women. In 1995 Dale made the revealingly titled film, *Blood & Donuts.*

—Cynthia Felando

COLETTE
French writer and actress

Born: Sidonie-Gabrielle Colette in Saint-Sauveur en Puisaye (Yvonne), France, 28 January 1873. **Education:** Received Primary Education Certificate. **Family:** Married (1) Henry Gauthier-Villars (known as Willy), 15 years her senior, 1893 (divorced 1907); (2) the newspaper editor Henry de Jouvenel, 1912 (divorced 1925), daughter, Colette ("Bel-Gazou"); (3) Maurice Goudeket, 17 years her younger, 1935. **Career:** 1900-1905—forced by husband Willy, a publisher, to spend four hours a day writing stories about her youth which he then published under his name (the "Claudine" novels); 1906-10—performed as a mime and dancer in music halls; 1911—began journalism career as drama critic; 1914—first film criticism; 1916—first film scenario based on her own novel, *La Vagabonde*; 1919—directed a play, *En Camarades,* in which she also performed; 1920—success of *Chéri* established her reputation as a novelist; 1924—began use of "Colette" only; 1932—opened a beauty salon selling her own line of products; 1942—suffered severe arthritis and oversaw the publication of the 15 volumes of her *Oeuvres complètes,* containing none of her film scripts and very little of her writing on cinema; assisted with film adaptations of her novels. **Awards:** Elected member, Belgian Royal Academy, 1936; elected member, Goncourt Academy, 1945; Grand Officer of the Legion of Honor, 1953. **Died:** In Paris, 3 August 1954.

Films as Writer

1918   *La Vagabonde* (*The Vagabond*) (Perego)
1920   *La Flamme cachée* (*The Hidden Flame*) (Musidora and Lion, produced in 1918)
1932   *La Vagabonde* (Bussi) (remake with additional scenes by Colette)
1935   *Divine* (Max Ophüls) (+ dialogue based on her *L'Envers du Music Hall*)

Films as Dialogue Writer

1934   *Lac-aux-Dames* (M. Allégret) (based on a 1932 novel by Vicki Baum)
1949   *Gigi* (Audry)
1950   *Chéri* (Billon)

Other Films Adapted from Her Novels (uncredited)

1916   *Minne* (Musidora) (adaption by Jacques de Baroncelli of *L'Ingénue libertine*; unreleased)
1937   *Claudine à l'école* (*Claudine at School*) (de Poligny)
1950   *Julie de Carneilhan* (Manuel); *Minne, l'Ingénue libertine* (*Minne, the Innocent Libertine*) (Audry)
1952   "L'Envie" ("Envy") ep. of *Les Sept péchés capitaux* (*The Seven Deadly Sins*) (Rossellini) (based on *La Chatte*)
1953   *Le Blé en herbe* (*The Game of Love*) (Autant-Lara)
1956   *Mitsou* (Audry)
1958   *Gigi* (Minnelli)

Publications by Colette

Novels

(Her numerous lyrical essays are not included as they never became a basis for films.)

Under the name of "Willy":

Claudine à l'école (*Claudine at School*), Paris, 1900.
Claudine à Paris (*Claudine in Paris*), Paris, 1901.
Claudine en ménage (*Claudine Married*), Paris, 1902.
Claudine s'en va (*Claudine and Annie*), Paris, 1903.
Minne, Paris, 1904.

Under the name of "Colette Willy":

La Retraite sentimentale (*The Retreat from Love*), Paris, 1907.
L'Ingénue libertine (*The Gentle Libertine*), Paris, 1909.
La Vagabonde (*The Vagabond*), Paris, 1910.

Under the name of "Colette (Colette Willy)":

L'Entrave (*The Shackle*), Paris, 1913.
Mitsou ou Comment l'esprit vient aux filles (*Mitsou and Music-Hall Sidelights*), Paris, 1919.
Chéri, Paris, 1920.

Under the name only of "Colette":

Le Blé en herbe (*The Ripening Seed*), Paris, 1923.
La Fin de Chéri (*The Last of Chéri*), Paris, 1926.

La Naissance du Jour (*Break of Day*), Paris, 1928.
La Seconde (*The Other One*), Paris, 1929.
Duo, Paris, 1934.
Bella-Vista (*The Tender Shoot*), Paris, 1937.
Le Toutounier (*The Toutounier*), Paris, 1939.
Chambre d'hôtel (*Chance Acquaintances*), Paris, 1940.
Julie de Carneilhan, Paris, 1941.
Le Képi (*The Tender Shoot*), Paris, 1943.
Gigi, Lausanne, 1944.

Publications on Colette:

Books

Crosland, Margaret, *Madame Colette: A Provincial in Paris,* London, 1953.
Marks, Elaine, *Colette,* New Brunswick, New Jersey, 1960.
Raaphorst-Rousseau, Madeleine, *Colette: sa vie et son art,* Paris, 1964.
Phelps, Robert, editor, *Colette: Autobiographie tirée des oeuvres de Colette,* Paris, 1966.
Colette at the Movies: Criticism and Screenplays, translated by Sarah W. R. Smith, edited by Alain and Odette Virmaux, New York, 1980; abridged ed. of *Colette au cinéma,* Paris, 1975.
Sarde, Michèle, *Colette: Free and Fettered,* translated by Richard Miller, New York, 1980.
Norell, Donna M., *Colette: An Annotated Primary and Secondary Bibliography,* New York, 1993.

Preface

Pichois, Claude, "Préface," *Colette, Oeuvres I,* Paris, 1984.

Film

Colette, documentary directed by Yannick Bellon, 1950.

* * *

During her lifetime, she was considered the greatest French female writer ever and was the first French female writer not of the aristocracy. Because Colette herself considered her role in cinema subservient to that of the novelist or playwright, it was largely overlooked by film histories until Alain and Odette Virmaux collected both her criticism and scripts into a single volume in 1975. Though participating actively in the later film adaptations of her novels, her influence on the new art was strongest in the era of silent films. Acting as film critic during the war years, she pointed out America's creative contribution to a cinematic language where European productions slavishly imitated theater. Whereas the rest of France saw only a pro-Japanese issue in Cecil B. DeMille's *The Cheat,* Colette underscored the significance of Sessue Hayakawa's internalized style of acting, more appropriate for cinema with its close-ups and the antithesis of exaggerated theatrical expression. She lauded filming in natural rather than studio settings and movies that dealt with ordinary daily life rather than dramatic and heroic plots.

When Philippe de Rothschild wanted a part in the cinematic enterprise as producer of *Lac-aux-Dames,* to be shot on location, he turned to his old acquaintance Colette for the dialogue. Though based on someone else's novel, she made it her own and much that is in her novels can be found in it: the combination of purity and provocation,

the male as object. *Divine* was based on her own novel, *L'Envers du Music Hall,* and directed by the then newcomer Max Ophüls. The star, an already famous French actress and producer, Simone Berriau, was a friend of Colette's and would play the music hall girl.

Colette's first-known newspaper article, written in 1914, praised the documentary character of *The Scott Expedition* and is worth quoting for its foresight as it reads like a commentary of television in the 1990s: "When Scott and his companions, before perishing at the South Pole, capture for the inhabited world living images, animated portraits of an unknown land, ... [the spectacle] honors—should we say rehabilitates?—the cinema ... [which] ceases in short to be merely a tool of vaudeville and grotesque imbroglios." Her "Short Manual for the Aspiring Scenario Writer" is still a valid satire of the artifice of many Hollywood studio films.

The qualities of her best novels—such as *Chéri* (1920) or *Le Blé en herbe* (1923)—are found in her films as well as her criticism. Like her novels, her films are primarily stories of love, both sought and feared by the principal characters, women. The female, however, like her mother Sido, is seen as subject, not object, in the relationship. The subject matter, as in all truly modern art since Impressionism, was not the most significant aspect of her work. From her mother she had learned to delight continually in plants and animals. This sense of renewed discovery and wonder within the everyday world is her hallmark. Her fresh approach often shocked by its naturalness, its lack of moral intent or attempt to instruct. Colette did not see people or things as black and white; she did not judge. Her world is firmly grounded in the five physical senses. Her dialogues express sensitivity through the use of peasant idioms or the often crude language of actresses, the demimonde. To affirm her liberation from her first husband Willy, she wrote her novels in the first person. As Claude Pichois succinctly observes, her stories tend to be collections of brief scenes, a succession of pleasures that, having no hierarchy, become prose poems, rendering plot subservient to the joy of self-expression. All physical pleasures delight and interest her—and they are in motion. The moving image was, therefore, already inherent in her novelistic orientation as were a succession of scenes; the adaptation of her novels to film was inevitable.

—Emily Zants

COMDEN, Betty
American writer and lyricist

Born: Betty Cohen in Brooklyn, New York, 3 May 1917. **Education:** Attended New York University, B.S. in drama, 1937. **Family:** Married Steven Kyle, 1942 (died 1979), children: Susanna and Alan. **Career:** 1940-44—with partner Adolph Green performed with Judy Holliday, John Frank, and Alvin Hammer in cabaret group The Revuers; 1944—wrote first Broadway musical, *On the Town* (later musicals include *Billion Dollar Baby,* 1945, *Bonanza Beyond,* 1947, *Two on the Aisle,* 1951, *Wonderful Town,* 1953, *Bells Are Ringing,* 1956, *Say Darling,* 1958, *Do Re Mi,* 1960, *Subways Are for Sleeping,* 1961, *Fade Out—Fade In,* 1964, *Hallelujah, Baby!,* 1967, *Applause,* 1970, *Lorelei, or Gentlemen Still Prefer Blondes,* 1974, *By Bernstein,* 1975, *On the Twentieth Century,* 1978, *A Doll's Life,* 1981, and *Will Rogers Follies,* 1991); 1947—first film as writers, *Good News;* 1953—first Academy Award nomination for Best Original Screenplay, for *The Band Wagon;* 1955—second Academy Award

Betty Comden and Adolph Green

nomination for Best Original Screenplay, for *It's Always Fair Weather.* **Awards:** Six Tony Awards, for *Wonderful Town,* 1953, *Hallelujah, Baby,* 1967, *Applause,* 1970, *On the Twentieth Century* (two), 1978, *Will Rogers Follies,* 1991; Writers Guild Awards, for *On the Town,* 1949, *Singin' in the Rain,* 1952, and *Bells Are Ringing,* 1960. **Agent:** ICM Agency, 40 West 57th Street, New York, NY 10019, U.S.A.

Films as Co-Writer and Co-Lyricist with Adolph Green

1947   *Good News* (Walters)
1948   *Take Me Out to the Ball Game (Everybody's Cheering)* (Berkeley) (lyricists only); *The Barkleys of Broadway* (Walters) (sc only)
1949   *On the Town* (Donen and Kelly)
1952   *Singin' in the Rain* (Donen and Kelly) (one song, "Moses Supposes")
1953   *The Band Wagon* (Minnelli) (sc only)
1955   *It's Always Fair Weather* (Donen and Kelly)
1958   *Auntie Mame* (da Costa) (sc only)
1960   *Bells Are Ringing* (Minnelli)
1964   *What a Way to Go!* (J. L. Thompson)

Films as Actress

1944   *Greenwich Village* (W. Lang)
1984   *Garbo Talks* (Lumet)
1989   *Slaves of New York* (Ivory) (as Mrs. Wheeler)

Publications by Comden

Books

With Adolph Green, *Singin' in the Rain* (script), New York, 1972.
With Adolph Green, *Comden and Green on Broadway,* New York, 1981.
With Adolph Green, *On the Twentieth Century* (play), New York, 1981.
Off Stage, (autobiography), New York, 1995.

Articles

With Adolph Green, *Cahiers du Cinéma* (Paris), January 1966, translated in *Cahiers du Cinéma in English,* no. 2, 1966.
With Adolph Green, *Positif* (Paris), no. 343, September 1989.

Publications on Comden

Books

Robinson, Alice M., *Betty Comden and Adolph Green: A Bio-Bibliography,* Westport, Connecticut, 1994.
The New York Musicals of Comden and Green, New York, 1996.

Articles

Film Comment (New York), Winter 1970-71.
Roddick, Nick, in *American Screenwriters,* 2nd series, edited by Randall Clark, Detroit, 1986.

* * *

With her longtime creative partner, Adolph Green, Betty Comden has co-written the scenarios and lyrics for two of the most beloved and entertaining of the classic MGM musicals, *Singin' in the Rain* and *The Band Wagon.* And her other credits are anything but chopped liver! Nevertheless, even with a string of musical film credits that reads like a Hollywood honor role, Comden has not transcended her identity as the other half of Adolph Green's enormous talent. (One cannot even call her Green's better half, since that role has been held by Phyllis Newman for close to 40 years.) Moviegoers have a sense that they know Adolph Green because they have seen him appear on-screen in various frenetic, sometimes self-parodying roles in *My Favorite Year* and *Lily in Love;* Green is so effusive that he practically jumps off the screen and into the viewer's lap. On the other hand, rare Comden screen performances have not been telling or expressive. In some ways, Comden is like Greta Garbo—whom she plays in the final scene of *Garbo Talks*—in that her film-going admirers have not had the opportunity to get to know her very well.

Hidden or perhaps guarded as she remains, the key to Comden actually is apparent to all who have seen the films she and Green wrote. Look closely at the original screen musicals *The Barkleys of Broadway, Singin' in the Rain,* and *The Band Wagon,* and you will recognize Comden in the vivacious, puckish, and well-developed female characters.

In *Barkleys* she is Dinah Barkley, an attractive, charming, and independent woman who is very close to what the French refer to as *d'un certain âge.* Dinah has lots of talent and a quick temper, which flares frequently as she vents frustration in being one half of a well-established creative partnership (even if the other half *is* Fred Astaire), rather than as a star in her own right with her name solely filling a marquee. A good deal of the scenario features Dinah complaining and plotting and finally striking out on her own as a serious dramatic actress—a metaphor, perhaps, for a fantasy of Comden's breaking loose from her Siamese coupling with Green in order to prove that her talents stand firm on their own.

As Kathy Selden in *Singin' in the Rain,* we may be seeing the early Comden, with a youthful positivism and collaborative spirit, trying to break into show business—as she did as one quarter of the cabaret act The Revuers. When Kathy has to sacrifice her own chance to be a movie star in order to save the motion picture, that is Comden as a happy team player, in love with show business and her fellow artists and primarily concerned with the success of the project. Whether it is the unique spirit of Debbie Reynolds in the role or the quality of the character as developed on the written page, Kathy has a freshness, vigor, drive, and camaraderie that are unusual to female characters of the post-World War II silver screen.

In *The Band Wagon,* Comden's alter-ego is Lily Marton, who with her husband Lester is writing a Broadway musical for a Hollywood star-pal. The Martons are as consolidated as Tweedledee and Tweedledum: a spunky, wisecracking couple who ache with separation pangs any time they do not share the frame. Lester is the homely, eccentric image of Green, and Lily is the pretty, sweet-natured, nurturing partner. This is the public image of Comden and Green—and, if you will, it is their legend. The showbiz-savvy, bubbly creations of Lily and Lester Marton, as concocted by Comden and Green, make for self-reflexive cinema that is uncommon in MGM musicals. This is the Comden imagined by most movie enthusiasts. She is a willing partner and good sport who complements the more famous, more capricious personality of Adolph Green.

Even with the publication of her memoir *Off Stage* in 1995, Betty Comden probably always will be remembered as one half of the successful creative team of Comden and Green. Perhaps this is destined by Comden. For after all, under her creative will, even tempestuous Dinah Barkley goes back to being one of the two *Barkleys of Broadway.*

—Audrey E. Kupferberg

COOLIDGE, Martha

American director

Born: New Haven, Connecticut, 1946. **Education**: Studied animation at Rhode Island School of Design; attended New York University to study filmmaking; took film classes at the School of Visual Arts, and Columbia Graduate School. **Career:** 1968—directed children's program for Canadian TV; 1972-75—made a series of radical feminist documentaries that were screened at film festivals; 1975—made the much-admired feminist feature, *Not a Pretty Picture*; 1978—hired by Francis Ford Coppola's Zoetrope Studio to develop the never-produced film *Photoplay*; 1982—directed first fiction feature *City Girl* (released in 1984); 1983—directed first commercially successful film, *Valley Girl*; 1991—directed the critically acclaimed independent feature, *Rambling Rose*. **Agent:** Ken Stovitz, Creative Artists Agency, 9830 Wilshire Boulevard, Beverly Hills, CA 90212, U.S.A.

Films as Director

1972	*David: Off and On* (+ pr, sc, ed)
1973	*More Than a School* (+ sc, ed)
1974	*Old-Fashioned Woman* (+ pr, sc, ed)
1975	*Not a Pretty Picture* (+ pr, sc, co-ed)
1978	*Bimbo* (+ pr, ed)
1979	*The Troubleshooters*
1980	*Strawberries and Gold* (for TV)
1983	*Valley Girl*
1984	*City Girl* (produced in 1982) (+ pr); *Joy of Sex*
1985	*Real Genius*
1986	*Hammered: The Best of Sledge* (for TV)
1988	*Plain Clothes*; *Roughhouse*
1989	*Trenchcoat in Paradise* (for TV)
1990	*The Friendly*; *Rope Dancing*
1991	*Bare Essentials* (for TV); **Rambling Rose**
1992	*Crazy in Love* (for TV)
1993	*Lost in Yonkers*
1994	*Angie*
1995	*Three Wishes*
1997	*Out to Sea*

Other Films

1971	*Passing Quietly Through* (pr, ed)
1990	*That's Adequate* (H. Hurwitz) (ro)
1994	*Beverly Hills Cop III* (Landis) (ro as security woman)

Publications by Coolidge

Articles

Interview with C. Chase, in *New York Times,* 6 May 1983.
Interview with Michael Singer, in *Film Directors: A Complete Guide*, edited by Michael Singer, Beverly Hills, 1984.
"Dialogue on Film—Martha Coolidge," in *American Film* (Washington, D.C.), June 1984.
Interview with Claire-France Perez, in *L.A. Woman* (Los Angeles), August 1985.
"Close Up," interview with Debby Birns, in *American Premiere* (Beverly Hills), September 1985.
"Dialogue on Film—Martha Coolidge," in *American Film* (Hollywood), December 1988.
"Film: Off Screen: Martha Coolidge Gets an 'A,'" interview with R. Shafransky, in *Village Voice* (New York), 13 August 1995.

Publications on Coolidge

Books

Quart, Barbara Koenig, *Women Directors: The Emergence of a New Cinema,* New York, 1988.
Acker, Ally, *Reel Women: Pioneers of the Cinema, 1896 to the Present,* New York, 1991.
Cole, Janis, and Holly Dale, *Calling the Shots: Profiles of Women Filmmakers,* Kingston, Ontario, 1993.
Foster, Gwendolyn Audrey, *Women Film Directors: An International Bio-Critical Dictionary,* Westport, Connecticut, 1995.

Articles

Schwann, S., "Close-ups: Martha Coolidge," in *Millimeter* (New York), September 1983.
Roddick, N., "Martha's Bag Full of Roles," in *Stills* (London) June/July 1984.
Attanasio, Paul, "The Road to Hollywood—Director Martha Coolidge's Long Trek to *Real Genius,*" in *Washington Post,* 1 August 1985.
Klapper, Zina, "Movie Directors: Four Women Who Get to Call the Shots in Hollywood," in *Ms.* (New York), November 1985.
Cook, P., "Not a Political Picture—Martha Coolidge," in *Monthly Film Bulletin* (London), December 1986.
Citron, Michelle, "Women's Film Production: Going Mainstream," in *Female Spectators: Looking at Film and Television,* edited by E. Deidre Pribram, London, 1988.
Bernstein, Sharon, "Women and Hollywood—It's Still a Lousy Relationship. But Is there Hope for the Future?," in *Los Angeles Times,* 11 November 1990.
Byars, Jackie, "Feminism, Psychoanalysis, and Female Oriented Melodrama of the 1950s," in *Multiple Voices in Feminist Film Criticism,* edited by Diane Carson, Linda Dittmar, and Janice Welsch, Minneapolis, 1994.
Chira, Susan, "Unwed Mothers: *The Scarlet Letter* Returns in Pink," in *New York Times,* 23 January 1994.
Sigesmund, B. J., "Feature Filmmaker," in *Independent Film and Video Monthly* (New York), June 1994.

*   *   *

Martha Coolidge

Martha Coolidge has proved to be one of Hollywood's most successful commercial directors, male or female. Early in her career, however, she garnered critical success as an independent documentary filmmaker. While still a film student at New York University, an instructor hired her to direct an hour-long documentary about a Long Island "free school," which was eventually screened on public television. Thereafter, she made several documentaries that were shown on the film festival circuit, one of which, *Not a Pretty Picture,* was widely respected. A semiautobiographical feature about a woman filmmaker directing a re-creation of a rape attack, *Not a Pretty Picture* now occupies an honored place in the feminist film canon. During this period, Coolidge was a vociferous champion of independent film and she wrote numerous articles about the obstacles to finding financial support and distribution deals.

Impressed by *Not a Pretty Picture,* Francis Ford Coppola invited Coolidge to develop a rock 'n' roll love story entitled *Photoplay* for his Zoetrope Studio. But, after working on it for two-and-a-half years, the financially strapped studio abandoned the project. Frustrated, Coolidge returned to Canada where she soon found work directing a television miniseries for the Canadian Broadcasting Corporation. While there, she was finally invited to direct her first fiction feature film, *City Girl,* a film she is proud to call a "woman's film." But, before *City Girl* found a distributor in 1984, Coolidge directed her breakthrough hit, the low-budget teenpic, *Valley Girl.*

Subsequently, Coolidge was offered numerous teen sex movies to direct. She finally agreed to make *Joy of Sex* (1984) for Paramount, a typical but unsuccessful teen comedy. To its predictably thin plot, she managed to provide some feminist perspective about the subjects of contraception, menstruation, and pregnancy. But, at the time, she implied in interviews that she really wanted to make other kinds of films. She ultimately left the project during postproduction and then tried to distance herself from the final product.

Next she directed a big-budget feature, the teen science-fiction comedy, *Real Genius.* With a nearly all-male cast, Coolidge's goal was to depict the young men as more vulnerable than she thought a male director would have, and to present the challenges of scientific conquest as fun, and more importantly, as respectable. *Real Genius* also marked the entry of females into the cherished multimillion dollar special effects' turf of male directors. Following *Real Genius,* however, she worked steadily in television and continued to pursue feature-film projects that would provide greater opportunities for artistic expression.

In 1991 she scored a critical hit with *Rambling Rose,* a coming-of-age story adapted by Calder Willingham from his novel. Upon discovering the script in a "dead script" file after it had been rejected by a series of Hollywood producers, Coolidge struggled for five years to get it made. It was Renny Harlin, known for directing action films, who finally agreed to produce the independent feature. With an impressive cast and quiet, thoughtful performances, the film treats the subject of feminine sexuality in the sexually constrained 1930s. It tells the story of Rose, a guilelessly promiscuous young woman hired to work as a housemaid for a Southern family who wants to prevent her from becoming a prostitute. Coolidge masterfully portrays Rose as a girl-woman who longs for affection, but confuses it with sex. *Rambling Rose* remains Coolidge's masterpiece, and it proved to be her ticket off the teenpic track.

The big-budget film *Angie,* a vehicle for the big-budget movie-star Geena Davis, restored Coolidge's reputation as a major studio director. It tells the story of a single, working-class Brooklynite who becomes unexpectedly pregnant. Coolidge's feminist touch permeates the movie, importantly, in her depiction of Angie as an engaging but, refreshingly, not always sympathetic heroine. The director also cleverly reworks the conventions of the melodrama by respecting rather than condemning Angie's pregnancy, by playing with the notion of the single girl who gets "in trouble," by implicating the fathers who fail to stick around, and by celebrating the community of women. Indeed, the film's most important relationship is between Angie and her best girlfriend.

Coolidge's 1997 feature film, *Out to Sea,* reunited Jack Lemmon and Walter Matthau in a shipboard sex farce that critics have praised as funny and smart about love and mortality. In addition to proving once again that Coolidge is a bankable, big-budget director, it is noteworthy for depicting one of Hollywood's most enduring taboos—against portraying older women as sexually desiring or desirable. Now a firmly established director, Coolidge's champions often note that she continues to bring fresh perspectives to her often predictable scripts; likewise, her body of work demonstrates a special talent for enabling inspired performances and for working with ensemble casts. Thus, as she explained in the early 1990s, her biggest lesson as a director was learning that she could express herself creatively, even under the most constrained filmmaking conditions.

—Cynthia Felando

LA COQUILLE ET LE CLERGYMAN

(The Seashell and the Clergyman)
France, 1928
Director: Germaine Dulac

Production: Delia Film (Dulac's company) may have produced it, but there is no concrete evidence to that fact; black and white, 35mm, silent; running time: 42 minutes, some sources list 38 minutes. Released 9 February 1928. Filmed at Studio de Ursulines in Paris.

Scenario: Antonin Artaud, revised by Germaine Dulac; **photography:** Paul Guichard; **editor:** Paul Parguel; **assistant editor:** Louis Ronjat.

Cast: Alex Allin (*Priest*); Bataille (*Officer*); Gerica Athanasiou (*Woman*).

Publications

Script

Artaud, Antonin, *La Coquille et le clergyman,* in *Nouvelle Revue Française* (Paris), November 1927.

Books

Curtis, David, *Experimental Cinema,* London, 1971.
Matthews, J. H., *Surrealism and Film,* Ann Arbor, Michigan, 1971.
Lawder, Standish D., *The Cubist Cinema,* New York, 1975.
Le Grice, Malcolm, *Abstract Film and Beyond,* Cambridge, Massachusetts, 1977.
Heck-Rabi, Louise, *Women Filmmakers: A Critical Reception,* Metuchen, New Jersey, 1984.

Articles

Dulac, Germaine, "Sur le cinéma visuel," in *Le Rouge et le noir* (Paris), July 1928.
Dulac, Germaine, "Jouer avec les bruits," in *Cinéma—Ciné pour tous* (Paris), 15 August 1929.
Ford, Charles, "Germaine Dulac," in *Anthologie du Cinéma 31* (Paris), January 1968.
Cornwell, Regina, "Maya Deren and Germaine Dulac: Activists of the Avant-Garde," in *Film Library Quarterly* (New York), Winter 1971-72.
Van Wert, W., "Germaine Dulac: First Feminist Filmmaker," in *Women and Film* (Santa Monica, California), vol. 1, nos. 5-6, 1974.
Dozoretz, Wendy, "Dulac vs. Artaud," in *Wide Angle* (Athens, Ohio), no. 1, 1979.
Travelling (Lausanne), Summer 1979.
Greene, N., "Artaud and Film: A Reconsideration," in *Cinema Journal* (Champaign, Illinois), Summer 1984.
Flitterman, Sandy, "Theorizing the Feminine: Women as the Figure of Desire in *The Seashell and the Clergyman,*" in *Wide Angle* (Athens, Ohio), vol. 6, no. 3, 1984.
Kolisnyk, M. H., "Surrealism, Surreptition: Artaud's Doubles," in *October* (Cambridge, Massachusetts), Spring 1993.

* * *

The Seashell and the Clergyman may now be regarded as the first surrealist film, released a year before Buñuel and Dali's *Un Chien andalou,* which contains the image of an eye sliced by a razor. In *The Seashell,* Germaine Dulac used trick photography to create the effect of an officer's head being split in half. The films share other surrealist devices as well.

Antonin Artaud wrote the scenario, and wanted to act the role of the priest, though he did not initially want to direct the film. He subsequently seems to have changed his mind, writing to Dulac of his annoyance that the shooting and editing of *The Seashell* were done without him. Dulac had revised his scenario, casting Alex Allin in the priest's role. The film represents the subconscious sexual cravings of the priest, and is set in dreamlike environments. In one notorious scene the priest is shown masturbating. In another, the priest encounters the frightening ghost of a woman in a ballroom. He runs away, pulling up the skirts of his cassock, which lengthens and stretches away like a tail behind him. The clergyman and the woman run through darkness, their progress marked by visions of the woman in varying forms, once with her tongue sticking out, another time with her cheek ballooning outward.

It is believed that Artaud was particularly infuriated by a scene in which the priest, wearing a frock coat, is in a wine cellar. He empties an array of glasses of red wine, then shatters all of them. With no transition, he is next seen crawling on his hands and knees in a Paris street.

Artaud criticized Dulac for softening the lean strength of his script. When Dulac premiered *The Seashell* as "a dream of Antonin Artaud," he denounced the film. According to Wendy Dozoretz, in her article in *Wide Angle,* it was André Breton who yelled out, as the film's credits appeared on the screen, "Mme. Dulac is a cow." Led by Artaud, critic Georges Sadoul, novelist Louis Aragon, and others stopped the film projector, threw objects at the screen and walked out in protest, leaving a bewildered audience behind. In Dozoretz's words, *The Seashell* was "the unique product of two incongruous minds."

Certain contemporary critics contend that Artaud's scenario was superior to Dulac's interpretation. David Curtis in *Experimental Cinema* faults Dulac's pictorial conceptions as oversimplified, and her editing as too well measured, subtracting from Artaud's visions. J. H. Matthews in *Surrealism and Film* affirms that Dulac did not comprehend Artaud's artistic intentions, and did distort his script: "She did not succeed altogether in emptying Artaud's scenario of surrealist content. For this reason alone, her *Seashell* deserves mention among the first Surrealist films."

Dozoretz admits that the feminist Dulac's direction of the film could have resulted in misinterpretation of Artaud's misogynistic scenario. Nevertheless, the optical tricks that Dulac used were those specified. As for Artaud's charge that Dulac "feminized" his script, Dozoretz agrees that Dulac probably did weaken the brutality of Artaud's vision.

The fact that *The Seashell* is currently well known and often shown is owed to Henri Langlois, former head of the Cinémathèque française, who rediscovered it after decades of oblivion. *The Seashell* has aged gracefully, its potency intact, secure in its deserved niche as a classic of surrealist cinema.

—Louise Heck-Rabi

CRAIGIE, Jill
British director and writer

Born: 7 March 1914. **Education:** Attended various boarding schools. **Family:** Married 1) the screenwriter, director, and novelist Jeffrey Dell; 3) member of Parliament Michael Foot, 1949. **Career:** 1932— journalist on teenage magazine, then for London branch of Hearst Newspapers; 1940-42—scriptwriter on documentaries for the British Council; 1944—signed up by producer Filippo del Giudice for Two Cities Film, directed first film, *Out of Chaos*; 1948—formed production company, Outlook; 1949—directed first feature film, *Blue Scar*; after 1951—gave up directing, but continued to write journalism, scripts for the BBC, and occasional film scripts. **Addresses:** c/o Michael Foot, The Labour Party, 150 Walworth Road, London SE17, England; and 308 Gray's Inn Road, London WC1X 8DY, England.

Films as Director

1944 *Out of Chaos* (doc, short) (+ sc)
1946 *The Way We Live* (doc) (+ sc, pr)
1948 *Children of the Ruins* (doc, short)
1949 *Blue Scar* (+ sc)
1951 *To Be a Woman* (doc, short) (+ sc, pr)
1994 *Two Hours from London* (doc for TV, produced 1992) (+ sc)

Other Films

1937 *Make-Up* (Zeisler) (ro as Tania)
1943 *The Flemish Farm* (Dell) (co-sc)
1953 *The Million Pound Note* (*Man with a Million*) (Neame) (sc)
1957 *Windom's Way* (Neame) (sc)

Publications by Craigie

Articles

"I Don't Believe Every Porter Needs a Halo," in *Sunday Express* (London), 20 February 1955.
"Underground Artist," in *Sunday Times Magazine* (London), 9 November 1986.

Publications on Craigie

Book

Foster, Gwendolyn Audrey, *Women Film Directors: An International Bio-Critical Dictionary,* Westport, Connecticut, 1995.

Articles

Medhurst, Andy, "*Blue Scar/Valley of Song,*" in *Raymond Williams: Film TV Culture,* edited by David Lusted, London, 1989.
Merz, Caroline, in *The Women's Companion to International Film,* edited by Annette Kuhn and Susannah Radstone, London, 1990.
Aitken, Ian, "Stop the Serbian Juggernaut," in *New Statesman and Society,* 16 December 1994.
Lennon, Peter, "Labour of Love," in *Guardian* (London), 17 July 1997.

* * *

Jill Craigie was not, as is sometimes claimed, the first British woman film director. That distinction should probably go to Dinah Shurey, director of patriotic features in the 1920s, followed by Mary Field, who made documentaries, children's films, and the occasional short feature in the 1930s. But Craigie was the first British woman to direct features that gained widespread distribution and publicity: *The Way We Live* is said to have had as many column inches devoted to it at the time of its release as Olivier's near-contemporary *Henry V.* And she was certainly the first British director—of either sex—to bring a consistently feminist and socialist viewpoint to her work.

Having worked as a journalist and—briefly—as an actress, Craigie spent the war years writing scripts for British Council documentaries. This, and the experience of working with her then-husband, the novelist and director Jeffrey Dell, on the script of *The Flemish Farm,* convinced her that she too could direct. "I developed a great urge to make a documentary for myself," she later recalled. "I did decide quite deliberately, why shouldn't a woman make a film? It was a male-dominated industry from top to bottom." She cut her teeth on a short subject not far different from those she had been scripting for the British Council. *Out of Chaos,* featuring interviews with such artists as Henry Moore and Graham Sutherland, was a pioneering attempt to use cinema to introduce people to modern art.

With the British documentary movement at its wartime-boosted height, Craigie ambitiously embarked on a feature-length documen-

Jill Craigie

tary intended for general distribution. She got backing from the open-minded impresario Filippo del Giudice, whose company Two Cities Films had released *Out of Chaos*, through the Rank Organisation. *The Way We Live* was something quite new: it set out to show how planning, that panacea of the postwar Labour government, affected the lives of "ordinary people"—and how they, in their turn, could influence the planning process. She chose to focus on the port city of Plymouth, shattered by wartime bombing, where enlightened town planners were proposing a radically redesigned housing system.

Focusing chiefly on one bombed-out family and working with an almost entirely amateur cast, Craigie set out "to show that Town Planning must be integrated with everyday life...I went to people and asked them what they really wanted...not what I wanted. The whole content of the film came from the people, from the architects, from the Town Councillors, and I was just the interpreter." The film climaxes in a procession of several thousand people to the Town Hall to demand that the new plan be put into effect, carrying banners with slogans derived from the vox populi comments Craigie had gleaned. The film exhilarates with its mood of buoyant postwar optimism, the sense that given the energy and will, anything is possible. But more, it was an exceptional—and in Britain, virtually unheard-of—ex-

ample of filmmaking as activism, the creative and political processes intertwining and advancing each other in a way that even the Soviet filmmakers of the 1920s had only rarely achieved.

After directing a documentary short, *Children of the Ruins,* on UNESCO's work to rehabilitate war-traumatized children, Craigie formed her own production company, Outlook, with the producer William McQuitty, to make a fiction feature, *Blue Scar.* A drama set—and largely filmed—in the mining valleys of South Wales, it mixed professional actors with local amateurs to tell the story of a young woman, a miner's daughter, enticed away from the valleys and her colliery sweetheart by the lure of a shallow social life in London. With the British film industry in crisis and Del Giudice ousted by hostile forces, financing proved elusive. Craigie and McQuitty raised the whole budget themselves with the help of friends, and converting a disused Welsh cinema into a studio, made the film with no distribution guarantee.

The film is uneven, often awkward—Craigie herself now dismisses it as "amateurish"—and betrays her inexperience in handling fictional drama. But, as Andy Medhurst observes, "what is so startling, and fascinating, about *Blue Scar*...is that it is a British feature film that is consciously political, avowedly socialist." It was certainly the politics, not the awkwardness, that led the major circuits to deny *Blue Scar* a booking, and the film was only shown after a skillful press campaign had roused public opinion in its favor.

But Craigie was increasingly disheartened by the dual struggle of being a female and independent director in an industry where the opinions were narrowing. After making a last documentary short for Outlook, *To Be a Woman,* a heartfelt plea for equal pay for women, she moved into screenwriting, scripting two comedies for Rank. In 1958 she suggested to Michael Balcon, head of Ealing, that she should make films for him featuring fully realized female characters—a rarity, she argued, in British films. Ealing, though, was nearing its last gasp, and nothing came of the idea. Craigie's filmmaking career seemed to be over.

Nevertheless, she unexpectedly returned to directing in 1992 with *Two Hours from London,* a documentary made for televi-sion. With her husband, the MP and former Labour leader Michael Foot, as on-screen presenter, it was a scathing and unashamedly partisan indictment of the passivity of the Western powers in the face of Serbian aggression in former Yugoslavia. The film had to wait 18 months before being transmitted by the BBC, and then only in a truncated form, but it proved that in her long absence from filmmaking Craigie had lost none of the deep-felt political and humanist passions. Too bad that her most cherished project, a fictionalized drama about the suffragette movement, never came to fruition; few directors could have been more ideally suited to the subject.

—Philip Kemp

DANCE, GIRL, DANCE
USA, 1940
Director: Dorothy Arzner

Production: RKO-Radio Pictures; black and white; running time: 90 minutes. Released September 1940.

Producers: Erich Pommer and Harry Edington; **screenplay:** Tess Slesinger and Frank Davis, from the novel by Vicki Baum; **assistant director:** James II. Anderson; **photography:** Russell Metty; **editor:** Robert Wise; **sound:** Hugh McDowell Jr.; **art director:** Van Nest Polglase; **associate art director:** Al Herman; **gowns:** Edward Stevenson; **music director:** Edward Ward; **dances:** Ernst Matray.

Cast: Maureen O'Hara (*Judy*); Louis Hayward (*Jimmy Harris*); Lucille Ball (*Bubbles*); Ralph Bellamy (*Steve Adams*); Virginia Field (*Elinor Harris*); Maria Ouspenskaya (*Madame Basilova*); Mary Carlisle (*Sally*), Katherine Alexander (*Miss Olmstead*); Edward Brophie (*Dwarfie*); Walter Abel (*Judge*); Harold Huber (*Hoboken Gent*); Ernest Truex (*Bailey 1*); Chester Clute (*Bailey 2*); Vivian Fay (*Ballerina*); Lorraine Krueger (*Dolly*); Lola Jensen (*Daisy*); Emma Dunn (*Mrs. Simpson*); Sidney Blackmer (*Puss in Boots*); Ludwig Stossel (*Caesar*), Erno Verebes (*Fitch*).

Publications

Books

Johnston, Claire, *Notes on Women's Cinema*, London 1973.
Rosen, Marjorie, *Popcorn Venus: Women, Movies and the American Dream*, New York, 1973.
Haskell, Molly, *From Reverence to Rape: The Treatment of Women in the Movies*, New York, 1974.
Johnston, Claire, editor, *The Work of Dorothy Arzner: Towards a Feminist Cinema*, London, 1975.
Smith, Sharon, *Women Who Make Movies*, New York, 1975.
Kay, Karyn, and Gerald Peary, editors, *Women and the Cinema: A Critical Anthology*, New York, 1977.
Slide, Anthony, *Early Women Directors*, South Brunswick, New Jersey, 1977; rev. ed. as *The Silent Feminists: America's First Women Directors*, Lanham, Maryland, 1996.
Heck-Rabi, Louise, *Women Filmmakers: A Critical Reception*, Metuchen, New Jersey, 1984.
Penley, Constance, editor, *Feminism and Film Theory*, London, 1988.

Articles

Crowther, Bosley, in *New York Times*, 11 September 1940.
Kine Weekly (London), 12 September 1940.
Monthly Film Bulletin (London), vol. 7, no. 81, 1940.
Feldman, J., and H. Feldman, "Women Directors," in *Films in Review* (New York), November 1950.
Pyros, J., "Notes on Women Directors," in *Take One* (Montreal), November/December 1970.
Henshaw, Richard, "Women Directors," in *Film Comment* (New York), November 1972.
Parker, F., "Approaching the Art of Arzner," in *Action* (Los Angeles), July/August 1973.
Velvet Light Trap (Madison, Wisconsin), Fall 1973.
Castle, W., "Tribute to Dorothy Arzner," in *Action* (Los Angeles), March/April 1975.
Kaplan, E. Ann, "Aspects of British Feminist Film Theory," in *Jump Cut* (Berkeley), nos. 12-13, 1976.
Glaessner, Verina, in *Focus on Film* (London), Summer/Autumn 1976.
Laemmle, Ann, in *Cinema Texas Program Notes*, 28 February 1978.
Bergstrom, J., "Re-reading the Work of Claire Johnston," in *Camera Obscura* (Berkeley), Summer 1979.
Forster, A., in *Skrien* (Amsterdam), September/October 1984.
Chell, S. L., "Dorothy Arzner's *Dance, Girl, Dance*," in *CineAction!* (Toronto), Summer/Fall 1991.

* * *

Dance, Girl, Dance is one of the few films directed by a woman in what is known as the "classical Hollywood" era, when, it has been argued, the conventional narrative codes of cinema were fixed. This unique position has inevitably informed the ways in which the film has been studied. Although Dorothy Arzner herself was not a feminist, it is due to feminism that she has been reassessed. In the mid-1970s feminist critics argued that while *Dance, Girl, Dance* may appear to be just one example of the popular musical comedies and women's pictures produced by RKO in the 1930s and 1940s, Arzner's ironic point of view questions the very conventions she uses.

The film was made in the relative flexibility of RKO's production system, whereby independent directors were contracted to work under minimal supervision. It was in this context that Arzner was reputedly able to rework a confusing and scrappy script to focus on the ambivalent relationship between the two strong, but very different, main female characters—Judy, an aspiring ballerina, and Bubbles, a gold-digging showgirl. Bubbles, after finding work in burlesque, brings Judy's "classy act" into her show, where Judy is humiliated as her stooge. One night, Bubbles announces that she has married Jimmy Harris, a weak heavy-drinking millionaire divorcé with whom Judy has fallen in love. Consequently, in a scene that has been much discussed, Judy, overwhelmed with frustration, furiously confronts her heckling audience. The standing ovation she receives infuriates Bubbles, and they fall into a vicious fight. Judy, unrepentant, is sent to jail, but the next day, Steve Adams, a ballet director who has been pursuing her, pays her bail and summons her

Dance, Girl, Dance

to his office. He intends to train her to be a professional ballerina and, it is implied, his wife.

Arzner's portrayal of the complex relationship between the two women is one of the ways in which the apparent opposition set up between art (offering "self-expression") and entertainment (imposing exploitation) is undermined. The ways in which each woman's dance numbers are presented subvert the stereotypes of a sexual Bubbles and an artistic Judy. For example, when Judy dances at the nightclub, Fitch, Steve's associate, comments in surprise at her impressive (i.e., artistic) footwork. Steve, however, leers that "her eyes aren't bad either." Arzner pinpoints with terrible clarity the tension between a woman's struggle for integrity and a male gaze that by its very nature undermines that struggle. Where, then, does this leave Bubbles? When she dances at the burlesque, the ironies of her performances are a real delight for the cinema audience. When she calls and points to her audience she is challenging them, from within the licensed confines of burlesque conventions, in a way that parallels Judy's later outburst. Both women challenge, from the stage, the men who watch them, and thereby resist their passive status. So while we are invited to gaze upon Bubbles as a non-artistic spectacle, she is also knowing, controlling, with a voice of her own. It is the sheer

power of this "voice," Bubbles's potent screen presence, that subverts her implied position as less worthy than Judy.

Much of the critical attention paid to Judy's furious speech has suggested that the artistic and moral criticism of the lecherous gaze of the burlesque audience also functions as a not-so-veiled attack on the cinema audience. The film has much invested, however, in drawing in its audience to enjoy the display of women's bodies, and this impulse arguably triumphs over the conflicting impulse to alienate the audience, or to chastise it for its voyeurism. Judy's gesture is thus defused by being applauded, and leading into the titillating catfight. But the irony is that she has found a voice and can defiantly assert, "I'm not ashamed," not within the structures of the ballet, but in those of the burlesque.

As in Arzner's earlier work, and within the conventions of the women's film, it is the scenes featuring women that are the most striking and subtle, and in contrast, the heterosexual romance appears hollow. Although a weak love-story element runs through the film, the women's desires are channeled less towards coupledom than independence. After a date with Jimmy, Judy wishes on a star that she might become a dancer too. She wants it all, romance *and* artistic integrity, and the latter is never submerged in the former. Bubbles, on the other hand, desires economic rather than artistic independence. Both her dancing and her sexual desires are grounded in a cynicism about heterosexual relationships that affords her one of the film's finest throwaway lines, describing the burlesque owner as "a great big capitalist in the artificial limbs business."

Nevertheless, the position of strong female protagonists in a Hollywood text is a precarious one, and it is in the final scene that this is tragically realized. Steve, in a humiliating tirade, asserts that Judy has been a silly, stubborn "girl." The incongruously huge hat that she wears in this scene hides her face until, as Steve embraces her and tells her to "go ahead and laugh," it is revealed that she is, in fact, weeping. Arzner's final irony offers the potential for a critique of the traditional boy-gets-girl resolution, and, implicitly, of the classical Hollywood text itself.

—Samantha Cook

DASH, Julie
American director and writer

Born: New York City, 1952. **Education:** Attended City College of New York, studying film production, B.A. 1974; American Film Institute, 1975; University of California, Los Angeles, M.F.A. 1986. **Career:** 1973-91—made a series of short films, including the critically well-received *Illusions*; 1978-80—worked for the Motion Picture Association of America's Classifications and Rating Administration, assigning ratings to films awaiting theatrical distribution in the United States; 1989—started production on her first feature film, *Daughters of the Dust*; 1992—*Daughters of the Dust* finally released; 1990s—directed music videos, including *Lost in the Night* (for Peabo Bryson), 1992, *Give Me One Reason* (for Tracy Chapman), and *More Than One Way Home*, 1996, *Thinking of You* (for Tony, Toni, Tone), 1997; and anthology television; 1996 directed an episode of the HBO series *Subway Stories*. **Awards:** Fulbright Fellowship, 1991; Dorothy Arzner Award, Women in Film, 1992; Best Film, Black Filmmaker's Hall of Fame, for *Daughters of the Dust,* 1992; Maya Deren Award, American Film Institute, 1993; John Simon Guggenheim Memorial Foundation Fellowship. **Address:** Geechee Girls Productions, Inc., 137 North Larchmont Boulevard, Box 244, Los Angeles, CA 90004, U.S.A.

Films as Director

1973   *Working Models of Success* (doc)
1975   *Four Women* (short)
1977   *Diary of an African Nun* (short)
1983   *Illusions* (short)
1988   *Breaking the Silence*
1989   *Preventing Cancer*; *Phillis Wheatley* (doc, short)
1990   *Relatives* (short, for TV)
1992   *Praise House* (short, for TV); *Daughters of the Dust* (+ pr)
1994   *Breaths* (short, for TV)
1997   *Grip Till It Hurts* (for TV)
1998   *Black South: The Life and Lifework of Zora Neale Hurston* (doc)

Publications by Dash

Books

Daughters of the Dust: The Making of an African-American Woman's Film, New York, 1991.
Daughters of the Dust (novel), New York, 1997.

Articles

Interview with Zeinabu irene Davis, in *Black Film Review* (Washington, D.C.), vol. 6, no. 1, 1990.
"*Daughters of the Dust*," interview with Zeinabu irene Davis, in *Wide Angle* (Baltimore, Maryland), vol. 13, no. 3/4, 1991.
"Movies in Their Blood," in *Interview* (New York), May 1993.

Publications on Dash

Books

Kuhn, Annette, and Susannah Radstone, editors, *Women in Film: An International Guide,* London, 1990.
Acker, Ally, *Reel Women: Pioneers of the Cinema, 1896 to the Present,* New York, 1991.
hooks, bell, *Black Looks: Race and Representation,* Boston, 1992.
Cole, Janis, and Holly Dale, *Calling the Shots: Profiles of Women Filmmakers,* Kingston, Ontario, 1993.
Foster, Gwendolyn Audrey, *Women Film Directors: An International Bio-Critical Dictionary,* Westport, Connecticut, 1995.
Foster, Gwendolyn Audrey, *Women Filmmakers of the African and Asian Diaspora,* Carbondale, Illinois, 1997.

Articles

Taylor, Clyde, "The LA Rebellion: New Spirit in American Film," in *Black Film Review* (Washington, D.C.), vol. 2, no. 3, 1986.
Harris, K., "New Images," in *Independent* (New York), December 1986.
Jackson, Lynne, and Karen Jaehne, "Eavesdropping on Female Voices: A Who's Who of Contemporary Women Filmmakers," in *Cineaste* (New York), vol. 16, no. 1/2, 1987-88.
"Biographical Notes," in *Undercut* (London), Spring 1988.
Tate, G., "Mood Indigo: Favorite Daughters: Julie Dash Films Gullah Country," in *Village Voice* (New York), 12 April 1988.
Huang, V., and Bérénice Reynaud, "Julie Dash: *Illusions*," in *Motion Picture* (New York), vol. 3, no. 3/4, 1990.
Reynaud, Bérénice, "Et Pourtant, elles tournent," in *24 Images* (Montreal), January/February 1991.
Tate, Greg, "Of Homegirl Goddesses and Geechee Women," in *Village Voice* (New York), 4 June 1991.
Thomas, D., and C. Saalfield, "Geechee Girl Goes Home: Julie Dash on *Daughters of the Dust*," in *Independent* (New York), July 1991.
Baker, Houston A., "Not without My Daughters," in *Transition: An International Review,* vol. 57, 1992.
Tate, Greg, and Arthur Jafa, "La Venus Negre," in *Artforum* (New York), January 1992.
Rule, S., "Director Defies Odds with First Feature, *Daughters of the Dust*," in *New York Times,* 12 February 1992.
Backstein, Karen, "The Cinematic Jazz of Julie Dash," in *Cineaste* (New York), Fall 1992.

Reid, Mark A., "Rebirth of a Nation: Three Recent Films Resist Southern Stereotypes of D. W. Griffith, Depicting a Technicolor Region of
Black, Brown and Gray," in *Southern Exposure,* Winter 1992.

Alexander, Karen, "*Daughters of the Dust,* and a Black Aesthetic,"
in *Women in Film: A Sight and Sound Reader,* edited by Pam Cook
and Philip Dodd, Philadelphia, 1993.

Jones, Jacquie, "The Black South in Contemporary Film," in *African
American Review,* Spring 1993.

Mellencamp, Patricia, "Haunted History: Tracey Moffatt and Julie
Dash," in *Discourse* (Bloomington, Indiana), Winter 1993-94.

Gibson-Hudson, Gloria, "Aspects of Black Feminist Cultural Ideol-
ogy in Films by Black Women Independent Artists," in *Multiple
Voices in Feminist Film Criticism,* edited by Diane Carson, Linda
Dittmar, and Janice Welsch, Minneapolis, 1994.

Weinraub, Bernard, "A Movie, Then a Book," in *New York Times,* 17
October 1997.

Lee, Felicia R., "Where a Filmmaker's Imagination Took Root," in *New
York Times,* 3 December 1997.

*   *   *

Independent filmmaker Julie Dash was the first African-American
woman to produce a full-length, theatrically released film, 1992's *Daughters of the Dust.* Born and raised in New York City, it was her uncle who
first gave her a camera, after which she studied film production in an
after-school program in Harlem, and in college at the City College of
New York, the American Film Institute, and the University of California,
Los Angeles. Subsequently, she made short films for several years
before she made her first feature, the critically acclaimed *Daughters of
the Dust.* Dash's avowed intentions are to correct the white distortions
that have predominated in Hollywood films, to reflect the realities of
black life and history, and to craft positive black images that will counter
those of the mainstream cinema. She specifically cites the novelists Alice
Walker, Toni Cade Bambara, and Zora Neale Hurston for providing
important inspiration.

Dash's early short films include *Diary of an African Nun,* an
adaptation of an Alice Walker short story, and *Four Women,* an
experimental dance poem based on a Nina Simone song. Her best-
known short film is *Illusions.* Like all of her work, it reveals an acute
sense of racial and sexual oppression and is concerned with the
images and identities of black women. *Illusions* has been the subject
of considerable critical attention and adulation, among feminists in
particular, for its unique examination of the issue of black female
identity in the realm of Hollywood's mythmaking. Set during World
War II, it tells the story of Mignon Dupree, a light-skinned black
woman who "passes" as white and thereby works her way to the
executive suites of a movie studio; and Ester Jester, a black woman
who is hired to dub the voice of a white Hollywood movie star. It is
only when she befriends Ester that Mignon realizes the irony of her
position, in terms of her participation in constructing Hollywood's
illusions and in maintaining the invisibility of black women and their
stories. Ultimately, she decides to stay to fight the system from
within. The film's compelling narrative confirms the means by which
the film industry has perpetuated racism and sexism by depicting
one-dimensional stereotypes that ignore the diversity of African
Americans and women. Accordingly, Dash's work suggests the
power of the medium of film to enlighten audiences about the realities and intersections of black history and women's history. Notably,
after she made *Illusions,* critics championed Dash, along with filmmaker Alile Sharon Larkin, as the forerunners of an emerging African-American cinema.

Dash's first feature film and reigning masterpiece is *Daughters of
the Dust,* a hauntingly poetic work that celebrates African culture,
the oral tradition, and the Gullah people. Focusing on a matriarchal
clan of a Gullah family (or Geechee—from the descendants of the
freed slaves who settled on the islands off the coast of South Carolina and Georgia), it tells the story of a turn-of-the-century gathering
that marks the occasion of some of the Peazant family's departure to
the mainland. Dash shot the film on the Sea Islands, a location of
enormous significance due to its isolation, which has meant the
retention of its West African cultural traditions. *Daughters* employs
a uniquely drawn combination of narrative and nonnarrative elements to illuminate issues of family, migration and exile, sex, race,
and nationality, and does so from personal, political, and historical
perspectives. Visually the film is highly stylized, using painterly
colors, natural lighting, and slowed action, to achieve a poetic sensuality. Dash has explained that she used slow motion, in particular, to
give viewers a sense of memory or déjà vu. Interestingly, she first
conceived of the film in 1975; then, after she made *Illusions* she
undertook extensive research for *Daughters*—collecting stories from
her relatives, and studying at the National Archives in Washington,
D.C., the Library of Congress, the Smithsonian Institution, Harlem's
Schomburg Center for Research in Black Culture, and at the Penn
Center on St. Helena Island. In addition, she struggled for several
years to raise the production money. Consequently, the film is a
remarkable achievement and evidence of her deep commitment to
capturing and celebrating the realistic and subtle details of African-
American cultures, especially the rituals and relationships of women.
Thus, as Dash put it, *Daughters* is "about abandoning your home,
but not your culture."

Dash notes that her films are about women facing pivotal moments in their lives; for example, those who are juggling complex
psyches and those who communicate with fractured sentences and
familiar gestures. That is, the kind of women who surrounded her as
a child. In addition, her work reflects her belief that our identities are
shaped by the intersections of histories and personal influences.
Accordingly, Dash proudly acknowledges the importance to her
work of the "old souls" who preceded her; in particular, she cites the
influence of largely forgotten filmmakers such as Oscar Micheaux
and Spencer Williams Jr. For example, the baptism scene in *Daughters of the Dust* was inspired by a scene in Williams's *The Blood of
Jesus.* Likewise, the enchanting tree scene in which Trula's legs
hang into the frame was inspired by a similar scene in Bill Gunn's
Ganja and Hess.

In recent years, Dash has directed a number of music videos,
including "Give Me One Reason" for Tracy Chapman, and "Lost in
the Night" for Peabo Bryson. She is currently writing for Dutton
Signet books, developing multimedia projects for her company,
Geechee Girls Productions, Inc., and planning a futuristic film (set
in 2050), to be called *Bone, Ash and Rose.*

—Cynthia Felando

DAVIS, Zeinabu irene
American director and producer

Born: Irene Davis in Philadelphia, 13 April 1961. **Education:** Attended Brown University, B.A., 1983; University of California, Los
Angeles, MA in African Studies, 1985, MFA in Motion Picture and

Television Production, 1989. **Family:** Married the screenwriter Marc Arthur Chéry. **Career:** 1987—selected as Most Promising Filmmaker by the National Black Filmmakers Hall of Fame; 1996—awarded tenure at Northwestern University. **Awards:** Best Drama, National Black Programming Consortium, Best of category (Experimental) Black Filmmakers Hall of Fame, for *Cycles,* 1989; Best Narrative, Lawrence Kasdan Award, 30th Ann Arbor Film Festival, Best Experimental Narrative, ETA Creative Arts Foundation (Chicago), for *A Powerful Thang,* 1991; Best Film and Video, Children's Jury, 12th Annual Chicago International Children's Fest, Best Short Feature, 6th New England Children's Film Festival, Best of Category, Chris Award, 34th Columbus International Film Festival, Silver Hugo, Chicago International Film and Video Festival, for *Mother of the River,* 1995. **Address:** Department of Radio-TV-Film, Northwestern University, 1905 Sheridan Road, Evanston, IL 60208, U.S.A.

Films as Director

1982   *Filmstatement* (+ pr, sc)
1983   *Recreating Black Women's Media Image* (doc)
1986   *Sweet Bird of Youth* (doc) (+ pr); *Crocodile Conspiracy*
1987   *Canta for Our Sisters* (+ pr)
1989   *Cycles* (short) (+ pr, cd); *Trumpetistically, Clora Bryant* (doc) (+ pr)
1990   *Kneegrays in Russia* (doc) (+ pr)
1991   *A Period Piece* (+ pr); *A Powerful Thang* (+ pr, sc, cd)
1995   *Mother of the River* (+ pr)
1997   *Compensation* (+ pr)

Publications by Davis

Articles

"Film Clips: Black Film at UCLA" and "Film Review: Too Much Eddie Murphy (*Beverly Hills Cop II*)," in *Black Film Review* (Washington, D.C.), vol. 3, no. 2, 1987.
"The Future of Black Film: The Debate Continues," in *Black Film Review* (Washington, D.C.), vol. 5, no. 4; reprinted as "Voices from *Black Film Review*: David Nicholson, Clyde Taylor, Zeinabu irene Davis," in *Wide Angle* (Baltimore, Maryland), vol. 13, nos. 3-4, 1989.
"Black Independent or Hollywood Iconoclast?—What Is the Right Thing?: A Critical Symposium on Spike Lee's *Do the Right Thing,*" in *Cineaste* (New York), vol. 17, 1990.
"Interview with Independent Filmmaker Julie Dash" and "Media Clips," in *Black Film Review* (Washington, D.C.), vol. 6, no. 1, 1990; reprinted and expanded as "An Interview with Julie Dash," in *Wide Angle* (Baltimore, Maryland), vol. 13, nos. 3-4, 1991.
"Woman with a Mission: Zeinabu irene Davis on Independent Filmmaking," in *VOICES of the African Diaspora* (Ann Arbor, Michigan), Fall 1991; reprinted from *Hot Wire,* vol. 7, no. 1, 1991.
"Daunting Inferno: Review of Fired-Up, a Video Installation by O. Funmilayo Makarah," in *Afterimage* (Rochester, New York), vol. 21, no. 1, 1993.
"Keeping Up with Video Technology," interview with Gloria Gibson-Hudson, in *Black Film Review* (Washington, D.C.), vol. 8, no. 1, 1994.
"Media News: Jackie Shearer, 1946-1993," in *Independent Film and Video Monthly* (New York), March 1994.

"FESPACO 97: Celebrating African and Diasporic Film," in *Black Camera: The Newsletter of the Black Film Center/Archive* (Bloomington, Indiana), Summer 1997.

Publications on Davis

Books

Reid, Mark, *Redefining Black Film,* Berkeley, 1993.
Foster, Gwendolyn Audrey, *Women Film Directors: An International Bio-Critical Dictionary,* Westport, Connecticut, 1995.
Foster, Gwendolyn Audrey, *Women Filmmakers of the African and Asian Diaspora,* Carbondale, Illinois, 1997.

Articles

Ventura, Jan, "Women's Work," in *Los Angeles Weekly,* 7-13 April 1989.
Springer, Christiana, "Waiting & Cleaning & Praying," in *Sojourner: The Women's Forum,* April 1990.
"Zeinabu irene Davis: La Femme doit être partout où est question du destin du monde," in *Amina,* June 1991.
Tate, Greg, "Cinematic Sisterhood," in *Village Voice* (New York), Film Supplement, 4 June 1991.
Lawson, Terry, "Thang Is Sex but Identity Is Film's Key," in *Dayton Daily News,* 29 September 1991.
Thomas, Kevin, "Three Provocative Works by Zeinabu Davis at Film Forum," in *Los Angeles Times,* 4 November 1991.
Filemyr, Ann, "Zeinabu irene Davis: Filmmaker, Teacher with a Powerful Mission," in *Angles* (Milwaukee), Winter 1992.
Welbon, Yvonne, "Calling the Shots: Black Women Filmmakers Take the Helm," in *Independent* (New York), March 1992.
Bambara, Toni Cade, "Reading the Signs, Empowering the Eye: *Daughters of the Dust* and the Black Independent Cinema Movement," in *Black American Cinema,* edited by Manthia Diawara, New York, 1993.
Abbe, Elfrieda, "Love's a Many-Splendored '*Thang*'," in *Milwaukee Sentinel,* 5 February 1993.
Ukadike, N. Frank, "Reclaiming Images of Women in Films from Africa and the Black Diaspora," in *Frontiers: A Journal of Women Studies,* vol. 1, 1994.
Mims, Sergio, "Critics Corner: *Mother of the River,*" in *Black Camera: The Newsletter of the Black Film Center/Archive* (Bloomington, Indiana), Winter 1995.
Shen, Ted, "Reel Life: New Lessons from African Folklore," in *Reader: Chicago's Free Weekly,* 5 July 1995.
Kurson, Bob, "Action! Chicago's Independent Filmmakers Make the Scene," in *Chicago Sun-Times,* 16 February 1997.

* * *

Equally talented in the mediums of film and video, Zeinabu irene Davis is an internationally renowned African-American producer and director who, rather than following conventional film form and narrative styles, works to create what she describes as "a visual language that is representative of the African American female experiences." A recipient of grants from such prestigious organizations as the Illinois Arts Council, the Rockefeller Foundation, the Paul Robeson Fund for Independent Media, the National Endowment for the Arts, the American Film Institute, and the National Black Programming Consortium, her work includes documentaries, short narratives, experimental pieces, and music videos. Though diverse in subject and style, Davis's productions are consistent in that they construct African-American female subjectivity through the everyday experience and draw upon the culture of the African diaspora through the use of music and symbols of Pan African spirituality.

As an undergraduate student of law at Brown University, Davis was introduced to media production while serving as an intern at WSBE, the Public Broadcasting Station in Providence, Rhode Island. Working closely with African-American Gini Booth—host and producer of the minority affairs program *Shades*—Davis became increasingly aware of the power media wields in the arenas of ideology and culture. Her interest in media was furthered in 1981, while studying in Kenya. During her year abroad, Davis worked with Kenyan playwright Ngugi wa Thiong'o on a multimedia staging of one of his works, and also observed European film crews shooting ethnographic films of "exotic" Africa. Determined to become a film director, Davis enrolled in UCLA's graduate program in African Studies, earning a Master's of Arts degree in 1985, and a Master of Fine Arts degree in Motion Picture and Television Production four years later.

The name of her production company, Wimmin with a Mission, reflects Davis's approach to film and video production. Her work differs significantly from the Hollywood tradition of movies and television not only in terms of form, but also because it focuses on the lives of women of color, particularly African-American women—presenting characters far from the characteristic misrepresentations and one-dimensional stereotypes common in the media. One can look to her most noted works, *Cycles, A Powerful Thang,* and *Mother of the River* to view representations of African-American women rarely seen, constructed in a style that Gwendolyn Foster characterizes as "poetic (re)constructions of time, the body, and an exploration of spatial configurations."

Cycles, a provocative and innovative black-and-white experimental short, explores an important aspect of women's lives—the act of waiting. The film combines live action, still photography, animation, and pixilation to reflect the mood and feelings of the protagonist Rasheeda Allen as she awaits the start of menstruation. A complex and dense film, *Cycles* gives voice to women's experiences through its multilayered soundtrack of dialogue spoken by several women. Through the use of music by such artists as South African Miriam Makeba, Haitian Martha Jean-Claude, and American trumpeter Clora Bryant and the images of a Haitian Veve, ground paintings drawn during Vodun ceremonies, Davis links the culture of African Americans to the larger diaspora.

Like *Cycles,* the first feature-length film directed by Davis, *A Powerful Thang,* also embraces Pan African culture. The performance of Afro-Haitian dance, the use of *djembe* drums and jazz in the soundtrack, and the braided hair of the lead female character Yasmine, illustrate the diversity and richness of culture in this film, which focuses on friendship and intimacy in the lives of an African-American couple.

A Powerful Thang is also illustrative of Davis's dedication as an educator. The film was produced while Davis worked as an assistant professor at Antioch College, the first African-American woman to teach at the institution. Working with her on the film were several professionals in the field: cinematographer S. Toriano Berry, art director Claudia Springer, and editor Casi Pacilio. But the crew also included several production students from the college's Institute of Communications and Media Arts. This inclusion was instrumental in demystifying the filmmaking process for the students, and provided an opportunity for them to gain production experience.

Like other filmmakers of color, Davis is concerned with the issue of invisibility. Given age, race, and gender, the group rendered in film most rarely are African-American girls. Davis and African-American women media artists such as Debra J. Robinson, Ayoka Chenzira, and Alile Sharon Larkin are filling the gap with productions that depict the lives and unique perspectives of African-American girls. In 1995 Davis directed a script written by her husband Marc Arthur Chéry. *Mother of the River,* produced for ITVS, the Independent Television Service, is 30-minute narrative based on an African coming-of-age folktale. It takes place on a plantation in the Southern United States, and concerns the relationship between an enslaved girl and a magical older woman, the Mother of the River. An innovative film, it is one of the first to present slavery from a girl's perspective.

Davis was once quoted as saying film is an articulation of voice and vision. Her work in the media arts, while giving voice to persons and issues not usually discussed in film and video, itself presents a distinct voice and unique vision. Her legacy as a filmmaker will be a great one, adding diverse perspectives, creative stylings, and serving as an inspiration to countless generations of filmmakers to come.

—Frances K. Gateward

DE CIERTA MANERA

(One Way or Another)
Cuba, 1977
Director: Sara Gómez

Production: Instituto Cubano del Arte e Industria Cinematográficos (ICAIC); black and white, 35mm, originally shot in 16mm; running time: 79 minutes; length: 2147 meters. Released 1977.

Producer: Camilo Vives; **scenario:** Sara Gómez and Tomas González Pérez; **screenplay:** Tomas Gutíerrez Alea and Julio García Espinosa; **assistant directors:** Rigoberto López and Daniel Díaz Torres; **photography:** Luis García; **editor:** Iván Arocha; **sound:** Germinal Hernández; **production designer:** Roberto Larraburre; **music:** Sergio Vitier; **songs:** Sara González.

Cast: Mario Balmaseda (*Mario*); Yolanda Cuellar (*Yolanda*); Mario Limonta (*Humberto*).

Publications

Articles

Chijona, Geraldo, in *Cine Cubano* (Havana), no. 93.
López, Rigoberto, "Hablar de Sara: *De cierta manera,*" in *Cine Cubano* (Havana), no. 93.
"Special Sections" of *Jump Cut* (Berkeley), December 1978 and May 1980.
Lesage, Julia, "*One Way or Another*: Dialectical, Revolutionary, Feminist," in *Jump Cut* (Berkeley), May 1979.
Marrosu, A., in *Cine al Día* (Caracas), June 1980.
Pym, John, in *Monthly Film Bulletin* (London), July 1980.
Chanan, M., "Otra mirada," in *Cine Cubano* (Havana), no. 127, 1989.

Lezcano, J. A., "*De cierta manera* con Sara Gómez," in *Cine Cubano* (Havana), no. 127, 1989.

Lopez, A. M., "Parody, Underdevelopment, and the New Latin American Cinema," in *Quarterly Review of Film and Video* (New York), nos. 1-2, 1990.

* * *

Here is a revolutionary film: dialectical in form and content, humble in the face of real human experience, proposing no final answers except the unending struggle of a people to make something out of what history has made of them. *One Way or Another* is that powerful hybrid—the fictional documentary set to a tropical beat—for which the cinema of revolutionary Cuba is justifiably famous. In this instance, the documentary deals with the destruction of slum housing and the struggle against the culture of marginality generated in such slums through the creation of a new housing project (Miraflores) and an accompanying educational program. The fictional embodiment of this historical process is seen in the clash of attitudes between Mario (a product of the slums), his lover Yolanda (a teacher who has come to Miraflores to help integrate such marginal elements into the revolution), and his friend Humberto (a fun-loving slacker). In the course of telling these stories and others, *One Way or Another* demolishes the categories of fiction and documentary, insisting that both forms are equally mediated by the intention of the filmmaker, and that both thus require a critical stance.

This insistence on a critical attitude is conveyed, first of all, in the dialectical resonance of the film, a structure characteristic of the best of the Cuban cinema. Visually this resonance is achieved through a rich blending of fictional present and historical recreation with documentary and semidocumentary. In fact, it becomes impossible to distinguish the different forms; fictional characters are set in documentary sequences where they interact with real people and real people reenact historical reconstructions which are not visually in accordance with their *own* telling of the stories. Further, the film repeats various sequences several times, twisting the film back on itself and requiring the audience to participate actively in analyzing the different perspectives offered on the problems posed by the film.

The sound track is as creatively textured as are the images, and is every bit as demanding of the audience. The film sets up a tension between the classical documentary and its omniscient narrator, cinema-verité interviews, and fictional cinema. The omniscient documentary provides sociological data on different facets of marginality. Although this data establishes one framework for the "fictional" core of the film, its deliberately pompous tone warns us that we must critically question even such "official" pronouncements.

The omniscient narrator is juxtaposed to the conversations which take place around different aspects of marginalism. The manifestations of the culture of marginality are seen to be manifold—work absenteeism, machismo, delinquency—and the problem is hotly debated by everyone. Humberto is criticized for taking off from work on an unauthorized four-day jaunt with a girl friend, while lying about his "sick mother." Mario is criticized for denouncing Humberto, not because his attitude was counter-productive, but because Humberto accused him of being an informer—a violation of male-bonding rules. Yolanda criticizes the mothers of children who misbehave in school, and is in turn criticized by her co-workers for her inability to empathize with women whose background is so different from her own. Although trenchant and acute, these critiques are also loving and constructive. Just as individuals in the film leave these confrontations with a clearer understanding of the revolutionary process to which they are committed, so too does the audience leave the film with a more precise notion of dialectical film.

At the end of the film, the factory workers meet where the fictional confrontation of Mario and Humberto took place and enter into a discussion of the case. They seem to rise up and incorporate themselves into the actual production of the film itself. This is as it should be, for this film demands the participation of all: real people and actors, workers and marginal elements, teachers and housewives, audience and filmmaker. The wrecking ball (in a sequence repeated several times during the film) is not only destroying the slums and (metaphorically) the slum mentality, it may also be demolishing some of the more cherished assumptions of moviegoers in bourgeois cultures.

—John Mraz

THE DECLINE OF WESTERN CIVILIZATION
USA, 1980
Director: Penelope Spheeris

Production: Nu-Image Film; color, 35mm; running time: 100 minutes. Released July 1981, New York. Filmed in Los Angeles.

Producer: Penelope Spheeris; **executive producers:** Jeffrey Prettyman and Gordon Brown; **photography:** Steve Conant, Bill Muerer, and Penelope Spheeris; **editors:** Charles Mullin, Peter Wiehl, and David Colburn; **sound:** Kevin Williams; **music recording and engineering:** Alan Kutner and Gary Hirstius.

Publications

Articles

Caldwell, Carol, "Rude Bitches," in *Sotto News,* 1 July 1981.

Rickey, C., "Film: Civilization and Its Malcontents," in *Village Voice* (New York), 1-7 July 1981.

Corliss, Richard, "Cinema: La Dolce Vita," in *Time* (New York), 27 July 1981.

Koechl, P., "*The Decline of Western Civilization,*" in *Film Journal* (New York), 10 August 1981.

* * *

Penelope Spheeris's directorial debut is an ambitious feature-length documentary that offers an unflinching look at some of the key and not-so-key figures in the Los Angeles punk music scene circa 1979. The film focuses specifically on seven bands: Black Flag, Alice Bag Band, Germs, Catholic Discipline, Circle Jerks, Fear, and X. Accordingly, it provides a valuable portrait—almost a cultural anthropology—of punk history that is alternately amusing and serious. The film betrays Spheeris's general fascination with marginal youths and their despair, rebellions, ennui, and occasional violence. The film combines a provocative mix of interviews with the musicians, their managers, club owners, music critics, and fans along with concert footage that gives an idea of the range of music, personalities, and dancing that were integral to the movement. It also provides glimpses of the occasionally violent and wretched hopelessness of at least a few of punk's participants.

The Decline of Western Civilization conveys Spheeris's intrepid determination and talent for going beyond the shocking details of punk with which the popular press was enormously preoccupied. But, the film does have some shocking bits, including an interview with Darby Crash, the lead singer of the Germs, whose giggling friend delightedly describes the time they discovered the corpse of a house painter in their backyard and then recruited their friends to pose with it for photographs. The scenes that feature the drunken, stumbling, and scarred Crash seem to anticipate his death from a drug overdose only a few months later. Other sequences display the rabid disdain of some of the performers for their own fans; thus, Claude Bessy, a singer and rock critic, declares that he wants the audience to hate him, because it makes him "feel good." Another punker proclaims somewhat loftier aims, "Nothing else is going on. We're the only form of revolution left."

Although Spheeris is a fan of the punks and their movement, she is to be credited for neither condemning nor championing them in her film. Another strength is the attention she pays to at least a few of the estimable women who helped develop the punk movement, and who garnered substantial power and profits from it. Especially the delightfully disheveled femme Exene Cervenka, the lead singer in the popular and critically acclaimed band X, such women discovered that punk music provided the means by which to express their unique political and artistic perspectives.

The live music featured in the film conveys its generic "speedrock" attributes, including a rigorous monotony, pessimistic, nearly incomprehensible lyrics (Spheeris sometimes includes English subtitles), and aggressive vocalizing. In terms of screen time, Spheeris favors the live, crowd-pleasing performances of X, which are raw yet rehearsed, and cleverly dissonant, as well as her interviews with the band members. Most engaging are the married leaders of X, Cervenka and John Doe, who are strange, intelligent, and sometimes silly, as they tattoo themselves and discuss a range of subjects, from the origins of their band and marriage to Cervenka's cherished and obsessive collection of Christian pamphlets.

Spheeris's preoccupation with rock 'n' roll youth subcultures is likely related to her tough childhood as the eldest child of the proprietors of a traveling carnival. Throughout the film, during the interviews, she is an audible but off-camera presence. The participants apparently trust her and they are typically respectful, which is radically different than the cynicism and contempt they communicate on stage. Spheeris remains nonplused by some of the more sordid stories she hears, and carefully asks for clarification about vague answers. For example, when a punk fan proudly announces that he attends concerts to do "something I'm good at," she asks simply, "What?" His quick response: "Beating people up."

Interestingly, many critics read the title of the *Decline of Western Civilization* literally, although Spheeris intended it ironically. Yet it could be literally applied to her subsequent features, such as the fiction films *Suburbia* (1984) and *The Boys Next Door* (1985), in which she returned to the subject of disaffected, mostly male, adolescence. In 1988 she produced a sequel to *Decline*, entitled *The Decline of Western Civilization Part II: The Metal Years*. Like its predecessor, it was a feature-length documentary set in Los Angeles that included music and interviews with several "heavy metal" rock bands. It compellingly revealed the outrageous, usually drunken

sexism of many of the bands, as well as of the venue owners who fed the insatiable sexist frenzy of both the musicians and their fans with near-nude "beauty contests." Perhaps more disturbing are the sequences that depict the scores of young women who were eager to be the objects of the men's noisy lust.

—Cynthia Felando

DE HIRSCH, Storm
American director

Born: Lillian Malkin in New Jersey, 9 December 1912. **Family:** Following a stormy relationship with her parents, she left home at an early age for an artistic life as a painter and poet in New York City, where she married an artist named De Hirsch, which lasted some 20 years; married (2) Louis Brigante one of the early editors of *Film Culture* magazine, during the latter part of their 25-year relationship which ended only with his death in 1975. **Career:** 1963—first film, *Goodbye in the Mirror,* feature-length narrative shot in Rome and later blown up to 35mm for possible showings in movie theaters, with disappointing results (Brigante assisted her on this and subsequent films); 1963-73—made a dozen or so short abstract animation and live-action films, using many experimental techniques including cameraless etching and painting directly onto film, multiple images, dual-screen projection, and in-camera masking; 1968—only woman winner of American Film Institute's first round of $10,000 grants to independent filmmakers; 1973—retrospective film showing at Whitney Museum of American Art; 1973-74—made ten or more very short, silent Super-8mm films and became a pioneer advocate of this low-cost, easily accessible medium of artistic expression. Throughout her film career, lectured and taught at major institutions throughout the United States, including a course in visionary film at New York's School of Visual Arts; forced to give up her studio after Brigante's death, in 1975, she made no more films and suffered a gradual decline in health that has turned into a long and tragically debilitating case of Alzheimer's disease.

Films as Director

1963   *Journey around a Zero*
1964   *Goodbye in the Mirror* (produced 1963)
c. 1965   *Newsreel: Jonas in The Brig*
1966   *Sing Lotus* (music of Manipur, Kashmir, and Nepal)
1968   *Trap Dance*; *Third Eye Butterfly* (dual screen projection)
1969   *The Tattooed Man*
1971   *An Experiment in Meditation*
1975   *Geometrics of the Kabballah* (16mm, silent)

"The Color of Ritual, The Color of Thought" Series—

1964-67   *Divinations*; *Shaman: A Tapestry for Sorcerers*; *Peyote Queen*

"Hudson River Diary" Series—

1967   *Cayuga Run*
1973   *Wintergarden*; *River-Ghost*

"Cine-Sonnets" Series (Silent Super-8mm)—

1973-74 *Lace of Summer*; *September Express*; *Charlotte Moorman's Avant-Garde Festival #9*; *Malevitch at the Guggenheim*; *Ives House: Woodstock*; *Deep in the Mirror Embedded*; *Silently, Bearing Totem of a Bird*; *A Reticule of Love*; *Aristotle*; *The Recurring Dream*

Publications by De Hirsch

Books

Alleh Lulleh Cockatoo (poetry), 1955.
Twilight Massacre (poetry), 1964.

Articles

"Roman Notebook," in *Film Culture* (New York), no. 25, 1962.
"Roman Notebook," in *Film Culture* (New York), no. 27, 1963.
"Astral Daguerreotype," in *Film Culture* (New York), no. 33, 1964.
"Walk a Little Faster" (poem), in *December* (Western Springs, Illinois), vol. 8, no. 1, 1966.
"'Female' Film-Making," interview with Shirley Clarke, in *Arts Magazine* (New York), April 1967.
"A Conversation—Shirley Clarke and Storm De Hirsch," in *Film Culture* (New York), no. 46, 1967-68.
"Storm De Hirsch, Independent Filmmaker," interview with Martyn K. Green, in *Super-8 Filmmaker*, January/February 1974.

Publications on De Hirsch

Books

Mekas, Jonas, *Movie Journal: The Rise of the New American Cinema, 1959-71,* New York, 1972.
Noguez, Dominique, *Un Renaissance du Cinéma: Le Cinéma "Underground" American,* Paris, 1985.

Articles

Markopoulos, Gregory, "Three Filmmakers" (Andy Meyer, Charles Boultenhouse, Storm De Hirsch), in *Film Culture* (New York), no. 35, 1964-65.
Patterson, Maggie, "Storm Takes Direct Path," in *Pittsburgh Press,* 16 April 1971.
Mekas, Jonas, review of *Cine Sonnets*, in *Village Voice* (New York), 29 November 1973.
"Making 'Reel' Art," in *Redding (Pennsylvania) Times,* 26 April 1976.

*   *   *

Storm De Hirsch made her first motion picture in 1963, two years after the untimely death of Maya Deren, the woman who had virtually masterminded the avant-garde film movement in the United States. Although De Hirsch was born five years earlier than Deren, she was a mature artist—over 40 years old—when she began her filmmaking career. Deren was only 25 when she made her first film—the classic *Meshes of the Afternoon*—and at the age of 44, she died.

Though they may never have known each other, they had quite a bit in common. Both women had created new names and personas for themselves; Deren's were earthy and radical, De Hirsch's more imposing and regal. Both had backgrounds in poetry and other arts; they were also deeply involved with primitive cultures and the occult. In making their first films, both were supported by their husbands. In Maya Deren's case, it was an inspired artistic collaboration with Alexander Hammid in a short-lived marriage; Storm De Hirsch's first professional collaboration with Louis Brigante was disappointing, but the personal relationship endured. Both women made lasting contributions to the American avant-garde film scene, within the limits of their times and talents.

The 1960s offered Storm De Hirsch many more options than the 1940s had offered Deren, allowing her to start big, with an ambitious feature-length story about three young women, living is Rome, loosely based on a poem she had written and on her own experiences. Brigante was associate director. Called *Goodbye in the Mirror,* part scripted, part improvised, it was shot on 16mm and later blown up to 35mm, at a total cost of some $20,000. *Variety*'s reviewer found it too uneven for a feature, and thought it might have been a sharp, incisive short. Even before its release, De Hirsch already had begun making short films that were much more suited to her painterly and poetic roots.

Independent, cheaply made underground films, she later said, were not merely a futile rebellion against Hollywood's slickness, but were spontaneous efforts to create the equivalent of off-Broadway theater in the medium of film. De Hirsch's first short film, *Journey around a Zero,* was made without a camera, simply because she did not have one. Using old black-and-white film stock and some rolls of 16mm sound tape, she painted and etched images of her imagination with a variety of discarded surgical instruments and the sharp edge of a screwdriver. Compared to the $20,000 cost of *Goodbye in the Mirror, Journey*'s cost was cheap indeed—practically zero. The visuals were pure abstract animation, which De Hirsch described as "a phallic invocation." In her writing and especially in making her animation abstractions De Hirsch felt she became both man and woman, or either one—not for lack of sexual identification but with an awareness of a cosmic sexuality.

De Hirsch's trilogy entitled *The Color of Ritual, The Color of Thought,* explored relationships of abstract animated imagery (this time in color) with live photography and what she called "voyages into buried continents of the self." The very titles indicated her penchant for magic, myth, and ritual: *Divinations, Shaman: A Tapestry for Sorcerers, Peyote Queen.* In 1968 Storm De Hirsch was awarded $10,000 in the American Film Institute's first round of grants to independent filmmakers—the only woman among the winners. With the money she made a mini-feature called *The Tattooed Man,* based on her poem of the same name; it was more episodic than her first film had been, like a "happening" more than a dramatic film, and more representative of her times. For her tenth film, *Third Eye Butterfly,* De Hirsch used dual screens, side-by-side, creating a 70mm effect. One critic wrote that this encouraged the viewer's mind to give the two horizontal images a third meaning, as Eisenstein's montage of two images on a strip of film gave them an implied third meaning.

In 1973, for her Hudson River Diary series, De Hirsch used a handheld 16mm camera to create cinematic landscapes and waterscapes shot from a moving train (*Cayuga Run*) or walking along the frozen water's edge (*Wintergarden*). These films began to look more like visual poems than movies based on poems or films for which she had written poetic descriptions. Sometimes for convenience or safety's sake, she shot on Super-8 which later was blown up to 16mm. When she was given a cartridge loading Super-8 camera to take to the Venice Film Festival, she began her Cine-Sonnets series. Filmed in England's Heathrow Airport, on the train from Rome to Venice, or in her Venice hotel room, each was three or four minutes long, short and edited in the camera. No random shots of this and that—as her first European film had been—each carefully selected shot was framed by her eye and mind and hand, beautifully lighted by nature or perhaps by God Himself. As the films outwardly became shorter and simpler, inwardly they grew richer and more revealing.

With Louis Brigante's death in 1975, Storm De Hirsch lost not only her much-loved companion of some 25 years, but also the studio where they had worked, much of her creative energy, and ultimately her health. As she succumbed slowly to Alzheimer's disease, eventually she lost all memory of her achievements in film—the retrospectives at New York's Whitney Museum and the Museum of Modern Art; her classes in visionary filmmaking at the School of Visual Art; lectures and screenings in Pennsylvania and Ohio, Vancouver, and Brussels, and at many film festivals and women's programs. At the time of this writing, Storm De Hirsch continues to survive in a Manhattan nursing home with this long and devastating illness. Her fascinating role in independent cinema has yet to be well documented and assessed.

Comparison with Maya Deren deserves these further comments. Deren was something of a genius, far ahead of her times in virtually everything she did. Storm De Hirsch was an extremely talented filmmaker of her time, exploring many aspects of film as an artist's medium. The very title of her film, *Peyote Queen,* shows her to be an outspoken product of those times—the rebellious sixties, the Beat Generation, the hallucinatory decade. It is a sad footnote to those times that although P. Adams Sitney played a major role in one of her major films (*The Tattooed Man,* 1968), Sitney's seminal book on American avant-garde cinema (*Visionary Films,* 1974) does not even mention her name.

—Cecile Starr

DEITCH, Donna
American director

Born: 8 June 1945. **Education:** Studied painting and photography as an undergraduate; studied film production as a University of California, Los Angeles, graduate student. **Career:** 1970s—made a series of documentary films; 1975—gained recognition from feminists for the documentary, *Woman to Woman*; 1986—directed first feature film, *Desert Hearts*; 1989—directed TV miniseries *The Women of Brewster Place*; 1990s—worked as a television director on series including: *Murder One, NYPD Blue,* and *ER.* **Awards:** Honorable Mention, Sundance Film Festival, for *Desert Hearts,* 1986. **Agent:** William Morris Agency, 151 El Camino Drive, Beverly Hills, CA 90212, U.S.A. **Address:** c/o Desert Heart Productions, 685 Venice Boulevard, Venice, CA 90291, U.S.A.

Films as Director

1968   *Berkeley 12 to 1*
1969   *Memorabilia P P 1*
1970   *She Was a Visitor*
1972   *Portrait*
1975   *"For George, Love Donna"* (short); *Woman to Woman* (doc)
1978   *The Great Wall of Los Angeles* (doc)
1986   *Desert Hearts* (+ pr, ro as Hungarian gambler)
1991   "Esperanza" ep. of *Prison Stories: Women on the Inside* (for TV)
1992   *Sexual Advances* (for TV)
1994   *Criminal Passion*

Publications by Deitch

Articles

Interview with Pat Aufderheide, in *Cineaste* (New York), vol. 15, no. 1, 1986.
"Deitch Makes Feature Debut with Drama of Self-Discovery," interview with E. Gordon, in *Film Journal* (New York), February 1986.
"Not the Only Game in Town," interview with J. Root, in *Monthly Film Bulletin* (London), August 1986.
"The Queen of *Desert Hearts,"* interview with N. Norman, in *Photoplay Movies & Video* (London), September 1986.

Publications on Deitch

Books

Russo, Vito, *The Celluloid Closet: Homosexuality in the Movies,* New York, 1987.
Maio, Kathi, *Feminist in the Dark,* Freedom, California, 1988.
Quart, Barbara Koenig, *Women Directors: The Emergence of a New Cinema,* New York, 1988.
Acker, Ally, *Reel Women: Pioneers of the Cinema, 1896 to the Present,* New York, 1991.
Foster, Gwendolyn Audrey, *Women Film Directors: An International Bio-Critical Dictionary,* Westport, Connecticut, 1995.

Articles

Haskell, Molly, "Time to Judge Women's Films on Merit," in *Village Voice* (New York), 29 December 1975.
Kort, M., "Independent Filmmaker Donna Deitch Controls Her Whole Show," in *Ms.* (New York), November 1985.
Reitman, J., "In Production: Reno Roulette," in *Millimeter* (New York), March 1986.
Rich, B. Ruby, "*Desert Heart,"* in *Village Voice* (New York), 8 April 1986.
Pepe, Barbara, "Ten Years Gone," in *Advocate* (Los Angeles), 20 August 1996.

*   *   *

Feminist filmmaker Donna Deitch is known for making films that feature strong, cleverly nuanced female characters who find particular strength in the community of women. Her first feature was the independently produced *Desert Hearts,* which earned the praise of feminist critics for its unusual depiction of a lesbian love affair. Early in her career, Deitch worked as a still photographer, camerawoman, and editor, in addition to directing several documentaries, film shorts, and commercials. But, like many feminist filmmakers who started working in the 1970s, Deitch eventually moved from making documentary films to fiction features.

As a film student at UCLA, Deitch displayed a cheeky irreverence with her short film, *"For George, Love Donna,"* which consisted of a close shot of an erect penis that was meant to call attention to and challenge the sexism of her male student colleagues. Her interest in operating outside the conventions of male Hollywood directors is evident in her early documentaries as well, which include *Woman to Woman* about women's social roles, or, as Deitch put it, about "hookers, housewives, and other mothers"; and *The Great Wall of Los Angeles* about a mile-long mural in the Tujunga Wash of Los Angeles.

Her best-known film, *Desert Hearts,* was the product of more than two years of intensive fund-raising on Deitch's part to acquire $1.5 million in financing. She found most of her investors among women who sympathized with her desire to avoid the studio system and to retain control of her vision for the film. Indeed, Deitch was determined to deal with her subject frankly and realistically, in order to resist the depictions of lesbian relationships more typically found in American films. *Desert Hearts* tells the story of Columbia English professor Vivian Bell, a 30-something blond sophisticate who arrives in Reno in 1959 to get a divorce. In order to meet the state's residency requirements for divorce, she settles temporarily at a dude ranch run by a salty older woman. Though Vivian intends to spend her time studying, the openly lesbian and younger Cay Rivers, a lithe, bold, yet casual Westerner, attracts her attention. Vivian is not, however, initially comfortable with Cay's sexuality—or with her own. The emotions unleashed by their developing intimacy, and Vivian's ambivalence and insecurity about her feelings towards Cay, are played out against a rocky Western landscape usually associated with masculinity. Importantly, it is the female gaze that moves the film, as in a scene in which the two women eye each other while Cay dances with a man, but does not look at him. Also, more so than in the novel, Deitch effectively conveys Vivian's intrapersonal conflict, between the world of respectable heterosexuality and the challenges and rewards of a lesbian relationship.

Desert Hearts has been favorably compared to two other features from the 1980s about lesbian relationships: John Sayles's 1983 *Lianna* and Robert Towne's 1982 *Personal Best,* both of which feature less-than-happy endings for their lesbian heroines. Deitch explained that she wanted to make *Desert Hearts* because American films had failed to show a relationship between women that did not end with some "suicides, murders, or convoluted bisexual triangles." Adapted from Jane Rule's novel *Desert of the Heart,* Deitch's film is a sincere lesbian love story. Interestingly, before she agreed to sell them to Deitch, the novelist turned down a studio's offer to buy the rights to her novel, because she expected that they would alter her story beyond recognition. With its 1950s Reno setting, Deitch was drawn especially to Rule's tender love story and its key metaphor—gambling. That is, while people gamble with their money in the casinos, *Desert Hearts*'s two heroines gamble with their sexuality and social identities by pursuing a "taboo" but true love.

Critics praised *Desert Hearts*'s love scene for being highly erotic without resorting to the voyeurism or objectification of women's bodies that are typical of lesbian love scenes crafted for the "male gaze," such as *Personal Best,* whose exploitative sex scenes serve as a prelude for the heterosexual love scene; or, like *Lianna,* which means well but fails to convey any level of eroticism. Accordingly, B. Ruby Rich approvingly called *Desert Hearts* a "lesbian heart-throb movie." Indeed, as Deitch explained, "I wanted to make just a

Donna Deitch

love story, like any other love story between a man and a woman, handled in a frank and real way." Thus, her film is not heavy-handed about its sexuality or sexual politics; that is, it presents the women's relationship as fully romantic, healthy, and true without forcing the characters to take on the world's homophobia on any large scale.

Deitch's next film was for Oprah Winfrey, who recruited her to direct her pet project *Women of Brewster Place,* a four-hour television miniseries adapted from Gloria Naylor's award-winning novel. It tells the story of a strong community of seven black women, including a church woman, a welfare mother, and a yuppie lesbian couple. Their collective strength is tested by the city's attempt to thwart their neighborhood's newly thriving community by erecting a brick wall to separate it from the rest of the neighborhood.

More recently, Deitch directed *Criminal Passion,* a fairly conventional story about a detective who falls in love with her prime murder suspect, thus impossibly blurring the lines between passion and police work. In the 1990s, Deitch has found success as a television director, for both movies and episodic dramas, such as *Murder One* and *ER.* In addition, she directed one of the three episodes of the cable-television anthology *Prison Stories: Women on the Inside,* which aimed to bring attention to the problems prison mothers endure. Certainly, however, the independent films from the 1990s that have achieved success featuring lesbian relationships owe a debt of gratitude to Deitch's groundbreaking *Desert Hearts* and its affirmations of lesbian love.

—Cynthia Felando

DENIS, Claire
French director and writer

Born: Paris, France, 21 April 1948. **Education:** Attended Institut des Hautes Cinématographiques in Paris, graduated in 1972. **Career:** Mid-1970s to mid-1980s—worked on short films and was an assistant director for Costa-Gavras, Wim Wenders, and Jim Jarmusch; 1988—completed her first feature, the widely seen *Chocolat*; 1996—completed award-winning film, *Nénette et Boni*. **Awards:** Golden Leopard, Locarno International Film Festival, for *Nénette et Boni*, 1996. **Address:** c/o: Flach Pyramide International, 5 Rue Richepanse, 75008 Paris, France.

Films as Director

1973-74 *Chroniques de France*
1988 ***Chocolat*** (*Chocolate*) (+ co-sc)
1989 *Man No Run* (+ co-sc); *Jacques Rivette, Le Veilleur* (for TV)
1990 *S'en fout la mort* (*No Fear, No Die*) (+ co-sc)
1991 *Contre l'oubli* (*Against Oblivion*) (co, + co-sc); *Keep It for Yourself* (*Moyen Montrage*); *Ni Une, Ni Deux* (for TV)
1992 *La Robe à Cerceaux* (*The Hoop Skirt*) (for TV)
1993 *J'ai pas sommeil* (*I Can't Sleep*) (+ co-sc)
1994 *U.S. Go Home* (+ co-sc) (for TV)
1995 *Nice, Very Nice* (for TV)
1996 *Nénette et Boni* (*Nénette and Boni*) (+ co-sc)

Other Films

1978 *Mais où et donc Ornicar* (van Effenterre) (ro, asst d)
1984 *Paris, Texas* (Wenders) (asst d)
1986 *Down by Law* (Jarmusch) (asst d)
1987 *Der Himmel über Berlin* (*Wings of Desire*) (Wenders) (asst d)
1995 *En avoir (ou pas)* (*To Have [or Not]*) (Masson) (ro as Alice's mother)

Publications by Denis

Articles

Interview with C. Piccino, in *Filmcritica* (Rome), June/July 1988.
Interview with T. Jousse and F. Strauss, in *Cahiers du Cinéma* (Paris), May 1994.
Interview with J. Valot and J. M. Lalanne, in *Mensuel du Cinéma* (Paris), June 1994.
"French Cancan," in *Cahiers du Cinéma* (Paris), July/August 1994.
"Awakenings," interview with Ira Sachs, in *Filmmaker* (Los Angeles), Fall 1997.

Publications on Denis

Books

Tomaselli, Keyan, *The Cinema of Apartheid: Race and Class in South African Films,* New York, 1988.
Diawara, Manthia, *African Cinema: Politics and Culture,* Bloomington, Indiana, 1992.

Petrie, Duncan, editor, *Screening Europe: Image and Identity in Contemporary European Cinema,* London, 1992.
Foster, Gwendolyn Audrey, *Women Film Directors: An International Bio-Critical Dictionary,* Westport, Connecticut, 1995.

Articles

O'Shea, Stephen, "Claire Denis," in *Premiere* (Des Moines, Iowa), March 1989.
Chutkow, Paul, "This *Chocolat* Is Bittersweet," in *New York Times,* 5 March 1989.
Strauss, Frederic, "Feminin Colonial," in *Cahiers du Cinéma* (Paris), July/August 1990.
Strauss, Frederic, "*S'en fout la mort,*" in *Cahiers du Cinéma* (Paris), September 1990.
Murphy, Kathleen, "The Color of Home," in *Film Comment* (New York), September/October 1992.
Roth-Bettoni, D., "*J'ai pas sommeil,*" in *Mensuel du Cinéma* (Paris), May 1994.
Kelleher, E., "Real-Life Parisian Killing Spree Animates Denis' *I Can't Sleep,*" in *Film Journal* (New York), July 1995.
Limosin, J.-P., "Six Regards en contre champ," in *Cahiers du Cinéma* (Paris), July/August 1995.
Taubin, Amy, "Now, Voyeur," in *Village Voice* (New York), 22 August 1995.
Camhi, Leslie, "A French Director with a Taste for the Gritty and Unglamorous," in *New York Times,* 12 October 1997.

* * *

Over the course of the last ten years, Claire Denis has created an impressive body of work that ranges from narrative features and music documentaries to films for television. Known worldwide as an inspired director with a vivacious, trenchant perspective, she has been called "one of the great directors of our time," and enjoys a reputation as an extraordinarily inventive and influential independent filmmaker.

When she was two months old, Denis's parents moved to Africa, where, while her father worked in the French civil service, they lived in a series of countries until she was 14 years old. When she finished college, Denis took a position as a trainee at a company that made short educational films, whereupon she decided to attend film school in Paris. After she was graduated from film school in Paris, she worked her way from production assistant to assistant director for several highly esteemed filmmakers, such as Jacques Rivette, Constantin Costa-Gavras, Wim Wenders, and Jim Jarmusch. In a few years she was writing scripts; four years later she made her first feature film, the sublimely beautiful, much-praised, *Chocolat*. In general, her films are rich, complex combinations of intimate drama and acute sociological and political awareness.

It was while working as an assistant director on Wim Wenders's *Paris, Texas* in 1984 that she had the idea for her first feature film. The southwestern landscape prompted her memories of Africa, and the result was, *Chocolat,* a fictional rendering of her own experience as a privileged, white female in colonial West Africa and of the emotional conflicts generated by colonialism. It is an altogether subtle, sophisticated film that features the aptly named character, "France," a French woman who returns as an adult to her childhood home in postcolonial Cameroon, where her father had been a district officer in the late 1950s, during the last years of French colonialism. France's story and growing racial consciousness are revealed via a long flash-

Claire Denis (right)

back to her life as an eight-year-old girl. Denis has explained that the film was fictional rather than a documentary account of her own experiences, since "when you make fiction you talk about yourself."

After *Chocolat* Denis switched gears and made *Man No Run,* a documentary about the Cameroon band Les Têtes Brûlées on their first French tour. Her next feature was *No Fear, No Die,* which offered a brutal depiction of the strange and metaphorical realm of cockfighting. *I Can't Sleep,* based on a true story, is about the infamous "granny killer" of Paris. It features the beautiful Daiga, who has emigrated from Lithuania to Paris and is looking for work; Theo, a struggling musician; and Theo's brother Camille, a transvestite dancer. It is one of the three who might be linked to the serial killer who has been terrorizing Paris, but strangely, no one notices them. The film's loose narrative evokes the work of director Eric Rohmer, but is distinctively Denis's, inasmuch as characters are revealed via their brief intersections and subtle gestures.

U.S. Go Home was part of the series *Tous les garçons et les filles* [All the boys and girls in their time], a collection of ten coming-of-age movies by esteemed French directors. Denis's highly energetic contribution is set in 1965 France and considers the pervasive influence of American culture, especially upon 14-year-old heroine Marlene who attends a party with a single-minded goal—to lose her virginity. She fails at the party, but while hitchhiking home, she meets an American serviceman. Denis brilliantly conveys Marlene's

likable charm, as well as her ambivalence—both fascination and fear—of sex.

Denis routinely collaborates with Jean-Pôl Fargeau on the screenplays for her films. Her films share a commitment to examining racism and colonialism (as in *No Fear, No Die* and *Chocolat*). Further, several of her films feature characters who are siblings, including *U.S. Go Home, I Can't Sleep,* and *Nénette et Boni,* because she is drawn to the complexities, and, as she puts it, the weirdness of sibling relationships. Critics laud her moviemaking strategies, especially her knack for "committing the texture of life to film." Likewise, she has a canny sense of people and place, a compelling approach to film time and space, and she is known for her effective use of nonactors, such as the female leads in *U.S. Go Home,* and the male lead in *I Can't Sleep.*

Denis's most recent film is the award-winning *Nénette et Boni,* an impressionistic and hauntingly heartfelt, yet unsentimental look at sibling ties and immature teenage emotions. Notably, the film's characterizations and story are built in layers of metaphor and scene fragments. In the southern port city of Marseilles, Boni is a 19-year-old pizzeria worker with an active sex-fantasy life, and Nénette is his 15-year-old sister who discovers that she is pregnant and runs away from boarding school. When she unexpectedly arrives on Boni's doorstep, the two eye each other suspiciously. Both sister and brother are tough and uncompromising, as they are used to years of tribulations and coping with the legacy of their father, whom they hate. Slowly Nénette's pregnancy brings the two together, though Nénette is apparently indifferent to the baby, and it means perhaps too much to Boni.

Like Denis's other work, *Nénette et Boni* is deeply sensual. Indeed, all of her deeply evocative and unpredictable films avoid the slick production values of commercial cinema in favor of a sense of intimacy and sincerity. Nevertheless, they are remarkably varied, both visually and thematically. As a result, her many-layered films are always memorable—and occasionally haunting.

—Cynthia Felando

DEREN, Maya
American director

Born: Kiev, 1917, became U.S. citizen. **Education:** Attended the League of Nations School, Geneva, Switzerland; studied journalism at University of Syracuse, New York; New York University, B.A.; Smith College, M.A. **Family:** Married (second time) the Czech filmmaker Alexander Hackenschmied (Hammid), 1942 (divorced); later married Teijo Ito. **Career:** 1922—family emigrated to America; 1943—made first film *Meshes of the Afternoon*; 1946—traveled to Haiti; 1960—secretary for Creative Film Foundation. **Awards:** Guggenheim Fellowship for work in creative film, 1946. **Died:** Of a cerebral hemorrhage in Queens, New York, 13 October 1961.

Films as Director

1943   *Meshes of the Afternoon* (with Alexander Hammid) (+ ro); *The Witches' Cradle* (unfinished)
1944   *At Land* (+ ro)
1945   *A Study in Choreography for Camera*; *The Private Life of a Cat* (home movie, with Hammid)
1946   *Ritual in Transfigured Time* (+ ro)
1948   *Meditation on Violence*
1949   *Medusa*
1951   *Divine Horsemen*; *Ensemble for Somnambulists*
1959   *The Very Eye of Night*
1960   *Haiku* film project

Film as Writer

1961   *Maeva (Wahine)* (Bonsignori)

Publications by Deren

Books

An Anagram of Ideas on Art, Form, and the Film, New York, 1946.
The Divine Horseman: The Living Gods of Haiti, New York, 1953.
Divine Horsemen: Voodoo Gods of Haiti, New York, 1970.

Articles

"Choreography of Camera," in *Dance* (New York), October 1943.
"Cinema as an Art Form," in *Introduction to the Art of the Movies,* edited by Lewis Jacobs, New York, 1960.

"Cinematography: The Creative Use of Reality," in *Daedalus: The Visual Arts Today,* 1960.
"Movie Journal," in *Village Voice* (New York), 25 August 1960.
"Movie Journal," in *Village Voice* (New York), 1 June 1961.
"A Statement of Principles," in *Film Culture* (New York), Summer 1961.
"A Lecture ... ," in *Film Culture* (New York), Summer 1963.
"Notes, Essays, Letters," in *Film Culture* (New York), Winter 1965.
"A Statement on Dance and Film," in *Dance Perspectives* (New York), no. 30, 1967.
"Tempo and Tension," in *The Movies as Medium,* edited by Lewis Jacobs, New York, 1970.

Publications on Deren

Books

Hanhardt, John, and others, *A History of the American Avant-Garde Cinema,* New York, 1976.
Sitney, P. Adams, *Visionary Film,* 2nd ed., New York, 1979.
Clark, VeVe A., Millicent Hodson, and Catrina Neimans, *The Legend of Maya Deren: A Documentary Biography and Collected Works: Vol. 1, Pt. 1, Signatures (1917-1942),* New York, 1984.
Heck-Rabi, Louise, *Women Filmmakers: A Critical Reception,* Metuchen, New Jersey, 1984.
Wodening, Jane, *From the Book of Legends,* New York, 1989.
Mayne, Judith, *The Woman at the Keyhole: Feminism and Women's Cinema,* Bloomington, Indiana, 1990.
Acker, Ally, *Reel Women: Pioneers of the Cinema, 1896 to the Present,* New York, 1991.
Rabinovitz, Lauren, *Points of Resistance: Women, Power and Politics in the New York Avant-Garde Cinema, 1943-1971,* Urbana, Illinois, 1991.
Foster, Gwendolyn Audrey, *Women Film Directors: An International Bio-Critical Dictionary,* Westport, Connecticut, 1995.
Sudre, Alain-Alcide, *Dialogues theoriques avec Maya Deren: du cinema experimental au film ethnographique,* Paris, 1996.

Articles

Farber, Manny, "Maya Deren's Films," in *New Republic* (New York), 28 October 1946.
"Deren Issue" of *Filmwise,* no. 2, 1961.
Obituary, in *New York Times,* 14 October 1961.
Tallmer, Jerry, "For Maya Deren," in *Village Voice* (New York), 19 October 1961.
Arnheim, Rudolf, "To Maya Deren," in *Film Culture* (New York), no. 24, 1962.
Sitney, P. Adams, "The Idea of Morphology," in *Film Culture* (New York), nos. 53, 54, and 55, 1971.
Cornwell, Regina, "Maya Deren and Germaine Dulac: Activists of the Avant-Garde," in *Film Library Quarterly* (New York), Winter 1971/72.
Bronstein, M., and S. Grossmann, "Zu Maya Derens Filmarbeit," in *Frauen und Film* (Berlin), December 1976.
Hoberman, J., "The Maya Mystique," in *Village Voice* (New York), 15 May 1978.
Camera Obscura Collective, The, "Excerpts from an Interview with 'The Legend of Maya Deren' Project," in *Camera Obscura* (Berkeley), Summer 1979.

Mayer, T., "The Legend of Maya Deren: Champion of American Independent Film," in *Film News* (New York), September/October 1979.

"Kamera Arbeit: Der schopferische umgang mit der realitat," in *Frauen und Film* (Berlin), October 1984.

"Maya Deren Issue," of *Film Culture* (New York), nos. 72-75, 1985.

Millsapps, Jan L., "Maya Deren, Imagist," in *Literature Film Quarterly* (Salisbury, Maryland), January 1986.

Monthly Film Bulletin (London), June and July 1988.

* * *

Maya Deren was the best-known independent, experimental filmmaker in the United States during and after World War II. She developed two types of short, subjective films: the psychodrama and the ciné-dance film. She initiated a national nontheatrical network to show her six independently made works, which have been referred to as visual lyric poems, or dreamlike trance films. She also lectured and wrote extensively on film as an art form. Her films remain as provocative as ever, her contributions to cinematic art indisputable.

Intending to write a book on dance, Deren toured with Katherine Dunham's dance group as a secretary. Dunham introduced Deren to Alexander Hammid, and the following year the couple made *Meshes of the Afternoon*. Considered a milestone in the chronology of independent film in the United States, it is famous for its four-stride sequence (from beach to grass to mud to pavement to rug). Deren acted the role of a girl driven to suicide. Continuous action is maintained while time-space unities are severed, establishing a trancelike mood by the use of slow motion, swish-pan camera movements, and well executed point-of-view shots.

In her next film, *At Land,* a woman (Deren) runs along a beach and becomes involved in a chess game. P. Adams Sitney refers to this work as a "pure American trance film." The telescoping of time occurs as each scene blends with the next in unbroken sequence, a result of planned editing. *At Land* is also studded with camera shots of astounding virtuosity.

Other films include Deren's first ciné-dance film, the three-minute *A Study in Choreography for Camera.* Filmed in slow motion, a male ballet dancer, partnered by the camera, moves through a variety of locales. Continuity of camera movement is maintained as the dancer's foot changes location. Space is compressed while time is expanded. According to Sitney, the film's importance resides in two fresh observations: space and time in film are *created* space and time, and the camera's optimal use is as a dancer itself. *Ritual in Transfigured Time,* another dance-on-film, portrays psycho-dramatic ritual by use of freeze frames, repeated shots, shifting character identities, body movements, and locales. *Meditation on Violence* explores Woo (or Wu) Tang boxing with the camera as sparring partner, panning and zooming to simulate human response. *The Very Eye of Night* employed Metropolitan Ballet School members to create a celestial ciné-ballet of night. Shown in its negative state, Deren's handheld camera captured white figures on a total black background. Over the course of her four dance-films Deren evolved a viable form of ciné-choreography that was adapted and adjusted to later commercial feature films. In cases such as *West Side Story,* this was done with great skill and merit.

Deren traced the evolution of her six films in "A Letter to James Card," dated April 19, 1955. *Meshes* was her "point of departure" and "almost expressionist"; *At Land* depicted dormant energies in mutable nature; and *Choreography* distilled the essence of this natural changing. In *Ritual* she defined the processes of changing, while *Meditation* extends the study of metamorphosis. In *The Very Eye* she expressed her love of life and its living. "Each film was built as a chamber and became a corridor, like a chain reaction."

In 1946 Deren published *An Anagram of Ideas on Art, Form, and the Film,* a monograph declaring two major statements: the rejection of symbolism in film, and strong support for independent film after an analysis of industrial and independent filmmaking activities in the United States.

Although *Meshes* remains the most widely seen film of its type, with several of its effects unsurpassed by filmmakers, Deren had been forgotten until recently. Her reputation now enjoys a well-deserved renaissance, for as Rudolf Arnheim eulogized, Deren was one of film's "most delicate magicians."

—Louise Heck-Rabi

DESPERATELY SEEKING SUSAN
USA, 1985
Director: Susan Seidelman

Production: Orion; DeLuxe color; running time: 103 minutes. Released March 1985.

Producers: Sarah Pillsbury and Midge Sanford; **screenplay:** Leora Barish; **assistant directors:** Joel Tuber and David Dreyfuss; **photography:** Edward Lachman, **camera operator:** Francis Kenny; **editor:** Andrew Mondshein; **supervising sound editor:** Maurice Schell; **sound editors:** Peter Odabashian, Mark Rathus, and Lou Graf; **production designer:** Santo Loquasto; **art director:** Speed Hopkins; **music:** Thomas Newman, **music supervisors:** Danny Goldberg and Timothy R. Sexton, **music editor:** Lou Cerborino.

Cast: Rosanna Arquette (*Roberta Glass*); Madonna (*Susan*); Aidan Quinn (*Dez*); Mark Blum (*Gary Glass*); Robert Joy (*Jim*); Laurie Metcalf (*Leslie Glass*); Anna Levine (*Crystal*); Will Patton (*Wayne Noble*); Peter Maloney (*Ian*); Steven Wright (*Larry Stillman DDS*); John Turturro (*Ray*); Anne Carlisle (*Victoria*); José Santana (*Boutique Owner*); Giancarlo Esposito (*Street Vendor*); Richard Hell (*Bruce Meeker*); Rockets Redglare (*Taxi Driver*); Steve Bosh (*Newscaster*); Daisy Bradford (*Daisy*); Annie Golden (*Band Singer*); Richard Edson (*Man with Newspapers*); Ann Magnuson (*Cigarette Girl*); John Lurie (*Neighbour Saxophonist*); Mary Joy; Rosemary Hochschild (*Cocktail Waitresses*); Iris Chacon (*TV Singer*); Victor Argo (*Sergeant Taskal*); Shirley Stoler, J. B. Waters (*Jail Matrons*); Arto Lindsay (*Newspaper Clerk*); Michael R. Chin (*Choy*).

Award: British Academy Award for Best Supporting Actress (Arquette).

Publications

Book

Penley, Constance, *Feminism and Film Theory,* London, 1988.

Articles

Rickey, C., "Where the Girls Are," in *American Film* (Washington, D.C.), January/February 1984.

Hollywood Reporter, 25 March 1985.

Variety (New York), 27 March 1985.

Jaehne, Karen, "In Search of Susan: An Interview with Susan Seidelman," in *Stills* (London), May 1985.

Yakir, D., and others, in *Film Comment* (New York), May/June 1985.

Golden, P., "Susan Seidelman: An Interview," in *Films in Review* (New York), June/July 1985.

Elia, M., in *Séquences* (Montreal), July 1985.

Padroff, J., "Lachman Films *Desperately Seeking Susan,*" in *American Cinematographer* (Los Angeles), July 1985.

Koole, C., "*Desperately Seeking Susan*: Susan Seidelman in Madonna-land," in *Skoop* (Amsterdam), August 1985.

Steinborn, B., in *Filmfaust* (Frankfurt), August/September 1985.

Chevrie, M., in *Cahiers du Cinéma* (Paris), September 1985.

Cook, Pam, in *Monthly Film Bulletin* (London), September 1985.

Root, Jane, "Celine and Julie, Susan and Susan," in *Monthly Film Bulletin* (London), October 1985.

Frauen und Film (Berlin), December 1985.

Stacey, Jackie, "Desperately Seeking Difference," in *Screen* (London), Winter 1987.

* * *

At first glance, the film's plot (bored suburban housewife Roberta, intrigued by an ad in the personal columns, tracks down the free-spirited Susan, gets knocked out, suffers amnesia and believes she *is* Susan) could be read as just another mistaken identity comedy, notable, perhaps, in that its main protagonists are women. Susan Seidelman's film is, however, much more than this. In mainstream Hollywood, where the predominant relationships are either heterosexual or male "buddy" couples, the celebration of a female friendship is remarkable. When it is written, produced, and directed by women and features one of the most important female stars of the 1980s, it becomes highly significant. When, formulated as an art-house feature, it becomes a commercial hit, it is nothing short of momentous.

The film's star, Madonna, was crucial to this success. Little known when originally cast and a superstar when the film was released, she was renowned for her pop videos and witty pastiches of feminine sexuality. Her skill in working in the fleeting video medium and her spectacular yet accessible persona (young women worldwide copied her ragbag glamour) made her the ideal Susan—sexily itinerant and supremely in control. Susan Seidelman has commented that it was Madonna's sense of timing as a singer/dancer that made her perfect for the sassy quick-fire comedy, which owes as much to Howard Hawks as to the more laid-back New York-independent style of film-making used in Seidelman's earlier film *Smithereens*.

Although many of the film's pleasures come from a two-fold desire for Susan (through Roberta's wistful gaze and from our knowledge of the powerful Madonna persona), many contemporary (male) reviewers underplayed Madonna's role, categorizing the film as harmless comedy, comparing Seidelman unfavorably with screwball auteurs such as Hawks and finding the heroines inferior to Katharine Hepburn. While it is true that the film pays homage to earlier classics of the screwball genre, which traditionally gives space to anarchic women, *Desperately Seeking Susan* also broke ground and paved the way for a sequence of modern "yuppie-in-peril" screwballs (for example, *Something Wild, After Hours*)

in which women endangered the lives of straitlaced men. The difference is that this film does not focus on wacky women as a "problem," but on the pleasures and potential of their female anarchy. Seidelman reworks screwball conventions to bring the field of action and narrative into a particularly feminine sphere. It is around questions of femininity and femaleness that the film's special appeal rotates.

Some film theorists recognized in the representation of the women's fascination with each other and in the unabashed feminine arena for action an opportunity to open debates around the mobilization of positive pleasures for the female spectator. In one delightful swoop, the film defiantly challenges the accepted 1970s notion that if "woman as spectacle" is built into the apparatus of mainstream cinema, then the position of the female spectator can be, at best, only ambivalent. Although Seidelman claims her film is not a feminist text, but a film imbued with a female point of view, it offers an alternative to this argument. Its use of style, fashion, popular music, fairy-tale, and fantasy plays with femininity *and* feminism, illuminating them with a much overlooked device—fun. And it is this playfulness that challenges the notion that the female spectator is doomed to remain outside the pleasures offered by mainstream cinema.

One way in which the playfulness operates is by reworking the conventions of the women's picture, a genre which traditionally offers a feminine world as a context for narrative. Instead of constructing a milieu of feminine excess as a locus of neurosis or tragedy, all the emblems of female culture, so frequently scorned in patriarchy, are served up as magnificent spectacle. The sense of a female space, for example, in the ladies' toilet scene or the dressing room of the Magic Club, creates an imaginary world both familiar and glamorous, to be identified with and desired. The pleasures for the female spectator are the recognition not only of Susan's exciting world, but also of Roberta's pink-hued surroundings, beauty parlors, crying at soppy movies, and eating gateau in the middle of the night—not as peripheral concerns, not simply as sites of repression or claustrophobia, but as a context for action and adventure. There is real delight in having frequently derided female pleasures—a love of dressing-up, an all-consuming desire for particular clothes such as the spangled boots and pyramid jacket—served up as legitimate narrative devices. The very motive behind fashion, to put together different images and play visually with identities, translates into an impulse that allows entry into forbidden, exciting worlds so often inaccessible to women.

The closing shot of the film, the front-page newspaper photograph of the women, hands held and raised high, is an image of glorious triumph. It is not only Susan and Roberta who have triumphed. Seidelman, through a female point of view tempered with a sumptuous visual style and comic sense, transforms the feminine world into a feminist world, or, at the very least, a world in which feminists can have fun.

—Samantha Cook

DEUTSCHLAND, BLEICHE MUTTER
(Germany, Pale Mother)
West Germany, 1980
Director: Helma Sanders-Brahms

Production: Helma Sanders-Brahms, Literarisches Colloquium, Westerdeutscher Rundfunk, color, 35mm; running time: 129 minutes. Released February 1980, Berlin.

Deutschland Bleiche Mutter

Producer: Ursula Ludwig; **screenplay:** Helma Sanders-Brahms; **photography:** Jürgen Jürges; **editor:** Elfi Tillack; **sound editors:** Hartmut Eichgrün and Gerhard Jensen; **sound engineers:** Gunther Kortwich and Wolf Dietrich Peters; **art director:** Götz Heymann; **music:** Jürgen Knieper; **costume designer:** Janken Janssen.

Cast: Eva Mattes (*Helene, "Lene"*); Ernst Jacobi (*Hans*); Elisabeth Stepanek (*Hanne*); Angelika Thomas (*Lydia*); Rainer Friedrichsen (*Ulrich*); Gisela Stein (*Tante Ihmchen*); Fritz Lichtenhahn (*Onkel Bertrand*); Anna Sanders, Sonja Lauer, Miriam Lauer (*Anna*).

Publications

Script

Sanders-Brahms, Helma, *Deutschland, bleiche Mutter: Film-Erzahlung,* Hamburg, 1980.

Books

Möhrmann, Renate, *Die Frau mit der Kamera,* Munich, 1980.
Kaes, Anton, *From Hitler to Heimat: The Return of History as Film,* Cambridge, Massachusetts, 1989.

McCormick, Richard W., *Politics of the Self: Feminism and the Postmodern in West German Literature and Film,* Princeton, New Jersey, 1991.
Knight, Julia, *Women and the New German Cinema,* London, 1992.

Articles

Berthommier, Vivian, and Marie-Christine Questerbert, "Cinéma Allemand. Journal de Voyage II. Femmes et Cinéastes a Berlin," in *Cahiers du Cinéma* (Paris), February 1980.
Hiller, Eva, "Mutter und töchter," in *Frauen und Film* (Berlin), June 1980.
Münzberg, Olaf, "Schaudern vor der *bleichen Mutter,*" in *Medium,* July 1980.
Blumenberg, Hans-Christoph, "*Deutschland, bleiche Mutter* von Helma Sanders-Brahms. Ein Brief an Lene," in *Gegenschuss: Texte über Filmemacher und Filme 1980-1983,* Frankfurt, 1984.
Bammer, Angelika, "Through a Daughter's Eyes: Helma Sanders-Brahms' *Germany, Pale Mother,*" in *New German Critique,* Fall 1985.
Kaplan, E. Ann, "The Search for the Mother/Land in Sanders-Brahms's *Germany, Pale Mother,*" in *German Film and Literature: Adaptations and Transformations,* edited by Eric Rentschler, New York, 1986.

Seiter, Ellen, "Women's History, Women's Melodrama: *Deutschland, bleiche Mutter*," in *German Quarterly*, vol. 59.

Hyams, Barbara, "Is the Apolitical Woman at Peace? A Reading of the Fairy Tale in *Germany, Pale Mother*," in *Wide Angle* (Baltimore, Maryland), vol. 10, no. 3, 1988.

* * *

A single German word lightly captures Helma Sanders-Brahms's complex purpose: *Vergangenheitsbewältigung*, "coming to terms with the past," in this case the life of her parents who met in 1939. Her society scarcely encouraged this responsibility; her national cinema offered a thin template for initiating this depiction. Even literature offered few analogies, more often presenting sons as the recorders of their fathers' public history. Sanders-Brahms easily effaces this public/private dichotomy because her topic is wartime, when mothers and daughters routinely enter the public realm and when little is heard of fathers waging war, somewhere distant, and private. The film has two voices of mutual certification, the voice-overs of daughter Anna certifying what we see, and the director who shapes the historical narrative, scrupulously documenting her historical veracity.

Since history is traditionally verbal text—a combination of the general and the particular both literal and figurative, and inherently intertextual—Sanders-Brahms boldly opens her film with words as visual image, a Brecht poem that gives the film its title and its motif of sons who bleed the motherland of courage and integrity. Outside the poem the film reveals the other half of the story: women and mothers as silently complicitous and even actively so.

From the beginning Sanders-Brahms, director and writer, represents National Socialism as a disease of many symptoms simultaneously infecting public and private life. In the first scene, for example, we vividly see its painful effects upon the initial contact between Hans and Lene, Anna's parents-to-be. Correlatively we witness the amused indifference of Hans's Nazi buddy as other, puberty-plagued young Nazis harass Lene, undeterred by Hans's proximity. From the outset people are, at best, half-aware of their behavior. This scene of incipient romance is sullied by the men who serve as history's background rather than its foreground. Filling the foreground are the two women, mother Lene and daughter Anna, who live this history, striving mightily for a moral consciousness that sometimes eludes them.

Living history also specifies an important technical procedure. While the film's narrator is the director, reflecting on her mother's life and her own role in it, the narrator's voice is the director's daughter, continuing the sequence of generational connection. Paradoxically this very personal voice serves to distance the audience from events by creating a sensory disjunction between what we see and what we hear. Thus Sanders-Brahms doubly interrogates the past, both placing herself in her mother's shoes, and effectively asking her own daughter for the criticism that she directs lovingly and critically to her own progenitor.

Through this and other distancing devices the director obliges her audience to read and experience her history as preludes to understanding it. Avoiding easy judgment her camera coolly engages several perspectives. Each member of her family, for example, reads interactions differently. Necessary resolutions of these contradictory views lie with us, the audience, and our complex identifications yield complex conclusions.

Mother and daughter are closest in the middle section, the war period. Very young Anna is exceedingly happy, idyllically so, an infant deriving pleasure from her mother's intense involvement with her. Appropriately self-absorbed Anna remains oblivious to the painful growth and change in circumstances that her mother feels; by Herculean acts of will Lene hides the horrors of the time from her daughter, feeding Anna large doses of joy and delight.

This central third of the film begins with Lene giving birth to Anna during an air raid, which we see and hear in conspicuous cross-cutting. Our perspective is principally Anna's point of view as the pair trek across Germany's snow-shrouded countryside, expelled by bombs from home, from any urban structure. This section interpolates the most documentary footage, shows us more of the larger world, yet we focus most deeply on the mother-daughter relationship that we must read as both public and private, both personal and political as we cannot separate those dimensions from each other at any point in the film.

It is fairly hard to assign to the pigeonhole of realism a film whose first third predates the birth of the memoirist, and whose central third dilates in very adult ways on her infancy. Quite clearly this is a mediated representation of many parts: a daughter's memories and dreams, cultural history, allegory and more. It is best to view the film's structure as designed to approach the complexities of the world that it represents, as a tale told cross-generationally as an illustration, a multifaceted dialogue and rigorous interrogation of realities to which one can perhaps get no closer.

War's end returns mother and daughter to the home, the private sphere where to be sheltered is to be banished. The initially benign Hans now as father is embittered and hostile. In a nominally reconstructed Germany the marriage of Lene and Hans lies slain by the war's depredations, and by the patriarchal ideology that made it possible.

—Arthur G. Robson

DIABOLO MENTHE

(Peppermint Soda)
France, 1977
Director: Diane Kurys

Production: Les Films de l'Alma/Alexandre Films; Eastmancolor, 35mm; running time: 101 minutes. Released December 1977, Paris. Filmed in Paris, and on the Normandy coast.

Producer: Armand Barbault; **executive producer:** Serge Laski; **screenplay:** Diane Kurys; **photography:** Philippe Rousselot; **editor:** Joëlle Van Effenterre; **sound engineers:** Bernard Aubouy and Jean-Louis Ughetto; **sound editor:** Hervé de Luze; **art director:** Bernard Madelenat; **music:** Yves Simon; **costumes:** Thérèse Ripaud.

Cast: Eléonore Klarwein (*Anne Weber*); Odile Michel (*Frédérique Weber*); Anouk Ferjac (*Mme. Weber*); Michel Puterflam (*M. Weber*); Yves Rénier (Philippe); Robert Rimbaud (*M. Gazeau*); Marie-Véronique Maurin (*Muriel Gazau*); Corinne Dacla (*Pascal Carimil*); Coralie Clément (*Perrine Jacquet*); Valérie Stano (*Martine Dubreuil*); Anne Guillard (*Sylvie Le Garrec*); Véronique Vernon (*Evelyne Delacroix*); Françoise Bertin (*Mlle. Sassy*); Arlette Bonnard (*Mme. Poliakoff*); Dora Doll (*Mme. Clou*); Jacques Rispal (*Superintendent*); Jacqueline Boyen (*Mlle. Petitbon*); Tsilla Chelton (*Mme. Colotte*).

Diabolo menthe

Awards: Prix Louis Delluc.

Publications

Books

Lejeune, Paule, *Le Cinéma des femmes,* Paris, 1987.
Quart, Barbara Koenig, *Women Directors: The Emergence of a New Cinema,* Westport, Connecticut, 1988.

Articles

Interview with Diane Kurys, in *Film Français,* December 1977.
Chevallier, Jacques, in *Image et Son* (Paris), February 1978.
Pouillade, Jean-Luc, "Le naturalism souriant," in *Positif* (Paris), April 1978.
Gillett, John, in *Monthly Film Bulletin* (London), August 1980.

Murray, Scott, interview with Diane Kurys, in *Cinema Papers* (Melbourne), August/September 1980.

*   *   *

Diabolo menthe, Diane Kurys's directorial debut, launched the cycle of autobiographical films that to date have formed the central strand of her oeuvre. Drawing on her own life and that of her mother, these films display her strengths as a filmmaker—the charm, humor, and insight, the fresh, unforced naturalism of her style—as well as exploring her central concern with women achieving, and preserving, a sense of identity and self-expression in the teeth of an often repressive society.

Set in 1963-64, *Diabolo menthe* traces a year in the lives of 13-year-old Anne Weber and her 15-year-old sister Frédérique. Their parents (both Jewish) are divorced, and the two girls live with their mother in Paris and attend the local lycée. Each year they spend some weeks with their father on the Normandy coast, and the action of the film is framed between the last day of one such holiday and first day of the next.

The tone of the film—affectionate, but spiced with residual malice—is set by the on-screen dedication: "To my sister, who still hasn't given me back my orange sweater." Anne, the director's surrogate, both adores and resents her elder sister, envying Frédérique her more conventionally attractive looks and the greater savoir faire and success with boys that comes with two years' seniority. The relationship between the two is convincingly volatile: at one moment close and loving, co-conspirators against the adult world; the next spikily at odds, Frédérique turning bossy, Anne acting brattish. The parents are ambiguous figures, too, shown as well-meaning but frequently wrongheaded in their treatment of their daughters.

But the sharpest satire is reserved for the school episodes. Kurys contrived to shoot much of the film at her old lycée, vividly capturing the atmosphere of bleak, echoing corridors and imposed formality. The school comes across as a reactionary, self-satisfied institution, staffed by a fine gallery of monsters: the foul-tempered headmistress; the creepy, malicious janitor; the sadistic art mistress; the eccentric sports mistress in fur coat and turban. This is unashamedly a pupil's-eye view, harking back to Vigo's *Zéro de conduite*; and like Vigo, Kurys instinctively adopts the viewpoint of her young protagonists without condescension or sentimentality.

Working with 300 schoolgirls, none of whom—including those playing her young leads—had ever acted before, she draws from them engagingly immediate and unself-conscious performances. Giggling, gossiping, swapping breathless misinformation on sex ("I think it can get two meters long at least"), and fizzing with youthful ebullience, they scarcely seem to be acting. Altogether *Diabolo menthe* is strikingly assured for a first film, with the confidence that comes from drawing on direct personal experience. As Kurys herself explained: "I knew exactly what I wanted to see on the screen. When you really know what you want you're able to explain it, to put it across to the people around you, the actors and the technicians." Close-ups are rare; scenes play in mid-shots and two-shots, bringing out the links and tensions within groups.

Though the adolescent-rites-of-passage film had long been a French specialty, it had traditionally (as in Truffaut's *Les Quatre cents coups* or Malle's *Le Souffle au coeur*) adopted a male perspective. For the first time, *Diabolo menthe* revealed the female angle. The loose, episodic structure mirrors girls' adolescent experience: the friendships, feuds, and jealousies; the preoccupations with clothes and sex and first menstruation. On its release, the film's success showed how accurately Kurys had captured a universal experience; young audiences in particular identified with her heroines, disregarding the period differences and embracing the underlying affinities.

Diabolo menthe scored a huge hit, becoming the most successful French film of its year and winning the Prix Louis Delluc, French equivalent of an Oscar—the first cinematic debut to be awarded the prize since Malle's *Ascenseur pour l'échafaud* in 1958. Some critics slated the film for triviality, sentimentality, and lack of narrative structure. But reviewers who concentrated—approvingly or otherwise—on the film's undeniable charm missed the undertones of anger and resentment that rescue it from turning saccharine. In particular the episode when Frédérique, encountering anti-Semitic prejudice, takes her first steps toward political action, seethes with tangible indignation. "No politics in the school—especially not the girls!" shouts the outraged janitor, an attitude shared by nearly all the adults including Frédérique's mother. In these scenes Kurys's film, looking back at the early 1960s across the watershed of 1968, foreshadows

that year of upheaval—a political convulsion that would become the subject of her second film, *Cocktail Molotov* (1980).

—Philip Kemp

DILLON, Carmen
British art director

Born: Cricklewood, London, 1908. **Education:** Attended New Hall Convent, Chelmsford, Essex; qualified as architect. **Career:** Actress and designer for amateur dramatics; 1934—assistant to Ralph Brinton, Wembley Studios; then long association with Two Cities and Rank. **Awards:** Academy Award, for *Hamlet,* 1948; Venice Festival prize, for *The Importance of Being Earnest,* 1952.

Films as Art Director

1937 *The Five Pound Man* (Albert Parker)
1938 *Who Goes Next?* (Elvey)
1939 *French without Tears* (Asquith) (asst); *The Mikado* (Schertzinger) (asst)
1940 *Freedom Radio* (*The Voice in the Night*) (Asquith)
1941 *Quiet Wedding* (Asquith)
1942 *Unpublished Story* (French); *The First of the Few* (*Spitfire*) (L. Howard); *Secret Mission* (French)
1943 *The Gentle Sex* (L. Howard); *The Demi-Paradise* (*Adventure for Two*) (Asquith)
1945 *Henry V* (Olivier); *The Way to the Stars* (*Johnny in the Clouds*) (Asquith)
1946 *Carnival* (Haynes); *School for Secrets* (Ustinov)
1947 *White Cradle Inn* (*High Fury*) (French)
1948 *Vice Versa* (Ustinov); *Woman Hater* (T. Young); *Hamlet* (Olivier)
1949 *Cardboard Cavalier* (Forde)
1950 *The Reluctant Widow* (Knowles); *The Woman in Question* (*Five Angles on Murder*) (Asquith); *The Rocking-Horse Winner* (Pelissier)
1951 *The Browning Version* (Asquith)
1952 *The Story of Robin Hood and His Merrie Men* (*The Story of Robin Hood*) (Annakin); *The Importance of Being Earnest* (Asquith); *Meet Me Tonight* (Pelissier)
1953 *The Sword and the Rose* (Annakin); *Rob Roy, the Highland Rogue* (French)
1954 *Doctor in the House* (Thomas); *One Good Turn* (Carstairs)
1955 *Richard III* (Olivier); *Doctor at Sea* (Thomas)
1956 *Simon and Laura* (M. Box); *The Iron Petticoat* (Thomas) *Checkpoint* (Thomas)
1957 *The Prince and the Showgirl* (Olivier); *Miracle in Soho* (Amyes)
1958 *A Tale of Two Cities* (Thomas)
1959 *Sapphire* (Dearden)
1960 *No Kidding* (*Beware of Children*) (Thomas); *Watch Your Stern* (Thomas); *Carry on Constable* (Thomas); *Please Turn Over* (Thomas); *Kidnapped* (Stevenson); *Make Mine Mink* (Asher)
1961 *The Naked Edge* (M. Anderson); *Raising the Wind* (*Roommates*) (Thomas)

1962 *Carry on Cruising* (Thomas); *Twice 'round the Daffodils*
      (Thomas)
1963 *The Iron Maiden* (*The Swingin' Maiden*) (Thomas)
1964 *The Chalk Garden* (Neame)
1965 *The Battle of the Villa Fiorita* (Daves); *The Intelligence Men*
      (*Spylarks*) (Asher)
1966 *Sky, West, and Crooked* (*Gypsy Girl*) (Mills)
1967 *Accident* (Losey)
1968 *A Dandy in Aspic* (A. Mann and Harvey); *Otley* (Clement)
1969 *Sinful Davey* (J. Huston)
1970 *The Rise and Rise of Michael Rimmer* (Billington)
1971 *Catch Me a Spy* (Clement); *The Go-Between* (Losey)
1973 *Lady Caroline Lamb* (Bolt); *A Bequest to the Nation* (*The*
      Nelson Affair) (J. C. Jones)
1974 *Butley* (Pinter)
1975 *In This House of Brede* (Schaefer—for TV); *Love among*
      the Ruins (Cukor—for TV)
1976 *The Omen* (R. Donner)
1977 *Julia* (Zinnemann)
1978 *The Sailor's Return* (Gold)
1979 *The Corn Is Green* (Cukor—for TV)

Publications by Dillon

Article

"The Function of the Art Director," in *Films and Filming* (London),
May 1957.

Publications on Dillon

Articles

Picturegoer (London), 16 July 1949.
Cinema Studio (London), November 1951.
McGillivray, D., "Bequest to the Nation," in *Focus on Film* (London),
Spring 1973.

*   *   *

Carmen Dillon was born in 1908 in London. As did so many art
directors, she originally studied architecture. Dillon worked as a set
dresser and art director on many pictures for Two Cities and Rank,
and for nearly a quarter of a century she was the only woman art
director working in English films.

Early in her career Dillon collaborated with the great British art
directors Paul Sheriff and Roger Furse. She assisted Sheriff on
Olivier's *Henry V*, and the sets of Olivier's *Hamlet* were by Dillon
with design by Furse. These two pictures were very significant in
the history of film design. *Henry V* changed style from a "realistic"
look at an historic (Elizabethan) time, to an historic theatrical setting,
and finally to a re-creation of the style, color, and spatial sense of
medieval illuminated manuscripts. It was a daring and successful
undertaking. As a contrast to the highly colored spectacle of *Henry V*,
Olivier filmed the tragedy of *Hamlet* in black and white. The impression was that of an etching. The design emphasized spaces, with
ominous repeating arches and geometric platforms, giving a sense of
modern minimal theater as well as that of a dark and drafty castle.

Dillon did several historical reconstruction films. *The Importance
of Being Earnest* and *The Go-Between* amply illustrate her skills as a

Carmen Dillon

researcher. In 1977 Dillon worked with Gene Callahan and Willy
Holt on *Julia*. This film had great potential as a costumer. Art Deco
was enjoying a revival and there were enough scenes of the wealthy,
the bohemians, and the decadents for some standard streamlining
and a bit of neon here and there. But the picture had none of that.
Except for a calendar on the wall and the political events taking place
it could have represented any time. This is critical. It gives the film a
timeless meaning that speaks beyond a particular era and style. This
story does not only tell specifically about Julia fighting Nazi atrocities but also how a brave human can stand up against injustice and
evil. It is not just about the author Lillian Hellman and her deep
relationship with a childhood companion, but of the strength of
loving friendships. Furthermore, this film concerns nonmaterialistic
characters who care more about feelings and ideas than decor. Dillon
must convey that tone.

Julia uses clean simple lines. Dillon emphasizes few objects, and
only then with the precision of a still life. Objects, when shown,
have specific relationships to the story. They are never there just for
local color. Again, the sets are painted with the sparsity of a modern
minimalist stage set. Often, particularly in the scenes of Hellman and
Dashiell Hammett, darkness forms a cover. At times it serves as a
protective blanket, at others as a threat of the unknown. Sometimes it
serves for dramatic composition. Light also plays many roles—
exposing, attacking, enlightening. Scene after scene features silhouettes and outlines, lamps and lighting fixtures. Ceilings are shown,
giving a feeling of claustrophobia.

Dillon characterizes Julia's childhood in strongly lit reflective surfaces broadcasting to the viewer the opulent wealth of her family.

There are few objects—the highly polished silver, the crystal chandeliers, the red velvet chairs. The rest of the house is almost bare, even the few hanging paintings blend into the blankness of the walls. The tall arches throughout oppress and intimidate. The staircase at the end of the film serves a similar function. Julia's room, in contrast, feels cozy, an all-white interior which symbolizes purity rather than coldness.

In *Julia* Dillon's free use of space and lighting as key elements in design goes back to her earlier work on *Hamlet.* These elements project inner feelings and serve a purpose other than that of decorative surface trappings. Dillon's versatility allows her to use detail or to eliminate it, in her pursuit of achieving an appropriate narrative effect.

—Edith C. Lee

DÖRRIE, Doris
German director and writer

Born: Hanover, West Germany, 26 May 1955. **Education:** Studied theater at the University of the Pacific in Stockton, California; philosophy, psychology, and semantics at the New School for Social Research in New York; and film and television at the Hochschule für Film und Fernsehen in Munich, where she received a diploma in directing. **Career:** 1976-86—wrote film criticism for *Süddeutsche Zeitung*; 1979-86—directed documentaries for German television; 1983—directed her first feature, *Straight through the Heart*; 1986— won international acclaim for directing *Men....* **Address:** Tengstrasse 16, 8000 Munich 40, Germany. **Agent:** ICM, 40 West 57th Street, New York, NY 10019, U.S.A.

Films as Director and Writer/Co-Writer

1976   *Ob's stürmt oder schneit (Come Rain or Shine)* (co-d)
1977   *Ene, mene, mink* (short)
1978   *Der Erste Walzer (The First Waltz)* (short); *Hättest was Gescheites gelernt* (for TV); *Alt werden in der Fremde*
1979   *Paula aus Portugal*
1980   *Von Romantik keine Spur (No Trace of Romanticism)* (for TV); *Katharina Eiselt*
1981   *Dazwischen (In Between)* (co-d with Reichel—for TV); *Unter Schafen (Among Noisy Sheep)*
1983   *Mitten ins Herz (Straight through the Heart)* (for TV)
1985   *Im Innern des Wals (In the Belly of the Whale)*
1986   *Männer... (Men...)*; *Paradies (Paradise)*
1987   *Ich und Er (Me and Him)*
1989   *Geld (Money)*; *Love in Germany*
1991   *Happy Birthday Türke! (Happy Birthday!)*
1993   *What Can It Be*
1994   *Keiner Liebt Mich (Nobody Loves Me)*

Other Films

1977   *Der Hauptdarsteller* (Hauff) (ro)
1984   *King Kongs Faust* (Stadler) (ro)
1987   *Wann—Wenn Nicht Jetzt?* (Juncker) (sc)

Publications by Dörrie

Books

Was wollen sie von mir?: und 15 andere Geschichten, Zurich, 1987; published as *What Do You Want from Me?: And Fifteen Other Stories,* translated by John E. Woods, New York, 1991.
Liebe, Schmerz und das ganze verdammte Zeug: vier Geschichten, Zurich, 1989; published as *Love, Pain and the Whole Damn Thing: Four Stories,* translated by John E. Woods, New York, 1989.
Der Mann meiner Träume: Erzählung, Zurich 1991.
Für immer und ewig: enie Art Reigen, Zurich, 1991.
With Volker Wach, *Love in Germany: Deutsche Paare im Gespräch mit Doris Dörrie,* Zurich, 1992.
Bin ich schön: Erzählungen, Zurich, 1994.
Samsara: Erzählungen, Zurich, 1996.

Articles

Interview with Scott Bradfield, in *Elle* (New York), June 1991.
Interview in *Short Story* (Cedar Falls, Iowa/Brownsville, Texas), Fall 1994.

Publications on Dörrie

Books

Angier, Carole, "Monitoring Conformity: The Career of Doris Dörrie," in *Women and Film: A Sight and Sound Reader,* edited by Pam Cook and Philip Dodd, Philadelphia, 1993.
Foster, Gwendolyn Audrey, *Women Film Directors: An International Bio-Critical Dictionary,* Westport, Connecticut, 1995.

Articles

Pally, Marcia, "Open Dörrie," in *Film Comment* (New York), September/October 1986.
Diehl, Siegfried, "Doris Dörrie: The Women behind *Men...*," in *World Press Review,* October 1986.
Root, Jane, "*In the Belly of the Whale* and Sharing Flats with Men: Doris Dörrie Discusses Her Researches with Jane Root," in *Monthly Film Bulletin* (London), November 1986.
Haskell, Molly, "Doris Dörrie: More Realist than Feminist," in *Vogue* (New York), December 1986.

* * *

Doris Dörrie's most consistent cinematic themes are sexual politics and the chasms existing between men and women. In her films, it is almost as if the opposite sexes have evolved from different species. Women are looking for emotional honesty and sexual pleasure in relationships, and attempt to connect with men in what are fated to be hapless, luckless searches for everlasting love. Men, on the other hand, are emotionally unavailable. They are obsessed with the power of their sex organs, yet become sexually unresponsive once they are married (or, for that matter, regularly sharing the same bed with the woman they have so ardently pursued). Dörrie's heroines may be unable to break through to the men in their midst, but they are not perfect either. They might be flaky or self-absorbed, and this adds resonance to her work. Furthermore, Dörrie's films are consistently offbeat. Her characters in the best of them, while existing in real worlds and facing genuine emotional dilemmas, respond to situations in altogether humorous, original, and unusual ways.

Men..., Dörrie's biggest hit to date, is a razor-sharp feminist satire. It is a farcical portrait of the manner in which a pompous middle-class married man responds upon learning that he is being cheated on by his sexually ignored wife. By having this affair, she has struck a blow for independence after years of devotion to a womanizing husband. An outlandish scenario unfolds, involving the cuckold befriending his wife's lover and transforming him into a clone of himself, knowing full well that his wife will become bored. *Men...* is an astute portrayal of the casual attitudes many men have toward women and the manner in which men view each other, all filtered through the sensibilities of a woman writer/director.

Unfortunately, Dörrie has been unable to repeat the international box-office success and win the critical raves achieved by *Men... Me and Him,* her follow-up to *Men...,* was a major let-down: a stupefyingly unfunny parody—based, no less, on a novel by Alberto Moravia—about an architect whose penis begins offering him guidance on how to live his life. In *In the Belly of the Whale* and *Paradise,* Dörrie repeats the plot structure of *Men...*: a third party comes to play a key role in a less-than-sound two-person, opposite-sex familial relationship. The cornerstone of *In the Belly of the Whale* is the sadomasochistic connection between a 15-year-old girl and her policeman father. The girl runs away, in search of her mother (who also was physically abused by her father), and becomes involved with a young man who previously had conflicted with the father. *Paradise* is the story of a married couple who are more concerned with their hobbies and professions than with each other; furthermore, the husband is disinterested in satisfying the wife sexually. The third party here is the wife's former schoolmate.

Men..., however, is far from Dörrie's lone artistic success. *Straight through the Heart,* her debut feature (after working for German television and making shorts and documentaries), is a sharply observed exploration of the relationship between a pair of lonely neurotics: a 20-year-old woman seeking her identity and a reclusive middle-aged dentist. While the latter is willing to pay the former to move in with him, he offers her no companionship; he is interested solely in a lively female presence in his life. She becomes psychologically connected to him, but is unsuccessful in her attempt to make him love her.

In *Happy Birthday, Türke!,* an entertaining noirish detective film (as well as Dörrie's one major thematic departure), the filmmaker touches on the issue of ethnic identity. It is the story of a Turkish-born private eye who was raised by German parents and speaks only German; as a result, he is mistrusted by the Turkish community and subjected to ethnic slurs by Germans. He is hired by a Turkish woman to locate her missing husband, and becomes immersed in a scenario involving murder, prostitution, and police corruption.

Nobody Loves Me is a quirky chronicle of the trials of a lonely, death-obsessed airport security officer who is about to turn 30 and senses that life is passing her by. She declares she does not need a man, but still is desperate to find one. Her gay next-door neighbor (who is a psychic, as well as her kindred spirit) declares that she momentarily will meet her perfect love match. Could he be the new manager of their apartment building, whose primary interests are seducing attractive blonds and collecting the compensation to be gained by redoing the building into an extravagant living space?

In the end, Dörrie's heroine is left only with the companionship of her neighbor. One of the points of *Nobody Loves Me* is that, within the framework of heterosexual relations, it nearly is impossible for a man and a woman to be friends. In fact, the only male who can express compassion and remain loyal to a woman is a gay male; the emotional honesty that exists between the heroine and her neighbor is able to flourish because of the absence of sexual expectation.

Over the years, the heterosexual men in Dörrie's films have not changed. But the women have. The heroines in *Straight through the Heart* and *Nobody Loves Me* may be unsuccessful in their quests for love. In the former, the result is tragedy, while in the latter (which was made a decade later), the heroine undergoes a transformation, becoming less self-indulgent and more independent. This is her triumph, and it is one that reflects the evolution of Dörrie's view of the plight and fate of women.

—Rob Edelman

DULAC, Germaine
French director

Born: Charlotte Elisabeth Germaine Saisset-Schneider in Amiens, France, 17 November 1882. **Family:** Married Marie-Louis Albert Dulac, 1905 (divorced 1920). **Career:** 1909-13—writer and editor for feminist journal *La Française;* 1914—offered position as camerawoman on *Caligula* by actress friend Stacia de Napierkowska; formed production company with husband and scenarist Irène Hillel-Erlanger; 1915—directed first film, *Les Soeurs enemies;* 1921—traveled to United States to observe production techniques; from 1922—general secretary of Ciné-Club de France; 1930s—directed newsreels for Gaumont; formed production company, Delia Film. **Died:** In Paris, July 1942.

Films as Director

1915   *Les Soeurs enemies*
1916   *Géo le mystérieux; Vénus Victrix, Dans l'ouragan de la vie*
1917   *Ames de fous* (+ sc)
1918   *Le Bonheur des autres*
1919   *La Fête espagnole; La Cigarette* (+ co-sc)
1920   *Malencontre; La Belle dame sans merci*
1921   *La Mort du soleil*
1922   *Werther* (incomplete)
1923   *La Souriante Madame Beudet (The Smiling Madame Beudet); Gossette*
1924   *Le Diable dans la ville*
1925   *Ame d'artiste* (+ co-sc); *La Folie des vaillants*
1926   *Antoinette Sabrier*
1927   **La Coquille et le clergyman** (*The Seashell and the Clergyman*); *L'Invitation au voyage; Le Cinéma au service de l'histoire*
1928   *La Princesse Mandane; Disque 927; Thèmes et variations; Germination d'un haricot*
1929   *Etude cinégraphique sur une arabesque*

Other Films

1928   *Mon Paris* (Guyot) (supervision)
1932   *Le Picador* (Jacquelux) (supervision)

Publications by Dulac

Book

Écrits sur le cinéma: 1919-1937, Paris, 1994.

Articles

"Un Article? Mais que faut-il prouver?" in *Le Film* (Paris), 16 October 1919.

"Aux amis du cinéma," address in *Cinémagazine* (Paris), 19 December 1924.

"L'Art des nuances spirituelles," in *Cinéa-Ciné pour tous* (Paris), January 1925.

"Du sentiment à la ligne," in *Schémas,* no. 1, 1927.

"Les Esthètiques, les entraves, la cinégraphie intégrale," in *L'Art cinématographique,* Paris, 1927.

"Sur le cinéma visuel," in *Le Rouge et le noir* (Paris), July 1928.

"Jouer avec les bruits," in *Cinéa-Ciné pour tous* (Paris), 15 August 1929.

"Das Wesen des Films: Die Visuelle Idee," and "Das Kino der Avantgarde," in *Frauen und Film* (Berlin), October 1984.

Publications on Dulac

Books

Heck-Rabi, Louise, *Women Filmmakers: A Critical Reception,* Metuchen, New Jersey, 1984.

Buchsbaum, Jonathan, *Cinema Engage: Film in the Popular Front,* Urbana, Illinois, 1988.

Flitterman-Lewis, Sandy, *To Desire Differently: Feminism and the French Cinema,* Chicago, 1990.

Mayne, Judith, *The Woman at the Keyhole: Feminism and Women's Cinema,* Bloomington, Indiana, 1990.

Acker, Ally, *Reel Women: Pioneers of the Cinema, 1896 to the Present,* New York, 1991.

Foster, Gwendolyn Audrey, *Women Film Directors: An International Bio-Critical Dictionary,* Westport, Connecticut, 1995.

Articles

Obituary, in *New York Times,* 23 July 1942.

Ford, Charles, biography in *Anthologie du cinéma* (Paris), no. 31, January 1968.

Cornwell, Regina, "Maya Deren and Germaine Dulac: Activists of the Avant-Garde," in *Film Library Quarterly* (New York), Winter 1971/72.

Van Wert, W., "Germaine Dulac: First Feminist Filmmaker," in *Women and Film* (Santa Monica, California), vol. 1, nos. 5-6, 1974.

Dozoretz, Wendy, "Dulac versus Artaud," in *Wide Angle* (Athens, Ohio), vol. 3, no. 1, 1979.

Dozoretz, Wendy, and Sandy Flitterman, in *Wide Angle* (Athens, Ohio), vol. 5, no. 3, 1983.

Flitterman, Sandy, "Theorizing the 'Feminine': Women as the Figure of Desire in *The Seashell and the Clergyman,*" in *Wide Angle* (Athens, Ohio), vol. 6, no. 3, 1984.

Serra, R., "La prima scrittura femminile del cinema," in *Cinema Nuovo* (Bari), August/October 1984.

Tol, I., "Films van Germaine Dulac," in *Skrien* (Amsterdam), Winter 1985-86.

*   *   *

Before becoming a film director, Germaine Dulac had studied music, was interested in photography, and had written for two feminist journals—all of which played a role in her development as a filmmaker. There were three phases to her filmmaking career: in commercial production, in the avant-garde, and in newsreels. In addition, filmmaking was only one phase of her film career; she also was prominent as a theorist and promoter of the avant-garde film, and as an organizer of the French film unions and the ciné-club movement. The French historian Charles Ford wrote in *Femmes Cinéastes* that Dulac was the "heart" of the avant-garde in France, that without her there would have been no avant-garde. Her role in French film history has been compared to that of Maya Deren in the United States three decades later.

Dulac learned the rudiments of filmmaking by assisting a friend who was making a film in 1914. The following year she made her first film, *Les Soeurs enemies,* which was distributed by Pathé. It was the ideal time for a woman to enter commercial production, since many men had been called into the army. After directing several other conventional story films, Dulac became more and more drawn to the avant-garde cinema, which she defined in 1927 as "lines, surfaces, volumes, evolving directly without contrivance, in the logic of their forms, stripped of representational meaning, the better to aspire to abstraction and give more space to feelings and dreams—INTEGRAL CINEMA."

It is generally reported that Dulac was introduced to the French film avant-garde movement through her friendship with Louis Delluc; but Ester Carla de Miro claims that it was in fact through Dulac that he became involved in film. Delluc wrote that Dulac's first film was worth "more than a dozen of each of her colleagues.... But the cinema is full of people ... who cannot forgive her for being an educated woman ... or for being a woman at all."

Dulac's best-known and most impressive film (of the few that have been seen outside France) is *The Smiling Madame Beudet,* based on a play by André Obey. It depicts the life and dreams of a small-town housewife married to a coarse, if not repulsive, businessman. The film created a sensation in its day. Dulac succeeded with what was, at the time, signal originality in expressing by pictorial means the atmosphere and implications of this study of domestic conflict.

Showings of *The Seashell and the Clergyman,* based on an original screenplay by Antonin Artaud, have generally been accompanied by program notes indicating Artaud's outrage at Dulac's "feminized" direction. Yet as P. Adams Sitney points out in his introduction to *The Avant-Garde Film,* Artaud praised the actors and thanked Dulac for her interest in his script in an essay entitled "Cinema et l'abstraction." (Wendy Dozoretz has pointed out that the protest aimed against Dulac at the film's Paris opening in 1928 was based on a misunderstanding; at least one protester, Georges Sadoul, later said he had thought he was protesting against Artaud.)

At the other end of the cinema spectrum, Dulac began to use time-lapse cinematography to reveal the magical effects of tiny plants emerging from the soil with leaf after leaf unfolding and stretching to the sun. "Here comes Germaine Dulac and her lima bean," became a popular joke among film-club devotees, a joke that did not exclude admiration.

The last decade of Dulac's life was spent directing newsreels for Gaumont. She died in 1942, during the German occupation. Charles Ford, who has collected her articles, indicates that she expressed ideas in "clear and accessible language" which others often set forth "in hermetic formulas." One American writer, Stuart Liebman, sums up the opposing view: "Despite their undeniable importance for the film culture of the 1920s, the backward-looking character of Dulac's film theory, constituted by her nostalgia for the aesthetic discourse of the past, both defines and delimits our interest in her theoretical contributions today." The final assessment of Germaine Dulac's life and work as filmmaker and theorist may depend on the arrival of a well-documented biography, and greater access to all her writings (some short pieces are now available in English translations) and all her existing films.

—Cecile Starr

DURAS, Marguerite
French director and writer

Born: Marguerite Donnadieu in Giadinh, French Indo-China, 2 April 1914. **Education:** Educated in mathematics, law and political science at the Sorbonne, Paris. **Career:** 1943—published first novel, *Les Impudents*; subsequently novelist, journalist and playwright; 1966—directed first film, *La Musica*. **Awards:** Prix Goncourt for novel *L'Amant*, 1984, Ritz Paris Hemingway, Paris, 1986. **Died:** In Paris, 3 March 1996.

Films as Director

1966   *La Musica* (co-d with Seban, sc)
1969   *Détruire, dit-elle* (*Destroy, She Said*) (+ sc)
1971   *Jaune le soleil* (+ pr, co-ed, sc, from her novel *Abahn, Sabana, David*)
1972   *Nathalie Granger* (+ sc, music)
1974   *La Femme du Ganges* (*Woman of the Ganges*) (+ sc)
1975   ***India Song*** (+ sc, voice)
1976   *Des journées entières dans les arbres* (*Days in the Trees*) (+ sc), *Son nom de Venises dans Calcutta désert* (+ sc)
1977   *Baxter, Vera Baxter* (+ sc); *Le Camion* (*The Truck*) (+ sc, ro)
1978   *Le Navire Night* (+ sc)
1978/79 *Aurélia Steiner* (4-film series): *Cesarée* (1978) (+ sc); *Les Mains négatives* (1978) (+ sc); *Aurélia Steiner—Melbourne* (1979) (+ sc); *Aurélia Steiner—Vancouver* (1979) (+ sc)
1981   *Agatha et les lectures limitées* (*Agatha*) (+ sc)
1983   *Il Dialogo di Roma* (doc) (+ sc)
1985   *Les Enfants* (*The Children*)

Other Films

1958   *La Diga sul Pacifico* (*This Angry Age*; *The Sea Wall*) (Clémént) (st only)
1959   *Hiroshima mon amour* (Resnais) (sc)
1960   *Moderato Cantabile* (P. Brook) (sc, co-adapt from her novel)
1961   *Une Aussi longue absence* (*The Long Absence*) (Colpi) (co-sc from her novel)
1964   *Nuit noire, Calcutta* (Karmitz) (short) (sc)
1965   "Les rideaux blancs" (Franju) episode of *Der Augenblick des Friedens* (*Un Instant de la paix*) (for W. German TV) (sc); *Mademoiselle* (Richardson)
1966   *10:30 P.M. Summer* (*Dix heures et demie du soir en été*) (Dassin) (co-sc uncredited, from her novel); *La Voleuse* (Chapot) (sc, dialogue)
1967   *The Sailor from Gibraltar* (Richardson) (st only)
1992   *The Lover* (Annaud) (st only)

Publications by Duras

Screenplays

Hiroshima mon amour, Paris, 1959.
Moderato Cantabile, with Gérard Jarlot and Peter Brook, 1960.
Une Aussi longue absence, with Gérard Jarlot, Paris, 1961.
La Musica, Paris, 1966.
Les rideaux blancs, Paris, 1966.
10:30 P.M. Summer, with Jules Dassin, Paris, 1966.
Détruire, dit-elle, Paris, 1969; as *Destroy, She Said,* New York, 1970.
Jaune le soleil, Paris, 1971.
Nathalie Granger, suivi de La Femme du Gange, Paris, 1973.
India Song—texte—theatre—film, Paris, 1975; as *India Song,* New York, 1976.
Des journées entières dans les arbres, Paris, 1976.
Son Nom de Venises dans Calcutta desert, Paris, 1976.
Le Camion, Paris, 1977.
Le Navire Night, Césarée, Les Mains négatives, Aurélia Steiner, Paris, 1979.
Vera Baxter; ou, Les Plages de l'Atlantique, Paris, 1980.
Agatha, Paris, 1981.
Les Enfants, Paris, 1985.

Fiction

Les Impudents, Paris, 1943.
La Vie tranquille, Paris, 1944.
Un Barrage contre le Pacifique, Paris, 1950; as *The Sea Wall,* New York, 1952; as *A Sea of Troubles,* London, 1953.
Le Marin de Gibraltar, Paris, 1952; as *The Sailor from Gibraltar,* London and New York, 1966.
Les Petits Chevaux de Tarquinia, Paris, 1953; as *The Little Horses of Tarquinia,* London, 1960.
Des journées entières dans les arbres, Paris, 1954; as *Whole Days in the Trees,* New York, 1981.
Le Square, Paris, 1955.
Moderato Cantabile, Paris, 1958, and New York, 1987.
Dix heures et demi du soir en été, Paris, 1960; as *Ten-Thirty on a Summer Night,* London, 1962.
L'Après-midi de Monsieur Andesmas, Paris, 1962; as *The Afternoon of Monsieur Andesmas,* London, 1964.
Le Ravissement de Lol V. Stein, Paris, 1964; as *The Ravishing of Lol V. Stein,* New York, 1967; as *The Rapture of Lol V. Stein,* London, 1967.
Le Vice-consul, Paris, 1966; as *The Vice-Consul,* London, 1968, New York, 1987.
L'Amante anglaise, Paris, 1967, New York, 1968.
Abahn, Sabana, David, Paris, 1970.
Ah! Ernesto, with Bernard Bonhomme, Paris, 1971.
L'Amour, Paris, 1971.
La Maladie de la mort, Paris, 1983; as *The Malady of Death,* New York, 1986.
L'Amant, Paris, 1984; as *The Lover,* New York, 1985.
Les Yeux bleus cheveux noirs, Paris, 1987; as *Blue Eyes, Black Hair,* London and New York, 1988.
Emily L., Paris, 1987, New York, 1989.

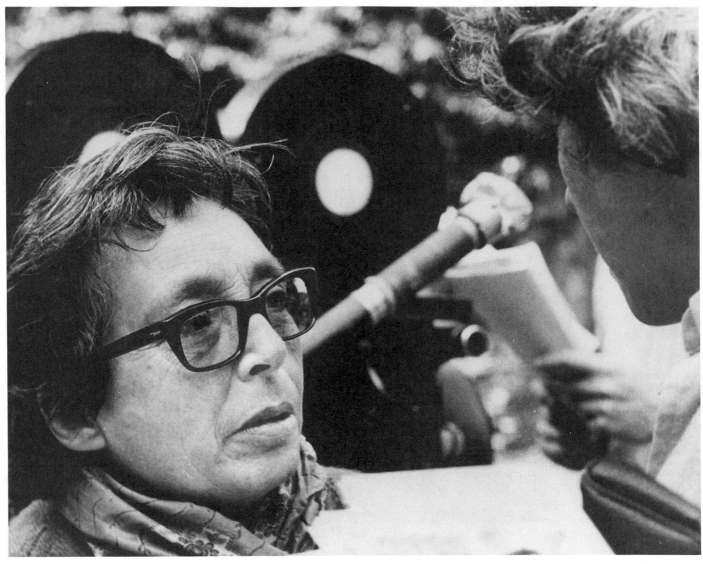

Marguerite Duras

Plays

Théâtre 1 (includes *Les Eaux et forets, Le Square, La Musica*), Paris, 1965.
Théâtre 2 (includes *Susanna Andler; Yes, peut-être; Le Shaga; Des journées entières dans les arbres; Un Homme est venu me voir*), Paris, 1968.
L'Homme assis dans le couloir, Paris, 1980.
L'Homme Atlantique, Paris, 1982.
Savannah Bay, Paris, 1982.
The Square, Edinburgh, 1986.
Yes, peut-être, Edinburgh, 1986.

Other Books

Les Parleuses, with Xaviere Gauthier, Paris, 1974.
Étude sur l'oeuvre littéraire, théâtrale, et cinématographique, with Jacques Lacan and Maurice Blanchot, Paris, 1976.
Territoires du féminin, with Marcelle Marini, Paris, 1977.

Les Lieux de Duras, with Michelle Porte, Paris, 1978.
L'Été 80, Paris, 1980.
Outside: Papiers d'un jour, Paris, 1981, Boston 1986.
The War: A Memoir, New York, 1986.
The Physical Side, London, 1990.

Articles

"Conversation with Marguerite Duras," with Richard Roud, in *Sight and Sound* (London), Winter 1959/60.
"Marguerite Duras en toute liberté," interview with F. Dufour, in *Cinéma* (Paris), April 1972.
"Du livre au film," in *Image et Son* (Paris), April 1974.
"*India Song,* a Chant of Love and Death," interview with F. Dawson, in *Film Comment* (New York), November/December 1975.
"*India Song* and Marguerite Duras," interview with Carlos Clarens, in *Sight and Sound* (London), Winter 1975/76.
Interview with J.-C. Bonnet and J. Fieschi, in *Cinématographe* (Paris), November 1977.

"Les Yeux verts," special issue written and edited by Duras, of *Cahiers du Cinéma* (Paris), June 1980.

Interview with D. Fasoli, in *Filmcritica* (Rome), June 1981.

Interview with A. Grunert, in *Filmfaust* (Frankfurt), February/March 1982.

"The Places of Marguerite Duras," interview with M. Porte, in *Enclitic* (Minneapolis), Spring 1983.

Interview with P. Bonitzer, C. Tesson, and Serge Toubiana, in *Cahiers du Cinéma* (Paris), July/August 1985.

Interview with Jean-Luc Godard, in *Cinéma* (Paris), 30 December 1987.

"The Life and Loves of Marguerite Duras, interview with Leslie Garis, in *New York Times Magazine,* 20 October 1991.

Publications on Duras

Books

Bernheim, N.-L., *Marguerite Duras tourne un film,* Paris, 1976.

Ropars-Wuillcumier, Marie-Claire, *La Texte divisé,* Paris, 1981.

Trastulli, Daniela, *Dalla parola all imagine: Viaggio nel cinema di Marguerite Duras,* Geneva, 1982.

Borgomano, Madeleine, *L'Écriture filmique de Marguerite Duras,* Paris, 1985.

Brossard, Jean-Pierre, editor, *Marguerite Duras: Cinéaste, écrivain,* La Chaux-de-Fonde, 1985.

Guers-Villate, Yvonne, *Continuité/discontinuité de l'oeuvre Durassienne,* Brussels, 1985.

Fernandes, Marie-Pierre, *Travailler avec Duras: La musica deuxième,* Paris, 1986.

Sclous, Trista, *The Other Woman: Feminism and Femininity in the Work of Marguerite Duras,* New Haven, Connecticut, 1988.

Acker, Ally, *Reel Women: Pioneers of the Cinema, 1896 to the Present,* New York, 1991.

Vircondelet, Alain, *Duras,* Paris, 1991.

Foster, Gwendolyn Audrey, *Women Film Directors: An International Bio Critical Dictionary,* Westport, Connecticut, 1995.

Harvey, Robert, *Marguerite Duras: A Bio-Bibliography,* Westport, Connecticut, 1997.

Articles

Gollub, Judith, "French Writers Turned Film Makers," in *Film Heritage* (New York), Winter 1968/69.

"Reflections in a Broken Glass," in *Film Comment* (New York), November/December 1975.

Lakeland, M. J., "Marguerite Duras in 1977," in *Camera Obscura* (Berkeley), Fall 1977.

Van Wert, W. F., "The Cinema of Marguerite Duras: Sound and Voice in a Closed Room," in *Film Quarterly* (Berkeley), Fall 1979.

Seni, N., "Wahrnehungsformen von Zeit und Raum am Beispiel der Filme von Marguerite Duras und Chantal Akerman," in *Frauen und Film* (Berlin), September 1979.

Andermatt, V., "Big Mach (on the truck)," in *Enclitic* (Minneapolis), Spring 1980.

"Marguerite Duras à l'action," in *Positif* (Paris), July/August 1980.

Lyon, E., "Marguerite Duras: Bibliography/Filmography," in *Camera Obscura* (Berkeley), Fall 1980.

Murphy, C. J., "The Role of Desire in the Films of Marguerite Duras," in *Quarterly Review of Film Studies* (Pleasantville, New York), Winter 1982.

Fedwik, P., "Marguerite Duras: Feminine Field of Nostalgia," in *Enclitic* (Minneapolis), Fall 1982.

Sarrut, B., "Marguerite Duras: Barrages against the Pacific," in *On Film* (Los Angeles), Summer 1983.

Murphy, C. J., "New Narrative Regions: The Role of Desire in the Films and Novels of Marguerite Duras," in *Literature Film Quarterly* (Salisbury, Maryland), April 1984.

Le Masson, H., "La voix tatouee," in *Cahiers du Cinéma* (Paris), January 1985.

McWilliams, D., "Aesthetic Tripling: Marguerite Duras's *Le Navire Night,*" in *Literature Film Quarterly* (Salisbury, Maryland), January 1986.

Holmlund, Christine Ann, "Displacing Limits of Difference: Gender, Race, and Colonialism in Edward Said and Homi Bhabha's Therorctical Models and Marguerite Duras's Experimental Films," in *Quarterly Review of Film and Video* (Pleasantville, New York), vol. 13, nos. 1-3, 1991.

Shields, Brooke, "Duras, Mon Amour," in *Harper's Bazaar* (New York), September 1992.

Obituary, in *New York Times,* 4 March 1996.

Obituary, in *Time* (New York), 18 March 1996.

*   *   *

As a writer, Marguerite Duras's work is identified, along with that of such authors as Alain Robbe-Grillet and Jean Cayrol, with the tradition of the New Novel. Duras began working in film as a screenwriter, with an original script for Alain Resnais's first feature, *Hiroshima mon amour.* She subsequently wrote a number of film adaptations from her novels. She directed her first film, *La Musica,* in 1966. If *Hiroshima mon amour* remains her best-known work in cinema, her later films have won widespread praise for the profound challenge they offer to conventional dramatic narrative.

The nature of narrative and the potential contained in a single text are major concerns of Duras's films. Many of her works have appeared in several forms, as novels, plays, and films. This not only involves adaptations of a particular work, but also extends to cross-referential networks that run through her texts. The film *Woman of the Ganges* combines elements from three novels—*The Ravishing of Lol V. Stein, The Vice-Consul,* and *L'Amour. India Song* was initially written as a play, taking characters from *The Vice-Consul* and elaborating on the structure of external voices developed in *Woman of the Ganges. India Song* was made as a film in 1975, and its verbal track was used to generate a second film, *Son nom de Venises dans Calcutta désert.*

This process of transformation suggests that all works are "in progress," inherently subject to being reconstructed. This is partly because Duras's works are more concerned with the quality or intensity of experience than with events per se. The films present narrative rather than a linear, unambiguous sequence of events. In *Le Camion,* two characters, played by Gérard Depardieu and Duras, sit in a room as the woman describes a movie about a woman who hitches a ride with a truck driver and talks with him for an hour and 20 minutes. This conversation is intercut with scenes of a truck driving around Paris, and stopping for a female hitchhiker (with Depardieu as the driver, and Duras as the hitchhiker). Thus, the verbal description of a potential film is juxtaposed by images of what that film might be.

An emphasis on the soundtrack is also a crucial aspect of Duras's films; her verbal texts are lyrical and are as important as the images. In *India Song,* sound and image function contrapuntally, and the audience must actively assess the relation between them, reading across the body of the film, noting continuities and disjunctions. The verbal text often refers in past tense to events and characters on screen, as the viewer is challenged to figure out the chronology of events described and depicted—which name on the soundtrack corresponds to which actor, whether the voices belong to on- or off-screen characters, and so forth. In this way the audience participates in the search for a story, constructing possible narratives.

As minimal as they are, Duras's narratives are partially derived from melodrama, focusing on relations between men and women, the nature or structure of desire, and colonialism and imperialism in both literal and metaphoric terms. In pursuing these issues through nonconventional narrative forms, and shifting the burden of discovering meaning to the audience, Duras's films provide an alternative to conventional ways of watching movies. Her work is seen as exemplifying a feminine writing practice that challenges the patriarchal domination of classical narrative cinema. In an interview, Duras said, "I think the future belongs to women. Men have been completely dethroned. Their rhetoric is stale, used up. We must move on to the rhetoric of women, one that is anchored in the organism, in the body." It is this new rhetoric, a new way of communicating, that Duras strived for in her films.

—M. B. White

ELEK, Judit
Hungarian director

Born: Budapest, 10 November 1937. **Education:** Graduated from
Hungary's Academy of Theater and Film Arts. **Career:** Early 1960s—
became a member of the Béla Balázs Studio of young Hungarian
filmmakers, a workshop for experimental film; 1963—directed her
first documentary, *Encounter*; 1968—directed her first fiction feature, *Island on the Continent*; **Awards:** Chevalier de l'Ordre des
Arts et des Lettres, 1987; Ecumenical Prize, Montreal World Film
Festival, for *Memoirs of a River,* 1988; main prize, Salerno Film
Festival, for *Awakening,* 1994.

Films as Director

1963   *Találkozás (Encounter)* (short)
1966   *Kastélyok lakói (Occupants of Manor Houses; Tenants of
        Castles; Inhabitants of Castles)* (short) (+ sc)
1967   *Meddig él az ember? (How Long Does Man Matter?)*
1968   *Sziget a szárazföldön (Island on the Continent; The Lady
        from Constantinople)*
1971   *Találkozunk 1972-ben (We'll Meet in 1972)* (short)
1974   *Istenmezején 1972-73 (A Hungarian Village)*
1975   *Egyszerű történet (A Simple Story; A Commonplace Story)*
        (+ sc)
1980   *Majd holnap (Maybe Tomorrow); Martinovics* (for TV)
1983   *Mária-nap (Maria's Day)*
1988   *Tutajosok (Memoirs of a River; The Raftsmen)* (+ sc)
1994   *Ébredés (Awakening)* (+ sc, ed)
1996   *Mondani a mondhatatlant: Elie Wiesel üzenete (To Speak the
        Unspeakable: The Message of Elie Wiesel)* (+ sc, ed)

Other Film

1976   *Árvácska* (G. Mészáros and Ranódy) (sc)

Publications by Elek

Articles

Interview with J. L. Heijs, in *Skrien* (Amsterdam), September
    1976.
Interview with F. Aude, in *Positif* (Paris), January 1982.
With G. Petho, "*Mária-nap,*" in *Filmkultura* (Budapest), no. 6,
    1983.
With G. Petho, "*Mária-nap,*" in *Filmkultura* (Budapest), no. 1,
    1984.
"A bengali vandor," in *Filmvilag* (Budapest), no. 2, 1987.

Publications on Elek

Books

Balski, Grzegorz, *Directory of Eastern European Film-Makers and
    Film, 1945-1991,* Westport, Connecticut, 1992.
Foster, Gwendolyn Audrey, *Women Film Directors: An International
    Bio-Critical Dictionary,* Westport, Connecticut, 1995.
Burns, Bryan, *World Cinema: Hungary,* Trowbridge, England, 1996.

Articles

Aude, F., "Le camera directe de Judit Elek: *Un village hongrois* et *Un
    simple histoire,*" in *Positif* (Paris), January 1979
Ember, M., "Tarlatvezetes Elek Judit filmjeirol," in *Filmkultura*
    (Budapest), May/June 1980.
"Le cinema avec ses si," in *Cahiers du Cinema* (Paris), Summer 1984.
"Filmrendezok valaszolnak," in *Filmkultura* (Budapest), no. 8, 1985.
"Svetovbi reziseri: Judit Elek, Bruce Beresford," in *Film a Doba*
    (Prague), February 1986.
Csepeli, G., "Europa kozepe," in *Filmvilag* (Budapest), no. 3, 1989.
Berczes, L., "Nem mas," in *Filmvilag* (Budapest), no. 2, 1995.
Mandelbaum, Jacques, "Sur les pas d'Elie Wiesel, de Sighet a
    Auschwitz," in *Monde* (Paris), May 1996.
Bori, Erzsebet, "Torte à la Russe: Ibolya Fekete (*Az Apokalipszis
    gyermekei, Bolshe Vita*), Judit Elek (*Mondani a mondhatatlant*) and
    Peter Gothar (*Hagyjallogva Vaszka*)," in *Hungarian Quarterly*
    (Budapest), Winter 1996.

* * *

The films of Judit Elek serve as textbook examples of art as a
reflection of personal experience and political/humanist commitment.
The works of many of our foremost contemporary filmmakers are
autobiographical: In his films, Woody Allen consistently focuses on
the neuroses of middle-class Jewish New Yorkers whose childhood
insecurities and Brooklyn roots forever affect their actions as adults;
the films of Martin Scorsese often spotlight the Italian-American
tough guys and tough-guy wannabes of the director's youth. Yet
Elek goes Allen and Scorsese one better as she combines autobiography with a sensitivity towards human suffering that is a direct
outgrowth of her own youthful experience.

As a child, World War II raged around her. Elek's father, a bookstore owner, was exiled to a Nazi labor camp, and she and her family
were confined to the Budapest ghetto until the Allied liberation in
1945. While they all survived, Elek did witness the obliteration of
her own community, not to mention the entire Eastern European
Jewish culture.

And so her films are both humanist and activist in content. They
serve as testimonials to the brutalization of the human spirit, as
historical records and heartfelt contemplations of anti-Semitism, and

as warnings of the folly of sitting idly by in the face of genocidal racial and ethnic hatred.

From the outset, Elek has been a trailblazer. She was the lone woman in her class at her country's Academy of Theater and Film Arts. In the early 1960s she and her fellow young Hungarian film makers, including István Szabó, Pál Gabór, Imre Gyongyossy, and Zsolt Kedzi-Kovács, were lauded as Hungary's "first generation" of filmmakers. This "generation of 1956" trained at the Béla Balázs Studio, a workshop that served as an experimental and bureau-cracy-free learning center for young directors. Summarily, Elek was acknowledged as one of the notable members of Hungary's "direct cinema" movement, whose constituents went about por-traying history in realistic and factual (rather than idealized, Hollywoodized) terms as they directly confronted the grisly re-alities of fascism and violence in their homeland's recent and distant past.

Throughout her career, Elek has directed both documentaries and fiction features. Thematically speaking, they spotlight individuals who most often are young, and who suffer through troubled child-hoods and summarily must struggle to overcome childhood con-straints. They are girls coming of age in a man's world, or girls and boys confronting the bleak realities of life in wartime or under totali-tarianism. By exploring the plight of abandoned or abused children and charting the harsh realities of the Holocaust, it is as if Elek is affirming her own survival and exorcising her own ghosts.

Occasionally, Elek's films explore the intricacies of familial relationships. *Maybe Tomorrow* is a portrait of a family devas-tated by resentment, brutality, and adultery. *Maria's Day* is a Chekhovian account of the familial and political tensions that arise during the summer reunion of an aristocratic family. Here, a recurring theme is the place and role of women within the patriar-chal family structure. Similarly, the docudramas *A Hungarian Village* and *A Simple Story* chart the plights of young women aspiring to dodge the limitations placed upon them because of their gender in a Hungarian village. Elek's approach to filmmaking is never casual. While making *A Hungarian Village* and *A Simple Story,* she relocated herself and spent four years in the village re-searching her subject.

The pressures on Elek's main characters also may result from events that transcend familial conflict. *Awakening* is the story of Kati, a young teenager coming of age in Stalinist Budapest during the 1950s. Upon the exile of her father and the death of her mother, she is forced to her own devices and ends up residing in a communal apartment. In order to get on with her life, she must face up to her growing loneliness and psychological isolation and come to terms with her mother's death.

Arguably Elek's most acclaimed film is *Memoirs of a River,* a commanding and haunting examination of anti-Semitism. Its fact-based story—one she had wanted to tell for two decades—is set in Austria-Hungary in 1882, with the core of its scenario involving the apprehension and persecution of a group of Jewish and non-Jewish loggers who are falsely accused of the ritualistic murder of a 14-year-old Christian girl. In *Memoirs of a River,* Elek contrasts pasto-ral countryside images with sudden and quick bursts of violence. She effectively re-creates a shtetl world—a world of her own ances-tors, if you will—which is devastated by anti-Semitism.

Elek had wanted to make *Memoirs of a River* for two decades. Significantly, when the film opened in Hungary, she was harassed by anonymous threats and hate mail, and her car was vandalized.

Her most recent film, *To Speak the Unspeakable: The Message of Elie Wiesel,* is a poignant documentary that charts the journey of Nobel Peace Prize-winner/Holocaust survivor Elie Wiesel back to his hometown in the Carpathian mountains. Wiesel recalls the destruction of his village by the Nazis, and the tragic plight of him and his family as they are deported to Auschwitz-Birkenau and Buchenwald. Wiesel in fact tours what remains of the con-centration camps, and his recollections are gut-wrenchingly pain-ful as he recounts his final memories of his sister and mother and how his father died. Yet Wiesel—as Elek—emerges as a survi-vor, a storyteller and a recorder of history, and this is their tri-umph.

Elek has noted that *To Speak the Unspeakable* is "dedicated to our children." She has also observed: "Although I haven't lost as much as Elie Wiesel, I have the feeling [that] despite all, we are like sister and brother. And I wish to share our common fate, our common responsibility, with the people who will see the film. We are both convinced our mission is to keep the memory alive and pass on to our children this history we've inherited from those who lost their life [sic]. It is the only way to protect the living and do the dead justice."

—Rob Edelman

EPHRON, Nora
American writer, director, and producer

Born: New York City, 19 May 1941; daughter of screenwriters and playwrights Phoebe and Henry Ephron; sister of the novelist Amy Ephron; sister of the journalist-novelist and her frequent screenwriting collaborator Delia Ephron. **Education:** Graduated from Beverly Hills High School, California, 1958, and Wellesley College, Massa-chusetts, 1962. **Family:** Married (1) Dan Greenburg, 1967 (di-vorced); (2) Carl Bernstein, 1976 (divorced 1979), two sons: Jacob and Max Bernstein; (3) Nicholas Pileggi. **Career:** 1963-68—worked as a newspaper journalist at the New York *Post*; 1968-78—wrote personally inflected social criticism for popular American maga-zines, including monthly columns as a contributing editor at *Esquire* (1972-73 and 1975-78) and *New York* (1973-74); published three books collecting these essays in the 1970s; 1978—wrote Lauren Bacall's telefilm debut, *Perfect Gentlemen*; 1983—published *Heart-burn,* a best-selling novel drawn from her marriage to Watergate muckraker Bernstein, and also co-wrote with Alice Arlen the screen-play of *Silkwood,* directed by Mike Nichols; 1986—wrote the screen-play for Nichols's film version of *Heartburn*; 1989—wrote and associate produced *When Harry Met Sally...,* directed by Rob Reiner, also made a cameo appearance in Woody Allen's *Crimes and Misde-meanors*; 1992—co-wrote with her sister Delia her own directorial debut, *This Is My Life,* did another Allen cameo in *Husbands and Wives*; 1993—co-wrote and directed *Sleepless in Seattle*. **Agent:** Sam Cohn, International Creative Management, 40 West 57th Street, New York, NY 10019, U.S.A.

Films as Director and Co-Writer

1992 *This Is My Life*
1993 ***Sleepless in Seattle***
1994 *Mixed Nuts*
1996 *Michael* (+ pr)

Nora Ephron

Films as Writer

1978   *Perfect Gentlemen* (Jackie Cooper—for TV)
1983   *Silkwood* (M. Nichols) (co-sc)
1986   *Heartburn* (M. Nichols)
1989   *Cookie* (S. Seidelman) (co-sc, + exec pr); *When Harry Met
        Sally ...* (R. Reiner) (+ assoc pr)
1990   *My Blue Heaven* (H. Ross) (+ exec pr)

Films as Actress

1989   *Crimes and Misdemeanors* (W. Allen) (as wedding guest)
1992   *Husbands and Wives* (W. Allen) (as dinner party guest)

Publications by Ephron

Books

Wallflower at the Orgy, New York, 1970.
Crazy Salad: Some Things about Women, New York, 1975.
Scribble Scribble: Notes on the Media, New York, 1978.
Heartburn, New York, 1983.

When Harry Met Sally ..., New York, 1990.
Nora Ephron Collected, New York, 1995.

Articles

"This Is Their Lives," interview with Wendy Wasserstein, in *Harper's
    Bazaar* (New York), June 1993.
"Nora Ephron: On the Front Lines of the Sexual Battlefield with the
    Writer and Director of *Sleepless in Seattle,*" interview with
    Lawrence Frascella, in *Rolling Stone* (New York), 8 July 1993.

Publications on Ephron

Books

McCreadie, Marsha, *The Women Who Write the Movies: From
    Frances Marion to Nora Ephron,* Secaucus, New Jersey, 1994.
Foster, Gwendolyn Audrey, *Women Film Directors: An International
    Bio-Critical Dictionary,* Westport, Connecticut, 1995.

Articles

Current Biography, New York, 1990.
Nonkin, Lesley Jane, "Take One," in *Vogue* (New York), January
    1992.
Wills, Garry, "How to Repossess a Life: Witty Nora Ephron Takes
    Control by Telling Her Story Her Way," in *Time* (New York), 27
    January 1992.
Coburn, Randy Sue, "An Affair to Inspire," in *Premiere* (New York),
    July 1993.
Fleming, Michael, "Nora Ephron," in *Variety* (New York), 19 July
    1993.

*   *   *

During the 1980s, Nora Ephron wrote or co-wrote five Hollywood features. So far in the 1990s she has directed four films. She is
one of the most prolific and commercially successful female filmmakers in Hollywood history.

In a 1972 essay called "Fantasies," Ephron wrote that the women's
movement helped her see the need for new types of stories which
would free women from sexual submissiveness (and men from constant dominance), but she felt hampered in her (culture's) ability to
think of any. Ephron's films give center stage to daughters of the
feminist revolution in that her heroines enjoy sex and happily pursue
careers which often grant them power and wealth. Nevertheless, her
women propel themselves fundamentally not toward self-sufficiency
or toward the affection of women friends but toward male approval.

Though Ephron's genre of choice is the romantic comedy, her
heroines suffer. They generally suggest, in Ephron's rapid-fire dialogue, that their tragedy is the inability of men and women to overcome gender differences—differences that the stories nonetheless
posit as essential to their own structures and thus to the viability of
the characters' love. A viewer who believes that a woman need not
look solely and unilaterally to men to secure her identity might feel
that the tinge of sadness to Ephron's movies comes from the heroines' constant efforts to employ a means of self-definition which
they know does not work.

Ephron's first script is anomalous in her oeuvre for its genre but
not its plot construction. *Silkwood,* directed by Mike Nichols and co-
written with Alice Arlen, builds from the true story of a nuclear

power plant worker (Meryl Streep) who died under suspicious circumstances while attempting to expose her bosses' abuses. The film expresses its passion for Silkwood's causes by training a sharp eye on the characters from a respectful distance. Still, the script shapes Silkwood's story into a thwarted quest for family, for one good man. Silkwood's work as a union leader (so threatening that someone at her plant deliberately contaminates her and her house with plutonium) functions in the film, however abstrusely, as a painful interruption to her romance with her boyfriend.

The subtlety (and resultant poignancy and realism) with which *Silkwood* approaches Ephron's central theme is abandoned in her later projects, which are consumed with Woman's search for Man to complete her. After Academy Award nominations all around for *Silkwood,* Ephron, Nichols, and Streep reprised their respective jobs in *Heartburn.* The film ends with its heroine finally leaving her husband, long after she discovers his ongoing affair during her second pregnancy. The story makes it hard to understand why she wants to be married to him from the start.

Heartburn was not a hit, but Ephron received a second Academy Award nomination for writing the popular *When Harry Met Sally ...* (directed by Rob Reiner). Famously, Sally (Meg Ryan) demonstrates to pal Harry (Billy Crystal)—who denies, with the film, that he can be "just" her pal—that women fake orgasm. The puncturing of a male ego is equaled by what may be taken as a celebration of female self-denial. Earlier in the film, Sally has humiliated herself in a similar diner setting by speaking too loudly about sex, while Harry never humiliates himself at all.

A second of Ephron's screenplays produced in 1989, *Cookie* (directed by Susan Seidelman), also finds humor in its heroine's humiliation. The title character is an adolescent girl (Emily Lloyd) who wins the respect of her long-lost father (Peter Falk), a gangster, by engineering his escape from his enemies and his legal wife of convenience, so that he can run off with her mother. Mother and daughter only bond via the daughter's facilitation of the mother's still-healthy lust for the father, and this androcentrism is rigidly enforced. Early on, her father slaps Cookie for defending her mother, and it is played for laughs as she falls backward over a rack of Santa suits to a jolly tune.

This Is My Life (1992), Ephron's directorial debut, allows for patriarchal failure within the familial framework it shares with *Cookie.* Its young heroines' absentee father turns out to be less than inspiring, and they return to their mother who—in a slant unaffected by feminists' then 20-year-old arguments that motherhood and working need not be mutually exclusive—has disappointed them by leaving their sides to become a stand-up comedy star. By the end, both the older daughter and the mother have paramours, and even the prepubescent younger girl has a present from the man on whom she has a crush. Even without the father, the (formerly) all-female family unit is undergirded by each member's relationship with a man.

Ephron's second directorial effort, *Sleepless in Seattle,* did wonderfully at the box office and won her a third Oscar nomination for writing. A love story about lovers who do not meet until the final scene, *Sleepless* represents its protagonists' passion as substanceless, formalizing a certain lack of conviction about its fantasy of ironclad romantic destiny. Some critics have suggested that Ephron's doubts about the old forms of storytelling which she favors make her films popular in an age where viewers want to have their fun and scoff at it too. Maybe it is to be expected that blockbusters about women's desire, still rare enough, should ask us to mock as well as identify with them. On the flip side, it may be not the active femininity of the characters but their exaggerated dependence on men which makes the ambivalence appear, and sell.

Since *Sleepless,* Ephron has directed two little-seen films. The most recent, *Michael,* uses its archangel fallen to Earth as a cupid, his other divine powers only spicing up the love story. *Mixed Nuts* is the second of Ephron's projects to star Steve Martin—she wrote *My Blue Heaven* in 1990—and both Martin films vary from Ephron's usual pattern. Her only films with male protagonists, both side with oddballs and underdogs, both create a community rather than just one couple, and both feature a midpoint dance between two men. Ephron's work studiously avoids homoerotic tension between women, but the men's dances infuse these films with energy—though all homoeroticism transmutes into hetero-romance. As one of Hollywood's biggest female hit-makers, Ephron seems in the position of an ultimate inside outsider. It would be interesting to see her expand the comparative mess and liveliness of her Martin films to bring more of the outside in.

—Susan Knobloch

EPSTEIN, Marie
French director, writer, and editor

Born: Marie-Antonine Epstein, 1899; sister of the director Jean Epstein. **Career:** 1923—assistant director and actress in Jean Epstein's avant-garde film *Coeur fidèle;* 1925-27—wrote screenplays and co-directed films for Jean Epstein; 1927—began collaboration with Jean Benoît-Lévy with film *Âmes d'enfants,* which she co-wrote, co-edited, and co-directed; 1933—co-scripted, co-edited, and co-directed best-known film *La Maternelle;* 1940-77—worked in film reconstruction and restoration as director of technical services at Cinémathèque Française, until she retired; 1953—sole director of *La Grande espérance.* **Awards:** Grand Prix du Film Français at French Exposition, for *La Mort du cygne,* 1937. **Died:** 1995.

Film as Director and Writer

1953   *La Grande espérance*

Films as Writer and Co-Director and Co-Editor with Benoît-Lévy

1927   *Âmes d'enfants* (*Children's Souls*) (co-sc)
1928   *Peau de pêche*
1929   *Maternité*
1930   *Jimmy Bruiteur*
1931   *Le Coeur de Paris*
1933   **La Maternelle** (*Children of Montmartre; The Nursery School*)
1934   *Itto*
1936   *Hélène*
1937   *La Mort du cygne* (*The Dying Swan*)
1938   *Altitude 3200* (*Youth in Revolt*)
1939   *La Feu de paille* (*Fire in the Straw; The Straw Fire*)

Other Films

1923   *L'Auberge rouge* (Jean Epstein) (ro); *Coeur fidèle* (Jean Epstein) (ro as Mlle. Marice)

1925   *L'Affiche* (Jean Epstein) (sc); *Mauprat* (Jean Epstein) (ro)
1927   *Six et demi-onze (6½ x 11)* (co-d with Jean Epstein, sc)

Publications on Epstein

Books

Benoît-Lévy, Jean, *The Art of the Motion Picture,* New York, 1946.
Fescourt, Henri, *La Foi et les Montagnes (ou le septième art au passé),* Paris, 1959.
Sadoul, Georges, *Le Cinéma Français (1890-1962),* Paris, 1962.
Abel, Richard, *French Cinema: The First Wave, 1915-1929,* Princeton, 1984.
Flitterman-Lewis, Sandy, *To Desire Differently: Feminism and the French Cinema,* Urbana, Illinois, 1990.
Museum of Modern Art, *Museum of Modern Art Circulating Film Library Catalogue,* New York, 1992.
Williams, Alan, *Republic of Images: A History of French Filmmaking,* Cambridge, Massachusetts, 1992.
Foster, Gwendolyn Audrey, *Women Film Directors: An International Bio-Critical Dictionary,* Westport, Connecticut, 1995.

Articles

Epardeaud, Edmond, *"L'Afiche* de Jean Epstein," in *Cinéa-Ciné pour tous* (Paris), 1 April 1925.
Culvile, G. M., "Alice Did and Does...Make Films," *Semiotica* (The Hague, Mouton), no. 1/2, 1993.
DeSanti, G. "Marie Epstein, l'amputazione del corpo," in *Cineforum* (Bergamo, Italy), June 1993.

*   *   *

Recently, film historians have rediscovered Marie Epstein's contributions to French cinema as one of the few French women filmmakers of the 1920s and 1930s. Although she worked as a screenwriter, director, and editor, she was typically unacknowledged in film histories in favor of her two collaborators, brother Jean Epstein and Jean Benoît-Lévy.

Marie Epstein began her film career as an actress, most notably as the crippled neighbor of the heroine in Jean's 1923 film *Coeur fidèle.* Her work as a screenwriter began when she won first prize in a scenario-writing competition with *Les Mains qui meurent,* which was never produced. Subsequently, she wrote two scripts for her brother, *L'Affiche* and *6½ x 11.* The compelling *L'Affiche* includes many of the themes that would characterize her subsequent films. It begins classically, with a woman's seduction and abandonment by a man; when the baby she conceives is born, she enters its photograph in a contest for the most beautiful baby in Paris, to be used in an extensive advertising campaign. Soon after winning, the baby dies and as the grieving woman wanders through Paris, she is besieged by images of her baby. The scenario was inspired by an actual soap advertisement, which illustrates Epstein's assertion that the best scenarios are discovered in "all the little details of life." It also demonstrates her interest in the still image, a theme taken up again in *6½ x 11,* whose title refers to the dimensions of a Kodak print.

Epstein's major work was produced in collaboration with Jean Benoît-Lévy, with whom she scripted, co-directed, and edited 11 films, although they are usually attributed to Benoît-Lévy alone. Their egalitarian professional relationship was one of the earliest and most productive in France. In addition, their films feature themes rarely depicted on screen, such as the desires of mothers for children and children for mothers. In *Maternité* a woman who regrets her decision not to have children discovers that there are equally rewarding opportunities to nurture the children of friends as well as the poor children in orphanages. Likewise, in *La Maternelle* an orphaned girl longs for a mother and ultimately finds one in a tenderhearted cleaning woman. And, *The Dying Swan* features a maternal relationship between a 12-year-old ballerina and the object of her adoration, the star dancer of a stage troupe.

Along with Epstein's interest in offering realistic depictions of motherhood, childhood, domesticity, and the friendship among females, the Epstein–Benoît-Lévy films also emphasize Benoît-Lévy's commitment to using film in the service of moral education. Consequently, *Children's Souls* extols the virtues of good parenting and sanitary healthy housing by contrasting two children of poor families—one neglected and the other carefully supervised. The Epstein–Benoît-Lévy films likewise address the issue of personal responsibility and moral choices, especially the weighty ethical dilemmas that accompany various social conditions. Thus, *Hélène* tells the story of a single woman who endeavors to raise her child on her own after the father commits suicide, though she must overcome a variety of obstacles. Nevertheless, despite their shared themes, the Epstein–Benoît-Lévy films looked different from one another, revealing Epstein's remarkable visual vocabulary and versatility. Indeed, she was especially interested in using poetic imagery and sophisticated, often avant-garde, cinematic techniques to convey the subjectivity of her characters.

Epstein and Benoît-Lévy's masterpiece and most successful work was *La Maternelle.* An early sound film loosely based on Léon Frapié's populist novel, its heartbreaking story takes place in the nursery school of a Paris slum. It looks like a documentary, much as the later Italian Neorealist and French "poetic realist" films did, and offers authentic observations of its largely nonprofessional cast—a group of actual slum children. A tender and haunting film, it tells the story of an newly orphaned little girl, Marie, who immediately develops an intense attachment to the new cleaning woman at her nursery school. Although the woman is lovingly attentive to her, Marie sees the school director propose to the woman and Marie becomes distraught anticipating a second abandonment. She tries to kill herself by flinging herself into a river, but she eventually reunites with her substitute *maternelle* and the film ends happily.

After World War II, Epstein and Benoît-Lévy made a short series of television documentaries about the ballet (*Ballets de France*). During the Cold War Epstein made a documentary about atomic power, *La Grande espérance.* Thereafter, she worked as a film archivist at the Cinémathèque Française, where she restored and reconstructed silent films, including some of her own, until she retired at age 76 in 1977.

—Cynthia Felando

EXPORT, Valie
Austrian director

Born: Waltraut Lehner in Linz, Austria, 1940. **Education:** Attended the Vienna College for Textile Art and Industry, B.A. 1964. **Family:** 1 daughter: Perdita. **Career:** Since 1967—created "expanded cinema" performances, often in collaboration with Peter Weibel; 1968—performed well-known "touch cinema" piece, *Tapp und Tastkino*, co-founded the Austrian Filmmakers Cooperative; 1970—began creating "video-actions" with *Split Reality*; 1975—was an associate founding member of the Graz Writers' Conference and a founding member of Film Women International (UNESCO); 1976—completed first feature-length film, *Invisible Adversaries*; 1989—professor of film and video, School of Fine Arts, University of Wisconsin, Milwaukee. **Awards:** Prize for most political film, Third Maraisiade, for *Ping Pong*, 1968; Special Jury Prize, Mostra Internationale de Film d'Autore, for *Invisible Adversaries*, 1976; Special Jury's Prize, 27th Bilbao International Film Festival, for *Syntagma*, 1983; Festival Prize, Daniel Wadsworth Memorial Video Festival, for *A Perfect Pair, or, Indecency Sheds Its Skin*, 1986.

Films as Director

1967   *Menstruationsfilm (Menstruation Film)*
1967-68 *Ars Lucis*; *Abstract Film No. 1*; *Cutting*
1968   *Ohne Titel Nr. 2 (Without Title No. 2)* (co-d with Weibel); *Ohne Titel xn (Without Title xn)* (co-d with Weibel); *Der Kuss (The Kiss)* (co-d with Weibel); *Ein Familienfilm von Waltraut Lehner (A Family Film by Waltraud Lehner)*; *Instant Film* (co-d with Weibel); *Valie Export* (co-d with Weibel); *Wor(l)d Cinema: Ein Sprachfest (Wor[l]d Cinema: A Festival of Languages)* (co-d with Weibel); *Gesichtsgrimassen (Facial Grimaces)*; *Ansprache Aussprache (Speak to, Speak Out)*; *Splitscreen-Solipsismus*; *Tapp und Tastkino (Touch Cinema)*; *333*; *Ping Pong*; *Sie Suesse Nummer: Ein Konsumerlebnis*; *Sehtext: Fingergedicht*; *Auf+Zu+Ab+An (Up+Down+On+Off)*; *Vorspann: Ein Lesefilm (Cast and Credits: A Film to Be Read)*
1969   *Proselyt (Proselyte)*; *Eine Reise ist eine Reise Wert (A Journey Is Worth the Trip)* (co-d with Weibel); *Das Magische Auge (The Magical Eye)* (co-d with Weibel); *Tonfilm (Sound Film)*; *Genitalpanik (Genital Panic)*
1970   *Split Reality*
1971   *Facing a Family*; *Eros/ion*
1971-72 *Interrupted Line*; *Stille Sprache (Silent Language)*
1973   *Hyperbulie (Hyperbulia)*; *Adjungierte Dislokationen (Adjoined Dislocations)*; *Asemie (Asemia)*; *Mann & Frau & Animal (Man, Woman and Animal)*; *... Remote ... Remote ...*; *Sehtext: Fingergedicht (Sight Poem: Finger Poem)*; *Die Süsse Nummer: Ein Konsumerlebnis (The Sweet One: A Consumer Experience)*; *Hauchtext: Liebesgedicht (1970) (Love Poem)*; *Touching (1970)*
1974   *Body Politics*; *Raumsehen und Raumhören (Seeing Space and Hearing Space)* (+ co-sound)
1976   *Unsichtbare Gegner (Invisible Adversaries)* (+ co-sc, pr); *Homometer II*; *Wann ist der Mensch eine Frau? (When Is a Human Being a Woman?)*; *Schnitte (Cuts)*
1977   *Delta: Ein Stück (Delta: A Piece)*
1978   *I [(Beat) It]*
1979   *Restringierter Code (Restricted Code)*; *Menschenfrauen* (+ co-sc, pr)
1982   *Das Bewaffnete Auge (The Armed Eye)* (doc) (+ sc)
1983   *Syntagma* (+ sc, pr)
1984   *Die Praxis der Liebe (The Practice of Love)* (+ sc, pr)
1985   *Tischbemerkungen-November 1985 (Table Quotes-November 1985)* (doc)
1986   *Die Zweiheit der Natur (The Duality of Nature)* (+ pr); *Ein Perfektes Paar oder die Unzucht wechselt ihre Haut (A Perfect Pair, or, Indecency Sheds Its Skin)* (+ sc, pr); *Yukon Quest* (co-d with I. Wiener, O. Weiner, and E. Forster)
1987   *Maschinenkörper-Körperraum-Körpermaschinen (Machine-Bodies/Body-Space/Body-Machines)*; *Mental Images, Oder der Zugang der Welt (Mental Images, or, the Gateway to the World)* (co-d)
1988   *Dokumente zum Internationalen Aktionismus*; *Unica*
1989   *Die Meta-Morphose (The Meta-Morphosis)* (+ co-sc)

Publications by Export

Books

With Peter Weibel, *Wien-Bildkompendium Wiener Aktionismus und Film*, Frankfurt, 1970.
With Hermann Hendrich, *Stadt: Visuelle Strukturen*, Vienna, 1973.
Austria, Biennale di Venezia, Vienna, 1980.
Dokumentations—Ausstellung des Österreichischen Beitrags zur Biennale Venedig 1980, Vienna, 1980.
Editor, with Silvia Eiblmayr and Monika Prischl-Maier, *Kunst mit Eigen-Sinn*, Vienna, 1985.
Das Reale und sein Double: Der Körper, Bern, 1987.

Articles

With Peter Weibel, "Women Working: *Invisible Adversaries*," in *Camera Obscura* (Berkeley), Summer 1979.
"Corpus More Geometrico," in *ConText* (Vienna), 1987.
"The Real and Its Double: The Body," in *Discourse* (Milwaukee), no. 1, 1988-89.
"Aspects of Feminist Actionism," in *New German Critique*, Spring/Summer 1989.
"Expanded Cinema as Expanded Reality," in *JAM*, July 1991.
Interview with Margret Eifler and Sandra Frieden, in *Gender and German Cinema: Feminist Intervention*, Volume 1, *Gender and Representation in New German Cinema*, edited by Sandra Frieden, Richard W. McCormick, Vibeke R. Petersen, and Laurie Melissa Vogelsang, Oxford, 1993.

Publications on Export

Books

de Lauretis, Teresa, *Technologies of Gender: Essays on Theory, Film, and Fiction*, Bloomington, Indiana, 1987.
Prammer, Anita, *Valie Export: eine multimediale Künstlerin*, Vienna, 1988.
Mayne, Judith, *The Woman at the Keyhole: Feminism and Women's Cinema*, Bloomington, Indiana, 1990.
Juro, Andrea, and V. Vale, editors, *Angrywomen*, San Francisco, 1991.
Lamb-Faffelberger, Margarete, *Valie Export und Elfriede Jelinek im Spiegel der Presse: zur Rezeption der Feministischen Avantgarde Österreichs*, New York, 1992.
Mueller, Roswitha, *Valie Export: Fragments of the Imagination*, Bloomington, Indiana, 1994.
Foster, Gwendolyn Audrey, *Women Film Directors: An International Bio-Critical Dictionary*, Westport, Connecticut, 1995.

MacDonald, Scott, *A Critical Cinema 3: Interviews with Independent Filmmakers,* Berkeley, 1998.

Articles

Mueller, Roswitha, "Through the Eyes of a Woman: Valie Export's Invisible Adversary," in *Substance,* no. 29, 1983.

Couder, M., "Valie Export: *Unsichtbare Gegner,*" in *Skrien* (Amsterdam), September/October 1984.

Koehler, M., "Filme von frauen (im wettberwerb und im forum)," in *Medien und Erziehung* (Munich), no. 2, 1985.

Kiernan, Joanna, "Films by Valie Export," in *Millennium* (New York), Fall/Winter 1986-87.

CP, "Eine kunst mit Eigen-Sinn um ein weibliches selbst zu erreichen," in *Blimp* (Graz, Austria), Fall 1989.

Cornwell, Regina, "Interactive Art: Touching the Body in the Mind," in *Discourse* (Milwaukee), Spring 1992.

Curry, Ramona, "The Female Image as Critique in the Films of Valie Export," and Margret Eifler, "Valie Export's *Invisible Adversaries*: Film as Text," in *Gender and German Cinema: Feminist Intervention,* Volume 1, *Gender and Representation in New German Cinema,* edited by Sandra Frieden, Richard W. McCormick, Vibeke R. Petersen, and Laurie Melissa Vogelsang, Oxford, 1993.

* * *

As Annie, a character in Valie Export's first feature film, *Invisible Adversaries,* explains, "images penetrate me like psychic meteors, they frighten me—but they mirror the reality that surrounds me as a paranoid." Throughout her long career as an artist, Export has emphasized the amazing power of images to shape psychic and external realities, especially when the images depict women's bodies. With an international reputation as a challenging and prolific avant-garde artist, Export has noted that her body of work includes "films, expanded movies, video, body actions (body-material-interactions), photography, drawings." In general, her work explores psychoanalytic themes regarding femininity, sexuality, and desire, and critics have complimented her imaginative use of film to counter the conventions of mainstream narrative films and their depictions of the female body.

In the 1960s Export earned recognition for her avant-garde performance pieces, films, videos, and installation work. She has explained that her work is linked to and inspired by the avant-garde movements of the first half of the 20th century and their developments after World War II. In addition, her artistic development is productively understood in relation to contemporary art trends in Vienna, especially to the work of progressive artists who sought to connect with prewar trends and deployed a variety of media in their work to question the relationship between and meanings of language, culture, and reality.

Export is the author of several brave and challenging works that suggest an acute interest in contemporary feminist film theoretical and critical attention to the function of the female body, along with a remarkable willingness to put her body on the line—literally. One of her most acclaimed "expanded films," *Tapp und Tastkino,* considered the kind of cinematic male voyeurism and fetishism of the female body that film scholar Laura Mulvey gained renown for writing about much later, in her 1975 article, "Visual Pleasure and Narrative Cinema." Export titled the piece "touch cinema" because it consisted of inviting a "spectator" to take pleasure in a real woman's body: Export's own. Specifically, she donned a "movie theater"—a box with curtains that contained her bare chest, while Peter Weibel encouraged passersby to participate by touching her breasts.

Indeed, much of Export's work uses the female body as a primary material element of film in order to suggest the interrelationships between the body and its social and cultural environments. ... *Remote ... Remote ...* and *Man, Woman, and Animal* are short 16mm films that depict the body as the site of psychological and sociological examination, via both pain and pleasure. *Man, Woman, and Animal* investigates women's pleasure by depicting a woman's genitals as she masturbates in the bath. ... *Remote ... Remote ...* shows a woman who methodically undertakes the bloody mutilation of her hands by cutting away her cuticles with an Exacto blade. At intervals, she washes the blood in a bowl of milk that sits in her lap. Significantly, she is linked symbolically to a poster-size black-and-white photograph of two infants who were abused by their parents and are apparently being exploited by their rescuers—the legal authorities who have permitted the children's pain to be recorded by a news photographer. The film foregrounds Export's interest in making internal states visible; as she puts it, she is preoccupied with "the pictorial representation of psychic conditions, with the responses of the body when its loses its identity."

The defining characteristics of Export's work are her emphasis on materials and objects, spontaneity and randomness, transgressions of the lines between art media and between life and art. Moreover, her aim is to alter the conventions that govern typical depictions of the female body and to intervene in the audience's passive consumption of more typical representations. Her expanded cinema pieces from the 1960s and 1970s experimented with new considerations of the film medium, and include a number of works that documented the multimedia events or "happenings" she created, occasionally with her collaborator Peter Weibel. Among her best-known expanded films are *Cutting,* and *Genital Panic,* in which she walked through a row of spectators with the front of her pants cut out. Likewise, her expanded films *Instant Film* and *The Magical Eye* elide the gap between production and consumption so as to force spectators out of their typically passive viewing modes into a more active engagement with the film experience. Thus, *Instant Film,* which Export also called an "object film," consists of a sheet of transparent plastic that viewers were encouraged to look through to create their own "films."

Export's first feature, *Invisible Adversaries,* enjoyed critical acclaim for its meditations on feminine identity and representation and for the refusal to provide unambiguous meanings. The film echoes *Invasion of the Body Snatchers* to the extent that it features a photographer, Anna, who is convinced that unknown forces are controlling the minds of the people around her. Specifically, she believes that Earth has been colonized by a foreign enemy, the Hyksos—an ancient Egyptian tribe known for sudden appearances and disappearances. Unlike the earlier film, however, the mind control to which Export's film refers is related to patriarchal attitudes about and representations of the female body. Accordingly, Anna, like Export, uses the tools of her trade to observe hidden "truths" that reveal how the female body has been "constructed" by male artists and medical discourses. For example, the men in the film either are uninterested in taking up Anna's system of understanding or they think she is crazy. Thus, when she confides her concerns about the "invisible adversaries," her doctor recommends drugs to control her "hallucinations."

Export's second feature, *Menschenfrauen,* works like a "consciousness-raising" film in its focus on the "true" life stories of four women. Her third feature film, *The Practice of Love* is about a professional journalist, Judith, who discovers during a criminal investigation that she is surrounded by corruption when she learns that one of her two lovers is an illegal arms dealer. Part of the film's task is to consider the integration of the public and private realms, a salient theme in much of Export's work.

In addition to her work as an artist, Export has written several published pieces on the subjects of contemporary art and feminist theory. Like her films and performances, her writing offers poetically jarring, direct challenges to the function of patriarchal language to deindividuate women and it exhorts viewers to challenge dehumanizing "realities." Accordingly, she has advised that "if sentences devoid of general meaning are spoken ... then it is no longer a question of testing a theory of existence but of saving individuation, naked existence in a reality of senseless destruction."

—Cynthia Felando

FAYE, Safi
Senegalese director and writer

Born: Dakar, Senegal, 22 November 1943. **Education:** Received teaching certificate from Rufisque Normal School, 1963; studied ethnology at the École Pratique des hautes Études and filmmaking at the Louis Lumière Film School during the 1970s; University of Paris, Ph.D. in Ethnology, 1979; degree in ethnology from the Sorbonne, 1988. **Family:** Daughter, Zeiba. **Career:** Ethnologist, filmmaker; 1963-69—teacher, Dakar school system; 1972—began filmmaking; 1979-80—guest lecturer, Free University of Berlin. **Awards:** Georges Sadoul Prize, Festival International du Film de l'Ensemble Francophone (Geneva), and International Film Critics Award, Berlin Film Festival, for *Kaddu Beykat,* 1975; Award, Carthage Film Festival, for *Fad'jal,* 1979; Special Prize, Leipzig Festival (Germany), for *Selbé One among Others,* 1982. **Addresses:** 12 Rue Morère, 75014 Paris, France; B P 1352, Dakar, Senegal.

Films as Director

1972   *La Passante (The Passerby)* (short) (+ sc, ro)
1973   *Revanche (Revenge)* (short)
1975   *Kaddu Beykat (Lettre paysanne; Peasant Letter; Letter from the Village)*
1979   *Fad'jal (Come and Work; Grand-père raconte)* (+ sc); *Goob na nu (La Récolte est finie; The Harvest Is In)* (short)
1980   *Man Sa Yay (I, Your Mother; Moi, ta mère)*
1981   *Les Âmes au soleil (Souls in the Sun)* (short)
1982   *Selbé et tant d'autres (Selbé One among Others)* (doc)
1983   *3 ans 5 mois (3 Years Five Months)* (short)
1984   *Ambassades Nourricières (Culinary Embassies)* (doc)
1985   *Racines noires (Black Roots)* (short); *Elsie Haas (Elsie Haas: Femme peintre et cinéaste d'Haiti)*
1989   *Tesito* (short)
1990   *Tournage Mossane* (short)
1996   *Mossane (Beauty)* (+ sc)

Film as Actress

1972   *Petit à petit ou Les Lettres persanes 1968 (Little by Little; 1968 Persian Letters)* (Rouch)

Publications by Faye

Articles

Interview with Françoise Maupin, in *Review du Cinéma, Image et Son* (Paris), February 1976.

Interview with Henry Welsch, in *Jeune Cinéma* (Paris), December 1976/January 1977.

Publications on Faye

Books

Vieyra, Paulin Soumanou, *Le Cinema au Senegal,* Brussels, 1983.
Pfaff, Françoise, *Twenty-five Black African Filmmakers,* New York, 1988.
Armes, Roy, and Lizbeth Malkmus, *Arab and African Film Making,* London, 1991.
Foster, Gwendolyn Audrey, *Women Film Directors: An International Bio-Critical Dictionary,* Westport, Connecticut, 1995.

Articles

Deye, Ben Diogaye, "Safi Faye, vedette du film *Petit à petit ou Les Lettres persanes 1968,*" in *Bingo,* January 1969.
Bernard, Jean, "Safi Faye comme elle se dit," in *Afrique Nouvelle,* 15 October 1975.
Eichenberger, P., "Safi Faye—une africaine derrière la camera," in *Unir Cinéma,* October/November 1976.
Bosseno, Christian, "*Lettre paysanne,*" in *Revue de Cinéma, Image et Son* (Paris), October 1977.
Ruelle, Catherine, "Faye, Safi," in *L'Afrique Litteraire et Artistique,* vol. 49, 3rd quarter, 1978.
Courant, Gerard, "*Fad'jal,*" in *Cinéma* (Paris), July/August 1979.
Martin, Angela, "Four Filmmakers from West Africa," in *Framework* (Norwich, England), vol. 11, 1979.
Traore, Moussa, "La Passion selon Safi Faye," in *Bingo,* August 1979.
Mangin, Marc, "J'aime filmer sur un rhyme africain," in *Droit et Liberté,* March 1980.
Schissel, Howard, "Africa on Film: The First Feminist View," in *Guardian,* 9 July 1980.
Haffner, Pierre, "Senegal," in *CinémAction* (Conde-sur-Noireau), special issue, 1982.
Petty, Sheila, "(Re)Presenting the Self: Identity and Consciousness in the Feature Films of Safi Faye," in *International Women's Writing,* edited by Anne E. Brown and Marjanne E. Gooze, Westport, Connecticut, 1995.
Petty, Sheila, "How an African Woman Can Be: African Women Filmmakers Construct Women," in *Discourse* (Berkeley), Spring 1996.

* * *

Considered the first woman filmmaker of sub-Saharan Africa, Safi Faye remains one of the few active black African women directors. Born in Dakar, Faye's family belongs to the Serer ethnic group, and comes from Fad'jal, the village upon which she would base her fourth film.

Safi Faye

Trained as an educator, Faye was introduced to filmmaking by Jean Rouch, the ethnographic filmmaker credited with the term cinema verité and known for films that Fatimah Tobing Rony, in her book *The Third Eye,* describes as "increasingly self-reflexive and collaborative cinema" that "gets beyond scientific voyeurism." Rouch and Faye met in 1966, while Faye was working as an official hostess for the 1966 Dakar Festival of Negro Arts. Her first entry into the cinema was not as a filmmaker, but as an actress. She appeared in Rouch's film *Little by Little.* The filmmaker encouraged Faye to pursue her interest in ethnographic film, and she did so in 1972, traveling to Paris to study both filmmaking and ethnology.

Her first film, *The Passerby,* in which she stars, was made while Faye was still a film student. The film is a critique of the neocolonialist introduction of agricultural monoculture; shifting farming from varied crops of use to the community to a single crop for export. As Sheila Petty states, this film, as well as *Fad'jal* "attempts to bring a feminist consciousness to African film by revealing rather than glossing over, certain structures or uses of structures that continue to deny women equality."

Using money earned from her first film, Faye shot her first feature-length docudrama with a budget of only $20,000, *Kaddu Beykat.* The film was completed three years later, and garnered international attention and awards. As Françoise Pfaff states, the film was "literally meant to give a voice to Senegalese peasants," and like *Fad'jal,* to "condemn the precariousness of base on the whims of peanut monoculture." But rather than focus solely on the role of foreign markets in the oppression of African people, the film also critiques the role of the Senegalese government. As Faye noted in the *Guardian,* "It is all too easy and convenient to place the blame for Africa's present ills uniquely on the past or on outside forces."

One of her best-known films is the documentary *Selbé One among Others* produced in 1982. This film was part of a unique and innovative program funded by UNICEF. Several filmmakers were chosen to direct films documenting the everyday experiences of women in different countries. Faye focused on her native Senegal, and Selbé

Diout, a 39-year-old woman struggling in a village for the survival of herself and her children. Selbé, whose husband has left the community for a job in the city, is only one of many women who are the sole providers for their families. With no jobs and no viable incomes, the women work endlessly making and selling goods, foraging for food, and tending small subsistence plots of land.

Faye's international reputation is defined not only by her vision, but also by her style, for she brought to African ethnographic film the perspective not of the "outsider" observing the exotic, but that of a member of the culture. Her method is participatory and as she herself states: "I do not work singlehandedly, but rather through and with people. I go to talk to farmers in their village, we discuss their problems and I take notes. Even though I may write a script for my films, I basically leave the peasants free to express themselves in front of a camera and I listen. My films are collective works in which everybody takes an active part."

—Frances K. Gateward

FERNÁNDEZ VIOLANTE, Marcela
Mexican director and writer

Born: Mexico City, 9 June 1941. **Education:** Centro Universitario de Estudios Cinematográficos (CUEC), Universidad Nacional Autonoma de México (UNAM). **Family:** Divorced; sons: Roberto and Jaime. **Career:** 1971 to present—professor at CUEC; 1974-75—feature film debut, *Whatever You Do, You Lose*; 1975—first woman to join Mexican film director's union; 1978-82—technical secretary, CUEC; 1988-91—director of CUEC; director, Sección de Autores del Sindicato de Trabajadores de la Industria Cinematográfica (Authors' Section, Film Industry Workers Union). **Awards:** Diosa de la Plata, critics' award for best experimental short, for *Blue,* 1966; Ariel, Best Documentary Short, Mexican Academy of Motion Picture Arts and Science, and Diosa de la Plata for best documentary short, for *Frida Kahlo,* 1971; Ariel, Best Feature Film, Mexican Academy of Motion Picture Arts and Science, for *Whatever You Do, You Lose,* 1975; Ariel, Best Feature Film, and Best Director, Mexican Academy of Motion Picture Arts and Science, and Jury's Special Award, Mystery International Film Festival, for *Mystery,* 1979. **Address:** c/oMexican Film Institute (IMCINE), Ateletas 2 Country Club, Coyoacán, DF 14220, Mexico.

Films as Director

1966   *Azul (Blue)* (experimental short)
1968   *Gayosso de descuentos* (unfinished short)
1971   *Frida Kahlo* (doc, short) (+ sc)
1975   *De todos modos Juan te llamas (In Any Case, Your Name Is Juan; Whatever You Do, You Lose; The General's Daughter)* (+ sc)
1977   *Cananea*
1979   *Misterio (Mystery)* (+ sc)
1980   *En el país de los pies ligeros (El niño Raramuri; The Raramuri Boy; In the Country of Fast Runners)* (+ co-sc)
1986   *Nocturno amor que te vas (Nocturnal Love That Leaves)*
1991   *Golpe de suerte (Stroke of Luck; Lucky Break)*

Other Film

1990 *My Filmmaking, My Life: Matilde Landeta* (P. Diaz and J. Ryder—doc) (appearance)

Publications by Fernández Violante

Articles

"Marcela Fernández Violante: A Filmmaker Apart," interview with John Mosier and Alexis Gonzales, in *Américas* (Washington, D.C.), January/February 1983.
"'We Are Losing Our Identity'", interview with Andrew Horton, in *Literature/Film Quarterly* (Salisbury, Maryland), vol. 15, no. 1, 1987.

Publications on Fernández Violante

Books

Pick, Zuzana M., editor, *Latin American Film Makers and the Third Cinema,* Ottawa, 1978.
Trelles Plazaola, Luis, editor, *Cine y mujer en América Latina: Directoras de Largometrajes de ficción,* Rio Piedras, Puerto Rico, 1991.
Foster, Gwendolyn Audrey, *Women Film Directors: An International Bio-Critical Dictionary,* Westport, Connecticut, 1995.

Articles

Vega, E. de la, "Fichero de cineastas nacionales," in *Dicine* (Mexico), March/April 1988.
Huaco-Nuzum, Carmen, in *The Women's Companion to International Film,* edited by Annette Kuhn and Susannah Radstone, London, 1990.

* * *

In each of its important moments, Mexican cinema has been able to boast at least one prominent woman producer, director, or screenwriter. In the 1970s, the woman of note was Marcela Fernández Violante, who wrote and directed award-winning short films and feature films. She studied at the film school at the Universidad Nacional Autonoma de México in the late 1960s, where she learned her trade from film professionals. In 1971 she was invited back to the university to be trained as a professor and to teach in the film program. Since then, Fernández Violante has taught film, eventually being promoted to the leadership of the department in 1988.

From the beginning, Fernández Violante caught Mexico's and the international film community's attention. She won the 1966 Diosa de la Plata's critics' award for her first directorial effort, an experimental short entitled *Blue.* Her 1971 documentary about Frida Kahlo preceded the deification of Kahlo as perhaps the greatest and most misunderstood of Mexico's women painters. Winning both an Ariel (Mexico's equivalent of the Academy Award) and a Diosa de la Plata for best documentary, *Frida Kahlo* arguably primed the public for Paul Leduc's magnificent biopic, *Frida* (1982).

Fernández Violante has directed five feature films, each one critically acclaimed. In 1975, after the release of *Whatever You Do, You Lose,* she became the first woman to join the Mexican director's union. Her first feature analyzes the role of the military in Mexico through its treatment of the Cristero War of 1926, a conflict that revolved around religious questions. According to Fernández Violante, the film looks at "how the revolution was betrayed and the different aspects of loyalty to one's convictions and how one betrays them." Written and produced during a tense moment in Mexico's contemporary history, *Whatever You Do, You Lose* allowed her to explore how Mexico's military has traditionally dealt with opposition while avoiding the sensitive contemporary issues of Marxism and the tumultuous era of student uprisings of the late 1960s. She believes that the film, which was funded by UNAM, was only possible because it was made during a period of political rapprochement under President Luis Echevarría. Although she was criticized for not dealing specifically with the betrayal of peasants, Fernández Violante made a strong and lasting impression on Mexican critics and audiences with this sensitive portrayal of Mexican army officers and their families.

Fernández Violante's subsequent feature films have won vast critical acclaim, but have not succeeded at Mexico's box offices. Her second feature film, *Cananea,* is based on the real experiences of William C. Greene, a U.S. entrepreneur whose copper mine, Cananea, suffered a workers' strike in 1906 which finally had to be settled by the Texas Rangers. In this film, Fernández Violante partnered with Mexico's premier cinematographer, Gabriel Figueroa, whose cinematography defined the Mexican Cinema's Golden Age from the mid-1930s to the 1950s.

In 1979 Fernández Violante turned toward contemporary Mexico as the setting for her next feature film *Mystery.* Adapted by Vicente Leñero from his own novel *Studio Q, Mystery* is a self-reflexive tale about a soap-opera actor whose life begins to mirror that of his screen character. *Mystery* is a complex, twisted story in which the perennial question "does life imitate art or does art imitate life?" resounds loudly. This third feature won eight Ariels, including best director and best feature film.

Despite financing problems and shifting governmental support of the Mexican film industry, Mexican filmmakers in the 1980s and early 1990s affected a slow but steady renaissance of Mexican cinema. Fernández Violante was instrumental in this rebirth, both as a filmmaker and as a professor of cinema and, from 1988 to 1991, the director of UNAM's film school. Her 1991 film, *Stroke of Luck,* achieved not only critical acclaim, but perhaps more important, successful commercial exhibition in Mexico. This triumph, coupled with the domestic success of *Like Water for Chocolate* (directed by Alonso Arau, 1992) and *Danzón* (directed by María Novaro, 1990), truly demonstrates that Mexicans are returning to their own films, reveling in the opportunity to see themselves on screen. Fernández Violante's perseverance has certainly contributed to the audience's newly reborn respect and enthusiasm for Mexican film.

—Ilene S. Goldman

FIELDS, Verna
American editor

Born: 1918. **Family:** Married the film editor Sam Fields (died 1954), two sons. **Career:** 1940s—assistant editor on Hollywood films; 1950s-early 1960s—assistant editor on TV series *The Whistler,* 1954-55, *The Lone Ranger,* 1954-57, *Death Valley Days,* 1955-58, *Sky*

King, 1955-58, *Wanted: Dead or Alive,* 1959-60, and *The Tom Ewell Show,* 1960-61; taught film editing, University of Southern California, Los Angeles; from 1960—film editor; 1976-82—vice-president of Feature Productions, Universal. **Awards:** Academy Award, for *Jaws,* 1975. **Died:** 30 November 1982.

Films as Editor

1944   *Belle of the Yukon* (Seiter) (asst); *Casanova Brown* (Wood) (asst); *The Woman in the Window* (F. Lang) (asst)
1945   *Along Came Jones* (Heisler) (asst)
1960   *The Savage Eye* (Maddow, Meyers, and Strick); *Studs Lonigan* (Lerner); *The Sword and the Dragon* (English-language version of *Ilya Mourometz*) (Ptushko)
1963   *An Affair of the Skin* (Maddow); *Cry of Battle* (Lerner) (supervisor)
1964   *The Bus* (Wexler) (co)
1966   *Country Boy* (Kane); *Deathwatch* (Morrow)
1967   *The Legend of the Boy and the Eagle* (Couffer) (co); *Search for the Evil One* (Kane); *Track of Thunder* (Kane)
1968   *The Wild Racers* (Haller) (co)
1969   *Medium Cool* (Wexler)
1971   *Point of Terror* (Nicol) (supervisor)
1972   *What's Up, Doc?* (Bogdanovich)
1973   *American Graffiti* (Lucas) (co); *Paper Moon* (Bogdanovich)
1974   *Daisy Miller* (Bogdanovich); *The Sugarland Express* (Spielberg) (co); *Memories of Us* (Dyal) (co)
1975   *Jaws* (Spielberg)

Other Films

1956   *While the City Sleeps* (F. Lang) (sound ed)
1958   *Snowfire* (D. & S. McGowan) (sound ed)
1961   *El Cid* (A. Mann) (sound ed)
1963   *The Balcony* (Strick) (sound ed); *A Face in the Rain* (Kershner) (sound ed)
1967   *Targets* (Bogdanovich) (sound ed)
1968   *Journey to the Pacific* (d)
1969   *It's a Good Day* (d)

Publications by Fields

Articles

American Film (Washington, D.C.), June 1976.
Films and Filming (London), February 1977.
Mise-en-Scène (Cleveland, Ohio), Spring 1980.
American Premiere (Los Angeles), vol. 3, no. 5, 1982.

Publications on Fields

Book

Acker, Ally, *Reel Women: Pioneers of the Cinema, 1896 to the Present,* New York, 1991.

Articles

Cinema (Beverly Hills), no. 35, 1976.

Film Comment (New York), March/April 1977.
Action (Los Angeles), January/February 1978.
Obituary, in *Variety* (New York), 8 December 1982.

* * *

Verna Fields became one of the American film industry's most famous editors during the 1970s, and in the process was able to accumulate considerable power. Since she had helped with so many blockbusters of the decade, including *Jaws* and *American Graffiti,* Fields was promoted by a grateful Universal Pictures into the executive suite as vice president of feature films. She held that post until her death in 1982.

Unfortunately all this fame and power at the end of her long career only served to remind close observers of the American film industry that like in other multibillion dollar institutions, few women ever accumulated a measure of true power. Since the beginnings of the film industry, however, film editing had been one of the few arenas open to women. Fields, like Margaret Booth before her (at MGM), used this opening to become a force at a major Hollywood studio.

Indeed during the heyday of the "Movie Brats" of the 1970s, many looked to Fields as a symbolic breakthrough. Here was a person who had worked on many a low-budget independent film being elevated into a real position of power. She was so "in" that in 1974 *Newsweek* featured an article on her—one of the few in a popular magazine about a film editor.

Verna Fields's father helped her move into the film industry. Through him she met her husband Sam Fields, who was a film editor, in the 1940s. Sam died in 1954, leaving two sons to support. Verna returned to work that year and learned her craft on television fare such as *The Lone Ranger, Wanted: Dead or Alive, Death Valley Days,* and *Sky King.* She made her big splash in Hollywood as the sound editor for *El Cid.*

But her greatest impact came when she began to teach film editing to a generation of students at the University of Southern California. She then operated on the fringes of the film business, for a time making documentaries for the Office of Economic Opportunity. The end of that federal agency pushed her back into mainstream Hollywood, then being overrun by her former students.

Cutting *What's Up, Doc?* for Peter Bogdanovich represented her return, but her real influence began when she helped a former USC student, George Lucas, persuade Universal to distribute *American Graffiti.* A grateful Lucas, the story goes, presented her with a brand new BMW automobile in return. *Jaws* for Steven Spielberg "made" Fields's career.

She was quoted in the 1970s, at the height of her influence, saying that she believed editing should be invisible. She sought to play down her own influence, preferring to let the director dictate the terms. Thus she worked in a variety of projects equally well—from melodrama to comedy to classic genre films. Certainly that is precisely what the new young Hollywood generation liked about her. She was a great technician who was sympathetic to their projects and visions. She wanted to help them—unlike the rest of the Hollywood establishment of the day which fought their very entry into the system. It is for this support that Verna Fields will long be remembered.

—Douglas Gomery

FILM D'AMORE E D'ANARCHIA
(Film of Love and Anarchy; Love and Anarchy)
Italy, 1973
Director: Lina Wertmüller

Production: Europ International (Italy); Technicolor, 35mm; running time: 108 minutes, some versions are 125 minutes. Released 1973. Filmed in Italy.

Producer: Romano Cardarelli; **screenplay:** Lina Wertmüller; **photography:** Giuseppe Rotunno; **editor:** Franco Fraticelli; **sound:** Mario Bramonti; **production designer:** Enrico Job; **music:** Carlo Savina; **songs:** Nino Rota; **costume designer:** Enrico Job.

Cast: Giancarlo Giannini (*Tunin*); Mariangela Melato (*Salomé*); Lina Polito (*Tripolina*); Eros Pagni (*Spatoletti*); Pina Cei (*Madame Aida*); Elena Fiore (*Donna Carmela*); Isa Bellini; Giuliana Calandra; Isa Danieli; Anna Bonaiuto; Mario Scaccia.

Award: Cannes Film Festival, Best Actor (Giannini).

Publications

Script

The Screenplays of Lina Wertmüller, translated by Steven Wagner, New York, 1977.

Books

Dokumentation: Lina Wertmüller/Martin Scorsese, edited by Filmstelle Vseth/Vsu, Zurich, 1986.
Michalczyk, John J., *The Italian Political Filmmakers,* Cranbury, New Jersey, 1986.
Jacobsen, Wolfgang, and others, *Lina Wertmüller,* Munich, 1988.

Articles

Delmas, J., in *Jeune Cinéma* (Paris), July/August 1973.
Rubinstein, L., in *Cineaste* (New York), no. 3, 1974.
Erens, Patricia, "*Love and Anarchy*: Passion and Pity," in *Jump Cut* (Chicago), July/August 1974.

Film d'amore e d'anarchia

Van Wert, W., "Love, Anarchy, and the Whole Damned Thing," in *Jump Cut* (Chicago), November/December 1974.

Gorbman, C., in *Movietone News* (Seattle), April 1975.

Jacobs, Diane, "Lina Wertmüller," in *International Film Guide* (London), 1977.

Sternborn, B., in *Filmfaust* (Frankfurt), April/May 1985.

* * *

Film of Love and Anarchy is Lina Wertmüller's fourth feature and the first work to bring her critical attention in the United States. The film reveals the influence of Federico Fellini for whom Wertmüller worked as an assistant director on *8½,* and it incorporates most of the elements that were to become trademarks of the Wertmüller canon. From Fellini she inherited a tendency towards comic exaggeration, both in creating types and in producing broad performances. Typical to her own concerns are the thematic interest in sexual politics, frequently set against a political backdrop; commanding heroines; and flawed, vulnerable heroes.

Love and Anarchy is framed by two scenes: the first depicts the childhood trauma of the peasant Tunin (Giancarlo Giannini). When Tunin's father, a rural anarchist, is shot by the police, the young boy assumes his father's mission to assassinate Mussolini. The second framing scene is his death in a Roman prison some decades later. The remainder of the film takes place in a Roman bordello where the adult Tunin meets Salome (Mariangela Melato), an anarchist sympathizer, and Tripolina (Lina Polito), a young prostitute.

As protector and lover, Salome provides Tunin with information that she extracts from a self-important client, Spatoletti, the head of Mussolini's secret police. Yet, gradually, Tunin falls in love with Tripolina. The climax of the film takes place on the day appointed for Mussolini's assassination. Tripolina hides the key to Tunin's bedroom; she hopes that by allowing him to oversleep, she will prevent both the deed and the punishment. She and Salome fight over the "key" to Tunin's fate: a struggle between love and anarchy. Finally Tripolina succeeds in convincing Salome that she should opt for personal happiness. But that is not to be; once Tunin discovers their collusion, he goes berserk, shooting widely at some policemen who have come to check the prostitute for VD. The film ends with Tunin's execution, as the police repeatedly strike Tunin's head against the stone walls of his cell.

Love and Anarchy is part of an outpouring of Italian films, released between 1969 and 1973, that examines the relations of individuals and institutions of authority, particularly during the fascist period. Included in this group are Bertolucci's *Il conformista* and *Strategia del ragno,* Bellocchio's *Nel nome del padre,* and Visconti's *La caduta degli dei.* In contrast to her compatriots or the Greek Costa-Gavras (*Z* and *The Confession,* also released at this time), Wertmüller provides only minimal insight into the workings of political tyranny. Further, it is difficult to decipher her position from the evidence of the film. At the film's conclusion, a quotation from the nineteenth-century anarchist Malatesta cautions against assassination as a political expedient; it refers to assassins as saints as well as heroes. Yet the one clear message of the film remains the certain failure of political naïveté and the ineffectuality of individual action.

The film's most original moments are three lyrical interludes which crystallize mood rather than further plot; they demonstrate Wertmüller's ability to expose humor in the midst of dark circumstances. The interludes include a break-neck motorcycle ride through the Italian countryside; a series of seduction scenes as the prostitutes

begin their day's business; and a filmic and poetic chronicle of a holiday that Tunin and Tripolina take before the final tragedy.

Love and Anarchy is most memorable for its spirited performances: the lusty Salome, the freckled and wide-eyed Tunin, the angelic Tripolina, and the bombastic Spatoletti. In addition, Giuseppe Rotunno's fluid camera work, Nino Rota's music, and Wertmüller's exuberant scenario combine to create an overall impression of a fine Italian opera.

—Patricia Erens

FOSTER, Jodie
American director and actress

Born: Alicia Christian Foster in Los Angeles, 19 November 1962. **Education:** Attended Lycée Français, Los Angeles; Yale University, B.A., 1985. **Career:** Acted in TV commercials from the age of three; 1969—acting debut on TV in *Mayberry R.F.D.*; 1972—feature film acting debut in *Napoleon and Samantha*; 1991—directorial film debut with *Little Man Tate*. **Awards:** U.S. National Film Critics Award, and Los Angeles Film Critics Award, for *Taxi Driver,* 1976; BAFTA Awards for Best Supporting Actress and Most Promising Newcomer, for *Taxi Driver* and *Bugsy Malone,* 1976; Academy Awards for Best Actress, for *The Accused,* 1988, and for *The Silence of the Lambs,* 1991; Chevalier dans l'Orde des Arts et de Lettres, 1995; Governors Award, American Society of Cinematographers, 1996. **Agent:** ICM, 8942 Beverly Boulevard, Beverly Hills, CA 90211, U.S.A.

Films as Director

1991 *Little Man Tate* (+ ro as Dede Tate)
1995 *Home for the Holidays* (+ co-pr)

Films as Actress

1970 *Menace on the Mountain* (McEveety—for TV) (as Suellen McIver)
1972 *Napoleon and Samantha* (McEveety) (as Samantha); *Kansas City Bomber* (Freedman) (as Rita)
1973 *Tom Sawyer* (Taylor) (as Becky Thatcher); *One Little Indian* (McEveety) (as Martha); *Rookie of the Year* (Elikann—for TV)
1974 *Alice Doesn't Live Here Anymore* (Scorsese) (as Audrey); *Smile Jenny, You're Dead* (Thorpe—for TV) (as Liberty)
1976 *Echoes of a Summer* (*The Last Castle*) (Taylor) (as Deirdre Striden); *Freaky Friday* (Nelson) (as Annabel Andrews); *Bugsy Malone* (Alan Parker) (as Tallulah); *Taxi Driver* (Scorsese) (as Iris Steensman)
1977 *The Little Girl Who Lives down the Lane* (Gessner) (as Rynn Jacobs); *Candleshoe* (Tokar) (as Casey Brown); *Il casotto* (*The Beach House*) (Citti) (as Teresina)
1978 *Moi, Fleur Bleue* (*Stop Calling Me Baby!*) (as Fleur Bleue)
1980 *Foxes* (Lyne) (as Jeanie); *Carny* (Kaylor) (as Donna)
1983 *O'Hara's Wife* (Bartman) (as Barbara O'Hara); *Le Sang des autres* (*The Blood of Others*) (Chabrol) (as Hélène); *Svengali* (Harvey—for TV) (as Zoe Alexander)

Jodie Foster directing *Little Man Tate*.

1984   *The Hotel New Hampshire* (Richardson) (as Franny Berry)
1986   *Mesmerized (Shocked)* (Laughlin) (as Victoria, + co-pr)
1987   *Siesta* (Lambert) (as Nancy)
1988   *Five Corners* (Bill) (as Linda); *The Accused* (Kaplan) (as Sarah Tobias); *Stealing Home* (Kampmann) (as Katie Chandler)
1989   *Backtrack (Catchfire)* (D. Hopper—released in U.S. in 1991) (as Anne Benton)
1991   *The Silence of the Lambs* (J. Demme) (as Clarice Starling)
1992   *Shadows and Fog* (W. Allen) (as prostitute)
1993   *Sommersby* (Amiel) (as Laurel); *It Was a Wonderful Life* (Ohayon—doc) (as narrator)
1994   *Nell* (Apted) (title role, + co-pr); *Maverick* (R. Donner) (as Annabelle Bransford)
1997   *Contact* (Zemeckis) (as Dr. Eleanor Arroway)

Publications by Foster

Articles

Interview in *Ciné Revue* (Paris), 1 July 1976.
Interview in *Screen International* (London), 8 October 1977.
Interview with Andy Warhol, in *Interview* (New York), June 1980.

Interview, by Foster, with Nastassia Kinski, in *Film Comment* (New York), September/October 1982.
"Why Me?," in *Esquire* (New York), December 1982.
Interview, by Foster, with Rob Lowe, in *Interview* (New York), May 1984.
Interview in *Time Out* (London), 8 November 1984.
Interview in *Interview* (New York), August 1987.
Interview with Linda R. Miller, in *American Film* (Los Angeles), October 1988.
"American Original," interview with Michael A. Lerner, in *Interview* (New York), September 1989.
Interview with Rod Lurie, in *Empire* (London), June 1991.
Interview with Ingrid Sischy, in *Interview* (New York), October 1991.
"Wunderkind," interview with Arion Berger, in *Harper's Bazaar* (New York), November 1991.

Publications on Foster

Books

Sinclair, Marian, *Hollywood Lolita: The Nymphet Syndrome in the Movies*, London, 1988.
Jodie Foster, Growing up On-screen: A Retrospective, Minneapolis, 1991.

Chunovic, Louis, *Jodie: A Biography,* Chicago, 1995.

Foster, Gwendolyn Audrey, *Women Film Directors: An International Bio-Critical Dictionary,* Westport, Connecticut, 1995.

Kennedy, Philippa, *Jodie Foster: A Life on Screen,* New York, 1996.

Smolen, Diane, *The Films of Jodie Foster,* Secaucus, New Jersey, 1996.

Foster, Buddy, *Foster Child,* New York, 1997.

Articles

Van Meter, Jonathan, "Child of the Movies," in *New York Times Magazine,* 6 January 1991.

Abramowitz, Rachel, "Loving a Lie," in *Premiere* (New York), March 1991.

Clark, John, filmography in *Premiere* (New York), March 1991.

Hirshey, Geari, "Jodie Foster," in *Rolling Stone* (New York), 21 March 1991.

Wilson, P., "The Changing Fortunes of Jodie Foster," in *Film Monthly* (Berkhamsted, England), July 1991.

Cameron, Julie, "Burden of the Gift," in *American Film* (Washington, D.C.), November/December 1991.

Rich, B. R., "Nobody's Handmaid," in *Sight and Sound* (London), December 1991.

Current Biography 1992, New York, 1992.

Nevers, C., "Jodie Foster," in *Cahiers du Cinéma* (Paris), no. 30, 1992.

Schnayerson, Michael, "Pure Jody," in *Vanity Fair* (New York), May 1994.

Abramowitz, Rachel, "Fearless," in *Premiere* (New York), January 1995.

Andrews, Suzanna, "Calling the Shots," in *Working Woman,* November 1995.

* * *

A wunderkind stage-managed by a pushy mother who enrolled her in a French-speaking school for gifted children and succeeded in bringing her to the notice of fledgling director Martin Scorsese, Jodie Foster has in many ways lived up to her early promise, winning Academy Awards for her performances in *The Accused* and *The Silence of the Lambs* and graduating with honors from Yale. After notable appearances as a child actress in *Alice Doesn't Live Here Anymore* and *Taxi Driver* (the only performance to inspire a would-be presidential assassin?), Foster suffered through the reactionary and overly conventional 1980s with few real opportunities to display her acting talents. Both *The Accused* and *Silence of the Lambs,* however, afforded her the opportunity once again to make an impression on mainstream cinema with finely crafted portraits of morally ambiguous women who, though victimized, maintain their integrity and self-respect.

Though urged by talent and inclination toward the director's chair, Foster has directed only two films. Perhaps too much was expected of her maiden effort (Foster appeared on the cover of *Time* immediately upon the release of *Little Man Tate,* which the magazine enthusiastically reviewed). Critics and audiences alike, however, generally did not like the film. Foster was undoubtedly attracted to the project to some extent by the subject matter, which has strong resonances with her own life and experiences. Fred Tate is also a wunderkind, whose only problem is that he needs more stimulation than his loving, though terribly low-brow, mother (played by Foster) is able to provide. Enter Jane Grierson, head of a school for gifted children, who wants to take charge of Fred's education. Dede Tate reluctantly agrees, and the remainder of the film treats the struggle between these two mothers, with their different parenting styles, for control of Fred.

Never a fan of mainstream cinema's glitz and fascination with (particularly) violent spectacle, Foster seems to have found in this story by Scott Frank the material for a dramatically effective small film. And yet Foster's handling (not discounting the problems in Frank's screenplay) does not do the material justice. Because Fred has no conflicts, except for finding a proper environment, he is rightly displaced from the story's center. And yet the conflict between the two women is not adroitly handled. Dede's decision to let Jane have Fred is not clearly dramatized; in fact, a number of scenes that begin with some promise of illuminating the similarities and differences of the two women end confusingly. Lacking the essential Aristotelian elements of a linear movement toward a conclusion and clearly drawn characters, the film becomes tedious and pointless; it is not rescued by an improbable conclusion and out-of-place melodramatic touches along the way. If Foster's point is to make some point about a mother's need to combine career aspirations for her child with unconditional elemental love and respect, the film only confusingly endorses such a position.

Foster waited four years before directing her follow-up effort, *Home for the Holidays,* in 1995. Continuing with the theme of parent-child relationships, the film stars Holly Hunter as the estranged daughter of a dysfunctional family who returns home to attempt to make peace. *Home for the Holidays* received mixed reviews, with some critics praising its dark humor and on-target picture of family life, while others claimed that the repeated clashes between parents and siblings made it difficult to watch. At any rate, the release of the film demonstrated that the multitalented Foster does intend to continue her pursuit of a directorial career.

—R. Barton Palmer

FRIEDRICH, Su
American director

Born: New Haven, Connecticut, 1954. **Education:** Attended the University of Chicago, 1971-72; Oberlin College, art and art history, B.A., 1975. **Career:** 1976—moved to New York; 1978—made her first film, *Hot Water*; part-time teacher of film production at the Millennium Film Workshop, New School for Social Research, and New York University; films have been the subject of retrospectives at numerous venues, including the Whitney Museum of American Art, National Film Theater (London), Stadtkino (Vienna), American Cinematheque (Los Angeles), and Anthology Film Archives (New York); active in many film-related and feminist endeavors. **Awards:** Special Merit Award, Athens Film Festival, for *Cool Hands, Warm Heart,* 1979; Best Experimental Film Award, Athens Film Festival, and Best Experimental Narrative Award, Atlanta Film Festival, for *Damned if You Don't,* 1987; Guggenheim Foundation Fellowship, 1989; Golden Gate Award, San Francisco Film Festival, Gold Juror's Choice Award, Charlotte Film and Video Festival, and Grand Prix, Melbourne Film Festival, for *Sink or Swim,* 1990; Rockefeller Foundation Fellowship, 1990; National Endowment for the Arts grant, 1994; Best Narrative Film Award, Athens International Film Festival, and Outstanding Documentary Feature, Outfest '97, for *Hide and Seek,* 1996; Alpert Award, 1996. **Address:** 222 East 5th Street, #6, New York, NY 10003, U.S.A.

Films as Director

1978 *Hot Water* (short) (+ sc, ph, ed)
1979 *Cool Hands, Warm Heart* (short) (+ sc, ph, ed); *Scar Tissue*
      (short) (+ sc, ph, ed)
1980 *I Suggest Mine* (short) (+ sc, ph, ed)
1981 **Gently down the Stream** (short) (+ sc, ph, ed)
1982 *But No One* (short) (+ sc, ph, ed)
1984 *The Ties That Bind* (+ sc, ph, ed)
1987 *Damned if You Don't* (+ sc, ph, ed)
1990 *Sink or Swim* (+ sc, ph, ed)
1991 *First Comes Love* (short) (+ sc, ph, ed)
1993 *Rules of the Road* (+ sc, ph, ed); *The Lesbian Avengers Eat
      Fire Too* (video) (co-d with Baus, + co-ed)
1996 *Hide and Seek* (+ co-sc, ed)

Publications by Friedrich

Scripts

"Script for a Film without Images," in *Feminism/Film*, no. 1, 1984.
"*Gently down the Stream*," in *Dreamworks*, Summer 1986.
"*Sink or Swim*," in *Cinematograph* (San Francisco) Spring 1991.

Articles

Photographs, fiction, essays, and film script, in *Heresies: A Feminist
    Journal on Art and Politics*, vols. 1-4, 6, 9, 16, 1977-83.
"On Margareta von Trotta's *The Second Awakening of Christa
    Klages*," in *Downtown Review*, Fall/Winter, 1979-80.
"Jennifer, Where Are You?," in *Downtown Review*, Fall/Winter/
    Spring, 1981-82.
Interview with Stephanie Deroes, in *Cinematograph* (San Francisco),
    no. 2, 1986.
"*Damned if You Don't*," interview with Scott MacDonald, in *After-
    image* (Rochester, New York), May 1988.
"Does Radical Form Require Radical Content?," in *Millennium* (New
    York), Winter/Spring 1989-90.
"Daddy Dearest: Su Friedrich Talks about Filmmaking, Family and
    Feminism," interview with Scott MacDonald, in *Independent* (New
    York), December 1990.
Interview with Sam McElfresh, in *American Federation of the Arts
    Newsletter*, Autumn 1991.
"Girls Out of Uniform," interview with Lydia Marcus, in *Release
    Print*, April 1997.

Publications on Friedrich

Books

Kuhn, Annette, *Women's Pictures: Feminism and Cinema*, London,
    1982; rev. ed., 1993.
de Lauretis, Teresa, editor, *Feminist Studies/Critical Studies*,
    Bloomington, Indiana, 1986.
Mellencamp, Patricia, *Indiscretions: Avant-Garde Film, Video and
    Feminism*, Bloomington, Indiana, 1990.
Kuhn, Annette, with Susannah Radstone, editors, *Women in Film: An
    International Guide*, New York, 1991.
Gever, Martha, John Greyson, and Pratibha Parmar, editors, *Queer Looks:
    Perspectives on Lesbian and Gay Film and Video*, New York, 1993.

Su Friedrich. Photograph by James Hamilton.

MacDonald, Scott, *Avant-Garde Film: Motion Studies*, New York,
    1993.
MacDonald, Scott, *A Critical Cinema 2*, Berkeley, 1993.
Stein, Arlene, editor, *Sisters, Sexperts, Queers: Beyond the Lesbian
    Nation*, New York, 1993.
Weiss, Andrea, *Vampires & Violets: Lesbians in the Cinema*, New
    York, 1993.
Foster, Gwendolyn Audrey, *Women Film Directors: An International
    Bio-Critical Dictionary*, Westport, Connecticut, 1995.
MacDonald, Scott, *Screen Writings: Scripts and Texts by Indepen-
    dent Filmmakers*, Berkeley, 1995.
Straayer, Chris, *Deviant Eyes, Deviant Bodies: Sexual Re-orienta-
    tions in Film and Video*, New York, 1996.
Holmlund, Chris, and Cynthia Fuchs, editors, *Between the Sheets, in
    the Streets: Queer, Lesbian, and Gay Documentary*, Minneapolis,
    1997.
Redding, Judith M., and Victoria A. Brownworth, *Film Fatales: In-
    dependent Women Directors*, Seattle, 1997.

Articles

Hanlon, Lindley, "Female Rage: The Films of Su Friedrich," in *Mil-
    lennium* (New York), Spring 1983.

MacDonald, Scott, "Text as Image," in *Afterimage* (Rochester, New York), March 1986.

Jenkins, Bruce, "*Gently down the Stream,*" in *Millennium* (New York), Fall/Winter 1986-87.

MacDonald, Scott, "Reappropriations," in *Film Quarterly* (Berkeley), Winter 1987-88.

Gever, Martha, "Girl Crazy," in *Independent* (New York), July 1988.

Sykora, Katharina, "When Form Takes as Many Risks as the Content," in *Frauen und Film* (Berlin), February 1989.

Galst, Liz, "A Woman on the Verge," in *Advocate* (Los Angeles), 26 February 1991.

Hoberman, J., "Life with Father," in *Premiere* (New York), December 1991.

Anker, Steve, "Unknown Territories: American Independent Film," in *Blimp,* 1992.

MacDonald, Scott, "From Zygote to Global Cinema via Su Friedrich's Films," in *Journal of Film and Video,* Spring/Summer 1992.

Lebow, Alisa, "Lesbians Make Movies," in *Cineaste* (New York), December 1993.

Holmlund, Chris, "Fractured Fairy Tales and Experimental Identities: Looking for Lesbians in and around the Films of Su Friedrich," in *Discourse* (Berkeley), Fall 1994.

Renov, Michael, "New Subjectivities: Documentary and Self-Representation in the Post-Verité Age," in *Documentary Box,* no. 7, 1995.

Olson, Jenni, "Child's Play," in *Out,* July 1997.

* * *

Su Friedrich is a New York-based independent filmmaker whose work is intensely personal and often centers around issues of feminism, gender, identity, family, body politics, and sexuality. Her work comes out of several key traditions within the American avant-garde such as structural, poetic, and autobiographical film. Friedrich's earliest short films in the late 1970s often revolved around specific female rituals such as shaving, or were primarily formal explorations concerned with the materiality of film. Friedrich achieved a certain maturity as a filmmaker with *Gently down the Stream* (1981), a film that combines formal experimentation and sophisticated film techniques with provocative subject matter. The film includes hand-scratched material (poetic text that was taken from a dream journal kept by the filmmaker over a period of several years), and photographed imagery that makes extensive use of the optical printer and rephotographed images. The film is primarily concerned with the emotional conflict between the filmmaker's Roman Catholic upbringing and her lesbian desires.

The hand-scratched poetic text and the lack of a soundtrack make watching *Gently down the Stream* a highly individuated experience since reading each word of scratched text as it is projected is an essential part of the viewing experience. The film is related in some ways to earlier structural films of the late 1960s and early 1970s by filmmakers such as Hollis Frampton and Owen Land (George Landow) whose films also contained rigorous structures and often involved the active participation of the viewer in similar forms of direct address. Friedrich's film has the added appeal of working with very emotional and intense subject matter. *Gently down the Stream* breaks new ground in its formal experimentation and the way it encourages a kind of cinematic stream of consciousness. This creates a particularly subjective film experience that also links Friedrich to Maya Deren and Stan Brakhage, who pioneered the experimental poetic form and also explored dream states in their films.

Friedrich's autobiographical explorations can be seen most clearly in *The Ties That Bind* (1984), one of her most well-known, longer-form films. This film is an evocative examination of the filmmaker's relationship to her mother. The film's structure revolves around Friedrich's mother answering the filmmaker's questions about her life in Germany in the 1930s and 1940s. The questions are once again scratched onto the celluloid. The photographed imagery not only includes footage of the filmmaker's mother at the present moment but images made while the filmmaker traveled in Germany, as well as footage from an antinuclear demonstration at a U.S. army base, archival war footage, home movies of Friedrich's parents together, footage from an early silent film, and other kinds of visual material. The sheer variety of photographed images in the film is astounding and is skillfully edited into a complex shape with the addition of the voice of the filmmaker's mother and scratched text. The complexities of the film extend to include an analysis of the filmmaker's views about war and the nature of human conflict, the positioning of women in society, and an examination of the filmmaker's German identity. The film is also significant within Friedrich's oeuvre in that the material is fairly accessible to an audience not necessarily familiar with or particularly interested in avant-garde cinema. But as Friedrich has stated, she herself enjoys "films that are both sensual and entertaining, that engage me emotionally as well as intellectually. I'm so bored by most films that are made in response to current film theory, and I've never felt obliged to use that sort of language in my own work."

Damned if You Don't, another key film from the 1980s, once again examines the filmmaker's Catholic upbringing and lesbian sexuality but in a more analytical way than the earlier films. It incorporates images from Pressburger and Powell's *Black Narcissus* (1947), one of the most sumptuous films made in the 1940s that, to some extent, depends on its extraordinary color photography for its aesthetic effect. Friedrich chooses to deliberately cut in black-and-white images from the film that have been transmitted on a television screen, thus neutralizing the aesthetic power of the Pressburger/Powell film almost entirely. The effect of this strategy is to allow Friedrich to explore the world of nuns in a more critical way and create her own discourse revolving around lesbian desire, the church, repression, and sexual politics. It is also a film that has a fair degree of humor in it, something absent from Friedrich's earlier work. The film offers the unstartling observation that some nuns suffer from sexual frustration and are attracted to other women. Whatever one may feel about the politics of the film and its critique, there is no denying that Friedrich created one of the most controversial and complex avant-garde films of the 1980s. Friedrich returned to specifically autobiographical investigations in one of her most recent long-form films, *Sink or Swim,* which is concerned with her relationship to her father. Once again Friedrich works with highly structured, rigorous forms, but as with all her work, the emotional, highly charged material makes watching the film a more engaging experience than earlier structuralist films.

Su Friedrich has undoubtedly created one of the most impressive bodies of work in recent years. Her explorations into cinematic form include exploring the film frame and screen surface, layering of the image and soundtrack, complex editing patterns, and the rhythmical possibilities of cinema. What sets her work apart, however, is that she never sacrifices emotional content in creating these complex forms. She is a filmmaker of great integrity and skill who continues to experiment with the film medium in ways that continually surprise and astonish audiences.

—Mario Falsetto

FUSES
USA, 1967
Director: Carolee Schneemann

Production: Color, 16mm; running time: 22 minutes.

Screenplay: Carolee Schneemann; **editor:** Carolee Schneemann; **photography:** Carolee Schneemann and James Tenney.

Cast: Carolee Schneemann; James Tenney.

Publications

Books

Youngblood, Gene, *Expanded Cinema,* New York, 1970.
Mekas, Jonas, *Movie Journal: The Rise of the New American Cinema 1959-1971,* New York, 1972.
Le Grice, Malcolm, *Abstract Film and Beyond,* Cambridge, Massachusetts, 1977.
Schneemann, Carolee, *More than Meat Joy,* New Paltz, New York, 1979; rev. ed., 1997.
MacDonald, Scott, *A Critical Cinema,* Berkeley, 1988.
Elder, R. Bruce, *The Body in Film,* Toronto, 1989.
Film-Makers Cooperative Catalogue No. 7, New York, 1989.
James, David E., *Allegories of Cinema: American Film in the 1960's,* Princeton, New Jersey, 1989.
Schneemann, Carolee, *Early and Recent Work: Two Catalogues of Retrospective Exhibition,* New York, 1993.

Articles

Schneeman, Carolee, "Through the Body: A Dialogue between Carolee Schneemann and Amy Greenfield," in *Field of Vision,* Fall 1978.
Montano, Linda, "Interview with Carolee Schneemann," in *Flue,* Summer 1982.
"Rolling in the Maelstrom: A Conversation between Carolee Schneemann and Robert Haller," in *Idiolects,* Spring 1984.
Schneeman, Carolee, "The Obscene Body/Politic," in *Art Journal,* Winter 1991.

*   *   *

Carolee Schneemann's *Fuses* is a key film of the 1960s avant-garde film movement. It is an example of those highly subjective, poetic films produced by many American experimental filmmakers in this period best exemplified by the work of Stan Brakhage and Bruce Baillie. What sets this film apart, however, is its avoidance of the generally phallocentric approach of male filmmakers at the time to the representation of the sexual act and the human body. The film is a powerful attempt to visually communicate the intimacy of heterosexual lovemaking, and how one feels during this most intense human activity. In some ways, it is a response to Stan Brakhage's 1956 film *Loving,* in which Schneemann appears making love in a field of grass with her lover, the composer James Tenney, which she felt did not capture the ecstasy of the lovemaking act.

In *Fuses,* Schneemann conceives of the screen as a flat surface rather than as a window onto the world, reflecting her extensive background as a painter and assemblage artist. Every part of the screen space is extensively explored and often the sense of three dimensionality is completely obliterated. The images in *Fuses* consist mostly of the filmmaker and Tenney engaged in highly charged, graphic acts of lovemaking. She films (or sets up the camera to film) the two bodies engaged in many positions of lovemaking in graphic close-up resulting in an extreme fragmentation of the human body. Tenney presumably filmed the moving camera shots of Schneemann alone in the frame. There are also external images of the filmmaker on a beach and shots of Tenney in a car, which act to amplify the sense of freedom that the uninhibited sexual images communicate and convey the sense of a world outside the interior space where most of the film was shot.

The visuals are highly abstracted through various collage techniques and multiple superimpositions, emphasizing the materiality of the filmmaking process that, in some ways, allude to abstract expressionist painting techniques of the 1950s. The superimpositions also have a way of destroying the integrity of the individual shot. In other words, it is extremely difficult to know where one shot begins and another ends. Also, it is virtually impossible much of the time to determine how many layers of film have been superimposed in any particular sequence. In an attempt to make a direct correlation between the energy of the human body and the filmic material, Schneemann has put the film stock through various physical procedures such as baking, staining, scratching, and painting. This sense of physically working on the filmic materials is a key aspect of Schneemann's process. The film has been organized with a complicated system of editing patterns and visual strategies, sometimes abstracting images of lights in an attempt to represent the ecstatic state of orgasm. This is related no doubt to Schneemann's avowed interest in Wilhelm Reich's psychoanalytic theories, especially as they relate to orgone theory.

There is an immediacy and directness about *Fuses* that has on occasion been misinterpreted as a kind of amateurism in its technique. But the diaristic approach and somewhat messy quality of the images should not be construed as ineptitude. The film has a remarkable sense of the immediate and the images are often gorgeous in some of their color saturations. There is also a fairly rigorous attack on the frame edge. Schneemann's unconventional approach is typical of other films at the time that were breaking barriers, both formally and in terms of subject matter, such as Brakhage's *Dog Star Man* and Baillie's *Quixote.* The film's soundtrack, which consists mainly of the sound of rolling waves, adds a hypnotic, rhythmical element that further intensifies the highly subjective experience elicited by the film.

Although many of the film's images are graphic in their sexual explicitness—shots of the penis and vagina were highly shocking at the time and almost never appeared in mainstream cinema—the variety of cinematic techniques employed by the filmmaker abstracts them to such an extent that they are often difficult to decipher. Yet the film's explicit images of the nude male and female body were considered outrageous for their time, perhaps because such images were normally associated with pornographic films. This often resulted in a kind of exclusion of Schneemann from official histories of the period. Schneemann's film was not always appreciated at the time, either by the male-dominated avant-garde film movement or by some feminists. The end result of this notoriety and critical neglect was that *Fuses* became a film that was simply difficult to see, and when it was screened it generally aroused controversy.

Schneemann's film is important because it dares to show the human body, both male and female, in all its complexity while com-

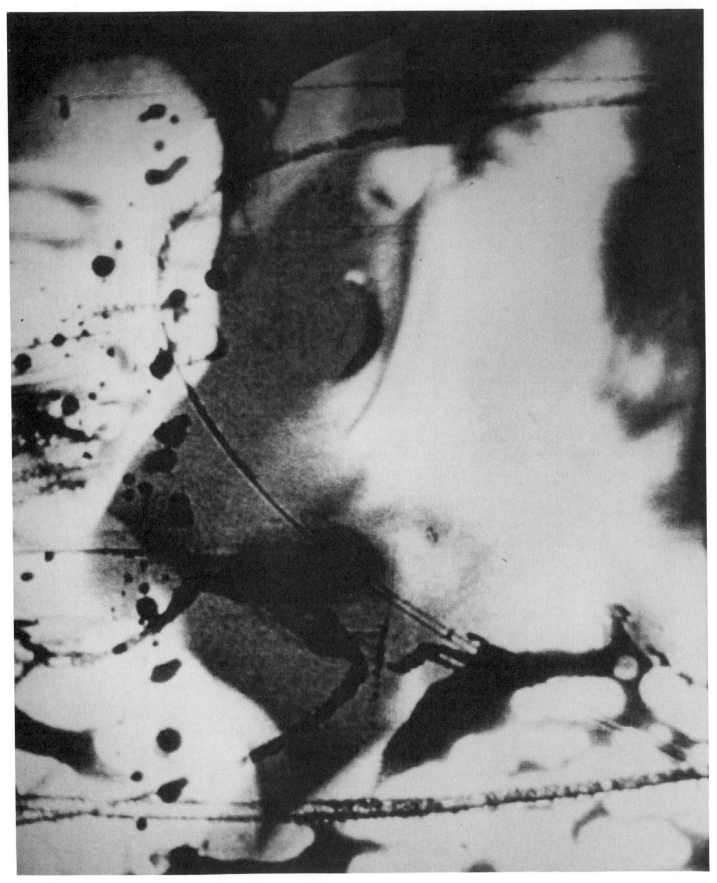

Fuses. Photograph by Carolee Schneemann.

pletely avoiding the voyeuristic. It is a daring film that celebrates the sexual potential of human beings and even today has the power to astonish audiences in its frankness. But it is always clear that Schneemann's main interest is to create a work of art not merely to shock. The film is also a radical attempt to forge a new relationship between filmmaker and the process of making a film. *Fuses* remains Carolee Schneemann's most impressive accomplishment as a filmmaker and a singular achievement in the history of American avant-garde cinema.

—Mario Falsetto

GENTLY DOWN THE STREAM
USA, 1981
Director: Su Friedrich

Production: Black and white, silent, 16mm; running time: 18 minutes at 18 frames per second; released 1981.

Screenplay: Su Friedrich; **editor:** Su Friedrich; **photography/optical effects:** Su Friedrich.

Cast: Su Friedrich.

Publications

Books

de Lauretis, Teresa, editor, *Feminist Studies/Critical Studies,* Bloomington, Indiana, 1986.
Film-makers' Cooperative Catalogue No. 7, New York, 1989.
Mellencamp, Patricia, *Indiscretions: Avant-Garde Film, Video and Feminism,* Bloomington, Indiana, 1990.
Canyon Cinema Catalogue 7, San Francisco, 1992.
Cook, Pam, and Philip Dodd, editors, *Women and Film: Sight and Sound Reader,* Philadelphia, 1993.
Gever, Martha, John Greyson, and Pratibha Parmar, editors, *Queer Looks: Perspectives on Lesbian and Gay Film and Video,* New York, 1993.
MacDonald, Scott, *A Critical Cinema 2,* Berkeley, 1993.
Weiss, Andrea, *Vampires & Violets: Lesbians in the Cinema,* New York, 1993.
Carson, Diane, Linda Dittmar, and Janice Welsch, editors, *Multiple Voices in Feminist Film Criticism,* Minneapolis, 1994.
Women Make Movies Catalogue, New York, 1994.
MacDonald, Scott, *Screen Writings: Scripts and Texts by Independent Filmmakers,* Berkeley, 1995.

Articles

Hanlon, Lindley, "Female Rage: The Films of Su Friedrich," in *Millennium* (New York), Spring 1983.
Jenkins, Bruce, "*Gently down the Stream,*" in *Millennium* (New York), Fall/Winter 1986-87.
MacDonald, Scott, "Reappropriations," in *Film Quarterly* (Berkeley), Winter 1987-88.

* * *

Gently down the Stream is a film made by Su Friedrich in 1981 that evolved out of Friedrich's dream journal. It revolves around two relationships of the filmmaker, one with a man, the other a woman. The film includes text that is hand-scratched directly onto the celluloid, as well as photographed imagery. Many of the images have been reworked on the optical printer and/or rephotographed off a screen. The text and the images work in a kind of mismatched way, and the images never directly illustrate the scratched text, functioning metaphorically. The film has many of the characteristics one associates with the "structural" cinema of the late 1960s and early 1970s. Because the film mixes several types of cinematic material and has such intense content revolving around the body and relationships it works somewhat differently than earlier structural films.

The genesis of the film is intriguing. Friedrich claims that the film evolved from "a succession of fourteen dreams taken from eight years of my journals.... I chose to work with dreams that were most troubling to me, that expressed my deepest fears, anxieties and longings." Some of the imagery in the film includes religious iconography (a statue of the Virgin Mary and Christ, and a nun), a woman on a rowing machine and a woman swimming in a pool (footage taken from Friedrich's first film *Hot Water,* 1978), shots of a body of water, and flicker effects. The dream texts are intriguing and often quite intense. They are scratched onto the film emulsion so as to highlight their graphic nature, and add an element of expressionism to the image. Generally the words are scratched one or two words at a time although there are exceptions to this. The lettering is not of uniform size and words are either capitalized or in small letters depending on the emphasis they are meant to convey. The act of reading (literally) becomes a key act in the viewing experience. The photographic images sometimes fill the whole frame and at other times they fill only a part of the screen. All these strategies tend to emphasize the material nature of the film medium.

Some of the dream texts are concerned with the body or sexual relationships as the following extracts reveal [all texts from the screenplay for *Gently down the Stream,* which attempts to visually approximate the rhythms of the poetry]:

> I make a second vagina
> beside my first one
> I look in surprise
> which
> is the original?"

> ****

> Woman on the bed shivers
> I wake her
> She is angry
> Smears spermicidal jelly
> on my lips

> NO!

The film also features poetic text that references the natural world as this extract illustrates:

A LEOPARD EATS TWO BLUE
two blue hummingbirds
humming
I feel the feathers
MY TONGUE
fl utter on my
BONES mutter HEARTS utter FEATHERS
humming   on my   tongue

These extracts give a flavor of the poetic text, its play with language and its emotional quality. Friedrich has mentioned that she is "more concerned with finding ways to integrate the (harsh) wisdom of dreams...than...in analyzing the structure and function of dreams through any given system (Freudian, Jungian, etc.)." The task of interpreting the film is thus perhaps more significant for the filmmaker than it is for the viewer. But as a cinematic experience *Gently down the Stream* undoubtedly breaks new ground in its formal experimentation and the way it encourages a kind of cinematic stream of consciousness. The film is also specifically concerned with an internal conflict between Friedrich's lesbian sexuality and her Roman Catholic upbringing. Most of the film's imagery, however, is not as specific as the Christian iconography and functions more poetically. This creates a particularly subjective film experience that resembles, in an odd way, the films of Maya Deren, which were also poetic, highly structured and concerned with dream states. Some have interpreted this film as filled with a "violent rage," but that seems a harsh reading. The vivid, almost visceral quality of the text coupled with the frenetic pace of the woman on the rowing machine no doubt encourages this interpretation.

The autobiographical nature of this important early work by Friedrich and the film's inherent ambiguity suggest that Friedrich is not interested in creating doctrinaire feminist films. As she has stated in an interview:

I wasn't saying that all women are good and it's only good to be with women. I was saying, well, you know, things are kind of messy in our private lives and in our dream worlds and that's just the way it is. At first it seemed that if I was going to be a "good" feminist I should show the relationship with the woman to be a good one as compared to the relationship with a man. But I couldn't because the dreams that I had about the relationship with the woman revealed a lot of problems. The dreams revealed that both relationships were pretty much failures, and that seemed more realistic than trying to sell some theory about how relationships should be.

Gently down the Stream is one of the strongest films to be made by an avant-garde filmmaker in the 1980s, and clearly illustrates that it is still possible to explore the film medium in innovative ways, and build on the achievements of earlier generations without being the least bit derivative.

—Mario Falsetto

GIRLFRIENDS
USA, 1978
Director: Claudia Weill

Production: Cyclops Film. Du Art color; 35mm; running time: 87 minutes. Released August 1978.

Producer: Claudia Weill; **associate producer:** Jan Saunders; **screenplay:** Vicki Polon; **photography:** Fred Murphy; **editor:** Suzanne Pettit; **sound:** Ed Rothkowitz, Hanna Wajshonig, and Emily Paine; **art director:** Patrizia von Brandenstein; **music:** Michael Small.

Cast: Melanie Mayron (*Susan Weinblatt*); Anita Skinner (*Anne Munroe*); Eli Wallach (*Rabbi Gold*); Christopher Guest (*Eric*); Amy Wright (*Ceil*); Gina Rogak (*Julie*); Viveca Lindfors (*Beatrice*); Bob Balaban (*Martin*); Mike Kellin (*Abe*); Russell Horton (*photo editor*); Tanya Berezin (*Rabbi's wife*); Roderick Cook (*Carpel*); Jean De Baer (*Terry*); Kenneth McMillan (*Cabbie*); Kristoffer Tabori (*Charlie*); Kathryn Walker (*Carpel's receptionist*).

Publications

Book

Kuhn, Annette, *Women's Pictures: Feminism and Cinema,* London, 1982.

Articles

Ahlander, L., "Traskor och diktatorer: rapport fran Cannes 78," in *Chaplin* (Stockholm), vol. 20, no. 4, 1978.
"Claudia Weill Pic for Cannes," in *Variety* (New York), 22 March 1978.
Variety Film Reviews (New York), 30 April 1978.
Dworkin, S., "*Girlfriends*: A Reality Fix," in *Ms.* (New York), August 1978.
Kauffmann, Stanley, "Small Film, Large Hurrah," in *New Republic* (Whitinsville, Massachusetts), August 1978.
Klemesrud, J., "*Girlfriends* Director on Female Friendship," interview with Claudia Weill, in *New York Times,* 4 August 1978.
Asahina, R., "On Screen: Good Things in Small Packages," in *New Leader* (New York), 14 August 1978.
Cocchi, J., "Claudia Weill Confident about Entry into Entertainment Feature Field," in *Boxoffice* (Kansas City, Missouri), 14 August 1978.
Schonberg, Harold C., in *New York Times,* 19 August 1978.
Denby, David, "A Nay for the 'Eyes,'" in *New York,* 21 August 1978.
Gilliatt, Penelope, "The Current Cinema: Proximity," in *New Yorker,* 21 August 1978.
Sarris, Andrew, "Films in Focus: Women Who Need No One," in *Village Voice* (New York), 21 August 1978.
Ansen, David, "Little Women; Antipasto," in *Newsweek* (New York), 28 August 1978.
Coe, R., "Vicki Polon: An Unburied Woman," in *Village Voice* (New York), 28 August 1978.
Rich, F., "Cinema: High Hopes," in *Time* (New York), 28 August 1978.
Schlesinger, A. M. Jr., "The Movies: One Feminist Film That Works," in *Saturday Review* (Des Moines, Iowa), 2 September 1978.
Coleman, J., "Love a Duck," in *New Statesman* (London), 29 September 1978.
Aude, F., "La Vibration du fugitif (*Girlfriends*)," in *Positif* (Paris), November 1978.
Tibbetts, J. C., "A Matter of Definition: Out of Bounds in 'The Girlfriends,'" in *Literature/Film Quarterly* (Salisbury, Maryland), vol. 7, no. 4, 1979.
Bailin, R. A., "*Girlfriends*: No Celebration of Female Bonding," in *Jump Cut* (Berkeley), May 1979.
Stefanoni, L., "Claudia Weill: *Girlfriends*," in *Cineforum* (Bergamo, Italy), December 1979.
Termine, L., "*Girlfriends*"; "L'amour viole," in *Cinema Nuovo* (Torino, Italy), December 1979.

Girlfriends

Bullitta, J. M., "Susan y Ana," in *Hablemos de Cine* (Lima), April 1980.
Charbonneau, C., and L. Winer, "Lesbians in 'Nice' Films," in *Jump Cut* (Berkeley), March 1981.
Quart, Barbara Koenig, "Friendship in Some Recent American Films," in *Film Criticism* (Edinboro, Pennsylvania), vol. 6, no. 2, 1982.
Kuhn, Annette, "Hollywood et les nouveaux women's films," in *CinémAction* (Conde-sur-Noireau), vol. 67, no. 2, 1993.

* * *

Girlfriends was a well-received independent fiction feature made by the filmmaker Claudia Weill, who had previously been known for her feminist documentaries. For *Girlfriends,* her first feature, Weill managed to secure grant money to make the film, about $140,000, which was originally conceived as a low-budget, $10,000 short that would be funded through a collection of grants, loans, and private donations. But, over the course of several years, the film developed into a full-length feature about the struggle to maintain a friendship between two young women. It earned enthusiastic praise at several film festivals, including Cannes, which led to a worldwide distribution deal with Warner Bros.

The film opens compellingly with a series of still photographs of the two fresh-out-of-college girlfriends' tightly framed faces, after which the heroine Susan Weinblatt, who is Jewish, is shown photographing her roommate Anne as she sleeps. The next scene further defines Susan as the central character and as a working woman, as she is shown photographing a bar mitzvah boy as he shakes hands with a rabbi. The character of Susan is well-developed and cleverly nuanced, and Weill presents her as a photographer by vocation and avocation. The story itself begins as Susan's gentile friend Anne, an occasional poet, moves out of their shared apartment to get married, whereupon a series of significant event take place in Susan's life, especially as she struggles to develop her professional photography career. Indeed, although the friendship between the women is the narrative thread that ties the film together, Weill conveys the myriad challenges of Susan's work, along with her professional insecurities and inexperience. Based on her own experience as a still photographer, Weill details the competitiveness, menial jobs, manipulations, and unappealing compromises Susan must make to survive, along with the manipulations of editors who alter her work without her approval.

In *Girlfriends,* it is the development of the characters that is more important than plot. As the *New York Times* reviewer explained,

"Nothing much happens in *Girlfriends*. Nothing much is supposed to happen." So, in terms of the girlfriends' relationship, Weill suggests the rewards as well as the sense of betrayal that some women feel when it seems that their friends have placed their friendship second to their marriages. Furthermore, in the context of the women's movement, the film offered a timely depiction of a woman who questions her feelings about whether or not to get married and have children, while pursuing her professional goals. In a fleeting image, one of Susan's photographs seems to refer to her own predicament, as it depicts a girl as she turns away from a bride who is totally covered as though wearing a shroud. At the same time, however, Weill avoids portraying living alone as an ideal situation; instead, she depicts it as often lonely—showing Susan crying alone as she watches television, and walking forlornly down the street past a kissing couple after the dissolution of her relationship with the rabbi. Consequently, Susan is compelled to pick up a spaced-out stray girl, the lesbian Ceil, who brings yet another set of problems, though not romantic ones, to Susan's already challenging life.

Critics enthusiastically praised Weill's deft technical skills, confident style, and authenticity. *Variety,* for example, described the film as a "warm, emotional and at times wise picture ... deserving of a wide audience." Others noted that although it is sentimental, it never degenerates into overwrought pathos. Ultimately, however, the film earned critical but not great commercial success, though it did enjoy some mainstream impact.

Critics further commended Weill's inspired casting choices and the actresses', especially Mayron's, natural performances. Weill employed actresses who were not then well known and whose ethnicity was palpable but not stereotypical. The anti-glamorous looks and personality that Mayron brought to the film are crucial; her Susan sports wild hair, awkward eyeglasses, crooked teeth, and a plump round face along with charm and intelligence that betray her longing for rich experiences and professional satisfaction. Interestingly, Weill cast Eli Wallach as the middle-aged rabbi who is Susan's occasional romantic interest. Weill also treats the male characters with a noteworthy sympathy. Thus, Susan's boyfriend Eric is a charming, playful man, and the rabbi, though married, is respectable and humane, and Susan often shares with him knowing winks and affectionate jokes about their Jewish world of weddings and bar mitzvahs.

Girlfriends does not have a simple, flashy, or tidy ending. Instead, it ends with the two friends endeavoring to share their lives despite their separation. The final scene shows them sitting in front of the fireplace as they laugh together, thus excluding Anne's husband. Strangely, Weill was unwilling to call *Girlfriends* a feminist film; but, feminist critics have pointed out the folly of her claim. Especially given that, at the time, male buddy films were quite prolific, while female friendships were extraordinarily rare on movie screens. Indeed, if it is not a feminist film, what film could be characterized as feminist?

—Cynthia Felando

GISH, Lillian

American director and actress

Born: Lillian Diana Gish in Springfield, Ohio, 14 October 1896 (some sources say 1893) sister of the actress Dorothy Gish. **Education:** Briefly attended Ursuline Academy, East St. Louis, Illinois.

Career: About 1902—stage debut in Rising Sun, Ohio, in *The Little Red Schoolhouse*; 1903-04—with mother and sister Dorothy, toured in *Her First False Step*; 1905—danced with Sarah Bernhardt production in New York City; 1908-11—lived with aunt in Massillon, Ohio, and with mother in East St. Louis, and briefly with father in Oklahoma; 1912—film debut as featured player, with sister, in *An Unseen Enemy* for D. W. Griffith; 1913—in Belasco production of *A Good Little Devil* starring Mary Pickford; collapsed during run of play with pernicious anemia; 1920—directed sister Dorothy Gish in *Remodeling Her Husband* for D. W. Griffith; 1921—last film under Griffith's direction, *Orphans of the Storm*; joined Inspiration Films; 1924—$800,000 contract with MGM; 1930—first talkie, *One Romantic Night*; resumed stage career in *Uncle Vanya*; 1930s—began working in radio; 1948—TV debut in Philco Playhouse production *The Late Christopher Bean*; 1969—began giving film lecture "Lillian Gish and the Movies: The Art of Film, 1900-1928." 1987—starred in her last film, with Bette Davis, in *The Whales of August*. **Awards:** Honorary Academy Award, "for superlative artistry and for distinguished contribution to the progress of motion pictures," 1970; Life Achievement Award, American Film Institute, 1984; D. W. Griffith Award, for "an outstanding career in motion pictures," 1987. **Died:** In New York City, 27 February 1993.

Film as Director

1920 *Remodeling Her Husband* (+ co-sc)

Films as Actress

1912 *An Unseen Enemy* (D. W. Griffith); *Two Daughters of Eve* (D. W. Griffith); *In the Aisles of the Wild* (D. W. Griffith); *The One She Loved* (D. W. Griffith); *The Musketeers of Pig Alley* (D. W. Griffith); *My Baby* (F. Powell); *Gold and Glitter* (F. Powell); *The New York Hat* (D. W. Griffith); *The Burglar's Dilemma* (D. W. Griffith); *A Cry for Help* (D. W. Griffith)

1913 *Oil and Water* (D. W. Griffith); *The Unwelcome Guest* (D. W. Griffith); *The Stolen Bride* (O'Sullivan); *A Misunderstood Boy* (D. W. Griffith); *The Left-Handed Man* (D. W. Griffith); *The Lady and the Mouse* (D. W. Griffith); *The House of Darkness* (D. W. Griffith); *Just Gold* (D. W. Griffith); *A Timely Interception* (D. W. Griffith); *Just Kids* (Henderson); *The Mothering Heart* (D. W. Griffith); *During the Round Up* (D. W. Griffith); *An Indian's Loyalty* (F. Powell); *A Woman in the Ultimate* (D. W. Griffith); *A Modest Hero* (D. W. Griffith); *So Runs the Way* (D. W. Griffith); *The Madonna of the Storm* (D. W. Griffith); *The Blue or the Gray* (Cabanne); *The Conscience of Hassan Bey* (Cabanne); *The Battle at Elderbush Gulch* (D. W. Griffith)

1914 *The Green-Eyed Devil* (Kirkwood); *The Battle of the Sexes* (D. W. Griffith); *The Hunchback* (Cabanne); *The Quicksands* (Cabanne); *Home, Sweet Home* (D. W. Griffith); *Judith of Bethulia* (D. W. Griffith) (as the young mother); *Silent Sandy* (Kirkwood); *The Escape* (D. W. Griffith); *The Rebellion of Kitty Belle* (Cabanne); *Lord Chumley* (Kirkwood); *Man's Enemy* (F. Powell); *The Angel of Contention* (O'Brien); *The Wife*; *The Tear that Burned* (O'Brien); *The Folly of Anne* (O'Brien); *The Sisters* (Cabanne); *His Lesson* (Crisp) (as extra)

1915 *The Birth of a Nation* (D. W. Griffith) (as Elsie Stoneman); *The Lost House* (Cabanne); *Enoch Arden (As Fate Ordained)* (Cabanne); *Captain Macklin* (O'Brien); *Souls Triumphant* (O'Brien); *The Lily and the Rose* (P. Powell)

1916 *Daphne and the Pirate* (Cabanne) (as Daphne); *Sold for Marriage* (Cabanne); *An Innocent Magdalene* (Dwan); *Intolerance* (D. W. Griffith); *Diane of the Follies* (Cabanne) (title role); *Pathways of Life*; *Flirting with Fate* (Cabanne); *The Children Pay* (Ingraham)

1917 *The House Built upon Sand* (Morrissey)

1918 *Hearts of the World* (D. W. Griffith) (as the Girl, Marie Stephenson); *The Great Love* (D. W. Griffith); Liberty Bond short (D. W. Griffith); *The Greatest Thing in Life* (D. W. Griffith); *The Romance of Happy Valley* (D. W. Griffith)

1919 *Broken Blossoms* (D. W. Griffith) (as Lucy Burrows); *True Heart Susie* (D. W. Griffith) (title role); *The Greatest Question* (D. W. Griffith)

1920 *Way Down East* (D. W. Griffith) (as Anna Moore)

1921 *Orphans of the Storm* (D. W. Griffith) (as Henriette Girard)

1923 *The White Sister* (H. King) (as Angela Chiaromonte)

1924 *Romola* (H. King) (title role)

1926 *La Bohème* (K. Vidor) (as Mimi); *The Scarlet Letter* (Seastrom) (as Hester Prynne)

1927 *Annie Laurie* (Robertson) (title role); *The Enemy* (Niblo)

1928 *The Wind* (Seastrom) (as Letty Mason)

1930 *One Romantic Night* (Stein) (as Alexandra)

1933 *His Double Life* (Hopkins and W. B. deMille) (as Mrs. Alice Hunter)

1942 *The Commandos Strike at Dawn* (Farrow) (as Mrs. Bergesen)

1943 *Top Man* (*Man of the Family*) (Lamont) (as Beth Warren)

1946 *Miss Susie Slagle's* (Berry) (title role); *Duel in the Sun* (K. Vidor) (as Mrs. Laura Belle McCanles)

1948 *Portrait of Jennie* (*Jennie*) (Dieterle) (as Mother Mary of Mercy)

1955 *The Cobweb* (Minnelli) (as Victoria Inch); *The Night of the Hunter* (Laughton) (as Rachel); *Salute to the Theatres* (supervisor: Loud—short) (appearance)

1958 *Orders to Kill* (Asquith) (as Mrs. Summers)

1960 *The Unforgiven* (J. Huston) (as Mattilda Zachary)

1963 *The Great Chase* (Killiam—doc)

1966 *Follow Me, Boys!* (Tokar) (as Hetty Seiber)

1967 *Warning Shot* (Kulik) (as Alice Willows); *The Comedians* (Glenville) (as Mrs. Smith); *The Comedians in Africa* (short) (appearance)

1970 *Henri Langlois* (Hershon and Guerra) (as guest)

1976 *Twin Detectives* (Day—for TV)

1978 *A Wedding* (Altman) (as Nettie Sloan)

1981 *Thin Ice* (Aaron—for TV)

1983 *Hobson's Choice* (Cates—for TV)

1984 *Hambone and Hillie* (Watts) (as Hillie)

1986 *Sweet Liberty* (Alda) (as Cecelia Burgess); *The Adventures of Huckleberry Finn* (Hunt)

1987 *The Whales of August* (L. Anderson) (as Sarah Webber)

Publications by Gish

Books

Life and Lillian Gish, with Albert Bigelow, New York, 1932.
The Movies, Mr. Griffith, & Me, with Ann Pinchot, Englewood Cliffs, New Jersey, 1969.
Dorothy and Lillian Gish, New York, 1973.
An Actor's Life for Me, as told to Selma Lane, New York, 1987.

Articles

"The Gish Girls Talk about Each Other," by Ada Patterson in *Photoplay* (New York), June 1921.
"Dorothy Gish, the Frankest Girl I Know," in *Filmplay Journal,* April 1922.
"We Interview the Two Orphans," by Gladys Hall and Adele Whitely Fletcher, in *Motion Picture Magazine* (New York), May 1922.
"My Sister and I," in *Theatre Magazine* (New York), November 1927.
"Birth of an Era," in *Stage,* January 1937.
"D. W. Griffith: A Great American," in *Harper's Bazaar* (New York), October 1940.
"Silence Was Our Virtue," in *Films and Filming* (London), December 1957.
"Conversation with Lillian Gish," in *Sight and Sound* (London), Winter 1957-58.
"Life and Living," interview, in *Films and Filming* (London), January 1970.
"Lillian Gish...Director," in *Silent Picture* (London), Spring 1970.
Interview with Y. Lardeau and V. Ostria, in *Cahiers du Cinéma* (Paris), November 1983.
Interview with Allan Hunter, in *Films and Filming* (London), August 1987.

Lillian Gish

"Conversazione con Lillian Gish," interview with N. Lodato, in *Filmcritica* (Rome), April 1993.

Publications on Gish

Books

Wagenknecht, Edward, *Lillian Gish: An Interpretation,* Seattle, 1927.
Lillian Gish: Actress, compiled by Anthony Slide, London, 1969.
Pratt, George C., *Spellbound in Darkness,* Connecticut, 1973.
Rosen, Marjorie, *Popcorn Venus,* New York, 1973.
Slide, Anthony, *The Griffith Actresses,* New York, 1973.
Affron, Charles, *Star Acting: Gish, Garbo, Davis,* New York, 1977.
Lillian Gish, edited by the Museum of Modern Art, New York, 1980.
Wagenknecht, Edward, *Stars of the Silents,* Metuchen, New Jersey, 1987.
Foster, Gwendolyn Audrey, *Women Film Directors: An International Bio-Critical Dictionary,* Westport, Connecticut, 1995.

Articles

Hall, Gladys, "Lights! Say Lillian!," in *Motion Picture Magazine* (New York), April/May 1920.
Brooks, Louise, "Women in Films," in *Sight and Sound* (London), Winter 1957-58.
Brooks, Louise, "Gish and Garbo: The Executive War on Stars," in *Sight and Sound* (London), Winter 1958-59.
Tozzi, Romano, "Lillian Gish," in *Films in Review* (New York), December 1962, see also issue for April 1964.
Bodeen, DeWitt, "Lillian Gish: The Movies, Mr. Griffith and Me," in *Silent Picture* (London), Autumn 1969.
Morley, Sheridan, "Lillian Gish: Life and Living," in *Films and Filming* (London), January 1970.
Current Biography 1978, New York, 1978.
Curran, T., "Lillian Gish: Tribute to a Great Lady," in *Films in Review* (New York), October 1980.
Kael, Pauline, "Lillian Gish and Mae Marsh," in *The Movie Star,* edited by Elisabeth Weis, New York, 1981.
Naremore, J., "True Heart Susie and the Art of Lillian Gish," in *Quarterly Review of Film Studies* (Pleasantville, New York), Winter 1981.
"Dossier: Lillian Gish," in *Cinématographe* (Paris), October 1983.
Brownlow, Kevin, "Glimpses of a Legend," in *Sight and Sound* (London), Spring 1984.
Brownlow, Kevin, "Lillian Gish," in *American Film* (Washington, D.C.), March 1984.
Slide, Anthony, "Filming Lillian Gish," in *American Cinematographer* (Los Angeles), June 1984.
Gomery, Douglas, "Lillian Gish: First Lady of Film," in *Modern Maturity* (Ojai, California), February/March 1993.
Obituary in *New York Times,* 1 March 1993.
Obituary in *Variety* (New York), 8 March 1993.
Collins, G., "Hundreds Gather to Mourn a Friend," in *New York Times,* 12 March 1993.
Kaplan, M., "Gish and Davis: Could the Two Work Together?" in *New York Times,* 18 April 1993.
Dyer, Richard, "A White Star," in *Sight and Sound* (London), August 1993.
Brownlow, Kevin, "Lillian Gish," obituary in *Griffithiana* (Baltimore, Maryland), October 1993.
Merrritt, Russell, "In and Around *Broken Blossoms,*" in *Griffitiana* (Baltimore, Maryland), October 1993.

Wolfe, R. H., "The Gish Film Theater and Gallery: The Ohio Roots of Dorothy and Lillian Gish," in *Journal of Popular Film and Television* (Washington D.C.), no. 2, 1994.

* * *

In 1919 Lillian Gish was one of Hollywood's most respected performers and D. W. Griffith's favorite actress. That year, confident that her knowledge of the movies was equal to his own, Griffith asked her to direct a movie starring her sister Dorothy for Paramount. Convinced that women had already proven to be proficient directors, Gish happily accepted the offer. Griffith gave her a $50,000 budget and total liberty in the production. He also asked, however, that she supervise the conversion of a recently acquired Long Island estate into a studio, which was far from properly equipped for film production. It proved to be an enormous task, but she completed both it and the film successfully.

Believing that Dorothy's considerable charm and comedic skills had never been fully captured on film by her directors, Lillian was committed to doing a better job. In addition, she wanted the production to be an "all-woman picture," so she recruited Dorothy Parker to bring her immense wit to the task of writing the intertitles, a first for Parker. The Gish sisters worked together to develop a comedy scenario that was inspired by a "little piece of business" that Dorothy had discovered in a magazine. The result was *Remodeling Her Husband,* which provides a clever take on the notions of male prerogative and feminine "charms," with a heroine who was quite different from the fragile, demure, and often-victimized heroines Lillian usually played. Specifically, a husband complains that his wife is so dowdy that she never attracts the admiring gazes of men. Furious, the wife determines to teach him a lesson by insisting that he follow her as she walks down the street. Each time she passes a man she makes amusing or seductive faces at him, which her husband cannot see. Consequently, each man turns to stare intently at her and she successfully convinces her surprised husband that he is wrong about her lack of sex appeal. The film gently mocks masculine expectations about femininity as its heroine cleverly avoids making herself over to satisfy her husband—a common theme in films at the time. Instead, she uses her "natural" charms to entice the looks of men, and more importantly, to "remodel" her husband's opinion of her.

In addition to preparing Griffith's studio for film production in general, Gish recalled her overwhelming responsibilities during the production of *Remodeling Her Husband,* including designing and furnishing all of the sets, coordinating the costumes, negotiating the hazards of filming in winter, and calming the frazzled nerves of the cinematographer—a shell-shocked war veteran. One of Gish's favorite anecdotes about the production involved learning the day before shooting one of the film's most complicated scenes that a police permit was required. Set in downtown Manhattan—where a bus on which Dorothy was riding would pass a taxicab that held her husband and another woman—the scene was crucial to the narrative. So, because it would take several days to acquire one, and because she was without the budget to pay her crew in the meantime, Gish decided to film the scene as scheduled. Risking jail, the film company agreed to the plan. Their gamble paid off, with the help of a sympathetic policeman—a fan of Lillian's—who allowed the cast and crew to continue shooting after he discovered them breaking the law. In the end, she was able to complete the film for $58,000 and it netted more than $460,000. Interestingly, the film erroneously credited Gish with being the first woman director; that is, it included an introductory title card that suggested that because the modern woman was becoming active in all of the arts, it was time for her to undertake motion picture directing.

When *Remodeling Her Husband* was completed, Griffith praised Lillian's work but the critics were less kind, suggesting that Dorothy's performance was its only strength. In any event, the film marked the beginning and the end of Lillian Gish's career as a director. She subsequently told an interviewer that she thought directing was "no career for a lady," mostly because she was not enamored of the myriad administrative details it requires. By the time she left Griffith's employ, Gish had acquired considerable filmmaking expertise, and her subsequent studio contracts gave her unusual power in the production of her films; at both the smaller Inspiration Pictures studio and later for MGM, she had script control and her choice of directors. Thus, in the mid-1920s, she made two of her most memorable films, which were directed by two virtuoso directors: *La Bohème* directed by King Vidor, and *The Scarlet Letter* directed by Victor Seastrom. In addition, she diligently scouted locations and sought to bring authenticity to her films and performances.

—Cynthia Felando

GLYN, Elinor
British director and writer

Born: Elinor Sutherland in Jersey, England, 17 October 1864; sister of the fashion designer Lady Lucy Duff Gordon. **Education:** Taught at home by a series of governesses until age 14. **Family:** Married Clayton Glyn, 1892 (died 1915), daughters: Margot and Juliet. **Career:** 1900—published first novel, *The Visits of Elizabeth*; 1907—gained fame as a novelist with *Three Weeks*; 1920—wrote first screenplay, *The Great Moment*; 1921—gained fame in Hollywood for second screenplay, *Beyond the Rocks*; 1928—helped adapt her 1926 novel, *It*, for the screen; 1930—directed two films in England, both were failures that precipitated her retirement from the movies, 1936—published her autobiography, *Romantic Adventure*. **Died:** In London, 23 September 1943.

Films as Director

1930   *Knowing Men* (+ pr, co-sc); *The Price of Things* (+ pr, sc)

Films as Writer

1920   *The Great Moment* (Woods)
1921   *Beyond the Rocks* (Woods)
1923   *Six Hours* (Rabin); *Three Weeks* (*The Romance of a Queen*) (Crosland)
1924   *His Hour* (K. Vidor)
1925   *Man and Maid* (Schertsinger); *Love's Blindness* (Dillon)
1926   *The Only Thing* (Conway)
1927   *Ritzy* (Rosson)
1928   *It* (Badger) (+ ro as herself, co-pr); *Red Hair* (Badger)

Film as Actress

1921   *The Affairs of Anatol* (C. B. DeMille) (as bridge player)

Elinor Glyn

Publications by Glyn

Books

The Visits of Elizabeth, London, 1900.
The Reflections of Ambrosine, London, 1902.
The Damsel and the Sage, London, 1903.
The Vicissitudes of Evangeline, London, 1905.
Beyond the Rocks, London, 1906.
Three Weeks, London, 1907.
Sayings of Grandmamma, London, 1908.
Elizabeth Visits America, London, 1909.
His Hour, London, 1910.
The Reason Why, London, 1911.
Halcyone, London, 1912.
The Contrast and Other Stories, London, 1913.
The Sequence (1905-1912), London, 1913.
Letters to Caroline, London, 1914.
The Man and the Moment, London, 1915.
Three Things, London, 1915.
The Career of Katherine Bush, London, 1917.
Destruction, London, 1918.
The Price of Things, London, 1919.
Points of View, London, 1920.
Man and Maid, London, 1922.
The Great Moment, London, 1923.
The Philosophy of Love, Auburn, New York, 1923.
Six Days, London, 1924.

Letters from Spain, London, 1924.
This Passion Called Love, London, 1925.
Love's Blindness, London, 1926.
The Wrinkle Book, London, 1927.
It, New York, 1927.
Love—What I Think of It, London, 1928.
The Flirt and the Flapper, London, 1930.
Love's Hour, London, 1932.
Glorious Flames, London, 1932.
Saint or Satyr? and Other Stories, London, 1933.
Sooner or Later, London, 1933.
Did She? London, 1933.
Romantic Adventure (autobiography), New York, 1937.
The Third Eye, London, 1940.

Articles

"'It Isn't Sex—It's Good Pictures,'" interview with I. St. Johns, in
   Photoplay (New York), March 1926.
"How to Get a Man and How to Hold Him," in *Photoplay* (New York),
   July 1928.

Publications on Glyn

Books

Glyn, Anthony, *Elinor Glyn—A Biography,* New York, 1955.
Etherington-Smith, Meredith, and Jeremy Pilcher, *The "It" Girls:
   Lucy, Lady Duff Gordon, the Couturière "Lucile," and Elinor Glyn,
   Romantic Novelist,* London, 1986.
Hardwick, Joan, *Addicted to Romance: The Life and Adventures of
   Elinor Glyn,* London, 1994.
Foster, Gwendolyn Audrey, *Women Film Directors: An International
   Bio-Critical Dictionary,* Westport, Connecticut, 1995.

Articles

"Elinor Glyn in Talking Act, 'Love.'" in *Weekly Variety* (New York)
   12 August 1921.
Spensley, Dorothy, "What Is IT?" in *Photoplay* (New York), February 1926.
Ahrens, Gertine, "The 'No' Woman," in *Photoplay* (New York),
   September 1928.
Larkin, Mark, "What Is IT?" in *Photoplay* (New York), June 1929.
Obituary in *New York Times,* 24 September 1943.
Fowler, Marian, "Would You Sin with Elinor Glyn?," in *Saturday
   Night,* November 1996.

*   *   *

Elinor Glyn was one of Hollywood's most famous screenwriters
in the 1920s, when she was known for her bold and sexy scenarios.
She began her writing career as a romantic novelist, and in 1908
when her immensely popular novel *Three Weeks* was published, she
earned a salacious notoriety in the United States. The novel scandal-
ized conservatives at the time for featuring a married woman's passionate and illicit love affair—conducted atop a tiger skin rug. During the 1910s and 1920s, Glyn enjoyed continued fame for her
daring novels and "expert" advice on the subjects of love, femininity,
and most importantly, "sex appeal."

Based on her immense popularity as a novelist, in 1920, at the age
of 56, Glyn was invited to Hollywood by Jesse Lasky of Famous

Players-Lasky to write and supervise the production of a scenario.
She was part of the wave of well-known authors, including F. Scott
Fitzgerald and Somerset Maugham, who were recruited to the film
capital to write original scenarios or to adapt their existing works for
the movies so as to lend Hollywood a tone of sophistication. Although she had no practical knowledge about filmmaking, Glyn
proved to be one of the most adaptable and successful at the venture.

Credited with putting "sex appeal" on screen, Glyn's early screenplays were tremendous hits, including *The Great Moment* written
especially for Gloria Swanson, *Beyond the Rocks* (adapted from her
novel) with Swanson and Rudolph Valentino, and the screen adaptation of *Three Weeks. The Great Moment* featured the adventures of
an English socialite who falls in love with a macho Westerner who
saves her from a rattlesnake bite and discovers the wild gypsy streak
she inherited from her mother. Although she returns home with her
father and finds a millionaire to marry, she is miserable until her
reunion with her rugged hero, who has in the meantime become
wealthy. Like *The Great Moment,* Glyn's early screenplays were all
lush, extravagantly costumed, and overwrought romances set in
mythical pasts, which shared her favorite themes—of love, passion,
sex, and danger. But the formula eventually lost its appeal, and after
the failure of *Man and Maid* and *The Only Thing* she attempted to
modernize her screenplays. The result was *Ritzy,* an absurd farce
about a young woman hunting a duke in Paris, who is duped by an
duke who loves her but masquerades as poor to teach her a lesson. It
was a box-office failure.

But, in 1926, Glyn's popular reputation was restored when her
serialized novella *It* was published. Although nearly everyone knew
that "It" translated as sex appeal, Glyn took credit for discovering it,
thus prompting widespread discussions about what "It" was, who
had "It," and how to cultivate "It." She then reached the height of her
Hollywood career in 1928 after Famous Players-Lasky purchased
the movie rights to *It* and she was linked with Clara Bow's quickly
rising star. Intended as a comedy vehicle for Bow specifically, the
film has almost nothing in common with the novel other than a
seductive title, but it includes Glyn's campy "grande dame" cameo
appearance in which she explains the meaning of "It." The movie's
credits list Glyn as "author and adaptor" [sic], and the writing team
of Hope Loring and Louis D. Lighton received the "scenario" credit.
Jesse Lasky confirmed in his memoirs that it was Loring and Lighton,
the studio's top writing team, who were responsible for the screenplay. In any event, the film was a popular phenomenon of huge
proportions, and since then it has been fixed in popular memory as
the quintessential "Jazz Age"—and Elinor Glyn—movie. In addition, *It* was both a smash hit and a distinctive example of Hollywood's
"flapper movies." Its extraordinary success was due, in large part, to
Bow's compelling performance as a sexy, free-spirited shop-girl
who is smitten by and ultimately wins her boss, a department-store
heir. Glyn's last Hollywood film, *Red Hair,* was another comedy
vehicle for Bow with a slim story meant to demonstrate the passion
of red-haired people.

In addition to her screenwriting success, Glyn was famous for
cultivating an aristocratic star persona, which Hollywood's elite
obliged by dubbing her "Madame Glyn." But, in literary circles she
was decidedly less celebrated and critics disparaged her novels and
scenarios as simple, melodramatic potboilers. Nevertheless, Glyn
audaciously lamented that her literary skills were less valued in Hollywood than her famous name. After *Red Hair,* Glyn left Hollywood
to return to England, where she financed and directed the film *Knowing Men.* About an heiress who pretends to be her aunt's penniless
companion in order to ascertain the character of her beaux, the film

was an abysmal, amateurish failure, against which the screenwriter Edward Knoblock brought legal action to prevent its release. Nevertheless, she made one more film, the never-released *The Price of Things*. Both films were old-fashioned and slow-paced affairs that exhausted her finances and hastened Glyn's return to writing novels and articles for magazines and newspapers.

—Cynthia Felando

GODMILOW, Jill
American director

Born: Philadelphia, 1943. **Education:** Attended the University of Wisconsin, B.A., 1965. **Career:** Late 1960s—worked as a freelance editor on commercials and industrial films, and for San Francisco's KQED; 1973—co-directed her first documentary feature, *Antonia: A Portrait of the Woman*, which received an Academy Award nomination; 1970s-80s—directed videos and documentaries for television; 1992—associate professor, then full professor, Communication & Theatre, at the University of Notre Dame, teaching film and video production. **Awards:** Best Documentary, Independent New York Film Critics Awards, Emily Award, American Film Festival, for *Antonia: A Portrait of the Woman*, 1973; Red Ribbon, American Film Festival, for *Nevelson in Process*, 1976; Grand Jury Prize, Sundance Film Festival, for *Waiting for the Moon*, 1987. **Address:** Department of Communication and Theatre, University of Notre Dame, 320 O'Shaughnessy Hall, Notre Dame, IN 46556, U.S.A.

Films as Director

1967   *La Nueva Vida* (co-d—doc, incomplete)
1969   *Tales* (co-d—doc short)
1973   *Antonia: A Portrait of the Woman* (co-d with J. Collins)
1974   *Where Have All the Mentally Ill Gone?* (doc short)
1976   *Nevelson in Process* (co-d) (doc short)
1977   *The Popovich Brothers of South Chicago* (doc)
1979   *With Grotowski at Nienadowka* (short)
1980   *The Vigil* (short); *The Odyssey Tapes* (*Odyssey*) (short)
1981   *Far from Poland*
1984   *The Theory of Ideas* (co-d—short)
1987   *Waiting for the Moon* (+ sc)
1995   *Roy Cohn/Jack Smith*
1996   *What's Underground about Marshmallows*
1997   *What Farocki Taught* (short)

Other Film

1976   *Pleasantville* (Locker) (ed)

Publications by Godmilow

Articles

Interview with Patricia Erens, in *Women and Film* (Berkeley), no. 7, 1975.
"The Making of *Antonia*," interview with J. McNally, in *Filmmakers' Newsletter* (Ward Hill, Massachusetts), April 1975.
"Far from Documentary," interview with Wendy Patterson, in *Afterimage* (Rochester, New York), February 1986.
"A Little Something on Narrativity," in *Independent* (New York), April 1986.
"[Un]Documenting History," interview with Lynn C. Miller, in *Text Performance Quarterly*, vol. 17, no. 3, 1997.

Publications on Godmilow

Book

Foster, Gwendolyn Audrey, *Women Film Directors: An International Bio-Critical Dictionary*, Westport, Connecticut, 1995.

Articles

Hulser, Kathleen, "*Far from Poland*, Made in USA," in *Independent* (New York), October 1983.
Breitbart, Eric, "The Awful Truth: *Far from Poland*," in *American Film* (Washington, D.C.), November 1984.
Darnton, Nina, "At the Movies," in *New York Times* (New York), 6 March 1987.
Rodman, H. A., "In Production...," in *Millimeter* (Cleveland, Ohio), June 1987.
"Jill Godmilow," in *American Film* (Hollywood), June 1989.

*   *   *

Jill Godmilow won her initial acclaim for co-directing (with folksinger Judy Collins) *Antonia: A Portrait of the Woman*, a documentary look at the life of pioneer orchestra conductor Antonia Brico. The film is a compelling portrayal of Brico, who was 73 when the film was released, and how her desire to conduct a major symphony orchestra was continually thwarted because of sexism and discrimination. Brico poignantly describes how a musician who is not part of an orchestra at least may practice on her own to hone her skills, but a conductor whose instrument is her orchestra is not allowed the same luxury. At the time of its release, just as the women's movement was beginning to make headway among the masses of American baby boomers, *Antonia: A Portrait of the Woman* served as a valuable feminist testament of how sexism thwarts personal ambition.

Godmilow's most challenging undertaking is *Far from Poland*, the title of which alludes to *Far from Vietnam*, a French-made anti-war film consisting of individual meditations on the war in Southeast Asia. *Far from Poland* started out as a documentary on the then-burgeoning Solidarity movement. When martial law was declared in Poland, however, Godmilow was denied access to the country. Rather than abandon the project, she resolved to make a film about her experience. The result unfolds in three acts and an epilogue, with each consisting of a dramatic re-creation of the contents of published interviews, given during Solidarity's ascendance—by a shipyard laborer, a coal miner, and a government censor. Also included are a mix of fake documentary footage and real interviews and newsreel footage, and a conjured up ending in which Solidarity triumphs over its enemies. The result not only interprets a time and place in history but explores the same question posed in *Far from Vietnam*: What can a filmmaker do to aid a peoples' struggle against tyranny?

On a more theoretical/cinematic level, this question segues into the issue of documentary objectivity: Does a recorder of events need to be impartial about those events as she selects the material that will appear on screen, along with the order in which it will be presented?

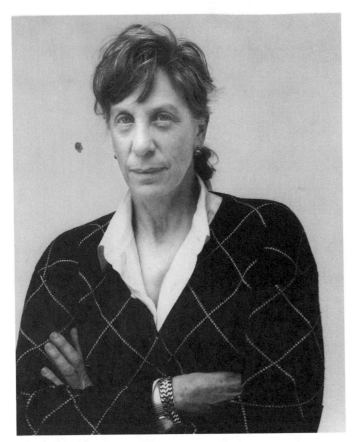

Jill Godmilow

Indeed, is it possible for a filmmaker to remain impartial while researching and recording controversial events? What is the effect of her imprint on the material? What happens when it is altered, or reinterpreted? Finally, what is the effect of the filmmaker's decision to appear on screen—as Godmilow does in *Far from Poland*?

Godmilow entered the realm of feature-length narrative filmmaking with *Waiting for the Moon,* an account of the lasting friendship and complex relationship between Gertrude Stein and her secretary-companion, Alice B. Toklas. *Waiting for the Moon* was a disappointment: a slow, lifeless semi-biography. The film also caused a minor controversy in that it is clear that Stein and Toklas are a couple, yet their romantic/sexual relationship is not depicted on screen. Godmilow's other major feature is *Roy Cohn/Jack Smith,* which may be linked to *Far from Poland* as an interpretation of real-life experience via performance. *Roy Cohn/Jack Smith* is a record of actor/performance artist Ron Vawter's theatrical exploration of the lives of two very dissimilar individuals who are linked in that both were gay, and died of AIDS (as did the actor who plays them). The first is Roy Cohn, the right-wing lawyer and Joseph McCarthy underling who refused to acknowledge his sexual preference while publicly condemning gay lifestyles; in the film, the hypocritical Cohn offers a lecture at a banquet for an organization called the American Society for the Protection of the Family. The second is Jack Smith, the legendary (as well as unabashedly out-of-the-closet) underground filmmaker, who appears in drag in a campy Arabian Nights setting. *Roy Cohn/Jack Smith* is worth seeing for the contrasts and ironies of its subjects. But the film is dramatically and visually static, with Godmilow unable to overcome the obstacle of transforming a stage performance into visually arresting cinema.

Prior to *Antonia: A Portrait of the Woman,* Godmilow started (but did not complete) her first film, *La Nueva Vida,* a documentary about New York's Spanish Harlem. Beyond *Antonia* and the ambitious and provocative *Far from Poland,* her best work has been her documentaries in which she explores diverse subject matter. Her topics have ranged from perspectives on sexuality (*Tales*) to the mental health establishment (*Where Have All the Mentally Ill Gone?*), fine artists and their creativity (*Nevelson in Process,* a portrait of artist Louise Nevelson) to musical traditions (*The Popovich Brothers of South Chicago,* a chronicle of Serbian dance music over a 50-year period).

—Rob Edelman

GÓMEZ, Sara

Cuban director

Born: Havana, 1943. **Education:** Attended the Conservatory of Music, Havana. **Career:** 1961 on—assistant director at Instituto Cubano del Arte e Industria Cinematograficos (ICAIC), under Tomás Gutiérrez Alea, Jorge Fraga, and Agnès Varda; 1964—directed first film, *Iré a Santiago;* 1974—shot and edited first feature, *De cierta manera;* original negative, damaged in processing, restored under supervision of Gutiérrez Alea and Rigoberto López, 1974-76. **Died:** Of acute asthma, 2 June 1974.

Films as Director

1964   *Iré a Santiago (I Shall Go to Santiago)*
1965   *Excursion a Vueltabajo (Outing to Vueltabajo)*
1967   *Y tenemos sabor (And We've Got "Sabor")*
1968   *En la otra isla (On the Other Island)*
1969   *Isla del tesero (Treasure Island)*
1970   *Poder local, poder popular (Local Power, People's Power)*
1971   *Un documental a proposito del transito (A Documentary about Mass Transit)*
1972   *Atencion prenatal (Prenatal Care in the First Year); Año uno*
1973   *Sobre horas extras y trabajo voluntario (About Overtime and Voluntary Labor)*
1977   ***De cierta manera** (One Way or Another)*

Publications on Gómez

Books

Chanan, Michael, *The Cuban Image,* London, 1985.
Foster, Gwendolyn Audrey, *Women Film Directors: An International Bio-Critical Dictionary,* Westport, Connecticut, 1995.

Articles

Chijona, Geraldo, and Rigoberto López, in *Cine Cubano* (Havana), no. 93.
Burton, Julianne, "Individual Fulfillment and Collective Achievement," in *Cineaste* (New York), January 1977.
Burton, Julianne, "Introduction to the Revolutionary Cuban Cinema," and Carlos Galiano, "*One Way or Another*: The Revolution in Action," in *Jump Cut* (Chicago), December 1978.

LeSage, Julia, "*One Way or Another*: Dialectical, Revolutionary, Feminist," in *Jump Cut* (Chicago), May 1979.

* * *

We shall never know all that Sara Gómez might have given to us. We have her one feature film, the marvelous *De cierta manera,* and a few short documentaries to indicate what might have been had she lived beyond the age of 31. But we will never really know all that this prodigiously talented woman was capable of.

Sara Gómez could be seen as prototypical of the new Cuban directors. Entering the Cuban Film Institute (ICAIC) at an early age, she worked as assistant director for various cineastes, including Tomás Gutiérrez Alea, whose influence marked her work as it has so many young directors. During a ten-year period (1964-74) she fulfilled the usual apprenticeship among Cuban cineastes by directing documentary films. Documentaries are seen as an important training ground for Cuban directors because they force them to focus on the material reality of Cuba and thus emphasize the use of cinema as an expression of national culture. As Gutiérrez Alea noted, "the kind of cinema which adapts itself to our interests, fortunately, is a kind of light, agile cinema, one that is very directly founded upon our own reality." This is precisely the kind of cinema Sara Gómez went on to produce, beginning work on *De cierta manera* in 1974 and finishing the editing of the film shortly before her death of acute asthma.

Gómez's early training in documentaries and the influence of Gutiérrez Alea is evident in *De cierta manera.* The film combines the documentary and fiction forms so inextricably that they are impossible to disentangle. Through this technique, she emphasized the material reality that is at the base of all creative endeavor and the necessity of bringing a critical perspective to all forms of film.

In choosing this style, which I call "dialectical resonance," Gómez appeared to follow Gutiérrez Alea's example in the superb *Memories of Underdevelopment.* But there is a crucial difference between the two films—a difference that might be said to distinguish the generation of directors who came of age before the triumph of the revolution (e.g., Gutiérrez Alea) from those who have grown up within the revolution. In spite of its ultimate commitment to the revolutionary process, *Memories* remains in some ways the perspective of an "outsider" and might be characterized as "critical bourgeois realism." Nevertheless, *De cierta manera* is a vision wholly from within the revolution, despite the fact that every position in the film is subjected to criticism—including that of the institutionalized revolution, which is presented in the form of an annoyingly pompous omniscient narration. Thus, the perspective of Gómez might be contrasted to that of *Memories* by calling it "critical socialist realism." The emphasis on dialectical criticism, struggle, and commitment is equally great in both films, but the experience of having grown up within the revolution created a somewhat different perspective.

Despite its deceptively simple appearance—a result of being shot in 16mm on a very low budget—*De cierta manera* is the work of an extremely sophisticated filmmaker. Merely one example among many of Gómez's sophistication is the way in which she combined a broad range of modern distanciation techniques with the uniquely Cuban tropical beat to produce a film that is at once rigorously analytic and powerfully sensuous—as well as perhaps the finest instance to date of a truly dialectical film. Although we are all a little richer for the existence of this work, we remain poorer for the fact that she will make no more films.

—John Mraz

GOODRICH, Frances
American writer

Born: Belleville, New Jersey, 1890. **Education:** Attended Passaic Collegiate High School, graduated 1908; Vassar College, Poughkeepsie, New York, graduated 1912; New York School of Social Work, 1912-13. **Family:** Married 1) the actor Robert Ames, 1917 (divorced 1923); 2) the writer Henrik Willem Van Loon, 1927 (divorced 1930); 3) Albert Hackett, 1931. **Career:** 1913—stage debut in Massachusetts; 1916—Broadway debut in *Come Out of the Kitchen*; 1927—actress in a Denver stock company, in which Albert Hackett was also a member; 1930—first writing collaboration with Hackett, on the play *Up Pops the Devil*; 1933-39—writers for MGM, and for Paramount, 1943-46, and MGM again after 1948. **Awards:** Writers Guild Award, for *Easter Parade,* 1948; *Father's Little Dividend,* 1951; *Seven Brides for Seven Brothers,* 1954; and *The Diary of Anne Frank,* 1959; Pulitzer Prize (for drama), for *The Diary of Anne Frank,* 1956. **Died:** Of cancer, in New York City, 29 January 1984.

Films as Co-Writer with Albert Hackett

1933 *The Secret of Madame Blanche* (Brabin); *Penthouse (Crooks in Clover)* (Van Dyke)
1934 *Fugitive Lovers* (Boleslawsky) (co); *The Thin Man* (Van Dyke); *Hide-Out* (Van Dyke)
1935 *Naughty Marietta* (Van Dyke) (co); *Ah, Wilderness!* (C. Brown)
1936 *Rose Marie* (Van Dyke) (co); *Small Town Girl* (Wellman) (co); *After the Thin Man* (Van Dyke)
1937 *The Firefly* (Leonard)
1939 *Another Thin Man* (Van Dyke); *Society Lawyer* (Ludwig) (co)
1943 *Doctors at War* (Shumlin—short)
1944 *Lady in the Dark* (Leisen); *The Hitler Gang* (Farrow)
1946 *The Virginian* (Gilmore); *It's a Wonderful Life* (Capra) (co)
1948 *The Pirate* (Minnelli); *Summer Holiday* (Mamoulian); *Easter Parade* (Walters) (co)
1949 *In the Good Old Summertime* (Leonard) (co)
1950 *Father of the Bride* (Minnelli)
1951 *Father's Little Dividend* (Minnelli); *Too Young to Kiss* (Leonard)
1954 *Give a Girl a Break* (Donen); *Seven Brides for Seven Brothers* (Donen) (co); *The Long, Long Trailer* (Minnelli)
1956 *Gaby* (Bernhardt) (co)
1958 *A Certain Smile* (Negulesco)
1959 *The Diary of Anne Frank* (Stevens)
1962 *Five Finger Exercise* (Daniel Mann)
1980 *The Diary of Anne Frank* (Sagal)

Publications by Goodrich (with Albert Hackett)

Plays

Up Pops the Devil, New York, 1933.
The Great Big Doorstep, Chicago, 1943.
The Diary of Anne Frank, New York, 1958.

Publications on Goodrich

Book

Acker, Ally, *Reel Women: Pioneers of the Cinema, 1896 to the Present,* New York, 1991.

Articles

Film Comment (New York), Winter 1970-71.
Films in Review (New York), October 1977.
Ehrlich, Evelyn, in *American Screenwriters,* edited by Robert E. Morsberger, Stephen O. Lesser, and Randall Clark, Detroit, 1984.
Obituary in *New York Times,* 31 January 1984.
Obituary in *Variety* (New York), 1 February 1984.

* * *

Although the screenwriting team of Frances Goodrich and Albert Hackett received critical and popular acclaim for the 1959 adaptation of their Pulitzer Prize-winning stage play, *The Diary of Anne Frank,* most of their creative efforts were not "serious" works. Schooled in the sophisticated stage comedies of the late 1920s and early 1930s, Goodrich and Hackett adapted *The Thin Man* in 1934, and it is a work that now as then is considered to be the best of the cinema's detective comedies. They followed this exceptional adaptation with an excellent *After the Thin Man* and an effective *Another Thin Man,* in both of which they succeeded in translating the work of Dashiell Hammett to the screen while managing to maintain the quality of his stories.

While it might appear that these screenplays owed much of their wit to the novelist, Goodrich and Hackett contributed the dramatic sense and skills they developed from almost two decades of working as actors and writers on the theatrical stage. The co-adapters could translate from one verbal medium to another, developing the story through dramatic dialogue. It was a special talent that both executed in unison so that it was difficult to trace which one contributed the most to a specific scene. One of their early collaborations on an original story was a sophisticated comedy stage play, *Up Pops the Devil* (1930) which was converted to a screenplay in 1931 and revised in a successful remake as a Bob Hope vehicle, *Thanks for the Memory* (1938).

From their sophisticated comedy background on the stage and screen, Goodrich and Hackett moved to the adaptation of the so-called light opera of the past. They were not happy with this assignment, but it was part of their MGM contract. In the mid 1930s they adapted two vehicles for Jeanette MacDonald and Nelson Eddy, *Naughty Marietta* and *Rose Marie,* reworking some of the stilted dialogue and simplifying the plots from the stage versions so that the works were more contemporary and more fluid. The pair also produced two splendid screen musicals—the flashy, colorful *The Pirate* in the late 1940s and the innovative *Seven Brides for Seven Brothers* in the mid-1950s. Less inventive musicals were their *Easter Parade* (1948) and *In the Good Old Summertime* (1949).

In the 1940s the couple's credits for director Frank Capra's *It's a Wonderful Life* seemed to be unusual for their background. The work's warmth and humanity seemed more likely to have been the work of Robert Riskin, Capra's frequent collaborator, than that of Goodrich and Hackett. Critics now regard *It's a Wonderful Life* as an outstanding achievement—for its screenplay as well as its execution. It was certainly a major film in Capra's career (coming ironically just when his fortunes were on the wane with the Hollywood establish-

ment), and it is certainly one of the couple's significant contributions to the movies.

A switch in handling another comedy genre emerged in the early 1950s when the screenwriters integrated social commentary into the humorous works *Father of the Bride* and *Father's Little Dividend.* The originally released *Father* focused on a rite of passage, marriage, while the sequel rite stressed the event of becoming a grandfather. The two films provided a boost to the career of Spencer Tracy in the lead role.

Only two movie adaptations seemed to be beyond the scope of the writers. These works were a Western, *The Virginian* (1946) starring Joel McCrea and a slapstick farce, *The Long, Long Trailer* (1954), featuring Lucille Ball and Desi Arnaz. The genre most effectively executed by the screenwriters proved to be variations of comedy: the sophisticated, witty comedy; the musical; and the genteel, humorous drama. There were a few exceptions, namely *The Diary of Anne Frank,* a drama that they wrote for the stage in 1958 and adapted to cinema in 1959.

An evaluator today probably could discern the specific contribution of Frances Goodrich by examining the strong female portraits, such as Nora Charles in the 1936 *The Thin Man* and Anne Frank. Goodrich's best work gives her a place as one of the leading writers for the screen. *Wonderful Life, Anne Frank,* and *The Thin Man* are works that meet high standards of dramatic writing with excellent dialogue and characters. The fresh handling of plot and character in the designed-for-the-screen musicals, *The Pirate* and *Seven Brides,* also serves to suggest that Goodrich and Hackett still remain the most eclectic screenwriters that Hollywood has produced. Their scope has not yet been matched by any other team.

—Donald W. McCaffrey

GORDON, Bette
American director

Born: 1950. **Education:** Attended the University of Wisconsin, Madison, B.A. in French, 1972, M.A. in radio, television, and film, 1975, and M.F.A. in film, 1976. **Family:** Married the filmmaker James Benning (divorced), one daughter, Lili. **Career:** 1970s— began making experimental films with James Benning while a graduate student, and also on her own; 1976-79—assistant professor at the School of Fine Arts, University of Wisconsin, Milwaukee; 1979— moved to New York City; 1979-94 adjunct professor and assistant professor, Hofstra University; from 1980—edits television films and documentaries, directs plays and stage readings, and directs music videos and films for television, including episodes in Laurel Entertainment's *Monsters* series, Playboy Channel's "Director's Showcase," and short films for HBO and Showtime; 1990s—contributing editor of *BOMB* magazine; from 1991—adjunct professor and associate professor in Columbia University Graduate Film Division; 1993-95—instructor at the School of Visual Arts; 1996—*Variety* and *Empty Suitcases* presented as part of the Whitney Museum's "New York/No Wave" retrospective; 1997—began principal photography on feature film *History of Luminous Motion.* **Awards:** Director's Choice Award, Sinking Creek Film Celebration, for *Still Life,* 1975. **Address:** School of Arts, Columbia University, 512 Dodge Hall, MC 1805, 2960 Broadway, New York, NY 10027, U.S.A.

Films as Director

1973 *Michigan Avenue* (co-d—short)
1974 *1-94* (co-d—short)
1975 *Still Life* (short); *United States of America* (co-d—short)
1976 *Noyes* (short)
1977 *An Algorithm* (short)
1979 *Exchanges* (short)
1980 *Empty Suitcases* (+ sc, ed, pr, sound recording, voice, ro)
1983 *What Is It, Zach* (short—for TV)
1984 *Variety* (+ original st, additional ph)
1987 "Greed" ep. of *Seven Women, Seven Sins* (for TV) (co-sc)

Other Film

1985 *The Boy Next Door* (Schidor) (asst d)

Publications by Gordon

Articles

"*Variety*: The Pleasure in Looking," in *Pleasure and Danger: Exploring Female Sexuality,* edited by Carole S. Vance, Boston, 1984.
"Women X," interview with Jane Root, in *Monthly Film Bulletin* (London), May 1984.
"Il Scenario," in *Cahiers du Cinéma* (Paris), October supplement, 1987.
With Betsy Sussler, "Al Pacino," in *BOMB* (New York), Fall 1990.
"*Variety*: The Pleasure in Looking," in *Issues in Feminist Film Criticism,* edited by Patricia Erens, Bloomington, Indiana, 1991.
With Karyn Kay, "Look Back/Talk Back," in *Dirty Looks: Women, Pornography, Power,* edited by Pamela Church Gibson and Roma Gibson, London, 1993.
"Allison Anders," in *BOMB* (New York), Winter 1994.
"Mike Leigh," in *BOMB* (New York), Winter 1994.
"Going Dutch," in *Independent Film and Video Monthly* (New York), May 1995.
"Mike Figgis," in *BOMB* (New York), Winter 1996.

Publications on Gordon

Book

Foster, Gwendolyn Audrey, *Women Film Directors: An International Bio-Critical Dictionary,* Westport, Connecticut, 1995.

Articles

Kay, Karyn, "Notes on the Films of Bette Gordon," in *Camera Obscura* (Bloomington, Indiana), vol. 5, 1980.
Taubin, Amy, "As Long as She Pleases: Bette Gordon's *Variety,*" in *Village Voice* (New York), 15 May 1984.
"Le cinéma avec ses si," in *Cahiers du Cinéma* (Paris), Summer 1984.
Lardeau, Y., "Du cote de la pornographie," in *Cahiers du Cinéma* (Paris), February 1985.
Armatage, Kay, "The Seven Sins of Bette Gordon's *Variety,*" in *CineAction!* (Toronto), Spring 1986.
Fields, S., "The State of Things," in *Monthly Film Bulletin* (London), January 1987.
Hershman, L., "Lust and Anger: The Commodification of Marginality," in *Cinematograph* (San Francisco), no. 3, 1988.

Taubin, Amy, "In the Money," in *Village Voice* (New York), 10 December 1996.

* * *

Bette Gordon is a feminist filmmaker/theorist whose special concerns are sexual subjugation and the sexual politics that sully male-female relations. To date, her best-known film is *Variety,* a low-budget, independently produced allegory about female empowerment linked to the manner in which men watch women on celluloid, and a chronicle of the manner in which pornographic images affect both sexes.

Variety is the story of Christine, unemployed and desperate to find a job, who is hired as a cashier in a New York City porn movie theater: a venue where men come to be voyeurs, to stare in silence at a screen and watch pornographic images of women. Two questions immediately become apparent. How will these men view Christine, as they purchase their $2 tickets? How will her duties, and her surroundings, influence Christine?

On her first day at work, Christine takes a break in the theater lobby. As she paces back and forth and smokes, she cannot help but overhear a woman oohing and aahing on screen, and a male voice declaring, "You're a whore, aren't you." She then peeks in on the film, which upsets her so that she promptly spills a soda she has purchased.

Because of Christine's sex, she is supposed to be passive. As she sits in the ticket booth, men may fantasize about her: What sort of woman would take such a job? One even attempts to grab her hand as he purchases his ticket. At one point Christine observes that the patrons see her as "some sort of attraction." At another, she receives an obscene phone call on her answering machine.

Christine turns the tables and takes control upon being approached by Louis, one of the customers, a well-dressed man who rides around in a chauffeured car. Louis is mysterious and patronizing as he not so much asks as orders her to join him for an evening at Yankee Stadium, and wants her to admit that she enjoys watching the porn movies. Christine eventually begins following him around, spying on him and his activities. In so doing, the woman becomes the aggressor, the voyeur, while the man becomes the passive visual object, who is spied on by prying eyes.

By the very nature of her employment, Christine already has become a voyeur. "I sit in a glass booth between the lobby and the street," is how she describes her job. In so doing, she has become a watcher of men as she handles their admission fees. But her presence in the booth still is demeaning. Her pay is low; she must receive permission to take a break; and she is scrutinized by the men who enter the theater. Only when Christine takes charge, and begins following Louis, does she become in any way empowered.

Variety is a story of sexual politics, and the silent, invisible walls existing between men and women. Just about all of the men in the story view Christine as an object. Even her co-worker at the theater, who initially is a sympathetic character, eventually hits on Christine. When she tells her boyfriend about her new job, he hardly reacts, and then leaves. The only genuine communication is between women: Christine and her bartender friend, and the various women who hang out in the latter's saloon.

At the same time, *Variety* depicts the impact of pornography on a woman's soul. Christine's job and surroundings affect her psyche. She becomes obsessed/disturbed by the sounds and images of pornography. She begins frequenting porn parlors, blurting out erotic stories, dressing as a seductress/whore. At one point, she even imagines herself and Louis in a porn movie.

While an individual may receive instant gratification from pornography, that gratification is not the result of real sexual/human contact. And so, as her attraction to pornographic images becomes imbedded within her, Christine is disconnected from her life. What will be her plight, and her fate? Gordon chooses to leave this up in the air, as the film concludes on an ambiguous note.

Despite all these subtexts, the ultimate theme of *Variety* is voyeurism. This is apparent at the film's outset, as Christine and her bartender friend chat in a locker room while the latter removes her clothes. So even here, as the camera records these images, the viewer becomes a voyeur.

Gordon's other directorial credits range from early experimental short films made on her own and in conjunction with former husband James Benning; to her subsequent work for television; to her direction of the "Greed" episode in *Seven Women, Seven Sins*, produced for German television, in which seven women filmmakers examine the seven deadly sins. Especially outstanding are the two films she made upon coming to New York in 1979, both of which are thematically linked to *Variety* in that they explore and deconstruct female images. *Exchanges* depicts various women switching clothes, resulting in a demystification of the image of women undressing; the 50-odd-minute-long, semiautobiographical *Empty Suitcases* explores the view of women as seductive objects as it presents a single woman who is at once a mistress, terrorist, struggling artist, and professor.

After *Variety*, Bette Gordon spent several years working on an adaptation of Catherine Texier's novel, *Love Me Tender*, a project which was not realized. It was not until 13 years after the release of *Variety* when she began principal photography on her next feature, *History of Luminous Motion*. This enormous time gap is a pity, if only because of the combination of intelligence and potential she demonstrated in *Variety*.

—Rob Edelman

GORRIS, Marleen
Dutch director and writer

Born: Holland, 1948. **Education:** Studied English and theater in Holland; attended the University of Birmingham, England, master's in drama. **Career:** 1981—directed acclaimed groundbreaking debut feature *A Question of Silence*; 1995—earned international renown with *Antonia's Line*. **Awards:** Best Feature, Dutch Film Days, Women's Festival Prize, Sceaux, France, for *A Question of Silence*, 1981; Best Foreign Language Film, Academy Award, Best Picture, Toronto International Film Festival, Best Screenplay, Chicago International Film Festival, and Best Director, Hampton's International Film Festival, for *Antonia's Line*, 1995. **Address:** c/o First Look Pictures, 8800 Sunset Boulevard, Los Angeles, CA 90069, U.S.A.

Films as Director

1981   *De Stilte Rond Christine M (A Question of Silence)* (+ sc)
1984   *Gebroken Spiegels (Broken Mirrors)* (+ sc)
1991   *The Last Island* (+ sc)
1993   *Tales from a Street* (for TV)
1995   *Antonia (Antonia's Line)* (+ sc)
1997   *Mrs. Dalloway*
1998   *Come West with Me*

Publications by Gorris

Articles

"Het speelfilm-regiedebuut van Marleen Gorris: stijfkopje zet door," in *Skoop* (Amsterdam), May/June 1981.
"Nuchtere observatie en betrokkenheid," interview with A. Forster, in *Skrien* (Amsterdam), November/December 1984.
"Avantpop: Film Fatale," in *Village Voice* (New York), 8 January 1985.
Interview with C. Cornioley, in *Filmviews* (Melbourne), Spring 1985.
Interview with Judy Stone, in *Eye on the World: Conversations with International Filmmakers*, Los Angeles, 1997.

Publications on Gorris

Books

Quart, Barbara Koenig, *Women Directors: The Emergence of a New Cinema*, New York, 1988.
Foster, Gwendolyn Audrey, *Women Film Directors: An International Bio-Critical Dictionary*, Westport, Connecticut, 1995.

Articles

Kottman, P., "*De Stilte rond Christine M.*: een parel voor de zwijnen," in *Skoop* (Amsterdam), April/May 1982.
Johnston, Sheila, "*De Stilte Rond Christine M (A Question of Silence)*," in *Monthly Film Bulletin* (London), February 1983.
Rickey, Carrie, "Three Women Kill a Man—'For No Reason,'" in *San Francisco Sunday Examiner and Chronicle*, 21 October 1983.
Rickey, Carrie, "Euro-girls," in *American Film* (Washington, D.C.), January/February 1984.
Roodnat, J., "Ik zeg niet dat alle mannen psychopaten zijn," in *Skoop* (Amsterdam), August 1984.
Stockbridge, S., "Marleen Gorris," in *Filmviews* (Melbourne), Winter 1985.
Gentile, Mary C., "Feminist or Tendentious? Marleen Gorris' *A Question of Silence*," in *Film Feminisms: Theory and Practice* (Westport, Connecticut), 1985.
Murphy, Jeanette, "*A Question of Silence*," and Jane Root, "Distributing *A Question of Silence*—A Cautionary Tale," in *Films for Women*, edited by Charlotte Brundson, London, 1987.
Jackson, Lynne, and Karen Jaehne, "Eavesdropping on Female Voices: A Who's Who of Contemporary Women Filmmakers," in *Cineaste* (New York), vol. 16, no. 1/2, 1987-88.
Ippel, M., "Meer dan alleen realiteit," in *Skoop* (Amsterdam), November 1990.
Reincke, Nancy, "Antidote to Dominance: Women's Laughter as Counteraction," in *Journal of Popular Culture*, Spring 1991.
Ramanathan, Geetha, "Murder as Speech: Narrative Subjectivity in Marleen Gorris' *A Question of Silence*," in *Genders*, Winter 1992.
Straayer, Chris, "Sexual Representation in Film and Video," and Linda Williams, "A Jury of Their Peers: Marleen Gorris' *A Question of Silence*," in *Multiple Voices in Feminist Film Criticism*, edited by Diane Carson, Linda Dittmar, and Janice Welsch, Minneapolis, 1994.
Bear, Liza, "Marleen Gorris: In the Name of the Mother," in *Ms.* (New York), March/April 1996.

* * *

Dutch director and screenwriter Marleen Gorris has several respected and commercially successful feature-film credits to her name—all of which express her abiding interest in women-centered stories and feminist issues. Her work treats themes of female identity, strength, and solidarity in the face of male oppression and exploitation, though she leavens them with sharp doses of wry, self-reflective humor. Interestingly, Gorris freely acknowledges her feminist perspective, "both by temperament and intellect," and that her films inevitably are influenced by that perspective, but she denies that she emphasizes "political or moral lessons." Yet more than a few, usually male, critics insist that her films are "anti-male."

Without any previous film experience, Gorris took her screenplay for *A Question of Silence* to the Dutch government and was given the funding to finance the project. As her directorial debut, it was her best-known work until 1995's *Antonia's Line. A Question of Silence* was commercially successful and enjoys a well-deserved reputation as a feminist classic. Its conventional, easily accessible narrative structure belies its status as a notoriously subversive film that expresses anger about a capitalist system that functions to demean and oppress women. The story concerns three women who spontaneously come together to viciously murder a man, though they are all strangers at the time. At first, the women seem a rather disparate group: a zaftig, jolly middle-aged divorcée working as a waitress; a dowdy housewife with a stiff, silent demeanor; and an attractive and smart executive secretary. It is while engaging in a typically feminine pursuit, shopping in a dress boutique, that the women join forces: when the housewife boldly lifts an item and the smug male shopkeeper attempts to retrieve it from her bag, she resists and the other two women boldly begin shoplifting too until, together, they beat him to death. Thereafter, they, and four strangely calm women who have silently witnessed their deed, each leave the shop. After their arrest, the three women, each of whom refuses to deny her deed or to reveal her motives, come under the purview of a female, court-appointed psychiatrist who is expected to evaluate their sanity. Soon, however, the psychiatrist loses her professional "objectivity" and develops a deep identification with the women. Her conclusion: that the women are all sane but wearied by the constraints and abuses of male domination.

The title of *A Question of Silence* works on several levels. First, it suggests the patriarchal refusal to hear women's voices: at business meetings, the secretary's insights are ignored; the waitress routinely endures her male customers' sexist remarks; and the housewife bears a poignant isolation and melancholy. The title also alludes to the women's shared silence, suggesting that it can function as a tool of solidarity and empowerment. Indeed, in the film's courtroom scene, Gorris cleverly underscores the myriad connections between the three women with a series of exchanged looks, with each other and with the four unidentified women who witnessed the killing. When the prosecutor makes the absurd declaration that it would make no difference if it had been three men who had killed one woman, rather than vice versa, it provokes peels of laughter among the women, including the psychiatrist. Nevertheless, the men involved in the case (cops, lawyers, judges) simply fail to understand the women's motivations. Although the women's shared act of violence can be read metaphorically, as symbolic of the potential power of women to fight sexism, not a few film critics (including some feminists) were shocked by the violence and rejected it as "extreme," especially the murder scene, which includes an offscreen genital mutilation. Not surprisingly, male critics were generally angered or confused by the film and produced vitriolic reviews.

Gorris's second feature was *Broken Mirrors*, a much darker film about seven prostitutes and a psychopath who beats and imprisons them until they die of hunger. It was not as well-received critically or commercially as *A Question of Silence*. Her third film, *The Last Island*, is about a group of plane-crash survivors who find themselves stranded on a desert island; they eventually come to the conclusion that they might be the last people on Earth. The men in the group thereby begin pressuring the only potential child-bearing woman in the group to breed so as to ensure the survival of the human race. Soon, however, she becomes frustrated as she watches the men argue and endeavor to destroy each other.

Antonia's Line brought Gorris international fame as a gifted, award-winning filmmaker. It is indeed a visually rich, beautiful film. On the last day of her life, 90-year-old Antonia lies quietly and recalls her return, shortly after World War II, to the village of her birth. Gorris traces the subsequent 50 years in Antonia's eventful life, including its dark secrets, violence, humor, and intense emotions—along with the array of eccentric female descendants who constitute her "line." The film differs from Gorris's earlier works in that the female characters are strong and happy, and the tone is generally warmer and lighter. The extraordinary success of *Antonia's Line* gave Gorris the cachet to direct the adaptation of Virginia Woolf's novel, *Mrs. Dalloway*. At a party she is hosting in her elegant home, Mrs. Dalloway is surprised by a former suitor whom she rejected over 30 years earlier. His sudden appearance prompts her to consider what might have been had she accepted rather than feared his passionate love, and chosen him instead of the dull, reliable, and respectable Mr. Dalloway. Both *Antonia's Line* and *Mrs. Dalloway* treat the subject of memory and the complex human emotions that characterize women's lives, and both films indicate Gorris's ability to direct women-centered films that speak to larger audiences. Accordingly, her next film suggests the confidence the major studios have in her continued success; she is currently at work on Twentieth Century-Fox's romance/drama, *Come West with Me*, from Beth Henley's play *Abundance*.

—Cynthia Felando

GRAYSON, Helen
American director

Born: Helen Steel Grayson, 1902. **Education:** Privately tutored in France in her early years; graduated from Bryn Mawr College, 1926. **Career:** Late 1920s-early 1930s—studied acting with Maria Ouspenskaya at New York's American Laboratory Theatre; became a dress and costume designer for New York avant-garde artists; later in the depression years, an adviser to the to Federal Theatre Costume Workshop, an unemployment relief project; film career began during World War II at the Office of War Information in New York, as an assistant on the production *Salute to France*, and on the filming of a tour of the United States by a group of French journalists that included the young Jean-Paul Sartre; 1945—first directing assignment, the OWI's *The Cummington Story*; 1953—directed the U.S. State Department's most widely shown films, a trio of documentaries on American history and culture; late 1950s-early 1960s—spent her last half-dozen years as an unofficial U.S. representative at film festivals in Europe and Canada, writing articles, and attempting unsuccessfully to find sponsors for two films she was eager to direct: one on Balanchine's young New York City Ballet and one on Benjamin Franklin in France. **Died:** Of cancer, in New York City, 5 May 1962.

Films as Director

1945   *The Cummington Story*
1947   *Starting Line*
1948   *Bryn Mawr College*
1949   *Wings to Hawaii*
1951   *The House in Sea Cliff*
1953   *The New World*; *To Freedom*; *A Nation Sets Its Course*

Other Films

1943   *Salute to France* (asst to producers)
1944   Newsreel sequence on American tour of visiting French journalists (asst d)

Publications by Grayson

Articles

"Films for Education," in *Bryn Mawr Alumnae Bulletin,* Bryn Mawr, Pennsylvania, April 1946.
"The American Picture," in *Festival* (Edinburgh), 1954.
"The French Scene," in *Saturday Review* (New York), September 1954.
"Edinburgh Festival Notes," in *Saturday Review* (New York), 16 October 1954.

Publications on Grayson

Articles

Flaherty, Frances Hubbard, "The Bryn Mawr Film," in *Bryn Mawr Alumnae Bulletin,* Bryn Mawr, Pennsylvania, April 1948.
Starr, Cecile, description of plans for Grayson's film on Benjamin Franklin in Paris (to be co-produced with William Novik), in *Saturday Review* (New York), 22 September 1956.
Screen Directors International Guild, *Directory of Directors,* New York, 1961-62.
Obituary in *New York Times,* 8 May 1962.
Starr, Cecile, "Helen Grayson, Documentary Film Director," in *Sightlines* (New York), Summer 1976.
Starr, Cecile, "Distaff Documentarians: Three American Pioneers," in *Documentary* (Los Angeles), July/August 1995.

*   *   *

Although virtually unknown today, Helen Grayson was prominent among the first generation of American women who directed documentary films. As was typical of the 1940s and 1950s, most of Grayson's films were shot on 35mm film by all-male crews, with little or no sync sound—with real people reenacting scripted versions of realistic situations in real locations. Her friend and colleague, Ricky Leacock, called it "the dark ages of documentary." Within these and other limitations, in their day Grayson's films ranged form average (*Bryn Mawr College*) to outstanding (*The Cummington Story*).

Most of the men she worked with in her ten-year career described her in glowing terms. Guy Glover, who produced and scripted the premature babies film, *Starting Line,* called her "a Beautiful Person—intelligent, kind, civilized and knowledgeable about film—a rare combination." Glover spent the rest of his life as a leading producer at the National Film Board of Canada. George Justin, who shot the same film, remembered Grayson as a "sensitive, artistic director...brilliantly organized [with] a fine sense of drama...camera...and all the technical things that go into making a film." Justin eventually became an executive production manager at Orion Pictures and later senior vice president at MGM. Ricky Leacock, who photographed the American history series Grayson directed, called her "a joy to work with...imaginative...and responsive to the ideas of those she worked with." Leacock later became an international icon for his role in helping develop the new documentary technique called cinema verité, and a longtime film teacher and guru at the Massachusetts Institute of Technology.

Anyone who was not close to the New York documentary-film scene in those early years might well wonder why the career of this capable woman came to a sudden halt. For one reason there were virtually no female mentors, models, or allies Grayson could turn to for a hand-up. Most of the women filmmakers who had preceded her (Osa Johnson, Frances Flaherty, Margaret Mead) worked only, or mainly, with their husbands. Lee Burgess Dick, who set up her own company to produce and direct documentary films in the late 1930s, soon abandoned it to work as an editor and occasional director for a commercial production company in New York. Virginia Bell, who became a highly successful filmmaker in the 1950s—in a company she had founded with her husband Robert—adopted the androgenous name of Tracy Ward to disguise her female identity. Shirley Clarke, who briefly joined Leacock, Donn Pennebaker, and Willard Van Dyke in a loose affiliation called Filmmakers, Inc., soon found herself on her own while the others moved on to more rewarding opportunities.

For another reason, Grayson was more than 50 years old when she directed her last film in an era when women that age were rarely considered employable. Remember that Dorothy Arzner was only 43 when she directed her last Hollywood feature. Yet in the mid-1950s, Grayson set out to find sponsorship for two films that would have capitalized on her early ties to Europe. One was in George Balanchine's new, exciting New York City Ballet, and the other (which she hoped to co-produce with the French filmmaker William Novik) on the charismatic Benjamin Franklin's years in Paris. Despite her endeavors, funding was not forthcoming.

Instead, Grayson spent those last years as unofficial goodwill ambassador, selecting and promoting America's outstanding documentaries for European film festivals—and vice versa. During her frequent stays in Paris, she often attended Jean-Paul Sartre's weekly literary circle—and was said to be the only American he ever invited. In New York she remained an active member of the Screen Directors Guild, as she had been for more than a dozen years. Helen Grayson died of cancer in New York City in 1962, after several years' illness. The Prix Helen Grayson was established that year at the Annecy (France) Animation Festival, and her good friend Jay Leyda dedicated to her his book, *Films Beget Films.*

Some years later, research on pioneer American women filmmakers revealed some of the obstacles Grayson had faced in her film career. "We were cruel to her," Larry Madison admitted to one researcher, recalling how he and some of the technical crew had tried to undermine her authority when she was directing *The Cummington Story.* He had already asked for and in some publications received co-credit as the film's director. To set the record straight, Grayson had published in the *Bryn Mawr Alumnae Bulletin* a lengthy account of her work as director and his as director of photography. (Later, Frances Flaherty published a full-page report on Grayson's *Bryn*

Mawr film in that same publication, and later still Grayson's close friend Claire Parker wrote of her work in pinboard animation with Alexander Alexeieff. Lee Burgess, another pioneer filmmaker, also attended Bryn Mawr, an all-women's college, which specialized in the arts.)

Although he was the producer of many films Grayson had directed, Willard Van Dyke stated after her death that Grayson's sole significance was that she had directed "one quite good documentary." Unfortunately for her, that film and others she directed have rarely been shown in the United States. Perhaps it is for this reason that Helen Grayson's name is rarely found in any film books, even those devoted only to women filmmakers.

—Cecile Starr

GREENWALD, Maggie
American director and writer

Born: 23 June 1955. **Career:** Began her career as an actor then a dancer; in her early twenties spent a year at film school, subsequently made several short films and moved into the postproduction phase of the film industry; she was a picture editor for several years and then shifted to sound editing; 1987—made her first feature, *Home Remedy*; 1989—made *The Kill-Off*, from the novel by Jim Thompson, 1993—made the highly acclaimed *The Ballad of Little Jo*; mid-1990s—adjunct associate professor, Columbia University School of the Arts. **Awards:** Best Director Award, Turin Film Festival, for *The Kill-Off*, 1989; Special Jury Award, Rome-Florence Film Festival, for *The Ballad of Little Jo,* 1994. **Address:** c/o Sloss Law Offices, 170 Fifth Avenue, 8th Floor, New York, NY 10010, U.S.A.

Films as Director and Writer

1987   *Home Remedy*
1989   *The Kill-Off*
1993   *The Ballad of Little Jo*

Publications by Greenwald

Articles

"Cowgirls," in *Sight and Sound* (London), October 1994.
"Our Heroes Have Sometimes Been Cowgirls," interview with Tania Modleski, in *Film Quarterly* (Berkeley), Winter 1995.

Publications on Greenwald

Books

Cook, Pam, and Philip Dodd, editors, *Women and Film: A Sight and Sound Reader,* Philadelphia, 1993.
Francke, Lizzie, *Script Girls: Women Screenwriters in Hollywood,* London, 1994.
Foster, Gwendolyn Audrey, *Women Film Directors: An International Bio-Critical Dictionary,* Westport, Connecticut, 1995.

Articles

Peary, Danny, "The Crooked Cue," in *Daily News Magazine* (New York), 27 August 1989.
Dewey, Fred, "The Dark Secret of Jim Thompson and Maggie Greenwald," in *Montage-IFG/West* (Los Angeles), November 1989.
Cameron-Wilson, James, "Deadlier than the Male," in *Film Review* (London), 1990.
Walter, Natasha, "An Unusual Film for a Woman," in *Guardian* (London), February 1990.
"The Kill-Off," in *New York Times,* 19 October 1990.
"The Kill-Off," in *Village Voice* (New York), 23 October 1990.
Aufderheide, P., "Maggie Greenwald," in *Angles* (Milwaukee), vol. 2, nos. 6-7, 1993.
Lee, Linda, "When Men Were Men (and So Were Women)," in *New York Times,* 15 August 1993.
Travers, Peter, *"The Ballad of Little Jo,"* in *Rolling Stone* (New York), 19 August 1993.
Holden, Stephen, "Feminist Cross-Dresser in the Old West," in *New York Times,* 20 August 1993.
Rich, B. Ruby, "At Home on the Range," in *Sight and Sound* (London), November 1993.
Miller, Lynn C., "Rewards High in Cross-Dressing Western," in *Texas Triangle,* 10 November 1993.
Francke, Lizzie, "Western Women," in *Guardian Weekend* (London), 4 December 1993.
Bartlett, J., "Pistol-Packing Mama," in *Time Out* (London), 2 March 1994.

Maggie Greenwald

Dowell, P., "The Mythology of the Western: Hollywood Perspectives on Race and Gender in the 90's," in *Cineaste* (New York), vol. 21, nos. 1-2, 1995.

Kitses, Jim, "An Exemplary Post-Modern Western: *The Ballad of Little Jo,*" in *The Western Reader,* 1998.

* * *

Best known for the cross-dressing, revisionist Western *The Ballad of Little Jo* (1993), Maggie Greenwald began her artistic career as a dancer and actor before embarking on a career in the film industry. Greenwald made several short films before gaining experience as a picture editor and sound editor. Her first feature as a director was the 1987 *Home Remedy,* followed by *The Kill-Off* (1989). According to Greenwald, it took five years to get the $200,000 needed to finance *Home Remedy.* Her first two films had short commercial lives with neither film making much of an impression on commercial critics. *The Kill-Off* is interesting because it represents Greenwald's first foray into a traditionally male genre, the film noir. Based on a Jim Thompson novel, Greenwald claims to have been attracted to the material by Thompson's use of language, his exploration of "low-lifes," and the opportunity to work on characters from an internal perspective. As she states, "You are reading stories about people who are doing incredibly vicious things, you are inside of them and experiencing the world from their point of view of being vulnerable and fragile. And I consider that perspective to be very feminine."

Greenwald is also one of the few women film directors to work in the traditionally male Western genre. Modleski claims *Little Jo* is the "first Western written and directed by a woman since the silent era." The strengths of this revisionist, feminist Western lie in Suzy Amis's compelling portrait of a 19th-century Eastern society woman who is ostracized from her community after the illegitimate birth of a child. The character ends up in the Far West where she encounters poverty and attempted rape and finally decides the only way to survive is to pass as a man. Eventually Jo becomes a miner then a sheepherder and falls in love with a Chinese man, Tinman (David Chung). Although they privately live as man and woman, the rest of the world believes Jo to be a man until her secret is discovered after her death. The central conceit of cross-dressing might have come across as a gimmick in less capable directorial hands, but added to the persuasive, sensitive performance by Amis, the film is genuinely moving and convincing. The film also features a surprisingly strong performance from Bo Hopkins, best known for his work in Peckinpah's *The Wild Bunch.* It also features, not surprisingly, a wonderfully detailed performance by Ian McKellen as Percy, a character who struggles with his own sexuality and displays a strong hatred for women.

The inspiration for this tale was a real individual although Greenwald claims that the only things she knew for certain about Josephine Monaghan are what was published in newspaper articles at the time of her death. Greenwald has taken the basic facts of the character's beginnings and the end of her life and imagined much of the rest. But that seems fair and honest within the context of a fiction film. *Little Jo* harkens back to earlier films like the Jack Nicholson/ Monte Hellman "existential" Westerns of the mid-1960s *Ride in the Whirlwind* and *The Shooting* in its level of realism. There is good attention to period detail in the film as well as an accuracy in the dialogue, which nicely captures the flavor and speech idioms common to the period. The re-creation of Ruby City is particularly well done and there is a real sense of life lived in the town scenes. One feels that people could very well have lived like this at the time and

the viewer actually learns something about the Old West. Greenwald claims that most of the research for the film was based on looking at photographs— unlike the Nicholson Westerns, which were inspired by real cowboy diaries.

Little Jo is strong in its visual style and montage, and nicely captures the sense of expanse and lyricism of the landscape. Viewer involvement is also enhanced by a lovely, emotional music score. Another strength of the film is the sudden shifts in tone and mood that occur within a scene. One particularly fine example occurs when the character played by Ian McKellen goes mad and attacks a deaf, mute whore. The sense that death or physical harm could explode at any instant in this world is well communicated by this scene. The sequence also communicates the character's self-loathing as well as his misogynistic streak. The film's pacing is leisurely but maintains interest throughout.

To say that the film is flawless, however, would be inaccurate. There are occasionally awkward moments, and the film's ideological project is at times too pat and obvious. One major flaw in the film is Jo's lack of an interior life. The film might have gained in complexity if it had tried to illustrate what this intriguing character felt or thought about her life, but that never happens. Greenwald's interest in the subjectivity of the noir genre might well have been transposed to this film. Nonetheless, *The Battle of Little Jo* is a serious contribution to the contemporary Western genre and offers a genuinely fresh spin on some well-worn territory. The film may not be as subversive as some have claimed, but it is a genuine accomplishment. Greenwald has a sure command of the medium and is clearly a director who merits attention.

—Mario Falsetto

GUILLEMOT, Agnès
French editor

Born: Agnès Perche in Roubaix, 1931. **Education:** Attended IDHEC, Paris, 1956-57. **Family:** Married the director Claude Guillemot. **Career:** 1956-57—editor for Télévision Canadienne (Télé-France); 1957-59—assistant editor at IDHEC; 1960—worked on TV news series, and then on series *L'Education sentimentale,* 1971, *L'Amour du métier,* 1972, *La Clé des champs,* 1973, and *Les Secrets de la Mer Rouge,* 1974; since 1980—teacher of film editing at IDHEC.

Films as Editor

1953   *La Faute des autres* (Guez—short)
1955   *Walk into Paradise* (*L'Odyssée du Capitaine Steve*) (Robinson and Pagliero) (asst)
1958   *Vous n'avez rien contre la jeunesse* (Logereau—short); *Voyage en Boscavie* (Herman—short)
1959   *Voiles à Val* (Perol—short)
1960   *Le Gaz de Lacq* (Lanoe—short); *Thaumetopoea* (Enrico—short); *Un Steak trop cuit* (Moullet—short)
1961   *La Quille* (Herman—short); *Une Femme est une femme* (*A Woman Is a Woman*) (Godard)
1962   *Une Grosse Tête* (De Givray); *Vivre sa vie* (*My Life to Live*) (Godard); "Il Nuovo mondo" ep. of *Rogopag* (Godard)

1963   *Le Petit Soldat* (*The Little Soldier*) (Godard—produced 1960) (co);
        Les Hommes de la Wahgi (Villeminot—short); *Les Carabiniers*
        (Godard); *Le Mépris* (*Contempt*) (Godard); "Le Grand Escroc"
        ep. of *Les Plus Belles Escroqueries du monde* (*The Beautiful
        Swindlers*) (Godard); *Jérôme Bosch* (Weyergans—short); *Une
        Semaine en France* (C. Guillemot and Chambon—short)

1964   *Bande à part* (*Band of Outsiders*) (Godard); *Une Fille à la
        dérive* (Delsol); *Rues de Hong Kong* (C. Guillemot—short);
        La Jonque (C. Guillemot—short); *Les Tourbiers*
        (Weyergans—short); *De l'amour* (Aurel); *Une Femme
        mariée* (*The Married Woman*) (Godard) (co)

1965   *Alphaville* (*Une étrange aventure de Lemmy Caution*;
        Alphaville: A Strange Adventure of Lemmy Caution; *Tarzan
        versus I.B.M.*) (Godard)

1966   *Masculin-féminin* (*Masculine-Feminine*) (Godard); *Dialectique*
        (C. Guillemot—short); *Le Chien fou* (Matalon); *Nature morte*
        (C. Guillemot—short); *Made in U.S.A.* (Godard)

1967   "Anticipation" ep. of *Le Plus Vieux Métier du monde* (*The Oldest
        Profession*) (Godard); *La Chinoise* (Godard); *Weekend* (Godard)

1968   *Les Gauloises bleues* (Cournot); *Baises volés* (*Stolen Kisses*)
        (Truffaut); *One Plus One* (*Sympathy for the Devil*)
        (Godard); *La Trêve* (C. Guillemot)

1969   "L'amore" ep. of *Amore e rabbia* (*Vangelo '70*) (Godard);
        La Sirène du Mississippi (*Mississippi Mermaid*) (Truffaut);
        L'Enfant sauvage (*The Wild Child*) (Truffaut)

1970   *Domicile conjugal* (*Bed and Board*) (Truffaut)

1974   *L'Age tendre* (Laumet)

1975   *Le Grand Matin* (C. Guillemot—short); *Cousin cousine*
        (Tacchella)

1976   *Un Type comme moi ne devrait jamais mourir* (Vianey); *Le
        Pays bleu* (*The Blue Country*) (Tacchella)

1977   *Monsieur Badin* (Ceccaldi); *Jean de la lune* (Villiers); *Les
        Violons parfois* (Ronet)

1978   *Folies douces* (Ronet); *Le Concierge revient de suite* (Wyn)

1979   *Il y a longtemps que je t'aime* (Tacchella)

1982   *Invitation au voyage* (Del Monte)

1983   *La Diagonale du fou* (*Dangerous Moves*) (Dembo)

1985   *Escalier C* (Tacchella)

1987   *La Brute* (C. Guillemot); *Fuegos* (C. Guillemot)

1988   *La Lumière du lac* (Comencini)

1990   *Un Week-End sur deux* (*Every Other Weekend*) (N. García);
        Sale comme un ange (*Dirty Like an Angel*) (Breillat)

1995   *N'oublie pas que tu vas mourir* (*Don't Forget You're Going
        to Die*) (Beauvois); *Memoires d'un jeune con* (Aurignac)

Publications by Guillemot

Articles

Cinématographe (Paris), March 1985.
Cahiers du Cinéma (Paris), November 1990.

Publications on Guillemot

Articles

Chaplin (Stockholm), December 1968.
Film Comment (New York), March/April 1977.

* * *

Agnès Guillemot's 45-year career places her as one of France's most important, respected, and influential editors. She teaches editing at IDHEC in Paris, edits television series, documentaries, and narrative features, and through the 1960s, established the basic editing style of modernist filmmaking, contemporary television commercials, and music videos. She began cutting film during the Nouvelle Vague and remains strongly associated with that era.

As Jean-Luc Godard's favorite editor, Guillemot edited all of his films from 1961 to 1969, with the exceptions of *Pierrot le fou*, *Deux ou trois choses que je sais d'elle* (both edited by one of her former assistants, Françoise Collin), and *Le Gai savoir*. Collaborating with Godard on 13 features and four episodes of compilation films, and having an assistant edit two others, she must share responsibility for the deconstructive narrative techniques and reflexive visual style usually credited to Godard. Although the similarity of the editing strategies in *Deux ou trois choses* and *Pierrot le fou* to all Godard's other films suggests the director's overriding influence, and Guillemot herself admits that an editor must embrace the personal rhythm of each director and not impose her own, Guillemot's reification of Godard's theories cannot be underestimated. By introducing a sense of musical rhythm and a disregard for spatial and temporal continuity, her work with Godard avoided the realist dictates of linear narrative and provided a locus for ideological analysis. This radicalizing of conventional editing eventually emerged as her most important legacy.

Within any one film, Guillemot's editing appears contradictory, or perhaps dialogic; in any case, her work seems, at first glance, an impossible melange of styles. She combines or juxtaposes the formal symmetry of long takes, the precise rigor of classical match-action editing and shot/reverse shot, the playfulness of reflexivity, and the spontaneity of jump cuts. These characteristics exactly demonstrate the musical and open narrative signature of the Nouvelle Vague. Guillemot cites her strongest work as *A Woman Is a Woman*, with its interplay of words and music as in an opera, and *Les Carabiniers* for the crescendo of the postcard sequence. In *Alphaville*, she reinforces Godard's parody of American science fiction by employing standard editing techniques only to abandon them at moments of highest narrative expectation. In *Contempt*, she uses jump cuts sparingly as a metaphor for Camille's confused mind, ironically embedding them in a fluid pattern of graceful tracking shots. In *Masculine-Feminine*, she plays off the symmetrical tension of the title to visually explore the energy of romance; initially, fast-paced jump cutting represents a new love, slowing to long takes as the romance dissolves. In *Weekend*, she summarizes her collaboration with Godard by fully exhibiting her varied and "contradictory" style of editing, a style perfectly suited for encapsulating Godard's "end of cinema."

Guillemot's late career allowed her to adapt radical Nouvelle Vague modernism for more mainstream cinema; as New Wave stylistics became accepted and standardized, she expanded the confining logic and limitations of classic linear narrative. She edited films for François Truffaut (including two of the Antoine Doinel series), Jean-Charles Tacchella (including the Oscar-nominated *Cousin cousine*), and Richard Dembo (the Academy Award-winning *Dangerous Moves*). By comparing these films to her Godard period, one can easily see Guillemot's influence on contemporary film editing. Eschewing only the reflexivity of her Godard period, she employs the other techniques (especially visual and aural jump cuts) to stress spatial and temporal ellipses. Contained within classical match action and shot/reverse shot sequences and countered with long takes, these ellipses open up a narrative, regardless of how confining (*Dangerous Moves*'s chess match) or how limited (*Cousin cousine*'s conventional love story) and offer the potential for social critique. Her editing on *La Lumière du lac* and *Every Other Weekend* accomplishes exactly this—expanding the parameters of linear narrative with humorous spontaneity, rhythmic pacing, and critical observations of modern society. She has also edited ten shorts and features by her husband Claude Guillemot, alternating between traditional documentary style and her Nouvelle Vague techniques.

Agnès Guillemot's New Wave cutting also influenced most contemporary film and television editing. Even though the link between her editing during the 1960s and today's television commercials and music videos loses its political edge, the continuation of her style in these formats seems incontrovertible (the 1989 Lee Jeans ads, particularly, acting as a direct homage). The formal symmetry of shot/reverse shot placed within long takes, invisible match-action editing alternating with jump cuts, a playful reflexivity, and loosely structured "nonnarratives" are now accepted as standard practice (almost every music video is edited this way). Like most historical avant-garde artists, her work seems much less radical today because of its wide appropriation. Nevertheless, Guillemot must be credited with modernizing editing during the 1960s, an accomplishment which continues to influence visual media today.

—Greg S. Faller

GUY, Alice
French director and writer

Pseudonym: Also known as Alice Guy-Blaché and Alice Blaché. **Born:** Saint-Mandé, 1 July 1873. **Education:** Attended the Convent du Sacré-Coeur, Viry, France 1879-85; religious school at Ferney, and brief term in Paris; studied stenography. **Family:** Married Herbert Blaché-Bolton, 1907 (divorced 1922), two children. **Career:** 1895—secretary to Léon Gaumont; 1896 (some sources give 1900)—directed first film, *La Fée aux choux*; 1897-1907—director of Gaumont film production; 1900—using Gaumont "chronophone," made first sound films; 1907—moved to United States with husband, who was to supervise Gaumont subsidiary Solax; 1917—ceased independent production, lectured on filmmaking at Columbia University; 1919-20—assistant director to husband; 1922—returned to France; 1964—moved to United States. **Awards:** Legion of Honor, 1953. **Died:** In Mahwah, New Jersey, 24 March 1968.

Films as Director and Writer

1896   *La Fée aux choux* (*The Cabbage Fairy*)
1897   *Le Pêcheur dans le torrent*; *Leçon de danse*; *Baignade dans le torrent*; *Une nuit agitée*; *Coucher d'Yvette*; *Danse fleur de lotus*; *Ballet Libella*; *Le Planton du colonel*; *Idylle*; *L'Aveugle*
1897/98 *L'Arroseur arrosé*; *Au réfectoire*; *En classe*; *Les Cambrioleurs*; *Le Cocher de fiacre endormi*; *Idylle interrompue*; *Chez le magnétiseur*; *Les Farces de Jocko*; *Scène d'escamotage*; *Déménagement à la cloche de bois*; *Je vous y prrrends!*
1898/99 *Leçons de boxe*

1899/1900 *Le Tondeur de chiens*; *Le Déjeuner des enfants*; *Au cabaret*; *La Mauvaise Soupe*; *Un Lunch*; *Erreur judiciaire*; *L'Aveugle*; *La Bonne Absinthe*; *Danse serpentine par Mme Bob Walter*; *Mésaventure d'un charbonnier*; *Monnaie de lapin*; *Les Dangers de l'acoolisme*; *Le Tonnelier*; *Transformations*; *Le Chiffonier*; *Retour des champs*; *Chez le Maréchal-Ferrant*; *Marché à la volaille*; *Courte échelle*; *L'Angélus*; *Bataille d'oreillers*; *Bataille de boules de neige*; *Le marchand de coco*
1900   *Avenue de l'Opéra*; *La petite magicienne*; *Leçon de danse*; *Chez le photographe*; *Sidney's Joujoux* series (nine titles); *Dans les coulisses*; *Au Bal de Flore* series (three titles); *Ballet Japonais* series (three titles); *Danse serpentine*; *Danse du pas des foulards par des almées*; *Danse de l'ivresse*; *Coucher d'une Parisienne*; *Les Fredaines de Pierrette* series (four titles); *Vénus et Adonis* series (five titles); *La Tarantelle*; *Danse des Saisons* series (four titles); *La Source*; *Danse du papillon*; *La Concierge*; *Danses* series (three titles); *Chirurgie fin de siècle*; *Une Rage de dents*; *Saut humidifié de M. Plick*
1900/01 *La Danse du ventre*; *Lavatory moderne*; *Lecture quotidienne*
1900/07 (Gaumont "Phonoscènes," i.e., films with synchronized sound recorded on a wax cylinder): *Carmen* (twelve scenes); *Mireille* (five scenes); *Les Dragons de Villars* (nine scenes); *Mignon* (seven scenes); *Faust* (twenty-two scenes); *Polin* series (thirteen titles); *Mayol* series (thirteen titles); *Dranem* series of comic songs (twelve titles); Series recorded in Spain (eleven titles); *La Prière* by Gounod
1901   *Folies Masquées* series (three titles); *Frivolité*; *Les Vagues*; *Danse basque*; *Hussards et grisettes*; *Charmant FrouFrou*; *Tel est pris qui croyait prendre*
1902   *La fiole enchantée*; *L'Equilibriste*; *En faction*; *La Première Gamelle*; *La Dent récalcitrante*; *Le Marchand de ballons*; *Les Chiens savants*; *Miss Lina Esbrard Danseuse Cosmopolite et Serpentine* series (four titles); *Les Clowns*; *Sage-femme de première classe*; *Quadrille réaliste*; *Une Scène en cabinet particulier vue à travers le trou de la serrure*; *Farces de cuisinière*; *Danse mauresque*; *Le Lion savant*; *Le Pommier*; *La Cour des miracles*; *La Gavotte*; *Trompé mais content*; *Fruits de saison*; *Pour secourer la salade*
1903   *Potage indigeste*; *Illusioniste renversant*; *Le Fiancé ensorcelé*; *Les Apaches pas veinards*; *Les Aventures d'un voyageur trop pressé*; *Ne bougeons plus*; *Comment monsieur prend son bain*; *La Main du professeur Hamilton ou Le Roi des dollars*; *Service précipité*, *La Poule fantaisiste*; *Modelage express*; *Faust et Méphistophélès*; *Lutteurs américains*; *La Valise enchantée*; *Compagnons de voyage encombrants*; *Cake-Walk de la pendule*; *Répétition dans un cirque*; *Jocko musicien*; *Les Braconniers*; *La Liqueur du couvent*; *Le Voleur sacrilège*; *Enlèvement en automobile et mariage précipite*
1903/04 *Secours aux naufragés*; *La Mouche*; *La Chasse au cambrioleur*; *Nos Bon Etudiants*; *Les Surprises de l'affichage*; *Comme on fait son lit on se couche*; *Le Pompon malencontreux 1*; *Comment on disperse les foules*; *Les Enfants du miracle*; *Pierrot assassin*; *Les Deux Rivaux*
1904   *L'Assassinat du Courrier de Lyon*; *Vieilles Estampes* series (four titles); *Mauvais coeur puni*; *Magie noire*; *Rafle de chiens*; *Cambrioleur et agent*; *Scènes Directoire* series

(three titles); *Duel tragique*; *L'Attaque d'un diligence*; *Culture intensive ou Le Vieux Mari*; *Cible humaine*; *Transformations*; *Le Jour du terme*; *Robert Macaire et Bertrand*; *Electrocutée*; *La Rêve du chasseur*; *Le Monolutteur*; *Les Petits Coupeurs de bois vert*; *Clown en sac*; *Triste fin d'un vieux savant*; *Le Testament de Pierrot*; *Les Secrets de la prestidigitation dévoilés*; *La Faim ... L'occasion ... L'herbe tendre*; *Militaire et nourrice*; *La Première Cigarette (The First Cigarette)*; *Départ pour les vacances*; *Tentative d'assassinat en chemin de fer*; *Paris la nuit ou Exploits d' apaches à Montmartre*; *Concours de bébés*; *Erreur de poivrot*; *Volée par les bohémiens (Rapt d'enfant par les romanichels)*; *Les Bienfaits du cinématographe*; *P tissier et ramoneur*; *Gage d'amour*; *L'Assassinat de la rue du Temple (Le Crime de la rue du Temple)*; *Le Réveil du jardinier*; *Les Cambrioleurs de Paris*

1905 *Réhabilitation*; *Douaniers et contrebandiers (La Guérité)*; *Le Bébé embarrassant*; *Comment on dort á Paris!*; *Le Lorgnon accusateur*; *La Charité du prestidigitateur*; *Une Noce au lac Saint-Fargeau*; *Le Képi*; *Le Pantalon coupé*; *Le Plateau*; *Roméo pris au piége*; *Chien jouant á la balle*; *La Fantassin Guignard*; *La Statue*; *Villa dévalisée*; *Mort de Robert Macaire et Bertrand*; *Le Pavé*; *Les Maçons*; *La Esmeralda*; *Peintre et ivrogne*; *On est poivrot, mais on a du cœur*; *Au Poulailler!*

1906 *La Fée au printemps*; *La Vie du marin*; *La Chaussette*; *La Messe de minuit*; *Pauvre pompier*; *Le Régiment moderne*; *Les Druides*; *Voyage en Espagne series (15 titles)*; **La Vie du Christ** *(25 tableaux)*; *Conscience de prêtre*; *L'Honneur du Corse*; *J'ai un hanneton dans mon pantalon*; *Le Fils du garde-chasse*; *Course de taureaux à Nîmes*; *La Pègre de Paris*; *Lèvres closes (Sealed Lips)*; *La Crinoline*; *La Voiture cellulaire*; *La Marâtre*; *Le Matelas alcoolique*; *A la recherche d'un appartement*

1907 *La vérité sur l'homme-singe (Ballet de Singe)*; *Déménagement à la cloche de bois*; *Les Gendarmes*; *Sur la barricade (L'enfant de la barricade)*

1910 *A Child's Sacrifice (The Doll)*

1911 *Rose of the Circus*; *Across the Mexican Line*; *Eclipse*; *A Daughter of the Navajos*; *The Silent Signal*; *The Girl and the Bronco Buster*; *The Mascot of Troop "C"*; *An Enlisted Man's Honor*; *The Stampede*; *The Hold-Up*; *The Altered Message*; *His Sister's Sweetheart*; *His Better Self*; *A Revolutionary Romance*; *The Violin Maker of Nuremberg*

1912 *Mignon or The Child of Fate*; *A Terrible Lesson*; *His Lordship's White Feather*; *Falling Leaves*; *The Sewer*; *In the Year 2000*; *A Terrible Night*; *Mickey's Pal*; *Fra Diavolo*; *Hotel Honeymoon*; *The Equine Spy*; *Two Little Rangers*; *The Bloodstain*; *At the Phone*; *Flesh and Blood*; *The Paralytic*; *The Face at the Window*; *A Detective's Dog*; *Canned Harmony*; *The Girl in the Armchair*; *The Making of an American Citizen*; *The Call of the Rose*; *Winsome but Wise*

1913 *The Beasts of the Jungle*; *Dick Whittington and His Cat*; *Kelly from the Emerald Isle*; *The Pit and the Pendulum*; *Western Love*; *Rogues of Paris*; *Blood and Water*; *Ben Bolt*; *The Shadows of the Moulin Rouge*; *The Eyes that Could Not Close*; *The Star of India*; *The Fortune Hunters*; *A House Divided*; *Matrimony's Speed Limit*

1914 *Beneath the Czar*; *The Monster and the Girl*; *The Million Dollar Robbery*; *The Prisoner of the Harem*; *The Dream Woman*; *Hook and Hand*; *The Woman of Mystery*; *The Yellow Traffic*; *The Lure*; *Michael Strogoff or The Courier to the Czar*; *The Tigress*; *The Cricket on the Hearth*

1915 *The Heart of a Painted Woman*; *Greater Love Hath No Man*; *The Vampire*; *My Madonna*; *Barbara Frietchie* (co-d)

1916 *What Will People Say?*; *The Girl with the Green Eyes*; *The Ocean Waif*; *House of Cards*

1917 *The Empress*; *The Adventurer*; *A Man and the Woman*; *When You and I Were Young*; *Behind the Mask*

1918 *The Great Adventure*; *A Soul Adrift*

1920 *Tarnished Reputations*

Other Films

1919 *The Divorcee* (asst d); *The Brat* (asst d)
1920 *Stronger than Death* (asst d)

Publications by Guy

Book

Autobiographie d'une pionnière du cinéma 1873-1968, Paris, 1976; published as *The Memoirs of Alice Guy-Blaché*, edited by Anthony Slide, Metuchen, New Jersey, 1986.

Articles

"Woman's Place in Photoplay Production," in *The Moving Picture World* (New York), 11 July 1914.
Letter in *Films in Review* (New York), May 1964.
"La Naissance du cinéma," in *Image et Son* (Paris), April 1974.
"Tournez, mesdames ...," in *Ecran* (Paris), August/September 1974.

Publications on Guy

Books

Slide, Anthony, *Early Women Directors*, New York, 1977.
Heck-Rabi, Louise, *Women Filmmakers: A Critical Reception*, Metuchen, New Jersey, 1984.
Elsaesser, Thomas, and Adam Barker, editors, *Early Cinema: Space-Frame-Narrative*, London, 1990.
Flitterman-Lewis, Sandy, *To Desire Differently: Feminism and the French Cinema*, Urbana, Illinois, 1990.
Acker, Ally, *Reel Women: Pioneers of the Cinema, 1896 to the Present*, New York, 1991.
Bachy, Victor, *Alice Guy-Blaché: 1873-1968: la première femme cinéaste du monde*, Perpignan, 1993.
Foster, Gwendolyn Audrey, *Women Film Directors: An International Bio-Critical Dictionary*, Westport, Connecticut, 1995.

Articles

Levine, H. Z., "Madame Alice Blaché," in *Photoplay* (New York), March 1912.
Ford, Charles, "The First Female Producer," in *Films in Review* (New York), March 1964.
Smith, F. L., "Alice Guy-Blaché," in *Films in Review* (New York), April 1964.
Lacassin, Francis, "Out of Oblivion: Alice Guy-Blaché," in *Sight and Sound* (London), Summer 1971.

Mitry, Jean, "A propos d'Alice Guy," in *Ecran* (Paris), July 1976.

Deslandes, J., "Sur Alice Guy: polémique," in *Ecran* (Paris), September 1976.

Peary, Gerald, "Czarina of the Silent Screen," in *Velvet Light Trap* (Madison, Wisconsin), Winter 1977.

Vincendeau, Ginette, "Feminism and French Cinema," in *Screen* (London), Winter 1990.

Film

The Lost Garden, 1995.

* * *

Alice Guy was the first person, or among the first, to make a fictional film. The story-film was quite possibly "invented" by her in 1896 when she made *The Cabbage Fairy.* Certain historians claim that films of Louis Lumière and Georges Méliès preceded Guy's first film. The question remains debatable; Guy claimed precedence, devoting much effort in her lifetime to correcting recorded errors attributing her films to her male colleagues, and trying to secure her earned niche in film history. There is no debate regarding Guy's position as the world's first woman filmmaker.

Between 1896 and 1901 Guy made films averaging just 75 feet in length; from 1902 to 1907 she made numerous films of all types and lengths using acrobats, clowns, and opera singers as well as large casts in ambitious productions based on fairy and folk tales, Biblical themes, paintings, and myths. The "tricks" she used—running film in reverse and the use of double exposure—were learned through trial-and-error. In this period she also produced "talking pictures," in which Gaumont's Chronophone synchronized a projector with sound recorded on a wax cylinder.

One of these sound films, *Mireille,* was made by Guy in 1906. Herbert Blaché-Bolton joined the film crew of *Mireille* to learn directing. Alice Guy and Herbert were married in early 1907. The couple moved to the United States, where they eventually set up a studio in Flushing, New York. The Blachés then established the Solax Company, with a Manhattan office. In its four years of existence, Solax released 325 films, including westerns, military movies, thrillers, and historical romances. Mme. Blaché's first picture in the United States was *A Child's Sacrifice* (in 1910), which centers on a girl's attempts to earn money for her family. In her *Hotel Honeymoon* of 1912, the moon comes alive to smile at human lovers, while in *The Violin Maker of Nuremberg,* two apprentices contend for the affections of their instructor's daughter.

The Blachés built their own studio at Fort Lee, New Jersey, a facility with a daily printing capacity of 16,000 feet of positive film. For its inauguration in February of 1912, Mme. Blaché presented an evening of Solax films at Weber's Theatre on Broadway. In that year she filmed two movies based on operas: *Fra Diavolo* and *Mignon,* each of which were three-reelers that included orchestral accompaniment. Her boldest enterprises were films using animals and autos.

Cataclysmic changes in the film industry finally forced the Blachés out of business. They rented, and later sold, their studio, then directed films for others. In 1922 the Blachés divorced. Herbert directed films until 1930, but Alice could not find film work and never made another film. She returned to France, but without prints of her films she had no evidence of her accomplishments and could not find work in the French film industry either. She returned to the United States in 1927 to search the Library of Congress and other film depositories for her films, but her efforts were in vain: only a half-dozen of her one-reelers survive. In 1953 she returned to Paris, where, at age 80, she was honored as the first woman filmmaker in the world. Her films, characterized by innovation and novelty, explored all genres and successfully appealed to both French and American audiences. Today she is finally being recognized as a unique pioneer of the film industry.

—Louise Heck-Rabi

HAMMER, Barbara
American director and writer

Born: 1939. **Education:** Attended University of California, Los Angeles, B.A. in psychology, 1961; San Francisco State University, M.A. in English literature, 1963, M.A. in film, 1975. **Family:** Married once (divorced c. 1968); domestic partner, Florrie Burke, 1988. **Career:** After undergraduate study, taught at Marin County Juvenile Hall; after graduate study in film, began career as avant-garde, feminist filmmaker whose body of work has become known for its exploration and articulation of lesbian concerns; has taught at State University of New York at Binghamton; Columbia College, Chicago; San Francisco State University; San Francisco Art Institute; California College of Arts and Crafts; University of Iowa, Iowa City; Art Institue of Chicago; New School for Social Research; School for Visual Arts, New York; and School of the Museum of Fine Arts, Boston. **Awards:** First Prize, Ann Arbor Film Festival, for *Optic Nerve,* 1985; First Prize, Black Maria Film Festival, and First Prize, Bucks County Film Festival, for *Endangered,* 1988; Atlanta Film/Video Festival, Women in Film Award, for *Still Point,* 1989; Jurors' Award, Black Maria Film Festival, and Best Experimental Film, Utah Film Festival, for *Vital Signs,* 1991; Polar Bear Award for Lifetime Contribution to Lesbian/Gay Cinema, Berlin International Film Festival, 1993; Isabel Liddell Art Award, Ann Arbor Film Festival, and Director's Choice, Charlotte Film Festival, for *Tender Fictions,* 1995. **Address:** 55 Bethune Street, #114G, New York, NY 10014, U.S.A.

Films and Videotapes as Director and Writer

1968   *Schizy*
1969   *Barbara Ward Will Never Die*
1970   *Traveling: Marie and Me*
1972   *The Song of the Clinking Cup*
1973   *I Was/I Am*
1974   *Sisters!; A Gay Day; Dyketactics; X; Women's Rites or Truth Is the Daughter of Time; Menses*
1975   *Jane Brakhage; Superdyke; Psychosynthesis; Superdyke Meets Madame X* (co-d with Almy)
1976   *Moon Goddess* (co-d with Churchman); *Eggs; Multiple Orgasm; Women I Love; Stress Scars and Pleasure Wrinkles*
1977   *The Great Goddess*
1978   *Double Strength; Home; Haircut; Available Space; Sappho*
1979   *Dream Age*
1980   *See What You Hear What You See*
1981   *Our Trip; Arequipa; The Lesbos Film; Machu Picchu; Pictures for Barbara; Pools* (co-d with Klutinis); *Sync Touch*
1982   *Pond and Waterfall; Audience*
1983   *Bent Time; New York Loft; Stone Circles*

1984   *Doll House; Pearl Diver; Bamboo Xerox*
1985   *Optic Nerve; Tourist; Parisian Blinds; Would You Like to Meet Your Neighbor?; Hot Flash*
1986   *Bedtime Stories*
1987   *Place Mattes; No No Nooky TV*
1988   *Endangered; The History of the World According to a Lesbian; Two Bad Daughters* (co-d with Levine)
1989   *Hot Flash; Snow Job: The Media Hysteria of Aids; Still Point; T.V. Tart*
1990   *Sanctus*
1991   **Vital Signs***; Dr. Watson's X-Rays*
1993   *Nitrate Kisses*
1994   *Out in South Africa*
1995   *Tender Fictions*
1997   *The Female Closet*

Publications by Hammer

Articles

"Body-Centered Film," in *Cinemanews* (San Francisco), November/December 1977.

"Use of Time in Women's Cinema," in *Heresies,* Fall 1979.

"From *Women's Images in Film,*" in *Cinemanews* (San Francisco), no. 1/2, 1980.

"Sara Kathryn Arledge," in *Cinemanews* (San Francisco), no. 6/1, 1980-81.

"Women's Images in Film," in *Women's Culture: The Women's Renaissance of the Seventies,* edited by Gayle Kimball, Metuchen, New Jersey, 1981.

"Lesbian Filmmaking: Self-Birthing," in *Film Reader* (Evanston, Illinois), no. 5, 1986.

Interview with Yann Beauvais, in *Spiral,* January 1986.

"The Function of Art in Culture Today," in *High Performance,* Spring/Summer 1988.

"Taking as Alternative Living/Art-Making: Or Why I Moved to the Big City," in *Millennium* (New York), Winter/Spring 1989-90.

"The Politics of Abstraction," in *Queer Looks: Perspectives on Lesbian and Gay Film and Video,* edited by Martha Gever, Pratibha Parmar, and John Greyson, London, 1993.

"Spontaneous Combustion," interview with Cylena Simonds, in *Afterimage* (Rochester, New York), December 1993.

"Ages of the Avant Garde," in *Performing Arts Journal,* no. 46, 1994.

"Diary: June 10, 1993," in *One Day in the Life of World Cinema,* edited by Willis and Wollen, London, 1994.

"Middle-Aged and Still Going Strong," in Special Section: Ages of the Avant-Garde, in *Performing Arts Journal,* January 1994.

"Uncommon History," interview with Holly Willis, in *Film Quarterly* (Berkeley), Summer 1994.

Barbara Hammer. Photograph by Glenn Halverson.

"Lesbian/Gay Media Comes Out in South Africa," in *Release Print,* September 1994.

MacDonald, Christine, "Sharing *Tender Fictions*: New Work by Leasian Filmmaker Barbara Hammer," in *Sojourner,* February 1997.

"Re/Constructing Lesbian Auto/biographies in *Tender Fictions* and *Nitrate Kisses,*" interview with Gwendolyn Foster, in *Post Script, Essays in Film and the Humanities* (Commerce, Texas), Summer 1997.

Interview with Kate Haug, in *Wide Angle* (Baltimore, Maryland), April 1998.

Publications on Hammer

Books

Kaplan, E. Ann, *Women and Film: Both Sides of the Camera,* New York, 1983.

Roth, Moira, editor, *The Amazing Decade: Women and Performance Art in America, 1970-1980,* Los Angeles, 1983.

de Lauretis, Teresa, *Alice Doesn't: Feminism, Semiotics, Cinema,* Bloomington, Indiana, 1984.

Dyer, Richard, *Now You See It: Studies on Lesbian and Gay Film,* London, 1990.

Kuhn, Annette, editor, with Susannah Radstone, *Women in Film: An International Guide,* New York, 1990.

Weiss, Andrea, *Vampires & Violets: Lesbians in Film,* New York, 1993.

Pramaggiore, Maria Therese, *Seeing Double(s): Performance and Self-Representation in the Films of Maya Deren, Barbara Hammer, and Yvonne Rainer,* Ann Arbor, Michigan, 1994.

Foster, Gwendolyn Audrey, *Women Film Directors: An International Bio-Critical Dictionary,* Westport, Connecticut, 1995.

Wilton, Tamsin, *Immortal, Invisible: Lesbians and the Moving Image,* New York, 1995.

Dixon, Wheeler Winston, *The Exploding Eye: A Re-visionary History of 1960s American Experimental Cinema,* Albany, New York, 1997.

Redding, Judith M., and Victoria A. Brownworth, *Film Fatales: Independent Women Directors,* Seattle, 1997.

Articles

Springer, Gregory, "Barbara Hammer: The Leading Lesbian behind the Lens," in *Advocate* (Los Angeles), 7 February 1980.

Weiss, Andrea, "*Women I Love* and *Double Strength*: Lesbian Cinema and Romantic Love," in *Jump Cut* (Berkeley), March 1981.

Zita, Jacquelyn, "Films of Barbara Hammer: Counter-Currencies of a Lesbian Iconography," in *Jump Cut* (Berkeley), March 1981.

Schusler, R. W., "Wouldn't You Like to Meet Your Neighbor?," in *High Performance,* vol. 9, no. 1, 1986.

Gorbman, Claudia, "Recent Work of Barbara Hammer: Bodies Displaced, Places Discovered," in *Jump Cut* (Berkeley), April 1986.

Ventura, Jan, "Barbara Hammer: Woman of Vision," in *High Performance,* Spring/Summer 1988.

Huang, V., and B. Reynaud, "Barbara Hammer: *No No Nooky TV,*" in *Motion Picture* (New York), vol. 3, no. 3/4, 1990.

Meyers, Ellen, and Toni Armstrong, "A Visionary Woman Creating Visions: Barbara Hammer," in *Hot Wire* (Chicago), May 1991.

Tamblyn, Christine, "No More Nice Girls: Recent Transgressive Feminist Art," in *Art Journal,* Summer 1991.

Guthmann, Edward, "Gay Culture, History Explored in *Kisses,*" in *San Francisco Chronicle,* 29 October 1992.

Ehrenstein, David, "Kisses for Barbara Hammer," in *Advocate* (Los Angeles), 17 November 1992.

Rich, B. Ruby, "Reflections on a Queer Screen," in *GLQ: A Journal of Lesbian & Gay Studies,* vol. 1, 1993.

Ayscough, Suzan, "*Nitrate Kisses,*" in *Variety* (New York), 1 February 1993.

Dargis, Manohla, "Trying to Mix It Up," in *Village Voice* (New York), 16 March 1993.

Wilmington, Michael, "A Look at Lesbian Sensibility at the Nuart," in *Los Angeles Times,* 20 May 1993.

Freuh, Joanna, "The Erotic as Social Security," in *Art Journal,* Spring 1994.

Davis, K. D., "Life in the Nonlinear Lane," in *Independent Film and Video Monthly* (New York), April 1994.

Brownworth, Victoria A., "*Out in South Africa,*" in *Advocate* (Los Angeles), 7 February 1995.

Gaiter, Colette, "Private Broadcasts/Public Conservations," in *Public Art Review,* Fall/Winter 1995.

Levy, Emanuel, "*Tender Fictions,*" in *Variety* (New York), 26 February 1996.

* * *

The impressive body of work created by Barbara Hammer during the last three decades exists at the intersection of developments in contemporary American avant-garde film/video practice, and the proactive lesbian feminist community that emerged in the 1970s. Consistently engaged in exploring alternative means of expression, Hammer has moved from experimental film to performance art to feature-length projects to designing sites in cyberspace. Pursuing a path consciously at odds with commercial cinema and structures endemic to patriarchal society, Hammer has worked to generate audience participation, and to that end has employed a collection of strategies—from post-screening discussions, to projection arrangements that create not just moving but mobile images, to website construction that invites visitors to contribute to cyberspace archives. Throughout her career, Hammer's writings, interviews, and screening performances have not only allowed her to provide a context for her creative work, they have also underscored the autobiographical character of her projects, and further, the role her creative work has played in the development of her identity as someone who, as she explained to Holly Willis in 1993, has dedicated her life to advancing film and lesbian studies.

After getting a bachelor's degree in psychology in 1961, and a master's in English literature in the mid-sixties, Hammer took stock of her life, caught the culture's wave of discontent and experimentation, and left her husband and the United States in 1968 to set off on a global tour with her lesbian lover. She returned to San Francisco in 1972, enrolled in graduate school—this time in cinema—and in the next few years, became one of the central figures of lesbian feminist cinema. Hammer's early trilogy, composed of *I Was/I Am* (1973), *X* (1974), and *Psychosynthesis* (1975) recounts, as Jacqueline Zita aptly explains, a transition from "anger directed outward [to] a synthesis of selves collaged in the symbol of Jungian archetypes." In making that transition, these (and other Hammer) films embrace central features of lesbian feminist art of the 1970s, for they are marked by—autobiographical and participatory, as opposed to voyeuristic, representations of lesbian sexuality; a focus on the lesbian body as beautiful, as opposed to abhorrent; an exploration of women's lives and women's bodies as being in touch with nature and spirituality, as opposed to being sites of artifice and deviance.

Hammer's body-centered films of the 1970s include a series of landmark films. *Dyketactics* (1974), a four-minute film in which each image focuses our attention on the sense of touch, is recognized as the first representation of lesbian sexuality by a lesbian. *Multiple Orgasm* (1977), with its celebration of the female genitalia, confirmed lesbian feminists' emphasis on sexuality—rather than procreativity—as the core of women's identity. *Women I Love* (1976), which emerged from Hammer's personal experience, explored and thus gave credence to women's sexuality as well as women's domain (cooking, craft work, gardening). *Double Strength* (1978), which recalled Hammer's relationship with trapeze artist Terry Sendgraff, not only created and valorized images of female power, like parallel strategies in other Hammer films, its use of sepia tones and muted colors helped to define an alternative aesthetic. Perhaps what is most remarkable is that Hammer's work during this time (as in later periods) ranged from the humor of such films as *Superdyke* (1975), to the spirituality of films such as *Moon Goddess* (1976).

As Hammer explains in her essay, "Politics of Abstraction," a 1979 Film Forum program in Los Angeles was the first time her work was screened "outside the supportive lesbian feminist community." That moment also serves as marker for a shift in her creative work, for in contrast to the 1970s, throughout the 1980s Hammer's more abstract films emphasize the role of the filmmaker in creating meaning. In this collection of work, films such as *Parisian Blinds*

(1985), *Tourist* (1985), *Optic Nerve* (1985), *Place Mattes* (1987), and *Endangered* (1988) represent some of Hammer's best and well-known work.

In 1993 Hammer created her 50th film, *Nitrate Kisses*. Her first feature-length piece, *Nitrate Kisses* is, as Holly Willis points out, a "critique of the marginalization of gays and lesbians from 'common history,'" and an account of lesbian and gay culture that "attempts to show the processes of history-making." The film creates complex levels of meaning by intercutting, among other things, quotes from the texts that helped shape her conception of the film; archival footage from *Lot in Sodom* (1930), perhaps the first gay film made in America; and footage she shot in Super 8 of places that held the dramatic stories of ordinary lesbians—from long-closed, off-limit bars to sites of former concentration camps. After completing *Nitrate Kisses*, Hammer has continued to produce lengthier pieces. In 1994 she documented the first gay and lesbian film festival in Africa in her work, *Out of South Africa*, and in 1995 she completed an autobiographical work entitled *Tender Fictions*.

Most recently, Hammer has been engaged in creating a website which she describes as a "Lesbian Community in Cyberspace." The site's interactive character and its role in making lesbian experience visible emerge from concerns that have informed Hammer's work from the beginning. In very practical terms, the site makes possible projects she has been working towards for some time. As early as 1982 Hammer sought to make an international compilation film consisting of women expressing what for them was erotic. Today, one component of the website's continuously developing archive is a collection of diverse expressions of women who have visited the website (www.echonyc.com/~lesbians).

Barbara Hammer is not the first American filmmaker to explore women's sexuality—Hammer has acknowledged the influence of American avant-garde filmmaker Maya Deren—nor is she the only filmmaker whose work helps to write the history of lesbian experience. She is, however, a pioneer, a force to be reckoned with, for, as she has explained to Jacqueline Zita, "to live a lesbian life, to make it real, to validate it in film, is a revolutionary act." As Zita convincingly suggests, we should see Barbara Hammer as "a woman artist struggling to redefine the medium in a form and content commensurate with the requirements of a new lesbian aesthetic."

—Cynthia Baron

HÄNSEL, Marion
French/Belgian director and writer

Born: Marseille, France, 12 February 1949; moved to Antwerp, Belgium, as a child. **Education:** Studied acting and mime; attended the French Circus School; studied at the Lee Strasberg Actor's Studio, New York. **Career:** 1970s—worked as an actress, and worked briefly with the Fratellini circus act in Paris; 1977—established her own company, Man's Films, and directed her first short film, *Equilibres*; 1979—directed three documentaries, *Gongola, Hydraulip*, and *Bakti*; 1982—directed her first feature, *The Bed*; 1987—named Belgium's Woman of the Year; 1988—elected president of the Belgium Film Selection Board. **Awards:** Silver Lion, Venice International Film Festival, for *Dust*, 1985. **Address:** Man's Films, 65 avenue Mostinck, 1150 Brussels, Belgium.

Films as Director

1977 *Equilibres* (short)
1979 *Sannu batture* (*Welcome, Foreigner*) (short); *Gongola*;
      Hydraulip; *Bakti*
1982 *Le Lit* (*The Bed*) (+ sc, pr)
1985 *Dust* (+ sc, co-pr)
1987 *Les Noces barbares* (*Cruel Embrace*) (+ co-sc, pr)
1989 *Il Maestro* (*The Maestro*; *Musical May*) (+ co-sc)
1993 *Sur la terre comme au ciel* (*Between Heaven and Earth*; *In
      Heaven as on Earth*; *Entre el cielo y la tierre*) (+ co-sc, co-
      pr)
1995 *Between the Devil and the Deep Blue Sea* (*Li*) (+ co-sc, co-
      pr)

Other Films

1976 *De guerre lasse* (Grospierre) (ro); *Berthe* (Ledoux)
1977 *L'Une chante l'autre pas* (*One Sings, the Other Doesn't*)
      (Varda) (ro); *Ressac* (L. Buñuel) (ro); *La belle affaire*
      (Arago) (ro)
1987 *Love Is a Dog from Hell* (Deruddere) (co-assoc pr)
1988 *Baptême* (Feret) (assoc pr)
1989 *Blueberry Hill* (De Hert) (assoc pr)

Publication by Hänsel

Article

"Equilibre," interview with J. Aubenas, in *Visions* (Brussels), 15
   February 1983.

Publications on Hänsel

Book

Foster, Gwendolyn Audrey, *Women Film Directors: An International
   Bio-Critical Dictionary,* Westport, Connecticut, 1995.

Articles

Wauters, J.-P., "Marion Haensel & *Le Lit*," in *Film en Televisie* (Brussels), October 1982.
Gobthals, G., "Marion Hänsel," in *Andere Sinema* (Antwerp), January 1984.
Blanchet, C., and others, "Onze cinéastes belges pour les années 80,"
   in *Cinéma* (Paris), July/August 1985.
Eddi, A., "Cinéma et litterature," in *Cinéma* (Paris), February 1987.
Horni, J., "Gespraech mit Marion Hänsel," in *Filmbulletin* (Zurich),
   no. 4, 1988.
Buruiana, M., "Marion Hänsel," in *Séquences* (Montreal), January
   1988.

* * *

Marion Hänsel makes intricately detailed and deeply personal
films that most often explore adult-child relationships. She primarily
is concerned with the manner in which adults relate to (and learn
from) children and, on the downside, the emotional dependence of a
child—even one who has grown to adulthood—on even the most
cruelly insensitive parent. Her films often are punctuated by lengthy
shots and long silences, with cameras lingering on scenes and recording their details or slowly tracking across landscapes.

Hänsel's most characteristic films fit into two groupings: those
that explore positive, hopeful adult-child connections (*Between Heaven
and Earth* and *Between the Devil and the Deep Blue Sea*); and those
that explore tumultuous relationships between parent and offspring
(*Dust* and *Cruel Embrace*). *Between Heaven and Earth* is the story
of Maria, a high-powered and unmarried television journalist who
has devoted herself to her career and ignored the ticking of her
biological time clock. After an erotic encounter in a stalled elevator,
Maria finds herself pregnant. She feels she can effortlessly juggle
motherhood and career, and so she decides to have the child. Notwithstanding, as her pregnancy progresses Maria begins to question
her decision to bring a human being into the world. While completing some job-related research, she watches a videotape of emaciated
children. She covers a bomb blast at a university and is jarred by the
sight of terrorized young people and how this place of learning—
where her child just might be in 20 years—can be rocked by violence
and death. She also comes in touch with the more general issue of
how mankind is mistreating the environment, and is no longer in
harmony with nature.

The most telling relationship in *Between Heaven and Earth* is
between Maria and Jeremy, a little boy whose parents recently moved
into her apartment building. They are never around (and are not seen
on camera), and Maria observes Jeremy's resentment over his situation. Maria and Jeremy bond and, despite his youth, he takes on the
role of her teacher. She feels that she can leave her baby at a nursery;
he points out that maybe the baby would not want to be abandoned in
such a way.

Then Maria comes to believe that her fetus is communicating with
her, and telling her that it does not want to be born into a world that
is so hostile to children. After refusing an induced labor and endan-
gering the life of the baby, Maria realizes that, despite the world's
ills, giving birth is an affirmation, an act of faith. At the finale she has
her baby, with whom she shares the kind of harmony she could not
have conceived scant months earlier.

Between Heaven and Earth is a profoundly intellectual film. Hänsel
points out that, on one hand, science has allowed mankind to produce test-tube babies. Yet in a society in which adults are increasingly career-oriented and self-involved, there is no longer room for
children: witness Jeremy, who is all by himself and has neither a
place to play nor children with whom to be friends.

The closeness and understanding that develops between Maria
and Jeremy mirrors the primary relationship in *Between the Devil
and the Deep Blue Sea,* which chronicles the passing friendship
between Nikos, a rootless, opium-addicted sailor whose ship docks
in Hong Kong, and Li, a bright ten-year-old who earns her living by
cleaning the ships in the harbor. Li is an involuntary participant in a
sampan subculture in which she is little more than an indentured
servant. Yet despite her plight, her optimism has allowed her to
preserve her innocence. Here, too, the adult learns from the child.
When Nikos asks Li why she takes on responsibility, she responds,
"That's what life is all about."

Between Heaven and Earth and *Between the Devil and the Deep
Blue Sea* make stark contrasts to *Dust* and *Cruel Embrace*. *Dust*
(which, tellingly, Hänsel dedicates "to my father") is a psychological
portrait of Magda, a woman who lives with her father (who is name-
less) in a remote region of South Africa, where they tend a small
sheep farm. Magda's life is not so much one of isolation as frustration and regret. At the outset, she expresses her thoughts about how,

over the years, she and her father have faced each other in silence. She craves his love and attention, yet her connection to him is strictly servile. In their first scene together he barks out her name. She promptly enters the room, offers him a drink, and removes his boots.

"I should have been a man," Magda declares. "I would have spent my days in the sun, doing whatever it is that men do." Rather than leaving her father and going off to make her own life, Magda is living a self-imposed prison sentence with her father as her jailor: a situation that results in her growing psychological breakdown, and her eventually murdering him after watching him seduce the shy wife of their farm's foreman. Magda cannot bear that her father is giving this young woman the attention—sexual and otherwise—that she covets.

Cruel Embrace also depicts a less-than-idyllic parent-child relationship. It is the story of a boy named Ludovic, who is despised by Nicole, his emotionally tormented and alcoholic mother, because he was conceived while she was brutally raped. Ludovic first is locked in an attic, and then is committed to an insane asylum. Yet like Magda, his need for, and love of, his parent transcends the manner in which he is so heartlessly treated.

In *Between Heaven and Earth* and *Dust,* Hänsel explores the interior lives and complex emotional states of women. In this regard, they are linked to *The Bed,* her debut feature, the story of a desperately ill man and the two women, his first and present wives, who are at his bedside as he approaches death.

In most of her films, however, Hänsel's primary concern is a fascination with children and their world views, and the manner in which they cope within their often hostile environments. "Childhood...clear of mind, unprejudiced and uncompromising," she has declared, "children with their courage (which we adults lack) have the power to change us...the world. To watch them, to listen and to stay close to them, reassures, guides and helps me to make my films."

—Rob Edelman

HARLAN COUNTY, U.S.A.
USA, 1976
Director: Barbara Kopple

Production: Cabin Creek Films; color; running time: 103 minutes. Released October 1976, New York. Filmed in Harlan County, Kentucky.

Producer: Barbara Kopple; **photography:** Hart Perry, Kevin Keating, Phil Parmet, Flip McCarthy, and Tom Hurwitz; **editors:** Nancy Baker, Mary Lampson, Lora Hays, and Mirra Bank; **sound engineers:** Barbara Kopple, Tim Colman, Bob Gates, and Josh Waletsky; **music:** Phyllis Boyens, Hazel Dickens, Sarah Gunning, David Morris, Merle Travis, and Nimrod Workman.

Awards: Academy Award for Best Documentary, 1976.

Publications

Articles

Kaplan, E. Ann, "*Harlan County, U.S.A.:* The Documentary Form," in *Jump Cut* (Chicago), no. 15, 1977.

Eder, Richard, "*Harlan County* Stirring Movie about Miners," in *New York Times,* 24 January 1977.

Simon, J., "Movies: Truth—No Stranger than Fiction," in *New York Magazine,* 24 January 1977.

Sarris, Andrew, "Films in Focus: In the Winter of His Discontent," in *Village Voice* (New York), 31 January 1977.

Canby, Vincent, "Documentaries: From Mining Coal to *Pumping Iron,*" in *New York Times,* 6 February 1977.

Maslin, Janet, "Bombs Away," in *Newsweek* (New York), 21 February 1977.

Westerbeck, C. L., "Women's Work," in *Commonweal,* 4 March 1977.

Crist, Judith, "They Say in Harlan County/There Are No Neutrals There...," in *Saturday Review* (New York), 5 March 1977.

Fitzgerald, F., "Harlan County: Generations of Strikers and Scabs," in *Ms. Magazine* (New York), April 1977.

McNally, Judith, "The Making of *Harlan County, U.S.A.,*" in *Filmmakers Newsletter* (Ward Hill, Massachusetts), May 1977.

Coleman, J., "Crying Out Loud," in *New Statesman* (London), 2 June 1978.

Sloan, W., "*Harlan County, U.S.A.,*" in *Film Library Quarterly* (New York), vol. 12, no. 2/3 1979.

Pierce, W., "*Harlan County, U.S.A.,*" in *Film Library Quarterly* (New York), vol. 13, no. 1, 1980.

King, Noel, "Recent 'Political' Documentary: Notes on *Union Maids* and *Harlan County, U.S.A.,*" in *Screen* (London) vol. 22, no. 2, 1981.

Ferrario, D., "*Harlan County, U.S.A.* di Barbara Kopple," in *Cineforum* (Bergamo, Italy), January 1981.

* * *

Barbara Kopple's debut film *Harlan County, U.S.A.* is a stirring documentary portrait of the 1973 coal miners' strike against the Brookside Mine in Harlan County, Kentucky, which was prompted by the company's refusal to sign a contract with its newly unionized employees. Present for the duration of the bitter strike that lasted more than a year, Kopple effectively conveys the hardships the miners endured not only due to lost wages, but also to the intimidation and violent retaliations from gun-toting company thugs. But she also demonstrates the means by which the community of striking miners and their wives remained closely knit and undeterred.

Director Kopple effectively places the strike within its larger context by providing background about the long and bloody history of the Kentucky mine workers during their struggles for unionization, as well as evidence of the greedy, insensitive, and sometimes criminal undertakings of the mine bosses. Archival film and still photographs offer poignant testimony of the mine conditions and earlier strikes, and contemporary footage conveys the camaraderie and power of the strikers as they continue to fight for safe, humane working conditions and hopeful futures for their children.

Harlan County, U.S.A. opens dramatically with an amazing sequence in which mine workers lying on their bellies are lowered via conveyor belt into the pit of a mine, where they work in seemingly impossible conditions. Then, Nimrod Workman, a quietly dignified retired mine worker begins to relate the story of his life with a touching understatement: "Coal mining was rough." The film is frequently punctuated by the coal miners' sad, timeworn folk songs that describe tragic tales and spirited struggles. A particularly touching scene shows the legendary and prolific folk songwriter, Hazel Dickens, elderly but still ferociously committed to the union as she sings her classic composition, "Which Side Are You On?" The film

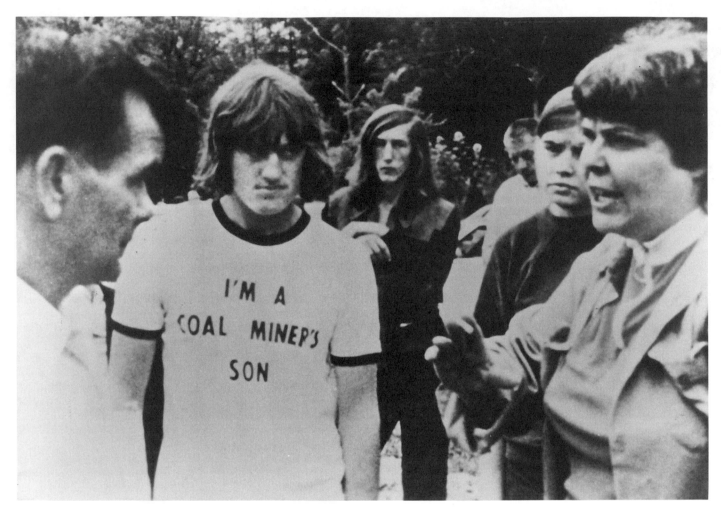

Harlan County, U.S.A.

is visually compelling, and at times quite subtle; one touching scene suggests the shared hopes and dreams of two seemingly disparate workers; in both long-shot and then in more intimate close-ups, Kopple shows a friendly, spontaneous chat between a tall, thin, weathered miner who is picketing on Wall St., and a shorter, beefier, upbeat, and thoroughly union-protected New York City cop. Their conversation is about the miner's struggle for an only moderately improved future and the cop's sympathy for him, in the face of his own bright and secure future.

The film is a testament to Kopple's and her crew's remarkable courage—to the point of dodging bullets—in order to record the strikers' efforts. Notably, Kopple avoids adhering to notions of documentary "objectivity"; her politics are clear—she stands with the strikers, often literally. The film is organized as an argument, in which the claims of the coal-mine operators and their officials (e.g., "the unions are running the U.S.") are juxtaposed with interview testimony of current and former miners. The miners describe horrific abuse, including the slow-death of black-lung disease, mine collapses, the realities of living in housing without plumbing or heat, and working without any health or retirement benefits. But Kopple provides no easy answers to the questions her film asks. For example, she demonstrates that, like the mine managers, the union managers are occasionally corrupt. Thus, she includes footage from a charged union election, between long-time leader Tony Boyle and

Joseph Yablonski, which resulted in the murder of Yablonski and his family and the conviction and imprisonment of Boyle for ordering the hit.

Although she is an invisible presence, Kopple's relationship with her film's "subjects" is clearly the result of their shared trust, and her efforts to convey the hardships, determination, and dignity of the miners and the strong-as-steel cadre of miners' wives who support them. Indeed, she pays considerable attention to the women, demonstrating their indomitable spirit as they struggle for their constitutional rights by marching on the picket line, and conducting strategy sessions and morale-boosting rallies during the long months of the strike. All of the women seem to be survivors of coal-miner fathers, husbands, brothers, or sons who were killed in the mines or are slowly dying from the long exposure to thick coal dust; though their experiences have embittered them, they have been empowered to fight for workers' rights. In a chilling sequence, a woman sweetly describes her decision to start carrying a gun, as she pulls it from her bosom. Immediately thereafter, Kopple includes shots of a mine foreman as he shoots a gun into the midst of the strikers and film crew.

Harlan County, U.S.A. was a hit when it screened at the 1976 New York Film Festival, but subsequent reviewers either effusively praised or disparaged its tight, fictionlike organization and generic elements, especially its gun-toting villains, dishonest and unscrupulous bosses, violent outbursts, and murder. Yet, it is a combination that Kopple employed again, to an equally riveting effect, with her more recent documentary, 1993's *Fallen Champ: The Untold Story of Mike Tyson.*

—Cynthia Felando

HARRIS, Leslie
American director

Born: Cleveland, Ohio, 1959. **Education:** Attended Denison University, M.F.A. in painting. **Career:** 1980s—moved to New York and worked for an advertising agency; directed television commercials. **Awards:** Special Jury Prize for a First Feature, Sundance Film Festival, for *Just Another Girl on the I.R.T.,* 1993; Open Palm, Independent Feature Project Gotham Award, 1993.

Film as Director, Writer, and Producer

1992   *Just Another Girl on the I.R.T.*

Publication by Harris

Article

Interview, in *Angles* (Milwaukee), vol. 2, no. 1, 1994.

Publications on Harris

Book

Foster, Gwendolyn Audrey, *Women Film Directors: An International Bio-Critical Dictionary,* Westport, Connecticut, 1995.

Articles

Taubin, Amy, "Working Girls," in *Village Voice* (New York), 24 November 1992.
Abbe, E. M., "Leslie Harris' Gritty Portrayal of a Young Woman," in *Angles* (Milwaukee), no. 1, 1993.
"Strength through Diversity," in *American Premiere* (Los Angeles), no. 1, 1993.
Phillips, Julie, "Growing Up Black and Female: Leslie Harris' *Just Another Girl on the I.R.T.,*" in *Cineaste* (New York), vol. 19, no. 4, 1993.
"Filmmaker Harris Puts Girls N the Hood in Focus," in *Ms.* (New York), no. 5, 1993.
Weinraub, Bernard, "A Trip Straight out of Brooklyn to the Sundance Film Festival," in *New York Times,* 26 January 1993.
Hruska, Bronwen and Graham Rayman, "On the Outside, Looking In," in *New York Times,* 21 February 1993.
Pryor, Kelli, "Not Just Another Girl from Ohio," in *Entertainment Weekly* (New York), 19 March 1993.
Coleman, Beth, "She's Gotta Do It," in *Village Voice* (New York), 23 March 1993.

Tate, Greg, "*Just Another Girl*: Flygirl on Film," in *Village Voice* (New York), 23 March 1993.
Southgate, Martha, in *Essence* (New York), April 1993.
Chambers, Veronica, and Holly Millea, "Young at Art," in *Premiere* (New York), May 1993.
Taubin, Amy, "Mirror, Mirror," in *Village Voice* (New York), 20 July 1993.
Taubin, Amy, "Girl in the Hood," in *Sight and Sound* (London), August 1993.

*   *   *

At the end of *Just Another Girl on the I.R.T.*—independently produced and shot in 17 days—the audience is informed that they have just sat through "A Film Hollywood Dared Not Do." This is true insofar as Hollywood has denied access to African-American women filmmakers, and *Just Another Girl on the I.R.T.* was directed, produced, and scripted by an African-American woman, Leslie Harris. Prior to its release, among the tens of thousands of films made in Hollywood across the decades, Euzhan Palcy's *A Dry White Season* was the *lone* one directed by a black woman. This fact speaks volumes about racism and sexism in Hollywood and American history.

Nevertheless, any film made by any filmmaker whether inside or outside the cinema mainstream must be held to artistic and technical standards. A film should not automatically be financed and released, critically acclaimed and showered with prizes solely because its maker is a woman or a person of color, and its content is politically correct.

In the case of *Just Another Girl on the I.R.T.,* it would fair to surmise that the movie industry powers that-be passed on it not because of a conspiracy to silence the voices of African-American women filmmakers. Instead, maybe they nixed it because its script was appallingly simplistic, and annoyingly manipulative.

Just Another Girl on the I.R.T., which to date is Harris's only feature, is significant insomuch as it tells the story of a black adolescent female who is more than on-screen window dressing in a male-dominated scenario. She is Chantel (Ariyan Johnson, whose likable performance is the film's sole saving grace), a spirited 17-year-old African American and child of inner-city hip-hop culture who desires to flee her stifling Brooklyn housing project by heading off to college, and then to medical school. But her plans are altered when she discovers she is pregnant.

Cinematically, *Just Another Girl on the I.R.T.* is astonishingly amateurish. The climactic scene, in which Chantel gives birth, is especially embarrassing as it is so poorly staged. And what of Harris's script? It is shrill and one-note, as well as racially loaded. For one thing, Harris hypocritically depicts her only two white characters in broad, mean-spirited terms. One is a snooty lady, a customer in the store in which Chantel works after school. This character acts as if she is the mistress of an antebellum plantation. The other is a narrow-minded Jewish history instructor who only wants to teach his all-black class about the Holocaust. He does not cite instances in which blacks have been discriminated against over the centuries. He responds to Chantel's complaints with a shrug, as he notes that he only is teaching what is in his curriculum.

In the production notes of *Just Another Girl on the I.R.T.,* Harris is quoted as follows: "It's time that we start seeing characters on the screen that are real." Yet the manner in which she depicts the customer and history teacher is broadly cliched, and serves as evidence that an African-American filmmaker can be as thoughtless, insensitive, and racist as a white one.

Chantel may be 17, with her bravado masking a child-woman who is scared and confused, but it is hard to feel anything for her but contempt. This is because, ultimately, she is a fraud. This shining beacon of feminism spouts rhetoric about a woman's right to self-determination. Yet she dumps her boyfriend, Gerard, who is as poor as she is and only can take her out on dates on the subway. What is her attraction to her new boyfriend, Tyrone? He has money. He drives a jeep. And, conveniently, the actor who plays him is attractive and charming, while the actor cast as Gerard is comically goofy.

After impregnating Chantel, Tyrone gives her $500 for an abortion. What does Chantel do with the money? She irresponsibly squanders it in one afternoon, on a shopping spree with a girlfriend.

Just Another Girl on the I.R.T. may be compared to *Girls Town,* another film which depicts the experience of inner city adolescent females. *Girls Town,* directed by Jim McKay, is a vivid slice-of-life about an interracial quartet of working-class teens who are completing their senior year in high school. At the outset, one of the group—a bright and attractive African American—inexplicably commits suicide. There is much soul-searching and sharing of feelings among the survivors; on one level, watching *Girls Town* is like taking a peek at a group therapy session involving these characters.

Girls Town is a story of female bonding, and female friendship. The few adults in the film have had little impact on the characters' lives. Furthermore, their involvement with males mostly is contentious. Boys either do not understand them, or regard them merely as receptacles for physical and verbal abuse and sex. *Girls Town* is extremely effective as a feminist tract about how girls can be as tough and self-sufficient as boys. They must not allow themselves to be victimized by boys. In fact, they must demand nothing less than respect from the opposite sex.

Unlike *Just Another Girl on the I.R.T., Girls Town* is emotionally honest. It portrays the confusion of youth without making excuses for its characters' lack of judgment or life experience.

In the 1990s, a list of films, directed by African-Americans, which offer illuminating, multilayered scenarios and characterizations just begins with *Boyz N the Hood, Menace II Society, Dead Presidents, Daughters of the Dust, To Sleep with Anger, Clockers, Malcolm X, Get on the Bus.* While these films vary in quality and subject matter, all have what *Just Another Girl on the I.R.T.* sorely lacks: maturity and integrity. As film critic Gene Seymour, in his *Newsday* review of the film, observed, "The best you could say about *I.R.T.* is that it gives you a view of life you don't often see in the movies. But as the African-American film movement continues to grow in ambition and achievement, just getting these stories on screen won't be enough. Thinking them through and making them sturdy will."

—Rob Edelman

HARRISON, Joan
British writer and producer

Born: Guildford, Surrey, England, 20 June 1909. **Education:** Attended the Sorbonne, Paris; Oxford University, B.A. **Family:** Married the writer Eric Ambler, 1958. **Career:** Secretary; 1935—began working as Alfred Hitchcock's secretary; 1937—first film as writer for Hitchcock, *Young and Innocent*; accompanied Hitchcock to the United States; 1944—first film as producer, *Phantom Lady*; 1953-64—producer of the TV series *Alfred Hitchcock Presents*; 1964—co-founder, Tarantula Productions. **Died:** 14 August 1994.

Films as Writer

1937 *Young and Innocent (The Girl Was Young)* (Hitchcock)
1939 *Jamaica Inn* (Hitchcock)
1940 *Rebecca* (Hitchcock); *Foreign Correspondent* (Hitchcock)
1941 *Suspicion* (Hitchcock)
1942 *Saboteur* (Hitchcock)
1943 *Shadow of a Doubt* (Hitchcock)
1944 *Dark Waters* (de Toth)

Films as Producer

1944 *Phantom Lady* (Siodmak) (+ co-sc)
1945 *Uncle Harry (The Strange Affair of Uncle Harry)* (Siodmak)
1946 *Nocturne* (Marin) (+ co-sc)
1947 *They Won't Believe Me* (Pichel); *Ride the Pink Horse* (Montgomery) (+ co-sc, uncredited)
1949 *Once More, My Darling* (Montgomery)
1950 *Your Witness (Eye Witness)* (Montgomery) (+ co-sc); *Circle of Danger* (J. Tourneur)

Publications by Harrison

Article

Studio Review, November 1950.

Publications on Harrison

Book

Acker, Ally, *Reel Women: Pioneers of the Cinema, 1896 to the Present,* New York, 1991.

Articles

New York Times, 27 June 1943.
Current Biography 1944, New York, 1944.
Chaplin (Stockholm), December 1968.
Obituary in *Los Angeles Times,* 24 August 1994.
Obituary in *New York Times,* 25 August 1994.
Obituary in *Time* (New York), 5 September 1994.

* * *

Those who think that there were no women producers in the old Hollywood studio system have perhaps never heard of the remarkable Joan Harrison. A wise woman who always made the most of her opportunities, the young Harrison took a job as secretary to Alfred Hitchcock, a reduction in salary and status from her former position in an advertising department of a London newspaper. ("I am probably the worst secretary Hitch ever had," she once told *Modern Screen* magazine.) Working for Hitchcock in the British film industry, she was able to invade every department and learn all aspects of the business, so when her opportunity to become a Hollywood producer came along, she was more than prepared. In her eight years with Hitchcock, she collaborated with him on several of his best screenplays: *Rebecca, Foreign Correspondent, Suspicion,* and *Saboteur* among them. Ultimately she returned to work with him as the producer of his acclaimed television series, *Alfred Hitchcock Presents.*

Harrison's mark was made in various types of crime films, particularly those which featured a woman in jeopardy. She had always been interested in criminal cases, and had followed many of England's more colorful examples through the courts of London. (She married the famous spy genre author Eric Ambler.) Her first film away from Hitchcock in Hollywood, as writer and associate producer, was *Dark Waters,* directed by Andre de Toth. It established the Harrison style in that it was a story about a young woman (Merle Oberon) caught in a *Gaslight* situation, being driven mad by a group of false relatives. Harrison's first feature as full producer was the much respected low-budget film noir *Phantom Lady,* directed by Robert Siodmak, starring Ella Raines as a fearless secretary bent on proving her boss did not actually murder his wife. These two excellent small pictures illustrate what would always be true of Harrison's work—she was a totally competent producer capable of making stylish mystery films from the woman's angle. They also illustrate a handicap she was never able to overcome in terms of critical acceptance: she seemed forever destined to remain in Hitchcock's shadow. In addition, her solo productions are almost all directed by men such as de Toth and Siodmak, who, like Hitchcock, are well known for a personal vision. Thus, it was not only difficult to identify what might be her touch, but no one seemed willing to try to do so. Perhaps the outstanding thing that can be said for Harrison is that the films she produced were often complimented for "being in the Hitchcock tradition." This meant that she had learned her lessons well from the master, and that she *was* capable of putting that stamp on her movies. All of Harrison's films have these qualities in common: excellent women characters, who are frequently intrepid in their response to danger and death; a low-key, subtle suggestion of violence rather than overt blood and gore; and elegant production values, with handsome sets and modish costumes.

A thoughtful woman who always utilized what she had learned in her experience with Hitchcock, Harrison commented on what made an effective suspense thriller by saying:

> There is a difference between violence and action. The two are not synonymous. This is a very important point to consider. Displayed violence, blow-by-blow account violence is irresponsible, unnecessary, and unworthy of creativity. Action, on the other hand, cannot be totally implied or merely suggested. For whodunits, no action is pretty bloody dull. Many persons equate in their minds action and violence. They speak of one when they mean the other. Each is an individual property, and suggested violence is much more interesting. I see no point in plunging a dagger in someone's chest and the viewer watching this unfold. One should see the dagger in the hand of the manipulator and then shift—the horror that results! This way is suspenseful and the audience gets involved.

Although her list of films is small, it displays subtle, tasteful suspense work in well-photographed, stylish films. It is also unique because few women achieved her status. Commenting on her unusual role as Hollywood's top female producer in the 1940s, Harrison remarked, "We women have to work twice as hard to be recognized in our own fields. But today there is more recognition of women's talents than ever before. Those women who want a career can certainly have one." The most obvious thing to say about Harrison's career is that what is remarkable about it is that it exists at all. Her work, however, is of a level of taste and intelligence that qualifies her as something more than an oddity or a footnote, and certainly has

earned her the right to be seen separately from, if not equal to, Alfred Hitchcock.

—Jeanine Basinger

HEAD, Edith
American costume designer

Born: Edith Claire Posener in San Bernardino, California, 28 October 1897. **Education:** Attended elementary school in Redding, California to 1911; schools in Los Angeles; University of California, Berkeley; Stanford University; also attended classes at Otis Art Institute and Chouinard Art School, both in Los Angeles. **Family:** Married 1) Charles Head (divorced 1938); 2) the designer Wiard Ihnen, 1940 (died 1979). **Career:** 1923—French, Spanish, and art teacher at Bishop School for Girls, La Jolla, California, and at Hollywood School for Girls; 1924-27—sketch artist; 1927-38—assistant to Travis Banton; 1938-66—head of design, Paramount; then chief designer at Universal until her death; also designed for other studios, for stage shows, and for commercial companies; 1945-52—regular appearances on the radio show *Art Linkletter's House Party* (and on TV, 1952-69); 1949-51—lecturer, University of Southern California, Los Angeles (also in 1973); 1978—designed for the TV miniseries *Little Women.* **Awards:** Academy Awards, for *The Heiress,* 1949, *Samson and Delilah,* 1949, *All about Eve,* 1950, *A Place in the Sun,* 1951, *Roman Holiday,* 1953, *Sabrina,* 1954, *The Facts of Life,* 1960, and *The Sting,* 1973. **Died:** In Los Angeles, 24 October 1981.

Films as Costume Designer

1924 *Peter Pan* (Brenon) (co)
1925 *The Golden Bed* (C. B. DeMille) (co); *The Wanderer* (Walsh) (co)
1926 *Mantrap* (Fleming)
1927 *Wings* (Wellman)
1929 *The Saturday Night Kid* (Sutherland) (co); *The Virginian* (Fleming); *The Wolf Song* (Fleming)
1930 *Along Came Youth* (Corrigan and McLeod); *Follow the Leader* (Taurog); *Only the Brave* (Tuttle); *The Santa Fe Trail* (Brower and Knopf)
1932 *The Big Broadcast of 1932* (Tuttle); *A Farewell to Arms* (Borzage) (co); *He Learned about Women* (Corrigan); *Hot Saturday* (Seiter); *Love Me Tonight* (Mamoulian); *The Sign of the Cross* (Banton) (co); *Two Kinds of Women* (W. de Mille); *Undercover Man* (Flood); *Wayward* (Sloman)
1933 *A Cradle Song* (Leisen) (co); *Crime of the Century* (Beaudine) (co); *Duck Soup* (McCarey); *Gambling Ship* (Gasnier and Marcin); *Hello, Everybody* (Seiter); *I'm No Angel* (Ruggles) (co); *She Done Him Wrong* (L. Sherman); *Sitting Pretty* (H. Brown); *Strictly Personal* (Murphy); *White Woman* (Walker) (co)
1934 *Ladies Should Listen* (Tuttle); *Little Miss Marker* (Hall); *Many Happy Returns* (McLeod); *The Notorious Sophie Lang* (Murphy) (co); *The Pursuit of Happiness* (Hall); *The Witching Hour* (Hathaway); *You Belong to Me* (Werker)

1935 *The Big Broadcast of 1936* (Taurog); *Car 99* (Barton); *The Crusades* (C. B. DeMille) (co); *Father Brown, Detective* (Sedgwick); *Four Hours to Kill* (Leisen); *The Glass Key* (Tuttle); *Here Comes Cookie* (McLeod); *Hold 'em, Yale* (Lanfield); *The Last Outpost* (Barton and Gasnier); *The Lives of a Bengal Lancer* (Hathaway) (co); *Man on the Flying Trapeze* (Bruckman); *Men without Names* (Murphy); *Mississippi* (Sutherland); *People Will Talk* (Santell); *Peter Ibbetson* (Hathaway); *Ruggles of Red Gap* (McCarey) (co); *Stolen Harmony* (Werker); *Two for Tonight* (Tuttle); *Wings in the Dark* (Flood)

1936 *The Accusing Finger* (Hogan); *The Big Broadcast of 1937* (Leisen); *Border Flight* (Lovering); *College Holiday* (Tuttle); *Collegiate* (Murphy); *Hollywood Boulevard* (Florey); *The Jungle Princess* (Thiele); *Lady Be Careful* (Reed); *The Milky Way* (McCarey); *Murder with Pictures* (Barton); *Poppy* (Sutherland); *The Return of Sophie Lang* (Archainbaud); *Rhythm on the Range* (Taurog); *Rose Bowl* (Barton); *The Texas Rangers* (K. Vidor); *Thirteen Hours by Air* (Leisen); *Three Cheers for Love* (McCarey); *Till We Meet Again* (Florey); *Too Many Parents* (McGowan); *Wedding Present* (Wallace); *Wives Never Know* (Nugent) (co); *Woman Trap* (H. Young)

1937 *Arizona Mahoney* (Hogan); *Artists and Models* (Walsh) (co); *The Barrier* (Selander); *Blonde Trouble* (Archainbaud); *Blossoms on Broadway* (Wallace); *Borderland* (Watt); *Born to the West* (Barton); *Bulldog Drummond Comes Back* (L. King); *Bulldog Drummond Escapes* (Hogan); *Bulldog Drummond's Revenge* (L. King); *Clarence* (Archainbaud); *The Crime Nobody Saw* (Barton); *Daughter of Shanghai* (Florey); *A Doctor's Diary* (C. Vidor) (co); *Double or Nothing* (Reed); *Easy Living* (Leisen) (co); *Ebb Tide* (Hogan); *Exclusive* (Hall); *Forlorn River* (Barton); *Girl from Scotland Yard* (Vignola); *The Great Gambini* (C. Vidor); *Her Husband Lies* (Ludwig) (co); *Hideaway Girl* (Archainbaud); *Hills of Old Wyoming* (Watt); *Hold 'em, Navy* (Neumann); *Hopalong Rides Again* (Selander); *Hotel Haywire* (Archainbaud); *Interns Can't Take Money* (Santell); *John Meade's Woman* (Wallace) (co); *King of Gamblers* (Florey); *The Last Train from Madrid* (Hogan); *Let's Make a Million* (McCarey); *Love on Toast* (Dupont); *Make Way for Tomorrow* (McCarey); *Midnight Madonna* (Flood); *Mind Your Own Business* (McLeod); *Mountain Music* (Florey); *Murder Goes to College* (Riesner); *Night Club Scandal* (Murphy); *A Night of Mystery* (Dupont); *North of the Rio Grande* (Watt); *On Such a Night* (Dupont); *Outcast* (Florey); *Partners in Crime* (Murphy); *Partners of the Plains* (Selander); *Rustler's Valley* (Watt); *She Asked for It* (Kenton); *She's No Lady* (C. Vidor); *Sophie Lang Goes West* (Riesner) (co); *Souls at Sea* (Hathaway); *Texas Trail* (Selman); *This Way, Please* (Florey); *Thrill of a Lifetime* (Archainbaud); *Thunder Trail* (Barton); *True Confession* (Ruggles) (co); *Turn Off the Moon* (Seiler); *Waikiki Wedding* (Tuttle); *Wells Fargo* (Lloyd); *Wild Money* (L. King)

1938 *The Arkansas Traveler* (Santell); *Bar 20 Justice* (Selander); *Artists and Models Abroad* (Leisen) (co); *The Big Broadcast of 1938* (Leisen); *Booloo* (Elliott); *The Buccaneer* (C. B. DeMille); *Bulldog Drummond in Africa* (L. King); *Campus Confessions* (Archainbaud); *Bulldog Drummond's Peril* (Hogan); *Cassidy of Bar 20* (Selander);

Coconut Grove (Santell); *College Swing* (Walsh); *Dangerous to Know* (Florey); *Doctor Rhythm* (Tuttle) (co); *The Frontiersman* (Selander); *Give Me a Sailor* (Nugent); *Heart of Arizona* (Selander); *Her Jungle Love* (Archainbaud); *Hunted Men* (L. King); *Illegal Traffic* (L. King); *In Old Mexico* (Venturini); *King of Alcatraz* (Florey); *Little Orphan Annie* (Holmes); *Men with Wings* (Wellman); *The Mysterious Rider* (Selander); *Pride of the West* (Selander); *Prison Farm* (L. King); *Professor Beware* (Nugent); *Ride a Crooked Mile* (A. E. Green); *Say It in French* (A. L. Stone); *Scandal Sheet* (Hogan); *Sing, You Sinners* (Ruggles); *Sons of the Legion* (Hogan); *Spawn of the North* (Hathaway); *Stolen Heaven* (A. L. Stone); *The Texans* (Hogan); *Thanks for the Memory* (Archainbaud); *Tip-Off Girls* (L. King); *Tom Sawyer, Detective* (L. King); *Touchdown Army* (Neumann); *Tropic Holiday* (Reed); *You and Me* (F. Lang)

1939 *All Women Have Secrets* (Neumann); *Arrest Bulldog Drummond* (Hogan); *Back Door to Heaven* (W. K. Howard); *The Beachcomber* (Pommer); *Beau Geste* (Wellman); *Boy Trouble* (Archainbaud); *Bulldog Drummond's Bride* (Hogan); *Café Society* (E. Griffith); *Bulldog Drummond's Secret Police* (Hogan); *The Cat and the Canary* (Nugent); *Death of a Champion* (Florey); *Disbarred* (Florey); *Disputed Passage* (Borzage); *Geronimo* (Sloane); *The Gracie Allen Murder Case* (A. E. Green); *Grand Jury Secrets* (Hogan); *The Great Victor Herbert* (A. L. Stone); *Heritage of the Desert* (Selander); *Honeymoon in Bali* (E. Griffith); *Hotel Imperial* (Florey); *Invitation to Happiness* (Ruggles); *Island of Lost Men* (Neumann); *I'm from Missouri* (Reed); *King of Chinatown* (Grinde); *The Lady's from Kentucky* (Hall); *Law of the Pampas* (Watt); *The Llano Kid* (Venturini); *The Magnificent Fraud* (Florey); *Man about Town* (M. Sandrich); *Man of Conquest* (Nicholls) (co); *Midnight* (Leisen) (co); *Million Dollar Legs* (Grinde); *Never Say Die* (Nugent); *The Night of Nights* (Milestone); *Night Work* (Archainbaud); *$1,000 a Touchdown* (Hogan); *Our Leading Citizen* (Santell); *Our Neighbors, the Carters* (Murphy); *Paris Honeymoon* (Tuttle); *Persons in Hiding* (L. King); *Range War* (Selander); *The Renegade Trail* (Selander); *Rulers of the Sea* (Lloyd); *Silver on the Sage* (Selander); *Some Like It Hot* (Archainbaud); *The Star Maker* (Del Ruth); *St. Louis Blues* (Walsh); *Sudden Money* (Grinde); *The Sunset Trail* (Selander); *Television Spy* (Dmytryk); *This Man Is News* (McDonald); *Undercover Doctor* (L. King); *Union Pacific* (C. B. DeMille); *Unmarried* (Neumann); *What a Life* (Reed); *Zaza* (Cukor)

1940 *Adventure in Diamonds* (Fitzmaurice); *Arise, My Love* (Leisen) (co); *The Biscuit Eater* (Heisler); *Buck Benny Rides Again* (M. Sandrich); *The Cherokee Strip* (Selander); *Christmas in July* (P. Sturges); *Comin' round the Mountain* (Archainbaud); *Dancing on a Dime* (Santley); *Doctor Cyclops* (Schoedsack); *Emergency Squad* (Dmytryk); *The Farmer's Daughter* (Hogan); *French without Tears* (Asquith) (co); *Golden Gloves* (Dmytryk); *The Ghost Breakers* (George Marshall); *The Great McGinty* (P. Sturges); *Hidden Gold* (Selander); *I Want a Divorce* (Murphy); *Knights of the Range* (Selander); *Light of Western Stars* (Selander); *The Light That Failed* (Wellman); *Love Thy Neighbor* (M. Sandrich); *Moon over Burma* (L.

Edith Head (left) with Arlene Dahl

King); *Mystery Sea Raider* (Dmytryk); *A Night at Earl Carroll's* (Neumann); *Northwest Mounted Police* (C. B. DeMille) (co); *Opened by Mistake* (Archainbaud); *A Parole Fixer* (Florey); *The Quarterback* (Humberstone); *Queen of the Mob* (Hogan); *Rangers of Fortune* (Wood); *Remember the Night* (Leisen); *Rhythm on the River* (Schertzinger); *Road to Singapore* (Schertzinger); *Safari* (E. Griffith); *Santa Fe Marshal* (Selander); *Seventeen* (L. King); *The Showdown* (Bretherton); *Stagecoach War* (Selander); *Texas Rangers Ride Again* (Hogan); *Those Were the Days* (Reed); *Three Men from Texas* (Selander); *Typhoon* (L. King); *Untamed* (Archainbaud); *Victory* (Cromwell); *The Way of All Flesh* (L. King); *Women without Names* (Florey); *World in Flames* (Richard)

1941　*Aloma of the South Seas* (Santell); *Among the Living* (Heisler); *Bahama Passage* (E. Griffith); *Ball of Fire* (Hawks); *Birth of the Blues* (Schertzinger); *Border Vigilantes* (Abrahams); *Buy Me That Town* (Forde); *Caught in the Draft* (D. Butler); *Doomed Caravan* (Selander); *Flying Blind* (McDonald); *Forced Landing* (Wiles); *Glamour Boy* (Tetzlaff); *Henry Aldrich for President* (Bennett); *Here Comes Mr. Jordan* (Hall); *Hold back the Dawn* (Leisen); *I Wanted Wings* (Leisen); *In Old Colorado* (Bretherton); *Kiss the Boys Goodbye* (Schertzinger); *The Lady Eve* (P. Sturges); *Las Vegas Nights* (Murphy); *Life with Henry* (Reed); *The Mad Doctor* (Whelan); *The Monster and the Girl* (Heisler); *New York Town* (C. Vidor); *The Night of January 16th* (Clemens); *Nothing But the Truth* (Nugent); *One Night in Lisbon* (E. Griffith); *The Parson of Panamint* (McGann); *Pirates on Horseback* (Selander); *Power Dive* (Hogan); *Reaching for the Sun* (Wellman); *Road to Zanzibar* (Schertzinger); *Roundup* (Selander); *Secret of the Wastelands* (Abrahams); *Shepherd of the Hills* (Hathaway); *Skylark* (M. Sandrich) (co); *Sullivan's Travels* (P. Sturges); *Virginia* (E. Griffith); *There's a Magic in the Music* (Stone); *West Point Widow* (Siodmak); *Wide-Open Town* (Selander); *World Premiere* (Tetzlaff); *You Belong to Me* (Ruggles); *You're the One* (Murphy)

1942　*Are Husbands Necessary?* (Taurog); *Beyond the Blue Horizon* (Santell); *The Fleet's In* (Schertzinger); *The Gay Sisters* (Rapper) (co); *The Glass Key* (Heisler); *The Great Man's Lady* (Wellman); *Henry Aldrich, Editor* (Bennett); *Holiday Inn* (M. Sandrich); *I Married a Witch* (Clair); *The Lady Has Plans* (Lanfield); *Lucky Jordan* (Tuttle); *The Major and the Minor* (Wilder); *Mrs. Wiggs of the Cabbage Patch* (Murphy); *My Favorite Blonde* (Lanfield); *My Heart Belongs to Daddy* (Siodmak); *The Palm Beach Story* (P. Sturges) (co); *The Remarkable Andrew* (Heisler); *Road to Morocco* (D. Butler); *Star-Spangled Rhythm* (George Marshall); *This Gun for Hire* (Tuttle); *Wake Island* (Farrow); *Young and Willing* (E. Griffith)

1943　*China* (Farrow); *The Crystal Bell* (Nugent); *Five Graves to Cairo* (Wilder); *Flesh and Fantasy* (Duvivier) (co); *For Whom the Bell Tolls* (Wood); *The Good Fellows* (Graham); *Happy Go Lucky* (Bernhardt); *Henry Aldrich Gets Glamour* (Bennett); *Hostages* (Tuttle); *Henry Aldrich Haunts a House* (Bennett); *Lady Bodyguard* (Clemens); *Lady of Burlesque* (Wellman) (co); *Let's Face It* (Lanfield); *Night Plane from Chungking* (Murphy); *No Time for Love* (Leisen) (co); *Riding High* (George Marshall); *Salute for Three* (Murphy); *Tender Comrade* (Dmytryk) (co); *They*

Got Me Covered (D. Butler) (co); *True to Life* (George Marshall)

1944　*And Now Tomorrow* (Pichel); *And the Angels Sing* (George Marshall); *Double Indemnity* (Wilder); *Going My Way* (McCarey); *The Great Moment* (P. Sturges); *Hail the Conquering Hero* (P. Sturges); *Henry Aldrich's Little Secret* (Bennett); *The Hitler Gang* (Farrow); *Here Come the Waves* (M. Sandrich); *The Hour before the Dawn* (Tuttle); *I Love a Soldier* (M. Sandrich); *I'll Be Seeing You* (Dieterle); *Lady in the Dark* (Leisen) (co); *The Man in Half Moon Street* (Murphy); *Ministry of Fear* (F. Lang); *The Miracle of Morgan's Creek* (P. Sturges); *National Barn Dance* (Bennett); *Rainbow Island* (Murphy); *Our Hearts Were Young and Gay* (L. Allen); *The Uninvited* (L. Allen); *Standing Room Only* (Lanfield); *Till We Meet Again* (Borzage); *You Can't Ration Love* (Fuller)

1945　*The Affairs of Susan* (Seiter); *The Bells of St. Mary's* (McCarey); *Bring on the Girls* (Lanfield); *Christmas in Connecticut* (Godfrey) (co); *Duffy's Tavern* (Walker) (co); *Hold That Blonde* (George Marshall); *Incendiary Blonde* (George Marshall); *The Lost Weekend* (Wilder); *Love Letters* (Dieterle); *Masquerade in Mexico* (Leisen); *A Medal for Benny* (Pichel); *Miss Susie Slagle's* (Berry) (co); *Murder, He Says* (George Marshall); *Out of this World* (Walker); *Road to Utopia* (Walker); *Salty O'Rourke* (Walsh); *The Stork Club* (Walker); *You Came Along* (Farrow)

1946　*The Blue Dahlia* (George Marshall); *Blue Skies* (Heisler) (co); *The Bride Wore Boots* (Pichel); *Monsieur Beaucaire* (George Marshall); *My Reputation* (Bernhardt) (co); *Notorious* (Hitchcock); *Our Hearts Were Growing Up* (Russell); *The Perfect Marriage* (L. Allen); *The Strange Love of Martha Ivers* (Milestone); *To Each His Own* (Leisen); *The Virginian* (Gilmore); *The Well-Groomed Bride* (Lanfield)

1947　*Blaze of Noon* (Farrow); *Calcutta* (Farrow); *California* (Farrow) (co); *Cross My Heart* (Berry); *Cry Wolf* (Godfrey) (co); *Dear Ruth* (Russell); *Desert Fury* (L. Allen); *Easy Come, Easy Go* (Farrow); *I Walk Alone* (Haskin); *The Imperfect Lady* (L. Allen) (co); *My Favorite Brunette* (Nugent); *The Other Love* (de Toth) (co); *The Perils of Pauline* (George Marshall); *Ramrod* (de Toth); *Road to Rio* (McLeod); *The Trouble with Women* (Lanfield); *The Two Mrs. Carrolls* (Godfrey) (co); *Variety Girl* (George Marshall) (co); *Welcome Stranger* (Nugent); *Where There's Life* (Lanfield); *Wild Harvest* (Garnett)

1948　*The Accused* (Dieterle); *Arch of Triumph* (Milestone) (co); *Beyond Glory* (Farrow); *The Big Clock* (Farrow); *Dream Girl* (Leisen); *The Emperor Waltz* (Wilder) (co); *Enchantment* (Reis) (co); *A Foreign Affair* (Wilder); *Isn't It Romantic?* (McLeod); *June Bride* (Windust) (co); *Miss Tatlock's Millions* (Haydn); *My Own True Love* (Bennett); *The Night Has a Thousand Eyes* (Farrow); *Saigon* (Fenton); *Rachel and the Stranger* (Foster); *The Sainted Sisters* (Russell); *The Sealed Verdict* (L. Allen); *So Evil My Love* (L. Allen) (co); *Sorry, Wrong Number* (Litvak); *Whispering Smith* (Fenton) (co)

1949　*The Great Gatsby* (Nugent); *Beyond the Forest* (K. Vidor); *The Great Lover* (Hall); *The Heiress* (Wyler) (co); *Malaya* (Thorpe) (co); *Manhandled* (Foster); *My Foolish Heart* (Robson) (co); *My Friend Irma* (George Marshall); *Red, Hot, and Blue* (Farrow); *Rope of Sand* (Dieterle); *Samson and Delilah* (C. B. DeMille) (co); *Song of Surrender* (Leisen)

1950 *All about Eve* (J. Mankiewicz) (co); *Copper Canyon* (Farrow) (co); *The Dark City* (Dieterle); *Fancy Pants* (George Marshall); *The File on Thelma Jordan* (Siodmak); *The Furies* (A. Mann); *Let's Dance* (McLeod); *Mr. Music* (Haydn); *My Friend Irma Goes West* (Walker); *Paid in Full* (Dieterle); *No Man of Her Own* (Leisen); *Riding High* (Capra); *September Affair* (Dieterle); *Sunset Boulevard* (Wilder)

1951 *The Big Carnival* (Wilder); *Branded* (Maté); *Crosswinds* (Foster); *Darling, How Could You?* (Leisen); *Dear Brat* (Seiter); *Detective Story* (Wyler); *Here Comes the Groom* (Capra); *Hong Kong* (Foster); *The Last Outpost* (Foster); *The Lemon Drop Kid* (Lanfield); *My Favorite Spy* (McLeod); *Payment on Demand* (Bernhardt) (co); *Peking Express* (Dieterle); *A Place in the Sun* (Stevens); *Rhubarb* (Lubin); *Silver City* (Haskin); *The Stooge* (Taurog); *Submarine Command* (Farrow); *That's My Boy* (Walker); *When Worlds Collide* (Maté)

1952 *Aaron Slick from Punkin Crick* (Binyon); *Caribbean* (Ludwig); *Anything Can Happen* (Seaton); *Carrie* (Wyler); *Come Back, Little Sheba* (Daniel Mann); *Denver and Rio Grande* (Haskin); *The Greatest Show on Earth* (C. B. DeMille) (co); *Hurricane Smith* (J. Hopper); *Jumping Jacks* (Taurog); *Just for You* (Nugent) (co); *My Son John* (McCarey); *Red Mountain* (Dieterle); *Road to Bali* (Walker); *Ruby Gentry* (K. Vidor); *Sailor Beware* (Walker); *The Savage* (George Marshall); *Somebody Loves Me* (Brecher); *Something to Live For* (Stevens); *Son of Paleface* (Tashlin); *This Is Dynamite* (Dieterle); *The Turning Point* (Dieterle)

1953 *Arrowhead* (Warren); *The Caddy* (Taurog); *Forever Female* (Rapper); *Here Come the Girls* (Binyon); *Houdini* (George Marshall); *Jamaica Run* (Foster); *Little Boy Lost* (Seaton); *Off Limits* (George Marshall); *Pleasure Island* (Hugh); *Pony Express* (J. Hopper); *Roman Holiday* (Wyler); *Sangaree* (Ludwig); *Scared Stiff* (George Marshall); *Shane* (Stevens); *Stalag 17* (Wilder); *The Stars Are Singing* (Taurog); *Those Redheads from Seattle* (L. R. Foster); *Thunder in the East* (C. Vidor); *Tropic Zone* (Foster); *The Vanquished* (Ludwig); *War of the Worlds* (Haskin)

1954 *About Mrs. Leslie* (Daniel Mann); *Alaska Seas* (J. Hopper); *The Bridges at Toko-ri* (Robson); *The Country Girl* (Seaton); *Elephant Walk* (Dieterle); *Jivaro* (Ludwig); *Knock on Wood* (Panama and Frank); *Living It Up* (Taurog); *Money from Home* (George Marshall); *Mr. Casanova* (McLeod); *The Naked Jungle* (Haskin); *Rear Window* (Hitchcock); *Red Garters* (George Marshall) (co); *Sabrina* (Wilder); *Secret of the Incas* (J. Hopper); *Three-Ring Circus* (Pevney); *White Christmas* (Curtiz)

1955 *Artists and Models* (Tashlin); *Conquest of Space* (Haskin); *The Desperate Hours* (Wyler); *The Far Horizon* (Maté); *The Girl Rush* (Pirosh); *Hell's Island* (Karlson); *Lucy Gallant* (Parrish); *The Rose Tattoo* (Daniel Mann); *Run for Cover* (N. Ray); *The Seven Little Foys* (Shavelson); *Strategic Air Command* (A. Mann); *To Catch a Thief* (Hitchcock); *The Trouble with Harry* (Hitchcock); *You're Never Too Young* (Taurog)

1956 *Anything Goes* (R. Lewis); *The Birds and the Bees* (Taurog); *The Come-On* (Birdwell); *The Court Jester* (Panama and Frank) (co); *Hollywood or Bust* (Tashlin); *The Leather*

Saint (Ganzer); *The Man Who Knew Too Much* (Hitchcock); *The Mountain* (Dmytryk); *Pardners* (Taurog); *The Proud and the Profane* (Seaton); *The Rainmaker* (Anthony); *The Scarlet Hour* (Curtiz); *The Search for Bridey Murphy* (Langley); *The Ten Commandments* (C. B. DeMille) (co); *That Certain Feeling* (Panama and Frank); *Three Violent People* (Maté)

1957 *Beau James* (Shavelson); *The Buster Keaton Story* (Sheldon); *The Delicate Delinquent* (McGuire); *The Devil's Hairpin* (Wilde); *Fear Strikes Out* (Mulligan); *Funny Face* (Donen) (co); *Gunfight at the O.K. Corral* (J. Sturges); *Hear Me Good* (McGuire); *The Joker Is Wild* (C. Vidor); *The Lonely Man* (Levin); *Loving You* (Kanter); *The Sad Sack* (George Marshall); *Short Cut to Hell* (Cagney); *The Tin Star* (A. Mann); *Wild Is the Wind* (Cukor); *Witness for the Prosecution* (Wilder)

1958 *As Young as You Are* (Gerard); *The Buccaneer* (Quinn) (co); *The Geisha Boy* (Tashlin); *Hot Spell* (Daniel Mann); *Houseboat* (Shavelson); *Maracaibo* (Wilde); *I Married a Monster from Outer Space* (Fowler); *King Creole* (Curtiz); *The Matchmaker* (Anthony); *Me and the Colonel* (Glenville); *The Party Crashers* (Girard); *Rock-a-Bye Baby* (Tashlin); *Separate Tables* (Delbert Mann) (co); *St. Louis Blues* (Reisner); *Teacher's Pet* (Seton); *Vertigo* (Hitchcock)

1959 *Alias Jesse James* (McLeod); *The Black Orchid* (Ritt); *But Not for Me* (W. Lang); *Career* (Anthony); *The Hangman* (Curtiz); *Don't Give Up the Ship* (Taurog); *The Five Pennies* (Shavelson); *A Hole in the Head* (Capra); *The Jayhawkers* (Frank); *Last Train from Gun Hill* (J. Sturges); *That Kind of Woman* (Lumet); *Too Young for Love* (Girard); *The Trap* (Panama); *The Young Captives* (Kershner)

1960 *The Bellboy* (J. Lewis); *A Breath of Scandal* (Curtiz); *Cinderfella* (Tashlin); *The Facts of Life* (Frank) (co); *G.I. Blues* (Taurog); *Heller in Pink Tights* (Cukor); *It Started in Naples* (Shavelson); *Pepe* (Sidney); *The Rat Race* (Mulligan); *A Touch of Larceny* (Hamilton); *Visit to a Small Planet* (Taurog)

1961 *All in a Night's Work* (Anthony); *Blue Hawaii* (Taurog); *Breakfast at Tiffany's* (Edwards) (co); *The Errand Boy* (J. Lewis); *The Ladies' Man* (J. Lewis); *Love in a Goldfish Bowl* (Sher); *Mantrap* (O'Brien); *On the Double* (Shavelson); *The Pleasure of His Company* (Seaton); *Pocketful of Miracles* (Capra); *Summer and Smoke* (Glenville)

1962 *The Counterfeit Traitor* (Seaton); *Escape from Zahrain* (Neame); *A Girl Named Tamiko* (J. Sturges); *Girls! Girls! Girls!* (Taurog); *Hatari!* (Hawks); *It's Only Money* (Tashlin); *The Man Who Shot Liberty Valance* (Ford); *My Geisha* (Cardiff); *The Pigeon That Took Rome* (Shavelson); *Too Late Blues* (Cassavetes); *Who's Got the Action?* (Daniel Mann)

1963 *The Birds* (Hitchcock); *Come Blow Your Horn* (Yorkin); *Critic's Choice* (Weis); *Donovan's Reef* (Ford); *Fun in Acapulco* (Thorpe); *Hud* (Ritt); *I Could Go On Singing* (Neame); *My Six Loves* (Champion); *Love with the Proper Stranger* (Mulligan); *A New Kind of Love* (Shavelson) (co); *The Nutty Professor* (J. Lewis); *Papa's Delicate Condition* (George Marshall); *Who's Been Sleeping in My Bed?* (Daniel Mann); *Who's Minding the Store?* (Tashlin); *Wives and Lovers* (Rich)

1964 *The Carpetbaggers* (Dmytryk); *The Disorderly Orderly* (Tashlin); *A House Is Not a Home* (Rouse); *Lady in a*

Cage (Grauman); *Men's Favorite Sport?* (Hawks); *Marnie* (Hitchcock); *The Patsy* (J. Lewis); *Roustabout* (Rich); *Sex and the Single Girl* (Quine) (co); *Thirty-Six Hours* (Seaton); *What a Way to Go* (J. L. Thompson) (co); *Where Love Has Gone* (Dmytryk)

1965   *Boeing, Boeing* (Rich); *The Family Jewels* (J. Lewis); *The Great Race* (Edwards) (co); *The Hallelujah Trail* (J. Sturges); *Harlow* (G. Douglas) (co); *Inside Daisy Clover* (Mulligan) (co); *John Goldfarb, Please Come Home* (J. L. Thompson) (co); *Love Has Many Faces* (Singer); *Red Line 7000* (Hawks); *The Slender Thread* (Pollack); *The Sons of Katie Elder* (Hathaway); *Sylvia* (G. Douglas); *Who Has Seen the Wind?* (Sidney); *The Yellow Rolls-Royce* (Asquith) (co)

1966   *Assault on a Queen* (Donohue); *The Last of the Secret Agents* (Abbott); *Nevada Smith* (Hathaway); *Not with My Wife, You Don't!* (Panama); *The Oscar* (Rouse); *Paradise, Hawaiian Style* (Moore); *Penelope* (Hiller); *The Swinger* (Sidney); *This Property Is Condemned* (Pollack); *Torn Curtain* (Hitchcock); *Waco* (Springsteen)

1967   *Barefoot in the Park* (Saks); *The Caper of the Golden Bulls* (Rouse); *Chuka* (G. Douglas); *Easy Come, Easy Go* (Rich); *Hotel* (Quine) (co); *Warning Shot* (Kulik)

1968   *In Enemy Country* (Keller); *Madigan* (Siegel); *The Pink Jungle* (Delbert Mann); *The Secret War of Harry Frigg* (Smight); *What's So Bad about Feeling Good?* (Seaton)

1969   *Butch Cassidy and the Sundance Kid* (G. R. Hill); *Downhill Racer* (Ritchie); *Eye of the Cat* (Rich); *The Hellfighters* (McLaglen); *House of Cards* (Guillermin); *The Lost Man* (Arthur); *Sweet Charity* (Fosse); *Tell Them Willie Boy Is Here* (Polonsky); *Topaz* (Hitchcock); *Winning* (Goldstone)

1970   *Airport* (Seaton); *Colossus: The Forbin Project* (Sargent); *Myra Breckinridge* (Sarne) (co); *Skullduggery* (G. Douglas and Wilson); *Story of a Woman* (Bercovici)

1971   *Red Sky at Morning* (Goldstone); *Sometimes a Great Notion* (P. Newman)

1972   *Hammersmith Is Out* (Ustinov); *Pete 'n' Tillie* (Ritt); *The Screaming Woman* (Smight); *The Life and Times of Judge Roy Bean* (J. Huston) (co)

1973   *Ash Wednesday* (Peerce); *A Doll's House* (Losey) (co); *Divorce His, Divorce Hers* (Hussein); *The Sting* (G. R. Hill); *The Don Is Dead* (Fleischer); *The Showdown* (Seaton)

1974   *Airport '75* (Smight)

1975   *The Great Waldo Pepper* (G. R. Hill); *Rooster Cogburn* (Miller); *The Man Who Would Be King* (J. Huston)

1976   *The Bluebird* (Cukor); *Family Plot* (Hitchcock); *Gable and Lombard* (Furie); *W. C. Fields and Me* (Hiller); *The Disappearance of Aimee* (Harvey)

1977   *Airport '77* (Hiller); *Sex and the Married Woman* (Arnold); *Sunshine Christmas* (G. Jordan)

1978   *The Big Fix* (Kagen); *Olly Olly Oxen Free* (Colla); *Sextette* (Hughes)

1979   *The Last Married Couple in America* (Cates)

1982   *Dead Men Don't Wear Plaid* (C. Reiner)

Publications by Head

Books

With Jane Kesner Ardmore, *The Dress Doctor,* Boston, Massachusetts, 1959.

With Joe Hyams, *How to Dress for Success,* New York, 1967.
With Paddy Calistro, *Edith Head's Hollywood,* New York, 1983.

Articles

"A Costume Problem: From Shop to Stage to Screen," in *Hollywood Quarterly,* October 1946.
"Honesty in Today's Film Fashions," in *Show* (New York), 6 August 1970.
"Head on Fashion" series in *Holiday* (New York), January/February 1973; July/August 1973; September/October 1974; November/December 1974; January/February 1975; March 1975; September/October 1975; March 1976.
In *Hollywood Speaks! An Oral History,* by Mike Steen, New York, 1974.
Interview (New York), January 1974.
Films Illustrated (London), September 1974.
Take One (Montreal), October 1976.
American Film (Washington, D.C.), May 1978.
Ciné Revue (Paris), 19 April 1979.

Publications on Head

Book

Acker, Ally, *Reel Women: Pioneers of the Cinema, 1896 to the Present,* New York, 1991.

Articles

Films in Review (New York), February 1972.
In *Costume Design in the Movies,* by Elizabeth Leese, New York, 1976.
In *Hollywood Costume Design,* by David Chierichetti, New York, 1976.
In *In a Glamorous Fashion,* by W. Robert LaVine, New York, 1980.
Films (New York), May 1981.
The Annual Obituary 1981, New York, 1982.
The Velvet Light Trap (Madison, Wisconsin), no. 19, 1982.
Spoto, Donald, in *Architectural Digest,* vol. 49, April 1992.

*   *   *

For many people, Edith Head and film costume design are synonymous. Other designers may have been more flamboyantly creative, or more consistently original, but no one did more to earn this art form popular recognition. Her guiding principle was that costume should support, rather than compete with, story and character development. Better than most, perhaps, she understood that clothing is not merely a matter of adornment, but a potent method of communication working in tandem with a film's sound and other visual elements. Her longevity, her productivity, her frequent touches of genius, and her talent for self-promotion secured her a celebrity status rare among Hollywood's legions of production artists. Moviegoers have long remained oblivious to the identities of those who work in the shadow of the stars, but they seem to have found a place in their consciousness for this tiny, austere-looking woman who wove illusions out of beads and cloth.

Unlike most of her peers, Head entered film costuming without relevant training or experience. When Howard Greer, Paramount's chief designer, hired her as a sketch artist in 1923, she was a high school teacher of French and art looking for a way to supplement her income. She learned quickly, however, honing her skills by observing the masters at work. From Greer she learned the value of attention to detail. From Travis Banton, another outstanding member of Paramount's design team, she learned how to fabricate the highest standards of glamour and elegance.

In her early years at the studio, Head mainly dressed minor characters and animals, or generated wardrobes for the countless B pictures then in production. Gradually she progressed to creating costumes for stars with whom the senior designers lacked the time or inclination to work. Among her first major assignments were Clara Bow, Lupe Velez, and Mae West. Head became Paramount's chief designer in 1938, when Banton, who replaced Greer as head designer in 1927, left to start a couture business. She remained at the studio for another three decades, working with most of Hollywood's major actresses and some of its best-known actors. When Paramount was sold in 1967, she became chief designer at Universal, where she worked until her death.

During her career, which spanned nearly six decades, Head's productivity achieved legendary proportions. In 1940 alone, she supervised costumes for 47 films. She is estimated to have contributed to more than 1,000 movies during her lifetime. In terms of formal recognition, her record is equally staggering. She received 34 Academy Award nominations, of which eight resulted in an Oscar. Costume design did not become an Academy Award category until 1948. For the first 19 years in which this honor was given, Head was nominated at least once every year. Had the award been introduced earlier, she would surely have earned additional nominations for such distinctive creations as Dorothy Lamour's sarongs in *The Jungle Princess* or Barbara Stanwyck's Latin-inspired garments for *The Lady Eve*.

Much of her best work was executed in the 1950s, when glamour and high-fashion were the keynotes of costume design. Among the enduring images her designs helped promote were Grace Kelly's refined allure in *Rear Window* and *To Catch a Thief*, Elizabeth Taylor's incandescent sensuality in *A Place in the Sun*, Audrey Hepburn's chic individuality in *Sabrina*, Bette Davis's mature sophistication in *All about Eve*, and Gloria Swanson's anachronistic glamour in *Sunset Boulevard*. This was also an era in which Head's public visibility reached its zenith. Already a fashion magazine editor, columnist, and regular contributor to Art Linkletter's radio show *House Party,* Head now made frequent television appearances, acted as consultant for the Academy Awards show, and published her first book. The diversity of her activities helped to extend her influence well beyond the realm of motion pictures.

Perhaps her greatest asset was her adaptability. Entering the business when limitless spending permitted designers broad artistic license, she later had to adjust to the restrictions imposed by wartime shortages of luxury textiles and the government's L-85 ruling on the amount of materials which could be used in clothing manufacture. Following the return to glamour and clothing-as-special-effects during the 1950s, Head made yet another successful transition when the 1960s ushered in a new emphasis on realism.

Head was also able to adjust to widely varying ideas about her role among the directors with whom she worked. Attitudes ranged from Alfred Hitchcock and George Roy Hill's close involvement in design, to the laissez-faire approach of Joseph Mankiewicz. Describing herself on one occasion as "a better politician than costume designer," Head was expert at handling star temperament, preferring to yield ground on a neckline or dress length than engage in a battle of wills. The conservative, neutral-colored suits she perennially wore

symbolized her willingness to suppress her individuality in the interests of her craft. With the exception of a dispute over whether she or Givenchy deserved the credit for Audrey Hepburn's famous bow-tied neckline in *Sabrina,* her career was unruffled by controversy.

Although she created a number of outstanding designs for period movies, most notably *The Heiress* and *Samson and Delilah,* she preferred to dress films with a contemporary theme, believing that they afforded more scope for originality. She also preferred to dress men rather than women, on the grounds that they were easier to deal with. One of her most effective wardrobes was the clothing worn by Robert Redford and Paul Newman in *The Sting,* in which her subtle use of accessories, especially hats, was brilliantly executed. Her designs, on occasion, set fashion trends, but she did not deliberately set out to influence what the public wore. She placed far more importance on enabling stars to assume their characters' identities. She also believed it essential to create designs that would not cause a movie to date prematurely. This preference for a middle-of-the-road approach dates from 1947, when Dior's "New Look" exploded onto the fashion scene, making Head's streamlined designs seem instantly outmoded.

Head's excellence as a designer was augmented by her keen understanding of the technical constraints within which she operated. She was acutely aware of the different requirements created by variations in lighting, sound, and color. She also believed in close collaboration with her fellow production artists. Although she worked in an industry in which honors and public recognition are focused on individual achievement, Head truly was a team player. She may have enjoyed the celebrity status earned by her television appearances and writing, but when it came to practicing her craft, aligning her skills with the needs of directors, cinematographers, art directors, and others is what mattered most. It was her capacity for partnership that helped her become one of Hollywood's preeminent production artists

—Fiona Valentine

HECKERLING, Amy
American director

Born: In Bronx, New York, 7 May 1954. **Education:** Attended Art and Design High School, New York; studied film at New York University Film School; earned a master's degree from the American Film Institute. **Family:** Married the writer/director Neal Israel. **Career:** 1982—directed first feature film, the hit *Fast Times at Ridgemont High*; 1986—producer for TV series *Fast Times*; 1989—revived her feature film career with the commercially successful *Look Who's Talking*; 1995—directed the critically and commercially successful *Clueless*; 1996—executive producer for TV series *Clueless*. **Agent:** Richard Lovett, Creative Artists Agency, 9830 Wilshire Boulevard, Beverly Hills, CA 90212, U.S.A.

Films as Director

1977   *Getting It Over With*
1982   *Fast Times at Ridgemont High*
1984   *Johnny Dangerously*
1985   *National Lampoon's European Vacation*

1989 *Look Who's Talking* (+ sc)
1990 *Look Who's Talking Too* (+ co-sc)
1995 *Clueless* (+ sc)

Other Films

1985 *Into the Night* (Landis) (ro as ship's waitress)
1988 *Life on the Flipside* (for TV) (pr)
1997 *Frank Capra's American Dream* (Bowser—doc for TV) (ro as herself)
1998 *A Night at the Roxbury* (Fortenberry and Markle) (co-sc, co-pr)

Publications by Heckerling

Book

With Pamela Pettler, *The No-Sex Handbook,* New York, 1990.

Articles

Interview with K. M. Chanko, in *Films in Review* (New York), October 1982.
"Movie Directors: Four Women Who Get to Call the Shots in Hollywood," interview with Z. Klapper, in *Ms.* (New York), November 1985.
"From the Director's Chair," interview with Michael Singer, in *Film Directors: A Complete Guide,* edited by Michael Singer, Beverly Hills, 1987.
"High School Confidential," interview with Rich Cohen, in *Rolling Stone* (New York), 7 September 1995.

Publications on Heckerling

Books

Quart, Barbara, *Women Directors: The Emergence of a New Cinema,* New York, 1988.
Mayne, Judith, *The Woman at the Keyhole: Feminism and Women's Cinema,* Bloomington, Indiana, 1990.
Cole, Janis, and Holly Dale, *Calling the Shots: Profiles of Women Filmmakers,* Kingston, Ontario, 1993.
Foster, Gwendolyn Audrey, *Women Film Directors: An International Bio-Critical Dictionary,* Westport, Connecticut, 1995.

Articles

Pym, J., *"Getting It Over With,"* in *Monthly Film Bulletin* (London), May 1979.
Chase, D., "The Director Who Came in from the Cold," in *Millimeter* (New York), September 1984.
Stuart, J., "Heckerling Took Stepping Stone Route from College to Big Time," in *Variety* (New York), 5 December 1984.
Warren, Elaine, "Amy Heckerling," in *Moviegoer,* January 1985.
Seidenberg, R., "Out of N.Y.U. into Independence," in *New York Times,* 27 January 1985.
Jackson, Lynne, and Karen Jaehne, "Eavesdropping on Female Voices: A Who's Who of Contemporary Women Filmmakers," in *Cineaste* (New York), vol. 16, no. 1/2, 1988.
Matthews, T., "Baby Talk," in *Boxoffice* (Los Angeles), November 1989.

Feld, B., "Filmmaker and Stars Reunited on *Look Who's Talking* Sequel," in *Film Journal* (New York), November/December 1990.
Francke, Lizzie, "Men, Women, Children and the Baby Boom Movies," in *Women and Film: A Sight and Sound Reader,* edited by Pam Cook and Philip Dodd, Philadelphia, 1993.

*   *   *

Amy Heckerling is an enormously successful commercial Hollywood director whose forte is comedy filmmaking. After film school, she worked as a television editor where she learned to create effective comic rhythms. Subsequently, her first feature, the smash hit *Fast Times at Ridgemont High* was a career-making effort. The film was based on Cameron Crowe's novel about his return to high school to examine what contemporary teenagers were doing. A hilarious parody of high school teenpics, it was enthusiastically endorsed by several critics. It is also noteworthy as the film that introduced Sean Penn and Jennifer Jason Leigh to mainstream audiences.

Heckerling's second feature, however, *Johnny Dangerously,* performed poorly at the box office, though it is a clever comic spoof of the 1930s gangster movies, in which an honest man turns to crime to fund his mother's surgeries. Likewise, *National Lampoon's European Vacation,* a fluffy comedy with an anemic screenplay that seems to gently mock the all-American family, was not a box-office success. Nevertheless, Heckerling has demonstrated a tenacious will to succeed in Hollywood. For example, when her screenplay *My Kind of Guy* unsuccessfully made the rounds of the studios, from Warner Bros., to Universal, to MGM, she responded by working on another screenplay—for *Look Who's Talking,* which was inspired by her own pregnancy. It ultimately proved to be a smash hit and marked her career "comeback." In addition, it prompted two sequels, the first of which she also directed, *Look Who's Talking Too.* In *Look Who's Talking,* an unmarried woman played by Kirstie Alley pursues her quest to find the perfect father for her baby. She finds him, unexpectedly, in an unconventional candidate—a taxi driver (played by John Travolta). The film's hook is baby Mikey's amusing impressions of his experiences between the time of his conception and his first birthday.

Heckerling had another huge commercial and critical hit with *Clueless,* a charming contemporary adaptation of Jane Austen's *Emma.* Arguably, it represents a career summation film, one that evokes prevalent issues and themes from her earlier movies. Yet, it is utterly original. Her most feminist film, it features a heroine who is a spoiled yet engaging Beverly Hills incorrigible who indefatigably endeavors to arrange and manipulate the romances of her high school cohorts, while she puts her own love life in neutral. Much of its considerable appeal is due to its clever take on the fads, slang, and other preoccupations of teenagers, especially girls. Like *Fast Times at Ridgemont High,* and unlike most teenpics, it attracted both teen and adult audiences. But, whereas the earlier film had a more realistic look and tone, in addition to more explicit depictions of youthful sexuality, *Clueless* revels in bright colors, quick, witty repartee, and camp sensibilities—especially in terms of the slightly-over-the-top performances Heckerling elicited from the film's leads, including Alicia Silverstone in her career-making role.

Heckerling has spoken of the pressure she felt in Hollywood whereby male directors can make a string of bad films before they finally succeed and are considered "hot directors"—a path she had never seen a female director tread. Therefore, she felt compelled to work without stopping so that she would not be

Amy Heckerling (center) on the set of *Look Who's Talking Too* with John Travolta and Kirstie Alley.

forgotten in Hollywood. Her critics, therefore, often charge that her eye is focused entirely upon the box office. But, as she herself explained, it would be great if a woman director could make "tons of money" since the "best and the worst thing about this industry is that that's the bottom line." Furthermore, her critics complain that her films look as though they were directed by men—sometimes leering men. They point to her first film, *Fast Times at Ridgemont High,* in which it is only the males who are fully developed characters, while the girls are obsessed with their looks and with boys, and whose bodies are featured in various states of undress.

Despite such criticisms, Heckerling's comic scripts boast fast-paced dialogue and clever humor that occasionally point to the sexism and superficialities of American consumer culture, as they mock and celebrate the insipid yet well-intentioned values of suburbia, even in upscale Beverly Hills. Likewise, they include subversive feminine humor despite their big studio backing. Thus, in *Look Who's Talking,* the babies voice the absurdities of their adult companions, and in *Clueless,* the teenage heroine expresses a clever awareness of the superficialities of consumer obsessions and of sexism. Accordingly, astute critics have compared her films to those of Jerry Lewis and Frank Tashlin. They are well-produced, technically proficient, and engaging works that employ the narrative conventions and formulae that predominate in commercial Hollywood movies. In addition, they are testimony to Heckerling's considerable skill in evoking humorously engaging performances from her actors.

Heckerling's résumé includes directorial assignments for television, including several episodes of the series *Fast Times.* Currently, she is working as a producer on the feature film, *A Night at the Roxbury.*

—Cynthia Felando

HEIN, Birgit
German director

Born: West Germany, 1942. **Education:** Studied art history. **Family:** Married the filmmaker Wilhelm Hein. **Career:** Late 1960s to late 1970s—produced several abstract formalist films with Wilhelm Hein, in addition to collaborating on multimedia events, and performances; 1978—the Heins started to incorporate certain representative images into their nonrepresentative works; 1970s on—written and published extensively on the subjects of art history and avant-garde film.

Films as Co-Director with Wilhelm Hein

1967 *S&W; Ole; Und Sie?*

1968 *Grün; Werbefilm Nr. 1: Bamberg; Rohfilm; Reproductions*

1969 *625; Square Dance; Work in Progress Teil A (Work in Progress Part A); Sichtbarmachung der Wirkungsweise optischer Gesetze am einfachen Beispiel*

1970 *Work in Progress Teil B (Work in Progress Part B); Porträts I; Auszüge aus einer Biographie; Madison/Wis; Replay; Foto-Film; Filmraum: Reproduktionsimmanente Ästhetik*

1971 *Porträts. 4. Nina I-III; Autobahn. 2 Teile; Work in Progress Teil C (Work in Progress Part C); Work in Progress Teil D (Work in Progress Part D); Doppelprojektion I; I Want You to Be Rich; Altes Material; Zoom—lange Fassung; Zoom—kurze Fassung; Videotape I; Liebesgrüsse; Yes to Europe*

1972 *Porträts. Kurt Schwitters I, II, III; Porträts; Doppelprojektion II-IV; Aufblenden (Abblenden); Dokumentation; Fussball*

1973 *Ausdatiertes Material; God Bless America; Stills; London; Zu Lucifer Rising von Kenneth Anger*

1974 *Strukturelle Studien; Jack Smith; Künstlerfilme I; Künstlerfilme II*

1975 *Porträts II*

1976 *Materialfilme I; Materialfilme II*

1977 *Porträts III*

1978 *Kurt Kren. Porträt eines experimentellen Fulmmachers*

1978-79 *Verdammt in alle Ewigkeit (From Here to Eternity)*

1980 *Superman und Superwoman*

1981 *Die Medien und das Bild. Andy Warhol's Kunst*

1982 *Love Stinks—Bilder des taeglichen Wahnsinns; American Graffiti*

1984-85 *Verbotene Bilder*

1986 *Fusswaschung* (in *Jesusfilm*)

1987-88 *Die Kali-filme (The Kali Films)*

1992 *Die Unheimlichen Frauen (The Frightening Women)* (+ ed, ph, sc, pr)

1995 *Baby, I Will Make You Sweat* (+ ed, ph, sc)

Publications by Hein

Articles

"Expanded Cinema," in *Film als Film* (Cologne), 1978.

"The Avantgarde and Politics," in *Millennium* (New York), Spring/Summer 1978.

Interview with Mo Beyerle, Noll Brinckmann, and others, in *Frauen und Film* (Frankfurt), no. 37, 1984.

With Wilhelm Hein, "Dokumente 1967-1985: Fotos, Briefe, Texte," in *Kinematograph* (Frankfurt), no. 3, 1985.

"'Frauengefaengnisfilme,'" in *Frauen und Film* (Frankfurt), December 1987.

Interview with Spiegelungen, in *Frauen und Film* (Frankfurt), December 1987.

"Mara Mattuschka," in *EPD Film* (Frankfurt), March 1988.

"Bonn: Experi," in *EPD Film* (Frankfurt), February 1990.

Publications on Hein

Books

Knight, Julia, *Women and the New German Cinema*, London, 1992.

Frieden, Sandra, Richard McCormick, Vibeke R. Petersen, and Laurie Melissa Vogelsang, editors, *Gender and German Cinema: Feminist Intervention,* Volumes 1 and 2, Oxford, 1993.

Foster, Gwendolyn Audrey, *Women Film Directors: An International Bio-Critical Dictionary,* Westport, Connecticut, 1995.

Articles

Kiernan, Joanna, "Birgit & Wilhelm Hein: From Structural Studies to Now," in *Millennium* (New York), Spring 1980.

Hoberman, J., "Hearing Voices," in *Village Voice* (New York), 23 April 1985.

Tscherkassky, P., "An der front der Bilder: aktuelle Positionen der Filmavantgarde," in *Blimp* (Graz, Austria), Spring 1989.

* * *

Since the late 1960s, the internationally renowned German avant-garde artist Birgit Hein has collaborated with her husband Wilhelm Hein on experimental films, multimedia projects, and performances. Known for their difficult "structural-materialist" films, the Heins have created an impressive body of work with determinedly political intentions. Though Birgit declared in 1978 that "art cannot change society," she conceded that it did, however, have a significant part to play in the struggle for progressive goals by conveying ideas that cannot be conveyed via other means. In addition to her avant-garde motion-picture collaborations with Wilhelm, Birgit is also a well-known and often-published art historian and avant-garde film critic.

Like other experimental filmmakers in the 1960s, the Heins's early films used the medium to explore the language of cinema and to challenge viewers' perceptions, and they employed abstract formalist techniques to challenge the strategies of mainstream cinema. Such techniques included using scratched film, visible sprocket holes, and experimenting with purely formal notions. *625,* for example, consisted of several sequences produced by photographing a television screen at different speeds to reveal the television's bar line. The aptly titled *Strukturelle Studien* was a compilation of 33 shorts made over the course of many years, each of which demonstrates either a factor related to film's ability to produce the illusion of movement, such as persistence of vision, or to investigate the camera's fundamental functions, such as focus and zoom.

In 1978 Birgit wrote that the Heins's perspective on the social function of art was characterized by two extremes: a leftist political agenda and a formal, nonnarrative film aesthetic. But she noted that formal nonrepresentational art was being rejected on both sides of the political spectrum. Interested only in critics on the left, who charged that abstract work was a manifestation of reactionary bourgeois politics and, therefore, was socially irrelevant, Birgit countered that purely formal works cannot be characterized as either reactionary or progressive simply for being nonrepresentational. Instead, she insisted that it is solely how art is used that can be judged as progressive or reactionary. She acknowledged, however, that in order to appreciate abstract art it was necessary to learn how to "decode" the information it presented, and that she was often advised to combine film formalism with narrative to make their work more accessible. So, by 1980, the Heins announced that their recent works marked a move away from strict abstract formalism and included representational images. Their decision followed serious meditation about whether or not their formal film exercises had simply become self-perpetuating. Consequently, the Heins started incorporating into their works a variety of popular generic elements, which they called "emotion, sentiment, triviality." The films included attention to their personal lives and relationship, and offered weighty reflections about female sexuality. In addition, the Heins explored some of the more taboo areas of female sexuality such as those that countered passive femininity, such as aggressive feminine sexuality. For example, *The Kali Films* depict women using weapons to attack men, along with clips from horror movies and women-in-prison films. Their work suggests that female sexuality can exist outside the realm of masculine voyeurism, and can be explored productively by women and men together.

One of the Heins's most famous films, *Love Stinks,* was shot during a year the filmmakers spent in New York, and it cleverly conveys the experience of life in a foreign land. Subtitled "Pictures of Everyday Madness," it includes footage of marital sex and shots of their surroundings, from the Bowery to the downtown art scene to the Lower East Side, where they found the graffiti that inspired the film's subtitle. One of the film's tasks is to locate signs of Germany in the States, such as graffiti swastikas, decimated tenements, and a television broadcast of *Inside the Third Reich.* But at least one critic commended the Heins for providing a comically witty investigation of New York's subway graffiti, especially their study of a series of vandalized movie posters for *Mommie Dearest* and *Rocky III.*

From Here to Eternity is a multimedia piece whose title was inspired by the 1953 Hollywood film and which consists of the earlier film's dubbed German trailer, in addition to popular music, live performances by the Heins, and multiscreen projections of both representational and nonrepresentational films. One of the work's themes concerns the notion of role-playing as an act of masquerade or ritual. Accordingly, the Heins performed as Frankenstein, in matching black suits and masks, by first dancing together slowly and mechanically on stage, and then by jumping offstage to dance crazily to rock and roll. To add further complications, the work's soundtrack presents a disjunction between the voice and the body, includes film images of a Marilyn Monroe impersonator, long home-movie sequences, and segments of scratched celluloid. Critics have suggested, however, that the work's combination of disparate elements failed to illuminate any new understandings regarding the processes of film and seeing.

—Cynthia Felando

HENNING-JENSEN, Astrid
Danish director

Born: Astrid Smahl in Frederiksberg, Denmark, 10 December 1914. **Family:** Married the director Bjarne Henning-Jensen, 6 October 1938, son: Lars. **Career:** 1931-38—actress at "Riddersalen," Copenhagen; 1941—assistant director, then director, 1943, at Nordisk Films Kompagni; 1950-52—Norsk Film A/S, Oslo; early 1950s on—Astrid and Bjarne both worked as freelance writers and directors for film, theater, radio, and television. **Awards:** Director Prize, Venice Film Festival, for *Denmark Grows Up,* 1947; Cannes Film Festival Prize, for *Palle Alone in the World,* 1949; Catholic Film Office Award, Cannes Festival, and Technik Prize, for *Paw,* 1960; Best Director, Berlin Festival, for *Winter Children,* 1979. **Address:** Frederiksberg Allé 76, DK-1820 Copenhagen V, Denmark.

Films as Director

1945   *Dansk politi i Sverige* (*The Danish Brigade in Sweden*)
1947   *Denmark Grows Up* (co-d)
1949   *Palle alene i Verden* (*Palle Alone in the World*)
1951   *Kranes Konditori* (*Krane's Bakery Shop*)
1952   *Ukjent mann* (*Unknown Man*)
1954   *Ballettens børn* (*Ballet Girl*)
1955   *Kaerlighed pa kredit* (*Love on Credit*) (+ sc)
1959   *Hest på sommerferie* (*Horse on Holiday*); *Paw* (*Boy of Two Worlds*; *The Lure of the Jungle*) (+ co-sc)
1961   *Een blandt mange* (*One among Many*)
1965   *De blå undulater*
1966   *Utro* (*Unfaithful*)
1967   *Min bedstefar er en stok*
1968   *Nille*
1969   *Mej och dej* (*Me and You*; *Mig og dig*) (+ sc)
1978   *Vinterbørn* (*Winter Children*; *Winterborn*) (+ sc, ed)
1980   *Øjeblikket* (*The Moment*) (+ sc)
1985   *Hodja fra Pjort*
1986   *Barndommens gade* (*Street of My Childhood*; *Early Spring*) (+ sc)

Films as Co-Director with Bjarne Henning-Jensen

1943   *S.O.S. Kindtand* (*S.O.S. Molars*)
1945   *Flyktingar finner en hamn* (*Fugitives Find Shelter*); *Folketingsvalg 1945*
1947   *Stemning i April* (*Impressions of April*); *De pokkers unger* (*Those Blasted Kids*)
1948   *Kristinus Bergman*
1950   *Vesterhavs drenge* (*Boys from the West Coast*)
1953   *Solstik* (+ st)
1954   *Tivoligarden spiller* (*Tivoli Garden Games*)
1991   *In Spite Of*
1995   *Bella, My Bella*

Other Films

1937   *Cocktail* (ro)
1943   *Naar man kun er ung* (*While Still Young*) (B. Henning-Jensen) (asst d)
1946   *Ditte Menneskebarn* (*Ditte: Child of Man*) (B. Henning-Jensen) (asst d)
1962   *Kort år sommaren* (*Short Is the Summer*) (B. Henning-Jensen) (co-sc)
1982   *Napló gyermekeimnek* (*Diary for My Children*) (Mészáros) (co-production supervisor)
1984   *Forbrydelsens Element* (*The Element of Crime*) (von Trier) (ro as Osborne's housekeeper)
1996   *Danske piger viser alt* (Blair and others) (as herself)

Publications by Henning-Jensen

Book

Øjeblikket: en filmhistorie med billeder, Skive, 1980.

Articles

"Om lengselens og fantasiens makt," interview with T. O. Svendsen and S. Sundby, in *Z Filmtidsskrift* (Oslo), vol. 5, no. 6, 1987.

Publications on Henning-Jensen

Books

Quart, Barbara, *Women Directors: The Emergence of a New Cinema,*
  New York, 1988.
Mayne, Judith, *The Woman at the Keyhole: Feminism and Women's
  Cinema,* Bloomington, Indiana, 1990.
Foster, Gwendolyn Audrey, *Women Film Directors: An International
  Bio-Critical Dictionary,* Westport, Connecticut, 1995.

Articles

Pedersen, B. T., "Astrid Henning-Jensen och 'Ogonblicket,'" trans-
  lated by R. Tereus, in *Filmrutan* (Liding, Sweden), vol. 23, no. 4,
  1980.
De Santi, G., "Cinema danese a Verona: la malinconia di guardarsi
  l'ombelico," in *Cineforum* (Bergamo, Italy), September 1983.
Mueller, T. S., "Gensyn med barndommen," in *Levende Billeder*
  (Copenhagen), 1 December 1986.
Iversen, E., "Astrid Henning-Jensen," in *Kosmorama* (Copenhagen),
  Summer 1987.
Iversen, G., "Den Klebrige tilvaerelsen," in *Z Filmtidsskrift* (Oslo),
  vol. 7, no. 38, 1989.
Koivunen, Anu, in *The Women's Companion to International Film,*
  edited by Annette Kuhn and Susannah Radstone, London, 1990.

*   *   *

Astrid Henning-Jensen's film career is closely linked with that of
her husband, the director Bjarne Henning-Jensen, but includes significant solo projects as well. Both started as stage actors, but shortly
after they married in 1938 they began working in films. Bjarne
Henning-Jensen directed several government documentaries beginning in 1940 and he was joined by Astrid in 1943. At that time the
Danish documentary film, strongly influenced by the British documentary of the 1930s, was blooming, and the Henning-Jensens played
an important part in this. In 1943 they made their first feature film,
Astrid serving as assistant director. *Naar man kun er ung* was a
light, everyday comedy, striving for a relaxed and charming style,
but it was too cute, and it was politely received. Their next film, *Ditte
Menneskebarn*—again with Astrid as assistant director—was their
breakthrough, and the two were instantly considered as the most
promising directors in the postwar Danish cinema. The film was an
adaptation of a neoclassical novel by Martin Andersen-Nexø. It was
a realistic story of a young country girl and her tragic destiny as a
victim of social conditions. The novel, published between 1917 and
1921, was in five volumes, but the Henning-Jensens used only parts
of the novel. The sentimentality of the book was, happily, subdued in
the film, and it is a sensitive study of a young girl in her milieu. The
film was the first example of a more realistic and serious Danish film
and it paralleled similar trends in contemporary European cinema,
even if one would refrain from calling the film neorealistic. It was a
tremendous success in Denmark and it also won a certain international recognition.

Astrid and Bjarne Henning-Jensen's film was a sincere attempt to
introduce reality and authentic people to the Danish film. They continued this effort in their subsequent films, but a certain facile approach, a weakness for cute effects, and a sensibility on the verge of
sentimentality made their films less and less interesting. In the 1950s
Bjarne Henning-Jensen returned to documentaries, while Astrid

Henning-Jensen—who had made her debut as a solo director in
1945—continued making films on her own. She made two carefully
directed and attractive films in Norway, and in the 1960s she tried to
keep up with the changing times in a couple of films. But it was not
until the late 1970s that she regained her old position. In 1978's
Vinterbørn, about women and their problems in a maternity ward,
and in 1980's *Øjeblikket,* treating the problems of a young couple
when it is discovered that the woman is dying of cancer, she worked
competently within an old established genre in Danish films, the
problem-oriented popular drama—in both cases writing the screenplay as well as directing.

—Ib Monty

HESTER STREET
USA, 1975
Director: Joan Micklin Silver

Production: Midwest Films; black and white, 35mm; running time:
92 minutes. Released October 1975. Filmed in New York City. Cost:
$320,000.

Producer: Raphael D. Silver; **associate producer:** David Appleton;
screenplay: Joan Micklin Silver, based on a story by Abraham
Cahan; **photography:** Kenneth Van Sickle; **editor:** Katherine
Wenning; **sound engineer:** William Daly; **sound editor:** Jack
Fitzstephens; **art director:** Edward Haynes; **music:** William Bolcom
and Herbert L. Clarke; **costumes:** Robert Pusilo.

Cast: Carol Kane (*Gitl*); Steven Keats (*Jake*); Mel Howard
(*Bernstein*); Dorrie Kavanaugh (*Mamie*); Doris Roberts (*Mrs.
Kavarsky*); Stephen Strimpell (*Joe Peltner*); Lauren Frost (*Fanny*);
Paul Freedman (*Joey*); Martin Garner (*Boss*); Leib Lensky (*Ped-
dler*); Zvee Scooler (*Rabbi*); Eda Reiss Merin (*Rabbi's wife*); with:
Robert Lesser; Joanna Merlin; Claudia Silver; Edward Crowley;
Philip Sterling; Sol Frieder; Joel Wolfe; Mordecai Lawner; Lin Shaye;
Anna Berger; Bert Salzman; Zane Laski.

Publications

Books

Cohen, Sarah Blacher, editor, *From* Hester Street *to Hollywood: The
  Jewish-American Stage and Screen,* Bloomington, Indiana, 1983.
Haskell, Molly, *From Reverence to Rape: The Treatment of Women
  in the Movies,* Chicago, 1987.
Quart, Barbara Koenig, *Women Directors: The Emergence of a New
  Cinema,* New York, 1988.
Acker, Ally, *Reel Women: Pioneers of the Cinema, 1896 to the
  Present,* New York, 1991.

Articles

Moskowitz, G., in *Variety* (New York), 14 May 1975.
Maupin, F., in *Revue du Cinéma* (Paris), June/July 1975.
Rosen, Marjorie, "Three Films in Search of a Distributor," in *Ms.*
  (New York), July 1975.

Hester Street

Alpert, H., "What I Really Want to Do Is Direct," in *Saturday Review,* 26 July 1975.

Perez, M., in *Positif* (Paris), July/August 1975.

Haskell, Molly, "How an Independent Filmmaker Beat the System (with Her Husband's Help)," in *Village Voice* (New York), 22 September 1975.

Silver, Joan Micklin, and Raphael Silver, "On *Hester Street,*" in *American Film* (Washington, D.C.), October 1975.

Kauffmann, Stanley, "Stanley Kauffmann on Films, Women at Work," in *New Republic* (New York), 18 October 1975.

Eder, Richard, in *New York Times,* 20 October 1975.

Simon, J., "Cinematic Illiterates," in *New York,* 20 October 1975.

Cocks, J., "Black-and-Tan Fantasy; Second Time Around; a Bintel Brief," in *Time* (New York), 27 October 1975.

Klain, S., in *Independent* (New York), 29 October 1975.

Coleman, J., "Gitl's Ghetto," in *New Statesman,* 31 October 1975.

Clouzot, Claire, in *Ecran* (Paris), November 1975.

Lajeunesse, J., and F. Maupin, in *Revue du Cinéma* (Paris), November 1975.

Predal, R., "Joan Micklin Silver: Les Immigrants d'*Hester Street,*" in *Jeune Cinéma* (Paris), November 1975.

Reed, Rex, in *Vogue* (New York), November 1975.

Goodman, Walter, "*Hester Street*—Overpraised and Overdone," in *New York Times,* 2 November 1975.

Haskell, Molly, in *Village Voice* (New York), 3 November 1975.

Kroll, J., "Sin and Sentimentality," in *Newsweek* (New York), 3 November 1975.

Crist, Judith, "A Cheer for Hollywood," in *Saturday Review,* 15 November 1975.

Kael, Pauline, "The Current Cinema: Becoming an American," in *New Yorker,* 24 November 1975.

Forbes, J., in *Monthly Film Bulletin* (London), December 1975.

Mack, D., in *Films in Review,* December 1975.

Forslund, B., in *Chaplin* (Stockholm), vol 18, no. 5, 1976.

Grown, G., in *Sight and Sound* (London), vol 45, no. 1, 1976.

Hirsch, P., in *Kosmorama* (Copenhagen), vol. 22, no. 131, 1976.

Lindeborg, L. "Kvinnobilder i Mannheim," in *Filmrutan* (Tyreso, Sweden), vol. 19, no. 1, 1976.

Gauthier, G., in *Revue du Cinéma* (Paris), January 1976.

Green, L., in *Films and Filming* (London), January 1976.

Halberstadt, I., in *Filmmakers Newsletter* (Ward Hill, Massachusetts), January 1976.

McBride, J., "Overcome Exhibs Fear of Yiddish, 1896: *Hester Street* Strictly Uphill," in *Variety* (New York), 25 February 1976.

Kurowski, U., and H. Adam, in *Medium* (Frankfurt), March 1976.

De Vos, J.-M., in *Film en Televisie* (Brussels), 28 March 1976.

Elia, M., in *Séquences* (Montreal), April 1976.

Quart, L., "On the East Side (*Hester Street*)," in *Times Educational Supplement* (London), April 1976.

Leirens, J., in *Amis du Film et de la Télévision* (Brussels), May/June 1976.

Schirmeyer-Klein, U., "Auch ein Stueck Amerika: *Hester Street,* ein Debutfilm von "Joan Micklin Silver," in *Film and Ton* (Munich), September 1976.

Garel, A., in *Revue du Cinéma* (Paris), October 1976.

Friedman, S., and S. Steinberg, "*Hester Street*: The Politics of Culture," in *Jump Cut* (Berkeley), 30 December 1976.

Michel, S., "*Yekl* and *Hester Street*: Was Assimilation Really Good for the Jews?," in *Literature/Film Quarterly* (Salisbury, Maryland), vol. 5, no. 2, 1977.

Skorecki, L., in *Cahiers du Cinéma* (Paris), December 1980.

Taconet, C., in *Cinéma* (Paris), December 1980.

Silver, Joan Micklin, in *Skrien* (Amsterdam), September/October 1984.

Hansen, H. J., "Store Jodiske Mor," in *Levende Billeder* (Copenhagen), May 1989.

Bordat, F., "Le Melting-Pot Americain et les Métèques Hollywoodiens," in *CinémAction* (Conde-Sur-Noireau), July 1990.

Glucksman, Mary, "Production Update," in *Filmmaker* (Los Angeles), Fall 1997.

* * *

Hester Street was the impressive first feature from feminist independent filmmaker Joan Micklin Silver, and it is the most respected of her films. Its simple, tenderly wrought story carefully blends humor and pathos. Adapted from Abraham Cahan's *Yekl, a Tale of the Ghetto* from 1896, it features a female rather than a male protagonist. *Hester Street* is about Russian-Jewish immigrants who settled in New York's Lower East Side during the huge wave of immigration to the United States in the 1890s, and features a loud, boisterous young married immigrant man, Jake, who works hard as a tailor and nurtures his urge to become an authentic "Yankee" with his flashy dress and roving eye. He is having an affair with a shapely neighborhood woman who runs a dance school that doubles as a social hangout, when his wife, Gitl, and son arrive from Russia to join him. Jake, whose favorite Yankee slang is "you betcha," is embarrassed about their Old World appearance, language, and customs, and in addition to changing his son's name to the quintessentially American "Joey," he repeatedly chastises Gitl to change herself to please him. But Gitl is disappointed to learn that he has forsaken his Old World culture as well as his family. Nevertheless, she endeavors to please Jake until she makes the decision that, fed up, she does not want him any longer. After they separate, Gitl finds a more suitable partner with the pious scholar who admires her, Mr. Bernstein, a former rabbinical student who also works as a tailor and lodges with Jake and Gitl. He is attracted to her because she embodies traditional values with her married woman's wig, the salt she puts in her son's pockets to defend against the evil eye, and her enormous respect for his tenacious studies after long days spent at his tailor's sewing machine. Indeed, while Bernstein teaches her son Joey the Hebrew alphabet, her husband Jake teaches him baseball and the finer points of being a "Yankee."

Although she is an avowed feminist, Silver has explained that she wanted *Hester Street* to be an homage to the strong Jewish women in her family, also immigrants from Russia, rather than an explicitly feminist endeavor. Further, she made the film thinking that it might be her last opportunity, so she wanted it to have a deeply personal resonance for her family. As a result, she did considerable research by reading immigrant literature and going to the Yiddish Institute to study a series of unpublished oral histories of immigrants. In the end, she was pleased when several older Jewish immigrants endorsed the film's vision. Its images are rendered beautifully in black and white with careful, inspired compositions, and successfully brings to mind period photographs from the turn of the century. Likewise, Silver includes many evocative scenes, such as when Jake collects his terrified wife from the crowded immigration center, and when an old peddler brings forth a surprising collection of goods from his bundles. Indeed, Silver's attention to period and cultural detail is outstanding; the screen is dense with the elements of immigrant ghetto life—kids, peddlers and their pushcarts, and horses and wagons, which vividly convey the pulse and challenge of immigrant life at the turn of the century. That is, Hester Street is where Eastern European Jews land before moving out of the ghetto and where old values bump into new ones, as does the cold realization that immigrant life means moving from a ghetto in the old country to a ghetto in the new country. Feminist critics, in particular, praised Silver's rendering of Gitl's transformation from meek self-consciousness to self-aware strength, as she defiantly retains most of her traditional values and rejects the American materialism so important to her husband Jake. As Silver explained, "It celebrates *shtetl* values above the new American values."

Silver's husband, real estate entrepreneur Raphael Silver, angered by her struggle to get a studio deal, determined to raise the money for her film after seeing her talents continually rejected. Together they formed Midwest Films to produce the movie. The film was a risky endeavor given its uncommercial profile; as Silver noted, the major studios were concerned that it was filmed in black and white, had Yiddish and subtitles, and no big stars; while the minor studios wanted to distribute it in 16mm to synagogues and colleges.

Nevertheless, the film was well received by critics, starting during Critics' Week at the Cannes Film Festival. But as Silver expected, distributors dubbed it a "Jewish film" and shied away. So, with help from Jeff Lipsky and the encouragement of the successful independent filmmaker John Cassavetes, the Silvers distributed it themselves. They sold the distribution rights to four countries, which enabled them to open the film in New York. Then, Carol Kane's Academy Award nomination garnered considerable publicity and helped the Silvers secure a wider distribution. The film eventually earned more than five million dollars. Joan Micklin Silver returned to some of the themes she worked in *Hester Street* with *Crossing Delancey* (1988), especially regarding the conflicts between old and new values.

—Cynthia Felando

THE HITCH-HIKER
USA, 1953
Director: Ida Lupino

Production: Filmakers; black and white; 35mm; running time: 71 minutes. Released March 1953.

Producers: Collier Young and Ida Lupino; **screenplay:** Collier Young and Ida Lupino, adaptation by Robert L. Joseph, based on a story by Geoffrey Homes; **photography:** Nicholas Musuraca; **editor:** Douglas Stewart; **special effects:** Harold Wellman; **art designers:** Albert S. D'Agostino and Walter E. Keller; **music composer:** Leith Stevens; **music director:** C. Bakaleinikoff.

Cast: Edmond O'Brien (*Roy Collins*); Frank Lovejoy (*Gilbert Bowen*); William Talman (*Emmett Myers*); José Torvay (*Captain Alvarado*); Sam Hayes (*himself*); Wendell Niles (*himself*); Jean Del Val (*Inspector General*); Clark Howat (*Government Agent*); Natividad Vacio (*José*); Rodney Bell (*William Johnson*); Nacho Galindo (*Proprietor*).

Publications

Book

Heck-Rabi, Louise, *Women Filmmakers: A Critical Reception,* Metuchen, New Jersey, 1984.

Articles

Variety (New York), 14 January 1953.
New York Times, 30 April 1953.
New Yorker, 9 May 1953.
Newsweek (New York), 11 May 1953.
Vermilye, Jerry, "Ida Lupino," in *Films in Review* (New York), May 1959.
Parker, Francine, "Discovering Ida Lupino," in *Action* (Los Angeles), July/August 1973.
Scheib, R., "Ida Lupino: Auteuress," in *Film Comment* (New York), January/February 1980.
Parker, Barry M., "Newsreel: Lost Lupino," in *American Film* (Washington, D.C.), June 1981.
Nacache, J., "Sur six films d'Ida Lupino," in *Cinéma* (Paris), October 1983.

* * *

Critics generally agree that *The Hitch-Hiker* is Ida Lupino's best directorial accomplishment; it was also her personal favorite. Made the same year as her impressive melodrama *The Bigamist*, this film is entirely different. With an all-male cast, the film was produced by Lupino and her husband's (Collier Young) film company, Filmakers and was released by RKO.

The Hitch-Hiker is an unrelentingly tense, grim melodrama about two California businessmen en route to a long-awaited fishing trip vacation in Mexico when they pick up a hitchhiker who is, unbeknownst to them, wanted for killing and robbing several helpful motorists. Thereupon, he takes them captive and forces them at gunpoint to accompany him for several days on his wild flight from the law by driving him through the southwest into Mexico until he no longer needs them. On the way to Baja California, the killer evades several police traps while leaving small clues for the shrewd Mexican police who are working with U.S. lawmen to find the trio. Notably, the police traps that ultimately lead to the murderer's capture are not excessive or unconvincing. Further, the conclusion is not unexpected in this cops-versus-killer story, so the lawmen eventually prevail. The film was interpreted by many critics as a warning to motorists about the dangers of picking up hitchhiker strangers. Indeed, it was a contemporary story that poignantly echoed the news stories about the misadventures and occasional murders that happened to well-intentioned people who aided hitchhikers. Not surprisingly, it was based on a real-life case—of William Cook, a 21-year-old hitchhiker/kidnapper who murdered six people. Accordingly, Lupino included a prologue that admitted the film was fictional, but that "its facts are actual."

Technically impressive, the film demonstrates Lupino's skill at creating fully developed characters. For example, Lupino depicts O'Brien's victim in terms of a gradual breakdown that is due to the strain of many days of forced association with the gun-wielding murderer, and also to his role as the boss at an automobile service and repair station—where he is used to giving the orders, so that he is easily and quickly vexed by the crazy killer. The

The Hitch-Hiker

other victim, however, conveys a compelling strength that is prompted by the harrowing ordeal, and that is based on his white-collar job where he is comfortable taking orders. Similarly, Lupino depicts the psychopathic murderer as a boaster who taunts his victims, mocking their weaknesses; his chilling conclusion: "you can get anything at the end of a gun." Interestingly, Lupino portrays his twisted, manic criminality as the result of his parents' hatred, and to a birth defect that has left one of his eyes heavy-lidded and unattractive. In addition, Lupino demonstrates a deft hand at crafting a dismal noir atmosphere, both in terms of the tight, claustrophobic confines of the car that contrasts with the vast, emptiness of the desert. Indeed, she effectively depicts the rugged, arid Mexican landscape in order to underscore the two men's seemingly hopeless plight. Lupino also movingly reveals the changes in the victimized men's relationship as they argue about what to do; further, she suggests that their survival depends on sustaining their union more than anything else. As with her other feature films, Lupino elicited riveting performances from her performers, and she managed to avoid the clichés of other suspense films while methodically and slowly building a riveting suspense. Likewise, as Lupino typically avoided fancy produc-

tion values in favor of realistic and moving stories that had short production schedules and little-known actors, *The Hitch-Hiker* is a high quality, yet low-budget film about a provocative subject.

Critiques that accompanied the film's release are rather different from more recent assessments. Early critics tended to focus on the inspiration for the story and Lupino's rendering of suspense. Some complained that its sense of suspense is so relentless that it verges on parody, and others claimed that it fails to reflect the story's basis in reality. Likewise, they contended that its psychological explanations for the characters' behavior are too facile. Still others, however, praised the film as a taut, "crisp thriller," which was predictable but realistically chilling. But, subsequent to its release, critics have tended to place it within the context of Lupino's body of work as a whole, and have characterized it as her most commendable, if not feminist, film—especially for her skillful, fast-paced, yet orderly, building of a terrifying tension that was conveyed in part via her eloquent cinematic compositions, dynamic editing, and the effective rendering of the contrasts between dark and light, and inside and outside—both physical and emotional. One critic, for example, suggested that these elements are present in all of Lupino's films and they are instrumental in terms of conveying the mysterious emotions that historians have attributed to her work.

—Cynthia Felando

HOLLAND, Agnieszka
Polish director and writer

Born: Warsaw, Poland, 28 November 1948. **Education:** Graduated from the Filmova Akademie Muzickych Umeni (FAMU) film school in Prague, 1971, where she studied directing. **Career:** 1970—maintained her studies in Prague even after the Soviet invasion; was jailed by the authorities after months of harassment by police; 1972—returned to Poland and became member of film collective "X," headed by Andrzej Wajda; 1973—began career as a production assistant to director Krzysztof Zanussi on *Illumination*; 1970s—worked in Polish theater and television; 1979—began writing scripts for films directed by Wajda; directed first feature, *Provincial Actors*; 1981—moved to Paris after the declaration of martial law in Poland, and began making documentaries for French television; 1985—earned first major international acclaim for *Angry Harvest*; member of board of directors of Zespoly Filmowne; member of board of directors of Polish Filmmakers Association. **Awards:** Golden Globe Award, Best Foreign Language Film, National Board of Review, Best Foreign Language Film, 1990, for *Europa, Europa*. **Agent:** William Morris Agency, 151 El Camino Drive, Beverly Hills, CA 90212, U.S.A.

Films as Director and Writer

1974   *Wieczór u Abdona* (*Evening at Abdon's*; *An Evening at Abdon*) (for TV)
1976   *Niedzielne Dzieci* (*Sunday Children*) (for TV)
1977   *Zdjecia próbne* (*Screen Tests*) (ep. in sketch film); *Cós za cos* (*Something for Something*) (for TV—co-d with Wajda)
1979   *Aktorzy prowincjonalni* (*Provincial Actors*)
1981   *Goraczka* (*Fever*; *The Fever: The Story of the Bomb*)
1982   *Kobieta samotna* (*A Woman Alone*; *A Lonely Woman*) (co-d)
1985   *Bittere ernte* (*Angry Harvest*)
1988   *To Kill a Priest* (*Le complot*) (co-sc)
1990   *Europa, Europa*
1991   *Olivier, Olivier*

Films as Director

1990   *Largo Desolato* (co-d with Zizka—for TV)
1993   *The Secret Garden*
1995   *Total Eclipse*
1997   *Washington Square*

Other Films

1978   *Dead Case* (sc); *Bez znieczulenia* (*Without Anesthesia*; *Rough Treatment*) (Wajda) (sc)
1981   *Czlowiek z Zelaza* (*Man of Iron*) (Wajda) (sc)
1982   *Przesluchanie* (*The Interrogation*) (Bugajski—released 1990) (ro as Witowska)

1983   *Danton* (Wajda) (co-sc)
1984   *Ein Liebe en Deutschland* (*A Love in Germany*) (Wajda) (co-sc)
1987   *Anna* (Bogayevicz) (sc); *Les Possedes* (sc)
1988   *La Amiga* (*Die Freundin*) (Meerapfel) (co-sc)
1990   *Korczak* (Wajda) (sc)
1993   *Trois Coleurs: Bleu* (*Three Colors: Blue*) (Kieslowski) (additional dialogue)
1994   *Trois Coleurs: Blanc* (*Three Colors: White*) (Kieslowski) (co-sc)

Publications by Holland

Books

Korczak: opowiesci filmowe, Warsaw, 1991.
Olivier, Olivier, Portsmouth, New Hampshire, 1996.

Articles

"Agnieszka Holland: le cinéma polonais cintinue d'exister mais un lui a coupe le souffle," interview with P. Li, in *Avant-Scène Cinéma* (Paris), December 1983.
"Lessons from the Past," interview with Peter Brunette, in *Cineaste* (New York), no. 1, 1986.
"Off screen: A Pole Apart," interview with J. Hoberman, in *Village Voice* (New York), 18 March 1986
"Dialogue on Film: Agnieszka Holland," in *American Film* (New York), September 1986.
"Lekja historii," interview with J. Wroblewski, in *Kino* (Warsaw), August 1989.
"Felix dia Wajdy," in *Kino* (Warsaw), April 1991.
"Spotkanie z Agnieszka Holland," interview with T. Lubelshi, in *Kino* (Warsaw), April 1991.
"Nowa gra," interview with Z. Benedyktow, in *Kino* (Warsaw), 16 February 1992.
"Holland," interview with E. Krolikowska-Avis, in *Kino* (Warsaw), October 1992.

Publications on Holland

Books

Quart, Barbara, *Women Directors: The Emergence of a New Cinema*, New York, 1988.
Foster, Gwendolyn Audrey, *Women Film Directors: An International Bio-Critical Dictionary*, Westport, Connecticut, 1995.

Articles

Warchol, T., "The End of a Beginning," in *Sight and Sound* (London), no. 3, 1986.
Stone, Judy, "Behind *Angry Harvest*: Polish Politics and Exile," in *New York Times*, 16 March 1986.
Taubin, Amy, "Woman of Irony," in *Village Voice* (New York), 2 July 1991.
Quart, Barbara, "Three Central European Women Directors Revisited," in *Cineaste* (New York), no. 4, 1993
Blinken, Antony J., "Going to Extremes," in *Harper's Bazaar* (New York), February 1993.

Cohen, Roger, "Holland without a Country," in *New York Times Magazine*, 8 August 1993.

Taubin, Amy, "Imagination among the Ruins," in *Village Voice* (New York), 17 August 1993.

Clark, John, and Henry S. Hample, "Filmographies," in *Premiere* (New York), September 1993.

Quart, Barbara, "The Secret Garden of Agnieszka Holland," in *Ms. Magazine* (New York), September/October 1993.

Gaydos, Steven, "For Holland, Less Is More," in *Variety* (New York), October 30, 1995.

* * *

The death camps were liberated decades ago. Auschwitz and Birkenau, Chelmno and Dachau—the ABCDs of the Final Solution—have long been silent memorials to the mass murder of millions. Despite this passage of time—and despite the media-induced impression that Steven Spielberg's *Schindler's List* is the only movie ever made which confronts the mass extermination of a people during World War II—the Holocaust has long been a topic for filmmakers. One such filmmaker is director Agnieszka Holland.

Holland is a Polish Jew who was born scant years after the end of World War II. The legacy of that era has influenced her life, and her work. She is not so much interested in the politics of the war, in how and why the German people allowed Hitler to come to power. Rather, a common theme in her films is the manner in which individuals responded to Hitler and the Nazi scourge. This is most perfectly exemplified in what is perhaps her most distinguished film to date: *Europa, Europa*, a German-made feature based on the memoirs of Salamon Perel, who as a teenaged German Jew survived World War II by passing for Aryan in a Hitler Youth academy. This thoughtful, tremendously moving film was the source of controversy on two accounts: it depicts a Jew who compromises himself in order to ensure his survival; and it was not named as Germany's official Best Foreign Language Film entrant, making it ineligible in that category for an Academy Award. Nevertheless, it did earn Holland a nomination for Best Screenplay (based on material from another medium).

Even though Holland only wrote the screenplay for *Korczak*—the film was directed by her mentor, Andrzej Wajda—it too is one of her most impassioned works. Her simple, poignant script chronicles the real-life story of a truly gentle, remarkable man: Janusz Korczak (Wojtek Pszoniak), a respected doctor, writer, and children's rights advocate who operated a home for Jewish orphans in Warsaw during the 1930s. Korczak's concerns are people and not politics. "I love children," he states, simply and matter-of-factly. "I fight for years for the dignity of children." In his school, he offers his charges a humanist education. And then the Nazis invade his homeland. Given his station in life, Korczak easily could arrange his escape to freedom. But he chooses to remain with his children and do whatever he must to keep his orphanage running and his children alive, even after they all have been imprisoned in the Warsaw Ghetto.

After directing several theatrical and made-for-television features in Poland, Holland came to international attention in 1985 with *Angry Harvest*, a superb drama about a wealthy farmer who offers to shelter a Jewish woman in his cellar in World War II Poland. His repressed sexuality transforms this act of kindness into one of hypocrisy, as he attempts to abuse his guest. Films such as *Angry Harvest*, *Korczak*, and *Europa, Europa* serve a necessary, essential purpose: they are tools that can be used to educate young people, Jew and non-Jew alike, about the exploitation and extermination of a race. They are monuments—as much to the memory of generations past as to the survival of generations to come.

Not all of Holland's films have dealt directly with the Holocaust. Another of her themes—which also may be linked to the Holocaust by its very nature—is the loss of innocence among children that occurs not by the natural progression of growing into adulthood, but by odd, jarring circumstances. *Olivier, Olivier*, like *Europa, Europa* and *Korczak*, also is a narrative based on fact. It is the intricate account of a country couple whose youngest offspring, Olivier, mysteriously disappears. Six years later he "reappears," but is no longer the special child who was a joy to his family. Rather, he is a Parisian street hustler who claims to have forgotten his childhood. One also can understand Holland's attraction to *The Secret Garden*, an adaptation of the Frances Hodgson Burnett children's story about a ten-year-old orphan who revitalizes a neglected garden in her uncle's Victorian mansion.

Most of Holland's films have been artistically successful. Two exceptions have been *To Kill a Priest*, an ambitious but ultimately clumsy drama about an ill-fated activist priest in Poland; and *Total Eclipse*, about the relationship between French poets Arthur Rimbaud and Paul Verlaine (and based on a play by Christopher Hampton), which was a fiasco—one of the more eagerly anticipated yet disappointing films of 1995. Thankfully, however, these failures comprise the minority of Holland's filmic output.

—Rob Edelman

HUBLEY, Faith Elliott
American animator, producer, and director

Born: Faith Chestman in New York City, 16 September 1924. **Education:** Attended Art Students League, New York City. **Family:** Married (second) the animator John K. Hubley, 1955 (died 1977), four children: Mark, Ray, Emily, Georgia. **Career:** 1943-55—film editor, script supervisor, music editor; 1955-president, The Hubley Studio; 1972—senior critic, Yale University School of Art. **Awards:** Academy Award (with John Hubley), Best Short Subjects, Cartoons, for *The Hole*, 1962; Academy Award (with John Hubley), Best Short Subjects, Cartoons, for *Herb Alpert and the Tijuana Brass Double Feature*, 1966; honorary doctorate, Columbia College, Chicago, 1990; honorary doctorate, Hofstra University, 1995; 14 CINE Golden Eagle awards. **Address:** Hubley Studio Inc., 2575 Palisade Avenue, Apartment 12L, Riverdale, NY 10463-6127, U.S.A.

Films as Co-Producer and Co-Director with John Hubley

1956 *Adventures of an **
1957 *Harlem Wednesday*
1958 *The Tender Game*
1959 *Moonbird*
1960 *Children of the Sun*
1961 *Of Stars and Men* (+ ed)
1962 *The Hole*
1964 *The Hat*
1966 *Herb Alpert and the Tijuana Brass Double Feature*; *Urbanissimo*
1968 *Windy Day*

1969   *Of Men and Demons*
1970   *Eggs*
1972   *Dig: A Journey into the Earth*
1973   *Cockaboody*
1974   *Voyage to Next*
1975   *People People People*
1976   *Everybody Rides the Carousel*
1977   *The Doonesbury Special* (for TV) (+ co-sc)

Films as Producer and Director

1975   *W.O.W. (Women of the World)*
1976   *Second Chance: Sea*
1977   *Whither Weather*
1978   *Step by Step*
1980   *Sky Dance*
1981   *The Big Bang and Other Creation Myths*; *Enter Life*
1983   *Starlore*
1984   *Hello*
1985   *The Cosmic Eye* (+ sc)
1987   *Time of the Angels*
1988   *Yes We Can*
1989   *Who Am I*
1990   *Amazonia*
1991   *Upside Down*
1992   *Tall Time Tales*
1993   *Cloudland*
1994   *Seers & Clowns*
1995   *Rainbows of Hawai'i*
1996   *My Universe Inside Out*
1997   *Beyond the Shadow Place*

Other Films

1957   *Twelve Angry Men* (Lumet) (script supervisor)
1966   *The Year of the Horse* (Sunasky) (co-sc)

Publications by Hubley

Books

With John Hubley, *Zuckerkandl!,* New York, 1968.
With John Hubley, *Dig! A Journey under the Earth's Crust,* New York, 1973.
With John Hubley, *The Hat,* New York, 1974.
With Elizabeth Swados, *Lullaby,* New York, 1980.
With Elizabeth Swados, *Sky Dance,* New York, 1981.

Article

Interview with Pat McGilligan, in *Film Quarterly* (Berkeley), Winter 1988-89.

Publications on Hubley

Books

Smith, Sharon, *Women Who Make Movies,* New York, 1975.
Trudeau, Garry, *John & Faith Hubley's A Doonesbury Special: A Director's Notebook,* Kansas City, Kansas, 1978.

Commire, Anne, editor, *Something about the Author, Facts and Pictures about Authors and Illustrators of Books for Young People,* vol. 48, Detroit, 1978.
Horn, Maurice, editor, *Contemporary Graphic Artists: A Bibliographical, Biographical, and Critical Guide to Current Illustrators, Animators, Cartoonists, Designers, and Other Graphic Artists,* vol. 1, Detroit, 1986.
Chadwick, Whitney, and Isabelle de Courtivron, editors, *Significant Others: Creativity and Intimate Partnership,* London, 1993.
Pilling, Jayne, editor, *Women and Animation: A Compendium,* London, 1993.
Foster, Gwendolyn Audrey, *Women Film Directors: An International Bio-Critical Dictionary,* Westport, Connecticut, 1995.

Articles

Durkin, Tish, "A Cel of One's Own," in *New York,* 12 April 1993.
Saccoccia, Susan, "Legendary Animator Carries on Tradition," in *Christian Science Monitor,* 24 November 1995.

Film

Camera Three. The Fine Art of Film Animation—John and Faith Hubley, directed by Ivan Cury, 1972.

* * *

When Faith Elliott married John Hubley in 1955, they agreed that they would make one independently financed short film a year, and that they would always eat dinner at the table with their children. They upheld their agreement for 22 years, co-directing and co-producing films and animated shorts. After John's death in 1977, Faith Hubley—in spite of a lengthy battle with breast cancer—continued to produce and direct on her own. By then her own children had grown up, and several were working with her, while she continued to raise new generations of "children": her students at Yale.

In Hell's Kitchen as a young woman, Faith Chestman's parents had wanted her to become a dentist, and conflicts became heated when they realized that she had other plans. She showed ability as a visual artist, but she drifted toward theater work instead: already a dedicated radical, Chestman worked in People's Theatre in New York while studying with the New Theatre League. After a brief, failed marriage that left her with little more than the new surname of Elliott, she moved to Los Angeles, where she went to work in a factory. By that time, the Soviet Union had entered World War II against Nazi Germany, so she had become an enthusiastic proponent of the war, and she was fired for being overly zealous in organizing the workers to make war against fascism.

Faith Elliott got a job as a messenger for a film studio, where the war had opened up more film jobs for women. Over the next decade, she progressed through a variety of jobs at Columbia, Goldwyn, and Republic, gaining experience by working with The Three Stooges—and she met John Hubley, a Disney animator who had worked on such classics as *Dumbo* and *Bambi*. John helped form United Productions of America, where Faith first worked with him on an educational film about menstruation—hardly typical subject matter in the 1940s.

John Hubley had left Disney after a 1941 strike, and as he and Faith became collaborators in life and work, Disney's negative influence would become a significant motivating factor for both of them. The animated films the Hubleys made, from the 1950s on, would mark a dramatic departure from the glossy style of Disney. Instead of bright, sharp colors, they used muted tones influenced not only by cubist art, but by ancient cave paintings and children's drawings. Those three influences—modernism, primitivism, and a celebration of the child—would become the pillars of the couple's joint projects and later of Faith Hubley's solo work.

Given John's work as an animator and Faith's earlier explorations in visual art, animated shorts made a natural basis for the Hubley Studio, formed in 1955, the year of their marriage. These were usually outlandish films such as *The Hole* (featuring their friend Dizzy Gillespie), in which two construction workers in a manhole discuss the future of the world. *The Hole* was decades ahead of its time, prefiguring the style of 1990s television shows such as *Seinfeld* with their concentration on quirky dialogue over plot, and it won an Academy Award.

But the Hubleys also showed a talent for innovation in their more commercial work—projects they did chiefly to pay the bills and finance their experimental and avant-garde projects. One of the most famous "films" to come out of the Hubley Studio, in fact, was the "Markie Maypo" cereal commercial in 1959. Hubley later described it as a "non-commercial," and like *The Hole,* it belonged more to the 1990s than the 1950s. Using the voice of their own son, the Hubleys created the character of "Markie Maypo," who despises Maypo cereal and dismisses it with a "Yuck!" This form of anti-selling proved enormously popular with the public, yet it did not gain common usage until the 1990s, with "anti" campaigns employed by Sprite, McDonald's (for the Arch Deluxe burger), and others.

In spite of such successes, or the acclaim given to other commercial works such as a 1966 documentary about Herb Alpert's Tijuana Brass or a 1977 television special based on the *Doonesbury* cartoon, the Hubleys' first love was their cutting-age, sardonic, and highly innovative animation work. Just as they visually contrasted with Disney cartoons, the Hubleys' cartoons were markedly different in their political and "progressive" undertones. A number of films emphasized feminist themes, including *Windy Day* (1968), which used their daughters' voice-overs; and 1975's *W.O.W.* Faith Hubley's later work, such as *Amazonia* (1990) and *Rainbows of Hawai'i* (1995), explores environmental issues.

Ironies abound in Faith Hubley's lengthy career. A feminist married to a man who shared her views, she saw their joint efforts routinely categorized as "Films by John Hubley" or "John Hubley *with* Faith Hubley." A communist sympathizer in the Stalin era and a "progressive" in the years since, she has routinely eschewed public grants for her films, financing them through her own efforts. (She has also described herself as "not [a] very populist person.") Finally, there is the irony of her films' distributorship. In the 1990s, a number of the animated shorts from earlier decades became available on video from Pyramid Films, but before that, their chief distributor had been the Hubleys' arch-nemesis, Disney.

—Judson Knight

HUI, Ann
Chinese/Hong Kong director

Pseudonyms: Xu Anhua, Hsu An-hua, Ann Huio On-Wah. **Born:** Anshan, Liaoning province, Manchuria, China, 23 May 1947; moved to Hong Kong in 1952. **Education:** Attended Hong Kong University, graduated with a degree in English and comparative literature; attended the London Film School for two years. **Career:** 1975-77—worked as assistant to Hong Kong director King Hu and directed drama series and short documentaries for the TVB television station; 1977—produced and directed six one-hour films for Hong Kong's Independent Commission against Corruption; 1978—directed three episodes for the RTHK series *Below the Lion Rock*; 1979—directed first feature, *The Secret*; 1997—Fellow, Academy for Performing Arts. **Awards:** Best Picture and Best Director, Hong Kong Film Awards, for *Boat People*, 1982; Best Film, Asian Pacific Festival, Best Film, Rimini Festival, for *Song of the Exile*, 1990; Best Picture and Best Director, Hong Kong Film Awards, Best Picture and Best Director, Golden Bauhinia Awards, Best Picture, Hong Kong Film Critics Society, Golden Horse Award, Taipei Golden Horse Film Festival, Best Film, Creteil International Festival of Women's Films, for *Summer Snow*, 1994; awarded MBE (Member of British Empire), 1997. **Address:** 1-7 Shell Street, 7B, Hong Kong.

Films as Director

1979 *Feng Jie* (*The Secret*)
1980 *Zhuang Dao Zheng* (*The Spooky Bunch*; *Xiaojie Zhuang Dao Gui*)
1981 *Hu Yueh Te Ku Shih* (*The Story of Woo Viet*; *Huyue de gushi*)
1982 **T'ou-Pen Nu-Hai** (*Boat People*; *Tou Bun No Hoi*)
1984 *Qing Cheng Zhi Lian* (*Love in a Fallen City*)
1987 *Xiang Xiang Gong Zhu* (*Princess Fragrance*) (+ sc); *Shu Jian En Chou Lu* (*The Romance of Book & Sword*) (+ co-sc)
1988 *Jinye Xingguang Canlan* (*Starry Is the Night*)
1990 *Ketu Qiuhen* (*Song of the Exile*); *Xiao Ao Jiang Hu* (*Swordsman*; *Siu Ngo Gong Woo*) (co-d)
1991 *Jidao Zhuizhong* (*Zodiac Killer*)
1992 *Shanghai Jiaqi* (*My American Grandson*) (+ sc)
1994 *Xiatian de Xue* (*Nuren sishi*; *Summer Snow*) (+ co-pr)
1996 *Ah Kam* (*A Jin de gu shi*; *The Stunt Woman*; *Stuntwoman Ajin*)
1997 *Personal Memoir of Hong Kong: As Time Goes By* (+ co-pr, sc); *Sixteen Springs*

Other Films

1993 *Fong Sai-Yuk* (*The Legend of Fong Sai-Yuk*) (Yuen Kwai) (production)
1994 *Tianguo Niezi* (*The Day the Sun Turned Cold*) (Yim Ho) (co-pr)
1996 *He Liu* (*The River*) (Tsai Ming-liang)
1997 *Yi Sheng Yitai Xi* (*A Little Life-Opera*) (Fong) (exec pr)

Publications by Hui

Articles

Interview with H. Niogret, in *Positif* (Paris), May 1983.
Interview with O. Assayas and C. Tesson, in *Cahiers du Cinéma* (Paris), September 1983.
Interview with Karen Jaehne, in *Cineaste* (New York), no. 2, 1984.
"Shanghai jiaqu," with T. Sato, in *Cinemaya* (New Delhi), Summer 1992.

Publications on Hui

Books

Foster, Gwendolyn Audrey, *Women Film Directors: An International Bio-Critical Dictionary,* Westport, Connecticut, 1995.
Browne, Nick, Paul G. Pickowicz, Vivian Sobchack, and Esther Yau, editors, *New Chinese Cinema: Forms, Identities, Politics,* Cambridge, England, 1997.

Articles

Rayns, Tony, "In the Picture: Across the Border," in *Sight and Sound* (London), no. 4, 1982.
Tesson, C., "Tu n'as rien vu a Da-nang," in *Cahiers du Cinéma* (Paris), September 1983.
Kennedy, Harlan, "*Boat People,*" in *Film Comment* (New York), September/October 1983.
"Hui Sees Fest-Fave *Boat People* as 'Non-Political' Cry for Rights," in *Variety* (New York), 12 October 1983.
Elhem, P., and C. Tatum, "Ann Hui: simple comme une tragedie," in *Visions* (Brussels), 15 April 1984.
Assayas, O., and C. Tesson, "Le contrat," in *Cahiers du Cinéma* (Paris), September 1984.
Assayas, O., and F. Huguier, "Une journée sur le tournage de Ann Hui," in *Cahiers du Cinéma* (Paris), September 1984.
Rayns, Tony, "Chinese Changes," in *Sight and Sound* (London), Winter 1984-85.
Rayns, Tony, "The Position of Women in New Chinese Cinema," in *East-West Film Journal* (Honolulu), no. 2, 1987.
Francia, L. H., "Off Screen: Ann Hui: Nothing Is What It Seems," in *Village Voice* (New York), 21 April 1987.
Hoberman, J., "Film: What Women Want," in *Village Voice* (New York), 21 April 1987.
Jaivin, L., "Cinema and China: The Woman from Hong Kong," in *Cinema Papers* (Victoria, Australia), November 1987.
Kaplan, E. Ann, "Problematizing Cross-Cultural Analysis: The Case of Women in the Recent Chinese Cinema," in *Wide Angle* (Baltimore), no. 2, 1989.
Roggemans, J., and others, "*La romance du livre et de l'épée,*" in *Grand Angle* (Mariembourg, Belgium), January 1990.
Bernstein, R., "Grappling with Modern China," in *New York Times,* 17 March 1991.
Nientied, A., "Schreeuwen tegan de ondergaande zon," in *Skoop* (Amsterdam), June 1991.
Romano, H., and A. Kieffer, "Cretail 91: regards d'Extreme-Orient," in *Jeune Cinéma* (Paris), July/August 1991.
Rafman, C., "Imagining a Woman's World: Roles for Women in Chinese Films," in *Cinémas* (Montreal), no. 2/3, 1993.
Hoare, S., "Romance du livre et du film: l'adaptation de la *Romance du livre et de l'épée* par Ann Hui," in *Cinémas* (Montreal), no. 2/3, 1993.
Abbas, A., "The New Hong Kong Cinema and the Deja Disparu," in *Discourse* (Bloomington, Indiana), Spring 1994.

* * *

Ann Hui is one of the most distinguished directors in the first new wave of Hong Kong film making, which emerged on the international cinema scene during the 1980s. While many of the period's films are Eastern variations on the popular gangster and action-adventure genres of Hollywood, Hui's best work is more personal in nature. Her films reflect on cultural displacement, and the effect on individuals who are uprooted from one country and culture and planted in another, either by personal choice or political or economic necessity. Hui is especially concerned with how her characters respond to their new surroundings, and how they are affected when they return—also by choice or necessity—to their homelands.

Hui also has directed films that are more generic in nature. *The Secret,* her first feature, is a based-on-fact suspense drama about a double murder. *The Spooky Bunch,* her follow-up, is a satiric ghost story. Her major cinematic concerns emerged in *The Story of Woo Viet,* a drama about a South Vietnamese refugee in Manila, and *Boat People,* her most lauded early film, a semidocumentary account of the plight of downtrodden Vietnamese after the 1975 Liberation, whose only hope for survival lies in their becoming boat people.

Familial conflict is a key theme in Hui's work. In the two-part historic epic *Princess Fragrance* and *The Romance of Book & Sword,* she focused on the dissension between two brothers, one a Manchurian emperor and the other the head of the secret anti-Manchu Red Flower Society. *My American Grandson* is the story of an elderly Chinese man looking after his 12-year-old American grandson. Here, Hui acutely examines the cultural differences between East and West, the manner in which American-reared Chinese have lost touch with their native culture, and the importance of understanding that culture. By far her best recent film is *Summer Snow,* a family comedy-drama about May Sun, a working woman with a husband and teenage son, who has never gotten along with her father-in-law but must take him in upon the death of his wife. The scenario follows May Sun's struggle to deal with the situation, which is exacerbated when the father-in-law is afflicted with Alzheimer's disease.

To date, *Song of the Exile* is Hui's most intensely intimate work, if only because it so obviously is semiautobiographical. This slice-of-life, set in 1973, tells the story of Hueyin, a 25-year-old woman who (like Hui) was raised in Hong Kong and, at the scenario's outset, completes a film school education in London. Hueyin returns to Hong Kong to attend her younger sister's wedding, where she recalls the supportive grandparents with whom she spent much of her childhood and clashes with her manipulative mother who attempts to stifle her dreams and her individuality.

For Hueyin, the cultural revolution in China and the war in Vietnam are little more than news items reported on television. As such, she pays them no mind. Yet in the wake of such events, families are separated and individuals are forced to flee their homes and become refugees. If she ever is to attain self-understanding, Hueyin must realize that the wars and revolutions of the recent past, coupled with economic realities, have separated, and affected, the various members of her family.

On the surface, *Song of the Exile* chronicles the clashing personalities and value-systems of a mother and daughter. But more to the point, it is the story of a displaced family and the cultural and nationalistic barriers that isolate its members. Hueyin's mother was born in Japan, lived most of her adult life in Hong Kong, and in the film's final section returns to Japan. Hueyin's grandparents reside in Canton, and resent her mother because she is Japanese. Hueyin spent her youth in Canton as well as Hong Kong, studied in London, returns to Hong Kong, travels with her mother to Japan, and visits her grandparents in Canton. Upon her marriage, Hueyin's sister and her husband emigrate to Canada.

When an individual moves to a foreign country out of choice, as Hueyin did when she went off to study in London, it can be an enlightening experience. But when you are forced to move, the result is altogether different as the individual sadly and tragically feels displaced and loses touch with native culture and familial roots. Hueyin comes in touch with this differentiation as she spends time with her mother, and journeys with her back to Japan. At the outset of *Song of the Exile,* Hueyin merrily romps through the London streets with her classmates. She is an idealistic schoolgirl, with the promise of a happy life before her. But in the course of the story, she changes as she becomes more worldly and realizes there is much more between herself and her mother than superficial generational conflict. She comes to understand the source of her mother's unhappiness and frustration. Indeed, in the last shot of the film, Hueyin is crying.

During the 1990s, Ann Hui has gravitated to directing commercial genre films, and working in behind-the-scenes capacities for other filmmakers. One of her latest works, *The Stunt Woman,* tells the story of Ah Kam, a movie stuntwoman. But even here, the theme of displacement is present: Ah Kam is born in China but comes to Hong Kong to pursue her career; she is separated from her family, and struggles to acclimate herself to her new environment. In the mid-1990s, Hui unsuccessfully attempted to raise money for an ambitious, potentially controversial project: a film about the people of Hong Kong at the time of the Tiananmen Square massacre.

—Rob Edelman

HUILLET, Danièle
French director

Born: France, 1 May 1936. **Education:** Studied film at universities in Nancy and Strasbourg. **Family:** Married the director Jean-Marie Straub, 1959. **Career:** 1954—began collaboration with Jean-Marie Straub; 1959—Straub and Huillet moved to Munich; 1963—collaborated on their first film, *Machorka-Muff;* 1969—moved to Italy. **Address:** c/o French Film Office, 745 5th Avenue, New York, NY 10151, U.S.A.

Films as Co-Director with Jean-Marie Straub

1963   *Machorka-Muff* (+ sc, co-ed, co-sound)
1965   *Nicht versöhnt oder Es hilft nur Gewalt, wo Gewalt herrscht* (*Es hilft nicht, wo Gewalt herrscht; Not Reconciled*) (+ sc, co-ed, co-ph)
1968   *Chronik der Anna Magdalena Bach* (*Chronicle of Anna Magdalena Bach*) (+ sc); *Der Bräutigam, die Komödiantin und der Zuhälter* (*The Bridegroom, the Comedienne and the Pimp*) (+ sc, co-ed)
1969   *Othon* (*Les Yeux ne veulent pas en tout temps se fermer ou Peut-être qu'un jour Rome se permettra de choisir à son tour; Die Augen wollen sich nicht zu jeder Zeit schliessen oder Vielleicht eines Tages wird Rom sich erlauben, seinerseits zu wählen; Eyes Do Not Want to Close at All Times or Perhaps One Day Rome Will Permit Herself to Choose in Her Turn, Othon*) (+ sc, co-ed); *Einleitung zu Arnold Schoenberg Begleit Musik zu einer Lichtspielscene* (*Introduction to Arnold Schoenberg's Accompaniment for a Cinematographic Scene*) (for TV) (+ sc, co-pr, co-ed)
1972   *Geschichtsunterricht* (*History Lessons*) (+ sc, co-pr, co-ed)
1975   *Moses und Aron* (*Moses and Aaron*) (+ sc, co-ed)
1976   *Fortini/Cani* (*I cani del Sinai; The Dogs of Sinai*) (+ sc, co-ed)
1977   *Toute révolution est un coup de dés* (*Every Revolution Is a Throw of the Dice*) (+ sc, ed)
1979   *Della nube alla resistenza* (*From the Cloud to the Resistance*) (+ sc, ed)
1982   *En Rachachant*
1983   *Trop tot, trop tard* (*Zu früh, zu spät; Too Early, Too Late*)
1985   *Klassenverhältnisse* (*Class Relations*) (+ co-sc, ed)
1986   *Der Tod des Empedokles* (*The Death of Empedocles*) (+ ed, costumes)
1989   *Schwarze Sunde* (*Black Sins*) (+ ed); *Cézanne*
1992   *Antigone*
1994   *Lothringen!* (+ ed)

Publications by Huillet (with Jean-Marie Straub)

Book

Klassenverhältnisse, edited by Wolfram Schütte, Frankfurt, 1984.

Articles

"Frustration of Violence," in *Cahiers du Cinéma in English* (New York), January 1967.
"*Moses und Aron* as an Object of Marxist Reflection," interview with J. Rogers, in *Jump Cut* (Berkeley), no. 12-13, 1976.
"Decoupage di Fortini/Cani," in *Filmcritica* (Rome), November/December 1976.
Interview with R. Gansera, in *Filmkritik* (Munich), September 1978.
Interview with Serge Daney and J. Narboni, in *Cahiers du Cinéma* (Paris), November 1979.
Interview with H. Hurch and B. Brewster, in *Undercut* (London), Spring 1983.
Interview with H. Farocki, in *Filmkritik* (Munich), May 1983.
Interview with S. Blum and J. Prieur, in *Camera/Stylo* (Paris), September 1983.
Interview with E. Bruno and R. Rosetti, in *Filmcritica* (Rome), September 1984.
Interview with M. Blank and others, in *Filmkritik* (Munich), September/October 1984.
Interview with A. Bengala and others, in *Cahiers du Cinéma* (Paris), October 1984.
Interview with P. Toulemonde, in *Cinématographe* (Paris), November 1984.
Interview with E. Szekely, in *Filmvilag* (Budapest), vol. 28, no. 8, 1985.
Interview with G. Baratta and G. Latini, in *Filmcritica* (Rome), January/February 1987.
Interview with C. Desbarats, in *Cinéma 88* (Paris), 6-13 January 1988.
Interview with H. Hurch, in *Andere Sinema* (Antwerp), September/October 1989.
Interview with P. Willemsen, in *Andere Sinema* (Antwerp), September/October 1989.

Publications on Huillet

Books

Roud, Richard, *Jean-Marie Straub,* London, 1971.

Walsh, Martin, *The Brechtian Aspect of Radical Cinema,* London, 1981.

Franklin, James, *New German Cinema: From Oberhausen to Hamburg,* Boston, 1983.

Rosetti, Riccardo, editor, *Straub-Huillet Film,* Rome, 1984.

Elsaesser, Thomas, *New German Cinema: A History,* London, 1989.

Byg, Barton, *Landscapes of Resistance: The German Films of Danièle Huillet and Jean-Marie Straub,* Berkeley, 1995.

Foster, Gwendolyn Audrey, *Women Film Directors: An International Bio-Critical Dictionary,* Westport, Connecticut, 1995.

Articles

"Moses und Aron Issue" of *Cahiers du Cinéma* (Paris), October/November 1975.

"Straub and Huillet Issue" of *Enthusiasm* (London), December 1975.

Dermody, S., "Straub/Huillet: The Politics of Film Practice," in *Cinema Papers* (Melbourne), September/October 1976.

"Danièle Huillet Jean-Marie Straub's *Fortini/Cani,"* special issue of *Filmkritik* (Munich), January 1977.

Simsolo, Noel, "Jean-Marie Straub et Danièle Huillet," in *Cinéma* (Paris), March 1977.

Bennett, E., "The Films of Straub Are Not 'Theoretical'," in *Afterimage* (Rochester, New York), Summer 1978.

Rosenbaum, Jonathan, "Jean-Luc, Chantal, Danièle, Jean-Marie and the Others," in *American Film* (Washington, D.C.), February 1979.

Daney, Serge, "Le Plan Straubien," in *Cahiers du Cinéma* (Paris), November 1979.

Magisos, M., "Not Reconciled: The Destruction of Narrative Pleasure," in *Wide Angle* (Athens, Ohio), vol. 3, no. 4, 1980.

Sauvaget, D., in *Revue du Cinéma* (Paris), April 1980.

Blank, R., in *Skrien* (Amsterdam), Summer 1981.

Durgnat, Raymond, "From Caligari to Hitler," in *Film Comment* (New York), Summer 1981.

Graziani, G., and others, in *Filmcritica* (Rome), September/October 1981.

Goldschmidt, D., in *Cinématographe* (Paris), March 1982.

Mitry, Jean, in *Cinématographe* (Paris), September 1982.

Simons, J., in *Skrien* (Amsterdam), September 1982.

Lange, M., and others, in *Filmkritik* (Munich), January 1983.

Ranieri, N., in *Cinema Nuovo* (Torino), August/October 1983.

Turim, Maureen, "Jean-Marie Straub and Danièle Huillet: Oblique Angles on Films as Ideological Intervention," in *New German Filmmakers: From Oberhausen through the 1970s,* edited by Klaus Phillips, New York, 1984.

Maderna, M., in *Segnocinema* (Vicenza), January 1984.

Hoberman, J., "Once upon a Time in Amerika," in *Artforum* (New York), September 1984.

Bergala, A., in *Cahiers du Cinéma* (Paris), October 1984.

Ehrenstein, D., and others, "Reagan at Bitburg: Spectacle and Memory," in *On Film* (Los Angeles), Spring 1985.

Rosetti, R., in *Filmcritica* (Rome), October 1985.

Kamiah, J., in *Filmcritica* (Rome), January/February 1987.

Chevrie, M., in *Cahiers du Cinéma* (Paris), April 1989.

Dominicus, M., and J. de Putter, in *Skrien* (Amsterdam), February/March 1990.

Petley, Julian, "Straub/Huillet's *Empedocles,"* in *Sight and Sound* (London) Summer 1990.

* * *

In Ephraim Katz's *Film Encyclopedia,* Jean-Marie Straub is given his own entry, in which he is described as "a leading voice in the New German Cinema." Meanwhile, the entry for his wife and co-creator, Danièle Huillet, is cross-referenced to Straub. She is not mentioned until the final sentence, which reads, "His wife, Danièle Huillet, collaborates on his films as producer and writer."

In *Cinema: A Critical Dictionary,* an anthology edited by Richard Roud, Straub is cited on 13 pages. Huillet is mentioned only on one, in Roud's essay on Straub, and it is an ever-so casual citation.

Is this lack of attention the result of an assumption that the male automatically is the more important contributor in a male-female collaboration? Or is it an offshoot of the auteurist theory that Straub, as the officially credited director, is the foremost contributor to a film while Huillet, as collaborator/producer/writer, is rendered merely an asterisk?

In these post-feminist times, the latter would seem to be the case, if only because contemporary women directors (rather than their male scriptwriters, producers, or "collaborators") are the ones who take center stage at film festivals and are the focus of press interviews and critical analysis. And after all, the direction of Straub and Huillet's earliest films *was* credited only to Straub. For example, *Nicht versöhnt oder Es hilft nur Gewalt, wo Gewalt herrscht,* based on a novel by Heinrich Böll, is listed as a Straub-Huillet production, directed by Straub and scripted by Straub and Huillet.

Still, there is more-than-ample evidence pointing to Huillet's omission as a case of wholesale sexism. This is because, from the early 1970s on, Huillet has shared directorial credit with Straub. They are listed as co-directors of *Geschichtsunterricht,* based on Bertolt Brecht's *The Affairs of Mr. Julius Caesar.* Yet in the body of the *Variety* review, only Straub is cited. Huillet may be mentioned in the *Variety* critique of *Moses und Aron,* an adaptation of Arnold Schoenberg's biblical opera, but she is immediately referred to as "Mrs. Straub," while Straub alone is the focus of the critical commentary. This dismissal directly segues into the space (or lack of) devoted to Huillet by Katz and Roud.

As with many intimate, long-lasting two-person collaborations, the boundaries of who does what over the course of many years and many films often becomes fuzzy. So the point really is not who directed what, who scripted what, who photographed what—and who was credited with what. Straub and Huillet are equal partners. When one discusses one, one certainly must cite the other.

Beyond giving acknowledgment where acknowledgment is due, it is reasonable to assume that Straub and Huillet never will be as celebrated as fellow New German filmmakers Rainer Werner Fassbinder, Volker Schlöndorff, Werner Herzog, or Wim Wenders. Nevertheless, their unconventionally structured, gloriously uncommercial experimental minimalist films, which more often than not spotlight German literature and music, are sharply visual and mind-massagingly cerebral. They abandon naturalism and conventional narrative and combine images, sounds, and words to create impressions and emotions, with the use of music taking on a special emphasis as a tool of communication.

Most significantly, Straub and Huillet place demands on their audiences to interact with and respond to their work. Some critics and film goers have written off their efforts as static, uncinematic, even downright boring. But as Dave Kehr so succinctly put it in a review of *Moses und Aron,* "Straub and Huillet's investigation of the medium is an important experience for anyone interested in the way film represents reality—or fails to."

—Rob Edelman

HUNGERJAHRE
(Years of Hunger; Years of Famine)
Germany, 1980
Director: Jutta Brückner

Production: ZDF (West German television), black and white, running time: 114 minutes.

Producer: Jutta Brückner; **photography:** Jörg Jeshel; **editor:** Anneliese Krigar; **music:** Johaness Schmölling.

Cast: Britta Pohland (*Ursula*); Sylvia Ulrich (*Mother*); Claus Jurichs (*Father*).

Publications

Book

Knight, Julia, *Women and the New German Cinema,* London, 1992.

Articles

"*Hungerjahre,*" in *Variety* (New York), 5 March 1980.
Harbord, Patricia, "Interview with Jutta Brückner," in *Screen Education,* vol. 40, 1981-82.
Mayne, Judith, Helen Fehervary, and Claudia Lensson, "Female Narration, Women's Cinema," in *New German Critique,* Fall/Winter 1981-82.
Brückner, Jutta, "Women behind the Camera," in *Feminist Aesthetics,* edited by Gisela Ecker, translated by Harriet Anderson, Boston, 1986.
Silberman, Marc, "Women Filmmakers in West Germany: A Catalogue," in *Camera Obscura* (Berkeley), Fall 1990.
Kosta, Barbara, "Representing Female Sexuality: Jutta Brückner's Film *Years of Hunger,*" and Marc Silberman, "Interview with Jutta Brückner: Recognizing Collective Gestures," in *Gender and Ger-*

Hungerjahre

man Cinema: Feminist Interventions, Volume 2, German Film History/German History on Film, edited by Sandra Frieden, Richard W. McCormick, Vibeke R. Petersen, and Laurie Melissa Vogelsang, Oxford, 1993.

* * *

Jutta Brückner's 1980 film Years of Hunger arises directly out of the efflorescence of feminism experienced in West Germany in the late 1970s. The title of the film refers to the social, spiritual, and psychological deprivation of the postwar decade, and also alludes to the eating disorder experienced by the film's protagonist, Ursula.

The film commences in 1953, the era known in Germany as "The Economic Miracle." While the (West) German economy was expanding at an astonishingly rapid rate, the populace, after the hardships of World War II, became increasingly enchanted by consumerism. Years of Hunger focuses on family unit that yearns for the profits of the postwar era—better housing, new appliances, smarter clothing, in short, the accoutrements of petit-bourgeois existence. At the same time, their household is engulfed by an equally pervasive, but more insidious product of the war. There is almost complete silence about the war, the fascists regime, and the Holocaust. Ursula, the adolescent only child of the family becomes the focal point for the dis-ease of both the family, and by extension, of Germany itself. The notion of suppression is further implanted by Brückner's intercutting of documentary footage of brutal police containment of pro-communist uprisings that punctuated the period.

Years of Hunger represents one popular type of feminist filmmaking, the koerperfilme, or body film, which treats women's issues such as abortion, menstruation, birth, and body image. These issues are deeply tied to ideas about identity and family. Near the beginning of Years of Hunger, Ursula experiences her first menstruation, an event that is acknowledged by the women in her family with contradictory reactions. (It was also apparently a struggle for Brückner to be able to display a sanitary napkin on screen, no less a bloody one, even the [male] cameraperson objected to filming the scene. {Harbord, p. 53.}) Ursula is told by her mother that "it's nice to be a woman," but at the same time, told her activities are now restricted—she must no longer play with boys, bathe while menstruating, or change her underclothes. (Kosta in Frieden and others, p. 251.) In general, silence surrounds the process. But Ursula—like any adolescent—is full of questions, which her mother avoids, suggesting they will be answered in her biology class. Ursula is depicted as thoroughly ill-at-ease with her body and her blossoming sexuality. Her mother suppresses her daughter's natural instincts at every turn, refusing to let her engage in normal teenage activities, particularly those which might involve sexual contact of the mildest kind. Her mother's attitude toward sexuality is extreme. After making love with her husband—which she clearly performs as a duty—she douches in the bathtub (another of the film's confrontational images), and says, "we should be able to tear out our ovaries." Ursula is taught to hate and disown who and what she is. As Ursula suffers under her mother's rigid surveillance, she becomes more isolated, depressed, and self-destructive. Desperately longing for self-confirmation, she seeks solace in nighttime secret eating binges, and the use of laxatives. Quickly, she moves on to other forms of self-mutilation, in a powerful wish to obliterate her own body. Her negative perception of her physicality, sexuality, and self-image achieve a nadir when her first sexual experience becomes a quasi-rape. She meets and empathizes with an Algerian soldier who lifts his caftan to reveal his war wounds—doubling Ursula's less visible wounds. When she rejects his sexual advances he blackmails her, saying, "You don't like colored people?" His victimization becomes hers, as he forces himself on her. The link between internalized, personal, and sociopolitical oppression is made clear. The silence and suppression of questions concerning Germany's fascist past, which return obsessively throughout the film, are conflated with Ursula's growing neuroses about her body and identity; they become part of her personal history. The inaccessibility of Ursula's mother—as a loving body or role model—becomes a metaphor for the silence of the German state apparatus. Ursula's mother rejects her "sick" child, replicating the Nazi repudiation and eradication of the mentally and physically ill. Eventually, Ursula attempts suicide by consumption, eating and drinking pills, food, and whiskey, a representation of simultaneous lack and plenitude that addresses the psychic and economic condition of the 1950s in West Germany. The film ends with the girl's photograph being annihilated by flames. But we know, because the film is narrated by the adult Ursula, that the child has survived her crucible intact. It is a powerful image, but one which suggests the beginning of healing.

Brückner's strongly autobiographical work (Harbord, p. 51) is thematically provocative; it is a hallmark study, as well, of eating disorders, which, to my knowledge, had never received treatment in a film prior to Years of Hunger. It is also a formally interesting work that interweaves documentary (shots of nuclear test sites, beauty contests through which we witness the social pressure of the adolescent Ursula to model herself after culturally acceptable images of beauty—and footage of pro-communist riots) with the film's fictive world, voice-over narration, nursery rhymes, poetry, extracts from dime-store romance novels, interior monologues, day dream/fantasy sequences, that create a complex access to the narrative material. Years of Hunger creates a rich tapestry that examines an apocalyptic experience that is at once personal and political.

—Carole Zucker

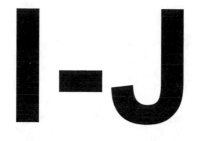

I-J

INDIA SONG

France, 1975
Director: Marguerite Duras

Production: Sunchild, Les Films Armorial, S. Damiani and A. Cavaglione; color, 35mm. Released 1975.

Producer: Stephane Tchalgaldjeff; **screenplay:** Marguerite Duras; **photography:** Bruno Nuytten; **editor:** Solange Leprince; **sound:** Michel Vionnet; **original music:** Carlos D'Alessio, recording at the ORTF: Gaston Sylvestre, Beethoven selection: Gerard Fremy, "India Song Blues" interpreted by: Raoul Verez.

Cast: Delphine Seyrig (*Anne-Marie Stretter*); Michel Lonsdale (*Vice-Counsel of France*); Matthieu Carriere (*Young Attaché to the Ambassador*); Didier Flamand (*Young Escort to Stretter*); Claude Mann (*Michael Richardson*); Vernon Dobtcheff (*Georges Crawn*); Claude Juan (*A Guest*); Satasinh Manila (*Voice of the Beggar*); Nicole Hiss, Monique Simonet, Viviane Forrester, Dionys Mascolo, and Marguerite Duras (*Voices of Time*); François Lebrun, Benoit Jacquot, Nicole-Lise Bernheim, Kevork Kutudjan, Daniel Dobbels, Jean-Claude Biette, Marie-Odile Briot, and Pascal Kane (*Voices from the Reception*).

Publications

Script

Duras, Marguerite, *India Song: Texte—theatre—filme,* Paris, 1973; translated as *India Song,* New York, 1976.

Books

Bernheim, Nicole-Lise, *Marguerite Duras tourne un film,* Paris, 1976.

Ropars-Wuilleumier, Marie-Claire, *La Texte divisé,* Paris, 1981.

Trastulli, Daniela, *Dalla parola all imagine: Viaggio nel cinema di Marguerite Duras,* Geneva, 1982.

Borgomano, Madeleine, *L'Ecriture filmique de Marguerite Duras,* Paris, 1985.

Brossard, Jean-Pierre, editor, *Marguerite Duras: Cineaste, écrivain,* La Chaux-de-Fonde, Switzerland, 1985.

Guers-Villate, Yvonne, *Continuité/discontinuité de l'oeuvre durassienne,* Brussels, 1985.

Articles

Clouzot, C., in *Ecran* (Paris), April 1975.
Amiel, M., in *Cinéma* (Paris), June 1975.

Moskowitz, G., in *Variety* (New York), 18 June 1975.

Amengual, Barthélemy, "Les Yeuxs fertiles," in *Positif* (Paris), July/August 1975.

Bonitzer, Pierre, in *Cahiers du Cinéma* (Paris), July/August 1975.

Lanol, A., in *Jeune Cinéma* (Paris), July/August 1975.

Dawson, Jan, "*India Song,* a Chant of Love and Death: Marguerite Duras Interviewed," in *Film Comment* (New York), November/December 1975.

Clarens, Carlos, in *Sight and Sound* (London), Winter 1975-76.

Tarantino, M., interview with Marguerite Duras, in *Take One* (Montreal), no. 4, 1976.

"Marguerite Duras," in *Film en Televisie* (Brussels), November 1976.

McWilliams, D., in *Wide Angle* (Athens, Ohio), no. 4, 1977.

Straram, P., "Tanner and Duras," in *Cinéma Quebec* (Montreal), no. 10, 1977.

Pym, John, in *Monthly Film Bulletin* (London), November 1977.

Schepelern, P., in *Kosmorama* (Copenhagen), Summer 1978.

"*India Song* Issue" of *Avant-Scène du Cinéma* (Paris), 1 April 1979.

Escudero, I., in *Cinema 2002* (Madrid), October 1979.

Forster, A., "Marguerite Duras," in *Skrien* (Amsterdam), September 1980.

Duras, Marguerite, and E. Lyon, in *Camera Obscura* (Berkeley), Fall 1980.

De Kuyper, E., in *Skrien* (Amsterdam), May 1981.

Undercut (London), nos. 2-5, August 1981/July 1982.

Porte, M., "The Places of Marguerite Duras," in *Enclitic* (Minneapolis), Fall 1983.

Loutti, M. A., "Duras' India," in *Literature Film Quarterly* (Salisbury, Maryland), vol. 14, no. 3, 1986.

Murphy, C. J., "Duras' New Narrative Regions: The Role of Desire in the Films and Novels of Marguerite Duras," in *Literature Film Quarterly* (Salisbury, Maryland), vol. 14, no. 3, 1986.

Holmlund, C. A., "Displacing Limits of Difference: Gender, Race, and Colonialism in Edward Said and Homi Bhabha's Theoretical Models and Marguerite Duras's Experimental Films," in *Quarterly Review of Film and Video* (New York), nos. 1-3, 1991.

Williams, B., "Splintered Perspectives: Counterpoint and Subjectivity in the Modernist Film Narrative," in *Film Criticism* (Meadville, Pennsylvania), no. 2, 1991.

* * *

India Song is radical in both form and content. Like Alain Resnais's *L'année dernière à Marienbad,* Marguerite Duras's film offers an ambiguity of narrative—a type of enigma which paradoxically calls for a reading and yet makes any reading tentative. The film asks, who is Anne-Marie Stretter, the protagonist? What is her relation to men? To India? Or to a beggar woman whose destiny somehow parallels her own? In answering these questions or, more precisely, in eluding any definitive answer, the film expresses some important feminist perspectives while making innovations in film narrative.

India Song

Duras, in this film, finally puts into full practice what Sergei Eisenstein posed in theory 45 years earlier—non-synchronous sound. She separates the verbal track of the film from the visual track in such a way that either the narrator or the dialogue is over-voiced with images that do not correspond on a simple story level. Both the verbal and visual tracks offer us fragmented and disparate pieces of the puzzle of Anne-Marie Stretter that the viewer must reassemble.

Duras has structured the plot in layers. Madame Stretter, wife of the French Ambassador to colonial India, has a doppelgänger in an insane beggar woman who haunts the embassy gardens. While we never see the woman, we hear her distant off-camera cries. Often these cries are juxtaposed with the restrained stance and expression of Madame Stretter. It is as if these cries spring from Madame Stretter's inner self, which has no outlet in the oppressive society she inhabits. The beggar woman, whom we learn has followed Madame Stretter from French Indo-China, perhaps is emblematic of India or other lands burdened by European imperialism; her cries may also be theirs.

A sense of the oppressive lends unity to the film. While we never see colonial India beyond the embassy walls, Duras conveys, through actors' movements and details in the mise-en-scène, the oppressively humid atmosphere. Colonialism is shown oppressing not only the Indians but the Europeans who seem in power. There is a double meaning in Madame Stretter's sexual enslavement of the men around her—all members of the apparent ruling-class. She and India are ineluctable forces that elude and, even to some degree, control the male hierarchy which only seems to oppress them.

Duras explores stasis in all of its forms and ramifications. The characters often remain immobile under the influence of both the sultry atmosphere and class-imposed decorum. *India Song* treats death and life at once, or more precisely, death in life; for Madame Stretter lives a death amid a mise-en-scène filled with funeral objects and flowers. Further, since sound and visuals do not match in a realistic sense, narration and dialogue seem something vaguely heard from beyond the tomb.

Interlacing the destiny of one woman with another and then comparing their situation to nations occupied by foreigners suggests that *India Song* be read as a film about political oppression on all levels—from personal to national. While some might find Duras's view—

that women and, by extension, nations are able to transcend oppression—somewhat naive, the innovative techniques she uses gives this work a haunting quality beyond mere polemics.

—Rodney Farnsworth

IRENE

American costume designer

Born: Irene Lentz in Montana, 1901. **Family:** Married the screenwriter Elliot Gibbons. **Career:** 1932—first costume designs for film *The Animal Kingdom*; 1942-50—chief designer for MGM; 1950—formed own design manufacturing company, with some freelance film work in early 1960s. **Died:** (Suicide) in Hollywood, 15 November 1962.

Films as Costume Designer

1932 *The Animal Kingdom* (E. H. Griffith) (co)
1933 *Goldie Gets Along* (St. Clair); *Flying Down to Rio* (Freeland) (co)
1936 *The Unguarded Hour* (Wood)
1937 *Vogues of 1938* (Cummings) (co); *Shall We Dance* (M. Sandrich); *Topper* (McLeod) (co)
1938 *Algiers* (Cromwell); *Merrily We Live* (McLeod) (co); *There Goes My Heart* (McLeod); *Trade Winds* (Garnett) (co); *Vivacious Lady* (Stevens) (co); *You Can't Take It with You* (Capra) (co); *Blockade* (Dieterle); *Service De Luxe* (R. V. Lee)
1939 *Bachelor Mother* (Kanin); *Eternally Yours* (Garnett); *Intermezzo* (Ratoff); *Topper Takes a Trip* (McLeod); *Midnight* (Leisen) (co); *The Housekeeper's Daughter* (Roach); *In Name Only* (Cromwell) (co)
1940 *Arise My Love* (Leisen) (co); *Lucky Partners* (Milestone) (co); *Seven Sinners* (Garnett) (co); *The House Across the Bay* (Mayo); *He Stayed for Breakfast* (Hall) (co); *Too Many Husbands* (Ruggles)
1941 *That Uncertain Feeling* (Lubitsch); *Skylark* (M. Sandrich) (co); *Sundown* (Hathaway) (co); *Escape to Glory (Submarine Zone)* (Brahm); *Bedtime Story* (Hall); *This Thing Called Love* (Hall); *Mr. and Mrs. Smith* (Hitchcock)
1942 *The Lady Is Willing* (Leisen); *The Palm Beach Story* (P. Sturges); *The Talk of the Town* (Stevens); *They All Kissed the Bride* (Hall); *To Be or Not to Be* (Lubitsch) (co); *Twin Beds* (Whelan) (co); *Take a Letter, Darling (The Green Eyed Woman)* (Leisen) (co); *Reunion in France (Mademoiselle France)* (Dassin); *You Were Never Lovelier* (Seiter); *Tales of Manhattan* (Duvivier) (co); *The Wife Takes a Flyer (A Yank in Dutch)* (Wallace)
1943 *Three Hearts for Julia* (Thorpe); *Song of Russia* (Ratoff); *The Heavenly Body* (Hall); *Cry Havoc* (Thorpe); *Lost Angel* (Rowland); *The Youngest Profession* (Buzzell); *Above Suspicion* (Thorpe); *Thousands Cheer* (Sidney); *Slightly Dangerous* (Ruggles); *The Human Comedy* (C. Brown); *The Man from Down Under* (Leonard); *Dr. Gillespie's Criminal Case* (Goldbeck); *Whistling in Brooklyn* (Simon); *Cabin in the Sky* (Minnelli) (co); *Assignment in Britanny* (Conway) (co); *Du Barry Was a Lady* (Del Ruth) (co); *Swing Shift Maisie (The Girl in Overalls)* (McLeod); *Best

Foot Forward (Buzzell) (co); *No Time for Love* (Leisen) (co); *Broadway Rhythm* (Del Ruth) (co)
1944 *Between Two Women* (Goldbeck); *The Seventh Cross* (Zinnemann); *Two Girls and a Sailor* (Thorpe); *An American Romance* (K. Vidor); *Nothing but Trouble* (Taylor); *Andy Hardy's Blonde Trouble* (Seitz); *A Guy Named Joe* (Fleming); *See Here, Private Hargrove* (Ruggles); *Maisie Goes to Reno* (Beaumont); *Kismet* (Dieterle); *Mrs. Parkington* (Garnett) (co); *The White Cliffs of Dover* (C. Brown) (co); *Meet the People* (Riesner) (co); *Two Girls and a Sailor* (Thorpe) (co); *Bathing Beauty* (Sidney) (co); *Gaslight (Murder in Thornton Square)* (Cukor) (co); *Three Men in White* (Goldbeck); *The Thin Man Goes Home* (Thorpe) (co); *Marriage Is a Private Affair* (Leonard) (co); *Blonde Fever* (Whorf); *Thirty Seconds over Tokyo* (LeRoy) (co); *Music for Millions* (Koster) (co); *Dragon Seed* (Conway and Bucquet) (co); *National Velvet* (C. Brown) (co)
1945 *The Picture of Dorian Gray* (Lewin) (co); *Adventure* (Fleming); *The Sailor Takes a Wife* (Whorf) (co); *Weekend at the Waldorf* (Leonard) (co); *This Man's Navy* (Wellman) (co); *Keep Your Powder Dry* (Buzzell) (co); *Anchors Aweigh* (Sidney) (co); *The Clock (Under the Clock)* (Minnelli) (co); *Without Love* (Bucquet) (co); *Son of Lassie* (Simon); *Valley of Decision* (Garnett) (co); *Thrill of a Romance* (Thorpe) (co); *Twice Blessed* (Beaumont) (co); *The Hidden Eye* (Whorf) (co); *Our Vines Have Tender Grapes* (Rowland) (co); *Abbott and Costello in Hollywood* (Simon) (co); *Dangerous Partners* (Cahn) (co); *She Went to the Races* (Goldbeck); *What Next Corporal Hargrove?* (Thorpe)
1946 *Up Goes Maisie (Up She Goes)* (Beaumont); *Bad Bascomb* (Simon); *Easy to Wed* (Buzzell) (co); *Holiday in Mexico* (Sidney) (co); *Undercurrent* (Minnelli) (co); *Two Smart People* (Dassin) (co); *Courage of Lassie* (Wilcox); *Boys' Ranch* (Rowland); *Lady in the Lake* (Montgomery); *Love Laughs at Andy Hardy* (Goldbeck); *The Secret Heart* (Leonard); *No Leave No Love* (Martin); *The Green Years* (Saville) (co); *Faithful in My Fashion* (Salkow) (co); *The Postman Always Rings Twice* (Garnett) (co); *Little Mister Jim* (Zinnemann) (co); *Three Wise Fools* (Buzzell) (co); *Undercurrent* (Minnelli); *My Brother Talks to Horses* (Zinneman) (co); *The Mighty McGurk* (Waters) (co); *Till the Clouds Roll By* (Whorf); (co); *The Yearling* (C. Brown) (co); *The Harvey Girls* (Sidney); *The Hoodlum Saint* (Taurog) (co); *Ziegfeld Follies* (Minnelli) (co)
1947 *Fiesta* (Thorpe) (co); *This Time for Keeps* (Thorpe) (co); *The Arnelo Affair* (Obeler); *The Beginning of the End* (Taurog); *Undercover Maisie* (Beaumont); *Dark Delusion* (Goldbeck); *High Barbaree* (Conway); *Desire Me* (Cukor and others—uncredited); *The Hucksters* (Conway); *Cynthia (The Full Rich Life)* (Leonard); *Merton of the Movies* (Alton) (co); *Living in a Big Way* (La Cava) (co); *Song of Love* (Franklin and Marion) (co); *The Romance of Rosy Ridge* (Rowland) (co); *Song of the Thin Man* (Buzzell) (co); *The Unfinished Dance* (Koster) (co); *Green Dolphin Street* (Saville) (co); *10th Avenue Angel* (Rowland); *If Winter Comes* (Saville); *Cass Timberlane* (Sidney)
1948 *Summer Holiday* (Mamoulian); *Three Daring Daughters* (Wilcox); *State of the Union* (Capra); *Easter Parade* (Walters) (co); *Julia Misbehaves* (Conway); *On an Island with You* (Thorpe); *B.F.'s Daughter* (Leonard)

Irene

1949   *The Bribe* (Leonard); *The Great Sinner* (Siodmak) (co);
        Neptune's Daughter (Buzzell); *Malaya* (Thorpe) (co); *The
        Barkleys of Broadway* (Walters); *In the Good Old Sum-
        mertime* (Leonard) (co); *The Sun Comes Up* (Thorpe);
        The Shadow on the Wall (Jackson); *The Scene of the Crime*
        (Rowland)
1950   *Please Believe Me* (Taurog); *Key to the City* (Sidney)
1960   *Midnight Lace* (Miller)
1961   *Lover Come Back* (Delbert Mann)
1963   *A Gathering of Eagles* (Delbert Mann) (co)

Film as Actress

1922   *A Tailor Made Man* (De Grasse)

Publications on Irene

Articles

Chierichetti, David, in *Hollywood Costume Design*, New York, 1976.
Leese, Elizabeth, in *Costume Design in the Movies*, New York, 1976.
LaVine, Robert, in *In a Glamorous Fashion*, New York, 1980.

* * *

Irene's first work in Hollywood was as a movie extra, but after
studying at the Wolfe School of Design, she opened a dress shop at
the University of California, Los Angeles, which attracted the likes
of Lupe Velez and Dolores Del Rio. The actresses loved Irene's
elegant evening gowns and gladly recommended her to their celebrity friends. Following a trip to Europe, where she studied the couturier collections in search of inspiration, Irene opened an even larger
boutique, catering to scores of Hollywood starlets. Her reputation
soon landed her a position as head of Bullock's Wilshire Custom
Salon, and while there she often received commissions to dress such
clients as Ginger Rogers, Myrna Loy, Rosalind Russell, Irene Dunne,
and Claudette Colbert for their film roles. Her designs lent the actresses
the level of taste and sophistication they sought to exude, both privately
and on screen, and, in turn, the starlets were willing to champion Irene's
work in film. By 1942 Irene had signed a seven-year contract with
MGM to be Adrian's successor as executive designer

Irene's film specialty was an extension of her boutique work—the
fabulous evening gown. Her soufflé gowns were soft and classic,
draped elegantly, and would cling in such a way as to accentuate the
flowing lines of the women she dressed. Those women were often
likened to moving sculptures, and are best represented by Claudette
Colbert in *The Palm Beach Story* and Rita Hayworth in *You Were
Never Lovelier.* Irene was not limited to one style, though. Among
her most famous works was Lana Turner's midriff blouse/turban/hot
pants ensemble from *The Postman Always Rings Twice.*

Irene was one of the most prolific designers in the screwball
comedy genre. She dressed the actresses in confident-yet-feminine
outfits that the strong female characters in these films begged for,
such as with Carole Lombard in *Mr. and Mrs. Smith* and Claudette
Colbert in *Midnight.* In addition, Irene perfected the sensible career
gal look, which she favored for herself. Her suits were worn with
flair by Rosalind Russell in *Take a Letter, Darling* and Joan Crawford
in *They All Kissed the Bride.*

Unfortunately, Irene's costumes had a reputation for being quite
costly. A custom tailored Irene gown sold for double what a Paris

original of equal quality did, and her film designs were often just as
extravagant. One failed outlandish outfit for *Kismet* had Marlene
Dietrich wearing pants made entirely of hundreds of tiny gold chains,
a creation that fell apart once Dietrich began performing in them. The
mistake raised the ire of Irene's boss, Louis B. Mayer, who felt his
executive designer wasted too much money. Irene's penchant for
costly designs is very apparent in her period dresses. Because she
was not comfortable with historical costumes, her designs were as
indicative of the times Irene lived as of the times they were meant to
depict. *The Great Sinner,* which took place in Germany in the 1800s,
featured elegant gowns in the soft fabrics popular in the 1940s, not
the stiff silk used in the era. Period pictures dressed by Irene (such as
the Oscar nominated *Mrs. Parkington*) were noted for their asymmetrical rayon crepe gowns draped with layered chiffon and other
couture fabrics, resembling creations out of her own boutiques. But
what Irene lacked in authenticity, she more than made up for in
beauty, with her sharp inventiveness in costuming.

Obviously suited for more personal and singular design work,
and convinced her stint with MGM had been a mistake, Irene left
the field of costume design almost completely in 1949, preferring
to devote her full attentions to her boutiques, which she had
launched in 1947. She was lured back on a few occasions, most
notably to dress Doris Day in a couple of films in the early 1960s.
In *Midnight Lace,* Irene created a very popular and memorable
black-lace negligee for Day to wear, earning the designer an Academy Award nomination. In *Lover Come Back,* Irene furthered
Day's cheerleader chic image with more white hats, dresses, and
gloves, as well as favorable use of furs. Her last film *A Gathering
of Eagles* was completed shortly before her suicide in 1962. By
the time Irene leapt from the Knickerbocker Hotel, the era of
glamour which she had helped clothe so immaculately was long
gone.

—John E. Mitchell

JAKUBOWSKA, Wanda
Polish director

Born: Warsaw, 10 October 1907. **Education:** Studied architecture
and arts. **Career:** 1930—co-founder of Society of Devotees of the
Artistic Film (START); 1930s—made short documentary films;
1937—co-founder of the Cooperative of Film Authors (SAF); 1939—
directed first feature film, *On the Neman River*—which has been
lost; 1942—arrested by German Nazis and imprisoned in concentration camps Oswiecim (Auschwitz) and Ravensbrück; 1947—first
feature film after the war, *The Last Stop*; 1949-74—lecturer at Lódz
Film School; 1955-68—artistic director of START film unit.

Films as Director

1932   "Impresje jesienne" ("Autumn Impressions") ep. of *Reportaz
        nr 1 (Reportage no. 1)* (co-d with Cekalski and Zarzycki—
        doc, short); *Morze (The Sea)* (co-d with Cekalski and
        Wohl—doc, short)
1934   *Budujemy (We Are Building)* (co-d with Cekalski, Emmer,
        and Maliniak—doc, short)
1937   *Ulica Edisona (Edison Street)* (doc, short)

1939   *Nad Niemnem* (*On the Neman River*) (co-d with Szolowski—unreleased)
1946   *Budujemy nowe wsi* (*We Are Building New Villages*) (doc, short)
1947   *Ostatni etap* (*The Last Stop; The Last Stage*) (+ co-sc)
1953   *Zolnierz zwyciestwa* (*The Soldier of Victory*) (+ sc)
1954   *Opowiesc Atlantycka* (*The Atlantic Story*)
1956   *Pozegnanie z diablem* (*Farewell to the Devil*) (+ co-sc)
1957   *Król Macius I* (*King Matthias I; King Matthew I*)
1960   *Spotkania w mroku* (*Begegnung im Zwielicht; Encounters in the Dark*) (+ co-sc); *Historia wspólczesna* (*Modern Story*)
1963   *Koniec naszego swiata* (*The End of Our World*) (+ sc)
1965   *Goraca linia* (*The Hot Line*)
1971   *150 na godzine* (*150 km per Hour*)
1978   *Bialy mazur* (*The White Mazurka; Dance in Chains*) (+ sc)
1986   *Zaproszenie* (*The Invitation*) (+ sc)
1988   *Kolory kochania* (*The Colors of Love*) (+ co-sc)

Other Film

1962   *Wielka Wielksza Najwielksza* (*The Great Big World and Little Children*) (Sokolowska) (production supervisor)

Publications by Jakubowska

Articles

Interview in *Film und Fernsehen* (Berlin), September 1975.
"Sprawa poczucia odpowiedzialnosci," in *Kino* (Warsaw), January 1976.
"Um die Freihat—das heisst um Polen: ein Gespraech mit Wanda Jakubowska," interview with W. Wertenstein, in *Film und Fernsehen* (Berlin), vol. 7, no. 10, 1979.
"Wiernosc sobie: rozmowa z Wanda Jakubowska," interview with B. Mruklik, in *Kino* (Warsaw), May 1985.
"Ja po prostu swojej partii ufalam," interview in *Kino* (Warsaw), August 1991.

Publications on Jakubowska

Books

Historia filmu polskiego I-V, Warsaw, 1966-85.
Ryszard Koniczek: Polski film fabularny, 1947-67, Warsaw, 1967.
Janicki, Stanislaw, *Film polski od A do Z,* Warsaw, 1977.
Kinematografia w Polsce ludowej, Warsaw, 1980.
Kuhn, Annette, *Women's Pictures: Feminism and Cinema,* London, 1982.
Twórcy polskiego filmu, Warsaw, 1984.
Quart, Barbara Koenig, *Women Directors: The Emergence of a New Cinema,* New York, 1988.
Balski, Grzegorz, *Directory of Eastern European Film-Makers and Film, 1945-1991,* Westport, Connecticut, 1992.
Attwood, Lynn, editor, *Red Women on the Silver Screen: Soviet Women and Cinema from the Beginning to the End of the Communist Era,* London, 1993.
Foster, Gwendolyn Audrey, *Women Film Directors: An International Bio-Critical Dictionary,* Westport, Connecticut, 1995.

Articles

Armatys, L., "Wanda Jakubowska," in *Polish Film Polnaise* (Warsaw), no. 2, 1979.

"Wanda Jakubowska," in *Avant-Scène Cinéma* (Paris), December 1983.
Piatek, W., "*Zaproszenie,*" in *Filmowy Serwis Prasowy* (Warsaw), vol. 32, no. 8, 1986.
Jewiewicki, W., "Polscy filmowcy I Oswiecim," in *Kino* (Warsaw), September 1987.
Malatynska, M., "Portret slowem rysowany," in *Kino* (Warsaw), July/August 1994.
Liebman, Stuart, and Leonard Quart, "Lost and Found: Wanda Jakubowska's *The Last Stop,*" in *Cineaste* (New York), Fall 1996.

* * *

Wanda Jakubowska decided to become a film director at a time when this occupation was rather unusual for a woman. It was even more unusual in a country such as Poland where the economical and technical conditions for film development were lacking. In spite of that fact, towards the end of the silent film many people appeared who were enchanted by the medium of film and at the same time realized its social and artistic power. Those enthusiasts, Jakubowska among them, founded an avant-garde group, START (Society of Devotees of the Artistic Film), which began to bring to life—from the theoretical to the practical—their ideas of how to elevate the film. They found their models in the Soviet documentary film, especially those of Dziga Vertov, and later within the British documentary school.

Under the influence of those trends, Jakubowska shot her first short films and her first feature film, *On the Neman River.* The latter never reached an audience. The premiere should have taken place in September 1939, the very month that World War II began with the attack on Poland. In the apocalypse that followed, the film was entirely lost. Jakubowska was soon arrested and imprisoned in Auschwitz and Ravensbrück.

Shortly after the war she directed her most famous film, *The Last Stop,* which was based on the horror of the concentration camps. It was one of the first films about the fascist "death factories." Jakubowska had started to work on the film in 1946, at a time when there were still rows of prison houses, when an Auschwitz commander waited for his verdict, and when the new and more horrible crimes of fascism were still being revealed at the Nuremberg Tribunal. Although the recent past was alive, Jakubowska was able to keep her recollections in check and collect facts using a strict selection. She consciously refused to shock spectators with drastic scenes and decided to convey the testimony of modest and nonpathetic heroes who even under the pressure of suffering and fear managed to keep their human dignity and sensitivity. On the other hand she did not conceal the truth about those who had been broken by a cruel system. A few trite, unbelievable motives and too pathetic an end disturb a bit the integrity of the film.

But for all that, *The Last Stop* is a significant piece of art born out of real suffering, from love of people and the desire to fight to stay alive. Thanks to this desire Jakubowska survived: "I might owe my life to my desire to shoot this film. This desire saved me from going through my experience in Auschwitz too subjectively, it allowed me to perceive everything around me as a special kind of documentation" (*Historia filmu polskiego III* 1966-85).

Jakubowska devoted all her active life to film. For decades she was active in various organizations, involved with education, and continued in film production. At the same time she stayed faithful to the main principles of START, which aimed to create socially useful and committed films. Following *The Last Stop,* she unfortunately was not able to realize these principles with a sufficient artistic might.

The gigantic two-part epopee about General Swierczewski (*The Soldier of Victory*) was schematic and false, tributary to the aesthetics of socialist realism. Her effort to express up-to-date contemporary problems was converted to a direct political proclamation (*Modern Story*). Even the films where she evoked her experience from the war lacked an artistic persuasiveness and impressiveness. Perhaps only *King Matthias I* is worth mentioning for its design.

Only *The Last Stop* guarantees a place for Jakubowska in film history—this is more significant than it might seem. With this film, Jakubowska opened the way for Polish film to reach the world. Only in its wake came the "Polish film school" of the fifties and sixties.

—Blazena Urgošíková

JAWS
USA, 1975
Director: Steven Spielberg
Editor: Verna Fields

Production: Universal Pictures; Technicolor, 35mm; running time: 124 minutes. Released 20 June 1975. Filmed summer 1974 on location on Martha's Vineyard.

Producers: Richard D. Zanuck and David Brown with William S. Gilmore Jr.; **screenplay:** Peter Benchley and Carl Gottlieb, from the novel by Benchley; **production design:** Joe Alves; **photography:** Bill Butler; **editor:** Verna Fields; **set decorator:** John Dwyer; **special effects:** Robert A. Mattey; **sound:** Robert L. Hoyt, Roger Herman, Earl Madery, and John Carter; **music:** John Williams; **technical adviser:** Manfred Zendar.

Cast: Roy Scheider (*Martin Brody*); Robert Shaw (*Quint*); Richard Dreyfuss (*Matt Hooper*); Lorraine Gary (*Ellen Brody*); Murray Hamilton (*Larry Vaughan*); Carl Gottlieb (*Meadows*); Jeffrey Kramer (*Hendricks*); Susan Backlinie (*Chrissie Watkins*); Jonathan Filley (*Cassidy*); Ted Grossman (*Estuary victim*); Chris Rebello (*Michael Brody*); Jay Mello (*Sean Brody*); Lee Fierro (*Mrs. Kintner*); Jeffrey Voorhees (*Alex Kintner*); Craig Kingsbury (*Ben Gardner*); Dr. Robert Nevin (*Medical examiner*); Peter Benchley (*Interviewer*).

Awards: Academy Awards for Best Sound, Best Editing, and Best Original Score, 1975.

Publications

Books

Gottlieb, Carl, *The* Jaws *Log,* New York, 1975.
Blake, Edith, *On Location on Martha's Vineyard: The Making of the Movie* Jaws, New York, 1975.
Monaco, James, *American Film Now: The People, the Power, the Money, the Movies,* Oxford, 1979.
Pye, Michael, and Lynda Myles, *The Movie Brats: How the Film Generation Took Over Hollywood,* London, 1979.
Daly, David Anthony, *A Comparison of Exhibition and Distribution Patterns in Three Recent Feature Motion Pictures,* New York, 1980.

Kolker, Robert Phillip, *A Cinema of Loneliness: Penn, Kubrick, Scorsese, Spielberg, Altman,* Oxford, 1980; revised edition, 1988.
Crawley, Tony, *The Steven Spielberg Story,* London, 1983.
Goldau, Antje, and Hans Helmut Prinzler, *Spielberg: Filme als Spielzeug,* Berlin, 1985.
Mott, Donald R., and Cheryl McAllister Saunders, *Steven Spielberg,* Boston, 1986.
Smith, Thomas G., *Industrial Light and Magic: The Art of Special Effects,* London, 1986.
Weiss, Ulli, *Das neue Hollywood: Francis Ford Coppola, Steven Spielberg, Martin Scorsese,* Munich, 1986.
Godard, Jean-Pierre, *Spielberg,* Paris, 1987.
Sinyard, Neil, *The Films of Steven Spielberg,* London, 1987.

Articles

Riger, R., "On Location with *Jaws*—Tell the Shark We'll Do It One More Time," in *Action* (Los Angeles), July/August 1974.
"What Directors Are Saying," in *Action* (Los Angeles), September/October 1974.
Cribben, M., "On Location with *Jaws*," in *American Cinematographer* (Los Angeles), March 1975.
Murphy, A. D., in *Variety* (New York), 18 June 1975.
Magill, M., in *Films in Review* (New York), August/September 1975.
Shear, D., in *Film Heritage* (Dayton, Ohio), Autumn 1975.
Milne, Tom, in *Monthly Film Bulletin* (London), December 1975.
Monaco, James, in *Sight and Sound* (London), no. 1, 1975-76.
Blacher, R., "Le Point de vue d'un psychiatre sur *Les Dents de la mer*," in *Cinéma* (Paris), April 1976.
Bonitzer, P., and S. Daney, in *Cahiers du Cinéma* (Paris), April/May 1976.
Fieschi, J., "La Religion du monstre," in *Cinématographe* (Paris), April/May 1976.
Paini, D., "Toujours à propos des *Dents de la mer*," in *Cinéma* (Paris), May 1976.
Martin, Marcel, and others, "Vérités et mensonges du cinéma américain," in *Ecran* (Paris), September 1976.
Dagneau, G., in *Revue du Cinéma* (Paris), October 1976.
Cumbow, R. C., "The Great American Eating Machine," in *Movietone News* (Seattle), 11 October 1976.
Michalek, B., in *Kino* (Warsaw), December 1976.
Dworkin, M. S., "In the Teeth of Jaws," in *Ikon* (Milan), January/March 1977.
Kapralov, G., in *Iskusstvo Kino* (Moscow), October 1977.
Caputi, J. E., "Jaws as Patriarchal Myth," in *Journal of Popular Film and Television* (Washington, D.C.), no. 4, 1978.
Verstappen, W., in *Skoop* (Amsterdam), February 1978.
"Readers' Forum," in *Journal of Popular Film and Television* (Washington, D.C.), no. 2, 1979.
Erickson, Glenn, in *Magill's Survey of Cinema 2,* Englewood Cliffs, New Jersey, 1980.
Vega, F., in *Casablanca* (Madrid), July/August 1981.
Fauritte, A., "Super Star Jaws," in *Revue du Cinéma* (Paris), April 1984.
Fried, B., in *Chaplin* (Stockholm), 1985.
Noel, J., "Steven Spielberg (Suite No. 3)," in *Grand Angle* (Mariembourg, Belgium), July 1990.
Sheehan, H., "The Panning of Steven Spielberg," in *Film Comment* (New York), May/June 1992.
Torry, R., "Therapeutic Narrative: *The Wild Bunch, Jaws,* and Vietnam," in *Velvet Light Trap* (Austin, Texas), Spring 1993.

Griffin, Nancy, "In the Grip of *Jaws*," in *Premiere* (New York), October 1995.

* * *

Jaws, directed by Steven Spielberg, was one of the smash-hit summer movies of 1975. Its setting: a normally safe and secure beach community, not unlike countless similar resorts across the world, where vacationers soak up sun, stroll in the sand, and swim in the ocean. Its premise: one such community is instantaneously transformed into a panic-stricken hell when a ravenous killer shark begins dining on the flesh of unsuspecting bathers.

This scenario is established in the film's celebrated opening sequence. Late one evening, an effervescent young woman playfully swims out into the deep. Her youthfulness and attractiveness (not to mention lack of swim wear) might lull the viewer into thinking he is watching an R-rated 1970s beach-party movie. The water is calm; the setting is peaceful, and lit only by moonlight. The woman is shown in a mixture of long shots and close-ups, and from different camera angles. As she swims she is a black silhouette surrounded by deep blue. Then, the music becomes tense. In a flash, she is pulled at by a powerful force beneath her, a force which neither she nor the audience can see. She screams, and attempts to swim away. For a moment, she is able to cling to a buoy before disappearing beneath the blue. Then, in yet another instant, all is again calm. This young American beauty has been transformed into fish-food by the film's villain: an ominous, carnivorous Great White Shark.

Much of the tension in *Jaws* is derived from similar sequences, featuring unruffled soon-to-be victims who are unaware that their lives are about to become violent and terror-filled (if not end altogether). They may not know what is about to befall them, but *we* do, because of the manner in which the film has been directed, edited, scored. For a major part of *Jaws,* the entire shark remains unseen. During subsequent onslaughts, the viewer is made privy to its presence via rhythmically edited subjective camera shots as the shark zooms in on its prey, combined with shots of its various parts. Meanwhile, the graphic bloodletting transpires off-camera; just enough is seen in snippets to terrorize the viewer, with shots of severed hands serving as evidence of the human toll of the shark's attacks.

Some of the connecting shots in *Jaws* are ironic, and even humorous. A short sequence in which the town's mayor persuades its police chief not to close the beaches upon the death of the girl is followed by one of an obese woman wading into the ocean. Then there are the various false alarms that add to the suspense. Shots of swimmers and sunbathers are edited together, accompanied by such beach-sounds as a radio playing, water splashing, and a din of conversation. Suddenly, a dark object approaches a woman floating in the water. Could it be the shark's fin? No, it is instead the top of a bathing cap worn by a man swimming underwater. Later on, a fin is seen heading toward a group of swimmers. There is mass panic, conveyed via close-ups and medium shots of bathers and their torsos and ankles as they rush to safety. Then the "danger" is revealed to be a cardboard fin, carried by two young boys swimming underwater.

Still, the most potent scenes in the first part of *Jaws* are those that end in the deaths of innocent bathers. They come in short bursts: there is calm, then panic and violence, then calm again. In the concluding section, a trio of "experts" and "protectors"—a grizzled shark hunter, a college-educated shark authority, and the police chief—set out to hunt down the killer and soon come face-to-face with their prey. It is here where the shark is first seen in its entirety, and full enormity. This lengthy sequence is fluidly edited, with the visuals, as they are pieced together, telegraphing the action as much as the dialogue or the emotions expressed by the actors. If Alfred Hitchcock's *Psycho* made viewers apprehensive about taking showers, *Jaws* succeeded in making them second-guess their decisions to vacation by the sea. Such was the impact of these two classic thrillers.

Jaws helped cement Steven Spielberg's fame as a director of highly entertaining and thrill-packed blockbusters. An estimable number of them, from *Jaws* through *Jurassic Park,* rank among the highest-grossing films of all time. *Jaws*—Spielberg's second theatrical feature—was his first such success. It was made for $8.5 million, earned $130 million, and until *Star Wars* in 1977 was the all-time top-grossing film. This phenomenal box-office performance helped usher in the age of the Hollywood megabuck movie, and alter the manner in which the industry perceived its business practices.

Without the indispensable contribution of Spielberg's editor, Verna Fields, *Jaws* might not have been such a surefire entertainment. Despite this fact, one would be hard-pressed to find Fields listed in the very same movie encyclopedias that prominently chart the accomplishments of Spielberg. This is not so much the end result of sexism as the pervasive auteurist view that directors and directors alone are responsible for their films, and the contributions of editors, cinematographers, composers, or, lest we forget, screenwriters, are slight at best.

With this in mind, it is imperative to recall that major obstacles hampered the production of *Jaws,* beginning with the inability to function on the part of the mechanical shark that was built for the film. In fact, *Jaws* was 100 days over schedule, and Spielberg almost was replaced during the shoot. While in its various stages of production, there even was a certain apprehension that the film never would be completed, let alone released. Even as it was being previewed, Spielberg still was tinkering with it. At one point, he went about shooting additional footage in Fields's swimming pool. And today, while carefully watching *Jaws* (and replaying its individual scenes) on video, it becomes evident that a considerable number of shots within sequences do not quite match.

And so a question arises: Taking into consideration that so much of Spielberg's footage was disconnected, given the existing pressures during which it was filmed, how much of *Jaws* was "created" by Spielberg and Fields in the editing room, rather than during its filming? Over the years, film historians and critics have offered contradicting answers. Suffice to say that the most authoritative commentary should come from Spielberg himself. In a 20-years-later retrospective on the film, published in *Premiere* magazine, Spielberg observed: "There's no way we could match the shots in postproduction. I just took a big deep breath and accepted the fact that some days the water was rough, some days it was calm in the same sequence. (Cinematographer) Bill Butler did the best he could to even out the shots, and Verna did a great job editing. She's a great film editor. Mother Cutter, we used to call her."

Summarily, the success of *Jaws* as an edge-of-your-seat entertainment, despite its production problems, attests to Verna Fields's editing room acumen. Her editing—she was honored with an Academy Award for her work—is as much a star of *Jaws* as Spielberg's direction, or Bill Butler's cinematography, or John Williams's score, or the solid performances by its cast. One of Fields's rewards for doing such an outstanding job: she was moved up to a senior executive post at Universal Pictures, thus becoming one of the rare female movie executives of the 1970s—and one of the most powerful women in Hollywood.

—Rob Edelman

Jaws

JEAKINS, Dorothy
American costume designer

Born: San Diego, California, 11 January 1914. **Education:** Attended Otis Art Institute, 1931-34; Guggenheim fellowship, to Japan, 1961. **Family:** Married Raymond Eugene Dane, 1940 (divorced 1946), sons: Peter Dane and Stephen Dane. **Career:** Stage and TV designer; 1948—first film as costume designer, *Joan of Arc*; 1967-70—curator of textiles, Los Angeles County Museum of Art. **Awards:** Academy Awards, for *Joan of Arc*, 1948, *Samson and Delilah*, 1950, and *The Night of the Iguana*, 1964. **Died:** In Santa Barbara, California, 21 November 1995.

Films as Costume Designer

1948   *Joan of Arc* (Fleming) (co)
1949   *Samson and Delilah* (C. B. DeMille) (co)
1952   *Belles on Their Toes* (Levin); *The Big Sky* (Hawks); *The Greatest Show on Earth* (C. B. DeMille) (co); *Les Misérables* (Milestone); *Lure of the Wilderness* (Negulesco); *My Cousin Rachel* (Koster); *The Outcasts of Poker Flat* (J. Newman); *Stars and Stripes Forever* (Koster); *Treasure of the Golden Condor* (Daves)
1953   *Beneath the Twelve Mile Reef* (Webb); *City of Bad Men* (H. Jones); *Inferno* (R. W. Baker); *The Kid from Left Field* (H. Jones); *Niagara* (Hathaway); *Titanic* (Negulesco); *White Witch Doctor* (Hathaway)
1954   *Three Coins in the Fountain* (Negulesco)
1956   *Friendly Persuasion* (Wyler)
1957   *The Ten Commandments* (C. B. DeMille) (co)
1958   *South Pacific* (Logan)
1959   *Green Mansions* (M. Ferrer)
1960   *Elmer Gantry* (R. Brooks); *Let's Make Love* (Cukor); *The Unforgiven* (J. Huston)
1961   *The Children's Hour* (Wyler)
1962   *All Fall Down* (Frankenheimer); *The Music Man* (da Costa)
1964   *The Best Man* (Schaffner); *Ensign Pulver* (Logan); *The Night of the Iguana* (J. Huston)
1965   *The Fool Killer* (*Violent Journey*) (Gonzalez); *The Sound of Music* (Wise)
1966   *Any Wednesday* (R. E. Miller); *Hawaii* (G. R. Hill) (+ ro as Hepzibah Hale)
1967   *The Flim-Flam Man* (Kershner); *Reflections in a Golden Eye* (J. Huston)
1968   *Finian's Rainbow* (F. F. Coppola); *The Fixer* (Frankenheimer); *The Stalking Moon* (Mulligan)
1969   *True Grit* (Hathaway)
1970   *Little Big Man* (A. Penn); *The Molly Maguires* (Ritt)
1972   *Fat City* (J. Huston); *Fuzz* (Colla)
1973   *The Iceman Cometh* (Frankenheimer); *The Way We Were* (Pollack) (co)
1974   *Young Frankenstein* (M. Brooks)
1975   *The Hindenburg* (Wise); *The Yakuza* (Pollack)
1977   *Audrey Rose* (Wise)
1978   *The Betsy* (Petrie)
1979   *North Dalls Forty* (Kotcheff); *Love and Bullets* (Rosenberg)
1981   *The Postman Always Rings Twice* (Rafelson); *On Golden Pond* (Rydell)
1987   *The Dead* (*The Dubliners*) (J. Huston)

Publications on Jeakins

Articles

Chierichetti, David, in *Hollywood Costume Design,* New York, 1976.
Obituary, in *Los Angeles Times,* 28 November 1995.
Obituary, in *New York Times,* 30 November 1995.

* * *

Dorothy Jeakins was abandoned by her natural parents for unknown reasons, and had an unhappy childhood. She lived with a foster mother who frequently whipped her and threatened to send her to reform school. Often left alone, as a young child she would roam the streets of Los Angeles and ask people for free food and clothes. She called it a "Dickensian existence." She has described herself as "pathologically shy and neurotically modest," but very secure in her sense of taste and style, with the "sensitive soul of an artist." Perhaps as a result of her shyness, virtually nothing has been written about Jeakins or her impressive film credits.

At Fairfax High School she found plays to be a "sweet escape into fantasy." Encouraged into drama by sympathetic teachers, she discovered her vocation when she visited a costume house and found a means of interpreting the plays she loved through costume. She attended Otis Art Institute on a scholarship and continued to frequent the public library to read and illustrate the characters of plays.

She worked for the WPA at the age of 19 during the Great Depression, and then moved on to Disney studios as an illustrator for $16 a week until a strike left her unemployed. She next became an illustrator of fashion layouts for I. Magnin's advertising department. Eventually a studio art director saw her sketches and hired her as an assistant designer for *Joan of Arc*—her first major film for which she won her first Oscar. (She had also been an assistant to the designer Ernst Dryden for *Dr. Rhythm,* 1938.)

Jeakins had an impressive number of credits, almost equally divided between the theater and motion pictures, and some plays she designed for Broadway she later designed as films, such as *South Pacific* and *The Sound of Music*.

Jeakins's noted specialty was for ethnic and period costumes, and also for her use of color. With each film Jeakins considered how she could use costume in a new way, and when searching for inspiration for the color scheme would consider such natural elements as "wet stones or peonies or pullet-eggs beige and white or Chinese-coolie blues." The designer Edith Head once commented that Jeakins had a particularly good eye for color. On a separate occasion, Jeakins said candidly of Edith Head that "her work is extremely mediocre ... but Edith deserves a lot of credit for hanging in there." Jeakins was also budget-conscious when she worked on films and could make elegant costumes with inexpensive muslin. As a designer, she said of herself, "I'm dependable, experienced, organized, aesthetic, creative."

—Susan Perez Prichard

JEANNE DIELMAN, 23 QUAI DU COMMERCE, 1080 BRUXELLES
Belgium-France, 1975
Director: Chantal Akerman

Production: Paradise Films (Brussels) and Unité Trois (Paris), in association with Le Ministère de la Culture française du

Belgique; color; running time: 201 minutes; length: 7,232 feet. Released 1975.

Producers: Evelyne Paul and Corinne Jenart; **screenplay:** Chantal Akerman; **assistant directors:** Marilyn Watelet, Serge Brodsky, and Marianne de Muylder; **photography:** Babette Mangolte; **editor:** Patricia Canino; **assistant editors:** Catherine Huhardeaux and Martine Chicot; **sound editor:** Alain Marchall; **sound recordists:** Benie Deswarte and Françoise Van Thienen; **sound re-recordist:** Jean-Paul Loublier; **art director:** Philippe Graff; **assistant art editor:** Jean-Pol Ferbus; **music extract:** "Bagatelle for Piano," No. 27, op. 126 by Ludwig van Beethoven.

Cast: Delphine Seyrig (*Jeanne Dielman*); Jan Decorte (*Sylvain Dielman*); Henri Storck (*1st Caller*); Jacques Doniol-Valcroze (*2nd Caller*); Yves Bical (*3rd Caller*); Chantal Akerman (*Voice of Neighbor*).

Publications

Articles

Rosenbaum, Jonathan, in *Sight and Sound* (London), Winter 1975-76.

Maupin, Françoise, in *Image et Son* (Paris), February 1976.

Alemann, C., and H. Hurst, interview with Chantal Akerman, in *Frauen und Film* (Berlin), March 1976.

Bertolina, G., "Chantal Akerman: Il cinema puro," in *Filmcritica* (Rome), March 1976.

Dubroux, Daniele, in *Cahiers du Cinéma* (Paris), March/April 1976.

Creveling, C., "Women Working," in *Camera Obscura* (Berkeley), Fall 1976.

Villien, Bruno, and P. Carcassone, "Chantal Akerman," in *Cinématographe* (Paris), June 1977.

Kinder, Marsha, in *Film Quarterly* (Berkeley), Summer 1977.

Mairesse, E., "Apropos des films de Chantal Akerman: Un Temps atmosphère," in *Cahiers du Cinéma* (Paris), October 1977.

Loader, Jayne, in *Jump Cut* (Berkeley), November 1977

Patterson, Patricia, and Manny Farber, "Kitchen without Kitsch," in *Film Comment* (New York), November/December 1977.

Bergstrom, Janet, in *Camera Obscura* (Berkeley), Autumn 1978.

Martin, Angela, "Chantal Akerman's Films," in *Feminist Review*, no. 3, 1979.

Perlmutter, Ruth, "Feminine Absence: A Political Aesthetic in Chantal Akerman's *Jeanne Dielman*," in *Quarterly Review of Film Studies* (New York), Spring 1979.

Pym, John, in *Monthly Film Bulletin* (London), April 1979.

Lakeland, M. J., "The Color of *Jeanne Dielman*," in *Camera Obscura* (Berkeley), Summer 1979.

Seni, N., in *Frauen und Film* (Berlin), September 1979.

Jayamanne, L., "Modes of Performance in Chantal Akerman's *Jeanne Dielman*," in *Australian Journal of Screen Theory* (Kensington, New South Wales), no. 8, 1980.

Orellana, M., "Notas sobre un nuevo cine: El de Chantal Akerman," in *Cine* (Mexico City), January/February 1980.

Perlmutter, Ruth, "Visible Narrative, Visible Woman," in *Millenium* (New York), Spring 1980.

Aranda, I., and A. Pagaolatos, interview with Chantal Akerman, in *Contra campo* (Madrid), March 1981.

Singer, B., in *Millennium* (New York), Winter/Spring 1989-90.

von Bagh, P., "Keskusteluvuorossa: Chantal Akerman," in *Filmihullu* (Helsinki), no. 4, 1991.

* * *

Chantal Akerman, a 25-year-old French-speaking Belgian from a Jewish family, made in *Jeanne Dielman*—which is perhaps the most prestigious Belgian film—an emblematic masterpiece of the feminist cinema of the 1970s. With no camera movement whatsoever, and very rarely departing from a single medium-long shot per scene, the 201-minute film scrutinizes the rigorously methodical life of a woman approximately 50 years old and her teenage son over three days. The fastidious rituals of her daily existence include prostitution with what appears to be a regulated sequence of men who come to her apartment, presumably without the son's knowledge, on weekly appointments.

Inspired by Michael Snow's cinematic investigations of space and time and the ritualized gestures of Resnais's and Duras's films, Akerman radically understated the dramatic dimension of her film even though it culminates in the unexpected murder of a client after a day in which Dielman's defensive and psychically anesthetizing rituals go awry. The filmmaker's careful compositions, abetted by Babette Mangolte's brilliantly cool cinematography, so frequently recall the features of paintings of seventeenth-century interiors (Vermeer, De Hooch, Metsu, Ter Borch) that she seems to be commenting on the Netherlandish art of representing women cleaning house, preparing food, reading letters, grooming children, sewing, listening to music, and entertaining men. *Jeanne Dielman* recasts that treasury of lucid images in rigorously geometrical settings from the perspective of a participating woman, interpreting them as compulsive displacements of anxiety.

Akerman so protracted and extenuated the pace of her film that the subtle shifts in Dielman's behavior as the film progresses seem to occur at the threshold of attention. The long-held distant shots, with vivid natural sounds but no movie music, and the rhythmical editing that follows the heroine around her house and at times onto the streets, remaining for a few seconds on a location she has left, or anticipating her arrival, inure the viewer to her underplayed emotions. Furthermore, the shot changes so often mark ellipses, and the dialogue is so sparse, that the viewer may become deeply enmeshed in the film before realizing the significance of a scene that occurred much earlier. For instance, the film opens with the departure of one of Dielman's afternoon clients. But it is possible to think that he is her husband, departing for a week and giving her spending money, until the next client appears more than an hour later.

Two intertitles, "End of the first day" and "End of the second day," divide the film into three parts. On the second day Dielman's polished routine begins to show some roughness: she mistimes dinner and overcooks the potatoes, but it is not until the third day that minute misfunctions begin to indicate an imminent breakdown: she skips a button on her housecoat, drops a shoe brush and some silverware, washes the same dishes twice, goes too early to the post office and too late to her customary café, fails to untie a package. These minor lapses prepare us to see the orgasm she experiences while coolly having intercourse with her afternoon client as a massive deviation from her routine of self-control. In the next shot, she drives the scissors she had to use to get her package open into his throat.

Through most of the film we watch Dielman alone. Even when she is with her son or a neighbor, she says very little. The very sparseness of speech gives weight to the rare instances of it. In this way, the recitation of Baudelaire's poem of the ravages of time, "L'Ennemi," which Jeanne helps her son to memorize, takes on importance. But most of all, it is his brief bedtime discussions of love, sex, and Oedipal rage against his dead father which suggest that the sexual maturing of her son might be the catalyst for the fatal disruption of her defensive compulsions.

—P. Adams Sitney

JHABVALA, Ruth Prawer
American writer

Born: Cologne, Germany, of Polish parents, 7 May 1927; emigrated to England as a refugee, 1939; naturalized, 1948; became U.S. citizen, 1986. **Education:** Attended Hendon County School, London; Queen Mary College, University of London, M.A. in English literature, 1951. **Family:** Married Cyrus Jhabvala, 1951, three daughters. **Career:** 1951-75—lived in India; 1955—first novel published; 1963—began association with producer Ismail Merchant and director James Ivory: first collaborative film, *The Householder*; 1975—moved to New York. **Awards:** Booker Prize, 1975; British Academy Award, for *Heat and Dust*, 1983; Academy Awards, for *A Room with a View*, 1986, and *Howards End*, 1992. **Address:** 400 East 52nd Street, New York, NY, 10022, U.S.A.

Films as Writer for Director James Ivory

1963	*The Householder*
1965	*Shakespeare Wallah*
1968	*The Guru*
1970	*Bombay Talkie*
1975	*Autobiography of a Princess* (co)
1977	*Roseland*
1978	*Hullabaloo over Georgie and Bonnie's Pictures*
1979	*The Europeans*
1980	*Jane Austen in Manhattan*
1981	*Quartet*
1983	*Heat and Dust*
1984	*The Bostonians*
1986	*A Room with a View*
1990	*Mr. and Mrs. Bridge*
1992	*Howards End*
1993	*The Remains of the Day*
1995	*Jefferson in Paris*
1996	*Surviving Picasso*
1998	*A Soldier's Daughter Never Cries* (co)

Other Films as Writer

1982	*The Courtesans of Bombay* (Merchant—doc)
1988	*Madame Sousatska* (Schlesinger) (co)

Publications by Jhabvala

Fiction

To Whom She Will, London, 1955, as *Amrita*, New York, 1956.
The Nature of Passion, London, 1956.
Esmond in India, London, 1958.
The Householder, London, 1960.
Get Ready for Battle, London, 1962.
Like Birds, Like Fishes and Other Stories, London, 1963.
A Backward Place, London, 1965.
A Stronger Climate: Nine Stories, London, 1968.
An Experience of India, London, 1971.
A New Dominion, London, 1972, as *Travelers*, New York, 1973.
Heat and Dust, London, 1975.
How I Became a Holy Mother and Other Stories, London, 1976.

Ruth Prawer Jhabvala

In Search of Love and Beauty, London, 1983.
Out of India: Selected Stories, New York, 1986.
Three Continents, London, 1987.
Poet and Dancer, London, 1993.
Shards of Memory, London, 1995.

Other Books

Meet Yourself at the Doctor (nonfiction), London, 1949.
Shakespeare Wallah (script), London, 1973.
Autobiography of a Princess (script), London, 1975.

Articles

Sight and Sound (London), Winter 1978-79.
Interview (New York), December 1983.
"Novel Scribe," interview with Daniel S. Moore, in *Variety* (New York), 28 October 1996.

Publications on Jhabvala

Books

Williams, H. M., *The Fiction of Ruth Prawer Jhabvala*, Calcutta, 1973.
Shahane, Vasant A., *Ruth Prawer Jhabvala*, New Delhi, 1976.

Gooneratne, Yasmine, *Silence, Exile, and Cunning: The Fiction of Ruth Prawer Jhabvala*, New Delhi, 1983.

Pym, John, *The Wandering Company*, London, 1983.

Sucher, Laurie, *The Fiction of Ruth Prawer Jhabvala*, London, 1989.

Bailur, Jayanti, *Ruth Prawer Jhabvala: Fiction and Film*, New Delhi, 1992.

Crane, Ralph J., *Ruth Prawer Jhabvala*, New York, 1992.

Articles

"*Quartet* Issue" of *Avant-Scène Cinéma* (Paris), 1 October 1981.

Atlas, James, "A Cinematic Sensibility," in *Vogue* (New York), March 1993.

Hart, Josephine, "The Book of Ruth," in *Vanity Fair* (New York), March 1993.

* * *

Since the 1960s, Ruth Prawer Jhabvala has enjoyed a unique position among screenwriters as one of the principal collaborators in Merchant Ivory Productions, the independent film company headed by the Indian producer Ismail Merchant and the American director James Ivory. Jhabvala has supplied the scripts for a majority of the company's productions, in a happy blend of narrative styles and thematic concerns that has proven so seamless it is often difficult to tell where the writer's influence ends and the filmmaker's begins.

Jhabvala was born in Germany and emigrated with her parents to England in 1939. She later married the architect Cyrus Jhabvala and moved with him to India, where she lived for 24 years. (She eventually was to divide her time between India and New York City.) Her life in India became the source of many of her richest early works, and fostered within her a fascination with the country which she shares with Ivory. Beginning with *The Householder*, an adaptation of one of her own novels, Jhabvala wrote a series of films for Merchant Ivory Productions which helped establish both the company itself and James Ivory's reputation as a director. All of these films are set in India and deal with cultural clashes of one kind or another, a theme that would become a hallmark of the company's output. The best known of the group, *Shakespeare Wallah*, follows the fortunes of a British touring theatrical company, sadly out of place in modern India yet determined to hang on to their traditional way of life. Conflicts between East and West, tradition and change, or simply different strata of the same society recur throughout the Jhabvala-Ivory collaborations, with the stories' characters trying—and often failing—to reconcile themselves to their differences in culture and class.

Ivory's films are exquisite, leisurely portraits of minutely observed people and places, and Jhabvala's screenplays lend themselves admirably to the director's style. Subtle nuances of dialogue reveal shifts in a character's thoughts or emotions, while the story is allowed to unfold through delicately sketched character interaction rather than dynamic physical activity. The themes that mark the team's earliest films were applied on a more diverse scale in their collaborations between the mid-1970s and mid-1980s, with *The Europeans*, adapted from Henry James's novel, exploring the conflicts between British and American culture; *The Bostonians*, again adapted from James, examining the problematic interplay between men and women; and *Roseland* depicting the gulf between reality and imagination in its stories of the people who frequent an outmoded New York ballroom. *Autobiography of a Princess* and *Heat and Dust* find Jhabvala and Ivory returning again to the Anglo-Indian cultural conflict, with a particular emphasis on the differences between present-day India and the India of the British Raj.

Merchant-Ivory's 1986 adaptation of E. M. Forster's *A Room with a View* introduced new audiences to the style of filmmaking that had won them a hitherto select—but devoted—following. Its story of a young Englishwoman's emotional and sexual awakening in the face of the beauty and passion of Florence was ideally suited to Ivory's and Jhabvala's long-standing concerns, and the latter's witty, literate script is alive with carefully shaded characterizations. The same can be said for *Howards End*, also based on Forster, which explores class distinctions in 1910 England (and is considered the penultimate Merchant-Ivory-Jhabvala collaboration); and *The Remains of the Day*, adapted from Kazuo Ishiguro's novel, about an efficient, mindlessly selfless professional servant, in which most of the narrative occurs between the World Wars. Less successful (but no less ambitious) were *Mr. and Mrs. Bridge* (about the manner in which the passage of time affects a Midwestern couple) and *Jefferson in Paris* (chronicling Thomas Jefferson's experiences while serving as the U.S. ambassador to France).

In the 1990s, the ever-thinning line between Hollywood and the world of independent cinema may be best symbolized by Merchant-Ivory's inking a three-film pact with the Walt Disney Company. Nonetheless, Merchant-Ivory—and Ruth Prawer Jhabvala have sustained the conviction that the tradition of the intelligent, thoughtful film, brimming with observations on the complexities of human nature, a conviction which seems so out of place in contemporary Hollywood, remains safe and alive in their hands.

—Janet Lorenz/Rob Edelman

K

KAPLAN, Nelly
Argentinean/French director and writer

Born: Buenos Aires, Argentina, 1936. **Education:** Studied economics at the University of Buenos Aires. **Career:** 1954—met and became assistant of the French director Abel Gance; 1961—directed a series of prize-winning short documentaries about artists; 1967—directed feature *Le Regard Picasso* for a retrospective on Picasso's 85th birthday; 1969—directed first full-length fiction feature, *La Fiancée du pirate*. **Awards:** Golden Lion Award, Venice International Film Festival, for *Le Regard Picasso*, 1967; Chevalier dans l'Ordre National de la Légion d'Honneur, 1996. **Address:** Cythere Films, 34 Champs Elysees, 75008 Paris, France.

Films as Director

1961   *Gustave Moreau* (doc short) (+ sc, ed); *Rodolphe Bresdin 1825-1885* (doc short) (+ sc, ed)
1963   *Abel Gance, hier et demain* (doc short) (+ sc, ed)
1965   *À la source, la femme aimée* (doc short) (+ sc, ed)
1966   *Les Années 25* (+ sc, ed); *La Nouvelle orangerie* (+ sc, ed); *Dessins et merveilles* (doc short) (+ sc, ed)
1967   *Le Regard Picasso* (+ sc, ed)
1969   *La Fiancée du pirate* (*A Very Curious Girl*; *Dirty Mary*) (+ co-sc, co-ed)
1971   *Papa les petits bateaux* (+ co-sc, ro as Belen)
1976   *Néa* (*A Young Emmanuelle*) (+ co-sc, ro as librarian)

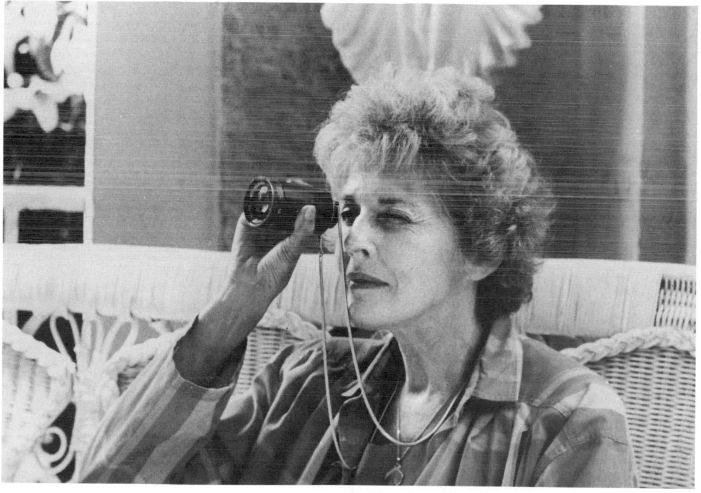

Nelly Kaplan

1979   *Charles et Lucie* (+ ro as Belen)
1983   *Abel Gance et son Napoléon* (+ sc, pr)
1986   *Pattes de Velours*
1994   *Plaisir d'amour*

Other Films

1954   *La Tour de Nèsle* (Gance) (ro)
1960   *Austerlitz/Napoleone ad Austerlitz* (*The Battle of Austerlitz*)
       (Gance) (asst d, ro)
1963   *Cyrano et d'Artagnan* (Gance) (co-d)
1964   *La prima donna* (Lifchitz) (ro)
1974   *Au Verre de l'amitié* (Makovski) (co-sc)
1975   *Il faut vivre dangereusement* (Makovski) (co-sc)
1980   *Livingstone* (Chapot—for TV) (co-sc)
1981   *La Tentation d'Antoine* (Chapot—for TV) (co-sc); *Un Fait
       d'hiver* (Chapot—for TV) (co-sc)
1982   *Ce fut un bel été* (Chapot—for TV) (co-sc, ro)
1984   *Regard dans le miroir* (Chapot—for TV) (co-sc)
1992   *Honorin et la Lorelei* (Chapot—for TV) (co-sc); *Polly West
       est de retour* (Chapot—for TV) (co-sc)
1993   *Honorin et l'Enfant prodigue* (Chapot—for TV) (co-sc)
1994   *Les Mouettes* (Chapot) (co-sc)

Publications by Kaplan

Books

Manifeste d'un Art Nouveau: la Polyvision, 1954.
Le Sunlight d'Austerlitz, 1960.
Le Réservoir des sens (written under pseudonym Belen), 1966.
Le Collier de Ptyx, 1972.
Memoirs d'une Liseuse de Draps (written under pseudonym Belen),
    1974.
La Jardienne du Temps, 1995.

Articles

"A nous l'histoire d'une de nos folies," in *Revue du Cinéma* (Paris),
    April 1974; translated by B. H. Martineau in *Women and Film*
    (Berkeley), vol. 2, no. 7, 1975.
"The *Film Journal* Interviews Nelly Kaplan about *Charles and Lucie,*"
    interview with E. Perchaluk, in *Film Journal* (New York), August
    1980.

Publications on Kaplan

Books

Kuhn, Annette, *Women's Pictures: Feminism and Cinema,* London, 1982.
Williams, Alan, *Republic of Images: A History of French Filmmak-
    ing,* Cambridge, Massachusetts, 1992.
Foster, Gwendolyn Audrey, *Women Film Directors: An International
    Bio-Critical Dictionary,* Westport, Connecticut, 1995.
Sebbag, Georges, *Le point sublime: André Breton, Arthur Rimbaud,
    Nelly Kaplan,* Paris, 1997.

Articles

Kay, K., "The Revenge of Pirate Jenny," in *Velvet Light Trap* (Madi-
    son, Wisconsin), Summer 1973.

Waldman, D., "The Eternal Return of Circe," in *Velvet Light Trap*
    (Madison, Wisconsin), Summer 1973.
Elley, D., "Hiding It under a Bushel," in *Films and Filming* (London),
    January 1974.
Lindeborg, L., "Kvinnorna och filmen," in *Chaplin* (Stockholm), vol.
    17, no. 6, 1975.
Johnston, Claire, "Myths of Women in the Cinema," in *Women and
    the Cinema: A Critical Anthology,* edited by Karyn Kay and Gerald
    Peary, New York, 1977.
Lennard, E., and N. L. Bernheim, "A Portfolio of European Directors,"
    in *Ms.* (New York), January 1977.
Buckley, T., "At the Movies," in *New York Times,* 9 May 1980.
Godin, N., "*Charles et Lucie,*" in *Amis du Film et de la Télévision*
    (Brussels), April 1981.
"Kaplan Winds 'Gance and Napoleon,' Hour-Long Documentary for
    All Media," in *Variety* (New York), 30 November 1983.
"The Director," in *Film* (London), January 1984.
"Nelly Kaplan," in *Film Dope* (London), March 1984.
Godin, N., "Nelly Kaplan," in *Visions* (Brussels), 15 June 1984.
Holmlund, Chris, "The Eyes of Nelly Kaplan," in *Screen* (London),
    Winter 1996.

*   *   *

The controversial French feminist filmmaker Nelly Kaplan is
known for her fantastic films that utilize her unique combination of
gentleness, grotesquerie, vulgarity, boldness, and contradiction.
Kaplan came to filmmaking by way of her work as an archivist for
the Argentine cinematheque. After traveling to Paris to represent her
native Argentina at an International Congress of film archivists, she
decided to remain to work as a correspondent for Argentinean film
journals. In 1954 she met the legendary French director Abel Gance
and became his assistant. He taught her film production—though
they had different ideological perspectives—and they worked together on four films. In the early 1960s, Kaplan directed her first
short films, including the short documentaries about artists *Gustave
Moreau, Rodolphe Bresdin, Dessins et merveilles, Abel Gance, hier
et demain,* and *À la source, la femme aimée.* Subsequently she
gained renown as a successful feminist feature-film director. Kaplan's
renderings of feminine sexuality celebrate female fantasies of desire
and do so with lovely and slightly surreal images that suggest the
power of feminine pleasure and the possibility that fantasy may be a
liberating urge. But her films have provoked considerable controversy among feminists, with some charging that her films are nothing more than commercial pornography.

Kaplan's first feature film, *La Fiancée du pirate* tells the story of
a young Gypsy girl who returns to her small village to exact a
sometimes hilarious revenge upon the people who sexually enslaved
her. She becomes the village whore and makes herself up with makeup,
scents, sexy attire, and an amusing collection of cheesy consumer
items in order to showcase her sexuality and to conquer and destroy
her enemies, while making them pay for it, pitting them against each
other, and destroying the community's economy. The film was distributed as soft-core pornography, but Kaplan has said that her aim
was to make an allegorical fantasy of the avenging archetypal witch/
prostitute woman. As she explained, "I wanted to tell a story in
which witches burn the others." Her second feature likewise depicted a woman in revolt. *Papa les petits bateaux* is a satirical, indi-
rect tribute to Tex Avery and Betty Boop that has a relentlessly
improbable cartoonish fantasy of a luscious heiress, Cookie, who is
kidnapped by a gang of ugly bumblers who hold her in a suburban

house. Despite their imagined macho, Cookie manages with her single-minded determination and rapier wit rather than violence to eliminate them one by one, and thus to emerge victorious. Further, she succeeds in getting her father's ransom for herself and then decides to "kidnap Daddy" himself. Kaplan's first two features both have strong fantastic elements because Kaplan preferred to avoid neorealist strategies in order to employ myths, and because she believed it is possible to focus on realistic subjects in fantastic ways.

Néa reveals the feminist politics that characterizes all of Kaplan's work. One feminist critic described it as a feminist "erotic art" movie in which its adolescent heroine unabashedly seeks sexual experiences. Accordingly, it is vastly different from the pornography made for male spectators that depicts women as the passive objects of male sexual desires. Nevertheless, in England *Néa* received an "adults only" rating, was retitled *A Young Emmanuelle,* and was screened in soft-core pornography theaters. Its heroine Sybille is the daughter of wealthy straight-arrow parents from Geneva who finds personal liberation by writing an erotic novel. Constrained by her prejudiced father and a hypocritical family existence, she becomes determined to publish the novel anonymously, to urge her lesbian mother to leave her father for her lover, and to take her own lover in order to attain the experiences she lacks. During the course of her writing, Sybille sees and experiences a panoply of sexual activities, and she is presented as having supernatural powers that she deploys to get precisely what she desires. In the whimsical *Charles et Lucie,* a romantic comedy, an elderly working-class couple tries to secure a fortune and happiness by gambling, though they are swindled to the point of pennilessness. They are hunted by the law through the south of France so that they must use their wits to survive. Ultimately, their unhappiness with each other is replaced by a rekindling of their love. Although the film is sentimental, Kaplan brings her usual ironic sense of humor and a surreal absurdity to her offbeat story.

Some critics allege that Kaplan is a technically proficient film-maker, but that her work fails to challenge conventional filmmaking. Her early films were influenced by surrealism and by Freud. An admitted feminist, Kaplan also has confessed to a weakness for animated cartoons, humor, audacity, nonsense, and the absurd, in order to counter the more familiar stereotypical ideas about women depicted on-screen. She explained that to combat 40 centuries of "slavery," any extreme was permitted. Further, her films are not only radical but generous, clever, and engaging. In her recent work, Kaplan has moved toward less radical themes though her stories are still generally female dominated. For example, her film, *Plaisir d'amour* concerns three generations of women. In addition, although she has not gained wide recognition in the United States, Kaplan continues to enjoy success in the arena of feminist commercial filmmaking in France.

—Cynthia Felando

KIDRON, Beeban
British director

Born: London, 1961. **Education:** Studied film at Britain's National Film and Television School. **Career:** 1970s—worked as an assistant to photographer Eve Arnold; 1981—made a short film, *With or Without (Sugar),* as part of a three-day film course at the South Bank Poly, London; 1983—co-directed (with Amanda Richardson) the documentary *Carry Greenham Home* while a student at the National Film and Television School; 1986—directed a second documentary, *Global Gamble,* for the BBC; 1988—directed *Vroom,* her first feature; 1991—her success with *Antonia & Jane* led to her coming to Hollywood to make *Used People,* 1992. **Awards:** Hugo Award, Chicago Film Festival, for *Carry Greenham Home,* 1983; Audience Award for Best Feature, San Francisco International Lesbian and Gay Film Festival, and Cable ACE Award, for *Oranges Are Not the Only Fruit,* 1989. **Agent:** United Talent Agency, 9560 Wilshire Boulevard, 5th Floor, Beverly Hills, CA 90212, U.S.A.

Films as Director

1981	*With or Without (Sugar)* (short)
1983	*Carry Greenham Home* (co-d with A. Richardson—doc)
1985	*Alex* (unfinished)
1986	*Global Gamble* (doc)
1988	*Vroom*
1989	*Itch*; *Oranges Are Not the Only Fruit*
1991	*Antonia & Jane*
1992	*Used People*
1993	*Hookers, Hustlers, Pimps and Their Johns* (doc); *Great Moments in Aviation* (*Shades of Fear*)
1995	*To Wong Foo, Thanks for Everything! Julie Newmar*
1997	*Swept from the Sea* (+ co-pr)

Publications on Kidron

Book

Foster, Gwendolyn Audrey, *Women Film Directors: An International Bio-Critical Dictionary,* Westport, Connecticut, 1995.

Articles

D'Erasmo, S., "A Love Bizarre," in *Village Voice* (New York), 5 November 1991.

Kelleher, E., "MacLaine, Mastroianni Topline Kidron's *Used People,*" in *Film Journal* (New York), December 1992.

Slate, L., "Close-ups," in *American Premiere* (Beverly Hills), no. 1, 1993.

James, Caryn, "Film View: Assaying Holiday Movies: After the Pitch, the Reality," in *New York Times,* 3 January 1993.

Farber, Stephen, "Oscar Bait," in *Movieline* (Escondido, California), January/February 1993.

Swanson, Annie Gerson, "Beeban Kidron," in *Premiere* (New York), February 1993.

La Polla, F., "*Antonia e Jane,*" in *Cineforum* (Bergamo, Italy), May 1993.

Pede, R., "Beeban Kidron," in *Film en Televisie + Video* (Brussels), May 1993.

Delval, D., "*Used People,*" in *Grand Angle* (Mariembourg, Belgium), June 1993.

"Filmografie," in *Segnocinema* (Vicenza, Italy), July/August 1993.

Marshment, Margaret, and Julie Hallam,"String of Knots to Orange Box: *Oranges Are Not the Only Fruit,*" in *Jump Cut* (Berkeley), June 1994.

Chambers, Veronica, and Holly Millea, "Wings of Desire," in *Premiere* (New York), October 1994.

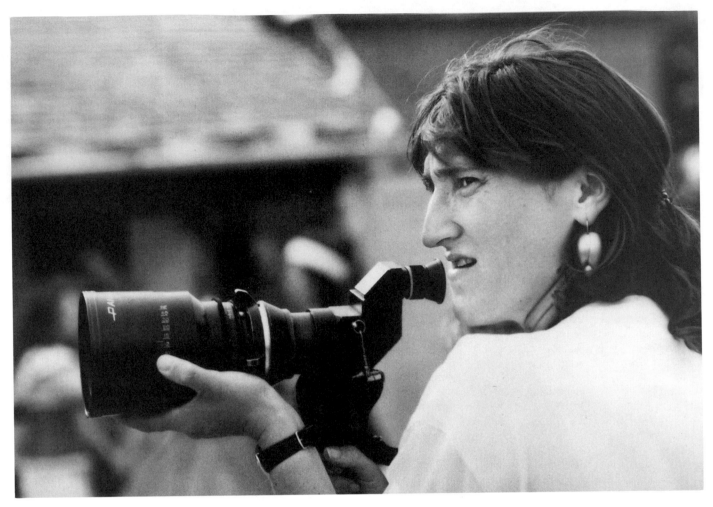

Beeban Kidron

Brown, Corie, "Hell on Heels," in *Premiere* (New York), September 1995.

* * *

Throughout her career, Beeban Kidron has made films that explore the need for individuals to be who they are, and take and maintain control of their lives. They might be young heterosexual women (*Antonia & Jane*) or older heterosexual women (*Used People*), gay women (*Oranges Are Not the Only Fruit*) or gay men (*To Wong Foo, Thanks for Everything! Julie Newmar*).

To date, two of Kidron's best films—as well as those that established her international reputation—are among her first: *Oranges Are Not the Only Fruit* and *Antonia & Jane,* low-budget, character-oriented dramas made for British television. Both depict complex, tug-of-war relationships between two distinctly different women. In *Oranges Are Not the Only Fruit,* they are a stridently religious mother and her adopted daughter, who grows up to be a lesbian; in *Antonia & Jane,* they are two contemporaries who form an unlikely friendship despite their polar-opposite personalities.

Oranges Are Not the Only Fruit, adapted by lesbian writer Jeanette Winterson from her semiautobiographical first novel, is the story of Jess, who is depicted in the scenario at ages seven and 16. Jess is brought up by a strict, fanatically religious foster mother who spends her life at revival meetings and constantly spouts on about how she "met the lord" and gave "my heart to Jesus." The mother refuses to allow the daughter any friends her own age, and maintains that school is little more than a "den of vice." She wants Jess to grow up to be a missionary. "The world is full of sin," she declares. "You can change the world."

As an impressionable seven year old, Jess is little more than a receptacle for her mother's fanaticism. But by the time she is 16, she has developed into a headstrong young woman who knows her own mind, exudes a zest for life, and verbalizes her feelings about the narrow-mindedness in her midst. Additionally, Jess is in the process of realizing that she is physically attracted to her own sex. To date, her sole friend in the world is 82-year-old Elsie, the lone member of her mother's religious group who attempts to understand her and give her space in which to grow. Then Jess meets Melanie, who becomes her first friend her own age—as well as her first lover. Their relationship is discovered and exposed, leading to bitter conflict with her mother, and her church.

According to the church, Jess's love for Melanie is an "illness," and "the devil inside her." But Jess has become acutely aware that the love is natural, joyous, and of her own free will. So as Jess comes to separate herself from her mother and church—at the film's finale she is accepted at Oxford, where she will "read a lot more books than the Bible" and her life truly will begin—*Oranges Are Not the Only Fruit* becomes a story of sexual and spiritual liberation triumphing over sexual and spiritual repression.

Antonia & Jane chronicles the relationship between two friends, Antonia McGill and Jane Hartman, who are a study in contrast and irony. Jane, who is unmarried, is plain, obsessive, unassertive. "At parties, I always get stuck with the resident loser," she tells her therapist (whom she unknowingly shares with Antonia). Whenever she is treated rudely, Jane is incapable of complaining, and only can smile meekly. It is no understatement when she admits, "I've always had difficulty expressing my feelings."

Jane is envious of Antonia, who is pretty and outwardly successful. Antonia is married to Howard, Jane's first-ever boyfriend; Antonia and Howard had an affair when he and Jane were supposed to be "ecstatically in love." Jane even went to the wedding, and watered Antonia's plants while she and Howard were on their honeymoon.

Nonetheless, Antonia's life really is not so perfect. Her marriage and publishing industry job are less ideal than she lets on to Jane, and she is jealous of the latter's freedom. "Jane always makes me feel middle-aged," Antonia observes. "Every time we meet, she's into something new ... I'm in a rut, and she keeps moving." Unlike Jane, Antonia may be able to say what she feels. But then she acts in a manner that is diametrically opposed to what she says, and how she feels.

Antonia & Jane is a carefully realized examination of the manner in which these two characters perceive each other, and the boundaries and subtleties of female friendship. But primarily (and like *Oranges Are Not the Only Fruit*), it is about the need for women (or, actually, anyone) to take and maintain control of their lives. It also mirrors the manner in which people perceive each other. You might expect a plain Jane to be jealous of an attractive Antonia, yet the latter also might think she has a legitimate reason to envy the former.

Kidron's success with *Oranges Are Not the Only Fruit* and *Antonia & Jane* led to her coming to Hollywood. The two American films she has made to date, *Used People* and *To Wong Foo, Thanks for Everything! Julie Newmar*, are, thematically speaking, way outside the movie industry mainstream. They are similar to her earlier work in that they focus on human relationships and unlikely personal connections. *Used People* chronicles the courtship of a middle-aged, just-widowed Jewish woman, who is surrounded by neurotic relatives, by an Italian gentleman who for decades has loved her from afar. *To Wong Foo...* is the story of three drag queens driving cross-country and their positive impact on the inhabitants of a small town. Neither film is particularly successful. *Used People* is dramatically heavy-handed, and none-too convincing. *To Wong Foo...*, a poor relation of *The Adventures of Priscilla, Queen of the Desert*, is simplistic and infuriatingly uneven (not to mention highly improbable). Both films are Hollywood "product," lacking the natural flow and believability of *Oranges Are Not the Only Fruit* and *Antonia & Jane*.

To her credit, Kidron has not abandoned her cinematic roots. Since heading for Hollywood, she has returned to England to direct *Great Moments in Aviation*, scripted by Jeanette Winterson and set in the 1950s, whose main character is a young woman bent on becoming a flyer; and *Hookers, Hustlers, Pimps and Their Johns*, a documentary (made for Britain's Channel 4) about New York City's multibillion-dollar prostitution industry, in which Kidron offers a nonjudgmental portrait of her subject. Her most recent project is *Swept from the Sea*, inspired by the Joseph Conrad novella *Amy Foster*.

—Rob Edelman

KOPPLE, Barbara
American director

Born: New York City, 30 July 1946. **Education:** Graduated from Northeastern University with degree in psychology. **Career:** Assisted documentary filmmakers as an editor, sound recordist, and camerawoman; 1973-76—spent four years in coal fields of Harlan County, Kentucky, recording struggles of unionized miners for documentary *Harlan County, U.S.A*; 1996—directed episode of TV series *Homicide: Life on the Streets.* **Awards:** Academy Award, Best Feature Documentary, designation by Congress as American Film Classic in National Film Registry, for *Harlan County, U.S.A.,* 1976; National Endowment for the Arts Fellowships, 1970s and 1980s; Academy Award, Best Feature Documentary, Best Feature Documentary, Directors Guild of America, for *American Dream,* 1991; John Simon Guggenheim Memorial Foundation Fellowship, 1992; Dorothy Arzner Directing Award, Women in Film, 1993; Outstanding Directorial Achievement, Directors Guild of America, for *Fallen Champ,* 1993; Maya Deren Award, American Film Institute, 1994. **Address:** 58 East 11th Street, New York, NY 10003, U.S.A. **Agent:** William Morris Agency, 151 El Camino Drive, Beverly Hills, CA 90212, U.S.A.

Films as Director

1972 *Winter Soldier* (co-d)
1976 **Harlan County, U.S.A.** (+ sound, pr)
1981 *No Nukes* (co-d with Wexler)
1983 *Keeping On* (+ exec pr)
1989 *Civil Rights: The Struggle Continues* (+ pr)
1990 *Out of Darkness* (co-d)
1991 *American Dream* (+ sound, co-pr)
1992 *Beyond JFK: The Question of Conspiracy* (co-d); *Locked Out: Ravenswood*
1993 *Fallen Champ: The Untold Story of Mike Tyson* (for TV) (+ pr)
1994 *Century of Women* (segment d)
1995 *Prisoners of Hope* (co-d)
1997 *With Liberty and Justice for All*
1998 *Wild Man Blues*

Other Films

1974 *Richard III* (pr, sound, ed)
1986 *Hurricane Irene* (pr)
1995 *Nails* (segment pr)

Publications by Kopple

Articles

Interview with Chuck Kleinhans, in *Jump Cut* (Chicago), no. 14, 1977.
"Filming in Harlan," interview with Gary Crowdus, in *Cineaste* (New York), Summer 1977.
Interview with J. Aghed, in *Positif* (Paris), October 1977.
Interview with M. Martin, in *Ecran* (Paris), 15 October 1977.
Interview with S. Le Peron and L. Skorecki, in *Cahiers du Cinéma* (Paris), November 1977.

"American Dreams," interview with Richard Porton, in *Cineaste* (New York), vol. 18, no. 4, 1991.

Interview with L. A. Winokur, in *Progressive* (Madison, Wisconsin), November 1992.

"Barbara Kopple: A Firebrand Documentary Filmmaker Moves to TV to Tackle Her Latest Subject: Iron Mike Tyson," interview with Pope Brock, in *People Weekly* (New York), 15 February 1993.

Publications on Kopple

Books

Rosenthal, Alan, *The Documentary Conscience: A Casebook in Film Making,* Berkeley, 1980.

Shulevitz, Judith, *The Women's Companion to International Film,* edited by Annette Kuhn and Susannah Radstone, Berkeley, 1994.

Foster, Gwendolyn Audrey, *Women Film Directors: An International Bio-Critical Dictionary,* Westport, Connecticut, 1995.

Articles

Dunning, Jennifer, "A Woman Film Maker in the Coal Fields," in *New York Times,* 15 October 1976.

Biskind, Peter, "*Harlan County, U.S.A.:* The Miners' Struggle," in *Jump Cut* (Chicago), no. 14, 1977.

Kaplan, E. Ann, "*Harlan County, U.S.A.:* The Documentary Form," in *Jump Cut* (Chicago), no. 15, 1977.

McNally, Judith, "The Making of *Harlan County, U.S.A.,*" in *Film-makers Newsletter* (Ward Hill, Massachusetts), May 1977.

Giraud, T., "*Harlan County, U.S.A.,*" in *Cahiers du Cinéma* (Paris), July 1977.

Henry, M., "*Harlan County, U.S.A.,*" in *Positif* (Paris), July/August 1977.

Thirard, P. L., "*Harlan County, U.S.A.,*" in *Positif* (Paris), November 1977.

Odebrant, P., and Ohlsson, J., "*Harlan County, U.S.A.,*" in *Chaplin* (Stockholm), vol. 20, 1978.

Vrdlovec, Z., "Harlanski revir," in *Ekran* (Paris), vol. 3, 1978.

Heijs, J., "*Harlan County, U.S.A.,*" in *Skrien* (Amsterdam), May 1978.

Forbes, J., "*Harlan County, U.S.A.,*" in *Sight and Sound* (London), Summer 1978.

King, Noel, "Recent 'Political' Documentary: Notes on *Union Maids* and *Harlan County, U.S.A.,*" in *Screen* (London), vol. 22, no. 2, 1981.

Ferrario, D., "*Harlan County, U.S.A.* di Barbara Kopple," in *Cineforum* (Bergamo, Italy), January 1981.

McCall, A., and A. Tyndall, "Sixteen Working Statements: Notes from Work on a Film in Progress," in *Millennium* (New York), Spring/Summer 1978.

Hoberman, J., "The Non-Hollywood Hustle," in *American Film* (Washington, D.C.), October 1980.

Kaplan, E. Ann, "Theories and Strategies of the Feminist Documentary," in *Millennium* (New York), Fall 1982/Winter 1983.

Penley, Constance, "Documentary/Documentation," in *Camera Obscura* (Berkeley), Spring/Summer 1985.

Sorensen, S., "Dokumentarisme," in *Film & Kino,* no. 4, 1987.

Rossi, U., "Per una comunicazione attiva," and "Due scioperi da Oscar nel cinema off Hollywood," in *Cineforum* (Bergamo, Italy), September 1991.

Weinberg, Joel, "Union Maid," in *New York,* 9 March 1992.

Rule, S., "In Film, a Career of Trying to Balance the Inequalities of Life," in *New York Times,* 24 March 1992.

Brown, G., "O Say Can You See?," in *Village Voice* (New York), 24 March 1992.

Klawans, Stuart, "*American Dream,*" in *Nation* (New York), 30 March 1992.

Kelleher, E., "Kopple's Oscar-Winning *Dream* Explores Harsh Labor Dispute," in *Film Journal* (New York), April 1992.

Linlield, Susie, "Barbara Kopple," in *Premiere* (New York), April 1992.

Schickel, Richard, "Which Side Are You On?," in *Time* (New York), 6 April 1992.

Powers, John, "Food for Thought," in *New York,* 13 April 1992.

Roberts, S., "*American Dream* Charts Labor's Loss," in *New York Times,* May 1992.

Christgau, Georgia, "The Spirit of Resistance and the Second Line," in *Labor History,* Winter 1993.

Espen, Hal, "The Documentarians," in *New Yorker,* 21 March 1994.

Orvell, Miles, "Documentary and the Power of Interrogation: *American Dream* and *Roger and Me,*" in *Film Quarterly* (Berkeley), Winter 1994/95.

*   *   *

Barbara Kopple got her start in film working for Albert and David Maysles. In order to make films, she decided it was necessary to learn all aspects of their production. At the Maysles' studio, she became familiar with the craft—from getting coffee to reconstituting trims, no job was trivialized. She became an assistant editor for the Maysles and began working as editor and sound recordist for other producers.

After gaining enough experience and confidence, Kopple decided it was time to direct her own films. Her crews consisted of a camera operator and sound recordist, of which she was the sound recordist. As with most documentaries, such a small crew was an economic necessity, but it also enhanced the filmmaker's intimacy with the subject. According to Kopple, recording sound brought her "deeper into what was happening"; she was "hearing" and participating in the filmic process on multiple levels. As a technician, interviewer, and director, she is both observer and participant. In supervising post-production she becomes the storyteller.

Most of Kopple's independent films require her constant attention to fund-raising. Winning the Academy Award for Best Feature-length Documentary for *Harlan County, U.S.A.* did not ensure funds for another project. While shooting *American Dream,* rather than process film, she bought freezers to store the exposed rolls until money could be raised for lab expenses. Kopple thinks "small crews are great, but sometimes it's better to have money and hire a sound recordist."

Kopple was influenced by the Maysles brothers and D. A. Pennebaker, exponents of Direct Cinema. Her method of filmmaking, though owing much to her predecessors, is very much a result of form following content. Though her style may differ slightly from film to film because of the organic strategy she employs for each story, there is an overriding consistency to her work. She gives those not normally heard a voice—the audience of most films are her subjects. Her documentaries have become emblematic of social change films.

Most of Kopple's films have no simple beginning—we enter a story that has already begun. The audience may know the outcome, yet we are engaged in the suspense of how we arrived at that point. Her films examine the antecedents of power relationships, how people are affected, respond, and make sense of their own actions and those of others. Though the chronology of a film may shift through history, intercutting past events with the contemporary, we experience the action in the present tense. Her endings are never clean, sometimes with story updates occurring under the end credits. Kopple's films create a discourse that cuts through historical time in an attempt to understand where we are today.

Kopple's films create such intimacy of identity that we feel sure she lived the experience. Nevertheless, *Harlan County, U.S.A.* took only 13 months to make. After reading about the death of Joseph Yablonski, his wife, and daughter, and the formation of Miners for Democracy, she decided to make the film and secured a $10,000 loan from Tom Brandon. The film develops small stories to contextualize a larger narrative.

The Consolidation Coal Mannington Mine Disaster of 1968, the Yablonski family murder in 1970, and the union election places the Harlan strike in a national relationship. History is seen as a growing organism and montage moves the discourse through time. John L. Lewis is cut against Carl Horn, president of Duke Power, as though they were engaged in debate. Yet the film is faithful to and references the chronology of the Harlan strike.

Kopple uses music to remind the audience of our folk storytelling tradition. In geographically isolated regions such as Harlan, music has been a way of sharing experience, creating a unifying identity. In the film music functions to evoke cultural memory and meaning. Though we may be thousands of miles from Harlan, we share a common heritage of labor struggle. The voice of the film is the voice of many. There is no one hero, but a common chorus of purpose uniting gender and race.

"Which Side Are You On" functions as *Harlan County, U.S.A.*'s theme song. The film is about choice. Kopple is asked by Duke Power's thugs to identify herself; there is no question of her allegiance. Kopple thinks that being a woman may have contributed to the local police letting her film in jail. They did not consider her a threat. There is no question that the film threatened Duke Power; the camera is beaten. And the film is very much about violence: everyday life seems harsh, and the strike heightens the brutality. The audience must look at the conflict's viscera—pieces of lung and brains in the dirt—and ultimately the death of striker Lawrence Jones. The strike may be won, but it is a momentary victory. The struggle continues without end through the credits.

Kopple continues themes developed in *Harlan County, U.S.A.* in *American Dream,* but the story and issues have become more complicated. Again she films a strike, a labor crisis, and documents the crisis of labor. At issue is whether the union movement will be destroyed by Reaganism, or whether it will transform and once again play an active role in the American drama. The film follows Local P-9 of the United Food and Commercial Workers International Union as the rank and file struggles with the International leadership and dissidents among its own membership, as well as labor's traditional antagonist, in this case Hormel and Company.

Again a strike is the motivating force for communality. But because labor is divided—brother pitted against brother—*American Dream* evokes the heartbreak of the Civil War. The labor movement has lost its innocence, yet Local P-9 seems naive. They lack a historical perspective to labor negotiations. When the strike is going well they are enthusiastic, but they succumb to moral self-righteousness when frustrated. Recognizing stasis in the International, they hire an outside labor consultant, Ray Rogers of "Corporate Campaign," whose strategy is to effect economic distress on Hormel, build solidarity with other locals, and make the strike "newsworthy." He packages the strike for television, but we are not sure which side of the camera he prefers to be on; as he seems to be playing a role from *Norma Rae* (Rogers was the organizer at J. P. Stevens). Authenticity becomes problematic.

As in *Harlan County, U.S.A.,* there is no doubt that Kopple's camera is on the side of labor. In *American Dream,* however, the camera repositions itself to show the conflicting points of view within the labor movement. The camera is with Local P-9 leader Jim Guyette, then with Lewie Anderson, director of the International Union's Meatpacking Division. It is in a car with dissidents as they defy the Local and go back to work. But the camera does not cross the picket line with them; it watches the dissidents go through the gate from the vantage point of the strikers.

In *American Dream,* Kopple utilizes various documentary styles. Direct Cinema techniques are combined with conventional sit-down interviews and narration. The voice of the film is that of labor, but unlike *Harlan County, U.S.A., American Dream* employs narration. Guyette and Anderson provide commentary for their own stories. And Kopple personally announces voice-over information necessary to move the story forward. As the film proceeds to its end, we are aware of a distance and dislocation of voice and character not experienced in *Harlan County, U.S.A.* The grand narrative of American labor is fractured, and we wonder if the Dream can ever be reconstructed. The film ends with an *American Graffiti*-style montage of character updates. But it is the 1980s, and although there may be personal change, one story remains the same: company profits continue to grow while workers are paid less.

Kopple thinks of herself as a filmmaker of traditional dramas, examining how people behave in moments of crisis and change. Her films question the construct of the "American Dream" and the price we pay in its attainment; how this "Dream" influences and informs our collective and individual identity and what we value; and how we are equipped to deal with and interpret issues of justice and change.

—Judy Hoffman

KROKODILLEN EN AMSTERDAM
(Crocodiles in Amsterdam)
Netherlands, 1990
Director: Annette Apon

Production: Nederlandse Films Stichting Coproductiefonds Binnenlandse Omroep in co-production with NOS Televisic; color; 35 mm; running time: 84 mins. Released 1990.

Producer: Rolf Orthel; **screenplay:** Annette Apon, Yolanda Entius, and Henriette Remmers; **photography:** Bernd Wouthvysen; **editor:** Danniel Danniel; **production design:** Ruben Schwartz and Serge van Opzeeland; **music:** Henk van der Meulen.

Cast: Joan Nederlof (*Gino*); Yolanda Entius (*Nina*); Hans Hoes (*Jacques*); Marcel Musters (*Jerry*); Trudie Lute (*Charlotte*); Jaap ten Holt (*Peter*); Evert van der Meulen (*Adje*); Olga Zuiderhoek (*Mevrouw Top*); Cahit Olmez (*Alex*).

Publications

Articles

Stratton, David, in *Variety* (New York), 7 March 1990.
Stam, H., in *Skoop* (Amsterdam), April 1990.

Lucas, F., "De kleur van krokodillen," in *Skrien* (Amsterdam), June/July 1990.

Gilles, M., "Die Einsamkeit der Spielfilmerin," in *Filmfaust* (Frankfurt), July/October 1990.

* * *

Crocodiles in Amsterdam is a personal, idiosyncratic female bonding movie, a fable of an emerging friendship between two outwardly different young women. Its point of view is that the developing relationship at the core of the story very well may be the most meaningful human contact each of these characters will have for their entire lives.

The film opens with the nocturnal fantasies of its two heroines, Gino and Nina. Gino (Joan Nederlof) dreams of a man parachuting through the sky, flying freely through space. Upon landing, he presents her with a bouquet which she smilingly accepts. This symbolically establishes Gino as a passive character, a receiver (rather than giver) of material objects.

All of Gino's romantic relationships are casual, and unsatisfactory. At the outset, one of her lovers brings her breakfast in bed—but alas, it is a meal for one, as he immediately is on his way. She has a crush on another man, for whom she declares she would sacrifice her all, but he too is emotionally distant and romantically unavailable.

Gino takes no responsibility for her life, as evidenced by her passivity in relationships and in expecting her wealthy Uncle Victor to pay for a new motorcycle. And symbolically, she keeps changing her name. To Nina, she is Gino, while others know her as Mildred, Elsa, Magdalena.... (Throughout the film, it never becomes clear what her actual name is.) Gino is not grounded, and her plans alter with the direction of the wind. At the film's beginning, she intends to travel around the world. Yet in an instant, she revises these plans and begins negotiating the purchase of a house.

While she is spoiled and self-centered, Gino always tries to be nice and agreeable. Also near the film's outset, as she sells an old motorbike, the cycle dealer tellingly observes, "You're easy to please."

Gino's dream is contrasted to that of Nina: cartoon images in which she is participating in an act of sabotage—described later on as a "bomb attack on an arms factory"—which culminates in a fiery explosion. It quickly becomes apparent that, unlike Gino, Nina wears her emotions on her sleeve, and is perfectly capable of asserting herself and expressing her feelings. With three cronies—two males and a female—she has been plotting a robbery, and she spews anger over the woman's having backed out of the job. Nina declares (in an observation which also might pit her against Gino), "Dammit! I hate people who don't do what they say!"

Nina is constantly angry, for reasons both political and personal. Her ire stems from the reality that she does not live in what she describes as "a just world." Still, the key to her personality may be discerned in a revealing sequence in which she visits her mother, who spurns her touch when Nina attempts to hug her.

Gino and Nina meet—it so happens that Nina and her cronies' intended victim is Uncle Victor—and their friendship seems unlikely in that they are such a study in contrast. They have different temperaments and lifestyles, and even styles of hair and dress. Gino is blond, and feminine. Nina has short dark hair, and is masculine in appearance. Her sexual preference is only alluded to in the scenario, and never becomes a factor in her evolving relationship with Gino.

Yet they are destined to become fast friends, and share a series of spirited, comical misadventures which become increasingly surreal. The union between Gino and Nina is complex, in that they argue as much as they laugh. But their impact on each other is immediate and telling as Nina's character becomes softer (though no less assertive), while Gino becomes more aggressive. As the two women bond, *Crocodiles in Amsterdam* becomes a chronicle of the magnitude and meaning of female friendship.

In a more predictable, politically/sexually loaded film, Gino and Nina somehow would end up in bed. This does not happen, however. *Crocodiles in Amsterdam* is a story of female friendship, not sexuality. Perhaps in the future, Gino will hook up romantically with a man. But the point is that no male ever will be able to bring to her the kind of companionship and, more to the point, complex shared relationship and understanding she can have with Nina.

Structurally, *Crocodiles in Amsterdam* is whimsical, and is never grounded in reality. Director Annette Apon constantly cuts away to shots which express her characters' hopes and desires, or illustrate whatever is on their minds. Even more specifically, shots of animals—especially different types of dogs—are interspersed throughout. Dogs know nothing of their breeds. They live by their instincts, and frolic together despite their superficial differences in size, color or shape. Humans, meanwhile, may be more complicated in that they think and feel, and the memories of their pasts impact on their present lives. But despite their differences, they are just as capable of bonding, and positively influencing each other—if only they allow themselves to do so.

—Rob Edelman

KRUMBACHOVÁ, Ester

Czech costume designer, writer, and director

Born: Brno, Czechoslovakia, 12 November 1923. **Education:** Studied at the University of the Arts, finishing in 1948. **Family:** Married the director Jan Nemec, 1965 (divorced 1968). **Career:** From 1954—worked at Czech theaters; from 1961—began work in the cinema; 1970—first and last feature film as director, *Murder of Mr. Devil*; also worked in television. **Died:** 13 January 1996.

Films as Costume Designer

1961   *Ztracená revue* (*The Lost Revue*) (Podskalský—for TV)
1962   *Zivot bez kytary* (*Life without a Guitar*) (Hanibal)
1967   *Muz, který stoupl v cene* (*A Man Who Rose in Price*) (Moravec); *Ta naše písnicka ceská* (*Love with a Song*) (Podskalský)
1969   *Ezop* (*Aesop*) (Valczanov)
1970   *Archa bláznu aneb Vyprávení z konce zivota* (*Ark of Fools*) (Balada); *Vrazda ing. Certa* (*Murder of Mr. Devil*) (+ d, co-sc)
1971   *Psi a lidé* (*Dogs and People*) (Schorm); *Slamený klobouk* (*Straw Hat*) (Lipský); *Tajemství velikého vypravece* (*The Secret of the Great Story-Teller*) (Kachyna)
1989   *Království za kytaru* (*The Kingdom for a Guitar*) (Králová)
1990   *Poslední motýl* (*The Last Butterfly*) (Kachyna)
1996   *Marian* (Václav) (+ set designer)

Films as Artistic Collaborator

1961   *Muz z prvního století (The Man from the First Century)*
        (Lipský); *Medved (A Bear)* (Fric—for TV)
1962   *Král Králu (The King of Kings)* (Fric); *Transport z ráje (A
        Convoy Leaving Paradise)* (Brynych); *Slzy, které svet nevidí
        (The Tears That the World Doesn't See)* (Fric—for TV)
1963   *Ikarie XB 1 (Icarus XB 1)* (Polák); *Usporená libra (A Saving
        Pound)* (Svitácek and Rohác—for TV)
1964   *Démanty noci (Diamonds of the Night)* (Nemec); *Kdyby tisíc
        klarinetu (If a Thousand Clarinets ...)* (Rohác and
        Svitácek); *... a pátý jezdec je Strach (The Fifth Horseman
        Is Fear; ... and the Fifth Rider Is Fear)* (Brynych) (+ co-sc)
1965   *At zije republika (Long Live the Republic!)* (Kachyna); *Nikdo
        se nebude smát (Nobody Gets the Laugh)* (Bocan)
1966   *Hotel pro cizince (Hotel for Strangers)* (Máša); *Kocár do
        Vídne (A Carriage Going to Vienna)* (Kachyna); *Mucedníci
        lásky (Martyrs of Love)* (Nemec) (+ co-sc); *O slavnosti a
        hostech (The Party and the Guests)* (Nemec) (+ co-sc);
        Romance pro krídlovku (Romance for Cornet) (Vávra);
        Sedmikrásky (Daisies) (Chytilová) (+ co-sc)
1967   *Pension pro svobodné pány (Boarding House for Single Gentle-
        men)* (Krejcík); *Mother and Son* (Nemec—short) (+ co-sc)
1968   *Všichni dobrí rodáci (All Good Countrymen ...)* (Jasný);
        Náhrdelník melancholie (Necklace of Melancholy)
        (Nemec—for TV)
1969   *Kladivo na carodejnice (The Witch Hunt)* (Vávra) (+ co-sc);
        *Ovoce stromu rajských jime (The Fruit of Paradise, We Eat
        the Fruit of the Trees of Paradise)* (Chytilová)
1970   *Ucho (The Ear)* (Kachyna); *Uz zase skácu pres kaluze (I
        Can Jump over Puddles Again)* (Kachyna); *Valerie a týden
        divu (Valerie and a Week of Wonders)* (Jireš) (+ co-sc)
1973   *Dny zrady (The Days of Betrayal)* (Vávra)
1975   *O neposedném knoflícku (A Fidgety Little Bouton)* (Scko—
        animated short)
1976   *Malá morská víla (Little Mermaid)* (Kachyna)
1981   *O Honzovi, Jakubovi Kosteckovi a papírovém okénku (Honza,
        Jakub Kostecvka and a Little Paper Window)* (Bocik—
        animated short) (+ co-sc)
1983   *Faunovo prilis pozdni odpoledne (The Very Late Afternoon
        of a Faun)* (Chytilová) (+ co-sc); *O statecném kovári (Brave
        Blacksmith)* (Švéda)
1984   *Shoe show aneb Botky mají pré (Shoe Show)* (Scko—ani-
        mated short)
1987   *O zivej vode (Live Water)* (Balada)
1988-89 *Pravdivý príbeh Josta Buergiho (The True Story of Jost
        Buergi)* (Havas—doc for TV)
1996   *Co delat? (Cesta z Prahy do Ceského Krumlova aneb Jak
        jsem sestavoval novou vládu; What to Do?)* (Vachek)

Other Films

1968   *Trináctá komnata (The Thirteenth Chamber)* (Vávra) (words
        of songs)
1985   *Leoš Janácek* (Havas—doc) (co-sc)
1986   *Figure behind the Glass* (Stevens) (co-sc)
1995   *Genus: Zivot Jitky a Kvety Válových (Genus: The Life of
        Jitka and Kveta Válovy)* (d, sc—doc, short, for TV); *Ge-
        nus: Zivot divadelníka Oty Ornesta (Genus: The Live of
        Theater Maker Ota Ornest)* (d, sc—doc, short, for TV);
        Winner Takes All (d of musical clip)

Publications by Krumbachová

Book

První knízka Ester, Prague, 1994.

Article

"Kino, magiia I protivostoianie," in *Iskusstvo Kino* (Moscow), no. 7,
1994.

Publications on Krumbachová

Books

Liehm, A. J., *Generace,* Prague, 1990.
Škvorecký, Josef, *Všichni ti bystrí mladí muzi a zeny: Osobní historie
   ceského filmu,* Prague, 1991.
Komárek, Martin, *Gen,* Olomouc, Czech Republic, 1994.
Komárek, Martin, *Gen—100 Cechu dneška,* Prague, 1994.
Ester Krumbachová mucednice filmové lásky, Hradec Králové, Czech
   Republic, 1996.

Film

Gen: Ester Krumbachová, television documentary, directed by Jan
   Nemec, 1993.

*   *   *

Czechoslovakian filmmaking became considerably well known
abroad in connection with the so-called Czech New Wave in the
1960s. In that time—actually a span of just a few years—many films
were shot in Czechoslovakian film studios, and they have been shown
at cinemas and various retrospective programs into the present day.
Not just men, but women too found success in this new trend.
Probably the best known is the director, Vera Chytilová, but another
remarkable Czech woman filmmaker was Ester Krumbachová, whose
influence upon the Czech New Wave is undoubted. Her former colleagues said that she was imbued with a versatile talent; they compare her to a renaissance type of an artist, and she was in fact a
costume designer, scriptwriter, and director.

Krumbachová was most active in the artistic area of filmmaking,
which was natural because she had studied at the University of the
Arts, in the art and graphics branch. After finishing her studies, she
worked as a set designer and a costume designer in a few Czech
theaters. Then in 1961 she began her film career, also in art and
costume design, helping to give a new and modern face to Czech
film. She participated in the films of the most significant directors
and worked in different genres—contemporary, historical, science-
fiction settings. Her participation was always welcomed because for
each film Krumbachová approached the problem of design from a
global view. Her costumes together with the idea of the work shaped
the necessary atmosphere, enforced the story, and defined each character. She had an extraordinary developed sense of material and
color thanks to inspiration from painting. She also managed to work
with a wide scale of shades in black-and-white films. For example,
in Jaromil Jireš's *Valerie and a Week of Wonders,* Krumbachová
effectively brought black-and-white sequences into harmony with
colored ones; in the process, an imaginative story clearly came out of
the contours of narrative levels.

Another chapter in Krumbachová's career is her work as a scriptwriter, which directly influenced the essence of the Czech New Wave. She co-wrote such significant films as *Martyrs of Love, The Party and the Guests,* and *Daisies.*

The versatility of her talent—the separate elements of which complemented each other—led her to work as an independent director. In 1970 she finished the comedy *Murder of Mr. Devil,* the first and last film she would direct for the cinema. Krumbachová not only directed the film, but also wrote the script and served as the art designer and the costume designer. The film was truly her own. *Murder of Mr. Devil* is a rather peculiar story with morbid elements about a woman who is gatecrashed by the very Devil under the pretext of marrying her. But the Devil is more interested in good food and drinks and the woman must get rid of him later.

If we look back at Krumbachová's lifetime of work we find that the high point came in the 1960s. During that time she absorbed the atmosphere of permissive politics and the ideas of the Prague Spring of 1968; in turn, her work influenced the politics of the day. Her opinions on life, the status of man in society, and freedom had their own moral dimension. Krumbachová did not change them, either after the Soviet occupation or during the ominous years that followed. Therefore she could not devote herself entirely to her work and develop her talent to its full extent. Unfortunately, her modest contributions to film during the 1990s stopped entirely and suddenly with her death in early 1996.

—Blazena Urgošíková

KURYS, Diane

French director and writer

Born: Lyon, 3 December 1948, to Russian-Jewish immigrants. **Education:** Attended Lycée Jules Ferry, Paris. **Family:** Married to the director-producer Alexandre Arcady. **Career:** 1970—joined Jean-Louis Barrault's theater group; 1977—directed first feature film, *Peppermint Soda,* the year's largest-grossing film in France; 1983—international success of *Entre nous.* **Awards:** Prix Louis Delluc, Best Picture, for *Peppermint Soda,* 1977. **Agent:** William Morris Agency, 151 El Camino Drive, Beverly Hills, CA 90212, U.S.A.

Films as Director and Writer

1977　*Diabolo menthe* (*Peppermint Soda*)
1980　*Cocktail Molotov* (*Molotov Cocktail*)
1983　*Coup de foudre* (*Entre nous*; *Between Us*; *At First Sight*)
1987　*A Man in Love* (*Un Homme amoureux*) (co-sc, + pr)
1990　*La Baule-les-Pins* (*C'est la vie*) (+ pr)
1992　*Après l'amour* (*Love after Love*) (co-sc)
1994　*À la folie* (*Alice et Elsa*; *Six Days, Six Nights*; *To the Limit*)

Other Films

1972　*Poil de carotte* (*Carrot Top*) (Graziani) (ro as Agathe); *Elle court, elle court la banlieue* (Pirès) (ro)
1976　*Casanova* (*Il Casanova di Federico Fellini*) (Fellini) (ro)
1992　*Pour Sacha* (*For Sasha*) (Arcady) (co-pr)

Publications by Kurys

Book

With Olivier Cohen, Coup de foudre*: le rêve des années cinquante,* Paris, 1983.

Articles

Interview in *Film Français,* December 1977.
Interview with Scott Murray, in *Cinema Papers* (Melbourne), August/September 1980.
"Come Hither—But Slowly: Dessert with Diane Kurys," interview with Marcia Pally, in *Village Voice* (New York), 31 January 1984.
"Like Eating a Lot of Madeleines," interview with Ginette Vincendeau, in *Monthly Film Bulletin* (London), March 1991.

Publications on Kurys

Books

Quart, Barbara Koenig, *Women Directors: The Emergence of a New Cinema,* New York, 1988.
Foster, Gwendolyn Audrey, *Women Film Directors: An International Bio-Critical Dictionary,* Westport, Connecticut, 1995.
Austin, Guy, *Contemporary French Cinema: An Introduction,* Manchester, 1996.
Straayer, Chris, *Deviant Eyes, Deviant Bodies: Sexual Re-orientations in Film and Video,* New York, 1996.

Articles

Insdorf, Annette, "A Women's Wave," in *American Film* (Washington, D.C.), January/February 1980.
Holmlund, Christine, "When Is a Lesbian not a Lesbian: The Lesbian Continuum and the Mainstream Femme Film," in *Camera Obscura* (Berkeley), January/May 1991.
Lipman, Amanda, "*Après l'amour,*" in *Sight and Sound* (London), September 1993.

* * *

It is not unusual for young independent filmmakers to create an autobiographical first or second feature: perhaps a tale of struggling adolescence on the model of Truffaut's *The Four Hundred Blows.* But *Peppermint Soda,* Diane Kurys's first film, a resounding critical and box-office success in France, was highly unusual in 1977 for having a female perspective on teenage rites of passage. It also initiated a remarkable group of films—one that does not follow the same characters through a series of sequels, à la Truffaut's Antoine Doinel cycle, but focuses upon essentially the same family (with slightly different names and played by different actors), rather the way some novelists and playwrights have circled around the same traumatic event, catching it from different angles, different characters' viewpoints, in work after work. Though Kurys has created some other striking films—concerned chiefly with self-defeating sexual games—her most enduring works to date may be those about a divorce in a French-Jewish family and the children who witness the breakup.

The title of that first film refers to the "grown-up" drink young Anne Weber orders in a café—until Frédèrique, her older sister and sometime confederate, humiliatingly sends her home. This and many

Diane Kurys

other painful moments of budding youth are presented—sometimes with heartfelt intensity, sometimes with a cool comic edge—in vignettes that take us into the sisters' Paris lycée (schoolyard secrets, wretched teachers) and their lives outside it (mother-daughter conflicts, reluctant encounters with the divorced father, and most disturbingly, Frédèrique's near-seduction by a school-friend's father). Politics intersect with private life (the year is 1963, marked by Kennedy's assassination): a girl tells of witnessing a police riot, and Frédèrique's antifascist student group is disparaged by her principal as well as attacked by neo-Nazi thugs. Quiet observations of character, sudden explosions of emotion, unexpected turns of plot, touches of ironic humor—such hallmarks of Kurys's later work are already evident in this first feature.

Molotov Cocktail, at least a peripheral chapter in the family saga, is marked as a sequel by the title's ironic echo of the first film's less potent concoction, and by the name of the young protagonist. We are now in May 1968, though ironically Anne is off on an excursion with two male friends, exploring sexuality and independence from her mother, while missing the political events back in Paris. Nevertheless, Kurys's third film, *Entre nous,* is more directly a prequel, centering upon the girls' mother and her intense friendship with another woman, with the subsequent breakups of both their marriages. The film became Kurys's greatest international success to date and certainly her most controversial film.

Entre nous has been admired by some as a superbly powerful and subtle drama, gorgeously realized, while others have dismissed it as too vague in its sexual politics, too chic, too conservative in its filmmaking style. Much of the debate over the film centered upon the question of whether it should be categorized as a "lesbian film." The original title ("Stroke of Lightning," an idiom for love at first sight) may suggest as much, and several scenes between Lena and Madeleine certainly have an erotic charge, though the women are never shown to make love. Lena's husband accuses her of leaving him for a "dyke," but his outrage is colored by Madeleine's earlier rejection of his sexual advances.

A sympathetic reading of the film—or more, an argument that it is a major achievement in French cinema of recent years—might stress its refusal to reduce love relationships to the binary "sexual/nonsexual," or to make characters simply likable or dislikable. Lena's husband is heroic in rescuing her from probable death in a concentration camp, tender with his daughters, and quite vicious with Madeleine. The women, memorably played by Isabelle Huppert and Miou-Miou, are seen as both admirable in their quest for independence and selfish—or curiously absentminded—in their consideration of others; sometimes the viewer's sympathies seem intended to shift not just from scene to scene but from shot to shot. (Consider the episode of Lena losing little Sophie on the bus, or her encounter with the soldiers on the train and later confession to Madeleine.) The dramatic canvas is broad, with its wartime prologue, crosscutting

between Michel's rescue of Lena (which has its comic moments) and the violent death of Madeleine's first husband; the women's first meeting in the 1950s and ultimate decision to move to Paris; and the startling shift to an autobiographical mode (Sophie's point of view) in the film's last moments. Kurys's consistently brilliant use of widescreen Panavision, whether in the epic views of a Pyrenees prison camp or the languid reclinings of the two women, is essential to the film's overall effect, as is the attention to period detail, particularly fashions and music, as a way of dramatizing the 1950s context (the war years seemingly long past, the possibilities for women's independence largely in the future) and underlining the women's interest in fashion as a career. Perhaps most striking, though difficult to pinpoint, is the film's ability to present scenes with a full sense of immediacy and yet as if we were watching a reenactment of family legends from a distance.

The story is once again told in *C'est la vie,* named after the seaside resort where the entire film takes place. The daughters are once again the central characters, while Madeleine has metamorphosed into Lena's stepsister (though the same actor, the one carryover, plays her husband), and Lena is having an affair with another man. The film records the usual lazy amusements of a long summer at the beach, but also the girls' growing anxiety over their parents' impending separation. Lena is cruelly distant (literally and figuratively) at times, warmly affectionate at others. The eruption of violence in this film, when Michel attacks his wife, is truly shocking in its suddenness and brutality (i.e., in the staging of the scene, the editing, the performances); yet the placidities of beach life continue for the children, for some weeks/scenes to come, as they might indeed in life.

A Man in Love, made in between *Entre nous* and *C'est la vie,* is equally interested in passion at first sight, adultery, and flares of temper, and has a similar eye for wide-screen compositions, but this international co-production has quite a different setting: the glamour world of international filmmaking, where an American movie star, hired to play Cesare Pavese in an Italian biopic, has a steamy affair with his co-star, who abandons her French lover though the American will not give up his wife. The film has a great many fine moments which, however, do not add up to a coherent whole, and the actor remains uninterestingly egocentric, thanks to some combination of the screenwriting and Peter Coyote's wooden performance. A more successful, though certainly peculiar, tale of people involved in ludicrously neurotic love relationships is *Love after Love,* in which a cluster of affluent Parisians make themselves miserable by oscillating between their old and new lovers. One can only assume the tone is one of detached amusement, as one assumes too of *Six Days, Six Nights,* in which a house guest disrupts a pair of lovers. Whether Kurys can find a new theme which can bring out the full range of talent displayed in *Entre nous* is yet uncertain.

—Joseph Milicia

LANDETA, Matilde Soto
Mexican director and writer

Born: Mexico City, 20 September 1910. **Education:** Attended Colegio de las Damas del Sagrado Corazón in San Luis Potosí (Mexico); boarding schools in St. Louis, Missouri, and Mexico City. **Family:** Married Martín Toscano, a colonel in the Mexican army, 1933 (divorced 1942). **Career:** 1933-45—continuity person for several Mexican producers, including Films Mundiales; 1945-48—assistant to various directors, including Emilio Fernández, Mauricio Magdaleno, Julio Bracho, and Alfredo Crevena; 1948—directed first film, *Lola Casanova;* 1953—directed 110 half-hour children's television programs; 1950s-70s—taught screenwriting, wrote scripts, worked in television, ran a movie theater, worked as government liaison on foreign films shot in Mexico; 1975—"rediscovered" when her *The Black Angustias* was screened during "The Woman Filmmaker" series, part of the International Woman's Year celebrations; 1991—returned to feature filmmaking with *Nocturne for Rosario.* **Awards:** Ariel, for best screenplay, Mexican Academy of Motion Picture Arts and Science, for *Los Caminos de la vida,* 1956; lifetime achievement award, Mexican film institute (IMCINE), 1992.

Films as Director

1948   *Lola Casanova* (+ pr, co-sc)
1949   *La Negra Angustias (The Black Angustias)* (+ pr, co-sc)
1951   *Trotacalles (Streetwalker)* (+ pr, co-sc)
1990   *Islas Revillagigedo (Revillagigedo Islands)*
1991   *Nocturno a Rosario (Nocturne for Rosario)* (+ sc)

Films as Writer

1956   *Los Caminos de la vida* (Corona Blake)
1957   *Siempre estaré contigo* (co)

Publication by Landeta

Article

"Mexico's Feminist Pioneer," interview with Moira Soto, in *World Press Review,* September 1990.

Publications on Landeta

Books

García Elio, Diego, editor, *6 mujeres cineastas mexicanas,* Mexico City, 1987.

Trelles Plazaola, Luis, editor, *Cine y mujer en América Latina: Directoras de Largometrajes de ficción,* Rio Piedras, Puerto Rico, 1991.
Foster, Gwendolyn Audrey, *Women Film Directors: An International Bio-Critical Dictionary,* Westport, Connecticut, 1995.

Articles

Ayala Blanco, Jorge, "Matilde Landeta, nosotros te amamos," in *Siempre!* (Mexico City), 23 July 1975.
Huaco-Nuzum, Carmen, "Matilde Landeta: An Introduction to the Work of a Pioneer Mexican Filmmaker," in *Screen* (London), vol. 28, no. 4, 1987.
Rollo, Leticia, "Matilde Landeta: Aquí estoy," in *México en el arte,* Fall 1987.
Paranagua, P. A., "Pioneers: Women Film-makers in Latin American," in *Framework* (Norwich, England), no. 37, 1989.

Film

Matilde Landeta: My Filmmaking, My Life, documentary directed by Patricia Diaz and Jane Ryder, 1990.

*   *   *

The only woman to have broken into the male-dominated Mexican film industry during its "golden age" (1930-50s), Landeta directed three successful fictional features but was forced to give up her career by male bias. Estranged from filmmaking for 40 years, she was rediscovered as a pioneer woman filmmaker in the 1970s and 1980s and finally received national tributes and many international acknowledgments (at festivals in such locations as Havana, London, Tokyo, Barcelona, Créteil, Buenos Aires, and San Francisco).

Born into a distinguished family the same year that the Mexican revolution broke out, Landeta was orphaned early and she and her brother Eduardo were raised in the family's grand ancestral home in San Luis Potosí by their maternal grandmother. Eventually but separately, both were sent to the United States to study, but Landeta and her brother reunited in Mexico City in the 1930s, a time of great postrevolutionary ferment in the arts and culture. Eduardo became a film actor and Landeta, although still a schoolgirl, decided that she also wanted a career in the movies. Despite her family's protests, she became a "script girl" (continuity person) and went on to work with some of the Mexican cinema's greatest directors and stars. After working on more than 75 feature films, she fought her way through the professional hierarchy of the Mexican film-workers union to become an assistant director, working on 14 films. She eventually succeeded in becoming the first recognized woman director in the Mexican film industry—and the first female in Latin America to direct within a studio-based production system—though she had to attend a union meeting dressed as a man in order to get the promotion.

Working in a highly competitive industrial system, Landeta co-scripted, produced, and directed three feature films before hostile producers and distributors blocked her from the industry. All of her three films adopt a clear women-centered perspective and simultaneously work within and against the predominant genres of the Mexican industry at the time. Each film invokes a distinct moment in Mexican history—the Spanish colony in *Lola Casanova,* the Mexican revolution in *The Black Angustias,* and modern urbanization in *Streetwalker*—with narratives centered upon a conflicted heroine who assumes a contestatory social position. In *Lola Casanova,* for example, a tale of Creole gentry captured by Indians, the captured heroine (Meche Barba, successfully cast against type) does not attempt to either civilize the Indians or escape and chooses instead to remain with them and adapt to their ways. In the revolutionary melodrama *The Black Angustias,* the mulatta Angustias (María Elena Marquez), an outcast in her own village, redefines the role of women in the Mexican revolution not as a *soldadera* (camp follower), but as a powerful leader of men in battle. The film addresses not only questions of gender, but also explores the tensions produced by racial and class differences. *Streetwalker* works within the *fichera* or prostitute melodrama subgenre. The narrative focuses on the parallel stories of two sisters, María (Edna Peralta), a prostitute who is exploited and abused by Rodolfo, her pimp, and Elena (Miroslava), the pampered wife of a rich older businessman who begins an affair with Rodolfo unaware of his relationship to her sister. In a clear reversal of the prevailing bourgeois morals, Landeta positions the married woman as the real prostitute, both within and outside her marriage.

In the 1950s Landeta had a fourth film in the works, a script that she had long nurtured entitled *Tribunal de menores*; a duplicitous producer, however, tricked her into ceding him the rights to the script and it was filmed by Alfonso Corona Blake as *Los Caminos de la vida.* Landeta had to sue to get her name included in the credits, and the Ariel prize (the Mexican equivalent of the Oscar) she won for the script was a most bittersweet triumph. As a result of her confrontations with the director of the National Cinema Bank, she was effectively barred from the industry.

Although eagerly awaited, her 1990s comeback film, *Nocturne for Rosario,* was not well received by critics. Its evocation of end-of-the-century romanticism through the failed love affair between a poet and a powerful and seductive older woman failed to impress even Landeta's most ardent supporters. Landeta is currently working on her memoirs.

—Ana M. López

LARKIN, Alile Sharon
American director

Born: Chicago, 6 May 1953. **Education:** Attended the University of Southern California, B.A. Humanities (creative writing); University of California, Los Angeles, M.F.A., film and television production. **Career:** 1979—began filmmaking career with *Your Children Come Back to You*; co-founder of Black Filmmakers Collective; educator-writer-activist and advocate of children's educational television; 1982—directed *A Different Image*; 1989—formed NAP productions. **Awards:** First prize, Black American Cinema Society, for *A Different Image,* 1982.

Films as Director

1979 *Your Children Come Back to You*
1982 *A Different Image*
1984 *My Dream Is to Marry an African Prince* (for TV)
1986 *What Color Is God?* (doc—for TV)
1987 *Miss Fluci Moses* (doc—for TV)

Publications by Larkin

Articles

"New Images: An Interview with Julie Dash and Alile Sharon Larkin," interview with Kwasi Harris, in *Independent* (New York), December 1986.
"Black Women Film-makers Defining Ourselves: Feminism in Our Own Voice," in *Female Spectators: Looking at Film and Television,* edited by E. Deidre Pribram, London, 1988.

Publications on Larkin

Books

Gray, John, *Blacks in Film and Television: A Pan-African Bibliography of Films, Filmmakers, and Performers,* Westport, Connecticut, 1990.
Acker, Ally, *Reel Women: Pioneers of the Cinema, 1896 to the Present,* New York, 1991.
Klotman, Phyllis Rauch, editor, *Screenplays of the African American Experience,* Bloomington, Indiana, 1991.
Foster, Gwendolyn Audrey, *Women Film Directors: An International Bio-Critical Dictionary,* Westport, Connecticut, 1995.

Articles

Campbell, Loretta, "Reinventing Our Image: Eleven Black Women Filmmakers," in *Heresies,* vol. 16, no. 4, 1983.
hooks, bell, "Black Women Filmmakers Break the Silence," in *Black Film Review* (Washington, D.C.), Spring 1986.
Wali, Monona, "L.A. Black Filmmakers Thrive Despite Hollywood's Monopoly," in *Black Film Review* (Washington, D.C.), Spring 1986.
Jackson, Lynne, with Karen Jaehne, "Eavesdropping on Female Voices: A Who's Who of Contemporary Women Filmmakers," in *Cineaste* (New York), vol. 16, no. 1/2, 1987-88.
Reid, Mark A., "Dialogic Modes of Representing Africa(s): Womanist Film," in *Black American Literature Forum,* Summer 1991.
Bambara, Toni Cade, "Reading the Signs, Empowering the Eye: *Daughters of the Dust* and the Black Independent Cinema Movement," and Manthia Diawara, "Black Spectatorship," in *Black American Cinema,* edited by Manthia Diawara, New York, 1993.

*   *   *

African-American independent filmmaker Alile Sharon Larkin burst onto the fresh and electrifying world of the black cinema movement in 1979 when she completed her production of *Your Children Come Back to You* while still a film student. After studying creative writing and earning a bachelor's at the University of Southern California, Larkin entered the M.F.A. program in film and television production at the University of California, Los Angeles. Along with classmates Barbara McCullough and Carroll Blue, together they helped form the second wave of black "womanist" filmmakers.

Her 1979 film explores issues concerned with the "blind" assimilation of Western culture. Larkin is perhaps best known, however, for her award-winning 1982 production of the film, *A Different Image*. Simple in construction but powerful in message, *A Different Image* explores the exploitation of women's bodies and the sexism and racism of Western culture—all against a backdrop of "Pan-African consciousness."

It is the story of Alana, a young, free-spirited African-American woman, and her best friend Vincent. Though their relationship has always been platonic, Vincent allows himself to become influenced by an older male friend, who teases him about not having "gotten over" on Alana. Vincent's world is the real world: billboards adorned with erotic images of scantily clad women dot the highway; men's magazines exploit the sacredness of the female body. Larkin intersperses this imagery of sexism and exploitation with a montage of other images; that of photographs of black American and African women of all shapes, sizes, hues, dress, and ethnicity—including women of cultures where various states of undress are the norm and not a means of exploitation and for the selling of products.

In a moment of supreme weakness, Vincent attempts to molest a tired and sleeping Alana who accuses him of rape. He has violated the sanctity of their friendship. Noting his stack of Penthouse magazines, she cries at him in desperation: "We see you! Why can't you see us?"

A Different Image received a great deal of well-deserved accolades and a good measure of recognition, including a first place award from the Black American Cinema Society. Though largely well-received, Larkin's work has also endured some criticism. As she has noted in various interviews, she was sometimes maligned by "radical feminists," who would have preferred that her work contain more of a general condemnation of black men. Some felt that she should align herself with white women against patriarchy. Larkin is very clear in her position on these and other issues in her essay on black women filmmakers that appears in a book edited by E. Deidre Pribram, "White feminists' insistence that black women condemn Black men is seen by many of us as a tactic ... to divide and conquer us as a people." Further, she states, "many Black women see feminism as a 'white women's movement,' not at all separate from the rest of white society."

Like her contemporaries, Larkin concerns herself with much more than simply "women's stories," but seeks to explore themes rarely dealt with realistically by the mainstream film industry. Issues of assimilation, Western beauty standards, sexism, stereotyping, and the history of the African-American experience are appropriate fodder for her work, just as they are for many black women filmmakers. Black women filmmakers, too, share the same difficulties, most notably the challenge of procuring funding for their work.

In addition to her work in film, Larkin is a videographer and has produced or co-produced material for television. Larkin is a co-founder of the Black Filmmakers Collective. This group of independent filmmakers, with a grant from the California Foundation for Community Service Cable Television, produced the 1984 cable program *My Dream Is to Marry an African Prince*. It focused on the effects that racial stereotyping has on the psyche of young black children. "I believe it is important for Black people to control their own image," she states, "Black people working in the established 'Western' film industry do not have the power that we [independent filmmakers] have." In 1985 she began an examination of racism and sexism in contemporary Christianity in the production of *What Color Is God?*

In 1987, through a commission from the Woman's Building, she produced *Miss Fluci Moses,* a documentary of the life of African-American poet and educator Louise Jane Moses. This presentation was screened on cable television. Larkin, a stanch advocate of children's education television in 1989 formed NAP productions for the purpose of producing quality education children's television and video.

—Pamala S. Deane

LAW, Clara
Chinese director

Born: Clara Law Chuck-Yiu, in Macao, China, 29 May 1957. **Education:** Studied English literature at the University of Hong Kong, graduated; attended National Film and Television School in England, 1982-85. **Family:** Married the screenwriter Eddie Ling-Ching Fong. **Career:** 1978—production assistant with Radio Television Hong Kong (RTHK); 1978-81—directed 12 single-episode television dramas; 1985—directed first feature, the student film, *They Say the Moon Is Fuller Here*; returned to Kong Kong to continue working for RTHK directing fiction and docudramas; 1988—directs first professional feature, *The Other Half and the Other Half*; 1990—migrated to Australia. **Awards:** Golden Leopard, Locarno International Film Festival, for *Autumn Moon,* 1992; Silver Leopard, Locarno International Film Festival, for *Floating Life,* 1996. **Address:** c/o Southern Star Film Sales, Level 10, 8 West Street, North Sydney, NSW 2060, Australia.

Films as Director

1985   *They Say the Moon Is Fuller Here*
1988   *Wo ai tai kung ten (The Other Half and the Other Half)*
1989   *Pan jin lian zhi qian shii jin sheng (The Reincarnation of Golden Lotus)*
1990   *Ai zai biexiang de jijie (Farewell China); Yes! Yi zu (Fruit Bowl; Fruit Punch)*
1991   *It's Now or Never*
1992   *Qiuyue (Autumn Moon)* (+ co-pr)
1993   *You seng (Temptation of a Monk)*
1994   "Wonton Soup" ep. of *Erotique* (for TV)
1996   *Floating Life* (+ co-sc)

Publications on Law

Articles

"Farewell China," in *Variety* (Los Angeles), 25 April 1990.

Lee, S., "Clara Law: Unsettled in Hong Kong," in *Angles* (Milwaukee), vol. 2, no. 1, 1993.

Laden, T., and J. Painter, "Dirty Dames," in *Film Threat* (Beverly Hills), June 1994.

See, K. T., and others, "Clara Law," in *Cinemaya* (New Delhi), Autumn/Winter 1994-95.

Yue, A., "Postmodern Orientalism: Clara Law's *Temptation of a Monk*," in *Filmnews* (Kings Cross, New South Wales, Australia), vol. 25, no. 2, 1995.

*   *   *

Internationally acclaimed director Clara Law was born in Macao, China, raised in Hong Kong, and emigrated to Australia as an adult. As a filmmaker, she is an esteemed part of Hong Kong's thriving and enormously creative film industry. She has been directing films since the mid-1980s, and has proven to be an important, provocative, and inventive director who is praised for her intimate modern dramas. Starting with her student feature film, her work has been screened throughout the world on the film-festival circuit. In addition, she has been characterized as a representative of the so-called "diasporic multicultural cinema." Indeed, themes of anxiety about emigration are present in *Floating Life* and *Autumn Moon.* Moreover, her first professional film, *The Other Half and the Other Half,* explored the problems of married couples who live apart due to emigration. In general, Law's films have complex, metaphorically charged narratives, and although, on occasion, mainstream U.S. critics have expressed dissatisfaction with her pacing and characterizations, her films have been the subject of enthusiastic praise at film festivals.

The Reincarnation of Golden Lotus, Law's most successful film in Hong Kong, is about China's ancient myth of the notorious fallen woman, which is integrated with a contemporary love story. The mythical fallen woman is reincarnated as Lotus, though she, like her forebear, is fated for tragedy due to her innocent desires. In the political turbulence of 1966 Shanghai, Lotus is unfairly labeled a counterrevolutionary and thus her tragic story begins again. When the 20th-century Lotus reads the old myth, the two stories join for a romantic yet tragic ending. Much of Law's focus in the film is the connectedness of the political and personal.

Farewell China is Law's fourth feature, whose themes concern cultural dislocation and individual disconnection. Filmed on location in New York, it stars the beautiful and hugely popular Hong Kong star Maggie Cheung. It tells the compelling story of Li, who, after many failed attempts to get a visa to the United States, finally succeeds and makes the trip. Although she expects that her husband and child will eventually join her, within a year she writes home for a divorce. But her husband illegally immigrates to search for her. With a Chinese-American teenager as his guide, he discovers the people and places Li has known, and it is not until he finally begins to get on with his life that the two meet again. But Li has changed, with ultimately tragic results.

Law's first costume drama, *Temptation of a Monk,* demonstrates her skillful blending of two genres—art film and action film. It is a historical allegory set in early Tang dynasty China (A.D. 626), which is based on a story by popular Hong Kong writer Lilian Lee. It is a richly textured accomplishment, despite a relatively small budget, in which Law employs and intensifies the imagery of sword films and conveys a tasteful and even-handed eroticism. In addition, it deftly juxtaposes disparate elements—quiet contemplation and chaotic violence, the spiritual and worldly. According to Law, she wanted the film to be theatrical, with masklike makeup and stiff body movements, and a stagelike delivery of dialogue in order to expose the thoughts rather than faces of the characters. It tells the story of two imperial princes who are fighting for the old emperor's throne as he is dying. The hero is General Shi, who serves one of the brothers but believes his master is incompetent to rule the empire and inevitably will destroy it. Therefore, Shi betrays the prince and subsequently his former master is brutally murdered. Shi's guilt about his treason prompts him to leave the princess he loves and escape to his ancestral home. But he is pursued by his nemesis, General Huo, and much bloody battling ensues—whose slow motion sequences evoke Peckinpah's scenes of cine-violence. Eventually Shi seeks refuge in an isolated Buddhist monastery where he develops a deep self-aware-

ness and decides to become a monk, but his evil past and pursuers continue to haunt him. As Law explained: "With the present world, where chaos reigns, values are confused, and countries are deep in turmoil ... only a return to the origin can lend us clarity."

Law gained international acclaim with *Autumn Moon,* a study of alienation in modern Hong Kong. Along with its beautiful cinematography, Law carefully combines humor and nostalgia. The film traces two parallel love affairs, but Law's focus is really on Hong Kong's erasure of its past and the alienation of its modern conveniences and pastimes, as well as the encroachment of foreign, especially Western, influences, which is underscored by the presence of three languages. *Autumn Moon* expresses Law's concern for modern Chinese children: "As our culture fades away, what will they remember? Will they be nomadic modernists that wander, with no attachments, no memories, no dreams?"

Floating Life is Law's most recent film and her first Australian project, which has personal resonances given her emigration to Australia from Hong Kong with her husband in the early 1990s. The film is also noteworthy as the first Australian feature film that was not mostly in English. With her husband, she wrote the screenplay, which draws from their own experiences. Set in the context of the Chinese takeover of Hong Kong, the film examines what it means to live as an exile from a home country as well as the meaning of "home" itself. It tells the story of the Chan family—father, mother, and two sons—who emigrate to their second daughter's home in Australia out of anxiety about Beijing's leaders. In Australia, their domineering daughter tries to run their lives and to frighten them with tales of the country's dangers, including dogs and criminals. Law treats the cultural gaps and stresses between the emigrants and their new country in depth. Visually she underscores the disparities by contrasting the daughter's brightly lit, sterile, and mechanized home with the warm overcrowding of Hong Kong.

The themes Law explores in her work include migration, exile, loyalty, love and sensual pleasures, and family. Despite their shared themes, each of Law's films is quite different. Indeed, her work has been praised for its assured use of a broad range of visual styles, genres, and narrative rhythms.

—Cynthia Felando

LEAF, Caroline
American/Canadian animator and director

Born: Seattle, 12 August 1946. **Education:** Studied art at Radcliffe College, 1964-68. **Career:** 1968—while at college, invented the technique of creating animated movement with sand on glass; 1972—moved to Montreal, and started work in the animation department of the National Film Board of Canada, serving as a staff animator and director from 1979 until she left in 1991; 1977—received Academy Award nomination for *The Street*; 1990s—focused on painting in oils and mixed media; has done several 30-second animation commercials; 1997—visiting lecturer, Harvard University. **Awards:** Wendy Michener Award, Canadian Film Awards, 1976; Grand Prix, Ottawa International Animation Festival, for *The Street,* 1976; Grand Prix, Melbourne Film Festival, for *Interview,* 1979; Grand Prix, and Best Story Award, Ottawa International Animation Festival, for *Two Sisters,* 1990; Norman McLaren Award, Ottawa, 1994; Life Achievement Award, Zagreb, 1996. **Agent:** Acme Filmworks, 6525 Sunset Boulevard, Garden Suite 10, Hollywood, CA 90028, U.S.A.

Films as Animator/Director (shorts and commercials)

1969   *Sand or Peter and the Wolf*
1972   *Orfeo*; *How Beaver Stole Fire*
1974   *Le Mariage du Hibou* (*The Owl Who Married a Goose*)
1976   *The Street*
1977   *The Metamorphosis of Mr. Samsa*
1979   *Interview* (co-animator, co-d with V. Soul)
1983   *War Series* title
1988   *Paradise Found*
1990   *Entre Deux Soeurs* (*Two Sisters*) (+ sc)
1991   *I Met a Man*
1993   *Bell Partout*
1994   *Fleay's Fauna Centre*
1995   *Brain Battle*; *Radio Rock Detente*

Other Films

1981   *The Right to Refuse?* (co-sc, co-pr); *Kate and Anna McGarrigle* (doc, short) (d, co-ed)
1982   *An Equal Opportunity* (short) (d, co-sc)
1983   *Pies* (Cohen—animation) (pr)
1985   *The Owl and the Pussycat* (d, designer, pr)
1986   *The Fox and the Tiger* (d, designer); *A Dog's Tale: A Mexican Parable* (short) (d)

Publications by Leaf

Articles

"Talking with Caroline Leaf," interview with Thelma Schenkel, in *Film Library Quarterly* (New York), vol. 10, no. 182, 1977.
Interview with Maurice Elia, in *Séquences* (Montreal), January 1978.
"A Conversation with Caroline Leaf," interview in *Storytelling in Animation*, vol. 2, edited by John Canemaker, Los Angeles, 1988.

Publications on Leaf

Books

Russett, Robert, and Cecile Starr, editors, *Experimental Animation*, New York, 1976.
Laybourne, Kit, *The Animation Book*, New York, 1979.
Halas, John, *Masters of Animation*, Topsfield, Massachusetts, 1987.
Bendazzi, Gianalberto, *Cartoons: Il cinema d'animazione, 1888-1988*, Venezia, 1988.
Culhane, Shamus, *Animation from Script to Screen*, New York, 1988.
Pilling, Jayne, editor, *Women & Animation: A Compendium*, London, 1993.
Bendazzi, Gianalberto, *Cartoons: 100 Years of Animation*, translated by Anna Taraboletti-Segre, Bloomington, Indiana, 1994.
Foster, Gwendolyn Audrey, *Women Film Directors: An International Bio-Critical Dictionary*, Westport, Connecticut, 1995.

Articles

Canemaker, John, "Redefining Animation," in *Print*, March/April 1979.
Munro, Grant, "Sand Beads and Plasticine," in *Wide Angle* (Baltimore, Maryland), vol. 3, no. 2, 1979.

Levitin, Jacqueline, "Caroline Leaf et le cinéma d'animation," in *Femmes et Cinéma Québécois*, edited by L. Carrière, Montreal, 1983.
Schenkel, Thelma, "A Child's Perception of Death and Its Ritual—Caroline Leaf's Film Adaptation of Mordecai Richler's *The Street*," in *Proceedings of the Ninth World Congress of Jewish Studies*, Division D, vol. II, Jerusalem, 1986.

*   *   *

Serendipity is the hallmark of this animated life, ironically because Caroline Leaf plans so well. Her professional serendipity and planning began at Harvard when as a Radcliffe College senior she ambled into the Harvard classroom of Derek Lamb. Having previously taken no film courses, unskilled at drawing, surely unaware that her teacher would become the head of the English animation division of the National Film Board of Canada (NFBC), unsure whether this course was preferable to the documentary course she also considered, Leaf responded just as casually to an early homework assignment, "Bring an object to class tomorrow, something we can animate." Her classmates brought the expected: things that easily fit in one's pocket. Leaf brought sand, which she photographed on an opaque glass lit from below. Six months later she had completed her first film, *Sand*, in tribute to the unusual medium. To praise it as a first film is insufficient since its virtuosity well exceeds this definition. Already she understood the need to personalize her material, to control her medium, to invent as a complement to planning, and to grasp instinctively animated motion's secret ingredient, timing.

After a year of drawing in Italy, a Harvard postdoc (*Orfeo*), and St. Louis freelancing (*How Beaver Stole Fire*), she began work at the NFBC in the Arctic, where for a year and a half she worked with an Eskimo legend and twice daily collaborated with an Eskimo artist (*The Owl Who Married a Goose*).

The Street required a comparably arduous 18 months that she spent finger-painting tempera watercolors and oil on glass. Her dabbing and erasing create stunningly mobile transitions that whirl the viewer through a complex overlay of emotionally moving characters and richly colored moods. The soundtrack interacts gracefully with the ever-changing visuals, anticipating and reading what we feel we see. Across decades buildings, cars, families, porches, stairs, and furniture all speak to us with tradition-rich insistence. In animation people are somehow more human for losing the fixity of time and space that binds literal bodies. Here both the visual and aural tracks continually re-create reality with force and power that challenge our minds and hearts. Ten minutes on Mordecai Richler's St. Urbain Street becomes timeless. Of all her highly honored films, this one has earned the most awards, and the ambiguous benefice of an Academy Award nomination.

Although Franz Kafka persuaded his publisher not to illustrate his short story about a man turned into an insect, the problem of literal representation has never existed for Leaf. In *The Metamorphosis of Mr. Samsa* external shape poses no barrier to our emotional identification with the soul of this allegorical fantasy. Caroline Leaf herself now undergoes metamorphosis, pursuing for ten years a series of cinematic projects and experiments that derive from her earlier work with animation and prepare her for new directions.

A strong sense of individuality and difference drive her and other women animators, often of her generation. They usually avoid the studio worlds of Hollywood and New York, rejecting Disneyfication and the soul-shackling prescriptions of its assembly-line laws. Rather than devising cartoon ideas, she and they begin with a feeling and create personal connections between altogether elective forms and content. This freedom arises from a college milieu rather than from a cartoon studio.

Defining employment as a means to new, creative directions Leaf has continued to experiment plastically, with new definitions of documentary, interactions between it and animation, between theater and animation, between theater, film, and music. In the nineties she has created the emotionally and dramatically compelling *Two Sisters* by scratching her color images directly on 70mm film. A staunch promoter of independent animation, she has traveled the world doing screenings and animation workshops.

—Arthur G. Robson

LENNART, Isobel
American writer

Born: Brooklyn, New York, 18 May 1915. **Family:** Married the actor John Harding, one son and one daughter. **Career:** 1939-45—twice member of the Communist Party (testified before the House committee, 1952); 1943—first film as writer, *A Stranger in Town*; 1964—wrote successful Broadway play *Funny Girl*. **Awards:** Writers Guild Award for *Love Me or Leave Me*, 1955; *Funny Girl*, 1968. **Died:** In an automobile accident in California, 25 January 1971.

Films as Writer

1943   *A Stranger in Town* (Rowland); *The Affairs of Martha* (*Once upon a Thursday*) (Dassin); *Lost Angel* (Rowland)
1945   *Anchors Aweigh* (Sidney)
1946   *Holiday in Mexico* (Sidney)
1947   *It Happened in Brooklyn* (Whorf)
1948   *The Kissing Bandit* (Benedek)
1949   *Holiday Affair* (Hartman)
1950   *East Side, West Side* (LeRoy); *A Life of Her Own* (Cukor)
1951   "Rosika, the Rose" ep. of *It's a Big Country* (C. Vidor)
1952   *Skirts Ahoy!* (Lanfield); *My Wife's Best Friend* (Sale)
1953   *The Girl Next Door* (Sale); *Latin Lovers* (LeRoy)
1955   *Love Me or Leave Me* (C. Vidor)
1956   *Meet Me in Las Vegas* (Rowland)
1957   *This Could Be the Night* (Wise)
1958   *Merry Andrew* (Kidd); *The Inn of the Sixth Happiness* (Robson)
1960   *The Sundowners* (Zinnemann); *Please Don't Eat the Daisies* (Hill)
1962   *Period of Adjustment* (G. R. Hill); *Two for the Seesaw* (Wise)
1967   *Fitzwilly* (Delbert Mann)
1968   *Funny Girl* (Wyler)

Publications by Lennart

Play

Funny Girl, New York, 1964.

Publications on Lennart

Articles

Obituary, in *New York Times,* 26 January 1971.
Slater, Thomas, in *American Screenwriters,* 2nd series, edited by Randall Clark, Detroit, 1986.

* * *

Isobel Lennart began writing Hollywood screenplays in the 1940s and specialized in frothy entertainments such as *Anchors Aweigh, Holiday in Mexico, It Happened in Brooklyn,* and *The Kissing Bandit* and an occasional melodrama such as *East Side, West Side.* Finally, in 1955, with Daniel Fuchs, she fashioned the gritty and often bitter screenplay *Love Me or Leave Me,* based on the life of Ruth Etting, the popular singer of the 1920s and 1930s. This sadomasochistic love story between Etting (Doris Day) and her crippled, racketeer husband (James Cagney) was a far cry from the whitewashed musical biographies so familiar to moviegoers. With Charles Vidor directing, and a score of such excellent musical standards as "Ten Cents a Dance," "You Made Me Love You," "Mean to Me," and the title song, the film is a hard-hitting and true-to-life look at show business. Lennart and Fuchs received Academy Award nominations for best screenplay, and Fuchs won an Oscar for best original story.

Lennart seemed to hit her stride with screen biographies, and her next good script was for *The Inn of the Sixth Happiness,* based on the life of Gladys Aylward, the English servant girl who becomes a missionary in China. Unlike *Love Me or Leave Me,* this script *was* a romanticized biopic, but was saved by the excellent acting of Ingrid Bergman and Robert Donat. Two years later Lennart adapted for the screen the Jon Cleary novel *The Sundowners.* This rambling story of an Irish sheepdrover and his itinerant family in Australia was beautifully directed by Fred Zinnemann, expertly acted by Deborah Kerr and Robert Mitchum (probably his best screen performance), and earned Lennart a second Academy Award nomination.

Following *Fitzwilly,* Lennart created her greatest work, *Funny Girl,* the Barbra Streisand tour de force. Drawing upon the style used in *Love Me or Leave Me,* Lennart wrote the original Broadway play version of this life of the great comic Fanny Brice, focusing on her tempestuous love affair with the gangster Nicky Arnstein. The Broadway version made Streisand a star, and the film version, for which Lennart wrote the screenplay and which William Wyler directed, made Fanny Brice's story a permanent part of Hollywood musical history.

—Ronald Bowers

LEVIEN, Sonya
American writer

Born: Near Moscow, Russia, 25 December 1888; emigrated to the United States with her parents when she was a child. **Education:** Attended New York University, law degree. **Family:** Married the writer Carl Hovey, 1917 (died 1956), children: Tamara and Serge. **Career:** Practiced law briefly; 1916-20—staff member, *Woman's Journal* and *Metropolitan* magazines; 1919—first film writing credit, *Who Will Marry Me?*; 1929-41—writer for 20th Century-Fox, and

for MGM, 1941-56; 1956—joined George Sidney Productions.
Award: Screen Writers Guild, Laurel for Achievement Award, 1953;
Academy Award, for *Interrupted Melody,* 1955. **Died:** Of cancer, in
Hollywood, 19 March 1960.

Films as Writer

1919   *Who Will Marry Me?* (Powell)
1921   *Cheated Love* (Baggot); *First Love* (Campbell)
1922   *The Top of New York* (Taylor); *Pink Gods* (Stanlaws)
1923   *The Snow Bride* (Kolker); *The Exciters* (Campbell)
1925   *Salome of the Tenements* (Olcott)
1926   *The Love Toy* (Kenton); *Christine of the Big Top* (Mayo)
1927   *The Princess from Hoboken* (Dale); *The Heart Thief*
          (Chrisander); *A Harp in Hock* (R. Hoffman)
1928   *A Ship Comes In* (*His Country*) (W. K. Howard); *The
          Power of the Press* (Capra); *Behind that Curtain*
          (Cummings); *The Younger Generation* (Capra); *Trial
          Marriage* (Kenton); *Lucky Star* (Borzage); *They Had to
          See Paris* (Borzage); *South Sea Rose* (Dwan); *Frozen
          Justice* (Dwan)
1930   *Song o' My Heart* (Borzage); *So This Is London* (Blystone)
1931   *Delicious* (D. Butler)
1932   *She Wanted a Millionaire* (Blystone); *After Tomorrow*
          (Borzage)
1933   *State Fair* (H. King); *Warrior's Husband* (W. Lang); *Berke-
          ley Square* (Lloyd); *Mr. Skitch* (Cruze)
1934   *Change of Heart* (Blystone); *The White Parade* (Cummings)
1935   *Here's to Romance* (A. E. Green); *Navy Wife* (Dwan); *Paddy
          O'Day* (Seiler) (st only)
1936   *The Country Doctor* (H. King); *Reunion* (Taurog)
1938   *In Old Chicago* (H. King); *Kidnapped* (Werker); *Four Men
          and a Prayer* (Ford)
1939   *Drums along the Mohawk* (Ford); *The Hunchback of Notre
          Dame* (Dieterle)
1941   *Ziegfeld Girl* (Leonard)
1943   *The Amazing Mrs. Holliday* (Manning); *Rhapsody in Blue*
          (Rapper); *State Fair* (W. Lang)
1946   *The Green Years* (Saville); *The Valley of Decision* (Garnett);
          Ziegfeld Follies (Minnelli)
1947   *Cass Timberlane* (Sidney)
1948   *Three Daring Daughters* (Wilcox)
1951   *The Great Caruso* (Thorpe)
1952   *The Merry Widow* (Bernhardt)
1954   *The Student Prince* (Thorpe)
1955   *Hit the Deck* (Rowland); *Interrupted Melody* (Bernhardt);
          Oklahoma! (Zinnemann); *Bhowani Junction* (Cukor)
1957   *Jeanne Eagels* (Sidney)
1960   *Pepe* (Sidney)

Films as Co-writer with S. N. Behrman

1930   *Lightnin'* (H. King); *Liliom* (Borzage); *The Brat* (Ford);
          Surrender (W. K. Howard)
1931   *Daddy Long Legs* (Santell)
1932   *Rebecca of Sunnybrook Farm* (Santell); *Tess of the Storm
          Country* (Santell)
1933   *Cavalcade* (Lloyd)
1934   *As Husbands Go* (MacFadden)
1935   *Anna Karenina* (C. Brown)

1938   *The Cowboy and the Lady* (H. C. Potter)
1951   *Quo Vadis* (LeRoy)

Publications on Levien

Books

Acker, Ally, *Reel Women: Pioneers of the Cinema, 1896 to the
    Present,* New York, 1991.
Ceplair, Larry, *A Great Lady: A Life of the Screenwriter Sonya Levien,*
    Lanham, Maryland, 1996.

Articles

Obituary, in *New York Times,* 20 March 1960.
Film Comment (New York), Winter 1970-71.
Hurwitz, Edith, in *American Screenwriters,* 2nd series, edited by
    Randall Clark, Detroit, 1986.

* * *

Throughout the golden era of the Hollywood studio system,
Sonya Levien wrote enough screenplays (sometimes as many as
five per year) to qualify her as a guaranteed professional name,
but on most of her films she shared the writing credit, so that
identifying her personal trademarks becomes difficult. Nevertheless, despite a minimum of biographical knowledge and no opportunity to examine the evolution of any single screenplay she
worked on, it is still possible to assume three primary characteristics to her career: a strong tendency toward co-authorship, a
talent for adaptation, and a flair for creating women characters
who are intelligent, noble, and independent, but who are also
searching to define their particular roles in life.

When Levien was paired with an established male author, it
seems possible to assume she was hired to represent the feminine
point of view, and to enhance the female characters. For instance,
she was paired more than once with such different writers as S.
N. Behrman, Lamar Trotti, and William Ludwig. As might be
expected, the Behrman films are sophisticated comedies, the Trotti
are prestige productions of an epic scale, and the Ludwig are
musical adaptations. Since in all three cases she is working with
an established writer with a personal style, her contribution is an
enrichment of the leading female roles. The best example is probably the Trotti-Levien adaptation of *Drums along the Mohawk,* in
which the central role of Lana, played by Claudette Colbert, is a
classic example of the pioneer wife, feminine and attractive but
strong enough to survive the dangers and hardships presented in
the story line.

Levien's association with what were termed "quality" projects
led her to work on many adaptations of novels, plays, and musicals. One of her most successful solo efforts was her adaptation
of Sinclair Lewis's *Cass Timberlane,* in which the plot was restructured to reflect the postwar era in which it was released by
including a character who sold faulty war materials for profit.
Her skill at updating projects is also reflected in the three versions of *State Fair* she worked on, as well as in her refurbishing
of such older musicals as *The Merry Widow* and *The Student
Prince.* In all cases, she maintains the essential characters and
overall ambience of the original, while removing outdated attitudes, particularly toward women and sex.

Given the number of collaborations Levien was involved in, it is difficult to identify exactly what she might have contributed to a specific characterization. Nevertheless, it is obvious that the assignments she was given—and took—are frequently stories about women. It must have been assumed that her name and her talent enhanced a project that would feature a leading actress. Thus, her work for Greer Garson in *The Valley of Decision,* and Eleanor Parker in *Interrupted Melody,* created strong roles for which both actresses were nominated for Oscars. In addition, such sex symbols as Lana Turner, Ava Gardner, and Kim Novak found parts that stretched their reputations and abilities in *Cass Timberlane* and *Ziegfeld Girl, Bhowani Junction,* and *Jeanne Eagels,* respectively. The difficulty of untangling "who is responsible for what" in Sonya Levien's prolific and successful career points to the problems of historical research, and illustrates how much is yet to be learned about many of Hollywood's most influential writers.

—Jeanine Basinger

LITTLETON, Carol
American editor

Born: Oklahoma, c. 1948. **Education:** Attended University of Oklahoma; received Fulbright Fellowship, Paris, France. **Family:** Married the cinematographer John Bailey. **Career:** 1972-77—owned company which made commercial ad spots; 1977—began as editor with director Karen Arthur on *Legacy,* followed by Arthur's *The Mafu Cage* in 1978 before her first major commercial release with 1979's *French Postcards*; 1982—Academy Award nomination for editing Steven Spielberg's *E.T.—The Extraterrestrial*; 1987—elected president of Editors Guild Local 776 (West Coast); member, Board of Governors, Academy of Motion Picture Arts & Sciences. **Agent:** c/o United Talent, 9560 Wilshire Boulevard, Suite 500, Beverly Hills, CA 90212, U.S.A.

Films as Editor

1977 *Legacy* (Arthur)
1978 *The Mafu Cage (My Sister, My Love)* (Arthur)
1979 *French Postcards* (Huyck)
1980 *Roadie* (Rudolph)
1981 *Body Heat* (Kasdan)
1982 *E.T.—The Extraterrestrial* (Spielberg)
1983 *The Big Chill* (Kasdan)
1984 *Places in the Heart* (Benton)
1985 *Silverado* (Kasdan)
1986 *Brighton Beach Memoirs* (Saks)
1987 *Swimming to Cambodia* (J. Demme)
1988 *Vibes* (Kwapis); *The Accidental Tourist* (Kasdan)
1990 *White Palace* (Mandoki)
1991 *The Search for Signs of Intelligent Life in the Universe* (Bailey); *Grand Canyon* (Kasdan)
1993 *Benny & Joon* (Chechik)
1994 *China Moon* (Bailey) (co); *Wyatt Earp* (Kasdan)
1996 *Diabolique* (Chechik)
1998 *Twilight* (Benton)

Publications on Littleton

Books

Acker, Ally, *Reel Women: Pioneers of the Cinema, 1896 to the Present,* New York, 1991.
Oldham, Gabriella, *First Cut: Conversations with Film Editors,* Berkeley, 1992.

Articles

Padroff, J., "Close-ups: Off-Screen Romance," in *Millimeter* (Cleveland, Ohio), February 1986.
Lee, N., "The Art of Light and Rhythm," in *American Cinematographer* (Los Angeles), May 1987.

*   *   *

Editor Carol Littleton's music training is evident in the lyrical images that open *Places in the Heart.* Pictures of people populating a dust-bowl town during the Great Depression may epitomize her work, a gentle evocation of humanity undergoing some emotionally trying struggle of common rather than Herculean tests.

Her greatest achievements in structuring film images seem to fall into quiet, understated imagery. Even with the fantastical elements of *E.T.,* for which she received an Academy Award nomination for her editing, Littleton emphasized the simple magic of the friendship between the boy, Elliott, and his alien visitor in a manner suitable to François Truffaut. While it may have been an unlikely approach to science-fiction fantasy, it surely had much to do with why audiences responded to the fable. Even hardened audiences warmed to this sentimental and charming story.

With frequent collaborator Lawrence Kasdan, Littleton has helped bring warmth to *The Accidental Tourist* and the entertaining *The Big Chill,* two of his successes. The stylish *Body Heat,* revisiting Hollywood's film noir, brought imitation after imitation, perhaps including Littleton's own collaboration with her husband, cinematographer John Bailey, in his foray as director with *China Moon.* Kasdan and Littleton also worked together on two Westerns, *Silverado* and *Wyatt Earp,* the former a superficial homage to childhood oaters and the latter windy, dry, and far too long.

Littleton has said that simplicity is the key and that, while many editors have great technical knowledge, those that "can make a film purely emotional at the same time" are rarer. And in fact Littleton's best work seems simple on the surface but has an underlying emotional core that strikes a real note for audiences. Friendship could be said to be at the heart of *E.T., Places in the Heart,* and most of her work with director Kasdan—and this is some of her most successful work artistically.

Even in the less-pleasing films Littleton has edited, such as *Vibes, Brighton Beach Memoirs,* and the recent remake of *Diabolique,* critics take note of the assistance that she has given the work. The film may not be good but Littleton as editor has helped make it a little better.

The editor's role is unspecific and anonymous, according to Littleton; it is much like that of a symphony conductor who pulls diverse elements together in an attempt to make a cohesive whole. Her best work seems to emphasize affection and humanity that is clearly heartfelt.

—Allen Grant Richards

LIVINGSTON, Jennie

American director

Born: Los Angeles, 1960. **Education:** Graduated from Yale University, with a major in art, 1983; took summer school filmmaking class at New York University. **Career:** 1985—moved to New York City; 1986—began working on, and raising funds to complete, what was to be the documentary feature, *Paris Is Burning*; early 1990s—wrote *Not for Profit,* her first screenplay, which was not produced; mid-1990s—at work on two film projects, *Prenzlauerberg* and *Who's the Top?* **Awards:** Grand Jury Prize, Best Documentary, Sundance Film Festival, Best Documentary, New York Film Critics Circle, Best Documentary, Los Angeles Film Critics, Best Documentary, National Society of Film Critics, Open Palm, Independent Feature Project Gotham Award, Teddy Award for Best Documentary, all for *Paris Is Burning,* 1990; Vito Russo Film Award, GLAAD Media Awards, 1992. **Agent:** William Morris Agency, 151 El Camino Drive, Beverly Hills, CA 90212, U.S.A.

Films as Director

1990   *Paris Is Burning* (doc) (+ co-pr, still ph, co-sound recording)
1993   *Hotheads* (short)

Publications by Livingston

Articles

"The Fairer Sex," in *Aperture* (New York), Fall 1990.
"New Rage," in *Village Voice* (New York), 8 October 1991.

Publications on Livingston

Books

Butler, Judith, *Bodies That Matter: On the Discursive Limits of "Sex,"* New York, 1993.
Cvetkovich, Ann, "The Powers of Seeing and Being Seen: *Truth or Dare* and *Paris Is Burning,*" in *Film Theory Goes to the Movies,* edited by Jim Collins, Hilary Radner, and Ava Preacher Collins, New York, 1993.
Foster, Gwendolyn Audrey, *Women Film Directors: An International Bio-Critical Dictionary,* Westport, Connecticut, 1995.

Articles

Howell, John, "Exits and Entrances," in *Artforum* (New York), February 1989.
Jones, W., "Burning Voices," in *International Documentary* (Los Angeles), Spring 1991.
Hoberman, J., "Burning Crosses and Lamé Dresses," in *Premiere* (New York), March 1991.
Dunning, Jennifer, "An Exotic Gay Subculture Turns Poignant under Scrutiny," in *New York Times,* 23 March 1991.
Minx, P., "House Frau," in *Village Voice* (New York), 26 March 1991.
Crisp, Quentin, "A Place Where Love Becomes a Chronic Invalid," in *New York Times,* 7 April 1991.
Dekle, N., "Deep in Vogue," in *Dance Magazine* (New York), April 1991.

Toumarkine, Doris, "*Paris Is Burning*: Documentary Explores Voguing Subculture," in *Film Journal* (New York), April/May 1991.
Dale, A., "Jennie Livingston," in *Millimeter* (Cleveland, Ohio), May 1991.
Goldsby, Jackie, "Queens of Language," in *Afterimage* (Rochester, New York), 11 May 1991.
Crisp, Quentin, "Love Lies Bleeding," in *New Statesman and Society* (London), 9 August 1991.
Kuflik, A., "Cross-Dressed for Success," in *Newsweek* (New York), 12 August 1991.
Henderson, Lisa, "*Paris Is Burning* and Academic Conservatism," in *Journal of Communication,* no. 2, 1992.
Larner, J., "The Natural, the Real & the Significant," in *Dissent* (New York), no. 2, 1992.
Waters, J., "Truth or 'Realness,'" in *Jump Cut* (Berkeley), July 1992.
Paul, R., "*Paris Is Burning,*" in *Premiere* (New York), October 1992.
Bick, I. J., "To Be Real: Shame, Envy, and the Reflections of Self in Masquerade," in *Discourse,* Winter 1992-93.
Dean, T., "Transsexual Identification, Gender Performance Theory, and the Politics of the Real," in *Literature and Psychology* (Providence, Rhode Island), no. 4, 1993.
Green, Jesse, "Paris Has Burned," in *New York Times,* 18 April 1993.
Harper, P. B., "The Subversive Edge: *Paris Is Burning,* Social Critique and the Limits of Subjective Agency," in *Diacritics: A Review of Contemporary Criticism* (Baltimore, Maryland), no. 2/3, 1994.
Crowe, Patrick, "No Place Like Home: Homelessness, Identity and Sexuality in American Queer Cinema," in *CineAction!* (Toronto), August 1994.
Sandell, Jillian, "Shopping for a Change: *The House of Mirth* and *Paris Is Burning,*" in *Bad Subjects* (Berkeley), January/February 1994.
Kasindorf, Jeanie Russell, "The Drag Queen Had a Mummy in Her Closet," in *New York Magazine,* 2 May 1994.
Gomez, Gabriel, "Homocolonialism: Looking for Latinos in *Apartment Zero* and *Paris Is Burning,*" in *Post Script* (Commerce, Texas), no. 1/2, 1994-95.

*   *   *

To date, Jennie Livingston is a one-film filmmaker. But what a film it is! *Paris Is Burning* is an exemplary documentary, a vivid and ultimately bittersweet portrait of an authentic American/New York City subculture and one of the most acclaimed early examples of 1990s New Queer Cinema.

The blacks and Latinos in *Paris Is Burning* are outside the mainstream because they are minorities, and they are poor—and they are outcasts from their families because they are transsexuals and drag queens. So they exist within their own subculture in which they establish extended families and join different "houses" which serve to forge their identities. They not only fit in and find acceptance here but attend competitive, dress-up drag balls. Going to one, and vogueing at one (or dancing and striking poses in imitation of high-fashion images), is the closest they ever will come to experiencing "the way rich people live." As they walk at a ball, they live out the "fantasy of being a superstar." And by winning a trophy, they attain a certain kind of fame within the subculture.

These balls have their own history. Decades ago, drag queens attended them garbed as Las Vegas showgirls. In the 1970s, participants attempted to imitate movie stars like Marilyn Monroe and Elizabeth Taylor. In the 1980s, they were copying supermodels, like Christie Brinkley and Iman.

Participants also dress up to resemble (and take on the superficial personalities of) character types they never could be in the real world: preppie college students and smartly dressed business executives, wealthy ladies of leisure and immaculately uniformed military personnel. The point is to create a sense of "realness," to capture "the great white way of living or looking or dressing or speaking," to look so authentic as to be able to blend in on Wall Street or a military base or a college campus without revealing sexual preference. As one of the participants pointedly observes: "The fact that you are not an executive is merely because of the social standing of life.... Black people have a hard time getting anywhere. Those that do are usually straight. In a ballroom you can be anything you want.... You're showing the straight world that I can be an executive. If I had the opportunity, I could be one ... and that is like a fulfillment."

Nevertheless, there is a melancholy edge to *Paris Is Burning*, in that many of those depicted feel cheated because of their "sad backgrounds," their coming from "broken homes, or no homes at all." After a ball is over, they do not retire to limousines and Park Avenue duplexes. Unlike wealthy New York gays, they do not own West Village brownstones or summer in chic beach communities. Rather, they often are homeless, and come to balls starving. The fantasies they create for themselves are affectations, which exist only for a short time; within them remains a yearning for permanency which never can be fulfilled. Person after person, they talk about making it in the "real world" as models or dancers or actors, and attaining the affluence they see as being an intrinsic part of straight, white America. Yet their view of affluence is distorted. It comes not from real life experience but from watching television shows such as *Dynasty* and perusing ads in slickly designed high-fashion magazines.

The one true realist in the group is Dorian Corey, an aging drag queen who is well aware that her dreams of mainstream stardom can never be achieved. It is "a small fame," she declares, of her status within the subculture: "But you accept it. And you like it." Later on, she adds, "As you get older, you aim a little lower." Age has taught her that "you've left a mark on the world if you just get through it, and a few people remember your name."

The most tragic of *Paris Is Burning*'s subjects is Venus Xtravaganza, a petite blond boy-girl who declares: "I would like to be a spoiled rich white girl. They get what they want, whenever they want. They really don't have to struggle with finances." Venus wants a sex change operation, which will make her "complete." She admits that, to make money, she has turned tricks. Near the finale, she adds, "I want a car. I want to be with the man I love. I want a nice home, away from New York City, up the Peekskills [sic] or maybe in Florida, somewhere far away where no one knows me ... I want to get married in church, in white...I want to be a complete woman." It then is revealed that Venus was murdered in a sleazy hotel room. She was strangled, and her body went undiscovered for four days.

The violent death of Venus is of course unplanned, and lamentable. But it adds an unexpected resonance—and an uncompromising dose of reality—to *Paris Is Burning.*

The film was not without controversy. An organization called the Christian Film and Television Commission announced that "all moral Americans" should boycott *Paris Is Burning,* indicting it as a "homosexual propaganda film." Nonetheless, it is anything but a gay indoctrination tract. The lives depicted on screen are not glorified, but rather are tinged with sadness, and the film is as much about cultural and economic disenfranchisement as sexual preference.

Unfortunately, the success of *Paris Is Burning* has not translated into a prolific directorial career for Jennie Livingston. In 1993 she

made *Hotheads,* a three-minute video on the subject of violence against women. She wrote *Not for Profit,* her first screenplay, which she described to filmmaker Sarah Jacobson as being about "a rapist of indeterminate gender who attacks famous straight white guys.... There's this fundraising PR agency where this Jewish girl works, and they get approached by this coven of witches who want to better the image of pagans in the eyes of the public. The Jewish girl falls in love with the witch who is head of the coven." Livingston was unable to raise the funds to have *Not for Profit* produced. By the mid-1990s she had two projects in the works: *Prenzlauerberg,* "an ensemble piece, like a *Nashville* or *Short Cuts.* It takes place among artists and writers in Berlin—some of whom are informants for the secret police—and among artists and writers in New York during the kind of art boom of the 1980s, just before the stockmarket crashed"; and *Who's the Top?,* a lesbian sex comedy which is "kind of like *She's Gotta Have It* meets *Belle du Jour* meets *8½.* The theme is how do you live in a world where maybe you have one partner, you have one girlfriend, and you know your fantasies and possibilities are endless. What decisions do you make and how do you deal with that when those fantasies comes to call?"

—Rob Edelman

LOOS, Anita
American writer and producer

Born: Corinne Anita Loos in Sissons (now Mount Shasta), California, 26 April 1888. **Education:** Attended schools in San Francisco and San Diego. **Family:** Married 1) Frank Pallma Jr., 1915 (divorced 1915); 2) the director and writer John Emerson, 1920 (died 1956), one adopted daughter. **Career:** Child actress briefly; 1912—first film as writer, *The New York Hat,* followed by a large number of films for D. W. Griffith; 1916—collaborator with Emerson, and co-producer with Emerson from 1919; 1925—published the novel *Gentlemen Prefer Blondes* (play version, 1926, film version, 1928); other plays include *The Whole Town's Talking, The Fall of Eve, The Social Register, Happy Birthday, Gigi, The Amazing Adèle, Chéri, Gogo Love You;* 1963—one-woman show, *An Evening of Theatrical Reminiscences.* **Died:** In New York City, 18 August 1981.

Films as Writer

1912   *The New York Hat* (D. W. Griffith); *My Baby* (F. Powell); *The Musketeers of Pig Alley* (D. W. Griffith)
1913   *The Power of the Camera; The Telephone Girl and the Lady* (D. W. Griffith—short); *A Horse on Bill* (Powell); *The Hicksville Epicure* (Henderson); *Highbrow Love* (O'Sullivan); *Pa Says* (Henderson); *The Widow's Kids* (Powell); *The Lady in Black; His Hoodoo* (Powell); *A Fallen Hero* (Powell); *A Cure for Suffragettes* (Kirkwood); *The Suicide Pact* (Powell); *Bink's Vacation* (Bink Runs Away); *How the Day Was Saved* (Powell); *The Wedding Gown* (Powell); *Gentleman or Thief; For Her Father's Sins* (O'Brien); *A Narrow Escape; The Mother; The Lady and the Mouse* (D. W. Griffith) (short); *The Mistake* (D. W. Griffith) (short)

1914 *Hickville's Finest*; *His Awful Vengeance*; *The Saving Grace* (Cabanne); *A Bunch of Flowers*; *When a Woman Guides*; *The Road to Plaindale*; *The Saving Presence*; *The Meal Ticket*; *The Suffering of Susan*; *Nearly a Burglar's Bride*; *Some Bull's Daughter*; *The Fatal Dress Suit*; *The Girl in the Shack*; *The Stolen Masterpiece* (Pollard); *A Corner in Hats*; *The Million Dollar Bride*; *A Flurry in Art*; *Billy's Rival* (*Izzy and His Rival*) (Taylor—short); *The Last Drink of Whiskey* (Dillon); *Nell's Eugenic Wedding*; *The White Slave Catchers*; *The Deceiver* (Dillon); *How to Keep a Husband*; *The Gangsters of New York* (Cabanne and Kirkwood) (short); *The Hunchback* (Cabanne); *A Lesson in Mechanics*

1915 *The Deacon's Whiskers* (Dillon); *The Tear on the Page*; *Pennington's Choice* (Lund); *Sympathy Sal*; *Mixed Values* (Dillon); *The Fatal Finger Prints* (Dillon); *Lord Chumley* (Kirkwood); *The Sisters* (Cabanne) (short); *A Ten-Cent Adventure* (short); *When the Road Parts* (short); *Double Trouble* (Cabanne); *The Lost House* (Cabanne)

1916 *The Little Liar* (Ingraham); *A Corner in Cotton* (Balshofer); *Intolerance* (D. W. Griffith); *Macbeth* (Emerson); *Stranded* (Ingraham); *Wild Girl of the Sierras* (Powell); *A Calico Vampire*; *Laundry Liz*; *The French Milliner*; *The Wharf Rat* (Withey); *The Half-Breed* (Dwan); *American Aristocracy* (Ingraham); *A Daughter of the Poor* (Dillon)

1917 *Wild and Woolly* (Emerson); *Down to Earth* (Emerson); *The Deadly Glass of Beer*

1927 *Stranded* (Rosen); *Publicity Madness* (A. Ray)

1932 *Red-Headed Woman* (Conway); *Blondie of the Follies* (E. Goulding)

1933 *The Barbarian* (Wood); *Hold Your Man* (Wood); *Midnight Mary* (Wellman)

1934 *Biography of a Bachelor Girl* (E. Griffith); *The Merry Widow* (Lubitsch) (uncredited)

1935 *Riffraff* (Ruben)

1936 *San Francisco* (Van Dyke)

1937 *Mama Steps Out* (Seitz); *Saratoga* (Conway)

1939 *The Women* (Cukor)

1940 *Susan and God* (*The Gay Mrs. Trexel*) (Cukor)

1941 *They Met in Bombay* (C. Brown); *Blossoms in the Dust* (LeRoy); *When Ladies Meet* (Leonard)

1942 *I Married an Angel* (Van Dyke)

Films as Co-writer with John Emerson

1916 *His Picture in the Papers* (Emerson); *Manhattan Madness* (Powell); *The Matrimaniac* (P. Powell); *The Social Secretary* (Emerson)

1917 *In Again, Out Again* (Emerson); *Reaching for the Moon* (Emerson); *The Americano* (Emerson)

1918 *Let's Get a Divorce* (Giblyn); *Hit-the-Trail Holliday* (Neilan); *Come on In* (Emerson) (+ co-pr); *Good-bye-Bill* (Emerson) (+ co-pr)

1919 *Oh, You Women!* (Emerson); *The Isle of Conquest* (Jose); *Under the Top* (Crisp); *Getting Mary Married* (Dwan) (+ co-pr); *A Temperamental Wife* (Emerson) (+ co-pr); *A Virtuous Vamp* (Kirkland) (+ co-pr)

1920 *In Search of a Sinner* (Kirkland) (+ co-pr); *The Perfect Woman* (Kirkland); *The Love Expert* (Kirkland) (+ co-pr); *Two Weeks* (Franklin); *The Branded Woman* (Albert Parker)

1921 *Dangerous Business* (Neill); *Mama's Affair* (Fleming); *A Woman's Place* (Fleming)

1922 *Polly of the Follies* (Emerson); *Red Hot Romance* (Fleming) (+ co-pr)

1923 *Dulcy* (Franklin)

1924 *Three Miles Out* (Willat)

1925 *Learning to Love* (Franklin)

1928 *Gentlemen Prefer Blondes* (St. Clair)

1929 *The Fall of Eve* (Strayer)

1931 *The Struggle* (D. W. Griffith)

1934 *The Girl from Missouri* (*One Hundred Percent Pure*) (Conway)

Films Based on Loos's Writings

1926 *The Whole Town's Talking* (Edward Laemmle)

1931 *Ex-Bad Boy* (Moore)

1934 *The Social Register* (Neilan)

1953 *Gentlemen Prefer Blondes* (Hawks)

1955 *Gentlemen Marry Brunettes* (Sale)

Publications by Loos

Fiction

Gentlemen Prefer Blondes, New York, 1925 (play version, with John Emerson, New York, 1926)

But Gentlemen Marry Brunettes, New York, 1928.

A Mouse Is Born, New York, 1951.

No Mother to Guide Her, New York, 1961.

Other Books

With John Emerson, *How to Write Photoplays* (includes script *The Love Expert*), New York, 1920.

With John Emerson, *Breaking into the Movies* (includes script *Red Hot Romance*), New York, 1921.

With John Emerson, *The Whole Town's Talking* (play), New York, 1925.

With Jane Murfin, *The Women* (script), in *Twenty Best Film Plays,* edited by John Gassner and Dudley Nichols, New York, 1943.

Happy Birthday (play), New York, 1947.

Gigi (play), New York, 1952.

With D. W. Griffith, *Intolerance* (script), New York, 1955.

A Girl Like I (autobiography), New York, 1966.

The King's Mare (play), London, 1967.

With Helen Hayes, *Twice over Lightly: New York Then and Now,* New York, 1972.

Kiss Hollywood Good-by, New York, 1974.

Cast of Thousands, New York, 1977.

The Talmadge Girls: A Memoir, New York, 1978.

San Francisco (script), edited by Matthew J. Bruccoli, Carbondale, Illinois, 1979.

Fate Keeps on Happening: Adventures of Lorelei Lee and Other Writings, edited by Ray P. Corsini, New York, 1984.

Articles

Close Up (London), April 1928.

Inter/View (New York), July 1972.

Anita Loos (right) with Jean Harlow

Publications on Loos

Books

Carey, Gary, *Anita Loos: A Biography,* New York, 1988.
Acker, Ally, *Reel Women: Pioneers of the Cinema, 1896 to the Present,* New York, 1991.

Articles

Schmidt, Karl, "The Handwriting on the Screen," in *Everybody's* (New York), May 1917.
Carey, Gary, in *The Hollywood Screenwriter,* edited by Richard Corliss, New York, 1972.
Cinema (Beverly Hills), no. 35, 1976.
Quarterly Journal of the Library of Congress (Washington, D.C.), Summer/Fall 1980.
Obituary, in *Newsweek* (New York), 31 August 1981.
The Annual Obituary 1981, New York, 1982.
Grant, Thomas, in *American Humorists 1800-1950,* edited by Stanley Trachtenberg, Detroit, 1982.

Yeck, Joanne, in *American Screenwriters,* edited by Robert E. Morsberger, Stephen O. Lesser, and Randall Clark, Detroit, 1984.

*   *   *

At the early age of 16, Anita Loos began her career in films by scripting more than 100 scenarios for D. W. Griffith's Biograph Company. She is credited with writing the subtitles for *Intolerance* (1916), and is regarded as one of the first screenwriters to employ intertitles to silent films. Although she wrote serious plots for silent films (*Wild Girl of the Sierras* and *Stranded*), her early success came as a satirist of everyday events. Indeed, her original use of intertitles provided her with the opportunity to let loose with her wisecracks that teased the picture. She was also proficient in slapstick comedy and wrote a number of half-reels featuring the Keystone Kops.

It was Loos, with her husband, the director John Emerson (who assumed much of the credit for her creative endeavors) who first realized that Douglas Fairbanks's acrobatics were an extension of his effervescent personality. Loos, Emerson, and Fairbanks worked as a unit in Griffith's company and parlayed Fairbanks's natural athletic ability into swashbuckling adventure roles. Never missing a chance for satire, Loos (the "O'Henrietta of the Screen") parodied not only the nouveau riche American industrialist but also Fairbanks's own star persona in *American Aristocracy*. The scenario for the film is typical of Loos's humor: Fairbanks foils a buccaneer who is sending powder to Mexico in the guise of malted milk and as the result of his adventurous exploits wins the heart of a hat-pin king's daughter. In pursuit of the villain, Fairbanks vaults a dozen walls and fences. He readies himself to leap at a window ten feet above the ground when he suddenly decides to take the easy way out and opens a basement window, climbing in the building like an ordinary mortal. Loos wrote other humorous films that firmly established Fairbanks as a major leading man of the American screen. Americans' love of publicity was ridiculed in *His Picture in the Papers* and pacifism was satirized in *In Again, Out Again*.

Loos left the Griffith studio in 1925 and moved east with her husband. During her brief "retirement" from the film colony she wrote the durable story of Lorelei Lee, *Gentlemen Prefer Blondes*. The story was quite successful as a novel, Broadway musical, and film. Loos and Herman J. Mankiewicz co-wrote the intertitles for the original silent film version directed by Mal St. Clair in 1928. Howard Hawks's *Gentlemen Prefer Blondes* (1953) was an adaptation of the stage play and featured Marilyn Monroe as Lorelei and Jane Russell as her dark-haired girlfriend. Through the perils of Lorelei, the amoral and dim-witted young blond from Little Rock, Loos poked fun at male-female relationships. The blond's flirtations and the gullible millionaires who surrounded her provided Loos with rich material gleefully to expose the merchandising of sexuality.

Loos returned to Hollywood and worked for MGM during the Irving Thalberg reign. She took over the writing duties from F. Scott Fitzgerald on the Harlow vehicle *Red-Headed Woman*. She also wrote *Hold Your Man* starring Harlow and Clark Gable. Gable, Jeanette MacDonald, and Spencer Tracy were featured in the Loos script for *San Francisco*. This large-scale Hollywood soap opera evolved around San Francisco at the time of the great earthquake. Loos and the veteran MGM scriptwriter Jane Murfin adapted Clare Boothe Luce's venomous comedy *The Women* to the screen; it featured an all-woman cast including Norma Shearer, Rosalind Russell, Paulette Goddard, and Joan Crawford.

—Doreen Bartoni

LUPINO, Ida
American director and actress

Born: London, 4 February 1918; daughter of the actor Stanley Lupino and the actress Connie Emerald; became U.S. citizen in 1948. **Education:** Attended Clarence House School, Hove, Sussex; Royal Academy of Dramatic Art, London. **Family:** Married 1) the actor Louis Hayward, 1938 (divorced 1945); 2) the writer Collier Young, 1948 (divorced 1951); 3) the actor Howard Duff, 1951 (divorced 1972), daughter: Bridget. **Career:** Stage debut at Tom Thumb Theatre, London, at age 12; late 1920s—extra in films for British International Studios; 1932—first lead role in *Her First Affaire*; 1933-37—contract with Paramount; 1939—success in *The Light that Failed*: contract with Warner Brothers; 1949—co-founder, with Anson Bond, Emerald Productions: producer, co-director, and co-scriptwriter of *Not Wanted*; 1950—director of the film *Never Fear*; 1950-80—co-owner, with Collier Young, Film-makers Company;

1952—co-founder, with Dick Powell, Charles Boyer, and David Niven, Four Star Productions for television; 1956—director for TV series *On Trial*; 1957-58—in TV series *Mr. Adams and Eve*; 1957-66—worked exclusively in television. **Awards:** Best Actress, New York Film Critics, for *The Hard Way*, 1943. **Died:** Of cancer, in Burbank, California, 3 August 1995.

Films as Director

1949 *Not Wanted* (co-d with Clifton, + pr, co-sc)
1950 *Never Fear (The Young Lovers)* (+ pr, co-sc); *Outrage* (+ co-pr, co-sc)
1951 *Hard, Fast, and Beautiful* (+ co-pr)
1953 **The Hitch-Hiker** (+ co-pr, co-sc); *The Bigamist* (+ co-pr, ro as Phyllis Martin)
1966 *The Trouble with Angels* (+ co-pr)

Films as Actress

1932 *Her First Affaire* (Dwan) (as Anne)
1933 *Money for Speed* (Vorhaus) (as Jane); *High Finance* (G. King) (as Jill); *The Ghost Camera* (Vorhaus) (as Mary Elton); *I Lived with You* (Elvey) (as Ada Wallis); *Prince of Arcadia* (Schwartz) (as Princess)
1934 *Search for Beauty* (Kenton) (as Barbara Hilton); *Come on, Marines!* (Hathaway) (as Esther Cabot); *Ready for Love* (Gering) (as Marigold Tate)
1935 *Paris in Spring* (Milestone) (as Mignon De Charelle); *Smart Girl* (Scotto) (as Pat Reynolds); *Peter Ibbetson* (Hathaway) (as Agnes)
1936 *Anything Goes (Tops Is the Limit)* (Milestone) (as Hope Harcourt); *One Rainy Afternoon (Matinee Scandal)* (R. V. Lee) (as Monique Pelerin); *Yours for the Asking* (Hall) (as Gert Malloy); *The Gay Desperado* (Mamoulian) (as Jane)
1937 *Sea Devils* (Stoloff) (as Doris Malone); *Let's Get Married* (A. E. Green) (as Paula Quinn); *Artists and Models* (Walsh) (as Paula Sewell); *Fight for Your Lady* (Stoloff) (as Marietta)
1939 *The Lone Wolf Spy Hunt* (Godfrey) (as Val Carson); *The Lady and the Mob* (Stoloff) (as Lila Thorne); *The Adventures of Sherlock Holmes* (Werker) (as Ann Brandon); *The Light that Failed* (Wellman) (as Bessie Broke)
1940 *They Drive by Night* (Walsh) (as Lana Carlsen)
1941 *High Sierra* (Walsh) (as Marie Garson); *The Sea Wolf* (Curtiz) (as Ruth Webster); *Out of the Fog* (Litvak) (as Stella Goodwin); *Ladies in Retirement* (C. Vidor) (as Ellen Creed)
1942 *Moontide* (Mayo) (as Ada); *The Hard Way* (V. Sherman) (as Helen Chernen); *Life Begins at 8:30 (The Light of Heart)* (Pichel) (as Kathi Thomas)
1943 *Forever and a Day* (Clair and others) (as Jenny); *Thank Your Lucky Stars* (D. Butler) (appearance)
1944 *In Our Time* (V. Sherman) (as Jennifer Whittredge); *Hollywood Canteen* (Daves) (appearance)
1945 *Pillow to Post* (V. Sherman) (as Jean Howard)
1946 *Devotion* (Bernhardt) (as Emily Brontë); *The Man I Love* (Walsh) (as Petey Brown)
1947 *Deep Valley* (Negulesco) (as Libby); *Escape Me Never* (Godfrey) (as Gemma Smith)
1948 *Road House* (Negulesco) (as Lily Stevens)

1949 *Lust for Gold* (Simon) (as Julia Thomas); *Woman in Hiding*
        (Gordon) (as Deborah Chandler Clark)
1951 *On Dangerous Ground* (N. Ray) (as Mary Malden)
1952 *Beware, My Lovely* (Horner) (as Mrs. Helen Gordon)
1953 *Jennifer* (Newton) (as Agnes)
1954 *Private Hell 36* (Siegel) (as Lilli Marlowe, + co-sc)
1955 *Women's Prison* (Seiler) (as Amelia Van Zant); *The Big Knife*
        (Aldrich) (as Marion Castle)
1956 *While the City Sleeps* (F. Lang) (as Mildred); *Strange In-*
        truder (Rapper) (as Alice)
1969 *Backtrack* (Bellamy) (as Mama Delores)
1972 *Junior Bonner* (Peckinpah) (as Elvira Bonner); *Deadhead*
        Miles (Zimmerman) (as herself); *Women in Chains*
        (Kowalski—for TV) (as Tyson); *The Strangers in 7A*
        (Wendkos—for TV) (as Iris Sawyer)
1973 *Female Artillery* (Chomsky—for TV) (as Martha Lindstrom);
        I Love a Mystery (L. Stevens—for TV) (as Randolph
        Cheyne); "Dear Karen" ep. of *The Letters* (Krasny—for
        TV) (as Mrs. Forrester)
1975 *The Devil's Rain* (Fuest) (as Mrs. Preston)
1976 *Food of the Gods* (B. I. Gordon) (as Mrs. Skinner)
1978 *My Boys Are Good Boys* (Buckalew)

Publications by Lupino

Articles

"The Trouble with Men Is Women," in *Silver Screen* (New York), April
    1947.
"Who Says Men Are People?," in *Silver Screen* (New York), Octo-
    ber 1948.
"I Cannot Be Good," in *Silver Screen* (New York), June 1949.
"Me, Mother Directress," in *Action* (Los Angeles), May/June 1967.
"This Was My Favorite Role," in *Movie Digest,* November 1972.
Interview with D. Galligan, in *Interview* (New York), February
    1976.
"Moi, la mere metteur en scene," in *Positif* (Paris), March 1986.
Interview with Graham Fuller, in *Interview* (New York), October
    1990.

Publications on Lupino

Books

Kline, Richard, *The Hollywood Way to a Beautiful Body,* Greenwich,
    Connecticut, 1937.
Koszarski, Richard, *Hollywood Directors 1941-1976,* New York,
    1977.
Vermilye, Jerry, *Ida Lupino,* New York, 1977.
Stewart, Lucy, and Ann Liggett, *Ida Lupino as Film Director, 1949-*
    1953: An Auteur Approach, Ann Arbor, Michigan, 1979.
Kowalski, Rosemary, *A Vision of One's Own: Four Women Film*
    Directors, Ann Arbor, Michigan, 1980.
Parish, James, and Don Stanke, *The Forties Gals,* Westport, Connecti-
    cut, 1980.
Heck-Rabi, Louise, *Women Filmmakers: A Critical Reception,*
    Metuchen, New Jersey, 1984.
Scharres, Barbara, Taorimina Film Festival Catalogue, 1988.
Acker, Ally, *Reel Women: Pioneers of the Cinema, 1896 to the*
    Present, New York, 1991.
Foster, Gwendolyn Audrey, *Women Film Directors: An International*
    Bio-Critical Dictionary, Westport, Connecticut, 1995.
Kuhn, Annette, editor, *Queen of the 'B's: Ida Lupino behind the*
    Camera, Westport, Connecticut, 1995.
Donati, William, *Ida Lupino: A Biography,* Lexington, Kentucky,
    1996.

Articles

Current Biography, New York, 1943.
"Director Only?," in *Films and Filming* (London), January 1955.
Vermilye, Jerry, "Ida Lupino," in *Films in Review* (New York), May
    1959.
Gardner, Paul, "Ida Lupino in Comeback after Fifteen Years," in *New*
    York Times, 10 October 1972.
Parker, Francine, "Discovering Ida Lupino," in *Action* (Los Angeles),
    July/August 1973.
Haskell, Molly, "Women Directors: Toppling the Male Mystique," in
    American Film (Washington, D.C.), June 1976.
Siclier, J., and O. Eyquem, "Le Cinéma feminin d'Ida Lupino," in
    Cahiers de la Cinémathèque (Perpignan, France), no. 28, 1979.
Scheib, R., "Ida Lupino: Auteuress," in *Film Comment* (New York),
    January/February 1980.
Rickey, Carrie, "Lupino Noir," in *Village Voice* (New York), 29 Oc-
    tober-4 November 1980.
Parker, Barry M., "Newsreel: Lost Lupino," in *American Film* (Wash-
    ington, D.C.), June 1981.
Films in Review (New York), October 1982.
Interim, L., "Une Femme dangereuse," in *Cahiers du Cinéma* (Paris),
    May 1983.
Nacache, J., "Sur six films d'Ida Lupino," in *Cinéma* (Paris), Octo-
    ber 1983.
Dozoretz, W., "The Mother's Lost Voice in *Hard, Fast, and Beauti-*
    ful," in *Wide Angle* (Athens, Ohio), vol. 6, no. 3, 1984.
Ida Lupino section of *Positif* (Paris), March 1986.
Agan, P., "'Warner's Reluctant Queen': Ida Lupino," in *Hollywood*
    Studio (Los Angeles), July 1987.
Paskin, S., "Alternative Images 1: Not Wanted in Hollywood," in
    Monthly Film Bulletin (London), August 1987.
Lyden, P., "Action Shots," in *Classic Images* (Muscatine, Iowa),
    February 1990.
Briggs, C., "Ida Lupino and Howard Duff," in *Hollywood: Then and*
    Now (Los Angeles), January 1991.
White, P., "Ida in Wonderland," in *Village Voice* (New York), 5 Feb-
    ruary 1991.
Chiacchiari, F., "Ida Lupino," in *Cineforum* (Bergamo, Italy), May
    1991.
Hallensleben, S., "Ida Lupino," in *EPD Film* (Frankfurt), April 1993.
Mallory, M., "Ida Lupino," in *Scarlet Street,* Winter 1994.
Lambert, G., "Ida Lupino in Brentwood," in *Architectural Digest,* April
    1994.
Flint, Peter B., obituary, in *New York Times,* 5 August 1995.
Obituary in *Variety* (New York), 14 August 1995.
Scorsese, Martin, "Behind the Camera, a Feminist," in *New York Times*
    Magazine, 31 December 1995.

*   *   *

One of the few female directors to enjoy success in Hollywood in
the 1950s, Ida Lupino was perhaps destined to work in the realm of
entertainment, as she was descended from ancestors who had worked

as performers during the Renaissance. After studying at London's Royal Academy of Dramatic Art, she went to Hollywood in 1934 and enjoyed a successful career as a film actress before she embarked upon a career as a film director. Specifically, during a period of suspension from Warner Bros. and of general frustration as an actress after she was unable to work for 18 months in the mid-1940s, Lupino was inspired to direct movies rather than to star in them, as she put it to "fill the time." With her second husband, Collier Young, she founded her own film company, Film-makers, for which she controlled the production, direction, and screenplays of its films. Between 1949 and 1954, she made six feature films. She took over the directorial duties on her first film, *Not Wanted,* when director Elmer Clifton had a heart attack. She was uncredited, however. Subsequently, she and Collier co-wrote and co-produced, and she directed, each of their films.

As a film director Lupino can be characterized as a social realist because she relished tackling daring topics that were usually overlooked in Hollywood at the time. Critics have praised her as an *auteur* (i.e., as the author of her films) because her work reveals a consistency of themes and motifs. Certainly she often selected controversial social issues as the subjects of her films, such as rape, promiscuity, single motherhood, and bigamy, though she provided no easy answers and the films themselves often end ambiguously. Typically, her characters are from the working class, and often her male characters are the dangerous or questionable figures who are usually portrayed in film noir by women. In addition, her films explore the themes of feminine sexuality, independence, and dependence, and her female characters are as likely to be villains, or at least morally questionable, as they are to be heroines. Likewise, her films convey the tensions of disillusioned characters who are trapped by their surroundings. For example, *Never Fear* concerns the travails of a female dancer who is stricken by polio; *Not Wanted* is about unwed mothers, and tells the story of a promiscuous teenage girl who takes up with men she meets in bars, thus becoming pregnant in the process. *Hard, Fast, and Beautiful* is about a bored mother filled with dreams for her tennis-champion daughter, though the film denounces her for what it suggests are her unhealthy ambitions and the daughter ultimately chooses marriage over her tennis career. *Outrage* treats the subject of rape by focusing on the trauma endured by a rape victim who finds comfort in the arms of a paternal man. And, in *The Bigamist* the central character is a man who is driven by his wife's professional ambitions to an affair and it earned the praise of critics for its empathetic account of the ambiguous origins of a couple's double affair. Critics have pointed out that for Lupino's characters, the problem is not about the difficulties of being reintegrated into the mainstream of society, but rather about the superficiality of that mainstream.

Critics generally agree that *The Hitch-Hiker* is Lupino's best directorial accomplishment; it was her biggest critical and commercial success. Made the same year as her impressive melodrama *The Bigamist,* this film is nonetheless entirely different. It is an unrelentingly tense story of two businessmen on a fishing holiday who pick up a hitchhiker—a murdering psychopath—and are held as his captives. They are forced at gunpoint to drive him through the southwest and into Mexico until he no longer needs them. Lupino demonstrated a deft hand at crafting a dismal noir atmosphere, in coaxing riveting performances, and avoiding suspense-film clichés. She also effectively revealed the changes of the victimized men's relationship as they argue about what to do, and she suggests that their survival depends on their union more than anything else.

Ida Lupino

Lupino's technically proficient films boasted small budgets, usually less than $200,000, and no stars; they were usually shot in about 13 days. Not surprisingly, given her extensive acting experience, actors especially appreciated her directorial skills. Nonetheless, Lupino proclaimed distinctly antifeminist aims and ultrafeminine means, to the chagrin of many feminist film scholars. She freely admitted to using a soft touch as a director; i.e., she cooed instructions to her cast and crew, and encouraged them to call her "mother" because she wanted her productions to operate like a big, happy family. Nevertheless, she approached her duties with determination and extensive preparation. And, though she was apparently rhetorically unconcerned with feminist issues, in her own life she worked prolifically, and critics have astutely noted that her rhetoric about feminism was belied by the way she conducted her own life. In her later years, however, Lupino softened her rhetoric and lamented that there were not more women working as directors and producers in Hollywood.

Lupino and Collier's mistake was going into distribution, a move to which she objected because she considered herself a creative worker rather than a businessperson. But, when their film company folded in 1954, Lupino went to work in television. Initially reluctant, she was persuaded to work as an actress for two years. She loved it. Eventually, she moved into television directing and ultimately, she directed at least a hundred episodes for series television, though she claimed to have directed hundreds. She was praised for her use of a mobile camera during a time when camera work tended to be static. Among the series she directed were *Gunsmoke, Have Gun Will Travel, Sunset Strip, The Untouchables,* and *Alfred Hitchcock Pre-*

sents. Interestingly, as a television director, Lupino became pigeon-holed as a director who was best at Westerns and action shows, though she longed to do a love story. Eventually, she directed Anne Baxter and Ronald Reagan in a teleplay for *General Electric Theater.* After a lengthy period directing for television, Lupino returned to feature film work with *The Trouble with Angels,* a frothy movie about an all-girls religious academy whose educational goals are compromised by the high jinks of a pair of wild, boy-crazy girls. It was her last Hollywood feature film.

—Cynthia Felando

LYELL, Lottie

Australian director and actress

Born: Lottie Edith Cox in Sydney, 23 February 1890. **Family:** Married the director Raymond Longford, 1925. **Career:** 1907—professional stage debut as the female lead in *An Englishman's Home*; 1911—appeared on-screen for the first time, in a supporting role with Raymond Longford in *Captain Midnight, the Bush King*; made her first film with Longford, *The Fatal Wedding*; 1919—her masterpiece, *The Sentimental Bloke* was released; 1922—Longford and Lyell formed the Longford-Lyell Australian Picture Productions Limited in order to fight Australia's ongoing problems of exhibition and distribution; 1924—Longford and Lyell re-formed their production company as Longford-Lyell Productions. **Died:** Of tuberculosis, in Australia, 21 December 1925.

Films as Actress

1911   *Captain Midnight, the Bush King* (Rolfe) (as Thelma); *Captain Starlight*; *The Life of Rufus Dawes*

(all films directed by Longford)

1911   *The Fatal Wedding*; *The Romantic Story of Margaret Catchpole* (title role)
1912   *The Tide of Death*; *The Midnight Wedding*
1913   *Australia Calls*; *Pommy Arrives in Australia*; *'Neath Austral Skies*
1914   *The Swagman's Story*; *Trooper Campbell*; *Taking His Chance*; *The Silence of Dean Maitland*
1915   *We'll Take Her Children in Amongst Our Own*; *Ma Hoggan's New Boarder*
1916   *A Maori Maid's Love* (+ sc); *The Mutiny of the Bounty* (as Nessie Heywood, + sc, ed)
1917   *The Church and the Woman*
1918   *The Woman Suffers* (as Marjorie Manton)
1919   *The Sentimental Bloke* (as Doreen, + sc, art d, ed, production asst)
1920   *Ginger Mick* (+ sc)
1921   *Rudd's New Selection* (as Nell)
1923   *The Dinkum Bloke* (+ co-d, sc, pr)

Other Films

1921   *The Blue Mountains Mystery* (co-d with Longford, sc, ed)
1923   *Australia Calls* (sc); *An Australian by Marriage* (sc, + possibly ro)

1924   *Fisher's Ghost* (sc, pr)
1925   *The Bushwackers* (sc, pr)
1926   *Peter Vernon's Silence* (sc, pr); *The Pioneers* (Longford) (sc)

Publications on Lyell

Books

Pike, Andrew, and Ross Cooper, *Australian Film: 1900-1977,* Melbourne, 1980.
Shirley, Graham, and Brian Adams, *Australian Cinema: The First Eighty Years,* Sydney, 1981.
Tulloch, John, *Legends on the Screen: The Australian Narrative Film, 1919-1929,* Sydney, 1981.
Amery, Kerryn L., *Hidden Women: Locating Information on Significant Australian Women,* Melbourne, 1986.
Wright, Andrée, *Brilliant Careers: Women in Australian Cinema,* Sydney, 1986.
Bertrand, Ina, editor, *Cinema in Australia: A Documentary History,* Sydney, 1989.
Foster, Gwendolyn Audrey, *Women Film Directors: An International Bio-Critical Dictionary,* Westport, Connecticut, 1995.

Articles

Long, J., "Part 1 of a Historical Survey of Women in Australian Film Production," in *Cinema Papers* (Melbourne), June/July 1976.
Shirley, G., and A. Andrée Wright, "Kelly: Hit or Myth," in *Cinema Papers* (Melbourne), July 1987.

*   *   *

Lottie Lyell is credited with being the first Australian movie star, but she is also noteworthy as a director, producer, writer, art director, and editor. For more than a decade, during the 1910s and early 1920s, she enjoyed a productive personal and professional partnership with filmmaker Raymond Longford. Nevertheless, her long career was overlooked by Australian film historians, despite her status as a cinema pioneer. Indeed, as film historian Andrée Wright contends, Lyell is "the outstanding Australian personality of early film."

Lyell's acting career began in the theater in 1907, and by 1909 she was performing on stage with Longford. Then, in 1911 she and Longford made a momentous decision—to make movies. Together, they made 28 films and Lyell starred in 21 of them, although only a few survive. Film historians have bemoaned the fact that primary evidence about Lyell's early career is so sparse, but she is presumed to have combined her role as an actress with that of director for many years. Reportedly, Lyell co-directed all of her films, though such accomplishments went uncredited. Indeed, many of her production colleagues steadfastly maintained that she was the primary director of the Lyell-Longford productions. Her contributions were so great, that one of her acting colleagues alleged that she, rather than Raymond, had the skills to direct a film alone, and further credited her with using her power with "reserve and discretion."

During a period when screen roles for women were fairly narrow, Lyell enacted an important depiction of Australian femininity that was both demure and defiant, quiet and daring—the "girl of the bush," in films such as *The Tide of Death* and *'Neath Austral Skies.*

In the latter film she rides to the rescue of a trooper who has been bound and tossed into a river by cattle thieves. While her man takes care of the gang, Lyell, with knife clenched between her teeth, dives to the rescue. Critics at the time enthusiastically characterized Lyell as like the "all-Australian heroine" she often played, especially for her skills as a horsewoman. Notably, more recent film critics have observed the tendency for Lyell's heroines to blur the distinction between good and evil. In other words, in the Longford-Lyell films it was the men who caused women to go "wrong." Thus, in the most-cited example, *The Woman Suffers,* two women are seduced and abandoned after they become pregnant. The first woman commits suicide in desperation, while the second (played by Lyell) attempts a self-induced abortion without success. But rather than ensuring a hopeless future, her act leads her lover to acknowledge his wrong and to marry her, which seems to guarantee a happy future.

Despite considerable opposition from critics and investors, Lyell and Longford determined to adapt C. J. Dennis's popular 1915 book *The Songs of a Sentimental Bloke* for the screen. *The Sentimental Bloke,* a romantic comedy about the working class, proved to be their masterpiece, and moreover, it achieved legendary status as the earliest Australian feature to be considered a classic. It successfully blends love story, social comedy, and a working-class setting—though without featuring the extreme class conflict as did other films of the time that featured the poor. Like Dennis's volume, nearly all of the film's titles consist of dialected verse from the Bloke's point of view, which lent considerably to its Australian humor and spirit. The film is largely unknown outside Australia, though local historians consider it one of the world's best films made before 1920. Among its other noteworthy attributes, it is considered innovative for its realistic ambience and an unusually respectful depiction of the working poor, unlike other films that associated the city with vice and the country with virtue. Lyell played the Bloke's true love, the sweet factory-girl Doreen for whom he goes straight. Most of the movie's narrative concerns their courtship, which is broken when they argue about a rival for Doreen's affection. After they reconcile and marry, the Bloke goes astray from his vow to give up drinking and gambling with his pub mates. Eventually Doreen's uncle arrives and presents the couple with an enticing opportunity—to take over his country orchard, where they find happiness in hard work. When their baby boy is born, their future seems assuredly idyllic.

When it was released, *The Sentimental Bloke* made more money than any previous Australian film and it earned enormous praise. Indeed, in Australia it was considered a landmark of quality until the end of the silent era. Its performances are especially noteworthy, in large part, due to Lyell's restrained, sympathetic, and realistic style of acting. She has been credited with being one of the first Australian performers to adapt her performance style to the film medium, by avoiding the exaggerated gestures that were necessary on stage but not on-screen. In addition, reportedly, Longford encouraged the actors to spend time in a working-class Sydney suburb to prepare for their roles. After *The Sentimental Bloke,* Longford and Lyell made two sequels, *Ginger Mick* and *The Dinkum Bloke,* which no longer survive, though historians have presumed they followed the formula established in *The Sentimental Bloke.*

Lyell's first screen credit for directing did not come until 1921's *The Blue Mountains Mystery,* for which she also adapted the script from Harrison Owen's novel, *The Mount Maranga Mystery.* The film features an innocent young heroine who is contrasted with the mean and mysterious sophisticate, Belle Vere. The sophisticate, however, was not entirely irredeemable, as she eventually confesses her role in falsely convicting the innocent woman of manslaughter, and then kills herself.

In the early 1920s, Lyell started to experience diminishing health due to tuberculosis; then, after living together for 13 years, Longford secured a divorce and married her only weeks before her death at the age of 35. One obituary appropriately described her passing as "a distinct blow to the motion picture industry of this country and the loss of one who has left the mark of her genius on Australia's screen progress." After her death, Longford directed *The Pioneers* from a script Lyell had written, though without her other skills, his career declined rapidly thereafter.

—Cynthia Felando

MACLEAN, Alison

Canadian/New Zealander director

Born: Ottawa, Ontario, Canada, 31 July 1958; moved to New Zealand in 1972. **Education:** Attended Auckland University, BFA, majored in sculpture. **Career:** 1982—directed first short film, *Taunt,* the year she was graduated from Auckland University; 1989—moved to Sydney, Australia; 1992—directed her first feature, *Crush;* 1992—directed "Greed," an episode of the Australian TV series *The Seven Deadly Sins;* moved to New York City; 1990s—contributing editor of *BOMB* magazine; 1995—directed *The Adventures of Pete & Pete* for Nickelodeon; 1996—directed "Subway Kick," an episode of the HBO series *Subway Stories;* mid-1990s—in development on several projects, including a remake of *Bedlam,* originally produced by Val Lewton and starring Boris Karloff, *Iris,* produced by Good Machine, and an untitled "Chrome Dragon" project, an action film set in Bangkok; 1997—directed episode of TV series *Homicide: Life on the Streets.* **Awards:** Best Short Film, New Zealand Film and Television Awards, for *Talkback,* 1987; Best Short Film, New Zealand Film Awards, for *Kitchen Sink,* 1989. **Agent:** William Morris Agency, 151 El Camino Drive, Beverly Hills, CA 90212, U.S.A.

Films as Director

1982   *Taunt* (short) (+ sc)
1985   *Rud's Wife* (short) (+ co-sc)
1987   *Talkback* (short) (+ co-sc)
1989   *Kitchen Sink* (short) (+ sc)
1992   *Crush* (+ co-sc)
1993   *Positive* (short)

Publications by Maclean

Articles

"Tom Noonan," in *BOMB* (New York), Fall 1994.
"Todd Haynes," in *BOMB* (New York), Summer 1995.

Publications on Maclean

Book

Foster, Gwendolyn Audrey, *Women Film Directors: An International Bio-Critical Dictionary,* Westport, Connecticut, 1995.

Articles

Clarke, J., "*Kitchen Sink,*" in *Illusions* (Wellington, New Zealand), November 1985.

Logan, C., "First Crush," in *Onfilm* (Auckland, New Zealand), no. 9, 1991.
Taubin, Amy, "Object Choices," in *Village Voice* (New York), 10 September 1991.
"*Variety* Vets *Brain, Crush,*" in *Onfilm* (Auckland, New Zealand), no. 6, 1992.
"*Sink, Snail* on the Road," in *Onfilm* (Auckland, New Zealand), no. 10, 1992.
Baddiley, M., "Behind the Scenes in *Crush,*" in *Filmnews* (New South Wales), no. 4, 1993.
"Open Arms for *Crush* and *AWOL,*" in *Onfilm* (Auckland, New Zealand), no. 4, 1993.
Bilbrough, M., "Car *Crush* Views," in *Illusions* (Wellington, New Zealand), Winter 1993.
Bourget, E., "*Crush,*" in *Positif* (Paris), January 1993.
Ciment, Michel, "Crash and *Crush,*" in *Positif* (Paris), January 1993.
Francke, Lizzie, "Dark Side—*Crush,*" in *Sight and Sound* (London), April 1993.
Glaessner, Verina, "*Crush,*" in *Sight and Sound* (London), April 1993.
Macaulay, Scott, "Under Pressure," in *Filmmaker* (New York), Summer 1993.
Brown, Georgia, "B Happy," in *Village Voice* (New York), 14 September 1993.
Chua, Lawrence, "*Crush* Groove," in *Village Voice* (New York), 28 September 1993.
Dieckmann, Katherine, "Accident," in *Film Comment* (New York), September/October 1993.
James, Caryn, "A Distinctive Shade of Darkness," in *New York Times,* 28 November 1993.
Dargis, Manhola, "Down under the Rainbow," in *Village Voice* (New York), 30 November 1993.
Morton, Lisa, "*Crush* and *Sweetie*: The Female Grotesque in Two Contemporary Australasian Films," in *Deep South* (Dunedin, New Zealand), Spring 1995.
Taubin, Amy, "In the Money," in *Village Voice* (New York), 10 December 1996.

*   *   *

Alison Maclean is one of a group of Australasian women filmmakers—the list only begins with Jane Campion, Gillian Armstrong, and Jocelyn Morehouse—who have brought distinctly female perspectives to a male-dominated movie industry. In her films, Maclean has exhibited a special concern for gender roles and empowerment; words and their meanings; and the manner in which women communicate (as well as lack of communication and its ramification).

All of these issues are articulated in *Talkback,* one of Maclean's earlier short films, the story of a female talkback radio producer who replaces a male host. The producer must acclimate herself to her new role, and her new power to communicate, as she converses with her callers. Maclean's follow-up, *Kitchen Sink,* is a small masterpiece: a riveting—and wordless—12-minute-long surreal horror film about a woman and the man-monster/paramour who emerges from the hair in her sink. *Kitchen Sink* works as an exploration of an evolving male-female relationship and a textbook example of the often over-looked power of the short film. It is tightly directed, and exudes a nonstop energy that would be impossible to maintain in a feature-length film.

Maclean's debut feature is *Crush,* an oddly compelling psychological thriller. *Crush* is the story of New Zealander Christina, a literary critic who has set up an interview with Colin, a reclusive writer. Her American womanfriend Lane is at the wheel as the pair drive to meet Colin. Seemingly inexplicably, Lane begins speeding. The car crashes. Christina is nearly killed; she ends up hospitalized, comatose, and with massive head injuries. Lane leaves the accident scene without summoning help. She shows up at the home of Colin, where she encounters his unpolished 15-year-old daughter, Angela. Both Angela and Colin are attracted to Lane, who begins seducing her way into their lives.

This triangle is dissolved upon the reappearance of Christina. Angela, who is confused by her conflicting feelings and her father's developing relationship with Lane, switches her attention to Christina. The adolescent visits the invalid in the hospital, assists in her therapy, and contaminates her mind against Lane. Christina's physical condition improves to the point where she can spend a weekend with Colin, Angela, and Lane; however, she is bound to a wheelchair, and her speech is slurred.

The film concludes with the characters spending a day by a waterfall, with Lane aspiring to clear the air with both Angela and Christina (who is still in her wheelchair). When the others are not around, Christina rises from the chair and shoves Lane to her death over the waterfall cliff.

During the course of the film, many questions emerge. Exactly what is the nature of Lane and Christina's relationship? Are they merely friends, or have they been lovers? What spurred on Lane's actions in the car? Had she and Christina had some kind of spat just before the film opens? Has Lane abandoned Christina out of selfishness or thoughtlessness, or has she been psychologically jarred (if not physically damaged) by the accident?

Why does Lane relate to Colin and Angela in the manner in which she does? And what is the true extent of Christina's injuries? Can she think clearly, and is unable to communicate because of her physical limitations, or has the accident shattered her mind and memory? (More clear are Angela's motivations for her connecting with Lane and Christina. She is no manipulative devil, but rather a lonely, attention-seeking innocent who seeks female camaraderie with Lane and at the same time is dazzled by her and attracted to her because of her fear of heterosexual sex. When Angela sees Lane linking romantically with her father, and thus becoming a rival for his affection, she switches her attention to Christina. As Christina has been rendered mute and physically helpless, Angela can exercise power in her presence.)

At the outset, Lane's actions make her appear to be the rogue, while helpless Christina suffers dearly because of Lane. As the scenario develops, however, these roles become more ambiguous. At the end, it is purposefully unclear which character truly is the villain and which is the victim—or, indeed, if either one can be labeled or judged as "good" or "evil."

These questions—and their lack of answers—are what gives *Crush* its appeal. Maclean does not in any way transform Lane or Christina into feminist heroines. She does not define their motivations; the viewer has to figure them out. The result is a tale of deep and complex emotions, which is at its most compelling when exploring the intricate connection between Lane, Christina, and Angela. Meanwhile, a masculine point of view is practically missing from the film, as the role of Colin is more of a catalyst for the actions of the other characters.

Crush is a highly unconventional film, and Alison Maclean is a gifted cinematic voice. As of mid-1997 she was living in New York, where she was "in development" on several projects (one of which is a remake of the 1946 Val Lewton-produced chiller, *Bedlam*). One hopes that her promising feature film career will not end with *Crush*.

—Rob Edelman

MACPHERSON, Jeanie

American writer, director, and actress

Born: Boston, 18 May 1884. **Education:** Attended Mademoiselle DeJacque's School, Paris. **Career:** 1907-14—stage and film actress: member of the chorus, Chicago Opera House, film debut in *Mr. Jones at the Ball,* 1908, and in road companies of *Cleopatra* and *Strongheart* and on Broadway in *Havana*; 1912—directed and appeared in new version of lost film, *The Tarantula*; 1915—began long association with Cecil B. DeMille. **Died:** Of cancer, in Hollywood, 26 August 1946.

Films as Writer for Director Cecil B. DeMille

1915   *The Unafraid; The Captive* (+ ro); *Chimmie Fadden Out West; The Golden Chance*
1916   *Maria Rosa; Temptation; The Trail of the Lonesome Pine; The Heart of Nora Flynn; The Dream Girl*
1917   *Joan the Woman; A Romance of the Redwoods; The Little American; The Woman God Forgot; The Devil Stone*
1918   *The Whispering Chorus; Old Wives for New; Till I Come Back to You*
1919   *Don't Change Your Husband; For Better, for Worse; Male and Female*
1920   *Something to Think About*
1921   *Forbidden Fruit; The Affairs of Anatol*
1922   *Saturday Night; Manslaughter*
1923   *Adam's Rib; The Ten Commandments*
1924   *Triumph*
1925   *The Golden Bed; The Road to Yesterday*
1927   *The King of Kings*
1929   *The Godless Girl; Dynamite*
1930   *Madam Satan*
1935   *The Crusades*
1936   *The Plainsman*
1938   *The Buccaneer*
1939   *Land of Liberty* (doc); *Union Pacific*
1940   *Northwest Mounted Police*
1942   *Reap the Wild Wind* (uncredited)
1944   *The Story of Dr. Wassell*

Other Films as Writer

1912   *The Tarantula* (+ d, ro)
1913   *The Sea Urchin* (E. August) (+ ro as lover); *Red Margaret, Moonshiner* (Dwan)

Jeanie Macpherson with Cecil B. De Mille

1914   *The Ghost Breaker* (+ d); *The Lie* (Dwan)
1916   *The Love Mask* (Reicher) (co)
1926   *Red Dice* (W. K. Howard); *Young April* (Crisp); *Her Man o' War* (Reicher)
1933   *Fra Diavolo* (*The Devil's Brother*) (Roach and Rogers)

Films as Actress for Director D. W. Griffith

1908   *Mr. Jones at the Ball*; *The Fatal Hour*; *The Vaquero's Vow*; *Father Gets in the Game*; *The Devil*; *Concealing a Burglar*; *The Curtain Pole*; *The Clubman and the Tramp*; *Mrs. Jones Entertains*; *The Test of Friendship*; *A Wreath in Time*; *Tragic Love*
1909   *Mr. Jones Has a Card Party*; *Trying to Get Arrested*; *The Medicine Bottle*; *Lady Helen's Escapade*; *A Rude Hostess*; *Confidence*; *The Peach Basket Hat*; *The Faded Lilies*; *The Message*; *The Seventh Day*; *With Her Card*; *Lines of White on the Sullen Sea*; *A Midnight Adventure*; *The Death Disc*; *A Corner in Wheat*; *The Call*
1910   *The Newlyweds*; *The Way of the World*; *A Victim of Jealousy*; *An Affair of Hearts*; *The Impalement*; *A Flash of Light*; *In Life's Cycle*; *The Iconoclast*; *Winning Back His Love*; *A Wreath of Orange Blossoms*; *Heart Beats of Long Ago*
1911   *Fisher Folks*; *The Spanish Gypsy*; *Enoch Arden*; *The Blind Princess and the Poet*; *The Last Drop of Water*; *Out from the Shadow*
1914   *The Desert's Sting* (d unknown)

Other Films as Actress

1914   *Rose of the Rancho* (C. B. DeMille); *The Ghost Breaker* (C. B. DeMille and Apfel); *The Merchant of Venice* (Weber and Smalley) (as Merrissa)
1915   *The Girl of the Golden West* (C. B. DeMille); *Carmen* (C. B. DeMille)
1923   *Hollywood* (Cruze) (as herself)

Publications by Macpherson

Articles

"Development of Photodramatic Writing," in *Moving Picture World*, 21 July 1917.

"Functions of the Continuity Writer," in *Opportunities in the Motion Picture Industry,* Los Angeles, 1922.

"The Subtitle: Friend and Foe," in *Motion Picture Director* (Hollywood), November 1926.

Publications on Macpherson

Book

Acker, Ally, *Reel Women: Pioneers of the Cinema, 1896 to the Present,* New York, 1991.

Articles

Cinema (Beverly Hills), no. 35, 1976.

Foreman, Alexa L., in *American Screenwriters,* 2nd series, edited by Randall Clark, Detroit, 1986.

Obituary, in *New York Times,* 27 August 1946.

* * *

Jeanie Macpherson was not a screenwriter when she was introduced to Cecil B. DeMille. She had been a director at Universal at one time, but when she met DeMille she was concentrating on acting. Due to her dark features, however, she was being typecast as either a gypsy or a Spaniard. Macpherson was cast by DeMille to act in a few of his features (*Rose of the Rancho, The Girl of the Golden West, Carmen,* and *The Captive*—the last of which she also wrote) before she decided to turn exclusively to screenwriting. There was mutual attraction between Macpherson and DeMille from the start: she loved the challenge of working with a hard-driving perfectionist; he was drawn to her spirit and courage. It was a partnership that would last more than 25 years.

Macpherson and DeMille held a common belief that would be the basis for every screenplay on which they collaborated: they despised weakness in men and women. In Macpherson's scripts, weak men were taken advantage of and degraded, and weak women were shallow, gold-digging, and destructive creatures who went from one rich man to the next. The screenwriter believed that men and women could learn from experience, however, and change weak or evil ways, and she demonstrated this in her early social dramas. Both Macpherson and DeMille celebrated the hero and the heroine—biblical, historical, or fictional—and praised their courage and perseverance.

Macpherson's strength was writing historical dramas. When she began her work for DeMille, she assisted the director in writing features for Geraldine Farrar, the operatic star, including *Maria Rosa, Temptation,* and *Joan the Woman.* This last was based on the life of Joan of Arc. While DeMille created the huge frame around the French girl's life with his grandiose settings and hundreds of extras, Macpherson fashioned a human drama with which the audience could identify. Thus, while Joan was part of a spectacular event, upon a closer look she was seen as a frightened young girl driven by her spiritual beliefs. The title, Macpherson's idea, emphasized the view of Joan as a human being rather than an indestructible saint. This same viewpoint was used in the DeMille epic *The King of Kings.* Based on the life of Jesus Christ, the film portrayed Mary Magdalene as a woman who was not evil but misguided, and Jesus as a virile and strong man.

The end of World War I ushered in the era of the Roaring Twenties and by then Macpherson had begun writing contemporary drama rather than historical projects. The liberal moral climate gave rise to the flapper, the sexually aware young woman who rejected conventional mores. Some of the best films DeMille and Macpherson created were responses to America's change in mood and fashion: *Old Wives for New, Don't Change Your Husband, Male and Female, The Affairs of Anatol, Manslaughter,* and *Adam's Rib. Male and Female,* an update of the play *The Admirable Crichton,* introduced a new element into Macpherson's screenplays: the blending together of past and present stories. Macpherson interwove episodes from history and the Bible into modern dramas to demonstrate moral lessons. These lessons warned audiences of the excesses of the 1920s and what the future would hold if the warnings were not heeded. Flashbacks were used as lessons, such as the prologue to *The Ten Commandments* which concerned Moses and the story of the commandments (this version of *Ten Commandments* had a modern-day plot). *Male and Female* contained a flashback to Babylon, *Manslaughter* to ancient Rome, *Adam's Rib* to prehistoric times, *Triumph* to Romeo and Juliet, and *The Road to Yesterday* to 17th-century England. These screenplays offered audiences not only an admonishment for their money, but also the attraction of seeing stars in the period costumes that each flashback required.

In 1933, while DeMille was busy with other projects, Macpherson wrote the screenplay for *Fra Diavolo* for Laurel and Hardy, before rejoining the director for several films celebrating heroes: King Richard the Lionhearted in *The Crusades,* Wild Bill Hickok in *The Plainsman,* Jean Lafitte in *The Buccaneer,* the men who started the transcontinental railroad in *Union Pacific,* Canadian Mounties in *Northwest Mounted Police,* and Dr. Corydon E. Wassell in *The Story of Dr. Wassell.* In 1939 she co-wrote and narrated the DeMille film *Land of Liberty,* a historical look at America for the New York World's Fair. These last research and writing projects were done mostly without credit. Before she could finish her research work on *Unconquered* for DeMille, Macpherson died of cancer in 1946. Her screenplays had gone full circle from the early escapist and historical films to realistic and social dramas and back to escapist and historical pictures again.

—Alexa L. Foreman

MADAME X—EINE ABSOLUTE HERRSCHERIN
(Madame X—An Absolute Ruler)
Germany, 1977
Director: Ulrike Ottinger

Production: Color, 16mm; running time: 141 minutes. First screened on ZDF, 13 April 1978. Filmed in Lake Konstanz, Konstanz, Germany.

Producer: Ulrike Ottinger; **associate producer:** Tabea Blumenschein; **screenplay:** Ulrike Ottinger; **photography:** Ulrike Ottinger; **editor:** Ulrike Ottinger; **costume designer:** Tabea Blumenschein.

Cast: Tabea Blumenschein (*Madame X*); Roswitha Jantz (*Noa-Noa*); Irena von Lichtenstein (*Blowup*); Yvonne Rainer (*Josephine de Collage*); Claudia Skoda (*Flora Tannenbaum*); Monika von Cube (*Klara*

Freud-Goldmund); Lutze (*Betty Brillo*); Mona (*Omega Zentauri*); Mackay Taylor (*Belcampo*); with: Cynthia Beatt.

Publications

Script

Ottinger, Ulrike, *Madama X—eine absolute Herrscherin: Drehbuch,* Berlin, 1979.

Books

Silverman, Kaja, *The Acoustic Mirror: The Female Voice in Psycho-analysis and Cinema,* Bloomington, Indiana, 1988.
Mayne, Judith, *The Woman at the Keyhole: Feminism and Women's Cinema,* Bloomington, Indiana, 1990.
Weiss, Andrea, *Vampires and Violets: Lesbians in Film,* New York, 1993.

Articles

Steinwachs, Ginka, "Madame X. Ein Versuch zur Archäologic der Subjektivitat von Ulrike Ottinger und Tabea Blumenschein," in *Die Schwarze Botin,* no. 6, 1979.
Schlungbaum, Barbara, and Claudia Hoff, "Eindruck—Ausdruck: Tabea Talks," in *Frauen und Film* (Frankfurt), no. 26, 1980.
Silberman, Marc, "Ciné-Feminists in West Berlin," in *Quarterly Review of Film Studies* (Pleasantville, New York), vol. 5, no. 2, 1980.
Sartor, F., "Ulrike Ottinger," in *Film en Televisie* (Brussels, Belgium), May/June 1980.
Treut, Monika, "Ein Nachtrag zu Ulrike Ottinger's Film *Madame X,*" in *Frauen und Film* (Frankfurt), vol. 28, 1981.
Mueller, Roswitha, "Interview with Ulrike Ottinger," in *Discourse* (Berkeley), Winter 1981-82.
McRobbie, Angela, introduction, "Interview with Ulrike Ottinger," by Erica Carter, translated by Martin Chalmers, in *Screen Education* (London), Winter/Spring 1982.
Fritze, Christoph, Georg Seeblen, and Claudium Weil, "Totenkopf und weisse Segel: Der Piratenfilm," in *Der Abenteurer, Geschichte und Mythologie des Abenteuer-Films,* Reinbek, 1983.
Ottinger, Ulrike, "Der Zwang zum Genrekino: Von der Gefährdung des Autoren-Kinos," in *Courage,* no. 4, 1983.
White, Patricia, "*Madame X: An Absolute Ruler,*" in *Screen* (London), Autumn 1987.
Hake, Sabine, "'Gold, Love, Adventure': The Postmodern Conspiracy of Madame X," in *Discourse,* Fall/Winter 1988-89.
Bergstrom, Janet, "The Theatre of Everyday Life: Ulrike Ottinger's *China—The Arts—Everyday Life,*" in *Camera Obscura* (Berkeley), September 1988.
Grisham, Therese, "Twentieth Century Theatrum Mundi: Ulrike Ottinger's *Johanna d'Arc of Mongolia,*" in *Wide Angle* (Baltimore, Maryland), April 1992.
Silberman, Marc, "Interview with Ulrike Ottinger: Surreal Images," in *Gender and German Cinema: Feminist Intervention,* Volume 1, *Gender and Representation in New German Cinema,* edited by Sandra Frieden, Richard W. McCormick, Vibeke R. Petersen, and Laurie Melissa Vogelsang, Oxford, 1993.

* * *

Madame X—An Absolute Ruler is a campy postmodern pirate movie about an eponymous heroine, the beautiful, ruthless, "uncrowned ruler of the China Seas," who persuades women to give up their boring everyday lives with men for the promise of "gold, love, and adventure" aboard a ship of women. The film is the rarely screened first feature from lesbian filmmaker Ulrike Ottinger who, since then, has earned a reputation for parodying art cinema and for generally problematizing cinema conventions while endeavoring to find new ways to represent women on film. Funded by ZDF, German public television, *Madame X* is part of the 1970's German New Wave and has been praised by at least some critics for its clever linking of feminist surrealism and queer cinema.

A feminist allegory that subverts the pirate film's conventions and glories in resisting cinema realism, *Madame X* stars underground film icon Tabea Blumenschein playing a dual role as the leather-clad dominatrix pirate captain and as the ship's living figurehead. (She also designed the films extravagant costumes.) On board the junk *Orlando,* Madame X with her servant Hoi-Sin has lured a motley crew of familiar feminine types, "from all walks of life," each sporting exaggerated costumes—including a cover girl, a dowdy housewife, a psychologist, an outdoorswoman, a bush pilot, a disenchanted artist, and a beautiful "native." Each has received the captain's message in a manner that suits her circumstance; for example, the Polynesian Noa-Noa discovers the message in a bottle while canoeing, housewife Betty Brillo finds it on a coupon in a soap box, and the model Blowup receives a phone call in her limousine. Their adventures include rescuing a shipwrecked hermaphrodite manicurist who has been thrown overboard a luxury yacht, the *Hollyday,* and then boarding the very same yacht to kill all the passengers and loot its showy treasures. Ultimately, however, the women's desires and jealousies become overwhelming, and Madame X orders the deaths of all but Noa-Noa and the rescued manicurist. But, undeterred, Madame X secures a new crew, the same women in new costumes, to embark on new adventures assisted by "favorable winds."

Upon its release, *Madame X* offended many critics who considered it nothing more than a voyeuristic display of the female body and lesbian sadomasochism that reiterates patriarchal constructions. Since then, the critical response has shifted somewhat as it has attained cult status, and as more recent critics have undertaken complex reevaluations of the film and its feminist provocations. Certainly, *Madame X* cleverly subverts the conventional cinema's "male gaze," in part, by refusing to depict lesbian sexuality with a weighty seriousness. The sex scenes between Madame X and her protégé Noa-Noa are played with an exaggerated theatrical absurdity. In addition, the film refuses to offer simplistic utopian visions, as the ship's women ultimately adopt the masculine power structures they sought to escape. As Ottinger has noted, her film plays with the desires of women, for violence and sex, in a comedic way, and it was intended to provoke reflection about the emerging women's movement and its own power structures. She further claimed it is entirely unrealistic to depict a women's revolt in which the women "triumph gloriously" and unproblematically.

In general, Ottinger's film avoids the structures of conventional linear storytelling by using a variety of experimental film strategies, including the use of a complex nonsynchronous soundtrack and the refusal to provide narrative closure, simple identification, and easily discerned hierarchies of meaning. Interestingly, Ottinger herself appears in a flashback as Madame X's lost lover. Also, feminist filmmakers Cynthia Beatt and Yvonne Rainer appear in the film. Rainer plays an artist who is unhappy with the art world and so decides to embark on the high-seas adventure, on roller skates, after pausing long enough to pronounce her profound disillusionment with art to a reporter—in a monologue she wrote herself.

As its critics have noted, *Madame X* includes complex references to Orientalism; for example, in addition to the Chinese cook and South Pacific "native," Ottinger's discovery of a historical Chinese woman pirate, Lai Cho San, provided a model for the character of Madame X. (Orientalism is a theme that continues to preoccupy Ottinger—as her most recent film's title suggests: *Exit Shanghai*.) Critics also have noted the film's indebtedness to the tradition of camp with its excesses of irony; antirealist acting; exaggerated gestures and costuming, color and textures—black leather, airy chiffon, feathers, flowers, cosmetics, jewelry. Likewise, *Madame X* has an abundance of elements that have provoked the interest of psychoanalytic film critics, from the captain's phallic blade-spiked, leather stump that conceals her castrated hand, to her double—the figurehead that has the power to speak, gaze, and kill—to the film's representation of pre-Oedipal lesbian desire. Finally, critics have noted the film's many references to Virginia Woolf's novel *Orlando*, which features a hero/heroine who changes his/her sex at the age of 30. Certainly, it is likely that *Madame X*'s multilayered ambiguities, including its many literary and filmic references and subversions, will continue to attract the attention of film critics and scholars.

—Cynthia Felando

MÄDCHEN IN UNIFORM

(Girls in Uniform)
Germany, 1931
Director: Leontine Sagan with Carl Froelich

Production: Deutsches Film Gemeinschaft; black and white, 35mm; running time: 98 minutes; length: 8799 feet. Released 1931. A new, reconstructed print was released in the 1970s.

Screenplay: Christa Winsloe and F. D. Andam, from the play *Yesterday and Today* by Christine Winsloe; **photography:** Reimar Kuntze and Franz Weihmayr; **music:** Hansom Milde-Meissner.

Cast: Dorothea Wieck (*Fraülein von Bernburg*); Hertha Thiefe (*Manuela von Meinhardis*); Emilie Unda (*Headmistress*); Ellen Schwanneke (*Ilse von Westhagen*); Hedwig Schlichter (*Fraülein von Kosten*); Gertrud de Lalsky (*Manuela's Aunt*).

Publications

Books

Kracauer, Siegfried, *From Caligari to Hitler: A Psychological History of the German Film*, Princeton, 1947.
Klinowski, Jacek, and Adam Garbicz, *Cinema, The Magic Vehicle: A Guide to Its Achievement: Journey One: The Cinema through 1949*, Metuchen, New Jersey, 1975.

Articles

Close Up (London), March 1932.
Herald Tribune (New York), 21 September 1932.
New York Times, 21 September 1932.
National Board of Review Magazine (New York), September/October 1932.
Hardy, Forsyth, interview with Leontine Sagan, in *Cinema Quarterly* (London), Winter 1932.
Potamkin, Harry, "Pabst and the Social Film," in *Hound and Horn* (New York), January/March 1933.
Jahier, Valerio, "42 ans de cinema," in *Le Role intellectuel du cinéma*, Paris, 1937.
Kael, Pauline, in *Kiss Kiss Bang Bang*, Boston, 1968.
Kjborup, S., in *Kosmorama* (Copenhagen), December 1972.
Scholar, N., in *Women in Film* (Berkeley), Summer 1975.
Rich, B. Ruby, "From Repressive Tolerance to Erotic Liberation," in *Jump Cut* (Chicago), March 1981.
Schlüpmann, H., and K. Gramann, "Vorbemerkung," in *Frauen und Film* (Berlin), June 1981.
Thiefe, Hertha, "Gestern und Heute" (interview), in *Frauen und Film* (Berlin), June 1981.
Lefanu, Mark, in *Monthly Film Bulletin* (London), January 1982.

* * *

Girls in Uniform was directed by Leontine Sagan under the supervision of Carl Froelich in 1931; it was based on the play *Yesterday and Today* by Christine Winsloe. Its subversive antifascist, antipatriarchal themes seem astonishing when one realizes that the film was shot in Germany just two years before Hitler's rise to power.

Girls in Uniform achieved great popularity in Paris, London, and Berlin, but it was later banned in Germany by Goebbels, Hitler's cultural minister, for its unhealthy moral conclusions. For the next few decades, the film was almost forgotten and received little critical attention. It seems to have been lost somewhere in film history between German expressionism and the Nazi cinema. In the early 1970s interest in the film was revived by women's film festivals; it has come to be seen as the first truly radical lesbian film; and in the last decade *Girls in Uniform* has finally received the recognition it deserves.

The structure of the film is a mixture of montage and narrative sequences which inform each other and create an atmosphere which perhaps could not have been achieved by the use of one of these methods alone. The montage sequence at the beginning of the film—stone towers, statues, and marching soldiers—sets up a compliance and strength, a tone that introduces the audience to the life of the girls at school. From the constricting montage shots, the camera turns immediately to the girls' school. Periodically, still shots of the militaristic, patriarchal world outside the school are interspersed with the narrative. The audience is reminded that although the school is a feminine space (indeed, there are no male characters in the film), it is surrounded and even permeated by ubiquitous male authority. Yet, that authority is itself called into question by the narrative, the defiance that continues despite the prevalence of authoritarianism. By its structure, the film succeeds in creating a feminine space enclosed in the literal walls (as exemplified by the montage) of the outside world.

In her utilization of the new sound medium, Sagan was the most advanced director in pre-war Germany. Lotte Eisner said: "With this work, the German sound film reached its highest level." Not only Sagan's precise use of dialogue but also her use of sound as metaphor (the sounding trumpet at the beginning and end of the film) and her creation of atmosphere, the whispers of the girls exchanging secrets, their final desperate chanting of Manuela's name—all attest to the accuracy of Eisner's statement.

Mädchen in Uniform

Siegfried Kracauer also praised Sagan for her cinematography. He noted her ability to impart the "symbolic power of light" to her images. Sagan's use of shadows adds not only depth to the flat screen but also meaning and atmosphere. Sagan's cinematography is an excellent example of what Eisner calls "*stimmung*" (emotion), which suggests the vibrations of the soul through the use of light. The lighting and shooting of the stairway is a notable example. Its ascending shadows and its center depth create a tension in which the girls must operate, for the front, well-lighted stairs are off limits to them. The staircase is then a symbol of the girls' confinement, and its darkness literally shadows all of their activities.

Sagan also pioneered the cinematic convention of superimposition of one character's face over that of another to symbolize a deep psychological connection between them. She uses this technique in the film to convey moments of deep attraction between the teacher Fräulein von Bernburg and her student Manuela. The fusion of their images suggests the strength of their bond. It was a technique used 30 years later by Bergman in *Persona* to achieve the same effect.

Girls in Uniform was the first film in Germany to be cooperatively produced. The Deutsches Film Gemeinschaft was created especially for this project—a cooperative film company formed by the cast and crew in which shares rather than salaries were distributed.

—Gretchen Elsner-Sommer

MADISON, Cleo
American director and actress

Born: Bloomington, Indiana, 1883. **Career:** 1900s —worked as an actress on the legitimate stage and in vaudeville; 1910s—moved to California and acted with the Santa Barbara Stock Company; 1913—made her screen debut as an actress; 1914—won stardom for her performance in *The Trey O'Hearts*; 1915—began directing and co-directing Universal shorts and features; 1924—retired from movies. **Died:** Burbank, California, 11 March 1964.

Films as Actress and/or Director

(+ d is listed where direction by Madison has been confirmed)

1913 *The Trap* (August—short); *The Heart of a Cracksman* (Reid and Robards—short); *Cross Purposes* (short); *The Buccaneers* (short); *Captain Kidd* (short); *Shadows of Life* (Weber—short); *His Pal's Request* (+ d, uncredited—short); *Under the Black Flag* (short)

1914 *The Trey O' Hearts* (W. Lucas—serial) (as Ruth/Judith); *Samson* (J. F. Macdonald) (as Jasmine, the Philistine); *Damon and Pythias* (Turner) (as Hermion); *The Master*

Key (serial); *Dead Man Who Killed* (*Eye for an Eye*; *The Dead Man That Kills*) (short); *The Feud* (short); *The Last of Their Race* (short); *The Law of Their Kind* (short); *The Love Victorious* (short); *The Man Between* (short); *The Mexican's Last Raid* (short); *The Mystery of Wickham Hall* (short); *Sealed Orders* (short); *The Severed Hand* (short); *The Strenuous Life* (short); *Unjustly Accused* (short)

1915   *The Pine's Revenge* (DeGrasse—short); *A Mother's Atonement* (DeGrasse—short) (as Alice/Jen); *The Fascination of the Fleur de Lis* (DeGrasse—short) (as Lisette); *Alas and Alack* (DeGrasse—short) (as Wife); *Agnes Kempler's Sacrifice* (short); *Liquid Dynamite* (+ d—short); *The Ring of Destiny* (+ d—short); *The Power of Fascination* (+ d—short); *The Dancer* (Park—short); *Extravagance* (Giblyn—short); *Faith of Her Fathers* (Giblyn—short); *A Fiery Introduction* (Giblyn—short); *The Flight of a Nightbird* (Giblyn—short); *The People of the Pit* (Giblyn—short); *A Wild Irish Rose* (Giblyn—short); *Haunted Hearts* (short); *The Mother's Instinct* (short); *Their Hour* (short); *The Ways of a Man* (short); *A Woman's Debt* (short)

1916   *A Soul Enslaved* (as Jane, + d); *The Chalice of Sorrow* (Ingram) (as Lorelei); *Her Bitter Cup* (as Rethna, + d, sc); *Her Defiance* (+ co-d with J. King—short); *Alias Jane Jones* (+ co-d—short); *Along the Malibu* (+ co-d with Mong—short); *His Return* (+ d—short); *Eleanor's Catch* (+ d—short); *Virginia* (+ d—short); *When the Wolf Howls* (+ co-d—short); *The Crimson Yoke* (+ co-d with Mong—short); *Priscilla's Prisoner* (+ d—short); *The Girl in Lower 9* (+ co-d—short); *The Guilty One* (+ co-d—short); *The Triumph of Truth* (+ d—short); *To Another Woman* (+ co-d with Mong—short); *Cross Purposes* (short); *The Heart's Crucible* (+ co-d with Kerrigan—short); *The Mystery Woman* (short); *Tillie, the Little Swede* (+ co-d with Mong—short)

1917   *Black Orchids* (Ingram) (as Marie De Severac/Zoraida); *The Girl Who Lost* (Cochrane—short); *The Web* (Cochrane—short); *The Woman Who Would Not Pay* (Baldwin—short); *The Sorceress* (short)

1918   *The Romance of Tarzan* (Meredyth and W. Lucas) (as La Belle Odine); *The Flame of the West* (short)

1919   *The Girl from Nowhere* (W. Lucas) (as "Gal")

1919-20   *The Great Radium Mystery* (R. F. Hill and Broadwell—serial)

1920   *The Price of Redemption* (Fitzgerald) (as Anne Steel)

1921   *Ladies Must Live* (Tucker) (as Mrs. Lincourt); *The Lure of Youth* (Rosen) (as Florentine Fair)

1922   *The Dangerous Age* (Stahl) (as Mary Emerson); *A Woman's Woman* (Giblyn) (as Iris Starr)

1923   *Gold Madness* (Thornby) (as Olga McGee); *Souls in Bondage* (Clifford) (as The Chameleon)

1924   *Discontented Husbands* (Le Saint) (as Jane Frazer); *The Lullaby* (Bennett) (as Mrs. Marvin); *The Roughneck* (Conway) (as Anne Delaney); *True as Steel* (Hughes) (as Mrs. Parry); *Unseen Hands* (Jaccard) (as Mataoka)

Publications on Madison

Books

Slide, Anthony, *Early Women Directors,* South Brunswick, New Jersey, 1977; rev. ed. published as *The Silent Feminists: America's First Women Directors,* Lanham, Maryland, 1996.

Acker, Ally, *Reel Women: Pioneers of the Cinema, 1896 to the Present,* New York, 1991.

Foster, Gwendolyn Audrey, *Women Film Directors: An International Bio-Critical Dictionary,* Westport, Connecticut, 1995.

Articles

Henry, William M., "Cleo, the Craftswoman," in *Photoplay* (New York), January 1916.

Chic, Mlle., "The Dual Personality of Cleo Madison," in *Moving Picture Weekly,* 1 July 1916.

Obituary in *Hollywood Reporter,* 12 March 1964.

Rainey, Buck, "Buck Rainey's Filmographies: Cleo Madison," in *Classic Images* (Davenport, Iowa), May 1987.

*   *   *

Cleo Madison found a steady job acting and writing for Carl Laemmle at Universal studios in 1913. She appeared in a steady flow of short films, serials, and occasionally a feature length drama, working with a stream of skilled technicians, including pioneer women directors Lois Weber and Ida May Park who would become mentors to Madison. Particularly in the 1914 serial *The Trey O' Hearts,* Madison won the hearts of fans starring in the dual role of an innocent but resilient heroine Ruth, and her evil identical twin Judith. As such, she remarkably survived through 15 episodes of apparently relentless action, including a car crash, forest fire, shooting, and death-threatening curse. As Madison became established as an on-screen personality, she became self-confident that she could do equally well working behind the camera. According to a fan magazine story of the mid-teens, she asked the company bosses to allow her to direct, and when they refused she became so difficult to work with—a prima donna à la Sarah Bernhardt—that they finally relented and gave her her own small production company.

As a combination film star and director, Madison was living in the limelight, bringing a number of feminist cinema pieces to the screen, and receiving a steady paycheck. Yet life at Universal was a mixed blessing. As silent-film historian Richard Koszarski has pointed out, Universal was one of the low-paying Hollywood studios. Perhaps that is why they hired so many women for directorial jobs that the other studios offered only to men. If you could bring a picture in on time and under budget and make it a crowd-pleaser to boot, then "Uncle Carl" Laemmle was happy to have you on the director's payroll. By 1915 there was an outstanding group of capable women directing at Universal, including Weber and Park, Nell Shipman, Ruth Ann Baldwin, Grace Cunard and others. Most of these women did their most prolific and effective work before and during the World War I years when men were in uniform. And while it cannot be said that women obtained director jobs before the war because men were not available, an argument can be made that some of these women lost their jobs when the war ended and a population of males sought to replace military duty with private-sector jobs.

Between 1915 and the end of 1916, Madison directed, or co-directed, and also starred in close to 20 films at Universal. Most were two-reeler shorts. Of these, very few survive due to the fact that Universal, in a classic example of corporate shortsightedness, burned its silent film material (shot on flammable and chemically unstable nitrate film stock) because they foresaw no further financial gain to be had from silent product. The surviving evidence of her film work shows that Madison was concerned with telling stories of social significance that center on the plight of working-class women.

A Soul Enslaved, a feature starring and directed by Madison, is about Jane, a poor girl working in a factory, who has a brief affair with the rich factory owner. As a result, years after her marriage to another man, she is castigated by her husband for being "damaged goods." *Her Bitter Cup*, a feature in which Madison starred as well as directed and wrote, relates the story of yet another factory laborer, Rethna, who organizes her fellow workers against a merciless factory owner. While a romance between Rethna and the factory owner's son provides the audience with entertainment, there also is a strong message that women working in factories must band together to fight for improved working conditions. One of the few films directed by Madison that does survive is a 23-minute short entitled *Her Defiance*. In this photoplay, a young woman (Madison) becomes pregnant by a lover who appears to abandon her. She chooses to bear the bastard child and then finds work as a cleaning woman to support herself and baby, rather than follow her brother's instructions to marry a wealthy old man. Film historian and archivist Eileen Bowser comments on this film in the Museum of Modern Art Circulating Film Library Catalog, "[it is] noteworthy for its own defiance of thematic taboos and its avoidance of a stereotypical portrayal of women." From these examples, it is clear that Madison, as Lois Weber did before her, was creating a body of work devoted to a social and moralistic view of lower- and middle-class women's lifestyles, paying detailed attention to the individual rights of women and society's power to control women's destinies.

After 1916 Madison either quit or was asked to leave the Universal lot. One can imagine an argument over a much deserved raise or perhaps a desire to work on more carefully structured features, rather than an assembly line of shorts, as reason for her termination. Or perhaps she, or the physically disabled sister for whom she took responsibility, became ill. In any case, there are no director credits for her in 1917. After that, she appears to have taken work wherever it could be found. She appeared in a single feature for a variety of studios and independent producers. She even returned to work as a lead in a Universal serial in 1919—quite a challenge for a 36-year-old veteran.

Age actually may have been Madison's worst enemy. And the Hollywood system has never had much patience with women aging. By 1924 she was playing the part of an Indian woman in a rather undistinguished scenario. Then she disappeared from the Hollywood scene. As happened with so many of the men and women pioneers of the silent screen, her skills lay dormant as sound films took over, and new, younger talents were imported to Hollywood. Only with the recent rise of interest in feminist cinema has Cleo Madison's name been resurrected. One only hopes that archivists will recover any privately held prints of the films she created—examples of an early feminist cinema—one that predates the Jazz Age, before women got the vote. Only then will her body of work be viewed with authority, and only then will her creativity and message truly be recognized.

—Audrey E. Kupferberg

MALDOROR, Sarah
French director

Born: Sarah Ducados, in Condom, Gers, France. **Education:** Attended École Dramatique de la rue Blanche, Paris, 1958-60; studied with Mark Donskoï at University Lomonosov, All-Union State Institute of Cinematography (VGIK), Moscow, 1961-62. **Family:** Companion to the president/founder of the Popular Movement for Angolan Liberation (MPLA) Mario de Andrade (died 1990), two daughters: Anna Ginga and Heinda Lucia. **Career:** 1960-62—founded the black theater company Les Griots in which she also worked as director and actor; 1965—assistant to Gillo de Pontercorvo on *The Battle of Algiers*; 1969—directed her first short in Algeria, *Monangambée*; 1970—directed her first feature in Guinea-Bissau, *Guns for Banta*. **Awards:** First Prize, Dinard Film Festival, and Best Director Award, Carthage Film Festival, for *Monangambée,* 1969; Golden Tanis, Carthage Film Festival, and International Catholic Film Office award, Ouagadougou Film Festival, Upper Volta, for *Sambizanga,* 1972; Label de la Qualité, for *Vlady-Peintre,* 1988; First Prize, Milan Film Festival, and Jury Prize and Critics Prize, Cairo Film Festival, for *Léon G. Damas,* 1996. **Address:** 14, Avenue Jean Moulin, Bat B1, Appt. 22, 93200 Saint Denis, France.

Films as Director

1969   *Monangambée* (short)
1970   *Des Fusils pour Banta (Guns for Banta)*
1971   *Carnaval en Guinée-Bissau (Carnival in Guinea-Bissau)* (short); *Saint-Denis sur Avenir (The Future of Saint Denis)* (featurette)
1972   **Sambizanga**
1977   *Un carnaval dans le Sahel (Carnival in Sahel)* (short); *Fogo, Ile de Feu* (short); *Et les Chiens se taisaient (And the Dogs Kept Silent)* (short); *Un Homme, une Terre (A Man, a Country)* (featurette)
1980   *La Basilique de Saint Denis* (short); *Un dessert pour Constance (A Dessert for Constance)* (featurette—for TV)
1981   *Le Cimetière du Père Lachaise* (short); *Miró* (short); *Alberto Carliski, Sculpteur* (short)
1982   *Robert Lapoujade, Peintre* (short); *Toto Bissainte, Chanteuse* (short); *René Depestre, Poète* (short); *L'hôpital de Leningrad (Leningrad Hospital)* (featurette—for TV)
1983   *La littérature tunisienne de la Bibliothèque Nationale (Tunisian Literature at the National Library)* (for TV); *Un Sénégalais en Normandie (A Senegalese in Normandy)* (for TV); *Robert Doisneau, Photographe* (for TV); *Le racisme au quotidien (Daily-Life Racism)* (for TV)
1985   *Le passager du Tassili (The Tassili Passenger)* (for TV)
1986   *Aimé Césaire, le masque des mots (Aimé Césaire, Words as Masks)* (short)
1988   *Emmanuel Ungaro, Couturier* (short); *Louis Aragon—Un Masque à Paris* (short); *Vlady, Peintre* (short)
1996   *Léon G. Damas* (short)
1997   *L'enfant-cinéma (Cinema-Child)* (short)
1998   *La tribu du bois de l'é (The Tribe of the "E" Wood)*

Publications by Maldoror

Articles

With Sylvia Harvey, Nadja Kasji, and Elin Clason, "Third World Perspectives: Focus on Sarah Maldoror," in *Women and Film* (Santa Monica, California), vol. 1, nos. 5-6, 1974.

"We Have to Take Television by Storm," interview with Jadot Sezirahiga, in *Ecrans d'Afrique/African Screen,* vol. 4, no. 12, 1995.

Publications on Maldoror

Books

Kuhn, Annette, and Susannah Radstone, editors, *The Women's Companion to International Film,* London, 1990.
Ukadike, Nwachukwu Frank, *Black African Cinema,* Berkeley, 1994.
Foster, Gwendolyn Audrey, *Women Film Directors: An International Bio-Critical Dictionary,* Westport, Connecticut, 1995.

Article

Lipinska, Suzanne, "Cinéma chez les Balantes," in *AfricAsia,* 6 July 1970.

* * *

There are unsolved questions, gaps, mysteries, misunderstandings (willful or not) in Sarah Maldoror's career and biography, that are best summarized by the origin of her name: Maldoror is the title of one of the "venomous" flowers of French culture, *The Songs of Maldoror,* a book-length descent into hell written by 19th-century-poet Lautréamont. By choosing this name as an alias, Maldoror posited herself within French culture—claiming some of its most sophisticated, albeit slightly elitist aspects—while simultaneously embracing its iconoclastic tradition (Lautréamont is hailed as an ancestor to Rimbaud and the Surrealists). In one word, she paid homage to the dilemma of the French-speaking black intellectual: in love with and a part of French culture, yet deeply aware that he/she will never belong to the "mainstream." Another tantalizing question: where does Maldoror come from? Even though she made some of her better-known movies in Africa, she was born in France, and is discreet about the nature of her West Indian (Guadeloupean) descent. The point is, like many children of mixed parentage, Maldoror proudly claims her black heritage, and identifies with it. The most puzzling question: why wasn't Maldoror given the opportunity to direct more feature films after *Sambizanga?* As it stands now, her filmography is particularly impressive, as she has turned her camera, her incisive and generous gaze, her sense of rhythm and poetry, to a number of subjects, from the history of the Saint Denis Cathedral to African immigration in Paris, from the work of poets, fashion designers, sculptors, and singers (including the legendary Haitian Toto Bissainte, one of the four members of the theater group "Les Griots" she founded in the early 1960s), to adaptation of literary works (such as *L'hôpital de Leningrad,* from a short story by Victor Serge, or *Le passager du Tassili,* from a novel by Akli Tadjer). Yet, after *Monangambée, Guns for Banta,* and mostly *Sambizanga,* our appetite was whetted, and we were expecting more African revolutionary movies from Sarah Maldoror. Not only because there are still so few women working as directors in the African continent, but because *Sambizanga,* combining a superb mastery of cinematic language with a unique sensibility, both Pan-African and feminine, expressed a new, powerful voice in world cinema: African women had never been shown with such compassion, understanding, and love, with such a keen attention to detail, body language, and modes of communication.

When Maria's husband is brutally kidnapped by the police, she is immediately surrounded by a group of village women of all ages who cry and mourn with her, comfort her, eventually pacify her. After a long and exhausting journey in her search for her jailed husband, she arrives at the home of friends, where she is welcomed by a community of women; one of them takes Maria's baby in her arms and suckles him. bell hooks wrote: "[in *Sambizanga*] there are black women imaged, constructed there so differently from what i had seen before. i remember the cries of these black women in their sister bonding ... their cries haunt me these mourning black women, their grief unmediated, different."

Yet Maldoror's life also articulates the essential *displacement* which defines women in the African diaspora; her own situation is made more complex by her involvement with Mario de Andrade, a complex, charismatic figure who was a writer, artist, and poet as well as a political leader who contributed to the Revolution in Angola. In the early 1960s, they received scholarships to go to Moscow (where she studied with Mark Donskoï and met Ousmane Sembene, the "father" of African cinema), as the Soviet Union sought to play a role in the emerging African countries and train its new elites. Then, the left-wing intelligentsias in Europe, Latin America, and Africa believed that only the "Third World" could foster world revolution. This was a time of struggle and utopia. For some African essentialists, though, Maldoror is still considered a "foreigner," only redeemed by "her long service to the black and African causes and her marriage [sic] to a prominent African nationalist." Significantly, the same writer adds that "[*Sambizanga*'s] deliberate feminist slant ... dilutes the impact of the film's concern with armed guerrilla struggle," forgetting to mention that *Sambizanga* is one of Angela Davis's personal favorites.

When Maldoror came back to live in France and started working for television in the late 1970s, she was faced with another aspect of this cultural dilemma (characterized by the French as *métissage*): as she claims at once French, West Indian, and African cultures, she is considered from neither place (not African enough for some, too black for others), and, as a woman, she has to fight across-the-border prejudices at a professional level. Moreover, French television is not known for the cultural diversity of its programs, as it postulates an average white *téléspectateur.* It is, therefore, a testimony to Maldoror's stamina, strength, and determination that, as funding for another feature film keeps eluding her, she has managed to work within a variety of formats (shorts, TV films, featurettes), and, among a series of more or less commissioned works, insert the object of her real desire, the telling, uncovering, and celebration of the stories, myths, traditions, memories of a multifaceted African diaspora. In Martinique, she shot *Aimé Césaire, Words as Masks,* a multi-voiced, sensual, impressionist portrait of the French-speaking poet/playwright/ politician who developed the concept of *négritude.* In Guyana, another documentary, *Léon G. Damas* was filmed. In Réunion Maldoror made *The Tribe of the "E" Wood.* And she is still trying to raise money for *Colonel Delgrès,* a feature about a colonel from the West Indies, who loved classical music, fought in Napoleon's armies, came to believe in the ideas of liberty, equality, fraternity, but found, upon returning to his native island of Guadeloupe, that slavery has been reestablished. A man who, like Maldoror, knew the price of treading the narrow line between races and cultures.

—Bérénice Reynaud

MALLET, Marilú
Chilean director and writer

Born: Santiago, Chile, 1945. **Education:** Attended Université de Montréal, received M.A., working on Ph.D., in literature and cinema. **Family:** Married, one son. **Career:** 1973—fled Chile for Montreal; made films with the support of the National Film Board of Canada; two collections of short stories published in French; 1980—co-founder with Dominique Pinel, Les Films de l'Atalante; assistant professor of cinema, University of Montreal, Concordia University. **Awards:** Festival awards, Locarno Film Festival, Strasbourg Film Festival, for *There Is No Forgetting*, 1975; Filmmaking Award, John Simon Guggenheim Fellowship; Meilleur Documentaire d'Essai à Création, FIPA, for *Dear America*, 1989. **Address:** Department of Cinema, Concordia University, Sir George Williams Campus, 1455 De Maisonneuve Boulevard West, Suite VA 035-1, Montreal, PQ H3G 1M8, Canada.

Films as Director

1971 *Amuhuelai-Mi* (doc)
1972 *A.E.I.* (doc)
1973 *Donde voy a encontrar otra Violeta* (*Where Am I Going to Find Another Violeta*) (unfinished)
1974 *Lentement* (*Slowly*)
1975 *Il n'y à pas d'oubli* (*There Is No Forgetting*) (doc) (co-d with Fajardo and R. González)
1978 *Los Borges* (doc)
1979 *L'évangile à Solentiname*; *Musique d'Amérique latine* (doc)
1986 *Journal inachevé* (*Unfinished Diary*) (doc)
1988 *Mémoires d'un enfant des Andes* (*Child of the Andes*) (doc)
1989 *Chère Amérique* (*Dear America*) (doc)
1995 *2, Rue de la Memoire*

Publications by Mallet

Books

Les Compagnons de l'horloge-pointeuse: nouvelles, Montreal, 1981; published as *English Voyage to the Other Extreme: Five Stories*, translated by Alan Brown, Montreal, 1985.
Miami Trip: Nouvelles, translation of *El embajador de la triple mirada*, translated by Louise Anaouïl, Montreal, 1986.

Publications on Mallet

Book

Foster, Gwendolyn Audrey, *Women Film Directors: An International Bio-Critical Dictionary*, Westport, Connecticut, 1995.

Articles

Longfellow, Brenda, "Feminist Language in *Journal inachevé* and *Strass café*," in *Words and Moving Images: Essays on Verbal and Visual Expression in Film and Television*, edited by W. C. Wees and M. Dorland, Montreal, 1984.
Pick, Zuzana M., "Chilean Cinema in Exile (1973-1986)," in *Framework* (Norwich, England), no. 34, 1987.
Deschamps, Y., and others, "Cinéma et architecture: notre espace au cinéma," in *24 Images* (Montreal), Fall 1988.
Euvrard, M., "Les cineastes neo-quebecois," in *CinémAction* (Conde-sur-Noireau), July 1990.
Pick, Zuzana M., "The Politics of the Personal: *Unfinished Diary*," in *The New Latin American Cinema: A Continental Project*, Austin, Texas, 1993.

* * *

Chilean-born Marilú Mallet began her filmmaking career during the Popular Unity government led by Salvador Allende (1970-73). Like many of her compatriots, Mallet fled Chile in the wake of the 1973 military coup that installed the repressive regime of General Pinochet. She settled in Montreal, Quebec, and embarked on a dual career of filmmaking and writing. In addition to making documentary films and working for television, Mallet has published two collections of short stories.

Mallet's oeuvre is marked by a continual exploration of the condition and experience of the immigrant-exile and the process of adjusting to a new country and trying to make it one's own. She blends fiction with documentary discourse, allowing her characters to react to situations from the depth of their own experiences. In the process of unraveling her own painful isolation, Mallet has created a personal, poetic film language which uses everyday behavior as a lens through which to examine gender, language, immigration, and exile. One sees how the subjective, personal experiences blends with and/ or abuts collective experience. Mallet's innovative filmmaking carries on a pan-American dialogue with other feminist filmmakers and with Latin American political documentary. As one of a handful of prominent Chilean women making films in exile, Mallet also contributes to an international Chilean cinema that, especially in its early years (1973-79), concerned itself with identity issues and with the hope of returning to a Chile where economic and social disparities might be eradicated.

Mallet's most well-known film, *Unfinished Diary* exemplifies her aesthetic and political approach to film. Made as part of the filmmaker's own struggle with alienation and language, *Unfinished Diary* reveals Mallet's relationship with her English-speaking husband, himself a prominent filmmaker, and with their young Quebec-born son who speaks only French. Verbal language separates and unites this family, creating gender boundaries when Mallet reverts to her native Spanish. Moreover, her husband's objective approach to filmmaking clashes with Mallet's more personal, subjective style. When he criticizes her use of film language, we understand the profundity of linguistic and emotional isolation Mallet feels. Interviews with the writer Isabel Allende and other Chilean exiles uncover the universality of these language and gender problems within the female exile community.

Ultimately *Unfinished Diary* is both an analysis of and a product of exile culture. The film reveals the process of exile—a journey that begins with separating from one's home for political or ideological reasons and that can lead to a permanent struggle to balance one's identity with one's new surroundings. It is about negotiating the slippages of identity, gender, language, and exile, about ambivalence and resistance, and about getting through.

Many of Mallet's films focus on the exile or the immigrant condition in Quebec. In *Les Borges* she documents the small Portuguese community in Montreal, centering particularly on the family of Manuel Borges who arrived in Montreal in 1967. The Borges family's personal experiences serve as a meditation on how immigrants learn to live in a country that they wish to make their own. Ten years later Mallet continues to struggle with questions of how an individual consciously alters his or her life's course—in her 1989 *Dear America* two women from Montreal talk about their lives and the choices they have made. The younger, Quebec native Catherine, has the very contemporary dream of having children without neglecting her musical career. Céleste, a Portuguese woman, considers how she sacrificed her children's love by leaving them in Portugal while she sought her fortune in America. Ultimately, like most of Mallet's documentary subjects and protagonists, Catherine and Céleste struggle for happiness.

—Ilene S. Goldman

MANNER...
(Men...)
West Germany, 1985
Director: Doris Dörrie

Production: Olga Film in cooperation with Second German Television (ZDF); color; 35 mm; running time: 99 mins. Released 1985.

Producer: Helmut Rasp; **screenplay:** Doris Dörrie; **assistant director:** Michael Juncker; **photography:** Helge Weindler; **editor:** Raimund Barthelmes; **assistant editor:** Jeanette Magerl; **sound:** Berthold Posch and Michael Etz; **set designer:** Jörg Neumann; **music:** Claus Bantzer; **costume design:** Jörg Trees; **makeup:** Werner A. Püthe.

Cast: Heiner Lauterbach (*Julius Armbrust*); Uwe Ochsenknecht (*Stefan Lachner*); Ulrike Kriener (*Paula Armbrust*); Janna Marangosoff (*Angelika*); Dietmar Bar (*Lothar*); Marie-Charlott Schuler (*Marita Strass*); Edith Volkmann (*Frau Lennart*); Louis Kelz (*Florian*); Cornelia Schneider (*Caro*); Sabine Wegener (*Juliane Zorn*).

Publications

Articles

Review in *Variety* (New York), 13 November 1985.

Goodman, Walter, "Ribbing Adam," in *New York Times,* 30 July 1986.

McHenry, S., in *Ms.* (New York), 4 August 1986.

Kauffmann, Stanley, in *New Republic* (Washington, D.C.), 25 August 1986.

Haskell, Molly, in *Vogue* (New York), September 1986.

Kael, Pauline, in *New Yorker,* 8 September 1986.

Pally, Marcia, in *Film Comment* (New York), September/October 1986.

Boyum, Joy Gould, in *Glamour* (New York), October 1986.

Diehl, Siegfried, in *World Press Review,* October 1986.

Gardner, James, in *New Leader* (New York), 12-26 January 1987.

*   *   *

Manner... (*Men...*) is a satire that chides the behavior of men, and the manner in which they relate to each other and to women. It is a farcical portrait of two males: Julius Armbrust (Heiner Lauterbach),

a pompous, self-involved middle-class advertising executive; and Stefan Lachner (Uwe Ochsenknecht), a scruffy illustrator who is the lover of Julius's wife, a situation that offends Julius (even though he is himself an inveterate womanizer). What makes the film both entertaining and unique is the manner in which this cuckold schemes to exact revenge, and win back his wife. Furthermore, the film is an astute portrayal of the casual attitudes men often have toward women and the manner in which men view each other, all filtered through the sensibilities of a woman writer/director, Doris Dörrie.

Julius has been married for 12 years, and his relationship with his wife, Paula (Ulrike Kriener), is stagnant. He carries on as a single man, shamelessly cheating on Paula with his pretty secretary and ogling an attractive young woman while in his car. Another, older subordinate must remind Julius of his upcoming wedding anniversary. He purchases some expensive jewelry to mark the occasion; it is not so much a token of his feelings or a way of celebrating their union as a means of buying Paula off. In the office, Julius will enjoy quickie sex with his secretary, but at home he is inattentive to Paula. She attempts to snuggle up to him in bed, yet he snores away and admonishes her for bothering him. At one point their young daughter asks them if they are still "madly" in love. Their response is a stony silence, rather than affirmation or reassurance.

So it is no surprise that Paula has been carrying on her affair with Stefan. Upon learning this, Julius becomes unstrung and acts the part of a hurt little boy. His infidelities are different, he declares, because he is a man. It almost is expected for him to cheat on his mate, in order to affirm his manhood. But how could Paula betray him? What could her lover possibly have that he lacks? His temperature soars as he spies on Paula and Stefan as they happily frolic. Julius first envisions a divorce, in which he will receive most of their possessions (two of which are their children). Now that he is in danger of losing Paula, however, he realizes that he really wants to keep her. He tells her that he "loves her so," not because of his feelings for her but because he wants her attention. When this ploy fails, he concocts a scheme that will enable him to win her back.

Julius conspires to meet and befriend Stefan, and become his roommate without divulging his identity. Superficially, the men are polar opposites. Julius is a well-groomed establishment product who wears $500 Italian suits and relishes playing the games men play to get ahead in business. Stefan, on the other hand, is a long-haired counterculture type who hangs out in punk bars, lives as if he is still a student, and shows no interest in credit cards, Rolexes, or a nine-to-five lifestyle. Julius, who thinks that all women want in relationships is security, cannot comprehend how Paula could be attracted to a man like Stefan, whom he regards as a failure.

But Julius does come to understand why Paula has rejected him, and this forms the crux of his scheme. He sets out to re-create Stefan in his own image by playing on the illustrator's deeply hidden desires for financial success and recognition. Julius convinces Stefan that he possesses the talent to become a hot-shot ad-agency art director. For Stefan, this translates into a new haircut, a new wardrobe, a new attitude. What Julius has created, then, is a Frankenstein monster who quickly becomes too immersed in his job and in acquiring possessions to supply Paula with the attention she craves. Paula then rejects Stefan—she explains that "he got boring, like most men"— and Julius is there waiting for her. But Julius too has undergone a transformation. As Stefan (who of course is unaware of Julius's identity) talks "man-to-man" about Paula and their sexual relationship, he is mirroring Julius's own casual view of women. This is disturbing to Julius. He does come away with insight into his own boorish behavior.

What makes *Men...* so effective as satire is that Dörrie zaps across her points about male ego and behavior without becoming strident or preachy. As Julius attempts to follow Stefan by riding a bicycle that is a bit too small for his frame, he is a comical caricature of an overgrown boy-man. In order to conceal his identity when Paula comes to Stefan's apartment, Julius dons a gorilla mask and grunts and paws at her. It is Dörrie's view not so much that man is descended from the apes as man all-too-often absurdly acts the part of an ape.

Meanwhile, Dörrie does convey that women are as sexually needy (not to mention deserving) as men. While her character is secondary to Julius and Stefan, the point of Paula's involvement with Stefan is that women also can play the game of infidelity if their sexual needs are not met. And women can regard men in as graphically physical/ sexual terms as men objectify women. At one point Julius asks a young woman named Angelica what her first impression of him would be if she saw him in the street. Her response is that she would notice that he has a nice ass.

It is this very honesty and irreverence, coupled with the tongue-in-cheek nature of the goings on—at the finale, as Stefan learns Julius's true identity, both men end up laughing hysterically at the situation— that allowed *Men...* to become a smash hit with audiences and critics worldwide.

—Rob Edelman

MARION, Frances

American writer

Born: Frances Marion Owens in San Francisco, 18 November 1890. **Education:** Attended Hamilton Grammar School; St. Margaret's Hall; University of California, Berkeley. **Family:** Married 1) Wesley De Lappé, 1907 (divorced 1909); 2) Robert Pike, 1910 (divorced); 3) Fred Thomson (died 1928), sons: Fred Jr. and Richard; 4) the director George William Hill, 1930 (divorced 1931). **Career:** 1909— reporter, *San Francisco Examiner*; then commercial artist, advertising designer, model, and poster painter for Oliver Morosco's Theatre; 1914—assistant to Lois Weber; 1915-17—writer for World Company Films (association with Mary Pickford), and Paramount; 1918-19—war correspondent in France; after 1920, wrote for Hearst's Cosmopolitan Studios, MGM, and Columbia; 1925—first novel published; 1940—retired from screenwriting, taught scriptwriting at the University of Southern California, Los Angeles. **Awards:** Academy Awards, for *The Big House*, 1929-30, and *The Champ*, 1931-32. **Died:** In Los Angeles, 12 May 1973.

Films as Writer

1915 *Camille* (Capellani); *'Twas Ever Thus* (Janis) (+ ro); *Nearly a Lady* (Janis) (+ ro); *Fanchon, the Cricket* (Kirkwood)
1916 *The Foundling* (O'Brien); *The Yellow Passport* (E. August); *Then I'll Come Back to You* (Irving); *The Social Highwayman* (E. August); *The Feast of Life* (Capellani); *Tangled Fates* (Vale); *La Vie de Bohème* (Capellani); *The Crucial Test* (J. Ince and Thornby); *A Woman's Way* (O'Neil); *The Summer Girl* (August); *Friday, the 13th* (Chautard); *The Revolt* (O'Neil); *The Hidden Scar* (O'Neil); *The Gilded*

Cage (Knoles); *Bought and Paid For* (Knoles); *All Man* (Chautard); *The Rise of Susan* (S. E. Taylor); *On Dangerous Ground* (Thornby); *The Heart of a Hero* (Chautard)
1917 *A Woman Alone* (Davenport); *Tillie Wakes Up* (Davenport); *The Hungry Heart* (Chautard); *A Square Deal* (Knoles); *A Girl's Folly* (M. Tourneur); *The Web of Desire* (Chautard); *The Poor Little Rich Girl* (M. Tourneur); *As Man Made Her* (Archainbaud); *The Social Leper* (Knoles); *Forget-Me-Not* (Chautard); *Darkest Russia* (Vale); *The Crimson Dove* (Fielding); *The Stolen Paradise* (Knoles); *The Divorce Game* (Vale); *The Beloved Adventuress* (Brady and Cowl); *The Amazons* (Kaufman); *Rebecca of Sunnybrook Farm* (Neilan); *A Little Princess* (Neilan); *The Pride of the Clan* (M. Tourneur)
1918 *Stella Maris* (Neilan); *Amarilly of Clothes-Line Alley* (Neilan); *M'Liss* (Neilan); *How Could You, Jean?* (W. Taylor); *The City of Dim Faces* (Melford); *Johanna Enlists* (W. Taylor); *He Comes Up Smiling* (Dwan); *The Temple of Dusk* (J. Young); *The Goat* (Crisp)
1919 *Captain Kidd, Jr.* (W. Taylor); *The Misleading Widow* (Robertson); *Anne of Green Gables* (W. Taylor); *A Regular Girl* (J. Young); *The Dark Star* (Dwan)
1920 *The Cinema Murder* (G. D. Baker); *Pollyanna* (P. Powell); *Humoresque* (Borzage); *The Flapper* (Crosland); *The Restless Sex* (Leonard and d'Usseau); *The World and His Wife* (Vignola)
1921 *Just around the Corner* (+ d); *The Love Light* (+ d); *Straight Is the Way* (Vignola)
1922 *Back Pay* (Borzage); *The Primitive Lover* (Franklin); *Sonny* (H. King); *East Is West* (Franklin); *Minnie* (Neilan and Urson); *The Eternal Flame* (Lloyd)
1923 *The Voice from the Minaret* (Lloyd); *The Famous Mrs. Fair* (Niblo); *The Nth Commandment* (Borzage) (+ artistic supervisor); *Within the Law* (Lloyd); *The Love Piker* (E. M. Hopper); *Potash and Perlmutter* (Badger); *The French Doll* (Leonard)
1924 *The Song of Love* (+ co-d with Franklin, co-ed); *Through the Dark* (G. Hill); *Abraham Lincoln* (Rosen); *Secrets* (Borzage); *Cytherea* (Fitzmaurice); *Tarnish* (Fitzmaurice); *In Hollywood with Potash and Perlmutter* (*So This Is Hollywood*) (Green); *Sundown* (Trimble and Hoyt)
1925 *A Thief in Paradise* (Fitzmaurice); *The Lady* (Borzage); *The Flaming Forties* (Forman); *His Supreme Moment* (Fitzmaurice); *Zander the Great* (G. Hill); *Lightnin'* (Ford); *Graustark* (Buchowetzki); *The Dark Angel* (Fitzmaurice); *Lazy Bones* (Borzage); *Thank You* (Ford); *Simon the Jester* (Melford) (+ pr); *Stella Dallas* (H. King)
1926 *The First Year* (Borzage); *Partners Again* (H. King); *Paris at Midnight* (E. M. Hopper) (+ pr); *The Son of the Sheik* (Fitzmaurice); *The Scarlet Letter* (Sjöström); *The Winning of Barbara Worth* (H. King)
1927 *The Red Mill* (Goodrich); *The Callahans and the Murphys* (G. Hill); *Madame Pompadour* (Wilcox); *Love* (E. Goulding)
1928 *Bringing Up Father* (Conway); *The Cossacks* (G. Hill); *Excess Baggage* (Cruze); *The Wind* (Sjöström); *The Awakening* (Fleming); *The Masks of the Devil* (Sjöström)
1929 *Their Own Desire* (E. M. Hopper and Forbes)
1930 *Anna Christie* (C. Brown); *The Rogue Song* (L. Barrymore); *The Big House* (G. Hill); *Let Us Be Gay* (Leonard); *Good News* (Grinde and MacGregor); *Min and Bill* (G. Hill); *Wu Li Chang* (Grinde)

Frances Marion

1931   *The Secret Six* (G. Hill); *The Champ* (K. Vidor)
1932   *Emma* (C. Brown); *Blondie of the Follies* (E. Goulding);
          Cynara (K. Vidor)
1933   *Secrets* (Borzage); *Peg o' My Heart* (Leonard); *Dinner at
          Eight* (Cukor); *The Prizefighter and the Lady* (Van Dyke);
          Going Hollywood (Walsh)
1935   *Riffraff* (Ruben)
1937   *Camille* (Cukor); *Love from a Stranger* (R. V. Lee); *Knight
          without Armour* (Feyder); *The Good Earth* (Franklin) (un-
          credited)
1940   *Green Hell* (Whale)

Films as Writer, Actress, and Editor/Assistant Editor

(All directed by Lois Weber)

1914   *False Colors*; *Hypocrites*; *It's No Laughing Matter*; *Like
          Most Wives*; *Traitor*
1915   *Sunshine Molly*

Films as Actress

1915   *Caprices of Kitty* (Janis); *Betty in Search of a Thrill* (Janis);
          A Girl of Yesterday (Dwan) (as Rosanna Danford); *City
          Vamp*; *The Wild Girl from the Hills*; *Captain Courtesy*
          (stunt double)

Publications by Marion

Books

Minnie Flynn (novel), New York, 1925.
The Scarlet Letter (script) in *Motion Picture Continuities,* by Frances
  Patterson, New York, 1929.
The Cup of Life (play) in *Hollywood Plays,* edited by Kenyon
  Nicholson, New York, 1930.
The Secret Six (novel), New York, 1931.
Valley People (novel), New York, 1935.

How to Write and Sell Film Stories (nonfiction), New York, 1937.
Molly, Bless Her (novel), New York, 1937.
Westward the Dream (novel), New York, 1948.
The Powder Keg (novel), Boston, Massachusetts, 1954.
Off with Their Heads! (autobiography), New York, 1972.

Articles

Film Weekly (London), 10 November 1935.
"Scenario Writing," in *Behind the Screen,* edited by Stephen Watts, London, 1938.

Publications on Marion

Books

Acker, Ally, *Reel Women: Pioneers of the Cinema, 1896 to the Present,* New York, 1991.
McCreadie, Marsha, *The Women Who Write the Movies: From Frances Marion to Nora Ephron,* Secaucus, New Jersey, 1994.
Beauchamp, Cari, *Without Lying Down: Frances Marion and the Powerful Women of Early Hollywood,* New York, 1997.

Articles

Tully, Jim, in *Vanity Fair* (New York), January 1927.
Bodeen, Dewitt, in *Films in Review* (New York), February and March 1969, additions in April 1969 and August/September 1973.
Film Comment (New York), Winter 1970-71.
Obituary, in *New York Times,* 14 May 1973.
Obituary, in *Variety* (New York), 16 May 1973.
Bodeen, Dewitt, in *More from Hollywood,* South Brunswick, New Jersey, 1977.
Uhn, Joyce, in *American Screenwriters,* 2nd series, edited by Randall Clark, Detroit, 1986.

*   *   *

Generally ranked with the leading screenwriters of all time, Frances Marion had more than 130 screen credits during her 25-year career, spanning the years 1915 to 1940, from the rise of the star-laden silent features to the height of the Golden Age of talkies. Her work encompasses such diversities as the 1915 *Camille* starring Clara Kimball Young and the 1937 Garbo version; *The Poor Little Rich Girl* with Mary Pickford in 1917 and *Riffraff* with Jean Harlow in 1935; but she was best known for her "four-handkerchief" pictures (*Stella Dallas, The Champ*) and high dramas (*The Big House, Dinner at Eight*).

Frances Marion arrived in Los Angeles from San Francisco in 1913 at age 23, twice married and divorced, talented and ambitious, having already worked as a journalist, artist's and photographer's model, commercial artist/illustrator, and writer of published stories and verse. She got into film work under a system that today would be called "networking," when her close friend Adela Rogers St. Johns introduced her to director-producer-writer Lois Weber, who took Marion into Bosworth studios as her protégée, doing a little bit of everything—acting, writing, cutting, publicity. There Marion met actor Owen Moore who introduced her to his wife, Mary Pickford; Marion and Pickford became and remained the best of friends, and frequent colleagues, for life.

If that sounds like the start of a heartwarming movie script, one could add other similar episodes. Friendship was one of Frances Marion's special talents, so when Lois Weber died penniless and forgotten after a significant career, it was Marion who, at the peak of her own fame and fortune, arranged and paid for Weber's funeral. When Marie Dressler, another old friend, could not get work on stage or screen, Marion revitalized her career with lively hand-tailored scripts—and helped get her cast as Marthy in *Anna Christie* which Marion had also scripted. After that, there was no stopping Dressler, who consulted Frances Marion at every turn. Among other close friends for whom Marion wrote scripts were Alice Brady, Elsie Janis, Billie Burke, and Marion Davies. She also wrote vehicles for Ronald Colman, Rudolph Valentino, John Gilbert, and Wallace Beery, and helped discover Gary Cooper and Clark Gable.

Although by tradition Hollywood writers usually travel in their own circles, Frances Marion also had many good friends among producers: William A. Brady, who gave her a writing contract at $200 a week in 1917; William Randolph Hearst, who let her direct her first film, *Just around the Corner,* in 1921; Joe Kennedy, who encouraged her third husband, the ex-chaplain and college athlete Fred Thomson, to star in Westerns; Samuel Goldwyn, her favorite producer, who called her his favorite scriptwriter; Irving Thalberg, who over several years sought her advice on production problems and on other writers' scripts.

What distinguished Marion's scripts, according to DeWitt Bodeen (who researched and interviewed Frances Marion in her later life), were her original characters with their dramatic but genuinely human conflicts, and her eye-minded stories, written always with the camera in mind. Her screenplays *moved,* and could be *acted,* Bodeen wrote. As one of the few scriptwriters who made a successful transition from silent films to talkies, Marion often wrote sequences without any dialogue, relying on pantomime (and the especially expressive faces of Garbo, Beery, and Dressler) to reach audiences more effectively than words could.

Soon after Marion started a long-term $3,500-a-week contract at MGM, as one of Hollywood's highest paid scriptwriters, tragedy came into her life: her husband died suddenly of tetanus, leaving their two young sons for her to raise alone. A later short-lived marriage to George W. Hill, a director-friend, was followed by his suicide a few years after their divorce. Already feeling vulnerable, as screenwriting was being handled more and more on an assembly-line basis, Marion decided that she would have to be a writer-director or writer-producer to maintain the integrity of her scripts.

She had already tried directing and it seemed to go nowhere. Following her first effort for Hearst in 1921, Marion had directed Mary Pickford in *The Love Light.* A few years later, when the film's director was too ill to work, Marion had finished directing her own script for *The Song of Love,* a Norma Talmadge production. But her efforts to produce her own scripts in the late 1930s and 1940s never got off the ground. She turned instead to magazine stories and serials. Her book *How to Write and Sell Film Stories* emphasizes visual over verbal communication, stresses simplicity and detail, colorful personalities, and everyday emotions. Her later book of reminiscences, *Off with Their Heads!,* tells more about her friends than about herself. She mentions merely in passing that she directed three films but writes nothing about her experiences or why she stopped.

—Cecile Starr

MARSHALL, Penny
American director and actress

Born: New York City, 15 October 1942 (some sources say 1943). **Education:** Attended the University of New Mexico, majored in math and psychology. **Family:** Married 1) Michael Henry (divorced), one daughter, Tracy; 2) the actor/director Rob Reiner, 1971 (divorced 1979). **Career:** 1960s—began acting, appearing in stock productions; 1967-68—network acting debut on *The Danny Thomas Hour*; 1970—auditioned unsuccessfully for the role of Gloria on the television sitcom *All in the Family*; 1971-75—initially attracted notice for recurring role as Jack Klugman's secretary on TV's *The Odd Couple*; 1970s—acted on television series, including *The Mary Tyler Moore Show, Taxi, Mork and Mindy,* and *Happy Days*; 1976—became a television star on *Laverne & Shirley*; late 1970s-1980s—directed commercials, several episodes of *Laverne & Shirley,* two episodes of *The Tracey Ullman Show,* and TV pilot *Working Stiffs*; 1985—made stage debut in off-Broadway play *Eden Court*; 1986—directed first feature, *Jumpin' Jack Flash*; 1990—signed a three-picture deal with Columbia Pictures. **Agent:** c/o Todd Smith, Creative Artists Agency, 9830 Wilshire Boulevard, Beverly Hills, CA 90212, U.S.A.

Films as Director

1986	*Jumpin' Jack Flash*
1988	***Big***
1990	*Awakenings* (+ co-exec pr)
1992	*A League of Their Own* (+ exec pr)
1994	*Renaissance Man* (+ co-exec pr)
1996	*The Preacher's Wife*

Films as Actress

1968	*The Savage Seven* (Rush) (as Tina); *How Sweet It Is!* (Paris) (as tour girl)
1970	*The Grasshopper* (Paris) (as Plaster Caster)
1971	*The Feminist and the Fuzz* (Paris—for TV)
1972	*Evil Roy Slade* (Paris—for TV) (as bankteller); *The Crooked Hearts* (J. Sandrich—for TV); *The Couple Takes a Wife* (Paris—for TV)
1975	*How Come Nobody's on Our Side?* (Michaels) (as Theresa); *Let's Switch* (Rafkin—for TV)
1978	*More than Friends* (Burrows—for TV)
1979	*1941* (Spielberg) (as Miss Fitzroy)
1984	*Love Thy Neighbor* (Bill—for TV) (as Linda)

Penny Marshall on the set of *Big*.

1985   *Movers & Shakers* (Asher) (as Reva); *Challenge of a Life-
         time* (Mayberry—for TV)
1991   *The Hard Way* (Badham) (as Angie)
1993   *Hocus Pocus* (Ortega)
1995   *Get Shorty* (Sonnenfeld) (as herself)

Other Films

1993   *Calendar Girl* (Whitesell) (exec pr)
1996   *Getting Away with Murder* (H. Miller) (co-pr)

Publications by Marshall

Articles

Interview with Burt Prelutsky, in *TV Guide* (Radnor, Pennsylvania),
    22 May 1976.
Interview with Marty Friedman, in *New York,* 26 October 1981.
"The Marshall Plan," interview with Carol Caldwell, in *Interview* (New
    York), January 1991.
Interview with Iain Blair, in *Chicago Tribune,* 3 February 1991.
Interview with Larry Rohter, in *New York Times,* 17 March 1991.
Interview in *Vanity Fair* (New York), May 1994.
"Penny Marshall Marshals Her Wits and Fishes for Dish with Car-
    rie Fisher," interview with Carrie Fisher, in *Interview* (New York),
    May 1994.
"Marshall Arts," interview with Carrie Fisher, in *Harper's Bazaar*
    (New York), December 1996.

Publications on Marshall

Books

Acker, Ally, *Reel Women: Pioneers of the Cinema, 1896 to the
    Present,* New York, 1991.
Edelman, Rob, *Great Baseball Films,* New York, 1994.
Foster, Gwendolyn Audrey, *Women Film Directors: An International
    Bio-Critical Dictionary,* Westport, Connecticut, 1995.

Articles

Cunneff, Tom, "Penny Marshall," in *People* (New York), 15 August
    1988.
Walters, Harry F., in *New York Woman,* December 1990.
Morgenstern, Joseph, "Penny from Heaven," in *Playboy* (Chicago),
    January 1991.
Current Biography 1992, New York, 1992.
Orenstein, Peggy, "Making It in the Majors," in *New York Times
    Magazine,* 24 May 1992.
Wolf, Jeanne, "*Laverne & Shirley's* Strange Brew," in *TV Guide*
    (Radnor, Pennsylvania), 13 March 1995.
Diamond, Jamie, "Penny Marshall: 1988 the First Woman Director
    to Break $100 Million at the Box Office," in *Working Woman,*
    November/December 1996.

*   *   *

Had Penny Marshall not had show business connections—she is
the younger sister of director-producer-writer Garry Marshall—she
might not have been allowed the opportunities she received first as
an actress, then as a director. But this can be said for any second- or
third-generation Hollywood name, from Bridges to Fonda, Carradine
to Sheen. Besides, had Marshall lacked the requisite abilities, her
career might not have flourished as it has in both venues. Marshall
has become one of a generation of actors—Ron Howard and Rob
Reiner, her former husband, are others who come to mind—who
first earned popularity as stars of television situation comedies, and
then went on to forge major careers behind the cameras.

Marshall cut her teeth as an actress, appearing first in a handful of
features and made-for-television movies, then in a quartet of television
situation comedies: *The Odd Couple* (as Myrna Turner, 1971-75, co-
produced by brother Garry); *The Bob Newhart Show* (as Miss Larson,
1972-73); *Paul Sand in Friends and Lovers* (as Janice Dreyfuss, 1974-
75); and, most notably, *Laverne & Shirley* (as Laverne De Fazio, 1976-
83, co-created and produced by brother Garry), a spin-off of *Happy
Days.* The success of the latter made Marshall a household name. In
1978 she co-starred with Reiner in *More than Friends,* a made-for-
television romantic comedy based on their courtship.

Marshall initially began directing episodes of *Laverne & Shirley.* Her
feature-film directorial debut, *Jumpin' Jack Flash,* was inauspicious:
one of Whoopi Goldberg's pitifully unfunny post-*Color Purple* fiascos.
More recently, Marshall made *Renaissance Man,* an overlong (at 129
minutes), generic comedy about an advertising man (Danny DeVito)
who finds himself suddenly unemployed, and accepts a job tutoring a
bunch of none-too-bright Army recruits. In between, however, Marshall
made a trio of popular features that firmly established her as a leading
Hollywood director. Each is a commercially viable film that combines
solid entertainment value with a humanistic, life-affirming story line.

Big is by far the best in a string of late 1980s fantasy-comedies
(including *Like Father, Like Son; Vice Versa;* and *18 Again!*) which are
variations on the same theme: the souls of young people are transferred
into the bodies of their elders (and vice versa). *Big* is the story of a
preteen boy who, like many kids, wishes he were older. Miraculously,
this request is granted—and the boy, now trapped in the body of a man
almost three times his age, is thrust into the adult world. The adult is
played by Tom Hanks, giving a performance which earned him his first
Academy Award nomination and solidified his status as an A-list movie
star. The based-on-fact *Awakenings* features superlative performances
by Robin Williams (as Oliver Sacks, a reticent research doctor working
in a hospital ward which houses the chronically ill) and Robert De Niro
(as a patient who awakens from a 30-year coma). *A League of Their
Own* mixes fiction with fact as it tells the story of the trailblazing women
athletes who played professional baseball in the All-American Girls
Professional Baseball League during the 1940s and 1950s.

Along with fellow television refugees Reiner and Howard, Marshall
has been able to entertain audiences while making them think and
feel: an impressive accomplishment in an era dominated by crass, in-
your-face, assembly-line Hollywood product.

—Rob Edelman

LA MATERNELLE

(Children of Montmartre; The Nursery School)
France, 1933
Directors: Marie Epstein and Jean Benoît-Lévy

Production: Max Laemmle Universal; black and white, 35mm; running time: 83 minutes. Released September 1933, Paris.

La Maternelle

Screenplay: Marie Epstein and Jean Benoît-Lévy, based on the novel by Léon Frapié; **photography:** Georges Asselin; **editors:** Marie Epstein and Jean Benoît-Lévy; **music:** Edouard Flament; **songs:** Alice Verlay.

Cast: Madeleine Renaud (*Rose*); Paulette Elambert (*Marie*); Mady Berry (*Mme. Paulin*); Alice Tissot (*Directrice*); Henri Debain (*Dr. Libois*); Mariane (*Teacher*); Gaston Severin (*Inspectrice*); Sylvette Fillacier (*Marie's mother*); Alex Bernard (*Professor*); Ed van Deele (*Father Pantin*).

Publications

Book

Flitterman-Lewis, Sandy, *To Desire Differently: Feminism and the French Cinema,* Chicago, 1990.

Article

Flitterman-Lewis, Sandy, "Nursery/Rhymes: Primal Scenes in *La Maternelle,*" in *Enclitic* (Minneapolis), Fall 1981/Spring 1982.

* * *

La Maternelle is an early French sound film that was produced by the long and fruitful collaboration between filmmakers Marie Epstein and Jean Benoît-Lévy. Loosely based on Léon Frapié's populist novel, its heartbreaking story takes place in the nursery school of a Paris slum. It is the only film produced by Epstein and Benoît-Lévy that was distributed in the United States, where its depictions of gaunt, sad orphans were vastly different than the pudgy, indomitable, and effervescent orphans that Shirley Temple played.

A tender and tragically beautiful film, it tells the story of a young woman, Rose, who loves children and fears she might never have any of her own. Despite a college degree, she gets a job as a cleaning woman in a nursery school where an orphaned little girl, Marie, immediately develops an intense attachment to her. Although Rose is lovingly attentive to her, Marie witnesses the school director asking Rose to marry him. Marie becomes distraught as she relives the trauma of her mother's recent abandonment of her for a man she has met in a cabaret. Anticipating a second abandonment, Marie unsuccessfully tries to kill herself by flinging herself into a river. But she reunites with Rose, accepts her fiancé, and the film ends happily.

La Maternelle marks a culmination of the themes and issues present in Epstein's earlier films, especially her concern with female identity and its relation to the social milieus. In addition, her work offers sensitive portrayals of children's lives and illustrates her interest in psychological realism. Specifically, all of the main characters in *La Maternelle* are female and the primary dramatic concern is the deep emotional bond between the child Marie and the maternal figure Rose. The film looks very much like a documentary, much as the later Italian Neorealist and French "poetic realist" films did, and the filmmakers provide touchingly authentic observations of the largely nonprofessional cast—a group of actual slum children. Yet, it also employs elements of an earlier film style, specifically impressionism. For example, among *La Maternelle*'s most compelling sequences are those that depict Marie's point of view, especially her longing for a mother and her fear of desertion. In one shocking scene, a pained Marie watches as her mother flirts shamelessly with a man she has only just met in a tawdry bar. The film's climax is the attempted suicide of young Marie, which is conveyed subjectively and poetically via a quick succession of images. They reveal a jumble of her actual memories and fantasies about the adult couples who seem not to care about her. Marie tries desperately to escape the images by first throwing stones into the water and then herself. As the film progresses, the filmmakers work to build the viewer's identification with Marie until it culminates with the poignant suicide scene. Indeed, unlike the typical classical Hollywood movie that is organized to favor the male gaze, usually at women, and with which the viewer is encouraged to identify, *La Maternelle* inverts this organization in favor of a female point of view.

Epstein's work can be understood in the context of the 1930's "Poetic Realist" movement in French cinema, which typically provides an aesthetic balance between character and atmosphere that reduces the importance of plot. Thus, in *La Maternelle* Epstein reveals her interest in the ordinary details and intimate themes of everyday life, as well as her attention to the interdependency of economic and social factors. The filmmakers cast nonprofessional actors to enhance the film's atmosphere of vitality and naturalism, which purportedly enabled the professional actors to give more realistic performances. They depict a cross-section of orphans, from a little boy who never learned to smile, to the children whose desperate longing to be nurtured with affection is etched in their thin faces. In addition, the characters in *La Maternelle* frequently use slang terms, which contributes to the film's Parisian ambiance and further illustrates Epstein's attention to naturalistic detail. Indeed, the sets for the film reveal a careful attention to details; they were precise replicas of the schools Epstein and Benoît-Lévy visited during several months of preproduction research. Epstein's skill at directing virtuoso performances is evidenced by the beautifully rendered performance of Paulette Elambert as Marie. Usually shown wearing a pathetic little paper crown, Elambert looks the part of a lonely, despairing waif, and her skillful range and expression of emotion is stunning—alternately heartbreaking and delightful. Among the film's most gripping images are those in which little Marie gazes directly into the camera—an exceedingly rare occurrence in fiction films; with an almost unbearable intimacy, she directly addresses the audience, as though implicating it in her pain, or at least challenging its complacency about the social conditions that produce such wretched lives for impoverished children.

When it was exhibited in the United States in 1935, critics praised *La Maternelle* as one of the best French films ever exhibited. Further, they reassured viewers who were not fluent in French that it was so simply told that, even without subtitles, they would understand and appreciate its story. The *New York Times* reviewer enthusiastically endorsed its authenticity and sensitivity, saying that it had "great subtlety and almost unendurable power," and was a film "of extraordinary insight, tenderness, and tragic beauty." Indeed, critics were so impressed with the film that they loftily judged its narrative and performances as superior examples of what other French films should aspire to be.

—Cynthia Felando

MATHIS, June
American writer

Born: Leadville, Colorado, 1892. **Family:** Married the director Silvanio Balboni, 1924. **Career:** 1910-16—stage and vaudeville actress; 1918—hired at Metro as writer; 1919—appointed head of script department; associated with the performers Nazimova, Valentino, and Colleen Moore, and the director Rex Ingram during the next few years; 1923—edited von Stroheim's *Greed* down from 18 to 10 reels. **Died:** In New York City, 26 July 1927.

Films as Writer

1917   *Red, White and Blue Blood* (Brabin); *Blue Jeans* (Collins); *Aladdin's Other Lamp* (Collins)
1918   *To Hell with the Kaiser* (Irving); *An Eye for an Eye* (Capellani); *Social Quicksands* (Brabin)
1919   *Out of the Fog* (Capellani); *The Red Lantern* (Capellani); *The Brat* (Blaché); *Satan Junior* (Blaché and Collins); *The Microbe* (Otto); *The Man Who Stayed at Home* (Blaché); *The Island of Intrigue* (Otto); *The Divorcee* (Blaché)
1920   *Old Lady 31* (J. Ince); *Hearts Are Trumps*; *Polly with a Past* (De Cordova); *The Saphead* (Blaché); *The Right of Way* (Dillon); *Parlor, Bedroom and Bath* (Dillon)
1921   *The Four Horsemen of the Apocalypse* (Ingram); *The Conquering Power* (Ingram); *A Trip to Paradise* (Karger); *Camille* (Smallwood); *The Idle Rich* (Karger)
1922   *Turn to the Right* (Ingram); *Kisses* (Karger); *Hate* (Karger); *Blood and Sand* (Niblo); *The Young Rajah* (Rosen)
1923   *Three Wise Fools* (K. Vidor); *The Spanish Dancer* (Brenon); *In the Palace of the King* (Flynn); *Greed* (von Stroheim) (re-write, re-edit)
1924   *Three Weeks* (Crosland) (+ cd)
1925   *Sally* (A. E. Green); *The Desert Flower* (Cummings); *Classified* (Santell); *We Moderns* (Dillon)
1926   *Ben-Hur* (Niblo); *Irene* (A. E. Green); *The Greater Glory* (Rehfeld); *The Masked Woman* (Balboni); *The Magic Flame* (H. King)

Film as Actress

1923   *Souls for Sale* (R. Hughes) (as celebrity)

Publications by Mathis

Book

Greed, edited by Joel W. Finler, London, 1972.

June Mathis

Article

"Tapping the Thought Wireless," in *Moving Picture World,* 21 July 1917.

Publications on Mathis

Book

Acker, Ally, *Reel Women: Pioneers of the Cinema, 1896 to the Present,* New York, 1991.

Articles

Photoplay (New York), October 1926.
Obituary, in *New York Times,* 27 July 1927.
Cinema (Beverly Hills), no. 35, 1976.
Slater, Thomas, in *American Screenwriters,* 2nd series, edited by Randall Clark, Detroit, 1986.

*   *   *

June Mathis in her short but brilliant career (she died in her mid-thirties) was one of the most influential women in Hollywood production during the silent film era, becoming chief of Metro's script department in 1919 when she was only 27. Her family had a background in the theater, and she had already be-gun to write for the theater when she secured a job with Metro as scenario-writer in 1918, and was immediately responsible for scripting a range of films with titles such as *To Hell with the Kaiser, An Eye for an Eye, Hearts Are Trumps,* and *Polly with a Past.* This initial work culminated in her notable adaptation of the famous war novel by Vicente Blasco Ibáñez, *The Four Horsemen of the Apocalypse.* By this stage she was influential enough to succeed in her insistence with Metro on the appointment of her young friend Rex Ingram (aged 29) as the film's director, though his postwar reputation rested only on the direction of a few minor features, and on the casting of Rudolph Valentino (then only a bit-player) as the star, so establishing his meteoric career (like hers, to be only too short) as the embodiment of the erotic imaginings of the mass international female film-going public. Mathis went on to script and supervise a range of Valentino's subjects, including *Camille, Blood and Sand,* and *The Young Rajah.*

Mathis, it would appear, had by now extended her status in the studios to that of an associate producer, and she was to assume a similar responsibility of scripting and cutting (then often a producer's prerogative) over a considerable range of films. According to Lewis Jacobs, in his authoritative book *The Rise of the American Film,* she was the "most esteemed scenarist in Hollywood." Her strength lay in careful preparation of the shooting script along with the director, cutting out waste in production while at the same time sharpening narrative continuity. She became in effect head, or one of the heads, of the Metro and Samuel Goldwyn units, and joined with other youthful women writers (such as Anita Loos and Bess Meredyth) in establishing the importance of the basic screenplay-scenario in silent American film. It was she who was in good measure responsible for persuading Metro-Goldwyn to agree to sponsor Erich von Stroheim's celebrated film *Greed,* and so became notorious among film devotees, who see the company she represented as "betraying" one of the greatest artists of silent cinema, and all but destroying one of its potentially greatest films. *Greed* as initially shot and assembled by Stroheim ran to 42 reels (ten hours), following every detail of Frank Norris's novel *McTeague*; Stroheim himself reduced this to 24 reels (six hours), hoping the film could then be screened with intermissions in two successive evenings. But Metro-Goldwyn-Mayer (as the company had now become) demanded more drastic cutting. At Stroheim's request, his close friend Rex Ingram reduced it to 18 reels (4½ hours). But Mathis was instructed to reduce the film on her own initiative (without consultation with Stroheim) to ten reels (2½ hours), which she undertook with the aid of a routine cutter, Joseph W. Farnham, "on whose mind was nothing but a hat," as Stroheim put it. The exact nature of this drastic cutting of an overlong masterpiece of realistic, psychological cinema is detailed by Joel W. Finler in his edition of Stroheim's full-scale original script *Greed.*

Mathis went on to script and supervise the adaptation of the "epic" *Ben-Hur* for Goldwyn, finally after much trouble directed by Fred Niblo and starring Francis X. Bushman and Ramon Novarro. Mathis, however, was withdrawn from the film by MGM while on location in Italy, but in any case she disowned what had initially been shot by the film's first director, Charles Brabin, whom she had chosen. Her final films included *Irene* for Colleen Moore and *The Magic Flame* with Ronald Colman and Vilma Banky. Mathis died suddenly in 1927.

—Roger Manvell

MAY, Elaine
American writer, director, and actress

Born: Elaine Berlin in Philadelphia, 21 April 1932; moved to Los Angeles, California, 1942; daughter of the theater director Jack Berlin and the actress Jeannie Berlin. **Education:** Attended University of Chicago and Playwrights Theatre in Chicago, 1950. **Family:** Married 1) Marvin May, 1949, daughter: Jeannie Berlin; 2) the lyricist Sheldon Harnick, 1962 (divorced 1963). **Career:** 1947—studied acting under Maria Ouspenskaya; 1953-57—member of the improvisational theater group, the Compass Players, where began partnership with Mike Nichols; 1957—performed in New York clubs with Nichols, made several TV appearances; 1960—Broadway debut in the revue *An Evening with Mike Nichols and Elaine May*; 1960s—wrote, directed, and acted in the theater, also wrote and performed for radio; recorded comedy albums; 1971—directed her first feature film, *A New Leaf.* **Address:** c/o Julian Schlossberg, Castle Hill Productions, 1414 Avenue of the Americas, New York, NY 10019, U.S.A.

Films as Writer

1971   *Such Good Friends* (Preminger) (under pseudonym Esther Dale)
1978   *Heaven Can Wait* (Beatty and Henry) (co)
1982   *Tootsie* (Pollack) (co—uncredited)
1995   *Dangerous Minds* (J. Smith) (co—uncredited)
1996   *The Birdcage* (M. Nichols)
1998   *Primary Colors* (M. Nichols)

Films as Writer and Director

1971   *A New Leaf* (+ ro as Henrietta Lowell)
1976   *Mikey and Nicky*
1987   *Ishtar*

Film as Director

1972   *The Heartbreak Kid*

Films as Actress

1966   *Enter Laughing* (C. Reiner) (as Angela)
1967   *Luv* (C. Donner) (as Ellen Manville); *Bach to Bach* (Leaf—short)
1978   *California Suite* (Ross) (as Millie Michaels)
1990   *In the Spirit* (Seacat) (as Marianne Flan)

Publications by May

Book

The Birdcage: The Shooting Script, New York, 1996.

Articles

Millimeter (New York), vol. 3, no. 10, October 1975.
"Elaine May Finishes Off New Age," interview with Marlo Thomas, in *Interview* (New York), April 1990.

"She's a Beginner, but What Connections," in *New York Times,* 1 April 1990.
Interview with Walter Matthau, in *New Yorker,* 25 November 1996.

Publications on May

Books

Acker, Ally, *Reel Women: Pioneers of the Cinema, 1896 to the Present,* New York, 1991.
Foster, Gwendolyn Audrey, *Women Film Directors: An International Bio-Critical Dictionary,* Westport, Connecticut, 1995.

Articles

Kaminsky, Stuart, "Eight Comedy Directors of the Last Decade," in *Film Reader* (Evanston, Illinois), no. 1, 1975.
Malm, Linda, in *American Screenwriters,* 2nd series, edited by Randall Clark, Detroit, 1986.
Blum, David, "The Road to *Ishtar,* in *New York,* 16 March 1987.
Biskind, Peter, "Inside *Ishtar,*" in *American Film* (Hollywood), May 1987.
Jackson, L., and Karen Jaehne, "Eavesdropping on Female Voices," in *Cineaste* (New York), vol. 16, no. 1-2, 1987-88.
Film Dope (London), no. 41, March 1989.
"One More Death-Defying Act," in *New York Times Magazine,* 5 March 1995.

*   *   *

Elaine May's historical importance as a female writer/director pioneer in the 1970s has not been diminished by her inability to live up to her reputation as a groundbreaking filmmaker such as Ida Lupino or Dorothy Arzner. Because May carved a niche for herself out of a traditionally male workplace, contemporary Hollywood hyphenates such as Penny Marshall and Barbra Streisand owe her a debt of gratitude. Despite her unassailable originality, however, May's post-*Heartbreak Kid* assignments (*Mikey and Nicky,* 1976, and *Ishtar,* 1987) have been exercises in character-driven chaos that yielded mixed results. Scattering her talent through the fields of screenwriting, directing, playwriting, and performing, this comic iconoclast has not been able to channel her energies safely and commercially like her more successful, less inspiring, former partner Mike Nichols.

Having been a child actress with the Yiddish Theater run by her father, Jack Berlin, May attended the University of Chicago and joined the Compass Players, a precursor of the Second City Troupe. May's formative years in sketch comedy inform all her subsequent work. Paired with the equally deadpan Mike Nichols, May shot to stardom as half of a droll duo, whose improvisation-derived material remains more sophisticated than today's stand-up acts. After conquering cabaret, television, and Broadway, Nichols and May amicably parted company. Hailed for his directorial achievements in New York, in 1966 Nichols became Hollywood's fair-haired boy with *Who's Afraid of Virginia Woolf?* (Nichols and May later starred in a stage version of the play at the Long Wharf Theatre in 1980.)

Throughout the sixties, May honed her playwriting skills, most notably with the one-act *Adaptation.* As a screen comedienne, she offered two bewitchingly offbeat interpretations of urban insecurity in *Enter Laughing* and *Luv.* Considering May's estimable behind-the-scenes accomplishments, a preference for her performing talent may seem like heresy. In her directorial debut, *A New Leaf* (1971),

Elaine May on the set of *A New Leaf*.

she also stars, with virtuoso skill, as a wallflower heiress victimized by her lawyer, her servants, and her gaslighting husband, but protected from harm by cosmic clumsiness. This endearingly wacky directorial bow plays like a riff on the Charlie Chaplin/Martha Raye rowboat scene in *Monsieur Verdoux.* In 1990 May replanted herself in front of the cameras in the slapdash female buddy comedy, *In the Spirit,* which she did not direct. As Marianne Flan, a shopaholic stripped of consumer power, May wings it with a jubilantly hilarious turn. Her study of fraying equanimity is a classic comic tour de force.

It is her love for actors, and her insistence on allowing them breathing space that is the one constant of May's filmmaking style. Her penchant for thespic improvisation, and her directorial curiosity in permitting characters to reach the end of their rope, is an essential element of May's moviemaking modus operandi. Unfortunately, such freewheeling methods fly in the face of Hollywood convention. Right off the bat, May resisted Hollywood logic. Having crafted a zany update on thirties screwball comedy with *A New Leaf,* May handed in a 180-minute black comedy that the studio cut and sweetened into a 102-minute weird romance. May had the last laugh with her next film, *The Heartbreak Kid,* an exhilarating soufflé whipped up from potentially sour ingredients. In a dazzling tightrope walk, with pathos and slapstick on either side, May maintained perfect comic balance. Although screenwriter Neil Simon had been knocked for his formulaic style, May dived headfirst into the wisecracking neurosis that made him a household name and emerged with a literally painfully funny exposé of romantic self-absorption. In essence, *The Heartbreak Kid* was a series of sharply written sketches cemented by Simon's professionalism and May's risk-taking. She created an off-kilter comic momentum as the film's self-deluded characters talked themselves into corners marked "Be Careful What You Wish For." Despite the cruel treatment of the heroines in these films, May's sympathies lie with the passive martyrs of *A New Leaf* and *The Heartbreak Kid;* the more her male protagonists wrangle and prevaricate, the deeper a hole they dig for their own happiness.

The assurance of May's first two films has never been recaptured. Based on her unproduced play, *Mikey and Nicky* emerged as a John Cassavetes film without that maverick director's edge. This bleak fable about a small-time gangster marked for sacrifice attracted a cult following, but May's collaboration with her actors rambled on without a focus. For May, exercising a variety of choices became a liability. You can feel her confidence wane as *Mikey and Nicky* unravels before your eyes.

Pilloried in the press as an example of fiscal mismanagement and ego-fueled disorder, the floundering *Ishtar* struck critics as less defensible than the equally undisciplined *Mikey and Nicky.* Heralded as a May-Day version of a Hope-Crosby "Road" picture, *Ishtar* offered further proof of May's fussiness as a director and her deteriorating knack for following through on ideas as a writer. Although the movie's early scenes sparkled with show biz savvy, May proved to be incompatible with the adventure-flick elements of her own screenplay about Middle East intrigue. *Ishtar* revisited a dead genre known for vaudevillian energy and re-killed it with feeble directorial pacing and two over-intellectualized leading performances that lacked personality-powered oomph.

As a writer-for-hire, May remains highly regarded. Having won an Oscar nomination for updating *Here Comes Mr. Jordan* as *Heaven Can Wait* and having won industry plaudits for doctoring the script of *Tootsie,* May contributed greatly to her reunion with Mike Nichols on *The Birdcage.* Astutely relocating the classic French farce *La Cage aux Folles* to South Beach, Florida, May incorporated contemporary broadsides that made *The Birdcage* politically correct if sexually backward in its treatment of gay stereotypes. In director Nichols's hands, May's screenplay was a polished laugh-getter, although their remake is neither as liberatingly amusing nor as moving as the original. It is rather dispiriting to conclude that after all these embattled years, feisty May may be poised to follow in the less audacious footsteps of her one-time foil, Nichols. They are scheduled for re-teaming on *Primary Colors.*

Whatever May's filmmaking shortcomings were, they never stemmed from commercial compromise. When her skewered world-view sustained itself in *A New Leaf* and *The Heartbreak Kid,* the audience became willing participants in comic hijackings that May transformed into joyrides. Even when her failures of nerve produced the spotty *Ishtar* and the protracted *Mikey and Nicky,* May's bracing originality always flickered. Bolstered by the acclaim of *The Birdcage,* May is set to star on Broadway in 1998 in one acts co-written by Alan Arkin and herself. Perhaps, she will rekindle her film directing desire with a screenplay written by a sympathetic co-conspirator, a script that May could translate into her own wacky vernacular.

Wonderfully expressive as a wordsmith, and provisionally gifted as a moviemaker, May is irreplaceable as a comic voice and as a comedienne. In front of or behind the cameras, she is a modern screwball born in a trunk and raised on an analyst's couch.

Unlike some of her directorial successors (e.g., Jane Campion, Claudia Weill), filmmaker May was never obsessed with feminist causes. Her distinctively hapless heroines are doormats ruled by dumb luck. Her gallery of spineless males includes ineffectual hoods (*Mikey and Nicky*), boobish songwriters (*Ishtar*), a larcenous gold digger (*A New Leaf*), and a shiksa-obsessed social climber (*The Heartbreak Kid*). In these oddball films, the battle of the sexes is a draw. In May's male-dominated universe, women are either prizes or obstacles, but men are fools for not being able to recognize who is which.

—Robert Pardi

The McDONAGH Sisters

Australian actress (Isobel), producer, writer and art director (Phyllis); director and writer (Paulette)

ISOBEL. Pseudonym: Marie Lorraine. **Born:** Isobel Mercia McDonagh in Sydney, 1899. **Education:** Attended Kincoppal, the Convent of the Sacred Heart, Elizabeth Bay. **Family:** Married Charles Stewart, 1932, three children. **Career:** Worked as a nurse; co-founded a photographic studio; modeled for the painter, Thea Proctor; 1924—billed as "Marie Lorraine," she made her film debut in *Joe*; 1933—starred in her last film, *Two Minutes Silence*; 1959—appeared with her three children in Tennessee Williams's play, *Orpheus Descending.* **Died:** In London, 4 March 1982.

PHYLLIS. Born: Phyllis Glory McDonagh in Sydney, 1900. **Education:** Attended Kincoppal, the Convent of the Sacred Heart, Elizabeth Bay. **Family:** Married Leo O'Brien, 1941. **Career:** 1933—retired from filmmaking; mid-to-late 1930s worked as editor of New Zealand newspaper *Truth*; after 1941—worked as a freelance journalist and short story writer; 1960-78—worked as social editor of *North Shore Times.* **Died:** In Sydney, 17 October 1978.

PAULETTE. Born: Paulette de Vere McDonagh in Sydney, 1901. **Education:** Attended Kincoppal, the Convent of the Sacred Heart, Elizabeth Bay; studied acting at P. J. Ramster School. **Career:** 1924—worked as an extra in *The Mystery of a Hansom Cab*; 1926—co-directed first feature film *Those Who Love*; 1934—unsuccessfully tried to produce another film. **Died:** In Australia, August 1978.

1926—the sisters earned widespread attention in Australia for their first feature film collaboration, *Those Who Love*; 1933—the sisters produced their final film together, *Two Minutes Silence*. **Awards:** The sisters received the Australian Film Institute's Raymond Longford Award for significant contributions to the Australian film industry, 1978.

Films as Collaborators

(Paulette: director and writer; Phyllis: production manager, co-writer, art director, and titles; Isobel [billed as Marie Lorraine]: actress)

1926   *Those Who Love* (Paulette, co-d with Ramster)
1928   *The Far Paradise*
1930   *The Cheaters*
1933   *Two Minutes Silence*

Films as Actress (Isobel)

(billed as Marie Lorraine)

1924   *Joe* (B. Smith)
1925   *Painted Daughters*

Other Films (Paulette)

1924   *The Mystery of a Hansom Cab* (Shirley) (ro as extra)
Early 1930s   *Australia in the Swim* (co-d with Macken—doc, short); *How I Play Cricket* (co-d with Macken—doc, short); *The Mighty Conqueror* (co-d with Macken—doc, short)

Publications on the McDonagh Sisters

Books

Weaver, John T., *Twenty Years of Silents, 1908-1928,* Metuchen, New Jersey, 1971.
Tulloch, John, *Legends on the Screen: The Australian Narrative Film, 1919-1929,* Sydney, 1981.
Edmondson, Ray, and Andrew Pike, *Australia's Lost Films,* Canberra, 1982.
Long, Joan, and Martin Long, *The Pictures That Moved,* Melbourne, 1982.
Ryan, Penny, and Margaret Eliot, *Women in Australian Film Production,* Sydney, 1983.
Matthews, Jill, *Good and Mad Women: The Historical Construction of Femininity in Twentieth Century Australia,* Sydney, 1984.
Wright, Andrée, *Brilliant Careers: Women in Australian Cinema,* Sydney, 1986.
Murray, Scott, editor, *Australian Cinema,* St. Leonards, Australia, 1994.
Foster, Gwendolyn Audrey, *Women Film Directors: An International Bio-Critical Dictionary,* Westport, Connecticut, 1995.

Article

Shirley, Graham, "McDonaghs of Australian Cinema," in *Film News* (New York), December 1978.

* * *

The McDonagh sisters were a trio of Australian filmmakers who funded and produced four feature films that reflected their admiration for Hollywood movies. In a truly unique partnership, the sisters worked together as a production team between 1926 and 1933: Paulette was the screenwriter and director; Phyllis was the production manager and collaborated on the stories and titles; and Isobel, billed as Marie Lorraine, starred in each of the films. They are noteworthy as the first women in Australia to produce feature films; it was not until Gillian Armstrong's 1979 film *My Brilliant Career* that their accomplishment would be repeated.

The McDonagh sisters' father worked as the honorary surgeon to J. C. Williamson's theatrical companies, so as children they became quite familiar with show business. Paulette worked as a movie extra in *The Mystery of a Hansom Cab,* after which she wrote two scenarios, *Those Who Love* and *The Greater Love.* Then, she studied film acting briefly with P. J. Ramster. Yet Paulette learned about filmmaking by assiduously watching Hollywood films; she would go to a movie in the morning and if she liked it, she would return for the afternoon and evening screenings to study the techniques more closely. In addition, the cinematographer Jack Fletcher, who had worked briefly in Hollywood, helped teach her camera and editing techniques in order to craft the more delicate rhythms and moods that she favored. Paulette employed her acting teacher Ramster to direct their first film, *Those Who Love.* But, she soon took the director's reins herself in order to produce the effects she envisioned. The film proved to be commercially successful, and was commended by critics for its dramatic qualities and technical standards, especially compared to other Australian films. The press trumpeted the story that the Governor de Chair cried at its premiere. Their second film, *The Far Paradise,* was also critically applauded and is considered one of the best-directed of the pre-sound Australian films.

The sisters' aim was to counter the prevailing Australian genres. Paulette, in particular, objected to the vulgarities of the popular bush comedies and their macho sensibilities as well as the social issue films. She disliked Australian films in general for what she considered their technical limitations, their overly melodramatic qualities, and their overwrought acting styles. Instead, she chose to make cosmopolitan society dramas and she carefully studied Hollywood techniques for creating more delicate rhythms and moods.

The McDonagh sisters' films were low-budget affairs that featured the themes of family antagonism, the longing for vengeance, the power of beauty, and the joys and torments of love. In addition, Phyllis paid careful attention to the art direction and the sisters favored grand settings, including the family's colonial home, Drummoyne House, which was brimming with antiques and spectacular furnishings and came in handy for *Those Who Love* and *The Far Paradise.* In 1928, an Australian journalist suggested that the McDonaghs would be challenged and nurtured in Hollywood, especially Isobel whose career would benefit by the possibility of appearing in more films than was possible in Australia.

Critics and film historians generally praise the sisters' films for their authenticity and Paulette's skill in framing, lighting, and editing her films, as well as Isobel's "natural" and restrained performances. Their heroines are typically innocent victims of their fathers' efforts to keep them from their lovers, though they are usually reunited after considerable trials and tribulations. Both *The Far Paradise* and *The Cheaters* featured heroines who were torn by their loyalty to their criminal fathers versus the men they loved. *The Far Paradise* tells the story of Cherry who returns home from finishing school to discover that her father is a drunken swindler and the proclaimed nemesis of her lover's father. *Those Who Love* tells the story of a dancer Lola who willingly sacrifices her lover when she learns their relationship will mean the loss of his inheritance.

In *The Cheaters* the heroine is a safe-cracking thief who eventually realizes the wrongs of her cheating life and so confesses her reluctance to her father, a criminal patriarch. But *The Cheaters* was troubled by the coming of the "talkies"; originally produced as a silent film, before its release it was converted to a part-talkie by substituting a number of synchronized sound sequences and by embellishing other scenes with music. The effect was disappointing. One of the film's investors recalled that it "died a horrible death" at the premiere, in part because several recording mistakes produced howls of laughter from the audience. In 1931 it was converted to a full-talkie and some sequences were re-shot. The changes, however, failed to produce box-office profits. The story is occasionally overwrought and the style a bit slow, and the ending is too facile—as it is revealed that the cheating daughter is not really related to her criminal father, but rather to her adopted lover's father! Yet, her characterizations reveal more complexity and cynicism than was the case in Australia's earlier star-crossed romances.

The last film the McDonagh sisters made was *Two Minutes Silence,* a sound epic adapted from the antiwar play by Leslie Haylen that featured the painful memories of four people as they participate in the two-minutes silence customary on Armistice Day. It is noteworthy as the first Australian talkie that focused on a social issue and as the film of which Paulette was most proud. But the newspaper *Sunday Sun and Guardian* criticized the film for its deadly serious subject and for the failure to depict Australian characterizations, though outraged fans deluged the paper with letters supporting the film. Nevertheless, its failure at the box office meant the retirement of the team.

Before the sisters made *Two Minutes Silence* Paulette made a series of documentary shorts with Neville Macken that featured Australian sports heroes, including *Australia in the Swim* with the Olympic swim team, *How I Play Cricket,* and *The Mighty Conqueror* with the race horse Phar Lap. Only two of the four feature films produced by the McDonaghs are still extant, *The Far Paradise* and *The Cheaters.* In the 1970s, as feminist historians began to resurrect the work of noteworthy yet overlooked women, these two films were restored and the silent version of *The Cheaters* was widely screened as the work of a pioneering woman director.

—Cynthia Felando

MEERAPFEL, Jeanine
Argentinean director and writer

Born: Buenos Aires, Argentina, 14 June 1943. **Education:** Received German Academic Exchange Service (DAAD) scholarship, Academy of Art and Design, Ulm, Germany, 1964. **Career:** 1964—moved to Germany to pursue film studies; lecturer for Adult Education Center in Ulm and Goethe Institute in various countries. **Awards:** Golden Ducat, Mannheim Film Festival, for *In the Country of My Parents,* 1981; Prize for Young Filmmaker, San Sebastian Film Festival, FIPRESCI Award (International Film Critics), Cannes Film Festival, and First Prize, Chicago International Film Festival, for *Malou,* 1981; Interfilm Award and Otto Dibielius Award, Berlin International Film Festival, for *Die Kümmeltürkin geht,* 1985; Hessen-Film Award, for *Zwickel auf Bizykel,* 1997.

Films as Director

1964-68 *Distanciamiento* (short); *Diario Regional* (doc, 16mm)
1966 *Abstand*
1967 *Regionalzeitung*
1968-97 *Zwickel auf Bizykel* (co-d)
1969 *Team Delphin*; *Am Ama am Amazons*
1981 *Im Land miener Eltern* (*In the Country of My Parents*) (doc) (+ sc); *Malou* (+ sc)
1983 *Solange es Europa noch gibt—Fragen an den Freiden* (*As Long as There's Still a Europe—Questions on Peace*) (video) (co-d with Schäfer)
1985 *Die Kümmeltürkin geht* (*Melek Leaves*) (doc) (+ sc)
1987 *Die Verliebten* (*Days to Remember*) (+ sc)
1988 *La Amiga* (+ sc)
1989 *13 Minuten vor zwölf in Lima* (doc—for TV) (co-d with Chiesa); *Desembarcos* (*Es Gibt Kein Vergessen*; *When Memory Speaks*) (doc) (co-d with Chiesa, + co-sc)
1990 *Im Glanze dieses Glückes* (doc) (co-d)
1993-95 *Amigomío* (co-d with Chiesa, + co-sc)

Other Film

1995 *Die Nacht der Regisseure* (*The Night of the Filmmakers*) (Reitz—doc) (appearance)

Publication by Meerapfel

Article

"Einen behutsamen Dialog herstellen," interview with M. Ulbrich, in *Film und Fernsehen* (Berlin), vol. 16, no. 11, 1988.

Publications on Meerapfel

Articles

King, John, "Assailing the Heights of Macho Pictures: Women Film Makers in Contemporary Argentina," in *Essays on Hispanic Themes in Honour of Edward C. Riley,* edited by Jennifer Lowe and Philip Swanson, Edinburgh, 1989.
"Amigomío," in *Kino* (Munich), no. 1, 1994.

*   *   *

By the end of the 1930s Argentinean cinema had flourished, leading the film industry in Latin America and regaining its foothold in the international Spanish-language film market. The tango, that quintessential Argentinean musical form, had propelled this success. Tango's tragic legendary hero, Carlos Gardel, gave the tango its lasting sophistication and brought it to the big screen as its romantic hero. His contract with Paramount Pictures, resulting in seven feature-length films, gave Argentinean cinema international prominence, heightened by the star's untimely death in a 1935 airplane collision. The Argentinean cinema's meteoric rise, however, was curtailed by World War II—Argentina's neutrality, seen as veiled support of the Axis powers, brought the wrath of the United States, the only country then producing raw film stock. Cut off from necessary resources and poorly managed, the film industry collapsed.

In the 1940s, President Péron set up several initiatives to bolster the film industry. Most of these, however, did little to support its continuation and the industry saw further decline. In the early 1970s, when Péron returned from exile to lead his country once more, the film industry responded favorably to the new atmosphere and optimism of Argentina. Péron died in office and in 1976 the government that succeeded him was overthrown by a military junta. The military dictatorship imposed strict censorship on the mass media, seeing popular culture as related to politics and as a potential source of resistance. Once again, Argentinean cinema was stymied. This time, however, its filmmakers were blacklisted, "disappeared," or went into exile.

The return of democracy after the brutal military dictatorship brought with it the resurgence of Argentinean cinema. President Raúl Alfonsín (1983-89) could count among his successes the international acclaim and critical acceptance of Argentinean cinema. In the 1980s, Argentina's filmmakers, both the stars and the newcomers, explored the extent of their new expressive freedom in films that addressed national identity, conflicts raised by national history and by being part of the bourgeoisie. These films cannot easily be characterized in brief terms, but, as John King has noted, a great energy and inventiveness accompanied filmmakers' explorations of their new political freedom. Further, many of the films of this period directly address the traumas of recent history, perhaps most notably the Academy Award-winning film *The Official Story* (directed by Luis Puenzo, 1985).

Jeanine Meerapfel's work in many ways epitomizes the issues—economic, political, and emotional—with which Argentinean directors have grappled in the past two decades. Born in Buenos Aires, Meerapfel left Argentina in 1964 to study cinema in Ulm, Germany, and has resided in Germany ever since. Her films, however, frequently return to her Argentinean heritage. Meerapfel approaches exile, distance, and memory directly as in her documentary *When Memory Speaks* about how Argentina deals with its past. Similar themes crop up in her 1981 feature *Malou,* which shows the life of a woman (modeled on the experience of Meerapfel's mother), who follows her husband into a lonely exile in Argentina, an ocean away from her own native land. Again in 1993, Meerapfel approaches exile and the search for identity in *Amigomío,* a road movie in which a father and son flee Argentina after the disappearance of the boy's politically active mother.

We note in all of Meerapfel's work the continual struggle to reconcile exile, rootlessness, liminality, history, memory, and the continual quest for identity. These thematic touchstones connect Meerapfel's work to that of other contemporary Argentinean filmmakers (especially María Luisa Bemberg, Fernando Solanas, and Luis Puenzo). Meerapfel's artistic search also relates to that of Chilean filmmakers in exile, and now in Chile, who struggle with similar issues and their own tortuous experience with a repressive dictatorship.

Like many Latin American filmmakers, Meerapfel has found co-production to be the only secure route to a finished film and, as the German titles indicate, many of her films have been German-Argentinean co-productions. These factors, as well as her continued

residence in Germany coupled with the Argentinean themes and setting of some of her films, create in Meerapfel a thoroughly Latin American filmmaker, one who cannot be pigeonholed as "feminist" or "Argentinean" and whose films resonate not only across Latin America, but throughout the contemporary world.

Meerapfel's most acclaimed and best-known film is *La Amiga.* Made in 1988, *La Amiga* concentrates on Argentina's painful recent history through its depiction of the formation and development of the political movement, Las madres de Plaza de Mayo (the Mothers of the Plaza de Mayo). As chronicled in the award-winning documentary *Las madres de la Plaza de Mayo* (directed by Susana Muñoz and Lourdes Portillo, 1986), Las madres began as a small group of women who in 1977 organized to protest the disappearance of their children and family members. Not able to cut through legal and bureaucratic red tape, Las madres began to demonstrate once a week in front of the government building, Casa Rosada, in Buenos Aires's main plaza. Growing in size and strength, the group defied political pressure to disband and gained worldwide media attention. By the 1980s, Las madres had evolved into a sophisticated human-rights organization. *La Amiga,* the first feature fiction film devoted to Las madres, centers on two friends, María and Raquel, who have grown apart due to Raquel's exile during the dictatorship. Their reunion is set against the backdrop of Las madres, for which María is the main spokeswoman, and the complexity of renegotiating identities and relationships in post-dictatorship Argentina.

Like María Luisa Bemberg's *Camila* (1984), *La Amiga* is a significant film not just because of its poignant story and strong filmmaking. In the late 1980s, Argentina's Radical government had declared an official end to the trials of military leaders accused of human-rights atrocities during the dictatorship. *La Amiga* is Meerapfel's contribution to the ongoing struggle, a loud refusal to let the human-rights debate end or to forget or forgive the crimes against Argentina by her own military. As Meerapfel herself said in an interview with John King, "Those who forget their story, repeat their story. Identity is formed by keeping memory alive."

—Ilene S. Goldman

MEHTA, Deepa
Indian/Canadian director

Born: Amritsar, India, 1950. **Education:** Earned a degree in philosophy from the University of New Delhi; learned the basics of filmmaking while working for a documentary film company in India. **Family:** Married the Canadian filmmaker Paul Saltzman (divorced 1983), daughter: Devyani. **Career:** Introduced to film as a child by her father, a film distributor in India; obtained a job with a documentary film company and wrote scripts for children's films; 1973—emigrated to Canada and co-founded Sunrise Films Ltd., with her husband, Paul Saltzman, and her brother, photojournalist Dilip Mehta; 1970s-80s—directed film and television documentaries; 1988—directed *The Twin,* a half-hour television drama, and acted in another episode of this (as well as other) series; 1988-89—directed four episodes of the television series *Danger Bay*; 1992—directed an episode of the television series *Young Indiana Jones Chronicles*; 1995—directed the final episode of *Young Indiana Jones Chronicles.* **Awards:** Etrog Award, Best Documentary, for *At 99: A Portrait of Louise Tandy Murch,* 1975; Best Feature Film, International Women's Film Festival, for *Martha, Ruth & Edie,* 1988; Special Prize of the Jury, International Filmfest Mannheim-Heidelberg; Most Popular Canadian Film, Vancouver International Film Festival, for *Fire,* 1996.

Films as Director

1975   *At 99: A Portrait of Louise Tandy Murch* (doc, short); *What's the Weather Like Up There* (doc, short)
1985   *K.Y.T.E.S.: How We Dream Ourselves* (doc)
1986   *Travelling Light: The Photojournalism of Dilip Mehta* (doc)
1988   *Martha, Ruth & Edie* (co-d with Bailey and Suissa, + pr)
1991   *Sam & Me* (+ co-pr)
1994   *Camilla*
1996   *Fire* (+ co-pr, sc)

Other Films

1974   *The Bakery* (Saltzman—doc) (sc, ed)
1994   *Skin Deep* (Onodera) (exec pr)

Publications on Mehta

Book

Cole, Janis, and Holly Dale, *Calling the Shots,* Kingston, Ontario, 1993.

Articles

Ruet, E., "Deepa Mehta, realisatrice coleur," in *Cinema* (Paris), June 1991.
Turbide, Diane, "Georgia on Their Minds," in *Maclean's* (Toronto), 28 June 1993.
Cormier, Jim, "Mehta Morphosis," in *Chatelaine,* November 1993.
"Deepa Mehta: 11 Million Dollar Director," in *Take One* (Toronto), Fall 1994.
Vasudev, A., "Deepa Mehta," in *Cinemaya* (New Delhi), Autumn/Winter 1994-95.
Johnson, Brian D., "Forbidden Flames," in *Maclean's* (Toronto), 29 September 1997.
Sidhwa, Bapsi, "Playing with Fire," in *Ms.* (New York), November/December 1997.

* * *

In her films, Deepa Mehta has mostly been concerned with the lives of women, and the manner in which women communicate on the deepest and most intimate levels. A common theme has been the unlikely union developing between two disparate individuals who end up transcending age differences and cultural barriers as they strike up a friendship, and an understanding. Another of her recurring topics is the depiction of older women as vital and active. This is evident in her very first film, the documentary short *At 99: A Portrait of Louise Tandy Murch,* in which her subject is shown doing yoga and making music and otherwise relishing her life.

Working with two other women filmmakers, Norma Bailey and Daniele J. Suissa, Mehta directed *Martha, Ruth & Edie,* consisting

of a trio of vignettes in which the title characters attend a self-help conference and end up examining their innermost emotions. *Sam & Me,* Mehta's first solo feature, is an exception to her other work in that its protagonists are male. And it is her best film to date: a compassionate slice-of-life about Nikhil, a young Indian who comes to Toronto under the sponsorship of a manipulative uncle. Nikhil ends up looking after Sam Cohen, a cantankerous, elderly Jew. Despite their dissimilarities, Nikhil and Sam are united in that they are outcasts. Eventually, they develop a bond. Tragically, however, peer and family pressures on both sides result in the termination of their friendship. *Sam & Me* works as an indictment of those within ethnic communities who are more concerned with custom and convention than human interaction.

Camilla, her follow-up feature, is a redo of *Sam & Me* as an exploration of intergenerational camaraderie. Only here, the characters are women—and the end result is well-intentioned but deeply flawed. The title character, Camilla Cara (played by Jessica Tandy in her cinematic swan song), is an aged concert violinist who is lorded over by her fat, pompous son. She becomes the friend of, and mentor to, a young musician who desires a career as a composer and is weighed down by a thoughtless, patronizing husband.

Camilla often is obvious and silly, as the two women set out on the road and share experiences. But it is never uninteresting whenever Tandy is on screen. She rises above the film's shortcomings, and is especially luminous in her brief scenes with her husband Hume Cronyn (playing Camilla's long-ago lover). These sequences transcend the film, becoming a celebration of Tandy and Cronyn, their talent and their lives together.

The focus of *Fire,* Mehta's next feature, also is on the evolving relationship between two women who are victimized by unfeeling males—but with a decidedly sexual twist. And with *Sam & Me,* it serves as a lambasting of the stifling constraints of tradition.

The film (along with Mira Nair's *Kama Sutra: A Tale of Love,* which made the film-festival rounds with *Fire*) deals with a subject rarely seen on Western movie screens: sexuality and Indian women. It is the story of Sita, an innocent young bride in an arranged marriage. The future seems to hold little for Sita, as her husband disregards her and prefers the company of his Chinese mistress. At one point he patronizingly orders Sita to occupy herself with "needlework," or by taking "a beauty course or something."

The other woman in the story is Radha, Sita's new, long-married sister-in-law. Radha may be a devoted wife, but because she has been unable to conceive a child she has brought shame to her husband. Both women are bound by custom and ritual, and their lives of drudgery, frustration, and isolation seem preordained. But each has a restless spirit; each yearns for freedom and liberation. And they are certain to cause contention in their household when they are drawn together out of their shared loneliness and yearning for tenderness, and eventually find solace in each other's arms.

Fire is valuable as a mirror of social change in contemporary India. Dramatically speaking, however, it is like a virulent 1970s feminist tract. The characters are one-dimensional stereotypes: *All* the men in the story are boorish, perverted, or good old-fashioned male chauvinist pigs, while the women are downtrodden and victimized. And there is plenty of shallow symbolism. It just so happens that Biji, Sita and Radha's elderly mother-in-law, is mute—this is meant to symbolize the state of women throughout Indian history—and thus is unable to cry out as a sleazy household servant watches X-rated videos in her presence.

Mehta has stated that she means for *Fire* to be "about the intolerance in class, culture and identity. And how we can cope with [the] burdens of society and the tug of war between tradition and the voice of personal independence." Despite the worthiness of these goals, the result is a superficial drama that lacks fully fleshed-out characters and a multilayered scenario.

Nonetheless, *Fire* serves as an example of how a woman filmmaker may go about exploring a topic—sex—that stereotypically is the domain of men. In India, the film was considered highly controversial. When it was presented at an Indian film festival, Mehta reported that "a lot of the [older] men wanted to shoot me dead....They feel it is threatening their masculinity."

Fire is scheduled as the first of a trilogy, to be followed by *Earth* and *Water.*

—Rob Edelman

MENKEN, Marie
American director

Born: New York, 1910, of Lithuanian immigrant parents. **Family:** Married the poet and filmmaker Willard Maas, 1937. **Career:** Early 1930s—began painting; mid-1930s—received a residence grant from the Yaddo art colony, where she met Willard Maas; 1943—first film experience, photographing *Geography of the Body,* a film directed by Maas; 1945—first film as director *Visual Variations on Noguchi;* mid-1950s—founded the Gryphon Film Group with Willard Maas, Stan Brakhage, and Ben Moore; also worked at Time-Life most of her married life. **Awards:** Special Citation, Creative Film Foundation for *Dwightiana,* 1959. **Died:** New York, 29 December 1970.

Films as Director

1945   *Visual Variations on Noguchi*
1957   *Hurry! Hurry!*; *Glimpse of the Garden*; *Dwightiana*
1960   *Faucets* (unfinished)
1961   *Eye Music in Red Major*; *Arabesque for Kenneth Anger*; *Bagatelle for Willard Maas*
1962   *Moonplay*; *Here and There with My Octoscope and Zenscapes* (unfinished)
1963   *Go! Go! Go!*; *Mood Mondrian*; *Notebook*; *Drips and Strips*
1964   *Wrestling*
1965   *Andy Warhol*
1966   *Lights*; *Sidewalks*
1967   *Watts with Eggs*
1968   *Excursion*

Other Films

1943   *Geography of the Body* (Maas) (ph)
1966   *The Chelsea Girls* (*The Trip*) (Warhol) (ro as Mother); *Life of Juanita Castro* (Warhol) (ro)

Publication by Menken

Article

Filmwise, no. 5-6, 1967. (Special issue devoted to Menken and Willard Maas; includes an interview with Menken by P. Adams Sitney.)

Publications on Menken

Books

Brakhage, Stan, *Metaphors of Vision,* New York, 1963.
Renan, Sheldon, *An Introduction to the American Independent Film,* New York, 1967.
Mekas, Jonas, *Movie Journal,* New York, 1972.
The American Federation of the Arts, editors, *A History of the American Avant-Garde Cinema,* New York, 1976.
Sitney, P. Adams, *Visionary Film,* New York, 1979.
Film-Makers' Cooperative Catalogue 6, New York, 1987.
Brakhage, Stan, *Film at Wit's End,* Edinburgh, 1989.
Acker, Ally, *Reel Women: Pioneers of the Cinema, 1896 to the Present,* New York, 1991.
Rabinovitz, Lauren, *Points of Resistance: Women, Power and Politics in the New York Avant-Garde Cinema, 1943-71,* Urbana, Illinois, 1991.
Canyon Cinema Catalogue 7, San Francisco, 1992.
Foster, Gwendolyn Audrey, *Women Film Directors: An International Bio-Critical Dictionary,* Westport, Connecticut, 1995.

Articles

Goodman, Paul, "Statement on Marie Menken," in Exhibition Catalogue, Betty Parsons Gallery, New York, 1949.
Myers, Louis Budd, "Marie Menken Herself," in *Film Culture* (New York), Summer 1967.
Obituary in *New York Times,* 31 December 1970.
Wolf, Reva, "Collaboration as Social Exchange: Screen Tests/A Diary by Gerard Melanga and Andy Warhol," in *Art Journal,* Winter 1993.
Brakhage, Stan, "Stan Brakhage on Marie Menken (Innis Film Society, Nov. 19, 1992)," in *Film Culture* (New York), Summer 1994.
MacDonald, Scott, "Cinema 16: Documents toward a History of the Film Society Part 1," in *Wide Angle* (Baltimore, Maryland), vol. 19, no. 1, 1997.
MacDonald, Scott, "Cinema 16: Documents toward a History of the Film Society Part 2," in *Wide Angle* (Baltimore, Maryland), vol. 19, no. 2, 1997.

*   *   *

Along with key experimental filmmakers such as Maya Deren, Sidney Peterson, and Kenneth Anger, Marie Menken formed a part of that generation of American avant-garde filmmakers who emerged in the early to mid-1940s. Menken was a painter/collagist and filmmaker whose first film experience was photographing *Geography of the Body* (1943), a film made by her husband, Willard Maas, that featured poetic text by George Barker. It was made with a 16mm camera left with Menken by animator Frances Lee when she went into the army, and features distorted images of the human body produced by dime-store magnifying glasses taped to the camera lens. Although Menken's contribution to the film was substantial, it does not reflect the kind of films she would eventually make on her own.

Menken's true first film was the beautiful *Visual Variations on Noguchi* (1945), which was made in the artist's studio and features several techniques that we now associate with Menken's visual style, in particular exhilarating handheld camera work and rhythmical editing patterns. In later films such as *Hurry! Hurry!* (1957), *Notebook* (1963), *Moonplay* (1962), and *Arabesque for Kenneth Anger* (1961),

Menken would add to her visual repertoire such techniques as "nightwriting" (night lights filmed with such speed that they seem to be dancing) and fast motion photography (achieved by under-cranking the camera), which in *Moonplay* make the moon appear to be dancing in the night sky. Menken's films are short, lyrical, and poetic. She also helped create a new form of experimental film: the poetic, diary film.

One of her most notorious films, *Hurry! Hurry!,* was made from footage of spermatozoa shot in microscopic close-up. This found-footage film incorporated scientific footage not shot by the filmmaker, but the film is made her own by the addition of a complex formal structure and editing patterns. The resulting film is one of Menken's most impressive. *Eye Music in Red Major* (1961) creates a symphony of color, shape, and movement through the rhythmical photographing and editing of Christmas-tree decorations. Equally appealing is *Arabesque for Kenneth Anger,* made while traveling with the filmmaker in Alhambra. The references to music and dance in these films are not casual. Menken's films have a musical quality, and they often involve a dance between the camera and its subject. At times camera movement is the guiding structural principle, as in *Moonplay,* and at others it is the movement of the object within the frame. *Notebook,* a film constructed from footage dating to the late 1940s though not given final shape until the early 1960s, is a fine example of Menken's editing strategies of cutting on shape, color, and length of shot. Though Menken's films represent serious investigations into the rhythmical possibilities of cinema, her work always remains exuberant and playful.

Menken's films also bear the imprint of the economy of means that went into their making. The simplicity of her shooting and editing techniques is one of their great charms and connects her to other women artists working in different media, as well as to many other experimental filmmakers. Stan Brakhage describes how Menken's editing process involved hanging strips of film and looking at the shapes within the frame to determine the length of each shot visually (Brakhage 1989). He relates her work to collage techniques in painting. Menken rarely used an editing machine, and it was only when the films were projected that she could judge if the film was in its final shape. The handcrafted aspect of her films emphasizes the filmic material and the physicality of making art.

It can be argued that her influence on other filmmakers such as Stan Brakhage and Jonas Mekas, and her encouragement of others such as Kenneth Anger and Andy Warhol, is as great a legacy as the body of work she left behind. P. Adams Sitney in *Visionary Film* credits Menken as being a key influence on the lyrical film of the 1950s and 1960s, which reached its apotheosis in the great lyric films of Brakhage and Bruce Baillie. Menken's attachment to Andy Warhol's Factory in the mid-1960s undoubtedly had some influence on the films produced by Warhol in this period as well. Additionally, Menken turns up in several of Warhol's key films, most notably in *Life of Juanita Castro* and *The Chelsea Girls*. Despite this certain influence on other filmmakers, the power and accomplishment of Menken's own work as a filmmaker should not be underestimated. Menken's films have been undervalued to some extent because of their seeming simplicity and naive faith in the power of cinema to produce a fresh perspective of the world. They are also not as readily available or as well known as they should be.

Menken's personal life was noteworthy in that her long marriage to poet and filmmaker Willard Maas was notoriously tempestuous in part due to Maas's homosexuality. Menken's Catholicism prevented her from seeking a divorce, although Brakhage argues that Menken could not bear to leave Maas because "she loved him, all the same"

(Brakhage 1989). Menken's difficult personal life was also exacerbated by alcohol. Notwithstanding her turbulent personal history, Marie Menken's impact on experimental film is substantial. She is a key figure whose work deserves a wider audience and critical re-evaluation.

—Mario Falsetto

MEREDYTH, Bess
American writer and actress

Born: Helen MacGlashan in Buffalo, New York, 1890. **Family:** Married the director Michael Curtiz, 1928 (died 1962). **Career:** 1911—extra for Griffith at Biograph; first role in *A Sailor's Heart,* 1912; 1917—first feature film as writer, *The Midnight Man*. **Died:** In Woodland Hills, California, 13 July 1969.

Films as Writer

1913   *At Midnight* (Lucas); *The Honor of the Regiment* (Lucas)
1914   *The Forbidden Room* (Dwan); *The Love Victorious* (Lucas); *The Mystery of Wickham Hall*; *The Outlaw Reforms*; *The Smuggler's Daughter*; *The Trey of Hearts* (Lucas—serial)
1915   *The Blood of the Children* (McRae); *Their Hour*; *The Mystery Woman*; *Stronger than Death* (DeGrasse); *The Fascination of the Fleur de Lis* (DeGrasse)
1917   *Three Women of France* (Baldwin); *The Midnight Man* (Clifton); *Scandal* (Giblyn); *Pay Me* (DeGrasse)
1918   *The Romance of Tarzan* (+ co-d with Lucas); *Morgan's Raiders* (+ co-d with Lucas)
1919   *The Man from Kangaroo* (+ co-d)
1921   *The Fighting Breed* (Lucas); *The Grim Comedian* (Lloyd); *The Shadow of Lightning Ridge* (Lucas)
1922   *The Dangerous Age* (Stahl); *Grand Larceny* (Worsley); *One Clear Call* (Stahl); *Rose o' the Sea* (Niblo); *The Song of Life* (Stahl); *The Woman He Married* (Niblo)
1923   *Strangers of the Night* (Niblo)
1924   *The Red Lily* (Niblo); *Thy Name Is Woman* (Niblo)
1925   *The Love Hour* (Raymaker); *The Slave of Fashion* (Henley); *The Wife Who Wasn't Wanted* (Flood)
1926   *Ben-Hur* (Niblo); *Don Juan* (Crosland); *The Sea Beast* (Webb)
1927   *Irish Hearts* (Haskin); *The Magic Flame* (H. King); *Rose of the Golden West* (Fitzmaurice); *When a Man Loves* (Crosland)
1928   *The Little Shepherd of Kingdom Come* (Santell); *The Mysterious Lady* (Niblo); *Sailors' Wives* (Henabery); *The Scarlet Lady* (Crosland); *A Woman of Affairs* (C. Brown); *The Yellow Lily* (A. Korda)
1929   *Wonder of Women* (C. Brown)
1930   *Chasing Rainbows* (*The Road Show*) (Reisner); *In Gay Madrid* (Leonard); *The Sea Bat* (Ruggles); *Our Blushing Brides* (Beaumont); *Romance* (C. Brown)
1931   *Laughing Sinners* (Beaumont); *Phantom of Paris* (Robertson); *The Prodigal* (*The Southerner*) (Pollard); *Cuban Love Song* (Van Dyke)

1932   *Strange Interlude* (*Strange Interval*) (Leonard); *West of Broadway* (Beaumont)
1933   *Looking Forward* (C. Brown)
1934   *The Affairs of Cellini* (La Cava); *The Mighty Barnum* (W. Lang)
1935   *Folies Bergère* (Del Ruth); *Metropolitan* (Boleslawsky); *Charlie Chan at the Opera* (Humberstone); *The Iron Duke* (Saville)
1936   *Half Angel* (Lanfield); *Under Two Flags* (Lloyd)
1937   *The Great Hospital Mystery* (Tinling)
1940   *The Mark of Zorro* (Mamoulian)
1941   *That Night in Rio* (Cummings)
1947   *The Unsuspected* (Curtiz)

Films as Actress

1912   *A Sailor's Heart* (Lucas)
1914   *The Magnet*; *Bess the Detectress, or The Old Mill at Midnight*; *When Bess Got in Wrong*; *The Little Autogomobile*; *Father's Bride*; *Willie Walrus and the Awful Confession*; *Bess the Detectress, or The Dog Watch*; *Bess the Detectress in Tick, Tick, Tick*; *Her Twin Brother*; *The Desert's Sting*

Publications by Meredyth

Book

With Gene Fowler, *The Mighty Barnum* (script), New York, 1934.

Publications on Meredyth

Article

Obituary, in *New York Times,* 15 July 1969.

* * *

Bess Meredyth was one of the solid core of first-class screen-writers, the majority of whom were women, who began their careers in the silent era and continued to enjoy success on into the coming of sound. Like many of the other women writers, Meredyth had early work in short-story and newspaper writing, as well as in vaudeville and stage acting. She began her career in films as an actress, starting in 1911 as an extra for D. W. Griffith at Biograph in New York, and soon went to Hollywood. Her screen-acting work for Biograph, Universal, and other studios includes the Western *The Desert's Sting,* in which she played the woman with whom the white husband of an Indian—played by Jeanie Macpherson—falls in love; both Macpherson and Meredyth would go on to successful screenwriting careers.

Meredyth had success writing and selling scenarios as early as 1913. In 1915 she was selected to be assistant to Joseph Vance in the preparation of all scripts for Fiction Pictures Inc., following several months during which she worked with Vance in the preparation of the 30-reel serial picture *The Trey o' Hearts* (Vance writing the story, Meredyth the scenario). By this time, Meredyth had written some 140 scenarios. In 1918 she co-directed with Wilfred Lucas *The Romance of Tarzan* (sequel to *Tarzan of the Apes*) for the National Film Corporation.

Meredyth later wrote for MGM, Warner Bros., Columbia, and other major studios; her scripts included vehicles for stars such as John Barrymore, Greta Garbo, Joan Crawford, and Clark Gable. Notable screenwriting credits include the Roman epic *Ben-Hur,* starring Ramon Novarro, and directed by Fred Niblo (with whom Meredyth would work on other productions). Bess Meredyth and Carey Wilson were hired to replace scenarist June Mathis; the high budget (more than $4.5 million) spectacle, shot in Italy, and incorporating two-color Technicolor sequences, proved to be a big success for MGM. Meredyth was also the scenarist on another hit, *Don Juan,* a lavish costume drama starring John Barrymore and directed by Alan Crosland. Warners' first feature film using the revolutionary Vitaphone sound process, the film began with a synchronized speech, and featured an elaborate recorded orchestral score performed by the New York Philharmonic.

Other notable work among Meredyth's many screen credits includes *The Mysterious Lady* (starring Greta Garbo), *Strange Interlude* (with Norma Shearer and Clark Gable), *The Mighty Barnum* (co-written with Gene Fowler for Darryl F. Zanuck), *Folies Bergère* (starring Maurice Chevalier and Ann Sothern), *Under Two Flags* (Ronald Colman and Claudette Colbert), and *That Night in Rio* (with Alice Faye, Don Ameche, and Carmen Miranda).

—Virginia M. Clark

MESHES OF THE AFTERNOON
USA, 1943
Director: Maya Deren

Production: Black and white, 16mm; running time: 18 minutes, some sources list 14 minutes. Released 1943.

Screenplay: Maya Deren and Alexander Hammid; **editor:** Maya Deren; **photography:** Alexander Hammid.

Cast: Maya Deren (*Woman*); Alexander Hammid (*Man*).

Publications

Books

Deren, Maya, *An Anagram of Ideas on Art, Form, and the Film,* New York, 1946.
Jacobs, Lewis, editor, *Introduction to the Art of the Movies: An Anthology of Ideas on the Nature of Movie Art,* New York, 1960.
Tyler, Parker, *Underground Film,* New York, 1969.
Sitney, P. Adams, *Visionary Film,* New York, 1974; rev. ed., 1979.
A History of the American Avant-Garde Cinema, New York, 1976.

Articles

Farber, Manny, "Maya Deren's Films," in *New Republic* (New York), 28 October 1946.
Tyler, Parker, "Experimental Film: A New Growth," in *Kenyon Review* (Gambier, Ohio), no. 1, 1949.
"Writings of Maya Deren and Ron Rice," in *Film Culture* (New York), Winter 1965.

Cornwell, Regina, "Maya Deren and Germaine Dulac: Activists of the Avant-Garde," in *Film Library Quarterly* (New York), vol. 5, no. 1, 1971.

Sitney, P. Adams, "The Idea of Morphology," in *Film Culture* (New York), nos. 53-55, 1972.

Mayer, T., "The Legend of Maya Deren: Champion of the American Independent Film," in *Film News* (New York), September/October 1979.

* * *

Meshes of the Afternoon launched the American avant-garde film movement after World War II. Made in collaboration by Maya Deren and her husband Alexander Hammid, the film depicts a woman's imaginative dream and the way it eventually destroys the woman herself. The film established dream imagery and visual poetic devices as the chief type of cinematic language for a new generation of postwar filmmakers and their audiences.

The story of *Meshes* is this: a woman (played by Deren) enters her home and falls asleep in a chair. As she sleeps and dreams, she repeatedly encounters a mysterious hooded figure whom she chases but cannot catch. With each failure, she reenters her house, where the household objects she employs in her waking state—a key, a knife, a flower, a phonograph, and a telephone—assume intensifying potency in an environment that becomes increasingly disoriented. Through such filmic means as creative editing, extreme camera angles, and slow motion, the movie creates a world in which it is more and more difficult for the woman to master the space and rooms around her. Finally, multiplied into three versions of herself, the woman attempts to kill her sleeping body. But she is awakened by a man (played by Hammid) only to find that physical reality, too, gives away to the dream logic of her imagination, ultimately causing her death.

Made privately in Deren and Hammid's home over a few weeks and for a few hundred dollars, *Meshes of the Afternoon* revived a European cinematic tradition established in the 1920s a tradition in which Hammid participated in his native Czechoslovakia. *Meshes of the Afternoon* sustained and developed the cinematic style of such leading European avant-garde filmmakers of the 1920s as Germaine Dulac, Luis Buñuel, and Jean Cocteau.

Meshes is a landmark film that has provided an important model, setting the tone and style for other individual efforts over the next decade. It launched Deren's career as one of the leading avant-garde filmmakers of the 1940s and 1950s. She showed the film at colleges, museums, and film societies across Canada and the United States. Her numerous bookings encouraged many younger artists interested in a personal cinema controlled by the individual artists. The film consequently inspired poetic self-exploratory films by such other filmmakers as Kenneth Anger, Stan Brakhage, and Willard Maas.

Meshes of the Afternoon is still one of the most popular of all American experimental films. It is revered as a classic mood poem which investigates a person's psychological reality.

—Lauren Rabinovitz

MÉSZÁROS, Márta
Hungarian director

Born: Budapest, 19 September 1931. **Education:** Attended VGIK (film school), Moscow, 1957. **Family:** Married 1) 1957 (divorced 1959); 2) the director Miklós Jancsó, 1960 (divorced 1973), three children; 3) the actor Jan Nowicki. **Career:** 1936—emigrated with family to U.S.S.R.; 1946—returned to Hungary; 1954—worked at Newsreel Studio, Budapest; 1957-59—worked for the Alexandru Sahia documentary studio, Bucharest, Romania; 1959-68—made science popularization shorts and documentary shorts, Budapest; mid-1960s—joined Mafilm Group 4; 1968—directed first feature. **Address:** c/o MAFILM Studio, Lumumba utca 174, Budapest, 1149 Hungary.

Films as Director

(short films in Hungary)

1954   *Ujra mosolyognak* (*Smiling Again*)
1955   *Albertfalvai történet* (*A History of Albertfalva*); *Tul a Kálvintéren* (*Beyond the Square*); *Mindennapi történetek* (*Everyday Stories*)
1956   *Országutak vándora* (*Wandering on Highways*)
1959   *Az élet megy tovább* (*Life Goes On*)
1960   *Az eladás müvészete* (*Salesmanship*); *Riport egy TSZ-elnökröl* (*Report on the Chairman of a Farmers' Co-Operative*); *Rajtunk is mulik* (*It Depends on Us Too ...*)
1961   *Szivdobogás* (*Heartbeat*); *Vásárhelyi szinek* (*Colors of Vásárhely*); *Danulon gyártás* (*Danulon Production*); *A szár és a gyökér fejlödése* (*The Development of the Stalk and the Root*)
1962   *Tornyai János* (*János Tornyai*); *Gyermekek, könyvek* (*Children, Books*); *Kamaszváros* (*A Town in the Awkward Age*); *Nagyüzemi tojástermelés* (*Mass Production of Eggs*); *A labda varásza* (*The Spell of the Ball*)
1963   *1963.julius 27.szombat* (*Saturday, July 27, 1963*); *Munka vagy hivatás?* (*Work or Profession?*); *Szeretet* (*Care and Affection*)
1964   *Festök városa Szentendre* (*Szentendre—Town of Painters*); *Bóbita* (*Blow-Ball*); *Kiáltó* (*Proclamation*)
1965   *15 perc 15 évröl* (*Fifteen Minutes on Fifteen Years*)
1966   *Borsós Miklós* (*Miklós Borsós*); *Harangok varosa— Veszprém* (*Veszprém—Town of Bells*)

(short films in Romania)

1957   *Sa zimbeasca toti copiii*
1958   *Femeile zilelor noastre*; *Popas in tabara de vara*
1959   *Schimbul de miine*

(feature films)

1968   *Eltávozott nap* (*The Girl*) (+ sc); *Mészáros László emlékére* (*In Memoriam László Mészáros*) (short); *A "holdudvar"* (*Binding Sentiments*) (+ sc)
1970   *Szép Iányok, ne sirjatok* (*Don't Cry, Pretty Girls*)
1971   *A lörinci fonóban* (*Woman in the Spinnery*; *At the Lörinc Spinnery*) (short)
1973   *Szabad lélegzet* (*Riddance*; *Free Breathing*) (+ sc)
1975   *Örökbefogadás* (*Adoption*) (+ co-sc)
1976   *Kilenc hónap* (*Nine Months*) (+ co-sc)
1977   *Ök ketten* (*Two Women*; *The Two of Them*)
1978   *Olyan, mint otthon* (*Just Like at Home*)
1979   *Utközben* (*En cours de route*; *On the Move*)

Márta Mészáros

1980 *Örökseg* (*The Heiresses*; *The Inheritance*)
1981 *Anya és leánya* (*Mother and Daughter*) (+ co-sc)
1982 *Nema Kiáltás* (*Silent Cry*) (+ sc); ***Napló gyermekeimnek***
        (*Diary for My Children*) (+ sc)
1983 *Délibábok országa* (*The Land of Mirages*)
1987 *Napló szerelmeimnek* (*Diary for My Loves*) (+ sc)
1988 *Piroska és a farkas* (*Bye-Bye Red Riding Hood*) (+ co-sc)
1989 *Utinapló* (doc)
1990 *Napló apámnak, anyámnak* (*Diary for My Father and My
        Mother*)
1992 *Edith és Marlene* (for TV)
1993 *A Magzat* (*Fetus*)
1995 *Siódmy pokój* (+ co-sc)

Publications by Mészáros

Book

Napló magamrol, Budapest, 1993.

Articles

Interviews in *Filmkultura* (Budapest), November/December 1972 and
    March/April 1977.
Interview in *Hungarofilm Bulletin* (Budapest), no. 2, 1977.
Interview with T. Giraud and D. Villain, in *Cahiers du Cinéma* (Paris),
    January 1978.
Interview with C. Clouzot and others, in *Ecran* (Paris), 15 January
    1979.
Interview with L. Bonneville, in *Séquences* (Montreal), September
    1988.
Interview with A. Troshin, in *Film und Fernsehen* (Berlin), vol. 18,
    no. 9, 1990.

Publications on Mészáros

Books

Acker, Ally, *Reel Women: Pioneers of the Cinema, 1896 to the
    Present,* New York, 1991.

Portuges, Catherine, *Screen Memories: The Hungarian Cinema of Márta Mészáros,* Bloomington, Indiana, 1993.

Foster, Gwendolyn Audrey, *Women Film Directors: An International Bio-Critical Dictionary,* Westport, Connecticut, 1995.

Articles

Elley, Derek, "Hiding It under a Bushel: Breaking Free," in *Films and Filming* (London), February 1974.

Elley, Derek, "Márta Mészáros," in *International Film Guide 1979,* London, 1978.

Martineau, Barbara Halperin, "The Films of Márta Mészáros or, the Importance of Being Banal," in *Film Quarterly* (Berkeley), Fall 1980.

"Hungarian Film Section" of *Filmfaust* (Frankfurt), January/February 1984.

Malik, Amita, "Hungary's Dissenters," in *World Press Review,* March 1985.

"*Diary for My Loves,*" in *Hungarofilm Bulletin* (Budapest), no. 2, 1987.

Portuges, C., "Retrospective Narratives in Hungarian Cinema: The 1980s 'Diary' Trilogy of Márta Mészáros," in *Velvet Light Trap* (Madison, Wisconsin), Spring 1991.

Quart, Barbara, "Three Central European Women Directors Revisited," in *Cineaste* (New York), no. 4, 1993.

Waller, Marguerite R., "*Fetus,*" in *American Historical Review,* October 1994.

*   *   *

Márta Mészáros is one of few contemporary woman filmmakers consistently making films both critically and commercially successful for an international audience. Her eight feature films made from 1968 to 1979 are concerned with the social oppression, economic constraints, and emotional challenges faced by Hungarian women. Mészáros explains, "I tell banal, commonplace stories, and then in them the leads are women—I portray things from a woman's angle."

Trained in filmmaking on a scholarship at Moscow's film school, she worked at Newsreel Studios in Budapest, made four short films at the Bucharest Documentary Studios, married a Romanian citizen in 1957, and was divorced in 1959. She returned to Budapest, where she made more than 30 documentaries before attempting a feature. Mészáros's documentaries deal with subjects as diverse as science (*Mass Production of Eggs*), a Hungarian hero (*Saturday, July 27, 1963*), orphans (*Care and Affection*), and artists (*Szentendre—Town of Painters,* which she considers her best documentary.)

In the mid-1960s Mészáros joined Mafilm Group 4, where she met Miklós Jancsó, whom she later married. She wrote and directed her first feature, *The Girl,* in 1968. A hopeless mood pervades this story of the quest by an orphan girl for her biological parents, who had abandoned her. The girl leaves her textile-factory job to comfort her mother, who introduces her as her niece to her husband and relatives. The girl meets a man whom she believes is her father. The man neither confirms nor denies this. The girl returns home and attends a factory dance where she meets a young man who is interested in her. As with most Mészáros features the film is open-ended, lacking a conventional plot. Dialogue is sparse. Derek Elley asserts that *The Girl* is a model to which Mészáros adheres in her subsequent features; her visual compositions are "carefully composed, rarely showy," and "characterisation never remains static."

In *Binding Sentiments* the conflicts between an aging mother and her son's fiancée are delineated with understated solemnity and subtle humor. A semi-musical, *Don't Cry, Pretty Girls,* lightheartedly captures the romance between a rural girl and a city musician in a hostel and youth-camp setting. Mészáros's short *Woman in the Spinnery* studies the working status and conditions of the factory worker, the same subjects that she explores in *Riddance.* In this generation gap tale, a pair of lovers must deceive the young man's parents, who object to his love for a girl who was raised in a children's home with no family. *Riddance* urges assertiveness and truth to oneself, and shows little sympathy for the older generation.

A fortyish woman wants a child from her unmarried lover in *Adoption.* She meets a teenager raised by the state who wants to marry her boyfriend. The relationship which develops between these two women and the man in their lives becomes the subject of Mészáros's most illuminating work.

A factory woman with one child has an affair with an engineer in *Nine Months.* The conflicts in their relationship are never resolved; they cannot agree on the terms and conditions of a life together; neither can surrender enough self to form a partnership. The woman leaves him to bear her second child alone. The actual birth of Lila Monari's child was photographed for the film.

The aptly titled *Two Women* depicts a friendship. Juli has a daughter and a husband attempting to find a cure for his alcoholism. Mari directs a hostel for working women, and tolerates a lackluster husband. Juli and Mari enjoy a greater rapport with each other than with the men in their lives. Situations depicting humiliation of and discrimination against women recur. The subject of Mészáros's next film, about a young man's attraction to a little girl, makes *Just Like at Home* a departure from her focus on women. In this film, Andras returns to Budapest after study in the United States and strikes up a friendship with a ten-year-old Zsuzsi, whose parents agree that she live with Andras in Budapest and be educated there. Their chaste friendship endures despite the intrusion of Andras's lady friend. Andras learns more from Zsuzsi than she learns from him, to the bewilderment of their parents.

In *The Heiresses* Mészáros used a period setting for the first time. A young, sterile woman marries a military officer during the World War II era. Because she needs an heir to inherit her father's money, she persuades a Jewish woman to bear a child sired by her husband. After the birth, the woman and her husband become deeply attached, and a second child is born. Then the wife "turns in" the Jewish woman (Jews were deported from Hungary in 1944), the husband is arrested, and the wife is given custody of the second child.

Mészáros's films deal with realities usually ignored in Eastern European cinema: the subordination of women, conflicts of urban and rural cultures, antagonism between the bureaucracy and its employees, alcoholism, the generation gap, dissolution of traditional family structures, and the plight of state-reared children. In her unpretentious works, she creates a composite picture of life in Hungary today.

In Derek Elley's words, she "has created a body of feature work which, for sheer thematic and stylistic homogeneity, ranks among the best in current world cinema." Her features examine emotional struggles "in the search for human warmth and companionship in a present-day, industrialised society."

—Louise Heck-Rabi

MIRÓ, Pilar
Spanish director and writer

Born: Pilar Miró Romero, in Madrid, 20 April 1940. **Education:** Studied law and journalism, University of Madrid; attended Escuela Oficial de Cinematografí [Official school of cinematography], Madrid, graduating in screenwriting, 1968. **Family:** One son: Gonzalo. **Career:** 1960—began working as program assistant for Radiotelevisión Española, Spain's state television; 1964—wrote screenplay for first of two films directed by Manuel Summers, *The Girl in Mourning*; 1966—directed made-for-TV movie *Lilí,* becoming the first woman to direct dramas for Spanish TV; subsequently made more than 300 programs for Spanish TV, primarily directing dramas based on noted literary works; 1976—directed first feature film, *The Engagement Party,* which was briefly banned; 1976—joined Socialist Party, member until 1989; 1979—directed *The Crime at Cuenca,* which after being banned for two years because of scenes depicting torture at the hands of the Civil Guard was released in 1981 and became a top box-office attraction; 1982—directed Bizet's opera *Carmen* in Madrid, one of her occasional forays into directing plays and operas; during general elections, served as media adviser to Felipe González in his successful campaign to become Spain's prime minister, an event ushering in almost 14 years of Socialist Party rule; 1982-85—served as director general of cinematography for the Culture Ministry; 1984—helped enact the "Miró Law," which provided generous subsidies to Spanish filmmakers; 1985—resigned from government post to return to directing, making the 1986-released *Werther*; 1986-89—served as director general of Radiotelevisión Española, resigning in 1989 under controversy, cleared of wrongdoing in 1992 following lengthy court case; 1990—directed first of two video documentaries, *Velázquez* (also *Nacho Duato—la danza* [*Nacho Duato—The Dance*], 1992); 1993—directed Christopher Hampton's play *Dangerous Liaisons* in Barcelona; 1995—directed Spanish state television coverage of the royal wedding in Seville of Princess Elena, eldest daughter of Spain's King Juan Carlos; her acclaimed *The Dog in the Manger* is released, a film that won seven prizes at the 1997 Goya Awards; 1996—her final film, *Your Name Poisons My Dreams,* is released; 1997—in October, two weeks prior to her death, directed Spanish state television coverage of the royal wedding in Barcelona of Princess Cristina, daughter of the king. **Awards:** "Antena de oro" award for her overall work for Spanish state television, 1972; Sindicato Nacional de Espectáculo [National entertainment syndicate] award for best screenplay, and Círculo de Escritores Cinematográficos [The screenwriters' circle] award for best new director, for *The Engagement Party,* 1976; Silver Bear, Berlin International Film Festival, for *Beltenebros,* 1991; Best Film, Mar del Plata Film Festival, 1996, and Goya Film Award for Best Director, 1997, for *The Dog in the Manger.* **Died:** In Madrid, of a heart attack, 19 October 1997.

Films as Director

1976   *La petición* (*The Engagement Party; The Request; The Betrothal*) (+ co-sc)
1981   *El crimen de Cuenca* (*The Crime at Cuenca; The Cuenca Crime*) (produced 1979) (+ co-sc); *Gary Cooper que estás en los cielos* (*Gary Cooper Who Art in Heaven*) (+ co-sc, co-pr)
1982   *Hablamos esta noche* (*Let's Talk Tonight*) (+ co-sc, co-pr)

1986   *Werther* (+ co-sc, pr)
1991   *Beltenebros* (*Prince of Shadows*) (+ co-sc)
1993   *El pájaro de la felicidad* (*The Bird of Happiness*)
1995   *El perro del hortelano* (*The Dog in the Manger*) (+ sc)
1996   *Tu nombre envenena mis sueños* (*Your Name Poisons My Dreams*) (+ co-sc)

Other Films

1964   *La niña de luto* (*The Girl in Mourning*) (Summers) (sc)
1965   *El juego de la oca* (*Snakes and Ladders*) (Summers) (sc, st); *Luciano* (Claudio Guerín Hill) (dialogue writer)

Publications by Miró

Book

With Mario Camus and Juan Antonio Porto, *Beltenebros: la película,* Gijón, Spain, 1994.

Articles

"El cine español bajo la dictadura y después," in *España 1975-1980: conflictos y logros de la democracia,* edited by José L. Cagigao, John Crispin, and Enrique Pupo-Walker, Madrid, 1982.
Interview with J. Jurka, in *Film a Doba* (Prague), October 1982.
Interview with C. de Bechade, in *Revue du Cinéma* (Paris), April 1984.
"Diez añoz de cine español," in *La cultura española en el postfranquismo: diez añoz de cine, cultura y literatura en España,* edited by Samuel Amell and Salvador García Catañeda, Madrid, 1988; published as "Ten Years of Spanish Cinema," in *Literature, the Arts, and Democracy: Spain in the Eighties,* edited by Samuel Amell, translated by Alma Amell, Rutherford, New Jersey, 1990.
Interview with S. Pylvanainen, in *Lahikuva* (Turku, Finland), no. 2, 1993.
Interview with Salvador Llopart, in *La Vanguardia* (Barcelona), 6 May 1993.
Prologue, in *Morirás en Chafarinas: la película,* by Pedro Olea and Fernando Lalana, Saragossa, Spain, 1995.

Publications on Miró

Books

Besas, Peter, *Behind the Spanish Lens: Spanish Cinema under Fascism and Democracy,* Denver, 1985.
Hopewell, John, *Out of the Past: Spanish Cinema after Franco,* London, 1986.
Schwartz, Ronald, *Spanish Film Directors (1950-1985): Twenty-One Profiles,* Metuchen, New Jersey, 1986.
Higginbotham, Virgina, *Spanish Film under Franco,* Austin, Texas, 1988.
Kuhn, Annette and Susannah Radstone, editors, *The Women's Companion to International Film,* London, 1990.
Thompson, Owen, *Beltenebros: historia secreta de un rodaje,* Barcelona, 1991.
Pérez Millán, Juan Antonio, *Pilar Miró: directora de cine,* Madrid, 1992.
Kinder, Marsha, *Blood Cinema: The Reconstruction of National Identity in Spain,* Berkeley, 1993.

Monterde, José Enrique, *Veinte años de cine español: un cine bajo la paradoja, 1973-1992,* Barcelona, 1993.

España, Rafael de, compiler and editor, *Directory of Spanish and Portuguese Film-Makers and Films,* Westport, Connecticut, 1994.

Merino Acebes, Azucena, *Diccionario de directores de cine español,* Madrid, 1994.

Romaguera i Ramió, Joaquim, *Diccionario filmográfico universal-I: de directores de España, Portugal y Latinoamérica,* Barcelona, 1994.

Colmeiro, José, and others, editors, *Spain Today: Essays on Literature, Culture, Society,* Dartmouth, Massachusetts, 1995.

Foster, Gwendolyn Audrey, *Women Film Directors: An International Bio-Critical Dictionary,* Westport, Connecticut, 1995.

Vincendeau, Ginette, editor, *Encyclopedia of European Cinema,* New York, 1995.

D'Lugo, Marvin, *Guide to the Cinema of Spain,* Westport, Connecticut, 1997.

Hamilton, Jayne, *Gender Representation and Textual Strategies in the Films of Pilar Miró,* Newcastle upon Tyne, England, 1997.

Kinder, Marsha, editor, *Refiguring Spain: Cinema/Media/Representation,* Durham, North Carolina, 1997.

Articles

Markham, James M., "Spanish Regime in First Film Ban," in *New York Times,* 6 January 1980.

"Pilar Miró Indicted; Pic 'Insult' Alleged," in *Variety* (New York), 23 April 1980.

"Delayed *Cuenca Crime* Makes Profit," in *Variety* (New York), 30 September 1981.

McCarthy, Todd, "Miró Moves to Correct Spain's Production and Distribution Ills," in *Variety* (New York), 18 April 1984.

Besas, Peter, "Pilar Miró Blasts Local Producers, Reviews 1st Yr.," in *Variety* (New York), 9 May 1984.

Besas, Peter, "Miró Ankles as Spain's Top Govt. Film Honcho; Had Stormy Tenure," in *Variety* (New York), 15 January 1986.

"Pilar Miró Named to Director's Post at Spain's TV Web," in *Variety* (New York), 22 October 1986.

Meulen, H. van der, "Gedömde liefdes," in *Skrien* (Amsterdam), Summer 1987.

"Spanish TV Topper Miró Gets Sacked," in *Variety* (New York), 18 January 1989.

Moore, Linda, "Miró Cleared of Money Misuse," in *Variety* (New York), 13 July 1992.

Martí-Olivella, Jaume, "Toward a New Transcultural Dialogue in Spanish Film," in *Spain Today: Essays on Literature, Culture, Society,* edited by José Colmeiro and others, Hanover, New Hampshire, 1995.

Martí-Olivella, Jaume, "La piedad profana de Pilar Miró," in *Cine-Lit II: Essays on Hispanic Film and Fiction,* edited by George Cabello-Castellet, Jaume Martí-Olivella, and Guy Wood, Corvallis, Oregon, 1996.

Obituary in *Diário de Notícias* (Portugal), 20 October 1997.

Goodman, Al, obituary in *New York Times,* 21 October 1997.

*   *   *

Pilar Miró was undoubtedly one of the most important figures of the late-20th-century Spanish entertainment industry. In addition to winning acclaim—and enduring some controversy—for her direction of nine motion pictures from 1976 to 1996, Miró was also an award-winning and prolific director for Spanish television. Her more than 300 small-screen credits include made-for-television movies, dramatic series, plays, operas, and perhaps most famously the televising of the royal weddings of the two daughters of Spain's King Juan Carlos, whom she had befriended when they were both law students in Madrid in the late 1950s. In a more sporadic vein, Miró made occasional forays into the theater to direct plays and operas and made two video documentaries.

Miró, who had joined the Socialist Party as soon as it was legal to do so in 1976 and remained a member until 1989, also played a key role as media adviser to Felipe González in his victory in the 1982 general elections, after which the Socialists ruled for nearly 14 years. González then persuaded Miró to become director general of cinematography for the Culture Ministry starting in 1983, making her the first industry figure in what had been a post occupied only by political appointees. During her three years in the position, Miró achieved some success in improving the quality—if not the quantity—of Spanish films, mainly through what was known as the "Miró Law." In effect, from 1984 through 1989, the law provided generous subsidies to Spanish filmmakers, including such notables as Pedro Almodóvar and Fernando Trueba. Following her resignation from this post to direct *Werther* (based on a Goethe novel), Miró served as head of state radio and television from 1986 through 1989. She resigned under a cloud of controversial expenditures she had made for clothing and gifts, but was cleared of all charges in 1992 (during the last few years of her life, when she attended awards ceremonies, she wore tuxedo-like clothing as an effective form of silent protest over the obviously sexist accusations).

Beyond the overall quality of her creations, Miró the film director helped raise the technical bar for Spanish filmmaking through innovative use of Steadicams and other modern gadgets. She also played an important role in expanding the range of what could be depicted on the Spanish screen. Her very first film, *The Engagement Party*—adapted from an Émile Zola story called "For a Night of Love"—centered around a wealthy, sadistic, sexually voracious, and ultimately murderous woman ably and erotically played by Ana Belén. Although Spanish cinemas of the time were filled with the usual assortment of popular, low-budget sex comedies, Miró's decidedly feminist portrayal of a strong sexually aggressive woman told from the woman's perspective—ran afoul of the censors of post-Franco Spain. A ban on the film was soon lifted after a press campaign emphasized the film's artistic merit.

Miró then encountered more serious difficulties with her follow-up to *The Engagement Party,* the 1979-produced *The Crime at Cuenca.* In depicting the true story of a rather obscure 1912 case of two anarchists falsely accused of murder, the film includes graphic scenes of the men being tortured into confession by the notorious Spanish Civil Guard. This politically explosive film was taken by the Civil Guard to be an attack on them, and Miró and the film's producer were indicted by a military court in early 1980 for "insults to the Civil Guard." *The Crime at Cuenca* was banned in Spain, although a print had already made its way to the February 1980 Berlin film festival, helping to make the film an international cause célèbre. Eventually the Guard was persuaded to let the case against Miró be shifted to a civil court, which soon dropped the charges. Upon its release in Spain in 1981, *The Crime at Cuenca* was an enormous hit, in part thanks to its notoriety, and it set a record in Spain for box-office gross receipts for a domestically made movie.

Of her films that followed *The Crime at Cuenca,* several of them were semiautobiographical in nature, with Mercedes Sampietro serving as Miró's cinematic alter ego. In the 1981 film *Gary Cooper Who*

Art in Heaven—which has been noted for its similarities to Agnès Varda's *Cleo from 5 to 7*—Sampietro portrays a television director who must undergo an abortion after learning she has ovarian cancer. The film covers a three-day period prior to and including the day of the operation (although it ends before the operation begins), during which time the character examines what she feels has been an unsuccessful life. The story draws upon and effectively—and realistically, even grimly—depicts the difficulties Miró faced in the male-dominated entertainment industry, as well as upon her own 1975 heart surgery (which would be followed by a second heart surgery in 1985). *Gary Cooper* is also noteworthy as the first film Miró produced herself, having been forced to do so when no one in the industry would work with her because of her then still-pending *Cuenca* trial.

In 1993, Miró, with Sampietro again as her stand-in, returned to depict another unfulfilled middle-aged woman taking stock of her life in *The Bird of Happiness*. Beginning with the character being robbed and nearly raped in Madrid, the film shows the character gradually escaping from various familial and communal ties to a remote rural village where at the end it appears that she will contentedly raise—alone—her grandson who has been abandoned to her. In addition to being a depiction of a woman finding an inner peace on her own, *The Bird of Happiness* also represents Miró's disillusionment with socialism in the 1990s.

Although *The Bird of Happiness* is perhaps her greatest achievement, Miró received much acclaim for her next-to-last film, *The Dog in the Manger*. It won seven Goya Awards, including best director, as well as the $650,000 first prize at the 1996 Mar del Plata Film Festival in Argentina. Based on a play by Lope de Vega, this period comedy is noteworthy for its depiction of a strong, complex woman (agilely played by Emma Suárez). Not as autobiographical as her earlier films, *The Dog in the Manger* nonetheless has at its center a woman who breaks with the female archetypes of her time, just as Miró during her most impressive and pioneering career broke through numerous barriers to create a new archetype for future women filmmakers the world over.

—David E. Salamie

MURATOVA, Kira
Russian/Ukrainian director and writer

Born: Kira Georgievna Korotkova, in Soroca, Romania (now Moldova), 5 November 1934. **Education:** Attended Moscow State University for one year; attended All-Union State Institute of Cinematography (VGIK), studying with the director Sergei Gerasimov, graduating with a degree in directing, 1962. **Family:** Married 1) the director Alexander Muratov (divorced); 2) Yevgeni Golunbenko. **Career:** 1963—made her directing debut with her diploma film, *By the Steep Ravine,* co-directed by her then-husband Muratov; 1967—her solo directing debut, *Brief Encounters,* receives only a limited release to film clubs and is otherwise banned; 1971—her film *Long Farewells* is banned and she is barred from directing for several years; 1979—allowed to return to directing with *Getting to Know the World*; 1983—*Among the Grey Stones* is heavily reedited after she completes it, prompting her to have her name removed from the film, the directing of which is credited to "Ivan Sidorov"; 1987—comes to international attention following the general release of *Brief*

Encounters and *Long Farewells,* which are shown widely at international film festivals, and with the release of her new film *A Change of Fate*; 1989—her widely acclaimed *The Asthenic Syndrome* is initially banned, then released in 1990. **Awards:** Grand Prix, USSR Festival, and Fipressi Prize, Locarno International Film Festival, for *Long Farewells,* 1987; Silver Bear, Special Jury Prize, Berlin Film Festival, and Nika Award, for *The Asthenic Syndrome,* 1990; Best Director Nika Award, for *Passions,* 1994. **Address:** Proletarsky Boulevard 14B, Apartment 15, 270015 Odessa, Ukraine.

Films as Director

1963   *U krutogo yara* (*By the Steep Ravine*; *The She-Wolf*) (co-d with A. Muratov, + co-sc)

1964   *Nash chestnyi khleb* (*Our Honest Bread*; *Honest Bread*) (co-d with A. Muratov)

1967   *Korotkiye vstrechi* (*Brief Encounters*) (released 1987) (+ co-sc, ro as Valentina Ivanova); *Braslet-2*

1971   *Dolgie provody* (*Long Farewells*) (released 1987)

1972   *Russia*

1979   *Poznavaya belyi svet* (*Getting to Know the World*) (released 1980)

1983   *Sredi serykh kamnei* (*Among the Grey Stones*) (credited as Ivan Sidorov—released 1987) (+ sc)

1987   *Peremena uchasti* (*A Change of Fate*) (+ sc)

1989   *Astenicheskii Sindrom* (*The Asthenic Syndrome*; *The Weakness Syndrome*) (released 1990) (+ co-sc)

1992   *Chuvstvitel'nyi militsioner* (*The Sentimental Policeman*) (+ co-sc)

1994   *Uvletschenia* (*Passions*; *Avocations*; *Obsessions*) (+ sc)

1997   *Tri istorii* (*Three Stories*)

Other Film

1985   *Ya tebya pomnyu* (*I Remember You*) (Khamrayev) (ed)

Publications by Muratova

Articles

Interview with V. Bozhovich, in *Iskusstvo Kino* (Moscow), no. 9, 1987.

"Eloge de la tanacite," interview with F. Sabouraud, in *Cahiers du Cinéma* (Paris), December 1987.

Interview with B. Pelka, in *Filmowy Serwis Prasowy* (Warsaw), vol. 34, no. 19, 1988.

Interview with B. Bollag and M. Ciment, in *Positif* (Paris), February 1988.

Interview with Viktor Bozhovich, in *Soviet Film* (Moscow), no. 4, 1990.

Interview with C. Taboulay, in *Cahiers du Cinéma* (Paris), April 1991.

Interview with M. Dominicus and J. de Putter, in *Skrien* (Amsterdam), April/May 1991.

"Faire voir, refleter, rien de plus," interview with F. Aude, in *Positif* (Paris), May 1991.

"Iskusstvo—eto utekha, otrada i opium," in *Iskusstvo Kino* (Moscow), no. 7, 1992.

Interview with I. Mantsov, in *Iskusstvo Kino* (Moscow), no. 8, 1994.

Interview with P. Sirkes, in *Iskusstvo Kino* (Moscow), no. 2, 1995.

Interview in *Novoe russkoe slovo* (New York), 15-16 April 1995.

Interview, in *Eye on the World: Conversations with International Filmmakers,* by Judy Stone, Los Angeles, 1997.

Publications on Muratova

Books

Bozhovich, Viktor, *Kira Muratova: tvorcheskii portret,* Moscow, 1988.

Galichenko, Nicholas, *Glasnost—Soviet Cinema Responds,* Austin, Texas, 1991.

Balski, Grzegorz, compiler and editor, *Directory of Eastern European Film-Makers and Films 1945-1991,* Westport, Connecticut, 1992.

Horton, Andrew, and Michael Brashinsky, *The Zero Hour: Glasnost and Soviet Cinema in Transition,* Princeton, New Jersey, 1992.

Attwood, Lynn, *Red Women on the Silver Screen: Soviet Women and Cinema from the Beginning to the End of the Communist Era,* London, 1993.

Foster, Gwendolyn Audrey, *Women Film Directors: An International Bio-Critical Dictionary,* Westport, Connecticut, 1995.

Vincendeau, Ginette, editor, *Encyclopedia of European Cinema,* New York, 1995.

Articles

Alexandrova, Nellie, "Coming Attraction: Kira Muratova," in *Soviet Film* (Moscow), no. 10, 1987.

Film a Doba (Prague), October 1987.

Fainaru, Edna, "Muratova's Coming Out Was a Locarno Fest Revelation," in *Variety* (New York), 21 October 1987.

Okszana, B., "Kira Muratova 'provincialis mozija,'" in *Filmkultura* (Budapest), no. 1, 1988.

Zaporowski, J., "Dlugie pozegnania," in *Filmowy Serwis Prasowy* (Warsaw), vol. 34, no. 19, 1988.

Bollag, B., "Kira Muratova," in *Positif* (Paris), February 1988.

Silvestri, S., "Schegge dell'Est: Il cinema di Kira Muratova," in *Filmcritica* (Rome), May 1989.

"Three Soviet Film Makers Take Their Work on Tour," in *New York Times,* 20 October 1989.

Navailh, F., "Muratova la survivante," in *Cinéma* (Paris), April 1990.

Yampolsky, Mikhail, "In Defence of Somnolence," in *Soviet Film* (Moscow), May 1990.

Revue du Cinéma (Paris), November 1990.

Vinogradov, I., "Lik, lido i lichina naroda," in *Iskusstvo Kino* (Moscow), no. 5, 1991.

Gul'chenko, V., "Mezhdu 'ottepeliami,'" in *Iskusstvo Kino* (Moscow), no. 6, 1991.

Dominicus, M., "Kunst is altijd agressief," in *Skrien* (Amsterdam), February/March 1991.

Graffy, Julian, "Private Lives of Russian Cinema," in *Sight and Sound* (London), March 1993.

Taubman, Jane A., "The Cinema of Kira Muratova," in *Russian Review* (Columbus, Ohio), July 1993.

Roll, Serafima, "Fragmentation and Ideology in Kira Muratova's *The Asthenic Syndrome* and Arto Paragamian's *Because Why,*" in *Canadian Journal of Film Studies* (North York, Ontario), Spring 1996.

Film

Women in Soviet Cinema: I Am an Ox, I Am a Horse, I Am a Man, I Am a Woman, television documentary directed by Sally Potter, 1988.

* * *

Though Kira Muratova's career as a film director was seriously hindered by the censors of the Brezhnev-to-Gorbachev-era Soviet Union, she still managed to emerge as one of the leading figures in contemporary Russian cinema. She was born in 1934 in Soroca, Romania (which is now part of Moldova), with her family background being partly Western. Raised by a Russian grandmother while her parents were in prison for their Communist activities, Muratova moved to the Soviet Union in 1954, attended Moscow State University for one year, then studied under the director Sergei Gerasimov at the Soviet state film school (VGIK). She then joined the Odessa Film Studio (located in what is now the Ukraine), where she has made most of her films. Having co-directed two films with her then-husband Alexander Muratov, in 1967 she solo-directed *Brief Encounters,* a love-triangle tale with Muratova as one of the three in the only acting role of her career, and then in 1971 directed *Long Farewells,* which centers around a middle-class mother-son relationship. Both of these black-and-white films were effectively banned from general release, although *Brief Encounters* did receive a very limited release to some film clubs. On the surface, it seems puzzling why two intensely personal, relationship-oriented films would run afoul of the censor. But Muratova in all of her films has been intent upon depicting daily life in an honest manner, warts and all, and it was evidently the details that she included—water shortages in Odessa, stockings that run, contractors who cheat their clients—that made them threatening. *Long Farewells* was additionally condemned for its rather gloomy ending and its bourgeois sensibilities.

Long Farewells also led to Muratova being stripped of her VGIK degree and blacklisted from directing. She worked at a variety of jobs for the next several years, and tried without success to gain permission to film a couple of her scenarios. In 1978, Lenfilm invited Muratova to direct any of several scenarios they had on hand. She chose a story about another love triangle, this one taking place at the construction site of a huge new tractor factory. This was the 1979-produced, 1980-released (rather limitedly) *Getting to Know the World,* Muratova's first film in color. Though not banned outright, the authorities criticized the director for depicting negative types of characters, and she was barred from filming contemporary subjects.

Even when Muratova did then draw on a literary classic for her next film, 1983's *Among the Grey Stones,* she ran into trouble. An adaptation of an 1883 story by Russian writer Vladimir Korolenko, the film is a story of haves meeting have-nots, specifically a neglected son of a powerful judge befriending a strange community of hobos who live among the ruins of a castle. Again criticized for making a pessimistic film, Muratova saw her film mutilated in the postproduction editing, leading her to request that her name be taken off the film.

The turning point in Muratova's career came with the advent of glasnost and the 1986-initiated review of banned films by the Filmmakers Union's Conflict Commission. This led to the 1987 release of all of her banned films, and *Brief Encounters* and *Long Farewells* in particular received long-overdue acclaim both at home and abroad.

That same year, Muratova directed the aptly titled *A Change of Fate,* which she adapted from another literary classic, Somerset Maugham's short story "The Letter."

It was her next film, however, that has come to be considered her masterpiece. *The Asthenic Syndrome* is one of the key films of the glasnost period, and in its withering portrayal of a society in moral decay even managed to be briefly banned. In Muratova's vision, the syndrome of the title—which manifests itself in the face of extreme stress—implies not only a torpor as in the dictionary definition of "asthenic" but also extreme aggression. The film is extremely complex in its construction, including a film-within-a-film (which is in black and white), an innovative use of documentary style, and a long second sequence which is largely plotless and consists of a variety of vignettes that surreally and effectively depict a society largely out of control. Yet as much as it is of its late-glasnost time and place, *The Asthenic Syndrome* is actually much more universal; its critique can be seen as applying perfectly to contemporary Western society, whose stressed-out public face alternates between mean-spirited aggression and excessive apathy.

With this rather apocalyptic film behind her, Muratova next offered some hope in the amusing comedy *The Sentimental Policeman,* which was filmed as the Soviet Union was collapsing. The title character is a young policeman who finds an abandoned baby (in a cabbage patch!), takes her to the station house, and later returns with his wife after the couple decides they wish to adopt the child; complications then arise. Though set in the same indifferent society as her previous film, *The Sentimental Policeman* offers portraits of a few people persevering in a positive way through this chaotic world.

In the post-Soviet period, Muratova has continued to experiment with the cinematic form—though somewhat more obscurely, in an ironic twist. As she has throughout her career, Muratova continues to work with little-known actors, to rely on the spontaneity of these nonprofessionals, and to heavily utilize montage—her favorite cinematic device. *Passions* is a largely plotless, difficult to fathom film, centering around male jockeys and female circus trainers and their obsessions with horses. *Three Stories* consists of three episodes linked by the motif of violent death; the crimes in each episode, however, are not solved and the perpetrators are not brought to justice. Muratova has said that she wanted to simply lay out the events as they occurred and let the audience make their own judgments. This inherently noncommercial approach is typical of Muratova, who has also said that she is not a director who can please a large audience. Rather, she is one "who is able to please a small, indeed very small, number of viewers, but really please them."

—David E. Salamie

MURFIN, Jane
American writer

Born: Quincy, Michigan, 1893. **Family:** Married the actor and director Donald Crisp, 1932 (divorced 1944). **Career:** Playwright from 1908, often with (and for) the actress Jane Cowl: *Lilac Time, Daybreak, Information Please,* and *Smilin' Through* (using the joint pseudonym Allan Langdon Martin); other plays include *The Right to Lie* and *Stripped;* 1919—first film as writer, *The Right to Lie;* also produced some of her scripts in the early 1920s. **Died:** In Brentwood, California, 10 August 1955.

Films as Writer (selected list)

1919   *The Right to Lie* (Carewe); *Marie, Ltd.* (Webb)
1921   *The Silent Call* (Trimble)
1922   *Brawn of the North* (Trimble) (+ co-pr)
1924   *The Love Master* (Trimble) (+ co-pr); *Flapper Wives* (+ co-pr, co-d)
1925   *White Fang* (Trimble); *A Slave of Fashion* (Henley)
1926   *The Savage* (Newmeyer); *Meet the Prince* (Henabery)
1927   *The Notorious Lady* (Baggot); *The Prince of Headwaiters* (Dillon)
1929   *Half Marriage* (Cowen); *Street Girl* (Ruggles); *Dance Hall* (M. Brown); *Seven Keys to Baldpate* (Barker)
1930   *The Pay Off* (L. Sherman); *Leathernecking* (Cline); *Lawful Larceny* (Dwan); *The Runaway Bride* (Crisp); *Too Many Crooks* (G. King)
1931   *Friends and Lovers* (Schertzinger); *White Shoulders* (M. Brown)
1932   *What Price Hollywood?* (Cukor); *Young Bride* (Seiter); *Rockabye* (Cukor); *Way Back Home* (Seiter)
1933   *After Tonight* (Archainbaud); *Ann Vickers* (Cromwell); *Double Harness* (Cromwell); *Our Betters* (Cukor); *The Silver Cord* (Cromwell); *Little Women* (Cukor)
1934   *Crime Doctor* (Robertson); *The Fountain* (Cromwell); *The Life of Vergie Winters* (Santell); *The Little Minister* (Wallace); *Romance in Manhattan* (Roberts); *Spitfire* (Cromwell); *This Man Is Mine* (Cromwell)
1935   *Alice Adams* (Stevens); *Roberta* (Seiter)
1936   *Come and Get It* (Hawks and Wyler)
1937   *I'll Take Romance* (Griffith)
1938   *The Shining Hour* (Borzage)
1939   *Stand Up and Fight* (Van Dyke); *The Women* (Cukor) (co)
1940   *Pride and Prejudice* (Leonard) (co)
1941   *Andy Hardy's Private Secretary* (Seitz)
1943   *Flight for Freedom* (Mendes)
1944   *Dragon Seed* (Conway and Bucquet)

Publications by Murfin

Plays

With Jane Cowl, *Smilin' Through,* New York, 1924.
With Anita Loos, *The Women* (script), in *Twenty Best Film Plays,* edited by John Gassner and Dudley Nichols, New York, 1943.

Publications on Murfin

Book

Acker, Ally, *Reel Women: Pioneers of the Cinema, 1896 to the Present,* New York, 1991.

Articles

Obituary, in *New York Times,* 12 August 1955.
Film Comment (New York), Winter 1970-71.

*   *   *

Jane Murfin had a successful career as a playwright on Broadway before being lured to Hollywood in the late 1910s to become an equally successful screenwriter for many years. Murfin's first stage play, *The Right to Lie,* was produced in 1908; it was later turned into a motion picture, under the direction of Edwin Carewe. Other stage plays were written in collaboration with actress Jane Cowl: *Daybreak,* 1917 (filmed the same year); *Lilac Time* (filmed with Colleen Moore in 1928); *Smilin' Through* (filmed with Norma Talmadge in 1922, Norma Shearer in 1932, and Jeanette MacDonald in 1941).

Coming to Hollywood in the late 1910s, Murfin wrote numerous stories and screenplays, alone or in collaboration, mostly romantic comedies and dramas for RKO and MGM; she believed that human interest was the key to a successful story. Murfin had started writing scripts for Famous Players-Lasky while still in New York; in Hollywood, she wrote some 60-odd scripts, directing or producing a few of them. In one of her earliest projects, Murfin sponsored, and wrote a series of pictures for Strongheart—a German shepherd dog who had formerly served in a Red Cross unit in the army. Starting in 1922, five pictures were made for First National. Aided by the direction of dog trainer, writer, and producer Larry Trimble, Strongheart's success as a canine star in the 1920s was rivaled only by that of Rin-Tin-Tin.

Murfin wrote frequently for RKO, for directors such as George Cukor, and for stars such as Constance Bennett (*What Price Hollywood?* and *Rockabye*), Katharine Hepburn (*Little Women*), and Irene Dunne (*The Silver Cord*). In 1934 Pandro Berman appointed Murfin to be the first woman supervisor of motion pictures at RKO; some of her first writing projects included *The Little Minister* (starring John Beal and Katharine Hepburn) and the sparkling Jerome Kern musical *Roberta* (featuring Irene Dunne, Randolph Scott, Fred Astaire, and Ginger Rogers).

In 1935 Murfin severed ties with RKO, and signed a long-term contract with Samuel Goldwyn. Some of the outstanding films that she wrote or co-wrote for MGM include *Come and Get It* (starring Edward Arnold and Frances Farmer and directed by William Wyler and Howard Hawks), *The Women* (co-written with Anita Loos; starring Norma Shearer, Joan Crawford, Rosalind Russell and Paulette Goddard and directed by George Cukor), and *Pride and Prejudice* (co-written with Aldous Huxley; starring Laurence Olivier and Greer Garson; directed by Robert Z. Leonard). Later work ranged from *Andy Hardy's Private Secretary* to *Dragon Seed.*

—Virginia M. Clark

MURPHY, Brianne

British/American cinematographer and director

Pseudonyms: Sometimes credited as Geraldine Brianne, Bri Murphy, G. B. Murphy, and Geraldine Brianne Murphy. **Born:** London, 1 April 1937. **Education:** Studied at Neighborhood Playhouse, 1952-54; Brown University, M.A., 1962. **Family:** Married Ralph Brook, 1958 (deceased). **Career:** 1952-55—actress, various other jobs; from 1955—cinematographer; has served as cinematographer for TV series, including: *Breaking Away, Square Pegs, For Love and Honor, Highway to Heaven, In the Heat of the Night, Shades of L.A.,* and *Love and War,* and episodes of *The Next Generation, Shortstories,* and *ABC Afterschool Special*; 1973—admitted to cameraman's union; first woman member of the American Society of Cinematographers; 1995—ASC president, Columbia College, Hollywood. **Awards:**

Emmy Award, Best Cinematography, for *Five Finger Discount,* 1978; Academy Award, Scientific or Technical Achievement, for design of the MISI camera insert safety car and trailer, 1982. **Address:** c/o American Society of Cinematographers, 1782 North Orange Drive, Hollywood, CA 90028, U.S.A.

Films as Cinematographer

1955   *Man Beast* (J. Warren) (+ script supervisor)
1960   *The Barrier*
1961   *Chivato (Rebellion in Cuba)* (Gannaway)
1962   *Panchito y El Gringo*
1972   *Pago*
1973   *Pocket Filled with Dreams*
1976   *Secrets of the Bermuda Triangle*
1978   *Like Mom, Like Me* (Pressman—for TV)
1979   *Five Finger Discount* (for TV); *Before and After* (K. Friedman—for TV)
1980   *Fatso* (Bancroft)
1983   *Little House: Look Back to Yesterday* (French—for TV)
1985   *There Were Times, Dear* (Malone—for TV)
1988   *Destined to Live: 100 Roads to Recovery* (for TV)
1990   *In the Best Interest of the Child* (David Greene—for TV)
1991   *This Old Man*

Films as Director

1957   *Virgins from Venus* (+ sc)
1958   *Teenage Zombies* (sc, ro as Pam)
1962   *Magic Tide*
1968   *Single Room Furnished* (uncredited)
1972   *Blood Sabbath* (+ ph)
1992   *To Die, to Sleep (Mortal Danger; Turn Your Pony Around)* (+ ph)

Other Films

1960   *The Incredible Petrified World* (J. Warren) (production supervisor, dialog d)
1961   *Bloodlust!* (Brooke) (production manager)
1965   *House of the Black Death (Blood of the Man Devil; Night of the Beast)* (H. Daniels) (script asst)
1981   *Cheech and Chong's Nice Dreams* (Chong) (additional ph)

Publications on Murphy

Books

Acker, Ally, *Reel Women: Pioneers of the Cinema, 1896 to the Present,* New York, 1991.

Rooney, Terrie M., editor, *Contemporary Theatre, Film and Television,* vol. 13, Detroit, 1995.

Krasilovsky, Alexis, *Women behind the Camera: Conversations with Camerawomen,* Westport, Connecticut, 1997.

Articles

Lee, Nora, "Voigtlander & Murphy on *Highway to Heaven,*" in *American Cinematographer* (Los Angeles), April 1986.

"The Boss Said She'd Get in Over His Dead Body, and by Golly She Did," in *People Weekly* (New York), Special Issue, Spring 1991.

Wibking, Angela, "Murphy Breaks Stereotypes in Cinematography," in *Nashville Business Journal,* 20 May 1996.

* * *

Perhaps the best understanding of Brianne Murphy's career as a cinematographer does not lie in a study of her camera work as such, because she does not seem to have had a full opportunity to explore her creative abilities. Even in 1996, Murphy—who has often used non-gender-specific aliases such as G. B. Murphy in order to increase her chances of getting jobs—was one of only four women belonging to the American Society of Cinematographers. With men dominating her profession more thoroughly than they have most other realms of film work, Murphy's talents have been relegated to television, or to light features such as *Cheech and Chong's Nice Dreams.*

Therefore the true essence of Murphy's career as a cinematographer lies in the story—which she tells with characteristic good humor—of how she broke into the "man's world" surrounding the operation of cameras. The first female member of the feature-film union, the International Alliance of Theatrical and Stage Employees (IATSE), Murphy fought a long battle, not for recognition, but simply for the right to work alongside men.

One of the principal themes of Murphy's story is her ability to turn a supposed disadvantage—that of being a woman—into an advantage. In her early Hollywood days, she would often quiz cameramen about what they did, and they would happily brag to her about their abilities, never dreaming that she was actually taking mental notes. Because she was a woman, she recalled: "I could take a cameraman out to lunch and ask him all kinds of questions. I think he felt flattered ... whereas if a young man had taken him out and asked all these questions, he'd find some way to say 'Go find out for yourself.'"

Murphy has never considered herself above admitting it when she does not know something, and she has seldom disdained the advice of others. From the beginning of her film career, before she managed to find a place for herself behind the camera, she made it a point to get to know everyone on the set—to find out what they did, how they did it, and if she could help them. That same attitude helped her win an Oscar, when she used the assistance of race-car drivers to develop a newer, safer camera car. Up until that time, cameras had been mounted on conventional pick-up trucks, and they could become so top-heavy that they could overturn and kill someone—as one did her camera assistant Rodney Micchell in 1980. After this tragic event, while Murphy was in Georgia working on the television series *Breaking Away,* she talked to some race-car drivers on the NASCAR circuit about an idea that ultimately became the Micchell Camera Car, winner of a 1982 technical Academy Award.

Outgoing by nature and well-inclined to win friends and influence people, Murphy seemed in her early years to lead a charmed life. As a little girl in Bermuda, fleeing the Nazi bombing of her native Britain during World War II, she was "discovered" for a theater role as Emily in *Our Town.* Later producer Elia Kazan took an interest in her, and again and again in her later career, she seemed to have a talent for being at the right place at the right time. For instance, when she went to work on her first feature, the low-budget *Man Beast* in 1955, she came on the set as a props and wardrobe person, but ended up taking control of the camera because the cameraman was the only member of the crew who could fit into the monster suit needed for a

particular scene. Even divine justice seemed to work in her favor, as in her oft-told story of the IATSE union boss who told her a woman would only get into the union over his dead body: he suddenly died.

Yet her story was not as smooth as it might have seemed. Her parents had divorced when she was young, and with no man around the house, she had grown up knowing how to take care of herself. "My sister asked me what I wanted for Christmas," Murphy commented. "I told her power tools. I never had a man around as a copout." And though she seemingly had people opening doors for her, those opportunities did not just happen: Murphy made them happen with her unbridled chutzpah. As a young woman, she got her first camera job working for the Ringling Brothers Circus, and she got it by dressing up as a clown and joining the circus parade when it came through town. Later, on the set of *Man Beast,* she told the film's backer that she could make two movies for the price of the one film, which she considered a staggering budget at $30,000. Suddenly she found herself in the driver's seat on *Virgins from Venus* and *Teenage Zombies.* Murphy delivered, and became one of a select-few female directors—even if the material was not exactly classic. (Though it was certainly classic schlock cinema.)

Again and again, Murphy managed to find herself at the right place, at the right time. In 1979 NBC needed a woman to shoot footage for a documentary on breast cancer in which the female patients refused to allow a male cameraman into the room. The choice was not difficult, since there was only one female cinematographer in Hollywood. Actress Anne Bancroft, when she was making *Fatso* in 1980, hired Murphy because, according to Murphy: "she couldn't give orders to men.... I was a woman and not fat [so] she chose me."

But for every time she got a job because she was a woman, she missed out on countless other ones for the same reason. "It's a sad thing," Murphy has said, "but it's true—as a woman, you just have to be better." She offers this advice to both women and men: "I think if you work cheap enough, come in early enough, and stay late enough, you can always get a job." Though she eschews any sort of role as a movement leader or spokeswoman, Murphy has been a pioneer for women, and because of her efforts, women will one day "man" the cameras of Oscar-winning blockbusters.

—Judson Knight

MUSIDORA
French director, writer, and actress

Born: Jeanne Roques in Paris, 23 February 1889. **Education:** Studied art at Académie Jullian, Atelier Schommer, and École des Beaux Arts. **Family:** Married Clément Marot, 1927 (divorced 1944), one son. **Career:** After deciding on stage career, took name "Musidora" from heroine of Théophile Gautier's novel *Fortunio*; 1910—stage debut in vaudeville *La Nuit de noces,* Paris; 1910-12—member of troupe Théâtre Montparnasse; 1912—music-hall star, appearing at Ba-ta-clan and the Châtelet; 1913—film acting debut in production of syndicalist cooperative Le Cinéma du Peuple, a film protesting exploitation of domestic workers, *Les Misères de l'aiguille*; 1914—hired by Feuillade for Gaumont company; 1915—began working on first of Feuillade serials, *Les Vampires*; created French version of much-imitated "vamp" character; 1916—first directing effort, adaptation of Colette's *Minne,* reportedly unreleased and no longer in existence; 1916-17—made several films for André Hugon; 1918—

in first film adaptation of Colette novel, *La Vagabonde*; 1919—first film as director released, *Vicenta*, produced by her own production company, La Société des Films Musidora; 1921-26—lived principally in Spain; 1926—last commercial film appearance in *Les Ombres du passé*; after 1926—active as writer of fiction, stage and radio plays, and popular songs; 1944—through Henri Langlois, actively involved with film preservation efforts of Cinémathèque Française; 1950—directed her last film *La Magique image*. **Died:** 11 December 1957.

Films as Director and Actress

1916   *Minne* (incomplete or not distributed)
1917   *Le Maillot noir* (*The Black Leotard*) (as herself, + co-sc)
1918   *La Vagabonde* (*The Vagabond*) (Perego) (as Renée Néré, co-adapt only)
1919   *Vicenta* (title role, + sc)
1920   *La Flamme cachée* (*The Hidden Flame*) (co-d with Lion, ro as Anne Morin, + sc, ed—produced 1918)
1921   *Pour Don Carlos* (*La Capitana Allegria*) (co-d with Lasseyre, ro as Allegria Detchard, + sc)
1922   *Una aventura de Musidora en España* (*Musidora en Espagne*) (+ sc); *Soleil et ombre* (*Sol y sombra*; *Sun and Shadow*) (co-d with Lasseyre, ro as Juana/blond stranger, + sc)
1924   *La Tierra de los toros* (*La Terre des Taureaux*; *Land of the Bulls*) (+ sc)
1926   *Le Berceau de Dieu*
1950   *La Magique image* (+ sc—16mm compilation short)

Films as Actress

1913   *Les Misères de l'aiguille* (Clamour)
1914   *La Ville de Madame Tango*; *Severo Torelli* (Feuillade) (as Portia); *Le Calvaire* (Feuillade) (as Bianca Flor); *Tu n'épouseras jamais un avocat* (Feuillade) (as Estelle); *Les Fiancés de 1914* (Feuillade)
1915   *Sainte Odile* (Ravel), *Les Trois rats* (Ravel) (as young ballerina); *La Bouquetière des Catalans* (Ravel); *Les Leçons de la guerre* (Ravel); *La Petite refugiée* (Ravel); *L'Autre Victoire* (Ravel); *Bout de Zan et l'espion* (Feuillade); *Le Colonel Bontemps* (Feuillade); *L'Union sacrée* (Feuillade) (as the typist); *Celui qui reste* (Feuillade) (as Suzanne Gerson); *Le Coup du fakir* (Feuillade); *Deux Françaises* (Feuillade) (as Mme. Castel); *Fifi tambour* (Feuillade); *L'Escapade de Filoche* (Feuillade) (as Mme. Pichepin); *Les Noces d'argent* (Feuillade); *Le Roman de la midinette* (Ravel); *Le Sosie* (Feuillade); *Triple Entente* (Ravel); *La Barrière* (Feuillade); *Le Fer à cheval* (Feuillade); *Le Collier de perles* (Feuillade); *Le Trophée du zouave* (Ravel); *Le Grand Souffle* (Ravel); *Bout de Zan et le poilu* (Feuillade); *Une Page de gloire* (Perret)
1915-16   *Les Vampires* (Feuillade—serial) (as Irma Vep)
1916   *Le Troisième Larron*; *Jeunes Filles d'hier et d'aujourd'hui* (Feuillade); *Coeur fragile*; *Le Pied qui étreint* (Feyder—serial) (as Irma Vep); *Les Mariés d'un jour* (Feuillade); *Les Fourberies de Pingouin* (Feuillade); *Les Fiançailles d'Agenor* (Feuillade) (as Amélie); *Le Poète et sa folle amante* (Feuillade); *Fille d'Eve*; *Si vous ne m'aimez pas* (Feuillade) (as Simone); *La Peine de talion* (Feuillade) (as Rosa Larose); *Lagourdette, gentleman cambrioleur* (Feuillade); *Judex* (Feuillade—serial) (as Diana Monti/Marie Verdier)
1917   *C'est pour les orphelins!* (Feuillade); *Mon Oncle* (Feuillade); *Débrouille-toi* (Feuillade) (as Mlle. Friquette); *Les Chacals* (Hugon) (as Dolorès Melrose)
1918   *Johannès fils de Johannès* (Paglieri and Hugon) (as Gabrielle Baude)
1919   *Mam'zelle Chiffon* (Hugon) (title role)
1921   *La Geole* (Ravel—produced 1918) (as Marie-Ange Gaël)
1922   *La Jeune fille la plus méritante de France*
1926   *Les Ombres du passé* (Leroy-Granville)

Publications by Musidora

Books

Arabella et Arlequin (novel), Paris, 1929.
Paroxysmes (novel), Paris, 1934.
Auréoles (poems), Paris, 1940.
La Vie sentimentale de George Sand (play), with illustrations by Musidora, Paris, 1946.
Souvenirs sur Pierre Louys, Muizon, 1984.

Articles

"Ce que je suis devenue," in *Pour vous* (Paris), 8 June 1938.
"La Vie d'une vamp," in *Ciné-Mondial* (Paris), 12 June-24 July 1942.
In *L'Ecran Français* (Paris), 13 February 1950.
"Dialogues de jadis," in *Cahiers du Cinéma* (Paris), November 1964.

Publications on Musidora

Books

Delluc, Louis, *Cinéma et Cie*, Paris, 1919.
Kyrou, Ado, *L'Amour au cinéma*, Paris, 1957.
Fescourt, Henri, *La Foi et les montagnes ou Le 7e Art au passé*, Paris, 1959.
Fernández, Carlos, *Cuenca toros y toreros en la pantalla*, San Sebastian, 1963.
Kyrou, Ado, *Le Surréalisme au cinéma*, Paris, 1963.
Lacassin, Francis, *Musidora*, Paris, 1970.
Smith, Sharon, *Women Who Make Movies*, New York, 1975.
Cazals, Patrick, *Musidora: La Dixième Muse*, Paris, 1978.
Virmaux, Odette, and Alain Virmaux, editors, *Colette at the Movies*, New York, 1980.
Abel, Richard, *French Cinema: The First Wave, 1915-1929*, Princeton, New Jersey, 1984.
Armes, Roy, *French Cinema*, New York, 1985.
Acker, Ally, *Reel Women: Pioneers of the Cinema, 1896 to the Present*, New York, 1991.
Foster, Gwendolyn Audrey, *Women Film Directors: An International Bio-Critical Dictionary*, Westport, Connecticut, 1995.

Articles

Obituary in *Variety* (New York), 18 December 1957.
Lacassin, Francis, and Raymond Bellour, "Musidora et les quarante voleurs," in *Cinéma* (Paris), June 1961.

Beylie, C., and G. Braucourt, "Seven Women & Seven Women," in *Ecran* (Paris), August/September 1974.

* * *

One of the greatest stars of the French silent cinema, Musidora gained extraordinary fame playing France's first screen vamp, Irma Vep (an anagram of "vampire") in Louis Feuillade's 1915-16 film series, *Les Vampires*. She played its femme fatale with great aplomb, appearing in each of its ten semi-independent episodes in a different disguise—both male and female. In addition, her sexy villainess wore a provocative black leotard and expressed an unashamed sexuality. Her characterizations earned Musidora an amazing fame, and she was embraced enthusiastically by popular audiences as well as by the surrealists who appreciated her subversive androgynous eroticism. But, Musidora was something of a "Renaissance woman": in addition to her work as a film actress, she was a novelist, poet, dancer, painter, songwriter, and playwright. Yet very little historical attention has been paid to Musidora's offscreen film roles, despite the fact that she became a film director in the mid-1910s when very few women had such opportunities. When she died, she left behind seven unpublished screenplays and several films that she directed or co-directed.

Musidora had rather auspicious roots: her mother was a feminist who started the journal *Le Vengeur* in 1897, which was devoted to feminism, sociology, and the arts. Clearly influenced by her mother, after she gained fame in *Les Vampires,* Musidora earned a reputation for her flamboyant lifestyle and avant-garde friends, including Colette, Germaine Dulac, Louis Delluc, André Breton, Marcel L'Herbier, and other surrealists.

Musidora's early forays into the arena of film directing involved collaborations with the legendary French writer Colette, with whom she worked on three films—*Minne, La Vagabonde,* and *La Flamme cachée*. Musidora's first directorial effort was an adaptation of Colette's *Minne,* based on *The Innocent Libertine,* in which she also starred. It was reportedly based on Colette's life, though it never was finished and its footage no longer exists. Next, she made *Le Maillot noir,* which she wrote in collaboration with Germaine Beaumont, and in which she revisited the vampire image she had created for Feuillade. 1918's *La Vagabonde* was a pivotal film for Musidora because it was both popular and well-received by critics. She also starred in and adapted it with Eugenio Perego (who also directed); the scenario was written by Colette. With *La Flamme cachée* she collaborated with Colette on the script and the production was the first from her own company, La Société des Films Musidora. The film was a "drama in four parts" that Musidora starred in, adapted, edited, and co-directed (with Roger Lion), from a scenario by Colette. Musidora's recollections of the film were published in *L'Ecran Français* in 1950; she described it as a story of a student (played by Musidora) who marries a fellow student who is a millionaire, despite the fact she loves another man who is poor. Hoping to change her life and be with her true love, she tries to compel her husband to commit suicide, but she dies in an explosion after offending her lover.

In 1919 Musidora made and starred in *Vicenta,* from her original script. Between 1920 and 1923, she collaborated with Jacques Lasseyre on the direction of *Pour Don Carlos* and *Soleil et Ombre*. In 1924 Musidora wrote a feminist screenplay for *La Tierra de los toros,* which she shot in Spain. While in that country, Musidora reportedly determined to prove that women were courageous enough to be given voting rights—by demonstrating her own bravery in the bull ring.

In 1926 Musidora was celebrated as the "queen of the cinema," but her film career came to an end with the arrival of sound, except for the 1951 compilation short film, *La Magique image,* which included clips from her early films. After she retired from filmmaking, she became a journalist, writing several articles about cinema, and she wrote fiction and poetry as well. In 1946 she began working at the Cinémathèque Française. In France, Musidora's legend as a woman with a charged sexual persona endures. In the 1970s feminists began to acknowledge and embrace her achievements as a brave filmmaker, and in 1973 the Musidora Association was founded. In 1974 the association organized the first Musidora International Festival of Women's Films, where Musidora's only surviving film, *Soleil et ombre,* was screened. According to the Musidora Association, the primary goal of the festival was to make the point that films made by women actually existed.

—Cynthia Felando

MY BRILLIANT CAREER
Australia, 1979
Director: Gillian Armstrong

Production: New South Wales Film Corporation and Margaret Fink Films; Panavision, Eastmancolor; running time: 100 minutes; length: 9,005 feet. Released 1979.

Producer: Margaret Fink; **associate producer:** Jane Scott; **screenplay:** Eleanor Witcombe, from the novel by Miles Franklin; **assistant directors:** Mark Egerton, Mark Turnbull, and Steve Andrews; **photography:** Don McAlpine; **camera operators:** Louis Irving and Peter Moss; **editor:** Nicholas Beauman; **sound editor:** Greg Bell; **sound recordist:** Don Connolly; **production designer:** Luciana Arrighi; **art director:** Neil Angwin; **costume designer:** Anna Senior; **music:** Nathan Waks.

Cast: Judy Davis (*Sybylla Melvyn*); Sam Neill (*Harry Beecham*); Wendy Hughes (*Aunt Helen*); Robert Grubb (*Frank Hawden*); Max Cullen (*Mr. McSwat*); Pat Kennedy (*Aunt Gussie*); Aileen Britton (*Grandma Bossier*); Peter Whitford (*Uncle Julius*); Carole Skinner (*Mrs. McSwat*); Alan Hopgood (*Father*); Julia Blake (*Mother*); Tony Hughes (*Peter McSwat*); Tina Robinson (*Lizer McSwat*); Aaron Corrin (*Jimmy McSwat*); Sharon Crouch (*Sarah McSwat*); Robert Austin (*Willie McSwat*); Mark Spain (*Tommy McSwat*); Simone Buchanan (*Mary Anne McSwat*); Hayley Anderson (*Rosie Jane McSwat*); Marion Shad (*Gertie*); Suzanne Roylance (*Biddy*); Zelda Smyth (*Ethel*); Amanda Pratt (*Blanche Derrick*); Bill Charlton (*Joe Archer*).

Publications

Script

Witcombe, Eleanor, *My Brilliant Career,* St. Lucia, Queensland, 1992.

Books

Tulloch, John, *Australian Cinema: Industry, Narrative, and Meaning,* Sydney and London, 1982.

My Brilliant Career

McFarlane, Brian, *Words and Images: Australian Novels into Films,* Richmond, Victoria, 1983.

Hall, Sandra, *Critical Business: The New Australian Cinema in Review,* Adelaide, 1985.

Moran, Albert, and Tom O'Regan, editors, *An Australian Film Reader,* Sydney, 1985.

Mathews, Sue, *35mm Dreams: Conversations with Five Directors about the Australian Film Revival,* Ringwood, Victoria, 1987.

McFarlane, Brian, *Australian Cinema 1970-85,* London, 1987.

Articles

Metro, Spring 1979.

Fink, Margaret, and Gillian Armstrong, in *Cinema Papers* (Melbourne), March/April 1979.

Variety (New York), 23 May 1979.

McFarlane, Brian, in *Cinema Papers* (Melbourne), September/October 1979.

Adair, Gilbert, in *Monthly Film Bulletin* (London), February 1980.

Wallace, Melanie, in *Cineaste* (New York), Spring 1980.

Image et Son (Paris), November 1980.

Oakes, Philip, in *Listener* (London), 23 February 1984.

Bertrand, I., "Woman's Voice: The Autobiographical Form in Three Australian Filmed Novels," in *Literature Film Quarterly* (Salisbury, Maryland), no. 2, 1993.

"Gillian Armstrong," in *Current Biography 1995,* New York, 1995.

* * *

Gillian Armstrong's film of Miles Franklin's novel remains remarkably true to the spirit of the original which, almost unbelievably, considering the modernity of its sentiments and the ebullient confidence of its tone, was written by a young woman of 16 and first published in 1901. That it was not reprinted until 1966 can be explained partly by the fact that it was withdrawn by its author, who was annoyed at the "stupid literalness" with which it was taken to be her own autobiography. Nevertheless, the fact that the novel's sequel, *My Career Goes Bung,* was rejected by publishers as too outspoken and not published until 1946, also suggests that, even if it had not been withdrawn, *My Brilliant Career* would have stood little chance of establishing itself in the male-dominated pantheon of "great" Australian literature at the turn of the century.

The story centers on Sybylla Melvyn, a young woman living with her parents on a remote farm in the bush. She dreams of living a more intellectually and culturally rewarding life, and is writing a memoir. When she goes to stay on her grandmother's estate at Caddagat things improve somewhat, and she is also courted by Frank Hawden, a rather fatuous English immigrant, and Harry Beecham, a young landowner. She is attracted to the latter, and is faced with the choice of trying to pursue a "brilliant career" or getting married.

There are, of course, parallels with Miles Franklin's own life here—the dusty, arid Possum Gully is clearly modeled on Stillwater, the smallholding to which her family moved from a far more attractive cattle station in the mountains of New South Wales; and Caddagat is a fictional version of Talbingo, where her maternal grandmother lived and with whom she went to stay for a few years of her adolescence. But these are incidental details, and the real importance of both novel and film lies in their acute delineation of a young woman's feelings at a transitional moment in her life. As Carmen Callil has aptly noted, "Miles Franklin was decades ahead of her time, and *My Brilliant Career* was written for an audience not yet born. For in the character of Sybylla Melvyn, Miles Franklin created a character who mouths with incredible charm but deadly accuracy the fears, conflicts and torments of every girl, with an understanding usually associated with writers of the 1960s and 70s." All the qualities that Callil admires in the book have been triumphantly retained by the film which, it might be added, also manages to exclude some of the original's slightly less attractive qualities, such as its nationalism (which it shared with many of its literary contemporaries) and a certain tendency to let ebullience and exuberance overflow into gush and overly self-conscious romanticism. The dialogue, too, has been considerably updated and "de-literacized," but the *sentiments* expressed by Sybylla are very much those that animate her in the novel.

All credit must go here to Judy Davis, whose performance makes Sybylla utterly convincing and never allows her effervescence and high spirits to become wearying or trying. The only problem, per-

haps, is that in her hands Sybylla comes across as so attractive, capable, and accomplished that it sometimes becomes difficult to understand the oft-mentioned fact of her "plainness" and the various other negative judgments passed upon her by the other characters. Gillian Armstrong's mise-en-scène is also a triumph, not simply in its loving attention to period detail but in the way in which it is used to comment on or reflect Sybylla's feelings, and in particular her growing consciousness of herself as being different from those around her and as destined for higher things. Particularly important in this respect are the contrasts between Possum Gully and Caddagat, the latter making Sybylla more aware than ever of the possibilities of life beyond the bush. Significantly, when Sybylla plays the piano at home, with no one paying any attention, the effect is decidedly jangly, whereas at her grandmother's, with an appreciative audience, the change in style is most striking. At the same time, however, the elegance of some of the scenes at Harry Beecham's mansion suggest not simply the lifestyle which Sybylla desires but also the kinds of constraints and limitations that she fears may come with it.

Scenes such as these work extremely effectively to communicate the sense that Sybylla is still in the process of developing and maturing, that she is still trying to decide on her role in life, and is subject to all sorts of contradictory pressures, both internal and external. Important here, too, is the characterization of Harry, who is portrayed very much as a potential soul mate and worthy partner, thus facing Sybylla with a very real and difficult choice with which the spectator can clearly empathize. Indeed, although nothing actually "happens," some of the scenes between Sybylla and Harry contain a distinct sexual charge.

My Brilliant Career has been "rediscovered" as something of a proto-feminist text, which it undoubtedly is, but it is also very much a Bildungsroman which works remarkably well on both a particular and more general level. Like the best of all such works in the genre, it is both poignant and amusing and both of these qualities have been well served by Armstrong's meticulous and occasionally sumptuous mise-en-scène, Judy Davis's splendid performance, which never goes over the top, as it so easily could, and a score which makes poignant use of Schumann's *Scenes from Childhood*.

—Sylvia Paskin

N

NAIR, Mira
Indian director

Born: Bhubaneshwar, Orissa, India, 1957. **Education:** Studied sociology at Delhi University; studied sociology and cinema on scholarship at Harvard University, 1976. **Family:** Married (1) the cinematographer Mitch Epstein; (2) Mahmood Mamdani, son: Zohran. **Career:** 1979—made first documentary, *Jama Masjid Street Journal*; 1985—gained some notoriety for the controversial documentary, *India Cabaret*; 1988—garnered critical acclaim and commercial success with first fiction feature, *Salaam Bombay!*; 1996—created more controversy with the erotic *Kama Sutra*. **Awards:** Best Documentary, Global Village Film Festival in New York, for *India Cabaret,* 1985; Camera d'Or, Best First Feature, Cannes Film Festival, and Prix de Publique, Audience Favorite, Cannes Film Festival, for *Salaam Bombay!,* 1988; Ciak Award for Most Popular Film at the Festival, and Best Screenplay, Venice Film Festival, for *Mississippi Masala,* 1991; Muse Award for Outstanding Vision and Achievement, New York Women in Film and Television, 1997; Boston Film Video Association's Vision Award, 1997. **Agent:** Bart Walker, International Creative Management, 40 West 57th Street, New York, NY 10019, U.S.A. **Address:** Mirabai Films, 24 Belmont Avenue, Oranjezicht, Cape Town 8001, South Africa.

Films as Director

1979   *Jama Masjid Street Journal* (doc)
1983   *So Far from India* (doc)
1984   *Women and Development* (doc)
1985   *India Cabaret* (doc)
1987   *Children of Desired Sex* (doc)
1988   *Salaam Bombay!* (+ pr, co-sc)
1991   *Mississippi Masala* (+ pr, co-sc, ro as gossip)
1993   *The Day the Mercedes Became a Hat* (short video) (+ pr, co-sc)
1995   *The Perez Family* (+ ro as woman buying flowers)
1996   *Kama Sutra* (*Kama Sutra: A Tale of Love*) (+ pr, co-sc)
1997   *My Own Country* (+ ro as gossip)

Publications by Nair

Book

With Sooni Taraporevala, *Salaam Bombay!,* New Delhi, 1989.

Articles

"Star of India," interview with Brad Kessler and Mitch Epstein, in *Interview* (New York), September 1988.

"'Many Stories in India Are Just Crying Out to Be Made'—Mira Nair," interview with M. Purohit and S. Parmar, in *Cinema India-International* (Bombay), vol. 5, no. 3, 1988.

Interview with L. Vincenzi, in *Millimeter* (New York), March 1992.

"Capturing the Rhythms of Life," in *Film Journal* (New York), October/November 1994.

Publications on Nair

Books

Cole, Janis, and Holly Dale, *Calling the Shots: Profiles of Women Filmmakers,* Kingston, Ontario, 1993.

Foster, Gwendolyn Audrey, *Women Film Directors: An International Bio-Critical Dictionary,* Westport, Connecticut, 1995.

Articles

Shah, A., "Independents: A Dweller in Two Lands: Mira Nair, Filmmaker," in *Cineaste* (New York), vol. 15, no. 3, 1987.

Malcolm, D., "Lessons of the Street," in *Cinema in India* (Bombay), vol. 2, no. 3, 1988.

Purohit, M., "Mira Nair Scores a Unique Triumph," in *Cinema India-International* (Bombay), vol. 5, no. 3, 1988.

James, C., "Mira Nair Combines Cultures to Create a Film," in *New York Times,* 17 October 1988.

"Life Is a Cabaret, the Camera Is a Veil: A File on Mira Nair," in *Monthly Film Bulletin* (London), February 1989.

Van Gelder, L., "At the Movies," in *New York Times,* 10 March 1989.

Ochiva, D., "Mira Nair," in *Millimeter* (New York), January 1989.

Freedman, S. G., "One People in Two Worlds," in *New York Times,* 2 February 1992.

Outlaw, M., "The Mira Stage," in *Village Voice* (New York), 18 February 1992.

Simpson, Janice C., "Focusing on the Margins," in *Time* (New York), 2 March 1992.

Current Biography, New York, 1993.

Anderson, Erika Surat, "*Mississippi Masala,*" in *Film Quarterly* (Berkeley), Summer 1993.

Arora, Poonam, "The Production of Third World Subjects for First World Consumption: *Salaam Bombay!* and *Parama,*" in *Multiple Voices in Feminist Film Criticism,* edited by Diane Carson, Linda Dittmar, and Janice Welsch, Minneapolis, 1994.

Negi, M., "Mira Nair," in *Cinemaya* (New Delhi, India), Autumn/Winter 1994-95.

Chatterjee, V., "Mira Nair's Better Films," in *Deep Focus* (Bangalore, India), vol. 3, no. 1, 1996.

Patel, Vibhuti, "Making a Woman's *Kama Sutra,*" in *Ms.* (New York), May/June 1997.

* * *

Mira Nair. Photograph by Prabhuddo Dasgupta.

After spending three years working as a theater actress in New Delhi, the award-winning filmmaker Mira Nair was inspired to pursue a career in filmmaking after taking a course in documentary production at Harvard University. Subsequently, she made four documentaries in India that focused on her country's changing culture. For example, the controversial *India Cabaret* is about Bombay strippers and their male audiences, and effectively illuminates the marginalized lives of the strippers as well as the double standards and patriarchal values whereby women in general are never moved to question or challenge their lot as oppressed citizens. Nair intended that this film would present an Indian woman's perspective that was unknown in Indian cinema, one that depicts men and women, as she put it, "as they are, the way they speak." *Jama Masjid Street Journal* is a documentary about India's culture that served as Nair's thesis film; it was screened at New York's Film Forum in 1986. Yet another documentary, *So Far from India* is about an Indian-American subway newsstand salesman living in New York, while his wife awaits his return to India. Like many women filmmakers, Nair made several documentaries before turning to fiction feature production.

Nair's first fiction feature was *Salaam Bombay!* Her breakthrough film, it tells the compelling and heartrending story of the tremendous trials of a runaway boy from the country who survives in the mean streets and back alleys of Bombay with his wits, despite being surrounded by a proliferation of low-life hustlers, prostitutes, and junk-

ies. A powerful successor to Héctor Babenco's film about street children, *Pixote,* Nair's film is filled with both pathos and humor. She developed the film, in addition to discovering and training her principal actors, by arranging a series of improvisational theater workshops with street children in Bombay. In 1989 it was nominated for an Oscar for Best Foreign Film and enjoyed considerable box-office success in India and the West. Putting her money where her heart is, Nair gave part of the film's profits to a foundation in order to help educate homeless children in the city.

Nair garnered additional critical and commercial success with the dramatic feature *Mississippi Masala,* about an Indian family living in exile in the southern United States where they must endure the region's racism. In addition, despite their determined attempts to retain their Indian culture, the daughter becomes attracted to and falls in love with a young, handsome African-American man. Thus, the family must cope with the couple's budding affair, a situation Nair uses to help underscore the equally pervasive racism that exists between minority groups. Nevertheless, her film celebrates the mélange of cultures and the possibilities created by migration. As Nair has said, she herself identifies with the notion of *masala*—a term that refers to those who dwell in two lands.

The Perez Family proved to be another critical success for Nair. A romantic fable set within the context of the 1980 Mariel boat-lift of Cuban refugees, it tells the story of a newly released Cuban prisoner who goes to Miami in order to search for his long-lost wife and daughter. But he hooks up with a lusty young woman while his wife, who mistakenly believes he missed the boat, finally permits herself to fall in love with another man.

Nair's recent film, *Kama Sutra,* which is set in 16th-century India, did not enjoy the critical praise of her earlier work. It features two girls, one a lowly servant and the other a noble princess, who grew up together. As children they are inseparable companions, though the princess enjoys the privileges of her class position, while the servant is acutely aware of her position of subordination. Yet the servant uses her striking beauty and her precocious skills of seduction in order to exact her revenge on the sexually repressed princess by seducing her husband, a king, on their wedding day. So begins a vengeful struggle for power that leads the servant to become an accomplished courtesan well-versed in the lessons of the *Kama Sutra,* the Indian book of love. But, ultimately the women's dissension produces tragic results. Nair's evocation of the look and tone of 16th-century India is impressive; as she explained, it is incredible to know that so much style surrounding pleasure could exist in one part of the world, while Puritanism dominated elsewhere. Some critics charged that the film played like a Harlequin Romance, as a result of its many beautiful bodies alluringly arrayed and photographed, as well as its dramatic, contrived, and breathless emotions. Such critics suggested that despite its nearly explicit depictions of sex, the film fails on the level of passion. On the other hand, some critics praised it as a lush, beautiful, voluptuous tale that was compellingly expressed with a quiet and impressive eroticism. Interestingly, Nair was reportedly unable to get the film screened in India, which she says prohibits scenes of kissing but has no problem with scenes of rape and violence toward women.

In *Salaam Bombay!, Mississippi Masala,* and *The Perez Family,* Nair provided compelling combinations of history with provocative tales of the marginalized. In addition, her films each focus in some way on class issues and other cultural differences. Further, since *Salaam Bombay!* her films have shared a focus on female sexuality and sensuality; indeed, she is refreshingly unafraid to depict beautiful, lusty women who openly express their attraction to men.

—Cynthia Felando

NAPLÓ GYERMEKEIMNEK

(Diary for My Children)
Hungary, 1982
Director: Márta Mészáros

Production: Hungarofilm/Nordisk; black and white, 35mm; running time: 107 minutes. Premiered February 1984, Hungarofilm Film Festival, Budapest. Filmed in Budapest.

Producer: Ferenc Szohar; **production supervisors:** Bjarne Henning-Jensen and Astrid Henning-Jensen; **screenplay:** Márta Mészáros; **assistant director:** Dezsö Koza; **photography:** Miklós Jancsó Jr.; **editor:** Eva Kármentö; **sound editor:** György Fék; **production designer:** Éva Martin; **music:** Zsolt Döme; **costumes:** Fanni Kemenes; **literary consultant:** Endre Vészi .

Cast: Zsuzsa Czinkóczi (*Juli*); Anna Polony (*Magda*); Jan Nowicki (*Janos/Juli's Father*); Tamás Tóth (*Andras*); Mari Szemes (*Grandmother*); Pàl Zolnay (*Grandfather*); Ildikó Bánsági (*Mother*); with: Agnes Csere; Teri Földi; Sándor Oszter; Vilmos Kun; Eva Szabó; Eva Albert Almási; Kati Bus.

Awards: Special Jury Prize, Cannes Film Festival.

Publications

Books

Quart, Barbara Koenig, *Women Directors: The Emergence of a New Cinema,* Westport, Connecticut, 1988.
Portuges, Catherine, *Screen Memories: The Hungarian Cinema of Márta Mészáros,* Bloomington, Indiana, 1993.

Articles

Aude, Françoise, in *Positif* (Paris), December 1984.
Quart, Barbara Koenig, in *Film Quarterly* (Berkeley), Spring 1985.
Barrowclough, Susan, in *Monthly Film Bulletin* (London), June 1985.
Hibbin, Sally, in *Films and Filming* (London), September 1985.
Troschin, A., "Geschichte eines Hauses," interview with Márta Mészáros, in *Film und Fernsehen* (Berlin), vol. 18, no. 9, 1990 (abridged from *Iskustvo I kino* (Moscow), November 1989).

* * *

Diary for My Children is the first of what developed into a trilogy of autobiographical films from Hungary's leading woman director, Márta Mészáros. (The subsequent installments were *Diary for My*

Napló gyermekeimnek

Loves [1987] and *Diary for My Mother and My Father* [1990].) Mészáros's 12th feature, *Diary for My Children* was not only the most personal but the most political film she had made until then although, as she points out, "all my films are in some sense autobiographical," and all deal, though often indirectly, with politics.

Diary for My Children opens with the orphaned teenager Juli arriving in Budapest by plane from Russia in 1947 with her adoptive grandparents, to be met by her grandfather's younger sister Magda, with whom they are to live. The film covers the next six years, tracing the battle of wills between Magda, a senior Party official, and the increasingly independent-minded Juli. The personal and the political are closely interwoven: in struggling to assert herself Juli constantly comes up against the fear, hypocrisy, and denial engendered by the harsh Stalinist regime of the period. "Don't worry about grown-ups' problems," Magda tells her—and when Juli mentions her dead father she is warned, "Don't talk about it—do as you're told." What Magda demands of Juli is what the Rákosi government demands of the Hungarian people: silence, subservience, and unquestioning obedience.

But since Juli's father (like Mészáros's) was a noted sculptor arrested in the USSR in 1938 and never seen again, her very existence is a standing reproach to Stalinist repression. The more she is ordered to forget her past, the more stubbornly she clings to it, and the film is punctuated by flashbacks to memories of her parents. Lyrical scenes of love and happiness, of the family picnicking together in sunlit Russian woods, are crosscut with the bleak, snow-covered Hungarian landscape; images of Juli's mother (who died of typhoid during the war)—a warm, beautiful, laughing woman—contrast painfully with the severe, sharp-faced Magda in her close-buttoned uniform.

Yet Magda, in Anna Polony's subtle performance, is not merely a monster. Her attempts to become a foster mother to Juli, stiff and awkward though they are, reveal impulses of genuine frustrated affection; and now and again we see glimpses of the "lovely girl...full of life and all brains," remembered by her old friend and party comrade Janós. In Magda, Mészáros shows us a woman who has ruthlessly suppressed her emotional side in the name of party discipline, and still regrets it despite herself. Nor is Juli uncritically presented; manipulative and sly, she lies and steals without a qualm, and with the unthinking callousness of youth accuses both Janós and her grandfather of cowardice in the face of dangers far beyond her imagining.

Janós, Magda's old comrade and Juli's friend, is the film's key figure on both its personal and political levels. Politically, he stands for the humane, idealistic side of Communism, the starry-eyed revolution betrayed by Stalinism. "How we believed in the future then!" he sighs, recalling the youthful days when he, Magda, and his future wife fought and suffered for the cause. Linked to Juli by his own personal loss (his wife and daughter were killed, and his son crippled, by a bomb blast), he defends her against Magda and her apparatchik friends—an impulse that hastens his undoing. The unstated sexual attraction between him and Juli transcends their age difference; the ambivalence of the relationship is heightened by having the same actor (Jan Nowicki, Mészáros's third husband) play both Janós and—in flashback—Juli's father. Both men share the same fate, jailed for bringing into question the absolute wisdom of the Party, and Janós's arrest signals the extinction of any last hope for Communism as a benign system. Magda has triumphed, but in doing so has ensured her own (and her party's) eventual downfall. Meanwhile, the crude propagandist films that Juli sees in the course of her avid moviegoing provide an ironic commentary: massed choirs, beaming with synthetic happiness, singing "In Stalin's name we rebuild the world!"

Even though each main character in *Diary for My Children* can be readily aligned with a different political strand of the period, Mészáros's deep personal involvement in her material prevents it from ever feeling in the least schematic. The film brings together themes and preoccupations that recur throughout her earlier films: adoption, father-daughter relationships, young women struggling to assert their identities, children searching for their true parents. The actress who plays Juli, Zsuzsa Czinkóczi, previously starred for Mészáros in *The Two of Them* and *All the Way Home,* as well as in the subsequent *Diary* films, becoming the director's surrogate rather as Jean-Pierre Léaud was for Truffaut. In the light of *Diary for My Children,* all Mészáros's work leading up to it can be seen as fragments of a submerged autobiography. She herself described it as the film she had been wanting to make for 15 years—that is, since the very start of her directorial career.

Even in the more liberal climate of the early 1980s the Communist authorities were alarmed by the film's outspokenness; until then, no Hungarian filmmaker had dared refer openly to the arbitrary arrests and disappearances of the Stalin era. *Diary for My Children* was withheld from release for nearly two years. Its eventual emergence revealed—and perhaps even helped to hasten—the crumbling of the regime. In this, Mészáros fully achieved her aim when she set out to make the film, as she put it, "not just for *my* children, but for their whole generation."

—Philip Kemp

NEAR DARK
USA, 1987
Director: Kathryn Bigelow

Production: The Near Dark Joint Venture; color, 35mm; running time: 94 minutes. Premiered Septmber 1987, Toronto Film Festival. Filmed in Arizona and Oklahoma.

Producers: Steven-Charles Jaffe and Eric Red; **executive producers:** Edward S. Feldman and Charles R. Meeker; **production manager:** Mark Allan; **screenplay:** Kathryn Bigelow and Eric Red; **photography:** Adam Greenberg; **editor:** Howard E. Smith; **sound engineer:** Jonathan D. Evans; **sound editor:** R. J. Palmer; **special effects:** Steve Galich and Dale Martin; **production designer:** Stephen Altman; **art director:** Dian Perryman; **music:** Tangerine Dream; **costumes:** Joseph A. Porro; **makeup:** Davida Simon and Gordon Smith; **stunt co-ordinator:** Everett Creach.

Cast: Adrian Pasdar (*Caleb Colton*); Jenny Wright (*Mae*); Lance Henriksen (*Jesse*); Bill Paxton (*Severen*); Jenette Goldstein (*Diamondback*); Joshua John Miller (*Homer*); Marcie Leeds (*Sarah Colton*); Tim Thomerson (*Loy Colton*); Kenny Call (Deputy Sheriff); Ed Corbett (*Ticket Seller*); Troy Evans (*Plainclothes Officer*); Bill Cross (*Sheriff Eakers*).

Publications

Articles

Cook, Pam, in *Monthly Film Bulletin* (London), January 1988.
Norman, Neil, "Lady Roams the Badlands," in *Evening Standard* (London), 7 January 1988.

Near Dark

Johnston, Sheila, "Return from the Dead: The Vampire Bites Back,"
in *Independent* (London), 8 January 1988.

Oldfield, Helen, "Howling down the Highways," in *Guardian* (London), 8 January 1988.

Gray, Louise, "The Lady and the Vamps," in *New Musical Express*
(London), 9 January 1988.

Wigan, Michael, "Making Blood Run Cold," in *Scotsman*
(Edinburgh), 9 January 1988.

Hoberman, J., in *Village Voice* (New York), 26 April 1988.

Bergson, Philip, "Fangs Ain't What They Used to Be," in *What's On*
(London), 27 April 1988.

Guérif, François, interview with Kathryn Bigelow, in *La Revue du
Cinéma* (Paris), November 1988.

Powell, Anna, "Blood on the Borders—*Near Dark* and *Blue Steel,*"
in *Screen* (London), Summer 1994.

* * *

With *Near Dark,* her first solo feature as director, Kathryn Bigelow
stylishly and wittily extended the vampire movie into entirely new
territory—literally so.

Generic hybrids have always attracted Bigelow, and *Near Dark*
offers an especially rich mix. Essentially a vampire Western, it also
takes in elements of star-crossed-lovers romance and the counterculture road movie. Though it is not difficult to detect her sources—and
Bigelow herself, interviewed at the time, readily credited Peckinpah,
Dreyer's *Vampyr,* Kenneth Anger, and Walter Hill—these influences
are transmuted into a film with a flavor all its own, at once poetic,
scary, funny, erotic, and anything but derivative.

Set in the scoured flatlands of the American southwest, *Near
Dark* pivots around a series of archetypal opposites: light and dark,
love and death, nurturing and destroying. The young hero, Caleb, is
torn between his two families: on the side of light, his veterinarian
father and self-assured young sister, and lurking in the dark the
itinerant vampire clan into which he is inducted by the sensual Mae.
At the crisis of the action he is forced to choose between them, and
even rides off on horseback in classic Western-hero style to rescue
his sister; but the film is too subtle for any reductive assignation of
good and evil. In the film's most tender—and most voluptuously
erotic—moment Mae, having newly killed, slits her wrists so that
Caleb, craving blood but refusing to kill for himself, can suck ravenously from her.

As this scene suggests, the vampires—a motley group of society's outcasts and losers whose leader, Jesse, fought for the South in the Civil War—are treated with a certain sympathy. Even the most vicious of them, Severen, takes on the aspect of Caleb's dark twin, his shadow-side, and when Jesse and his mate Diamondback are finally consumed by the sun's rays the mood is one of pathos rather than triumph. Bigelow and her co-screenwriter, Eric Red, make a selective trawl through standard vampire lore, junking the hokier elements such as garlic, bats, crucifixes, and stakes through the heart, but retaining invulnerability, preternatural strength, and—most crucially—aversion to daylight, which causes the vampires' flesh to blacken, smoke, and finally combust.

The film makes vivid, almost tactile use of light; much of it takes place at dawn or twilight, and Adam Greenberg's cinematography invests these turning points with an eerie sense of expectation, with figures darkly silhouetted against the waning or encroaching glow. At a shoot-out in a motel cabin, spear shafts of light, far more harmful to the vampires than the bullets that caused them, stab through the punctured walls; and when a door is suddenly opened to the outside the stock is overexposed, conveying how the invasive daylight, to those inside, comes as searing, fire-edged pain. In the coda, when both Caleb and Mae have been rehumanized by blood transfusion and the rest of the clan destroyed, the sunlight falling harmlessly on the young couple's faces signals their redemption.

Bigelow combines a taste for action with a distinctive sense of lyricism, and in *Near Dark* several set-piece scenes are played against expectations. At a key juncture—the point at which Caleb very nearly goes over to the undead—the vampire clan trash a redneck bar and slaughter its customers. Instead of driving the violence hard and fast, with slam-bang editing and a pounding music track, Bigelow heightens the scene's impact by taking it slowly and deliberately, each gang member perpetrating mayhem in turn while the others watch and wait. The effect is of a courtly but lethal ritual, conducted according to age-old etiquette. By way of accompaniment we get the Cramps's rendition of the sultry old torch song "Fever," played quietly and sourced to the bar's ancient jukebox. Though never sacrificing tension, this measured pacing leaves room for black humor, "I hate 'em when they ain't bin shaved," cracks Severen as he sinks his teeth into a biker's neck.

On the film's release, many reviewers expressed surprise (in some cases bordering on alarm) that a woman should have co-scripted and directed "a hard-edged, violent actioner." By horror-movie standards, though, *Near Dark* is not exceptionally violent. What makes it stand out is not its treatment of violence, but Bigelow's subtle repositioning of the mythic elements, bringing to them an art-trained eye and a poetic sensibility, and affording her vampire clan a dignity that distances them from the usual cartoon monsters. The film set the pattern for her subsequent career as a director—both in her bold appropriation of the action genres previously considered an off-limits male preserve, and her fresh and individual approach to generic material.

—Philip Kemp

NELSON, Gunvor
Swedish/American director

Born: Gunvor Grundel in Stockholm, 1931; naturalized American. **Education:** Attended Humboldt State University, California, majoring in art, B.A. 1957; San Francisco Art Institute, studying painting and lithography with Nathan Olivera, 1957; Mills College, painting (with Richard Diebenkorn) and art history, M.F.A. 1958. **Family:** Daughter, the artist Oona Nelson. **Career:** Mid-1950s—came to United States to study art; pursued career in painting and filmmaking; made several films, especially in the mid-to-late 1960s and early 1970s, with Dorothy Wiley; late 1960s—began own 16mm films, several made in both the United States and Sweden, financed through grants from both countries; taught filmmaking for 24 years at the San Francisco Art Institute; since 1993—living and working in Sweden, based in Kristinehamn; now working with painting, collage, print-making, photography, video, and computer animation. **Awards:** Guggenheim Fellowship, 1973; American Association of University Women Fellowship, 1974; National Endowment for the Arts, 1975 and 1982; American Film Institute, 1977; Filmverkstan Fellowship, 1981 and 1987; Konstnarsnamden, 1982, 1990, and 1994; Swedish Short Film Fund, 1985; San Francisco Arts Commission Award, 1986; Western States Regional Media Arts Fellowship, 1987 and 1988; Marin Arts Council, 1988; Rockefeller Foundation, 1990. **Address:** Hovslagaregatan 2B, S 681 31, Kristinehamn, Sweden.

Films as Director

1965 *Schmeerguntz* (short) (co-d with Dorothy Wiley)
1967 *Fog Pumas* (co-d with Wiley)
1969 *Kirsa Nicholina* (short); *My Name Is Oona*
1971 *Five Artists: BillBobBillBillBob* (co-d with Wiley)
1972 *One and the Same* (short) (co-d with Freude Solomon-Bartlett); *Take Off* (short) (co-d with Magda)
1973 *Moons Pool* (short)
1973-76 *Trollstenen*
1979 *Before Need* (co-d with Wiley)
1984 *Frame Line* (short); *Red Shift*
1987 *Light Years* (short); *Light Years Expanding* (short)
1988 *Field Study #2* (short)
1990 *Natural Features* (short)
1991 *Time Being* (short)
1993 *Old Digs*; *Kristina's Harbor*
1995 *Before Need Redressed* (co-d with Wiley)

Publications on Nelson

Books

Vogel, Amos, *Film as a Subversive Act,* New York, 1974.
Sitney, P. Adams, *Visionary Film: The American Avant-garde, 1943-1978,* New York, 1979.
Film-Makers' Cooperative Catalogue No. 7, New York, 1989.
Fischer, Lucy, *Shot/Counter-Shot: Film Tradition and Women's Cinema,* Princeton, New Jersey, 1989.
Rabinovitz, Lauren, *Points of Resistance: Women, Power and Politics in the New York Avant-Garde Cinema, 1943-71,* Urbana, Illinois, 1991.
Canyon Cinema Catalogue 7, San Francisco, 1992.
Filmverkstan, Skeppsholmen, 1973-1993, Catalogue, Tryckgruppen, Stockholm, 1993.
Foster, Gwendolyn Audrey, *Women Film Directors: An International Bio-Critical Dictionary,* Westport, Connecticut, 1995.
MacDonald, Scott, *A Critical Cinema 3: Interviews with Independent Filmmakers,* Berkeley, 1998.

Articles

Richardson, Brenda, "An Interview with Gunvor Nelson and Dorothy Wiley," in *Film Quarterly* (Berkeley), Fall 1971.

Canyon Cinema News (San Francisco), no. 3, May/June 1974.

DiMatteo, Robert, "Gunvor Nelson: Capturing the Nether Regions of Femininity on Film," in *San Francisco Bay Guardian,* 15 October 1976.

* * *

Trained as a painter and lithographer, currently working in a variety of media but not film, Gunvor Grundel Nelson describes herself as an artist rather than as a director. Her films have been widely screened in festivals and one-woman shows around the United States and Europe. Marked by engagements with surrealist and personal avant-garde film, they all, though differently, meld attention to color, light, shape, form, and texture with a keen sense of rhythm and time. Emotion and mood predominate: although careful choreography, always of images and frequently also of sound, underpins her individual and her collaborative works, such structurings are more often viscerally felt than directly perceived. For Nelson, an openness to associations and an appreciation of transformations are key.

Interested in animation from the start, Nelson's five "field studies" in particular (*Frame Line, Light Years, Light Years Expanding, Field Study #2,* and *Natural Features*) are created thanks to an amateur animation camera that she designed to accommodate the mixing of a variety of media, including cut-outs, photographs, fluids, toys, and live-action footage. *Frame Line* and *Natural Features* revolve around footage shot in Stockholm while *Light Years* and *Light Years Expanding* move into the Swedish countryside, but all represent reflections on cross- and trans-cultural commutations, evoking spaces and times recaptured, remembered, and reshaped within and through film frames and fields. Of the five, only *Frame Line* is in black and white.

Two of Nelson's most recent films, *Kristina's Harbor* and *Old Digs,* engage with similar themes, but are not made with her amateur animation camera. Both present lyrical excavations and poetic reassemblages of bits and pieces of Kristinehamn, Nelson's hometown, where she is again based after living for more than 30 years in the United States. *Old Digs* uses sounds from *Kristina's Harbor* (looped voices of old people, now indecipherably murmuring and mumbling; clock tones; a rainstorm; electronic music) as a subterranean backdrop for images of dead birds, insects, clouds, water, cutouts, photographs, buildings, reflections. Shot with a different attitude, a lighter-weight camera, and no tripod, *Old Digs* varies appreciably in tone, seeming darker than *Kristina's Harbor* though equally, subtly, dramatic.

More overtly surrealist, *Schmeerguntz, Take Off, Fog Pumas, Before Need,* and *Before Need Redressed,* also explore the beauty in strange obsessions, and even decay, while mocking perfection as socially defined, limiting, and absurd, often through disjointed and absurd narratives and dialogue. In *Before Need* and *Before Need Redressed,* for example, close-ups and extreme close-ups of dental instruments and teeth are rendered with an eye to form and color, highlights and shadows, as are Faberge eggs, a block of ice melting under the impact of a hot iron, and more. Both films present viewers with a series of kaleidoscopic puzzles to be deciphered as, and if, they will. A recut and condensed version of *Before Need, Before Need Redressed* stands as a quite different film, because even though many of the whispered voice-over reflections of an older woman "character" and snatches of string music remain, and even though, like the images, these sounds are presented in the same order, many of the original images and much of the synchronized dialogue of non sequiturs have been excised.

Nelson's early works often generated interest because she was one of a handful of women filmmakers working among the largely male West Coast avant-garde in the 1960s and 1970s. *Schmeerguntz,* a collage send-up that juxtaposes recycled images of magazine model femininity with select footage of more everyday female experiences, and *Take Off,* an animated *cum* live-action film about a stripper who ends up stripping her own body parts, then rocketing off into space, were and continue to be hailed by some critics as "feminist"; in fact they were quite diversely received among feminists at the time.

Other films, including *My Name Is Oona, Red Shift, Time Being, Kirsa Nicholina, Five Artists, One and the Same,* and *Trollstenen,* center on family, friends, and/or self, and emotion. Like Nelson's other work in film, all exceed gender-based or gender-limited labels. The haunting *My Name Is Oona,* a ten-minute black-and-white short, casts Nelson's young daughter as playful child and fairy-tale princess via multilayered superimpositions of negative and positive images combined in varying speeds with choral and singular transformations of Oona's recorded voice, off, chanting, mantralike, "My name is Oona." The nearly feature-length *Red Shift* weaves exchanges among three generations of Grundel/Nelson women (Oona, Gunvor, and Gunvor's mother, Carin) together with the reflections of fictional characters and Calamity Jane's letters to her absent daughter, evoking some of the emotional connections experienced by mothers and daughters of differing ages, in differing epochs. *Time Being,* an eight minute silent, moves from still photos of Nelson's vibrantly athletic middle-aged mother, smiling on skis, to three long takes, the first in close-up, the second in medium shot, the third in long shot, of Carin in old age, nearly motionless on a nursing home or hospital bed, struggling to breathe. Interspersed gestural camera work and manipulations of light exposure powerfully suggest the intensities of observation and feeling to be found in waiting, and being.

—Chris Holmlund

NOTARI, Elvira
Italian director and writer

Born: Elvira Cody, in Salerno, Italy, 10 February 1875. **Family:** Married Nicola Notari, 1902, three children. **Career:** 1906—founded Film Dora (later called Dora Film) and started producing films; 1906-11—produced film shorts intended to open or close a cinema show; 1909—started producing longer films; 1920—due to popular demand, *'A Legge* screened for a full month rather than the usual two weeks; 1920s—Notari's films were censored and increasingly were shown in the United States; 1925-30—her company's film output declined drastically due to Italian censorship; 1930—made her last film, likely *Christian Triumph.* **Died:** In Italy, 1946.

Films as Director and Writer

1906-11 *Arrivederci* and *Augurali* (at least 27 episodes of varying lengths)
1909 *Capri Incantevole (Enchanting Capri); Posillipo da Napoli (Posillipo as Seen from Naples); L'Accalappiacani (The Dog Catcher); Il Processo Cuocolo (The Trial Cuocolo)*

1910   *La Fuga del Gatto (Escape of the Cat)*
1911   *La Corazzata San Giorgio (The Ship San Giorgio);
       Preparativi Guerreschi a Napoli (Preparing for the War
       in Naples); Bufera d'Anime (Blizzard of Passion); Carmela
       la Pazza (Carmela the Madwoman); Maria Rosa di Santa
       Flavia (Maria Rosa of Santa Flavia)*
1912   *Capri Pittoresco (Picturesque Capri); Caratteristica Guerra
       Italo-Turca Tra i Nostri Scugnizzi Napoletani (Italo-Turk-
       ish War among Our Neapolitan Urchins); Cattura di un
       Pazzo a Bagnoli (Capture of a Madman in Bagnoli); Rivista
       Navale Dell' 11 Novembre 1912 (Great Parade of the
       Fleet); L'Eroismo di un Aviatore a Tripoli (Heroism of an
       Aviator in Tripoli); La Figlia del Vesuvio (The Daughter of
       Vesuvius); I Nomadi (Nomadic People); Ritorna all'Onda
       (Return to the Wave)*
1913   *Povera Tisa, Povera Madre (Poor Consumptive! Poor
       Mother!); Il Tricolore (The Italian Flag); A Marechiaro ce
       sta 'na Fenesta (At Marechiaro There Is a Window)*
1914   *Fenesta che Lucive (Lighted Window)*
1915   *Addio Mia Bella Addio, l'Armata se ne va (Farewell, My Dear,
       Farewell...the Army Is Going); Figlio del Reggimento (Son of
       the Regiment); Sempre Avanti Savoia (Forward, Savoia)*
1916   *Carmela la Sartina di Montesanto (Carmela the Dressmaker
       of Montesanto); Ciccio il Pizzaiuolo del Carmine (Ciccio,
       the Pizzamaker of Carmine); Gloria ai Caduti (Glory to
       the Fallen Soldiers)*
1917   *Mandolinata a Mare (Mandolin Music at Sea); La Maschera
       del Vizio (The Mask of Vice); Il Nano Rosso (The Red Dwarf)*
1918   *Il Barcaiuolo d'Amalfi (The Boatman of Amalfi); Gnesella;
       Pusilleco Addiruso (Rimpianto; Urchins; Regret)*
1919   *Chiarina la Modista (Chiarina the Milliner); Gabriele il
       Lampionaio di Porto (Gabriele the Lamplighter of the Har-
       bor); La Medea di Porta Medina (The Medea of Porta Medina)*
1920   *A Piedigrotta (At Piedigrotta); 'A Legge ('O Festino e 'a
       Legge; The Law; The Feast and the Law); 'A Mala Nova
       (The New Criminal Underworld)*
1921   *Gennariello il Figlio del Galeotto (Gennariello the Son of the
       Convict); Gennariello Polizziotto (Gennariello the Police-
       man); Luciella (Luciella la Figlia Della Strada; Luciella;
       Luciella, the Daughter of the Street); 'O Munaciello (The
       House of Spirit)*
1922   *Cielo celeste; Cielo 'e Napule; E' Piccarella (The Little Girl's
       Wrong); Il Miracolo Della Madonna di Pompei (Mary the
       Crazy Woman); 'A Santa notte (The Holy Night)*
1923   *Core 'e Frata (Brother's Heart); 'O Cuppe' d'a Morte (The
       Carriage of Death); Pupatella (Waltzer Dream); Reginella
       (Little Queen); Scugnizza (Orphan of Naples); Sotto il
       Carcere di San Francisco (Beneath the Prison)*
1924   *A Marechiaro ce sta 'na Fenesta (At Marechiaro There Is a
       Window) (2nd version); La Fata di Borgo Loreto (The
       Fairy of Borgo Loreto); 'Nfama (Voglio a Tte; Infamous
       Woman; I Fancy You); Otto e Novanta (8 and 90); Piange
       Pierrot (Cosi Piange Pierrot; Pierrot Cries)*
1925   *Fenesta che Lucive (Lighted Window) (2nd version); Mettete
       l'Avvocato (Get a Lawyer)*
1927   *Fantasia 'e Surdata (Soldier's Fantasy); L'Italia s'è Desta
       (Italy Has Risen); Mother and Country (produced in 1925)*
1928   *Duie Paravise (Two Heavens); La Leggenda di Napoli (The
       Legend of Naples); La Madonnina del Pescatore (The Little
       Madonna of the Fisherman); Napoli Terra d'Amore
       (Naples, Land of Love)*

1929   *Napoli Sirena Della Canzone (Naples, Singing Mermaid)*
1930   *Passa a Bandiera (The Flag Passes By); Trionfo Cristiano
       (Christian Triumph)*

Publications on Notari

Books

Bruno, Giuliana, and Maria Nadotti, editors, *Off Screen: Women and
    Film in Italy,* London, 1988.
Bruno, Giuliana, *Streetwalking on a Ruined Map: Cultural Theory
    and the City Films of Elvira Notari,* Princeton, New Jersey, 1993.
Museum of Modern Art, *Notes from the Napoletana Images of a City
    Series,* New York, 1994.
Foster, Gwendolyn Audrey, *Women Film Directors: An International
    Bio-Critical Dictionary,* Westport, Connecticut, 1995.

Articles

Gili, J. A., "Elvira Notari," in *Positif* (Paris), July/August 1983.
Troianelli, E., "Elvira Notari, Pioniera del Cinema Napoletano," in
    Quaderni du Cinema (Florence, Italy), January/February 1987.
Bruno, Giuliana, "Le Films di Elvira Notari (1875-1946)," in *Lapis,*
    no. 2, 1988.
Bruno, Giuliana, "Streetwalking around Plato's Cave," in *October*
    (Cambridge, Massachusetts), Spring 1992.
Hoberman, J., "Napoletana: Images of a City," in *Village Voice* (New
    York), 16 November 1993.
Foster, Gwendolyn, "Giuliana Bruno: *Streetwalking on a Ruined
    Map,*" in *Post Script* (Commerce, Texas), Winter/Spring 1994.

*   *   *

Though her name is now largely forgotten, Elvira Notari was
Italy's first and most prolific woman filmmaker and her vast body of
work is considered an important antecedent of Italian neorealism.
Her films were distributed throughout Italy and other countries,
especially to New York City (where Dora Film had an office). Unfortunately, the bulk of her work no longer exists, though the fragments that remain suggest that she brought a richly textured female
perspective to her looks at love, violence, poverty, desire, and death.

After Notari finished school, unusual for a girl from the working
class, she went to Naples to work as a milliner. After she married Nicola
Notari, the couple supported themselves by hand-coloring photographs,
and soon they started coloring motion pictures. In 1906 they started
making their own films—shorts that were intended to open or close a
cinema show, and which were called, *Augurali* and *Arrivederci* films. In
addition, they made short documentaries that mostly consisted of brief
scenes of street life and expansive city and natural vistas, as well as
"actualities"—films of real events, including urban youth gang fights
(*Italo-Turkish War among Our Neapolitan Urchins*) and the arrest of a
madman (*Capture of a Madman in Bagnoli*). By 1909, under the name
Film Dora, they were releasing feature films (they changed the studio's
name in about 1915 to Dora Film). Their company was a family affair:
Nicola was responsible for the cinematography and sets, and he developed, printed, and edited the films with Elvira. In addition, their son
Edoardo appeared in nearly all of the films, playing the recurring character Gennariello.

During a career that spanned the years 1906 to 1930, Elvira directed and co-produced all of Dora Film's output, including about 60

feature films, as well as more than a hundred documentaries and shorts. She selected the stories and wrote the original screenplays as well as the scripts that were adapted from popular novels and songs. Interestingly, at Dora Film she was known as "the general" for her serious and precise working style. Apparently, her films were extraordinarily popular: in the Naples's arcade theaters where they were regularly screened, each of her films generally ran for two weeks, from the morning until late at night, and each was likely seen by thousands of theater patrons. Further, her films were popular in the United States among Italian immigrants. Until her career was resurrected by Giuliana Bruno, however, film history had forgotten her. Historians routinely had propagated misinformation about Dora Film, in particular that Nicola had directed all of the films. Nevertheless, a local critic in 1916 praised her films and noted that what audiences appreciated in particular was that "the suggestive drama develops against the enchanting panorama of the city of Naples."

During Elvira's career, the Italian film industry was divided between the lively film production of the South, which included the popular Dora Films, and Northern film production, mostly near Rome and Turin. In particular, the Southern Neapolitan cinema was associated with depictions of "crude local scenes of poverty and violence." Elvira's films were of their region; indeed, her "cinema of the street" was far different from the slick Italian "super-spectacles" of her Northern contemporaries that were dominant in Italian cinema, and preferred by commercial American distributors. Her distinctive style arguably foreshadowed neorealism, in terms, for example, of mise-en-scène and subject matter. That is, Elvira shot her melodramas on location in the streets of Naples, and often with nonprofessional performers. Accordingly, her films revealed the conditions of urban living among the poor, as well as her interest in the experiences of women. But her work was usually not explicitly political—she made tearful melodramas with exciting crimes of passion and betrayal. Notably, the subjects of her melodramas were inspired by Neapolitan popular culture, 19th-century popular literature, and Italian women's romantic fiction. Often, the titles of her films were taken from contemporary popular songs, including Fenesta che Lucive, A Marechiaro ce sta 'na Fenesta, and Pupatella. They often featured women who reject prevailing social expectations, including women who are mad, violent, and highly sexual; and they were populated by temptresses and vamps and weak men all too eager to commit horrible crimes for them. E' Piccarella, for example, was a melodrama about a woman who is pursued by two men, and who favors the sinister over the good man, with tragic results. Indeed, one of Elvira Notari's recurrent female characters was the matriarchal piccarella; as her film suggested, the term refers to a strong-willed, outspoken, and somewhat bad girl. In addition, Notari's films often depicted a betrayed and abandoned mother who is instrumental in reestablishing the Law, as in 'A Legge. Core 'e Frata, like many of her films, is a romance, but with a difference: it is about a woman who works as a lighthouse keeper and longs for a romance with a passionate assassin, instead of with her disinterested and drunken fiancé.

During the 1920s, with the rise of Italian Fascism, Dora Film increasingly experienced censorship problems because the films seemed to criticize the law, and because they depicted crime, neglect, and poverty, and employed authentic dialects, instead of adhering to the fascist regime's favored images of an ordered and honest Italy. Thus, for example, Notari's film Mother and Country was cut and reedited several times before the Italian censors finally approved it. Nevertheless, when her films were refused censorship visas by Rome's authorities, they often were smuggled into the United States and distributed to Italian immigrant communities in New York's Little Italy and other urban areas where they were quite popular. Continuing censorship problems and the coming of sound, however, marked the end of Elvira Notari's film career.

—Cynthia Felando

NOVARO, María
Mexican director and writer

Born: Mexico City, Mexico, 11 September 1951. **Education:** Studied sociology at the Universidad Autonoma de México (UNAM) and filmmaking at the Centro Universitario de Estudios Cinematográficos (CUEC). **Career:** Feature film debut, Lola, 1989. **Awards:** Ariel, Best Short Fiction, Mexican Academy of Motion Picture Arts and Science, for An Island Surrounded by Water, 1984; Ariel, Best Feature Debut and Best Film Script, Mexican Academy of Motion Picture Arts and Science, for Lola, 1989.

Films as Director

1981   Sobre las olas (Over the Waves) (short); De encaje y azucar (Of Lace and Sugar) (short); Lavaderos (Laundry Shed) (short); Es primera vez (For the First Time)
1982   Conmigo la pasas muy bien (With Me You Do Very Well) (short)
1983   Querida Carmen (Dear Carmen) (short); 7 AM (short)
1984   Una Isla rodeada de agua (An Island Surrounded by Water) (short)
1985   La Pervertida (Depraved) (short)
1988   "Azul celeste" ("Celestial Blue"; "Sky Blue") ep. of Historias de ciudad (co-d)
1989   Lola (+ sc)
1990   Danzón (+ co-sc, co-ed)
1992   Otoñal (Autumn) (short)
1994   El jardín del Edén (The Garden of Eden) (+ sc, ed)

Other Film

1990   My Filmmaking, My Life: Matilde Landeta (P. Diaz and J. Ryder—doc) (appearance)

Publications by Novaro

Book

With Beatriz Novaro, Danzón: The Screenplay, Mexico, 1994.

Articles

"De Lola a Danzon," interview with V. Bustos, in Dicine (Mexico), July 1991.
"Le città del cinema: Firenze," interview with M. Teatini, in Cinema & Cinema (Bologna, Italy), September/December 1992.

Publications on Novaro

Book

Foster, Gwendolyn Audrey, *Women Film Directors: An International Bio-Critical Dictionary,* Westport, Connecticut, 1995.

Articles

Huaco-Nuzum, Carmen, in *The Women's Companion to International Film,* edited by Annette Kuhn and Susannah Radstone, London, 1990.

Vega, E. de la, "Fichero de cineastas nacionales," in *Dicine* (Mexico), November 1990.

Fusco, C., "Dance and Remembrance," in *Village Voice* (New York), 27 August 1991.

Golden, T., "*Danzon* Glides to a Soft Mexican Rhythm," in *New York Times,* 11 October 1992.

* * *

The 1990s have been an exciting decade in Mexican cinema, especially for women filmmakers. Between 1989 and 1992, five women debuted feature films—María Novaro, Busi Cortés, Dana Rotberg, Marysa Systach, and Guita Schyfter. Most of these women made their second features within two years of their first. María Novaro contributed to this renaissance of Mexican cinema with the production of *Danzón,* her second feature, which earned international acclaim. Even more impressive, without exception films by these women have been among the nominees in several categories for the Ariel, Mexico's Academy Award, in the past ten years.

The decade did not begin auspiciously—rounding off the trouble in the industry in the 1980s, 992 theaters were closed between 1989 and 1991. Feature-film production dropped from 100 films in 1989 to 52 in 1990 and only 34 in 1991. The difficulties affected not only state-supported cinema, but Mexico's independent production as well. As Mexican cinema rose from the ashes, complete state production (through IMCINE, the Mexican film institute) was discontinued, giving bureaucrats a lesser hold on films, and co-productions between IMCINE, independent producers, and foreign countries increased.

Despite the crisis in the Mexican film industry, exacerbated by the country's economic crisis in 1990-91, Mexican filmmakers persevered. In fact, 1990-91 was a great year for Mexican cinema—a number of internationally acclaimed films were released, many produced by new, young filmmakers. Even more notable, perhaps, was the fact that the Mexican film-going audience flocked to see Mexican films, keeping them in the theaters longer than expected and creating new excitement and demand for domestic cinema.

María Novaro's films embody the spirit and the art of this new Mexican cinema. In the 1980s she produced a number of short films that were all well received. Novaro introduced in these shorts a number of aesthetic and political themes that resound throughout her oeuvre. She is unapologetically feminist, and continuously explores the role of women in Mexican society, gender inequity, the limits of fantasy and desire, and the political realities of being next-door neighbors with the mighty United States of America. In her combination of aesthetic and textual complexity, Novaro contributes to a strong movement of feminist filmmaking that began across Latin America in the late 1970s and continues today.

Her best-known short, *An Island Surrounded by Water,* lyrically narrates a young orphan girl's search for her mother. Its exquisite setting, Guerrero, on the coast of Costa Grande, enhances the girl's quest, which ultimately ends with two cameras—the filmmaker's and a portrait photographer's—presenting us with the girl's conflictual feelings about coming into womanhood. The search for her displaced mother becomes, in the end, a search for a guide into the next phase of life, or for the woman inside herself. The film received the Ariel for Best Fiction Short.

Novaro's other shorts examine distinct moments in the lives of Mexican women. *7 AM* (1983) allegorizes the contrast between the day of an average working woman and her fantasies of a life of leisure, informed by her experiences of mass media. This theme seemed to pulse throughout Latin America in the 1980s and, in fact, the Colombian feminist film and video collective Cine Mujer produced a very similar film in 1978 entitled *A primera vista* (*At First Glance*). Novaro's *Dear Carmen* (1983) also looks at the contradictions between reality and fantasy and the limits of desire, juxtaposing the life of a young professional woman with her fantasies about taming the Wild West as the legendary heroine Calamity Jane.

Novaro's feature-film debut, *Lola,* garnered several Ariel nominations including Best Feature Debut and Best Film Script. Like her subsequent films, *Lola* was written in collaboration with Novaro's sister, Beatriz. *Lola* is set in one of the shanty towns that surround Mexico City, just after the earthquake of 1985. Through its protagonists, a female street peddler and a "rockanrolero" (rock and roll fan), the film examines social and sexual politics.

In 1990 Novaro came to the attention of the international film community with *Danzón*. A beautiful and compelling film, *Danzón* tells the story of a telephone operator and single mother, Julia, whose ballroom dancing takes the place of any emotional life. She is devastated when her dancing partner disappears and she embarks on a dizzying quest to find him. As much inner voyage as odyssey, Julia's extraordinary journey is exuberant, difficult, and fulfilling. Novaro and actress María Rojo received Ariel nods, for Best Director and Best Actress respectively. The script, written with her sister Beatriz, was nominated for Best Original Screenplay. In a year seemingly jam-packed with exciting Latin American films, *Danzón* stands out as an uplifting tale about a woman's search for inner strength and happiness.

Novaro followed *Danzón* with a film about Mexicans in Tijuana struggling to cross the border into the United States. *El jardín de Edén* poignantly portrays the would-be emigrés as regular people, seeking a better life, and hoping to find it in "the Garden of Eden," the United States. Like the biblical garden, however, the mythical northern neighbor has hidden risks and dangers. Coinciding with the NAFTA agreement and the U.S. bailout of the Mexican economy, *El jardín de Edén* humanizes people who are generally portrayed by the U.S. press as dirty, backward, and subhuman, reminding us at the same time what it should mean to be a "neighbor."

—Ilene S. Goldman

UNE NUIT SUR LE MONT CHAUVE
(Night on Bald Mountain)
France, 1933
Directors: Alexander Alexeieff and Claire Parker

Production: Black and white, 35mm, animation; running time: 8 minutes, some sources list 9 minutes. Released 1933, Paris.

Narrative development: Alexander Alexeieff, inspired in part by Modest Moussorgsky's music and notes, and a short story based on a Slavic fairy tale by Gogol; **music:** Moussorgsky; **arrangement:** Rimski-Korsakov, "His Master's Voice" interpreted by: London Symphony Orchestra under the direction of Albert Coates; **animation:** Alexander Alexeieff and Claire Parker.

Publications

Books

Alexandre Alexeieff (catalog), Edinburgh, 1967.
Rondolino, G., *Alexandre Alexeieff,* Este, 1971.
Starr, Cecile, *Discovering the Movies,* New York, 1972.
Bendazzi, G., editor, *Alexandre Alexeieff,* Milan, 1973.
A. Alexeieff, C. Parker: Films et eaux-fortes (catalog), Annecy, 1975.
Russett, R., and Cecile Starr, *Experimental Animation,* New York, 1976.
A. Alexeieff; ou, La Gravure animée (catalogue), Annecy, 1983.
Bendazzi, G., editor, *Pages d'Alexeieff,* Milan, 1983.

Articles

Cheronnet, L., in *Art et Décoration* (Paris), no. 63, 1934.
Priacel, S., "Gravure animée," in *Art Vivant* (Paris), no. 188, 1934.
Grierson, John, in *Cinema Quarterly* (London), Autumn 1934.
Martin, A., "Alexandre Alexeieff et les cinémas possibles," in *Cinéma* (Paris), no. 81, 1963.
Alexeieff, Alexandre, "Reflections on Motion Picture Animation," in *Film Culture* (New York), no. 32, 1964.
Alexeieff, Alexandre, "The Synthesis of Artificial Movements in Motion Picture Projection," in *Film Culture* (New York), no. 48-49, 1970.
Arnault H., editor, "Le Chant d'ombres et de lumières de 1,250,000 épingles," in *Cinéma Pratique* (Paris), no. 123, 1973.
Jouvanceau, J. P., and Gaudillière, C., "A. Alexeieff," in *Banc-Titre* (Paris), no. 25, 1982.

* * *

The power of *Night on Bald Mountain* derives from the extraordinary versatility that Alexander Alexeieff and Claire Parker brought to their unusual medium. Their "pinboard" (*l'écran d'épingles*) is an upright perforated screen, three by four feet, with 500,000 (one million in later films) headless steel pins as its physical matrix. Images created on the pinboard take their character from the depth of the pins and their oblique lighting. Pushed forward, the pins create an entirely dark surface; when fully recessed, they produce a white ground. By varying the depth of the pins, one creates between the extremes of white and black a wide variety of subtle shades the brilliance and delicacy of which exceed that of engravings. The pinboard screen yields a single picture at a time which must be photographed as part of a sequence of thousands of such shots to shape the cumulative effect.

This frame-by-frame creation during the process of filming, rather than before it, is the earliest form of direct animation. Alexeieff acknowledges the pointillism of Seurat as analogous to the character of his images. The delicacy of this process of image-building becomes apparent when one realizes that four minutes of production requires a year of work. Since the artist can see only the current frame, the procedure is akin to writing a short story sentence-by-sentence and locking away each one until completion of the narrative. During the interactive process of creating and filming, the only original of a pinboard picture that remains is its photographic negative; there are almost 12,000 for this eight-minute film.

It is important to note that *Night on Bald Mountain* has about as much affinity to Walt Disney's evocation of the same Moussorgsky work in *Fantasia* (1940) as Lotte Reiniger's *Cinderella* has to Disney's version, i.e., the relationship is one of contrast more than of comparison. While Disney's *Fantasia* used cell animation in a direct and explicit way, which includes a sketching from life of Bela Lugosi as a Moussorgsky demon, Alexeieff and Parker employ indirection and impression, eminently conscious of art's power to universalize experience, of animation's power to create movement that is not "live" in the conventional ways of narrative, feature-length films. Their technique is most closely akin to the music that they visualize in their manipulation of time and space through shadowy referents. More physicists than engineers, their mobile structures reflect the changing character of thought and feeling, depict imaginary rather than static worlds. To photography and painting's laws of perspective they add the suggestive movement of implicit images. To the dance they add weightless figures whose unlimited metamorphoses invokes the license of Ovid's epic poem or the transitory, spatial and temporal fluidity of musical patterns. More than do other approaches to cinema, that of Alexeieff and Parker embody Suzanne Langer's description of cinema as a dream mode.

Night on Bald Mountain is a nightmare, a *Walpurgisnacht,* inspired by Moussorgsky's music and written notes, by childhood recollections, by the Russian short-story writer Gogol's record of an ages-old Slavic fairy tale, and by a dancing windmill in Pushkin's *Eugene Onegin.* The film's witches, demons, and skeletal horses, in contrasting day and night reflection of each other, create a feverish tone poem that Moussorgsky's music "describes" as powerfully as would a verbal sound track. The description, however, of both sight and sound is poetic and lyric rather than narrative and prosaic. The correlative and opposing patterns of visual and musical images create unexpected harmonies whose tonalities are both elastic and balanced. The clash of old and new realities, of expected and unexpected sights and sounds that regularly, rather than continually, complement each other provides the conceptual unity that is finally as satisfying as it is initially troubling. The audience comes to realize that the animation and the music are metaphorical equivalents to one another and that in combination they tell a tragicomic story of life and death, which calls upon the vertical complexity of poetic allusion and brevity for its thrilling and very temporary resolution of basic human contradictions.

The first pinboard was built in 1932, for *Night on Bald Mountain,* and was used by Alexeieff and Parker for all their noncommercial films. Jacques Drouin's *Le paysagiste* (*Mindscape:* National Film Board of Canada, 1976) continues their tradition. Because of the difficulty of the technique, however, Alexeieff and Parker have had many more admirers than cinematic descendants.

Following the traditional path of successful experimenters, they earned well-deserved critical acclaim, but the applause only gradually expanded beyond the ranks of film experts and film society aficionados. Initial success in Paris did not yield widespread distribution in spite of John Grierson's generous praise in the Autumn 1934 issue of *Cinema Quarterly.* In 1970 Norman McLaren proclaimed *Night on Bald Mountain* "first and foremost" on his list of the world's best animated films, and in 1980 it earned inclusion on a list of the eight best short animation films of all time.

—Arthur G. Robson

NÜREN DE GUSHI

(Women's Story)
People's Republic of China, 1987
Director: Peng Xiaolian

Production: Shanghai Film Studio; color, 35mm; running time: 96 minutes. Released 1989, in New York. Filmed in China. Language: Mandarin.

Producer: He Yijie; **screenplay:** Xiao Mao and Peng Xiaolian; **photography:** Liu Lihua; **editor:** Shen Chuanzeng; **sound engineer:** Tu Mingde; **music:** Yang Mao, Shanghai Film Orchestra; **music director:** Wang Yongji; **costume designer:** Wei Xiaoming; **lighting:** Wang Dexiang.

Cast: Zhang Wenrong (*Lai's Mother*); Zhang Min (*Xiao Feng*); Song Ruhui (*Jing Xiang*).

Awards: Special Jury Prize, Créteil International Women's Film Festival, Paris; People's Choice Award, Hawaii International Film Festival.

Publications

Books

Berry, Chris, "Interview with Peng Xiaolian," in *Camera Obscura* (Berkeley), vol. 18, 1988.

Li Mengxue, "Jianzao 'ziji de yijian wu': lu Hu Mei, Peng Xiaolian, Liu Miaomiao de diangying chuangzuo" [To build 'one's own room': on the film creation of Hu Mei, Peng Xiaolian and Liu Miaomiao], in *Film Art,* vol. 89, no. 3.

* * *

The collective hero of *Nüren de Gushi* is three women who struggle to define integrity in a world of competing, fundamental demands. "Lai's mother" ("L.M."), the oldest of the three, in her early 30s, has a husband whose brothers need to find wives in their poor village. The village lies both close to Beijing and, like other oral societies, massively isolated from it. "L.M." has no name of her own because her identity resides in her familial role. She will leave the village to raise money for her oldest brother-in-law's dowry by selling goods in the city. Planning to journey with "L.M." is Xiao Feng, the oldest of five daughters in a boyless family. Xiao Feng's city-derived income will support a family lacking patriarchal advantage.

Last to join the group is Jing Xiang. Although she is the youngest, the greatest burden is hers because she leaves to escape an arranged marriage. Since dowries are provided by the groom, who because he is mute must provide a sizable one, Jing Xiang's will pass to her brother, otherwise unable to marry. In this tiny society he looks forward to marrying the mute's sister. Thus Jing Xiang flees her family and its "needs," addressed by her mother on bended knee, needs which Jing Xiang regrets that she must rebuff.

Action, of which there is plenty, begins and ends in this anonymous oral world adjacent to the Great Wall, with few resources made more precious by the psychic constraints that hem them in. Everyone here is poor, barely surviving. A lone mule is harnessed to a mill to grind the community's grain. One herd of goats displays inordinate pride of place. Houses are shacks. Living this close to the bone, the women of the village freely voice their disdain for those whom they can construe as beneath them. Although everyone is well below the poverty line, those at the bottom are scorned by those less dreadfully off.

The Great Wall serves as the village's backdrop. While most locals see it as a dignified source of their isolation, the three woman read the edifice as a mark of civilization that inspires them, a screen of protection that also extends their horizons. In the beginning the Great Wall guides the three women away from their tight little world, serving them as a source of strength, stability, and direction. In the end the Great Wall is their cultural and historical reference that enables them to resist the impositions that two villagers would make upon them. It represents their resolve and their liberation.

The yarn that the trio will peddle in the big city, to which no one in the village has previously gone, is a political and an economic matter. In the latter respect sale of the yarn will enable three families to survive until spring. The trio leave in November and return proud, elated, and much wiser before the February New Year. The poverty of the village represents the failure of Maoist policies, a commune with no way to survive because Mao is not in any way providing. On the other hand, newly ascendant Deng Xiaoping's policies encourage entrepreneurship. Thus the "old boss," the head of the commune, passes enough Orlon yarn out the local factory's back door to lighten fractionally the poverty of three families.

Every woman in the village possesses voice, and yet lacks face, until the big city trio changes things. "Lai's mother" leaves the village of necessity rather than choice to serve the needs of her in-laws. While she leaves as their servant to provide them with income, she functions on the journey and in the city as a mother for the two younger women. At times she is a wise adviser; at times she scolds; and once she even expresses jealousy, quietly and almost humbly. Comparably subservient as a village woman, in fact more so because her family lacks a phallus, Xiao Feng provides a center to the urban narrative because of her place in the trio, neither weathered nor immature, and deeply committed to finding her way.

The trio's narrative of assimilation to urban worlds proceeds delicately and touchingly. Each place is a source of wonder and excitement, posing challenges to which they all rise, either through success or failure. Since the village has nurtured their voices, in unexpected ways, the world writ large proves addressable. Seasoned pride, a natural sense of possibilities, and homegrown voice enable them to convert obstacles into adventures. The sojourners return "home" as new people permanently changed, souls and imaginations with far greater scope that will never again be compressed. They are the new leaders, the future of their society. The women left home at dawn, and their return is a new dawn: one of reformed tradition and personal integrity.

—Arthur G. Robson

O

OBOMSAWIN, Alanis
Canadian director

Born: Lebanon, New Hampshire, 31 August 1932; moved to Canada in 1933 and was raised to age 9 on the Odonak Reserve in Quebec. **Family:** One child, Kisos. **Career:** Late 1950s—moved to Montreal, joining circle of writers, photographers, and artists; 1960—made professional singing debut at New York City's Town Hall; 1960s—traveled extensively throughout Canada, the United States, and Europe, earning a reputation as a singer, songwriter, storyteller, and activist; made several guest appearances on TV series *Sesame Street* (Canadian version); 1967—joined National Film Board of Canada as a consultant, beginning long-term relationship; 1971—directorial debut with the short, *Christmas at Moose Factory*; 1973—directed first of two multimedia education packages, *Manowan* (*L'ilawat* followed in 1976); 1977—made first feature-length documentary, *Mother of Many Children*; 1979—directed two shorts, *Old Crow* and *Gabriel Goes to the City*, for the educational TV series, *Sounds from Our People*; 1982—as a guest of the music department, taught a course on oral tradition at Dartmouth College; 1988—released "Bush Lady," an album of traditional Abenaki and original songs, sung in Abenaki, English, or French; 1993—directed *Kanehsatake: 270 Years of Resistance*, winner of 18 awards and international acclaim. **Awards:** "Outstanding Canadian of the Year," *Maclean's* magazine, 1965; Grand Prix, International Festival of Arctic Film (Dieppe, France), and Best Documentary, American Indian Film Festival (San Francisco), for *Mother of Many Children*, 1977; Order of Canada, 1983; Best Documentary, American Indian Film Festival (San Francisco), for *Richard Cardinal*, 1986; Best Documentary, American Indian Film Festival (San Francisco), for *No Address*, 1988; 125th Anniversary of the Confederation of Canada Medal, 1992; best Canadian feature award, Toronto Film Festival, for *Kanehsatake*, 1993; Award for Outstanding Achievement in Direction, Toronto Women in Film and Television, Toronto, 1994; Outstanding Contribution Award, Canadian Sociology and Anthropology Association, 1994; Taos Mountain Award, Taos Talking Pictures, 1997. **Address:** c/o National Film Board, Box 6100, Station A, Montreal, PQ, Canada H3C 3H5.

Films as Director

1971   *Christmas at Moose Factory* (short) (+ sc)
1977   *Mother of Many Children* (+ sc, co-pr, narrator); *Amisk* (+ co-pr)
1979   *Old Crow* (short—for TV); *Gabriel Goes to the City* (short—for TV); *Canada Vignettes: Wild Rice Harvest Kenora* (short) (+ sc); *Canada Vignettes: June in Povungnituk—Quebec Arctic* (short) (+ sc, narrator)
1984   *Incident at Restigouche* (+ sc, co-pr, narrator)
1986   *Richard Cardinal: Cry from a Diary of a Métis Child* (short) (+ sc, co-pr)
1987   *Poundmaker's Lodge: A Healing Place* (short) (+ sc, co-pr)
1988   *No Address* (+ sc, co-pr); *A Way of Learning* (+ sc, co-pr)
1991   *Le Patro Le Prévost 80 Years Later* (+ sc, co-pr)
1992   *Walker* (short)
1993   *Kanehsatake: 270 Years of Resistance* (+ sc, co-pr, narrator); *Voices of Experience, Voices for Change, Part 1* (compilation that includes *Richard Cardinal*)
1995   *My Name Is Kahentiiosta* (short) (+ sc, co-pr, co-ph)
1996   *Referendum—Take 2/Prise deux* (co-d)
1997   *Spudwrench—Kahnawake Man* (+ pr)

Other Film

1970   *Eliza's Horoscope* (appearance)

Publication by Obomsawin

Article

"Talking Heads," interview with K. Marginson, in *International Documentary* (Los Angeles), December 1993/January 1994.

Publications on Obomsawin

Books

Kuhn, Annette, and Susannah Radstone, editors, *The Women's Companion to International Film*, London, 1990.
Steven, Peter, *Brink of Reality: New Canadian Documentary Film and Video*, Toronto, 1993.
Foster, Gwendolyn Audrey, *Women Film Directors: An International Bio-Critical Dictionary*, Westport, Connecticut, 1995.
Notable Native Americans, Detroit, 1995.
Pallister, Janis L., *The Cinema of Québec: Masters in Their Own House*, Madison, New Jersey, 1995.

Articles

Alioff, M., and S. S. Levine, "The Long Walk of Alanis Obomsawin," in *Cinema Canada* (Montreal), May 1987.
Greer, Sandy, "Three Native Women," in *Turtle Quarterly* (Niagara Falls, New York), Spring 1991.

Video

Interview, in *Voices of Experience, Voices for Change, Part 1*, anthology of documentary films, National Film Board of Canada, 1993.

*   *   *

Documentarian Alanis Obomsawin has become one of Canada's leading native filmmakers—and has garnered international renown—in a career spanning more than a quarter of a century, a career that emerged out of unique background. Soon after her birth in New Hampshire, her family moved to Canada, where they initially lived on the Odonak Reserve, northeast of Montreal. There, Obomsawin learned the songs and stories of her people, the Abenaki. When she was nine, her family moved again, this time settling in Trois-Rivières, a small town 75 miles northeast of Montreal, where Obomsawin was the only native child and had to endure cultural isolation and racial discrimination—experiences that had a profound effect on her later filmmaking. Following this typically difficult native childhood, Obomsawin moved to Montreal in the late 1950s, where she eventually emerged as a singer and storyteller out of the circle of writers, photographers, and artists she had joined. During the 1960s she traveled widely throughout Canada, the United States, and Europe performing in universities, prisons, art centers, and at folk festivals for humanitarian causes; she even made several guest appearances on the Canadian version of the television series *Sesame Street,* and was named "Outstanding Canadian of the Year" in 1965 by *Maclean's* magazine. In 1967, Canada's National Film Board (NFB) invited her to work as an adviser on several film projects, leading to her entrance into documentary filmmaking and a long-term relationship with the NFB. Making this move was a natural one for Obomsawin, the storyteller; she has said that "to make a film you have to be able to tell a story. Filmmaking for me is really storytelling."

All of Obomsawin's films deal with one or more aspects of native life, culture, and customs, conveyed through the sensitive and perceptive prism of an insider (it is worth noting that she also writes and co-produces, and often narrates, her films). Her 1971 debut, *Christmas at Moose Factory,* tells the story of life at the Cree settlement of Moose Factory through the artwork of its native children. After directing two multimedia educational packages in 1973 and 1976, she returned to film in 1977 with the award-winning *Mother of Many Children,* her first feature-length documentary. For this film, Obomsawin traveled throughout Canada to document the seminal role that women play—by using language and storytelling to pass on their culture—in what are largely matrilineal societies.

Also in 1977 came *Amisk,* in which Obomsawin showcased native music and dancing at a concert that was part of a week-long festival. Held in Montreal, the purpose of the festival was to raise funds in support of the Cree people of James Bay, who were battling to save their land from a massive hydroelectric project being built by the government of Quebec. This was the first of several films in which Obomsawin documents conflicts between native peoples and the government, which is somewhat ironic given that she was awarded the prestigious Order of Canada in 1983. In fact, the year following this honor, Obomsawin directed *Incident at Restigouche,* which portrays a showdown over salmon fishing rights between the Micmac people on the Restigouche Reserve and the Ontario Provincial Police. Snappily edited, the film draws on television coverage of two police raids of the reserve, montaged news photographs, maps, courtroom drawings, shots of Micmac fishermen, on-camera interviews, and footage of salmon migrating and spawning. Although it plays down the issue of overfishing and is thus not entirely even-handed in its approach, *Incident at Restigouche*—like many of Obomsawin's films—gives voice to native peoples whose rights are too often trampled upon.

In *Richard Cardinal,* Obomsawin drew upon a diary left behind by the Métis title character who had committed suicide in 1984 at age 17 after being shuttled—incredibly—between 28 foster homes, group homes, and shelters in Alberta. To tell this story of abuse and neglect inflicted by the child-welfare system, Obomsawin intersperses quotes from his diary with scenes from his life reconstructed by actors, interviews with some of his foster parents, and depictions of the squalid settings the agencies placed him in.

Obomsawin's next films continued to portray the difficulties of native life in Canada but also highlighted the importance of collective action and tradition in efforts to help native peoples overcome these difficulties. *Poundmaker's Lodge* focuses on a treatment center in St. Albert, Alberta, where native people attempt to rebuild their substance abuse-devastated lives through mutual support, the sweat lodge and other rituals, and the rediscovery of their traditions. In *No Address* Obomsawin depicts the plight of native people who become part of the homeless population of Montreal soon after arriving there in search of a better life; it also looks, however, at the work of various organizations, such as the Montreal Native Friendship Centre, which attempt to help these individuals. In yet another portrayal of a community organization, *Le Patro Le Prévost 80 Years Later* showcases the 1909-founded Patro Le Prévost, a downtown Montreal religious-oriented center that brings people in the community together through various programs and activities.

In the 1990s, Obomsawin has spent much of her time documenting the summer and early fall 1990 confrontation in the Mohawk village of Kanehsatake near Oka, Quebec, between the Mohawks, the provincial police, and Canadian army—and this historic event's aftermath. She has so far made three films centering on the Oka crisis, with the first, the 1993-released *Kanehsatake: 270 Years of Resistance,* becoming her most-celebrated film yet. During the entire 78-day standoff—which grew out of a scheme to have the government take over Mohawk pine-forest land to build a golf course—Obomsawin lived with the Mohawks, thus very much imparting an insider's perspective to the film. But this film, unlike *Incident at Restigouche,* is more even-handed in its politics, with, for example, an army major being portrayed rather sympathetically. More importantly, Obomsawin in this two-hour-long film takes the time to put the Oka crisis into a historical context, namely the nearly three centuries of land-grabbing in and around Montreal at the expense of the Mohawks. This powerful documentary—winner of 18 international awards—thus fulfilled her intention of presenting a community to itself, at the same time that it provided to outsiders a complex record of an important event and its impact on the people involved.

Obomsawin next provided intimate portraits of two of the Mohawks involved in the Oka crisis through 1995's *My Name Is Kahentiiosta* and 1997's *Spudwrench—Kahnawake Man.* The former focuses on a young woman named Kahentiiosta, who is arrested during the crisis and then detained for longer than the other women because the government will not accept her aboriginal name in court. *Spudwrench* tells the story of Randy Horne, a high-steel worker who adopted the code name "spudwrench" during the crisis, and of the generations of Mohawk high-steel workers who have traveled around North America to work on some of the tallest buildings in the world. In both films, Obomsawin is careful to detail the reasons why these and other Mohawks were willing to risk their lives to save their sacred land.

Throughout her increasingly impressive career, Obomsawin has lived up to her goal of making documentary films both for her own community and for the outside world. She concisely summed up her approach when she said, "I make films for the world, [but] first of all I think of the people who I am documenting."

—David E. Salamie

OLYMPIA

(Olympische Spiele 1936)
Germany, 1938
Director: Leni Riefenstahl

Production: Tobis Cinema (Germany); black and white, 35mm; running time: Part I, 100 minutes, and Part II, 105 minutes; length: Riefenstahl's final cut was 18,000 feet. Released 20 April 1938. Filmed 20 July-4 August 1936 in Berlin at the Olympic Games. Cost 2.2 million Reichsmarks (approximately $523,810 in 1938).

Producers: Walter Traut and Walter Grosskopf; **screenplay:** Leni Riefenstahl; **photography:** Leni Riefenstahl, Hans Ertl, Walter Frentz, Guzzi Lantschner, Kurt Neubert, Hans Scheib, and Willy Zielk; **editor:** Leni Riefenstahl; **music:** Herbert Windt.

Awards: Biennale Film Festival, Venice, 1st Prize; State Prize (Staatspreis) of Germany; Polar Prize, Sweden.

Publications

Books

Riefenstahl, Leni, *Schönheit im Olympischen Kampf,* Berlin, 1937.
Riefenstahl, Leni, *Notes on the Making of Olympia,* London, 1958.
Sarris, Andrew, editor, *Interviews with Film Directors,* Indianapolis, Indiana, 1967.
Hull, David Stewart, *Film in the Third Reich,* Berkeley, 1969.
Mandell, Richard, D., *Nazi Olympics,* 1971.
Young, Vernon, *On Film: Unpopular Essays on a Popular Art,* Chicago, 1972.
Barsam, Richard, *Nonfiction Film: A Critical History,* New York, 1973.
Barnouw, Erik, *Documentary: A History of the Non-Fiction Film,* New York, 1974.
Johnson, Lincoln, F., *Film: Space, Time, Light, and Sound,* 1974.
Infield, Glenn, *Leni Riefenstahl, The Fallen Film Goddess,* New York, 1976.
Ford, Charles, *Leni Riefenstahl,* Paris, 1978.
Infield, Glenn, *Leni Riefenstahl et le 3e Reich,* Paris, 1978.
Berg-Pan, Renata, *Leni Riefenstahl,* Boston, 1980.
Welch, David, *Propaganda and the German Cinema,* Oxford, 1983; rev. ed., 1987.
Graham, Cooper C., *Leni Riefenstahl and Olympia,* Metuchen, New Jersey, 1986.
Downing, Taylor, *Olympia,* London, 1992.
Kubler, Manon, *Olympia,* Caracas, 1992.
Hoffmann, Hilmar, *Mythos Olympia: Autonomie und Unterwerfung von Sport und Kultur: Hitlers Olympiade, olympische Kultur, Riefenstahls* Olympia-*Film,* Berlin, 1993.
Riefenstahl, Leni, *Olympia,* New York, 1994.

Articles

New York Times, 9 March 1940.
Monthly Film Bulletin (London), no. 175, 1948.
Gunston, D., "Leni Riefenstahl," in *Film Quarterly* (Berkeley), Fall 1960.
Gardner, Robert, in *Film Comment* (New York), Winter 1965.
"Statement on Sarris-Gessner Quarrel about *Olympia,*" in *Film Comment* (New York), Fall 1967.
Swallow, Norman, interview with Leni Riefenstahl on *Olympia,* in *Listener* (London), 19 September 1968.
Corliss, Richard, "Leni Riefenstahl: A Bibliography," in *Film Heritage* (Dayton, Ohio), Fall 1969.
Richards, J., "Leni Riefenstahl: Style and Structure," in *Silent Pictures* (London), Autumn 1970.
"*Olympia* Issue" of *Film Culture* (New York), Spring 1973.
Barsam, Richard, "Leni Riefenstahl: Artifice and Truth in a World Apart," in *Film Comment* (New York), November/December 1973.
Barkhausen, H., "Footnote to the History of Riefenstahl's *Olympia,*" in *Film Quarterly* (Berkeley), Fall 1974.
Riefenstahl, Leni, "Notes on the Making of *Olympia,*" in *Nonfiction Film: Theory and Criticism,* edited by Richard Barsam, New York, 1976.
Interview with Leni Riefenstahl, in *Montreal Star,* 20 July 1976.
Vaughan, Dai, "Berlin versus Tokyo," in *Sight and Sound* (London), Autumn 1977.
Tyler, Parker, "Leni Riefenstahl's *Olympia,*" in *The Documentary Tradition,* edited by Lewis Jacobs, 2nd ed., New York, 1979.
Horton, W. J., "Capturing the Olympics," in *American Cinematographer* (Los Angeles), July 1984.
Foldenyi, F. L., "Felhotlen almok nyomaszto vilaga," in *Filmvilag* (Budapest), no. 2, 1993.
Graham, C. C., "*Olympia* in America, 1938: Leni Riefenstahl, Hollywood, and the Kristallnacht," in *Historical Journal of Film, Radio und Television* (Abingdon, Oxfordshire), no. 4, 1993.

* * *

Any film of the Olympic Games would be useless, Goebbels maintained, unless it could be shown a few days after they ended. Who could be interested after the excitement and the memory faded? Fortunately, director Leni Riefenstahl, with Hitler's approval, overrode any objections with astonishing results. While *Olympia* is a superb example of the sports documentary, it also stands on its own as an aesthetic achievement.

The fact its creator is a controversial figure whose alliance with the Nazi Party is still held up to scrutiny, and still as coolly contested by Riefenstahl, forces one to examine the boundaries of "artistic integrity" versus a very fundamental morality. One cannot view *Olympia* simply as film, or simply as propaganda.

There was almost as much preparation for *Olympia*'s shooting than for the Games themselves. For the best angles, uninterrupted by distracted participants, two steel towers were built in the stadium infield, and pits were dug for the sprinting and jumping events. Scaffolding platforms caught the rowing teams in their winning strokes thanks to cameras pulled along tracks by car. Hundreds of technicians and advisers were brought in, as were some of the best camera people. Several cameramen had previously worked with Riefenstahl on her earlier film, *Triumph of the Will,* a stunning record of Hitler's Nazi rallies, as well as the "mountain" films by Arnold Fanck that she had starred in. Despite Riefenstahl's total control, much of the look of *Olympia* was due to people such as Hans Ertl, for the celebrated diving sequences; Walter Frentz for the marathon, yachting events, and the romantic opening scenes in Part II; and Gustav Lantschner for the gymnastic, equestrian, and some of the diving.

Three kinds of film stock were used; one was good for half-tones, one flattering to outdoor scenes, a third for architecture. Over ten

Olympia

hours of film were shot each day during the 16-day Games. Including training footage (incorporated into the film) and reshooting (some winning athletes were delighted to re-create their finest moments), there were 250 hours for her, alone, to edit. Logging the film took a month, viewing the rushes more than two. According to the director, editing took a year and a half: "It was cut like a symphony...according to laws of aesthetics and rhythm." Adding the sound took another six weeks. It must be remembered that in 1936 and 1937 there were no zoom lenses, no soundproof cameras, no computer mixing—merely what was, to us now, primitive technology.

After nearly three years, Riefenstahl was finished. Her powerful 12-minute opening-sequence in Part I evokes the classical past, an analogy dear to Nazi propagandist hearts. Classical ruins—ironically to become Nazi ones—Wagnerian strains, whirling clouds and Greek statues; together with the human body celebrated in motion via the discus throw, the shot-put and the javelin, the epic stance is firmly established. The international foundation of the Games was exploited to produce a propaganda climax; in a series of shots, the torch aloft, carried from Greece, is ignited, the flame returns to life,

only in Germany, only under Hitler, who pronounces the Games open. With lab effects, the results are almost religious.

The high jump becomes a filmic ballet, with slow motion, different camera angles, and cross-cuts. Then follow the discus, hurdles, throwing the hammer, pole vaulting, relays. The long-jump is one of the more interesting pieces in the film, having a personal dimension. The competition is between Aryan Lutz Long and American (and, gallingly for the Games hosts) black star Jesse Owens. Riefenstahl, sensitive to the symbolism, accomplishes the drama effectively, incorporating the tension in the situation, the personal drive of the two contestants with honed slow-motion camera work, fast audience reaction shots (significantly, not Hitler's—who rarely appears applauding any but German athletes), the sharp timing. Primarily, her camera is not aimed at documenting history-making records, but at the athletes themselves. Interestingly, more of the slow-motion effect, with the result of making the bodies almost superhuman, is aimed at the German athletes, whether or not they win, although the film's content is not, presumably, out to confirm the superiority of the "master" race.

The bodies seem to add another dimension, almost bursting out of the flat screen, which is seemingly barely able to contain the exuberance, the strength. And while many sports event have, by their nature, repeated actions by series of contestants, Riefenstahl films each in a slightly different manner to keep the movements fresh by her choreography.

The handling of the marathon, the antidote to any possible flagging attention, is the high point of Part I. Taylor Downing, in her book *Olympia* refers to this segment, rightly, as "a film within a film. It creates a statement about achievement and endurance, and takes the viewer right inside the race itself. Rarely has a marathon been treated with such imagination on film." Using the distorted shadows of the runners, interspersed with shots of feet pounding the pavement, leg muscles pulsing, the viewer's own body tenses, feeling the strength flowing from, then, as the runners feel the exhaustion, draining out of their bodies; each frame fairly courses with energy, and with the constant drive. The marathon is not an event, in Riefenstahl's camera eye, it is each athlete's personal trial.

One of Riefenstahl's gifts is her ability to manipulate the range of responses (within the film, within the audience) through her use of music, content, editing, and tone, not only within each individual sequence but the combining/contrasting of them for the bigger effect. For example, the dramatic rowing sequence is then followed by the occasionally humorous riding event; the result is a dynamic, *filmic* flow. In Part II, she begins sensuously, with reflected pools of mist-layered water, the tiny details such as a bird's wing in flight, a drop of water trembling on a spider web, with violin music threading through shots of muscled male bodies bathing, birching one another...Aryan Fatherland and Mother Nature in harmony. She cuts—like a hit of ice—to the rousing ceremony march, then on to physical training, as the different nationalities get into their stride for the bustling day's events. A shot of mass gymnastics is a long pan; tens of thousands of women in endless regimented lines do push-ups. The result is oddly dehumanizing; like Busby Berkeley's routines, individual grace is transformed into a pop design. Here the effect is one of uneasiness, not thrill.

Part II also ends with a crescendo. The diving sequence is justly the most celebrated in the film, even in film history. Camera people Ertl and Dorothy Poynton-Hill had to adjust for distance during the dive, change exposure the second the diver hit the water, then reverse the process when the diver resurfaced. An elevator-type device mounted by the pool ensured a fluid movement. The divers become suspended, as the camera seemingly redefines the physical laws of motion, of space and of time. The divers appear in the sky from nowhere, defying gravity; in slow motion, they become surreal. Bodies twist, twirl, arc, and never descend. No commentary mars the effect. Once again, no matter how beautiful each movement, repetition with each contestant could visually numb. To avoid that, Riefenstahl matched each shot with the movement of the dive preceding it; at the end, to the dive following. Such grace shows the director at her best; one forgets the background outside the realm of pure artistry.

She has perennially maintained her political innocence, reminding us of the gold medal the Olympic Committee awarded her in 1948. To many people, her stance rings hollow. *Olympia* is a stunning, and reasonably accurate account of the Games. Nevertheless, she was only independent of the Propaganda Ministry because of Hitler's personal involvement. It partly transcends politics, but it was established for political motives for political propaganda. *Olympia* is not a product of the political naif (she would "borrow" a group of gypsies from a nearby concentration camp for a later film—then return

them when she was through), but a brilliant, ambitious director who wanted her work seen. Genius can work both ways.

—Jane Ehrlich

ONO, Yoko
Japanese director, composer, and actress

Born: Tokyo, 18 February 1933; permanent resident of the United States. **Education:** Attended Gakushuin School; studied at Gakuishin University, Japan, and Sarah Lawrence College, without completing a degree. **Family:** Married (1) Toshi Ichiyanagi, 1957 (divorced 1963); (2) Tony Cox, 1963 (divorced 1969), daughter: Kyoko Cox; (3) the musician John Lennon, 1969 (died 1980), son: Sean Ono Lennon. **Career:** 1960-61—held gatherings at her Lower Manhattan loft where experimental poets, composers, and performance artists, most later allied with the loose Fluxus group of "conceptual artists," plied their trades; 1961—had her first gallery show in Manhattan and performed "concerts" (her keening accompanying a woman shattering glass, for example) there; 1962—presented *Works of Yoko Ono* in Tokyo, a five and a half hour-long performance piece filmed for TV, to horrendous reviews, spent time in a mental hospital; 1963—recorded the soundtrack to Tasha Iimura's film *Love*; 1964—published *Grapefruit*, a series of "instruction paintings" or written recipes for artworks to be constructed in the audience member's head; presented a series of conceptual pieces in *Yoko Ono's Final Performance* in Tokyo and then left Japan for New York City; 1966—contributed her first film shorts to the omnibus *Fluxfilm Program*; exhibited at the Indica Gallery in London, attained some British notoriety for her first long film, *Bottoms*; 1966-71—shot a series of experimental films, often in collaboration with John Lennon; 1967—presented the exhibit *Half-a-Wind* at the Lisson Gallery in London, with partial underwriting by Lennon; 1968—recorded *Two Virgins* with Lennon, an experimental sound collage, the album's release brought horrendous reviews; from 1968 until the present, recorded and performed a unique and eventually fairly influential cross between avant-garde and rock music, with Lennon and on her own; late 1960s—Ono and Lennon also made antiwar, anti-hatred Happenings out of their world-famous love, such as the Acorn Event or the Bed-Ins for Peace; 1969—appeared in the cinema verité-styled *Honeymoon* short, about her seven days in (just postmarital) bed with Lennon surrounded by members of the press; 1970—presented Fluxfest, a festival of events and exhibits in Manhattan; 1971-72—showed a retrospective at Everson Art Museum, Syracuse, New York; 1980—released *Double Fantasy* in collaboration with Lennon, their last record before he was shot dead in front of her; 1988—Rykodisc released *Onobox*, a 6-compact-disc retrospective of the past two decades of her music; 1989—the Whitney Museum of American Art in New York City presented a retrospective of her films and installations, including some old pieces redone in bronze to reflect the impact of the 1980's zeitgeist on a 1960's spirit; 1992—appeared on TV comedy series *Mad about You* as herself in the "Yoko Said" episode about documentary filmmaking; 1994—wrote score and book for an off-Broadway musical, "New York Rock," about love and violence in a modern cityscape; 1995—appeared in *The Beatles Anthology,* a TV history of the band, also released on video. **Address:** c/o Starpeace, 1 West 72nd Street, New York, NY 10023, U.S.A.

Films as Director

1966   *Film No. 4* (*Bottoms*); *Match*; *Eyeblink* (shorts, all 3 part of
        Fluxfilm Program omnibus)
1967   *Film No. 4* (*Bottoms*) (80-minute version)
1968   *Film No. 5* (*Smile*) (co-d with Lennon); *Instant Karma* (mu-
        sic short); *Two Virgins* (co-d with Lennon)
1969   *Honeymoon* (co-d); *Film No. 6* (*Rape*); *Self-Portrait* (co-d
        with Lennon); *Apotheosis* (co-d with Lennon); *Cold Tur-*
        key (music short); *Apotheosis No. 2* (co-d); *Bed-In*
        (*Bedpeace*; *Give Peace a Chance*) (co-d with Lennon)
1970   *Up Your Legs Forever* (co-d with Lennon); *Fly*; *Erection*
        (co-d with Lennon)
1971   *Clock* (co-d with Lennon); *Imagine* (co-d with Lennon); *Free-*
        dom (short); *The Museum of Modern Art Show*
1981   *Walking on Thin Ice* (music video); *Woman* (music video)
1982   *Goodbye Sadness* (music video)

Films as Actress

1967   *Satan's Bed* (*Judas City*) (Marshall Smith) (as Ito)
1969   *The Magic Christian* (McGrath) (cameo)
1970   *Let It Be* (Lindsay-Hogg—doc)
1971   *Dynamite Chicken* (Pintoff)
1982   *Scenes from the Life of Andy Warhol* (Mekas—doc) (as her-
        self)
1988   *Imagine: John Lennon* (Solt—doc) (as herself)
1993   *The Misfits: 30 Years of Fluxus* (Movin—doc) (+ co-mus)
1994   *Jonas in the Desert* (Sempel—doc)
1996   *The Rolling Stones Rock-and-Roll Circus* (Lindsay-Hogg—
        doc for TV, produced in 1968)

Publications by Ono

Scripts

MacDonald, Scott, "Yoko Ono: Ideas on Film (Interview/Scripts),"
    in *Film Quarterly* (Berkeley), Fall 1989.
Grapefruit: A Book of Instructions, New York, 1970.

Books

Yoko Ono-One Woman Show: Dec. 1st-Dec. 15th, New York, 1972.
The Playboy Interviews with John Lennon and Yoko Ono, edited
    by G. Barry Golson, interview with David Sheff, New York,
    1981.
Objects, Films, New York, 1989.
In Facing, curated by Jon Hendricks, London, 1990.
To See the Skies, edited by Jon Hendricks, Milano, 1990.
Instruction Paintings, New York, 1995.
Pennyviews, Isla Vista, California, 1995.

Articles

"On Yoko Ono," in *Film Culture* (New York), Winter/Spring
    1970.
"The Ballad of Yoko: The B-52's Kate Pierson Talks with Yoko Ono,"
    interview with Kate Pierson, in *Rolling Stone* (New York), 19
    March 1992.
"Yoko Ono, 13 A.D.," in *New Yorker,* 13 December 1993.

Publications on Ono

Books

Mekas, Jonas, *Movie Journal: The Rise of a New American Cinema,*
    1959-1971, New York, 1972.
Hopkins, Jerry, *Yoko Ono,* New York, 1986.
Thomson, Elizabeth, and David Gutman, editors, *The Lennon Com-*
    panion: Twenty-Five Years of Comment, New York, 1987.
Goldman, Albert, *The Lives of John Lennon,* New York, 1988.
Hendricks, Jon, compiler, *Fluxus Codex,* Detroit, 1988.
Robertson, John, *The Art & Music of John Lennon,* New York, 1993.
Foster, Gwendolyn Audrey, *Women Film Directors: An International*
    Bio-Critical Dictionary, Westport, Connecticut, 1995.

Articles

Sontag, Susan, "Happenings: An Art of Radical Juxtaposition," in
    Against Interpretation, and Other Essays, New York, 1966.
McCormick, Carlo, "Yoko Ono Solo," in *Artforum* (New York),
    February 1989.
Taylor, Paul, "Yoko Ono's New Bronze Age at the Whitney," in *New*
    York Times, 5 February 1989.
Larson, Kay, "The Flux Stops Here," in *New York,* 27 February 1989.
MacDonald, Scott, "Putting All Your Eggs in One Basket: A Survey
    of Single-Shot Film," in *Afterimage* (Rochester, New York), March
    1989.
Hoberman, J., "*Rape,*" in *Village Voice* (New York), 14 March 1989.
Chin, Daryl, "Walking on Thin Ice: The Films of Yoko Ono," in *In-*
    dependent (New York), April 1989.
Johnson, Ken, "Yoko Ono at the Whitney," in *Art in America* (New
    York), June 1989.
Hainley, Bruce, "Oh Yoko!," in *Artforum* (New York), April 1996.

*   *   *

Scholars have only barely begun to investigate Yoko Ono's filmmaking. She is of course best known as John Lennon's widow.
Before the ex-Beatle was assassinated, she was cast as the "dragon
lady" who broke up the band. Though mean-spirited biographers
such as Albert Goldman continue to give a sleazy edge to her self-
confidence and wide-ranging appetites for both art and life, Ono has
candidly expressed her most intimate feelings—as visual artist, composer, lyricist, and performer as well as director—throughout her
life, before and after her time with her third husband.

Ono's filmmaking career grew out of her work as part of the
Fluxus group, an international collective of musicians, poets, visual
artists, and proto-performance artists, united by their commitment to
overturning ideas about what art is and what an audience does,
primarily by blurring boundaries between art and nonart, and between art forms. In 1966 the impresario at the heart of the loose
alliance of Dada-inspired artists, George Maciunas, acquired a fast-
speed movie camera and asked several artists to contribute to the
Fluxfilm Program. *Fluxfilm* was an omnibus of short film pieces,
including Ono's *Match, Eyeblink,* and *No. 4* (*Bottoms*). Avant-garde
film historian Scott MacDonald calls the latter two films the earliest-
known examples of "single-shot films," whose slow-motion action
consists of one take only: a blinking eye, a bare rear end walking
away from the camera.

In 1967 Ono elaborated *Bottoms* into an 80-minute version: she
placed a humorously notorious ad in a London paper asking for

performers willing to bare their behinds. Ono writes in *Grapefruit* that her aim with the film was both political/historical (to reflect the funny side of the antiauthority, convention-busting sixties) and formal. MacDonald calls the long *Bottoms* one of the first films with a "serial" structure. Ono tells him that her concept was to fill the screen completely with one moving object at a time, in a series of some 375 individual butts, each filling the frame for some 15 seconds. MacDonald notes the film's theme that human beings, precisely in their culturally proscribed, forbidden, or "ugly" aspects, are equal, united, and actually beautiful. This is an idea dear to Ono's heart across all her art.

In 1968 Ono made the 51-minute-long *Smile* with her new lover, Lennon. It consists of two shots, each of Lennon's face in slow motion. Lennon and Ono also collaborated that year on *Two Virgins*. This film's form parallels both the overlapping sound collage that Lennon's play with multitrack audio tape allows on the accompanying record project of the same title, and the multitracked form of rock-era music recording in general. The film superimposes, or visually "multitracks," images of Ono's and Lennon's faces, and images of nature, for its first part. (The second is a shot of the two lovers kissing.) *Two Virgins* reflects several themes also present in Ono's artwork and performance pieces: the idea that looking at nature with care makes it art, the idea that communication and blending between people is desirable if frightening, and the idea that techniques of looking, whether shaped by the form of a canvas or by a film's shot lengths and editing, can bring out beauty and eroticism in unexpectedly isolated and interconnected details of the everyday world, and everyday people. The effect of many of Ono's filmed ideas is much the same as her installations which ask the viewer to look at the sky or the room through a small eyehole in a canvas, or to reach out her or his hands through two holes in a canvas to greet new people. The art serves as the conduit toward an oddening, a freshening up, of the (only seemingly) mundane details of the natural, and the social.

In 1969 Ono and Lennon filmed *Bed-In,* a fairly conventional documentary of their second extended stay in bed, in touch with the media, for peace, in Montreal. Ono's film work as a whole—because it follows the Fluxus tradition of close focus upon one real-world object for extended periods, with an eye toward politics and toward the irritation/activation of the viewer—straddles the line between documentary and avant-garde, form-driven film. Also in 1969 Ono made the evil candid-camera film, *Rape,* wherein we watch a film crew chase a German-speaking girl around London for 77 minutes while she reacts to their unwanted intrusion. Again the themes of communication and its perils cross wires in Ono's work with the erotic politics of the gaze, here and in *Fly,* a 31-minute-long exploration of a female nude body—by the camera and also by, first, one and then several chloroformed-to-be-docile flies. At the end the camera "flies" out the window, the buried pun at once reinforcing and throwing up the parallel between the prying camera and the insects. Ono is similarly at once critiquing and reenergizing the typical cinematic form that takes the female form as its voyeuristic object. *Up Your Legs Forever* features such an unevenly unsettling pun only in its title. It is a serially structured film, this time about (some famous people's) thighs, up which the camera pans in what is edited to seem a continuum. Its levels of formal inventiveness and political shock value register lower than Ono's earlier efforts. *Apotheosis* is a seemingly single-shot film (actually edited once, unobtrusively) with a camera, mounted on a hot-air balloon, rising up past Ono's and Lennon's bodies, into the clouds, and finally above them into the sunlight.

Lennon and Ono's play with the sound/image relationship and with puns built on discrepancies between words and images, contin-

ued with their next films. *Erection* uses time-lapse photography to explore the raising of—not the Lennon penis that was the subject of *Self-Portrait,* but—a skyscraper. *Imagine* is silent except for an exchange of greetings at the start. Ono's *The Museum of Modern Art Show* details her "show which didn't exist" at the New York museum; sidewalk sign-bearers induce passersby to inquire for an installation that existed only in Ono's mind and advertising. In this stunt, the Fluxus-inspired Ono, who once offered as an art object a list of her own artworks' prices, devises objects of pure exchange and no-use value—inviting passersby to try to pay to see art so purely conceptual that its "catalogue" is all of it that exists. The gall and freedom to redefine the world, of course, is the "real" use value of such art—whose price turns out to be the viewers' investment of time and perhaps willingness to be shocked or humiliated by the unexpected directions in which Ono will take them.

Ono made no new films or art projects between 1972 and 1979 (though she and Lennon pulled off a form of concept art for billionaires in 1979 by running an obscurely motivated "love letter," preaching peace and brotherhood to their fans, in London, New York, and Tokyo newspapers). In the 1980s she directed several music videos for her own and the late Lennon's songs; they had collaborated on film shorts for several songs in their filmmaking period. MacDonald notes that the 1989 retrospective of her films and art at Manhattan's Whitney Museum was poised to lead to a redistribution of her films in the nineties. The prolific and yet evasive Ono is poised to receive the full measure of attention that it seems not only her unusual celebrity but her gender and race have prevented her filmmaking, and all her distinctive, affecting, and innovative art, from receiving thus far.

—Susan Knobloch

OTTINGER, Ulrike
German director

Born: Konstanz, Germany, 6 June 1942. **Education:** Attended Munich Academy of Arts, 1959-61. **Career:** 1962-66—worked independently as a painter, lived in Paris, learning engraving and photography; 1966—wrote first screenplay, *The Mongolian Double Drawer,* conceived as part animation and part live action; during this period also wrote the initial draft of *Laocoon and Sons;* 1969—returned to Germany, where she founded and ran a gallery, "Galerie-Press," and opened a film club in Konstanz, "Visuell," which operated until 1972; 1985—directed a theater play in Stuttgart. **Awards:** German Film Critics Award, for *China—The Arts—The People,* 1985; HDF Short Film Prize, for *Usinimage,* 1987; Federal German Film Gold Ribbon for Artistic Realization, for *Johanna d'Arc of Mongolia,* 1988. **Address:** Ulrike Ottinger Filmproduktion, Hasenheide 92, D-10967 Berlin, Germany.

Films as Director

1972-74 *Laokoon und Söhne (Laocoon and Sons)* (co-d with Blumenschein)
1973 *Vostell—Berlin-fieber (Berlin Fever—Wolf Vostell)*
1975 *Die Betörung der blauen Matrosen (The Enchantment of the Blue Sailors; The Bewitchment of the Drunken Sailors)* (co-d with Blumenschein)

1977 *Madame X—eine absolute Herrscherin* (*Madame X—An Absolute Ruler*)
1979 *Bildnis Einer Trinkerin—Aller jamais retour* (*Ticket of No Return*) (+ sc, ph)
1981 *Freak Orlando* (+ sc, ph, sets)
1984 *Dorian Gray in spiegel der Boulevardprsse* (*The Image of Dorian Gray in the Yellow Press*) (+ sc, ph, sets)
1985 *China—die Künste—der Alltag* (*China—The Arts—The People*) (doc) (+ ph)
1986 *Sieben Frauen—Sieben Sünden* (*Seven Women—Seven Sins*) (+ sc, ph)
1986-87 *Superbia—Der Stolz* (*Superbia—L'orgueil*; *Superbia—Pride*)
1987 *Usinimage*
1988 *Johanna d'Arc of Mongolia* (+ pr, sc, ph, ed, sets)
1990 *Countdown* (doc) (+ ph, sc)
1992 *Taiga* (doc) (+ pr, sc, ph)
1997 *Exil Shanghai* (doc) (+ pr, sc, ph)

Other Film

1995 *The Night of the Filmmakers* (Reitz—doc) (appearance)

Publications by Ottinger

Books

Madame X—eine absolute Herrscherin, Frankfurt, 1980.
Freak Orlando, Kleines Welttheater in fünf Episoden, Berlin, 1981.
Taiga, Eine Reise ins nördliche Land der Mongolen, Berlin, 1993.

Articles

"Cinéma d'Allemagne de l'Ouest: Cette Vieille Mentalité des Pirates: Entretien avec Ulrike Ottinger," interview with G. Hoffmann, in *Cinéma* (Paris), November 1979.
Interview with Roswitha Mueller, in *Discourse,* Winter 1981-82.
"Berlin Vu Par ... Ulrike Ottinger," interview with A. Ménil and C. Najaman, in *Cinématographe* (Paris), May 1983.
"The Pressure to Make Genre Films: About the Endangered *Autorenkino,*" in *West German Filmmakers on Film,* edited by Eric Rentschler, New York, 1988.
"Minorities and the Majority," interview with Roy Grundmann and Judith Shulevitz, in *Cineaste* (New York), vol. 18, no. 31, 1991.
"Twentieth Century Theatrum Mundi: Ulrike Ottinger's *Johanna d'Arc of Mongolia,*" interview with Therese Grisham, in *Wide Angle* (Baltimore, Maryland), April 1992.
"Real Time Travel," interview with Laurence Rickels, in *Artforum* (New York), February 1993.

Publications on Ottinger

Books

Women in German Yearbook 4, 1988.
Knight, Julia, *Women and the New German Cinema,* London, 1992.
Frieden, Sandra, Richard W. McCormick, Vibeke R. Petersen, and Laurie Melissa Vogelsang, editors, *Gender and German Cinema: Feminist Intervention,* Volume 1, *Gender and Representation in New German Cinema,* Oxford, 1993.

Queer Looks: Perspectives on Lesbian and Gay Film and Video, edited by Martha Gever, John Greyson, and Pratibha Parmar, New York, 1993.
Weiss, Andrea, *Vampires and Violets: Lesbians in Film,* New York, 1993.
Foster, Gwendolyn Audrey, *Women Film Directors: An International Bio-Critical Dictionary,* Westport, Connecticut, 1995.

Articles

Silberman, Marc, "Cine-Feminists in West Berlin," in *Quarterly Review of Film Studies* (Pleasantville, New York), vol. 5, no. 2, 1980.
Treut, Monika, "Ein Nachtrag zu Ulrike Ottinger's Film *Madame X,*" in *Frauen und Film* (Frankfurt), vol. 28, 1981.
Carter, Erica, "Introduction to Interview with Ulrike Ottinger," in *Screen* (London), Winter/Spring 1982.
Hansen, Miriam, "Visual Pleasure, Fetishism, and the Problem of Feminine/ Feminist Discourse: Ulrike Ottinger's *Ticket of No Return,*" in *New German Critique,* Winter 1984.
Lennsen, C., and others, "German Film Women," in *Jump Cut* (Berkeley), February 1984.
Perlmutter, R. "Two New Films by Helke Sander and Ulrike Ottinger," in *Film Criticism* (Meadville, Pennsylvania), Winter 1984-85.
Katsahnias, Iannis, "L'âme du Plan," in *Cahiers du Cinéma* (Paris), March 1986.
Kuhn, Annette, "Encounter between Two Cultures (A Discussion with Ulrike Ottinger)," in *Screen* (London), Autumn 1987.
White, Patricia, "*Madame X: An Absolute Ruler,*" in *Screen* (London), Autumn 1987.
Bergstrom, Janet, "The Theatre of Everyday Life: Ulrike Ottinger's *China—The Arts—Everyday Life,*" in *Camera Obscura* (Berkeley), September 1988.
Hake, Sabine, "'Gold, Love, Adventure': The Postmodern Conspiracy of Madame X," in *Discourse,* Fall/Winter 1988-89.
Silberman, Marc, "Women Filmmakers in West Germany: A Catalogue," in *Camera Obscura* (Berkeley), Fall 1990.
Dargis, M., "Price of Submission," in *Village Voice* (New York), 6 November 1990.
Holloway, R., "Ottinger Retrospective," in *Kino* (Warsaw), December 1990.
"*Countdown,*" in *Variety* (New York), 1 April 1991.
Knight, Arthur, "*Countdown,*" in *New Art Examiner,* May 1991.
Camhi, L., "No Place Like Home," in *Village Voice* (New York), March 1993.
Longfellow, Brenda, "Lesbian Phantasy and the Other Woman in Ottinger's *Johanna d'Arc of Mongolia,*" in *Screen* (London), Summer 1993.
Trumpener, K., "*Johanna d'Arc of Mongolia* in the Mirror of *Dorian Gray*: Ethnographic Recordings of the Aesthetic of the Masks in the Recent Films of Ulrike Ottinger," in *New German Critique,* Fall 1993.
Whissel, Kristen, "Racialized Spectacle, Exchange Relations, and the Western in *Johanna d'Arc of Mongolia,*" in *Screen* (London), vol. 37, 1996.

*   *   *

Ulrike Ottinger emerged from a tradition of the avant-garde visual arts as a painter, lithographer, and photographer. This differentiates her from other West German women filmmakers who came to prominence in the mid-to-late 1970s, who were more traditional left-wing feminists. Ottinger is also, and has always been, openly lesbian. Both of these factors have made her somewhat marginal in the feminist community, though certainly no less interesting, and often, a great deal more fun than her contemporaries. She shares few of the thematic concerns of the New German Cinema, and has often been compared with Werner Schroeter, because of her proclivity for stylization and exaggeration, artifice, and parody. When once asked where she positioned herself in relation to the then-burgeoning New German Cinema, she exclaimed, "I wouldn't know what I have in common with [them]."

Her work has polarized critics. The feminist journal *Frauen und film* criticized her for her retrograde, degenerate aesthetic agenda, whereas others have called her films "a celebration of Lesbian punk anti-realism."

Unlike many of her more earnest contemporaries, Ottinger's films are playful, with a strong element of fantasy. The director explains: "The tragic thing is that reality and fantasy are always separated: fantasy here, reality there. This separation, like the separation of forma and content of a work of art is the result of the invasion of certain areas by scientific thinking. Wishful dreaming and fantasy are the strongest forces in people's lives, the source of their actions. We have to stop rendering reality the way we see it, our surface perceptions of it. We have to learn how to deal with our wishes and our dreams as an integral part of ourselves."

Ottinger utilizes unusual juxtapositions of sound and image, highly saturated colors, nonnaturalistic performance styles, sometimes outrageous costume and set design, and disjunctive narrative, structures, to create a truly unique oeuvre. Those who claim her for feminism say she "radically subverts the terms in which patriarchal cinema has monopolized visual pleasure on behalf of the male gaze."

Ottinger's first feature film was *Madame X—An Absolute Ruler*, made in 1977. Seven women (including Yvonne Rainer) abandon their traditional roles to join the imperious, beautiful, lesbian pirate, the notorious Madame X, in a quest for love, adventure, and riches. The women have difficulty shedding their socialized roles, and under Madame X's ruthless domination, are eventually killed. Madame X searches for a new crew in her next port of call, and is rejoined by the same cast of characters—death has brought about renewal and change.

Highly stylized costume and set design (Madame X's severed hand is replaced by a decorative spike) and a series of bizarre performances are coupled with the imagery of sadism—chains and leather—making for a perverse, sexually charged, and ritualized atmosphere.

The director's next work was *Ticket of No Return,* once again starring Ottinger's sometime collaborator, and icon of the Berlin underground scene, Tabea Blumenschein (who also played Madame X). Blumenschein is introduced in the film as "a woman of antique grace and Raphaelic charm, a woman created like no other to be Medea, Madonna, Beatrice, Iphigenia, Aspasia"—in short, the classical, ideal Woman. Contrary to this euphoric introduction, "She" (known by no other name) buys a one-way ticket to Berlin with the specific project of drinking herself to death. The woman befriends a bag lady (Lutze—a well-known figure on the Berlin scene), and they

begin a tour of Berlin that would be unlikely for any travel guide, visiting a variety of locations, from underground clubs (where punk diva Nina Hagen graces them with a song), to the Banhof Zoo, to a traditional Bavarian-style beer hall. Throughout, the woman—who becomes increasingly disoriented as she fulfills her alcoholic program, wears a series of bizarre, but visually enticing costumes that serve to mock haute couture, and raise the issue of woman as an object to be looked at. The woman remains silent throughout the film, miming gestures in a ritualized fashion, heightening the film's sense of dissociation with reality, as well as encouraging associations with the woman's lack of voice in the patriarchy. Ottinger says: "In my opinion film should not be based on dialogue. It makes the film lack a certain sensuality which I find very important. Think of the beginnings of film, the expressionist silents. They spoke almost exclusively in images. The relation of image to objects is quite different than that of words to objects. This is not to say that I consider words or sound to be superfluous. To the contrary, I am making very conscious use of sound. I am working with twelve tracks to achieve the kind of sound rhythm I want. But again, this sound rhythm does not rely on language alone but equally as much on music and noises, also on fragment of various things."

Ottinger has always claimed to be an ethnographer, and indeed, the tour of the underbelly of Berlin speaks to this sensibility. But it is combined at the same time with Ottinger's typical stylization, providing an interesting aesthetic tension.

The filmmaker next made *Freak Orlando,* starring art cinema icon Delphine Seyrig. The film is a conflation of Tod Browning's 1932 classic, *Freaks,* with Virginia Woolf's meditation on gender, *Orlando.* It charts the time-travels of a mythic, androgynous figure, who challenges the patriarchy in various historical epochs. Ottinger says the film is "a history of freaks from the Middle Ages until now and analyzes power structures like the Inquisition and psychiatric power." *The Image of Dorian Gray in the Yellow Press* was Ottinger's next venture into filmmaking, and is a retelling of Fritz Lang's *Dr. Mabuse* films with, of course, a female cast. The director questions the objectivity of the press and stages a trial that humorously challenges the veracity of the fifth estate.

Ottinger shifted into a more documentary mode with *China—The Arts—The People,* a 4½ hour exploration of city life in China, as well as an investigation of the minorities inhabiting the outer perimeters of the country. In the film, Ottinger examines various art forms, both ancient and modern.

The director's next significant work was *Johanna d'Arc of Mongolia,* which again starred Delphine Seyrig, and presents a juxtaposition of the ancient and modern world, of Mongolia tribal culture and European mores, and of older and younger women. The film again combines ethnographic elements—as the assembled cast of women wander through Mongolia—with female-based rituals. Two of Ottinger's most recent films have been documentaries. *Countdown* deals with the fall of the Berlin wall, while in *Taiga* (a 501-minute epic), the director returns to Mongolia, detailing the nomadic tribes and their shamanic rites.

—Carole Zucker

PALCY, Euzhan

French West Indian director, writer, and producer

Born: In the French overseas department of Martinique, 1957. **Education:** Studied French literature at the Sorbonne in Paris, cinema at the Rue Lumière School. **Career:** 1974—wrote, directed, and acted in first locally produced film for Martinique television station; moved to Paris to study literature and film; 1983—wrote and directed internationally recognized feature, *Sugar Cane Alley*; 1989—co-wrote and directed *A Dry White Season*, the first Hollywood studio release directed by a black woman. **Awards:** Silver Lion, Venice Film Festival, and César for Best First Film, for *Sugar Cane Alley*, 1983; Orson Welles Prize for Special Cinematic Achievement, for *A Dry White Season*, 1989; Golden Keops, Ouagadougou Film Festival, Golden Senghor for Best Director, Special Jury Prize, Brussels Film Festival, Prix de la Jeunesse, Milan Film Festival, and Ban Zil Kreol Award, Montreal Film Festival, for *Simeon*, 1993. **Address:** Saligna and So On, 2435 21st Street, Santa Monica, CA 90405, U.S.A. **Agent:** Jeff Field, William Morris Agency, 151 El Camino Drive, Beverly Hills, CA 90212, U.S.A.

Films as Director and Writer

1974 *La messagère (The Messenger)* (doc—for TV)
1982 *L'atelier du diable (The Devil's Workshop)* (doc—for TV)
1983 *La Rue cases nègres (Sugar Cane Alley; Black Shack Alley)*
1989 *A Dry White Season*
1990 *Hassane* (doc—for TV)
1992 *Simeon* (+ pr)
1994 *Aimé Césaire: A Voice for History* (doc—for TV)
1997 *Ruby Bridges Story* (for TV) (+ pr)
1998 *Wings against the Wind* (co sc, + pr)

Publications by Palcy

Articles

"*Sugar Cane Alley*: An Interview with Euzhan Palcy," interview with Susan Linfield, in *Cineaste* (New York), vol. 13, no. 4, 1984.
"Euzhan Palcy: For All the Black Shack Alleys," interview with Mike Wilmington, in *LA Weekly* (Los Angeles), 11-17 May 1984.
"Tempest: Euzhan Palcy's *Dry White Season*," interview with Marlaine Glicksman, in *Film Comment* (New York), September/October 1989.
Interview with S. Brisset, in *Présence du Cinéma Français* (Paris), November/December 1992.
Interview with Janis Cole and Holly Dale, in *Calling the Shots: Profiles of Women Filmmakers*, Kingston, Ontario, 1993.
Interview with J. Zimmer, in *Mensuel du Cinéma* (Paris), 5 April 1993.

Publications on Palcy

Books

Quart, Barbara Koenig, *Women Directors: The Emergence of a New Cinema*, New York, 1988.
Acker, Ally, *Reel Women: Pioneers of the Cinema, 1896 to the Present*, New York, 1991.
Reid, Mark A., *Redefining Black Film*, Berkeley, 1993.
hooks, bell, "A Call for Militant Resistance," in *Multiple Voices in Feminist Film Criticism*, Minneapolis, 1994.
Kuhn, Annette, editor, with Susannah Radstone, *The Women's Companion to International Film*, Berkeley, 1994.
Foster, Gwendolyn Audrey, *Women Film Directors: An International Bio-Critical Dictionary*, Westport, Connecticut, 1995.

Articles

Canby, Vincent, "Third World Truths," in *New York Times*, 22 April 1984.
Denby, David, "*Sugar Cane Alley*," in *New York*, 30 April 1984.
Kauffmann, Stanley, "*Sugar Cane Alley*," in *New Republic* (New York), 30 April 1984.
Sarris, Andrew, "*Sugar Cane Alley*," in *Village Voice* (New York), 24 May 1984.
McKenna, Kristine, "Tough, Passionate, Persuasive: Euzhan Palcy Battled for Five Years to Put Her Vision of Apartheid on Screen, and then Lured Marlon Brando Back to Work—for Free," in *American Film* (Hollywood), September 1989.
"*A Dry White Season*," in *Variety* (New York), 13 September 1989.
Johnson, Brian, D., "*A Dry White Season*," in *Maclean's* (Toronto), 25 September 1989.
Schickel, Richard, "*A Dry White Season*," in *Time* (New York), 25 September 1989.
Easton, Nina J., "'Season' of Compromise Pays Off for Euzhan Palcy," in *Los Angeles Times*, 29 September 1989.
Rodman, Howard A., "Between Black and White," in *Elle*, October 1989.
Rosen, Marjorie, "A Woman for All Seasons: Euzhan Palcy—Director, Writer, Miracle Worker," in *Ms.* (New York), October 1989.
Denby, David, "*A Dry White Season*," in *New York*, 2 October 1989.
Kael, Pauline, "*A Dry White Season*," in *New Yorker*, 2 October 1989.
Travers, Peter, "*A Dry White Season*," in *Rolling Stone* (New York), 5 October 1989.
Kauffman, Stanley, "*A Dry White Season*," in *New Republic* (New York), 9 October 1989.
Simon, John, "*A Dry White Season*," in *National Review*, 27 October 1989.
Klawans, Stuart, "*A Dry White Season*," in *Nation* (New York), 30 October 1989.
Blake, Richard A., "*A Dry White Season*," in *America*, 18 November 1989.
Papineau, David, "*A Dry White Season*," in *Times Literary Supplement* (London), 26 January 1990.

Euzhan Palcy on the set of *A Dry White Season*.

Shipman, David, "A Dry White Season," in Contemporary Review, July 1990.

Carchidi, V., "Representing South Africa: Apartheid from Print to Film," in Film and History (Coral Gables, Florida), vol. 21, no. 1, 1991.

Nixon, R., "Cry White Season: Apartheid, Liberalism, and the American Screen," in South Atlantic Quarterly, vol. 90, no. 3, 1991.

Wellington, N., "Hollywood's Apartheid," in Jump Cut (Berkeley), May 1991.

Jowett, G. S., "Hollywood Discovers Apartheid," in Journal of Popular Film and Television (Washington, D.C.), vol. 19, no. 4, 1992.

O'Grady, Lorraine, "The Cave," in Artforum (New York), January 1992.

Magny, J., "Simeon," in Cahiers du Cinéma (Paris), January 1993.

Thirard, P. L., "Simeon," in Positif (Paris), January 1993.

Taillet, S., "Simeon," in Avant-Scène du Cinéma (Paris), February 1993.

Klady, Leonard, "Simeon," in Variety (New York), 25 October 1993.

Herndon, Gerise, "Auto-Ethnographic Impulse in Rue cases-nègres," in Literature/Film Quarterly (Salisbury, Maryland), July 1996.

Bustos, Roxann, "Sugar Cane Alley," in Library Journal (New York), 1 February 1997.

* * *

"For all the Black Shack Alleys of the world"—with these words, the opening dedication of her first feature, La Rue cases nègres (Sugar Cane Alley), Euzhan Palcy arrived on the scene of international filmmaking. The film not only garnered a César from the French Film Academy, and a Silver Lion from the Venice Film Festival, it also demonstrated that there was an audience for films with central black characters. The film proved to be remarkably successful in France; in Martinique, the setting of the story and Palcy's first home, Sugar Cane Alley outgrossed the Hollywood blockbuster of the year, E.T. The success of Palcy's initial feature led to her involvement in another landmark film, A Dry White Season, one of the few American films to depict the effects of South African apartheid, and, with Palcy at the helm, the first Hollywood production directed by a woman of color.

Growing up in Martinique, a French colony without local film or theater production—but swamped by an incessant flow of American media—Palcy became determined to be a filmmaker who created real images of her people. As a teenager, her success as a poet and songwriter led to her being asked to do a weekly poetry program on local television. While at the television station, Palcy—just 17 years old—wrote, directed, and performed in a 52-minute film entitled The Messenger. The drama, which centered on the relationship between a girl and her grandmother, and which explored the lives of workers on a banana plantation, was the first West Indian production mounted in Martinique.

Recognizing that to pursue a career as a filmmaker she would have to leave Martinique, Palcy moved to Paris in 1974. She went to film school, studied French literature at the highly competitive Sorbonne, worked as a film editor, and, for the first time, exchanged views with young African filmmakers. During this time she continued to revise her screenplay for Sugar Cane Alley. As she became acquainted with members of the French film community, Palcy received encouragement from New Wave filmmaker François Truffaut and his collaborator Suzanne Shiffman. Her work as an apprentice paid off. In 1982 the French government provided partial funding for the film. To secure funding from French television, one of the film's co-producers, Palcy wrote and directed a short entitled The Devil's Workshop,

which traced an outline of the story that would be told in Palcy's first feature.

Palcy seized upon the subject for her first full-length film when as a girl she read La Rue cases nègres, a novel by Martinique author Josef Zobel. As she has explained, reading the novel was an "event," for it was the first time in her life she had encountered work by a black writer, moreover, a black writer from her own country. Palcy's own experience growing up in Martinique, and her years of living with the story resulted in a production that was clearly the work of a filmmaker who, in the words of Stanley Kauffmann, "understands absolutely everything about the lives she is touching." After watching this story of a poor black boy's coming of age, who survives the effects of the French colonial system because of his grandmother's courage and the wisdom of Mr. M, an aged storyteller who introduces him to African and Afro-Caribbean traditions, critics such as Stuart Klawans rightly argue that "few films have conveyed so vividly the thrill of intellectual awakening."

Following the international success of Sugar Cane Alley, and returning to a subject that had been at the heart of another novel central to her growing up, Cry, the Beloved Country, Palcy worked to secure financing for a film that would, as Nina Easton explains, reveal "the horrors of apartheid through the eyes of a young black girl." Eventually recognizing that it was almost impossible to secure funding for a film without a central white character, Palcy became part of a project that took as its source André Brink's novel, A Dry White Season. Originally a Warner Bros. property and a David Puttnam production, the film, with a screenplay by Colin Welland and Euzhan Palcy was, in the end, distributed by MGM/UA and produced by Paula Weinstein, who, like her mother, Hannah Weinstein, was an experienced Hollywood executive and a champion of progressive filmmaking.

A Dry White Season, which follows a white South African schoolteacher as he is drawn into the antiapartheid movement, shows the filmmaker's efforts to bring the experience of black South Africans to the foreground—the film eliminates the novel's account of an affair between the schoolteacher (played by Donald Sutherland) and a proactive journalist (played by Susan Sarandon), and instead provides us with more detailed characterizations of the black South Africans involved. When the film was released, many reviewers argued that it was an emotionally potent film, and that it demonstrated—in contrast to other young directors whose second features represented a sellout—that Euzhan Palcy had remained true to her vision as a filmmaker. Other critics felt Palcy had not gone far enough to counter the commercial elements of the film.

Even Palcy's critics, however, recognize her remarkable ability to direct actors. For her performance in Sugar Cane Alley, veteran actress Darling Legitimus was named Best Actress at the Venice Film Festival, and in reviewing that film, Andrew Sarris argued that it was impossible to "overpraise the casting and acting which jumps out of the screen with an expressive vitality." Commenting on her direction of actors in A Dry White Season, Kauffmann underscores the fact that Palcy, who "deals empathetically with her cast ... works with economy and flair—[a] sense of movement as gesture."

In one of her most recent productions, Simeon, Palcy returned to a Caribbean setting, working to make, as she has always intended, films with real images of her people. While her work has been critiqued for individualizing narratives that explore social conditions, taken together, Euzhan Palcy's films represent a thoughtful and often brilliant response to the conventions of First World Cinema.

—Cynthia Baron

PARIS IS BURNING
USA, 1990
Director: Jennie Livingston

Production: Off White Productions. Shot in New York City, 1987 and 1989. Cost: $375,000. Funding sources included the New York State Council on the Arts, WNYC-TV, BBC-TV, and the National Endowment for the Arts. Shot on video and bounced up to 16mm (78 minutes, Todd AO sound). In 1990, a 58-minute video version screened at the New York New Festival of Gay and Lesbian Film; a short version also screened in the UK on BBC TV. The longer 16mm version premiered commercially at the Film Forum in New York City, 13-26 March 1991, and ran 17 weeks there; it opened nationwide in the United States in August 1991.

Producer: Jennie Livingston; **editor:** Jonathan Oppenheim; **co-producer:** Barry Swimar; **cinematographer:** Paul Gibson; **associate producers:** Claire Goodman and Meg McLagan; **sound recordists:** Catherine Calderon and Judy Karp; **second unit camera:** Mayrse Alberti; **additional camerawork:** William Megalos, Frank Prinzi, Alyson Denny, Ben Speth; **sound editor:** Stacia Thompson; **additional editing:** Kate Davis; **associate editor:** Carol Hillson; **production manager:** Natalie Hill; **production coordinator:** Elise Pettus; **additional associate producing:** Richard Dooley; **assistant editors:** Elizabeth Bouiss, Nancy Crumley, Melissa Hacker, Spike Lampros, Jacinta Orlando; **executive producers:** Nigel Finch for BBC Television, London, and Davis Lacy for WNYC Television, New York.

Cast (*as themselves*): Carmen, Brooke, Andre Christian, Dorian Corey, Paris Dupree, Pepper Labeija, Junior Labeija, Willi Ninja, Sandy Ninja, Kim Pendavis, Freddie Pendavis, Sol Pendavis, Avis Pendavis, Octavia Saint Laurent, Stevie Saint Laurent, Angie Xtravaganza, Bianca Xtravaganza, Danny Xtravaganza, David Xtravaganza, David Ian Xtravaganza, David the Father Xtravaganza, Venus Xtravaganza, and all of the Legendary Children and the Upcoming Children.

Awards: Los Angeles Film Critics Circle Award for Best Documentary; Grand Jury Prize for Best Documentary, Sundance Film Festival.

Publications

Book

Thernstrom, Stephan, and Abigail Thernstrom, *America in Black and White: One Nation Indivisible,* New York, 1997.

Articles

Livingston, Jennie, "The Fairer Sex," in *Aperture* (New York), Fall 1990.
Hoberman, J., "Burning Crosses and Lamé Dresses," in *Premiere* (New York), March 1991.
Brown, Joe, "*Paris Is Burning,*" in *Washington Post,* 4 August 1991.
hooks, bell, "Is Paris Burning?," in *Black Looks: Race and Representation,* Boston, 1992.
Henderson, Lisa, "*Paris Is Burning* and Academic Conservatism," in *Journal of Communication,* Spring 1992.

Waters, J., "Truth Or 'Realness,'" in *Jump Cut* (Berkeley), July 1992.
Bick, I. J., "To Be Real: Shame, Envy, and the Reflection of Self in Masquerade," in *Discourse,* Winter 1992-93.
Butler, Judith, "Gender Is Burning," in *Bodies That Matter: On the Discursive Limits of "Sex,"* New York, 1993.
Cvetkovich, Ann, "The Powers of Seeing and Being Seen: *Truth or Dare* and *Paris Is Burning,*" in *Film Theory Goes to the Movies,* edited by Jim Collins, Hilary Radner, and Ava Preacher Collins, New York, 1993.
Goldsby, Jackie, "Queens of Language," in *Queer Looks: Perspectives on Lesbian and Gay Film and Video,* edited by Martha Gever, John Greyson, and Pratibha Parmar, New York, 1993.
Taubin, Amy, "Queer Male Cinema and Feminism," in *Women and Film: A Sight and Sound Reader,* edited by Pam Cook and Philip Dodd, Philadelphia, 1993.
Gray, Louise, "*Paris Is Burning,*" in *Sight and Sound* (London), April 1993.
Harper, Philip Brian, "'The Subversive Edge': *Paris Is Burning,* Social Critique, and the Limits of Subjective Agency," in *Diacritics* (Ithaca, New York), Summer/Fall 1994.
Crowe, Patrick, "No Place Like Home: Homelessness, Identity and Sexuality in American Queer Cinema," in *CineAction!* (Toronto), August 1994.

* * *

Jennie Livingston was a Yale graduate in her mid-twenties when she began to collect the footage for her documentary *Paris Is Burning.* Raised in middle-class Los Angeles, Livingston had been exploring the terms of her own lesbianism, using photography to document gay lives. She first encountered black and Latino men voguing—adopting for themselves the appearance and poses of female fashion models, and transmuting them into competitive dance—at the Gay and Lesbian Community Center in Greenwich Village. The voguers explained to Livingston that, since the 1960s, gay men in Manhattan have been holding "balls," or fashion shows organized as contests. The goal is to see who can be most "real"—absolutely convincing—in an ever-widening range of "categories" of classed and gendered identity, such as "Femme Queen," for female impersonators, or business "Executive," for poor gay men in rich, male drag. Livingston wanted to use a movie to record her take on the balls: to capture the splendor of the (wo)men's bodies in motion, but also, she told Joe Brown, to allow the "children," as the ball-goers name themselves, to speak.

Paris Is Burning dwells at complicated intersections of gender, class, race, and sexuality which made its funding difficult. It suggests that gender is far more constructed than conventional ideas would dictate, without, however, feeding into the notion that, because gender is not rigidly congruent with biological sex, the gender identity of oneself or of one's desired objects is endlessly confused or in flux. *Paris* also presents painfully ironic evidence against the idea (currently fashionable among critics of affirmative action) that class differentiation is somehow the fault of the underclass and its inability to master the manners and mores of the dominant culture. When Stephan and Abigail Thernstrom suggest in 1997 that poor blacks should learn "how to dress" in order to find good work, Livingston's film jumps to mind. The legendary children know exactly how to dress, and how much dress makes the (wo)man. But knowing does not seem to end the racism and homophobia that keep them isolated from their biological families, from education, and from lucrative, legal jobs.

In liberal, humanist fashion, *Paris* negotiates the charge that its protagonists' desires just make them cultural dupes, as they re-embody all the social "categories" (supermodels, soldiers, suburban housewives, "buppies") whose privilege oppresses them. Both the film and, to varying degrees, its heroes seem aware that the voguers' intense wish to live out the American dream at once sustains them, gives them hope and community, and copes with but fails to change the system that (over)values whiteness, wealth, masculinity, and heterosexuality. The film presents the case that the benefits weigh at least as strongly as the deficits, however. Outcast by their relatives, the ball-goers find families in "houses," or groups all taking the same last name (from a famous designer or "legendary" ball walker). Each house has a father and, most powerful, a mother.

The ball-goers' identification with patriarchal gender roles, and with rich and famous, usually white, heterosexuals does keep them alienated from their "true" categories of identity, able to express their joys and solidarity as gay men of color only in code. But, even in its form as a double bind, their coding of their own energy and pride literally in costume gives them the means to express their systematically denied likeness, their fundamental human connection, to the supposedly superior "others." And it also expresses, however implicitly, the unfairness and the mutual danger of the dominant culture's refusal to recognize that likeness, or to allow unarbitrated differences to flourish.

The strains of the double bind linger around the edges of both the balls and the film. A prime example is the ball category of "bangee girl or boy"—or "the kid who robbed you on your way here tonight." The gay men and transsexuals—who sometimes "mop" or steal the designer clothes they need—take on the trappings of gay-bashing gang kids. Although it is otherwise never so open, such a looping catch-22 occurs in all the ball categories. Each one circles between self-empowerment and self-abnegation, with its convolutions interminable—until, of course, though the film never explicitly says it, laws and attitudes are changed to extend equal opportunities and protection to all.

Critic bell hooks faults Livingston for failing to either mark or question the limits of her own mediating presence as a white woman studying a black culture. It is true that *Paris* takes the form of a conventional, "objective" documentary with no visible author. But Livingston's use of title cards (usually terms that the interview subjects define), and, occasionally, of her own offscreen voice asking a brief question, combines with her sound-mixing strategy to formalize the idea that the film is not a transparent presentation but a structure. The sound/image relationships especially suggest that *Paris* is constructed by an authoring agency that literally wants to hear what the black and Latino voices have to say, (even if) from a position that is an outsider's with regard to the particular intersections of the social and the individual that shape their bodies.

At key moments the film's audio and video tracks work in a sort of counterpoint. Images of the balls predominate, but usually they are accompanied by a voice-over whose connection to the show-in-progress is less direct or organic than conceptual. Livingston uses synch sound to present the voices of her interview subjects, as they talk to the camera in their rooms or outdoors. They explain the history and language of their subculture, and its driving practices and desires. When Livingston cuts from a "talking head" speaker to the ballroom action, however, she mixes the ongoing voice-over at a louder volume than the sounds of the ball itself, the disco records and the MCs. Significantly, we hear very little from the performers themselves while they "walk" onstage or backstage at a ball. The viewer is thus kept at a certain remove from the balls proper, his or her perceptions of them always mediated through the ideas and sto-

ries—and socially enforced marginalization—of the interviewees. The movie presents its subjects' outsider status to the viewer as another, fellow outsider. About their extreme impoverishment and in empathy with their resilient resourcefulness, we are to take action as we will.

—Susan Knobloch

PARKER, Claire
American director and animator

Born: Boston, Massachusetts, 31 August 1906. **Family:** Married the director and animator Alexander Alexeieff, 1941 (died 1982). **Career:** 1931—with Alexander Alexeieff co-invented pinboard animation; 1933—co-creator of *Night on Bald Mountain,* a critical success, but commercially unmarketable; 1935-39—with Alexeieff and other collaborators (Georges Violet, Alexeieff's wife Alexandra Grinevsky, and others) collaborated on some 25 short advertising films that were shown in movie theaters, some with original musical scores by major composers such as Poulenc, Auric, and Milhaud; 1935-36—in Alexeieff's absence, directed documentary film on Rubens and one advertising film (*Étude sur l'harmonie des lignes*) on her own; 1940—emigrated to United States with Alexeieff and his family when Nazis invaded France; 1941—married Alexeieff soon after his divorce from Grinevsky, settled in White Plains, New York; 1943—created *En Passant,* second pinboard animation production, for the newly formed National Film Board of Canada; 1947—returned to Paris; 1952-64—created more advertising films with Alexeieff, using many different techniques, including "totalization" with compound pendulums; 1957—co-designed logo used on films of French distribution company Cocinor; 1962—co-produced pinboard prologue to Orson Welles's *The Trial*; 1962-79—worked with Alexeieff on three more pinboard films, *The Nose, Pictures at an Exhibition,* and *Three Moods,* and assisted him with pinboard illustrations for several books (Dostoyevsky's *The Gambler* and *Notes from Underground* and Pasternak's *Doctor Zhivago*). **Died:** 3 October 1981.

Films as Director

1935   *Étude sur l'harmonie des lignes* (advertising film)
1936   *Rubens* (art film)

Pinboard Animation Films as Co-Director and Co-Animator with Alexander Alexeieff

1933   ***Une Nuit sur le Mont Chauve*** (*Night on Bald Mountain*)
1943   *En Passant*
1962   Prologue to *Le Procès* (*The Trial*) (Welles)
1963   *Le Nez* (*The Nose*)
1972   *Tableaux d'une exposition* (*Pictures at an Exhibition*)
1980   *Trois Thèmes* (*Three Moods*)

Films as Co-Animator with Alexander Alexeieff and Others

(Advertising and Sponsored Films)

1935   *La Belle au bois dormant* (*Sleeping Beauty*) (puppet film)

1936-39 *Parade des chapeaux*; *Le Trône de France*; *Grands Feux*;
         La Crème Simon; *Les Vêtements Sigrand*; *Huilor*; *L'eau
         d'Evian*; *Les Fonderies Martin*; *Balatrum*; *Les Oranges
         de Jaffa* (3 films); *Les Cigarettes Davros*; *Gulf Stream*;
         Les Gaines Roussel; *Cenpa*; *Le Gaz* (unfinished)
1951-66 *Fumées* (first use of compound pendulum); *Masques*;
         Nocturne; *Pure beauté*; *Rîmes*; *Le Buisson ardent*; *La Sève
         de la terre*; *Quatre Temps*; *Bain d'X* (Bendix); *Constance*;
         Anonyme; *Osram* (for TV); *Cent pour cent*; Cocinor logo;
         Automation; *La Dauphine Java*; *Divertissement*; *L'eau*

Publications by Parker (with Alexander Alexeieff)

Books

A. Alexeieff, C. Parker: Films et eaux-fortes, 1925-75, exhibition
   catalogue, Chateau d'Annecy, 1975.
Entretien avec A. Alexeieff et C. Parker, by N. Salomon, Annecy, 1980.

Articles

"Circuit fermé!" in *Cinéma* (Paris), no. 14, 1957.
"L'Écran d'épingles," in *Technicien du Film* (Paris), no. 27, 1957.
"Reflections on Motion Picture Animation," in *Film Culture* (New
   York), no. 32, 1964.
Script, no. 10/12, 1964.
"Synthèse cinématographique des mouvements artificiels," in *IDHEC*
   (Paris), 1966.
Image et Son (Paris), no. 207, 1967.
"The Synthesis of Artificial Movements in Motion Picture Projection,"
   in *Film Culture* (New York), no. 48-49, 1970.
"Chère Marthe," in *Bulletin d'Information ASIFA,* no. 1, 1972.
"Alféoni par Alexeieff," edited by L. Olteanu, in *Nous Mêmes,* ASIFA,
   Bucharest, 1973.
"Le Chant d'ombres et de lumières de 1,250,000 épingles," edited by
   H. Arnault, in *Cinéma Pratique* (Paris), no. 123, 1973.
Giusti, M., "Cinema d'animazione: strategia e tattica," in *Filmcritica*
   (Rome), no. 31, 1980.

Publications on Parker

Books

Starr, Cecile, *Discovering the Movies,* New York, 1972.
Russett, R., and C. Starr, *Experimental Animation,* New York, 1976.
Acker, Ally, *Reel Women: Pioneers of the Cinema, 1896 to the
   Present,* New York, 1991.

Articles

Cheronnet. L., *"Une Nuit sur le Mont Chauve,* film en gravure animée par A.
   Alexeieff et C. Parker," in *Art et Décoration* (Paris), no. 63, 1934.
Alberti, Walter, in *Il cinema di animazione,* Rome, 1957.
Starr, Cecile, "Notes on *The Nose,*" in *Film Society Review* (New York),
   November 1965.
Rains, R. R., "The Road Less Travelled," in *Lens & Speaker* (Univer-
   sity of Illinois Visual Aids Service), 15 January 1977.
Obituary in *Revue du Cinéma* (Paris), December 1981.
Bendazzi, G., "Le courage de se nomer artiste," in *Plateau,* no. 5, 1984.
CinémAction (Conde-sur-Noireau), no. 51, April 1989.

Films

Alexeieff at the Pinboard, produced by Cinema Nouveau, Paris, 1960
   (English version produced by Cecile Starr, 1972).
Le Buisson ardent, 1962.
Pinscreen, produced by the National Film Board of Canada, 1972.
Annecy Impromptu, produced by S.F.P. Films, Paris, 1976.

* * *

Claire Parker's unique and memorable place in the history of
independent, non-cartoon animation is permanently and inextricably
linked to that of her partner/husband Alexander Alexeieff. For some
50 years Alexeieff and Parker worked together, first on the invention
of the world's first pinboard (1932); then on their celebrated *Night
on Bald Mountain* (1933) and later pinboard films; between times,
on a succession of innovative advertising films; and for many decades as promoters of animation as a fine art. Sometimes they introduced themselves as the artist and the animator, but even their close
friends have found it impossible to know exactly who did what.

Parker always maintained that Alosha (his Russian nickname)
was the genius, but without her many talents and steadfast dedication, his genius would certainly not have been expressed in motion-
picture animation. Although her role was secondary and supportive,
there is no indication that throughout their long relationship she
aspired to anything more.

On only two occasions, early in her career, did she assume full
filmmaking responsibilities: in 1936 when she shot a color art film
on the Rubens exhibition at the Orangerie in Paris, and later during
Alexeieff's absence when she directed a color advertising film of her
own. For the remainder of her career in film, Parker remained
Alexeieff's "constant collaborator."

When Parker and Alexeieff met in Paris in the late 1920s, she was
a young American studying painting and drawing abroad, and he
was a young Russian emigré already considered a master illustrator
of fine books. She asked him for lessons in engraving copper, wood,
and stone, but soon they were working together on a device he had
begun working on—a device to make "animated engravings" (*gra-
vures animées*), engravings that could move. The term was quickly
abandoned for "pinboard" animation, later changed to "pinscreen" (a
more accurate translation of the French *l'écran d'épingles*).

Their first "apparatus for producing images" was patented in Europe and the United States in Claire Parker's name alone, perhaps
because she, with help from her wealthy Boston family, had financed
the invention, along with the production of their first film. Both of
them felt sure that marketable uses of the pinboard would more than
repay Parker's investment and might also provide opportunities for
work in the highly paid film industry.

Their first film, *Night on Bald Mountain,* won wide acclaim in
European art circles, and is still considered one of the most important
animation films ever made. Parker's mathematical and musical talents helped her synchronize Alexeieff's images to a phonograph
recording of Moussorgsky's symphonic music "with the precision
of a twenty-fourth of a second." It could not have been easy, with
only the most primitive equipment at hand, just a few years after the
introduction of sound-on-film.

Program notes of the London Film Society's 1935 showing incor-
rectly gave Parker first billing ("Engravings by C. Parker and
Alexeieff"), but dozens of subsequent reviews and listings failed to
even mention her name. To be accurate and fair, it should be made
clear that the film's witches, goblins, and other creatures of the night,

disappearing and reappearing, come straight from Russian folklore and from Alexeieff's boundless imagination. But the careful filming of these images, the sound analysis, and synchronization were Parker's self-taught achievements—along with her operation of the reverse side of the pinboard.

But no commercial use was found for a short film, however magical, that had taken 18 months to complete. To earn enough money to support himself and his wife and daughter, Alexeieff began making advertising films, the first in color to be shown publicly in France. Here Claire Parker felt she made her major contribution, since she (a painter) worked more comfortably in color than he (a graphic artist). In the United States during World War II, Parker became Mrs. Alexeieff following his divorce from his first wife. On their return to France in 1947, she took on new roles as housekeeper, hostess, stepmother to his daughter Svetlana (and later step-grandmother to her four children—one of whom—Alexandre Rockwell—later became a filmmaker himself).

Having no children of their own, which had been part of their marriage agreement, Claire and Alosha welcomed into their animation family a young Canadian animator, Jacques Drouin, who had mastered the pinscreen technique and made a magical film called *Mindscape.* This may have spurred them on to even more intricate techniques in their own pinscreen films, using multiple in-camera loops, or a small pinscreen revolving in front of a larger one, techniques requiring even more patience and precision on Parker's part. For her the reward seemed to be that her hard work allowed her to become what she called the "spellbound spectator" of a true artist's visions and visual memories.

—Cecile Starr

PARMAR, Pratibha
British director

Born: 1955, to Indian parents in Kenya; family immigrated to England in 1967. **Education:** Postgraduate studies at the Centre for Contemporary Cultural Studies at the University of Birmingham. **Awards:** Audience award for Best Short Documentary, San Francisco Festival, for *Khush,* 1991; Best Historical Documentary, National Black Programming Consortium, for *A Place of Rage,* 1991; Frameline Award, 1993. **Address:** c/o 78 Fonthill Road, Finsbury Park, London N4 3HT, England.

Films as Director

1986   *Emergence* (short for TV)
1987   *A Plague on You* (for TV)
1988   *Sari Red* (short); *ReFraming AIDs* (doc)
1989   *Memory Pictures* (doc)
1990   *Flesh and Paper* (doc, short for TV)
1991   *Khush* (doc, short for TV) (+ pr); *A Place of Rage* (doc for TV)
1992   *Double the Trouble, Twice the Fun* (doc, short for TV)
1993   *Warrior Marks* (doc for TV) (+ pr)
1994   *The Colour of Britain* (doc)
1996   *Jodie: An Icon* (short)
1997   *Memsahib Rita* (short)

Publications by Parmar

Books

The Empire Strikes Back: Race and Racism in 70s Britain, London, 1982.
Editor, with Pearlie McNeill and Marie McShea, *Through the Break: Women in Personal Crisis,* London 1986.
Charting the Journey: Writings by Black and Third World Women, London, 1988.
Editor, with Martha Gever and John Greyson, *Queer Looks: Perspectives on Lesbian and Gay Film and Video,* London, 1993.
With Alice Walker, *Warrior Marks: Female Genital Mutilation and the Sexual Blinding of Women,* New York, 1993.

Articles

"Black Feminism: The Politics of Articulation," in *Identity: Community, Culture, Difference,* edited by Jonathan Rutherford, London, 1990.
With others, "Queer Questions," in *Sight and Sound* (London), September 1992.
"That Moment of Emergence," in *Queer Looks: Perspectives on Lesbian and Gay Film and Video,* edited by Martha Gever, Pratibha Parmar, and John Greyson, London, 1993.
With Joy Chamberlain, Isaac Julien, and Stuart Marshall, "Filling the Lack in Everyone Is Quite Hard Work, Really...," in *Queer Looks: Perspectives on Lesbian and Gay Film and Video,* edited by Martha Gever, Pratibha Parmar, and John Greyson, London, 1993.

Publications on Parmar

Books

Murray, Raymond, *Images in the Dark: An Encyclopedia of Gay and Lesbian Film and Video,* Philadelphia, 1994.
Foster, Gwendolyn Audrey, *Women Film Directors: An International Bio-Critical Dictionary,* Westport, Connecticut, 1995.
Foster, Gwendolyn Audrey, *Women Filmmakers of the African and Asian Diaspora,* Carbondale, Illinois, 1997.

Articles

Tsui, Kitty, "From Margin to Center," in *Advocate* (Los Angeles), 22 October 1991.
"Warrior Marks," in *off our backs,* December 1993.

* * *

Pratibha Parmar's films reflect her experiences as a woman of the Asian and African diaspora, as a lesbian, and as a political and cultural activist. She attributes her desire to be a filmmaker to the anger and rage kindled by her first playground encounter with "Paki-bashing" schoolmates. Her resistance to being defined as a "marginal" person, as someone who can be pigeonholed according to race, gender, or sexual orientation, is a constant theme in her work.

Parmar was one of the founding members of the first black lesbian group in Britain in 1984 and discovered within that group a sense of community based on shared experiences and cultural backgrounds. She came to filmmaking from a background of activism rather than from film or art school. In her first experimental video, *Emergence,*

Parmar uses interviews, poetry, and performance art, together with the juxtaposition of evocative images, to present issues of racial identity confronting women of the diaspora. The violence directed against these women is the subject of *Sari Red,* a short film commemorating Kalbinder Kaur Hayre who died when she and two other Asian women were run down by white racists. This film features the "look back," a confrontational technique used first on a poster created by the publishing house Black Women Talk, of which Parmar was also a founding member. The poster was one in a series called "In Our Own Image," and pictures a young South Asian woman practicing self-defense and confronting the viewer with the warning: "If anyone calls me a Paki, I'll bash their heads in." This "look-back" is a device used by Parmar in her films to redirect a gaze usually used as a means of domination back upon the viewer. In *Sari Red,* this gaze is found in the eyes of the mourners, of the three dolls symbolizing the victims of the racist attack, and in the eyes woven into the red sari featured in the film.

Parmar's choice of themes for her work has much to do with current issues, and reflects her own interest in activism. The British government's homophobic AIDS-awareness campaign of the 1980s inspired *A Plague on You,* produced by the Lesbian and Gay Media Group for British television, and *ReFraming AIDS.* The latter film brought Parmar criticism from fellow black lesbians because it included interviews with black and white gay men. *ReFraming AIDS* saw Parmar venture outside the black lesbian "community," and explore a broader territory.

This exploration continued in Parmar's next three works, *Memory Pictures, Flesh and Paper,* and *Khush,* which explore the attributes, histories, and eroticisms of individual lesbian and gay Asians. *Khush,* made for Channel 4's gay and lesbian series *Out on Tuesday,* won an award for Best Documentary Short at the San Francisco Festival in 1991, and has been shown at many lesbian and gay film festivals. In *Khush,* which is an Urdu word meaning "ecstatic pleasure," Parmar uses film clips, fantasy sequences, an erotic dance performance, and statements from western South Asian lesbians and gays to present the complexities of lesbian and gay identities. This interest in presenting the rich diversities that exist among gays and lesbians is further expressed in *Double the Trouble, Twice the Fun,* which features the gay Indian writer Firdaus Kanga, who also happens to be disabled.

A Place of Rage explores the role of women in the American civil rights movement, a study that Parmar undertook to further her understanding of racist violence and oppression. The documentary features interviews with Angela Davis, June Jordan, and writer Alice Walker, and is frequently screened at lesbian and gay film festivals. A collaboration with Walker on the documentary *Warrior Marks* followed in 1993. The film was inspired by Walker's book, *Possessing the Secret of Joy,* and treats the subject of female genital mutilation. Filming was done for *Warrior Marks* in Africa, Britain, and the United States and features interviews with women who have themselves endured this procedure, as well as those who perform it. In the book *Warrior Marks: Female Genital Mutilation and the Sexual Blinding of Women,* written by Walker and Parmar, which chronicles the making of the film, Parmar discusses the problems in making a documentary on such a complex issue, one which involves race, culture, and the rights of women and young girls. In *Warrior Marks,* as in *Sari Red, Flesh and Paper, A Place of Rage,* and *Khush,* dance is used as an enhancement of the theme, in this case expressing joy of sexuality as well as the sorrow of its loss.

Parmar must have found the making of *The Colour of Britain* very satisfying, as it features the work of South Asian artists who are having an impact on British culture. The documentary includes interviews with sculptor Anish Kapoor, choreographer Shobana Jeyasingh, and theater director Jatinder Verma, as well as examples of their work. Parmar has ventured into a new area of exploration with the short drama *Memsahib Rita,* made for BBC Television, a thriller in which questions of mixed race play a part.

—Jean Edmunds

PASCAL, Christine
French director, writer, and actress

Born: Lyons, France, 29 November 1953. **Family:** Married producer-writer Robert Boner. **Career:** 1973—made her film debut as an actress in *Black Thursday*; 1974—appeared in her first feature directed by Bertrand Tavernier, *The Clockmaker*; 1979—directed her first feature, *Felicité.* **Awards:** Best Script, Montreal Film Festival, and Louis Delluc Prize for Directing, for *The Little Prince Said,* 1992. **Died:** Suicide, outside Paris, 30 August 1996.

Films as Director and Writer/Co-Writer

1979 *Felicité* (+ ro)
1984 *La Garce* (*The Bitch*)
1988 *Zanzibar*
1992 *Le Petit prince à dit* (*The Little Prince Said*)
1995 *Adultere (mode d'emploi)* (*Adultery [A User's Manual]*)

Other Films

1973 *Les Guichets du Louvre* (*Black Thursday*) (Mitrani) (ro)
1974 *L'Horloger de Saint-Paul* (*The Clockmaker*) (Tavernier) (ro as Liliane Terrini)
1975 *Que la fête commence...* (*Let Joy Reign Supreme...*) (Tavernier) (ro as Emilie)
1976 *Le Juge et l'assassin* (*The Judge and the Assassin*) (Tavernier) (ro); *La Meilleure façon de marcher* (*The Best Way*) (C. Miller) (ro as Chantal)
1977 *Les Indiens sont encore loin* (*The Indians Are Still Far Away*) (Moraz) (ro); *Des enfants gâtés* (*Spoiled Children*) (Tavernier) (ro) (+ co-sc)
1979 *Panny z Wilka* (*The Girls from Wilko*) (Wajda) (ro as Tunia)
1980 *Pepi, Luci, Bom y otras chicas de montón* (Almodóvar) (ro); *Au bon beurre* (Molinaro) (ro)
1983 *Coup de foudre* (*Entre nous*; *Between Us*; *At First Sight*) (Kurys) (ro as Sarah); *Entre tinieblas* (*Into the Dark*; *The Sisters of Darkness*) (Almodóvar) (ro)
1984 *Train d'enfer* (Hanin) (ro as Isabelle)
1985 *Elsa, Elsa* (Haudepin) (title role); *Private Show* (Kayko) (pr); *Signé Charlotte* (*Sincerely Charlotte*; *Signed Charlotte*) (Huppert) (ro as Christine)
1986 *'Round Midnight* (*Autour de minuit*) (Tavernier) (ro as Sylvie)
1987 *Le Grand chemin* (*The Grand Highway*) (Hubert) (ro as Claire)
1988 *La Couleur du vent* (Granier-Deferre) (ro); *La Travestie* (Boisset) (ro as Christine)

1989 *Promis...Jure!* (Monnet) (ro)
1990 *The Island* (Leitao) (ro as Linda Walsh)
1991 *Rien que des mensonges* (*Nothing but Lies*) (Muret) (ro as Lise); *La Femme de l'amant* (Frank) (ro as Ludmilla)
1994 *Le Sourire* (*The Smile*) (C. Miller and Othenin-Girard) (ro); *Regarde les hommes tomber* (*See How They Fall*) (Audiard) (ro as Sandrine); *Les Patriotes* (*The Patriots*) (Rochant) (ro as Laurence)

Publications by Pascal

Articles

Interview with C. Arnaud, in *Revue du Cinéma* (Paris), June 1979.
Interview with P. Carcassonne and F. Cuel, in *Cinématographe* (Paris), June 1979.
Interview with F. Strauss and C. Taboulay, in *Cahiers du Cinéma* (Paris), November 1992.
Interview with M. Jean, in *24 Images,* December 1992/January 1993.
"*Adultere (mode d'emploi),*" in *Cahiers du Cinéma* (Paris), May 1993.
With others, "Ceux qui filment...," in *Cahiers du Cinéma* (Paris), March 1994.

Publications on Pascal

Books

Comédiennes aujourd'hui: Isabelle Adjani, Isabelle Huppert, Dominique Laffin, Miou Miou, Christine Pascal, Maria Schneider: au micro et sous le regard de Jean-Luc Douin, Paris, 1980.
Foster, Gwendolyn Audrey, *Women Film Directors: An International Bio-Critical Dictionary,* Westport, Connecticut, 1995.

Articles

Clouzot, C., "Entretien à trois roix; 2 femmes, 1 homme, 1 scenario," in *Ecran* (Paris), 15 October 1977.
"*La Meilleure façon de marcher,*" in *Revue du Cinéma* (Paris) no. 331, 1978.
Fuente, L. de la, "Propos d'auteur: Christine Pascal," in *Cinéma* (Paris), May 1979.
Mazurelle, J., "La pensées de Christine Pascal," in *Amis du Film de la Television* (Brussels), October 1979.
Derobert, E., "Christine Pascal," in *Positif* (Paris), February 1986.
Le Roux, H., "Christine Pascal," in *Cahiers du Cinéma* (Paris), June 1989.
Parra, D., "Christine Pascal," in *Mensuel du Cinéma* (Paris), April 1993.
Taboulay, C., "Christine Pascal à l'ecriture," in *Cahiers du Cinéma* (Paris), May 1993.
Obituary in *Variety* (New York), 7-13 October 1996.

* * *

From the mid-1970s through the early 1990s, Christine Pascal had starring or supporting roles as girlfriends and mothers, students and schoolteachers in more than two dozen European-made features. While never blossoming into a major international star, she lent charm and depth to films directed by Claude Miller, Pedro Almodóvar,

Andrzej Wajda, Diane Kurys, and, most especially, Bertrand Tavernier. She appeared in a half-dozen Tavernier films and, most significantly, co-scripted (as well as starred in) one, *Spoiled Children*. This blatantly autobiographical film casts Michel Piccoli as a famous filmmaker/writer named Bernardi who rents an apartment in a high-rise in order to work on a new script. The real world intrudes as he becomes involved in a landlord-tenant dispute and commences an affair with a neighbor (played by Pascal), a sensitive young woman who is half his age.

The six features Pascal directed (all of which she either scripted or co-scripted) also are heavily autobiographical. Collectively, they are disturbing, revealing, achingly personal psychological portraits. In them, Pascal elicits a fascination with male and female sexuality and the jumble of feelings people experience over sexual issues. The films are punctuated by raw emotion, and jarring sequences illustrating erotic sexual encounters with strangers. All of her characters—and especially her psychologically unhinged heroines—experience deep emotional turmoil, attempt to exorcise childhood demons, are haunted by death, act out sexually, or become consumed by sexual fantasies.

Pascal directed her first feature, *Felicité,* when she was 25 years old. It is her lone directorial effort in which she stars, and she casts herself in the title role: a young woman who is spending an evening with her lover, who meets a female friend whom he invites to join them. Felicité then is overcome by jealousy. She returns home by herself, at which point she begins drinking nonstop. Via hallucinations, she recalls her childhood and her domineering mother, and she plays out sexual fantasies (including some anonymous copulation and a striptease in a cheap club).

In *The Bitch,* Pascal's heroine is a young woman who jumps between her gangster boyfriend and a policeman. In *Zanzibar,* she is a drug-addicted actress. In *The Little Prince Said,* she is an emotionally unstrung actress. In *Adultery (A User's Manual),* she is a married, career-driven architect who plays extramarital sexual games with a friend. Pascal may only have produced *Private Show,* a film directed by Sixto Kayko, but its heroine—a young woman who dances in a private sex club in order to alleviate the pain of her child's death—is linked to those in her own films.

Pascal's two most mature films are her last. *The Little Prince Said* is a sincere and stirring drama about a ten-year-old girl who is diagnosed with a lethal brain tumor. While the child can accept her impending demise, the same cannot be said for her divorced parents: the actress, and a doctor who is used to being in command of his life. *Adultery (A User's Manual)* is a pungent exploration of the professional aspirations and personal/sexual/romantic needs of contemporary men and women. It is the story of married architects who work as a team and are awaiting word if they have won a major competition. As they do so, both characters act out their trepidation via sexual promiscuity.

Meanwhile, *Zanzibar* is effective as an exploration of the frenzied world of independent filmmaking—a world Pascal knew all-too-well—in a scenario that focuses on three characters: a producer who is attempting to secure financing for a project even though there is no script; the actress; and a tyrannical director. *Zanzibar* works as a reality test for anyone who might romanticize the "artistic" process of filmmaking.

In the program guide of the 1995 Toronto Film Festival, Kay Armatage ended her description of *Adultery (A User's Manual)* by noting that, "If there is a new breed of French cinema that combines Godard's street-smarts, Beineix's sexiness, post-modern cultural knowledge and an independent's immediacy, Christine Pascal is one director to watch." Tragically, Pascal was unable to exorcise her demons artistically or otherwise—and *Adultery (A User's Manual)* was to be her final film. A year after its release, she committed suicide, at age 42, as reported in *Variety,* by "throwing herself out the window of a clinic on the outskirts of Paris where she had apparently been battling depression."

—Rob Edelman

PENG Xiaolian
Chinese director

Born: Shanghai, 26 June 1953. **Education:** Attended Beijing Film Academy, 1978-82; visiting scholar at New York University, 1989-90. **Career:** 1969-78—sent to the countryside during the Cultural Revolution; 1976-78—actress in the Yi Chun County Opera Group; 1979—while in school directed her first television film, *Good-bye Yesterday,* then became assistant director for *Camel Xiang Zi;* 1982—upon graduation was appointed director at the Shanghai Film Studio; 1982-85—co-director and assistant director on four features; 1986—assigned to direct her first feature, a children's film, *Me and My Classmates;* 1989—her second feature, *Women's Story,* is temporarily banned in April by the Film Bureau; on 14 June her third feature, *Random Thoughts,* is canceled halfway through production. **Awards:** Bronze Medal, Chinese Television Competition, for *Good-bye Yesterday,* 1979; Best Film Script, Shanghai Young People's Cultural Competition, for *Come Back in the Summertime,* 1985; Golden Rooster Award, Best Children's Film, and Best Film and Best Director, Chinese Children's Film Competition, for *Me and My Classmates,* 1986; People's Choice Award, Hawaii International Film Festival, and Special Jury Prize, Créteil International Women's Film Festival, for *Women's Story,* 1987. **Address:** c/o International Film Circuit, Post Office Box 1151, Old Chelsea Station, New York, NY 10011, U.S.A.

Films as Director

1979   *Good-bye Yesterday* (for TV)
1982   *The Assistant Lawyer* (co-d)
1986   *Me and My Classmates* (+ co-sc)
1987   *Nüren de gushi* (*Women's Story*) (+ co-sc)

Other Films

1980   *Camel Xiang Zi* (asst d)
1983   *Golden Autumn* (asst d); *The Unusual Tourney* (asst d)
1985   *The Midnight Songs* (asst d); *Come Back in the Summertime* (sc)
1989   *The Last Trial* (sc)

Publication by Peng

Article

Interview with Chris Berry, in *Camera Obscura* (Berkeley), vol. 18, 1988.

Publication on Peng

Article

Berry, Chris, "The Viewing Subject and Chinese Cinema," in *New Chinese Cinemas: Forms, Identities, Politics,* edited by Nick Browne and others, Cambridge, England, 1994.

*   *   *

Along with Li Shaohong and Ning Ying, Peng Xiaolian is one of the few women who was graduated from the directing class of the Beijing Film Academy in 1982, and is therefore a member of the acclaimed "Fifth Generation" of Chinese directors. Born into a family of intellectuals (her father was a former Minister of Propaganda, her mother a translator) severely persecuted during the 1950s (her father was arrested when she was two and died in prison) and throughout the Cultural Revolution (during which her mother, then her brother were also arrested), Peng was sent to the countryside, like many "urban educated youths," and stayed there nine years. After the fall of the Gang of Four, schools and universities reopened, and, in order to escape the countryside, Peng applied to the Beijing Film Academy, where her schoolmates were other victims of the Cultural Revolution: Chen Kaige, Zhang Yimou, Tian Zhuangzhuang. Fifth Generation filmmakers shared the same experience of having had their childhood and teenage years cut short by the Cultural Revolution, and they all entered the Beijing Film Academy with hopes for a better, more creative life, and the possibility of pursuing artistic and formal experiments that were previously impossible.

Gender bias, however, still played a role and Peng found it was more difficult for a woman than for a man to be given a directing job. Her first assignment was a children's movie, whose original screenplay was "so bad" that she had to revise it six times. The film, however, was successful, which gave her credibility as a director, and allowed her to fight for her next production, a story she had co-written which was inspired by her intimate knowledge of peasant women. Criticized as a "bad movie" by most Chinese film critics, *Women's Story* was a huge success when screened at the Hawaii International Film Festival. Unfortunately, this attracted the attention of the Chinese Film Bureau, especially a newspaper article asserting that, since Peng was showing a peasant woman going into hiding to give birth to her second baby (in the hope of having a son), the film implicitly criticized China's one-child-per-family policy. The film was banned, but circulated in international circles in video form, and eventually the ban was lifted.

In *Women's Story,* only the point of view of the female protagonists is shown. Men are mostly kept off-screen. For the subject of the film is not how the three protagonists—Xiao Feng, "Lai's mother," and Jing Xiang—relate to the men in their lives, but how they find strength with or without them. Feng's one-night stand in the city is not an act of love, but a challenge to the life patriarchal society wants to impose on her as an "unmarriageable" girl. The older woman, defined only as "Lai's mother" (meaning she has borne a son), first reacts in a traditional way, upset at Feng's "shame." She eventually learns to respect the younger woman's decision, which implies a new understanding on her part. Xiang's revolt is clearer: arranged marriage is the stuff Chinese melodramas are made of. The socialist revolution eliminated the practice of selling girls as concubines or forcing them into marriage. But in the countryside, where kinship systems are economically determined and peasants are very poor, a young woman might have to accept her parents' decision in order to improve the family finances. Xiang's union to a man she abhors is a way to make her brother's marriage possible. A good Chinese daughter, she first tearfully submits. Later, she escapes to join Feng and "Lai's mother" when they leave the village to sell wool. Structurally, it is Xiang's story that brackets the often-humorous travels of the three women across China. What launches the narrative is her upcoming marriage; what closes it is the image of her husband arriving to retrieve his conjugal "property," while Feng and "Lai's mother" stand beside her. Will patriarchy win? Will Xiang be defeated? Significantly, the film stops here. *Women's Story* is situated within the space the three protagonists have created for themselves. When this space is threatened, the filmmaker remains silent.

After *Women's Story*, Peng spent two years researching a film about the writer Ba Jin, once a part of the May Fourth Movement of prerevolutionary intellectuals, who, in 1955, agreed to write an article attacking the poet Hu Feng (like Peng's father, Hu Feng was subsequently imprisoned for more than two decades). Later, Ba Jin courageously asserted, against the grain of political propaganda, that the Chinese people as a whole, and not only the reviled Gang of Four, bore responsibility for the excesses committed during the Cultural Revolution. Production for *Random Thoughts* started in the spring of 1989, and on 14 June, four days after the Tiananmen Square massacre, it was halted.

Peng received a fellowship to be a visiting scholar at New York University, and has lived mainly in the United States since. A prolific writer, she has continued publishing many stories in Chinese, and recently directed a television series in China.

— Bérénice Reynaud

PERRY, Eleanor
American writer

Born: Eleanor Rosenfeld in Cleveland, Ohio, 1915. **Education:** Attended Western Reserve University, Cleveland, M.A. in social work. **Family:** Married 1) Leo G. Bayer (divorced 1959), two children: Bill and Ann; 2) the director Frank Perry, 1960 (divorced 1971). **Career:** 1943—first of several books written with Leo Bayer; 1959—play (co-written with Bayer) produced in New York, *Third Best Sport*; 1962—first of several film scripts directed by Frank Perry, *David and Lisa*; also wrote for TV. **Died:** Of cancer, in New York City, 14 March 1981.

Films as Writer for Director Frank Perry

1962 *David and Lisa*
1963 *Ladybug, Ladybug*
1968 *The Swimmer*
1969 *Last Summer*; *Trilogy* (co)
1970 *Diary of a Mad Housewife*

Other Films as Writer

1970 *The Lady in a Car with Glasses and a Gun* (Litvak) (co)
1972 *La Maison sous les arbres* (*The Deadly Trap*) (Clément) (co)
1973 *The Man Who Loved Cat Dancing* (Sarafian) (co, + co-pr)

Publications by Perry

Fiction (co-written with Leo Bayer)

Paper Chase, New York, 1943.
No Little Enemy, New York, 1944.
An Eye for an Eye, New York, 1945.
Brutal Question, New York, 1947.
Dirty Hands across the Sea, Cleveland, Ohio, 1952.

Other Fiction

The Swimmer (novelization of script), New York, 1967.
With Truman Capote and Frank Perry, *Trilogy: An Experiment in Multimedia,* New York, 1969.
Blue Pages, Philadelphia, 1979.

Articles

In *The Hollywood Screenwriter,* edited by Richard Corliss, New York, 1972.
Cinema TV Today (London), 21 July 1973.
Women and Film, Summer 1975.
"Writers Profiled," in *American Film* (Washington, D.C.), April 1982.

Publications on Perry

Book

Acker, Ally, *Reel Women: Pioneers of the Cinema, 1896 to the Present,* New York, 1991.

Articles

Obituary, in *New York Times,* 17 March 1981.
Obituary, in *Variety* (New York), 18 March 1981.
Slater, Thomas, in *American Screenwriters,* 2nd series, edited by Randall Clark, Detroit, 1986.

* * *

Eleanor Perry was a writer of carefully crafted screenplays, mainly adaptations realized in collaboration with her second husband, the director Frank Perry. Their first film was a low-budget, independently produced feature, *David and Lisa,* which Perry adapted from psychiatrist Theodore Rubin's book. Her script was a faithful, accomplished and—due to the subject matter—necessarily brooding account of the love between two troubled adolescent patients in a mental hospital. Here Perry developed a penetrating style that would characterize her screen writing: a penchant for unflinchingly probing character and situation to the bone. The controversy that surrounded many of the Perrys' films was due in large measure to Eleanor's commitment to the honest adaptation of source material without cutting dramatic corners or pandering to audience expectations or societal norms. Though *The Swimmer, Diary of a Mad Housewife,* and even *David and Lisa* and *Last Summer* may appear dated today, in their time these films marked significant departures from standard American movie fare.

The Swimmer, based on John Cheever's short story, is too solemnly "artistic" for its own good, but Perry's screenplay deftly manages to capture the stunning looniness of Cheever's vision. At the same time it is a shrewd sociological study of affluent suburban life in the northeast of America. Since Cheever's story is very short, Perry added numerous scenes and incidents that flesh out the story as well as economically convey the character of the swimmer (played by Burt Lancaster). For example, to reveal him as a man driven to do things the hard way, like the character in the short story who "never used the ladder" to get out of a pool, Perry shows him swimming a pool the long way, diagonally, and racing a thoroughbred horse barefooted. These actions effectively exhibit the exacting (and ultimately insane) nature of the swimmer's personal code of masculinity. Owing both to the brilliance of Cheever's cockeyed conceit and Perry's accomplished translation, *The Swimmer* is an unforgettable, if flawed, film.

Last Summer, based on Evan Hunter's novel, essays the same social milieu as *The Swimmer,* focusing on four teenagers on their summer vacation on Fire Island. Once again Perry held true to her source material right down to its disturbing climax: the sexual assault of one of the characters by the others. Along with other independently produced American films released at about the same time, such as *Easy Rider* and *Medium Cool, Last Summer* helped alter the face of the American cinema. What was distinctive about *Last Summer* can be traced back to Eleanor Perry. Her script had the courage of its convictions, and she was willing to follow the narrative logic of the plot wherever it might lead without compromising the original material or softening the blow for the audience. The Perrys continued this new brand of realism in their next project, *Diary of a Mad Housewife,* based on the novel by Sue Kaufman. In retrospect, the film's feminism may seem dated (in later years Eleanor Perry thought so herself), but it exists as one of the first American films seriously to examine femininity in modern terms. As such, it is a groundbreaking film, more important today as a precedent than for any inherent quality. Three years after the film was released, Perry said she would have written the film differently, carrying "it one step further, to show Tina [the housewife] liberating herself, but not through a man."

In the late 1960s the Perrys, in collaboration with Truman Capote, also made short film adaptations for television of three of Capote's short stories. Two of them, *A Christmas Memory* and *A Thanksgiving Memory,* won Perry and her co-scenarist, Capote, best screenplay Emmy awards. The three films were later reedited and released as an anthology feature entitled *Trilogy.*

After her separation from her husband, Eleanor Perry co-produced and wrote a screenplay for *The Man Who Loved Cat Dancing.* She disowned the finished film, claiming that so many other writers—all male—had worked on the project (among them Robert Bolt, Bill Norton, Tracy Keenan Wynn, Steve Shagan, and Brian Hutton) that the resulting film bore little resemblance to her original intention, which was to tell a Western story from a woman's point of view.

Two years before she died, Perry published a thinly disguised roman à clef, *Blue Pages,* chronicling the exploitation of a woman screenwriter in the male-dominated American film industry. Among the myriad humiliations the female protagonist in the novel endures is being cajoled by her film-director husband to share a screenwriting credit with a "Great Writer" whose work she has been adapting, and whose contribution to the screenplay is nil, presumably to give the project credibility and stature.

In an introduction to the published screenplays of *Trilogy,* Perry wrote that she considered the two most important elements in developing literary material to film were "a deep empathy with the material, the author's theme, intention and view of life; and ... an unblocked imagination which is able to flow freely from the original source, playing, embroidering, ornamenting, extending and, in the most successful adaptations, even enriching the original material." At its best, Eleanor Perry's work exhibits this kind of sympathetic and enriching sensibility.

—Charles Ramírez Berg

THE PIANO

Australia, 1993
Director: Jane Campion

Production: Jan Chapman Productions, in association with CIBY 2000; Eastmancolor, 35mm; running time: 120 minutes. Filmed in New Zealand, 1992.

Producer: Jan Chapman; **screenplay:** Jane Campion; **photography:** Stuart Dryburgh; **editor:** Veronica Jenet; **assistant directors:** Mark Turnbull, Victoria Hardy, Charles Haskell, and Therese Mangos; **production design:** Andrew McAlpine; **music:** Michael Nyman; **sound editors:** Gary O'Grady and Jeanine Chialvo; **sound recording:** Tony Johnson, Gethin Creagh, and Michael J. Dutton; **costumes:** Janet Patterson.

Cast: Holly Hunter (*Ada*); Harvey Keitel (*Baines*); Sam Neill (*Stewart*); Anna Paquin (*Flora*); Kerry Walker (*Aunt Morag*); Genevieve Lemon (*Nessie*); Tungia Baker (*Hira*); Ian Mune (*Reverend*).

Awards: Cannes Film Festival, Palme d'or and Best Actress; Oscars for Best Actress (Hunter), Best Supporting Actress (Paquin), and Best Original Screenplay.

Publications

Script

Campion, Jane, *The Piano,* New York, 1993.

Articles

Bilbrough, M., *Cinema Papers* (Melbourne), May 1993.
Bourgignon, T., and others, *Positif* (Paris), May 1993.
Strauss, F., and others, *Cahiers du Cinéma* (Paris), May 1993.
Stratton, D., *Variety* (New York), 10 May 1993.
Ciment, Michel, and T. Bourgignon, *Positif* (Paris), June 1993.
Dumas, D., *Avant-Scène* (Montreal), July 1993.
Bruzzi, Stella, "Bodyscape," in *Sight and Sound* (London), October 1993.
Younis, R., *Cinema Papers* (Melbourne), October 1993.
Francke, L., *Sight and Sound* (London), November 1993.
Eggleton, D., "Grimm Fairytale of the South Seas," in *Illusions* (Wellington), Winter 1993.
Hardy, Ann, "The Last Patriarch," in *Illusions* (Wellington), Winter 1993.
"Jane Campion," in *Current Biography 1994,* New York, 1994.
Pearson, H., *Films in Review* (New York), nos. 3/4, 1994.
Quart, Barbara, *Cineaste* (New York), no. 3, 1994.
Greenberg, H., *Film Quarterly* (Berkeley), Spring 1994.

The Piano

Kerr, Sarah, "Shoot the Piano Player," in *New York Times Review of Books,* 3 February 1994.

* * *

Set in the 1800s, Jane Campion's *The Piano* is a tale of repression and sensuality. Ada (Holly Hunter) is a mute, who goes to New Zealand with her nine-year-old daughter to marry a man she has never met; essentially sold off by her father, Ada leaves Scotland for the wilderness and beauty of a new country. She comes to the country completely unprepared for her new life and armed only with her most beloved possessions: her daughter and her piano.

Music is Ada's way of communicating. She puts all of her repressed passion and sexuality into her piano playing. When her new husband Stewart (Sam Neill) refuses to bring the piano up to his house, Baines (Harvey Keitel), a man who has reportedly "gone native," buys the instrument and asks Ada to teach him how to play it. He trades her the piano one key at a time in return for sexual favors. Although initially disgusted and shocked by Baines's forwardness, when he finally gives her the piano, Ada goes to him and allows him to make passionate love to her.

The film portrays the absurdity of transferring the social niceties of Western society onto a wild and unknown environment. The rigidity of the European way of life is contrasted with the freedom of the native Maori culture—and the aboriginals' silent contempt and sardonic humor at the expense of Western culture.

When Stewart learns that Ada is sleeping with Baines, his response is unexpected and shocking. During Stewart's violent outburst, the audience thinks that his anger will be directed towards the piano—the symbol of Ada's hidden self—and is shocked and stunned when Stewart drags Ada out of their house and chops her finger off. This is the first expression of his feelings that Stewart has shown—illustrating that under his extremely constrained exterior he is a hotbed of seething passions.

After Stewart confronts Baines, in a scene reminiscent of the opening one in which Ada arrives on the island, Ada and her daughter leave the island with Baines—the piano strapped to the fragile boat. When the piano is thrown into the ocean to lighten the vessel's load, Ada purposely entangles her foot in a rope connected to the piano and plunges to a watery grave. Strapped to the piano Ada begins her long descent into the depths of the sea, but she struggles free and rises to the surface. Thus the piano, the symbol of her expression and repression, is no longer needed. Ada has liberated herself.

Ada is a willful, stubborn character. Half adult, half child, she combines an iron will with a deep and passionate nature. She has been mute since the age of six, for no apparent reason other than she simply does not wish to speak—she has retreated into a world in which the piano is her only friend and only source of expression. In the end it is ironic that it is the piano, or a part of it, which betrays her. She writes a message on one of the keys and gives it to her daughter to give to Baines. Flora, her daughter, gives it to Stewart instead, beginning the chain of tragic events which result in her mother's disfigurement. Yet in a sense, Ada's choice to withdraw into herself, to keep her voice inside her head, is also about control. She is a woman existing in a patriarchal society—who has no rights, even over herself. She is sold off by her father to Stewart, and is forced to go to a completely new world because of her sex. In choosing not to speak, Ada is exercising control over one of the few things left for her to control.

Stewart and Baines are contrasting images of masculinity and of European culture. While Stewart is tied to managing his female family and to his European social customs despite the inappropriateness of his behavior, Baines is dissolute and lewd. He consorts with the natives and lives a comparatively wild and lascivious life. While Stewart and his family are buttoned-up tightly in their oppressive clothes, Baines is seen naked, or dressed in stained, sweaty clothes.

Campion's *The Piano* is a superbly filmed piece of cinema. The scope and composition of the cinematography allows the viewer to witness New Zealand through Ada's eyes. The heat and oppressiveness of the climate and landscape are mirrored in the restrictiveness of Ada's apparel. As Ada gives in to passion and frees herself from her society's rules, she loosens her ties to the piano, and to her former silent self. At the end of the film, Ada is slowly shaping words, showing that she is rebuilding her world.

—A. Pillai

PICKFORD, Mary
Producer and actress

Born: Gladys Mary Smith in Toronto, Ontario, Canada, 8 April 1893. **Family:** Married 1) the actor Owen Moore, 1911 (divorced 1920); 2) the actor Douglas Fairbanks, 1920 (divorced 1936); 3) the actor Charles "Buddy" Rogers, 1937, two adopted children. **Career:** 1898—debut as child actress in stage play *Bootle's Baby*; played other roles in Valentine Stock Company, and toured with other companies; 1907—Broadway debut in *The Warrens of Virginia*; 1909—film debut as extra in *Her First Biscuits*; leading role in D. W. Griffith's *The Violin Maker of Cremona*: became known as "The Biograph Girl"; 1913-18—contract with Zukor; 1918—independent producer; 1919—co-founder, with Douglas Fairbanks, Charlie Chaplin, and D. W. Griffith, of United Artists; 1923-24—roles in *Rosita* and *Dorothy Vernon of Haddon Hall* attempted to break her "little girl" image; 1929—first sound film, *Coquette*; 1936—formed Pickford-Lasky Productions with Jesse Lasky; 1937—formed Mary Pickford Cosmetic Company; 1946-49—produced several films for a variety of companies; 1956—sold the last of her United Artists stock. **Awards:** Best Actress Academy Award, for *Coquette*, 1929; Special Career Academy Award, for her "unique contributions to the film industry and the development of film as an artistic medium," 1975. **Died:** Of cerebral hemorrhage, in Santa Monica, California, 29 May 1979.

Films as Producer

1919 *Daddy Long-Legs* (Neilan) (+ ro); *The Hoodlum* (+ ro); *Heart o' the Hills* (S. Franklin) (+ ro)
1920 *Pollyanna* (P. Powell) (+ title role); *Suds* (Dillon) (+ ro)
1921 *The Love Light* (Marion) (+ ro as Angela); *Through the Back Door* (A. E. Green and J. Pickford) (+ ro as Jeanne Budamere); *Little Lord Fauntleroy* (A. E. Green and J. Pickford) (+ title role)
1922 *Tess of the Storm Country* (Robertson) (+ title role)
1923 *Rosita* (Lubitsch) (+ title role); *Garrison's Finish* (Rosson) (co-sc titles only)
1924 *Dorothy Vernon of Haddon Hall* (Neilan) (+ title role)
1925 *Little Annie Rooney* (Beaudine) (+ title role)
1926 *Sparrows* (Beaudine) (+ ro as Mama Mollie)
1927 *My Best Girl* (Sam Taylor) (+ ro as Maggie Johnson)
1929 *Coquette* (Sam Taylor) (+ ro as Norma Besant); *The Taming of the Shrew* (Sam Taylor) (+ ro as Katherine)
1931 *Kiki* (Sam Taylor) (+ title role)
1933 *Secrets* (Borzage) (+ roles as Mary Marlow/Mary Carlton)
1936 *One Rainy Afternoon* (R. V. Lee); *The Gay Desperado* (Mamoulian)
1946 *Little Iodine* (Le Borg); *Susie Steps Out* (Le Borg)
1947 *The Adventures of Don Coyote* (Le Borg); *Stork Bites Man* (Endfield)
1948 *High Fury* (*White Cradle Inn*) (French); *Sleep, My Love* (Siodmak)
1949 *Love Happy* (D. Miller)

Films as Actress

(all films directed by D. W. Griffith unless noted)

1909 *Her First Biscuits*; *The Violin Maker of Cremona*; *The Lonely Villa*; *The Son's Return*; *The Faded Lilies*; *The Peach Basket Hat*; *The Way of Man*; *The Necklace*; *The Mexican Sweethearts*; *The Country Doctor*; *The Cardinal's Conspiracy*; *The Renunciation*; *The Seventh Day*; *A Strange Meeting*; *Sweet and Twenty*; *The Slave*; *They Would Elope*; *The Indian Runner's Romance*; *His Wife's Visitor*; *Oh Uncle*; *The Sealed Room*; *1776, or The Hessian Renegades*; *The Little Darling*; *In Old Kentucky*; *Getting Even*; *The Broken Locket*; *What's Your Hurry*; *The Awakening*; *The Little Teacher*; *The Gibson Goddess*; *In the Watches of the Night*; *His Lost Love*; *The Restoration*; *The Light That Came*; *A Midnight Adventure*; *The Mountaineer's Honor*; *The Trick That Failed*; *The Test*; *To Save Her Soul*
1910 *All on Account of the Milk* (Powell); *The Woman from Mellon's*; *The Englishman and the Girl*; *The Newlyweds*; *The Thread of Destiny*; *The Twisted Trail*; *The Smoker*; *As It Is in Life*; *A Rich Revenge*; *A Romance of the Western Hills*; *May and December*; *Never Again!*; *The Unchanging Sea*; *Love among the Roses*; *The Two Brothers*; *Romona*; *In the Season of Buds*; *A Victim of Jealousy*; *A Child's Impulse*; *Muggsy's First Sweetheart*; *What the Daisy Said*; *The Call to Arms*; *An Arcadian Maid*; *Muggsy Becomes a Hero*; *The Sorrows of the Unfaithful*; *When We Were in Our Teens*; *Wilful Peggy*; *Examination Day at School*; *A Gold Necklace*; *A Lucky Toothache*; *Waiter No. 5*; *Simple Charity*; *The Masher*; *The Song of the Wildwood Flute*; *A Plain Song*

1911   *White Roses; When a Man Loves; The Italian Barber; Three*
       Sisters; A Decree of Destiny; The First Misunderstanding
       (Ince and Tucker); *The Dream* (Ince and Tucker) (+ sc);
       Maid or Man (Ince); *At the Duke's Command; The Mir-*
       ror; While the Cat's Away; Her Darkest Hour (Ince); *Art-*
       ful Kate (Ince); *A Manly Man* (Ince); *The Message in the*
       Bottle (Ince); *The Fisher-maid* (Ince); *In Old Madrid*
       (Ince); *Sweet Memories of Yesterday* (Ince); *The Stam-*
       pede; Second Sight; The Fair Dentist; For Her Brother's
       Sake (Ince and Tucker); *Back to the Soil; In the Sultan's*
       Garden (Ince); *The Master and the Man; The Lighthouse*
       Keeper; For the Queen's Honor; A Gasoline Engagement;
       At a Quarter to Two; Science; The Skating Bug; The Call of
       the Song; A Toss of the Coin; The Sentinel Asleep; The
       Better Way; His Dress Shirt; 'Tween Two Loves (The Stron-
       ger Love); The Rose's Story; From the Bottom of the Sea;
       The Courting of Mary (Tucker); *Love Heeds Not the Show-*
       ers (Moore); *Little Red Riding Hood* (Moore); *The Caddy's*
       Dream (Moore)

1912   *Honor Thy Father* (Moore); *The Mender of Nets; Iola's*
       Promise; Fate's Inception; The Female of the Species; Just
       Like a Woman; Won by a Fish (Sennett); *The Old Actor; A*
       Lodging for the Night; A Beast at Bay; Home Folks; Lena
       and the Geese (+ sc); *The School Teacher and the Waif; An*
       Indian Summer; A Pueblo Legend; The Narrow Road; The
       Inner Circle; With the Enemy's Help; Friends; So Near, Yet
       So Far; A Feud in the Kentucky Hills; The One She Loved;
       My Baby; The Informer; The Unwelcome Guest; The New
       York Hat

1913   *In the Bishop's Carriage* (Porter); *Caprice* (Dawley)

1914   *A Good Little Devil* (Porter); *Hearts Adrift* (Porter); *Tess of*
       the Storm Country (Porter); *The Eagle's Mate* (Kirkwood);
       Such a Little Queen (Hugh Ford); *Behind the Scenes*
       (Kirkwood); *Cinderella* (Kirkwood)

1915   *Mistress Nell* (Kirkwood); *Fanchon, the Cricket* (Kirkwood);
       The Dawn of Tomorrow (Kirkwood); *Little Pal*
       (Kirkwood); *Rags* (Kirkwood); *Esmerelda* (Kirkwood);
       A Girl of Yesterday (Dwan); *Madame Butterfly* (Olcott)

1916   *The Foundling* (O'Brien); *Poor Little Peppina* (Olcott); *The*
       Eternal Grind (O'Brien); *Hulda from Holland* (O'Brien);
       Less Than Dust (Emerson)

1917   *The Pride of the Clan* (M. Tourneur); *The Poor Little Rich*
       Girl (M. Tourneur); *A Romance of the Redwoods* (C. B.
       DeMille); *Rebecca of Sunnybrook Farm* (Neilan) (title role);
       A Little Princess (Neilan)

1918   *Stella Maris* (Neilan) (title role/Unity Blake); *Amarilly of*
       Clothes-Line Alley (Neilan); *M'Liss* (Neilan); *How Could*
       You, Jean? (W. Taylor); *Johanna Enlists* (W. Taylor); *One*
       Hundred Percent American (Rossen)

1919   *Captain Kidd, Jr.* (W. Taylor)

1927   *The Gaucho* (F. R. Jones)

Publications by Pickford

Books

Pickfordisms for Success, Los Angeles, 1922.
Why Not Try God?, New York, 1934, as *Why Not Look Beyond?,*
   London, 1936.
Little Liar (novel), New York, 1934.

The Demi-Widow (novel), Indianapolis, 1935.
My Rendezvous with Life, New York, 1935.
Sunshine and Shadow, New York, 1955.

Articles

"What It Means to Be a Movie Actress," in *Ladies' Home Journal,*
   January 1915.
"The Body in the Bosphorus," in *Theatre,* April 1919.
"Greatest Business in the World," in *Chaplin* (Stockholm), 10 June
   1922.
"Mary Is Looking for Pictures," in *Photoplay* (New York), June 1925.
"Mary Pickford Awards," in *Photoplay* (New York), October 1925.

Publications on Pickford

Books

Cushman, Robert, *Tribute to Mary Pickford,* Washington, D.C., 1970.
Lee, Raymond, *The Films of Mary Pickford,* South Brunswick, New
   Jersey, 1970.
Niver, Kemp, *Mary Pickford: Comedienne,* Los Angeles, 1970.
Wagenknecht, Edward, *Movies in the Age of Innocence,* New York, 1971.
Rosen, Marjorie, *Popcorn Venus,* New York, 1973.
Windeler, Robert, *Sweetheart: The Story of Mary Pickford,* London,
   1973.
Carey, Gary, *Doug and Mary: A Biography of Douglas Fairbanks and*
   Mary Pickford, New York, 1977.

Mary Pickford

Herndon, Booto, *Mary Pickford and Douglas Fairbanks: The Most Popular Couple the World Has Ever Known,* New York, 1977.

Higashi, Sumiko, *Virgins, Vamps and Flappers: The American Silent Movie Heroine,* St. Alban's Vermont, 1978.

Eyman, Scott, *Mary Pickford: America's Sweetheart,* New York, 1990.

Whitfield, Eileen, *Pickford: The Woman Who Made Hollywood,* Lexington, Kentucky, 1997.

Articles

Johnson, Julian, "Mary Pickford, Herself and Her Career," in *Photoplay* (New York), November 1915/February 1916.

Belasco, David, "When Mary Pickford Came to Me," in *Photoplay* (New York), December 1915.

Cheatham, Maude, "On Location with Mary Pickford," in *Motion Picture Magazine* (New York), June 1919.

Russell, M. Lewis, "Mary Pickford—Director," in *Photoplay* (New York), March 1920.

St. Johns, Adela Rogers, "Why Does the World Love Mary?," in *Photoplay* (New York), December 1921.

Birdwell, Russell, "When I Am Old, as Told by Mary Pickford," in *Photoplay* (New York), February 1925.

St. Johns, Adela Rogers, "The Story of the Married Life of Doug and Mary," in *Photoplay* (New York), February 1927.

Whitaker, Alma, "Mrs. Douglas Fairbanks Analyzes Mary Pickford," in *Photoplay* (New York), March 1928.

St. Johns, Adela Rogers, "Why Mary Pickford Bobbed Her Hair," in *Photoplay* (New York), September 1928.

Harriman, M. C., "Mary Pickford," in *New Yorker,* 7 April 1934.

Current Biography 1945, New York, 1945.

Card, J., "The Films of Mary Pickford," in *Image* (Rochester, New York), December 1959.

Spears, J., "Mary Pickford's Directors," in *Films in Review* (New York), February 1966.

"Lettre de Paris sur Mary Pickford," in *Cahiers du Cinéma* (Paris), September 1966.

Scaramazza, Paul, "Rediscovering Mary Pickford," in *Film Fan Monthly,* December 1970.

Harmetz, Aljean, "America's Sweetheart Lives," in *New York Times,* 28 March 1971.

Gow, Gordon, "Mary," in *Films and Filming* (London), December 1973.

Obituary in *New York Times,* 30 May 1979.

"Album di Mary Pickford," in *Cinema Nuovo* (Turin), August 1979.

"Stars Attend Academy Tribute to Mary Pickford," in *Classic Film/ Video Images* (Muscatine, Iowa), January 1980.

Mitry, J., "Le Roman de Mary Pickford," in *Avant-Scène du Cinéma* (Paris), 1 November 1980.

Arnold, Gary, "Mary Pickford," in *The Movie Star,* edited by Elisabeth Weis, New York, 1981.

Brock, A., "Mary Pickford's Magic Conjured 'A Little Bit of Eternity,'" in *Classic Images* (Muscatine, Iowa), October 1983.

Fernett, G., "The Historic Film Studios: When Doug and Mary Had Their Own Studios," in *Classic Images* (Muscatine, Iowa), July 1984.

Howe, C., "Cliff's Classic Clips: When Pickfair Was Home," in *Classic Images* (Muscatine, Iowa), April 1985.

Bakewell, W., "Hollywood Be Thy Name," in *Filmfax* (Evanston, Illinois), March 1990.

Seville, J., "The Laser's Edge," in *Classic Images* (Muscatine, Iowa), June 1991.

Eyman, Scott, "Lubitsch, Pickford and the *Rosita* War," in *Griffithiana* (Baltimore, Maryland), May/September 1992.

Sherman, W. T., "From the Mailbag: Author's Apology," in *Classic Images* (Muscatine, Iowa), 4 July 1992.

Griest, Stephanie Elizondo, "Under Pickford's Curls, a Very Determined Mind," in *New York Times,* 7 July 1997.

* * *

Aptly dubbed "America's Sweetheart," Mary Pickford was the world's first motion-picture star. She was also an accomplished producer who successfully orchestrated a career that seemed, for a time, as though it would last forever. Very early in her movie career, Pickford demonstrated her business savvy by moving from one studio to another, negotiating each time for higher wages and greater creative control of her films. She was equally attentive to the importance of choosing roles that she thought would please her audience.

In 1918, when Pickford was renegotiating her contract with Adolph Zukor's Famous Players-Lasky company, she demanded more money, complete creative control of her movies, and that the studio act only as her distributor. But it was First National who agreed to meet her demands. Subsequently, she played only the roles she selected and she carefully controlled her star image in order to satisfy her audience's expectations. And she was very clear about the composition of her audience—mostly working-class women; she proudly declared, "I am a woman's woman. My success has been [because] women like the pictures in which I appear." Thus, her films were typically preoccupied with poverty and melodrama, and with plucky independent heroines who struggle relentlessly to survive in the harsh world. In addition, much of her success was due to her acute awareness of her star value, and her skill at picking directors and other crew members who would complement her talents and image.

In 1919 rumors made the rounds in Hollywood that Famous Players-Lasky and First National planned to merge. Seeking to avoid falling under the control of Zukor and losing control of her films, Pickford co-founded the United Artists Corporation (UA) with her fellow movie stars Charlie Chaplin and Douglas Fairbanks, and the star director D. W. Griffith. It was organized to distribute their high-end productions and to give them complete control of their films. Pickford's first film for UA was the sticky sweet *Pollyanna,* about the unfailingly optimistic little orphan girl who, despite a crippling accident, declares that because her grumpy aunt now loves her, she is happy she was hurt. Despite what critics called its uninspired direction, it was a huge hit. Her costume movie *Little Lord Fauntleroy* featured her in a dual role, and its box-office success confirmed Pickford's sense that her fans preferred her Victorian fables. She had moderate success with *Tess of the Storm Country,* a remake of an earlier Pickford hit; it featured one of her most exuberant performances in which she played a sweet, but bold girl who proves her mettle by tangling with swains and selflessly taking on the protection of orphaned babies.

Over time, Pickford produced films that were more and more elaborate, but they stuck with well-worn themes that were increasingly out of touch with the "Jazz Age." She tried to change her image by making *Rosita,* in which she played a gypsy heroine, but she and director Ernst Lubitsch continually clashed over their disparate conceptions of the film and the result was both mediocre and unpopular. She miscalculated again with *Dorothy Vernon of Haddon Hall,* an expensive costume romance set in the court of Elizabeth I in which Pickford played a grown-up woman instead of a girl. After *Dorothy Vernon of Haddon Hall,* she returned to her girlish persona with

Little Annie Rooney, an engaging, fluffy bit of fun, but weighty with ethnic stereotypes; it was a great hit. In the moderately successful Dickensian story *Sparrows,* Pickford played a guardian of ten children imprisoned on a baby farm who ultimately escorts the children to freedom. Her last silent film *My Best Girl* was a hit, in which she played a contemporary shop-girl who falls in love with the heir to the department store where she works. Her first sound film *Coquette* was a static, stagey film about the flighty daughter of a small-town doctor, but it was commercially successful and earned her the Academy Award for acting. Toward the end of her career, Pickford wanted to concentrate on classical roles, so she co-starred with her husband Douglas Fairbanks in an adaptation of *The Taming of the Shrew.* But it was overwrought with comedy gags, and although it returned a profit, it failed to meet her expectations and she claimed that she hated it. She had another "misadventure" with *Kiki,* in which she played a daring modern woman who ardently pursues the producer of her show; critics disparaged it and audiences were disinterested too.

More interested in commercial rather than artistic success, Pickford's career is characterized by her trepidation about alienating the audience. Consequently, she mostly hired directors who unquestioningly accepted her authority; in addition, she occasionally recut her movies according to her wishes. As the producer of her films, she freely exercised her extensive knowledge of and preferences for filmmaking. Charles Rosher recalled that she "knew everything there was to know about motion pictures," and often directed her own scenes while the official director did the crowd scenes. Pickford herself declared: "Nobody ever directed me, not even Mr. Griffith." According to Pickford, one of her most cherished filmmaking principles was that her function was not to educate her fans, but rather to entertain, and moreover, to "serve" them. In 1936, after she retired from acting, she formed Pickford-Lasky Productions, in order to produce "wholesome, healthy" movies that would counter Mae West's films, which Pickford thought were morally degrading to Hollywood. The partnership dissolved after only two films. During the late 1940s, however, she produced several films for different studios with her third husband, "Buddy" Rogers.

—Cynthia Felando

POIRIER, Anne-Claire

Canadian director and writer

Born: St. Hyacinthe, Quebec, Canada, 1932. **Education:** Attended University of Montreal, law degree; studied theater at the Conservatoire d'art dramatique. **Career:** 1960—began working for the French section of the National Film Board of Canada; 1963—directed *30 Minutes, Mister Plummer,* her first film for the NFB; 1968—directed her first feature, *Mother-to-Be,* the initial Quebec feature directed by a woman; 1972—with Jeanne Morazain and Monique Larocque, established "En tant que femmes," a program for women at the NFB, which lasted three years; 1975-78—served as executive producer of the Challenge for Change Société nouvelle program and as studio head in the French production branch; mid-1970s—produced a series of documentaries for other filmmakers; formed a working partnership with screenwriter Marthe Blackburn. **Awards:** Ordre national du Québec, 1985; Government of Quebec, Albert Tessier Award for lifetime achievement, 1988; Grand Prix

Hydro-Quebec, Festival du Cinema International, for *Salut Victor!,* 1988. **Address:** c/o National Film Board of Canada, P.O. Box 6100, Station Centre-Ville Montreal, PQ H3C 3H5, Canada.

Films as Director

1963   *30 Minutes, Mister Plummer* (doc, short) (+ sc, ed, narration)
1964   *La Fin des étés* (short) (+ co-sc, co-ed)
1965   *Les Ludions* (short)
1968   *De mère en fille (Mother-to-Be)* (+ sc)
1970   *L'Impot, et tout et tout* (short, revision)
1971   "1re partie" and "2e partie" of *Le savoir-faire s'impose* (shorts)
1974   *Les Filles du Roi (They Called Us "Les Filles du Roy")* (+ co-sc, co-pr)
1975   *Le Temps de l'avant (Before the Time Comes)* (+ co-sc, pr)
1979   *Mourir à tue-tête (A Scream of Silence)* (+ co-sc, co-pr)
1982   *La Quarantaine (Over Forty; Beyond Forty)* (+ co-sc)
1988   *Salut Victor!* (for TV) (+ co-sc, pr)
1989   *Il y a longtemps que je t'aime*
1997   *Tu as Crie (Let Me Go)* (+ co-sc)

Other Films

1962   *Jour apres jour (Day after Day)* (Perron—short) (ed)
1963   *Voir Miami* (Groulx—short) (co-sc, co-narration)
1973   *J'me marie, j'me marie pas* (Dansereau) (co-pr); *Souris, tu m'inquiétes* (Danis) (co-pr); *À qui appartient ce gage?* (Blackburn, Gibbard, Morazin, Saia, and Warny) (co-pr)
1974   *Les filles c'est pas pareil* (Girard) (pr)
1976   *Shakti—"She Is Vital Energy"* (Crouillere) (pr); *Surtout l'hiver* (Gagne) (pr); *Tie-Dre* (De Bellefeuille) (pr)
1977   *La P'tite Violence* (Girard) (pr); *Raison d'être* (Dion) (co-pr); *Quebec à vendre* (Garceau) (pr); *Le Menteur (1re partie)-L'Alcoholisme: la therapie* (Seguin) (pr); *Le Menteur (2e partie)-L'Alcoholisme: la maladie* (Seguin) (pr); *Famille et Variations* (Dansereau) (pr); *Les Heritiers de la violence* (Vamos) (pr)

Publications by Poirier

Articles

"Entretien avec Anne-Claire Poirier," interview with L. Bonneville, in *Séquences* (Montreal), July 1975.
"Carte blanche," in *Ciné-Bulles* (Montreal), no. 3, 1989.

Publications on Poirier

Articles

Hartt, L., "Anne-Claire Poirier: En tant que femmes," in *Cinema Canada* (Montreal), August/September 1974.
Prevost, F., and A. Reiter, "The Disturbing Dialectic of Anne-Claire Poirier," in *Cinema Canada* (Montreal), November/December 1982.
Prevost, F., "L'itineraire cinématographique d'Anne-Claire Poirier," in *Sequences* (Montreal), April 1984.
Beaudet, L., "Une femme armée," in *Copie Zero* (Montreal), February 1985.

Bersiank, L., "Tout ça c'est du cinéma," in *Copie Zero* (Montreal), February 1985.

Blackburn, Marthe, "En tant que femmes ..yyn. en tant qu'amies," in *Copie Zero* (Montreal), February 1985.

Jean, M., "Cinéma et conscience," in *Copie Zero* (Montreal), February 1985.

Jutras, P., "Anne Claire à une fa çon tres ouverte et affecteuse de diriger une equipe," in *Copie Zero* (Montreal), February 1985.

Marchessault, J., "Tourner à tue-tête," in *Copie Zero* (Montreal), February 1985.

Poupart, J.-M., "Lieux communs," in *Copie Zero* (Montreal), February 1985.

Veronneau, P., "Naissance d'une passion," in *Copie Zero* (Montreal), February 1985.

Bonneville, L., "Anne Claire Poirier," in *Séquences* (Montreal), January 1989.

* * *

Throughout her long career, Anne-Claire Poirier has consistently made films with feminist and humanist concerns. She explores serious issues facing young, contemporary women, from defining one's place in society and attaining personal satisfaction to dealing with the aftereffects of sexual violence. In the two outstanding fiction films she made in the 1980s, however, her characters are neither youthful nor fashionable. Rather, they respectively are aging, and aged.

Poirier's first film, *30 Minutes, Mister Plummer,* is a documentary portrait of actor Christopher Plummer as he prepares to play Cyrano de Bergerac; despite its title, the film actually runs 27-plus minutes. But she really hit her stride with her initial feature-length film, *Mother-to-Be,* a documentary about pregnancy and motherhood that provoked much debate about feminism in the Québécois cinema. In the film, Poirier explores the conflicting emotions of a young mother as she awaits the birth of her second child. *Mother-to-Be,* which was made in 1967, insightfully explores one of the key questions women were beginning to ask themselves as the modern feminist movement was taking shape: Can a woman attain self-fulfillment while devoting herself to a husband and children?

Through the 1970s Poirier's films focused on feminist issues. *They Called Us "Les Filles du Roy"* examines the roles of women in the history of Quebec, from squaw and settler's wife to self-sufficient member of the workforce. In the film, Poirier differentiates between the historical role of women as wives and mothers and their contemporary, postfeminist identity, while spotlighting the challenges couples must face if they are to work together and thrive. *Before the Time Comes* deals with the abortion issue, as it charts the plight of a happily married woman who already has three children. She finds herself pregnant and, with her husband, must make the torturous decision of whether to abort or have the baby. *A Scream of Silence* chronicles the rape and subsequent suicide of a nurse, whose sense of self is destroyed as a result of the brutality she experiences. Here, Poirier examines the reasons why women may feel they somehow are to blame for their sexual victimization.

In the 1980s Poirier expanded her thematic horizons and directed *Over Forty* and *Salut Victor!,* heartfelt, poetic dramas that sympathetically examine the lives of older characters. *Over Forty* is a *Return of the Secaucus Seven* and *The Big Chill* for those who grew up during the 1940s. It chronicles a reunion of The Gang, a clique of men and women who came of age together. After a three-decade-long separation, they meet one more time to sing, and recollect old times, and reveal the triumphs and disappointments of their lives.

Over Forty is an enchanting jewel of a movie about the nature of camaraderie, the passing of time, and the ability to forget one's dissatisfaction and live in the moment.

Salut Victor! charts the evolving friendship between two elderly residents of an old-age home: Philippe, a new arrival who no longer can care for himself, and who has come there to pass his remaining time and die; and Victor, talkative and spirited, who cherishes life yet is pragmatic about his surroundings. Victor also is proudly gay, and has suffered for his lifestyle; he had left his wife and children for a man, an airline pilot who was killed in a plane crash, and remains estranged from his family. He quickly befriends, and positively impacts on, the less outgoing, more pessimistic Philippe. The pair share some eloquent repartee, with Philippe eventually admitting that he too is gay, and has spent his life deeply hidden in the closet. But the crux of the story is the relationship between these two elderly gentlemen, and the warmth and solace they find in their friendship.

If *Over Forty* is a poignant story of characters at midlife, *Salut Victor!* is an equally eloquent account of how the elderly may be patronized (or downright ignored) by society despite their feelings, fears, desires—and their humanity.

In Poirier's earliest films, she deals thoughtfully and compassionately with women's issues. In *Over Forty* and *Salut Victor!,* made as she herself matured, she explores the emotions and attitudes of those who are no longer young. Notwithstanding, all of her films are united in that they have a way of reverberating inside even the most seasoned moviegoer for days after they have been seen.

—Rob Edelman

POOL, Léa
Swiss-Canadian director

Born: Geneva, Switzerland, 1950. **Education:** In 1975 traveled to Canada to study film and video production; graduated from the University of Quebec with a degree in communications. **Career:** Teacher in Switzerland; 1978-83—taught film and video at the University of Quebec; 1980—made first short film, the documentary *Un Strass café*; 1980-81—directed nine episodes of the "Planete" series for Radio Québec; 1980-83—directed a series of programs about cultural minorities for Quebec television; 1984—made her critically acclaimed debut feature film, *A Woman in Transit.* **Awards:** Critics Prize and International Critics Prize, Montreal World Film Festival, and Best Canadian Film, Toronto Festival of Festivals, for *A Woman in Transit,* 1984; First Prize, Namur Film Festival, and First Prize, Atlantic Film Festival, for *Straight for the Heart,* 1988. **Address:** c/o: Groupe MultiMédia du Canada, 525 Berri, Bureau 200, Montreal PQ H2J 2S4, Canada.

Films as Director

1978 *Laurent Lamerre, portier* (co-d)
1980 *Un Strass café* (doc, short) (+ sc, pr, ed)
1984 *La Femme de l'hôtel* (*A Woman in Transit*) (+ co-sc)
1986 *Anne Trister* (+ co-sc)
1988 *À corps perdu* (*Straight for the Heart*; *Straight to the Heart*) (+ co-sc)
1990 *Hotel Chronicles*

1991   *La Demoiselle sauvage* (*The Savage Woman*) (+ co-sc);
       "Rispondetemi" ep. of *Montréal vu par* (*Montreal Sextet*)
1992   *Blanche* (for TV)
1993   *C'était le 12 du 12 et chili avait les blues*
1994   *Mouvements du désir* (*Desire in Motion*) (+ sc)
1996   *Letter to My Daughter*
1997   *Marguerite Volant* (for TV)

Other Film

1993   *Cap Tourmente* (Langlois) (adviser)

Publication by Pool

Article

Interview with L. Bonneville, in *Séquences* (Montreal), January 1985.

Publications on Pool

Books

Cole, Janis, and Holly Dale, *Calling the Shots: Profiles of Women Filmmakers,* Kingston, Ontario, 1993.
Bertrand, Claudine, and Josée Bonneville, *La passion au féminin,* Montreal, 1994.
Foster, Gwendolyn Audrey, *Women Film Directors: An International Bio-Critical Dictionary,* Westport, Connecticut, 1995.

Articles

Longfellow, Brenda, "Feminist Language in *Journal inachevé* and *Un Strass café,*" in *Words and Moving Images: Essays on Verbal and Visual Expression in Film and Television,* edited by W. C. Wees and M. Dorland, Montreal, 1984.
Gaulin, S., "Pool's Splash," in *Cinema Canada* (Montreal), October 1984.
Laverdiere, S., "Léa Pool. Dire la dualite des êtres," in *24 Images* (Montreal), Fall/Winter 1984-85.
Horni, J., "Um Einen Film zu Lieben, Brauche ich nur Fuenf Oder Sechs Bilder, die Mich Ueberwaeltigen," in *Filmbulletin* (Zurich), vol. 28, no. 5, 1986.
Alemany-Galway, Mary, "Léa Pool's *Anne Trister,*" in *Cinema Canada* (Montreal), April 1986.
Longfellow, Brenda, "The Search for Voice: *La Femme de l'hôtel,*" in *Dialogue: Cinéma Canadien et Québécois/Canadian and Quebec Cinema,* edited by Pierre Véronneau, Michel Dorland, and Seth Fieldman, Montreal, 1987.
Madore, Edith, "'J'ai Besoin d'avoir un regard sur mon regard,'" in *Ciné-Bulles* (Montreal), vol. 8, no. 1, 1988.
Bonneville, L., "Léa Pool," in *Séquences* (Montreal), November 1988.
Pérusse, Denise, "Analyse spectrale autour de la représentation de la femme," in *Le Cinéma Québécois des Années 80,* edited by C. Chabot, M. Larouche, D. Pérusse, and P. Véronneau, Montreal, 1989.
Green, Mary Jean, "Léa Pool's *La Femme de l'hôtel* and Women's Film in Quebec," in *Quebec Studies,* no. 9, 1989-90.
Jean, M., "Le Point de Vue de Cineastes," in *24 Images* (Montreal), January/February 1990.
Euvrard, M., "Les Cineastes Neo-Quebecois," in *CinémAction* (Conde-sur-Noireau), July 1990.

Pallister, Janis L., "Léa Pool's Gynefilms," in *Essays on Quebec Cinema,* edited by Joseph I. Donohoe, East Lansing, Michigan, 1991.
Berube, B., "Creer pour Dire l'Indicible," in *24 Images* (Montreal), Autumn 1991.
Gingras, N., "Figures de la Melancolie," in *24 Images* (Montreal), Autumn 1991.
Loiselle, M. C., "Le Mal d'une Epoque," in *24 Images* (Montreal), Autumn 1991.
Loiselle, M. C., and C. Racine, "L'Ecran de la vie," in *24 Images* (Montreal), Autumn 1991.
Loiselle, M. C., and D. Perusse, "Léa Pool," in *24 Images* (Montreal), Autumn 1991.
Nadeau, Chantal, "Les Femmes frappees de disparition," in *24 Images* (Montreal), Autumn 1991.
Pérusse, Denise, "Deux ou Trois Choses que l'on Sait d'Elle," in *24 Images* (Montreal), Autumn 1991.
Garel, S., "Léa Pool, Retrouvailles Suisses," in *Cinéma* (Paris), October 1991.
Nadeau, Chantal, "Women in French-Quebec Cinema," in *CineAction!* (Toronto), Spring 1992.
Cloutier, M., "Le Film, c'est un outil de recherche et d'expression de soi," in *Ciné-Bulles* (Montreal), vol. 13, no. 2, 1994.
Beaulieu, J., "Les Chemins, de Léa Pool," in *Séquences* (Montreal), March 1994.

*   *   *

Léa Pool is a celebrated Canadian filmmaker who works in both film and video, fiction and documentary. Her work is highly intimate and introspective, refuses to follow familiar narrative conventions, and typically employs lengthy, subjective shots. Not surprisingly, she has expressed admiration for the films of her contemporary (and friend) Chantal Akerman. In addition, Pool has acknowledged that she is interested in images and perspectives of women, and she aligns herself with those filmmakers whose urges do not include the pursuit of commercial success by making Hollywood-style films. Indeed, she has lamented that, it is "very rare to see films that come from the heart" due to the commercial constraints of Hollywood.

After working as a teacher in her native Switzerland, Pool went to Montreal to study film production, where she garnered attention for a student film. Since 1975, she has lived in Quebec. After working on several student films, Pool made her first solo film, the low-budget experimental short documentary, *Strass café,* made at the National Film Board of Canada in 1980. It uses black-and-white cinematography and a poetic voice over to meditate upon the city, exile, solitude, identity, and a woman and man who desire but never meet each other.

Pool's debut feature was *A Woman in Transit,* an intense story of loneliness and creative frustration. Set in a downtown Montreal hotel, it features three female characters. Specifically, filmmaker Andrea returns to her native Montreal to make a musical drama; upon checking into her hotel, she briefly encounters a strange older woman who, distraught from a broken love affair, soon tries to commit suicide with drugs and alcohol. The film's third woman is an actress who has a part as a singer in Andrea's film. When Andrea and the older woman finally talk at length, it becomes clear that Andrea's film bears striking similarities to the older woman's life. Thus, the film treats the theme of life imitating art, and vice versa. In this film, Pool has explained that her intention was to address the three sides of a woman—the conscious, unconscious, and the combination of the two. To do so, she chose three different characters, and, as she put it, "each one is a side of me in a way." The film has a slow, contemplative pace, and critics generally praised it, calling it "introspective" and "arty." Significantly, its critical and popular success enabled Pool to raise the money for her next script very quickly.

Although *A Woman in Transit* alludes to lesbian desire, her second feature, *Anne Trister,* deals with the subject more explicitly. Funded by the National Film Board of Canada, it is the partly autobiographical tale of a Jewish woman who leaves her native Switzerland after the death of her father, in order to establish her own identity in Quebec, where she falls in love with an older woman. The film prompted considerable commentary for its subject matter at the Berlin Film Festival and it was lauded by Canadian critics. Moreover, although at the time gay and lesbian themes were considered commercially risky, it was an economic success. Some critics have disagreed, however, with Pool's portrayal of the lesbian relationship because it is decidedly unerotic. That is, the heterosexual love scene is more graphic than the lesbian love scene. The disparity was motivated by Pool's intention to express the desire that permeates a new love relationship, and to symbolically explore the primal mother-daughter love—a woman's "first love." Therefore, she chose to emphasize the women's emotions with their eyes and physical gestures rather than by using more sexually explicit means.

Pool's third feature, *Straight for the Heart,* is the story of Pierre, a photojournalist who returns to Montreal from an assignment in Nicaragua to discover that his ménage à trois of ten years has ended unexpectedly when his former lovers, David and Sarah, leave together. Pierre then nurtures his obsession to discover why they have deserted him, and undertakes a photographic study of Montreal's urban corrosion. Certainly, images of the city constitute a visual theme in Pool's work, as in *Un Strass café, A Woman in Transit,* and *Straight for the Heart.* In addition, her characters often exist in alienating transitional spaces; for example, the hotel in *A Woman in Transit,* and a train in *Desire in Motion.* Certainly, movement is an essential element of cinema—as is desire. Thus, in Pool's more recent film, *Desire in Motion,* she deploys the "strangers on a train" device, but with a difference—as the film's title suggests. The story concerns a woman who has recently ended a relationship and is traveling with her seven-year-old daughter on a train from Montreal to Vancouver. She meets a shy man traveling to meet his lover, but eventually the two strangers give full vent to their passion, to the chagrin of the little girl. The film's several surreal dream sequences and assortment of unusual characters are pure Pool. Critics called it "ultra steamy," and claimed it was her most "viewer friendly" film. Quebec critics, in particular, praised her juxtaposition of the tight, claustrophobic train interiors with the expansive Canadian landscapes.

Pool's films are better received in Europe than in English-speaking Canada or the United States. She is that rare Quebec filmmaker, however, whose films are screened in commercial theaters; and her success has prompted considerable attention from film critics and academics, particularly feminists. Notably, although mainstream film critics have characterized her films as feminist, many academic feminists have challenged them on the grounds that they are not clearly "feminist" because, for example, they tend to focus on individual, private tensions, rather than on the larger issue of the unequal distribution of power between men and women.

—Cynthia Felando

POTTER, Sally
British director

Born: London, 1947. **Education:** Attended London School of Contemporary Dance; St. Martin's Art School. **Career:** 1968—began making 8-millimeter films; 1974—performed and choreographed for the Strider Dance Company; founded Limited Dance Company; toured Britain and United States in performance shows, both solo and in collaboration, including the Feminist Improvising Group (FIG); 1979—released short feminist comedy, *Thriller,* funded by the Arts Council of Great Britain; 1980—formed Marx Bros. group with Lindsay Cooper and Georgie Born; choreographed solo dances for Maedee Dupres; lectured on feminism and feminism and cinema; 1983—made first feature film, *The Gold Diggers,* financed by the British Film Institute; 1980s—made films for television. **Address:** Adventure Pictures, Blackbird Yard, London E2, England. **Agent:** Alexandra Cann Representation, 337 Fulham Road, London SW10 9TW, England.

Films as Director

1968-73 *Hors d'oeuvres* (8mm short); *Play* (16mm short); *The Building* (expanded cinema event)
1979 *Thriller* (short) (+ pr, sc); *The London Story* (short) (+ pr, sc)
1983 *The Gold Diggers* (+ co-sc, co-ed, composer of lyrics, performer of song "Seeing Red," choreographer)
1986 *Tears Laughter Fear and Rage* (for TV)
1988 *I Am an Ox—Women in Soviet Cinema* (doc for TV)
1993 *Orlando* (+ sc, co-mus)
1997 *The Tango Lesson* (+ ro as Sally)

Publications by Potter

Articles

Camera Obscura (Berkeley), Spring 1980.
Interview with Valentina Agostinis, in *Framework* (Norwich, England), Spring 1981.
"Like Night and Day," interview with Sheila Johnston, in *Monthly Film Bulletin* (London), vol. 51, no. 604, 1984.
"*The Gold Diggers,*" interview with Pam Cook, in *Framework* (Norwich, England), Spring 1984.
"Gold Diggers and Fellow Travellers," in *National Film Theatre Programmes* (London), 1 May 1984.
"Das Schwarze in Weissen," interview with Claudia Hoff, in *Frauen und Film* (Berlin), October 1984.
"Immortal Longing," interview with Walter Donohue, in *Sight and Sound* (London), March 1993.
"Sally Potter: A Director Not Afraid of Virginia Woolf," interview with Manola Dargis, in *Interview* (New York), June 1993.
Interview with Peter Travers, in *Rolling Stone* (New York), 24 June 1993.
"Demystifying Traditional Notions of Gender," interview with Pat Dowell, in *Cineaste* (New York), July 1993.
"Debate: A Conversation with Sally Potter," interview with Penny Florence, *Screen* (London), Autumn 1993.
"Out of the Wilderness," interview with David Ehrenstein, in *Film Quarterly* (Berkeley), Fall 1993.

Publications on Potter

Books

Foster, Gwendolyn Audrey, *Women Film Directors: An International Bio-Critical Dictionary,* Westport, Connecticut, 1995.
MacDonald, Scott, *A Critical Cinema 3: Interviews with Independent Filmmakers,* Berkeley, 1998.

Articles

Glaessner, Verina, "Fire and Ice," in *Sight and Sound* (London), August 1992.
Lanouette, Jannine, "Potter's Yield," in *Premiere* (New York), July 1993.
Corliss, Richard, "A Film of One's Own," in *Time* (New York), 7 June 1993.

Film

Wendy Toye and Sally Potter: Two Directors, directed by Newson, 1985.

*   *   *

Sally Potter's career so far exemplifies the best and the worst features of British film culture: the best in its imaginativeness, inventiveness, and biting integrity; the worst in the extreme parsimony, both financial and critical, in which it existed. Potter's work in performance art, dance, and at the London Film Makers' Co-op was both culturally and financially "on the margins." Aware of these categories of "avant-garde" or "independent," "feminist" or "experimental," Potter has in quite serious ways never accepted them. Quite early on she spoke of herself as working within "avant-garde show business." Performance art and dance brought her into intimate contact with audiences, and she maintained this contact when she turned to film—regularly traveling with her films, watching and rewatching with different audiences, and involving herself in discussions afterwards. In various ways the idea of "the big screen" and the richness of the history of classical narrative cinema has been from the beginning part of her project. When making *Thriller,* a short but disconcerting deconstruction of *La Bohème,* she has said that she always asked herself, as she shot and then edited it, how it would look on the big screen in a Leicester Square cinema.

Changes in the structure of funding independent films in Britain during the 1980s enabled Potter to make her first feature film, *The Gold Diggers.* Using Colette Lafont, with whom she had worked in *Thriller,* and dramatic landscapes of "virginal purity" in Iceland, which she had visited with her performance group, she put together a film in which the circulation of finance and the circulation of images are both scrutinized. Lafont plays a computer programmer in a bank who becomes fascinated by gold—the touchstone of value, the basis of the calculations that appear daily on her screen. Julie Christie plays an actress on the run from her image. The film's radical quality extended to its mode of production. All participants took a salary of £30 per day and the film was shot with an all-women crew, including Babette Mangolte on camera, who had had previous experience with Chantal Akerman and Yvonne Rainer. The film was shot in black and white. Christie brought with her memories of her role within the traditional cinema epic, David Lean's *Doctor Zhivago,* but also a sense of the new, postwar woman from her work in British cinema of the sixties (*Billy Liar, Darling*). Lafont was deliberately cast against the stereotype of the black woman who is primarily a physical and sensual being. In the course of the action each woman attempts to locate a value system of her own, her own kind of gold. The film is full of affectionate references to cinema history and to the representations of women within it. Its very English quality lies in what has been called its narrative of "Alice in Wonderland-like inconsequentiality." In this lack of narrative seriousness, and in the sense in which its twin protagonists are experienced almost as a single entity, the film nicely prefigures *Orlando.*

With *Orlando* Potter seemed to be attempting to film the unfilmable, so much of the charm and persuasiveness of Virginia Woolf's thinly veiled love letter to Vita Sackville-West—and to history and to language—lies in its literary mode of address, the joy of words on paper. In the event Potter's intellectual adventurousness, allied to her equally strong awareness of the cinema's potential for magic, proved precisely right. Its rich, late-20th-century nouveau-rococo mise-en-scène (well within the English tradition of masque and display, explored also by Derek Jarman and Peter Greenaway), its quirky humor and laconic way with big themes, were purely cinematic. Central to the success of the film was the casting of Tilda Swinton as the protagonist who lives for 400 years, changing gender in the process—a role which Potter had envisaged for her from the beginning. The intelligent performance Swinton gives provides the film with an unshakable focus.

Financial necessity again nudged Potter towards radical production solutions. Funding was cobbled together from a handful of European sources, which included Russia. From Russia also came Elem Klimov's miraculous cinematographer Alexei Rodionov, the strange landscapes of Khiva, and St. Petersburg's snow. There is a sense in *Orlando* of everything—discourses on Englishness and the foreign, history and class, gender and identity—being thrown into the air to fall almost where they will. Gender, argues *Orlando,* is not central to the person but inconsequential. "Same person," says *Orlando,* "different sex."

Visual excitement comes not from narrative drive and the surrender to the merely sensational. "I edit," Potter has said, "not to narrative, but to an idea." Likewise her early work on performance and display inhibits her from an automatic recourse to the well-nigh ubiquitous language of the tight close-up with its concomitant fetishising of body parts at the expense of the person. Craft, a sense of timing, the awareness that an audience finds pleasure in a whole complex of feelings and ideas—"ethics too are pleasurable"—all play a part.

As the language of commercial cinema becomes more homogenous across the world, films that keep alive other ways of representation and response become increasingly valuable, and indeed necessary. Potter's work so far does so with considerable wit and aplomb.

—Verina Glaessner

PREOBRAZHENSKAYA, Olga
Russian director and actress

Born: Moscow, 1881. **Education:** Studied drama at the Moscow Art Theatre; was student of Konstantin Stanislavsky. **Family:** Married the film director Ivan Pravov. **Career:** Worked extensively as actress in provincial Russian theaters; 1913—became overnight success via her screen acting debut in Yakov Protazanov and Vladimir Gardin's immensely popular *The Keys to Happiness*; altogether, starred in more than 20 silent films, many directed by Protazanov and/or Gardin; 1916—made directing debut as co-director with Gardin of *The Lady Peasant,* becoming Russia's first female director; early 1920s—taught in the first Soviet film school, the State Cinema Technicum (GTK); 1927—filmed her masterpiece, *Peasant Women of Ryazan;* 1927-41—taught at the All-Union State Institute of Cinematography (VGIK); 1930s-early 1940s—worked primarily in a collaborative vein with Pravov; 1940s—career cut short by Stalin's purges. **Died:** 31 October 1971.

Films as Director

1916 *Baryshnia krestianka (The Lady Peasant; Miss Peasant)* (co-d with Gardin)
1917 *Viktoriya (Victoria)*
1923 *Slesar i kantzler (Locksmith and Chancellor)* (co-d with Gardin)
1925 *Fedka's Truth* (short)
1926 *Kashtanka*
1927 *Anya; Baby ryazanskie (Peasant Women of Ryazan; The Village of Sin; Women of Ryazan)*
1928 *Svetlyi gorod (Bright City; Luminous City)*
1929 *Poslednyi attraktzion (The Last Attraction)*
1930 *Tikhiy Don (Cossacks of the Don; The Quiet Don)* (co-d with Pravov, + sc)
1935 *Vrazhi tropi (Enemy Paths)*
1936 *Grain* (co-d with Pravov)
1939 *Stepan Razin* (co-d with Pravov)
1941 *Prairie Station; Paren iz taigi (Boy from the Taiga; Children of the Taiga)* (co-d with Pravov)

Films as Actress (selected)

1913 *Klyuchi shchastya (The Keys to Happiness)* (Protazanov and Gardin)
1915 *Petersburgskiye trushchobi (Petersburg Slums)* Protazanov and Gardin—serial); *Voina i mir (War and Peace)* (Protazanov and Gardin); *A Nest of Noblemen* (Gardin); *Plebei (Plebian)* (Protazanov)

Publications on Preobrazhenskaya

Books

Youngblood, Denise J., *Soviet Cinema in the Silent Era,* Ann Arbor, Michigan, 1985.
Kuhn, Annette, and Susannah Radstone, editors, *The Women's Companion to International Film,* London, 1990.
Youngblood, Denise J., *Movies for the Masses: Popular Cinema and Soviet Society in the 1920s,* Cambridge, England, 1992.
Attwood, Lynn, and others, *Red Women on the Silver Screen: Soviet Women and Cinema from the Beginning to the End of the Communist Era,* London, 1993.
Foster, Gwendolyn Audrey, *Women Film Directors: An International Bio-Critical Dictionary,* Westport, Connecticut, 1995.

* * *

Though little known in the West today, Olga Preobrazhenskaya was one of the pioneers of the Russian and early Soviet cinema.

Beginning as a Moscow Art Theatre- and Stanislavsky-trained actress for the stage, Preobrazhenskaya made a smashing screen debut in 1913's *The Keys to Happiness*—an adaptation of a popular novel by Anastasiya Verbitskaya, which was directed by Yakov Protazanov and Vladimir Gardin. Preobrazhenskaya played a young Russian woman who has a liaison with an older, Jewish businessman (at the time, she was in her early thirties, considered "too old" for starring roles by many filmmakers). Propelled by the film's stature as the greatest box-office success in Russia to date, Preobrazhenskaya went on to star in more than 20 other features, establishing herself as a leading actress of the pre-Revolutionary cinema in such "big-budget" films as the elaborate *War and Peace* (also directed by Protazanov and Gardin) and *Plebian,* an adaptation of August Strindberg's *Miss Julie* directed by Protazanov alone.

Like many other early cinematic actresses the world over, Preobrazhenskaya was not content with just performing but quickly moved behind the camera. In 1916 she became the first female director in Russia with her co-direction with Gardin of *The Lady Peasant,* which already represented two of the primary themes of her directing career: the place of women in Russian society and the lives of the Russian peasantry. In 1917—the year of the Russian Revolution—Preobrazhenskaya solo-directed for the first time with *Victoria.* After teaching at the first Soviet film school in the early 1920s, she returned to direct several films for and about children: *Fedka's Truth;* the popular *Kashtanka,* which was based on a Chekhov story; and *Anya.*

In 1927—the same year that she directed *Anya*—Preobrazhenskaya also returned to films for adults with what is generally considered her greatest film, the classically melodramatic *Peasant Women of Ryazan.* The film centers around two village women, one representing tradition (Anna) and the other change (Vassilisa). In a story based on *snokharchestvo* (the persistent problem in Russian villages of sexual abuse of daughters-in-law), Anna is raped by her vicious father-in-law—a kulak—after her husband leaves to fight in World War I. She bears the rapist's child, and in the end drowns herself when her husband returns and rejects her. In contrast, the independent-minded Vassilisa, daughter of the kulak, shacks up with the lowly blacksmith whom she loves, after her father refuses to give his consent to their marriage. Vassilisa also sets up an orphanage for homeless children in the country, thus completely establishing her as a "new Soviet woman"—nearly a proto-feminist. She even takes charge of Anna's child after the mother's suicide.

Although criticized by Soviet authorities at the time for—among other things—being "unrealistic," in particular for its cursory coverage of the Revolution and civil war, Preobrazhenskaya is now credited with making a masterpiece; Denise J. Youngblood has called it "a Soviet melodrama of the highest order." Following the launch of the Cultural Revolution in the spring of 1928, films about the collectivization campaign were encouraged, leading to a spate of "peasant films" in the 1930s; in this way, Preobrazhenskaya's *Peasant Women of Ryazan* was a pioneering film—Youngblood calls it "the only major Soviet film about peasant life made prior to the Cultural Revolution." *Peasant Women* also helped launch the career of Emma Tsesarskaya (in the role of Vassilisa), who became a star of the 1930s peasant films, including Preobrazhenskaya's own *Grain*—a 1936 film depicting Soviet collective farms battling on one hand with peasants clinging to the past and on the other with the standby-villain kulaks.

Grain was among several films that Preobrazhenskaya made from the late 1920s through 1941 in collaboration with her husband, Ivan Pravov. Among these, 1930's *Cossacks of the Don,* which was adapted from Mikhail Sholokhov's acclaimed novel *The Quiet Don,* is one of the best known. (Tsesarskaya has another starring role in this film.) Taking place during the civil war, it portrays the customs and morals of the Cossacks—and their role in the civil war—in a remarkably even-handed and realistic way, thus staying true to its novel source. A *New York Times* reviewer of the era raved: "The theme is one in which the tragic and the comic are well intermingled, and the ending—the dawn of a new era in Czarist-oppressed Russia—comes as a maturely conceived climax to a story of unusual merit." It is thus almost tragic that, following the completion of the historical epic *Stepan Razin* in 1939 and two more films in 1941, Preobrazhenskaya's career would come to an abrupt end via the Stalin-led purges of the 1940s, fading to black the vision of one of the most important women filmmakers of Russian and Soviet cinema.

—David E. Salamie

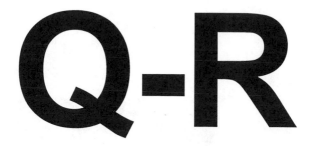

Q-R

QINGCHUNJI

(Sacrificed Youth)
People's Republic of China, 1985
Director: Zhang Nuanxin

Production: Beijing Film Academy Youth Studio; color; running time: 100 minutes. Released 1985. Filmed in Yunnan, PRC.

Producer: Zhao Yamin; **screenplay:** Zhang Manling and Zhang Nuanxin, based on the novella *You Yige Meili de Difang* [Such a beautiful place], by Zhang Manling; **photography:** Mu Deyuan and Deng Wei; **editor:** Zhao Yihua; **sound recording:** Ma Yuewen; **art directors:** Li Yongxin and Wang Yanjin; **props:** Xu Xianping; **music:** Liu Sula and Zhai Xiaosong; **conductor:** Hu Bingxu; **soloists:** Wu Jing and Zhai Xiaosong; **lighting:** Li Jingzhong and Lian Zhichen; **costumes:** Zhao Hui, **makeup:** Guo Shuyi; **consultants on Dai minority:** Yan Ha and Ming La.

Cast: Li Fengxu (*Li Chun*); with: Feng Yuanzheng; Song Tao; Guo Jianguo; Yu Da; Yu Shuai; Yan Hanmu; Zhu Lanfang; Wen Minhong; Yanhanmuha; Mao Xiang.

Publications

Books

Semsel, George, *Chinese Film: The State of the Art in the People's Republic,* New York, 1987.
Quart, Barbara Koenig, *Women Directors: The Emergence of a New Cinema,* New York, 1988.
Resource Book on Domestic Art Films 1949-1986, Hebei Film Studio, 1988.

Articles

"Ceaseless Explorations, Painstaking Innovations—Proceedings of the Symposium on Music in Film," in *Dianying Yishu Cankao Ziliao* [Reference materials on film art] (Beijing), 1985.
"Don't Repeat What Others Have Done, and Don't Repeat What You Yourself Have Done—Zhang Nuanxin Discusses the Filming and Interpretation of *Sacrificed Youth,*" in *Dianying Yishu Cankao Ziliao* [Reference materials on film art] (Beijing), 1985.
Han Shangyi, "As I See *Sacrificed Youth,*" in *Dianying Xinzuo* [New Cinema] (Beijing), 1986.
Clark, Paul, "Ethnic Minorities in Chinese Films," in *East-West Film Journal* (Honolulu), June 1987.
Wang, Yongwu, "Strolling through a Realm of Beauty: Reflections on *Sacrificed Youth,*" in *Zhongguo Dazhong Yingping Changbian* [Extended reviews of Chinese popular films], edited by Jin Zhongqiang and Zhang Xiangqing, Beijing, 1990.

Gladney, Dru C., "Representing Nationality in China: Refiguring Majority/Minority Identities," in *Journal of Asian Studies* (Milwaukee), February 1994.
Gladney, Dru C., "Tian Zhuangzhuang, the Fifth Generation, and Minorities Film in China," in *Public Culture* (Chicago), Fall 1995.

* * *

During the Cultural Revolution, a 17-year old girl named Li Chun, scion of an urban intellectual family, is sent to a remote mountainous village in a Dai (Thai) minority region in southern China for her mandatory period of "rural training." Assigned to the family of the head of the local cooperative, she is welcomed by its members—"Dadie" (father) and the 90-year-old "Yiya" (grandmother) who live alone, since the son (later called "Dage" [elder brother]) is away tending a kiln. She proves her worth by taking over the customarily female chore of fetching well water for household use. She also struggles to keep up with the brigade of young Dai women as they chop wood and bamboo. Soon, she grows envious of the relative uninhibitedness of these women, who dress in form-fitting sarongs and adorn themselves with silver ornaments, and end their days by singing flirtatious antiphonal songs with the unmarried men of the village, before slipping their sarongs turban-style around their heads to swim naked in the river.

When the Dai women attempt to banish Li Chun to work with the old people because of her drab, socialist clothing and her solemn demeanor, Li decides to "go native"—she changes into a sarong, accepts loans of ornaments to wear, and eventually begins to enjoy dancing by firelight and swimming without a bathing suit. By learning rudimentary first aid and medical techniques from a manual, she also gains a modest reputation as a healer within the community.

Trouble arises when Li befriends a young male Chinese intellectual named Ren Jia, and rejects the love of her Dai "older brother" upon his return. To avoid the ensuing hostilities, Li quietly departs the village, and settles elsewhere as a schoolteacher. From there she returns briefly to the village to mourn the passing of her "Yiya." Eventually she is given official leave to return to the city, but returns one last time to the village upon learning of catastrophic floods and mud slides in the region, that have, she discovers, leveled the village and killed both her Dai family and her Chinese friend.

Sacrificed Youth is filmed in a documentary style, on location, using mostly nonprofessional performers, and relying heavily on a first-person voice-over narrative to advance its simple story. The lighting is naturalistic, deriving from sun or fire, and the musical soundtrack consists largely of intradiegetic or offscreen ethnic songs and instrumental music. With the exception of a small number of early long shots to establish the lushness and verdancy of the context—subtropical trees and undergrowth, flowing water and torrential rain—much of the film is shot at eye level at a distance that ranges from objective to intimate: full shots of people at work in forest, field, or home, conversing before or after work, with close-ups to

Qingchunji

convey feelings and reactions. Occasional point-of-view shots reveal feet slipping into shoes, blades hacking at wood, hands implanting rice seedlings in a flooded field. Exceptions include two sequences near the end of the film, in which the subjects are viewed from a greater distance—once during the funeral procession of "Yiya," and again when a sobbing Li Chun stands alone amid the desolation that once was her forest home—when the distance and the barren landscape emphasize the loss of connection with what had once been close and intimate.

The film constitutes an intimate exploration of a young woman's feelings in self-reflection. Her examination proceeds on two planes. On one, the film contrasts her Han Chinese "civilized" but repressed self with an idealized primal and unfettered other. On the other, it relates her younger, past self—which was bonded with a nurturing environment and loving caregivers—to a present and future self which is less sentimental and more independent, but more alienated.

The self/other contrast is revealed in minor incidents (the village beauty passes by and Li Chun's voice-over narrative confides: "I always feel so insecure in her presence," as well as more extended sequences. In an often commented-upon scene, Li watches at a distance as the young Dai women first engage their

sweethearts in a melodic vocal exchange against the backdrop of a waterfall in the forest, then descend to swim naked in the river. Li's thoughts, conveyed once again in a sotto voce voice-over to hold the audience in confidence, focus on her own lack in the face of the Dai robustness: "I'm so tired. I can't work, I don't even know how to live. I'm filled with lethargy." But her transformation begins at this low point, as her voice-over continues: "Later I, too, learned to swim like they, and never again was willing to wear that sticky, clinging swimsuit."

At a socialist-style communal meeting shortly thereafter, Li sullenly realizes that, whereas most people were awarded ten points for their work performance, and she herself only earned six because she is "used to studying only, and doesn't know how to work," the village beauty was given 18 points largely because of her looks. "So beauty is worth points too?" After a lifetime of socialist conditioning, Li begins to attend to her own physicality, so that eventually she, too, can dance laughing with the others around a bonfire. But she retains enough of her Han intellectualism to realize the value of reading medical volumes in her spare time, as well as her basic Han reserve in the face of perceived tribal freedom. Late in the film, by the river in the moonlight, after a conversation about the relative desirability of Dai-style honesty and directness, Ren Jia asks her thoughts, and yet she refuses to divulge them, responding, "I ... think it's getting cool and we should go back." Although Li is charmed by the youthful sensuality of the culture of the other, she is also aware of its shortcomings—poverty, ignorance, seasons passed in backbreaking labor. She realizes that there is truth in the comment of her Han companion, "The beauty of youth only lasts a few years. When a Dai girl marries, she quickly becomes first a matron, and then an old woman." Han culture privileges age and the accumulation of wisdom over the attributes of the young; the treasures of youth, portrayed as particularly celebrated by the Dai, are short-lived.

Temporality is at the core of the film's second exploratory plane as well. Li's world in the Dai village is womblike, demarcated by familiar landmarks: an ancient tree, the river, the forest. Her relationship with her Dai family and her Han friend are close, nurturing, innocent, asexual, as intimate as the bond between a mother and child. In voice-over, she comments on her relationship with Ren Jia: "I had never become so close to a boy before. I told him everything. Whenever I parted from him, I felt bereft." Similarly, in a particularly tender sequence, Li and her Dai family are gathered at home, at night, companionably engaged in quiet chores by firelight. Contented, she begins to sing a Han song replete with images of nature and a domestic garden: grapes, a gentle moon, a fence, a sweet dawning sun, and the refrain—"Oooh, mama; oooh, mama." This song is reprised twice again in the film. When Li Chun lives alone as a schoolteacher, she teaches it to her charges, and finally, when the film's closing credits run, it appears again as the theme song, on the musical soundtrack.

Since she has otherwise made few references to her own mother (she and her mother together put her father on a train to the countryside; her mother now lives alone at home), the viewer has no grounds to posit a remarkable relationship between Li and her mother. Rather, this maternal invocation is best understood as referencing not a person but an abstracted emotional bonding, both to an environment as well as with individuals. The film is a haunted tribute to a lost state of grace, a condition once known but no longer attainable, in which the pre-sexual individual is content in the warm maternal embrace. Li's narration of her existence in the nurturing, womblike environment of the Dai village is a recollection of a childlike state, once loved and now discarded, in which her deepest bonds were both to the place and to the re-creation of a natal family—"Yiya" as grandmother, "Dadie" as father, Ren Jia as brother—and in which she chose not to see Ren Jia as a potential lover and explicitly rejected the sexual advances of "Dage." The maternal presence is something Li Chun both longs for in abstract but is repelled by in the concrete—her own mother is physically distant, and her Dai surrogate is not a mother (who has died) but a metaphorically distanced mother/grandmother. Li Chun leaves the Dai maternal environment of her own will, not to establish another bond elsewhere but to become independent. Upon departing the village, she intones in voice-over: "Now I have no home anywhere, but everywhere is my home." It is a reluctant but deliberate separation, which she mourns at the conclusion of the film—the place and all the people that constituted this re-creation of maternal engagement have been destroyed in flooding waters, just as passing time obliterates the child. That bonded state can now be evoked only in memory, as it is with the final rendition of the "Mama" theme song.

—Cynthia Y. Ning

RAGING BULL

USA, 1980
Director: Martin Scorsese
Editor: Thelma Schoonmaker

Production: United Artists; part in color, prints by Technicolor; running time: 129 minutes; length: 11,588 feet. Released November 1980.

Producers: Irwin Winkler and Robert Chartoff; **associate producers:** Hal W. Polaire and Peter Savage; **screenplay:** Paul Schrader and Mardik Martin, from the book by Jake La Motta with Peter Savage; **1st assistant directors:** Jerry Grandey and Allan Wertheim; **2nd assistant directors:** Elie Cohn and Joan Feinstein; **photography:** Michael Chapman; **editor:** Thelma Schoonmaker; **associate editor:** Susan E. Morse; **sound recordists:** Les Lazarowitz, Michael Evje, Walter Gest, and Gary Ritchie; **sound re-recordists:** Donald O. Mitchell, Bill Nicholson, and David J. Kimball; **sound effects supervising editor:** Frank Warner; **sound effects editors:** William J. Wylie and Chester Slomka; **special effects:** Raymond Klein and Max E. Wood; **production designer:** Gene Rudolf; **set decorators:** Philip Abramson and Frederic C. Weiler; **art directors:** Alan Manser, Kirk Axtell, and Sheldon Haber; **music editor:** Jim Henrikson; **costume design:** Richard Bruno; **makeup:** Michael Westmore; **stunt co-ordinator:** Jim Nickerson; **technical advisers:** Frank Topham and Al Silvani; **consultant:** Jake La Motta.

Cast: Robert De Niro (*Jake La Motta*); Cathy Moriarty (*Vickie La Motta*); Joe Pesci (*Joey La Motta*); Frank Vincent (*Salvy*); Nicholas Colasanto (*Tommy Como*); Theresa Saldana (*Lenore*); Mario Gallo (*Mario*); Frank Adonis (*Patsy*); Joseph Bono (*Guido*); Frank Topham (*Toppy*); Lori Anne Flax (*Irma*); Charles Scorsese (*Charlie, Man with Como*); Don Dunphy (*Himself*); Bill Hanrahan (*Eddie Eagen*); Rita Bennett (*Emma, Miss 48's*); James V. Christy (*Dr. Pinto*); Bernie Allen (*Comedian*); Michael Badalucco (*Soda fountain clerk*); Thomas Beansy Lobasso (*Beansy*); Paul Forrest (*Monsignor*); Peter Petrella (*Johnny*); Geraldine Smith (*Janet*); Mardik Martin (*Copa waiter*); Peter Savage (*Jackie Curtie*); Daniel P. Conte (*Detroit promoter*); Joe Malanga (*Bodyguard*); Allan Malamud (*Reporter at Jake's House*); D. J. Blair (*State Attorney Bronson*); Laura James (*Mrs. Bronson*); Richard McMurray (*J. R.*); Mary Albee (*Underage ID girl*); Candy Moore (*Linda*); Nick Trisko (*Bartender Curlo*); Lou Tiano (*Ricky*); Allan Joseph (*Jeweller*); Martin Scorsese (*Barbizon Stagehand*); Floyd Anderson (*Jimmy Reeves*); Johnny Barnes (*"Sugar" Ray Robinson*); Kevin Mahon (*Tony Janiro*); Eddie Mustafa Muhammad (*Billy Fox*); Louis Raftis (*Marcel Cerdan*); Coley Wallis (*Joe Louis*); Fritzie Higgins (*Woman with Vickie*); Johnny Turner (*Laurent Dauthuille*).

Awards: Academy Awards for Best Actor (De Niro) and Best Editing; British Academy of Film and Television Arts Award for Best Editing; Golden Globes for Best Actor, Drama (DeNiro); Los Angeles Film Critics Award for Best Film and Best Actor (DeNiro); National Board of Review for Best Actor (De Niro) and Best Supporting Actor (Pesci); National Society of Film Critics for Best Director, Best Supporting Actor (Pesci), and Best Cinematography; New York Film Critics Awards for Best Actor (De Niro) and Best Supporting Actor (Pesci).

Publications

Books

Kolker, Robert Phillip, *A Cinema of Loneliness: Penn, Kubrick, Coppola, Scorsese, Altman,* Oxford, 1980; rev. ed., 1988.

Arnold, Frank, and others, *Martin Scorsese,* Munich, 1986.

Bliss, Michael, *Martin Scorsese and Michael Cimino,* Metuchen, New Jersey, 1986.

Cameron-Wilson, James, *The Cinema of Robert De Niro,* London, 1986.

Cietat, Michel, *Martin Scorsese,* Paris, 1986.

Domecq, Jean-Philippe, *Martin Scorsese: Un Rève italo-américain,* Renens, Switzerland, 1986.

McKay, Keith, *Robert De Niro: The Hero Behind the Masks,* New York, 1986.

Weiss, Ulli, *Das neue Hollywood: Francis Ford Coppola, Steven Spielberg, Martin Scorsese,* Munich, 1986.

Wood, Robin, *Hollywood from Vietnam to Reagan,* New York, 1986.

Weiss, Marian, *Martin Scorsese: A Guide to References and Resources,* Boston, 1987.

Articles

Wiener, Thomas, "Martin Scorsese Fights Back," in *American Film* (Washington, D.C.), November 1980.

Variety (New York), 12 November 1980.

Georgakas, Dan, in *Cineaste* (New York), Winter 1980-81.

Thomson, David, "The Director as Raging Bull," in *Film Comment* (New York), January/February 1981.

Gentry, R., "Michael Chapman Captures *Raging Bull* in Black and White," in *Millimeter* (New York), February 1981.

Jenkins, Steve, in *Monthly Film Bulletin* (London), February 1981.

Millar, Gavin, in *Listener* (London), 26 February 1981.

"Dialogue on Film: Robert De Niro," in *American Film* (Washington, D.C.), March 1981.

"*Raging Bull* Section" of *Cahiers du Cinéma* (Paris), March 1981.

Combs, Richard, in *Sight and Sound* (London), Spring 1981.

"*Raging Bull* Section" of *Positif* (Paris), April 1981.

Rinaldi, G., in *Cineforum* (Bergamo, Italy), April 1981.

Sinyard, Neil, in *Films Illustrated* (London), May 1981.

Williams, A. L., in *American Cinematographer* (Los Angeles), May 1981.

Henry, M., in *Casablanca* (Madrid), June 1981.

Cook, Pam, "*Raging Bull:* Masculinity in Crisis," in *Screen* (London), September/October 1982.

Wood, Robin, "The Homosexual Subtext: *Raging Bull,*" in *Australian Journal of Screen Theory* (Kensington, New South Wales), no. 15-16, 1983.

Hemmeter, G. C., and T., "The Word Made Flesh: Language in *Raging Bull,*" in *Literature/Film Quarterly* (Salisbury, Maryland), April 1986.

Bruce, Bryan, "Martin Scorsese: Five Films," in *Movie* (London), Winter 1986.

Lane, J., "Martin Scorsese and the Documentary Impulse," in *Framework* (London), no. 1, 1991.

Sitney, P. Adams, "Cinematic Election and Theological Vanity," in *Raritan* (New Brunswick, New Jersey), no. 2, 1991.

Talty, Stephan, "Invisible Woman," in *American Film* (Hollywood), September/October 1991.

Librach, R. S., "The Last Temptation in *Mean Streets* and *Raging Bull,*" in *Literature/Film Quarterly* (Salisbury, Maryland), no. 1, 1992.

* * *

Martin Scorsese's *Raging Bull,* a chronicle of 23 years in the life of middleweight boxer Jake La Motta, was deservedly atop many critics' lists as the very best film of the 1980s. Beyond the story it tells, this stark, striking, black-and-white film is a visual spectacle, crammed with dazzling images and ironic juxtapositions which are the happy results of a seamless union of direction, camera work, and editing.

The flow of the visuals, resulting from the manner in which they are photographed (by Michael Chapman) and edited (by Thelma Schoonmaker), is evident from the film's very first sequences. The opening credits unravel over a poetic, slow-motion image of La Motta shadowboxing in a ring: a young bull, all nerve and energy, itching to strip off his robe and do damage to his opponent. Next, a title card informs us that it is 1964, in New York City. A puffy, punch-drunk, middle-aged La Motta—well past his physical prime and a jarring contrast to the lean boxing machine of the previous sequence—fumbles as he attempts to rehearse a nightclub monologue. In both sequences, the camera is still as it records these altogether different images of the same man, and there is a minimum of editing which allows the viewer to absorb their impact.

Next, another title card tells us that we are being transported back to 1941. La Motta, the young "Bronx Bull," is undefeated but in midst the fight of his life against Jimmy Reeves in the Cleveland Arena. Here, the editing becomes lively. The shots of La Motta and Reeves are at different angles. Some are stationary; in others, the camera glides across the ring, in the direction of both boxers. The shots come one after the other as the boxers flail away and a fight breaks out in the crowd. Energy is derived not only from the physical movement of the actors but the manner in which the contrasting pieces of film are edited. Indeed, in strictly visual terms, the most impressive sequences in *Raging Bull* are those that take place in the ring. Collectively, they are nothing short of electric. The film is loaded with them, and one is as exhilarating as the next. As the various pieces of film are edited together within each sequence, the result is a blow-by-blow view of boxing that is at once brutal and poetic.

The fast-paced editing parallels La Motta's exploding temper as he erupts at his first wife, beats up his brother in a jealous rage, or especially as he pummels his adversaries between the ropes. This is employed only in spurts, and counterpoints the longer shots in the film's more sedate, informational scenes. In a music video, where the fast-paced editing often is nonstop from beginning to end, the effect is at once visually dazzling but intellectually hollow: an exercise in style, with little concern for content or sustaining emotion. But in *Raging Bull,* Schoonmaker quite properly adapts her editing style to the dramatic pace of each sequence, and its purpose within the framework of the whole, resulting in a profound dramatic effect.

Additional cinematic technique adds to the film's visual power. When La Motta first spies Vickie, the woman whom he soon will seduce and who eventually will replace his first wife, slow-motion shots are edited next to regular-speed ones, with the result conveying in strict visual terms the manner in which this adolescent beauty captures La Motta's attention. In La Motta's bouts with Sugar Ray Robinson, slow-motion shots, regular-speed shots and even still shots coming after flashing ringside cameras are seamlessly joined together. Particularly as Robinson clobbers La Motta and strips him

Raging Bull

of his middleweight title—from a visual standpoint, the penultimate sequence in the film—Scorsese and Schoonmaker graphically and harrowingly capture the power and impact of one man's fist crashing into another's jaw as popping flashbulbs emit a blinding light.

From the opening sequences on, the power of so much of the imagery in *Raging Bull* is predicated upon irony. There are the choppily edited color home movies of La Motta, Vickie and their families, which visually record the progression of their lives during the 1940s. These short sequences are contrasted to black-and-white still images and slow-motion shots of La Motta's various bouts during the period. Even more to the point, the ring sequence in which La Motta finally wins the championship from Marcel Cerdan is followed by one in which he is back in the Bronx, in his sparsely furnished apartment, just another everyman attempting to adjust a primitive television set. A rare tender moment between La Motta and Vickie is followed by a fist smashing into his face during his next bout. The sequence in which he loses his championship to Robinson is immediately followed by one, set several years later, in which he is pudgy, and very retired. All of these images, those within each sequence and the sequences as they are connected together, are seamlessly united. The result is a film which is not so much watched as sensed and felt.

Schoonmaker and Scorsese, who met during the 1960s at New York University's film school, have a collaborative relationship that may be best described as a partnership. Throughout her career, Schoonmaker has labored almost exclusively for Scorsese. She worked on his first feature, *Who's That Knocking at My Door?*, and has edited all of his post-*Raging Bull* projects to date (from *The King of Comedy* and *After Hours* through *Casino* and *Kundun*). For her work on *Raging Bull*, Schoonmaker earned an Academy Award—and it is an Oscar well-deserved.

—Rob Edelman

RAINER, Yvonne
American director

Born: San Francisco, 1934. **Career:** From 1957—modern dancer, then choreographer, New York; 1962—co-founder of Judson Dance Theater; 1962-75—presented choreographic work in United States and Europe; 1968—began to integrate slides and short films into dance performances; 1972—completed first feature-length film, *Lives of Performers*; teacher at New School for Social Research, New York, California Institute of the Arts, Valencia, and elsewhere. **Awards:** Maya Deren Award, American Film Institute, 1988; Guggenheim Fellowship, 1969, 1989; MacArthur Fellowship, 1990-95; Wexner Prize, 1995. **Address:** 72 Franklin Street, New York, NY 10013, U.S.A.

Films

1967   *Volleyball (Foot Film)* (short)
1968   *Hand Movie* (short); *Rhode Island Red* (short); *Trio Film* (short)
1969   *Line*
1972   *Lives of Performers*
1974   *Film about a Woman Who...*
1976   *Kristina Talking Pictures*
1980   *Journeys from Berlin/1971*
1985   *The Man Who Envied Women*
1990   *Privilege*
1996   *Murder and Murder*

Films as Actress Only

1977   ***Madame X—eine absolute Herrscherin*** (*Madame X—An Absolute Ruler*) (Ottinger) (as Josephine de Collage)

Publications by Rainer

Books

Work 1961-73, New York, 1974.
The Films of Yvonne Rainer, by Rainer and others, Bloomington, Indiana, 1989.

Articles

"A Quasi Survey of Some 'Minimalist' Tendencies in the Quantitatively Minimal Dance Activity Midst the Plethora, or An Analysis of *Trio A,*" in *Minimal Art,* edited by Gregory Battcock, New York, 1968.
Interview in *Monthly Film Bulletin* (London), May 1977.
"More Kicking and Screaming from the Narrative Front/Backwater," in *Wide Angle* (Athens, Ohio), vol. 7, no. 1/2, 1985.
Interview with Mitch Rosenbaum, in *Persistence of Vision* (Maspeth, New York), Summer 1988.
"Demystifying the Female Body," interview with Scott MacDonald, in *Film Quarterly* (Berkeley), Fall 1991.
"A Legend Comes Out: Critically Acclaimed Filmmaker Yvonne Rainer," interview with Liz Kotz, in *Advocate* (Los Angeles), 5 November 1991.
"Script of Privilege," in *Screen Writings: Scripts and Texts by Independent Filmmakers,* edited by Scott MacDonald, Berkeley, 1995.

Publications on Rainer

Books

Acker, Ally, *Reel Women: Pioneers of the Cinema, 1896 to the Present,* New York, 1991.
Weiss, Andrea, *Vampires and Violets: Lesbians in Film,* New York, 1993.
Green, Shelley, *Radical Juxtaposition: The Films of Yvonne Rainer,* Metuchen, New Jersey, 1994.
Foster, Gwendolyn Audrey, *Women Film Directors: An International Bio-Critical Dictionary,* Westport, Connecticut, 1995.

Articles

Koch, Stephen, "Performance: A Conversation," in *Artforum* (New York), December 1972.
Borden, Lizzie, "Trisha Brown and Yvonne Rainer," in *Artforum* (New York), June 1973.
Michelson, Annette, "Yvonne Rainer: The Dancer and the Dance," and "Yvonne Rainer: *Lives of Performers,*" in *Artforum* (New York), January and February 1974.
"Yvonne Rainer: An Introduction, in *Camera Obscura* (Berkeley), Fall 1976.

Rosenbaum, Jonathan, "The Ambiguities of Yvonne Rainer," in *American Film* (Washington, D.C.), March 1980.

Rich, B. Ruby, "Yvonne Rainer," in *Frauen und Film* (Berlin), October 1984.

Cook, Pam, "Love and Catastrophe—Yvonne Rainer," in *Monthly Film Bulletin* (London), August 1987.

Vincendeau, Ginette, and B. Reynaud, "Impossible Projections," in *Screen* (London), Autumn 1987.

* * *

Although Yvonne Rainer made her first feature-length film in 1972, she had already been prominent in the New York avant-garde art scene for nearly a decade. She moved to New York from San Francisco in 1957 to study acting, but started taking dance lessons and soon committed herself to dance. By the mid-1960s, she emerged as an influential dancer and choreographer, initially drawing the attention of critics and audiences through her work with the Judson Dance Theater.

Rainer saw a problem inherent in dance as an art form, namely its involvement with "narcissism, virtuosity and display." Her alternative conception was of the performance as a kind of work or task, as opposed to an exhibition, carried out by "neutral 'doers'" rather than performers. Thus the minimalist dance that she pioneered, which depended on ordinary movements, departed radically from the dramatic, emotive forms of both its classical and modern dance precursors.

Rainer was not long content with merely stripping dance of its artifice and conventions. She became interested in psychology and sexuality, in the everyday emotions that people share, and grew dissatisfied with abstract dance, which she found too limited to express her new concerns. To communicate more personal and emotional content, Rainer began experimenting with combining movements with other media, such as recorded and spoken texts, slides, film stills, and music, creating a performance collage. Language and narrative became increasingly important components of her performance.

Rainer's first films, shorts made to be part of these performances in the late 1960s, were "filmed choreographic exercises," as she wrote in 1971, "that were meant to be viewed with one's peripheral vision ... not to be taken seriously." Her interest in the narrative potential of film and the director's dominance of the medium drew Rainer further into filmmaking.

Her first two feature films, *Lives of Performers* and *Film about a Woman Who ...*, both with cinematographer Babette Mangolte, originated as performance pieces. In these and her two other films, *Kristina Talking Pictures* and *Journeys from Berlin/1971*, Rainer interweaves the real and the fictional, the personal and the political, the concrete and the abstract. She preserves the collagist methods of her performances, juxtaposing personal recollections, previous works, historical documents, and original dialogue and narration, her soundtracks often having the same richness, and the same disjunction, as the visual portions of her films.

Like Brecht, Rainer believes that an audience should contemplate what they see; they should participate in the creative process of the film rather than simply receive it passively. Thus, instead of systematically telling a story, she apposes and layers narrative elements to create meaning. The discontinuity, ambiguity, and even contradiction that often result keep Rainer's audience at a distance, so they can examine the feminist, psychological, political, or purely emotional issues she addresses. Consistent with her dance and performance,

Rainer's films are theoretical, even intellectual, not dramatic, sentimental, or emotional, despite her subject matter, which is often controversial and emotion-laden.

—Jessica Wolff

RAMBLING ROSE
USA, 1991
Director: Martha Coolidge

Production: Seven Arts; DuArt and Deluxe, 35mm; running time: 112 minutes. Released September 1991. Filmed in Ivanhoe, North Carolina.

Producer: Renny Harlin; **executive producers:** Mario Kassar and Edgar J. Scherick; **screenplay:** Calder Willingham, based on his book; **photography:** Johnny E. Jensen; **editor:** Steven Cohen; **sound:** Richard Van Dyke; **sound editor:** Leslie Shatz; **production design:** John Vallone; **art director:** Christiaan Wagener; **set decorator:** Robert Gould; **music:** Elmer Bernstein; **costume designer:** Jane Robinson.

Cast: Laura Dern (*Rose*); Robert Duvall (*Daddy*); Diane Ladd (*Mother*); Lukas Haas (*Buddy*); John Heard (*Willcox "Buddy" Hillyer*), Kevin Conway (*Dr. Martinson*); Robert John Burke (*Dave Wilkie*); Lisa Jakub (*Doll Hillyer*); Evan Lockwood (*Waski Hillyer*); Matt Sutherland (*Billy*); D. Anthony Pender (*Foster*); David E. Scarborough (*Horton*); Robin Dale Robertson (*Young Salesman*); General Fermon Judd Jr. (*Shadrack*); Richard K. Olsen (*Chief of Police*); Michael Mott (*Man in Store*); James Binns (*Minister*).

Publications

Articles

Clendenin, Dudley, "*Rambling Rose* Blossoms for the Screen," in *New York Times,* 2 December 1990.

Meisel, M., "Coolidge Breaks Through with *Rambling Rose,*" in *Film Journal* (New York), September 1991.

James, C., "Sweet, Yes, but Wild at Heart," in *New York Times,* 20 September 1991.

Ansen, David, "Southern Hearts and Hormones," in *Newsweek* (New York), 23 September 1991.

Denby, D., "Mork and Terry," in *New York Magazine,* 30 September 1991.

Brown, G., "Driving Miss Rosebud," in *Village Voice* (New York), 1 October 1991.

Travers, Peter, "Why She's Gotta Have It," in *Rolling Stone* (New York), 3 October 1991.

Ball, E., "Neo-Dad," in *Village Voice* (New York), 26 November 1991.

Dupagne, M. F., "*Rambling Rose,*" in *Grand Angle* (Mariembourg, Belgium), February 1992.

* * *

Rambling Rose is the gem of Martha Coolidge's career as director. A breathtakingly beautiful film, it evokes the tender nostalgia of a sepia-tinted photograph. But, though nostalgic, it is never simple-minded. It is set in 1935 in the South, when the Great Depression was still palpable. "Daddy" and "Mother" Hillyer invite Rose, a young woman who is on the brink of a precarious future, likely as a prostitute, to care for their three children and to live with them as a member of the family in their spacious old mansion. But, easily able to charm men with her naive effervescence and desperately seeking their sincere affections, Rose repeatedly finds trouble and Daddy soon wearies of her rambling ways.

When it was released, critics overwhelmingly agreed that, in a virtual sea of male-themed films, *Rambling Rose* was a special treat. Perhaps not surprisingly, Coolidge spent five years seeking financial backing for the film, after discovering the screenplay in a "dead script" pile where it landed after 12 unsuccessful years of making the rounds of Hollywood producers. It has a quiet but never dull rhythm; along with lingering, loving shots of the Southern landscape, Coolidge uses long takes to enable virtuoso performances and rich collaborations between the actors. Further, its character-driven story conveys a sense of the manifold facets of femininity and sexuality, as well as some of their strengths and vulnerabilities. Yet, on another level, it is about youth, sexuality, and coming-of-age in a still sexually repressed, male-dominated era, and in a region apparently untouched by the Jazz Age and the proliferation of "modern women."

In this feminine Oedipal tale, Coolidge introduces the newly blossomed, 19-year-old heroine Rose (Laura Dern) in a memorable sequence, in which the newly pubescent boy Buddy studies—and becomes immediately smitten by—her flamboyant clothes and girl-woman gait as she arrives on their path slightly disheveled and sweaty from her journey. When she meets the ever-genteel Daddy, he welcomes her with a compliment—that she will bring a glow to the home's old walls. To underscore the point, Coolidge photographs Dern with a warm, golden light so that she indeed seems to glow. Though she falls hopelessly in love with Daddy, and at one point tests his will by flinging herself at him, she is a guileless young woman who discovers that she has a great deal in common with smart and eccentric Mother, herself a former orphan. When Rose gets into "trouble" with the town's young men, it is Mother who defends her because she understands her longing for love. Her thoughtful defense of Rose is crucial, especially when she saves the young woman from the operation that Daddy and her doctor agree would curtail her sexual desires and her attractiveness to men. In a striking scene, Mother chastises the men for their cruel audacity, demanding "is there no limit to which you will not go to keep your illusions about yourself?" On another occasion, Mother explains to Daddy that sexual pleasure is a gift from God: "You don't understand, it is a positive energy on this planet; it's what we do with it that makes it negative." The film further complicates the issue of feminine sexuality by alluding to the incest that Rose suffered as a child, which helps to account for her promiscuity. Indeed, one of the film's most memorable lines occurs when a heartbroken Rose, just discovered with a man in her bedroom, implores Daddy to understand that, "I am only a human-girl-person and I ain't always perfect."

Rambling Rose is framed by scenes that feature an adult Buddy upon his return home to visit his widower father. His musings about his childhood and the "damnable commotion" that Rose brought initiates the flashback and the film's main story. Critics noted with relief that although the opening hinted that what would follow would be improbably saccharine, it proved to be an honest, engaging, and thoroughly uncommon coming-of-age story. But other critics charged that the film's golden-hued nostalgia precluded serious consideration of the issues it raises.

The plot of *Rambling Rose* is far less important than its characters and situations, and Coolidge's direction beautifully evokes the period, but the film's charm does not dull its message. Critics, in particular, praised Coolidge's handling of the scene in which Rose acknowledges the emerging sexuality of her 13-year-old charge, Buddy; it is sweetly poignant and unnerving, without being voyeuristic or otherwise exploitative. Interesting, it faintly echoes brief moments in Coolidge's early teenpic films that, despite mostly male casts, render the complicated responses of young women to the challenges and disappointments of love. Finally, *Rambling Rose* suggests that female sexuality is neither simply "healthy" nor "harmful," but far more complicated than the bluenoses or pornographers—or most of the men in the film—would have it.

—Cynthia Felando

REINIGER, Lotte
British animator

Born: Berlin, 2 June 1899; became citizen of Great Britain. **Education:** Attended Max Reinhardt theater school, Berlin, 1916-17. **Family:** Married Carl Koch, 1921 (died 1963). **Career:** 1916—created silhouettes for intertitles of Paul Wegener's *Rübezahls Hochzeit;* 1918—introduced by Wegener to film group associated with Dr. Hans Cürlis; 1919—Cürlis's newly founded Institut für Kulturforschung, Berlin, sponsored Reiniger's first film; mid-1930s—with Koch moved to Britain, worked with G.P.O. Film Unit with Len Lye and Norman McLaren; 1936—made *The King's Breakfast,* first film in England; 1946—worked with Märchentheater of city of Berlin at Theater am Schiffbauerdamm; beginning 1950—lived and worked mainly for TV, in England; 1950s and 1960s—created sets and figures for English puppet and shadow theater Hoghart's Puppets; 1953—Primrose Productions set up, sponsored productions for American TV; 1975—began collaboration with National Film Board of Canada; 1979—*The Rose and the Ring* premiered at American Film Festival. **Awards:** Silver Dolphin, Venice Biennale, for *Gallant Little Tailor,* 1955; Filmband in Gold, West Germany, for service to German cinema, 1972; Verdienst Kreuz, West Germany, 1978. **Died:** 19 June 1981.

Films as Animator

1919   *Das Ornament des verliebten Herzens (The Ornament of the Loving Heart)*
1920   *Amor und das standhafte Liebespaar (Love and the Steadfast Sweethearts)*
1921   *Der fliegende Koffer (The Flying Coffer); Der Stern von Bethlehem (The Star of Bethlehem)*
1922   *Aschenputtel; Dornröschen*
1923-26 *Die Geschichte des Prinzen Achmed (Die Abenteuer des Prinzen Achmed; Wak-Wak, ein Märchenzauber; The Adventures of Prince Achmed)*
1928   *Der scheintote Chinese (originally part of Die Geschichte des Prinzen Achmed); Doktor Dolittle und seine Tiere (The Adventures of Dr. Dolittle) (in 3 parts: Abenteuer: Die Reise nach Afrika; Abenteuer: Die Affenbrücke; Abenteuer: Die Affenkrankheit)*

1930 *Zehn Minuten Mozart*
1931 *Harlekin*
1932 *Sissi* (intended as interlude for premiere of operetta *Sissi* by Fritz Kreisler, Vienna 1932)
1933 *Carmen*
1934 *Das rollende Rad*; *Der Graf von Carabas*; *Das gestohlene Herz* (*The Stolen Heart*)
1935 *Der kleine Schornsteinfeger* (*The Little Chimney Sweep*); *Galathea*; *Papageno*
1936 *The King's Breakfast*
1937 *Tocher*
1939 *Dream Circus* (not completed); *L'elisir d'amore* (not released)
1944 *Die goldene Gans* (not completed)
1951 *Mary's Birthday*
1953 *Aladdin* (for U.S. TV); *The Magic Horse* (for U.S. TV); *Snow White and Rose Red* (for U.S. TV)
1954 *The Three Wishes* (for U.S. TV); *The Grasshopper and the Ant* (for U.S. TV); *The Frog Prince* (for U.S. TV); *The Gallant Little Tailor* (for U.S. TV); *The Sleeping Beauty* (for U.S. TV); *Caliph Storch* (for U.S. TV)
1955 *Hansel and Gretel* (for U.S. TV); *Thumbelina* (for U.S. TV); *Jack and the Beanstalk* (for U.S. TV)
1956 *The Star of Bethlehem* (theatrical film)
1957 *Helen la Belle* (theatrical film)
1958 *The Seraglio* (theatrical film)
1960 *The Pied Piper of Hamelin* (interlude for theatrical performance)
1961 *The Frog Prince* (interlude for theatrical performance)
1962 *Wee Sandy* (interlude for theatrical performance)
1963 *Cinderella* (interlude for theatrical performance)
1974 *The Lost Son* (interlude for theatrical performance)
1976 *Aucassin et Nicolette* (Avoine) (interlude for theatrical performance) (short)
1979 *The Rose and the Ring* (interlude for theatrical performance)

Other Films

1916 *Rübezahls Hochzeit* (Wegener) (silhouettes for intertitles); *Die Schöne Prinzessin von China* (Glicse) (set decoration, props, and costumes)
1918 *Apokalypse* (Gliese) (silhouettes for intertitles); *Der Rattenfänger von Hameln* (*The Pied Piper of Hamelin*) (Wegener) (silhouettes for intertitles)
1920 *Der verlorene Schatten* (Gliese) (silhouette sequence)
1923 *Die Nibelungen* (F. Lang) (silhouette sequence, not used)
1929-30 *Die Jagd nach dem Glück* (*Running after Luck*) (Gliese) (co-story, co-sc, co-sound)
1933 *Don Quichotte* (Pabst) (opening silhouette sequence)
1937 *La Marseillaise* (Renoir) (created shadow theater seen in film)
1942 *Una Signora dell'ovest* (Koch) (co-sc)

Publications by Reiniger

Books

(Illustrator) *Das Loch im Vorhang,* Berlin, 1919.
Venus in Seide, Berlin, 1919.

Die Abenteuer des Prinzen Achmed, 32 pictures from film, with narration, Tubingen, 1926 (reprinted 1972; text translated into English by Carman Educational Associates, Pine Grove, Ontario, 1975).
Der böse Gutsherr und die guten Tiere, Berlin, 1930.
Wander Birds, Bristol, 1934.
Der ewige Esel, Zurich/Fribourg, 1949.
King Arthur and His Knights of the Round Table, London, 1952.
Mondscheingarten—Gedichte, Gütersloh, 1968.
Shadow Theatres and Shadow Films, London and New York, 1970.
Das gestohlene Herz, Tübingen, 1972.

Articles

"Scissors Make Films," in *Sight and Sound* (London), Spring 1936.
"The Adventures of Prince Achmed," in *Silent Picture* (London), Autumn 1970.
"Lotte Reiniger et les ombres chinoises," interview with L. Bonneville, in *Séquences* (Montreal), July 1975.

Publications on Reiniger

Books

White, Eric, *Walking Shadows,* London, 1931.
Russett, Robert, and Cecile Starr, *Experimental Animation,* New York, 1976.
Rondolino, Gianni, *Lotte Reiniger,* Torino, 1982.
Acker, Ally, *Reel Women: Pioneers of the Cinema, 1896 to the Present,* New York, 1991.
Pilling, Jayne, editor, *Women & Animation: A Compendium,* London, 1993.
Strobel, Christel, and Hans Strobel, *Lotte Reiniger,* 1993.
Foster, Gwendolyn Audrey, *Women Film Directors: An International Bio-Critical Dictionary,* Westport, Connecticut, 1995.

Articles

Weaver, Randolph, "*Prince Achmed* and Other Animated Silhouettes," in *Theatre Arts* (New York), June 1931.
Coté, Guy, "Flatland Fairy Tales," in *Film* (London), October 1954.
"She Made First Cartoon Feature," in *Films and Filming* (London), December 1955.
"The Films of Lotte Reiniger," in *Film Culture* (New York), no. 9, 1956.
Beckerman, H., "Animated Women," in *Filmmakers Newsletter* (Ward Hill, Massachusetts), Summer 1974.
Gelder, P., "Lotte Reiniger at Eighty," in *Sight and Sound* (London), no. 3, 1979.
Starr, Cecile, "Lotte Reiniger's Fabulous Film Career," in *Sightlines* (New York), Summer 1980.
Obituary, in *Cinématographie* (Paris), July 1981.
Hurst, H., "Zum Tode Lotte Reiniger," in *Frauen und Film* (Berlin), September 1981.
Sauvaget, D., "Lotte Reiniger au pays des ombres," in *Image et Son* (Paris), December 1981.
Filmihullu, no. 5, 1990.
Film a Doba (Prague), vol. 36, no. 1, January 1990.
Kotlarz, Irene, "Working against the Grain: Women in Animation," in *Women and Film: A Sight and Sound Reader,* edited by Pam Cook and Philip Dodd, Philadelphia, 1993.

* * *

Lotte Reiniger

Lotte Reiniger's career as an independent filmmaker is among the longest and most singular in film history, spanning some 60 years (1919-79) of actively creating silhouette animation films. Her *The Adventures of Prince Achmed* is the world's first feature-length animation film, made when she was in her mid-twenties and winning considerable acclaim.

Silhouette animation existed before 1919, but Reiniger was its preeminent practitioner, transforming a technically and esthetically bland genre to a recognized art form. Since childhood she had excelled at freehand cut-outs and shadow theaters. As a teenager at

Max Reinhardt's acting studio, she was invited by actor-director Paul Wegener to make silhouette decorations for the credits and intertitles of *The Pied Piper of Hamelin* (1918); she also helped animate the film's wooden rats, when live guinea pigs proved unmanageable. The rest of Reiniger's professional life was wholeheartedly devoted to silhouette animation, with an occasional retreat to shadow plays or book illustrations when money was not available for films.

Prominent among Lotte Reiniger's talents was her transcendence of the inherent flatness and awkwardness of silhouette animation through her dramatic mise en scène and her balletic movements. Her female characters are especially lively and original, displaying wit, sensuousness, and self-awareness rarely found in animated cartoons (from whose creative ranks women animators were virtually excluded until the 1970s). Few real-life actresses could match the expressiveness with which Reiniger inspired the gestures of her lead-jointed figures as she moved and filmed them fraction by fraction, frame by frame.

For more than four decades, Lotte Reiniger shared her professional life with her husband, Carl Koch, who designed her animation studio and, until his death in 1963, served as her producer and camera operator. "There was nothing about what is called film-technique that he did not know," Jean Renoir wrote in his autobiography. (In the late 1930s, Koch collaborated on the scripts and production of Renoir's celebrated *Grand Illusion* and *Rules of the Game,* and on *La Marseillaise* for which Reiniger created a shadow-play sequence.)

Aside from *The Adventures of Prince Achmed,* Reiniger ventured into feature filmmaking only once, in *Running after Luck,* the story of a wandering showman, part animation and part live-action, which she co-directed with Rochus Gliese. It was a critical and financial failure, perhaps because of its imperfect sound system. The rest of her films were shorts, mainly one or two reels in length.

Lotte Reiniger worked outside commercial channels, with minimal support. She said she never felt discrimination because she was a woman, but she did admit resenting that great sums were spent on films of little or no imagination while so little was available for the films she wanted to make. In the 1970s she was coaxed from her retirement to make two films in Canada; she also toured much of Europe, Canada, and the United States under the auspices of the Goethe House cultural centers of the West German government, showing her films and demonstrating her cut-out animation technique.

Hans Richter, who knew Reiniger in the early Berlin years, later wrote that she "belonged to the avant-garde as far as independent production and courage were concerned," but that the spirit of her work seemed Victorian. Jean Renoir placed her even further back in time, as "a visual expression of Mozart's music." It is more likely that, like the fables and myths and fairy tales on which many of her films are based, her work transcends time and fashion.

—Cecile Starr

REVILLE, Alma
British writer

Born: England, 14 August 1899. **Family:** Married the director Alfred Hitchcock, 1926 (died 1980), daughter: Patricia. **Career:** Early 1920s—editor's assistant, London Film, then Famous Players-Lasky, London; 1925—script girl on Hitchcock's *The Pleasure Garden,* then writer of many of his scripts, as well as scripts for other directors; 1939—emigrated to the United States with Hitchcock. **Died:** In Los Angeles, 6 July 1982.

Films as Co-writer for Director Alfred Hitchcock

1927   *The Ring*
1929   *Juno and the Paycock*

1930   *Murder*
1931   *The Skin Game*; *Rich and Strange* (*East of Shanghai*)
1932   *Number Seventeen*
1934   *Waltzes from Vienna* (*Strauss's Great Waltz*)
1935   *The 39 Steps*
1936   *The Secret Agent*; *Sabotage* (*A Woman Alone*)
1937   *Young and Innocent* (*The Girl Was Young*)
1938   *The Lady Vanishes*
1939   *Jamaica Inn*
1941   *Suspicion*
1943   *Shadow of a Doubt*
1947   *The Paradine Case*
1950   *Stage Fright*
1953   *I Confess* (uncredited)

Other Films as Co-writer

1928   *The Constant Nymph* (Brunel); *The First Born* (Mander)
1929   *After the Verdict* (Galeen); *A Romance of Seville* (N. Walker)
1931   *The Outsider* (Lachman); *Sally in Our Alley* (Elvey)
1932   *The Water Gipsies* (Elvey); *Nine till Six* (Dean)
1934   *Forbidden Country* (Rosen)
1935   *The Passing of the Third Floor Back* (Viertel)
1945   *It's in the Bag* (Wallace)

Films as Editor

1915   *The Prisoner of Zenda*
1923   *Woman to Woman* (Cutts)

Publications by Reville

Article

Sight and Sound (London), Autumn 1976.

Publications on Reville

Articles

Obituary, in *Times* (London), 15 July 1982.
Obituary, in *Variety* (New York), 21 July 1982.

*   *   *

Alma Reville's career is difficult to assess, since during most of it she worked exclusively on the films of her husband, director Alfred Hitchcock. Her contribution to his work fluctuated during the course of their 50-year marriage. It was sometimes that of a professional screenwriter or consultant, more often that of a supportive and knowledgeable wife.

Reville entered the British film industry even earlier than her husband, whose career spanned both the silent and sound eras. From the age of 16, Reville worked as a cutter (editor), first at the London Film Company, then at Famous Players-Lasky's English branch at Islington. Hitchcock's courtship of her began at the latter studio when he invited her to work as a cutter on *Woman to Woman,* an independent production that he was assistant directing under Graham Cutts at Islington; thus from the beginning, the couple's relationship was based on a combination of personal and professional interests. She shared her first

Alma Reville with Alfred Hitchcock

screenwriting credit with Hitchcock as co-writer of his boxing melodrama *The Ring* in 1927, while continuing to work with other directors as scriptwriter, continuity girl, and assistant director.

Ambitious and talented, Reville sought to move into the director's chair herself. But the birth of a daughter, Patricia Alma, in 1928 and the family's subsequent move to America altered her ambitions. Joan Harrison, whom Hitchcock hired as a secretary in 1935, quickly took over many of the routine production duties which had previously been Reville's responsibility, while Reville focused exclusively on preparation of her husband's scripts. Harrison eventually became involved in this capacity too, often sharing screen credit with Reville. When the Hitchcocks moved to America in 1939 so that Hitchcock could work under personal contract to David O. Selznick, Harrison went along.

The scripts Reville worked on for Hitchcock in Hollywood were *Suspicion,* a troubled project which was nearly not released; *The Paradine Case,* on which producer Selznick was more exasperating in his interference with Hitchcock than usual; *Stage Fright*; and *I Confess,* which was made on Reville's initiative, but proved to be a box-office failure. Three of these films concern a man who betrays a woman. Reville was partly responsible for this pattern, which probably reflected her attitude toward her husband, whose interest in her waxed and waned; the couple's marriage was reportedly celibate after the birth of their daughter as Hitchcock's romantic fancy attached itself silently and unreciprocally to the various glamorous blonds in his films.

In the mid-1950s, at the peak of Hitchcock's confidence and power, Reville retreated firmly into the background and stayed there. He still sought and respected his wife's judgment on potential projects and relied on her keen eye for detail during the editing process. A famous story about *Psycho* has it that Reville saved its most famous sequence from being marred by a significant blemish that no one else had caught during months of editing. As the final cut was being prepared for release, Hitchcock showed it to her. She alone spotted a single blink of Janet Leigh's eye as the actress lay "dead" following the notorious shower murder scene. The gaffe was replaced with a cutaway shot, and *Psycho* went out to theaters, the sequence shocking audiences around the world and making film history.

—Patricia Ferrara/John McCarty

RIEFENSTAHL, Leni
German director

Born: Helene Berta Amalie Riefenstahl in Berlin, 22 August 1902. **Education:** Studied Russian Ballet at the Mary Wigmann School for Dance, Dresden, and Jutta Klamt School for Dance, Berlin. **Family:** Married Peter Jacob, 1944 (divorced 1946). **Career:** From 1920—

dancer; from 1936—appeared in "mountain films" directed by Arnold Fanck; 1931—established own production company, Riefenstahl Films; 1932—first film, *Das blaue Licht,* released; 1933—appointed "film expert to the National Socialist Party" by Hitler; 1945-48—detained in various prison camps by Allied Forces on charges of pro-Nazi activity; 1952—charges dismissed by Berlin court, allowed to work in film industry again; 1956—suffered serious auto accident while working in Africa; 1972—commissioned by *The Times* (London) to photograph the Munich Olympics; 1974—honored at Telluride Film Festival, Colorado (festival picketed by anti-Nazi groups); 1993—was the subject of the documentary *The Wonderful, Horrible Life of Leni Riefenstahl,* directed by Ray Müller. **Awards:** Silver Medal, Venice Festival, for *Das blaue Licht,* 1932; Exposition Internationale des Arts et des Techniques, Paris, Diplome de Grand Prix, for *Triumph des Willens,* 1935; Polar Prize, Sweden, for *Olympia,* 1938. **Address:** 20 Tengstrasse, 80798 Munich, Germany.

Films as Director

1932 *Das blaue Licht* (*The Blue Light*) (+ co-sc, co-pr, ro as Junta)
1933 *Sieg des Glaubens* (*Victory of the Faith*)
1935 **Triumph des Willens** (*Triumph of the Will*) (+ pr, ed); *Tag der Freiheit: unsere Wermacht* (+ ed)
1938 **Olympia** (*Olympische Spiele 1936*) (+ sc, co-ph, ed)
1944 *Tiefland* (*Lowland*) (co-d with Pabst, + sc, ed, ro as Marta) (released 1954)

Films as Actress

1926 *Der heilige Berg* (Fanck) (as Diotima)
1927 *Der grosse Sprung* (Fanck)
1929 *Das Schiscksal derer von Hapsburg* (*The White Hell of Piz Palü* (Raffé); *Die woisses Hölle vom Piz Palü* (Fanck)
1930 *Stürme über dem Montblanc* (Fanck)
1931 *Der weiss Rausch* (Fanck)
1933 *S.O.S. Eisberg* (Garnett and Fanck)
1993 *Die Nacht der Regisseure* (*The Night of the Filmmakers*) (Reitz—doc) (appearance)

Publications by Riefenstahl

Books

Kampf in Schnee und Eis, Leipzig, 1933.
Hinter den Kulissen des Reichsparteitagsfilms, Munich, 1935 (uncredited ghost writer Ernst Jaeger).
Schönheit im Olympischen Kampf, Berlin, 1937.
The Last of the Nuba, New York, 1974.
Jardins du corail, Paris, 1978.
Memoiren, Munich, 1987 (also published as *The Sieve of Time: The Memoirs of Leni Riefenstahl,* London, 1992, and *Leni Riefenstahl: A Memoir,* New York, 1993).
Wonders Under Water, London, 1991.
Leni Riefenstahl: Life, Tokyo, 1992.
Olympia, London, 1994.

Articles

"An Interview with a Legend," with Gordon Hitchens, in *Film Comment* (New York), Winter 1965.

Interview with Michel Delahaye, in *Interviews with Film Directors,* edited by Andrew Sarris, New York, 1967.
"A Reply to Paul Rotha," with Kevin Brownlow, in *Film* (London), Spring 1967.
"Statement on Sarris-Gessner Quarrel about *Olympia,*" in *Film Comment* (New York), Fall 1967.
Interview with Herman Weigel, in *Filmkritik* (Munich), August 1972.
"Why I Am Filming *Penthesilea,*" in *Film Culture* (New York), Spring 1973.
"Leni Riefenstahl: A Memoir," in *New York,* 13 September 1993.

Publications on Riefenstahl

Books

Cadars, Pierre, and Francis Courtade, *Histoire du cinema Nazi,* Paris, 1972.
Fanck, Arnold, *Er furte Regie mit Gletschern, Sturmen, Lawinen,* Munich, 1973.
Hull, David Stewart, *Film in the Third Reich,* New York, 1973.
Leiser, Erwin, *Nazi Cinema,* London, 1974.
Barsam, Richard, *Filmguide to* Triumph of the Will, Bloomington, Indiana, 1975.
Infield, Glenn, *Leni Riefenstahl, the Fallen Film Goddess,* New York, 1976.
Ford, Charles, *Leni Riefenstahl,* Paris, 1978.
Hinton, David, *The Films of Leni Riefenstahl,* Metuchen, New Jersey, 1978, 2nd ed., 1991.
Infield, G. B., *Leni Riefenstahl et le troisieme Reich,* Paris, 1978.
Berg-Pan, Renata, *Leni Riefenstahl,* Boston, 1980.
Heck-Rabi, Louise, *Women Filmmakers: A Critical Reception,* Metuchen, New Jersey, 1984.
Graham, Cooper C., *Leni Riefenstahl and* Olympia, Metuchen, New Jersey, 1986.
Acker, Ally, *Reel Women: Pioneers of the Cinema, 1896 to the Present,* New York, 1991.
Deutschmann, Linda, Triumph of the Will: *The Image of the Third Reich,* Wakefield, New Hampshire, 1991.
Leeflang, Thomas, *Leni Riefenstahl,* Baarn, Netherlands, 1991.
Foster, Gwendolyn Audrey, *Women Film Directors: An International Bio-Critical Dictionary,* Westport, Connecticut, 1995.

Articles

"The Case of Leni Riefenstahl," in *Sight and Sound* (London), Spring 1960.
Gunston, David, "Leni Riefenstahl," in *Film Quarterly* (Berkeley), Fall 1960.
Berson, Arnold, "The Truth about Leni," in *Films and Filming* (London), April 1965.
Gregor, Ulrich, "A Comeback for Leni Riefenstahl," in *Film Comment* (New York), Winter 1965.
Brownlow, Kevin, "Leni Riefenstahl," in *Film* (London), Winter 1966.
Rotha, Paul, "I Deplore ...," in *Film* (London), Spring 1967.
Corliss, Richard, "Leni Riefenstahl—A Bibliography," in *Film Heritage* (Dayton, Ohio), Fall 1969.
Richards, J., "Leni Riefenstahl: Style and Structure," in *Silent Pictures* (London), Autumn 1970.
Alpert, Hollis, "The Lively Ghost of Leni," in the *Saturday Review* (New York), 25 March 1972.
"Riefenstahl Issue" of *Film Culture* (New York), Spring 1973.

Barsam, R. M., "Leni Riefenstahl: Artifice and Truth in a World Apart,"
in *Film Comment* (New York), November/December 1973.

Sontag, Susan, "Fascinating Fascism," in the *New York Review of Books,* 6 February 1975.

Sokal, Harry R., "Über Nacht Antisemitin geworden?," in *Der Spiegel* (Germany), no. 46, 1976.

"Zur Riefenstahl-Renaissance," special issue of *Frauen und Film* (Berlin), December 1977.

Fraser, J., "An Ambassador for Nazi Germany," in *Films* (London), April 1982.

Horton, W. J., "Capturing the Olympics," in *American Cinematographer* (Los Angeles), July 1984.

Loiperdinger, M., and D. Culbert, "Leni Riefenstahl, the SA, and the Nazi Party Rally Films, Nuremberg 1933-1934: *Sieg des Glaubens* and *Triumph des Willens,*" in *Historical Journal of Film, Radio and TV* (Abingdon, Oxon), vol. 8, no. 1, 1988.

Lopperdinger, M. and D. Culbert, "Leni Riefenstahl's *Tag der Freiheit:* The 1935 Nazi Party Rally Film," in *Historical Journal of Film, Radio and TV* (Abingdon, Oxon), vol. 12, no. 3, 1992.

Schiff, Stephen, "Leni's *Olympia,*" in *Vanity Fair* (New York), September 1992.

Harshaw, Tobin, "Why Am I Guilty?" in *New York Times Book Review,* 26 September 1993.

Corliss, Richard, "Riefenstahl's Last Triumph," in *Time* (New York), 18 October 1993.

Hoberman, J., "Triumph of the Swill," in *Premiere* (New York), December 1993.

Film

Die Macht der blier: Leni Riefenstahl (*The Wonderful, Horrible Life of Leni Riefenstahl*), documentary, directed by Ray Müller, 1993.

* * *

The years 1932 to 1945 define the major filmmaking efforts of Leni Riefenstahl. Because she remained a German citizen making films in Hitler's Third Reich, two at the Fuhrer's request, she and her films were viewed as pro-Nazi. Riefenstahl claims she took no political position and committed no crimes. In 1948, a German court ruled that she was a follower of, not active in, the Nazi Party. Another court in 1952 reconfirmed her innocence of war crimes. But she is destined to remain a politically controversial filmmaker who made two films rated as masterpieces.

She began to learn filmmaking while acting in the mountain films of Arnold Fanck, her mentor. She made a mountain film of her own, *The Blue Light,* using smoke bombs to create "fog." She used a red and green filter on the camera lens, over her cameraman's objections, to obtain a novel magical effect. This film is Riefenstahl's own favorite. She says it is the story of her own life. Hitler admired *The Blue Light* and asked her to photograph the Nazi Party Congress in Nuremburg. She agreed to make *Victory of the Faith,* which was not publicly viewed. Hitler then asked her to film the 1934 Nazi Party rally.

Triumph of the Will, an extraordinary work, shows Hitler arriving by plane to attend the rally. He proceeds through the crowded streets of Nuremburg, addresses speeches to civilians and uniformed troops, and reviews a five-hour parade. The question is: Did Riefenstahl make *Triumph* as pro-Nazi propaganda or not? "Cinematically dazzling and ideologically vicious," is R. M. Barsam's judgment. According to Barsam, three basic critical views of *Triumph* exist: 1)

those who cannot appreciate the film at all, 2) those who can appreciate and understand the film, and 3) those who appreciate it in spite of the politics in the film.

Triumph premiered 29 March 1935, was declared a masterpiece, and subsequently earned three awards. *Triumph* poses questions of staging. Was the rally staged so that it could be filmed? Did the filming process shape the rally, give it meaning? Riefenstahl's next film, *Olympia,* posed the question of financing. Did Nazi officialdom pay for the film to be made? Riefenstahl claims the film was made independently of any government support. Other opinions differ.

The improvisatory techniques Riefenstahl used to make *Triumph* were improved and elaborated to make *Olympia.* She and her crew worked 16-hour days, seven days a week. *Olympia* opens as *Triumph* does, with aerial scenes. Filmed in two parts, the peak of Olympia I is Jesse Owens's running feat. The peak of Olympia II is the diving scenes. In an interview with Gordon Hitchens in 1964, Riefenstahl revealed her guidelines for making *Olympia.* She decided to make two films instead of one because "the form must excite the content and give it shape.... The law of film is architecture, balance. If the image is weak, strengthen the sound, and vice-versa; the total impact on the viewer should be 100 percent." The secret of *Olympia*'s success, she affirmed, was its sound—all laboratory-made. Riefenstahl edited the film for a year and a half. It premiered 20 April 1938 and was declared a masterpiece, being awarded four prizes.

Riefenstahl's career after the beginning of World War II is comprised of a dozen unfinished film projects. She began *Penthesilea* in 1939, *Van Gogh* in 1943, and *Lowland* in 1944, releasing it in 1954. Riefenstahl acted the role of a Spanish girl in it while co-directing with G. W. Pabst this drama of peasant-landowner conflicts. Visiting Africa in 1956, she filmed *Black Cargo,* documenting the slave trade, but her film was ruined by incorrect laboratory procedures. In the 1960s, she lived with and photographed the Mesakin Nuba tribe in Africa.

Riefenstahl's *Triumph of the Will* and *Olympia* are two of the greatest documentaries ever made. That is indisputable. And it also is indisputable that they are among the most notorious and controversial. Each has been lauded for its sheer artistry, yet damned for its content and vision of Adolf Hitler and a German nation poised on the edge of totalitarian barbarism. After years as a name in the cinema history books, Riefenstahl was back in the news in 1992. *Memoirnen,* her autobiography, was first published in English as *The Sieve of Time: The Memoirs of Leni Riefenstahl,* and she was the subject of a documentary, Ray Müller's *The Wonderful, Horrible Life of Leni Riefenstahl.* Clearly, Riefenstahl had written the book and participated in the documentary in an attempt to have the final word regarding the debate over her involvement with Hitler and the Third Reich.

The documentary, which is three hours in length, traces Riefenstahl's undeniably remarkable life, from her success as a dancer and movie actress during the 1920s to her career as a director, her post-World War II censure, and her latter-day exploits as a still photographer. Still very much alive at age ninety-five, Riefenstahl is shown scuba diving, an activity she first took up in her seventies.

Riefenstahl is described at the outset as a "legend with many faces" and "the most influential filmmaker of the Third Reich." The film goes on to serve as an investigation of her life. Was she an opportunist, as she so vehemently denies, or a victim? Was she a "feminist pioneer, or a woman of evil?" Riefenstahl wishes history to view her as she views herself: not as a collaborator but as an artist first and foremost, whose sole fault was to have been alive in the

Leni Riefenstahl

wrong place at the wrong moment in history, and who was exploited by political forces of which she was unaware.

Upon meeting Hitler, she says, "He seemed a modest, private individual." She was "ignorant" of his ideas and politics, and "didn't see the danger of anti-Semitism." She claims to have acquiesced to making *Triumph of the Will* only after Hitler agreed that she would never have to make another film for him. To her, shooting *Triumph* was just a job. She wanted to make a film that was "interesting, one that was not with posed shots.... It had to be filmed the way an artist, not a politician, sees it." The same holds true for *Olympia,* which features images of perfectly proportioned, God-like German athletes. When queried regarding the issue of whether these visuals reflect a fascist aesthetic, Riefenstahl refuses to answer directly, replaying again that art and politics are separate entities.

"If an artist dedicates himself totally to his work, he cannot think politically," Riefenstahl says. Even in the late 1930s, she chose not to leave Germany because, as she observes, "I loved my homeland." She claims that she hoped that reports of anti-Semitism were "isolated events." And her image of Hitler was "shattered much too late.... My life fell apart because I believed in Hitler. People say of me, 'She doesn't want to know. She'll always be a Nazi.' [But] I was never a Nazi."

"What am I guilty of?" Riefenstahl asks. "I regret [that I was alive during that period]. But I was never anti-Semitic. I never dropped any bombs." Explained director Müller, after a New York Film Festival screening of the film, "She was an emancipated woman before there was even such a term. She has a super ego, which has been trod upon for half a century.... [She is] an artist and a perfectionist. I believe that she was purposefully blind not to look in the direction that would get her into trouble."

In this regard, *The Wonderful, Horrible Life of Leni Riefenstahl* ultimately works as a portrait of denial. As Müller so aptly observes, "Any artist has a great responsibility. Anyone who influences the public has this. She is possessed with her art. She says, 'I'm only doing my thing.' I think this is irresponsible. She may be obsessed and possessed, and a genius. But that does not exempt her from responsibility."

In 1995 Riefenstahl briefly resurfaced in Edgar Reitz's *The Night of the Filmmakers,* consisting of interviews with German filmmakers from Frank Beyer to Wim Wenders. Eric Hansen, writing in *Variety,* summed up the essence of her appearance by noting, "Names like the ninety-two-year-old Leni Riefenstahl and young director Detlev Buck are allowed only a few self-glorifying or sarcastic comments."

Perhaps the final word on Riefenstahl is found in Istvan Szabo's *Hanussen,* a 1988 German-Hungarian film. Much of *Hanussen* is set in Germany between the World Wars. One of the minor characters is a celebrated, egocentric woman artist, a member of the political inner circle, who surrounds herself with physical beauty while remaining callously unconcerned with all but her own vanity. Clearly, this character is based on Riefenstahl.

—Louise Heck-Rabi/Rob Edelman

ROSE, Helen

American costume designer

Born: Chicago, c. 1904. **Education:** Attended Chicago Academy of Fine Arts. **Family:** Married Harry Rose, 1929, daughter: Jode. **Ca-**

reer: Worked for Lester Costume Company and Ernie Young's costume house, Chicago; designer for Fanchon and Marco's Ice Follies, 14 years; 1942—costume designer for MGM until her retirement, 1966. **Awards:** Academy Awards, for *The Bad and the Beautiful,* 1952, and *I'll Cry Tomorrow,* 1955. **Died:** In Palm Springs, California, 9 November 1985.

Films as Costume Designer

1943   *Coney Island* (W. Lang) (co); *Hello Frisco, Hello* (Humberstone) (co); *Stormy Weather* (A. L. Stone)

1946   *The Harvey Girls* (Sidney) (co); *Two Sisters from Boston* (Koster) (co); *Ziegfeld Follies* (Minnelli) (co); *Till the Clouds Roll By* (Whorf) (co)

1947   *Good News* (Walters) (co); *Merton of the Movies* (Alton) (co); *The Unfinished Dance* (Koster)

1948   *A Date with Judy* (Thorpe); *Homecoming* (LeRoy); *Words and Music* (Taurog) (co); *Luxury Liner* (Whorf) (co); *The Bride Goes Wild* (Taurog); *Big City* (Taurog)

1949   *Act of Violence* (Zinnemann); *On the Town* (Kelly and Donen); *The Red Danube* (Sidney); *The Stratton Story* (Wood); *Take Me Out to the Ball Game* (Berkeley) (co); *East Side, West Side* (LeRoy); *That Midnight Kiss* (Taurog)

1950   *A Life of Her Own* (Cukor); *Nancy Goes to Rio* (Leonard); *Pagan Love Song* (Alton); *Summer Stock* (Walters) (co); *Three Little Words* (Thorpe); *To Please a Lady* (*Red Hot Wheels*) (C. Brown); *The Toast of New Orleans* (Taurog) (co); *The Reformer and the Redhead* (Panama and Frank); *Annie Get Your Gun* (Sidney) (co); *Father of the Bride* (Minnelli) (co); *The Duchess of Idaho* (Leonard); *The Big Hangover* (Minnelli); *Grounds for Marriage* (Leonard); *Two Weeks with Love* (Rowland) (co); *Right Cross* (J. Sturges); *Three Guys Named Mike* (Walters)

1951   *Father's Little Dividend* (Minnelli); *The Great Caruso* (Thorpe) (co); *The Light Touch* (R. Brooks); *Texas Carnival* (Walters); *The Unknown Man* (Thorpe); *Excuse My Dust* (Rowland) (co); *No Questions Asked* (Kress); *Strictly Dishonorable* (Panama and Frank); *The Strip* (Kardos); *Too Young to Kiss* (Leonard); *Callaway Went Thataway* (Frank and Panama); *The People against O'Hara* (J. Sturges) (co); *Love Is Better Than Ever* (Donen); *Rich, Young and Pretty* (Taurog); *Bannerline* (Weis)

1952   *The Girl in White* (J. Sturges) (co); *Because You're Mine* (Hall); *Above and Beyond* (Panama and Frank); *Glory Alley* (Walsh); *The Bad and the Beautiful* (Minnelli); *Invitation* (Bernhardt); *Holiday for Sinners* (Mayer); *The Merry Widow* (Bernhardt) (co); *Million Dollar Mermaid* (LeRoy) (co); *Skirts Ahoy!* (Lanfield); *The Belle of New York* (Walters) (co); *Washington Story* (Pirosh); *Everything I Have Is Yours* (Leonard)

1953   *Dangerous When Wet* (Walters); *Dream Wife* (Sheldon) (co); *Jeopardy* (J. Sturges); *Latin Lovers* (LeRoy) (co); *Mogambo* (Ford); *Sombrero* (N. Foster); *The Story of Three Loves* (Reinhardt and Minnelli); *Torch Song* (Walters); *I Love Melvin* (Weis); *Small Town Girl* (Kardos); *Remains to Be Seen* (Weis); *Easy to Love* (Walters); *Give a Girl a Break* (Donen) (co); *The Girl Who Had Everything* (Thorpe); *Escape from Fort Bravo* (J. Sturges)

1954   *Athena* (Thorpe) (co); *Executive Suite* (Wise); *Green Fire* (Marton); *Her Twelve Men* (Leonard); *The Last Time I*

Saw Paris (R. Brooks); *Rhapsody* (C. Vidor); *The Long, Long Trailer* (Minnelli); *Rogue Cop* (Rowland); *Rose Marie* (LeRoy) (co); *The Student Prince* (Thorpe) (co); *The Glass Slipper* (Walters) (co); *The Flame and the Flesh* (R. Brooks)

1955   *Bedevilled* (Leisen) (co); *Deep in My Heart* (Donen) (co); *Hit the Deck* (Rowland); *I'll Cry Tomorrow* (Daniel Mann); *Interrupted Melody* (Bernhardt); *It's Always Fair Weather* (Kelly and Donen); *Jupiter's Darling* (Sidney) (co); *Love Me or Leave Me* (C. Vidor); *The Rains of Ranchipur* (Negulesco) (co); *The Tender Trap* (Walters)

1956   *Forbidden Planet* (Wilcox) (co); *Gaby* (Beaumont); *High Society* (Beaudine); *Meet Me in Las Vegas* (Rowland); *The Opposite Sex* (Miller); *The Power and the Prize* (Koster); *Ransom!* (Segal); *The Swan* (C. Vidor); *Tea and Sympathy* (Minnelli); *These Wilder Years* (Rowland)

1957   *Designing Woman* (Minnelli); *Don't Go Near the Water* (Walters); *The Seventh Sin* (Neame); *Silk Stockings* (Mamoulian); *Something of Value* (R. Brooks); *Tip on a Dead Jockey* (Thorpe); *Ten Thousand Bedrooms* (Thorpe); *This Could Be the Night* (Wise)

1958   *Cat on a Hot Tin Roof* (R. Brooks); *Party Girl* (N. Ray); *The High Cost of Loving* (J. Ferrer); *Saddle the Wind* (Parrish); *The Reluctant Debutante* (Minnelli) (co); *The Tunnel of Love* (Kelly); *Torpedo Run* (Pevney)

1959   *Ask Any Girl* (Walters); *Count Your Blessings* (Negulesco); *It Started with a Kiss* (George Marshall); *The Mating Game* (George Marshall)

1960   *All the Fine Young Cannibals* (M. Anderson); *Butterfield 8* (Daniel Mann); *The Gazebo* (George Marshall); *Never So Few* (J. Sturges)

1961   *Ada* (Daniel Mann); *Bachelor in Paradise* (Arnold); *Go Naked in the World* (MacDougall); *The Honeymoon Machine* (Thorpe); *Two Loves* (Walters)

1963   *The Courtship of Eddie's Father* (Minnelli)

1964   *Goodbye Charlie* (Minnelli)

1966   *Made in Paris* (Sagal); *Mister Buddwing* (*Woman without a Face*) (Delbert Mann); *The Singing Nun* (Koster)

1968   *How Sweet It Is!* (Paris)

Publications by Rose

Books

"Just Make Them Beautiful": The Many Worlds of a Designing Woman, Santa Monica, California, 1976.
The Glamorous World of Helen Rose, Palm Springs, California, 1983.

Publications on Rose

Articles

Chierchetti, David, in *Hollywood Costume Design,* New York, 1976.
Leese, Elizabeth, in *Costume Design in the Movies,* New York, 1976.
LaVine, W. Robert, in *In a Glamorous Fashion,* New York, 1980.
Obituary, in *Variety* (New York), 13 November 1985.

*   *   *

Helen Rose was born on Chicago's south side on a yet undetermined date (Rose came from an era when women felt compelled not

to reveal their true age). Dates vary from 1904 to 1918. Because of this, she often appears as precocious as Mozart with her list of early achievements. It is most likely, however, that Rose started her career in her late teens.

She began studies at Chicago Academy of Fine Arts. While still in school she got a job at the Lester Costume Company creating "girlie" costumes for vaudeville and nightclub extravaganzas. She developed tremendous versatility turning chorus girls into, amongst other things, dancing cupcakes. She then worked at Ernie Young's costume house for three years gaining more experience and earning a highly regarded reputation as a theatrical designer. She expanded creatively and technically working for Young and at other companies, and learned the difficult art of chiffon design, a skill that she would later find useful in Hollywood. Continuing in the costume business, Rose moved to Los Angeles in 1929 to a company that supplied wardrobes for film studios. For several months she worked at 20th Century-Fox until a political upheaval in their costume department put an end to that assignment. She then became designer for the Ice Follies and stayed with them for 14 years. She was content with this work until MGM gave her a financial offer she could not refuse. The studio was still searching for a replacement for Adrian and did not feel confident that any of their current designers had taken his place. Irene was working at MGM at the time and Rose was assigned to design clothes only for the younger stars. Nevertheless, while the two designers were jointly doing a film for director Joe Pasternak, he so openly preferred Rose that Irene angrily left the studio.

Pasternak was not the only one who favored Rose. Even in their private lives, stars would ask for her. She created wedding gowns for Liz Taylor, Ann Blyth, Jane Powell, Pier Angeli, and Debbie Reynolds. It greatly upset Edith Head when Head's good friend Grace Kelly requested a Helen Rose gown for her marriage to the Prince of Monaco. Rose was also a favorite of Louis B. Mayer, who referred to her as "my sweetheart Rose." In general she was well-liked at the studio and dressed almost every major actress for MGM. Others who wore her costumes in addition to those mentioned above were Ava Gardner, Deborah Kerr, Cyd Charisse, Jane Powell, and Lena Horne.

Rose's designs were well structured with a strong emphasis on the silhouette. She kept her use of decoration simple and subdued. Her designs were elegant and understated, yet innovative, looking natural in spite of their theatrical nature. Like her rival at Paramount, Edith Head, Rose used designs that suited the new demands of the 1950s. They were more practical than fanciful; the sort of clothes a nice upper-middle-class suburbanite might wear. These clothes were also a goal to which less affluent members of the audience could aspire. Rose was not limited to the contemporary look, however, and could equally design excellent and accurate period costuming, as in *The Swan.*

Clothing manufacturers were not blind to the fact that Rose's designs were popular with the public. Her wedding dress for *Father of the Bride* was extensively copied by New York fashion designers. Her inventive bathing suits for the Esther Williams pictures, made of light new fabrics, influenced bathing-suit manufacturers such as Catalina, Jantzen, and Rose Marie Reid. In the 1958 film *Cat on a Hot Tin Roof,* Liz Taylor's white chiffon gown with the revealing décolletage caused a sensation. The star asked for a copy for her personal wardrobe and Rose received so many additional requests for copies that she decided to enter the wholesale garment business. Her expensive ready-to-wear was sold under franchise to exclusive department stores and speciality shops across the country. In making this move Rose may have reasoned that she could express herself more creatively and make a better living as a ready-to-wear designer. She might have also suspected, however, that the time of the great studio costume designers was coming to an end.

By the time she left the studio in 1966, Helen Rose had designed more than 200 pictures and had received two Academy Awards, for *The Bad and the Beautiful* and *I'll Cry Tomorrow*.

—Edith C. Lee

LA RUE CASES-NÈGRES

(Sugar Cane Alley; Black Shack Alley)
Martinique-France, 1983
Director: Euzhan Palcy

Production: SU.MA.FA./ORCA/NEF Diffusion; Fujicolor; 35mm; running time: 105 minutes. Released September 21, 1983, France. Filmed in Martinique.

Producers: Michel Loulergue, Jean-Luc Ormières, and Alix Régis; **production manager:** Christine Renaud; **screenplay:** Euzhan Palcy, based on the novel by Joseph Zobel; **assistant director:** Fred Runel; **photography:** Dominique Chapuis; **editor:** Marie-Josephe Yoyotte; **sound:** Pierre Befve and Yves Osmu; **production design:** Thanh At Hoang; **music:** Groupe Malavoi; **costumes:** Isabelle Filleul; **makeup:** Marie-France Vassel.

Cast: Garry Cadenat (*José*); Darling Légitimus (*Amantine/M'Man Tine*); Douta Seck (*Medouze*); Laurent St. Cyr (*Leopold*); Joby Bernabé (*M. Saint-Louis*); Marie-Ange Farot (*Mme. Saint-Louis*); Henri Melon (*M. Roc*); Francisco Charles (*The Supervisor*); Marie-Jo Descas (*Leopold's Mother*); Eugène Mona (*Twelve-Toes*); Joël Palcy (*Carmen*).

Awards: Silver Lion, Venice Film Festival: Best First Feature, Best Actress (Légitimus); César for Best First Film.

Publications

Books

Quart, Barbara Koenig, *Women Directors: The Emergence of a New Cinema,* New York, 1988.
Cham, Mbye, editor, *Ex-iles: Essays on Caribbean Cinema,* Trenton, New Jersey, 1992.
Cole, Janis, and Holly Dale, *Calling the Shots: Profiles of Women Filmmakers,* Kingston, Ontario, 1993.
Zaniello, Tom, *Working Stiffs, Union Maids, Reds, and Riffraff: An Organized Guide to Films about Labor,* Ithaca, New York, 1996.

Articles

Linfield, Susan, "Sugar Cane Alley: An Interview with Euzhan Palcy," in *Cineaste* (New York), vol. 13, no. 4, 1984.
Canby, Vincent, "Third World Truths," in *New York Times,* 22 April 1984.

McKenna, Kristine, "Tough, Passionate, Persuasive: Euzhan Palcy Battled for Five Years to Put Her Vision of Apartheid on Screen, and then Lured Marlon Brando Back to Work—for Free," in *American Film* (Hollywood), September 1989.
Hendron, Gerise, "Auto-ethnographic Impulse in *Rue cases-nègres,*" in *Literature/Film Quarterly* (Salisbury, Maryland), July 1996.

*   *   *

Based upon a novel of education by the Martinique writer Joseph Zobel, *La Rue cases-nègres* was an internationally celebrated debut film. In the United States its 1984 showing in the Museum of Modern Art's New Directors/New Films series, under the nonliteral but perhaps more euphonious title *Sugar Cane Alley,* occasioned rave reviews from the *New York Times* and other periodicals, and led to its successful distribution on the American art-house circuit. Though a cynic might have attributed the film's initial popularity to the "novelty value" of its writer-director being not only young but black, female, and Third World (and the setting "exotic" to European and American viewers), more recent viewers have continued to praise Euzhan Palcy for the strong overall assurance with which she tells her tale of a youth and his "black shack" community in the still-colonial Martinique of 1930. What impresses most about *Sugar Cane Alley* is not any one element—though one could single out the performances, the handsome though unflashy photography, the effectively varied, never slack pacing, or the convincing period detail—but the seeming ease with which Palcy has brought everything together.

The story told by *Sugar Cane Alley* is familiar enough: a gifted but impoverished child pursues a good education, with the help of a dedicated, hardworking parental figure who wants the child to break out of the cycle of poverty. (The film ends with the death of the boy's grandmother; the novel continues with the youth's entrance into a middle-class world from which he can look back upon his home world with a writer's perspective and mixed emotions.) *Sugar Cane Alley* presents this story in the context of the African diaspora. In one scene the wise elder Medouze tells young José of his longing for "*Afrique—le pays de mon papa,*" and of their people's years of slavery, triumphant revolt against the French overlords, and grim return to the cane fields, the *maître* having simply become the *patron.* In an important subplot, young Leopold, the illegitimate son of a black woman and an aristocratic overlord (who keeps his dependents in luxury until a fatal injury destines them for poverty), is forbidden to play with "those black children" but reacts with political defiance after his father refuses to bestow his grand French name upon him.

Palcy gives us scenes that are classic to the tale of the struggling youth and his working-class community: a sugarcane worker having his pay docked for urinating in the fields during working hours; a pompous teacher wrongly accusing the brilliant young student in front of the whole class of plagiarizing an essay; the boy arriving home to find his self-sacrificing grandmother seriously ill. But Palcy's special achievement is to tell this story freshly, as if it had never been told before. The payday scene, outdoors with a village crowd just beyond the whites' table, is bustling with varied activity caught by the moving camera: some workers venting their anger over their exploitation while others are joking and selling refreshments. Medouze's campfire speech that night is no mere polemic: hypnotic to the wide-eyed José, it is no less so to the viewer, with the actor's fierce expression in

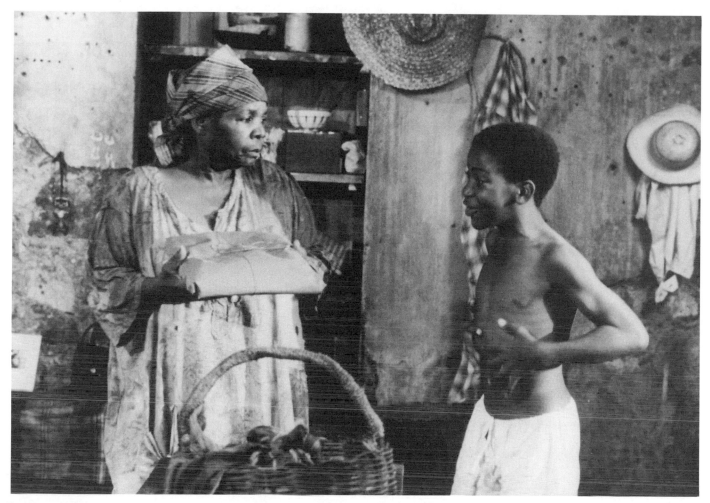

Rue cases-nègres

tight close-up glowing in the darkness, and with African-Caribbean drums and dancing of the payday revelers in the background. The accusatory teacher is arrogant without being melodramatized as a villain. And Darling Légitimus as the loving grandmother never slips into a stereotypical "mammy" role: perhaps it is a certain French "dryness" that tempers her displays of affection and disapproval, or simply a quiet dignity conveyed by both actor and director.

That the film has the air of an authentic re-creation of history is due not only to the talented costume and production designers but to Palcy's seemingly casual unfolding of events (such as the improvisation of a work chant in one scene) and her refusal to dwell on period props too long. The camera work is fluid and unobtrusively handsome, with only an occasional grand effect, such as the torchlight search for a missing Medouze. Never is there a nostalgic glaze spread over a past that could hardly have been idyllic. To be sure, the opening-credits sequence, with its sepia historic photos and ragtime piano soundtrack, does suggest that an exercise in nostalgia will follow, but in the body of the film Palcy and her collaborators re-create a partially vanished world without cloying sentiment. In the early scenes, young José's village playmates are never cute—rather they are somewhere between engagingly mischievous and appallingly undisciplined. A shot of M'Man Tine coming home from the fields against a pinkish-gold sky is not held before us as monumental,

though we may indeed be moved by the glimpses of her wearied, beautiful face.

Palcy leavens her story with considerable humor, or drollery, as when José unexpectedly sneaks away from school—where he is being made to stand outside of his classroom for tardiness—to throw rocks at a set of dishes drying in the sun. (The dishes, or rather their owner, were the cause of the tardiness.) She also achieves a drier irony, as when, following the accusation of cheating, José runs to his kindly adult friend Carmen, boatman and porter to a rich family: instead of advice Carmen (again quite unexpectedly) gives the now silent boy a tour of his patroness's opulent boudoir, where, lounging on the bed, he brags of being her lover.

In interviews Palcy has told of wanting to make a film of Zobel's novel since she first read it at the age of 14—when its portrayal of her own land from a black perspective made a lasting impression on her—and of writing her first script at 17. The completed film (released when she was 28), in its ability to tell a moving story not just of a child but of an entire community in its political context, achieves a significance far beyond its historical role as an early voice in a developing Caribbean cinema.

—Joseph Milicia

RUSSELL, Shirley
British costume designer

Born: Shirley Ann Kingdon in London, 1935. **Education:** Attended Royal College of Art, London. **Family:** Married the director Ken Russell, 1957 (divorced 1979), sons: Alex, James, Xavier, and Toby, daughter: Victoria. **Career:** Worked as costume designer on documentary, then on feature films directed by Ken Russell, and for other directors. **Awards:** Academy Award, for *Yanks,* 1979.

Films as Costume Designer

1963 *French Dressing* (K. Russell)
1967 *Billion Dollar Brain* (K. Russell); *Dante's Inferno* (K. Russell—for TV)
1969 *Women in Love* (K. Russell)
1970 *The Music Lovers* (K. Russell); *The Boys in the Band* (Friedkin)
1971 *The Devils* (K. Russell); *The Boy Friend* (K. Russell)
1972 *Savage Messiah* (K. Russell)
1974 *Mahler* (K. Russell); *Tommy* (K. Russell); *The Little Prince* (Donen)
1975 *Lisztomania* (K. Russell); *Inserts* (Byrum)
1977 *Valentino* (K. Russell)
1978 *Clouds of Glory* (K. Russell—2 parts, for TV)
1979 *Yanks* (Schlesinger); *Cuba* (Lester); *Agatha* (Apted)
1981 *Reds* (Beatty); *Lady Chatterley's Lover* (Jaeckin)
1982 *The Return of the Soldier* (Bridges)
1983 *Wagner* (Palmer)
1984 *The Razor's Edge* (Byrum); *Greystoke: The Legend of Tarzan, Lord of the Apes* (Hudson)
1985 *The Bride* (Roddam)
1987 *Hope and Glory* (Boorman)
1996 *Gulliver's Travels* (Sturridge—for TV)
1997 *Illumination* (Sturridge)

Publications by Russell

Articles

"Shirley Russell: Filmmaking a Family Affair," interview with M. McAndrew, in *Cinema* (Beverly Hills), no. 35, 1976.
"Them and Us," interview with G. Gow, in *Films and Filming* (London), October 1977.

* * *

Shirley Russell rose to prominence as a costume designer during the 1960s and 1970s working with her then-husband, the director Ken Russell. Her work remained precisely detailed and delicately stylized even as that of her husband became more extreme and outrageous. In *Women in Love,* Shirley Russell's costumes are brilliantly accurate not only in rendering the Edwardian period in general, but in sketching crucial class distinctions and even in lampooning characters' social aspirations. The clearest indication of her talents is in the differences of garb between the Brangwens and the Criches, but even more persuasive are the small nuances of costume, in the film's early scenes, that demarcate the contrasting styles of Rupert's and

Shirley Russell

Gerald's dandyism. In *The Music Lovers,* the character of Nina Tchaikovsky seems almost as much a product of Russell's costumes as of Glenda Jackson's exquisite performance. Nina's descent from fresh-faced maiden to besotted madwoman is aptly reflected in the explosions of color and texture of her early costumes that gradually give way, as she becomes more frustrated and unhappy, to monochromatic rags. *The Devils* was very much a turning point in its director's career, but it was also a turning point in his collaboration with Shirley Russell. While Ken Russell's vision becomes ever more Baroque, Shirley Russell remains concerned with minute observations of specific social manners. In *The Devils,* Russell's costumes expertly match Derek Jarman's wildly stylized production design, from the stark, hauntingly jet-gray robes of Sister Jeanne to the imperious attire of Grandier. At the same time, however, the intricacy of Shirley Russell's costumes may begin to seem out of keeping with the much broader strokes—to put it mildly—of her husband's direction.

After the end of their collaboration, Ken Russell's directorial strokes—to continue putting it mildly—become even broader, and many of his period pieces lack the flavor that had been provided by the meticulously exact costumes of his ex-wife. Perhaps sensing this lack, Russell even went so far as to set his adaptation of Bram Stoker's *The Lair of the White Worm* in the present, with predictably disastrous results. Shirley Russell, meanwhile, seemed very much at home in such comparatively realistic projects as Schlesinger's *Yanks* or Warren Beatty's *Reds,* continuing to explore the social and personal ramifications of costume.

—James Morrison

SAGAN, Leontine
Austrian director

Born: Leontine Schlesinger in Vienna, Austria, 1899 (some sources say 1889); moved to Johannesburg with her family. **Education:** Trained with Max Reinhardt in Berlin. **Family:** Married Dr. Victor Fleischer. **Career:** 1910s-20s—won her initial fame as a stage actress and director in Germany and Austria; 1931—won international fame with her debut feature, *Mädchen in Uniform*; 1932—went to England to direct her next feature, *Men of Tomorrow,* for Alexander Korda; mid-1930s—worked at Korda's studios; returned to working on the stage in England; 1939-on—moved to South Africa, where she had spent her childhood, and became one of the key directors in South African theater, and co-founded the National Theatre in Johannesburg. **Died:** In Pretoria, South Africa, 23 May 1974.

Films as Director

1931   *Mädchen in Uniform* (*Girls in Uniform*; *Maidens in Uniform*)
1932   *Men of Tomorrow* (co-d with Z. Korda, + ed)
1946   *Gaiety George* (*Showtime*) (co-d with G. King and F. Carpenter)

Publications by Sagan

Book

Lights & Shadows: The Autobiography of Leontine Sagan, edited by Loren Kruger, Johannesburg, 1996.

Article

Cinema Quarterly (London), Summer 1933.

Publications on Sagan

Books

Acker, Ally, *Reel Women: Pioneers of the Cinema, 1896 to the Present,* New York, 1991.
Ohm, Lisa, "The Filmic Adaptation of the Novel *The Child Manuela*: Christa Winslow's Child Heroine Becomes a *Girl in Uniform,*" and B. Ruby Rich, "From Repressive Tolerance to Erotic Liberation: *Mädchen in Uniform,*" in *Gender and German Cinema: Feminist Interventions, Vol. 2,* edited by Sandra Frieden, Richard McCormick, Vibeke R. Petersen, and Laurie Melissa Vogelsang, Oxford, 1993.
Foster, Gwendolyn Audrey, *Women Film Directors: An International Bio-Critical Dictionary,* Westport, Connecticut, 1995.

Articles

Hardy, Forsyth, in *Cinema Quarterly* (London), Winter 1932.
Kraszna-Krausz, "4 Films from Germany," in *Close Up* (London), March 1932.
Potamkin, Harry Alan, "Pabst and the Social Film," in *Hound and Horn* (New York), January/March 1933.
Jahier, Valerio, "42 ans de cinema," in *Le Role intellectuel du cinema* (Paris), 1937.
Kjorup, S., "Piger i uniform," in *Kosmorama* (Copenhagen), December 1972.
Obituary in *Times* (London), 23 May 1974.
"*Mädchen in Uniform,*" in *Bianco e Nero* (Rome), September/December 1974.
Scholar, Nancy, "*Mädchen in Uniform,*" in *Women and Film* (Berkeley), no. 7, 1975.
Dias, A., "Lembrar e relembrar," in *Celluloide* (Portugal), May 1975.
Slide, Anthony, "The Talkies: The First Women Directors," in *Films in Review* (New York), April 1976.
Rich, B. Ruby, "From Repressive Tolerance to Erotic Liberation," in *Jump Cut* (Chicago), March 1981.
Schlupmann, H., and K. Gramann, "Vorbemerkung," in *Frauen und Film* (Berlin), June 1981.
Lefanu, M., "*Mädchen in Uniform,*" in *Monthly Film Bulletin* (London), January 1982.
Pally, Marcia, "Women in Love," in *Film Comment* (New York), March/April 1986.
Hein, B., "Fraueng ef aeng nisfilme," in *Frauen und Film* (Frankfurt), December 1987.
Dyer, Richard, "Less Is More than Women and Men: Lesbian and Gay Cinema in Weimar Germany," in *New German Critique,* Fall 1990.
Rother, R., "Rueckblick auf Preussen?," in *Filmwaerts* (Hanover, Germany), May 1992.

*   *   *

Throughout her long career, most of which was spent as a stage director, Leontine Sagan directed only three films. The latter two were made in England, and are all but forgotten: *Men of Tomorrow,* chronicling the travails of a rebellious young Oxford University student; and *Gaiety George,* a biography of Irish-born stage producer George Edwardes (who is inexplicably called "George Howard" on screen).

But Sagan's first, *Mädchen in Uniform,* is a classic of pre-Hitler German cinema, a profoundly antifascist political tract as well as a groundbreaking and liberating depiction of a crystal-clear eroticism between women.

Mädchen in Uniform is the story of Manuela, a pretty 14-year-old who arrives at a Potsdam boarding school run in a strict, militaristic manner by Prussian Frau Oberin, the headmistress. "I demand absolute discipline," declares Oberin. Many of her charges are the children of Prussian soldiers, she observes, and hopefully they will grow up to be the wives of Prussian soldiers. Her Prussianism is ever-apparent upon her declaration, as the girls gripe about their lack of food, that "through discipline and hunger, hunger and discipline, we shall rise again."

Despite their preordained destiny as dutiful soldiers' wives, there are hints of romantic attachments (if not downright physical relations) between the girls. Upon her arrival, one of her fellow students tells Manuela, "Well, don't fall in love...." Meanwhile, all the girls have developed crushes on Fräulein von Bernburg, their sole sympathetic, nonauthoritarian teacher/housemistress.

On one level, the students are like typical adolescents as they act girlishly silly, talk about movie stars, and comically imitate their teachers. Yet it seems as if every last one has formed a romantic or physical attachment within the boundaries of their school. They have made such connections not necessarily because they are lesbians; these girls are lonely and desperate for affection, and are turning to each other because they live in a world completely devoid of boys and men.

The female-to-female eroticism in *Mädchen in Uniform,* both implied and obvious, is unmistakable throughout. There is much talk (as well as footage) of the girls dressing and undressing. Girls constantly walk hand-in-hand, or arm-in-arm. There is an emphasis on the girls' developing bodies. At one point, a girl rehearses dialogue for a school play while another sits at her feet, stroking her naked leg.

Fräulein von Bernburg is depicted as a responsible and caring adult who is deeply concerned with the welfare of the students, and who tells Manuela to make up her mind to be happy at school. Yet her involvement with the girls is not restricted to disseminating kindly advice. Each night, as they are about to retire, von Bernburg presents each girl with a kiss on the forehead. It becomes clear that a special attachment is developing between von Bernburg and Manuela when, after bidding goodnight to the others, she kisses the youngster on the lips.

From that point on, Manuela is enraptured by the Fräulein. Manuela does well in every other class but von Bernburg's, because she is so distracted by the teacher. She announces that, at night, she would like to enter von Bernburg's room, talk with her, and hold her hand.

Mädchen in Uniform ends on an idealistically upbeat note. Upon Manuela's publicly declaring her feelings toward her cherished teacher, Oberin pronounces that she is to be isolated from the others and blames von Bernburg for the "revolutionary ideas" instilled inside the girls. After the girls ignore Oberin and collectively save Manuela from committing suicide, the headmistress is shown walking down a flight of stairs in defeat, which symbolizes her loss of power and influence.

Mädchen in Uniform is a film about physical and spiritual liberation, in which caring, warmth, and intimacy triumph over blind authority, militarism, and repression. Unfortunately, just as the film was playing in movie houses, it was the Frau Oberins who were seizing power in Germany. Two years after its release, Hitler became the nation's chancellor—and dictator. While *Mädchen in Uniform* initially was greeted enthusiastically by critics in Germany and abroad, it eventually was banned by Goebbels. But the film remains significant not just for its antiauthoritarianism/militarism theme and fe-male-to-female imagery. By way of its union of dialogue and sound, gleaned from her formidable theatrical experience, Sagan displayed a mastery of the then-new sound film medium. Her use of visuals is equally impressive. By superimposing the images of Manuela and Fräulein von Bernburg, she communicates their intense psychological association.

Soon after directing *Mädchen in Uniform,* Sagan abandoned Germany for England, and eventually became a preeminent stage director in South Africa. But with this film, her place in the history of both German and gay cinema is assured.

—Rob Edelman

SALAAM BOMBAY!
India-France-Great Britain, 1988
Director: Mira Nair

Production: National Films Development Corporation (New Delhi)-Cadrage (Paris)-Channel 4 (London). A Mirabi Films production; in color; running time: 113 minutes; length: 10,271 feet. Released 1988. Filmed in Hindi, with English subtitles.

Executive producers: Anil Tejani, Michael Nozik, and Gabriel Auer; **producer:** Mira Nair; **co-producer:** Mitch Epstein; **screenplay:** Sooni Taraporevala; **Hindi dialogue:** Hriday Lani; **photography:** Sandi Sissel; **editor:** Barry Alexander Brown; **supervising sound editor:** Margie Crimmins; **production designer:** Mitch Epstein; **art directors:** Nitish Roy and Nitin Desai; **costume designers:** Deepa Kakkar, Nilita Vachani, and Dinaz Stafford; **music:** L. Subramaniam; **children's workshop director:** Barry John; **film extract:** *Mr. India* (1987).

Cast: Shafiq Syed (*Krishna, "Chaipau"*); Raghubir Yadav (*Chillum*); Aneeta Kanwar (*Rekha*); Nana Patekar (*Baba*); Hansa Vithal (*Manju*); Mohnraj Babu (*Salim*); Chandrashekhar Naidu (*Chungal*); Chanda Sharma (*Solasaal, "Sweet Sixteen"*); Shaukat Kaifi (*Madame*); Sarfuddin Quarrassi (*Koyla*); Raju Barnad (*Keera*); Dinshaw Daji (*Parsi Bawaji*); Alfred Anthony (*Lalua Chor*); Ramesh Deshavani (*Murtaza*); Anjan Srivastava (*Superintendent*); Irshad Hashmi (*Chacha*); Yunus Parvez (*Hashimbhai*); Ameer Bhai (*Ravi, Rekha's Rich Cousin*); Sulbha Deshpande (*Hemlata Joshi*); Mohan Tanturu (*Chillum II*); Amrit Patel (*Circus Boss*); Murari Sharma (*Ticket Seller*); Ram Moorti (*Mad Man*); Kishan Thapa (*Nepali Middleman*); Haneef Zahoor (*Bouncer*); Ramesh Rai (*Barber*); Shaukut H. Inamdar (*Crawford Market Shopkeeper*); Irfan Khan (*Scribe*); Neil Gettinger (*American Big Dog*); Double Battery Stafford (*Sexy Woman in Movie Theater*); Rana Singh (*Sleazy Man in Movie Theater*); Ali Bhai (*Butcher at Crawford Market*); Jayant Joshi (*Tailor*); Prashant Jaiswal (*Crooner at Wedding*); Joyce Barneto (*Bride*); Hassan Kutty (*Bridegroom*).

Publications

Book

Nair, Mira, *Salaam Bombay,* with Sooni Taraporevala, New Delhi, 1989.

Salaam Bombay!

Articles

Variety (New York), 8 June 1988.

Nair, Mira, in *Première* (Paris), August 1988.

Revue du Cinéma (Paris), September 1988.

Nair, Mira, in *Film Comment* (New York), September/October 1988.

Dieckmann, Katherine, in *Village Voice* (New York), 11 October 1988.

Malcolm, Derek, "Street Credibility," in *Guardian* (London), 20 January 1989.

Interview with Mira Nair, in *City Limits* (London), 26 January 1989.

Parmar, Prathiba, "Mira Nair: Filmmaking in the Streets of Bombay," in *Spare Rib* (London), February 1989.

Pym, John, in *Monthly Film Bulletin* (London), February 1989.

Moore, Suzanne, in *New Statesman and Society* (London), 3 February 1989.

Ehrlich, L. C., "The Name of the Child: Cinema as Social Critique," in *Film Criticism* (Meadville, Pennsylvania), no. 2, 1990.

Arora, P., and K. Irving, "Culturally Specific Texts, Culturally Bound Audiences: Ethnography in the Place of Its Reception," in *Journal of Film and Video* (Los Angeles), nos. 1-2, 1991.

Virdi, J., "(Mis)representing Child Labor," in *Jump Cut* (Berkeley), July 1992.

"Mira Nair," in *Current Biography 1993,* New York, 1993.

* * *

It is difficult to distinguish Mira Nair's film about Bombay's street children, *Salaam Bombay!,* from its existence as a media event. In India, radio shows, newspaper advertising, and *Salaam Bombay!* T-shirts have been harnessed to "sell" the film in ways similar to the marketing of the usual western film industry product. This might account for the rather cool response of domestic reviewers; in addition, the expatriate status of the director and even certain inflections of the narrative have been cited as indices of the film's tainted, inauthentic "foreignness."

Nair's objective is evidently to promote the film, and she is prepared to use whatever means are at hand. Nevertheless, this unabashed approach to the promotion of what would ordinarily rank as a social problem film in the tradition of India's state-supported "middle" cinema does present problems.

To redress this uncertainty about the zone between strategy and message, it is important to acknowledge that *Salaam Bombay!* does exist at the level of a reforming social project. The seriousness of the filmmakers' engagement with their subject has been fully indicated. Nair and her colleagues undertook detailed research into the lives of the street children. They set up a *Salaam Bombay!* trust for them and a school for their education. Concern for the children has extended beyond the film in the monitoring of each child's development and the attempt to ensure that the children are given the opportunity of improving their situation.

There is, however, a complex relationship between this activity—one predicated on knowledge, commitment, and thereby trust—and the reordering of the performative and existential attributes of the film's subject. Nair has remarked that it was observing the facility of the street children performing for their living that set her thinking about the film. Workshops were used to channel the children's skills into realist conventions of acting; their urge to perform in terms of the Hindi popular cinema's excesses of gesture and "theatrically" articulated dialogue was discouraged. The film allows such "artificiality" only in strictly regulated contexts, notably those used to dramatize the humiliation of the individual by the group and the delineation of a kind of daydream make-believe. Otherwise there is an underplaying of performance in the representation of the individual, a stress on the imperative of "capturing" intimate psychological states rather than essaying broad melodramatic flourishes. This reeducation of the children's performative skills extended to the way in which even camera performance was registered; Nair has noted that lead child actor Shafiq Syed reprimanded another actor for disturbing spatial continuity between shots.

How relevant is the question of "true" representation to the attributes of the street children? Which was the "normal" mode of relating to their world—the melodramatic one which they first presented, or the realist one into which they were educated? What is interesting is the way in which the film reorders the children's perception of the way they should relate to the world. Nair's ability to bring this about is probably related to earlier documentary work in which she drew a responsive interaction from the people she was dealing with. She has used interview and cinema-verité techniques (*So Far from India*, 1982, *India Cabaret*, 1985), but in ways which suggest a complicity of the subjects in the construction of their image. In *Salaam Bombay!* it is the induction of the cinema-verité subject into an active fictionalization of his or her experience which leads not only to representation but, in a sense, reconstitution.

None of this is intended to suggest that the film is "inauthentic"; realist narration is certainly not an alien phenomenon in India, though it may be a minority one. Further, the rapport Nair and her crew struck up not only with individuals but with crowds is indicated by the vivid portrait the film presents of Bombay; in this context it may be placed alongside such documentary essays on the city as *Bombay, Our City* (Anand Patwardhan, 1985), about the struggle of street dwellers to protect their habitation.

As for the film's "foreignness," one may speculate that it is precisely the multiplicity of cultural positions that the director occupies that enables her to regard her characters with a peculiar, resonating effect. On the one hand the film draws upon the need of the children to find some kind of stability and affection. On the other, it shows this drive as frustrated and leading to violence. The duality here reenacts the recurrent, indeed obsessive concerns of the Hindi commercial cinema of the 1970s, though on very different representational terms. It also, interestingly, has another possible point of reference. The leading child character is obsessed with a teenage girl who is being inducted into prostitution by a pimp. The relationship between the girl and the man is ambiguous. The analogy with Scorsese's *Taxi Driver* is too striking to be missed. Perhaps the relationship lies within certain modern male obsessions and anxieties. Whatever the reason, it is likely that only an Indian living in New York could have drawn out these subterranean links between American modernism and Hindi "kitsch."

—Ravi Vasudevan

SAMBIZANGA
France-People's Republic of the Congo, 1972
Director: Sarah Maldoror

Production: Isabelle Film; Eastmancolor; 35mm; 103 minutes.

Screenplay: Sarah Maldoror, Mario Andrade, and Maurice Pone, adapted from the novel by Luandino Vieira; **photography:** Claude Agostini.

Cast: Domingos Oliveira; Elisa de Andrade; Dino Abeline.

Awards: Golden Tanis, Carthage Film Festival; International Catholic Film Office award, Ouagadougou Film Festival, Upper Volta.

Publications

Articles

Hennebelle, Guy, "Sambizanga," in *Écran* (Paris), no. 15, May 1973.
Harvey, Sylvia, Sarah Maldoror, Nadja Kasji, and Elin Clason, "Third World Perspectives: Focus on Sarah Maldoror," in *Women and Film* (Santa Monica, California), vol. 1, nos. 5-6, 1974.
Tallon, Brigitte, "L'an II du cinéma antillais," in *Autrement,* vol. 49, 1983.

* * *

Sarah Maldoror's first feature fiction film earns its place in the history of Caribbean cinema in several ways—first for its depiction of Angolan rebellion against Portuguese colonial rule; second, as one of the first feature films by an Antillean director; and third, for the discussions it elicits about its director's origins and national identity and about the political process it examines.

Sambizanga is set in Angola just before 4 February 1961, the celebrated first day of Angolan resistance against Portuguese rule. On this day, resistance fighters left their village of Sambizanga and began their march to the country's colonial capital, Luanda. Once in Luanda, they attacked the Portuguese prison, liberating many of the political prisoners. This day marked the beginning of the Angolan liberation movement which eventually overthrew Portuguese rule. Maldoror's film follows Maria, the wife of Domingos Xavier, an Angolan construction worker, as she travels from one village to another trying to find out what has become of her husband. Eventually, the audience learns that Xavier had refused to betray a white friend who had joined the resistance struggle. For his loyalty to his comrade, Xavier was kidnapped by the secret police, tortured, and finally killed. During her travels, Maria gains political awareness and enlightenment, learning from the people along her way about the arduousness of anticolonialist struggle.

Based on a true story and the novelization of that experience by Luandino Vieira, *Sambizanga* presents Maria as a woman who at first is unaware of the implications of political struggle and the depth of the brutality of colonialism. Her coming into awareness on some level allegorizes the transformation of the Angolan people, showing collective responsibility and sharing as their political strengths. For Maldoror, the film was a deliberate exercise in educating Europeans about the African struggles—as she told the editors of *Women and Film*, "to make you Europeans who hardly know anything about Africa, conscious of the forgotten war in Angola, Mozambique and Guinea-Bissau." Her challenging, almost taunting attitude here perhaps reveals the self-defensiveness of a woman who never has felt quite at home in any of her adopted lands. Born in France to Guadeloupean parents, Maldoror identifies more with the country of her heritage than the country of her birth. The companion of the late Mario de Andrade, the Angolan writer who was also known for his leadership of the Angolan liberation movement, Maldoror not only sympathizes with African freedom struggles, she has experienced and contributed to them firsthand. Maldoror has always felt like an outsider in France and the reception of her first feature only deepened that feeling. She notes that in the United States African-American cinema is a real force, whereas her films are seen as made by an outsider by each of their audiences—in Africa she has been omitted from festivals because she is not "African" while the Frenchman Jean Rouch was included in the same gatherings. In Guadeloupe they say she is French. And in France, she feels the isolation of blacks from French society.

Although Sarah Maldoror admires the films of Agnès Varda and Anna Karina, she also looks toward Chris Marker and Alain Resnais for inspiration. Maldoror does not set out to make feminist films nor does she believe that the films of women filmmakers necessarily share characteristics because of the sex of their director. In addition to the influences of the aforementioned modernist French filmmakers, Maldoror's own films are greatly informed by her politics and experience. *Sambizanga*'s Maria is a woman looking for her husband. Her experience could occur in any country, it is not unique to Angola. Her trek teaches her much about her country, its people's struggles for freedom, and the potential of her own role in the struggle. This story may take place in Angola in 1961, but certainly it resonates for many African and Latin American countries in the same crucial historical moment.

Although she has been making films about African struggles against imperialism since the 1960s, Maldoror has to date only completed this one feature fiction film. Following her studies at the film school in Moscow, Maldoror's first film *Monangambée* (1968), a short documentary that exposed the more hideous forms of torture used by the French against the Algerians in that liberation struggle, won international recognition at several film festivals. Another well-known film, *Aimé Césaire, Words as Masks* (1986), is a biography of the Martinican poet and writer best known for his contributions to the literary movement "negritude." For this film, she visited the Caribbean for the first time, immediately feeling a strong connection to her ancestral home. Currently, she is developing a feature film based on Louis Delgrès, a Guadeloupean-born French Army officer and revolutionary.

Ultimately, in addition to educating "Europeans" about Africans, Maldoror seeks to write Africans back into the official histories of the countries in which they have lived, fought, and been denied a true national identity. Certainly this is a mission that parallels Maldoror's own search for identity, but bigger than its creator, it is also a mission that dovetails with that of her many contemporary filmmakers from Africa, Latin America, and the Caribbean.

—Ilene S. Goldman

SANDER, Helke

German director and writer

Born: Berlin, 31 January 1937. **Education:** Attended drama school, studying with Ida Ehre, Hamburg, 1957-58; studied German and psychology at the University of Helsinki, 1960-62; studied at the Deutsche Film-und Fernsehakademie, Berlin, 1966-69. **Family:** Married the Finnish writer Markku Lahtela, 1959, one son: Silvio. **Career:** 1962—worked in Finnish theater; 1964—worked for Finnish television; 1965—returned to Germany; 1966—directed first short film *Subjectivity*; 1974—founded *Frauen und Film*; since 1981—professor at the Hamburg University for Visual Arts; co-director for the Bremen Institute for Film and Television. **Awards:** Women's Film Hyères, and Prix l'age d'or, Brussels, for *Redupers,* 1977; Golden Bear and German Film Prize, Filmband in Gold, for *No. 1—From the Reports of Security Guards and Patrol Services,* 1984. **Address:** Hochschule für Bildende Künste, Hamburg, Germany.

Films as Director and Writer

1966 *Subjektitüde (Subjectivity)*
1967 *Silvio*; *Brecht die Macht der Manipulateure (Crush the Power of the Manipulators)*
1969 *Kindergärtnerin, was nun? (What Now, Nursery Workers)*; *Kinder sind nicht Rinder (Children Are Not Cattle)*
1971 *Eine Prämie für Irene (A Bonus for Irene)* (co-d)
1972 *Macht die Pille Frei? (Does the Pill Liberate?)* (co-d)
1973 *Männerbunde (Male Bonding)* (co-d)
1977 *Die allseitig reduzierte Persönlichkeit (Redupers; The All-Around Reduced Personality)* (+ ro as Edda Chiemnyjewski)
1981 *Der subjektive Faktor (The Subjective Factor)*
1983 *Der Beginn aller Schrecken ist Liebe (The Trouble with Love)* (+ ro as lover)
1984 *Nr. 1—Aus Berichten der Wach—und Patrouillendienst (No. 1—From the Reports of Security Guards and Patrol Services)* (doc); *Nr. 8—Aus Berichten der Wach—und Patrouillendienst (No. 8—From the Reports of Security Guards and Patrol Services)* (doc)
1986 "Füttern" ("Gluttony") ep. of *Sieben Frauen—Sieben Sünden (Seven Women—Seven Sins)*
1987 *Felix* (co-d with Buschmann, Sanders-Brahms, and von Trotta)
1990 *Die Deutschen und ihre Männer (The Germans and Their Men)*
1992 *BeFreier und Befreite Krieg, Vergewaltigung, Kinder (Liberators Take Liberties: War, Rape, Children)* (doc)
1997 *Duzlak*

Other Films

1983 *Vater und Sohn (Father and Son)* (Mitscherlich) (ro)
1988 *Das schwache Geschlecht muss stärker werden (The Weaker Sex Must Become Stronger)* (ro as herself)
1992 *Des Lebens schönste Seiten (Life's Most Beautiful Sides)* (Heine—for TV) (ro as Neri)
1995 *Die Nacht der Regisseure (The Night of the Filmmakers)* (Reitz—doc) (appearance)

Publications by Sander

Books

Editor, with Eva Hiller and Gesine Strempel, *Cutterinen,* Berlin, 1976.

Helke Sander

Editor, with Claudia Lenssen and Gesine Strempel, *Filmpolitik,* Berlin, 1978.
With Gislind Nabakowski and Peter Gorsen, *Frauen in der Kunst,* Frankfurt, 1980.
Die Geschichte der drei Damen K, Munich, 1987; published as *The Three Women K,* translated by Helen Petzold, London, 1991.
Oh Lucy: Erzählung, Munich, 1991.
Editor, with Barbara Johr, *BeFreier und Befreite: Krieg, Vergewaltigungen, Kinder,* Munich, 1992.
With Roger Willemsen, *Gewaltakte: Männerphantasien und Krieg,* Hamburg, 1993.

Articles

"Sexismus in den massenmedien," in *Frauen und Film* (Berlin), vol. 1, 1974.
"Feminismus und Film: 'I Like Chaos, but I Don't Know Whether Chaos Likes Me'," in *Frauen und Film* (Berlin), vol. 5, 1979.
Interview with Renate Möhrmann, in *Frau mit der Kamera: Filmemacherinnen in der Bundesrepublik Deutschland,* Munich, 1980.
"Krankheit als sprache," in *Frauen und Film* (Berlin), vol. 23, 1980.
Interview with Marc Silberman, in *Jump Cut* (Berkeley), vol. 29, 1984.

Interview with Renate Fischetti, in *Das neue Kino: Acht Proträts von deutschen Regisseurinnen,* Dülmen-Hiddingsel, Germany, 1992.
"Prologue," in *Mass Rape: The War against Women in Bosnia-Herzegovina,* edited by Alexandra Stilgmayer, translated by Marion Faber, Lincoln, Nebraska, 1994.
"A Response to My Critics" and "Remembering and Forgetting," in *October* (Cambridge, Massachusetts), vol. 72, 1995.

Publications on Sander

Books

McCormick, Richard, *The Politics of the Self: Feminism and the Postmodern in West German Literature and Film,* Princeton, New Jersey, 1991.
Das neue Kino: acht Proträts von deutschen Regisseurinnen, Frankfurt, 1992.
Foster, Gwendolyn Audrey, *Women Film Directors: An International Bio-Critical Dictionary,* Westport, Connecticut, 1995.

Articles

Silverman, Kaja, "Helke Sander and the Will to Change," in *Discourse* (Berkeley), Fall 1983.
McCormick, Richard, "Re-Presenting the Student Movement: Helke Sander's *The Subjective Factor,*" in *Gender and German Cinema: Feminist Interventions,* Volume 2, *German Film History/German History on Film,* edited by Sandra Frieden, Richard W. McCormick, Vibeke R. Petersen, and Laurie Melissa Vogelsang, Oxford, 1993.
Special issue of *October* (Cambridge, Massachusetts), vol. 72, 1995.
Kosta, Barbara, "Rape, Nation and Remembering History: Helke Sander's *Liberators Take Liberties,*" in *Gender and Germanness,* edited by Patricia Herminghouse and Magda Mueller, Providence, Rhode Island, 1997.

*   *   *

Helke Sander's name has become synonymous with the advent of Germany's second wave women's movement and feminist filmmaking. Provocative in style and subject matter, her self-reflexive documentaries and later fictional explorations of women's experiences reveal the ambition to politicize the private sphere and to challenge habitual ways of seeing. Owing to her unconventional choice of topics, Sander received no funding for a period of about five years with the justification that her proposed themes addressed only women instead of appealing to a general public. It was not until 1977 that Sander was able to direct her break-through and best-known feature-length film, *Redupers* which focuses on the life of Edda, a freelance photographer, mother, and activist who faces the conflicting demands of her private and professional life and who confronts sexism in the media when a photoessay of women's views of Berlin, commissioned by a mainstream magazine, is rejected.

While still at the Film and Television Academy, Sander became active in the student movement. In her 1968 address at the Socialist Student's Association ("Speech by the Action Council for Women's Liberation"), Sander criticized the male Left for its disregard of women's issues and, more generally, for a political analysis that overlooks the private realm. Disaffected with the Left's blind spots, Sander co-founded the Council for Women's Liberation. This experience is reflected in *The Subjective Factor,* a work of memory that traces the beginnings of the women's movement in Germany and the break with the socialist student movement and the APO (extraparliamentary opposition). Interspersed with documentary footage, the subjective, autobiographical fiction challenges the claim of the objectivity of historical narration and the documentary genre. In *The Trouble with Love* the paradoxical politics of emotion are parodied when two liberated, though jealous, women vie for the same man and perform for his gaze. The film addresses the oppressive structures that shape interpersonal relations as well as collective histories commented on in a voice-over. *The Germans and Their Men* similarly explores the failure to link the deeply entrenched public and private divide in numerous interviews with men who neglect to contemplate their conduct toward women. In *Liberators Take Liberties,* an ambitious three-and-one-half-hour documentary film, Sander probes the stories of German women who were raped predominately by soldiers of the Red Army in the last days of World War II. A montage of present-day interviews breaks through the silence that has beleaguered personal and public memory. Sander's film *Duzlak,* a road movie/comedy, depicts chance meeting between Jenny and a skinhead whom she tries to help after he hits a tree with his car while driving under the influence.

Throughout her career, in her films, essays, and most recently in her short stories, Sander has remained provocative and unveering in her pursuit to expose the asymmetrical power structures that disadvantage women and the general resistance to an analysis of gendered relations. Besides her own filmmaking interests, her formidable accomplishments include founding the first, and only, feminist film journal in Europe, *Frauen und Film,* in 1974—recovering works of women directors, actors, and scriptwriters either forgotten or ignored by film history, addressing the conditions under which women make films and the policies and preferences of funding agencies, and supporting women filmmakers who found little backing or visibility. In 1974 she co-organized the International Women's Film Seminar to promote women's productions.

—Barbara Kosta

SANDERS-BRAHMS, Helma

German director and writer

Born: Helma Sanders in Emden, Germany, 20 November 1940; added her mother's maiden name to her own to differentiate herself from another New German Cinema filmmaker, Helke Sander. **Education:** Studied acting in Hanover, Germany; studied drama and literature at Cologne University. **Family:** Daughter, the actress Anna Sanders. **Career:** 1960s—worked as an announcer and interviewer for a Cologne television station; 1970-began directing shorts and documentaries for German television; 1971—directed first feature, *Gewelt;* 1974—made *Erdbeben in Chile,* her first film for the Filmverlag der Autoren, set up by 13 New German Cinema directors as a production and distribution co-operative.

Films as Director and Writer

1970 *Angelika Urban, Verkaüferin, Verlobt (Angelika Urban, Salesgirl, Engaged)* (short)
1971 *Gewalt (Violence)* (for TV); *Die industrielle Reservarmee (The Industrial Reserve Army)* (doc—for TV)
1972 *Der Angestellte (The Employee)* (for TV)
1973 *Die maschine (The Machine)* (doc)
1974 *Die letzten Tage von Gomorrah (The Last Days of Gomorrah)* (for TV); *Erdbeben in Chile (Earthquake in Chile)* (for TV)
1975 *Unter dem Pflaster ist der Strand (The Sand under the Pavement)*
1976 *Shirins Hochzeit (Shirin's Wedding)* (for TV)
1977 *Heinrich*
1980 ***Deutschland, bleiche Mutter (Germany, Pale Mother)*** (+ pr); *Vringsveedeler Triptichon (The Vringsveedel Tryptych)* (doc)
1981 *Die Berührte (No Mercy No Future; No Exit No Panic)* (+ pr, costumes, makeup)
1982 *Die Erbtöchter (The Daughters' Inheritance)* (co-d)
1984 *Flügel und Fesseln (L'Avenir d'Emilie; The Future of Emily)*
1985 *Alte Liebe (Old Love)* (doc—for TV) (co-sc)
1986 *Laputa*
1987 *Felix* (co-d with Buschmann, Sander, and von Trotta)
1988 *Geteilte Liebe (Divided Love; Manoever)* (+ pr)
1992 *Apfelbaume (Apple Trees)*
1995 *Lumière et compagnie (Lumière and Company)* (doc) (co-d); *Jetzt leben - Juden in Berlin*

Other Films

1981 *Der Subjektive Faktor* (ro)
1995 *Die Nacht der Regisseure (The Night of the Filmmakers)* (Reitz—doc) (appearance)

Publications by Sanders-Brahms

Books

Deutschland, bleiche Mutter: Film-Erzahlung, Hamburg, 1980.
Das Dunkle zwischen den Bildern: Essays, Porträts, Kritiken, Frankfurt, 1992.

Articles

"Misunderstood Mother and Forgotten Father," interview with Ginette Vincendeau, in *Monthly Film Bulletin* (London), May 1985.
Interview with C. Racine, in *Séquences* (Montreal), February 1987.
With S. Toubiana, "Menace à l'est," in *Cahiers du Cinéma* (Paris), September 1990.
Interview with Peter Brunette, in *Film Quarterly* (Berkeley), Winter 1990.
Interview with E. Richter and R. Richter, in *Film und Fernsehen* (Berlin), vol. 19, no. 8/9, 1991.

Publications on Sanders-Brahms

Books

Tast, Brigitte, editor, *Helma Sanders-Brahms,* 1980.
Mayne, Judith, *The Woman at the Keyhole: Feminism and Women's Cinema,* Bloomington, Indiana, 1990.
Foster, Gwendolyn Audrey, *Women Film Directors: An International Bio-Critical Dictionary,* Westport, Connecticut, 1995.

Articles

Silberman, Marc, "Women Filmmakers in West Germany: A Catalog," in *Camera Obscura* (Los Angeles), Autumn 1980.

Aude, F., in *Positif* (Paris), November 1981.

Silberman, M., "Women Working: Women Filmmakers in West Germany: A Catalog (Part 2)," in *Camera Obscura* (Los Angeles), Fall 1983.

Article in *Film a Doba* (Prague), June 1985.

Bammer, A., "Through a Daughter's Eyes: Helma Sanders-Brahms's *Germany, Pale Mother*," in *New German Critique,* Fall 1985.

Fjordholm, H., in *Z Filmtidsskrift* (Oslo), vol. 4, no. 5, 1986.

Desjardins, M., "*Germany, Pale Mother* and the Maternal: Towards a Feminist Spectatorship," in *Spectator,* vol. 8, no. 1, 1987.

Elsaesser, T., "Public Bodies and Divided Selves: German Women Filmmakers in the 1980s," in *Monthly Film Bulletin* (London), December 1987.

Hyams, B., "Is the Apolitical Woman at Peace? A Reading of the Fairy Tale in *Germany, Pale Mother*," in *Wide Angle* (Baltimore, Maryland), vol. 10, no. 3, 1988.

Kinder, M., "Ideological Parody in the New German Cinema: Reading *The State of Things, The Desire of Veronika Voss,* and *Germany, Pale Mother* as Postmodernist Rewritings of *The Searchers, Sunset Boulevard,* and *Blonde Venus*," in *Quarterly Review of Film and Video,* vol. 12, no. 1/2, 1990.

Kindred, Jack, "German Helmer Quits Fest over Yank Invasion," in *Variety* (New York), 14 February 1990.

*   *   *

The films of Helma Sanders-Brahms have been programmed with some amount of relish at film festivals and in art houses and cinematheques, but it is a safe bet that they never will be mainstream movie fare. They are not engrossing dramas in which the audience can become emotionally involved in the on-screen action. Instead, Sanders-Brahms presents, from a distance, observable archetypes of life, often with a deliberate pacing. Rather than directing actors to express emotion, she prefers "pent-up" performers who hide their real feelings. In fact, actor Heinrich Giskes found himself so emotionally "pent-up" while shooting a scene for *Heinrich* that he broke a glass over his director's head as soon as she yelled cut.

Sanders-Brahms is a rebel to Hollywood conventions. She avoids casting glamorous leading ladies or hunky actors in order to sell tickets, and her films are often very slowly paced. She does not make "road movies," because she does not revel in what she calls "the poetry of the road, the journey. The autobahn and the factory assembly line are the same thing, the same prison."

A producer and writer in addition to director, Sanders-Brahms is a member of the New German Cinema movement, and as such she builds her scripts around the concerns of the political left. Many of her films present themes pertaining to the plight of the worker in Germany: the inequities of modern working conditions; how workers have been pitted against one another in order to attain Germany's capitalist "economic miracle"; and how the Gastarbeiter ("guest worker," or foreign migrant worker in Germany) is exploited. *Shirin's Wedding* addresses the Gastarbeiter problem, focusing on the suffering of a Turkish woman. As a child, Shirin was betrothed to Mahmud, but he left for Germany to become a Gastarbeiter. To escape an arranged marriage, Shirin travels to Germany to find Mahmud. She obtains work in a factory in Cologne and later as a cleaner, a job that disappears after she is raped by her boss. She winds up a prostitute, with Mahmud paying to have sex with her.

Eventually, she is killed by a pimp's bullet. In *No Mercy No Future,* the daughter of a bourgeois family seeks sexual partners in the streets, including black migrant workers, derelicts, and aged, crippled cast-offs of society. In these neglected people, she sees the essence of Christ. Finally, *Apple Trees* shows the destruction of a family whose members are adversely affected by the politics of reunification.

Other motifs in Sanders-Brahms's work are the independent woman under fire and the mother-daughter relationship. She herself was raised by her self-reliant mother while her father was away fighting in Hitler's armies. He did not return until she was five years old. Much of her perception of her parents' relationship and her own childhood is depicted in *Germany, Pale Mother,* one of her best-known films. The mother is shown as a strong and independent woman who gives birth to her daughter (played by Sanders-Brahms's own baby girl) during an air raid. When the war ends, this woman is expected to file away her independence in order to be an obedient wife. She does so, but her frustrations take hold in the form of a disease which paralyzes her face and, in a gut-wrenching scene, calls for the removal of all her teeth. *The Future of Emily* tells of an actress who lives a single, unconventional lifestyle. She returns to her parents' home to retrieve her daughter, only to be told by her own mother that she is a bad influence on the child. In a powerful scene the actress and her little girl visit the beach, where they spin fantasy adventures with each other. The movie makes reference to the myth of an Amazon queen, a woman who has killed off the man she loves and is living quite nicely without the company of men. Sanders-Brahms's point is that, in modern society, there are women who also are living well without men, but they are brainwashed into thinking that they would be better off with male partners.

Sanders-Brahms's us-against-them brand of feminism mirrors the early 1970s, when the modern feminist movement was new and women who had grown up in a male-dominated society were feeling confrontational. Indeed, *Felix,* released in 1987, might have been made in the early 1970s. It is the politically loaded story of an egocentric, hypocritical modern male whose lack of self-awareness borders on the ridiculous. He has just been left by his lover, and he finds himself cast adrift in a world in which women no longer need men, or want men. *Felix* is filmed in four episodes, each shot by a different woman director—Christel Buschmann, Helke Sander, and Margarethe von Trotta, in addition to Sanders-Brahms. All are guilty of stereotyping men as jabbering idiots, and women as collectively sensitive, sensuous, and perceptive—practically perfect.

Sanders-Brahms's films are united in that they are reflective of the society in which she came of age. Along with her fellow members of the New German Cinema, she has a mission: to point out what is wrong with the world as she sees it.

— Audrey E. Kupferberg

SARMIENTO, Valeria
Chilean director, writer, and editor

Born: Valparaiso, Chile, 1948. **Education:** Studied film and philosophy at the Universidad de Chile, Viña del Mar. **Family:** Married the director Raúl Ruiz. **Career:** 1973—fled General Pinochet's Chile for Paris; began working as editor; 1975—directed *The Housewife,* her first documentary made in exile. **Awards:** San Sebastian International Film Festival award, for *Our Marriage,* 1984.

Films as Director

1968-69 *Sueño como de colores* (*I Dream in Color*) (doc, short)
1972 *Poesia popular: la teoría y la práctica* (*Popular Poetry: Theory and Practice*) (doc, short) (co-d with Ruiz, + co-pr, co-ed)
1973 *Nueva canción (chilena)* (*New Song [Chilean]*) (unfinished short) (co-d, + ed)
1975 *La Femme au foyer* (*La dueña de casa*; *The Housewife*) (doc, short)
1979 *Le Mal du pays* (*The Bad Thing about This Country*) (doc)
1980 *Gens de toutes partes, Gens de nulle parte* (*Gente de todas partes ... Gente de ninguna parte*; *People from Everywhere, People from Nowhere*) (doc)
1982 *El hombre cuando es hombre* (*A Man, When He Is a Man*) (doc)
1984 *Notre mariage* (*Our Marriage*)
1991 *Amelia Lópes O'Neill; Le planète des enfants* (*The Planet of Children*)
1992 *Latin Women* (doc—for TV)
1995 *Elle* (*She*) (+ sc)

Films as Editor

1971 *La Expropiación* (*The Expropriation*) (Ruiz)
1972 *Los Minuteros* (*The Minute Hands*; *The Street Photographer*) (Ruiz—doc, short) (+ co-pr)
1974 *Dialogue d'exilés* (*Diálogo de exiliados, Exiles' Dialogue*) (Ruiz) (+ ro)
1975 *Mensche verstreut und Welt verkehrt* (*El cuerpo repartido y el mundo al revés*; *The Body Repaired and the World in Reverse*) (Ruiz)
1976 *Sotelo* (Ruiz—doc, short)
1977 *La Vocation suspendue* (*The Suspended Vocation*) (Ruiz); *Colloque de chiens* (*Dog's Language*) (Ruiz)
1979 *Des Grandes événements et des gens ordinaires: les élections* (*Big Events and Ordinary People: Elections*) (Ruiz—doc); *Petit Manuel d'histoire de France, ch. 1 "Des ancêtres les Gaulois à la prise du pouvoir par Louis XIV"* (*Short History of France, ch. 1 "From the Gaulle Ancestors to the Taking of Power by Louis XIV"*) (Ruiz—doc, video)
1980 *Le Borgne* (Ruiz—for TV, 4 eps.); *Guns* (Kramer) (co)
1981 *Le Territoire* (*The Territory*) (Ruiz); *Le Toit de la Baleine* (*On Top of the Whale*; *The Whale's Roof*; *Het dak van de walvis*) (Ruiz—doc for TV)
1982 *Les Trois Couronnes du matelot* (*The Three Crowns of a Sailor*; *Las Tres coronas del marinera*) (Ruiz) (co)
1983 *La Ville des pirates* (*The City of Pirates*) (Ruiz)
1985 *Voyage autour d'une main* (*Voyage around a Hand*) (Ruiz—short)
1988 *Derrière le mur* (*Behind the Wall*) (Ruiz)
1994 *Il Viaggio clandestino* (*The Secret Journey*) (Ruiz)
1997 *Généalogies d'une crime* (*Geneologies of a Crime*) (Ruiz); *Le Film à venir* (*Film in the Future*) (Ruiz—doc, short)

Publications by Sarmiento

Articles

"Amérique Latine: les machos piéges par un caméra 'invisible,'" anonymous interview, in *Marie-Claire* (Paris), October 1981.

Interview with Françoise Audé, in *Positif* (Paris), October 1985.
"Dreaming Melodramas," interview with Coco Fusco, in *Afterimage* (Rochester, New York) December 1991.
"Le labyrinthe du melo et le dedale de Valparaiso," interview with P. A. Paranagua, in *Positif* (Paris), February 1992.
"Les chausson rouges," in *Positif* (Paris), June 1994.

Publications on Sarmiento

Books

Boorman, John, and Walter Donohue, editors, *Film-makers on Film-making,* London, 1995.
Foster, Gwendolyn Audrey, *Women Film Directors: An International Bio-Critical Dictionary,* Westport, Connecticut, 1995.

Articles

Pick, Zuzana M., "Chilean Cinema in Exile (1973-1986)," in *Framework* (Norwich, England), no. 34, 1987.
Lesage, Julia, "Women Make Media: Three Modes of Production," in *The Social Documentary in Latin America,* edited by Julianne Burton, Pittsburgh, 1992.
Pick, Zuzana M., "*Machismo* and Gender: *A Man, When He Is a Man,*" in *The New Latin American Cinema: A Continental Project,* Austin, Texas, 1993.

* * *

Although Chile's vibrant film culture gave birth in 1962 to the important international film festival at Viña del Mar, it is difficult to speak of a Chilean national cinema until the late 1960s. In the brief moment of Salvador Allende's presidency (1970-73), Chilean national cinema blossomed. Most of Chile's filmmakers supported Allende's Popular Unity coalition government. Despite political, ideological, and economic difficulties, they managed to make an unprecedented number of films, both independently and with state aid given through national universities, the Ministries of Agriculture and Education, and three state-owned television channels. In 1973 President Allende's government was ousted by a military coup. General Pinochet's repressive dictatorship brutally squelched opposition voices and many Chileans who had supported Allende fled their native land. Among those who went into exile were Chile's artists and filmmakers, most notably poet Pablo Neruda, novelist Isabel Allende, and filmmakers Miguel Littin, Raul Ruiz, his wife Valeria Sarmiento, and Marilú Mallet.

Chilean cinema in exile, particularly in the immediate postcoup years (1973-79), has been referred to as a Cinema of Resistance. These films, while not a movement in the traditional aesthetic, theoretical, or political sense, shared common themes and goals: a celebration of Chilean culture as it grew under Allende; building a consensus against the military junta; and the liberation of Chilean and Latin American peoples governed by repressive regimes.

Valeria Sarmiento is among this generation of Chilean filmmakers who began their careers in the 1960s and supported the Popular Unity government of Salvador Allende with their films. Her husband, Raul Ruiz, an internationally acclaimed filmmaker, was also politically active in the 1960s and throughout the Allende years. Sarmiento and Ruiz sought political asylum in Paris in the wake of the 1973 military coup. Sarmiento found it difficult to finance new film projects because she was not as well known as her husband.

Many potential funders felt that Sarmiento's work was derivative of Ruiz's and did not merit their investments. Although she was able to make a living as an editor, Sarmiento still speaks of this period as one of the most difficult and demoralizing of her career. Her first films made in exile dealt specifically with exile and the exile's identity struggle in an adopted land. Subsequent projects explored constructions of Latin American identity in a more general sense. Although many of her films examine women's and feminist issues, their constant concern with Latin American realities prohibits pigeonholing her work as "feminist."

Sarmiento's first directorial effort, *Sueño como de colores* was made in Chile during the Popular Unity years. A documentary about two striptease workers, the film was poorly received by critics who felt it did not deal with the important issues of the moment. Specifically, although its subjects are working-class women struggling to get ahead, reviewers commented that the film did not deal with class and economic stratification, problems that the Allende government was trying to resolve.

Sarmiento's first documentary made in exile, *The Housewife*, finally produced in 1975, explores how the opposition mobilized Chile's bourgeois women against Popular Unity. The film revisits the inequities of Chile's classist society, picking up the dialogue of the Popular Unity cinema. For the second time, however, critics found this film to be only tangential to the issues of Chilean exile cinema. Sarmiento's approach to political issues, looking at them through the position of marginalized social players, sets her work apart from other Chilean filmmakers. Further, her innovative formal and aesthetic play teases the politics out even as it searches for a personal film language. As a result, Sarmiento's films are both intimate and pan-Latin American, a difficult balance that she reaches expertly.

In *The Bad Thing about this Country* Sarmiento concerns herself with the exile of working-class Chilean children who fled Chile's slums for working-class French neighborhoods. It is a poignant portrait of children ages 5 to 8 who long for their homeland and yet recognize the vast improvement in their quality of life.

Sarmiento made an international name for herself with *A Man, When He Is a Man*, a feature-length documentary that explores the theme of "machismo" in Latin American culture. *A Man* analyzes how machismo is continued by the attitudes of both men and women. Filmed in Costa Rica and told largely from the perspective of men, the film also touches on romanticism in Latin American culture, demonstrating how romanticism and machismo overlap and feed each other. *A Man* uses the rites that mark different phases of a woman's life to examine how machismo is produced, maintained, and reproduced.

The critical success of *A Man* gave Sarmiento the opportunity to direct her first feature fiction film, *Our Marriage*. An adaptation of a novel by Corín Tellado, one of the most widely read romance novelists in Latin America, the film tells the story of a girl put into foster care because her father cannot afford to provide for her. Years later when her foster mother has died, her biological father gives the girl's foster father permission to marry her. In this and her subsequent feature films, Sarmiento matches her canny observations about Latin American and female identity with melodrama, perhaps the most beloved film and television genre in Latin America. Through melodrama she can throw into relief obsession, desire, sexuality, and morality—topics laid bare by Latin American melodrama, but paradoxically greatly repressed in Latin American polite society.

—Ilene S. Goldman

SAVOCA, Nancy
American director and writer

Born: New York, 1959. **Education:** Attended Queen's College (CUNY), and New York University Film School. **Family:** Married Richard Guay (her co-writer and producer on two films), 1980, three children. **Career:** While in film school, made two noteworthy films, *Renata* and *Bad Timing*; 1989—directed and co-scripted first feature film, *True Love*. **Awards:** Haig P. Manoogian Award for overall excellence, NYU Student Film Festival, 1984; Grand Jury Prize, U.S. Film Festival, for *True Love*, 1989. **Agent:** United Talent Agency, 9560 Wilshire Boulevard, Suite 500, Beverly Hills, CA 90212, U.S.A.

Films as Director

1983   *Bad Timing* (short) (+ co-sc)
1989   *True Love* (+ co-sc)
1991   *Dogfight*
1993   *Household Saints* (+ co-sc)
1996   "1952" and "1974" eps. of *If These Walls Could Talk* (for TV) (+ co-sc)
1998   *The 24 Hour Woman* (+ co-sc)

Other Film

1996   "1996" ep. of *If These Walls Could Talk* (Cher—for TV) (co-sc)

Publications by Savoca

Articles

"Nancy Savoca's New Movie, *Dogfight*, Takes a Wallop at Hollywood's Ideal of the Beautiful Woman," interview with John Heilpern, in *Vogue* (New York), November 1991.
"All That Heaven Allows," interview with N. Christopher, in *Filmmaker* (Santa Monica, California), vol. 2, no. 1, 1993.
"Nancy Savoca: Real-Life Films about Real-Life Dreams," interview with Jonathan Demme and Manohla Dargis, in *Interview* (New York), September 1993.

Publications on Savoca

Book

Foster, Gwendolyn Audrey, *Women Film Directors: An International Bio-Critical Dictionary*, Westport, Connecticut, 1995.

Articles

Travers, Peter, "Women on the Verge: Four Women Attempt to Infiltrate a Male Stronghold: The Director's Chair," in *Rolling Stone* (New York), 21 September 1989.
James, Caryn, "*Dogfight* Wears Camouflage," in *Film View*, 1991.
Nardini, Gloria, "Is It True Love? Or Not? Patterns of Ethnicity and Gender in Nancy Savoca," in *Voice in Italian Americana*, Spring 1991.
Atkinson, M., "The Queen of Independent Film," in *Movieline* (Escondido, California), April 1993.

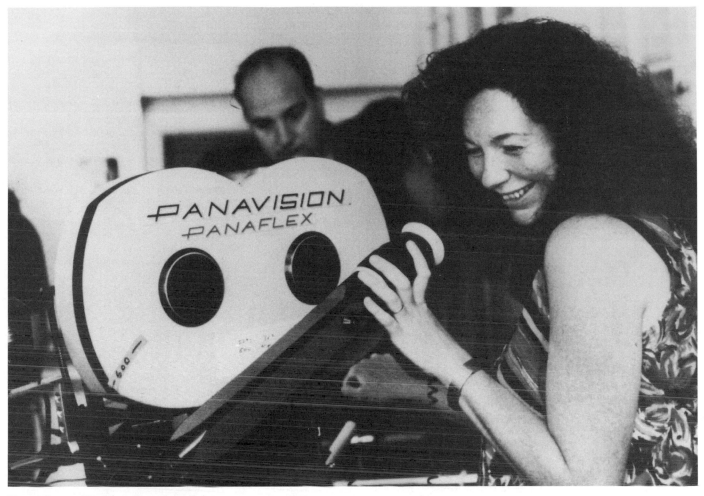

Nancy Savoca directing *Household Saints.*

Cleves, Grace, "Arc Angel," in *Premiere* (New York), October 1993.
Steinhauer, Jennifer, "A Director Who Films What She Knows Best,"
    in *New York Times,* 28 December 1997.

* * *

Nancy Savoca began as an amused chronicler of the courtship and wedding rituals of the Italian-American culture of her upbringing. Like her senior male counterparts, Coppola in the *Godfather* saga and Scorsese in *Mean Streets,* Savoca was inspired by the emotional volatility of such ferociously tight-knit communities. She works, however, on a more intimate cinematic scale, avoiding Coppola's expansive narratives and Scorsese's jittery manner in dramatizing how tribal life shapes, even deforms individual identity.

This drama is obviously not confined to any one ethnic group or community, and in fact, the social consciousness of Savoca's films extends beyond the confines of Italian-American culture, as *Dogfight* and her recent television work demonstrate. "I like," she revealed in an interview, "to look at people who are looking to follow the rules, looking desperately to get in." She is unsentimental, yet tactful in focusing on characters, usually of unexceptional looks, circumstances, and talents, who stand out in some small, but definitive way. The Group not only offers her characters a security that eludes them elsewhere, but promises them personal fulfillment in a socially sanctioned destiny—marriage in *True Love*; military camaraderie in *Dogfight. Household Saints* works a poignant reversal on this formula by giving us a heroine who takes the strictures of her Catholic upbringing so seriously that she aspires to sainthood, thus baffling the loving mother and tenderhearted, but secular father who want a less eccentric, self-denying life for her. Savoca's films observe a discrepancy between an established social consensus on the "good life" and the actual experience of men and women hampered in their desire to realize such a life.

This discrepancy, as Savoca understands and presents it, is mostly a comic one. But Savoca's comedy, like her irony, is gentle, even fragile, and on rare occasions is supplanted by pathos—as in the suicide of Michael, the emotionally dislocated and disabled Italian-American son of *Household Saints,* hopelessly adrift in the Orientalist fantasies spawned by *Madame Butterfly.* Still Savoca excels in revealing her characters not so much through their solitary moments as in their search for company or a night's diversion. Her films take on an invigorating satiric energy in representing boys on the town or hanging out at their favorite bar, women at a male strip club, or such ritual gatherings as family dinners and, of course, weddings.

True Love has the most contemporary feel of all of Savoca's work, although it is set in a community whose traditionalism makes it less susceptible to the convulsive changes that periodically rock American culture. Her second film, *Dogfight,* set in November 1963, ambitiously, if not always convincingly presents its story of a soldier on leave before being shipped off to Vietnam as an allegory of an America about to change its ways in the decade ahead. This film initially concerns a group of young soldiers who dub themselves "the four Bs," brought together, we suspect, primarily by the proximity of their names on the military rolls. On their last night Stateside, they stage a "dogfight," a party to which each soldier brings the ugliest girl—or dog—he can find, the winner to be determined by a panel of "judges" who rate the dogs as they take to the dance floor. It is a cruel game, but finally, one that only boys, especially those uncertain about their future, would play with such stupid intensity. Savoca seems to understand this, so while not excusing the game, she shows that a woman can be appreciative as Fellini of unsightly females. The "dogs" she rounds up for the competition are not freaks, however, but plain young women unused to male attention, so that when it comes their way, they are too grateful or surprised to question its sincerity.

Spiritedly playing, then renouncing the game is Eddie Birdlace, played winningly by River Phoenix, who settles on Lili Taylor's Rose. The second half of the film sweetly pursues the emotional adventures of this odd couple as they enjoy a "second" night on the town, having dinner at a restaurant they cannot afford, wandering through the romantic San Francisco streets until returning to her home to make awkward but fervent love. The film has two endings, both ambiguous. In the first we see Birdlace tear up Rose's address as he, reunited with his buddies, decides that his fate, if not his heart, is cast with the buddies on whom his life may one day depend. The second shows us the war-scarred Vietnam vet, returning four years later to a transformed city and a transformed, but still recognizable Rose, who welcomes him back in a quiet embrace.

Household Saints, based on Francine Prose's novel of the same name, is Savoca's most comically serene work to date. It genially takes its tone from those entertaining family legends recounted with droll solemnity after a hearty meal—in this instance, the story of how "it happened by the grace of God, that Joseph Santangelo won his wife in a pinochle game." It took, we learn, a perfect hand to win her, the first of many surreal occurrences that Savoca presents as co-existing imperturbably with commonplace happenings of everyday life. Tracey Ullman and Vincent D'Onofrio play the magically matched couple. Lili Taylor brings her talent for conveying spiritual insensity to the role as their daughter, whose religious ardor, denied any worldly outlet, surfaces as anorexia and culminates in a vision of a blond Christ who looks like a rock star and talks the King's English. Savoca never settles the question of whether Rose has suffered a mental breakdown (the official diagnosis) or has in fact been elected into a community of saints.

If These Walls Could Talk displays a talent for unadorned, even harrowing realism only vaguely hinted at in her earlier work. Her direction of the 1952 segment, featuring Demi Moore as a widow desperately seeking an abortionist, is unrelenting in showing us how a trained nurse might go about aborting herself. Nor does Savoca spare us the details of how an abortionist, making a house call with his seedy wares in hand, plies his trade on the kitchen table. The camera only pulls away in the final shot of Moore hemorrhaging and calling for help. Savoca does not pretend we can identify with such horror as easily as all that. Whether the matter before her be comic or grave, Savoca never slips into condescension or sanctimonious irony. Her gift is for understatement, trusting as she does to the surfaces of life to indicate the depths in which her characters are in danger of losing their footing, perhaps even drowning.

—Maria DiBattista

SCHILLER, Greta
American director

Born: Detroit, 21 December 1954. **Education:** Earned a BFA from the Picker Film Institute, City College, City University of New York. **Family:** Life partner of the filmmaker and film historian Andrea Weiss. **Career:** 1977—directed first film, *Greta's Girls,* while still a student at City College; 1984—with Andrea Weiss, founded Jezebel Productions; 1985—won international acclaim for the documentary, *Before Stonewall: The Making of a Gay and Lesbian Community.* **Awards:** Best Cultural or Historical Program, and Best Research, Emmy Awards, First Place, National Educational Film Festival, Best Film, Houston International Film Festival, and Best Documentary Feature, Los Angeles FILMEX, for *Before Stonewall,* 1985; Blue Ribbon, American Film and Video Festival, Audience Prize, Fest. International de Films de Femmes, Cretail, Prize of the International Jury, Oberhausen Short Film Festival, and Jury Prize, Leipzig International Documentary Festival, for *International Sweethearts of Rhythm,* 1986; Silver Plaque Award, Chicago International Film Festival, for *Tiny & Ruby: Hell-Divin' Women,* 1989; Fulbright Fellowship in Film, 1988-89; Film Fellowship, New York Foundation for the Arts, 1990; Best Documentary (Audience Prize), Fest. International de Films de Femmes, Cretail, and Best Documentary (Audience Prize), Berlin Film Festival, for *Paris Was a Woman,* 1996.

Films as Director

1977   *Greta's Girls* (co-d with Seid, + pr, ph); *Rape Prevention* (video short) (+ pr, ph)
1979   *Well, We Are Alive* (video short) (+ pr, ed, ph)
1985   *Before Stonewall: The Making of a Gay and Lesbian Community* (co-d with Rosenberg, + pr, co-sc, additional ph)
1986   *International Sweethearts of Rhythm* (short) (co-d, + co-pr, ph, ed)
1989   *Tiny & Ruby: Hell-Divin' Women* (short) (co-d with Weiss, + co-pr, ph); *Waking Up: A Lesson in Love* (video)
1991   *Maxine Sullivan: Love to Be in Love* (short) (+ pr, sc)
1994   *Woman of the Wolf* (short) (+ sc)
1996   *Paris Was a Woman* (+ co-pr, co-sc, ed, co-ph)
1998   *The Moffie Who Drove with Mandela* (+ pr)

Other Films

1981   *Greetings from Washington, D.C.* (short) (co-pr, camera)
1982   *Wild Style* (Ahearn) (camera operator)
1988   *Die Jungfrauen Maschine (The Virgin Machine)* (Treut) (asst d); *Charlotte Bunch: One Woman's Legacy* (promo tape) (pr, ed)
1994   *Age of Dissent* (short) (pr)
1997   *Seed of Sarah* (Weiss) (pr)
1999   *Escape to Life* (Weiss) (pr)

Publications by Schiller

Book

With Andrea Weiss, *Before Stonewall: The Making of a Gay and Lesbian Community,* Tallahassee, Florida, 1988.

Articles

"Manfred Salzgeber, Programmer and Distributor, 1943-1994," in *Independent* (New York), November 1994.

With Andrea Weiss, "*The International Sweethearts of Rhythm,*" interview with Rob Edelman, in *Cineaste* (New York), vol. 15, no. 4, 1987.

Publications on Schiller

Article

Shale, Arlene, "Women Filmmakers, Movie-Goers Descend on Small French Town: Two Americans Honored for Movie Success," in *off our backs,* June 1996.

* * *

In her most representative films, Greta Schiller documents the stories of spirited and single-minded individuals—many of whom have been lost in the pages of history—whose lives transcend social and sexual taboos. Her breakthrough documentary, co-directed with Robert Rosenberg, is *Before Stonewall: The Making of a Gay and Lesbian Community,* which outlines the beginnings of America's queer subculture. Using archival footage and interviews, Schiller and Rosenberg chart the history of the 1920s lesbian bar scene and gay GI experiences during World War II. In so doing, they portray queer lifestyles in the decades before the Stonewall rebellion of 1969, before gays and lesbians were celebrated on the covers of mainstream magazines, when oppression was the rule and gay-pride parades were unimaginable. As a full-bodied documentary exploration of its subject, *Before Stonewall* is a seminal work.

More often than not, Schiller's subjects have been connected to the arts or the entertainment industry. In collaboration with Andrea Weiss, she made *International Sweethearts of Rhythm,* which records the history of an interracial, all-woman jazz band that came to prominence during the 1940s, an era when female drummers, trombonists, and trumpet players were viewed as little more than novelties. One of the significant issues raised in *International Sweethearts of Rhythm* is that, had they not been women—let alone black women—a number of the band members might have enjoyed mainstream careers, and a more lasting fame. Another is that despite the prejudice of the time, these musicians experienced a freedom that then was rare for women, and that helped shape their lives.

An offshoot/companion piece to *International Sweethearts of Rhythm* is *Tiny & Ruby: Hell-Divin' Women,* which Schiller also directed with Weiss. The film's subjects are two larger-than-life personalities: jazz singer/trumpeter Ernestine "Tiny" Davis, a performer with the International Sweethearts (who, in the 1940s, was billed as "the female Louis Armstrong"), and her life partner, drummer Ruby Lucas. Another of Schiller's documentaries, *Maxine Sullivan: Love to Be in Love,* is a portrait of the black jazz singer whose prominence may have transcended that of the International Sweethearts of Rhythm but who nonetheless, because of her race and her sex, was denied the opportunity to cross over from radio to television during the 1950s.

One of Schiller's most recent films, *Paris Was a Woman,* records the lives of American expatriate women who, in the early 20th century, flocked to the Left Bank and created a community all their own. None fitted into mainstream society. None were defined by their relationships to men. All rejected the conventional social and sexual roles of women. In fact, many were lesbian and bisexual. All became writers and artists, publishers and editors, poets and photographers, journalists and salon hostesses. And all lived fiercely independent lives in an artistic community that flourished in the post-World War I years and ended upon the occupation of Paris by the German army in 1940.

Some of these women, such as Gertrude Stein, Alice B. Toklas, and Janet Flanner, are well-known today. Others, such as writer Djuna Barnes, have become cult figures. Still others, such as bookshop proprietresses Adrienne Monnier and Sylvia Beach and heiress/poet Natalie Barney, have been obscured by the course of time. It is the information on these women in particular that makes *Paris Was a Woman* so illuminating.

Schiller's documentaries, chock full of vintage clips and information, are meaningful as histories of times and places. Especially revealing are the found and filmed footage and recordings of many of her subjects. When the surviving members of the International Sweethearts of Rhythm recall their triumphs and difficulties, or when the effervescent personalities of Tiny and Ruby take hold, or when Gertrude Stein's voice fills the soundtrack and Janet Flanner's impressive presence fills the screen, these films becomes living, breathing histories.

An essay on Schiller would be incomplete without mention of her partner and frequent collaborator, Andrea Weiss, with whom she founded the New York/London-based Jezebel Productions in 1984. Weiss is, in her own right, an award-winning filmmaker and film historian. She was the research director of *Before Stonewall;* she produced (as well as co-directed) *The International Sweethearts of Rhythm* and *Tiny & Ruby: Hell-Divin' Women,* and wrote and produced *Paris Was a Woman.* In the immediate future, Schiller is scheduled to produce two films that Weiss will direct: *Seed of Sarah* and *Escape to Life.*

To date, Schiller's nondocumentary works are footnotes to her career. They include *Greta's Girls,* co-directed with Thomas Seid and made while a student at New York's City College, which chronicles the daily life of a lesbian couple; and *Waking Up: A Lesson in Love,* a drama about a promiscuous lesbian named Susan. Both films are notable for offering candid views of lesbian characters, whether at the beginning of a relationship (in *Greta's Girls*) or in the process of exploring sex in the hope of finding love (in *Waking Up*).

—Rob Edelman

SCHNEEMANN, Carolee
American director

Born: Fox Chase, Pennsylvania, 1939. **Education:** Attended Bard College, B.A.; University of Illinois at Urbana, M.F.A.; attended Columbia University School of Painting and Sculpture, New York, and New School for Social Research, New York. **Career:** Founded Kinetic Theatre, New York; has had numerous exhibitions in New York, Milan, Paris, California, and Vienna, including the Venice Biennale; the Museum of Modern Art, and the New Museum of Contemporary Art (retrospective, 1997), New York; San Francisco Museum of Modern Art; Centre Georges Pompidou, Paris; Frauen Museum, Bonn, Germany; the Museum of Contemporary Art, Los Angeles; and many other venues; has been an instructor of art at the Art Institute of Chicago, University of Colorado at Boulder, University of Ohio, Pratt Institute, New York, and University of California, Los Angeles. **Awards:** Individual Artist Grant, Gottlieb Foundation, 1987; Guggenheim Fellowship, 1993; Pollock-Krasner Grant, 1996. **Address:** 114 West 29th Street, New York, NY 10001, U.S.A.

Films as Director

1963   *Carl Ruggles' Christmas Breakfast*
1965   *Viet-Flakes*
1966   *Red News*
1967   **Fuses**
1971   *Plumb Line* (+ sound)
1971-72   *Reel Time* (co-d with McCall)
1973-78   *Kitch's Last Meal*
1982   *Up to and Including Her Limits* (video) (+ ed)
1992   *Vesper's Stampede to My Holy Mouth* (video) (co-d with Vesna)
1993   *Imaging Her Erotics: Carolee Schneemann* (video) (co-d with M. Beatty, + co-ed)
1995   *Interior Scroll - The Cave* (video) (co-d with M. Beatty)

Performance Documentation Films

1964   *Meat Joy* (Gaisseau and Giorgio)
1965   *Water Light/Water Needle* (3 films: Film 1 [J. Jones] [+ co-ed], Film 2 [Rocklin] [+ ed], Film 3 [Summers])
1966   *Snows* (Shilling)
1967   *Body Collage* (Bachmann); *Falling Bodies* (*Body Rotations*) (Whitehead)
1968   *Illinois Central* (Heinz); *Illinois Central Transposed* (Dacey)
1972   *Ices Strip Train Skating*; *American I Ching Apple Pie*
1973   *Acts of Perception*; *Cooking with Apes*
1975   *Interior Scroll* (Beskind—video)
1976-77   *ABC—We Print Anything—In the Cards* (Sharits and Morgan)
1977   *Homerunmuse* (Slater—video)

Appearances in Other Films

1957   *Daybreak* (Brakhage); *Whiteye* (Brakhage); *Loving* (Brakhage)
1959   *Cat's Cradle* (Brakhage)
1961   *Waves and Washes* (Vanderbeek—doc) (work by Oldenburg)

Publications by Schneemann

Books

Parts of a Body House, Devon, England, 1972.
Cezanne, She Was a Great Painter, New York, 1974.
ABC—We Print Anything—In the Cards, Holland, 1977.
More than Meat Joy, New Paltz, New York, 1979; rev. ed., 1997.
Video Burn, San Francisco, 1992.
Early and Recent Work: Two Catalogues of Retrospective Exhibition, New York, 1993.
Imaging Her Erotics: The Body Politics of Carolee Schneemann, edited by Jay Murphy, Cambridge, Massachusetts, 1999.
It Only Happens Once: Selected Letters and Performances of Carolee Schneemann, edited by Kristine Stiles, Baltimore, Maryland, 1999.

Articles

"Through the Body: A Dialogue between Carolee Schneemann and Amy Greenfield," in *Field of Vision,* Fall 1978.
Interview with Scott MacDonald, in *Afterimage* (Rochester, New York), March 1980.
"Kitch's Last Meal," in *Cinema News,* no. 81, 1982.
Interview with Linda Montano, in *Flue,* Summer 1982.
"Rolling in the Maelstrom: A Conversation between Carolee Schneemann and Robert Haller," in *Idiolects,* Spring 1984.
"The Function of Art in Society Today," in *High Performance,* Spring/Summer 1988.
"The Obscene Body/Politic," in *College Art Journal,* Winter 1991.
"Notes from the Underground: A Female Pornographer in Moscow," in *Independent* (New York), Winter 1992.
Interview with Carl Hayward, in *Art Papers,* January/February 1993.
"Ages of the Avant-Garde," in *Performing Arts Journal,* January 1994.
"Questions of Feminism: 25 Responses," in *October* (Cambridge, Massachusetts), Winter 1995.
Interview with Kate Haug, in *Wide Angle* (Baltimore, Maryland), April 1998.

Publications on Schneemann

Books

Youngblood, Gene, *Expanded Cinema,* New York, 1970.
Mekas, Jonas, *Movie Journal: The Rise of the New American Cinema 1959-1971,* New York, 1972.
Le Grice, Malcolm, *Abstract Film and Beyond,* Cambridge, Massachusetts, 1977.
Greenfield, Amy, editor, *Film Dance,* New York, 1984.
MacDonald, Scott, *A Critical Cinema,* Berkeley, 1988.
Elder, R. Bruce, *The Body in Film,* Toronto, 1989.
James, David E., *Allegories of Cinema: American Film in the 1960's,* Princeton, New Jersey, 1989.
Kuhn, Annette, and Susannah Radstone, editors, *Women in Film: An International Guide,* London, 1990.
MacDonald, Scott, *Avant-Garde Film: Motion Studies,* London, 1993.
Foster, Gwendolyn Audrey, *Women Film Directors: An International Bio-Critical Dictionary,* Westport, Connecticut, 1995.
Up to and Including Her Limits (retrospective catalogue), New Museum of Contemporary Art, New York, 1996.
Out of Actions: Between Performance and the Object, 1949-79, Museum of Contemporary Art, Los Angeles, 1998.

Articles

Glaessner, Verina, "Interviews with Three Filmmakers," in *Time Out* (London), March 1972.
Gibbs, Michael, "Introduction to Erotic Films by Women," in *Deciphering America,* Amsterdam, 1978.
Rich, B. Ruby, "Sex and Cinema," in *New Art Examiner,* Spring 1979.
Alloway, Lawrence, "Carolee Schneemann: The Body as Object and Instrument," in *Art in America,* March 1980.
MacDonald, Scott, "Carolee Schneemann's Autobiographical Trilogy," in *Film Quarterly* (Berkeley), Fall 1980.
Castle, Ted, "The Woman Who Uses Her Body for Art," in *Artforum* (New York), November 1980.
MacDonald, Scott, "Carolee Schneemann's *ABC*: The Men Cooperate," in *Afterimage* (Rochester, New York), April 1985.

McEvilley, Thomas, "Carolee Schneemann," in *Artforum* (New York), April 1985.

Lovelace, Carey, "The Gender and Case of Carolee Schneemann," in *Millennium* (New York), Fall/Winter 1986-87.

Joselit, David, "Projected Identities," in *Art in America,* November 1991.

Neiman, Catrina, "Women Pioneers of American Experimental Film," in *Feministische Streifzuge durch's Punkte-Universum,* Vienna, 1993.

Straayer, Chris, "The Seduction of Boundaries," in *Dirty Looks: Women, Pornography, Power,* London, 1993.

Glueck, Grace, "Of a Woman's Body as Both Subject and Object," in *New York Times,* 6 December 1996.

Princenthal, Nancy, "The Arrogance of Pleasure," in *Art in America,* October 1997.

*   *   *

Carolee Schneemann is a performance artist, filmmaker, writer, and assemblage artist who has been creating art since the early 1960s. Her work as an artist has been influenced by the psychoanalytical theories of Wilhelm Reich and Antonin Artaud's theater of cruelty. Schneemann is known for using a wide variety of materials in her artwork and performances such as paint, sand, glue, glass, flour, lights, and perhaps most significantly, the human body. As Schneemann said in speaking of her early performance work, she set out "to eroticise my guilt-ridden culture and further to confound this culture's sexual rigidities—that the life of the body is more variously expressive than a sex-negative society can admit." (*More than Meat Joy,* 1979). Schneemann is also known for her fierce independence and shock tactics as an artist. Her work, including many of her films, privileges the human body, the materiality of whatever medium she is working in and the experiential. She is concerned with an examination of the ecstatic in her art, and this is never so clear as in her best film, the controversial *Fuses.*

Fuses offers a radical approach to representations of the human body. It is a graphic attempt to represent the ecstatic in heterosexual lovemaking, and powerfully represents the emotional state of two individuals involved in the act of making love. Schneemann's approach to her filmmaking is similar to her work as a visual artist. She is interested in breaking down barriers, both in terms of cultural taboos and in her process of making films. The film fragments and abstracts the human body to such an extent that all traces of the voyeuristic are eliminated from the viewing experience. It incorporates multiple superimpositions and extreme collage techniques that have a way of blurring the discreteness of the individual shot. Schneemann's process also involves working with the filmic material by means of scratching, painting, and baking the celluloid. This results in an anti-illusionistic, reflexive kind of filmmaking that constantly reminds the viewer of the actual work involved in the art-making process and the physicality of working with one's materials. This physicality gives her films a directness and authenticity that is all too rare in the cinema. She stated in an interview that "she worked on that film the way I work on a canvas. It was like an overall immediacy put into a prolonged time duration, a way of working with film as one extended frame in time" (MacDonald, 1988).

The film's diaristic approach to documenting the intense activities of two individuals making love is radical and shocking for its time, and the film can still register strong reactions with an audience. In the first decade of its release, however, it was notorious for almost always creating controversy each time it was publicly screened, especially if the filmmaker was in attendance. This was due in part to the graphicness of the sexual imagery, which did involve many shots of the vagina and penis, as well close-ups of bodily fluids, images which had hitherto been the province of pornography. It was also due to the seemingly haphazard approach and messiness of the imagery in the film. *Fuses* does not have the cool elegance of many of the structuralist films at the time made by filmmakers such as Michael Snow or Hollis Frampton. Neither does it have the lyrical, mythopoeic complexity of Brakhage's best work.

It is true Schneemann's accomplishment is not of that order. But neither did it deserve the critical neglect or public attacks it generally received at the time. Schneemann recounts the astonishing story of how 40 young men at a screening in France in the late 1960s were so incensed by the film that they slashed the seats with razors, shredding and throwing the padding throughout the screening room (MacDonald, 1988). Where the film celebrates the potential of human sexuality some viewers were so enraged and fearful that they could only respond with anger. It is the mark of a truly subversive work of art that it can provoke such a hostile reaction, so totally out of proportion to any possible provocation. *Fuses* was a truly fresh, innovative attempt to graphically represent and celebrate the human body. The film has grown in stature as years have passed, and today it remains a bold, innovative film.

Carolee Schneemann continued to explore the film medium by incorporating her own life as subject matter in her next few films. *Plumb Line* differs from *Fuses* in that it was made after a relationship had disintegrated. Although an interesting film it does not have the radical groundbreaking quality of her earlier, best-known film. *Plumb Line* was made primarily to take control and give some sense of emotional balance to her life after the devastation of her break-up. *Kitch's Last Meal* is a Super-8, double-projection film based on the filmmaker's observations of her cat and the impressions it might have observed in the last days of its life. The film explores the daily routines of the filmmaker and her partner such as gardening, chopping wood, cleaning, cooking, reading, etc. It exists in several versions ranging in length from one hour to five hours. Neither of these films has been extensively screened over the years, and Schneemann's reputation as a filmmaker essentially rests on the not inconsiderable accomplishment of *Fuses.*

Carolee Schneemann is perhaps better known today as a visual artist and painter but her contribution to the history of the American avant-garde cinema, though small, remains a significant one. She proved that it was possible to create a truly radical film out of the dailiness of one's life, and in one astonishing film she explored human sexuality with more originality and creativity than most other filmmakers, male or female, mainstream or avant-garde could ever hope to achieve. Schneemann made a lasting contribution to the art of cinema, and *Fuses* remains one of the key films of the 1960s. Any discussion of sexuality in the cinema, as well as films that radically attempt to create a new way of seeing the world, must surely include her work.

—Mario Falsetto

SCHOONMAKER, Thelma
American editor

Born: Algiers, Algeria, 3 January 1940. **Education:** Attended Cornell University, studying political science and Russian, B.A., 1961; Columbia University, studying primitive art; New York University Film

School, six-week film course. **Family:** Married the director Michael Powell, 1984 (died 1990). **Career:** Met the director Martin Scorsese while both students at NYU; 1968—cut Scorsese's debut feature *Who's That Knocking at My Door?*; lack of union membership kept her from editing feature films until *Raging Bull,* 1980. **Award:** Academy Award, for *Raging Bull,* 1980. **Address:** c/o Cappa Productions, 445 Park Avenue, 7th Floor, New York, NY 10022, U.S.A.

Films as Editor

1965   *Finnegans Wake* (*Passages from James Joyce's Finnegans Wake*) (Bute) (co)
1968   *The Virgin President* (Ferguson) (co); *Who's That Knocking at My Door?* (Scorsese)
1970   *Street Scenes* (Scorsese—doc) (co); *Woodstock* (Wadleigh—doc) (chief ed, + asst d)
1979   *The Kids Are Alright* (Stein) (special consultant)
1980   ***Raging Bull*** (Scorsese); *Rockshow* (Cavalcanti—doc) (co)
1983   *The King of Comedy* (Scorsese) (+ production supervisor)
1985   *After Hours* (Scorsese)
1986   *The Color of Money* (Scorsese)
1988   *The Last Temptation of Christ* (Scorsese)
1989   "Life Lessons" ep. of *New York Stories* (Scorsese)
1990   *GoodFellas* (Scorsese); *Made in Milan* (Scorsese—doc, short)
1991   *Cape Fear* (Scorsese)
1993   *The Age of Innocence* (Scorsese)
1995   *Casino* (Scorsese)
1996   *Grace of My Heart* (Anders) (co)
1997   *Kundun* (Scorsese)

Publication by Schoonmaker

Article

"Ils ont travaille sur *Raging Bull,*" interview with O. Assayas and S. Toubiana, in *Cahiers du Cinéma* (Paris), March 1981.

Publications on Schoonmaker

Book

Acker, Ally, *Reel Women: Pioneers of the Cinema, 1896 to the Present,* New York, 1991.

Articles

Rafferty, T., "His Girl Friday: Thelma Schoonmaker Cuts Things Down to Size," in *Village Voice* (New York), 30 November 1982.
Arkush, Allan, "I Want My KEM-TV," in *American Film* (Washington, D.C.), December 1985.
Talty, Stephan, "Invisible Woman," in *American Film* (Hollywood), September/October 1991.
Morgan, D., "The Thriller in Scorsese," in *Millimeter* (New York), October 1991.
O'Neill, Michael, "Cinema Laureates," in *Premiere* (New York), 15 September 1993.
Current Biography, New York, 1997.

* * *

An axiom of Hollywood postproduction holds that the best editing maintains a seamless invisibility; that the best editors do not draw attention to their work. Thelma Schoonmaker simultaneously embodies and shatters that axiom. On one hand, she is certainly one of Hollywood's most self-effacing editors, perhaps understandably so working as Martin Scorsese's editor. Editing all his films from *Raging Bull* to *Casino,* she always claims the credit goes to Scorsese since he shoots for and edits with her. On the other hand, her editing is often far from self-effacing; although it functions within classical Hollywood parameters, it draws attention to itself as a fully realized art form and provides a compendium of what contemporary editing can accomplish. As Jeffrey Ressner says: *"Raging Bull, GoodFellas,* and *Casino* have pushed the editing craft into a postmodern, almost hallucinogenic art. They are what films can be."

Schoonmaker's "postmodern" editing synthesizes a number of different influences, approaches, and devices: Nouvelle Vague, music videos, classical continuity editing (particularly shot/reverse shot dialogue editing), long takes and intrasequence cutting, montage, freeze frames, dissolves, jump cuts, temporal ellipses, extreme close-ups, and irises. One might expect to see all these devices in a television commercial or a music video, yet Schoonmaker's films successfully employs them in narrative features. She established this "hallucinatory" battery of techniques in her first commercial narrative, *Raging Bull,* which according to Stephan Talty, "is one of the most obsessively crafted and exhaustively edited films in American cinema."

The techniques Schoonmaker initiated with *Raging Bull* won her an Oscar for best editing and she continued to use and expand them as her career progressed. Since 1980, her editing has become so innovative, complex, and continually evolving that addressing all aspects of it in a short essay is as unfair as it is impossible. Some of the above characteristics help describe her editorial signature.

Raging Bull appears documentary-like: shot in black and white, using subtitles to specify time and place, and telling the biography of Jake La Motta. Schoonmaker contributes to this appearance by utilizing long takes and intercutting "home movies" of La Motta and his friends and family. She also employs the naturalism associated with classical Hollywood editing by structuring much of the film around traditional shot/reverse shot dialogue sequences. But any sense of realism or naturalism these techniques may suggest shrinks behind the style she gives to the rest of the film. Most obviously, the eight fight sequences allow Schoonmaker to do anything she wants. She puts each sequence together in a different way with a different tempo, but all rely on montage and sound manipulation. Extreme close-ups are cut next to long shots; low angle shots are cut next to high angle shots; normal speed shots are cut next to slow and fast motion shots; long camera takes are cut next to split-second shots of camera flashes; the boxers and audience are cut next to objects (round cards, the bell, water buckets); freeze frames are cut next to Steadicam shots; sound intensifies, drops out, becomes subjective, becomes abstract. All of this makes each fight literally "explosive," especially when compared to the slower pacing of rest of the film. Schoonmaker explains that while working on "Round 13" of the third Sugar Ray Robinson fight, she first edited for narrative structure and then reworked the scene for movement, lighting, and effects—exactly the concerns that push her editing to the foreground.

Outside the fight sequences Schoonmaker employs subtler, but just as untraditional, editing techniques. Perhaps her most influential innovations occurred in this area: expanding the accepted boundary of the temporal ellipse and challenging the limitations of match-action editing. All editors eliminate unimportant information that a viewer can infer. For example, an editor will not bother showing a character getting into a car, driving to a new location, and then getting out of the car. Typically, we would see the character get into the car, drive out of the frame, and then exit the car at the new location. The viewer understands that the car was driven between two points without needing to see it. Schoonmaker pushes this in a number of ways, but most interestingly by using this technique when we do not expect to see it. For example, while standing at a poolside soda stand, La Motta first sees Vicki. Then a cut shows us Vicki in close-up (from La Motta's point of view). When another cut returns us to La Motta he is sitting down at a table. We do not see him move from the soda stand to the table, but we know he did. Later, during La Motta's courtship of Vicki, she accompanies him to his apartment. As he closes the refrigerator door, a cut shows him sitting down at a table across the room. Again, unorthodox but fully comprehendible.

Traditional match-action editing requires two things to make the cut "invisible": (1) cutting at the point of strongest action and (2) maintaining exact screen position and direction. Failure to follow these two conventions produces "bad editing" or "jump cuts." By traditional standards, Schoonmaker's editing borders on the "bad." But under contemporary editing aesthetics (heavily influenced by television and music videos) her editing delivers an excitement impossible under the strict parameters of match-action editing. Points of strongest action and exact screen position are replaced by jump cuts that produce a rhythmic pacing, an emphasis on character and dialogue (and actors' performances), and narrative intensification. In the many shot/reverse shot dialogue sequences, the street vernacular the characters speak, with its staccato tempo, perfectly complements and supports these editorial decisions and produces the edgy tension associated with Scorsese's films.

Schoonmaker also demonstrates a deft hand at intrasequence cutting. Brian Henderson defines intrasequence cutting as the linking of long takes to emphasize the rhythm and movement within a long duration shot. Each cut breaks that rhythm or movement but then replaces it with a different rhythm or movement of the next shot. Scorsese employs long takes usually with elaborate camera movements made possible by the Steadicam. In the Marcel Cerdan fight, the camera follows La Motta out of his dressing room, down a number of hallways, through the crowded arena, and into the ring as the camera (now on a crane) moves into a high angle shot. Schoonmaker uses such long takes in combination with her montage-inspired editing to break and establish different editing tempos.

Immediately before or after a montage sequence, cutting together long takes provides a needed respite from a taxing emotional or intensely physical scene. Combining long takes with shot/reverse shot editing allows characters to develop more naturally. The bookending sequences of La Motta in his dressing room set up the narrative and structure of the film with an efficiency no other editing technique could accomplish.

In *The King of Comedy,* she pushed the temporal ellipse to include a spatial aspect. Straight cutting on dialogue in a typical shot/reverse shot pattern we move freely between Rupert's basement and his (fantasized) luncheon at Sardi's with Jerry Langford. Rupert's first conversation with Rita at a bar does the same thing: on a line of continuous dialogue over a shot/reverse shot cut we relocate to a restaurant. Schoonmaker and Scorsese indulge in a bit of Nouvelle Vague reflexivity here. In the long takes and intrasequence cutting that structures this scene, a patron behind Rupert gazes at the camera and mocks Rupert's gestures and facial expressions. In a film that questions the thin line between reality and fantasy, this scene in particular demonstrates the impossibility of film to ever be real.

The opening title sequence of *The King of Comedy* superimposes credits over a freeze frame of Marsha's clawing hands. Schoonmaker develops the freeze frame until it becomes one of her signature devices. She uses the freeze frame extensively in *GoodFellas.* Whenever Henry Hill's voice-over makes an important point, Schoonmaker freezes the image. In *GoodFellas,* she also employs long takes (especially in the famous track-back/zoom-in-shot at the diner), intrasequence cutting (Karen and Henry and the Copacabana and the Saturday, 11 May sequence), spatial and temporal ellipses (all of the violence and the gifts of money at the wedding reception), and jump cuts (Karen at the beauty parlor and at Janet Rossi's apartment). Her work on *GoodFellas* earned her an Academy Award nomination.

In *The Color of Money,* she uses extreme close-ups of cue chalk, billiard balls, cigarettes, and money as a visual leitmotiv to stress the theme of the film. She balances long takes with montage sequences; Vincent's "Werewolves of London" pool-cue performance juxtaposed to the increased speed, overhead jump cuts, and extreme close-ups for a series of pool games. She plays much cutting on moving camera against a precise visual symmetry (the left/right balance of Vincent and Eddie's grudge match). In Vincent's game with Grady, Schoonmaker employs dissolves and superimpositions to convey the various deceits and facades of the two players.

Schoonmaker also develops the dissolve until it becomes another of her signature devices. She uses the dissolve extensively in *The Age of Innocence* and *Casino.* Whereas her earlier films used the dissolve traditionally (to indicate simultaneity or a passage of time), her later films use it to disorient. In *The Age of Innocence,* the opera sequence that opens the film immediately undercuts the period setting. Dissolves link shots that traditionally would be joined in one long take or through match action. Combining this unsettling technique with jump cuts (during the pan of the theater) and abandoned eye-line matches (an audience member looks up across the theater, yet the next shot is down to a performer on the stage) provides a commentary on the hidden meanings of exterior actions. Schoonmaker takes advantage of the period setting to employ irises. A silent-film device before editing used close-ups, an iris focused the viewer's attention on a specific part of the screen. Here Schoonmaker uses translucent irises as another visual metaphor for disguised appearances.

In *Casino,* Schoonmaker uses both devices but for different reasons. The dissolves work as point of view commentary (especially since the film is narrated in voice-over). For example, as Sam explains how he eliminated professional cheaters from the Tropicana we see him determine how two men have won $140,000 in blackjack. Schoonmaker presents this to us through dissolves that link Sam to the two tables involved in the scam. When Nicky and Jennifer first meet Ginger, we see her through Nicky's eyes in a three-shot dissolve that augments her approach. In *Casino,* the iris functions to suggest blindness. Sam is so obsessed with Ginger he cannot see the destruction their relationship will cause; an iris leads us to his head and then an extreme close-up of a flashbulb exploding. Both films also make extensive use of intrasequence cutting, temporal ellipses, cutting on moving camera, and montage.

These techniques also work well in the context of a suspense film. In *Cape Fear,* Schoonmaker melded her editing techniques with the action cutting demanded of a genre film. The result was a film that frightened and exhibited innovative twist on an old format. She used negative imagery to comment on the lack of clear difference between guilt and innocence. Her jump cutting and temporal ellipses added a new edge of terror and excitement to the final houseboat sequence (involving miniatures and special effects) as well as Sam Bowden's first sighting of Max Cady in town (three jump cuts from long shot to medium shot to close up on passing cars). Cady's seduction of Danielle on the school stage expertly demonstrates intrasequence cutting. Scorsese shot the improvised scene in one continuous, nine-minute take with two cameras. Schoonmaker seamlessly melded the two takes so it looks like a typical shot/reverse shot sequence even though she is linking long takes.

The approaches mentioned above outline the unique style of Schoonmaker's editing technique. Perhaps more than any other contemporary Hollywood editor, her distinct editorial signature positions her as an auteur. Working exclusively with Scorsese certainly supports this claim and demonstrates not only that editing must be viewed as an art but how film can function as a collaborative act of creativity.

—Greg S. Faller

SEIDELMAN, Susan
American director

Born: Near Philadelphia, Pennsylvania, 11 December 1952. **Education:** Attended school in Philadelphia; studied design and film at Drexel University; New York University Graduate School of Film and TV, 1974-77. **Career:** Directed first feature, *Smithereens*, 1982. **Address:** c/o Michael Shedler, 225 West 34th Street, Suite 1012 New York, NY 10122-0049, U.S.A. **Agent:** William Morris Agency, 151 El Camino Drive, Beverly Hills, CA 90212, U.S.A.

Films as Director

1976/77 *And You Act Like One, Too* (short); *Deficit* (short); *Yours Truly, Andrea G. Stern* (short)
1982 *Smithereens* (+ pr, st)
1985 ***Desperately Seeking Susan***
1987 *Making Mr. Right* (+ exec pr)
1989 *Cookie* (+ sc); *She-Devil* (+ co-pr)
1992 *Confessions of a Suburban Girl* (+ ro)
1995 *The Dutch Master* (short, released as ep. in *Tales of Erotica* in 1996) (+ co-sc); *The Barefoot Executive* (for TV)

Other Films

1982 *Chambre 666* (Wenders—doc, for TV) (appearance)
1993 *The Night We Never Met* (Leight) (co-assoc pr)

Publications by Seidelman

Articles

Interview with Richard Patterson, in *American Cinematographer* (Los Angeles), May 1983.
Interview with Don Yakir, in *Film Comment* (New York), May/June 1985.
Interview with Peter Golden, in *Films in Review* (New York), June/July 1985.
"Céline and Julie, Susan and Susan," interview with Jane Root, in *Stills* (London), October 1985.

Interview with R. Censi and G. A. Nazarro, in *Cineforum* (Bergamo, Italy), October 1992.

Publications on Seidelman

Books

Acker, Ally, *Reel Women: Pioneers of the Cinema, 1896 to the Present,* New York, 1991.
Foster, Gwendolyn Audrey, *Women Film Directors: An International Bio-Critical Dictionary,* Westport, Connecticut, 1995.

Articles

Hachem, S., "Susan Seidelman," in *Millimeter* (New York), August 1983.
Rickey, Carrie, "Where the Girls Are," in *American Film* (Washington, D.C.), January/February 1984.
Jaehne, Karen, "In Search of Susan," in *Stills* (London), May 1985.
Stacey, Jackie, "Desperately Seeking Difference," in *Screen* (London), Winter 1987.
Current Biography, New York, 1990.
Cook, Pam, "Good Girl/Bad Girl—Susan Seidelman," in *Monthly Film Bulletin* (London), May 1990.
Alion, Y., in *Revue du Cinéma* (Paris), September 1990.
Strauss, F., in *Cahiers du Cinéma* (Paris), December 1992.

* * *

Prior to directing *Smithereens,* her breakthrough independent feature, and *Desperately Seeking Susan,* the film that announced her as a major cinematic talent, Susan Seidelman made *Deficit,* a 40-minute drama about a young man who seeks revenge for a crime committed against his father. The film was funded in part by the American Film Institute Independent Filmmaker Program. Call it understatement or prophecy, but a comment on the film's evaluation form portended Seidelman's future, "The filmmaker shows a budding talent as a feature film director."

That talent was realized in *Smithereens* and *Desperately Seeking Susan.* Both are likably funky and keenly observed films featuring spirited, independent-minded but refreshingly unromanticized heroines: refugees from stifling suburbia who come to New York City's East Village where they forge identities within a subculture. Both films are knowing depictions of New York punk/New Wave/No Wave culture, and are clearly defined observations of hipness and pseudo-hipness.

Smithereens, made for $80,000, is a minor landmark in the history of the then-burgeoning American independent film movement; for one thing, it was the first such film accepted as an official in-competition entry at the Cannes Film Festival. *Smithereens* benefits from its low budget, which allows it an authentic feel for time and place. Its heroine is Wren, a rootless 19-year-old whose motto might be "Desperately Seeking Celebrity." She lives in a shabby East Village apartment, from which she is evicted for nonpayment of rent; she may be energetic and determined, but her dreams of achieving fame, which are connected to the rock music industry and an idealized Southern California lifestyle, are hazy at best. Instead of educating herself and working to realize them, Wren pastes xeroxed photos of herself on subway car and station walls and attempts to link up with a rock singer whom she foolishly regards as a meal ticket. She will say and do anything and manipulate anyone, even if it results in her

Susan Seidelman on the set of *Desperately Seeking Susan*.

own debasement. Her rationale for her behavior is a line she repeats throughout the scenario, "I got a million and one places to go."

Seidelman entered the realm of mainstream filmmaking with her follow-up feature: *Desperately Seeking Susan,* a stylish screwball comedy that remained faithful to the feeling of its predecessor and became a surprise box-office smash. In retrospect, it is one of the more entertaining films of the mid-1980s. There are two heroines in *Desperately Seeking Susan.* The first is Roberta, a bored suburban housewife who sets out on a comic odyssey upon becoming intrigued by a series of "Desperately Seeking Susan" personal ads. Roberta's counterpart, the Susan of the title, is a variation of Wren. She is a homeless but nonetheless ultrahip East Village free spirit who has various boyfriends and sexual liaisons, and who will think nothing of pilfering jewelry or stiffing a taxi driver. Roberta and Susan become immersed in a frantic, funny scenario involving mistaken identity, amnesia, and other plot devices. *Desperately Seeking Susan* is especially successful in capturing the appeal of Madonna, who plays the title role and who then was blossoming as one of the era's elite pop stars. Prior to her playing *Evita* 12 years later, Susan was her preeminent screen role.

Unfortunately, *Desperately Seeking Susan* was to be a career apex for Seidelman; it and *Smithereens* are her foremost films to date. The clever female-oriented humor that worked so well in *Desperately*

Seeking Susan simply is missing from *Making Mr. Right,* which attempts to squeeze laughs out of a supposedly successful career woman's inability to walk in high heels. The scenario (which is set in Miami Beach) has the heroine realizing she only can find true love with a robot. In *Smithereens* and *Desperately Seeking Susan,* the male characters run the gamut from boring and self-involved to sympathetic. In *Making Mr. Right,* the view of men is horribly clichéd and mean-spirited, and downright offensive in that a real man is insufficient as the heroine's romantic partner. Furthermore, the robot, which she has helped program, comes apart whenever it makes love.

In *She-Devil,* Seidelman directed one of the era's most distinguished film actresses (Meryl Streep) and popular television comediennes (Roseanne), and worked from an acclaimed feminist novel: Fay Weldon's *The Life and Loves of a She-Devil.* But the result, involving a frumpy housewife who seeks revenge after her husband leaves her, is slight and predictable. *Cookie,* which like *She-Devil* was scripted by Nora Ephron (working with Alice Arlen), is the story of a cheeky adolescent who forges a relationship with her mafioso father upon his release from jail. But the film was strictly formulaic, and paled beside Seidelman's earlier work. In these last three films, the feeling is that Seidelman abandoned her New York artistic roots, and in so doing lost her way as an idiosyncratic filmmaker.

In the 1990s Seidelman has been anything but prolific. But her films at least have been more than respectable, even if they have not established her as an A-list film maker. The luridly named *Confessions of a Suburban Girl,* whose title seems an attempted thematic throwback to *Smithereens* and *Desperately Seeking Susan,* actually is a revealing documentary account of the filmmaker and several of her friends as they parallel their youthful aspirations to the reality of their adult lives. *The Dutch Master,* a short film (which won Seidelman a Best Live Action Short Oscar nomination), is the story of New York dental hygienist who becomes fascinated by, and begins fantasizing about, a 17th-century painting.

If you are, say, Martin Scorsese or Woody Allen and you choose to direct a short, that work will be considered an exercise in creativity. But if you are Susan Seidelman, and you have not had a critical or commercial hit in a decade, your short film, however fine, will be viewed as a comedown. Tellingly, *The Dutch Master* was released commercially, along with three other shorts, under the throwaway title *Tales of Erotica.* It was paired with films by Ken Russell, Melvin Van Peebles, and Bob Rafelson—who, like Seidelman, are once-innovative filmmakers whose foremost works most likely are in their past.

—Rob Edelman

SERREAU, Coline

French director, writer, and actress

Born: Paris, 1947; daughter of theater director Jean-Marie Serreau. **Education:** Studied music, dance, and acrobatics. **Career:** 1970-76—actress for stage, film, and television; 1975—first documentary feature, *Mais qu'est-ce qu'elles veulent?;* 1977—first feature film, *Pourquoi pas?;* 1985—international success of *Trois hommes et un couffin.* **Awards:** César, Best Film and Best Screenplay, for *Trois hommes et un couffin,* 1985.

Films as Director

1976   *Le Rendez-vous* (short, for TV)
1977   *Pourquoi pas? (Why Not?)* (+ sc)
1978   *Mais qu'est-ce qu'elles veulent? (But What Do Women Want?)* (doc—produced 1975) (+ sc, sound)
1982   *Qu'est-ce qu'on attend pour être heureux! (What Are You Waiting for to Be Happy!)* (+ sc)
1985   **Trois hommes et un couffin** (*Three Men and a Cradle*) (+ sc)
1989   *Romuald et Juliette (Mama, There's a Man in Your Bed)* (+ sc)
1991   Ep. in *Contre l'oubli (Against Oblivion; Écrire contre l'oubli; Lest We Forget)*
1992   *La Crise (The Crisis)* (+ sc)
1996   *La Belle verte (The Green Planet)* (+ sc, mus, ro as Mila)

Other Films

1970   *Un Peu beaucoup, passionnément* (Enrico) (ro)
1973   *On s'est trompé d'histoire d'amour* (Bertucelli) (co-sc, ro as Anne)

1975   *Sept morts sur ordonnance* (Rouffio) (ro as Mme. Mauvagne)
1977   *Le Fou de Mai* (ro)
1987   *Three Men and a Baby* (Nimoy) (st)
1990   *Three Men and a Little Lady* (Ardolino) (technical adviser)

Publication by Serreau

Book

Quisaitout et Grobêta, Arles, France, 1993.

Publications on Serreau

Books

Foster, Gwendolyn Audrey, *Women Film Directors: An International Bio-Critical Dictionary,* Westport, Connecticut, 1995.
Austin, Guy, *Contemporary French Cinema: An Introduction,* Manchester, 1996.
Forbes, Jill, *The Cinema in France: After the New Wave,* Bloomington, Indiana, 1996.

Articles

Insdorf, Annette, "A Women's Wave," in *American Film* (Washington, D.C.), January/February 1980.
Seidenberg, Robert, "*Mama, There's a Man in Your Bed*: Coline Serreau—Remade in America," in *American Film* (Hollywood), March 1990.
Durham, Carolyn A., "Taking the Baby out of the Basket and/or Robbing the Cradle: 'Remaking' Gender and Culture in Franco-American Film," in *French Review,* April 1992.
Vincendeau, Ginette, "Coline Serreau: A High Wire Act," in *Sight and Sound* (London), March 1994.
Dalmolin, Eliane, "Fantasmes de maternité dans les films de Jacques Demy, Coline Serreau et François Truffaut," in *French Review,* March 1996.

* * *

Ginette Vincendeau's insightful survey of Coline Serreau's career calls it a "high wire act," but one might shift the metaphor a little to "balancing act," for Serreau has managed to keep a steady balance between feminism and commercial success, outright farce, and drama of sentiment, while keeping a cool eye on her typically obtuse—but educable—male protagonists.

Serreau's first film, a documentary interviewing women as socially and economically diverse as a Swiss church minister and a sex-film star, was named after Freud's famous expression of bafflement, "What do women want?" Her second and third features, both fiction, explored the utopian possibilities of (respectively) a ménage à trois and a group of actors rebelling against the commercial film they are making. To be sure, Serreau's own next feature was commercial enough: *Trois hommes et un couffin* was the most widely attended French film in 20 years, and garnered César awards for both Best Picture and Best Screenplay. Projects to direct American remakes of this and her fifth film, *Romuald et Juliette,* came to naught, but she has continued in France to be a successful maker of satiric comedies.

Trois hommes explores the comic—and sentimental—possibilities of three Parisian bachelors having to curtail their usual amorous activities, and indeed even their professional careers, to raise an abandoned infant. Farce is the engine that drives the plot at first: the writer-director seems to have asked herself what *could,* after all, induce three perennial swingers to settle down even unwillingly to such a task. But the latter part of the film manages to be touching without becoming treacly or preachy (or indulging in chase scenes) as did the American version that eventually got made. The film has been accused of misogyny, in that the men eventually seem to claim exclusive rights over the realm of child care, while there are no sympathetic females in the picture other than the infant. But Serreau's droll observations of the bachelors—both their vanity (as when one of them, citing all the books he has read, tells off the equally haughty "Seconde Maman") and their deep affection for the child behind their masks of detached "professionalism" (as when they sing "Au clair de la lune" in three-part harmony to get her to sleep)—suggest a more complex perspective.

The farcical setup is considerably more ingenious in *Romuald et Juliette,* in which a yogurt tycoon on the eve of his greatest financial coup is the victim of three different and coincidental plots at the same time: his executive protégé is having an affair with his wife, another executive sabotages the yogurt plant to make Romuald and the protégé/lover look culpable, and a third executive is using Romuald's secretary/mistress to trap the boss in a phony insider-trading scheme. All this is the means of igniting the unlikely romance of the title, between the tycoon and his office-cleaning woman, a black mother of five who lives in a cramped tenement. The *scène à faire,* in which Juliette tells her boss about one plot after the other that she has overheard, is truly hilarious, thanks not only to the explosive release of tension but to Daniel Auteuil's performance (and Serreau's direction), conveying genuine friendliness along with strained politeness and baffled incredulity. Equally brilliant is a later matching scene in which Juliette (the superb Firmine Richard) reacts to Romuald's marriage proposal with comparable astonishment but also indignation, even exasperation. Some have found the film's ending problematic, with Romuald's vast wealth seeming indeed to buy happiness, or at least serving to overcome Juliette's reservations, and with Juliette rather too neatly becoming an earth mother for the late 1980s. At least, in its delirious vision of family harmony despite racial and economic barriers it is consistent with Serreau's utopian/comic outlook.

La Crise follows to a considerable extent the pattern set by its predecessors. The opening crisis is actually a multiple one in which the protagonist loses his job, is deserted by his wife, and finds most of his friends and relatives having momentous quarrels with their spouses and lovers. In this case the outsider who leads the middle-class protagonist to reconciliation is not an infant girl or African woman but a lower-class sot who accompanies the "hero" on a sentimental journey. Most recently, *La Belle verte* carries Serreau's utopian proclivities a great deal further: in this comic fantasy the writer-director herself plays Mila, inhabitant of a "green planet," where everyone lives free of stress, pollution, and bureaucracy, while practicing vegetarianism and acrobatics. Mila's visit to Earth, armed with a device for "deprogramming" people so that they can be their "natural" selves (to the shock of other earthlings), allows Serreau herself to play the role of the beneficent outsider—to show up in her own cradle, as it were. Whether *La Belle verte* marks a new direction in her filmmaking or is a fanciful interlude amidst her more down-to-earth comedies remains to be seen.

—Joseph Milicia

SHARAFF, Irene
American costume designer

Born: Boston, 1910. **Education:** Attended the New York School of Fine and Applied Arts, Art Students League, New York, and La Grande Chaumiere, Paris. **Career:** 1928-30—assistant designer to Aline Bernstein, Civic Repertory Theatre Company; 1932—designer for Broadway plays, and for several ballet companies; 1943-45—costume designer, MGM, then freelance designer for films. **Awards:** Academy Awards, for *An American in Paris,* 1951; *The King and I,* 1956; *West Side Story,* 1961; *Cleopatra,* 1963; *Who's Afraid of Virginia Woolf?,* 1966. **Died:** In New York City, 16 August 1993.

Films as Costume Designer

1943   *Girl Crazy* (Taurog); *I Dood It* (Minnelli) (co); *Madame Curie* (LeRoy) (co)
1944   *Meet Me in St. Louis* (Minnelli)
1945   *Yolanda and the Thief* (Minnelli) (co)
1946   *The Best Years of Our Lives* (Wyler); *The Dark Mirror* (Siodmak)
1947   *The Bishop's Wife* (Koster); *The Secret Life of Walter Mitty* (McLeod); *A Song Is Born* (Hawks)
1948   *Every Girl Should Be Married* (Hartman)
1951   *An American in Paris* (Minnelli)
1953   *Call Me Madam* (W. Lang)
1954   *A Star Is Born* (Cukor) (co); *Brigadoon* (Minnelli)
1955   *Guys and Dolls* (J. L. Mankiewicz)
1956   *The King and I* (W. Lang)
1959   *Porgy and Bess* (Preminger)
1960   *Can-Can* (W. Lang)
1961   *Flower Drum Song* (Koster); *West Side Story* (Wise and Robbins)
1963   *Cleopatra* (J. L. Mankiewicz) (co)
1965   *The Sandpiper* (Minnelli)
1966   *Who's Afraid of Virginia Woolf?* (M. Nichols)
1967   *The Taming of the Shrew* (Zeffirelli) (co)
1968   *Funny Girl* (Ross)
1969   *Hello, Dolly!* (Kelly); *Justine* (Cukor)
1970   *The Great White Hope* (Ritt)
1973   *The Way We Were* (Pollack) (co)
1977   *The Other Side of Midnight* (Jarrott)
1981   *Mommie Dearest* (Perry)

Publications by Sharaff

Book

Broadway and Hollywood: Costumes Designed by Irene Sharaff, New York, 1976.

Articles

"Is Fashion an Art?," in *Metropolitan Museum of Art Bulletin* (New York), November 1967.
"Costume Drama," interview with Meredith Brody, in *Interview* (New York), August 1989.

Irene Sharaff (center) with Gene Kelly and Barbra Streisand on the set of *Hello, Dolly!*

Publications on Sharaff

Articles

Theatre Arts (New York), November 1949.

Chierchetti, David, in *Hollywood Costume Design,* New York, 1976.

Leese, Elizabeth, in *Costume Design in the Movies,* New York, 1976.

LaVine, W. Robert, in *In a Glamorous Fashion,* New York, 1980.

O'Connell, Bill, "Irene Sharaff Recreates Joan Crawford; Costumes for *Mommie Dearest,*" in *Theatre Crafts,* January 1982.

Obituary, in *New York Times,* 17 August 1993.

Obituary, in *Variety* (New York), 30 August 1993.

* * *

Making motion pictures often demands more from an artist than the duties suggested by an official title. Had "costume designer" Irene Sharaff merely sketched pretty dresses for stunning starlets, prestigious MGM studios would have slammed shut the pages of her drawing pad. But Sharaff's talent included a strong intellect, a fine eye, intuitive insights, and ingenious ability for original adaptation, and an integrating mind that united all into workable designs.

Sharaff succeeded quickly as a New York stage designer. She showed a clever use of color in her costumes for Irving Berlin's *Easter Parade.* For this stage revue, various shades of browns, tans, and other neutrals mimicked the pages of the *New York Times* rotogravure. Sharaff's designs for *Alice in Wonderland* won acclaim as reconstructions of the original Tenniel illustrations. These successes caught the attention of MGM filmmakers who hoped to translate Sharaff's theatrical skills into bankable Hollywood ventures. Specifically, they sought a suitable designer to deal with the new Technicolor process. Sharaff did not disappoint them after she joined the staff in 1942.

MGM designated Sharaff's skills to the Freed unit, which made some of the world's most memorable musicals. Almost immediately, her touch turned projects into screen gold. *Meet Me in St. Louis,* for instance, was a nostalgic valentine of lace, swiss dots, and ruffles. But the *An American in Paris* ballet sequence proved the costume designer's finest hour, as it utilized a multitude of her various talents. For this ballet, Sharaff based her visuals on a number of famous French painters. Paying homage to the Impressionists and several Post-Impressionists, she translated the colors and techniques of individual artists to set design and costume, even as she facilitated Gene Kelly's dances with garments constructed specifically for movement. Even the fabrics flowed with harmonizing rhythms.

Sharaff's career displayed considerable variety. *The King and I* sparkled with exotic ethnic dress. *Can-Can* offered an imaginative "Adam and Eve" ballet complete with guises from animal to insect. *West Side Story* glorified the uniforms of working-class New York toughs. A few years later, *The Sandpiper* peopled the beaches of Big Sur with contemporary bohemians. Sharaff often dressed Elizabeth Taylor, be it as Egyptian queen (*Cleopatra*), a brilliant but testy Renaissance jewel (*The Taming of the Shrew*), or an overweight, aging slob (*Who's Afraid of Virginia Woolf?*). Late in her career, Sharaff's designs for *Mommie Dearest* amplified the lurid luster of Hollywood glamour in the 1940s and 1950s.

Throughout her remarkable 50-year career, Irene Sharaff translated her visions from stage to screen, using all the artistries of the world as inspiration. Understanding the natures of film, the stage, and ballet, she recognized their similarities and differences. Starting with this knowledge, she splashed it with just the right colors and elevated each creation to optimum advantage. Sharaff will best be remembered for taking the superficial show out of show business and replacing it with the depth of fine art.

—Edith C. Lee/Denise Delorey

SHEPITKO, Larissa

Soviet Ukrainian director and writer

Born: Armtervosk, Eastern Ukraine, 1938 (some sources list 1939). **Education:** Studied with Alexander Dovzhenko at the VGIK (State Film Institute), from which she was graduated. **Family:** Married the director Elem Klimov. **Career:** 1958—assisted Yulia Solntseva, Alexander Dovzhenko's widow, in making *Poem of the Sea,* based on Dovzhenko's writings; early 1960s—directed the short films *The Blind Cook* and *Living Water* and the diploma feature *Heat* while at film school; 1978—a retrospective of her work presented at the Berlin Film Festival, where she was a member of the jury. **Awards:** Second Prize, Venice Film Festival, for *You and I,* 1971; Golden Bear and International Federation of Cinema Press, Berlin Film Festival, for *The Ascent,* 1977. **Died:** Near Moscow, July 1979.

Films as Director

1961   *The Blind Cook* (short)
1962   *Living Water* (short)
1963   *Znoy (Heat)* (+ co-sc)
1966   *Krylya (Wings)*
1968   *V trinadtsatom chasu (At One O'Clock)*
1971   *Ti I Ya (You and I)* (co-sc)
1977   *Voshojdenie (Kodiyettom; The Ascent)* (+ co-sc)
1987   *The Homeland of Electricity (Rodina Electrichestva)* (short—filmed in 1967 and released with *Angel,* a short directed by Andrei Smirnov, as *The Beginning of an Unknown Century*)

Other Films

1970   *Sport, Sport, Sport* (Klimov) (ro)
1981   *Proschanie s Matyoroy (Farewell; Farewell to Matyora)* (Klimov) (script concept)

Publications by Shepitko

Articles

"Sotnikov ni e nuzhen i dnes," in *Kinoizkustvo* (Sofia, Bulgaria), September 1977.

Interview with J. Vieira Marques and M. Martin, in *Ecran* (Paris), 15 March 1978.

With F. von Nostitz, "Obazana pered soboi i pered liudmi," in *Iskusstvo Kino* (Moscow), no. 1, 1988.

Publications on Shepitko

Books

Zemanova-Hojdova, Zuzana, *Larissa Sepitkova,* Prague, 1988.

Romanenko, A. R., *Elem Klimov and Larissa Shepitko,* translated by Natalia Shevyrinal, Moscow, 1990.

Foster, Gwendolyn Audrey, *Women Film Directors: An International Bio-Critical Dictionary,* Westport, Connecticut, 1995.

Articles

Elley, Derek, "Hiding It under a Bushel," in *Films and Filming* (London), March 1974.

Karakhan, L., "Krutoi put *Voskhozh deniia,*" in *Iskusstvo Kino* (Moscow), no. 10, 1976.

"Director Larissa Shepitko and Her New Film, *The Ascent,*" in *Soviet Film* (Moscow), no. 4, 1977.

"Four Directors So Respected They Can Evade Soviet 'Oversight'," in *Variety* (New York), 11 May 1977.

Simon, John, "Berlin Stories," in *New York,* 25 July 1977.

"Six Top Soviet Directors," in *Variety* (New York), 24 August 1977.

Kovic, B., "Pogovor z Larissa Shepitko," in *Ekran* (Yugoslavia), no. 5/6, 1978.

Herlinghaus, R., "Fuer Larissa Shepitko," in *Film und Fernsehen* (Berlin), no. 8, 1979.

Lotianu, E., obituary, in *Iskusstvo Kino* (Moscow), no. 12, 1979.

Obituary in *Cinématographe* (Paris), no. 50, 1979.

Holloway, Ron, obituary in *Variety* (New York), 25 July 1979.

Martin, M., obituary, in *Ecran* (Paris), 15 September 1979.

Nemes, K., "Larisza Sepityko (1938-1979)," in *Filmkultura* (Budapest), September/October 1979.

Obituary, in *Bianco e Nero* (Rome), September/December 1979.

Obituary, in *Cinéma* (Paris), November 1979.

Zemanova, Z, "Nespokojena maximalistka Larissa Shepitko," in *Film a Doba* (Prague), June 1982.

Pawlak, E., "W kregu pytan ostatecznych," in *Kino* (Warsaw), June 1983.

Abreu, T. G., "Ascension y permanencia de Larissa Shepitko," in *Cine Cubano* (Havana), no. 109, 1984.

Duarte, F., and M. F. Reis, "Larissa Chepitko (1938-1979): *Ascensao,*" in *Celuloide* (Portugal), October/November/December 1984.

Rosenberg, Karen, "Shepitko," in *Sight and Sound* (London), no. 2, 1987.

"Ohjaajat ja valvojat," in *Filmihullu* (Helsinki), no. 6, 1988.

Quart, Barbara, "Between Materialism and Mysticism: The Films of Larissa Shepitko," in *Cineaste* (New York), vol. 16, no. 3, 1988.

"Manchmal schwieg die Kritik," in *Film und Fernsehen* (Berlin), no. 1, 1989.

Holloway, Ron, "Larissa Shepitko: Her Life and Films," in *Cinema in India* (Bombay), no. 2, 1990.

Youngblood, Denise J., in *The Women's Companion to International Film,* edited by Annette Kuhn, with Susannah Radstone, Berkeley, 1994.

Wilmington, Michael, "A Chance to View Art of Shepitko," in *Chicago Tribune,* 12 September 1996.

Film

Larissa, short directed by Elem Klimov, 1980.

*   *   *

Barely two years after her greatest international triumph—winning the Golden Bear at the Berlin Film Festival for *The Ascent*—Ukrainian filmmaker Larissa Shepitko tragically died in an automobile accident. The Soviet cinema thus prematurely lost one of the major talents of its postwar generation, and the international film community was robbed of one of its emerging—and potentially most significant—creative lights. Summarily, Shepitko and her work pretty much have remained unknown and ignored in North America, despite a small but fervent cult of admirers (including Martin Scorsese and Stan Brakhage).

Shepitko's films are visually stunning, and loaded with images that eloquently communicate her characters' deepest feelings, concerns, and conflicts. They also are linked in that their settings are such disparate physical extremes as snow-covered landscapes, arid deserts and rugged wastelands. Nature itself presents a threat to human life, with the basics of survival often the primary challenge for her characters.

Furthermore, relationships in Shepitko's films mostly are strained. Characters have their own personal visions and opposing views on key issues. While her first films explore clear-cut political questions within Soviet society, her work evolved to deal more with moral and ideological concerns. Ultimately, her films reflect on the use of cinema as a means of exploring such issues—and, accordingly, serve as expressions of the essence of the human spirit.

In her all-too-short life—she was 40 years old when she died—Shepitko directed just four features. Her first, *Heat,* was her diploma work for the VGIK state film school, and was completed when she was 24 years old. It is set during the 1950s, on a small collective farm in the U.S.S.R.'s arid central Asian territory of Kirghizia, where two males from different generations quarrel over the manner in which agricultural procedures may be used to modernize the farm. This crisply directed film is especially successful in connecting its characters to their parched surrounding.

Wings, which Shepitko made three years later, examines the friction between Russians who survived World War II and their offspring. Its main character is a fabled female fighter pilot who has difficulty reconciling her past with her present job as a school administrator. She is entering middle age, her lone true love died in the war, and her memories of the war at once fill her thoughts and adversely affect her present-day relationships with her students and adopted daughter. From a political perspective, *Wings* is a provocative depiction of a character who views collectivism and obligation as the backbone of the Soviet Union and is troubled by what she views as an increase in individualism among the younger generation. Adding resonance to the story is the fact that she is neither a Stalinist heavy nor a well-intentioned visionary, but rather an all-too-human being who is attempting to clarify her present-day identity and follow her convictions. *You and I* is a companion piece to *Wings* in that its main character, a brain surgeon, has come to question his role in society and the significance of his life and his work. For this reason, he leaves his job and family and sets out on an odyssey through Siberia in search of himself. Both *You and I* and *Wings* are noteworthy as probing looks at moral dilemmas facing then-contemporary Soviet society.

Finally, *The Ascent,* Shepitko's masterwork, is a chilling drama about honor and corruption, devotion and duplicity, and human endurance under the most trying conditions. It is set during a snowy, dreary World War II winter in Byelorussia, the provincial Soviet region then controlled by the occupying Germans. The three pivotal characters are individuals who each must achieve a personal reconciliation as they fathom the meaning of their accountability while struggling to endure the bloodshed in their midst. The first is a German-speaking Russian—whose profession, ironically, is that of a schoolteacher—who collaborates with the enemy and toils as a torturer of his fellow citizens. The other two are partisans. The first gutlessly attempts to save himself by sacrificing his comrade; the second heroically refuses to cave into his captors' pressure and comes to view his imminent demise on a religious-mystical level, as a sacrifice in the wake of society's horrors. Among the other characters are a trio of innocents sentenced to death for allegedly favoring the partisans.

In July 1979, while driving to Moscow after looking over locations for her next film, Shepitko and four of her crew members lost their lives in an automobile accident. The film, which ironically was to be titled *Farewell,* was completed by Shepitko's husband, director Elem Klimov—who also filmed a documentary homage to her, titled *Larissa.*

That Shepitko's star was ascending on the international film scene is unquestionable. For this reason alone, her premature death is especially heartbreaking.

—Rob Edelman

SHIPMAN, Nell
Canadian director and actress

Born: Helen Foster-Barham in Victoria, British Columbia, Canada, 15 October 1892. **Family:** Married 1) the writer Ernest Shipman, 1911 (divorced 1920), son: the screenwriter Barry Shipman; 2) Charles Austin Ayers, 1925 (died 1964). **Career:** 1905—began appearing on stage in vaudeville and road shows; 1912—moved to Southern California and began writing for the screen, and serving as agent representing best-selling writers in their dealings with movie companies; 1916—had her first major on-screen success, *God's Country and the Woman;* 1920—formed her own production company, Nell Shipman Productions, which produced *The Girl from God's Country* and *The Grub Stake,* and moved to Priest Lake, Idaho; began co-directing films with Bert Van Tuyle; 1925—closed down her production company; 1985—National Archives of Canada premiered a restored print of *Back to God's Country;* 1987—her autobiography is published; 1989—a program of Shipman films is presented in New York at the Museum of Modern Art. **Awards:** A section of Priest Lake State Park at Priest Lake, Idaho, is named Nell Shipman Point, 1977. **Died:** Cabazon, California, 12 January 1970.

Films as Co-Director

1920   *Something New* (co-d with Van Tuyle, + ro as Nell Shipman, pr, sc); *The Trail of the Arrow*
1921   *The Girl from God's Country* (co-d with Van Tuyle, + ro as Neeka Le Mort/Marion Carslake, pr, sc, st); *A Bear, a Boy and a Dog* (*Saturday Off*) (co-d with Van Tuyle, + pr, sc)

Films as Actress

1916   *God's Country and the Woman* (Sturgeon) (as Jo Barton); *Through the Wall* (Sturgeon) (as Alice Kittredge); *Fires of Conscience* (Apfel) (as Nell Blythe)

1917   *The Black Wolf* (Reicher) (as Dona Isabel)
1918   *Baree, Son of Kazan* (Smith) (as Nepeese); *Cavanaugh of the Forest Rangers* (Wolbert) (as Virginia Wetherford); *A Gentleman's Agreement* (Smith) (as Theresa Kane) (+ sc); *The Girl from Beyond* (Wolbert) (as Cynthia Stewart); *The Home Trail* (Wolbert) (as Clara); *The Wild Strain* (Wolbert) (as Winifred Hollywood)
1919   *Back to God's Country* (Hartford) (as Dolores LeBeau, + pr, sc); *Tiger of the Sea* (+ sc)
1922   *The Grub Stake* (Van Tuyle) (as Faith Diggs, + pr, sc, st)
1923   *Little Dramas of the Big Places: Trail of the North Wind* (Van Tuyle) (+ pr, sc); *Little Dramas of the Big Places: The Light on Lookout* (Van Tuyle) (+ pr, sc); *Little Dramas of the Big Places: White Water* (Van Tuyle) (+ pr, sc)
1924   *Little Dramas of the Big Places: The Love Tree* (Van Tuyle), (+ pr, sc) (not completed)
1927   *The Golden Yukon* (shortened re-issue of *The Grub Stake*) (Van Tuyle) (as Faith Diggs, + pr, sc, st)

Other Films

1913   *Outwitted by Billy* (sc); *One Hundred Years of Mormonism* (sc, st)
1914   *Shepherd of the Southern Cross* (Butler) (sc)
1915   *The Pine's Revenge* (DeGrasse—short) (sc, st); *Under the Crescent* (King—serial) (sc, st)
1916   *The Melody of Love* (Kerrigan) (sc)
1917   *My Fighting Gentleman* (Sloman) (st)
1935   *Wings in the Dark* (Flood) (st)
1947   *The Story of Mr. Hobbs* (*The Clam-Digger's Daughter*) (Varney-Serrao) (uncredited pr)

Publications by Shipman

Book

The Silent Screen and My Talking Heart: The Autobiography of Nell Shipman, edited by Tom Trusky, Boise, Idaho, 1987.

Articles

"Me," in *Photoplay* (New York), February 1919.
"Fragments of Letters of Nell Shipman," in *Filmograph* (Orlean, Virginia), no. 2, 1974.

Publications on Shipman

Books

Slide, Anthony, *Early Women Directors,* South Brunswick, New Jersey, 1977; rev. ed. as *The Silent Feminists: America's First Women Directors,* Lanham, Maryland, 1996.
Morris, Peter, "Ernest Shipman and *Back to God's Country*," in *Embattled Shadows: A History of the Canadian Cinema,* Montreal, 1978.
Acker, Ally, *Reel Women: Pioneers of the Cinema, 1896 to the Present,* New York, 1991.
Foster, Gwendolyn Audrey, *Women Film Directors: An International Bio-Critical Dictionary,* Westport, Connecticut, 1995.

Articles

Fulbright, Tom, "Queen of the Dog Sleds," in *Classic Film Collector,* Fall 1969.

Smith, Judith, "Nell Shipman: Girl Wonder from God's Country," in *Cinema Canada* (Montreal), November/December 1978.

Martineau, B. H., "Leading Ladies behind the Camera," in *Cinema Canada* (Montreal), January/February 1981.

Trusky, Tom, "Nell Shipman: A Brief Biography," in *Griffithiana* (Italy), September 1988.

Everson, William K., "Rediscovery," in *Films in Review* (New York), April 1989.

Brauerhoch, A., "Nell Shipman," in *Frauen und Film* (Frankfurt), September 1989.

Trusky, Tom, "Nell Shipman: Eine kurze Biografie," in *Frauen und Film* (Frankfurt), September 1989.

"March Brings Nell Shipman Film Fest," in *Classic Images* (Muscatine, Iowa), February 1991.

Armatage, Kay, "Dog and Woman, Together at Last," in *CineAction!* (Toronto), Summer/Fall, 1991.

Newton, Mike, "Just Ask Mike: Nell Shipman: *The Girl from God's Country,*" in *Classic Images* (Muscatine, Iowa), December 1992.

Newton, Mike, "Just Ask Mike," in *Classic Images* (Muscatine, Iowa), October 1993.

Turner, D. J., "Who Was Nell Shipman and Why Is Everyone Talking about Her?," in *Archivist,* no. 110, 1995.

*   *   *

Between the mid-teens and early 1920s, Canadian-born and California-bred Nell Shipman had a fascinating but short-lived film career. During that period, which might be dubbed the brief but gilded age of women film pioneers, Shipman acted on-screen, directed, wrote screenplays and the stories upon which they were based, represented writers in their dealings with film companies, and even formed her own production company—thus becoming her own boss. She was a woman of incredible fortitude who insisted on shooting her films on location in the wilderness of Idaho and Canada, and was unafraid to take risks in order to realize her creative visions. As film historian William K. Everson has noted, however, "She was a maverick who ... tried to lick the Hollywood system and failed."

Shipman's best-known films have a shared theme: The woman's experience in the harsh regions of the north country. In fact, upon her initial success, *God's Country and the Woman,* she won the nickname "The Girl from God's Country." Contemporary writers have categorized Shipman as a purveyor of feminist stories because the heroines she created and portrayed are capable of fighting back and surviving the harsh destinies that befall them. True as that may be, a closer look at the films of her peak years shows as much of an emphasis on the woman as victim rather than champion. The focus is less on the triumph of the heroine than on her melodramatic predicament as she struggles with the beastly powerful male arch villain—and the typical Shipman heroine winds up in the arms of the good and loving man she first encountered at the opening of the story.

While she was at Vitagraph in the mid-teens, Shipman starred in two feature films based on popular novels of north country adventures by James Oliver Curwood. In *God's Country and the Woman,* her mother is raped and subsequently made pregnant by a dastardly cad. Years later, he returns to "God's Country" to tyrannize Shipman by kidnapping her and threatening her fragile marriage of convenience. During a fight between the cad and the husband, the villain is eaten by a pack of ravenous sledge dogs. To call this a feminist theme is taking a skewed look at the scenario. Instead, the film explores the subject of a woman as the victim of an evil-minded man.

In *Baree, Son of Kazan,* another Curwood concoction about the Canadian northwest, Shipman plays the "half-breed" daughter of a trapper. Alone in her cabin, she is sexually attacked by a brutish trading-post owner. It is left to her dog Baree to trap the bad man so that Shipman eventually can marry the good man of the story.

As Shipman gained more control over her films, she remained true to the themes in these melodramas. In *Something New,* the setting may be Mexico but the story is similar as an infamous Mexican *bandito* absconds with the heroine to his hideaway. With the help of the good man and his dog and Maxwell car, she is saved.

The triangular tale of the victimized yet spunky heroine, the villain and the good man continues in her later features. These include *The Girl from God's Country,* another north country tale about a young woman who saves the life of a millionaire roué who actually is her father (who sexually ruined her mother years earlier!). And in *The Grub Stake,* Shipman again combines her tried-and-true melodramatic theme with an appreciation for the north country wilderness and animals as a blackguard entices an innocent named Faith into a fake marriage in order to betray her honor.

Evidence of the brief success Shipman had as a filmmaker lies in two career milestones. The first is an offer of a seven-year contract from Samuel Goldwyn, which she later regretted turning down. The second came in 1920 when she established her own independent production company in Priest Lake, Idaho. Along with her co-director-lover Bert Van Tuyle, 200 animals, and a small contingent of actors and crew, she created a string of films over the next few years. Unfortunately, her failure to link her productions with a major distribution outlet appears to be the cause of the demise of her studio in 1925, when she shut the books on her production company and retired her animals to the care of the San Diego Zoo. Much to Shipman's credit, she not only loved animals but recognized the necessity for their protection decades before this notion entered the mainstream consciousness.

Part of Shipman's problem surely lay in her choice of stories, which were becoming redundant to those who made up her audience and perhaps were becoming passé to an America that had entered the Jazz Age. Also, Shipman was far from a classic beauty. She did not retain her looks with the passing years; as she approached the age of 30, she was no longer able to adequately play the "young girl" starring roles she created. William K. Everson politely noted, "Nell Shipman was an attractive woman, though a difficult one to photograph." Anthony Slide is harsher in his judgment, claiming that Shipman was "a poor actress, coy and with bad teeth." He goes on to describe her films as "amateurish in extreme." Yet when these films are projected for today's audiences, there is enthusiasm for Shipman's predictable melodramas, in spite of the contrived put-upon heroines; the black-hat, white-hat male characters; and the loyal animal defenders. The irony appears to be that today's viewers do not take these photoplays seriously—but Shipman did.

Sources state that much of Shipman's work remains uncredited, so it is impossible to completely evaluate her career at this time. Lastly, her autobiography, *The Silent Screen and My Talking Heart,* published in 1987, is based on memoirs that were discovered after her death.

—Audrey E. Kupferberg

SHUB, Esther
Soviet Ukrainian director

Born: Esfir Ilyianichna Shub in Chernigovsky district, Ukraine, 3 March 1894. **Education:** Studied literature, Moscow; Institute for Women's Higher Education, Moscow. **Career:** Administrator with Theatre Dept. of Narkompros (People's Commissariat of Education), collaborated on stage work with Meyerhold and Mayakovsky; 1922—joined film company Goskino, reediting imported films for Soviet distribution and producing compilation and documentary films; 1927—directed first "compilation film," *The Fall of the Romanov Dynasty*; 1933-35—taught montage for Eisenstein class at VGIK (film school); 1942—left Goskino to become chief editor of *Novosti Dnya* [The news of the day] for Central Studio for Documentary Film, Moscow. **Awards:** Honored Artist of the Republic, 1935. **Died:** In Moscow, 21 September 1959.

Films as Director

1927   *Padenye dinastii romanovykh (The Fall of the Romanov Dynasty)* (+ sc, ed); *Veliky put' (The Great Road)* (+ sc, ed)
1928   *Rossiya Nikolaya II i Lev Tolstoi (The Russia of Nicholas II and Lev Tolstoy)* (+ sc, ed)
1930   *Segodnya (Today)* (+ sc, ed)
1932   *K-SH-E (Komsomol—Leader of Electrification; Komsomol—The Guide to Electrification)* (+ sc, ed)
1934   *Moskva stroit metro (Moscow Builds the Subway; The Metro by Night)* (+ sc, ed)
1937   *Strana Sovietov (Land of the Soviets)* (+ sc, ed); *Turtsiia na podeme (Turkey at the Turning Point)*
1939   *Ispaniya (Spain)* (+ sc, ed)
1940   *Kino za XX liet (20 let sovetskogo kino; Twenty Years of Soviet Cinema)* (co-d, co-ed, sc)
1941   *Fashizm budet razbit (Fascism Will Be Destroyed; The Face of the Enemy)* (+ sc, ed)
1942   *Strana rodnaya (The Native Country)* (+ sc, ed)
1946   *Po tu storonu Araksa (Across the Araks)* (+ sc, ed); *Sud v Smolenske (The Trial in Smolensk)* (+ sc, ed)

Other Films

1922-25   Edited 200 foreign fiction films and ten Soviet films, final one being *The Skotinins* (Roshal)
1926   *Krylya kholopa (Wings of a Serf)* (Tarich) (ed); *Abrik Zaur* (Mikhin) (ed)

Publications by Shub

Books

Krupnyn planom [In the close-up], Moscow, 1959.
Zhizn moya—kinematogra [My life—cinema], Moscow, 1972.

Articles

"Road from the Past," in *Sovietskoye Kino* (Moscow), November/December 1934.

"Kuleshov, Eisenstein, and the Others: Part 1: On Kuleshov," interview with S. P. Hill, in *Film Journal* (New York), Fall/Winter 1972.

Publications on Shub

Books

Leyda, Jay, *Kino: A History of the Russian and Soviet Film,* New York, 1973.
Taylor, Richard, and Ian Christie, editors, *The Film Factory: Russian and Soviet Cinema in Documents 1896-1939,* London, 1988.
Mayne, Judith, *Kino and the Woman Question: Feminism and Soviet Silent Film,* Columbus, Ohio, 1989.
Acker, Ally, *Reel Women: Pioneers of the Cinema, 1896 to the Present,* New York, 1991.
Attwood, Lynn, *Red Women on the Silver Screen: Soviet Women and Cinema from the Beginning to the End of the Communist Era,* London, 1993.
Foster, Gwendolyn Audrey, *Women Film Directors: An International Bio-Critical Dictionary,* Westport, Connecticut, 1995.

Articles

Halter, R., "Esther Shub—ihre Bedeutung für die Entwicklung des Dokumentarfilms," in *Frauen und Film* (Berlin), October 1976.
Petric, Vlada, "Esther Shub: Cinema Is My Life," in *Quarterly Review of Film Studies* (Pleasantville, New York), Fall 1978.
Petric, Vlada, "Esther Shub: Film as a Historical Discourse," in *"Show Us Life": Toward a History of Aesthetics of the Committed Documentary,* edited by Thomas Waugh, Metuchen, New Jersey, 1984.

* * *

In Russia, as directors traditionally do their own editing, famous film editors are rare. A great exception to this rule was Esther Shub. After gaining her reputation and experience in the early 1920s on the strength of her reediting of foreign productions and a dozen Soviet features, she became, largely on her own initiative, a pioneer of the "compilation film," producing work that has seldom since been equaled. She brought to this genre far more than her speed, industry and flair; she brought a positive genius for using all sorts of ill-considered odd bits of old footage as a painter uses his palette, using them as if they had all been especially shot for her. In creating her first two brilliant compilations, *The Fall of the Romanov Dynasty* and *The Great Road,* about the first decade of the revolution (both released in 1927), she scavenged everywhere with indefatigable determination. Old newsreels, amateur footage shot by the imperial family and their friends, official footage from a pair of official imperial cinematographers, storage facilities (cellars, vaults, and closets) of wartime cameramen were all investigated by Shub. She even managed to purchase valuable material from the United States. All of this was against the original reluctance of her studios to go ahead with these projects, and they refused to recognize her rights as author when she had finished the films.

Shub originally planned a film biography of Tolstoy as her third work, but even she failed to dig out more than a few hundred feet of material. Undaunted, she wove the footage she did secure in with other early fragments with great effect, emerging with *The Russia of Nicholas II and Lev Tolstoy.*

With the advent of sound Shub made an abrupt change in her methods. For *K-SH-E (Komsomol—Leader of Electrification)* she created her own version of the Communist Hero—young, passionate and dedicated, complete with high-necked Russian blouse and leather jerkin. She forsook her cutting table to become a sort of investigative journalist, deliberately turning her back on archival material, sweeping generalizations, and bravura montage. Instead, she forged a new, original style of ultra-realism, predating by 30 years many of the practices and theories of cinema verité. Forty years later a Soviet film historian was to chide her for "indulging herself with a contemporary enthusiasm for the future of sound film and with the peculiar cult for film-apparatus." This was because she opened the film in a sound studio full of every kind of cinematic machinery with what she termed a "parade of film techniques," and occasionally cut back to this theme throughout the production. She purposely included shots in which people looked into the lens, screwed up their eyes at the arc-lamps, stumbled and stuttered in front of cameras and microphones visible in the scenes, and, in general, tried to augment reality by reminding the audience that the crew and camera were actually *there* instead of pretending that they were part of some all-seeing, omnipotent but unobtrusive eye.

Another important Shub film was *Spain,* a history of the Spanish Civil War. This work was seen once again as an "editor's film." Put together from newsreels and the frontline camera work of Roman Karmen and Boris Makaseyev, the film featured a commentary by Vsevolod Vishnevski, who also collaborated on the script. In the following year Pudovkin collaborated with Shub on her compilation *Twenty Years of Soviet Cinema,* a history of the Soviet industry. She continued her documentary work through the war years and into the late 1940s.

Although as a woman and an editor she perhaps suffered some bureaucratic indifference and obstruction ("they only join pieces of film together"), Shub was an influential filmmaker who deserves at least a niche in the Soviet film pantheon alongside such other originals (in both senses) as Pudovkin and Eisenstein, who certainly appreciated her work.

—Robert Dunbar

SILVER, Joan Micklin

American director

Born: Omaha, Nebraska, 24 May 1935. **Education:** Studied at Sarah Lawrence College, New York, B.A., 1956. **Family:** Married Raphael D. Silver, three daughters: the directors Marisa Silver and Claudia Silver, and the producer Dina Silver. **Career:** From 1967—freelance writer for an educational film company, New York; 1975—directed first feature, *Hester Street*; 1979—directed *Chilly Scenes of Winter* for United Artists, studio changed the title and the ending, but released it in its original form in 1982; 1980s—director for stage and TV, as well as film. **Address:** Silverfilm Productions, Inc., 510 Park Avenue, Suite 9B, New York, NY 10022-1105, U.S.A.

Films as Director

1972   *Immigrant Experience: The Long Long Journey* (short)
1975   **Hester Street** (+ sc)
1976   *Bernice Bobs Her Hair* (for TV)
1977   *Between the Lines*
1979   *Chilly Scenes of Winter (Head over Heels)* (+ sc)

1985   *Finnegan Begin Again* (for TV)
1988   *Crossing Delancey*
1990   *Loverboy*
1991   "Parole Board" ep. of *Prison Stories: Women on the Inside* (for TV)
1992   *Big Girls Don't Cry...They Get Even (Stepkids); A Private Matter* (for TV)
1997   *In the Presence of Mine Enemies* (for TV)
1998   *A Fish in the Bathtub*

Other Films

1972   *Limbo (Women in Limbo; Chained to Yesterday)* (Robson) (co-sc)
1979   *On the Yard* (R. Silver) (pr)

Publications by Silver

Books

A—*My Name Is Alice: A Musical Revue,* with Julianne Boyd, New York, 1985.
A—*My Name Is Still Alice: A Musical Revue,* with Julianne Boyd, London, 1993.

Articles

Interview in *Image et Son* (Paris), November 1975.
Interview with Graham Fuller, in *Independent* (London), 7 April 1989.
"Dialogue on Film: Joan Micklin Silver," in *American Film* (Los Angeles), May 1989.
Interview in *American Film* (Los Angeles), May 1989.

Publications on Silver

Books

Cohen, Sarah Blacher, *From* Hester Street *to Hollywood: The Jewish-American Stage and Screen,* Bloomington, Indiana, 1983.
Squire, Jason, E., *The Movie Business Book,* Englewood Cliffs, New Jersey, 1983.
Wood, Robin, *Hollywood from Vietnam to Reagan,* New York, 1986.
Quart, Barbara, *Women Directors: The Emergence of a New Cinema,* New York, 1988.
Acker, Ally, *Reel Women: Pioneers of the Cinema, 1896 to the Present,* New York, 1991.
Foster, Gwendolyn Audrey, *Women Film Directors: An International Bio-Critical Dictionary,* Westport, Connecticut, 1995.

Articles

Lichtenstein, Grace, "For Woman Director, *Hester Street* Is Victory," in *New York Times,* 15 October 1975.
Fleming, Michael, "Silvers Start N.Y. Indie Operation," in *Variety* (New York), 16 March 1992.

*   *   *

Undoubtedly, the impact of the feminist movement during the 1960s and early 1970s was instrumental in making it possible for women to establish themselves as directors by the latter half of the 1970s. Joan Micklin Silver was one of the first to do so. Silver's films are not explicitly feminist in content, but she consistently displays an awareness of and sensitivity to women's identities and concerns.

As in her initial effort, *Hester Street,* Silver's films have tended to be intimate character studies centered on heterosexual relationships that are in a transitional process. In several of the films, Silver, while not minimizing her significance, decenters the film's female protagonist: in *Finnegan Begin Again,* for example, the Robert Preston character dominates the narrative. But the two most striking examples are the films featuring John Heard, *Between the Lines* and *Chilly Scenes of Winter.* In both films, Heard plays a character with similar characteristics: a tendency to be possessive about the woman he professes to love and a casting of the relationship in the terms of romantic love. In *Chilly Scenes of Winter,* Heard imbues the film with his consciousness. His fantasy regarding a meeting with the Mary Beth Hurt character is visualized and he frequently directly addresses the viewer, providing access to his mental and/or emotional responses to a specific situation. By the film's conclusion, Heard has relinquished his romantic passion, but not without undergoing a considerable psychic and emotional strain. While Hurt rejects Heard and his overwhelming demands, she appears, on the other hand, to have no clearly formed idea of what she either wants or needs from a love relationship. Interestingly, the film does not imply that Hurt's uncertainty is a negative condition—she is just beginning to discover that she can explore the range of sexual and/or romantic involvements available to a contemporary woman.

In *Chilly Scenes of Winter,* the most complex and disturbing of her films, Silver indicates that from Hurt's point of view romantic love is oppressive and destructive; in *Crossing Delancey,* Silver employs a woman, the Amy Irving character, to investigate what could be called a romantic "perception" about possible relationships. Irving rejects the Peter Riegert character before she gets to know him on the grounds that the conditions of their meeting and his profession preclude the possibility of a romance between them. To an extent, Irving's rejection is motivated by her desire to distance herself from her Jewish ghetto origins. In Silver's films, a character's attitude to his or her origins, profession, etc., is often shown to be a contributing factor in the shaping of the romantic fantasy. In the Heard films, the character is frustrated by (*Between the Lines*) or indifferent to (*Chilly Scenes of Winter*) his professional life. In *Crossing Delancey,* it is only after Irving distinguishes between her romantic notions of appropriate partners and the reality of the Riegert character that a romance between the two can develop.

With *Loverboy,* Silver addresses another aspect of the thematic: a young man, played by Patrick Dempsey, learns gradually through his experiences as the paid lover of a number of frustrated married women that sexual desire, pleasure, and fulfillment are enriched by having a romantic attitude towards intimate relationships (in courting women, Dempsey's musical tastes move from heavy metal to Fred Astaire). Silver's films feature a continual probing of what the romantic means—the various dimensions of the concept and its possible significance to both of the sexes. As a concept, the romantic ideal is not gender specific, and it is treated as something that can be either negative or positive in application.

In *Hollywood from Vietnam to Reagan,* Robin Wood argues that *Chilly Scenes of Winter,* to be fully appreciated, needs to be read in relation to the generic expectations it in part fulfills but also undermines. Wood's contention that the film belongs to the classical Hollywood tradition of the light comedy is well-taken; essentially, the

Joan Micklin Silver. Photograph by Joyce Ravid.

same can be said of both *Crossing Delancey,* which is a reworking of the classical romantic comedy, and *Loverboy,* which has its antecedents in the 1930s screwball comedy. (Similarly, Silver's graceful but unobtrusive mise-en-scène is a reflection of the classical filmmaking tradition.) In making this claim, it is important to indicate that the films are not evoking these classical genres for nostalgic purposes; instead, the films, while utilizing the structural strengths and comic potentials of the generic formulas, are offering a contemporary vision of the tensions underpinning heterosexual relations, and Silver's films predominantly respond to these tensions in a progressive manner. From this perspective, Silver's films can be compared to Woody Allen's light romantic comedies (*Annie Hall, Manhattan, Broadway Danny Rose*), though of the two directors, Silver is much less sentimental and precious about her characters (particularly in her treatment of the films' male protagonists).

Silver mostly has been idle in the 1990s. Nevertheless, as more women directors emerge both outside and within the Hollywood establishment, she has come to be regarded as an elder statesman of women filmmakers. One of this new breed is her daughter, Marisa, whose films include *Old Enough, Permanent Record, Vital Signs,* and *He Said, She Said* (the latter co-directed with Ken Kwapis).

Silver's lone feature after *Loverboy* is *Big Girls Don't Cry...They Get Even,* released in 1992 but screened the preceding year as *Stepkids.* It is a comedy which charts the plight of Laura (Hillary Wolf), a teen with a large family—and big problems. While a genial, generally likable film, it is far from Silver's best work, as it often plays like a television situation comedy, complete with overly adorable or precocious children and a too neatly wrapped-up finale.

In the last 20 years, Silver has produced a small but personal and distinguished body of work. She remains an underrated filmmaker; in part, this may be due to the fact that her films are not big-budget projects or star vehicles. (Consistently, her films are conceived as ensemble pieces and contain beautifully judged performances.) It may also be due to the fact that the tone of Silver's films tends to be decidedly offbeat: although the films are clearly "serious" examinations of the complexities of heterosexual relations, Silver infuses the films with a slightly absurdist humor. On the one hand, this may produce a distancing effect that alienates the viewer. But it also allows the viewer to take a more contemplative attitude towards her depiction of the often aching pleasures involved in love relationships.

—Richard Lippe/Rob Edelman

ŠIMKOVÁ-PLÍVOVÁ, Vera

Czech director and writer

Pseudonym: Sometimes known as Vera Plívová-Šimková. **Born:** Lomnice nad Popelkou, Czechoslovakia, 29 May 1934. **Education:** Studied film direction at FAMU (Prague Film School), 1952-57, diploma film *Nez se rozhrne opona*. **Family:** Married Tomáš Šimek, one daughter, one son. **Career:** 1957-62—assistant to Jasný, Gajer, Kachyna, Vorlícek, Kašlík; 1964—first film as director, *Boys, Take Your Dancing Partners!*

Films as Director

1957   *Nez se rozhrne opona* (*Before the Curtain Goes Up*) (+ sc)
1958   *Touha* (*Desire*) (Jasn) (asst d); *Sny na nedeli* (*Dreams for Sunday*) (Gajer) (asst d)
1959   *Král Šumavy* (*Smugglers of Death*) (Kachyna) (asst d)
1960   *Prípad Lupínek* (*A Little Lupin's Investigation*) (Vorlícek) (asst d)
1962   *Rusalka* (*Water Nymph*) (Kašlík) (asst d)
1964   *Chlapci, zadejte se!* (*Boys, Take Your Dancing Partners!*) (short) (+ sc)
1965   *Káta a krokodýl* (*Katia and the Crocodile*) (+ co-sc)
1968   *Tony, tobe preskocilo* (*Tony, You Have a Bee in Your Bonnet*) (co-d with Králová, + co-sc)
1970   *Lišáci-myšáci a Šibenicák* (*Foxes, Mice and Gallows Hill*) (+ sc)
1972   *O Snehurce* (*Snow White*) (+ sc)
1973   *Prijela k nám pout* (*The Funfair Has Arrived*) (+ sc)
1975   *Páni kluci* (*Boys Will Be Boys*; *Gentlemen Boys*)
1977   *Jak se tocí Rozmarýny* (*Ring a Ring o' Roses*) (+ sc)
1979   *Brontosaurus* (+sc)
1980   *Krakonoš a lyzníci* (*The Mountain Giant and the Skiers*)
1982   *Mrkácek Ciko* (*Cziko, the Blinking Boy*) (co-d with Králová, + co-sc)
1985   *Hledám dum holubí* (*I Look for a House of Pigeons*) (+ sc)

1988   *Nefnukej, veverko!* (*Dear Squirrel, Don't Snivel*; *Katy and the Twins*) (+ sc); *Veverka a kouzelná mušle* (*Squirrel's Magic Shell*) (+ sc)
1990   *Houpacka* (*The Seesaw*) (+ sc)

Publications by Šimková-Plívová

Articles

"Hledam dum holubi," in *Film a Doba* (Prague), November 1985.
"Houpacka," in *Film a Doba* (Prague), July 1990.

Publications on Šimková-Plívová

Books

Ceskoslovenská kinematografie, Prague, 1981.
Ceskoslovenští filmoví reziséri sedmdesátých let, Prague, 1983.
Bartošková, Šárka, and Luboš Bartošek, *Filmové profily,* Prague, 1986.
Tibitanzlová, Ivana, *Vera Šimková-Plívová,* Prague, 1988.
Balski, Grzegorz, *Directory of Eastern European Film-Makers and Films, 1945-1991,* Westport, Connecticut, 1992.

Articles

Hrbas, J., "Vera Plívová-Šimková—Svet detských her a predstav," in *Film a Doba* (Prague), April 1973.
Carcedo, J., "Messieurs les gosses," in *Revue due Cinéma* (Paris), no. 331, 1978.
Prochazkova, J., "Scenare a filmy Very Plivove-Simkove," in *Film a Doba* (Prague), August 1983.
Smolinska, H., "Szukam golebnika," in *Filmowy Serwis Prasowy* (Warsaw), vol. 32, no. 18/19, 1986.
HN, "Vera Šimková-Plívová's Films for Children," in *Czechoslovak Film* (Prague), no. 3, 1988.
Wendt-Kummer, E., "Vera Šimková-Plívová," in *EPD Film* (Frankfurt), November 1990.

*   *   *

There are not many directors in international film history who have specialized in productions for children and teenagers and have done so with artistic success. This is understandable because this type of genre does not immediately bring enormous profits. In the former Czechoslovakia the regular production of films for children was ensured by the existence of a nationalized film industry which put aside a certain sum for these types of films. As a result of state support, numerous films of various genres were made for children. Among filmmakers we can find prestigious producers who turned to the children's world once or twice during their career, but there are few of them who chose to depict children's life on the film screen as a lifetime mission. Vera Šimková-Plívová belongs to the latter group and kept faithful to this genre from her debut in 1965 through the 1990s.

During this period Šimková-Plívová cinematized many films that delved from different directions into mysteries of children's souls, thinking, joys, and troubles. She was never interested in fairy tales; the stories of her films are set in the present and are usually based on reality. Šimková-Plívová devoted her attention as much to preschool children as to the troubles of teenagers. Her films are entertaining and thrilling but they do not hide either the raw reality of life or the complicacy of the world.

One of her best films—*Tony, You Have a Bee in Your Bonnet*—begins with an extraordinary scene: people carry two coffins containing the adoptive parents of a little boy to the graveyard. The boy's fate is endangered by the loss of his home. The film heroes and heroines of Šimková-Plívová must fight injustice, sorrow, and intolerance. For all that, she does not depict their world in dark or gray colors. Because she understands the children's world she also gives her heroes room for friendship, love, desires, and dreaming. She is able to advise children spontaneously of the values of good relationships with others, the variety of human characters, and the necessity to care for nature. Nevertheless, her films are not didactic.

Šimková-Plívová mastered her film profession. She wrote her scripts usually by herself and had a special ability to lead young "actors" to plausible performances. This ability also came from her life. Šimková-Plívová was born in a small town near the mountains. She rarely left this area, and far away from busy film studios, she shot most of her films there. Surrounded by forests, familiar houses, and familiar people, she explored—with her actors (many of whom came from this town)—the hidden problems of her heroes.

Her films were meant not only for children but for adults as well. She showed adults that children's fates can be complicated—more complicated than adults'—and that the suffering of children can be equal to the greatest of human tragedies. Šimková-Plívová chose a difficult branch of film voluntarily, "Because children haven't yet lost anything from their humanity."

—Blazena Urgošíková

SLEEPLESS IN SEATTLE
USA, 1993
Director: Nora Ephron

Production: Tri-Star; color, 35mm; running time: 104 minutes. Released June 1993. Filmed in Chicago, Seattle, and New York.

Producer: Gary Foster; **executive producers:** Patrick Crowley and Lynda Obst; **associate producers:** Jane Bartelme, Delia Ephron, and James W. Skotchdopole; **screenplay:** Nora Ephron, David S. Ward, and Jeffrey Arch (from a story by Arch); **photography:** Sven Nykvist; **editor:** Robert Reitano; **production designer:** Jeffrey Townsend; **set designers:** Clay A. Griffith, Charles Daboub Jr., Becky Weidner, and Roberta Holinko; **art designers:** Charley Beal and Gershon Ginsburg; **composer:** Marc Shaiman; **song producer:** Harry Connick; **costumes:** Judy Ruskin; **makeup:** Leonard Engelman; **stunt co-ordinator:** Conrad E. Palmisano; **title designers:** Walter Bernard and Milton Glaser.

Cast: Tom Hanks (*Sam Baldwin*); Meg Ryan (*Annie Reed*); Ross Malinger (*Jonah Baldwin*); Bill Pullman (*Walter*); Rosie O'Donnell (*Becky*); Rob Reiner (*Jay*); Rita Wilson (*Suzy*); Gaby Hoffmann (*Jessica*); Carey Lowell (*Maggie Baldwin*); Victor Garber (*Greg*); Calvin Trillin (*Uncle Milton*); Frances Conroy (*Irene Reed*); Dana Ivey (*Claire*); David Hyde Pierce (*Dennis Reed*); Tom Riis Farrell (*Rob*); Le Clanche Du Rand (*Barbara Reed*); Kevin O'Morrison (*Cliff Reed*); Valerie Wright (*Betsy Reed*); Tom Tammi (*Harold Reed*); Barbara Garrick (*Victoria*).

Publications

Articles

Lowry, Brian, in *Variety* (New York), 21 June 1993.

Canby, Vincent, "When Sam Met Annie, or When Two Meet Cute," in *New York Times,* 25 June 1993.

Lally, Kevin, in *Film Journal* (New York), July 1993.

Travers, Peter, "Date-Night Film Frenzy," in *Rolling Stone* (New York), 8 July 1993.

Frascella, Lawrence, "Nora Ephron: On the Front Lines of the Sexual Battlefield with the Writer and Director of *Sleepless in Seattle,*" in *Rolling Stone* (New York), 8 July 1993.

Simon, John, "Precarious Genres," in *National Review* (New York), 9 August 1993.

Gray, Marianne, in *Film Review* (London), September 1993.

Green, Roberta F., in *Magill's Cinema Annual 1994: A Survey of the Films of 1993,* edited by Frank N. Magill, Pasadena, California, 1994.

* * *

While evaluators in the 1990s seem to classify *Sleepless in Seattle* as a romantic comedy linked to the concept of the young woman who meets the young man movies of the forties and fifties, these critics have not dug into the past decades to see the revival of earlier comic genres. Part of the problem that leads to misclassification has been created by the screenwriters. *Sleepless in Seattle* contains constant references to *An Affair to Remember* and the use of clips from this 1950s movie. This film, created more than three decades before *Sleepless,* piques the interest of the young woman (Annie, played by Meg Ryan) in the contemporary meeting of lovers movie. When other characters—such as Suzy, enacted by Rita Wilson—in *Sleepless* express interest in the sentimental story of *An Affair to Remember,* it becomes a plot device for the 1993 movie.

A key to the comic tone the creators wanted to give this film rests with the way the characters react to the sentiment in the fifties work. One example, of at least three, develops when Suzy narrates the plot of *An Affair to Remember* to an audience of three males, tearfully breaking down with each turn of the story. Sam, portrayed by Tom Hanks, listens to her with a puzzled look. His son, Jonah, an eight year old, asks, "Are you all right?" After hearing Suzy's obsessively maudlin reaction to the fifties film, Sam and a male friend lampoon her with a sarcastic, weepy version of their reaction to the war movie, *The Dirty Dozen.* Obviously the filmmakers are not embracing the sentimentality of the romantic work of the past. They have created a lampoon, tongue-in-cheek version of the genre.

One of the most obvious plot devices in *Sleepless in Seattle* is Jonah's attempt to find a wife for his widowed father. The title of the film come from a radio lonely hearts "therapist" who gives Sam an identification based on his insomnia that is linked to the death of his wife. Director Nora Ephron and her co-writers employ the Mr. Fixit of the genteel and sentimental comedy to develop the story. Comedian Will Rogers, as early as 1920 in *Jubilo,* created a likable, homespun character who helps people when they are in a difficult predicament. He would continue as this comic Mr. Fixit in varied professions in such sound films as *Doctor Bull, State Fair,* and *David Harum.* The skill of advising people and even contriving events to solve problems for others was even passed to the moppet. For example, Shirley Temple became a Miss Fixit in many of her films—such as her efforts to mend relationships between two people on

Sleepless in Seattle

opposing sides of the Civil War in the 1935 *The Littlest Rebel.* Jonah, of course, becomes this type of Fixit child in *Sleepless in Seattle.* He is instigator of the search for a potential wife when he phones the radio "therapist." There are moments of sentiment between the father and son, proving that the writers are using some of the warmth of this genre. The constant advice of the son regarding the father's dates, however, causes the father, Sam, to "blow his top." He wants a sex life and does not care to provide a mother for Jonah. So, Hanks often utters sarcastic remarks about his son's meddling. To Victoria with whom he is having an affair, Sam says, with Jonah next to them, "All children are hideous at the age of eight. It's quite normal." As a result, the sentiment becomes a muted part of the screen drama and illustrates wit that is often employed in sophisticated comedy films.

Filmmaker Ephron and her two assistant screenwriters, David Ward and Jeff Arch, blend the genteel comedy with elements of the sophisticated comedy of the late thirties and early forties—a genre reaching its zenith with such Preston Sturges screen dramas as *Easy Living* (1937) and *The Lady Eve* (1941). The genre sometimes gets the label of screwball comedy because the couple, the man and woman, engaged in odd situations—sometimes even far-fetched ones on the level of the comedy farce genre. The potential lovers in *Sleepless* see each other from a distance two times, but are not united until the last reel. As if attached to a rubber band, they are almost drawn together by various circumstances and manipulations, usually by Jonah and by Annie's desire to meet the man she has heard only on a radio broadcast. As in the sophisticated comedy, the woman often may be very aggressive in her search for "Mr. Right." In this genre the woman evolves as an equal to the man or may possess traits that prove she is superior to the man.

As in so many of Preston Sturges's sophisticated works there exists a number of eccentric minor, comic portraits. Comedy in *Sleepless in Seattle* develops because of the allergy plagued fiancé of Annie. Sam dates a woman who has a laugh that jolts everyone around her. Sam's son, Jonah, states: "She laughs like a hyena." Already mentioned is the overly sentimental Suzy. Along with these minor characters, who are often comically naive, are the leads who make clever observations that come close to the effective wit that was already mentioned as a quality used in the sophisticated comedy.

The blend of two types of comedy does not always gel in this film or there would not be so many evaluators labeling it a romantic comedy. Maybe the creators realized this when they referred so much to *An Affair to Remember,* a true romantic comedy of past decades. A person needs to examine the music employed so liberally throughout the film. The songs of the past are a commentary and an abstraction to move the introspective movie created by movie makers to comedy. For example, the husky, gravel-voice of Jimmy Durante, via an old recording, sings the opening song, "As Time Goes By," and the closing song, "Make Somebody Happy." These two importantly placed renderings, plus most of the other songs, are executed by stylists who sell a song dramatically but do not possess the crooning mode so typical of romantic vocalists.

Sleepless in Seattle proved to be a very popular movie, drawing enthusiastic audiences on the level of the 1988 *A Fish Named Wanda.* Director Ephron helped give the Tri-Star film company nearly $200 million from this nineties work.

—Donald W. McCaffrey

SOLNTSEVA, Yulia
Russian director and actress

Born: Iuliia Ippolitovna Solntseva, Moscow, 7 August 1901. **Family:** Married the film director Alexander Dovzhenko, 1927 (died 1956). **Education:** Studied philosophy at Moscow University; graduated from the State Institute of Music and Drama in Moscow. **Career:** 1924—began her career as an actress, first appearing on-screen in Protazanov's *Aelita*; 1930—became the assistant and close collaborator of her husband, Alexander Dovzhenko; 1956—began directing the incomplete scripts of Dovzhenko at Mosfilm Studios after his death. **Awards:** Named an Honored Artist of the Republic, 1935; Lenin Prize, for *Poem of the Sea,* 1958, awarded the Dovzhenko Medal, 1972. **Died:** October 1989.

Films as Director

1939   *Shchors* (co-d)
1940   *Osvobozhdenie (Liberation)* (co-d); *Bukovyna-Zemlya (Bucovina-Ukrainian Land; Bucovina-Ukrainian Earth)*
1943   *Bytva za nashu Radyunsku Ukrayinu (The Battle for Our Soviet Ukraine; Ukraine in Flames)* (co-d)
1945   *Pobeda na pravoberezhnoi Ukraine i izgnanie Nemetskikh zakhvatchikov za predeli Ukrainskikh Sovetskikh zemel (Victory in Right-Bank Ukraine and the Expulsion of the Germans from the Boundaries of the Ukrainian Soviet Earth)* (co-d)
1948   *Michurin (Life in Bloom)* (co-d)
1953   *Egor Bulychov i drugie (Egor Bulytchev and Others; Igor Bulichov)* (two parts)
1955   *Revizory ponevole (Unwilling Inspectors; Reluctant Inspectors)* (short)
1958   *Poema o more (Poem of the Sea; Poem of an Inland Sea)*
1961   *Povest plamennykh let (Story of the Turbulent Years; The Flaming Years; Chronicle of Flaming Years)*
1965   *Zacharovannaya Desna (The Enchanted Desna)*
1968   *Nezabivaemoe (The Unforgettable; Ukraine in Flames)* (+ sc)
1969   *Zolotye vorota (The Golden Gate)* (+ co-sc)
1974   *Takie vysokie gory (Such High Mountains)*
1979   *Mir v treh izmerenijah (The World in the Three Dimensions)*

Other Films

1924   *Aelita (Aelita: Queen of Mars)* (Protazanov) (title role); *Papirosnitsa ot Mosselproma (Cigarette-Girl from Mosselprom)* (Zhelyabuzhsky) (ro)

1928   *Glaza, kotorye videli (Eyes That Saw; Motele the Weaver; A Simple Tailor)* (Vilner) (ro as Rosas, asst)
1930   *Zemlya (Earth; Soil)* (Dovzhenko) (ro as daughter, asst)
1932   *Ivan* (Dovzhenko) (asst)
1935   *Aerograd (Air City; Frontier)* (Dovzhenko) (asst)

Publications by Solntseva

Book

Compiler, *Polum'iane zhyttia: spogadi pro Oleksandr a Dovzhenka,* Kiev, 1973.

Articles

"Jivie otchi talanta," in *Ogoniok* (Moscow), no. 50, 1961.
"La Terre ukrainienne," in *Les Lettres francaises,* 25 May 1961.
"Pamiatnye dni," in *Iskusstvo Kino* (Moscow), no. 8, 1981.

Publications on Solntseva

Books

Dovzhenko, Alexander, *The Poet as Filmmaker: Selected Writings,* edited and translated by Marco Carynnyk, Cambridge, 1973.
Tolchenova, N., *Iuliia Solntseva,* Moscow, 1979.
Mayne, Judith, *Kino and the Woman Question: Feminism and Soviet Silent Film,* Columbus, Ohio, 1989.
Balski, Grzegorz, *Directory of Eastern European Film-Makers and Film, 1945-1991,* Westport, Connecticut, 1992.
Attwood, Lynn, *Red Women on the Silver Screen: Soviet Women and Cinema from the Beginning to the End of the Communist Era,* London, 1993.
Foster, Gwendolyn Audrey, *Women Film Directors: An International Bio-Critical Dictionary,* Westport, Connecticut, 1995.

Articles

Capdenac, M., "Julia Solntseva et la terre ukrainienne," in *Lettres francaises,* 25 May 1961.
Iakubovich, O. V., in *Iskusstvo Kino* (Moscow), no. 7, 1968.
Belyarski, O., "Time and Memory," in *Soviet Film* (Moscow), no. 9, 1974.
Roshal, G., "Julia Solntseva," in *Soviet Film* (Moscow), no. 2, 1976.
Roshal, G., "Vo imia luchshego," in *Iskusstvo Kino* (Moscow), no. 6, 1976.
Egiazarov, G., "Po veleniiu serdtsa," in *Iskusstvo Kino* (Moscow), no. 9, 1981.
Mashchenko, N., "Vernost," in *Iskusstvo Kino* (Moscow), no. 9, 1981.
Romanov, A., "Volia, masterstvo vdokhnovenie: Iu. I. Solntsevaoi," in *Iskusstvo Kino* (Moscow), no. 8, 1986.
Levin, E., "The Cinema of Our Lives: Lofty Calling," in *Soviet Film* (Moscow), no. 12, 1986.
Stroeva, V., "Iu. I. Solntseva," in *Iskusstvo Kino* (Moscow), no. 3, 1990.

* * *

One cannot consider the career of Soviet actress-filmmaker Yulia Solntseva without acknowledging the influence of her husband,

Alexander Dovzhenko, who with Eisenstein and Pudovkin is one of the virtuosos of the Russian cinema. After establishing herself on screen in the 1920s, Solntseva married Dovzhenko and, from then on, was inexorably linked to her husband. In this regard, Solntseva's work behind the camera is not that of an independent creative artist.

Solntseva had more of a self-contained identity during her relatively brief time before the camera than she did upon becoming Dovzhenko's deputy and, later, the director of his unfinished scripts. Most notably, she starred as the scantily clad title character in Protazanov's science-fiction melodrama *Aelita,* and as the cigarette girl in Zhelyabuzhsky's *Cigarette-Girl from Mosselprom.* Her role in the latter, that of a beauty who becomes a film actress and falls in love with a cameraman, foreshadowed her own relationship with her husband-to-be. Her final acting role was a supporting part in Dovzhenko's *Earth.*

Just about all of Solntseva's creative output reflects on Dovzhenko. She may be listed with him as co-director of *Shchors, Liberation,* and *Life in Bloom,* but the content and artistic vision of these films were dictated by Dovzhenko. Her credit does not mean that she was a creative equal; rather, the "co-director" acknowledgment is a generous one, and should be viewed as gratitude bestowed by Dovzhenko on a valued subordinate.

Solntseva's most notable early works are documentaries/compilation films involving the plight of the Ukraine from the late 1930s through mid-1940s, as war clouds hovered over her homeland. Yet even here, the serene, poetic imagery found in all these films, which are contrasted to those of war's devastation, clearly are reflective of Dovzhenko's aesthetic. The first film for which she earned sole directorial credit was the documentary *Bucovina-Ukrainian Land,* made as the Red Army moved into the Western Ukraine and Byelorussia in the wake of Germany's assault on Poland. The compilation film *Victory in Right-Bank Ukraine and the Expulsion of the Germans from the Boundaries of the Ukrainian Soviet Earth,* however, was co-directed with Dovzhenko; Solntseva co-directed another compilation film, *The Battle for Our Soviet Ukraine,* with Yakov Avdeyenko, but it was produced under the close supervision of Dovzhenko.

Dovzhenko already had completed preproduction on *Poem of the Sea,* which was scheduled as the first of a trilogy involving the evolution of a Ukrainian village, when he died of a heart attack. Solntseva not only took over the direction of *Poem of the Sea* but also filmed the two additional scripts. Here, too, whatever lyrical quality contained in these films—not to mention their focus on Ukrainian folklore—may be attributed to the vision of Dovzhenko. Solntseva simply was following his orders as it were, adding life to his cinematic blueprint.

Upon Dovzhenko's death, Solntseva declared, "I must complete (*Poem of the Sea*) in accordance with Dovzhenko's artistic conception, putting aside every trace of my own individual vision." When that film won the Lenin Prize, she demanded that the award be bestowed upon Dovzhenko. In viewing *Poem of the Sea* and its sequels, the point is not so much the manner in which they were visualized by Solntseva but what they might have been had Dovzhenko lived to direct them.

Not all of Solntseva's films were completed in conjunction with Dovzhenko. For instance, in the early 1950s, when Dovzhenko was still alive, she was one of a number of directors who made two-part filmed plays culled from the repertoires of prominent Russian theater groups. Even after completing her husband's Ukrainian trilogy, however, she remained dedicated to fleshing out his ideas. Solntseva scripted as well as directed *The Unforgettable,* a chronicle of the

Nazi occupation of the Ukraine, but the film was based on stories written by Dovzhenko. She directed and co-scripted *The Golden Gate,* a film in which she utilized her husband as subject matter. One exception to her Dovzhenko connection, in which she explored an independent theme, was *Such High Mountains,* which dealt with issues relating to contemporary education.

On one level, the fact that Solntseva directed films under her own name even before Dovzhenko's death may be viewed as a personal triumph, an act of individual liberation. Nevertheless, she closely aligned herself with Dovzhenko when he was alive, and after his death chose to work on projects based on his writing and ideas. The operative word here is "chose," and it is for this reason that Solntseva should not be viewed as a victim of sexism or creative repression. Her primary artistic motivation, after all, evolved from her respect for Dovzhenko as a cinema master.

Yulia Solntseva viewed herself as an interpreter of Dovzhenko's aesthetic vision. In the end, she made her creative choices, and apparently had no problem living with them.

—Rob Edelman

SPENCER, Dorothy
American editor

Nationality: American. **Born:** Covington, Kentucky, 2 February, 1909. **Career:** Hollywood film editor: first film, *Married in Hollywood,* 1929; 1939—received first of four Academy Award nominations, for *Stagecoach*; 1945-79—worked at 20th Century-Fox.

Films as Editor

1929   *Married in Hollywood* (Marcel Silver); *Nix on Dames* (Gallaher)
1934   *As Husbands Go* (McFadden); *Coming Out Party*; *She Was a Lady* (McFadden)
1935   *The Lottery Lover* (Thiele)
1936   *The Case against Mrs. Ames* (Seiter); *The Luckiest Girl in the World* (Buzzell); *The Moon's Our Home* (Seiter)
1937   *Stand-In* (Garnett); *Vogues* (*Vogues of 1938*) (Cummings)
1938   *Blockade* (Dieterle); *Trade Winds* (Garnett)
1939   *Eternally Yours* (Garnett); *Stagecoach* (Ford); *Winter Carnival* (Riesner)
1940   *Foreign Correspondent* (Hitchcock); *The House across the Bay* (Mayo); *Slightly Honorable* (Garnett)
1941   *Sundown* (Garnett)
1942   *To Be or Not to Be* (Lubitsch)
1943   *Happy Land* (Pichel); *Heaven Can Wait* (Lubitsch)
1944   *Lifeboat* (Hitchcock); *Sweet and Low-Down* (Mayo)
1945   *A Royal Scandal* (Lubitsch); *A Tree Grows in Brooklyn* (Kazan)
1946   *Cluny Brown* (Lubitsch); *Dragonwyck* (J. L. Mankiewicz); *My Darling Clementine* (Ford)
1947   *The Ghost and Mrs. Muir* (J. L. Mankiewicz)
1948   *The Snake Pit* (Litvak); *That Lady in Ermine* (Lubitsch)
1949   *Down to the Sea in Ships* (Hathaway)
1950   *Three Came Home* (Hathaway); *Under My Skin* (Negulesco)
1951   *Fourteen Hours* (Hathaway)

1952 *Decision before Dawn* (Litvak); *Lydia Bailey* (Negulesco); *What Price Glory?* (Ford)
1953 *Man on a Tightrope* (Kazan); *Tonight We Sing* (Leisen); *Vicki* (Horner)
1954 *Black Widow* (N. Johnson); *Demetrius and the Gladiators* (Daves); *Night People* (N. Johnson); *Broken Lance* (Dmytryk)
1955 *The Left Hand of God* (Dmytryk); *Prince of Players* (Dunne); *The Rains of Ranchipur* (Negulesco); *Soldier of Fortune* (Dmytryk)
1956 *The Best Things in Life Are Free* (Curtiz); *The Man in the Gray Flannel Suit* (N. Johnson)
1957 *A Hatful of Rain* (Zinnemann)
1958 *The Young Lions* (Dmytryk)
1959 *The Journey* (Litvak); *A Private's Affair* (Walsh)
1960 *From the Terrace* (Robson); *North to Alaska* (Hathaway); *Seven Thieves* (Hathaway)
1961 *Wild in the Country* (Dunne)
1963 *Cleopatra* (J. L. Mankiewicz)
1964 *Circus World* (Hathaway)
1965 *Von Ryan's Express* (Robson)
1966 *Lost Command* (Robson)
1967 *A Guide for the Married Man* (Kelly); *Valley of the Dolls* (Robson)
1969 *Daddy's Gone A-Hunting* (Robson)
1971 *Happy Birthday, Wanda June* (Robson)
1972 *Limbo* (*Women in Limbo*) (Robson)
1974 *Earthquake* (Robson)
1979 *The Concorde—Airport '79* (D. L. Rich)

Publication by Spencer

Article

"The Film Editing of *Earthquake*," in *American Cinematographer* (Los Angeles), November 1974.

Publications on Spencer

Articles

Winetrabe, Maury, "How Do You Edit an Earthquake?," *American Cinemeditor* (Los Angeles), Fall/Winter 1974-75.
"Silver Anniversary Eddie Awards," *American Cinemeditor* (Los Angeles), Spring 1975.
Sharples, W. Jr., and others, "Prime Cut: 75 Editors' Filmographies and Supporting Material," in *Film Comment* (New York), March/April 1977.

*   *   *

Dorothy Spencer's career as film editor spanned five decades in the industry. Beginning at the dawn of talking pictures, her work continued through the glory days of the Hollywood studio system to the widescreen extravagance of the 1950s and 1960s, working under such directors as John Ford, Alfred Hitchcock, Ernst Lubitsch, Henry Hathaway, and Mark Robson. Though her early days are affiliated with independent producer Walter Wanger, she involved herself exclusively with 20th Century-Fox from the late 1940s until her retirement in 1979. Despite a distinguished

and varied career, she was nominated for an Oscar only four times, losing out on each occasion.

Beginning her career at the age of 20, Spencer worked as cutter on many of Wanger's 1930s productions, including *The Case against Mrs. Ames* and *Winter Carnival.* She also found herself working with director Tay Garnett on *Stand-In, Trade Winds* and *Eternally Yours.* Her career with Wanger reached its peak with John Ford's seminal Western, *Stagecoach* and Hitchcock's *Foreign Correspondent.* In *Stagecoach* the editing principles of the Russian Formalists were deftly employed to convey suspense and pace. Most apparent is the chase sequence—in which the stagecoach is pursued by hostile Comanches—where the cutting is deliberately disorienting to convey the consternation of the passengers, while the crosscutting (alternating between the passengers' point of view and shots of the besetting Indians) increases the scene's tempo. The film was to earn Spencer her first Academy Award nomination.

In the early 1940s she began to work with Ernst Lubitsch, editing *To Be or Not to Be, Heaven Can Wait, A Royal Scandal* and *Cluny Brown.* She also completed work on her second (and final) Hitchcock film, the propagandist wartime drama, *Lifeboat.* Notable for its expert use of limited space (the entire film is set on a lone lifeboat in the middle of the Atlantic), the film is by and large muted. Nevertheless, two scenes do stand out—the harrowing buildup to a necessary amputation and the lynching of a German U-boat commander—both of which build to their climax through a methodical use of montage.

A Tree Grows in Brooklyn, directed by Elia Kazan, marked her first film for 20th Century-Fox. Among her early projects for the corporation were *Dragonwyck, The Ghost and Mrs. Muir,* and John Ford's broodingly low-key Western, *My Darling Clementine.* Lacking significant mood music, *Clementine* achieved its suspense—most spectacularly in the famous O.K. Corral gunfight sequence—in its editing, a tight, pared-down construction in which only the barest (and most pertinent) of information is conveyed.

In 1948 Spencer began the first of her two assignments under producer/director Anatole Litvak; the acclaimed *The Snake Pit* was followed by *Decision before Dawn,* a suspenseful espionage thriller which afforded Spencer her second Oscar nomination. It was her success in the latter that gave rise to Spencer's long association with big-budget actioners, an association that would direct the rest of her career. In the same year as *Decision before Dawn,* she edited *Lydia Bailey* and *What Price Glory?,* and shortly thereafter embarked upon a long list of the Fox-patented CinemaScope pictures, beginning with *Black Widow* in 1954.

Though the widescreen format brought an initial rethinking of the medium's form—traditional framing was reformulated for the wider format and the duration of scenes increased to allow audiences time to register the spectacle—such modifications were limited. By and large the editor's task remained unaltered and Spencer's work, from the mid-1950s onward, shows no apparent change in technique. She worked on a variety of pictures, from large-scale Biblical epics (*Demetrius and the Gladiators*) to Cold War anticommunist pictures (*Night People*) to war movies (*The Young Lions*). Her career in editing widescreen blockbusters reached its peak with Joseph L. Mankiewicz's labored epic *Cleopatra.* Taking more than four years to produce, with countless writers and a $40 million budget, the film provided Spencer with more than 70,000 feet (120 miles) of film to reduce to the final print's 22,000 feet. A gargantuan task on every level, the film won four Academy Awards with Spencer receiving her third nomination.

Many of Spencer's later efforts were under the direction of Mark Robson. In total they worked together on seven pictures, including

Von Ryan's Express, Valley of the Dolls and *Earthquake.* Expressing many of the concerns of the industry at the time, being big, expensive, and destructive, *Earthquake* marked the crowning achievement of Spencer's work in the 1970s. A huge success, the film managed to enthrall audiences with the scale and magnitude of its destruction, much of which depended on Spencer's competent skills as editor. In between her collaborations with Robson, Spencer worked with directors Henry Hathaway on *Circus World* and Gene Kelly on *A Guide for the Married Man,* and with David Lowell Rich on her final picture, *The Concord—Airport '79.*

After 50 years in the industry Dorothy Spencer retired. A consummate studio craftsperson, her work traced the rise and fall of the Hollywood system. Rejecting the reactionist editing styles that emerged in the late 1960s, such as Dede Allen's work on *Bonnie and Clyde* and Sam O'Steen's on *The Graduate,* she continued to employ the classical style formulated in the mid-teens. As with all editors, however, her impact on the films she edited is difficult to gauge. Since the editor's role is secondary to that of the director's, and subservient to the nature and style of the film itself, a critical analysis of her own individual input is difficult to realize. Some of her best work was under such autocrats as John Ford, Alfred Hitchcock, and Ernst Lubitsch, all of whom would have assumed complete responsibility for the style of the cutting employed. Nevertheless, despite the lack of any auteurist evidence, her competence in the field, her success within the industry, and her devotion to her craft remain uncontested.

—Peter Flynn

SPHEERIS, Penelope
American director

Born: New Orleans, Louisiana, 2 December 1945. **Education:** Attended School of Theater, Film, and Television, University of California at Los Angeles, M.F.A. **Family:** Daughter, Anna. **Career:** Voted Most Likely to Succeed by her high school classmates; early 1970s—made several short films while studying at UCLA; worked as an actress and film editor; 1974—founded Rock 'n' Reel, a company specializing in rock music promotion; mid-to-late 1970s—produced short films directed by Albert Brooks and presented on *Saturday Night Live;* 1979—entered the motion picture industry as producer of Brooks's feature *Real Life;* 1981—directed first theatrical feature, the documentary *The Decline of Western Civilization;* 1984—directed first fictional feature, *Suburbia;* 1993—co-created, co-wrote, and directed television series *Danger Theater.* **Agent:** The Gersh Agency, 232 North Canon Drive, Beverly Hills, CA 90210, U.S.A.

Films as Director

1981   *The Decline of Western Civilization* (doc) (+ sc, pr)
1984   *Suburbia (The Wild Side)* (+ sc)
1985   *The Boys Next Door*
1986   *Hollywood Vice Squad*
1987   *Dudes*
1988   *The Decline of Western Civilization Part II: The Metal Years* (doc) (+ sc)

1991   "New Chicks" ep. of *Prison Stories: Women on the Inside* (for TV)
1992   *Wayne's World; Lifers Group: World Tour* (doc short)
1993   *The Beverly Hillbillies* (+ co-pr)
1994   *The Little Rascals* (+ sc)
1996   *Black Sheep*
1998   *The Decline of Western Civilization Part III* (doc); *Senseless*

Other Films

1979   *Real Life* (A. Brooks) (pr)
1987   *Summer Camp Nightmare (The Butterfly Revolution)* (Dragin) (co-sc)
1990   *Wedding Band* (Raskov) (ro)

Publications by Spheeris

Articles

"Is There Life after Punk?," interview with Peter Occhiogrosso, in *American Film* (Washington, D.C.), April 1985.
"Western Civilization Declines Again," in *Premiere* (New York), June 1988.
"Dialogue on Film," with Danny Elfman, in *American Film* (New York), February 1991.

Publications on Spheeris

Book

Foster, Gwendolyn Audrey, *Women Film Directors: An International Bio-Critical Dictionary,* Westport, Connecticut, 1995.

Articles

Gold, Richard, in *Variety* (New York), 26 December 1984.
Wickenhaver, J., in *Millimeter* (New York), April 1987.
Occhiogrosso, Peter, in *Premiere* (New York), October 1987.
Milward, John, in *Newsday* (Melville, New York), 17 June 1988.
Maslin, Janet, "Film View: Penelope Spheeris Finds the Heart of Rock," in *New York Times,* 26 June 1988.
Clark, John, filmography in *Premiere* (New York), March 1992.
Willman, Chris, in *Los Angeles Times,* 1 March 1992.
Diamond, Jamie, "Penelope Spheeris: From Carny Life to *Wayne's World,*" in *New York Times,* 12 April 1992.
Cohn, Lawrence, "Truth-Tellers Start to Tell Tales," in *Variety* (New York), 11 May 1992.

*   *   *

Unlike many women directors, Penelope Spheeris does not make films that are sensitive at their core, that focus on women and their relationships and emotions. Rather, her films—at least the group she made in the first section of her career—are hard-edged and in-your-face brutal. In terms of subject matter, they often deal with male adolescent angst as it exists within a grim, realistic urban environment. If none are particularly distinguished, they certainly are linked thematically, and by their solemn and depressing outlook.

Suburbia, Spheeris's first nondocumentary feature, details the plight of a group of teen runaways residing on the edge of Los

Penelope Spheeris

the late 1970s punk rock scene in Los Angeles. Featured are groups with such names as Circle Jerks, Fear, X, and Catholic Discipline, which are made up of rockers who are alienated not only from the core of straight American society but from the established, old guard in the rock 'n' roll hierarchy; to these rockers, the Beatles, Rolling Stones, or Kinks are as much a part of the mainstream as Spiro Agnew. Six years later, Spheeris made *The Decline of Western Civilization Part II: The Metal Years,* which contrasted several veterans of the heavy metal scene (including Ozzy Osbourne, Gene Simmons, and members of Aerosmith) to younger punk wannabes. Indeed, Spheeris's attraction to individuals so far outside even the farthest degrees of the establishment may be traced to one of the films she made while a student at the UCLA Film School, *Hats Off to Hollywood,* about the romance between a drag queen and a lesbian.

Spheeris's first megahit came with *Wayne's World,* based on the nonsensical but nonetheless popular *Saturday Night Live* skit featuring Mike Myers and Dana Carvey as self-proclaimed "party dudes" who have their own cable TV show. Despite the film's box-office success, it is too often idiotic and dull. Her features since then, such as *The Beverly Hillbillies* and *The Little Rascals,* are even bigger disappointments, and far removed from the spirit of her earlier work: the first is a poorly done version of the silly but funny 1960s television sit-com, and the second a pale reworking of the beloved Hal Roach one- and two-reel comedies.

—Rob Edelman

Angeles. It opens with a pack of wild dogs tearing a baby to shreds. *The Boys Next Door* is the saga of two teen boys who become serial killers. It included footage which had to be edited out in order to avoid an X rating. *Dudes* focuses on some young urban punk rockers who cross paths with murderous Southwestern rednecks. Not all of Spheeris's young protagonists are male, however. One of the characters in *Hollywood Vice Squad* is a runaway girl who has become a heroin-addicted prostitute.

Spheeris has admitted that her preoccupation with alienation and brutality is directly related to the incidents in her life. "I look at violence in a realistic way because I've experienced a lot of it in my own life," she once told an interviewer. While she grew up in a traveling side show called the Magic Empire Carnival, there was nothing enchanted about her childhood. When she was seven years old, her father was murdered. Her younger brother died at the hands of a drunken driver. Her mother, an alcoholic, was married nine times. And her lover, the father of her daughter Anna, overdosed on heroin in 1974. Perhaps the infant being torn apart at the beginning of *Suburbia* is a representation of innocent young Penelope Spheeris, whose childhood purity was ripped from her at a too-young age.

As a child, Spheeris became captivated by rock music as an expression of youthful rebellion. This interest led her into a career in the music industry (as she formed her own company, Rock 'n' Reel, which produced short promotional films for such groups as the Doobie Brothers) and to the subject matter of her initial feature, the one that established her as a director. It is the 1981 documentary *The Decline of Western Civilization,* which records

STREISAND, Barbra
American director, actress, producer, and writer

Born: Barbara Joan Streisand in Brooklyn, New York, 24 April 1942. **Education:** Attended Erasmus Hall High School. **Family:** Married actor Elliott Gould, 1963 (divorced 1971), son: Jason Emanuel. **Career:** Singer in New York nightclub; 1961—professional stage debut in *Another Evening with Harry Stoones;* 1963 Broadway debut in *I Can Get It for You Wholesale;* recording star; 1964—phenomenal success in stage play *Funny Girl,* and later in film version, 1968; 1969—co-founder, with Paul Newman and Sidney Poitier, First Artists Productions; 1976—executive producer, *A Star Is Born;* 1983—producer and director, as well as actress, *Yentl;* 1995—executive producer for the TV film, *Serving in Silence.* **Awards:** Best Actress Academy Award, David Di Donatello award for Foreign Actress, and Golden Globe award for Best Actress, for *Funny Girl,* 1968; David Di Donatello award for Foreign Actress, for *The Way We Were,* 1973; Best Song Academy Award, and Golden Globe award for Best Song, for "Evergreen," in *A Star Is Born,* 1976; Golden Globe award for Best Director, Silver Ribbon (Italy) as Best New Foreign Director, for *Yentl,* 1983. **Agent:** International Creative Management, 8942 Wilshire Boulevard, Beverly Hills, CA 90210, U.S.A.

Films as Director

1983   *Yentl* (+ co-pr, co-sc, title role)
1991   *Prince of Tides* (+ co-pr, ro as Dr. Susan Lowenstein)
1996   *The Mirror Has Two Faces* (+ pr, mus, ro as Rose Morgan)

Films as Producer

1995   *Serving in Silence: The Margarethe Cammermeyer Story*
(Bleckner—for TV) (co-exec pr)
1997   *Rescuers: Stories of Courage—Two Women* (Bogdanovich—
for TV) (co-exec pr)

Films as Actress

1968   *Funny Girl* (Wyler) (as Fanny Brice)
1969   *Hello Dolly!* (Kelly) (as Dolly Levi)
1970   *On a Clear Day You Can See Forever* (Minnelli) (as Daisy
Gamble); *The Owl and the Pussycat* (Ross) (as Doris)
1972   *What's Up, Doc?* (Bogdanovich) (as Judy Maxwell); *Up the
Sandbox* (Kershner) (as Margaret Reynolds)
1973   *The Way We Were* (Pollack) (as Katie Morosky)
1974   *For Pete's Sake* (Yates) (as Henrietta)
1975   *Funny Lady* (Ross) (as Fanny Brice)
1976   *A Star Is Born* (Pierson) (as Esther Hoffman)
1979   *The Main Event* (Zieff) (as Hillary Kramer)
1981   *All Night Long* (Tramont) (as Cheryl Gibbons)
1987   *Nuts* (Ritt) (as Claudia Draper, + pr, mus)
1990   *Listen Up!: The Lives of Quincy Jones* (Weissbrod—doc)
1995   *Barbra Streisand: The Concert* (doc for TV) (+ co-pr)

Publications by Streisand

Articles

"'I Caught Myself Saying, Well, I'll Ask the Director. Then I Went,
Ohhh!',' interview with Dale Pollock, in *Los Angeles Times,* 16
October 1983.
"A Star Is Reborn," interview with Michael Shnayerson, in *Vanity Fair*
(New York), November 1994.
"The Artist as Citizen (Transcript)," in *New Perspectives Quarterly,*
Spring 1995.
"Barbra Streisand, Still Not Pretty Enough," interview with Bernard
Weinraub, in *New York Times,* 13 November 1996.

Publications on Streisand

Books

Castell, David, *The Films of Barbra Streisand,* London, 1974.
Spada, James, *Barbra: The First Decade,* Secaucus, New Jersey,
1974.
Black, Jonathan, *Streisand,* New York, 1975.
Jordan, René, *The Greatest Star: The Barbra Streisand Story,* New
York, 1975.
Brady, Frank, *Barbra: An Illustrated Biography,* New York, 1979.
Spada, James, with Christopher Nickens, *Streisand: The Woman and
the Legend,* New York, 1981.
Zec, Donald, and Anthony Fowles, *Barbra: A Biography of Barbra
Streisand,* New York, 1981.
Teti, Frank, photo-editor, and Karen Moline, *Streisand through the
Lens,* New York, 1982.
Considine, Shaun, *Barbra Streisand: The Woman, the Myth, the
Music,* New York, 1985.
Swenson, Karen, *Barbra: The Second Decade,* Secaucus, New Jer-
sey, 1986.

Gerber, Françoise, *Barbra Streisand,* Paris, 1988.
Kimbrell, James, *Barbra: An Actress Who Sings,* Boston, 1989.
Carrick, Peter, *Barbra Streisand: A Biography,* London, 1991.
Riese, Randall, *Her Name Is Barbra: An Intimate Portrait of the Real
Barbra Streisand,* Secaucus, New Jersey, 1993.
Bly, Nellie, *Barbra Streisand: The Untold Story,* New York, 1994.
Foster, Gwendolyn Audrey, *Women Film Directors: An International
Bio-Critical Dictionary,* Westport, Connecticut, 1995.
Spada, James, *Streisand: Her Life,* New York, 1995.
Waldman, Allison J., *The Barbra Streisand Scrapbook,* Secaucus,
New Jersey, 1995.
Vare, Ethlie Ann, editor, *Diva: Barbra Streisand and the Making of
a Superstar,* New York, 1996.
Dennen, Barry, *My Life with Barbra: A Love Story,* New York, 1997.
Edwards, Anne, *Streisand,* Boston, 1997.
Harvey, Diana Karanikas, and Jackson Harvey, *Streisand: The Pic-
torial Biography,* New York, 1997.

Articles

Maslin, Janet, "Barbra Streisand," in *The Movie Star,* edited by
Elisabeth Weis, New York, 1981.
Potok, Chaim, "Barbra Streisand and Chaim Potok," in *Esquire* (New
York), October 1982.
Singer, I. B, "I. B. Singer Talks to I. B. Singer about the Movie *Yentl,*"
in *New York Times,* 29 January 1984.
Pally, Marcia, "Kaddish for the Fading Image of Jews in Film," in *Film
Comment* (New York), February 1984.
Fernley, Allison, and Paula Maloof, "*Yentl,*" in *Film Quarterly* (Ber-
keley), Spring 1985.
Griffin, Nancy, "Shot by Shot, *The Prince of Tides,*" in *Premiere* (New
York), December 1991.
Current Biography, New York, 1992.
McDonagh, Maitland, "Psychiatrists Analyze Dr. Lowenstein," *New
York Times,* 19 January 1992.
Lieberman, Rhonda, "Glamorous Jewesses," in *Artforum* (New
York), January 1993.
Reed, Julia, "The Unguarded Barbra," in *Vogue* (New York), August
1993.
Zoglin, Richard, "The Way She Is," in *Time* (New York), 16 May 1994.
Carter, Bill, "Quiet Woman's Loud Message Will Be Heard in a TV
Movie," in *New York Times,* 2 February 1995.
Churchill, Bonnie, "Streisand Relishes 'Complete Control,'" in *Chris-
tian Science Monitor* (Boston), 13 December 1996.

* * *

Barbra Streisand's stardom as a singer and an actress underwrote
the first movie she directed, literally. She told Dale Pollock that her
previous success let her accept scale wages as director, no fee as co-
writer, and a low salary as star of *Yentl*. *Yentl* was publicized by
MGM/UA in 1983 as the first movie ever to feature one woman in
all the above-listed capacities, as well as in the role of co-producer.

It is clear that Streisand's star image also underwrites *Yentl*'s aesthetics. *Yentl* is a young woman in turn of the century Eastern Europe whose love of the Talmud drives her to masquerade as a boy, the
only way she can study the writings central to Judaism but prohib-
ited to females at the time. The grounding in Jewish culture, the
insistence upon women's rights, and the commitment to education all
are part of Streisand's persona, as the many biographies of her and
her philanthropic generosity detail. Formally, *Yentl* is a unique musi-

Barbra Streisand directing *Yentl.*

cal, predicated upon Streisand's grand, singular presence as a singer. At moments, Streisand sings Yentl's interior monologues, although (to the complaint of several critics) no one else in the film either sings or hears her.

At the yeshiva where s/he studies, Yentl meets Avigdor (Mandy Patinkin), and for love of him agrees to marry the girl he loves but cannot have, Hadass (Amy Irving). Allison Fernley and Paula Maloof make a strong case that Yentl's feelings of love and buried physical attraction for Hadass, in combination with Yentl's refusal at the end of the film to sacrifice her studies and retreat into a conventional marriage with Avigdor, mark *Yentl* as a uniquely feminist film. There was much speculation in the press that Streisand was refused an Oscar nomination for any of her work on the film, on sexist grounds.

Yentl shares a basic theme with Streisand's two subsequent directorial efforts: it is through each individual's ability to take on the roles and perspectives conventionally divided between genders that romantic love can best proceed between any two people, and that society can progress. Comparatively, however, the latter two films are less seditious in their promotion of this idea. *The Prince of Tides,* based upon Pat Conroy's novel, is a celebration of a strong woman's ability to reinvigorate a man by helping him admit past traumas, and by loving him for his vulnerability. Streisand cast herself as Lowenstein, psychotherapist to a suicidal (female) poet, and eventually lover to the poet's twin brother, Tom Wingo (Nick Nolte).

In *Yentl,* all three of the main characters serve as conduits between the other two. The crossed lines of desire, identification, and fear help all the characters grow, challenging norms of (especially female) gender and sexuality. But in *Prince,* while Lowenstein avails herself to Tom as the means whereby he can accept himself as he is and thus rekindle his love for his estranged wife, his daughters, and his teaching, Lowenstein remains a stranger to—unconnected and unconcerned with—these other females in his life. In the end, Tom and Lowenstein's play with conventional gender traits (she ordering a French dinner, he weeping in her arms) takes place only as temporary fantasy and dislocated experiment, much like their love itself, even though it is depicted as sexy and energizing.

Streisand's direction goes a long way toward contributing to that energy. She continues her preferred habit of using long takes wherever possible, allowing characters to overlap dialogue and react directly to one another. *Prince* bursts with characters—including, in a large sense, its South Carolina and New York City locations—and Streisand orchestrates a flow of full and active frames, in most of which Nolte is at the center.

Streisand's latest film integrates the personas and acting strengths of an impressively wide range of Hollywood, Broadway, and television stars, from Lauren Bacall, Brenda Vacarro, and Streisand's 1970 leading man George Segal, to Mimi Rogers and Pierce Brosnan. *The Mirror Has Two Faces* concerns Rose Morgan (Streisand), a Columbia English professor with a lackluster love life. Rose attracts the attention of a physically fit but priggish math professor (Jeff Bridges) so flustered by his desire, however well-met, that he now wants simply a companionate marriage. After he becomes her husband, he and Rose connect sexually as well as intellectually only after her mildly "unfeminine" style of dress—and love of learning, baseball, and her best pal—gives way, for a short period, to a "hyperfeminine" pursuit of physical beauty.

All three of Streisand's films are about an unconventionally gendered educator-student, at a crossroads in life, whose unexpected love for an intermediary enables her or him to (re)connect with a mate and find a future. The twist in *Mirror* is that the conduit figure for Rose is Rose herself, after a strenuous regimen of diet and exer-

cise. Thought-provoking and involving as it is, *Mirror* seems the least certain of Streisand's trio of films, perhaps because the transitory function of the buff, blond Rose is not completely clear. The film does leave itself open to the charge that it celebrates variations from norms of feminine appearance, comportment, and appetites only ambivalently, after lingering upon its heroine's capability to adhere to them.

—Susan Knobloch

SURNAME VIET, GIVEN NAME NAM
USA, 1989
Director: Trinh T. Minh-ha

Production: Women Make Movies/Idera Films; color, 16mm; running time: 108 minutes. Released April 1989.

Producer: Trinh T. Minh-ha; **associate producer:** Jean-Paul Bourdier; **screenplay:** Trinh T. Minh-ha; **photography:** Kathleen Beeler; **editor:** Trinh T. Minh-ha; **sound:** Linda Peckham; **art director:** Jean-Paul Bourdier.

Cast: Tran Thi Hien; Khien Lai; Ngo Kim Nhuy; Tran Thi Bich Yen; Lan Trinh.

Publications

Book

Foster, Gwendolyn Audrey, *Women Filmmakers of the African and Asian Diaspora,* Carbondale, Illinois, 1997.

Articles

Peckham, L., "*Surname Viet, Given Name Nam*: Spreading Rumors and Ex/changing Histories," in *Framework* (London), vol. 2, no. 3, 1989.
Canby, Vincent, "Women's Status in Vietnam in Documentary Form," in *New York Times,* 1 April 1989.
Hoberman, J., "Mekong Delta Blues," in *Village Voice* (New York), 11 April 1989.
Klawans, Stuart, in *Nation* (New York), 17 April 1989.
Gold, R., in *Variety* (New York), 9 September/3 October 1989.
Jayamanne, L., and A. Rutherford, "Why a Fish Pond," in *Filmnews* (Paddington, New South Wales, Australia), vol. 20, no. 10, 1990.
Higashi, Sumiko, in *American Historical Review,* October 1990.
Mayne, Judith, "From a Hybrid Place: An Interview with Trinh T. Minh-ha," in *Afterimage* (Rochester, New York), December 1990.
Lee, H., "The Subaltern Body," in *CineAction!* (Toronto), Summer/Fall 1991.
Reynaud, Bérénice, "Three Asian Films: For a New Cinematic Language," in *Cinematograph* (San Francisco), vol. 4, 1991.

* * *

Vietnamese filmmaker Trinh T. Minh-ha's best-known film, *Surname Viet, Given Name Nam* is a highly personal experimental work that explores the status of women in contemporary Vietnam with a deep understanding of the country's and the women's historical contexts. Trinh's work is known for prompting impassioned discussions, which have included denunciations of their "subjectivity," as well as praise for their refusals to adhere to ethnographic and documentary film conventions. That is, she generally blurs the line between fiction and documentary conventions, thus questioning the meanings and expectations of audiences (and filmmakers) about both kinds of filmmaking practices. Moreover, she seeks not only to question the notion of "ethnic identity" but also of "female identity"—indeed, she has said she considers them to be one issue that has been artificially separated.

Surname is extraordinary because, unlike documentary films, it makes no effort to present a specific argument or a specific "reality." Instead, Trinh works to destabilize both terms. Surname is not about Vietnam, rather it consists of interviews with Vietnamese women who tell of their experiences living in Vietnam during the war and then after the reunification of North and South under a communist government. But, the interviews are a mix of "fact" and "fake." That is, they are derived from interviews conducted by another Vietnamese woman in 1982; Trinh later recruited Vietnamese women in the United States to reenact the interviews for her film. In addition, after she cast the "actresses," Trinh asked them to help define their on-screen personas by choosing clothing and nonverbal gestures, as well as by collaborating on decisions about camera movement and lighting. Each of the actresses relates her story haltingly, as she describes her struggle for survival in the midst of corruption and economic hardship. Nevertheless, each woman expresses an enduring love for her country—thus the film's title. Trinh alludes to the notion that communist ascension to power had no effect on the subordinate status of women in Vietnamese society. Consequently, a woman's life still is believed to consist of three stages: unmarried "lady," married "maid," and after marriage, "monkey."

The "interviewees" are a doctor, an embassy maid, a former refugee, a student who was raised in the United States, and a woman whose husband was imprisoned when the communists took over South Vietnam. Despite their somewhat disparate backgrounds, each of the women shares the "four virtues" and "three submissions" that constrain Vietnamese women's male-dominated lives. The film combines several elements in unexpected ways. In addition to the "inter-

views," Trinh integrates scenes of folk dances and village life—boats, a wedding, in addition to archival film from the time of French colonialism and newsreels from the Vietnam War. Easy answers are complicated by the inclusion of folk songs and poetry, perhaps alluding to the timelessness of the five women's stories. Likewise, the layers of elements are not arranged to conform to the rules of Western logic; in addition to voice-overs (in English and untranslated Vietnamese), words appear on the screen—either with images or as intertitles. But, often the voice-overs and written text do not "match" the images.

Interestingly, at the beginning of the film it appears that the interviews are real, not staged for the camera. Thus, Trinh's project serves to question the meaning of documentary conventions and the truths documentary filmmakers purport to tell. Her inventive approach in Surname Viet, Given Name Nam echoes Michelle Citron's legendary film, Daughter Rite (1978), which also featured actresses who pose as documentary subjects in order to similarly question the documentary genre's "truth" claims. Likewise, Trinh alludes to her own presence in the filmmaking process via her own voice-over commentary and her use of highly stylized cinematography and editing.

Trinh has often spoken of the hostility Surname has inspired, noting that many viewers have been furious because they were not informed at the film's outset that they were watching performances. But her intention was precisely to highlight viewers' expectations and presuppositions about documentary films. Furthermore, the film complicates simple definitions of the concepts "Third World" and "women"—a complication that extends to other documentaries that endeavor to provide simple explanations of complex terms. In terms of the critical response to Surname, there has also been some hostility. Indeed, the well-known New York Times reviewer Vincent Canby complained that it over-used such photographic effects as stop motion and frame-masking, and for foregrounding Trinh's own presence and "upstaging the information"; thus, he entirely dismissed the film with his contention that it "make[s] one wish the director had never seen a movie or camera." But, a Variety reviewer embraced the film and its provocative style, saying that it had the "haunting resonance of the best documentaries." Though, as Trinh would note, Surname Viet, Given Name Nam is not really a documentary.

—Cynthia Felando

TANAKA, Kinuyo

Japanese director and actress

Born: Tokyo, 23 November 1910. (Other sources cite birthdate as 1907, or 29 December 1909, and birthplace as Shinomoseki City.) **Education:** Attended Tennoji Elementary School, Osaka; studied the musical instrument the *biwa* (a lute-like instrument), gained license 1919. **Family:** Married the director Hiroshi Shimizu, 1929 (divorced 1929); began relationship with the director Kenji Mizoguchi, 1947, which dissolved in the early 1950s. **Career:** 1920-23—member of the Biwa Shojo Kageki all-girl revue, Osaka; 1924—made film debut as actress in *Genroku onna*; 1925—joined Shochiku Kamata Studio, Tokyo; by 1930—had become Japan's top female star; continued acting in prominent roles until 1976, altogether appeared in more than 240 films; 1953—directed her first film, *Koibumi*. **Awards:** Japan Mainichi Eiga Concourse, 1947, 1948, 1957, 1960, 1974; Japan Kinema Jumpo Awards for Best Actress, for *Ballad of Narayama*, 1958, and *Sandakan, House No. 8*, 1974; Best Actress, Berlin Festival, for *Sandakan, House No. 8*, 1975. **Died:** Of a brain tumor, 21 March 1977.

Films as Director

1953 *Koibumi (Love Letters)* (+ ro as landlady)
1955 *Tsuki wa noborinu (The Moon Has Risen)* (+ ro as Yoneya); *Chibusa yo eien nare (The Eternal Breasts)* (+ ro as woman next door)
1958 *Ruten no ohi (The Wandering Princess)* (+ ro)
1961 *Onna bakari no yoru (Girls of the Night)*
1962 *O-gin sama (Love under the Crucifix)*

Films as Actress (selected)

1924 *Genroku onna* (Nomura) (as a maid)
1929 *Daigaku wa detakeredo (I Graduated, But...)* (Ozu) (as Machiko)
1930 *Ojosan (Young Miss)* (Ozu)
1931 *Rakudai wa shitakeredo (I Flunked, But...)* (Ozu) (as Sayoko); *Madamu to nyobo (Madame and Wife)* (Gosho) (as the wife)
1932 *Seishun no yume ima izuko (Where Now Are the Dreams of Youth?)* (Ozu) (as Oshige)
1933 *Izu no odoriko (Dancing Girl of Izu)* (Gosho) (as Kaoru); *Tokyo no onna (A Woman of Tokyo)* (Ozu) (as Harue); *Hijosen no onna (Dragnet Girl)* (Ozu) (as Tokiko)
1935 *Hakoiri musume (An Innocent Maid)* (Ozu); *Okoto to Sasuke (Okoto and Sasuke)* (Shimazu) (as Okoto)
1938 *Aizen katsura (Yearning Laurel)* (Nomura) (as Katsue Takaishi)
1940 *Naniwa ereji (Osaka Elegy)* (Mizoguchi) (as Ochika)

1941 *Kanzashi (Ornamental Hairpin)* (Shimizu)
1944 *Danjuro sandai (Three Generations of Danjuro)* (Mizoguchi) (as Okano); *Rikugun (The Army)* (Kinoshita) (as the mother); *Miyamoto musashi (Musashi Miyamoto)* (Mizoguchi) (as Shinobu)
1946 *Josei no shori (The Victory of Women)* (Mizoguchi) (as Hiroko); *Utamaro o mehuri go-nin no onna (Five Women around Utamaro)* (Mizoguchi) (as Okita)
1947 *Joyu Sumako no koi (Love of Sumako)* (Mizoguchi) (as Sumako Matsui)
1948 *Yoru no onna tachi (Women of the Night)* (Mizoguchi) (as Fusako); *Kaze no naka no mendori (A Hen in the Wind)* (Ozu) (as Tokiko Amamiya)
1949 *Waga koi wa moenu (My Love Has Been Burning)* (Mizoguchi) (as Eiko Hirayama)
1950 *Munekata shimai (The Munekata Sisters)* (Ozu) (as Setsuko)
1951 *Ginza gesho (Ginza Cosmetics)* (Naruse); *Oyu-sama (Miss Oyu)* (Mizoguchi) (title role); *Musashino fujin (Lady Musashino)* (Mizoguchi) (as Michiko Akiyama)
1952 *Nishijin no shimai (Sisters of Nishijin)* (Yoshimura); *Saikaku ichidai onna (Life of Oharu)* (Mizoguchi) (as Oharu); *Okasan (Mother)* (Naruse) (title role)
1953 *Entotsu no mieru basho (Four Chimneys)* (Gosho) (as Hiroko Ogata); *Ugetsu monogotari (Ugetsu)* (Mizoguchi) (as Miyaki)
1954 *Sansho dayu (Sansho the Bailiff)* (Mizoguchi) (as Tamaki); *Uwasa no onna (The Woman of Rumor)* (Mizoguchi) (as Hatsuko Mabuchi)
1956 *Nagareru (Flowing)* (Naruse)
1957 *Jotai wa kanashiku (Geisha in the Old City)* (Inagaki)
1958 *Narayama bushi-ko (Ballad of Narayama)* (Kinoshita) (as Orin)
1959 *Higanbana (Equinox Flower)* (Ozu) (as Kiyoko Hirayama)
1960 *Ototo (Her Brother)* (Ichikawa) (as stepmother)
1962 *Horoki (A Wandering Life; Lonely Lane)* (Naruse)
1963 *Taiheyo hitoribochi (Alone in the Pacific; My Enemy the Sea)* (Ichikawa)
1965 *Akahige (Red Beard)* (Kurosawa) (as Yasumoto's mother)
1974 *Sandakan hachi-ban shokan: Bokyo (Sandakan, House No. 8)* (Kumai) (as Osaki)

Other Film

1952 *Ani imoto (Older Brother, Younger Sister)* (Naruse) (asst d)

Publications on Tanaka

Books

Shindo, Kaneto, *Shoestu Tanaka Kinuyo* (fiction), Tokyo, 1983.
Yamuda, Joanne Y., in *The Women's Companion to International Film,* edited by Annette Kuhn and Susannah Radstone, London, 1990.

Foster, Gwendolyn Audrey, *Women Film Directors: An International Bio-Critical Dictionary,* Westport, Connecticut, 1995.

Articles

Gillett, John, "Kinuyo Tanaka: Portrait of an Actress/Director," in *NFT Programme Booklet* (London), July 1989.
Stimpson, Mansel, "One Woman's Achievement," in *What's On* (London), 12 July 1989.
Dargis, Manohla, in *Village Voice* (New York), 19 January 1993.
Johnson, William, "In Search of a Star: Kinuyo Tanaka," in *Film Comment* (New York), January/February 1994.
Tessier, Max, "Tanaka's Tales of Love and History," in *Cinemaya* (New Delhi), Autumn/Winter 1994.

*   *   *

For a woman to become accepted as a film director has rarely been easy, but in the Japan of the 1950s, a notoriously conventional society with rigidly traditional attitudes to the roles of the sexes, it was all but impossible. Only one woman achieved it, and then chiefly thanks to her status as Japan's most famous and respected cinema actress.

Kinuyo Tanaka's screen career began in the silent era, in 1924; still playing major roles, she made her last film in 1976, the year before she died. She starred in Japan's first talkie and first color film. Altogether she appeared in something more than 240 films and acted with almost every leading director of the period, starring in 10 films for Ozu and 14 for Mizoguchi. Yet despite her prestige she met with fierce opposition when she wanted to direct, and was able to make only six films as director. It says a lot for her talent and determination that not one of them is negligible, and that at their best they stand comparison with the finest films in which she acted.

Tanaka was inspired to take up direction on hearing that some of her female Hollywood contemporaries, such as Ida Lupino and Claudette Colbert, were contemplating directorial careers. In the winter of 1949-50 she visited Hollywood (in itself an audacious move for a Japanese actress) and came back resolved to work behind the camera. Her plan faced resistance from the directors' union, headed by Mizoguchi; though Tanaka's lover at the time, and director of some of the most sensitive films about women ever made (many of them starring Tanaka herself), he insisted that a woman should never direct. Other directors, including the supposed arch-traditionalist Ozu, were more supportive. Naruse took Tanaka on as assistant director to help her learn the ropes, Kinoshita scripted her first film, and Ozu co-scripted her second. (It was typical of Tanaka that even while battling on her own behalf she was ready to assist others. Her cousin, Masaki Kobayashi, always credited her with helping him launch his directorial career in 1952.)

As a director, Tanaka was not a formal innovator, and each of her six films fits into a prevailing genre such as *jidai-geki* (costume drama), *shomin-geki* (lower-middle-class melodrama), or *shin-geki* (realist drama). What distinguishes them is the female sensibility she brings to the established forms. Women, who take the key roles in all her films, are treated not just with sympathy, but with a humorous affection rare in Japanese cinema of the period. In *The Moon Has Risen* family relationships, and specifically father-daughter relationships, display a relaxed spontaneous warmth that feels refreshingly natural; the same goes for *Love under the Crucifix*—even more unusual in a *jidai-geki* film, where stiff formality between generations is the norm.

Two of Tanaka's films, *The Eternal Breasts* and *Girls of the Night,* were scripted by a noted feminist writer, Sukie Tanaka (no relation to the director), but a compassionate feminism suffuses all Kinuyo Tanaka's work. Often the action focuses on a young woman who, like Tanaka herself, refuses to conform to the rigid codes of behavior expected of Japanese women. In *The Moon Has Risen* it is the youngest of three daughters who bucks convention, a situation handled as gentle comedy. Kuniko, the ex-prostitute in *Girls of the Night,* finds herself the victim of prejudice at every level as she tries to build a new life on her own terms. And in *Love under the Crucifix* the heroine, trapped by implacable forces and unable to live the life she wants, chooses the dignity of death as the best available option.

The historical drama *The Wandering Princess* also centers on a woman trapped by convention—although since the princess in question, sister-in-law of the puppet emperor of Manchuria (as in Bertolucci's *The Last Emperor*) stands little chance of rebelling, the film misses something of the vitality of Tanaka's other work. But perhaps her most remarkable film is the clumsily titled *The Eternal Breasts.* Based on the biography of a young woman poet who contracted breast cancer, it brings to its subject a clear-eyed, unflinching physicality. Chilling, clinical images convey Fumiko's vulnerability and fear at the invasion of her body, first by the disease and then by a double mastectomy; while Tanaka celebrates the surge of sexuality her heroine experiences after the operation as a brief, defiant assertion of life and erotic joy in the face of approaching death.

Unlike many actor-directors, Tanaka never used her films to give herself plum starring roles. In the first three she takes small roles, scarcely even cameos, and in the others she does not appear at all. But all her films as director share the qualities of her screen persona (which by all accounts reflected her personality in real life): intelligent, tenacious, versatile, emotionally responsive, and unconcerned with spurious glamour. For all her tenacity, though, Tanaka finally abandoned the struggle to build a directorial career in the face of professional hostility and public indifference. Her last film, *Love under the Crucifix,* was her most ambitious in production terms, with 'scope, color, and a substantial historical subject set in a vividly re-created 16th century. Originally planned to follow *The Eternal Breasts,* it took six years to bring to the screen and, like its predecessors, met with no great response at the box office. Following its heroine's example, Tanaka chose to make a dignified exit, and in any case had her acting career. It would be many years before any other Japanese woman director ventured to follow her lead.

—Philip Kemp

THE THIN LINE
(The Thin Blue Line)
Canada, 1977
Directors: Janis Cole and Holly Dale

Production: Spectrum Films; color, 16mm; running time: 32 minutes. Released 1977. Filmed in Penetanguishene, Ontario, Canada. Cost: $12,000.

Producers: Janis Cole and Holly Dale; **photography:** John Clement and Joe Sutherland; **editors:** Janis Cole and Holly Dale; **narration:** Katherine Osborne.

Publications

Articles

Delaney, Marshall, "Brutal Art from Mean Streets," in *Saturday Night* (Toronto), June 1978.
Nelson, Joyce, in *Cinema Canada* (Montreal), September/October 1978.
"Street People," interview with G. C. Koller, in *Cinema Canada* (Montreal), September/October 1978.
Neher, Jack, "Social Concerns," in *Film News* (New York), Summer 1979.

* * *

The best-known film of Canadian filmmakers Janis Cole and Holly Dale is *The Thin Line,* about the maximum-security mental-health center at Penetang Prison in Ontario, and the treatment that "criminally insane" offenders receive there. The film is an extraordinary achievement, given its challenging subject matter and the youth of its makers: Cole and Dale were both 22 when they made it. They prepared for the project by spending six months at the facility in order to gain the friendship and confidence of inmate patients and therapists, and to obtain the administrators' permission to film. Then, partly supported by a $10,000 Canada Council grant they shot the documentary's footage. (They spent $2,000 of their own money to complete the film.) Cole and Dale used interviews and therapy sessions to reveal the understanding, humanity, and reality of men who are among society's most dangerous criminals. Interestingly, the film focuses on the stories of the inmates rather than on the administrators, therapists, and guards. Thus, it is the inmates—who are both threatening and reassuring—who judge the benefits of the institution's therapy methods and who enumerate the cruelties and inadequacies of the rest of Canada's penal system.

The filmmakers introduce viewers to several men who have perpetrated brutal crimes, including armed robbery, rape, assault, and murder, and who describe the dismal childhood experiences that likely influenced their criminal origins: "I was locked in a closet for a day-and-a-half at a time; while in the closet I had fantasies about killing my dad." Another man describes his criminal urge forthrightly: "Well it was a robbery. Yet I think it was part of my criminal nature to commit the ultimate crime—murder; the one you can be most respected for in the penitentiary and criminal society." Further, the men offer chilling confessions and poignant, crucial insights: "I stabbed the guy 42 times—in a way I was trying to kill myself." Indeed, many of the inmates speak of unhappy, deprived, and loveless early childhoods, especially of weak or absent fathers. This point is vividly underscored by the introduction of one young man's sad mother who is apparently unable to display any affection for her eight children, and who relates the difficulties of raising them alone. Yet the inmates also emphasize their desire to change with the help of therapy. Drug and alcohol treatment sessions reveal the processes by which patients begin to uncover why they committed their crimes.

Despite its difficult subject and its short length, the film retains Cole and Dale's optimism about the capacity of humans to recognize and work to solve their problems. They productively challenge viewers' likely preconceptions by focusing on thoughtful men working to analyze their problems, identify their weaknesses, and learn the social and psychological underpinnings of their criminal misdeeds. Moreover, the filmmakers emphasize the men's need for mutual caring, especially with regard to therapeutic methods. The patients endorse one treatment method in particular, a drastic and seemingly excessively grueling encounter session involving emotional release that is induced by alcohol or drugs, among other things. It takes place in a space of safety closely watched by other inmates, called the Capsule: a small isolation room into which two patients volunteer to be locked for two weeks—using an open toilet and taking nourishment through straws placed in the walls. Given speed, stripped to the waist, they talk almost continuously. For 24 hours each day, they are watched by the other patients and videotaped. Despite its bracing rigors, the patients believe that it helps them to resolve identity and other psychological problems.

Cole and Dale admittedly recognized that their positive approach to the Penetang facility might prompt criticism of *The Thin Line*; however, in general, it was well-received. Mental health professionals, for example, praised the film as one of the very few to treat prison rehabilitation programs positively. Jack Neher, a professional at the Mental Health Film Board and a film producer, reviewed the film and enthusiastically endorsed it, recommending it for criminology and social psychology courses and discussion groups because it shows the promising possibilities of careful, committed, humane treatment. Movie critics praised it as "threatening and reassuring," unlike most documentaries about mental-health facilities. Among its many strengths is the value it assigns to love, particularly in a seemingly hopeless place. In addition, it serves to question more conventional treatments for insanity. For example, Penetang does not tranquilize patients; rather it gives them speed and alcohol to enable them to confront their problems. That is, the facility attempts to treat the inmates' problems, though as one critic noted, in prisons criminal behavior is often reinforced.

Clearly, one goal of Cole and Dale was to humanize the people we generally only hear about, often in conjunction with discussions of capital punishment. *The Thin Line* also suggests the shortcomings of the larger penal system. That is, before arriving at Penetang, many of the men have been through several penal systems, which they recall candidly. In particular, they condemn the hostility of guards at most maximum security prisons: "The guards lined up with billy bats and beat us going down the hall all the way to our cells."

A number of critics attributed Cole and Dale's courage in undertaking *The Thin Line* to their "tough street backgrounds." And, the filmmakers themselves were forthright about their inspiration. As they explained, their similar backgrounds gave them a special bond and a unique perspective; i.e., they grew up in places that had unusual characters that "you don't meet in a nice middle class, suburban type of living situation. We understand criminals, hoods, people who had sex hangups, street people." Thus, according to Cole and Dale, their interest in documentary films is simple: "Reality is a lot more interesting than trying to write dramas about life."

—Cynthia Felando

T'OU-PEN NU-HAI

(Boat People; Tou Bun No Hoi)
Hong Kong, 1982
Director: Ann Hui

Production: Bluebird Movie Enterprises, Ltd.; color; 35 mm; running time: 111 minutes. Released 1982 in Hong Kong; 1983 elsewhere.

Producer: Chui Po-Chu; **screenplay:** K. C. Chiu; **story:** Tien Kor; **photography:** Chung Chi-Man; **editor:** Wong Yee-Sun; **music:** Law Wing-Fai.

Cast: George Lam Chi-Cheung (*Akutagawa*); Cora Miao (*The Madame*); Season Ma (*Cam Nuong*); Andy Lau (*To Minh*); Paul Chung (*Ah Thanh*); Wong Shau-Him (*Inoue*); Qu Mengshi (*Officer Nguyen*); Jia Meiying (*Comrade Le*); Lin Shujin (*Comrade Vu*); Hao Jialin (*Cam Nuong's Mother*).

Awards: Hong Kong Film Awards, Best Picture, Director, Screenplay, New Artist (Ma), and Art Direction; and New York Film Festival Award.

Publications

Articles

"*Boat People,*" in *Variety* (New York), 3 November 1982.

Mosier, J., "Politics and Excellence at Cannes," in *New Orleans Review,* no. 4, 1983.

Niogret, H., "Entretien avec Ann Hui," in *Positif* (Paris), May 1983.

Tobin, Y., "Pres du Vietnam," in *Positif* (Paris), May 1983.

Fougeres, R., "*Boat People* (Retour a Danang), in *Ciné Revue* (Brussels), 19 May 1983.

Tatum, C., "*Boat People,*" in *Visions* (Brussels), Summer 1983.

Roy, J., "*Boat People,*" in *Cinema 83* (Paris), July/August 1983.

Tesson, C., "Tu n'as rien vu a Da-nang," in *Cahiers du Cinéma* (Paris), September 1983.

Maslin, Janet, "Film Festival: Vietnam's Boat People," in *New York Times,* 27 September 1983; review reprinted 13 November 1983.

Kennedy, Harlan, "*Boat People,*" in *Film Comment* (New York), September/October 1983.

Shafransky, Renee, "Festival Film: Politics without History," in *Village Voice* (New York), 4 October 1983.

Sarris, Andrew, "Films in Focus: Art, Politics, and, Oh Yes, Talent," in *Village Voice* (New York), 11 October 1983.

"Hui Sees Fest-Fave *Boat People* as 'Non-Political' Cry for Rights," in *Variety* (New York), 12 October 1983.

Tobias, M., "*Boat People,*" in *Variety* (New York), 9 November 1983.

Corliss, Richard, "Cinema: Faraway Place," in *Time* (New York), 14 November 1983.

Hoberman, J., "Film: Far from Vietnam," in *Village Voice* (New York), 22 November 1983.

Sarris, Andrew, "Films in Focus: The Age of the Image," in *Village Voice* (New York), 22 November 1983.

"*Boat People,*" in *Ciné Revue* (Brussels), 24 November 1983.

Harvey, Stephen, "The 21st New York Film Festival: The Age of Calligraphy," in *Film Comment* (New York), November/December 1983.

Stein, Elliott, "The 21st New York Film Festival: Forbidden Revelations," in *Film Comment* (New York), November/December 1983.

Tarshis, J., "*Boat People,*" in *Film Journal* (New York), November/December 1983.

Reed, Rex, in *New York Post,* 14 November 1983.

Cuel, F., "*Boat People,*" in *Cinématographe* (Paris), December 1983.

Magny, J., "*Boat People,*" in *Cinéma 83* (Paris), December 1983.

Tessier, M., "*Boat People* (Passeport pour l'enfer)," in *Revue du Cinéma* (Paris), December 1983.

Ansen, David, "Movies: Death Watch," in *Newsweek* (New York), 5 December 1983.

Denby, David, in *New York Magazine* (New York), 5 December 1983.

Tournes, A., "*Boat People,*" in *Jeune Cinéma* (Paris), December 1983/January 1984.

Chevalier, J., "*Boat People,*" in *Revue du Cinéma* (Paris), vol. XXIX, 1984.

Gillett, John, and Mel Tobias, "Two Views of *T'ou-Pen Nu-Hai,*" in *International Film Guide* (London), 1984.

Jaehne, Karen, "*Boat People:* An Interview with Ann Hui," in *Cineaste* (New York), no. 2, 1984.

Sonet, H., and F. Jongen, "Derangeant vous avez dit derangeant...," in *Visions* (Brussels), 15 January 1984.

Marx, R., "*Boat People,*" in *Box Office* (Hollywood), 28 February 1984.

Thomas, Kevin, in *Los Angeles Times,* 11 April 1984.

Elhem, P., and C. Tatum, "Ann Hui: simple comme une tragedie," in *Visions* (Brussels), 15 April 1984.

Eysakkers, H., "*Boat People,*" in *Andere Sinema* (Antwerp), May/June 1984.

Goegbeur, E., "*Boat People,*" in *Film en Televisie* (Brussels), July/August 1984.

Francia, L. H., "Off-screen: Ann Hui: Nothing Is What It Seems," in *Village Voice* (New York), 21 April 1987.

* * *

The very existence of *Boat People* serves as evidence that not all products of the Hong Kong film industry are mindless escapist entertainment and imitations of Hollywood action-adventure fare. That the film was artistically and commercially successful only added to its luster, and helped cement the international reputation of its director, Ann Hui.

The scenario of *Boat People* reflects Hui's preoccupation with cultural displacement, and the impact on characters who become uprooted as they relocate from one nation and society to another. In fact, her previous feature, *The Story of Woo Viet,* charts the plight of an ex-South Vietnamese soldier who flees a Hong Kong refugee camp for Manila, where he becomes enmeshed in the local underworld.

Boat People is a grim, controversial depiction of a nation in despair, which Hui researched by interviewing Vietnamese boat people who began arriving in Hong Kong during the late 1970s. It chronicles the experiences of Akutagawa (George Lam Chi-Cheung), a Japanese photojournalist who returns to Vietnam three years after covering the 1975 victory march in honor of the liberation of Da Nang. What he finds is not an emancipated people, free of war and economic strife and enjoying the fruits of their "liberation." Instead, he unearths a nation wallowing in poverty, despair, and, even more telling, rampant hypocrisy.

During his trip, Akutagawa is guided by a representative of Vietnam's Cultural Bureau, whose mission is to show him only what she wants him to see. She first accompanies him to a New Economic Zone, in the vicinity of Da Nang, where he is exposed to propaganda: a group of cheerful schoolchildren who sing the praises of "Chairman Ho." At first, Akutagawa is ecstatic. He did not expect to return to this war-torn nation and find a new generation so hearty and content.

During the course of *Boat People,* Akutagawa moves about the country more freely and comes to realize that this image is a facade. Class distinctions glaringly exist in the "new" Vietnam; those who are poor, and must depend only on their own resources, have practically no chance to survive (let alone prosper). They have been left to languish and be victimized by widespread corruption and a gross abuse of human rights.

Most significantly, Akutagawa befriends Cam Nuong (Season Ma), a 14-year-old Da Nang girl who becomes his true guide through the "new" Vietnam. Cam's father had died during the war. Her mother has toiled as a prostitute; her kid brother is a rough-and-tumble, street-smart urchin who spouts American slang; the identity of the father of her infant brother is a mystery. In the film's most trenchant and unforgettable sequence, Cam Nuong escorts Akutagawa to a "chicken farm," where youngsters scavenge for valuables which may have been left on the rotting bodies of the freshly executed.

Among the other characters with whom Akutagawa mixes are "The Madame" (Cora Miao), an aging restaurant proprietress who has outlasted the Japanese, French, and Americans; and To Minh (Andy Lau), her boyfriend, who fantasizes about escaping Vietnam and setting her up in business elsewhere.

Akutagawa eventually backtracks to the same New Economic Zone seen at the beginning, where he discovers the same "happy" children living in squalor. That particular Zone, in fact, is specially designed for viewing by foreigners. New Economic Zones really are concentration camps for the politically incorrect, the most unfortunate of whom get to take apart land mines left over from the war.

There is a lone alternative for these sorrowful individuals: become "boat people," passengers on illegal vessels leaving Vietnam and heading for Hong Kong. But this is a hazardous and, often, fatal undertaking, as evidenced by the experience of To Minh, who (along with other refugees) is shot while trying to escape his homeland.

Boat People is a potent, uncompromising critique of life in postwar Vietnam. Scenes of the tranquil, beautiful Asian landscape are contrasted to the harsh and ugly reality of its characters, as observed in semidocumentary style through the eyes, lens, and sensibility of Akutagawa. As one would expect, the film was not shot on location, rather, it was filmed on Hainan Island and in the city of Zhanjiang, in cooperation with the Chinese government, and is a Hong Kong-Chinese co-production. One of the ironies of *Boat People* is that it is a story of a communist government's oppression against its citizenry, and it was made in cooperation with Chinese authorities who so often have been accused of similar tyranny.

Despite protests from the Vietnam government, *Boat People* was screened at the 1983 Cannes Film Festival. At Cannes, there was much controversy over the crux of its scenario and its implication that the Vietnamese state was violating the human rights of its most powerless citizens—who in turn were attempting to depart their homeland notwithstanding the danger and uncertainty of their becoming boat people.

Hui's view of the film may be summed up in the headline of a *Variety* piece reporting the controversy: "Hui Sees Fest-Fave *Boat People* as 'Non-Political' Cry for Rights." Her observation may be contrasted to critic David Ansen describing the film as "unabashedly one-sided"; J. Hoberman calling it "the most crudely anti-Communist agitprop since *The Green Berets*"; and Renee Shafransky labeling it "a lopsided, irresponsible, and reactionary picture of Vietnamese society."

Yet Ansen also characterized *Boat People* as "ferociously visceral," and Andrew Sarris noted that, while "Hui and her collaborators may not know beans about the history, politics, and economy of Vietnam (and) may have exaggerated the extent of the oppressiveness...they have not invented their victims. The boat people

are real even though many of us would like to pretend that they do not exist."

—Rob Edelman

TOYE, Wendy
British director

Born: London, 1 May 1917. **Career:** 1921—began working as a professional dancer, and performed at Albert Hall; 1927—staged a ballet, *Japanese Legend of the Rainbow,* at the London Palladium; 1930s—danced, choreographed, and acted on the London stage; late 1930s—performed on BBC television; 1946—began directing and producing plays and ballets for Sadler Wells, the Old Vic, and other British theater companies; 1947—formed her own ballet company, Ballet-Hoo de Wendy Toye; 1950—directed *Peter Pan* on stage in the United States; 1953—directed her first short film, *The Stranger Left No Card*; 1954—directed her first feature, *The Teckman Mystery*; 1950s-90s—directed and produced scores of stage plays, operas, operettas, and television productions. **Awards:** Best Short Fiction Film, Cannes Film Festival, for *The Stranger Left No Card,* 1953; awarded the Order of the British Empire, 1992. **Address:** Flat 5, 95 Lower Sloane Street, London LW1W S3Z, England.

Films as Director

1953   *The Stranger Left No Card* (short)
1954   *The Teckman Mystery*
1955   "In the Picture" ep. of *Three Cases of Murder*; *Raising a Riot*; *All for Mary*
1956   *On the Twelfth Day* (short)
1957   *True as a Turtle*
1962   *We Are in the Navy Now* (*We Joined the Navy*)
1963   *The King's Breakfast* (short)

Other Films

1931   *Dance Pretty Lady* (Asquith) (ro)
1935   *Invitation to the Waltz* (Herzbach) (ro as Signora Picci, choreographer)
1945   *I'll Be Your Sweetheart* (Guest) (ro)
1946   *Piccadilly Incident* (Wilcox) (choreographer)
1986   *Barnum!* (Coe and T. Hughes) (assoc pr)

Publications on Toye

Books

Dixon, Wheeler Winston, editor, *Re-Viewing British Cinema, 1900-1992: Essays and Interviews,* Albany, New York, 1994.
Foster, Gwendolyn Audrey, *Women Film Directors: An International Bio-Critical Dictionary,* Westport, Connecticut, 1995.

Articles

Paskin, S., "A Delicate but Insistent Trail of Confetti ...," in *Monthly Film Bulletin* (London), August 1986.

Wendy Toye

Paskin, S., "A Picasso for Every Season," in *Monthly Film Bulletin* (London), August 1986.

Cook, P., and S. Paskin, "The Director Left No Card—Wendy Toye," in *Monthly Film Bulletin* (London), September 1986.

Aude, F., "Creteil 1990," in *Positif* (Paris), January 1991.

Merz, Caroline, "The Tension of Genre: Wendy Toye and Muriel Box," in *Film Criticism* (Meadville, Pennsylvania), no.1/2, 1991/92.

Film

Wendy Toye and Sally Potter: Two Directors, directed by Newson, 1985.

* * *

Among the directors active in the British film industry during the 1950s were David Lean, Michael Powell, Emeric Pressburger, Carol Reed, Robert Hamer, Charles Crichton, Henry Cornelius, Alexander MacKendrick, John and Roy Boulting, Basil Dearden, Anthony Asquith, Ronald Neame, Guy Hamilton, Roy Ward Baker, Brian Desmond Hurst, Michael Anderson, Ralph Thomas ... and Wendy Toye.

Toye was not the only woman to direct a British film during the decade. Muriel Box (who, in the mid-1940s, won an Academy Award for co-scripting *The Seventh Veil* with her then-husband, Sydney Box) made over a dozen shorts and features between 1952 and 1964. Animator/producer Joy Batchelor and her husband, John Halas, created (among other films) an animated feature version of George Orwell's *Animal Farm* in 1954. Nevertheless, women directors back then practically were invisible, in England as well as elsewhere— and Toye only was to direct films for a decade, beginning in 1953.

Toye had no aspirations to make films. Her background was as a dancer/choreographer/dance and theater director, and she became involved with filmmaking due to the encouragement of producer Alexander Korda. Collectively, her feature films are unexceptional; none are among the very best British films produced during the decade. Her features include *The Teckman Mystery*, a drama about a writer investigating the supposedly accidental death of a pilot during a test flight, and a quartet of comedies: *Raising a Riot*, in which a wife/mother goes off to care for a sick parent, leaving her befuddled mate to cope with their hyperactive children; *All for Mary*, in which the title character is pursued by various men while on a Swiss vacation; *True as a Turtle*, about newlyweds who spend their honeymoon aboard a beat-up yacht; and her last feature, *We Are in the Navy Now*, in which a navy commander must reestablish his reputation after being relegated to training cadets.

It is tempting to decipher a subtle feminist agenda in *Raising a Riot*, in which a male character takes on a woman's role. After cooking, shopping, cleaning, and disciplining the children, this househusband declares, on his wife's return, "I wouldn't be a woman if the entire United Nations got down on their knees and begged me." In countless 1950s British comedies, however, male characters were feminized in order to evoke laughter. *Raising a Riot*, with its Brit-as-twit main character, is fashioned as a commercial entertainment. That it was directed by a woman is coincidental.

By far, Toye's best films were her short films. "In the Picture," her segment in *Three Cases of Murder*, is an eerie, surreal tale of terror in which a dead artist "resides" inside a house depicted in one of his paintings, which hangs in a museum. He emerges from the painting and lures a museum guide into it, and to his doom. *The Stranger Left No Card*, Toye's directorial debut—which she remade for television

in 1981—is her finest overall work: a nifty yarn about a murderous outsider who arrives in a village and is taken in by the citizenry. Jean Cocteau dubbed *The Stranger Left No Card* a masterpiece, while British film critic Leslie Halliwell labeled it a "smart little trick film which as a novelty has not been surpassed." Toye employed her ballet expertise in *On the Twelfth Day*, a dance-oriented visualization of the song "The Twelve Days of Christmas," which Halliwell called "a refreshing and extravagant novelty."

Toye remained active as a stage director well into the 1990s—30-plus years after making her last film. In retrospect, even her best screen work seems a footnote to her long and prolific stage career.

—Rob Edelman

TREUT, Monika
German director

Born: Dusseldorf, Germany, 6 April 1954. **Education:** Studied philosophy and literature in college, earning a Ph.D in literature, with a dissertation on the depiction of women in the Marquis de Sade's *Juliette* and Leopold von Sacher-Masoch's *Venus in Furs*. **Career:** 1970s-early 1980s—worked as an avant-garde performance artist, and made videos; 1985—co-directed *Verfuhrung: Die Grausame Frau*, her controversial feature debut, with Elfi Mikesch; co-founded the Women's Media Centre at Bildwechsel; 1996—visiting instructor at Vassar College.

Films as Director

1980	*Space Chaser* (short) (co-d)
1981	*Ich Brauche unbedingt Kommunikation* (*I Really Need Communication*) (short); *Bitchband* (short)
1983	*Bondage* (short)
1985	*Verfuhrung: Die grausame Frau* (*Seduction: The Cruel Woman*) (co-d with Mikesch, + co-sc, co-pr, video ph)
1988	*Die Jungfrauen Maschine* (*The Virgin Machine*) (+ sc, pr)
1989	*Annie* (short)
1991	*My Father Is Coming* (+ co-sc, co-pr)
1992	*Dr. Paglia* (short); *Max* (short); *Female Misbehavior* (+ pr)
1994	"Taboo Parlor" ep. of *Erotique* (+ sc, co-pr)
1996	*Danish Girls Show Everything*
1997	*Didn't Do It for Love*

Film as Actress

1993	*Domenica* (Kern) (as social worker)

Publications by Treut

Books

Die grausame Frau. zum Frauenbild bei de Sade und Sacher-Masoch [The Cruel Woman: the Portrayal of Women in de Sade and Sacher-Masoch], Basel, 1984.

"*Female Misbehavior*," in *Feminisms in the Cinema*, edited by Laura Pietropaolo and Ada Testaferri, Bloomington, Indiana, 1995.

Articles

"Man to Man," in *Sight and Sound* (London), May 1994.

"From 'Taboo Parlor' to Porn and Passing," interview with Gerd Gemuder, Alice Kuzniar, and Klaus Phillips, in *Film Quarterly* (Berkeley), Spring 1997.

Publications on Treut

Books

Beinstein, Krista, *Obszone Frauen: Mit Einen Essay v. Monika Treut,* Wein, 1986.

Foster, Gwendolyn Audrey, *Women Film Directors: An International Bio-Critical Dictionary,* Westport, Connecticut, 1995.

Articles

Carr, C., "Film: The Gay Film Festival: The Compleat Deviant," in *Village Voice* (New York), 14 January 1986.

Ang, I., and K. Manning, "De superieure lust van het sadomasochismo," in *Skrien* (Amsterdam), April/May 1986.

Carr, C., "Love Hurts," in *Village Voice* (New York), 28 February 1989.

Willis, Holly, "The Majestic Power of Play," in *Spectator* (Los Angeles), no. 2, 1991.

Minkowwitz, D., "Crossover Dreams," in *Village Voice* (New York), 10 December 1991.

Fox, Steve, "Coming to America," in *Cineaste* (New York), Winter 1992.

Knight, Julia, "Off Our Backs," in *Sight and Sound* (London), June 1992.

Knight, Julia, "*Female Misbehavior*: The Cinema of Monika Treut," in *Women and Film: A Sight and Sound Reader,* edited by Pam Cook and Philip Dodd, Philadelphia, 1993.

Vahtera, H., "Pahat niset," in *Filmihullu* (Helsinki), no. 5, 1993.

Dargis, Manhola, "*Female Misbehavior,*" in *Village Voice* (New York), 27 April 1993.

Hickethier, K., "*Female Misbehavior,*" in *EPD Film* (Frankfurt), May 1993.

Asselberghs, H., "*Female Misbehavior,*" in *Andere Sinema* (Antwerp), May/June 1993.

Saalfield, C., "Monika Treut: Documentarian," in *Independent* (New York), October 1993.

Eurrard, J., "Les intellectuels allemands ne savent plus ce qui se passe, il sont silencieux, sous le choc," in *Ciné-Bulles* (Montreal), no. 2, 1994.

Laden, T., and J. Painter, "Dirty Games," in *Film Threat* (Beverly Hills), June 1994.

* * *

To her supporters, the films of Monika Treut are daring and forceful, politically radical and groundbreaking in the manner in which they depict female sexuality. Her detractors, meanwhile, consider her most extreme works trashy and exploitive, even pornographic. These wildly divergent views crystallized during the world premiere, at the 1985 Berlin Film Festival, of this provocative filmmaker's very first feature: *Seduction: The Cruel Woman* (inspired by Sacher-Masoch's *Venus in Furs* and co-directed with her frequent collaborator, Elfi Mikesch), which was greeted with a combination of hearty applause and massive walkouts.

In her films, Treut suggests alternative—and highly radical—ideas and actions for fulfilling one's emotional needs. She portrays women as sexual aggressors. Men either are extraneous or undesirable sexually; they are completely missing from (and thus irrelevant to) sexual activity, or are victimized by the actions of women. Furthermore, a woman's sexual assertiveness is not depicted simply by having the female character on top of the male during the sexual act. In *Seduction: The Cruel Woman,* the main character is Wanda, an aloof, imperturbable dominatrix who operates a sex-performance gallery; she entices potential lovers of both sexes to her sanctuary of torture, where they become willing players in her sadistic erotic games. "It is my profession, being cruel," Wanda declares, simply and to-the-point.

The Virgin Machine and *My Father Is Coming* are stories of women who are struggling to find their identities, as well as someone to love. In the former, the main character, Dorothee, is addicted to romantic love, which only has brought her disappointment. She commences a sexual voyage that, geographically speaking, takes her from Hamburg to San Francisco. As she experiences various erotic encounters, she comes to grasp the lesbian aspect of her makeup.

My Father Is Coming is the story of Vicky, a German living in New York who waits tables while struggling to succeed as an actress. Like Dorothee, Vicky is desperate to find love. Her potential romantic partners are male—a female-to-male transsexual—and female. But more to the point, she has communicated to her father that she is happily married and a successful actress, and feels she must put up a front when he comes to New York for a visit. At its best, *My Father Is Coming* is an astute observation of the significance of learning to accept who you are, along with the diversity in others.

Female Misbehavior consists of four of Treut's short films: *Bondage,* in which a lesbian expounds on the enjoyment and feelings of security she experiences in her sadomasochistic contacts; *Annie,* in which porn star/performance artist/sexual activist Annie Sprinkle (who also is featured in *My Father Is Coming*) takes the viewer on a tour of her cervix; *Dr. Paglia,* an interview with Camille Paglia, the controversial academic, author, and egocentric "feminist fatale"; and *Max,* featuring ex-lesbian Anita, whose sex-change operation transformed her into Max, a heterosexual male.

"Taboo Parlor," Treut's episode in *Erotique* (which includes three other short films, directed by Lizzie Borden, Ana Maria Magalhaes, and Clara Law), is an allegory about women's sexual power. It involves two lesbian lovers, Claire and Julia, who pick up Victor, a "100 per cent hetero" hunk, in a S&M bar. Victor's sexual presence is more brutal than amorous, and his sense of eroticism is thus sorely limited; he is none-too-pleased when Claire straps on a dildo and initiates anal intercourse with him. Treut depicts most of the other males on screen as bystanders, who clearly feel left out as they observe Claire and Julia kissing by a swimming pool or in the throes of foreplay with Victor on a public bus.

Monika Treut's films shatter conceptions of "normal" sexuality. Such taboos as lesbianism, sadomasochism, and transsexuality are depicted frankly, and sympathetically. An unlikely union of antipornography feminists and members of the religious right might join in condemning Treut because of her stance that pornography is emotionally healthy for women as long as it is female-controlled. In *The Virgin Machine,* Dorothee has an amusing encounter with Susie Sexpert, a pseudonym for author-editor-performer-activist-sex educator Susie Bright, who displays an array of sex toys and passes out flyers advertising for-women-only strip shows featuring female strippers. Afterwards, Dorothee declares, "The sex industry is lousy because women have no say. Feminists should go there instead of being uptight. It's the perfect place to live out their fantasies."

On a more emotional level, Treut examines what it means to fall in love, or be feminine, or feel desire; in her films, characters who search for romantic love are destined to find only frustration. This is articulated in the very first bit of dialogue in *The Virgin Machine*: "For many lambs, love is worse than going to slaughter." What Treut offers as an antithesis to romantic love is passion and eroticism, as exemplified by a line from *Seduction: The Cruel Woman*: "Happiness consists of feeling different passions, and living different passions."

—Rob Edelman

TRINH T. Minh-Ha
American director

Born: Trinh Thi Minh-Ha, in Vietnam, 1953; came to the United States in 1970. **Education:** Studied music composition, ethnomusicology, and French literature at the University of Illinois, Champaign-Urbana, received M.F.A. and Ph.D. degrees. **Career:** Before becoming a filmmaker, she completed three years of ethnographic field research in West Africa and co-directed a research expedition there for the Research Expedition Program of the University of California, Berkeley; 1981—published first book *Un Art Sans Oeuvre*; 1982—completed first film *Reassemblage*; 1985—with Jean-Paul Bourdier published a second book (*African Spaces: Designs for Living in Upper Volta*) and made a closely related film (*Naked Spaces: Living Is Round*); from 1994—Film and Women's Studies professor at the University of California, Berkeley; 1995—completed her first fiction and 35mm feature film, *A Tale of Love*. **Awards:** Blue Ribbon Award for Best Experimental Feature, American International Film Festival, and Golden Athena Award for Best Feature Documentary, Athens International Film Festival, for *Naked Spaces*, 1985; Merit Award, Bombay International Film Festival, Film as Art Award, Society for the Encouragement of Contemporary Art, San Francisco Museum of Modern Art, and the Blue Ribbon Award, American Film and Video Festival, for *Surname Viet, Given Name Nam*; Best Documentary Cinematography, Sundance Film Festival, and Best Feature Documentary Award, Athens International Film Festival, for *Shoot for the Contents*, 1991; Maya Deren Award, American Film Institute, 1991. **Address:** Women's Studies Department, 2241 College #4, University of California, Berkeley, CA 94720, U.S.A.

Films as Director

1982   *Reassemblage* (+ pr, sc, ed)
1985   *Naked Spaces: Living Is Round* (+ pr, sc, ed)
1989   **Surname Viet, Given Name Nam** (+ pr, sc, ed)
1991   *Shoot for the Contents* (+ sc, ed)
1995   *A Tale of Love* (co-d with Bourdier, + pr, sc, ed)

Publications by Trinh

Books

Un Art Sans Oeuvre, or, L'anonymat dans les arts contemporains, Lathrup Village, Michigan, 1981.

With Bourdier, Jean-Paul, *African Spaces: Designs for Living in Upper Volta,* New York, 1985.
Woman, Native, Other: Writing Postcoloniality and Feminism, Bloomington, Indiana, 1989.
When the Moon Waxes Red: Representation, Gender, and Cultural Politics, New York, 1991.
Framer Framed, New York, 1992.
With Bourdier, Jean-Paul, *Drawn from African Dwellings,* Bloomington, Indiana, 1996.

Articles

"Mechanical Eye, Electronic Ear and the Lure of Authenticity," in *Wide Angle* (Athens, Ohio), vol. 6, no. 2, 1984.
Interview with Constance Penley and Andrew Ross, in *Camera Obscura* (Los Angeles), Spring/Summer 1985.
"*Reassemblage,*" in *Camera Obscura* (Los Angeles), Spring/Summer 1985.
"*Naked Spaces: Living Is Round,*" in *Motion Picture* (New York), no. 1, 1986.
"Questions of Images and Politics," in *Independent* (New York), May 1987.
Interview with R. Stephenson, in *Millennium* (New York), Fall/Winter 1987.
"Outside in Inside Out," in *Questions of Third Cinema,* edited by Jim Pines and Paul Willemen, London, 1989.
"*A Tale of Love,* interview with Gwendolyn Foster, in *Film Criticism* (Meadville, Pennsylvania), Spring 1997.

Publications on Trinh

Books

Mayne, Judith, *The Woman at the Keyhole: Feminism and Women's Cinema,* Bloomington, Indiana, 1990.
Foster, Gwendolyn Audrey, *Women Film Directors: An International Bio-Critical Dictionary,* Westport, Connecticut, 1995.
Foster, Gwendolyn Audrey, *Women Filmmakers of the African and Asian Diaspora,* Carbondale, Illinois, 1997.

Articles

Hulser, K., "Ways of Seeing Senegal," in *Independent* (New York), December 1983.
Peckham, L., "Peripheral Vision. Looking at the West through *Reassemblage,*" in *Cinematograph* (San Francisco), no. 2, 1986.
Kenny, L., "Theorizing Feminist Documentary," in *Afterimage,* April 1986.
Scheibler, S., "When I Am Silent, It Projects," in *USC Spectator* (Los Angeles), vol. 7, no. 2, 1987.

* * *

Originally trained as a musical composer, Trinh T. Minh-ha is a world-renowned feminist filmmaker, theorist, writer, and poet who is considered an expert on avant-garde and Third World, postcolonial film theory. Emigrating from Vietnam at the age of 17, she has developed a wide range of interests and talents that she consistently brings to her film work. Like the "theory films" of 1970's feminist filmmakers, Trinh's films offer theoretical musings into the subject of women, to which she adds the interrelated issue of ethnicity. She is known for such unique experimental documentaries as *Reassemblage,* about Senegalese village women and the aims of ethnography; *Surname Viet, Given Name Nam,* a film about identity and culture and the struggle of Vietnamese women; and *Shoot for the Contents,* a film about culture, art, and politics in China.

Trinh's films consistently prompt impassioned discussions, which have included denunciations of their "subjectivity," as well as praise for their refusals to adhere to ethnographic and documentary film conventions. That is, she generally blurs the line between fiction and documentary, thus questioning the meanings and expectations of audiences (and filmmakers) about both kinds of filmmaking practices. Moreover, she seeks not only to question the notion of "ethnic identity" but also of "female identity"—indeed, she has said she considers them as one issue that has been artificially separated. Trinh's affinity for music is also palpable in her films; she notes that her films' "non-expressive, non-melodic, non-narrative" aspects require a different kind of attention from its viewers, which hears "sound as sound, word as word, and sees images as image."

Her first film, *Reassemblage,* is a dynamic short film that refuses either to fit neatly into the categories of "documentary" or "fiction," or to provide easy answers to the questions it poses. Its style is highly experimental, using jump cuts, black leader, unfinished pans, fragmented compositions, multiple framings, and repetition. Accordingly, it challenges and comments on both the conventions of documentary film and ethnographic methodology. The soundtrack asks a suggestive question, "What can we expect from ethnology?" Later, it declares, "Filming in Africa means for many of us, colorful images, naked breast women, exotic dances and fearful rites, the unusual." Accordingly, Trinh dismisses the notion of "objectivity" among ethnographers who cannot help but express their personal values in their examinations of the "other," and she implies that ethnographers are unacknowledged voyeurs, not bias-free scientists.

Naked Spaces: Living Is Round is a feature-length film (Trinh calls it "exactly long") that was shot in rural Senegal, Mauritania, Mali, Burkina Faso, Togo, and Benin. It explores the relationships between people and their living environments. But her best-known film is *Surname Viet, Given Name Nam,* which is a highly personal documentary that explores the status of women in contemporary Vietnam from a historical perspective. Interestingly, it consists largely of confessional interviews with five contemporary Vietnamese women whose words have been translated by Trinh and are delivered by amateur actresses. Despite somewhat disparate backgrounds, each of the women shares the "four virtues" and "three submissions" that constrain Vietnamese women's male-dominated lives. Trinh thereby suggests, but never asserts, that the Communist ascension to power had no effect on the subordinate status of women in Vietnamese society. Nevertheless, the women express an enduring love for their country—thus the film's title.

A Tale of Love is Trinh's most-recent film, and also her first fictional narrative, which provides a meditation about the tangled meanings of love. It traces the intellectual and emotional musings of a young Vietnamese-American journalist who moonlights as a photographer's model, and who shares the name of the heroine in Vietnam's national poem, "The Tale of Kieu"—considered by many Vietnamese to be an allegory of the "motherland's" history of strife and foreign domination. Written in the early 19th century, it relates the misfortunes of Kieu, a martyred woman who sacrificed her "purity" and prostituted herself for the good of her family. The modern Kieu sees parallels between the poem's Kieu and her own search for her self, since she finds herself struggling between two cultures and her own desires, and using her body as an economic resource. The

film has a slow, contemplative pace and is peppered with painterly, often dreamy, images. Nevertheless, it is a challenging film that can be difficult to follow; that is, it has many scenes that have heavily didactic dialogue. In addition, the performances are stiff and amateurish, and Trinh contends that they are meant to be Brechtian. In large part, Trinh returns to feminist film theorist Laura Mulvey's important essay, "Visual Pleasure and Narrative Cinema," and its important thesis that Hollywood's movies are constructed for the pleasure of male viewers, largely, by fetishizing women's passive, glamorized bodies. Trinh extends Mulvey's thesis, however, by linking it to the subject of postcolonialism and the position of exile women.

In addition to her ongoing film career, since 1994 Trinh T. Minh-Ha has been a professor of women's studies and film at the University of California, Berkeley. As a professor, she aims to teach courses that, like her films, help to situate "women's work in the larger context of cultural politics, of post-coloniality, contemporary theory and the arts."

—Cynthia Felando

TRINTIGNANT, Nadine

French director and writer

Pseudonym: Some of her earlier work was done under the name Nadine Marquand. **Born:** Nadine Marquand in Nice, France, 11 November 1934; sister of the actors Serge and Christian Marquand. **Family:** Married the actor Jean-Louis Trintignant, 1960 (divorced), daughter: the actress Marie Trintignant, and son: Vincent. **Career:** 1949—dropped out of high school and began working in the film industry as a lab assistant; 1950s-60s—worked as a "script girl," assistant editor, and film editor; 1960s—began directing television programs; 1965—directed a short film, *Fragilité—ton nom est femme*; 1967—directed her first feature, *My Love, My Love.* **Address:** French Film Office, 745 Fifth Avenue, New York, NY 10151, U.S.A.

Films as Director and Writer/Co-Writer

1965   *Fragilité—ton nom est femme* (short)
1967   *Mon amour, mon amour (My Love, My Love)*
1969   *Le Voleur de crimes (The Crime Thief)*
1971   *Ça n'arrive qu'aux autres (It Only Happens to Others)*
1973   *Defense de savoir (Forbidden to Know)*
1976   *Le Voyage de noces (The Honeymoon Trip)*
1980   *Premier voyage (First Voyage)*
1985   *L'Été prochain (Next Summer)*
1986   *Tiroy senet*
1987   *Qui c'est ce garçon*
1988   *La Maison de jade (The House of Jade)* (co-sc)
1991   Ep. in *Contre l'oubli (Against Oblivion; Écrire contre l'oubli; Lest We Forget)*
1992   *Rè vense jeunesse*
1993   *Lucas*
1995   *Fugueuses (Runaways; Une Fille Galante)* (co-sc); *Lumière et Compagnie (Lumière and Company)* (co-d, one of 40)
1996   *L'Insoumise* (for TV) (co-sc)

Nadine Trintignant

Other Films

1960   *L'Eau à la bouche* (*A Game for Six Lovers*) (Doniol-Valcroze)
        (co-ed)
1961   *Léon Morin, prêtre* (*Leon Morin, Priest*) (Melville) (co-ed)
1962   *Le Coeur battant* (*The French Game*) (Doniol-Valcroze) (ed)
1963   *Le Petit Soldat* (*The Little Soldier*) (Godard—produced 1960)
        (co-ed); *Les Grands chemins* (*Of Flesh and Blood*) (C.
        Marquand) (ed)
1996   *Balade en ville* (Angelo) (sc)

Publications on Trintignant

Articles

Serre, C., "Les femmes du cinéma et la presse feminine," in *Revue du
    Cinéma* (Paris), April 1974.
Cardenas, F. de, and J. C. Huayhuaca, "Una cineasta francesa: Nadine
    Trintignant," in *Hablamos de Cine* (Lima), June 1981.
Parra, D., "*L'Été prochain*," in *Revue du Cinéma* (Paris), January 1985.

* * *

From the very beginnings of the career of Nadine Trintignant, the filmmaking process has been a family affair. One of her early credits, *Of Flesh and Blood,* on which she is the editor, was directed and co-scripted by her brother, actor-director Christian Marquand, and features another brother, actor Serge Marquand, in a supporting role. Trintignant's husband, from whom she separated during the 1970s, was actor-director Jean-Louis Trintignant; he frequently appeared in her films, beginning with a starring role in her debut feature, *My Love, My Love.* Their daughter is actress Marie Trintignant, who also has been a regular in her mother's films, first appearing as a nine year old in *It Only Happens to Others.* Little brother Vincent and Marie play the two children who are the focus of *First Voyage,* while *L'Insoumise,* a television movie that is one of Nadine Trintignant's most recent credits, is scripted by mother and son.

Trintignant's films explore the issues of trust and devotion within families and relationships. They occasionally examine the fragility of new romances, and how they are doomed by a lack of communication. But in the majority of her work, her concerns are the quandaries existing within family structures, from the impact of infidelities on both sides of marital relationships to the manner in which couples deal with life-and-death crises to the way in which children respond to the actions or fates of their parents. At their worst, Trintignant's films are unoriginal, and by-the-numbers: scenarios whose basics have been more profoundly explored by other, more distinguished directors. But at their best, they are genuinely emotional, and visually stylish.

After serving her apprenticeship as an editor or co-editor on several films, and directing a short film, *Fragilité—ton nom est femme,* Trintignant made her debut feature in 1967: *My Love, My Love,* a romantic drama about a young pop-singer wannabe who is having an affair with an idealistic architect; she becomes pregnant, but does not inform her lover. The relationship ends, and it remains unclear if the woman has an abortion. Trintignant's follow-up, *The Crime Thief,* is the based-on-fact account of a drab henpecked husband who observes a woman commit suicide. In order to gain attention, he claims responsibility for her death; eventually, he does in fact kill a young model. Murder also is of consequence in *Forbidden to Know*; among its characters is a woman charged with slaying her lover.

Trintignant's first truly intimate family-oriented feature is *It Only Happens to Others,* which chronicles the death of an 18-month-old girl and its impact on her anguished parents. *The Honeymoon Trip* is the story of a married couple who go on a second honeymoon, at which point their various infidelities are revealed. *First Voyage* charts the plight of two siblings whose mother abruptly dies and who set out in search of their father, who had abandoned them years earlier. *Next Summer* is a generational portrait of a large, diverse family. At its center is a couple, with six children, who break up because of the husband's faithlessness but are reunited at the finale; during the course of the story, the various family members must evaluate their lives and face up to their inadequacies. *The House of Jade* follows the relationship between an older woman and younger man; the woman's earlier marriage ended because of her inability to become a mother and her commitment to her writing career, and this romance is doomed when her lover resolves to also have a family. *Runaways* is the story of two young women who both have had harsh relations with men, and who meet and become fast friends. One is on her way to see her estranged father as she escapes an unhappy home life with her mother. Upon her drowning, the other takes over her identity.

Even when her films fit into genres—*Forbidden to Know* is a suspense drama about an ambulance-chasing lawyer battling political chicanery; *Runaways* is part female buddy movie, part psychological drama—the manner in which Trintignant's characters respond to familial dilemmas plays a key role in her scenarios. And beyond the fact that she casts family members in her films, quite a few clearly are autobiographical. *It Only Happens to Others,* arguably Trintignant's most deeply personal film, is based on a real-life occurrence in the lives of the filmmaker and her husband. *The Honeymoon Trip,* meanwhile, is based on an incident in their marriage, while the characters in *Next Summer* are modeled after those in Trintignant's family.

As they explore deeply imbedded emotions, Nadine Trintignant's films observe the flow of everyday life. This is reflected in the choice she made for her participation in *Lumière and Company,* an homage to the art of cinema, in which 40-odd filmmakers contribute 52-second-long "movies" shot with an original Lumière camera. Trintignant places her camera on a primitive dolly and glides it along an urban setting in which she captures an image of people sitting, standing, and walking in front of several buildings and water fountains. There may be strength in the image of the architecture, but the primary components to the shot are the people, and the panorama of life she records.

—Rob Edelman

TRIUMPH DES WILLENS
(Triumph of the Will)
Germany, 1935
Director: Leni Riefenstahl

Production: Universum Film Aktiengesellschaft (UFA); black and white, 35mm; running time: 120 minutes. Released March 1935. Filmed 4-10 September 1934 in Nuremburg at the Nazi Party Congress.

Producer: Leni Riefenstahl; **editor:** Leni Riefenstahl; **subtitles:** Walter Ruttmann; **photography:** Sepp Allgeier, Karl Attenberger, and Werner Bohne, plus several assistants; **architectural designs:** Albert Speer; **music:** Herbert Windt.

Awards: National Film Prize of Germany; Venice Biennale, Gold Medal (most sources do not list this award for *Triumph,* though David Gunston in *Current Biography* states that *Triumph* did receive this award); Exposition Internationale des Arts et des Techniques (Paris), Grand Prize

Publications

Books

Kracauer, Siegfried, *From Caligari to Hitler,* Princeton, New Jersey, 1947.

Hull, David Stewart, *Film in the Third Reich,* Berkeley, 1969.

Cadard, Pierre, and Francis Courtade, *Histoire du Cinema Nazi,* Paris, 1972.

Barsam, Richard, *Nonfiction Film: A Critical History,* New York, 1973.

Barnouw, Erik, *Documentary: A History of the Non-Fiction Film,* New York, 1974.

Barsam, Richard, *Filmguide to Triumph of the Will,* Bloomington, Indiana, 1975.

Infield, Glenn, *Leni Riefenstahl: Fallen Film Goddess,* New York, 1976.

Phillips, Baxter, *Swastika: The Cinema of Oppression,* New York, 1976.

Rhodes, Anthony, *Propaganda, the Art of Persuasion: World War II,* New York, 1976.

Ford, Charles, *Leni Riefenstahl,* Paris, 1978.

Hinton, David, *The Films of Leni Riefenstahl,* Metuchen, New Jersey, 1978.

Infield, Glenn, *Leni Riefenstahl et le 3e Reich,* Paris, 1978.

Berg-Pan, Renada, *Leni Riefenstahl,* edited by Warren French, Boston, 1980.

Nowotny, Peter, *Leni Riefenstahl's* Triumph des Willens*: zur Kritik dokumentarischer Filmarbeit im NS-Faschismus,* Dortmund, 1981.

Welch, David, *Propaganda and the German Cinema, 1933-1945,* Oxford, 1983; rev. ed., 1987.

Heck-Rabi, Louise, *Women Filmmakers: A Critical Reception,* Metuchen, New Jersey, 1984.

Loiperdinger, Martin, *Der Parteitagsfilm* Triumph des Willens *von Leni Riefenstahl: Rituale der Mobilmachung,* Opladen, 1987.

Riefenstahl, Leni, *Memoiren,* Munich, 1987.

Deutschmann, Linda, Triumph of the Will*: The Image of the Third Reich,* Wakefield, New Hampshire, 1991.

Triumph des Willens

Articles

Lewis, Marshall, in *New York Film Bulletin,* nos. 12-14, 1960.

Gunston, D., "Leni Riefenstahl," in *Film Quarterly* (Berkeley), Fall 1960.

Muller, Robert, "Romantic Miss Riefenstahl," in *Spectator* (London), 10 February 1961.

Berson, Arnold, "The Truth about Leni," in *Films and Filming* (London), April 1965.

"Issue on Riefenstahl," of *Film Comment* (New York), Winter 1965.

Delahaye, Michel, "Leni and the Wolf: Interview with Leni Riefenstahl," in *Cahiers du Cinéma in English* (New York), June 1966.

Corliss, Richard, "Leni Riefenstahl: A Bibliography," in *Film Heritage* (Dayton, Ohio), Fall 1969.

Richards, Jeffrey, "Leni Riefenstahl: Style and Structure," in *Silent Picture* (London), Autumn 1970.

Kelman, K., "Propaganda as Vision—*Triumph of the Will*," in *Film Culture* (New York), Spring 1973.

Barsam, Richard, "Leni Riefenstahl: Artifice and Truth in a World Apart," in *Film Comment* (New York), November/December 1973.

Gunston, David, "Leni Riefenstahl," in *Current Biography* (New York), May 1975.

Hinton, Davie, "*Triumph of the Will*: Document or Artifice?," in *Cinema Journal* (Evanston, Illinois), Fall 1975.

O'Donnell-Stupp, Vicki, "Myth, Meaning, and Message in *The Triumph of the Will*," in *Film Criticism* (Edinboro, Pennsylvania), Winter/Spring 1978.

Everson, William K., in *The Documentary Tradition,* edited by Lewis Jacobs, 2nd ed., New York, 1979.

Neale, Steve, "*Triumph of the Will*: Notes on Documentary and Spectacle," in *Screen* (London), no. 1, 1979.

Winston, B., "Was Hitler There? Reconsidering *Triumph des Willens,*" in *Sight and Sound* (London), Spring 1981.

"Cinema et Propaganda Issue" of *Revue Belge du Cinema* (Brussels), Summer 1984.

Gyurey, V., "A Harmadik Birodalom es a Fuehrer ket nezopontbol," in *Filmkultura* (Budapest), no. 6, 1989.

Wood, R., "Fascism/Cinema," in *Cineaction* (Toronto), Fall 1989.

Szilagyi, A., "Hitler Adolf szupersztar," in *Filmvilag* (Budapest), no. 1, 1990.

Foldenyi, F. L., "A birodalmi szepseg buvoleteben," in *Filmvilag* (Budapest), no. 12, 1991.

Doherty, Thomas, "The Filmmaker as Fascist," in *Boston Globe,* 13 December 1992.

Elsaesser, T., "Portrait of the Artist as a Young Woman," in *Sight and Sound* (London), February 1993.

Hoberman, J., "The Triumph of the Swill," in *Premiere* (New York), December 1993.

Winston, Brian, in *History Today,* January 1997.

* * *

Triumph of the Will is one of the greatest examples of film propaganda ever made. Commissioned by Hitler, Leni Riefenstahl recorded the 1934 Nuremberg National Socialist Party rally, transforming it through innovative editing, montage, and lighting into a frighteningly impressive work of indoctrination.

Riefenstahl maintains that the film is an accurate record of a historical event. In the French periodical *Cahiers du Cinéma,* the director commented that:

> In those days one believed in something beautiful....How could I know better than Winston Churchill, who even in 1935-36 was saying that he envied Germany its Führer?...you will notice if you see the film today that it doesn't contain a single reconstructed scene. Everything is real....It is history. A purely "historical" film.

What is surprising is that Riefenstahl was approached at all to create the film. Given the Nazi's chauvinistic attitude towards women—that they should act as wives and mothers before anything else—the fact that Hitler retained a female director to make such an important work is very interesting. Josef Goebbels, Hitler's Minister of Propaganda, hated Riefenstahl, and according to the director made filming *Triumph of the Will* as difficult as possible.

The film was viewed as an essential and important propaganda tool. The recent Rohm Purge which had resulted in the assassination of Ernst Rohm, head of the Sturmabteilung (S.A. or brownshirts), and his top men, on 30 June 1930 had effected Nazi morale. The S.A. was responsible for maintaining order at rallies, and controlling political opposition. Hitler had a major distrust of the S.A. leaders and of the German military, which he felt was dominated by the aristocracy. Rohm's murder divided the Nazi Party, which was unsure about Hitler's political direction. The film thus served as an important way of conveying to the world the Party's unity, and strength in the light of recent disruptions.

Out of the 96 propaganda films produced by Goebbels's ministry between 1933 and 1945, Riefenstahl's two films *Triumph of the Will* and the very beautiful *Olympia* have proved the most interesting examples and the most influential works on postwar cinema. The importance of this period to the Nazi Party is shown from the opening statement of the film:

> September 4, 1934. 20 years after the outbreak of World War I, 16 years after German woe and sorrow began, 19 months after the beginning of Germany's rebirth, Adolf Hitler flew again to Nuremberg to review the columns of his faithful admirers.

The aerial shot which tracks Hitler's arrival in his plane, and pans over the cheering crowds, military columns, and houses, focusing on a few happy, almost brainwashed looking people, creates the feeling that Hitler is a god descending from the heavens. This is emphasized by the shooting of scenes featuring Hitler from below using a low camera, which establishes the impression that the Führer is an Olympian creature, larger than life. In contrast the cheering masses are shot from above, signifying that they are Hitler's minions—and are inferior to the Führer.

The film's recurrent use of symbols: the swastika; the eagle; and flags, among them, help to control the audience by making it feel that it is participating in the action occurring on screen. The eagle, the symbol of the Party is most often seen silhouetted against the sky—again showing that the force and strength of the Party is divine.

Riefenstahl continuously intercuts images, alleviating the tediousness of the Party officials' speeches; emphasizing important words and phrases with relevant images. This technique is gleaned from Soviet propaganda films, particularly from the work of Eisenstein and Pudovkin, and is effective in retaining the audience's interest. The use of montage is also important because what the viewer sees on screen is a carefully created image rather than a natural reality.

The film emphasizes the godlike status of the Führer, the importance of the Volk and folk history, and the military strength of the Nazis. Long sweeping shots of the Hitler Youth, the military, and the Labor Movement, symbolically carrying spades instead of rifles, show the support that the Party enjoys.

Lutze, Rohm's successor, is also promoted by the film. William L. Shirer in *Berlin Diary* commented that Lutze was an unpopular successor to Rohm, but in *Triumph of the Will,* the S.A. leader is seen being mobbed by his men. Only the Führer receives the same kind of treatment in the film.

To shoot the film, Riefenstahl used a team of 16 cameramen with a further 16 assistants, using a total of 30 cameras. The two-hour film is a perfectly edited document of Nazi fanaticism. Accompanied by an impressively stirring sound track, which includes music by Wagner, *Triumph of the Will* is an example of how film can be used to manipulate and indoctrinate the masses.

Its influence on postwar cinema has been long-lasting, and the contemporary advertising industry employs many of the techniques used to such great effect in the film to capture the minds and thoughts of the audience: the repetition of motifs, montage, and a use of emotive and stirring music to manipulate the audience.

Triumph of the Will won a state award, and the Gold Medal at the Venice Bienniale of 1935, and the French Grand Prix at the film festival held in Paris.

—A. Pillai

TROIS HOMMES ET UN COUFFIN
(Three Men and a Cradle)
France, 1985
Director: Coline Serreau

Production: Flach Films/Soprofilms/TF1 Films Productions; Fujicolor, 35 mm; running time: 106 minutes. Released 18 September 1985, Paris. Filmed in Paris. Cost: 9.7 million francs.

Producers: Jean-François Lepetit; **screenplay:** Coline Serreau; **photography:** Jean-Jacques Bouhon and Jean-Yves Escoffier; **editor:** Catherine Renault; **sound:** Daniel Ollivier; **production de-**

Trois hommes et un couffin

oignt Yvan Maussion; **music:** Schubert: String Quintet in C; **costume designers:** Poussine Mercanton and Édith Vesperini.

Cast: Roland Giraud (*Pierre*); Michel Boujenah (*Michel*); André Dussollier (*Jacques*); Philippine Leroy Beaulieu (*Sylvia*); Dominique Lavanant (*Mme. Rapons*); Marthe Villalonga (*Antoinette*); Annick Alane (*Pharmacist*).

Awards: Césars for Best Film, Best Screenplay, and Best Supporting Actor (Boujenah).

Publications

Books

Fischer, Lucy, *Cinematernity: Film, Motherhood, Genre,* Princeton, New Jersey, 1995.
Austin, Guy, *Contemporary French Cinema: An Introduction,* Manchester, England, 1996.

Articles

Modleski, Tania, "Three Men and Baby M," in *Camera Obscura* (Berkeley), May 1988.
Carroll, Raymonde, "Film et analyse culturelle: le remake," in *Contemporary French Civilization,* Summer/Fall 1989.
Durham, Carolyn A , "Taking the Baby out of the Basket and/or Robbing the Cradle: 'Remaking' Gender and Culture in Franco-American Film," in *French Review,* April 1992.
Vincendeau, Ginette, "Coline Serreau: A High Wire Act," in *Sight and Sound* (London), March 1994.

* * *

Trois hommes et un couffin was a tremendous commercial and critical success in its native France: the most popular French-made film in 20 years, winner of three Césars, and France's official submission for the Academy Awards' Best Foreign Film category. Curiously, though the film was not well received in the United States, an American remake (*Three Men and a Baby*), based upon Coline Serreau's screenplay was itself a commercial sensation (though not in France), leading to much speculation about cultural differences in taste, especially when such matters as gender roles and parenthood are treated from a comic perspective.

In the tradition of farce, the plot of *Trois hommes* is set in motion by a misunderstood message. Before going off on vacation, a swinging (if we may be allowed the historical term) Parisian bachelor tells his two roommates to expect a package to be delivered to their door, for safekeeping for a few days. But shortly before the arrival of the package (heroin, unbeknownst to any of the three), a baby shows up on their doorstep—the vacationing bachelor's love child (also unknown to him), abandoned for six months by a fashion model off to the States. Multiple confusions between the heroin and heroine (the pun, never actually made explicit, is even more perfect in French: *l'héroïne*) arise in due course, as drug dealers arrive to pick up "their package," the police set up a surveillance team, and the returning vacationer is baffled by the tirade his outraged roommates launch at him. The drug subplot is disposed of fairly quickly, as the film focuses more completely upon its real concern: the transformation of the bachelors from clumsy, hostile babysitters to loving and superbly competent surrogate parents. (Comparison with the American remake, which follows the overall plot structure and uses many lines of Serreau's dialogue with minimal change, reveals cultural difference on every level, from the subtlest body language to larger changes in emphasis: e.g., the American film cannot simply let the bachelors get the drugs back to the dealers and forget the whole thing, but must show them comically apprehending the criminals for the police; and Jack's mother and latest girlfriend, unlike Jacques's, are not simply too self-involved to be interested in Baby Marie, but rather wisely lecture him on how he needs to take on "grown-up" responsibilities.)

The incompetence of men faced with dirty diapers and incessant wails is a time-honored subject for comedy, but to account for the remarkable success of *Trois hommes,* one must consider factors beyond the deft handling of standard comic tropes by Serreau and her three actors, plus the selection of a very cute baby—as important as these may be. Surely the film spoke to popular concerns and to feminist discourse of the mid-1980s, in France as elsewhere, about working mothers and men's parenting capabilities, though just what it had to say has been open to debate. A number of American academics have found the film misogynistic, noting that most of the film's women are either coldly scientific about child-raising (the pharmacist, the professional nanny) or downright hostile to the prospect (various girlfriends), while Sylvia, the actual mother, takes back the child but more or less neglects it while pursuing her career, and ends up "infantilized," curled up asleep in Marie's bed after having begged the bachelors to become co-parents. It has been argued that the men do not simply become good "fathers" or allow their "feminine side" to blossom, but actually co-opt the place of women, marginalizing them even beyond the usual condition under patriarchy. When Jacques, mournful after Sylvia first takes back Marie, drunkenly stuffs a pillow under his sweater and feels bitterly mocked by the story of Eve created from Adam's rib (since men really cannot give birth), one could ask whether this is an amusing reversal of the usual male self-satisfaction or a display of an arrogant desire to "have it all"—a desire fulfilled at the end of the film with the writer-director's evident approval.

Any detailed response to the charges of misogyny must involve itself in an investigation of French/American cultural differences on several levels: feminist theory, changing popular attitudes about child-rearing, and modes of comedy and satire. For now, one may simply suggest that any account of this film should take note of Serreau's generally cool detachment, her sense of drollery, in presenting the spectacle of her flustered male trio. The camera is often at a discreet distance, whether witnessing some sputtering outburst or watching Pierre sitting in rigid tension on a sofa, next to the cradle, waiting for the owner of the "package" to arrive, the only sound and movement coming from the baby's cheerful rattle peering just over the edge of the basket. (Thus all the more intense is Pierre's frantic rush though the devastated apartment, followed very closely by what seems to be

a deliberately unsteady Steadicam, to see if the drug dealers have harmed Marie—a scene whose drama is counterpointed on the soundtrack by the achingly tender slow movement of Schubert's String Quintet.) Other scenes worthy of study for Serreau's comic strategies: the confrontation between an almost hysterically turf-guarding Pierre and the haughtily defensive "Seconde Maman" from a child-care agency; and the final reunion of Marie and the bachelors, whose shirtless state (Sylvia having roused them all from sleep) seems a signifier of both their absurd masculinity and their emotional vulnerability.

—Joseph Milicia

TWO SMALL BODIES
Germany, 1993
Director: Beth B

Production: Castle Hill Productions, in cooperation with Samsa Film S.A.R.I., commissioned by ZDF/arte; color; 35mm; optical sound; running time: 85 minutes. Broadcast on French TV (Arte), summer 1993, and later on German TV (ZDF), screened in 1993 at Locarno and Toronto Film Festivals, released theatrically in the United States in 1994, included in a retrospective of Beth B's films in New York City in 1996; filmed in Frankfurt, Germany, in 19 days, completed in July 1993, for under one million dollars.

Producers: Daniel Zuta and Beth B; **associate producer:** Brigitte Kramer; **production manager:** Axel Unbescheid; **screenplay:** Beth B and Neal Bell, based on his play; **assistant directors:** Cornelia Dohrn van Rossum and Ulrike Bickelmann; **photography:** Phil Parmet; **editors:** Melody London and Andrea Feige; **sound editors:** Minka Maslowski and Britta Gotz; **sound engineer:** Kurt Eggmann; **art director:** Agnette Schlosser; **music:** Swans; **costume designer:** Bea Grossmann; **makeup:** Nicola Moczek.

Cast: Suzy Amis (*Eileen Mahoney*); Fred Ward (*Lieutenant Brann*).

Publications

Book

Bell, Neal, *Two Small Bodies: A Play,* New York, 1980.

Articles

Marchetti, Gina, and Keith Tishkin, "An Interview with Beth and Scott B," in *Millennium* (New York), Fall/Winter, 1981-82.
Taylor, Clarke, "Overview of Underground," in *Los Angeles Times,* 24 April 1983.
Reynaud, Bérénice, "German Co-Production: A Mixed Blessing for Sara Driver and Beth B," in *Independent Film and Video Monthly* (New York), December 1993.
Biskind, Peter, "Killer B," in *Premiere* (New York), January 1994.
James, Caryn, "*Two Small Bodies,*" in *New York Times,* 15 April 1994.
Silberg, Jon, "*Two Small Bodies,*" in *Boxoffice* (Chicago), July 1994.

Heartney, Eleanor, "Beth B at P.P.O.W. and The Crosby Street Project," in *Art in America* (New York), February 1996.
Frankel, David, "Beth B," in *Artforum* (New York), March 1996.

*   *   *

A Hollywood-style elaboration of Beth B's earlier underground work, *Two Small Bodies* is a highly rhetorical study of parenthood and heterosexuality. The film has the same style as its two protagonists, who bait each other throughout by offering what we later find to be falsehoods in a manner that seems all too possibly true.

Beth B first gained notice in 1970s downtown Manhattan, where she and her husband Scott (their last initial a tribute to trash culture and a refusal of matrimonial convention) made a series of Super 8 shorts about torture, sadomasochism, and crime, steeped in the punk-rock milieu. (*Bodies*'s score is by Swans, a post-punk New York band.) In the eighties, B began to direct 16mm films and music videos. Once a massage-parlor receptionist, B now creates multimedia museum installations, with which *Bodies* shares themes of eroticized violence and miscommunication, and formal strategies of repetition and surprise. B funded *Bodies* through German television, since American backing was hard to come by due to the film's subject.

B and Neal Bell adopted *Bodies*'s script from Bell's play, itself based on a murder case in 1977 New York City. A two-person set piece, the film takes place entirely in and around the house of Eileen, a young mother separated from her husband and working as a strip-club hostess. Eileen's two children have disappeared. Police Lieutenant Brann arrives, theorizing Eileen's possible involvement in the abduction and murder explicitly in terms of her maternal unfitness as a consequence of her job and her active sex life. He names and acts out the erotic impulses underlying his punishing interrogation, both performing and demanding uneasy stripteases. Her only defense is to repeat his ideas back to him, with a cold elaboration that only once or twice becomes a display of emotion "appropriate" to her situation. She confesses several times, but at the last minute he reveals that he has caught the true murderer elsewhere.

The moviegoer is predisposed toward identifying with these characters, especially the detective, by the familiarity of the situation, and the proficiency of the accomplished actors. But full complicity with either character is impossible, due to B's strategy of offering information about their inner lives only to take it back. After Eileen weeps, finally, Brann holds her but then says he does not believe her grief; after gently massaging his neck, she tells him—a lie—how she strangled her kids. B uses a fluid camera and long takes to inscribe the dysfunctional give and take between the characters in body language as well as words. When she mixes him an unsolicited drink, he does not touch it; when he takes a coffee cup for an ashtray, she grabs it away.

B told Bérénice Reynaud that *Bodies* appealed to her by showing how a woman and her children suffer from a socially imposed "contradiction between career and motherhood." Yet the film's plot could not retain the audience's interest if it did not, throughout its length, keep the audience wondering if Eileen really is guilty—if the detective's sexist logic equating her extra-domestic interests with infanticidal tendencies is true. In this sense, the story structure and the detective are in the same position regarding her, as in fact is Eileen herself. The plot allows her independence to maintain itself, perversely, by flaunting its own criminalization, as she refuses to let us understand why she agrees with and expands upon the detective's accusations.

It seems a similar double bind to the one some critics noted with regard to the film's play with the sexual pleasure of the interrogation, for both parties. B fluctuates between using the talk of sex realistically, to express emotions (even the ugly ones of his power-hunger and her self-abjection), and metaphorically, to vivisect patriarchal concepts of gender relations and motherhood. It is never certain if the metaphors are meant to undercut the emotions, or the reverse. The metaphors themselves are complex: Eileen claims she killed her children by teaching them that boys do not cry and males are bigger than females in all ways. This clear attack on patriarchal notions is confused by her otherwise blaming her children's death on her own excessive lust, or on her inversion of healthy mothering methods (teaching them to run with scissors and constantly watch television). Like the film as a whole, Eileen is sometimes a critic of patriarchy, and sometimes the alternatingly angry and enthralled embodiment of its constructs. She and Brann alike attack both the constraints upon her and herself in a uncertain dance between parody and undeserved but still terrible guilt.

Thus, only in flashes does B hint that it is the investigating man (and the male-dominated society behind him) who largely produces what he perceives as the woman's mystery, her sexual profligacy, and her criminality. "Think 'slut,'" he barks at her. "You'll have to tell me how," she says—and he does. In one shot, B visualizes the same idea. We see only Brann's midriff, with his tie and heavy belt, looming behind Eileen's head. Questioning her about finding the children gone, Brann mimics the motion of pushing open a door, and as his hand fills the space beside Eileen's head, its shadow blocks her face completely.

Inviting and then thwarting identification, *Bodies* is like a 1979 short by B and her husband called *Letters to Dad*. The short puts the audience in the place of a "dad" to whom the performers read loving words, which are finally revealed to have been written to the cult leader and mass murderer Jim Jones. *Bodies* is just far less clear about defining the social evil it wants to both align its viewers with unawares and (thus) condemn in the end. The final way in which the film complicates its impulse to social criticism is by suggesting that the characters are trapped not only by social roles but by existence itself. The dialogue equates gendered role playing in the nuclear family with death. It is not clear which element is meant as the greater evil, as nihilism runs neck and neck with social commentary, in circles. Reviewers generally found *Bodies* more discomfiting than cogent, an indication of B's success at memorably and distinctively slanting, if not subduing, the spiraling tangle of blocks and pleasures at which men and women, and Hollywood and patriarchy, intersect.

—Susan Knobloch

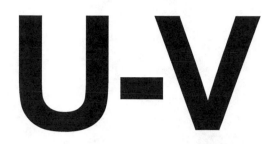

U-V

ULLMANN, Liv
Norwegian director, writer, and actress

Born: In Tokyo, 16 December 1939. **Education:** Studied acting in London; continued apprenticeship in repertory theater. **Family:** Married (1) Gappe Stang, 1960 (divorced 1965); five-year relationship with the director Ingmar Bergman, one child, Linne Ullmann; (2) Donald Saunders, 1985. **Career:** 1957—film debut; 1960—acted with National Theatre and Norwegian Theatre; 1966—role in *Persona,* the first of many performances in films by Ingmar Bergman; 1992—solo directorial debut; 1996—directed TV miniseries *Enskilda samtal* (*Private Confessions*). **Awards:** Swedish Gold Bug for Best Actress, for *Skammen,* 1968; Best Actress, New York Film Critics, for *Cries and Whispers* and *The Emigrants,* 1972; Best Actress, Golden Globe, for *The Emigrants,* 1972; Best Actress, New York Film Critics, for *Scenes from a Marriage,* 1973; Best Actress, New York Film Critics, for *Face to Face,* 1976; Seattle International Film Festival, New Directors Showcase, First Prize, for *Sofie,* 1992. **Agent:** Robert Lantz, 888 Seventh Avenue, New York, NY 10106, U.S.A.

Films as Director

1982   *Love* (co-d with Zetterling, Cohen, and Dowd)
1992   *Sofie* (*Sophie*) (+ co-sc)
1995   *Kristin Lavransdatter* (*Kransen*; *Kristin Lavransdotter*) (+ sc); *Lumière et compagnie* (*Lumière and Company*) (co, one of 40 directors)

Film as Actress

1957   *Fjols til Fjells* (*Fools in the Mountains*) (Carlmar)
1959   *Ung flukt* (*Young Escape*) (Carlmar)
1962   *Kort år sommaren* (*Short Is the Summer*) (B. Henning-Jensen) (as Eva)
1965   *De kalte ham Skarven* (*They Call Him Skarven*) (Gustavson) (as Ragna)
1966   *Persona* (I. Bergman) (as Elisabeth Vogler)
1968   *Vargtimmen* (*Hour of the Wolf*) (I. Bergman) (as Alma); *An-Magritt* (Skouen) (title role); *Skammen* (*Shame*) (I. Bergman) (as Eva Rosenberg)
1969   *En Passion* (*A Passion*; *The Passion of Anna*) (I. Bergman) (as Anna Fromm)
1971   *The Night Visitor* (Benedek) (as Esther Jenks)
1972   *Pope Joan* (*The Devil's Imposter*) (M. Anderson) (title role); *Viskningar och rop* (*Cries and Whispers*) (I. Bergman) (as a sister); *Utvandrarna* (*The Emigrants*) (Troell) (as Kristina)

1973   *Nybyggarna* (*The New Land*) (Troell) (as Kristina); *Lost Horizon* (Jarrott) (as Catherine); *40 Carats* (Katselar) (as Ann Stanley); *Scener ur ett äktenskap* (*Scenes from a Marriage*) (I. Bergman—for TV) (as Marianne)
1974   *Zandy's Bride* (Troell) (as Hannah Land); *The Abdication* (Harvey) (as Queen Christina); *L'uomo dalle due ombre* (*De la part des copains*; *Cold Sweat*) (T. Young) (as Fabienne); *Léonor* (Juan Buñuel) (title role)
1976   *Ansikte mot ansikte* (*Face to Face*) (I. Bergman—for TV) (as Jenny)
1977   *A Bridge Too Far* (Attenborough) (as Kate ter Horst); *The Serpent's Egg* (*Das Schlangenei*; *Örmens ägg*) (I. Bergman) (as Manuela Rosenberg)
1978   *Herbstsonate* (*Autumn Sonata*) (I. Bergman) (as Eva); *Couleur chair* (Wyergans)
1980   *The Gates of the Forest*
1981   *Richard's Things* (Harvey) (as Kate)
1983   *Children in the Holocaust* (Eisner—doc) (as narrator); *Jacobo Timerman: Prisoner without a Name, Cell without a Number* (*Prisoner without a Name, Cell without a Number*) (Yellen—for TV)
1984   *Jenny* (Bronken—for TV); *The Wild Duck* (Safran) (as Gina); *La Diagonale du fou* (*Dangerous Moves*) (Dembo) (as Marina Fromm)
1985   *The Bay Boy* (Petrie) (as Jennie Campbell); *Ingrid* (Annakin, Crabtree, and French)
1986   *Speriamo che sia femmina* (*Let's Hope It's a Girl*) (Monicelli) (as Elena)
1987   *Gaby: A True Story* (Mandoki) (as Sari Brimmer); *Mosca Addio* (*Moscow Goodbye*) (Bolognini) (as Ida Nudel)
1988   *La Amiga* (Meerapfel) (as Maria)
1989   *The Rose Garden* (Rademakers) (as Gabriele Schlueter-Freund)
1991   *Mindwalk* (B. Capra) (as Sonia Hoffman); *The Ox* (Nykvist) (as Maria)
1992   *The Long Shadow* (Zsigmond) (as Katherine)
1994   *Drømspel* (*Dreamplay*) (Straume) (as ticket seller); *Zorn* (G. Hallström) (as Emma Zorn)

Publications by Ullmann

Books

Changing (autobiography), London, 1977.
Choices (autobiography), New York, 1984.

Articles

Interview with Virginia Wright Wexman, in *Cinema Journal* (New Champaign, Illinois), Fall 1980.

Liv Ullmann with Anthony Harvey on the set of *The Abdication.*

"A New Career for Liv Ullmann," interview in *New York Times,* 4 October 1993.

Publications on Ullmann

Book

Segrave, Kerry, and Linda Martin, *The Continental Actress: European Film Stars of the Postwar Era,* London, 1990.

Articles

"*Love,*" in *Variety* (New York), 18 August 1982.
Ayscough, Suzan, "*Sofie,*" in *Variety* (New York), 14 September 1992.
Elia, M., "*Sofie,*" in *Séquences* (Montreal), November 1992.
Bjerkan, H., "*Sofie,*" in *Z Filmtidsskrift* (Oslo), no. 1, 1993.
Schick, T., "*Sofie,*" in *Filmnews,* no. 23, 1993.
Gaelen, H. van, "Liv Ullmann's Prachtig Regiedebut," in *Film en Televisie + Video* (Brussels), March 1993.
Delval, D., "*Sofie,*" in *Grand Angle* (Mariembourg, Belgium), April 1993.
Bartholomew, D., "*Sofie,*" in *Film Journal* (New York), May 1993.

Lally, Kevin, "Ullmann Turns to Directing with Period Saga of *Sofie,*" in *Film Journal* (New York), May 1993.
Holden, S., "Ullmann Directs an Extended Diary," in *New York Times,* 21 May 1993.
Kauffmann, Stanley, "Females of the Species," in *New Republic* (New York), 24 May 1993.
Brown, G., "Dutiful Daughters," in *Village Voice* (New York), 25 May 1993.
Kreps, K., "*Sofie,*" in *Boxoffice* (Chicago), June 1993.
Hinson, Hal, "*Sofie,*" in *Washington Post,* 18 June 1993.
James, C., "Film View: No Arnold. No T. Rex. Just Art," in *New York Times,* 20 June 1993.
Gerz, R., "*Sofie,*" in *EPD Film* (Frankfurt), August 1993.
Thompson, Ben, "*Sofie,*" in *Sight and Sound* (London), August 1993.
Andrews, David, "The Need to Belong," in *Christian Century,* 8 September 1993.
Edmunds, Marlene, "Ullmann Helms Norwegian Epic Slated for '95 Debut," in *Weekly Variety,* 31 October 1994.
Kieffer, A., "*Sofie,*" in *Jeune Cinéma* (Paris), January/February 1995.
Vivianai, C., "*Sofie,*" in *Positif* (Paris), February 1995.
Michel, A., "*Sofie* de Liv Ullmann," in *Avant-Scène du Cinéma* (Paris), March/April 1995.

Kelly, Brendan, "Montreal Fest Features a *Feast,*" in *Variety* (New York), 14 August 1995.

Lacey, Liam, "Ullmann's Direct Discourse," in *Globe and Mail* (Toronto), 14 May 1997.

Film

A Look at Liv, documentary directed by Richard Kaplan, 1979.

* * *

Liv Ullmann created a place for herself in cinema history with her performances in films such as *Persona, Cries and Whispers, Scenes from a Marriage,* and *Autumn Sonata.* As an actress, Ullmann's singular beauty and ability to convey meaning through subtle but expressive gesture brought grace and emotional resonance to the work of Ingmar Bergman, and, for three decades, to scores of film and theatre productions in Europe and America. In 1992 Ullmann began her own directorial career. Because her films have been thoughtful character studies that draw on the creative resources of cast and crew members considered part of a company established by Ingmar Bergman, Ullmann's films are often compared to Bergman's—or perhaps more accurately, to critics' memories of films directed by Bergman. Close study of Ullmann's films reveals, however, that while her work explores relationships, settings, and philosophical terrain found in Bergman's work, Ullmann invites us to see things through a slightly different filter, one which, in particular, offers us a more self-affirming vision of women.

Born in the opening months of World War II, Ullmann lived in Toronto with her family during the war in a community known as Little Norway. When the war ended, Ullmann returned to Norway with her widowed mother and older sister. As a young girl, Ullmann, an avid reader and prolific writer of condensed classics, formed a drama club for which she presented her first stage performances. Out of school, her first success as an actress was as the lead in a local repertory production of *The Diary of Anne Frank.* In 1972 she received an Academy Award nomination for her performance in *The Emigrants,* and in 1976 another nomination for her work in *Face to Face.* During this period Ullmann returned to her interest in writing, and published the first of two autobiographical works. While continuing to work as an actress, Ullmann began broadening her range in another direction—in the seventies and eighties she became actively involved in humanitarian projects.

In the 1990s Ullmann's growth as an artist has allowed her to bring together a range of experience. *Sofie* represents not only Ullmann's debut as a director, but as a screenwriter as well. The script, co-written by Ullmann and Peter Poulsen, is an adaptation of the 1932 novel, *Mendel Philipsen og søen,* by Danish author Henri Nathansen. Set in Denmark at the turn of the century, the film's thoughtful account of a woman's passage from daughter to wife to mother, and its detailed depiction of the rituals that create a sense of order for a small Jewish community living at a distance from Danish life, combine to offer us a deft portrayal of the way in which contentment—in Sofie's case, the contentment of her parents—can, as Hal Hinson aptly puts it, "destroy a life as profoundly as misery can." Yet the film is not only a clear-eyed look into the complexities of even nurturing domestic life. It also stands as a compelling alternative to commercial cinema. In much the same way orthodox tradition provides the characters with a sense of meaning not found in modern, secular Denmark, on a formal level, the film's muted colors, long-

take aesthetic, and casting of actors with "imperfect" features give audiences the opportunity to enter a richly detailed world of lifelike characters not found in productions driven by special-effects and star personas.

While *Sofie* has received the most critical attention and widest distribution of the films directed by Liv Ullmann, work following her directorial debut is also noteworthy. For her next project, an adaptation of the 1920s novel, *Kristin Lavransdatter,* by Nobel Laureate Sigrid Undset, Ullmann not only directed the film, but wrote the screenplay as well. While Ullmann's second film is set in the Christian world of medieval Norway, the narrative recalls dilemmas presented to *Sofie*'s central character, for again the direction of the woman's life is defined by the opposing demands of filial duty and passion. Here, however, the narrative explores the consequences of rejecting social convention.

Kristin Lavransdatter not only reveals thematic connections with Ullmann's earlier work—because the film's meaning is colored by the cinematography of Sven Nykvist—it also suggests a formal bridge to Ullmann's next piece, her contribution to the compilation film, *Lumière et compagnie,* for which Ullmann designed a self-reflective sequence in which Nykvist is seen filming the camera that films him. Produced in 1995 and shown at a collection of film festivals around the world, *Lumière et compagnie* celebrates the first 100 years of cinema with vignettes created by 40 filmmakers who produced work just as August and Louis Lumière had in 1895—using refurbished Lumière cameras, shooting films no longer than 52 seconds, and creating films using only natural light and nonsynchronous sound. Ullmann's contribution to the *Lumière* film echoes the economy of gesture one finds in her work as an actress and her direction of actors, for without fanfare, it invites us to acknowledge that film has always depended on the performance of brilliant cinematographers.

Ullmann's most recent project is a film/television miniseries, *Enskilda samtal (Private Confessions).* The film, based on a largely autobiographical screenplay by Ingmar Bergman, examines the domestic life of its central character, Anna. The project brings together several members of "Bergman's company," for Nykvist is the film's cinematographer and the cast includes Max von Sydow and Pernilla August. First shown in Sweden and Norway, the film was screened at the Cannes Film Festival in 1997 to accompany the awarding of the Palm of Palms to Bergman.

Ullmann acknowledges that, like Bergman, she is interesting in filmmaking that explores the geography of the human face. She points out, however, that she is concerned as well with figures in settings, and with what bodies as a whole can suggest about the inner lives of characters. Looking at Liv Ullmann's films as work that exists in its own right, what is perhaps most striking is that her aesthetic choices ask us to reckon with despair—and beyond that, they invite us to see the wonder and expressiveness of simple human gestures.

—Cynthia Baron

van DONGEN, Helen
Dutch editor and director

Born: Amsterdam, 5 January 1909. **Family:** Married Kenneth Durant, 1950. **Career:** 1928—assisted Joris Ivens on *The Bridge,* and later works; 1930—studied soundtrack recording and editing, Tobis Klangfilm Studios, and also studied at UFA, Berlin; 1934—assistant and observer at Joinville Studios, Paris, studied at the Academy of Cinematography, Moscow, under Eisenstein, Pudovkin, and Vertov, 1934-36, and observer in Hollywood studios, 1936; late 1930s—worked as producer on education films; abortive job as editor on film project of Nelson Rockefeller, the co-ordinator of Inter-American Affairs, during World War II; another abortive project as deputy commissioner for the Netherlands East Indies (Ivens was to serve as Commissioner); 1950—retired from filmmaking when she married.

Films as Editor

1928   *De brug (The Bridge)* (Ivens) (asst)
1929   *Regen (Rain)* (Ivens) (asst); *Wy brouwen (We Are Building)* (Ivens) (asst)
1931   *Philips-Radio (Industrial Symphony)* (Ivens); *Zuiderzee Dike* (doc); *Nieuwe polders* (doc); *Creosoot (Creosote)* (Ivens) (asst)
1933   *Zuyderzee* (Ivens)
1934   *Nieuwe Gronden (New Earth)* (Ivens); *Misère au Borinage (Borinage)* (Ivens)
1935   *Borza (The Struggle)* (von Wagenheim)
1936   *Spain in Flames* (+ pr)
1937   *The Spanish Earth* (Ivens)
1938   *You Can Draw* (+ d, ph)
1939   *The 400 Million (China's 400 Million)* (Ivens); *Pete Roleum and His Cousins* (Losey)
1940   *Power and the Land* (Ivens)
1942   *The Land* (Flaherty); *Russians at War* (compilation) (+ pr)
1943   *Netherlands America* (+ d); *Peoples of Indonesia* (+ d)
1945   *News Review No. 2* (compilation)
1946   *Gift of Green* (+ co-d—16 mm)
1948   *Louisiana Story* (Flaherty) (+ assoc pr)
1950   *Of Human Rights* (+ d)

Publications by van Dongen

Books

Joris Ivens, Berlin, 1963.
The Adirondack Guide-Book and Related Essays, Blue Mountain Lake, New York, 1971.

Articles

"350,000 Feet of Film," in *The Cinema 1951,* edited by Roger Manvell, London, 1951.
"Imaginative Documentary," in *The Technique of Film Editing,* by Karel Reisz, London, 1958.
"Notes on *Louisiana Story,*" "Robert Flaherty," and "Tonschnitt bei *Louisiana Story,*" in *Robert Flaherty,* edited by Wolfgang Klaue, Berlin, 1964.
"Robert J. Flaherty 1884-1951," in *Film Quarterly* (New York), Summer 1965.
Film Quarterly (New York), Winter 1976-77.

Publications on van Dongen

Articles

Films and Filming (London), December 1961.
Ivens, Joris, in *The Camera and I,* New York, 1969.
Skoop (Amsterdam), November 1978.

* * *

There is a famous story recounted by *Time* magazine's Richard Corliss in a 1980 essay on Robert Flaherty. Helen van Dongen, working as the editor of the filmmaker's *The Land,* showed him a sequence she had cut together and he fervently disapproved. A few days later she screened the same sequence for him and he said "Now you've got it." Van Dongen proved ably up to the task of working with Flaherty, transmuting the director's seemingly random and chaotic footage into, as Corliss writes, "a brilliant 'as told to' autobiography. If [Flaherty's] spirit informed their project, then [van Dongen's] will gave its final form."

In the truest spirit of the title, van Dongen was an editor whose techniques, honed by early work with Joris Ivens, extended beyond mere physical assemblage and continuity supervision to thoughtful documentary theory and to complex and creative sound work. In Flaherty's *Louisiana Story,* in which she served as editor and as associate producer, she worked closely with composer Virgil Thompson in creating specific themes for characters and sequences, and manipulated the soundtrack by disassembling sounds and then reconfiguring them: a scene on a bridge at night may contain up to 20 separate sounds (some of which were not endemic to the location) or a human scream could be a fusing of a dozen voices. Her exhaustive analysis of the film can be found in *The Technique of Film Editing* and is a fascinating look not only at how sequences were structured and sound was used, but also the reasons why—both the pragmatic and the dramatic.

Though her two World War II compilation documentaries, *Russians at War* and *News Review No. 2* were well received, having been compared favorably with the *World at War* series by Frank Capra, her two films with Flaherty have proven her most enduring works. Her extensive diaries of the production histories of *The Land* and *Louisiana Story* provide a telling memoir of working on location and in the editing room with the often opaque and stubborn Flaherty (he referred to her as his "Dutch mule"), while also revealing a uniquely productive and successful collaboration. Though certainly a tempestuous relationship, it was never overtly adversarial; in fact when van Dongen had to trick Flaherty into providing the narration for *The Land* because no narrator could capture his intonations (she earlier had corralled Ernest Hemingway into reciting his own written words on Ivens's *The Spanish Earth*), he was by all accounts incensed, but later conceded van Dongen was right because it benefited the film. While their goals were the same, van Dongen admitted her greatest challenge was in having to continually interpret and reinterpret Flaherty's admittedly elusive vision (which often led to gross continuity gaps and over- and undershooting) and then shape it into a cohesive and viewable motion picture. When she first began to work with Flaherty, she said she was "completely baffled by his method" and wrote to Ivens for help in understanding. Ivens's reply was equally cryptic: "Observe, look and listen and you'll find what he wants." Only when she was able to view the footage through Flaherty's realm of understanding, she said, and then decipher Flaherty's reaction while watching footage could she gauge the direction—and ultimately, the success—of the film. She wrote, "Had I myself gone to direct Flaherty's story, it would have looked quite different. But working with already filmed material, filmed under the influence of Flaherty ... essentially my editing would have resulted in approximately the same story and form. This would have been inevitable because, to use the random material to full value, the editor has to discover not only the inherent qualities of each shot but also must know the how's and why's, the director's reasoning behind each shot, or must know that no one else but Flaherty would have shot such a scene." Her ability to read the director in this way no doubt made her the best editor for Flaherty, but more importantly, made Flaherty's films better.

Though both *The Land* and *Louisiana Story* are prime examples of Flaherty's filmmaking sensibility, much of the beauty and emotional gravity of the films is owed to van Dongen's delicately focused sound and film editing. They move beyond what film history regards as documentary (and perhaps to a degree beyond what fiction can do as well), and into something ultimately more lyrical. In an interview with Ben Achtenberg, van Dongen herself resisted the label of documentary: "To me Flaherty is *not* a documentarian; he makes it all up. He does use the documentary style and background but, except for *The Land*, they are all, to a degree, stories....They are part of our history of filmmaking, but I do hesitate to call them documentaries. They are Flaherty-films, and worthwhile enjoying."

—Jon Lupo

VAN RUNKLE, Theadora
American costume designer

Born: c.1940. **Education:** Attended Chouinard Art Institute, Los Angeles. **Career:** Commercial artist; then sketch artist on *Hawaii*; 1967—first film as costume designer, *Bonnie and Clyde*, for which she received her first of three Academy Award nominations; 1983—costume designer for TV series *Wizards and Warriors*; 1997—costume designer for TV miniseries *The Last Don*. **Agent:** Darrin Sugar. **Address:** 8805 Lookout Mountain Road, Los Angeles, CA 90046, U.S.A.

Films as Costume Designer

1966   *Hawaii* (G. R. Hill) (sketch artist)
1967   ***Bonnie and Clyde*** (A. Penn)
1968   *Bullitt* (Yates); *The Thomas Crown Affair* (Jewison) (co); *I Love You, Alice B. Toklas!* (Averback); *Amanti* (*A Place for Lovers*) (De Sica) (co)
1969   *The Reivers* (Rydell); *The Arrangement* (Kazan)
1970   *Myra Breckenridge* (Sarne)
1971   *Johnny Got His Gun* (Trumbo)
1973   *Kid Blue* (Frawley); *Ace Eli and Rodger of the Skies* (Erman)
1974   *Mame* (Saks); *The Godfather, Part II* (F. F. Coppola)
1976   *Nickelodeon* (Bogdanovich)
1977   *New York, New York* (Scorsese)
1978   *Heaven Can Wait* (Beatty and Henry) (co); *Same Time, Next Year* (Mulligan)
1979   *The Jerk* (C. Reiner)
1981   *S.O.B.* (Edwards); *Heartbeeps* (Arkush) (co)

1982   *The Best Little Whorehouse in Texas* (Higgins)
1984   *Rhinestone* (Clark)
1986   *Peggy Sue Got Married* (F. F. Coppola)
1988   *Everybody's All-American* (Hackford); *Wildfire* (Z. King)
1989   *Troop Beverly Hills* (Kanew)
1990   *Stella* (Erman)
1991   *The Butcher's Wife* (T. Hughes)
1992   *Leap of Faith* (Pearce)
1995   *Kiss of Death* (Schroeder); *White Dwarf* (Markle—for TV)
1997   *Good-bye, Lover* (R. Joffé)

Publication by Van Runkle

Article

Cinema (Beverly Hills), no. 35, 1976.

Publication on Van Runkle

Article

Troy, Carol, "A Tale of Two Wardrobes," in *American Film* (Hollywood), September/October 1991.

* * *

In 1967 miniskirts maintained their hold on the world of women's fashions. With the release of *Bonnie and Clyde*, however, hemlines began to fall as fashion magazines featured the midi-look Theadora Van Runkle revived for that film. And while women were wearing midi-skirts with silk blouses, men began sporting wide lapelled, double-breasted suits.

Prior to *Bonnie and Clyde*, Van Runkle had worked as an ad illustrator before making her film debut as a sketch artist for Dorothy Jeakins on *Hawaii*. When Jeakins had to turn down *Bonnie and Clyde* due to a prior commitment, she recommended Van Runkle: it was a golden opportunity for the young designer with an admitted passion for 1930s clothing design. With her debut as a designer, Van Runkle was thrust into the spotlight: an Oscar nomination (she lost to John Truscott for *Camelot*), a Golden Tiberius from the Italian design industry, and numerous offers for more film work.

Bonnie and Clyde catapulted not only Van Runkle to fame, but Faye Dunaway as well; over the next few years, the star used Van Runkle to design her clothes both offscreen and on, establishing her fashion image as one based on soft silks which both reveal and disguise. In discussing her approach to dressing Dunaway for *The Thomas Crown Affair*, Van Runkle noted her use of accessories to counterpoint the outfit: Dunaway's passion is signified by her clothing, her control by her jewelry.

While Van Runkle has done a wide variety of period pieces, from the sock-hop styles of the 1950s in *Peggy Sue Got Married* to the hippie atrocities of *I Love You, Alice B. Toklas!*, she claims her favorite period is that from the beginning of World War I to the end of World War II. With *Mame* Van Runkle re-created a fashion obsession with hats that prompted the Millinery Institute of America to award her their Golden Crown, while with *New York, New York*, she redefined Liza Minnelli's fashion image by dressing her in tailored outfits. With *The Godfather, Part II* Van Runkle was able to cover much of the period between the wars, outfitting the mob in an exquisite array of tailored suits.

That tailored look remains one of her two favorites, the other being what she calls her "romantic" style: sensual satins, furs, lace, and velvet. With *The Best Little Whorehouse in Texas,* Theadora Van Runkle was allowed to indulge that latter penchant to great effect, director Colin Higgins agreeing with her that costumes are an effective shorthand to character. In that film Dolly Parton was never more appropriately, nor more lavishly attired: one costume, dubbed "Miss Mona Aflame with Passion," cost $7,000.

—Doug Tomlinson

VAN UPP, Virginia

American writer and producer

Born: Chicago, 1902. **Family:** Married (second) the former Paramount unit manager Ralph W. Nelson (divorced 1949); one daughter, Gay Harden, and one stepdaughter. **Career:** Began professional career as child actor in silent films; acted as script assistant, casting director, agent, scenarist, screenwriter; 1930s—scripted scenarios for Paramount Pictures, before moving to Columbia Pictures where she took the role of scriptwriter, producer, and executive producer and second-in-command to studio boss Harry Cohn; 1950s—while in West Germany, made propaganda films for the U.S. government; retired. **Died:** In Hollywood, of complications following an accident, 25 March 1970.

Films as Writer

1934 *The Pursuit of Happiness* (A. Hall) (co)
1936 *Timothy's Quest* (Barton) (co); *Poppy* (A. E. Sutherland) (co); *Easy to Take* (Tryon); *My American Wife* (H. Young) (co); *Too Many Parents* (McGowan) (co)
1937 *Swing High, Swing Low* (*The Dance of Life*) (Leisen) (co)
1938 *You and Me* (F. Lang)
1939 *Cafe Society* (E. H. Griffith); *St. Louis Blues* (*Best of the Blues*) (Walsh) (co); *Honeymoon in Bali* (*My Love for Yours*) (E. H. Griffith)
1941 *One Night in Lisbon* (E. H. Griffith); *Virginia* (E. H. Griffith); *Bahama Passage* (E. H. Griffith)
1943 *Young and Willing* (*Out of the Frying Pan*) (E. H. Griffith); *The Crystal Ball* (Nugent)
1944 *Cover Girl* (C. Vidor) (co); *The Impatient Years* (Cummings) (+ co-pr); *Together Again* (C. Vidor) (co-sc, + co-pr)
1945 *She Wouldn't Say Yes* (A. Hall) (co-sc, + co-pr)
1951 *Here Comes the Groom* (Capra) (co)

Film as Producer

1946 *Gilda* (C. Vidor)

Other Films

1941 *Come Live with Me* (C. Brown) (st)
1948 *The Lady from Shanghai* (Welles) (contributed to script and assumed role of producer, uncredited)
1952 *Affair in Trinidad* (V. Sherman) (co-st, assoc pr)

Publications on Van Upp

Books

Langman, Larry, *A Guide to American Screenwriters: The Sound Era, 1929-1982, Vol. I,* New York, 1984.
Eames, John Douglas, *The Paramount Story,* London, 1985.
McGilligan, Pat, editor, *Backstory: Interviews with Screenwriters of Hollywood's Golden Age,* Berkeley, 1986.
Hirschorn, Clive, *The Columbia Story,* New York, 1989.
Acker, Ally, *Reel Women: Pioneers of the Cinema, 1896 to the Present,* New York, 1991.
Dick, Bernard F., *The Merchant Prince of Poverty Row: Harry Cohn of Columbia Pictures,* Lexington, Kentucky, 1993.
Francke, Lizzie, *Script Girls: Women Screenwriters in Hollywood,* London, 1994.
McCreadie, Marsha, *The Women Who Write the Movies: From Frances Marion to Nora Ephron,* Secaucus, New Jersey, 1994.
Seger, Linda, *When Women Call the Shots: The Developing Power and Influence of Women in Television and Film,* New York, 1996.

Articles

Scheuer, Philip K., "Small Girl Makes Good in Large Job," in *Los Angeles Times,* 21 January 1945.
Obituary in *Variety* (New York), 15 April 1970.

* * *

Not until more than a decade after her death was the long and illustrious career of actress-screenwriter-producer Virginia Van Upp properly documented as a significant chapter of the history of Hollywood film. Her life was unique, multifaceted and singular. She was a producer, a studio executive, and an accomplished screenwriter with a significant body of work to her credit (and in some cases noncredit); her remarkable career in the Hollywood film industry spanned nearly half a century.

To some, she is considered a "first," perhaps the first woman to crash Hollywood's proverbial glass ceiling during a period when patriarchal studio bosses controlled their empires with an iron hand. The recent work of film scholars, however, most notably Ally Acker, attest to the fact that there were many women before Van Upp who assumed important positions in various facets of the early film industry. But whether she was truly a first or not, Van Upp's career was at the very least, states Acker, "unusual for the era in which she was working."

Van Upp was born in Chicago, Illinois, in 1902. As a child of perhaps seven, she appeared in silent films, working with directors Thomas Ince and Lois Weber and alongside such actors as film star John Gilbert. Her father, Harry Van Upp appears to have also had some connection with the film industry; her mother, Helen Van Upp, had been an editor and title writer for the Ince Company. As a young woman, Virginia Van Upp's life in motion pictures included a host of different occupations. She acted in the position of casting director for the 1925 production of *Ben Hur,* as an agent, as secretary for RKO-Pathé writer Horace Jackson, as a film cutter, and as a script assistant. Perhaps influenced by her work with Jackson, she discovered her true calling as a scriptwriter.

At Paramount Pictures in the 1930s, her co-written scripts and adaptations of stage plays and stories often explored in humorous terms, marital, interpersonal relationships, and comedies of

Virginia Van Upp

"romantic dilemma." Later, at Columbia, she was often paired with director-writer Edward H. Griffith on a number of wartime, "enjoyable trifles."

But more than simply being skilled in the art and craft of the motion-picture screenplay, Van Upp, by all accounts, possessed a certain measure of savvy that allowed her to move easily amongst the various operatives of film production. Van Upp "appreciated the myriad details involved in getting a movie made," writes Bernard Dick in his book on Harry Cohn; amongst these details was "the need to subject a script to a diversity of opinion."

In 1945 a writer for the *Los Angeles Times* wrote about Van Upp's success at Columbia Pictures, making a point of describing her as bespectacled and small in stature. Nevertheless, her small size had little relation to the enormous power she wielded in her position as executive producer and second-in-command to studio boss Harry Cohn. Working closely with Cohn, in 1945 she was directly responsible for the production of approximately 40 features and some $20 million of "stockholders coin."

Perhaps Van Upp's most remarkable achievement was Columbia's 1946 release of the film *Gilda,* starring World War II film-goddess Rita Hayworth. *Gilda* was a big picture with a big budget and Van Upp was in charge. In this picture, Van Upp solely is credited as the producer. The film, now considered an early archetype of the postwar film-noir style, was replete with a dark, sinister mood and overt sexual overtones. It went on to become one of the more commercially successful pictures of the year.

The post-World War II period was a turbulent one for the film industry as antitrust litigation, Communist witch-hunts, television, and the changing tastes of a society experiencing social upheaval, signaled the end of the so-called Golden Age of Hollywood. It is interesting to note Van Upp's involvement in the production of the 1948 classic, *Lady from Shanghai.* Considered filmmaker Orson Welles's masterpiece, the film may not have occurred at all had it not been for the intervention of Van Upp. Welles had gone well over budget. He erected elaborate sets and chose expensive on-location shooting in luxurious and expensive resorts in Acapulco. It was Van Upp who was assigned to save the day, patch the ragged script, and rein in Welles, the impetuous "Boy Wonder." One can only speculate how many other film "classics" occurred because of Virginia Van Upp's direct intervention.

In 1951 Van Upp co-wrote the screenplay for *Here Comes the Groom* and in 1952, for her last Hollywood film, she served as the associate producer for *Affair in Trinidad,* which was based on a story she co-wrote. A subsequent film for Republic Pictures was abandoned when Van Upp took ill.

Although one can only surmise what led to the end of Van Upp's professional career—the changing film industry and her poor health were most likely contributing factors—her career had already spanned almost 50 years. She had been a performer and had written or co-written more than a dozen respectable motion pictures. She had worked with internationally known directors from Fritz Lang to Frank Capra. She had saved *The Lady from Shanghai* from disaster and assumed one of the most powerful positions ever shouldered by a woman in modern film history. And notes Acker, it would be more than another 20 years before another woman would do the same.

—Pamala S. Deane

VARDA, Agnès
Belgian director

Born: Brussels, 30 May 1928. **Education:** Studied literature and psychology at the Sorbonne, Paris; studied art history at the École du Louvre; studied photography at night school. **Family:** Married the director Jacques Demy, 1962 (died 1990), son: Mathieu, daughter: Rosalie. **Career:** Stage photographer for Théâtre Festival of Avignon, then for Théâtre National Populaire, Paris, Jean Vilar; 1954—directed first film, *La Pointe courte*; 1955—accompanied Chris Marker to China as adviser for *Dimanche à Pekin*; 1968—directed two shorts in United States; 1977—founded production company Ciné-Tamaris. **Awards:** Prix Méliès, for *Cléo de cinq à sept,* 1961; Bronze Lion, Venice Festival, for *Salut les Cubains,* 1963; Prix Louis Delluc, David Selznick Award, and Silver Bear, Berlin Festival, for *Le Bonheur,* 1965; First Prize, Oberhausen, for *Black Panthers,* 1968; Grand Prix, Taormina, for *L'Une chante l'autre pas,* 1977; César Award, for *Ulysse,* 1983; Golden Lion, Venice Festival, Prix Méliès, and Best Foreign Film, Los Angeles Film Critics Association, for *Vagabond,* 1985; Commander des Arts et des Lettres, Chevalier Legion d'honneur. **Address:** c/o Ciné-Tamaris, 86 rue Daguerre, 75014 Paris, France.

Films as Director

1954   *La Pointe courte* (+ pr, sc)
1957   *O saisons, o châteaux* (doc short)
1958   *L'Opéra-Mouffe* (short); *Du côté de la Côte* (short)
1961   **Cléo de cinq à sept** (*Cleo from 5 to 7*) (+ sc)
1963   *Salut les Cubains* (*Salute to Cuba*) (+ text) (doc short)
1965   *Le Bonheur* (*Happiness*) (+ sc)
1966   *Les Créatures* (*Varelserna; The Creatures*) (+ sc); *Elsa*
1967   *Uncle Janco* (short); ep. of *Loin du Vietnam* (*Far from Vietnam*)
1968   *Black Panthers* (*Huey*) (doc)
1969   *Lions Love* (+ pr, sc)
1970   *Nausicaa* (for TV)
1975   *Daguerrotypes* (for TV) (+ pr); *Réponses de femmes* (8mm)
1977   *L'Une chante l'autre pas* (*One Sings, the Other Doesn't*) (+ sc, lyrics)
1980   *Mur Murs* (*Wall Walls; Mural Murals*) (+ pr)
1981   *Documenteur: An Emotion Picture* (+ pr)
1983   *Ulysse*
1984   *Les Dites cariatides*; *Sept P., Cuis., S. de B.,... a saisir*
1985   *Vagabonde* (*Sans Toit ni loi; Vagabond*)
1988   *Le Petit Amour* (*Kung Fu Master; Don't Say It*) (+ pr, sc); *Jane B. par Agnès V.* (doc) (+ appearance)
1991   *Jacquot de Nantes* (+ co-pr, sc)
1993   *Des demoiselles ont en 25 ans* (*The Young Girls Turn 25*) (doc)
1995   *Les cent et une nuits* (*A Hundred and One Nights*) (+ sc); *L'universe de Jacques Demy* (*The World of Jacques Demy*) (doc)

Other Films

1967   *Les Demoiselles de Rochefort* (*The Young Girls of Rochefort*) (Demy) (ro as nun)
1971   *Last Tango in Paris* (Bertolucci) (co-dialogue)

Agnès Varda. Photograph by Stephane Fefer.

1978 *Lady Oscar* (Demy) (pr)
1995 *Kulonbozo helyek* (*Different Places*) (doc short)

Publications by Varda

Book

Varda par Agnès, with Bernard Bastide, Paris, 1994.

Articles

"*Cléo de cinq à sept*: Script Extract," in *Films and Filming* (London), December 1962.
"Pasolini—Varda—Allio—Sarris—Michelson," in *Film Culture* (New York), Fall 1966.
"*Le Bonheur,*" in *Cinema* (Beverly Hills), December 1966.
"The Underground River," interview with Gordon Gow, in *Films and Filming* (London), March 1970.
"Mother of the New Wave," interview with J. Levitin, in *Women and Film* (Santa Monica, California), vol. 1, no. 5-6, 1974.
"*L'Une chante l'autre pas,*" interview with J. Narboni and others, in *Cahiers du Cinéma* (Paris), May 1977.
"*One Sings, the Other Doesn't,*" interview with R. McCormick, in *Cineaste* (New York), Winter 1977/78.
"Un cinéma plus 'partageable': Agnès Varda," interview with A. Tournés, in *Jeune Cinéma* (Paris), February 1982.
Interview with J. Sabine, in *Cinema Papers* (Melbourne), October 1982.
"Un jour sous le soleil," in *Monthly Film Bulletin* (London), December 1985.
"Traveling a Different Route," interview with Rob Edelman, in *Cineaste* (New York), vol. 15, no. 1, 1986.
Interview with Barbara Quart, in *Film Quarterly* (Berkeley), Winter 1986/1987.
Interview with F. Audé, in *Positif* (Paris), March 1988.
"Vers le visage de Jacques," in *Cahiers du Cinéma* (Paris), December 1990.

Publications on Varda

Books

Armes, Roy, *French Cinema since 1946: Vol. 2—The Personal Style,* New York, 1966.
Heck-Rabi, Louise, *Women Filmmakers: A Critical Reception,* Metuchen, New Jersey, 1984.
Flitterman-Lewis, Sandy, *To Desire Differently: Feminism and the French Cinema,* Urbana, Illinois, 1990.
Acker, Ally, *Reel Women: Pioneers of the Cinema, 1896 to the Present,* New York, 1991.
Foster, Gwendolyn Audrey, *Women Film Directors: An International Bio-Critical Dictionary,* Westport, Connecticut, 1995.

Articles

Strick, Philip, "Agnès Varda," in *Film* (London), Spring 1963.
Current Biography 1970, New York, 1970.
Pyros, J., "Notes on Women Directors," in *Take One* (Montreal), November/December 1970.
Roud, Richard, "The Left Bank Revisited," in *Sight and Sound* (London), Summer 1977.

Beylie, Claude, "Les Chardons ardents d'Agnès Varda," in *Ecran* (Paris), 15 April 1979.
Ranvaud, Don, "Travellers Tales," in *Monthly Film Bulletin* (London), May 1986.
Durgnat, Raymond, "Resnais & Co.: Back to the Avant-Garde," in *Monthly Film Bulletin* (London), May 1987.
Prédal, René, "Agnès Varda, une certaine idée de la marginalité," in *Jeune Cinéma* (Paris), October/November 1987.
Forbes, Jill, "Agnès Varda—The Gaze of the Medusa?," in *Sight and Sound* (London), Spring 1989.
Furlan, S., "*Jacquot de Nantes,*" in *Ekran* (Paris), vol. 16, no. 4/5, 1991.
Floret, M., and others, "Agnès par Varda," in *Jeune Cinéma* (Paris), April/May 1992.
Kelleher, E., "Director Varda's *Jacquot* Recalls Spouse Demy," in *Film Journal* (New York), May 1993.
Talton, Jana Meredyth, "Agnès Varda: Ahead of the Avant-Garde," in *Ms. Magazine* (New York), May/June 1993.

* * *

Agnès Varda's startlingly individualistic films have earned her the title "grandmother of the New Wave" of French filmmaking. Her statement that a filmmaker must exercise as much freedom as a novelist became a mandate for New Wave directors, especially Chris Marker and Alain Resnais. Varda's first film, *La Pointe courte,* edited by Resnais, is regarded, as Georges Sadoul affirms, as "the first film of the French nouvelle vague. Its interplay between conscience, emotions, and the real world make it a direct antecedent of *Hiroshima mon amour.*"

The use of doubling, and twin story lines; the personification of objects; the artistic determination of cinematic composition, color, texture, form, and time; and the correlation of individual subjectivity to societal objectivity to depict sociopolitical issues are denominators of Varda's films, which she writes, produces, and directs.

After *La Pointe courte* Varda made three documentaries in 1957 and 1958. The best of these was *L'Opéra-Mouffe,* portraying the Mouffetard district of Paris. Segments of the film are prefaced by handwritten intertitles, a literary element Varda is fond of using. In 1961-62 Varda began but did not complete two film projects: *La Cocotte d'azur* and *Melangite.* Her next film, *Cléo de cinq à sept,* records the time a pop singer waits for results of her exam for cancer. Varda used physical time in *Cléo*: events happening at the same tempo as they would in actual life. The film is divided into chapters, using tarot cards which symbolize fate. Varda next photographed 4,000 still photos of Castro's revolution-in-progress, resulting in *Salute to Cuba.*

Happiness is considered Varda's most stunning and controversial achievement. Critics were puzzled and pleased. Of her first color film, Varda says it was "essentially a pursuit of the palette.... Psychology takes first place." A young carpenter lives with his wife and children. Then he takes a mistress; when his wife drowns, his mistress takes her place. The film was commended for its superb visual beauties, the use of narrative in *le nouveau roman* literary pattern, and its tonal contrasts and spatial configurations. Critics continue to debate the film's theme.

Elsa is an essay portraying authors Elsa Triolet and her husband Louis Aragon. *The Creatures* uses a black-and-white-with-red color scheme in a fantasy-thriller utilizing an inside-outside plot that mingles real and unreal events. As in *La Pointe courte,* a young couple retreat to a rural locale. The pregnant wife is mute, due to an accident. Her husband is writing a book. He meets a recluse who operates a machine forcing people to behave as their subconscious would dictate. The wife gives birth, regaining her speech.

Visiting the United States, Varda and her husband Jacques Demy each made a film. Varda honored her *Uncle Janco* in the film so named. *The Black Panthers* (or *Huey*) followed. Both documentaries were shown at the London Film Festival in 1968. She next directed a segment of the antiwar short *Far from Vietnam*.

Using an American setting and an English-speaking cast, including the co-authors of the musical *Hair*, Varda made *Lions Love* in Hollywood. This jigsaw-puzzle work includes a fake suicide and images of a television set reporting Robert Kennedy's assassination. G. Roy Levin declared that it was hard to distinguish between the actual and the invented film realities. *Nausicaa* deals with Greeks living in France. Made for television, it was not shown, Varda says, because it was against military-ruled Greece.

In 1971 Varda helped write the script for *Last Tango in Paris*. Varda's involvement in the women's movement began about 1972; a film dealing with feminist issues, *Réponses de femmes,* has yet to be shown. Made for German television, *Daguerreotypes* has no cast. Varda filmed the residents and shops of the Rue Daguerre, a tribute to L. J. M. Daguerre.

In 1977 Varda made *One Sings, the Other Doesn't* and established her own company, Ciné-Tamaris, to finance it. This "family" of workers created the film. Chronicling the friendship of two women over 15 years, it earned mixed reviews, some referring to it as feminist propaganda or as sentimental syrup. But Varda, narrating the film and writing the song lyrics, does not impose her views. In *One Sings,* she wanted to portray the happiness of being a woman, she says.

Easily Varda's most potent film of the 1980s, and one of the best of her career, is *Vagabond,* an evocative drama about the death and life of a young woman, Mona (Sandrine Bonnaire). She is an ex-secretary who has chosen to become a drifter, and her fate is apparent at the outset. As the film begins, Mona has died. Her frost-bitten corpse is seen in a ditch. Her body is claimed by no one, and she is laid to rest in a potter's field. As *Vagabond* unfolds, Varda explores Mona's identity as she wanders through the rural French countryside hitching rides and begging for the necessities that will sustain her. The scenario also spotlights the manner in which she impacts on those she meets: truck drivers; a gas station owner and his son; a vineyard worker; a professor-researcher; and other, fellow drifters. Varda constructs the film as a series of sequences, some comprised of a single shot lasting several seconds, in which Mona passes through the lives of these people. The result is an eloquent film about one average, ill-fated young woman and the choices she makes, as well as a meditation on chance meetings and missed opportunities. On a much broader level, the film serves as an allegory of the travails a woman must face if she desires to completely liberate herself from the shackles of society.

Varda's most notable recent films have been valentines to her late husband, filmmaker Jacques Demy. *The Young Girls Turn 25* is a nostalgia piece about the filming of Demy's *The Young Girls of Rochefort; The World of Jacques Demy* is an up-close-and-personal documentary-biography consisting of interviews and clips from Demy's films.

A third title, *Jacquot de Nantes,* was the most widely seen. It is an exquisite film: a penetrating, heartrending account of the measure of a man's life, with Varda moving between sequences of Demy in conversation, filmed in extreme close-up; clips from his films; and a re-creation of his childhood in Nantes and the manner in which he

developed a passion for cinema. Varda illustrates how Demy's life and world view influenced his films; for example, his hatred of violence, which is ever so apparent in his films, was forged by his memories of Nantes being bombed during World War II. But *Jacquot de Nantes* (which was conceived prior to Demy's death) is most effective as a tender love letter from one life partner to another. Varda visually evokes her feeling towards her departed mate in one of the film's opening shots. She pans her camera across a watercolor, whose composition is that of a nude woman and man who are holding hands. With over three decades of filmmaking experience, Varda's reputation as a filmmaker dazzles and endures.

—Louise Heck-Rabi/Rob Edelman

DIE VERLORENE EHRE DER KATHARINA BLUM
(The Lost Honor of Katharina Blum)
West Germany, 1975
Directors: Volker Schlöndorff and Margarethe von Trotta

Production: Bioskop-Film and Paramount-Orion; color and black and white, 35mm; running time: 106 minutes. Released 1975. Filmed 1975 in Germany.

Screenplay: Volker Schlöndorff and Margarethe von Trotta, from the novel by Heinrich Böll; **photography:** Jost Vacano.

Cast: Angelika Winkler (*Katharina Blum*); Mario Adorf (*Beizmenne*); Dieter Laser (*Werner Toetgen*); Heinz Bennett (*Dr. Blorna*); Hannelore Hoger (*Trude Blorna*); Harald Kuhlmann (*Moeding*); Karl Heinz Vosgerau (*Alois Straubleder*); Jürgen Prochnow (*Ludwig Goetten*); Rolf Becker (*Hach*); Regine Lutz (*Else Woltersheim*); Werner Eichhorn (*Konrad Beiters*).

Publications

Script

Schlöndorff, Volker, and Margarethe von Trotta, *Die verlorene Ehre der Katharina Blum,* Tübingen, 1981.

Books

Sandford, John, *The New German Cinema,* Totowa, New Jersey, 1980.

Horton, Andrew, and Joan Magretta, *Modern European Filmmakers and the Art of Adaptation,* New York, 1981.

Bauschinger, Sigrid, and others, *Film und Literatur: Literarische Texte und der neue deutsche Film,* Munich, 1984.

Kilburn, R. W., *Whose Lost Honour? A Study of the Film Adaptation of Böll's "The Lost Honour of Katharina Blum,"* Glasgow, 1984.

Johansen, Annette, *Fra litteraturforlaeg til film: eksemplificeret ved Volker Schlondorffs og*

Margaretha von Trottas filmatisering af Die verlorene Ehre der Katharina Blum *efter Heinrich Bolls fortaelling af samme navn,* Copenhagen, 1987.

Elsaesser, Thomas, *New German Cinema: A History,* London, 1989.

Die Verlorene Ehre der Katharina Blum

Articles

Hawkins, R. F., in *Variety* (New York), 1 October 1975.

Anderson, W., in *Filmrutan* (Tyreso), no. 1, 1976.

Film und Fernsehen (East Berlin), no. 8, 1976.

Gersch, W., in *Film und Fernsehen* (East Berlin), no. 10, 1976.

Schirmeyer-Klein, U., in *Film und Ton Magazine* (Munich), January 1976.

Passek, J. L., in *Cinéma* (Paris), April 1976.

Kane, P., in *Cahiers du Cinéma* (Paris), May 1976.

Bonnet, J. C., in *Cinématographe* (Paris), June 1976.

Chavardes, B., in *Téléciné* (Paris), July/August 1976.

Dekeyser, H., in *Film en Televisie* (Brussels), July/August 1976.

Pellizzari, L., in *Cineforum* (Bergamo, Italy), July/August 1976.

Chevallier, J., in *Revue du Cinéma* (Paris), October 1976.

Wilson, D., in *Monthly Film Bulletin* (London), May 1977.

Elley, Derek, in *Films and Filming* (London), September 1977.

Friedman, L. D., "Cinematic Techniques in *The Lost Honor of Katharina Blum*," in *Literature Film Quarterly,* (Salisbury, Maryland), no. 3, 1979.

German Life and Letters, April 1979.

Holloway, Ronald, "Volker Schlöndorff," in *International Film Guide 1982,* London, 1981.

"Bio-filmographie de Volker Schlöndorff," in *Avant-Scène du Cinéma* (Paris), February 1984.

Bertin-Maghit, J.-P., and D. Sauvaget, "Volker Schlöndorff: Trouver l'acces au public...," in *Revue du Cinéma* (Paris), April 1984.

Helmetag, C. H., *The Lost Honor of Kathryn Beck:* A German Story on American Television," in *Literature Film Quarterly* (Salisbury, Maryland), October 1985.

* * *

The Lost Honor of Katharina Blum, co-directed by Volker Schlöndorff and Margarethe von Trotta, is based on the novel of the same name by Heinrich Böll, who worked closely with the directors in the transformation of his novel into film. Schlöndorff and von Trotta had worked together on several films prior to this one. Schlöndorff had directed von Trotta as an actress and she had also served as his scriptwriter. This was their first co-directed film, a credit which von Trotta had to demand. Their differences in style became obvious in this film as Schlöndorff concentrated on the action sequences, while von Trotta worked with the actors to bring out the power of their emotions. After this film they separated, though *Katharina Blum* was the most popularly successful of all their films.

Katharina Blum brought to the public's attention the extent of the political turmoil in West Germany. It followed closely on the heels of the murder of Hanns Martin Schleyer, a West German corporate leader and the prison deaths of three Baader-Meinhof terrorists. The film came at a time when the West German oppression of the left was quite harsh. The new Germany of the 1970s is shown in the film to be similar to Nazi Germany. In both the new and the old, the press, the church, and the state work closely together to smash any opposition to the policies of the government. Böll himself had been accused of harboring terrorists in his home and it is from this experience that the novel sprang. Although the film does not follow the exact pattern of the book, it carries the main theme as prescribed in the subtitle of the novel, "How Violence Develops and Where It Can Lead."

The main image of the film is one of spying. The opening sequence sets the tone for the whole film as the audience is introduced to Ludwig through the spying lens of the police camera. The film boldly switches from color to black-and-white images to make the audience aware of the sequences being observed by police. This subtle (there is no break in the action) yet startling technique dramatizes the unsuspected ubiquity of the police.

Characters are constantly looking at each other through glass partitions and other barriers that separate people but allow for no privacy. For privacy in this state is an illusion, both visually and literally, as exemplified by the invasion and distortion of Katharina's privacy by the press and the police.

The plethora of mirror and glass images, in which the characters are invited to look in and through in search of a clearer perception of themselves and those around them, is reminiscent of Lotte Eisner's comments concerning German Expressionists. In her book *The Haunted Screen,* she notes that such images suggest "visions nourished by moods of vague and troubled yearnings." Troubled yearnings are present in the film but they are anything but vague. The stereotyping of the characters into such categories as "bullying police chief," "wealthy clergyman," and "insensitive journalist" make it very clear to the audience exactly who the villains are and who the heroine is. Vincent Canby of *The New York Times* writes, "The corruption portrayed by the film is so pervasive that one expects it to challenge more. But it doesn't. Instead it has the effect of numbing us. Its single minded intensity nails the imagination to the floor."

Although the film is relatively undistinguished in technical and artistic terms, it does retain interest as a social document. The film managed to set before the German public a clear (albeit stereotyped and single-mindedly distorted) picture of present-day Germany.

—Gretchen Elsner-Sommer

LA VIE DU CHRIST

(Life of Christ)
France, 1906
Director: Alice Guy

Production: Gaumont and Company; black and white. Filmed at Gaumont Studios, outdoor scenes in forest of Fontainebleau.

Producer: Léon Gaumont; **associate director:** Victorin Jasset; **set designers:** Henri Ménessier and Robert-Jules Garnier.

Publications

Books

Slide, Anthony, *Early Women Directors,* South Brunswick, New Jersey, 1977; rev. ed. published as *The Silent Feminists: America's First Women Directors,* Lanham, Maryland, 1996.
Blaché, Alice Guy, *Autobiographie d'une pionnière du cinéma 1873-1968,* Paris, 1976; published as *The Memoirs of Alice Guy Blaché,* translated by Roberta and Simone Blaché, edited by Anthony Slide, Metuchen, New Jersey, 1986.

Articles

Blaché, Alice, "Woman's Place in Photoplay Production," in *Moving Picture World* (New York), 11 July 1914.
Ford, Charles, "The First Female Producer," in *Films in Review* (New York), March 1964.
Lacassin, Francis, "Out of Oblivion: Alice Guy-Blaché," in *Sight and Sound* (London), Summer 1971.

*   *   *

La Vie du Christ was arguably the first—and, measuring 600 meters—the longest historical spectacle attempted on film until then. It was also a film that tried to be faithful to the historical as well as spiritual realities that defined the life of "Christ among Men" (one of the film's subtitles). In her autobiography, Alice Guy remarks that the Biblical illustrations of James Tissot's "La Vie de Notre Seigneur Jésus-Christ," taken after sketches in the Holy Land, provided her "ideal documentation for decors, costumes, even local customs." But documentation is not conception, and the vision animating the Biblical tableaux was distinctly her own. Guy's visual signature, however, was not always legible, nor even self-evidently hers. Some film historians have doubted or diminished her part in making the film, a monumental undertaking for its time, involving more than 300 extras and 25 wooden sets designed by Henri Ménessier and Robert-Jules Garnier. Georges Sadoul attributed the film to Victorin Jasset (1862-1913), who himself had claimed credit for the work. Jean Mitry, noting the fluidity of terms and functions in those early days of film production, sensibly advised that we should not "apply present notions to designations applied to films before 1908, at time when the terms 'metteur en scène,' 'régisseur,' 'directeur' and even 'opérateur' (cameraman) referred to the same function world wide." Certainly the film could not have been made without the contribution of Jasset, a producer famed for the historical spectacles he staged at the Paris Hippodrome. Guy herself acknowledged Jasset's role in filming the outdoor scenes and in "administering" the extras. She nevertheless insisted the project remained primarily her own, citing the directorial credit she received (an uncommon practice at that time) when the film was presented at the Société de photographie de Paris. The film manifestly bears the imprimatur of a singular imagination adept in orchestrating divine with human elements. Whether that imagination is fundamentally or even marginally "female" is, of course, an open question, but also an unavoidable one, given Guy's pride of place as the founding mother of modern cinema.

While it is unnecessary to insist that *La Vie du Christ* is the work of a believer, it is unquestionably a devout work. Two of its alternate titles, *La Passion de Christ* or *La Passion,* convey the film's reverent interpretation of Christ's life as an irresistible martyrdom. Guy condenses the life into 25 episodes, three of which treat the birth and infancy of Christ, three his ministry before his triumphal entry into Jerusalem (Palm Sunday), and the rest the agony of the Passion, from the Last Supper to the Crucifixion and triumphant Resurrection. In dramatizing the crucial years of Christ's earthly ministry, Guy omits such initiatory episodes as the Baptism by St. John, the calling of the apostles, and the more public miracles and dramatizes those moments that confirm Christ's divine mission through his encounters with women: Christ and the Woman of Samaria, the raising of Jarius's daughter, and Mary Magdalene's anointing of Christ's feet. Both the Samaritan woman and Mary Magdalene are figures of sexual transgression whom Christ, unlike conventional moralists, neither shuns nor despises. His attitude toward them, rather than the Sermon on the Mount and the preaching of the Beatitudes, is taken to epitomize his radical religious teachings.

The film begins, however, on a traditional note with The Arrival in Bethlehem (all capitalized phrases are reproduced from intertitle cards in the restored version of the Museum of Modern Art). Family after family are shown stopping before an inn, seeking shelter but being turned away. Joseph and Mary, when they appear, seem like any other tired travelers, eager to find lodging and a night's rest. Only our knowledge of the story gives their arrival the mythic importance Guy initially refuses it; her naturalism entrusts the story to human history before it elevates it to divine narrative. But divinity is joyously acknowledged in the next panel, The Nativity and Adoration of The Wise Men. Jubilant commoners as well as the glorious Magi pour into the stable to rejoice in the birth of the Christ child, who, though only a few days, at most a few months old, is shown sitting up, clapping in delight at the celebration in his honor. The biological absurdity is redeemed by the boldness of Guy's psychological speculation that the Christ child, at this stage of his earthly existence, is no different than any other infant—adoration puts him in high spirits. Guy's interest in the psychology of Christ's double nature inspires the only "imagined" episode in the film, the sleep of the child Jesus, which shows him dreaming of doting angels.

Angels, in fact, attend Christ throughout his life, as the intertitle cards, framed by three angels, visually attest. They appear in crucial times of the Life, most movingly during Christ's vigil in the Garden of Gesthemene, to symbolize an agonized divinity that is beyond the reach of any human art to represent. Indeed Guy's "magical" or special effects generally tend to appear where we might expect to find them, but seldom in the way we might envision. Her treatment of the raising of Jarius's daughter is typical in this respect. Guy shows us the keen agitation of a household convulsed in grief, and then, as swiftly, transported by joy. The wailing of the household is rendered in the overly emphatic style favored by early cinema, yet the bringing of Jarius's daughter back to life is accomplished as undramatically as Guy dares. The girl simply rises from her deathbed. No theatrics, simply the awe-filled demonstration of Christ's power to make the transition from death to life as effortless as it is miraculous.

In such scenes, Guy shows herself a filmmaker as adept as Méliès in conjuring surreality and materializing fantasy (her first feature, *La Fée aux choux* [*The Cabbage Fairy*] had shown a whimsical ease in importing the supernatural into human domains), but one who is also imaginatively and emotionally rooted in the naturalistic world, the world of actual bodies and real environments. Perhaps nowhere is this so stunningly displayed than Guy's staging of the Deposition. Guy impresses upon our mind's eye the profound heaviness as well as pity of dead flesh as the body of Christ is laid tenderly, if helplessly, on the ground. His subsequent resurrection, accomplished by a superimposition of which Guy was especially proud, is much more visually startling than the raising of Jarius's daughter. Christ does not arise from the tomb by slow inclinations, but springs suddenly into an upright position, imposingly triumphant over the reality of the grave. A phantom throng of human mockers as well as angelic devotees flock around his risen body before he vanishes from view. The film concludes with angels and human disciples kneeling in prayer over the vacated tomb, gathered around the center of a mysterious reality invisible to the camera eye. There is nothing doctrinally objectional in Guy's *La Vie du Christ* and yet there is nothing orthodox about her manner of telling it.

—Maria DiBattista

VITAL SIGNS
USA, 1991
Director: Barbara Hammer

Production: Barbara Hammer Productions; 16mm, film/video collage; optical sound; running time: 8 minutes. Cost: $3,000.

Producer: Barbara Hammer; **screenplay:** Barbara Hammer; **photography:** Barbara Hammer; **editor:** Barbara Hammer; **sound:** Barbara Hammer.

Awards: Best Experimental Film, Utah Film Festival, 1992; Excellence Award, California State Fair, 1992; Jurors' Award, Black Maria Film Festival, 1992.

Publications

Book

Canyon Cinema Catalogue 7, San Francisco, 1992.

Articles

Dyer, Richard, "Lesbian Woman: Lesbian Cultural Feminist Film," in *Now You See It: Studies on Lesbian and Gay Film,* London, 1990.
Meyers, Ellen and Toni Armstrong Jr., "A Visionary Woman Creating Visions: Barbara Hammer, in *Hot Wire* (Chicago), May 1991.
Bornstein, Kate, "How Many Ways Can You Say 'Lesbian?,'" in *Bay Area Reporter* (San Francisco), 18 June 1992.
Hammer, Barbara, "The Politics of Abstraction," in *Queer Looks: Perspectives on Lesbian and Gay Film and Video,* edited by Martha Gever, Pratibha Parmar, and John Greyson, London, 1993.
Simonds, Cylena, "Spontaneous Combustion: An Interview with Barbara Hammer," in *Afterimage* (Rochester, New York), December 1993.

* * *

According to Barbara Hammer, the pioneering lesbian experimental filmmaker and creator of the film *Vital Signs,* "All of my work is focused on making the invisible, visible." Indeed, in a career that has produced more than 70 films and videos, Hammer's enduring goal has been to provide views of lesbian life, identity, and sexuality that counter those depicted in the conventional media as well as to promote a more active relationship between film and viewer.

Vital Signs is a complex, nonlinear, multimedia "collage" film/video that aims to deconstruct Western notions of death as terrible and frightful. She undertakes her task by literally embracing a symbol of death—a skeleton, which she feeds, dresses, and with which she walks and even dances. The film was inspired by Hammer's recognition, in middle age, of her own mortality and desire to examine the meanings attached to the Western "idea of death"—meanings that are embedded in our socialization by familial, educational, and religious institutions. She has explained that the Western fear of death represents a shift from the practices that predominated during the Middle Ages in Western Europe, when the dead were kept much closer to their communities and buried within the cities and neighborhoods where they had lived.

With *Vital Signs,* Hammer's hope was that a complex examination of the meanings of death might reveal other possibilities regarding our relationship to death. Yet, the filmmaker had a larger goal in mind; specifically, that if she could encourage viewers to consider multiple "realities" about death, then such a skill could be generalized to other issues and realities. Ideally, for Hammer, the "ability to hold several truths to be self-evident simultaneously, will be the determining factor in the survival of the human species." Further, *Vital Signs* employs a variety of media because Hammer considers it impossible for a single medium to communicate multiplicity or to signify the "end of unitary construction." Accordingly, the palette in *Vital Signs* is constituted by an exciting array of media and inventive strategies, including digital technologies, super 8mm and 16mm film, one-half-inch and three-quarters-inch videotape, optical printing, as well as found film footage that Hammer has manipulated and re-edited, including bits of Alain Resnais's 1959 film masterpiece, *Hiroshima, Mon Amour* (which she photographed off of a video monitor), in addition to text from the French theorist Michel Foucault's book *Birth of a Clinic.* Hammer deploys a collage technique to layer the variety of film and video images and sounds, in order both to avoid hierarchizing them and to avoid conveying the surface unity that filmmakers usually work to achieve. By presenting the images and sounds in this way, her intention is to disturb viewers' usual complacency; that is, Hammer believes that by experiencing a rapid succession of bits of information it becomes possible for viewers to create their own meanings, which thereby expands the possibilities for media to participate in changing society and viewers' perspectives.

Describing herself as an "experimental filmmaker and lesbian feminist," Hammer produces films that reflect her philosophy that "radical content deserves radical form." Accordingly, she eschews conventional cinema's preoccupation with classical narrative, believing that it cannot portray the experiences or issues of "lesbian and gay perceptions, concerns, and concepts."

Although her early 1970s films used strategies of "realism" to portray the lesbian body, Hammer later sought to explore other areas of expression, especially her love of abstraction. She argues that abstract films enable both filmmakers and viewers to actively engage the "pleasure of discovery" of multiple often challenging interpretations, so that they will become less passive in other, especially political, areas of life.

Hammer characterizes the experimental *Vital Signs* as a crucial link to her later works, *Nitrate Kisses* and *Tender Fictions,* which she describes as postmodern documentaries. That is, *Vital Signs*'s use of montage, varied textures, and shooting strategies to treat a central theme served as an antecedent to her subsequent longer works. Her first feature film, *Nitrate Kisses* (1993), explores the usually invisible history of lesbians and gays since 1930s Nazi Germany. The film focuses on four couples and uses both experimental and documentary modes of filmmaking, including segments of the first-known gay film in the United States, *Lot in Sodom* from 1933, and excerpts from German fiction and documentary films from the 1930s that are intercut, among many other sounds and images, with scenes of gay and lesbian sexuality, Castro Street, and New York City street life. According to Hammer, her goal with *Nitrate Kisses* was to illuminate the process by which history is created from fragments and historical interpretations of those fragments. The autobiographical *Tender Fictions* (1995) is an inventive personal exploration of the gay community and its challenge to craft a unique space within the homogeneity of American culture. The film's compelling montage includes home movies, experimental films, news segments, and excerpts from her mother's diary, to suggest the middle-class values and aspirations that characterized her family, and which Hammer has enthusiastically avoided via her emergence and development as a lesbian feminist and as an artist and activist.

—Cynthia Felando

VIVRE SA VIE
(My Life to Live; It's My Life)
France, 1962
Director: Jean-Luc Godard
Editor: Angès Guillemot

Production: Films de la Pléiade; black and white, 35mm; running time: 85 minutes. Released September 1962, Paris. Filmed 1960 in Paris.

Producer: Pierre Braunberger, **production manager:** Roger Fleytoux; **screenplay:** Jean-Luc Godard with additional narrative from Judge Marcel Sacotte's *Où en est la prostitution* and Edgar Allan Poe's "The Oval Portrait"; **assistant directors:** Jean-Paul Savignac and Bernard Toublanc-Michel; **photography:** Raoul Coutard; **editor:** Agnès Guillemot; **assistant editor:** Lila Lakshmanan; **sound:** Guy Vilette and Jacques Maumont; **sound editor:** Lila Lakshmanan; **music:** Michel Legrand; **costume designer:** Christiane Fage; **makeup:** Jackie Reynal.

Cast: Anna Karina (*Nana*); Sady Rebbot (*Raoul*); André S. Labarthe (*Paul*); Guylaine Schlumberger (*Yvette*); Gérard Hoffmann (*The Cook*); Monique Messine (*Elizabeth*); Paul Pavel (*Journalist*); Dimitri Dineff (*Dimitri*); Peter Kassowitz (*Young man*); Eric Schlumberger (*Luigi*); Brice Parain (*The Philosopher*); Henri Attal (*Arthur*); Gilles Quéant (*A Man*); Odile Geoffroy (*Barmaid*); Marcel Charton (*Policeman*); Jack Florency (*Bystander*); Gisèle Hauchecorne (*Concierge*); Jean-Luc Godard (*Voice*).

Awards: Venice Film Festival, Special Jury Prize, and the Italian Critics Prize, 1962.

Publications

Script

Godard, Jean-Luc, *Vivre sa vie,* in *Avant-Scène du Cinéma* (Paris), October 1962; "Scenario," in *Film Culture* (New York), Winter 1962.

Books

Collet, Jean, *Jean-Luc Godard,* Paris, 1963; New York, 1970.
Taylor, John Russell, *Cinema Eye, Cinema Ear: Some Key Filmmakers of the 60s,* New York, 1964.
Roud, Richard, *Jean-Luc Godard,* New York, 1967.
Mussman, Toby, editor, *Jean-Luc Godard: A Critical Anthology,* New York, 1968.
Cameron, Ian, editor, *The Films of Jean-Luc Godard,* London, 1969.
Mancini, Michele, *Godard,* Rome, 1969.
Brown, Royal, editor, *Focus on Godard,* Englewood Cliffs, New Jersey, 1972.
Godard on Godard, edited by Tom Milne, London, 1972; as *Godard on Godard: Critical Writings,* edited by Milne and Jean Narboni, New York, 1986.
Farassino, Alberto, *Jean-Luc Godard,* Florence, 1974.
Monaco, James, *The New Wave,* New York, 1976.
MacCabe, Colin, *Godard: Images, Sounds, Politics,* London, 1980.
Walsh, Martin, *The Brechtian Aspect of Radical Cinema,* London, 1981.
Lefèvre, Raymond, *Jean-Luc Godard,* Paris, 1983.
Bordwell, David, *Narration in the Fiction Film,* London, 1985.
Weis, Elisabeth, and John Belton, *Film Sound: Theory and Practice,* New York, 1985.

Articles

Sontag, Susan, in *Against Interpretation,* New York, 1961.
Sarris, Andrew, "A Movie Is a Movie Is a Movie Is a ...," in *New York Film Bulletin,* no. 5, 1962.
Shivas, Mark, in *Movie* (London), October 1962.
Truffaut, François, in *Avant-Scène du Cinéma* (Paris), October 1962.
Milne, Tom, in *Sight and Sound* (London), Winter 1962.
Collet, Jean, and others, "Entretien avec Jean-Luc Godard," in *Cahiers du Cinéma* (Paris), December 1962.
Films and Filming (London), December 1962.
Baker, Peter, in *Films and Filming* (London), January 1963.
Fieschi, Jean-André, "Godard: Cut-Sequence: *Vivre sa vie,*" in *Movie* (London), January 1963.
"Anna et les paradoxes," in *Cinéma* (Paris), July/August 1963.
Young, Colin, "Conventional/Unconventional," in *Film Quarterly* (Berkeley), Fall 1963.
Sarris, Andrew, in *Village Voice* (New York), 26 September 1963.
Carey, Gary, and Marilyn Goldin, "*My Life to Live:* Portrait of a Lady," in *Seventh Art* (New York), Winter 1963.
Sontag, Susan, "Godard," in *Partisan Review* (New Brunswick, New Jersey), Spring 1968.
Crofts, Stephen, "The Films of Jean-Luc Godard," in *Cinema* (London), June 1969.
Beh, Siew Hwa, in *Women and Film* (Santa Monica, California), no. 1, 1972.
Campbell, M., "*Life Itself: Vivre sa vie* and the Language of Film," in *Wide Angle* (Athens, Ohio), no. 3, 1976.

Baumgarten, Marjoric, in *Cinema Texas Program Notes* (Austin), 20 November 1977.
Conley, Tom, "Portrayals of Painting: Translations of *Vivre sa vie,*" in *Film Reader* (Evanston, Illinois), no. 3, 1978.
de Graaff, T., in *Skrien* (Amsterdam), Winter 1978-79.
Brown, R. S., "Music and *Vivre sa vie,*" in *Quarterly Review of Film Studies* (Pleasantville, New York), Summer 1980.
Ropars, Marie-Claire, "The Erratic Alphabet," in *Enclitic* (Minneapolis), no. 10-11, 1981.
"Godard Issue" of *Camera Obscura* (Berkeley), Fall 1982.
"Godard Issue" of *Revue Belge du Cinéma* (Brussels), Summer 1986.
van der Kooij, F., "Wo unter den Bildern sind die Klaenge daheim?," in *Cinema (Switzerland)* (Basel), no. 37, 1991.

* * *

Now you see it, now you don't. That is an apt way to describe the unobtrusive editing of Agnès Guillemot in *Vivre sa vie* (*My Life to Live*), a film conceived mainly of a series of lengthy shots presented in 12 distinct scenes.

For most of the film, the stunning, unorthodox visual style of director Jean-Luc Godard dominates as action is captured through a blend of notably odd camera placement and smooth, controlled camera movement. For instance, the first shot in the film is held for several minutes, and the camera never leaves the back of the head of the main character, Nana (Anna Karina), a record-store clerk who will become a prostitute, as she is talking to her ex-lover, Paul. When the camera eventually does move from the back of her head, it cuts to the back of Paul's talking head. Then this sequence is repeated. The viewer becomes somewhat involved with the action, but not with any help of editing. This involvement is the result of the unusual placement of the camera at a spot which, except for a vague distant mirror image, hides the faces of the characters.

There is almost no conspicuous editing in *My Life to Live* until scene four, which presents Nana in a darkened movie theater watching Carl Dreyer's *La Passion de Jeanne d'Arc.* In this segment, close-ups of Maria Falconetti as Jeanne d'Arc, and close shots of her male accuser, are intercut with close-ups of Nana's face. Whether the effect is to show Nana as a martyr, a victim, or a sad-faced romantic drawn into a lofty adventure is for speculation elsewhere. The point is that the cutting connects one cinematic character with another, via the unusual juxtaposition of two films.

Also in scene four, Nana is seen being questioned by a policeman. The sequence uses cuts to show Nana's face in close-up, then the policeman's face. Nana and the policeman do not share any frame, and so it seems that the cutting is used to isolate the characters in their own segments of the universe. This use of editing arises later in the film, in the sequence in which Nana speaks with an elderly philosopher at a cafe. Again, each character is shown alone within the frame, implying that each is an individual within his own slated territory. Ironically—or coincidentally—the main topics of conversation between the two in this scene are communication, philosophy, and love.

Towards the end of the film, Nana has a scene with a young man who is reading from a book by Edgar Allan Poe. Again, each is shown as a head within the frame. There are daring, abrupt cuts in this sequence from one close-up of Nana to another, with no attempt to match the angles or the lighting. Just as Nana seems to be most alone, however, the conversation becomes an expression of love, and eventually the two characters come together to share the frame.

Vivre sa vie **production still.**

In an unexpected change of pace, the excitement of rapid montage occurs during scene five in a series of shots showing Nana with her first paying customer. The editing style is brisk, with sharp cuts joining brief shots of objects and people that depict the business of a prostitute and her client. For instance, there is a quick shot of a bar of soap on a hotel dresser, and a quick shot of a man's hand in the front pocket of his trousers where his money is kept. The cuts join shots that have abrupt changes of angles in a manner that is jarring for the viewer, particularly when compared to the smooth-flowing style of the rest of the film. The effect is strong; the viewer sees only fleeting impressions of the prostitute and her client in the hotel. Because of the subject matter, it would be off-putting to hold the camera any longer on any of the shots.

This uncomfortable feeling towards the act of prostitution reoccurs in an energetic montage during scene seven where many fairly quick cuts are connected to show the action. First Nana and the man are in a hotel elevator. Then the bed is turned down. There is a payment of money. Nana is seen briefly on the telephone. Nana unfastens her shoes. A hand switches off the lamp next to the bed. The action continues in that vein, as if to make the statement that to dwell on any aspect of the prostitute's job would be superfluous to the scenario.

During scene six, a shooting occurs at a cafe where Nana is seated at a table where she had been conversing with a pimp named Raoul. At first, the viewer sees a close-up of Nana. There is a cut to the opening (by Nana) of Raoul's notebook of his prostitutes' schedules, and the shot is accompanied by absolute silence. Then there is the sound of a spray of gunshots, followed by a close shot of the notebook. Finally, there is a full shot of Nana at the table as loud gunfire is heard. The choice of images is a curious one to introduce the audience to a shooting; however, the results are very effective. By not actually cutting to the main action, Godard has put his viewers somewhere on the outside of the main event, having to crane their necks, so to speak, to gain entry to the action. The subtle, unconventional editing in this brief sequence is masterful.

The presentation of the backs of talking heads instead of their faces, the choice of montages of bits of action instead of lengthy, studied scenes of a prostitute and her men, and the showing of single talking heads in frames instead of more than one person, all serve to create a mood. *My Life to Live,* as the title tells the viewer, focuses on life in the singular. There are no supportive communities in the world being depicted. This is a lonely world, with other people often separated by doors (as Nana is shown trying to get past the concierge into her room, and as Nana tries to recruit a second prostitute into a sex act), or simply and conveniently placed outside the frame.

The viewer is presented with a realistic looking world, at times almost documentary in nature. Yet this world is skewed toward loneliness and alienation. Through the unusual cuts and montage work, Guillemot—who was to go on to edit a number of other key titles of the French New Wave—provides an integral part of the cinematic language that makes this world visually impressive.

—Audrey E. Kupferberg

von BRANDENSTEIN, Patrizia
American production designer

Born: Arizona. **Education:** Attended boarding school in Germany; Comedie Française school. **Family:** Married (second) the production designer Stuart Wurtzel, daughter: Kimberly. **Career:** Late 1960s-early 1970s—worked on stage productions for the American Conservatory Theater in San Francisco; assistant to production designer Stuart Wurtzel; 1975-77—served as art director on *Hester Street*; painted scenery for PBS; worked as costume designer on *Saturday Night Fever*; 1979—first major production-design work on *Breaking Away*. **Awards:** Academy Award for Art Direction, for *Amadeus,* 1984. **Agent:** Lawrence Mirisch, The Mirisch Agency, 10100 Santa Monica Boulevard, Suite 700, Los Angeles, CA 90067-4011, U.S.A.

Films as Costume Designer

1977   *Between the Lines* (J. Silver); *Saturday Night Fever* (Badham) (co)
1982   *A Little Sex* (Paltrow)

Films as Production Designer

1977   *The Gardener's Son* (for TV)
1978   **Girlfriends** (Weill); *Summer of My German Soldier* (Tuchner—for TV)
1979   *My Old Man* (Erman—for TV); *Breaking Away* (Yates)
1980   *Tell Me a Riddle* (L. Grant)
1981   *Heartland* (Pearce)
1983   *Silkwood* (M. Nichols); *Touched* (Flynn)
1984   *Amadeus* (Forman); *Beat Street* (Lathan)
1985   *A Chorus Line* (Attenborough)
1986   *The Money Pit* (Benjamin); *No Mercy* (Pearce)
1987   *The Untouchables* (De Palma)
1988   *Betrayed* (Costa-Gavras); *Working Girl* (M. Nichols)
1990   *The Lemon Sisters* (Chopra); *Postcards from the Edge* (M. Nichols); *State of Grace* (Joanou)
1991   *Billy Bathgate* (Benton)
1992   *Leap of Faith* (Pearce); *Sneakers* (Robinson)
1993   *Six Degrees of Separation* (Schepisi)
1995   *Just Cause* (Glimcher); *The Quick and the Dead* (Raimi)
1996   *The People vs. Larry Flint* (Forman)

Other Films

1972   *The Candidate* (Ritchie) (set designer)
1978   *The Last Tenant* (J. Taylor—for TV) (art d)
1980   *Hardhat and Legs* (Philips—for TV) (art d)
1981   *Ragtime* (Forman) (art d)

Publication by von Brandenstein

Article

Interview with Michael Larue, in *Theatre Crafts,* May 1987.

Publications on von Brandenstein

Articles

Smith, Ron, "Designing History," in *Theatre Crafts,* March 1984.
Kornbluth, Jesse, "One Singular Sensation," in *New York,* 14 January 1985.

Clarens, Carlos, and Mary Corliss, "'The Pit' and the Production
   Designer," in *Film Comment* (New York), March/April 1986.
Troy, Carol, "Architect of Illusions," in *American Film* (Hollywood),
   August 1990.
O'Neill, Michael, "Cinema Laureates," in *Premiere* (New York), 15
   September 1993.

* * *

Patrizia von Brandenstein made history in 1985 by becoming the
first woman ever to win an Oscar for production design, for Milos
Forman's ornate, pictorial *Amadeus.* But even if she had never won
an Oscar, or never worked on *Amadeus,* her versatility alone would
rank her at the top of her profession. Her credits show an astonishing range of subjects, styles, and periods: what does the low-budget,
break-dancing musical *Beat Street* have in common with the expensive plutonium-plant melodrama *Silkwood,* besides von Brandenstein?
Believing that a production designer can become as typecast as actors and actresses, and despite receiving Academy recognition only
for her big-budgeted period pieces (*Ragtime, Amadeus,* and *The
Untouchables*), von Brandenstein makes a concerted effort to avoid
repeating herself or latching onto familiar subjects. This openness to
challenge and diversity complicates any analysis of von
Brandenstein's designing "style," for she has worked in so many
genres her achievements resist categorization. Although not every
film she worked on was a success—critically or financially—the
enthusiasm she brings to such disparate pictures as *A Chorus Line*
and *The Quick and the Dead* is always visible: these films, however
flawed, catch the eye.

Von Brandenstein won some instant notoriety in 1977 as costume
designer on *Saturday Night Fever:* the white disco-dance outfit she
created for John Travolta appeared on the cover of *Newsweek,* spark-
ing a fad. But it was her association with Stuart Wurtzel, her production design mentor (and future husband) that established ties with
director Milos Forman. As Wurtzel's assistant on *Hair,* von
Brandenstein worked well with Forman, and later served as art director on *Ragtime,* supervising construction of a nickelodeon and a
lush rooftop garden that captured the film's nostalgic tone: they are
relics of a bygone era, still glowing and functional, as if dropped
from a time capsule. Her ability to establish historical verisimilitude
dominates *Ragtime* and later films such as *Amadeus, The Untouchables,* and *Billy Bathgate,* where the visual design is so vivid and
evocative the story and characters seem less interesting. For example, von Brandenstein and Forman scouted castles and palaces in
Czechoslovakia to select appropriate sets for *Amadeus,* and even
gained access to Prague's Tyl Theatre, where Mozart conducted the
premiere of *Don Giovanni* in 1787. With all this rich architecture as
background scenery, the dynamics of Peter Shaffer's stage play are
somewhat stifled; the viewer is too busy gawking at the sets to
concentrate on the vicious envy of F. Murray Abraham's mediocre
composer. Less problematic are *The Untouchables* and *The Quick
and the Dead,* period films by flamboyant directors uninterested in
the psychological dimensions of their characters: here, von
Brandenstein's bold re-creation of 1920s Chicago, and her hilarious
rendering of a rotting, ramshackle western town match the films'
comic-book plots and directorial flourishes.

Some of her best work, however, is not pure re-creation. Films
with contemporary settings can challenge von Brandenstein even
more than period pieces. She believes that for every picture, a production designer's main goal is to orchestrate visual material to establish the director's idea of the story's characters and central ideas,
whatever the setting. Two films directed by Mike Nichols show her
labors: in *Silkwood,* she conveys Karen Silkwood's paranoia and
feelings of entrapment by designing her home in the same feature-
less, pale-green hue as the plutonium plant where she works; only
Drew, Karen's freewheeling lover, brings life to the place with his
American flags and bright-red hot rod. And in *Postcards from the
Edge,* von Brandenstein plays illusion/reality games meant to represent the Hollywood heroine's disorientation: a tree-lined background
proves to be a set painting when a stagehand walks right through it;
a building shifts behind Dennis Quaid as Meryl Streep drives away,
but it is the building that is on wheels; and, most famously, Streep
hangs off a ledge over moving traffic, an illusion broken when
Streep lifts her hands and does not fall—both the ledge and the
traffic are fake. The viewer reads these images subconsciously, hardly
aware that von Brandenstein is building emotion with colors and
giant props. The sets are an outgrowth of the characters' personalities and conflicts, as in *The Money Pit,* where a crumbling mansion is
a comic metaphor for a crumbling marriage.

Von Brandenstein also enjoys tricking an audience with realistic
sets that, in terms of the plot and the characters, become absurd and
unsettling. The first half of Costa-Gavras's race-hate picture *Betrayed* depicts an underground network of paramilitary bigots as
deceptively simple country boys fond of beer, horses, and barbe-
cues, an extended conceit tailored to the subjective view of outsiders
like ourselves. (As soon as the country boys are exposed as out-and-
out racists, though, the picture loses tension and belabors the obvious Klan rallies and right-wing militia training exercises.) The eclectic *Six Degrees of Separation* extends the visual trickery to knock
down social barriers: vastly different New York environments (penthouse, hovel, bookstore, police station) are inhabited by the same
characters at various points, making everyone look slightly out of
place. A dirt-poor young actress, for instance, barges into a high-
priced apartment complex to meet a rich art dealer, who has to come
downstairs to a grubby little boiler room—it is a double clash of
cultures. The production design in *Six Degrees* achieves total authenticity, unlike the broad, expressionist *Silkwood;* but it is the authenticity of the locations that parodies the characters in their bizarre
explorations. The art dealer would not be laughable if the boiler
room did not look real.

A film designed by von Brandenstein is guaranteed to be visually
interesting, and von Brandenstein herself continues to expand her
territory. *The Quick and the Dead* is her first Western after 20 years
of movie work, and her memorable, dilapidated designs for that film
prove both her virtuosity and her readiness to take a risk.

—Ken Provencher

von HARBOU, Thea
German writer

Born: Tauperlitz, 27 December 1888. **Family:** Married 1) the actor
Rudolf Klein-Rogge (divorced); 2) the director Fritz Lang, 1924
(divorced 1934). **Career:** Actress in Dusseldorf, 1906, Weimar,
1908-10, Chemnitz, 1911-12, and Aachen, 1913-14; novelist; 1920—
first film script, *Die heilige Simplizie;* also wrote several scripts with
Lang; 1930s—joined Nazi party, and appointed official scriptwriter;
directed two films. **Died:** In Berlin, 1 July 1954.

Films as Writer

1920   *Die heilige Simplizie* (J. May); *Das wandernde Bild*
        (*Wandernder Held*; *Wandering Image*) (F. Lang)
1921   *Die Frauen von Gnadenstein* (Dinesen); *Kämpfende Herzen*
        (*Die Vier um die Frau*; *Four around a Woman*) (F. Lang);
        Das indische Grabmal (*The Indian Tomb*) (J. May); *Der
        müde Tod* (*Between Two Worlds*; *Beyond the Wall*) (F.
        Lang); *Der Leidensweg der Inge Krafft* (J. May)
1922   *Der brennende Acker* (*Burning Soil*) (Murnau); *Dr. Mabuse,
        der Spieler* (*Dr. Mabuse, the Gambler*) (F. Lang); *Phan-
        tom* (Murnau)
1923   *Die Austreibung* (*Driven from Home*; *The Expulsion*)
        (Murnau); *Die Prinzessin Suwarin* (Guter)
1924   *Die Finanzen des Grossherzogs* (*The Grand Duke's Fi-
        nances*) (Murnau); *Michael* (Dreyer); *Die Nibelungen* (F.
        Lang—2 parts)
1925   *Zur Chronik von Grieshuus* (*At the Grey House*) (von
        Gerlach)
1927   *Metropolis* (F. Lang)
1928   *Spione* (*Spies*) (F. Lang)
1929   *Die Frau im Mond* (*By Rocket to the Moon*; *The Woman in
        the Moon*) (F. Lang)
1931   *M* (F. Lang)
1932   *Das erste Recht des Kindes* (*Aus dem Tagebuch einer
        Frauenärztin*) (Wendhausen)
1933   *Das Testament des Dr. Mabuse* (*The Testament of Dr.
        Mabuse*) (F. Lang); *Der Läufer von Marathon* (Dupont)
1934   *Hanneles Himmelfahrt* (+ d); *Prinzessin Tourandot*
        (Lamprecht); *Was bin ich ohne Dich?* (Rabenalt)
1935   *Der alte und der junge König* (Steinhoff); *Ein idealer Gatte*
        (Selpin); *Ich war Jack Mortimer* (Froelich); *Der Mann
        mit der Pranke* (van der Noss)
1936   *Eine Frau ohne Bedetung* (*A Woman of No Importance*)
        (Steinhoff); *Eskapade* (*Seine offizielle Frau*) (Waschneck);
        Die unmögliche Frau (Meyer)
1937   *Der Herrscher* (*The Ruler*) (Harlan); *Versprich mir nichts!*
        (Liebeneiner); *Mutterlied* (Gallone); *Der zerbrochene Krug*
        (*The Broken Jug*) (Ucicky); *Solo per te* (Gallone)
1938   *Jugend* (*Youth*) (Harlan); *Verwehte Spuren* (Harlan); *Die Frau
        am Scheidewege* (von Báky); *Menschen im Variete* (von
        Báky)
1939   *Hurra! Ich bin Papa!* (Hoffmann)
1940   *Lauter Liebe* (Rühmann); *Wie konntest du, Veronika?*
        (Habich)
1941   *Annelie* (*Die Geschichte eines Lebens*) (von Báky); *Am Abend
        auf der Heide* (von Alten)
1942   *Mit den Augen einer Frau* (Külb)
1943   *Die Gattin* (Jacoby); *Gefährten meines Sommers* (Buch)
1944   *Eine Frau für drei Tage* (Kirchhoff)
1945   *Kolberg* (*Burning Hearts*) (Harlan) (co)
1948   *Fahrt ins Glück* (Engel—produced 1945); *Via Mala* (*Die
        Strasse des Bösen*) (von Báky—produced 1944)
1950   *Es kommt ein Tag* (Jugert); *Erzieherin gesucht* (Erfurth—
        produced 1944)
1951   *Angelika* (Hansen) (*Dr. Holl*; *Affairs of Dr. Holl*)
1953   *Dein Herz ist meine Heimat* (Häussler)

Film as Director

1934   *Elisabeth und der Narr*

Publications by von Harbou

Fiction

Die nach uns kommen, Stuttgart, 1910.
Von Engeln und Teufelchen, Stuttgart, 1913.
Der Krieg and Die Frauen, Stuttgart, 1913.
Die Masken des Todes, Stuttgart, 1915.
Der unsterbliche Acker, Stuttgart, 1915.
Aus Abend und Morgen ein neuer Tag, Heilbronn, 1916.
Gold in Feuer, Stuttgart, 1916.
Das Mondscheinprinzesschen, Stuttgart, 1916.
Der belagerte Tempel, Berlin, 1917.
Das indische Grabmal, Berlin, 1917.
Adrian Drost und sein Land, Berlin, 1918.
Sonderbare Heilige, Berlin, 1919.
Das Haus ohne Tür und Fenster, Berlin, 1920.
Legenden, Berlin, 1920.
Das Nibelungenbuch, Munich, 1923.
Mann zwischen Frauen, Leipzig, 1927.
Metropolis, Berlin, 1926, translated as *Metropolis,* London, 1927.
Frau im Mond, Berlin, 1928, as *The Girl in the Moon,* London, 1930.
Die Insel der Unsterblichen, Berlin, 1928.
Spione, Berlin, 1928, as *The Spy,* London, 1928.
Rocket to the Moon, New York, 1930.
Du bist unmöglich Jo, Berlin, 1931.
Aufblühender Lotos, Berlin, 1941.
Gartenstrasse 64, Berlin, 1952.

Other Books

Deutsche Frauen, Leipzig, 1914.
Die junge Wacht am Rhein, Stuttgart, 1915.
Die deutsche Frau im Weltkrieg, Leipzig, 1916.
Die unheilige Dreifaltigkeit, Heilbronn, 1920.
Liebesbriefe aus St. Florin, Leipzig, 1935.
Das Dieb von Bagdad, Holzminden, 1949.
With Fritz Lang, *M* (script), edited by Gero Gandert and Ulrich Gregor,
    Hamburg, 1963, translated as *M,* New York, 1968.
With Fritz Lang, *Metropolis* (script) in *Avant-Scène* (Paris), 1 Decem-
    ber 1977.

Publications on von Harbou

Book

Keiner, Reinhold, *Thea von Harbou und der deutsche Film bis 1933,*
    Hildesheim, 1984.

Articles

Mein Film (Vienna), 29 August 1952.
Filmblätter, 8 January 1954.
Chaplin (Stockholm), December 1968.

*   *   *

    Thea von Harbou worked as Fritz Lang's principal scenarist from
1924 to 1932, when she split with Lang on political matters, and
enthusiastically joined the Nazi Party. If we are to believe Fritz Lang's
later statements, made in the 1960s in America, it was von Harbou

who turned Lang in to Joseph Goebbels, the head of the Reich Propaganda Ministry.

Von Harbou's work as a scenarist for Lang includes her scripts for *Metropolis, By Rocket to the Moon, Dr. Mabuse, the Gambler,* and *Spies.* She also worked with Murnau, Dreyer, and Joe May. After writing the screenplay of Lang's most anti-Nazi film, *The Testament of Dr. Mabuse* (in which Hitler's words are put in the mouth of Dr. Mabuse, a criminal madman), von Harbou made a fatal decision, deciding for the nihilistic vision of the Nazis over the humanistic if sometimes brooding realism of the best of Lang's works. She worked continually up to her death on screen fare of decreasing distinction, ending her career with the screenplay for the mediocre film *Dein Herz ist meine Heimat.*

In all of von Harbou's screenplays, one can easily detect the strident notes of propaganda. Her work with Lang is the most restrained and fleshed-out of her long career, but, Lang later claimed that von Harbou was, at her best, merely a journeyman screenwriter who lacked the ability to get inside the motivations of her characters. Because von Harbou supported a regime that took a dim view of individualism or artistry without state direction, it is to be expected that her work under the Hitler regime, such as the screenplay for *Youth,* a study of the Hitler Youth Movement, would fail as both propaganda and cinematic art.

Between 1945 and 1951 von Harbou was prevented from working in the German cinema by order of the Nuremberg Tribunal, but clearly her major work, for better or worse, was long behind her. She also directed two films under the Nazis, *Elisabeth und der Narr* and *Hanneles Himmelfahrt.* Neither was a commercial or critical success. The same must be said of her work as a screenwriter between 1933 and 1945. That her resultant efforts were quickly forgotten by both the public and the critics seems an inescapable by-product of von Harbou's ardent espousal of the Nazi cause. For the researcher, prints of von Harbou's work during World War II are available for screening at the National Archive in Washington, D.C. Although von Harbou was undoubtedly one of the key figures in the Expressionist movement of the 1920s, her work from 1937 to 1945, founded as it inevitably was on a doctrine of racial hatred, simply has no place in a thoughtful or caring society.

—Wheeler Winston Dixon

von TROTTA, Margarethe
German director, writer, and actress

Born: Berlin, 21 February 1942. **Education:** Attended the Universities of Munich and Paris; studied acting in Munich. **Family:** Married the director Volker Schlöndorff, 1969 (divorced). **Career:** 1960s—actress in theaters in Dinkelsbül, Stuttgart, and Frankfurt; from 1969—worked only in TV and film; 1975—directed first film, *The Lost Honor of Katharina Blum.* **Awards:** Golden Lion, Venice Festival, for *The German Sisters,* 1981. **Address:** Bioskop-Film, Turkenstrasse 91, D-80799 Munich, Germany.

Films as Director

1975   *Die verlorene Ehre der Katharina Blum* (*The Lost Honor of Katharina Blum*) (co-d with Schlöndorff, co-sc)

1977   *Das zweite Erwachen der Christa Klages* (*The Second Awakening of Christa Klages*) (+ sc)

1979   *Schwestern oder Die Balance des Glücks* (*Sisters, or The Balance of Happiness*) (+ co-sc)

1981   *Die Bleierne Zeit* (*The German Sisters*; *Marianne and Juliane*; *Leaden Times*) (+ sc)

1983   *Heller Wahn* (*L'Amie*; *Sheer Madness*; *A Labor of Love*; *Friends and Husbands*) (+ sc)

1986   *Rosa Luxemburg* (+ sc)

1987   *Felix* (co-d with Buschmann, Sander, and Sanders-Brahms); *Eva*

1988   *Paura e amore* (*Love and Fear*; *Fuerchten und Liebe*) (+ co-sc)

1990   *Die Rückkehr* (*The Return*; *L'Africana*)

1993   *Il lungo silenzio* (*The Long Silence*); *Zeit des Zorns*

1994   *Das versprechen* (*The Promise*) (+ co-sc)

1997   *Winterkind* (for TV)

Other Films

1968   *Schräge Vögel* (Ehmck) (ro)

1969   *Brandstifter* (Lemke) (ro); *Götter der Pest* (Fassbinder) (ro as Margarethe)

1970   *Baal* (Schlöndorff) (ro as Sophie); *Der amerikanische Soldat* (*The American Soldier*) (Fassbinder) (ro as maid)

1971   *Der plötzliche Reichtum der armen Leute von Kombach* (Schlöndorff) (co-sc, ro as Heinrich's woman); *Die Moral der Ruth Halbfass* (Schlöndorff) (ro as Doris Vogelsang)

1972   *Strohfeuer* (*Summer Lightning*) (Schlöndorff) (ro as Elisabeth, co-sc)

1973   *Desaster* (Hauff) (ro); *Übernachtung in Tirol* (Schlöndorff) (ro as Katja)

1974   *Invitation à la chasse* (Chabrol—for TV) (ro as Paulette); *Georgina's Gründe* (Schlöndorff—for TV) (ro as Kate Theory)

1975   *Das andechser Gefühl* (Achternbusch) (ro as film actress)

1976   *Der Fangschuss* (*Coup de grâce*) (Schlöndorff) (co-sc, ro as Sophie von Reval)

1981   *Die Fälschung* (*The Forgery*; *Circle of Deceit*, *False Witness*) (Schlöndorff) (co-sc)

1984   *Blaubart* (*Bluebeard*) (Zanussi) (ro); *Unerreichbare Nähe* (Hirtz) (sc)

1995   *Die Nacht der Regisseure* (*The Night of the Filmmakers*) (Reitz—doc) (appearance); *Die Neugier immer weiter treiben* (Buchka—doc) (appearance)

Publications by von Trotta

Books

Die Bleierne Zeit, Frankfurt, 1981.
Heller Wahn, Frankfurt, 1983.
With Christiane Ensslin, *Rosa Luxemburg,* Frankfurt, 1986.

Articles

"*Die verlorene Ehre der Katharina Blum,*" in *Film und Fernsehen* (Berlin), no. 8, 1976.
"Gespräch zwischen Margarethe von Trotta und Christel Buschmann," in *Frauen und Film* (Berlin), June 1976.
"Frauen haben anderes zu sagen ...," interview with U. Schirmeyer-Klein, in *Film und Fernsehen* (Berlin), no. 4, 1979.

Margarethe von Trotta

Interview with Sheila Johnston, in *Stills* (London), May/June 1986.
Interview with Karen Jaehne and Lenny Rubenstein, in *Cineaste* (New York), vol. 15, no. 4, 1987.

Publications on von Trotta

Books

Franklin, James, *New German Cinema: From Oberhausen to Hamburg,* Boston, 1983.
Phillips, Klaus, editor, *New German Filmmakers: From Oberhausen through the 1970s,* New York, 1984.
Todd, Janet, editor, *Women and Film: Women and Literature,* New York, 1988.
Elsaesser, Thomas, *New German Cinema: A History,* London, 1989.
Acker, Ally, *Reel Women: Pioneers of the Cinema, 1896 to the Present,* New York, 1991.
Foster, Gwendolyn Audrey, *Women Film Directors: An International Bio-Critical Dictionary,* Westport, Connecticut, 1995.

Articles

Dormann, G., et al., "Le *Coup de grâce* Issue" of *Avant-Scène du Cinéma* (Paris), 1 February 1977.

Elsaesser, Thomas, "Mother Courage and Divided Daughter," in *Monthly Film Bulletin* (London), July 1983.
Dossier on von Trotta, in *Revue du Cinéma* (Paris), November 1983.
Moeller, H. B., "West German Women's Cinema: The Case of Margarethe von Trotta," in *Film Criticism* (Meadville, Pennsylvania), Winter 1984/85; reprinted Fall/Winter 1986/87.
Linville, Susan, and Kent Casper, "The Ambiguity of Margarethe von Trotta's *Sheer Madness,*" in *Film Criticism* (Meadville, Pennsylvania), vol. 12, no. 1, 1987.
Current Biography, New York, 1988.
Donough, Martin, "Margarethe von Trotta: Gynemegoguery and the Dilemmas of a Filmmaker," in *Literature/Film Quarterly* (Salisbury, Maryland), vol. 17, no. 3, 1989.
Kauffman, Stanley, "The Long Silence," in *New Republic* (New York), 30 May 1994.

* * *

An important aspect of Margarethe von Trotta's filmmaking, which affects not only the content but also the representation of that content, is her emphasis on women and the relationships that can develop between them. For example, von Trotta chose as the central theme in two of her films (*Sisters, or The Balance of Happiness* and *The German Sisters*) one of the most intense and complex relationships that can exist between two women, that of sisters. Whether von Trotta is dealing with overtly political themes as in *The Second Awakening of Christa Klages* (based on the true story of a woman who robs a bank in order to subsidize a day-care center) and *The German Sisters* (based on the experiences of Christine Ensslin and her "terrorist" sister) or with the lives of ordinary women as in *Sisters, or The Balance of Happiness* or *Sheer Madness,* von Trotta shows the political nature of relationships between women. By paying close attention to these relationships, von Trotta brings into question the social and political systems that either sustain them or do not allow them to exist.

Although the essence of von Trotta's films is political and critical of the status quo, their structures are quite conventional. Her films are expensively made and highly subsidized by the film production company Bioskop, which was started by her husband Volker Schlöndorff and Reinhard Hauff, both filmmakers. Von Trotta joined the company when she started making her own films. She did not go through the complicated system of incentives and grants available to independent filmmakers in Germany. Rather, she began working for Schlöndorff as an actress and then as a scriptwriter, and finally on her own as a director and co-owner in the production company that subsidizes their films.

Von Trotta has been criticized by some feminists for working too closely within the system and for creating characters and structures that are too conventional to be of any political value. Other critics find that a feminist aesthetic can be found in her choice of themes. For although von Trotta uses conventional women characters, she does not represent them in traditional fashion. Nor does she describe them with stereotyped, sexist clichés; instead, she allows her characters to develop on screen through gestures, glances, and nuances. Great importance is given to the psychological and subconscious delineation of her characters, for von Trotta pays constant attention to dreams, visions, flashbacks, and personal obsessions. In this way, her work can be seen as inspired by the films of Bresson and Bergman, filmmakers who also use the film medium to portray psychological depth.

"The unconscious and subconscious behavior of the characters is more important to me than what they do," says von Trotta. For this reason, von Trotta spends a great deal of time with her actors and actresses to be sure that they really understand the emotions and motivations of the characters that they portray. This aspect of her filmmaking caused her to separate her work from that of her husband, Volker Schlöndorff. During their joint direction of *The Lost Honor of Katharina Blum,* it became apparent that Schlöndorff's manner of directing, which focused on action shots, did not mix with his wife's predilections for exploring the internal motivation of the

characters. Her films are often criticized for paying too much attention to the psychological, and thus becoming too personal and inaccessible.

Von Trotta has caused much controversy within the feminist movement and outside of it. Nevertheless, her films have won several awards not only in her native Germany but also internationally, drawing large, diverse audiences. Her importance cannot be minimized. Although she employs the commonly used and accepted structures of popular filmmakers, her message is quite different. Her main characters are women and her films treat them in a serious and innovative fashion. Such treatment of women within a traditional form has in the past been undervalued or ignored. Her presentation of women has opened up possibilities for the development of the image of women on screen and contributed to the development of film itself.

Von Trotta's films have continued to express other concerns that were central to her earlier work as well. These include examinations of German identity and the impact of recent German history on the present; the view of historical events through the perceptions of the individuals those events affect; the personal risks that individuals take when speaking the truth or exposing the hypocrisy of those in power; and, in particular, the strengths of women and the manner in which they relate to each other and evolve as their own individual selves.

Rosa Luxemburg is a highly intelligent, multifaceted biopic of the idealistic, politically committed, but ill-fated humanist and democratic socialist who had such a high profile on the German political scene near the beginning of the 20th century. *Love and Fear,* loosely based on Chekhov's *The Three Sisters,* is an absorbing (if sometimes overdone) allegory about how life is forever in transition. It focuses on a trio of sisters, each with a different personality. The senior sibling is a scholarly type who is too cognizant of how quickly time goes by; the middle one lives an aimless life, and is ruled by her feelings; the junior in the group is a fervent, optimistic pre-med student.

The Long Silence is the story of a judge whose life is in danger because of his prosecution of corrupt government officials. After his murder—an unavoidable occurrence, given the circumstances—his gynecologist wife perseveres in continuing his work. *The Promise,* which reflects on the downfall of communism and the demise of the Berlin Wall, tells of two lovers who are separated in 1961 during a failed attempt to escape from East to West. With the exception of a brief reunion in Prague in 1968, they are held apart until 1989 and the death of communism in East Germany.

—Gretchen Elsner-Sommer/Rob Edelman

WANDA

USA, 1970
Director: Barbara Loden

Production: Foundation for Filmmakers; Kodachrome, 35mm blown up from 16mm; running time: 100 minutes. Released January 1971, London. Filmed in and around Scranton, Pennsylvania.

Producer: Harry Shuster; **screenplay:** Barbara Loden; **photography:** Nicholas T. Proferes; **editor:** Nicholas T. Proferes; **sound engineer:** Lars Hedman; **sound editor:** Harvey Greenstein.

Cast: Barbara Loden (*Wanda Goronski*); Michael Higgins (*Norman Dennis*); Dorothy Shapenes (*Wanda's Sister*); Peter Shapenes (*Wanda's Brother-in-law*); Jerome Thier (*Wanda's Husband*); Marian Thier (*Miss Godek*); Anthony Rotell (*Tony*); M. L. Kennedy (*Judge*); Gerald Grippo (*Court Clerk*); with: Milton Gittleman; Lila Gittleman; Arnold Kanig.

Awards: International Critics Prize, Venice.

Publications

Book

Smith, Sharon, *Women Who Make Movies*, New York, 1975.

Articles

Tallenay, Jean-Louis, interview with Barbara Loden, in *Télérama* (Paris), 5 September 1970.
Malcolm, Derek, interview with Barbara Loden, in *Guardian* (London), 9 December 1970.
Taylor, John Russell, in *Sight and Sound* (London), Winter 1970-71.
Billington, Michael, "Barbara Loden," in *Times* (London), 16 January 1971.
Andrews, Nigel, in *Monthly Film Bulletin* (London), March 1971.
Sarris, Andrew, "*Wanda* and the Women's Angle," in *Village Voice* (New York), 18 March 1971.
Kael, Pauline, in *New Yorker*, 20 March 1971.
Ritter, Jess, in *Rolling Stone* (New York), 27 May 1971.
Melton, Ruby, interview with Barbara Loden, in *Film Journal* (New York), Summer 1971.
Butterfield, Marni, "After a Long Silence, Barbara Loden Speaks on Film," interview with Barbara Loden, in *Show* (New York), July 1971.
Changas, Estelle, in *Film Quarterly* (Berkeley), Fall 1971.
Haskell, Molly, "We've Yet to Catch Up with *Adam's Rib*" (panel discussion chaired by Haskell), in *Village Voice* (New York), 21 October 1971.

Madison Women's Media Collective, "Barbara Loden Revisited," interview with Barbara Loden, in *Women and Film* (Santa Monica, California), 1974.
Kleinhans, Chuck, "Seeing through Cinema Verité," in *Jump Cut* (Chicago), May/June 1974.
Ciment, Michel, interview with Barbara Loden, in *Positif* (Paris), April 1975.

* * *

Wanda was the first—and, as it turned out, only—feature film directed by actress Barbara Loden. Loden, who had taken supporting roles in *Wild River*, *Splendor in the Grass*, and *The Swimmer*, came to fame on Broadway playing Maggie, the character closely based on Marilyn Monroe, in Arthur Miller's *After the Fall* (1964). Otherwise—apart from two short films she directed for television—she was best known as the second wife of the film director Elia Kazan. When *Wanda* was premiered, with little pre-publicity, at the 1970 Venice Festival, it came as a revelation: a wholly personal, distinctive, and assured work from a director who clearly knew exactly what she wanted.

Those who assumed, on hearing of Loden's film, that it would betray the influence of Kazan (if not his uncredited participation) were wide of the mark. *Wanda* shares nothing of Kazan's didacticism, nor his often overheated theatricality. According to Loden herself, his main input was to have his advice ignored. "I'd ask him about some scene and he'd say do it one way, then I'd think about it and say hell no, that's wrong, I'm going to do it totally different."

Right from its opening shot, as the camera pans dispassionately across a ravaged, quarried-out industrial wasteland, *Wanda* signals its rejection of all notions of conventional glamour and Hollywood pacing. The color—16mm stock blown up to 35mm—is grainy and faded; the lighting, especially in interiors, often neon-garish. (The film was all shot on location, with a $115,000 budget, using available light sources.) Loden favors long, considered takes: even in the action scenes (the kidnap of the bank manager, the bank robbery) the framing is matter-of-fact, the cutting deliberate and unhurried. This is a drab world, where even violent crime lacks much in the way of excitement, and *Wanda* presents it with unblinking honesty.

Wanda herself (played by Loden with no trace of actorly self-indulgence) seems as depleted as the landscape she inhabits, a woman utterly devoid of any sense of self-worth. At her divorce hearing she concedes every charge made against her by her husband, listlessly admits to being a useless wife and mother, and when the judge asks if she wants to claim custody of the children, responds, "I reckon they'd be better off with him." Sacked from her sweatshop job and bilked of the pitiful few bucks she is owed, or brutally dumped at the roadside by a casual pickup, she shows no surprise or resentment. Such treatment is no more than she expects, or feels she deserves. As she tells her small-time crook lover, Mr. Dennis, "Never did have anything, never will have anything. I'm stupid.... I'm just no good."

As played by Michael Higgins, the only other professional actor in the cast, the bookish-looking Dennis makes a hopelessly inept criminal. He meets Wanda when she drifts into a bar he is robbing, and takes her along because he cannot think what else to do with her. Taciturn, irritable, callous, Dennis is even more emotionally dysfunctional than Wanda herself, yet an oddly diffident regard develops between them. Wanda's tremulous smile when he tells her "You did good. You're really something," is moving in its incredulity; this is the first compliment she has heard in years. But it is also his last word to her: he heads off to rob the bank, while she loses him in traffic and arrives only to see his corpse being carried out. Alone again, she slumps back into her hapless existence.

This ending, too uncompromisingly flat even to be downbeat, typifies the film's strength. Compassionate but not for a moment sentimental, *Wanda* resists the temptation to offer its heroine any specious ray of hope. Nor is the film simplistic in its politics: though Wanda is evidently the product of her society, of a ground-down way of life that never gave her the chance of self-respect, Loden advocates no easy solutions, or indeed any solutions at all. "I wanted to make an antimovie," she explained, "to present a story without manipulating the audience and telling them what their response should be." The contrast with Kazan, intentional or not, could scarcely be greater. Where Brando's Terry Malloy in *On the Waterfront*, for all that he laments he "coulda been a contender," is finally shown taking control of his destiny, *Wanda* dares to suggest that some people—many of them women—cannot and never will.

Though widely acclaimed, *Wanda* came under attack from feminist critics who objected to the heroine's passivity and felt she should have been shown making positive moves to change her life. Loden responded that the film was drawn from her own childhood experience: "I was very passive and resigned to numbness, very much like Wanda, except that I had more emotional poverty than physical poverty in my youth." Such critics, she felt, "wouldn't want me to exist, and they would say that I was not valid or that I shouldn't be heard.... The whole point of why I wanted to make the film was that [women such as Wanda] never get a chance; nobody knows about their experience."

The exceptional promise shown by *Wanda* was never to be fulfilled. While setting up her second feature, an adaptation of Kate Chopin's 1899 proto-feminist classic, *The Awakening*, Barbara Loden was diagnosed with breast cancer, from which she died at the age of 48.

—Philip Kemp

WEBER, Lois

American director

Born: Allegheny City, Pennsylvania, 13 June 1882. **Family:** Married the director and actor Phillips Smalley, 1906 (divorced 1922). **Career:** 1890s—touring concert pianist, then Church Home Missionary in Pittsburgh; 1905—actress in touring melodrama *Why Girls Leave Home* for company managed by future husband Smalley; from 1908—writer and director (then actor) for Gaumont Talking Pictures; teamed up with Smalley, moved to Reliance, then Rex, working for Edwin S. Porter; 1912—the Smalleys (as they were known) took over Rex, a member of the Universal conglomerate, following Porter's departure; 1914—joined Hobart Bosworth's company; 1915—Universal funded private studio for Weber at 4634 Sunset Boulevard; 1917—founded own studio; 1920—signed contract with Famous Players-Lasky for $50,000 per picture and a percentage of profits; 1921—dropped by company after three unprofitable films, subsequently lost company, divorced husband, and suffered nervous collapse; late 1920s briefly resumed directing; 1930s—script-doctor for Universal. **Died:** In Hollywood, 13 November 1939.

Films as Director

(partial list—directed between 200 and 400 films)

1912   *The Troubadour's Triumph* (co-d); *The Japanese Idyll* (co-d)
1913   *The Eyes of God* (co-d); *The Jew's Christmas* (co-d, + sc, ro); *The Female of the Species* (+ ro); *Suspense* (co-d); *His Brand*
1914   *The Merchant of Venice* (co-d with Smalley, + ro as Portia); *Traitor*; *Like Most Wives*; *Hypocrites!* (+ sc); *False Colors* (co-d, + co-sc, ro); *It's No Laughing Matter* (+ sc); *A Fool and His Money* (+ ro); *Behind the Veil* (co-d, + sc, ro); *The Leper's Coat*; *The Career of Waterloo Peterson*
1915   *Sunshine Molly* (co-d, ro, sc); *Scandal* (co-d, + sc, ro); *Jewel*; *A Cigarette, That's All* (co-d, + sc)
1916   *Discontent* (short); *Hop, the Devil's Brew* (co-d, + sc, ro); **Where Are My Children?** (co-d, + sc); *The French Downstairs*; *Alone in the World* (short); *The People vs. John Doe* (+ ro); *The Rock of Riches* (short); *John Needham's Double*; *Saving the Family Name* (co-d, ro); *Shoes*; *The Dumb Girl of Portici* (co-d); *The Flirt* (co-d); *Idle Wives*; *Wanted—a Home*
1917   *The Hand that Rocks the Cradle* (co-d, + pr, ro); *Even as You and I*; *The Mysterious Mrs. M*; *The Price of a Good Time*; *The Man Who Dared God*; *There's No Place Like Home*; *For Husbands Only* (+ pr)
1918   *The Doctor and the Woman*; *Borrowed Clothes*
1919   *When a Girl Loves*; *Mary Regan*; *Midnight Romance* (+ sc); *Scandal Mongers*; *Home*; *Forbidden*
1921   *Too Wise Wives* (+ pr, sc); *What's Worth While?* (+ pr); *To Please One Woman* (+ sc); *The Blot* (+ pr, sc); *What Do Men Want?* (+ pr, sc)
1923   *A Chapter in Her Life* (+ co-sc)
1926   *The Marriage Clause* (+ sc)
1927   *Sensation Seekers* (+ sc); *The Angel of Broadway*
1934   *White Heat* (+ co-sc)

Publications by Weber

Articles

"How I Became a Motion Picture Director," in *Static Flashes,* 24 April 1915.
Interview with Aline Carter, in *Motion Picture Magazine* (New York), March 1921.

Publications on Weber

Books

Heck-Rabi, Louise, *Women Filmmakers: A Critical Reception,* Metuchen, New Jersey, 1984.

Lois Weber (left) with Billie Dove

Slide, Anthony, *Early Women Directors,* South Brunswick, New Jersey, 1977; rev. ed. as *The Silent Feminists: America's First Women Directors,* Lanham, Maryland, 1996.

Acker, Ally, *Reel Women: Pioneers of the Cinema, 1896 to the Present,* New York, 1991.

Foster, Gwendolyn Audrey, *Women Film Directors: An International Bio-Critical Dictionary,* Westport, Connecticut, 1995.

Slide, Anthony, *Lois Weber: The Director Who Lost Her Way in History,* Westport, Connecticut, 1996.

Articles

Obituary in *New York Times,* 14 November 1939.

Pyros, J., "Notes on Women Directors," in *Take One* (Montreal), November/December 1970.

Koszarski, Richard, "The Years Have Not Been Kind to Lois Weber," in *Women and the Cinema,* edited by Karyn Kay and Gerald Peary, New York, 1977.

"Lois Weber—Whose Role Is It Anyway?" in *Monthly Film Bulletin* (London), May 1982.

Ostria, V., "Lois Weber, cette inconnue," in *Cahiers du Cinéma* (Paris), April 1985.

"Lois Weber Issue" of *Film History* (Philadelphia), vol. 1, no. 4, 1987.

Acker, Ally, "Lois Weber," in *Ms. Magazine* (New York), February 1988.

*   *   *

Lois Weber was a unique silent film director. Not only was she a woman who was certainly the most important female director the American film industry has known, but unlike many of her colleagues up to the present, her work was regarded in its day as equal to, if not a little better than that of most male directors. She was a committed filmmaker in an era when commitment was virtually unknown, a filmmaker who was not afraid to make features with subject matter in which she devoutly believed, subjects as varied as Christian Science (*Jewel* and *A Chapter in Her Life*) or birth control (*Where Are My Children?*). *Hypocrites!* was an indictment of hypocrisy and corruption in big business, politics, and religion, while *The People vs. John Doe* opposed capital punishment. At the same time, Lois Weber was quite capable of handling with ease a major spectacular feature such as the historical drama *The Dumb Girl of Portici,* which introduced Anna Pavlova to the screen.

During the 1910s, Lois Weber was under contract to Universal. While at Universal, she appears to have been given total freedom as to the subject matter of her films, all of which where among the studio's biggest moneymakers and highly regarded by the critics of the day. (The Weber films, however, did run into censorship problems, and the director was the subject of a vicious attack in a 1918 issue of *Theatre Magazine* over the "indecent and suggestive" nature of her titles.) Eventually the director felt the urge to move on to independent production, and during 1920 and 1921 she released a series of highly personal intimate dramas dealing with married life and the types of problems which beset ordinary people. None of these films was particularly well received by the critics, who unanimously declared them dull, while the public displayed an equal lack of enthusiasm. Nonetheless, features such as *Too Wise Wives* and *The Blot* demonstrate Weber at her directorial best. In the former she presents a study of two married couples. Not very much happens, but in her characterizations and attention to detail (something for which Weber was always noted), the director is as contemporary as a Robert Altman or an Ingmar Bergman. *The Blot* is concerned with "genteel poverty" and is marked by the underplaying of its principals—Claire Windsor and Louis Calhern—and an enigmatic ending which leaves the viewer uninformed as to the characters' future, an ending unlike any in the entire history of the American silent film. These films, as with virtually all of the director's work, were also written by Lois Weber.

Through the end of her independent productions in 1921, Lois Weber worked in association with her husband Phillips Smalley, who usually received credit as associate or advisory director. After the two were divorced, Lois Weber's career went to pieces. She directed one or two minor program features together with one talkie, but none equaled her work from the 1910s and early 1920s. She was a liberated filmmaker who seemed lost without the companionship, both at home and in the studio, of a husband. Her career and life were in many ways as enigmatic as the ending of *The Blot*.

—Anthony Slide

WEILL, Claudia
American director

Born: New York City, 1947; distant cousin of the composer Kurt Weill. **Education:** Studied photography at Radcliffe College, degree in photography, 1969; studied painting with Oskar Kokoschka in Salzburg; studied still photography with Walker Evans at Yale. **Career:** 1972—co-directed landmark feminist short for PBS, *Joyce at 34*; 1978—directed and co-wrote the critically well-received independent feature *Girlfriends*; 1980—directed bigger-budget feature *It's My Turn* for Columbia; 1980s-1990s—worked as a director of television movies and series television, including episodes of the TV series *Once a Hero*, *thirtysomething*, *My So-Called Life*, and *Chicago Hope*. **Awards:** Emmy Award, Best Afterschool Special, for *The Great Love Experiment*, 1984. **Agent:** Walter Teller, Esq., Hansen, Jacobsen, Teller, & Hoberman, 450 North Roxbury Drive, 8th Floor, Beverly Hills, CA 90210, U.S.A.

Films as Director

1968   *Metropole*; *Radcliffe Blues*
1969   *Putney School*

1971   *This Is the Home of Mrs. Levant Grahame* (doc, short); *IDCA—1970*; *Roaches' Serenade* (doc, short)
1972   *Belly Dancing Class*; *Commuters*; *Joyce at 34* (co-d with Chopra—short); *Lost and Found*; *Marriage*; *Yoga*
1974   *Matine Horner—Portrait of a Person* (doc—short); *The Other Half of the Sky: A China Memoir* (doc—co-d with MacLaine, + ph, co-ed)
1978   *Girlfriends* (+ co-sc, pr)
1980   *It's My Turn*
1984   *The Great Love Experiment* (for TV)
1986   *Johnny Bull* (for TV)
1988   *Once a Hero*
1991   *Face of a Stranger* (for TV)
1992   *A Child Lost Forever* (for TV)
1996   *Critical Choices* (for TV)

Other Films

1973   *The Year of the Woman* (ph)
1978   *The Scenic Route* (ro)
1988   *Calling the Shots* (Cole and Dale—doc) (ro as herself)

Publications by Weill

Articles

"*Girlfriends* Director on Female Friendship," interview with J. Klemesrud, in *New York Times,* 4 August 1978.
"Claudia Weill: From Shoestring to Studio," interview with Cecile Starr, in *New York Times,* 6 August 1978.
"Warner Proves Girl's Best Friend: Claudia Weill Went to Hollywood Convinced of Certainty of Brushoff," interview with S. Klain, in *Variety* (New York), 9 August 1978.
"A Woman's Turn," interview with B. Riley, in *Film Comment* (New York), November/December 1980.
"A Conversation with Claudia Weill," interview with Beverly Gray, in *Performing Arts,* February 1981.
"En fri kvinde," interview with E. Iversen, in *Kosmorama* (Copenhagen), April 1981.

Publications on Weill

Books

Quart, Barbara Koenig, *Women Directors: The Emergence of a New Cinema,* New York, 1988.
Fischer, Lucy, *Shot/Countershot: Film Tradition and Women's Cinema,* Princeton, New Jersey, 1989.
Acker, Ally, *Reel Women: Pioneers of the Cinema, 1896 to the Present,* New York, 1991.
Foster, Gwendolyn Audrey, *Women Film Directors: An International Bio-Critical Dictionary,* Westport, Connecticut, 1995.

Articles

"Claudia Weill Joins Venezuelan Special for Women in Pics," in *Variety* (New York), 24 December 1975.
Viertel, J., and D. Colker, "The New New Hollywood: Steven Spielberg, Watch Your Ass," in *Take One* (Montreal), vol. 6, no. 10, 1978.

Honeycutt, Kirk, "Women Film Directors: Will They, Too, Be Allowed to Bomb?," in *New York Times,* 6 August 1978.

Cocchi, J., "Claudia Weill Confident about Entry into Entertainment Feature Field," in *Boxoffice* (Kansas City, Missouri), 14 August 1978.

"Director Claudia Weill: Making a Film for a Major Is Like 'Being in a Playpen with $7 Million,'" in *Film Journal* (New York), December 1980.

Winfrey, Carey, "Claudia Weill: It's Her Turn Now," in *New York Times,* 7 December 1980.

Egan, C., "Grand Time at the Grand Hotel," in *Sightlines* (New York), vol. 14, no. 4, 1981.

Kuhn, Annette, "Hollywood and New Women's Cinema," in *Films for Women,* edited by Charlotte Brunsdon, London, 1987.

Jackson, Lynne, and Karen Jaehne, "Eavesdropping on Female Voices," in *Cineaste* (New York), vol. 16, no. 1/2, 1987-88.

*   *   *

Director Claudia Weill started making amateur films as a student at Radcliffe College, and thereafter worked for a decade as a cinema-tographer. In addition, she made a variety of experimental and documentary shorts, including *This Is the Home of Mrs. Levant Grahame* and *Roaches' Serenade,* and directed 20 segments for *Sesame Street* as well as several other PBS television programs. She gained visibility as a filmmaker with her best known short, *Joyce at 34,* which she co-directed with her friend and colleague Joyce Chopra for public television.

Joyce at 34, features filmmaker Joyce Chopra as she contemplates her social conditioning and repressed anger at having to balance the conflicting demands of her life as a mother and as a professional. Its feminist perspective is evident in its suggestion that women can find some relief and moral community in their shared experiences. Subsequently, the actress Shirley MacLaine recruited Weill for *The Other Half of the Sky: A China Memoir,* which Weill co-directed, photographed, and co-edited, and which earned an Academy Award nomination.

The attention that *The Other Half of the Sky* garnered was instrumental in enabling Weill to secure the grant money that helped her piece together a small $140,000 budget to make her first fiction feature, *Girlfriends.* Using a conventional narrative structure, the

Claudia Weill (right) with Jill Clayburgh on the set of *It's My Turn.*

film was considered groundbreaking for its depiction of female friendship and the divergence that arises between two best friends when one chooses to pursue a career as a photographer and the other as a housewife. Its enthusiastic reception when it was screened at the Cannes Film Festival in 1978 prompted Warner Bros. to pick it up for distribution. But, although it was a critical success, it was not a great commercial success. Nevertheless, Weill subsequently was offered a number of big studio directorial assignments and she chose Columbia Studio's seven-million dollar project, *It's My Turn.* The film's heroine is a successful math professor, played by Jill Clayburgh, stuck in an unsatisfying long-term relationship with a self-absorbed, noncommittal man. When she attends her father's wedding, she becomes attracted to the son of her father's bride, a sensitive and handsome former baseball player. The film reflected Hollywood's efforts to produce films that featured women who expressed the challenges, choices, and pleasures of contemporary feminism. Written by Eleanor Bergstein, it echoed the earlier *Joyce at 34* and *Girlfriends* in terms of its focus on women who desire professional lives that satisfactorily complement their personal and family lives. As Weill put it, "It's hard to do everything, but I think it's important to try." The film's poor performance at the box office, however, inspired Weill to turn to directing several plays in New York.

Currently, Weill works in television where she has directed episodes for such critically acclaimed series as *thirtysomething, Chicago Hope,* and *My So-Called Life,* in addition to several made-for-television movies, and an after-school special. Earlier in her career, critics suggested that Weill had been hampered because she was unfairly stigmatized by being labeled a "feminist filmmaker." Perhaps not surprisingly then, after she made *Girlfriends* (prior to which she unhesitatingly acknowledged her feminist ideals), she denied altogether that she was a feminist. Although she has not achieved enormous success as a feature-film director, Weill has been involved in television film projects that have featured strong actresses playing women who are committed to women and women's issues. For example, *Face of a Stranger* stars Tyne Daly and Gena Rowlands as two apparently disparate women who find strength with each other in their time of need. After the death of her husband, Pat discovers that he squandered all of their savings and she is now nearly destitute. To the horror of her daughter who wants to marry a rich man, Pat helps the homeless woman who lives in a cardboard box near her building and they become friends. Subsequently, Weill directed the television movie about child abuse, *A Child Lost Forever,* in which a teenager who gives her baby up for adoption attempts, 19 years later, to contact her son only to learn that he died under questionable circumstances when he was three years old. More recently, Weill directed *Critical Choices* about a woman who operates the only abortion clinic in Madison, Wisconsin, and another woman who is an avid abortion-rights supporter; their views are countered by a woman who is a right-wing antiabortionist. Testimony to the film's evenhandedness is that although their views differ dramatically, their dedication and respect for each other remains strong.

—Cynthia Felando

WERTMÜLLER, Lina
Italian director and writer

Born: Arcangela Felice Assunta Wertmüller von Elgg Spanol von Braueich in Rome, 14 August 1928. **Education:** Attended several Catholic schools; Academy of Theatre, Rome, 1947-51. **Family:** Married the artist Enrico Job, 1968. **Career:** 1951-52—joined Maria Signorelli's puppet troupe; from 1952—actress, stage manager, set designer, publicist, and writer for theater, radio and TV; 1962—assistant to Fellini on *8½*; 1963—directed first feature, *I basilischi*; 1973—first film to be given U.S. release, *Film d'amore e d'anarchia*; hired by Warner Bros. to direct four films, contract terminated after financial failure of first film. **Address:** Piazza Clotilde 5, 00196 Rome, Italy.

Films as Director and Writer

1963   *I basilischi (The Lizards)*
1965   *Questa volta parliamo di uomini (Now Let's Talk about Men; This Time Let's Talk about Men)*
1967   *Non stuzzicate la zanzara (Don't Tease the Mosquito)*
1972   *Mimi metallurgio ferito nell'onore (The Seduction of Mimi; Mimi the Metalworker; Wounded in Honour)*
1973   **Film d'amore e d'anarchia, ovvero stamattina alle 10 in Via dei fiori nella nota casa di toleranza** *(Film of Love and Anarchy, or This Morning at Ten in the Via dei fiori at the Well-Known House of Tolerance)*
1974   *Tutto a posto e niente in ordine (Everything's in Order but Nothing Works; All Screwed Up)* ; *Travolti da un insolito destino nell'azzurro mare d'agosto (Swept Away...by an Unusual Destiny in the Blue Sea of August; Swept Away...)*
1976   *Pasqualino settebellezze (Pasqualino: Seven Beauties; Seven Beauties)*
1978   *The End of the World in Our Usual Bed in a Night Full of Rain (La Fine del mondo in una notte piena di poggia; A Night Full of Rain); Shimmy lagarno tarantelle e vino; Fatto di sangue fra due uomini per causa di una vedova (Blood Feud; Revenge)*
1979   *Belle Starr (under name "Nathan Wich"—for TV)*
1981   *E una Domenica sera di novembre (for TV)*
1983   *Scherzo del destinoin aqquato dietro l'angelo come un brigante di strada (A Joke of Destiny, Lying in Wait around the Corner Like a Street Bandit) (co-sc)*
1984   *Sotto, Sotto (co-sc)*
1986   *Camorra (Vicoli e delitti; Un complicato intrigo di donne, vicoli e delitti; The Naples Connection) (co-sc); Notte d'estate, con profilo Greco, occhi amandorla e odore di basilico (Summer Night with Greek Profile, Almond Eyes and Scent of Basil)*
1989   *In una notte di chiaro luna (In a Full Moon Night)* ; *Il Decimo clandestino*
1990   *Saturday, Sunday, Monday*
1994   *Io speriamo che me la cavo (Ciao, Professore!) (co-sc)*
1996   *Ninfa plebea* ; *Metal meccanico e parrucchiera in un turbine di sesso e di politica*

Other Films

1963   *Otto e mezzo (8½)* (Fellini) (asst d)
1966   *Rita la zanzara (Rita the Mosquito)* (d musical numbers only, sc)
1970   *Quando de donne avevano la coda (When Women Had Tails)* (Festa Campanile) (co-sc); *Città violenta (Violent City; The Family)* (Sollima) (co-sc)
1972   *Fratelli sole, sorella luna (Brother Sun, Sister Moon)* (Zeffirelli) (co-sc)

Lina Wertmüller

Publications by Wertmüller

Books

The Screenplays of Lina Wertmüller, translated by Steven Wagner, New York, 1977.
The Head of Alvise, London, 1983.

Articles

Interview in *Woman and Film* (Santa Monica, California), no. 5-6, 1974.
Interview in *Interview* (New York), March 1975.
"Look, Gideon—Gideon Bachmann Talks with Lina Wertmüller," in *Film Quarterly* (Berkeley), Spring 1977.
"Lina Sweeps In," interview with G. Ott, in *Cinema Canada* (Montreal), March 1978.
Interview with C. J. Rotondi, in *Film in Review* (New York), November 1984.
Interview with B. Steinborn, in *Filmfaust* (Frankfurt), April/May 1986.

Publications on Wertmüller

Books

Dokumentation: Lina Wertmüller/Martin Scorsese, Zurich, 1986.
Michalczyk, John J., *The Italian Political Filmmakers,* Cranbury, New Jersey, 1986.
Bruno, Giuliana, and Maria Nadotti, editors, *Off Screen: Women and Film in Italy,* London, 1988.
Jacobsen, Wolfgang, and others, *Lina Wertmüller,* Munich, 1988.
Foster, Gwendolyn Audrey, *Women Film Directors: An International Bio-Critical Dictionary,* Westport, Connecticut, 1995.

Articles

Durgnat, Raymond, in *Films and Filming* (London), October 1964.
Biskind, Peter, "Lina Wertmüller: The Politics of Private Life," in *Film Quarterly* (Berkeley), Winter 1974-75.
Willis, Ellen, "Is Lina Wertmüller Just One of the Boys?," in *Rolling Stone* (New York), 25 March 1976.
Quacinella, L., "How Left Is Lina?," in *Cineaste* (New York), Fall 1976.
Jacobs, Diane, "Lina Wertmüller," in *International Film Guide 1978,* London, 1977.
Tutt, Ralph, "*Seven Beauties* and the Beast: Bettelheim, Wertmüller, and the Uses of Enchantment," in *Literature Film Quarterly* (Salisbury, Maryland), vol. 17, no. 3, 1989.
"Missing Persons Corner," in *Variety* (New York), 29 July 1991.
Manera, P., in *Cineforum* (Bergamo, Italy), December 1991.
Filmography, in *Segnocinema* (Vicenza, Italy), January/February 1993.
Samueli, A., "Fellini au travail," in *Cahiers du Cinéma* (Paris), December 1993.

* * *

By the mid-1970s, Lina Wertmüller had directed a series of sharply observed (though, in retrospect, markedly uneven) features that made her one of the shining lights of European cinema. At their best, her films were crammed with pointed humor, astute social commentary, and outrageous sexuality. In 1976 she even became the first woman to win a Best Director Academy Award nomination, for *Seven Beauties.*

In recent years, Wertmüller's critical reputation has been tarnished. For one thing, the quality of her work has sharply deteriorated. For another, her detractors have dubbed her a reactionary, labeling her films as grotesque and self-absorbed, with little love for humanity. Meanwhile, her champions hail her as a defender of the downtrodden, an idealistic anarchist who realizes anarchy is impractical yet still cherishes the notion of total individual freedom. Upon examining her films, one might decide that most of her characters are caricatures, or might consider them sympathetic human beings. It all depends on the interpretation.

Wertmüller's films most characteristically focus on the eternal battle between the sexes, fought with noisy screaming matches and comical seductions in a class-warfare setting. Her most typical features—those that cemented her reputation—may be found in the midsection of her filmography, from *The Seduction of Mimi* through *Swept Away....* All are imperfect: for every inspired sequence—most notably, in *The Seduction of Mimi,* Giancarlo Giannini's antics between the sheets with a ridiculously obese woman—there are long stretches of repetitious ax-grinding on sex, love, anarchy, fascism, and the class struggle. All but *All Screwed Up* star Giannini, Wertmüller's favorite actor. His characters think they are suave, but they really are stubborn and stupid, in constant trouble both politically and sexually. An example: in *Film of Love and Anarchy,* set in 1932, Giannini plays an anarchist, hiding in a brothel, who plans to assassinate Mussolini but instead falls for a prostitute. Wertmüller's women, on the other hand, are not politically aware, and are uninterested in struggling for self-sufficiency.

Seven Beauties, filled with stunning images, is Wertmüller's penultimate feature: a searing drama about survival in a surreal, insane world. It chronicles the odyssey of a Don Juan (Giannini) through the horrors of World War II, with the highlight a typically gruesome Wertmüllian seduction sequence in which the "hero" entices a piggish female concentration-camp commandant.

Over the decades, the reputation of *Seven Beauties* has suffered because most of the features Wertmüller has made in its wake have been misfires. *The End of the World in Our Usual Bed in a Night Full of Rain,* her first English-language effort, is a verbose marital boxing match pitting journalist/communist Giannini and photographer/feminist Candice Bergen. *Revenge,* also known as *Blood Feud,* is the overbaked tale of a radical lawyer (Marcello Mastroianni) and a gangster (Giannini) who love widow Sophia Loren during the early years of Fascist rule in Italy. Both were released in the late 1970s, and were followed by close to a dozen forgettable films made over the next two decades.

Easily Wertmüller's most accessible later-career films are *Sotto, Sotto* and *Ciao, Professore!* Thematically speaking, *Sotto, Sotto* is related to her earlier work in that it is a tale of sexual combat, but with a twist. It is the story of a married woman who becomes romantically attracted to her best (female) friend, which predictably piques her brutally sexist husband. *Ciao, Professore!* is a social comedy about a Northern Italian grade-school teacher, used to working with affluent children, who is mistakenly assigned to an impoverished village near Naples, with the scenario detailing how he influences his students and how they impact on him. While not as disappointing as her other post-*Seven Beauties* features, *Sotto, Sotto* and *Ciao, Professore!* are by-the-numbers stories whose best moments cannot compare to their counterparts in *Love and Anarchy, Swept Away...,* and, most certainly, *Seven Beauties.*

Wertmüller's films have remained consistent in one regard: many have lengthy, flowery titles. The complete name of *Swept Away...* is *Swept Away...by an Unusual Destiny in the Blue Sea of August.*

Joining it and *The End of the World...* are *A Joke of Destiny, Lying in Wait around the Corner Like a Street Bandit*; and *Summer Night with Greek Profile, Almond Eyes and Scent of Basil*.

Once upon a time, these titles might have seemed clever and unique. Given the declining quality of Wertmüller's work, they now are overindulgent and pretentious.

—Rob Edelman

WEST, Mae

American writer and actress

Born: Brooklyn, New York, 17 August 1892. **Education:** Attended Brooklyn public schools to age 13. **Family:** Married the entertainer Frank Wallace, 1911 (divorced 1942). **Career:** Child entertainer: joined Hal Clarendon's stock company, Brooklyn, at age eight; toured with Frank Wallace; 1911—Broadway debut in the revue *A la Broadway and Hello, Paris*; then returned to vaudeville tour with star billing; 1907-18—frequently rewrote her vaudeville acts; early 1920s—toured in nightclub act with Harry Richman; 1926—on Broadway in her own play *Sex* (later plays produced include *The Drag*, 1926, *The Wicked Age*, 1927, *Diamond Lil*, 1928 and several revivals, *The Pleasure Man*, 1928, *The Constant Sinner*, 1931, and *Catherine Was Great*, 1944); 1932—film debut in *Night After Night*: contract with Paramount; 1933—adapted her stage hit *Diamond Lil* for the movie, in which she also starred, *She Done Him Wrong*; 1933-40—starred in a series of popular films in the 1930s for which she often wrote the screenplay; 1954-56—toured with nightclub act; 1955—first of several albums of her songs, *The Fabulous Mae West*; 1970—returned to the screen in *Myra Breckenridge*. **Died:** In Los Angeles, 22 November 1980.

Films as Writer and Actress

1933   *She Done Him Wrong* (L. Sherman) (as Lady Lou); *I'm No Angel* (Ruggles) (as Tira)
1934   *Belle of the Nineties* (McCarey) (as Ruby Carter)
1935   *Goin' to Town* (A. Hall) (as Cleo Borden)
1936   *Klondike Annie* (Walsh) (co-sc, as the Frisco Doll/Rose Carlton); *Go West, Young Man* (Hathaway) (as Mavis Arden)
1938   *Every Day's a Holiday* (A. E. Sutherland) (as Peaches O'Day/Mademoiselle Fifi)
1940   *My Little Chickadee* (Cline) (co-sc, as Flower Belle Lee)

Films as Actress

1932   *Night after Night* (Mayo) (as Maudie Triplett)
1943   *The Heat's On* (*Tropicana*) (Ratoff) (as Fay Lawrence)
1970   *Myra Breckenridge* (Sarne) (as Leticia Van Allen, +co-dialogue)
1978   *Sextette* (K. Hughes) (as Marlo Manners)

Publications by West

Books

Babe Gordon (novel), New York, 1930; as *The Constant Sinner*, New York, 1931.

Diamond Lil (novel), New York, 1932; as *She Done Him Wrong*, New York, 1932.
Goodness Had Nothing to Do with It, New York, 1959; rev. ed., New York, 1970.
The Wit and Wisdom of Mae West, edited by Joseph Weintraub, New York, 1967.
On Sex, Health, and ESP, New York, 1975.

Articles

Interview with C. Robert Jennings, in *Playboy* (Chicago), January 1971.
"Mae West," interview with W. S. Eyman, in *Take One* (Montreal), January 1974.
"Mae West: The Queen at Home in Hollywood," interview with A. Huston and P. Lester, in *Interview* (New York), December 1974.

Publications on West

Books

Rosen, Marjorie, *Popcorn Venus*, New York, 1973.
Tuska, Jon, *The Films of Mae West*, Secaucus, New Jersey, 1973; rev. ed., as *The Complete Films of Mae West*, 1992.
Parish, James Robert, and William T. Leonard, *The Funsters*, New Rochelle, New York, 1979.
Cashin, Fergus, *Mae West: A Biography*, London, 1981.
Eells, George, and Stanley Musgrove, *Mae West*, New York, 1982.
Chandler, Charlotte, *The Ultimate Seduction*, New York, 1984.
Bergman, Carol, *Mae West*, New York, 1988.
Ward, Carol Marie, *Mae West: A Bio-Bibliography*, New York, 1989.
Acker, Ally, *Reel Women: Pioneers of the Cinema 1896 to the Present*, New York, 1991.
Leonard, Maurice, *Mae West: Empress of Sex*, London, 1991.
Sochen, June, *Mae West: She Who Laughs, Lasts*, Arlington Heights, Illinois, 1992.
Baxt, George, *The Mae West Murder Case* (novel), New York, 1993.
Malachosky, Tim, and James Greene, *Mae West*, California, 1993.
Curry, Ramona, *Too Much of a Good Thing: Mae West as Cultural Icon*, Minneapolis, 1995.
Hamilton, Marybeth, *"When I'm Bad, I'm Better": Mae West, Sex, and American Entertainment*, New York, 1995.
Robertson, Pamela, *Guilty Pleasures: Feminist Camp from Mae West to Madonna*, Durham, North Carolina, 1996.
Leider, Emily Wortis, *Becoming Mae West*, New York, 1997.

Articles

Troy, William, "Mae West and the Classic Tradition," in *Nation* (New York), 8 November 1933.
Arbus, Diane, "Mae West: Emotion in Motion," in *Show* (Hollywood), January 1965.
Current Biography 1967, New York, 1967.
Christie, George, "Mae West Raps," in *Cosmopolitan* (New York), May 1970.
Braun, Eric, "Doing What Comes Naturally," and "One for the Boys," in *Films and Filming* (London), October and November 1970.
Passek, J.-L., "Hommage: Mae West: Sex transit gloria mundi," in *Cinéma* (Paris), November 1973.
Mellen, Joan, "The Mae West Nobody Knows," in *Women and Their Sexuality in the New Film*, London, 1974.

Mae West

Adair, G., "Go West, Old Mae," in *Film Comment* (New York), May/June 1980.

Obituary in *New York Times,* 23 November 1980.

McCourt, James, obituary in *Film Comment* (New York), January/February 1981.

Kobal, John, "Mae West," in *Films and Filming* (London), September 1983.

Curry, Ramona, "Mae West as Censored Commodity," in *Cinema Journal* (Champaign, Illinois), Fall 1991.

Clayton, J., "Mae West: The Biggest Blonde of Them All," in *Classic Images* (Muscatine, Iowa), March 1993.

Alexander, R., "Peel Her a Grape," in *New York Times,* 22 August 1993.

Haskell, Molly, "Mae West's Bawdy Spirit Spans the Gay '90's," in *New York Times,* 15 August 1993.

Robertson, Pam, "The Kinda Comedy that Imitates Me," in *Cinema Journal* (Austin, Texas), Winter 1993

Frank, M., "Mae West at the Ravenswood," in *Architectural Digest* (Los Angeles), April 1994.

Pierpont, Claudia Roth, "The Strong Woman: What Was Mae West Really Fighting For?," in *New York Times,* 11 November 1996.

* * *

Mae West was Hollywood's most flamboyant symbol of sexual satire in the 1930s, though she was known perhaps more for her swagger than for writing the witty screenplays for the films in which she starred. In 1933 Paramount invited West to adapt her enormously popular play *Diamond Lil* for the screen—despite the studio's reservations that its Gay Nineties setting would be hopelessly out-of-sync with the tastes of the all-important youth audience. But her bawdy humor struck a profitable chord with a vast audience. West had a shrewd sense of comic timing, and the determination to tap into and extend contemporary themes and rhythms, especially, of course, about sex. The ribald one-liners that peppered her scripts were endlessly repeated, and attest to their simple brilliance, including "I used to be Snow White, but I drifted."

By the time she arrived in Hollywood, West was already well known. From the age of five, she worked as a performer, and by her teens she was doing vaudeville routines that attracted attention for her scandalous dances, especially the "shimmy." By the mid-1920s, she was writing stage plays with sexual themes, such as *The Constant Sinner.* The play that assured her fame was 1926's sensation, *Sex,* which she wrote, produced, and directed on Broadway. Huffy critics lambasted it as "disgusting," but audiences adored it. After 385 performances, it was raided and West was charged and jailed briefly for obscenity. It was her Broadway hit *Diamond Lil'* that proved to be her ticket to Hollywood.

In 1932, at the age of 40, West made her movie debut in *Night after Night,* though it employed her acting rather than her writing skills. Yet, in her brief but much-noticed appearance, she uttered a now-famous line: to a coat-check girl's exclamation, "Goodness! What lovely diamonds!," West drawled, "Goodness had nothing to do with it." Her second film was her adaptation of *Diamond Lil,* retitled *She Done Him Wrong.* Her most noteworthy film, it features West as a saloon songstress in the Gay Nineties; Cary Grant plays the undercover cop who has been assigned to haul her in. But, West has other plans; she entices him to "Come up sometime and see me," thus ensuring a successful seduction. Although the film ends with the promise of West's marriage, there is no suggestion that she will be a docile wife. Her screenplay was a surprising combination of sexual satire and moral uplift that toyed mercilessly with conventional masculine and feminine sex roles. Thus, not a few critics have related her flamboyant sexuality to the excesses of camp. *She Done Him Wrong*

was a smash hit, and West followed it with another, *I'm No Angel,* which also starred Cary Grant. The character she wrote for herself was a familiar provocateur; she plays a lion tamer with an uncanny ability to separate wealthy old men from their money. One of the film's highlights is a courtroom scene in which West acts as her own attorney and proves to be a disruptingly seductive presence, especially to the judge.

In addition to writing or collaborating on the scripts for her films, Paramount gave West enormous control over their production, including final cut, full creative control, and her choice of directors and leading men. West's films not only reiterated the cheeky "sex goddess" persona she had cultivated on Broadway, they also rescued Paramount from the threat of bankruptcy. Plot was less important in her scripts than her quips and characterizations. They capitalized on her image—curvaceous figure, big blond hair, tight corset, and suggestive saunter, and usually featured her in roles in which she played independent adventurers, often entertainers, who unashamedly express their desire for the hunks who catch her gaze. Her characters are never subservient to men, and it is the pleasure of sex rather than the security of romantic love that her characters seek. Further, they refuse to reform by film's end, in the manner of other "modern women" heroines; instead, her films flaunted her sexuality and its myriad rewards—men, money, freedom, and irreverence. Indeed, her scripts brim with her witticisms and innuendo, which temporarily confounded Hollywood's censors. But, Depression-era audiences were both titillated and charmed by the sexual suggestiveness of her films, along with their implication that anyone could succeed if he or she had enough stubborn determination.

Following the enormous success of *She Done Him Wrong,* conservatives and reformers who thought her work was morally despicable prompted the Production Code Administration to demand that she tame her scripts. *She Done Him Wrong,* in particular, is routinely cited as one of the key reasons that the Production Code—Hollywood's moral code—was restructured. Eventually, West's trademark sexual parody and double entendre were diluted and her films sold fewer tickets. Her script for *Belle of the Nineties,* for example, was rewritten extensively to conform to the new Code, and many local censors trimmed it even further. By the end of the 1930s, she was called "box-office" poison by a major exhibitor, but she bounced back with the minor classic, *My Little Chickadee,* in which she traded quips with W. C. Fields. In 1943, after her disappointing film *The Heat's On,* West retired from Hollywood and returned to the stage. In the 1970s she made two more films for which she wrote her own lines. The ill-conceived and realized *Myra Breckenridge* was a failure at the box office, but succeeded in renewing West's popularity. At the age of 85, she made her last film, *Sextette.*

Film critics have long been preoccupied with the question of whether West's films have feminist intentions, or merely pander to male fantasies about sex-obsessed women. Such questions, however, are a tribute to the rich and wry complexity of her work, especially her clever parodies of her own sex-symbol persona.

—Cynthia Felando

WHERE ARE MY CHILDREN?
USA, 1916
Co-director: Lois Weber

Production: Universal; black and white, 35mm; running time: 5 reels. Released 27 April 1916.

Producer: Universal Film Manufacturing Company/Lois Weber Productions; **story:** Lucy Payton and Franklyn Hall; **screenplay:** Lois Weber and Phillips Smalley; **photography:** Stephen S. Norton and Allen G. Siegler.

Cast: Tyrone Power (*Richard Walton*); Helen Riaume (*Mrs. Walton*); Marie Walcamp (*Mrs. Brandt*); Cora Drew (*Walton's housekeeper*); Rene Rogers (*Lillian, her daughter*); A. D. Blake (*Roger*); Juan De La Cruz (*Dr. Malfit*); C. Norman Hammond (*Dr. Homer*); William J. Hope (*Eugenic husband*); Marjorie Blynn (*Eugenic wife*); William Haben (*Dr. Gilding*).

Publications

Books

Rosen, Marjorie, *Popcorn Venus: Women, Movies and the American Dream,* New York, 1973.

Heck-Rabi, Louise, *Women Filmmakers: A Critical Reception,* Metuchen, New Jersey, 1984.

Brownlow, Kevin, *Behind the Mask of Innocence: Sex, Violence, Prejudice, Crime: Films of Social Conscience in the Silent Era,* New York, 1990.

* * *

Lois Weber was a major director in the 1910s, when she made several films about women's issues, including child labor, prostitution, birth control, and abortion, as well as a number of more conventional melodramas. *Where Are My Children?* was described in publicity as "a five-part argument advocating birth control and against race suicide." According to historians, *Where Are My Children?* disparaged married women who failed to choose motherhood. Yet, feminist historians claim that the film endorsed the nobility of motherhood but questioned its inevitability and considered its alternatives, like abortion and birth control.

Where Are My Children? is about the rich women who patronize an abortionist without their husbands' knowledge. It features a district attorney and his selfishly childless wife. When the wife's cad brother seduces and impregnates the housekeeper's young daughter, the wife recommends he take the girl to her doctor, who is also an abortionist. When the girl dies, the district attorney eagerly prosecutes him. The abortionist, however, claims he was benefiting humanity by "preventing motherhood for vain, pleasure-seeking women and degenerates." Nevertheless, he is convicted and sentenced to 15 years of hard labor, but he bitterly advises the prosecuting attorney to "see to your own household." The district attorney then discovers a fifty dollar invoice from the abortionist to his wife for "services rendered." He is stunned, and when he arrives at home he finds his wife in the company of her also-childless friends. He angrily denounces them and orders them to leave, after which he beseechingly implores his wife, "Where are my children?," and she collapses as he laments that he must shield a "murderess." Subsequently, the wife goes to church to pray for motherhood, but to no avail as intertitles reveal that she has "perverted nature so often," she is physically unable to get pregnant.

Notably, *Where Are My Children?* attacked abortion, but defended birth control, thus echoing the aims of Margaret Sanger, renowned at the time as the most vociferous promoter of birth control for women. In addition, its underlying theme of eugenics endorsement reveals its racist implications, in terms of its allusions to abortion as "race suicide." The film's power is due to its subject matter rather than to its formal qualities, though it features an effective closing scene of the couple sitting before the fire as a title indicates that the wife has spent a lonely lifetime haunted by the silent question, "Where are my children?" In this scene, she imagines that a little girl climbs onto her husband's lap, and that when he's old three grown children happily gather behind his chair. Furthermore, it is well-shot, and convincingly renders the upper-class environs of the district attorney and his wife.

Universal was greatly concerned about the film's subject matter, and the National Board of Review initially rejected it for mixed audiences. The studio expected the wrath of local censors, so it opened it with an exclusive engagement at New York's Globe Theater, where it did record business. It got excellent reviews and the National Board of Review reconsidered it, ultimately approving it for adult screenings. The film created a scandal and was banned by Philadelphia's Board of Censors. The trade press quoted the famous conservative reformer, Dr. Ellis P. Oberholtzer, one of the board members who expressed his disgusted judgment that, "It is not fit for decent people to see." Another board member, the spiritual director of the Federation of Catholic Societies objected to its suggestion of immorality, though he conceded that it was not openly immoral. Likewise, in 1917, the fan press alleged that Weber's respectable film had prompted numerous "nasty-minded imitators."

Interestingly, Weber was reluctant to pledge adherence to the suffragettes or other special interest groups, but she did profess her interest in telling tales of morality. Thus, *Hypocrites* was about religious hypocrisy and the corruption of the modern world, *Shoes* is about child labor, and *The People vs. John Doe* opposed capital punishment. But, *Where Are My Children?* was Weber's favorite and most famous film.

The American version of the film alluded to Sanger in a long opening title that suggested Weber's "careful dramatization" had been inspired by the widespread discussion of birth control, after which a prologue of swirling clouds and huge gates opening with baby angels flying about preceded the appearance of a bright Christian cross, along with a title that suggested the evil of abortion as the babies who would have been born were "marked with the approval of the Almighty." It also featured a scene about a young doctor accused and convicted of distributing indecent material that advocated birth control as a palliative for abortion. Thereafter, when an abortion occurs in the film, Weber communicated the event by depicting a soul ascending to heaven.

Not surprisingly perhaps, the publicity about the controversy that was inspired by *Where Are My Children?* produced a box-office bonanza as the curious filled the theaters screening the film. It ultimately grossed three million dollars for Universal Studios, and studio chief Carl Laemmle proudly declared that he would trust Weber with any amount of money she deemed necessary for any movie she wanted to make.

—Cynthia Felando

WHO KILLED VINCENT CHIN?
USA, 1988
Directors: Christine Choy and Renee Tajima

Production: Film News Now Foundation and WTVS Detroit; color, 16mm; running time: 87 minutes. Released 11 March 1988, in New York. Filmed in Detroit, Michigan.

Producer: Robert Larson; **executive producer:** Juanita Anderson; **associate producer:** Nancy Mei-Yu Tong; **photography:** Christine Choy, Nick Doob, Kyle Kibbe, and Al Santana; **editor:** Holly Fisher; **sound editor:** Ira Spiegel; **sound engineers:** Mark Rance and Sylvie Thouard; **music:** Ge Gan Ru.

Publications

Articles

Goldman, D., "Focus: Independents," in *American Film* (Washington D.C.), 1988.

Hoberman, J., "Film: Standing on Ceremonies," in *Village Voice* (New York), 15 March 1988.

Turim, M., "Panels on Women in Asian Film—Parts I and II," in *Asian Cinema* (Hamden, Connecticut), vol. 4, nos. 1 and 2, 1988/89.

Cohan, C., "*Who Killed Vincent Chin?*," in *Cineaste* (New York), vol. 17, no. 1, 1989.

Kaplan, D. A., "Film about a Fatal Beating Examines a Community," in *New York Times,* 16 July 1989.

Huang, V., and B. Reynaud, "Christine Choy/Renee Tajima: *Who Killed Vincent Chin?*," in *Motion Picture* (New York), vol. 3, no. 3/4, 1990.

* * *

Who Killed Vincent Chin? is a solidly constructed and politically compelling documentary that recounts the murder of Vincent Chin, a Chinese-American engineer who was mistaken as Japanese and slain by an assembly-line auto worker who blamed him for the failing auto industry. Yet, Chin's killer spent only one night in jail. Accordingly, the documentary offers a detailed analysis of how the killer and his accomplice escaped justice, and it charts the development of an emotionally charged civil rights protest.

Born in China, Vincent Chin was adopted and brought to America as a five year old by a Chinese-American father and Chinese immigrant mother. In the summer of 1982, at age 27, he was an accomplished auto engineer looking forward to marriage. While celebrating with a small group of friends at a strip club, Chin brawled briefly with a pair of thugs—an auto worker, Ronald Ebens, and his stepson, Michael Nitz. Witness accounts differed dramatically about what precipitated the fight, but most of them agreed that an auto worker "beat up a Chinese guy who he thought was Japanese." What seems clear is that the murderer, assuming Chin was Japanese, considered him a symbol of the failure of the U.S. automobile industry and the loss of jobs due to Japanese competition. So, when Chin left the bar in the aftermath of the altercation, Ebens and Nitz chased and caught him, and Ebens repeatedly bludgeoned him with a baseball bat. Chin died several days later. Though two police officers and several other witnesses saw the beating, Ebens pleaded guilty to manslaughter charges and was given a shockingly light sentence: three years probation and a $3,000 fine. But Asian-American activists across the country were mobilized by the outcome and successfully pressured the federal government to file civil rights charges against the murderer and his stepson. They were acquitted after two trials.

The filmmakers examine the case from the perspective of the American Dream—with both its costs and rewards. Using clips of commercials, still photographs, and home movies, the filmmakers relate the history of Asian immigrant families in the 1950s who struggled to achieve the Dream, especially for their children. They further imply that Vincent was a near-perfect embodiment of the immigrants' hard work and success. The devastating loss of Vincent is written on his mother Lily's grief-scarred face, which the filmmakers use to underscore the outrage of Vincent's family and friends. In addition, the film features news footage and interviews to illuminate the effects of the Reagan-era demonization of Japan and the reluctance of authorities to address issues of racism. One amazing news clip features a procession of Detroit auto workers sledgehammering a Toyota to express their rage at the Japanese auto makers. But the filmmakers tell more than a story of racism and murder; they reveal how a masculine culture that encourages drinking, sexism, and strip clubs—what a friend of the murderer calls "working hard and playing hard"—feeds a violent and sexist culture. Indeed, its opening shots depict the facade of the strip club where Vincent and his murderer started fighting, as a stripper's voiceover describes what she saw that night; its last shot is a close-up of a stunned, desperate Lily Chin speaking at a press conference, after the federal acquittal, as she beseechingly begs for justice "for Vincent." Not surprisingly, director Choy has said that the film was not organized logically, but rather emotionally; her hope: that once viewers respond to the emotion of the film, they'll discover its logic.

The filmmakers have explained that they were compelled by the disparities between the media and witness accounts of the crime, to convey it as a Rashomon-like story. Strangely, the murderer, a farm boy turned auto worker, willingly agreed to sit for an extensive interview in which he coolly admits to killing Vincent, though he claims the act was neither premeditated nor racist: "it just happened." Moreover, he arrogantly paints himself as a victim—of media distortions. His story is countered by those told by an assortment of witnesses, including Vincent's best friend, the strippers, the police, and passersby. But, the filmmakers foreground Vincent's inconsolable mother above all else, and they are entirely candid about their sympathy for her; they forthrightly admit their commitment to the social function of the independent documentary filmmaker, whom they argue should keep "an ear to the ground" to discover important, but neglected or unpopular, stories that have larger social or political resonances. Their impetus for making the film was not only their outrage about the murder and subsequent miscarriage of justice, but also about the lack of media attention being paid to the subject of racism in general in the United States in the early 1980s. The title of the film is, of course, ironic; indeed, it is immediately clear who committed the murder, yet the film suggests that the larger community was also guilty of aiding and abetting the murderer's racism, and therefore, his crime. As a neighbor explains, "It could happen to anyone."

—Cynthia Felando

WIELAND, Joyce
Canadian director

Born: Toronto, 30 June 1931. **Education:** Attended Central Technical Vocational High School, Toronto. **Family:** Married the artist Michael Snow, 1957. **Career:** 1950s—independent artist and commercial artist, Toronto; 1955-56—animator for Jim McKay and George Dunning's Graphic Films; 1963—with Snow moved to New York City; 1964—formed company Corrective film; 1971—moved back to Toronto; instructor at Nova Scotia College of Art; 1971-76—worked on funding, producing and directing *The Far Shore*; 1979-

82—taught at Arts Sake, Toronto; 1985-86 —instructor at the San Francisco Art Institute; from 1987—continues working as visual artist; retrospective of art and films at Art Gallery of Ontario. **Awards:** Three Canadian film awards, 1977. **Address:** 497 Queen Street East, Toronto, Ontario M5A 1V1, Canada.

Films as Director

1958   *Tea in the Garden* (co-d)
1959   *A Salt in the Park* (co-d)
1963   *Larry's Recent Behaviour*
1964   *Peggy's Blue Skylight*; *Patriotism* (Parts 1 and 2)
1965   *Watersark*; *Barbara's Blindness* (co-d with B. Ferguson)
1967   *Bill's Hat*; *Sailboat*; *1933*; *Hand-tinting*
1968   *Catfood*; *Rat Life and Diet in North America*
1969   *La Raison avant la passion* (*Reason over Passion*); *Dripping Water* (co-d with Snow); *One Second in Montreal* (co-d with Snow)
1972   *Pierre Vallières*; *Birds at Sunrise*
1973   *Solidarity*
1976   *The Far Shore* (+ co-pr)
1984   *A & B in Ontario* (co-d with Frampton)
1985   *Birds at Sunrise*; *Wendy and Joyce* (incomplete)

Other Films as Actress

1967   *Sky Socialist* (Jacobs); *Wavelength* (Snow); *Standard Time* (Snow)
1972   *Knocturne* (George and Mike Kuchar); *"Rameau's Nephew" by Diderot (Thanx to Dennis Young) by Wilma Schoen* (Snow)

Publications by Wieland

Books

True Patriot Love/Veritable Amour patriotique, with interview with Pierre Théberge, Ottawa, 1971.
Joyce Wieland: A Decade of Painting: Dix Ans De Peinture, Montreal, 1985.
Joyce Wieland: Art Gallery of Ontario, Musée des beaux-arts de l'Ontario, Toronto, 1987.
Joyce Wieland: Twilit Record of Romantic Love: 18 December 1994 to 26 March 1995, Kingston, Ontario, 1995.

Articles

"North America's Second All-Woman Film Crew," in *Take One* (Montreal), December 1967.
"Jigs and Reels," in *Form and Structure in Recent Film,* edited by Dennis Wheeler, Vancouver Art Gallery, 1972.
"Kay Armatage Interviews Joyce Wieland," in *Take One* (Montreal), February 1972.
Interview with Lauren Rabinovitz, in *Afterimage* (Rochester, New York), May 1981.

Publications on Wieland

Books

Reid, Alison, *Canadian Women Film Makers,* Ottawa, 1972.
Rabinovitz, Lauren, *Points of Resistance: Women, Power & Politics in the New York Avant-Garde Cinema, 1943-71,* Urbana, Illinois, 1991.

Foster, Gwendolyn Audrey, *Women Film Directors: An International Bio-Critical Dictionary,* Westport, Connecticut, 1995.

Articles

Farber, Manny, "Joyce Wieland," in *Artforum* (New York), February 1970.
Sitney, P. Adams, "There Is Only One Joyce," in *ArtsCanada* (Toronto), April 1970.
McPherson, Hugo, "Wieland: An Epiphany of North," in *ArtsCanada* (Toronto), August/September 1971.
Cornwell, Regina, "'True Patriot Love': The Films of Joyce Wieland," in *Artforum* (New York), September 1971.
Martineau, Barbara Halpern, "*The Far Shore*: A Film about Violence, a Peaceful Film about Violence," in *Cinema Canada* (Montreal), April 1976.
Delaney, Marshall, "Wielandism: A Personal Style in Full Bloom," in *Canadian Film Reader,* edited by Feldman and Nelson, Ontario, 1977.
Martineau, Barbara Halpern, "Ragged History and Contemporary Scatterings," in *Cinema Canada* (Montreal), January/February 1981.
Rabinovitz, Lauren, "The Development of Feminist Strategies in the Experimental Films of Joyce Wieland," in *Film Reader* (Evanston, Illinois), no. 5, 1982.
McCarty, L. M., "The Experimental Films of Joyce Wieland," in *Cine-Tracts* (Montreal), Summer/Fall 1982.
Scott, Jay, "Full Circle," and Susan M. Crean, "Notes from the Language of Emotion," in *Canadian Art,* Spring 1987.
O'Pray, Michael, "Joyce Wieland: In Search of the Far Shore," in *Art Monthly* (London), March 1988.

Films

A Film about Joyce Wieland, directed by Judy Steed, 1972.
Artist on Fire, directed by Kay Armatage, 1972.

* * *

Joyce Wieland achieved her reputation as one of a group of experimental filmmakers who contributed to the creation of an avant-garde film style in the middle and late 1960s. Wieland's films formally investigate the limitations and shared properties of several media while they developed increasingly pointed themes regarding Canadian nationalism and feminism.

When Toronto developed into a leading Canadian art center in the late 1950s and 1960s, Wieland became the only woman who achieved artistic prominence among the new group of Canadian painters influenced by Abstract Expressionism and Pop Art. Concerned about being even closer to the most recent developments among vanguard artists, Wieland and her husband Michael Snow moved to New York City in 1963. Although they remained expatriates until 1971, Wieland continued to exhibit her work throughout Canada and established a reputation during the next decade as the country's leading woman artist.

In New York City, Wieland became friendly with many members of the "underground" film community, a group whose bohemian behavior and outrageously styled home movies were gaining increased notoriety. Influenced by underground filmmakers Harry Smith, Ken Jacobs, and George Kuchar, Wieland began making short, personal films, and her movies were soon included in the group's regular Greenwich Village screenings.

The cinematic style that evolved out of several underground film-makers' works became known by the late 1960s as "structural film." These films addressed the nature of the film viewing experience itself and created self-reflexive statements about such basic materials of filmmaking as projected light, celluloid, and the camera apparatus. Structural filmmaking paralleled painterly developments in minimal art and received international recognition as the new radical forefront of avant-garde film. Wieland's films—often grouped and discussed with those by such other structural filmmakers as Snow, Jacobs, Hollis Frampton, and Ernie Gehr—played at museums, film festivals, and colleges in Europe and North America.

In 1969 Wieland directed a feature-length movie that wedded the highly conceptual and experimental concerns of structural film with her own political feelings regarding Canada. The result, *Reason over Passion,* is an experimental documentary film about the country of Canada and Canadian culture and identity. Following the film's release, Wieland expressed and developed the same themes in an art show entitled "True Patriot Love" at the National Gallery of Canada in 1971. The show's Pop Art-styled quilts, embroideries, and knittings served as patriotic banners for nationalism and feminism.

Because of the direction her work was taking, and because of her increased involvement in Canadian artists' political groups and causes, Wieland returned in 1971 to Toronto. There she completed two additional short structural documentaries. *Pierre Vallières* is about a French-Canadian revolutionary and the problems between French and English Canada. *Solidarity* is about a labor strike at an Ontario factory whose workers were mostly women. At the same time, Wieland co-wrote, co-produced, and directed a theatrical feature-length film. *The Far Shore* is a romantic melodrama that tells the story of a French-Canadian woman whose failing marriage to a stuffy Toronto bourgeois results in her liberating affair with a Canadian painter. The film was not commercially successful but has subsequently been featured at film festivals, colleges, and museums in North America and Europe. After the completion of *The Far Shore,* Wieland returned primarily to drawing, painting, and printmaking and has since produced several series of new works. In 1987 the Art Gallery of Ontario hosted a retrospective of her art and films. It was the museum's first such honoring a living woman artist.

—Lauren Rabinovitz

WORKING GIRLS
USA, 1986
Director: Lizzie Borden

Production: Lizzie Borden/Alternate Current; color; 35mm; running time: 90 minutes. Released 27 February 1987, New York.

Producers: Lizzie Borden and Andi Gladstone; **screenplay:** Lizzie Borden and Sandra Kay; **photography:** Judy Irola; **editor:** Lizzie Borden; **sound:** J. T. Takagi; **sound editors:** Toby Shimin, Cindy Friedman, Christine Legoff, and Sandy Gerling; **production design:** Kurt Ossenfort; **art director:** Leigh Kyle; **music:** Roma Baran and David van Tieghem; **costumes:** Elisabeth Ross.

Cast: Louise Smith (*Molly*); Ellen McElduff (*Lucy*); Amanda Goodwin (*Dawn*); Marusia Zach (*Gina*); Janne Peters (*April*); Helen Nicholas (*Mary*); Deborah Banks (*Diane*); Liz Caldwell (*Liz*); Boomer Tibbs (*Bob*).

Publications

Book

Maio, Kathi, *Feminist in the Dark: Reviewing the Movies,* Freedom, California, 1988.

Articles

Wickenhaver, J., "Production Focus: *Working Girls,*" in *Millimeter* (New York), May 1986.
Hoberman, J., "'Tis Pity She's a Whore," in *Village Voice* (New York), 10 March 1987.
Kauffman, Stanley, "Daughters of Joy," in *New Republic* (Washington, D.C.), 16 March 1987.
Williamson, J., "Career Opportunities," in *New Statesman* (London), 20 March 1987.
Ansen, David and others, "Hollywood Goes Independent," in *Newsweek* (New York), 6 April 1987.
Snitow, A., "Sex on the Job," in *Ms. Magazine* (New York), May 1987.

*   *   *

Lizzie Borden's second independent feature, *Working Girls* focuses on the sexual politics of middle-class prostitution. Released three years after her much-discussed debut *Born in Flames,* it is a well-realized, fascinating, and occasionally amusing account of a workday in the lives of ten prostitutes in an upmarket Manhattan brothel. Along with a procession of male clients, the film gives a sense of the mundane rituals and preparations necessary for the brothel's brief sexual-economic exchanges. Its trenchant "slice-of-life" look at the often mythologized world of prostitution effectively demystifies the trade itself and denies the male fantasy of mutual ecstasy offered in Hollywood's more conventional depictions. Interestingly, Borden chose the title *Working Girls* to honor the pioneering woman director Dorothy Arzner and her 1931 film of the same name.

Indeed, the film's feminist difference is communicated immediately, with a framing device that reveals the protagonist Molly is a lesbian who lives a quiet life with her lover and a child. An Ivy-League graduate with degrees in English literature and art history, Molly has aspirations to become a professional photographer. In the meantime, she has been making a lucrative living for two months working as a prostitute for a few days each week. Her co-workers are a fairly disparate assortment of women, most of whom have plans for crossover work, including Dawn who attends law school, Gina who wants to own a beauty salon, and April who is reluctantly turning to drug dealing as prostitution becomes less profitable in her middle age. But what the women share is a lack of illusions about their work.

In this film, characterizations are more important than plot, and much is revealed as Molly and her colleagues chat about their personal lives and dreams, as well as their annoyances with work and their clients. Their conversations are interrupted by a parade of johns who are seeking everything from conversation and sloppy kisses, to unusual positions or light bondage. But, of course, for the prostitutes the point of such encounters is the exchange of money. Indeed, Borden shrewdly de-eroticizes the sex, in part, by depicting the prostitutes as they fake pleasure, make jokes about the johns, and otherwise remain emotionally detached from their work. Likewise,

Borden depicts but avoids objectifying the nude women, to focus instead on the mundane and occasionally demeaning details of their work. Further, the film's dramatic conflict is not between the prostitutes and their johns, but between the brothel's Madame Lucy and her "working girls." Herself a former working girl, Lucy is self-absorbed and constantly nags the girls about their sloppy housekeeping, impolite manners, or inattention to the bordello's lifeline, the telephone. Borden's portrayals of the johns are not disparaging, though she does not encourage viewers to either identify with or pity them. In addition, her choice to make Molly a lesbian seems intended to suggest that at least some prostitutes are well-adjusted lesbians, than to suggest, as Hollywood often does, that prostitutes inevitably become man-haters.

A low-budget film, *Working Girls* eschews slick production values in favor of documentary-style cinematography and characterizations that seemed snatched from life. Constructed with long takes and simple camera angles, the film's style evokes Frederick Wiseman's apparently objective cinema verité explorations of American institutions. Yet, its fictional story is more conventionally organized around a central character (Molly). When it was released many feminist critics objected to Borden's efforts to present the prostitutes' point of view, and suggested that her female characters were as stereotyped as those offered by Hollywood. Other critics objected to the film's suggestion that prostitution is not much different from being a secretary or flight attendant, and charged that Borden had sacrificed the opportunity to show how such work "sexually abuses" women. At the time of the film's release, Borden forthrightly attempted to answer such accusations by explaining that *Working Girls* was about prostitution as work, rather than as moral or psychological problem.

Further, instead of adhering to the media's typical rendering of the prostitute-as-glamour-girl or as hopeless streetwalker, Borden favors a feminist perspective that considers prostitution as far more complex, though her film suggests that it can function as a viable economic alternative in a social system that typically marginalizes and underpays women's work. Borden was inspired to make *Working Girls* after visiting some actual brothels, the result of her association with COYOTE (Cast Off Your Old Tired Ethics), which is a radical coalition of prostitutes and labor activists working for the legalization of prostitution. Thus, she effectively challenges the perspective of those feminists who disdain prostitutes as willing victims of an oppressive system, in order to fulfill a larger goal—to open a dialogue between a wide range of women so that they might come together as feminists working toward shared goals of liberation.

—Cynthia Felando

Y-Z

YAMASAKI, Tizuka

Brazilian director

Born: Porto Alegre, Brazil, 12 May 1949. **Education:** Studied architecture and then transferred to communications with a specialty in film at the Universities of Brasilia, 1970-72, and Federal Fluminense in Rio de Janeiro, 1972-75. **Career:** 1973 and 1977—assistant director to Nelson Pereira dos Santos; 1978—assistant director to Glauber Rocha; 1980—first feature film, *Gaijin: Road to Freedom*; 1989—directed TV miniseries *Kananga du Japão*. **Awards:** Gran Premio Coral, Havana International Film Festival, for *Gaijin*, 1980.

Films as Director

1973 *Bon Odoni* (short)
1978 *Viva 24 de Maio* (short) (co-d, + co-pr)
1980 *Gaijin: Caminhos da Liberdade* (*Gaijin: Road to Freedom*) (+ co-sc)
1981 *Cinéma: Embaixada do Brasil* (*The Cinema's Embassy*) (doc) (+ ed); *Alcool, alternativa para o furturo* (doc)
1983 *Parahyba Mulher-macho* (*Parahyba, a Macho Woman*) (+ co-sc)
1985 *Patriamada* (*Beloved Motherland*) (+ sc)
1991 *Fica Comigo, O noivo Rebelde*

Other Films

1973 *O Amuleto de Ogum* (Pereira dos Santos) (asst d)
1977 *Tenda Dos Milagros* (Pereira dos Santos) (asst d)
1978 *A Idade de Terra* (Rocha) (asst d)

Publication by Yamasaki

Article

"Sing, the Beloved Country: An Interview with Tizuka Yamasaki on *Patriamada*," interview with Julianne Burton, in *Film Quarterly* (Berkeley), Fall 1987.

Publications on Yamasaki

Book

Trelles Plazaola, Luis, editor, *Cine y mujer en América Latina: Directoras de Largometrajes de ficción,* Rio Piedras, Puerto Rico, 1991.

Articles

Nygren, Scott, "Boundary Crossings: Japanese and Western Representations of the Other," in *Quarterly Review of Film and Video* (Langhorne, Pennsylvania), vol. 14, no. 3, 1993.
Pick, Zuzana M., "Immigration and Identity: *Gaijin: The Road to Liberty,*" in *The New Latin American Cinema: A Continental Project,* Austin, Texas, 1993.

* * *

A Brazilian-born daughter of Japanese immigrants, Tizuka Yamasaki embodies one of Brazil's most complicated identity matrices. Negotiating her own identity means juggling her gender, race, and nationality to arrive at a "Brazilian" balance. Not surprisingly, many of Yamasaki's films deal with gender and racial identity, immigration, the hybridity of Brazilian culture, and democracy. In questioning country, patria, and culture, Yamasaki asks repeatedly, "What is it to be Brazilian?"

Yamasaki was born in Porto Alegre and grew up São Paulo. Her parents lived from the land and tried to make a good life for their children. Both geographically and ideologically, a career in filmmaking seemed out of place in such a context. Yamasaki began, instead, to study architecture. She quickly found that she was drawn to filmmaking and changed academic tracks. There was for Yamasaki a tangible risk in choosing filmmaking in the early seventies in Brazil. As she told Luis Trelles Plazaola in a recent interview, the cinema guaranteed her nothing.

After university, Yamasaki began her career under the tutelage of two of Brazil's most important filmmakers and contributors to its politically oriented Cinema Novo movement of the 1960s. As assistant director to Nelson Pereira dos Santos on two films, Yamasaki was given enough responsibility and trust to be able to explore her own relationship to the camera and to the films' subject. From these experiences she learned to rediscover the familiar, taking note of everyday gestures and recognizing how to integrate them into a poetic film language. With new eyes, she began for the first time to really see her country and understand its complexities. Glauber Rocha taught her the formal nuances of the medium, such as camera position and composition. Under his wing Yamasaki learned the basic tenets of the Cinema Novo and learned to fictionalize reality, to "turn it into cinema."

Yamasaki's approach to filmmaking combines these lessons from Brazil's master filmmakers with her own poetic and feminine instincts. The result, she believes, is that she can think of film as a feeling. An audience can watch the film, absorb the expression and the emotion, and then carry it with them, to think about later.

Yamasaki's first feature film, *Gaijin: Road to Freedom,* won her international acclaim and a Gran Premio Coral at the Second Annual International Festival of New Latin American Cinema in Havana, Cuba. Set at the turn of the century, *Gaijin* presents an intimate portrait of Japanese emigration to Brazil through the story of one family who come to seek their fortune on Brazil's coffee plantations. While her protagonists are Japanese, their story resonates for many other ethnic and national groups who toiled in the plantations at the turn of the century.

Her next feature, *Parahyba, a Macho Woman,* is about Anayde Beiriz, a Brazilian "any-woman," who wishes to be able to express herself and to love freely, defying the patriarchal, prejudiced, and moralistic society in which she lives. Set in 1930, the film sets Anayde's personal revolution within the political friction between conservatives and liberals in the northeast state of Parahyba. Anayde's personal struggle, then, allegorizes the struggle of this state to achieve modernity and autonomy.

In *Beloved Motherland,* Yamasaki looks at contemporary Brazil, combining fiction and documentary in a stunning portrait of Brazil's return to democracy following 20 years of military dictatorship. The film's fictional characters are Goias, a filmmaker documenting the impressive Candelaria demonstration in favor of popular presidential elections, and Lina, a reporter whom Goias has asked to interview celebrities in the crowd. Reportedly, the actress playing Lina, Debora Bloch, got so involved in her role that she pushed real reporters out of the way in order to "get her story." *Beloved Motherland* was made without a written script—the actors and director collaborated on writing scenes responding to daily events. In the end, this process allowed *Beloved Motherland* to reflect both the exhilaration and the ambiguity Brazilians experienced in this crucial moment.

Despite the critical success of her films, Yamasaki has not had many production options for further feature films. This is due, in large part, to the difficulties the Brazilian film industry suffered in the 1980s. During this time Yamasaki turned to television soap operas and even directed a stage production of the opera *Madame Butterfly* in Bello Horizonte. She has directed several projects for Embrafilme and a miniseries, *Kananga du Japão.*

—Ilene S. Goldman

ZETTERLING, Mai (Elisabeth)

Swedish director and actress

Born: Västerås, 24 May 1925. **Education:** Attended Ordtuery Theatre School, 1941; Royal Dramatic Theatre School, Stockholm, 1942-45. **Family:** Married 1) the ballet dancer Tutte Lemkow (divorced), two sons: Etienne and Louis; 2) the writer David Hughes (divorced). **Career:** 1941—stage debut and film debut; 1942-44—in repertory with the Royal Dramatic Theatre, Stockholm; 1960—turned director with the BBC documentary *The Polite Invasion*; 1960s—began collaborating on television documentaries with husband Hughes; 1990—directed episode of *Mistress of Suspense* for television. **Awards:** Golden Lion, Venice Festival, for *The War Game,* 1961. **Died:** Of cancer, in London, 15 March 1994.

Films as Director

1960   *The Polite Invasion* (short, for TV)
1961   *Lords of Little Egypt* (short, for TV); *The War Game* (short) (+ pr)

1962   *The Prosperity Race* (short, for TV)
1963   *The Do-It-Yourself Democracy* (short, for TV)
1964   *Älskande par* (*Loving Couples*) (+ co-sc)
1966   *Nattlek* (*Night Games*)
1967   *Doktor Glas* (co-d with D. Hughes)
1968   *Flickorna* (*The Girls*) (+ co-sc)
1971   *Vincent the Dutchman* (co-d with D. Hughes, + pr—doc for TV)
1973   "The Strongest" ep. of *Visions of Eight* (co-d with D. Hughes)
1976   *We har manje namn* (*We Have Many Names*) (+ ro, sc, ed)
1977   *Stockholm* (for TV) (+ ro)
1978   *The Rain's Hat* (for TV) (+ ed)
1980   *Of Seals and Men* (co-d)
1982   *Love* (co-d, + co-sc—for TV)
1983   *Scrubbers* (+ co-sc)
1986   *Amorosa* (+ sc, co-ed)
1990   *Sunday Pursuit*

Other Films

1941   *Lasse-Maja* (Olsson) (ro)
1943   *Jag drapte* (Molander) (ro)
1944   *Hets* (*Torment; Frenzy*) (Sjöberg) (ro as Bertha Olsson); *Prins Gustaf* (Bauman) (ro)
1946   *Iris och Lojtnantshjarta* (*Iris and the Lieutenant*) (Sjöberg) (ro as Iris); *Driver dagg faller Regn* (*Sunshine Follows Rain*) (ro)
1947   *Frieda* (Dearden) (title role)
1948   *Musik i moerker* (*Music in Darkness; Night Is My Future*) (I. Bergman) (ro as Ingrid); *Nu borjar livet* (Molander) (ro); *The Bad Lord Byron* (Macdonald) (ro as Teresa Guiccioli); *Portrait from Life* (*The Girl in the Painting*) (Fisher) (ro as Hildegarde)
1949   "The Facts of Life" ep. of *Quartet* (Smart and others) (ro as Jeanne); *The Romantic Age* (*Naughty Arlette*) (Gréville) (ro as Arlette)
1950   *Blackmailed* (Marc Allégret) (ro as Carol Edwards); *The Lost People* (Knowles and Box) (ro as Lili)
1951   *Hell Is Sold Out* (M. Anderson) (ro as Valerie Martin)
1952   *The Tall Headlines* (*The Frightened Bride*) (T. Young) (ro as Doris Richardson); *The Ringer* (*The Gaunt Stranger*) (Hamilton) (ro as Lisa)
1953   *Desperate Moment* (Bennett) (ro as Anna de Burgh)
1954   *Dance Little Lady* (Guest) (ro as Nina Gordon); *Knock on Wood* (Frank and Panama) (ro as Ilse Nordstrom)
1955   *A Prize of Gold* (Robson) (ro as Maria)
1956   "Ett dockhem" ("A Doll's House") ep. of *Giftas* (Henriksson) (ro)
1957   *Abandon Ship!* (*Seven Waves Away*) (Sale) (ro as Julie)
1958   *The Truth about Women* (Box) (ro as Julie); *Lek pa regnbagen* (Kjellgren) (ro)
1959   *Jet Storm* (Endfield) (ro as Carol Tilley)
1960   *Faces in the Dark* (Eady) (ro as Christiane Hammond); *Piccadilly Third Stop* (Rilla) (ro as Christine Pready);
1961   *Offbeat* (Owen) (ro as Ruth Lombard)
1962   *The Man Who Finally Died* (Lawrence) (ro as Lisa); *Only Two Can Play* (Gilliat) (ro as Elizabeth Gruffydd Williams); *The Main Attraction* (Petrie) (ro as Gina)
1963   *The Bay of St. Michel* (Ainsworth) (ro as Helene Bretton)
1965   *The Vine Bridge* (Nykvist) (ro)
1988   *Calling the Shots* (Cole—doc) (appearance)

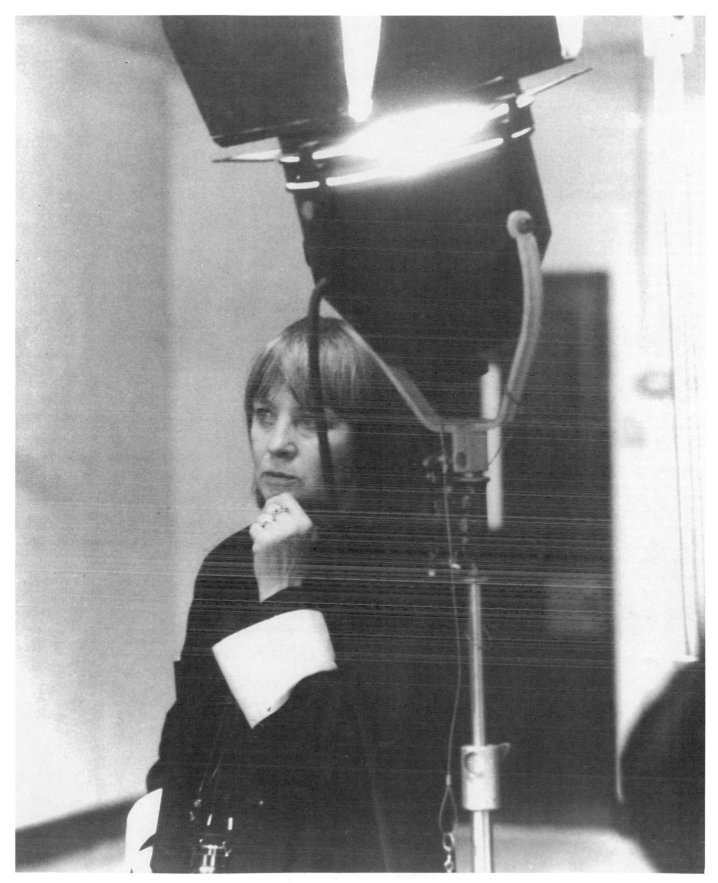

Mai Zetterling on the set of *Scrubbers*.

1990 *The Witches* (Roeg) (ro as Helga); *Hidden Agenda* (Loach) (ro as Moa)
1993 *Morfars Resa* (*Grandfather's Journey*) (Staffan Lamm) (ro as Elin Fromm)

Publications by Zetterling

Books

Shadow of the Sun (short stories), New York, 1975.
Bird of Passage (novel), New York, 1976.
Ice Island (novel), New York, 1979.
Rain's Hat (children's book), New York, 1979.
All Those Tomorrows (autobiography), London, 1985.

Articles

"Some Notes on Acting," in *Sight and Sound* (London), October/ December 1951.
Interview in *Cahiers du Cinéma* (Paris), April 1966.
"Mai Zetterling at the Olympic Games," interview in *American Cinematographer* (Los Angeles), November 1972.
"Mai Zetterling," interview with A. Jordahl and H. Lahger, in *Chaplin* (Stockholm), vol. 34, no. 3, 1992.

Publications on Zetterling

Books

Bjorkman, Stig, *Film in Sweden, the New Directors,* London, 1979.
Heck-Rabi, Louise, *Women Filmmakers: A Critical Reception,* Metuchen, New Jersey, 1984.
Acker, Ally, *Reel Women: Pioneers of the Cinema, 1896 to the Present,* New York, 1991.
Foster, Gwendolyn Audrey, *Women Film Directors: An International Bio-Critical Dictionary,* Westport, Connecticut, 1995.

Articles

"Meeting with Mai Zetterling," in *Cahiers du Cinéma in English* (New York), December 1966.
Pyros, J., "Notes on Women Directors," in *Take One* (Montreal), November/December 1970.
McGregor, C., "Mai Is behind the Camera Now," in *New York Times,* 30 April 1972.
Elley, Derek, "Hiding It under a Bushel: Free Fall," in *Films and Filming* (London), April 1974.
Modrzejewska, E. "Wiedzmy," in *Filmowy Serwis Prasowy,* vol. 37, no. 11/12, 1991.
Obituary in *New York Times,* 19 March 1994.
Obituary in *Variety* (New York), 28 March/3 April 1994.

* * *

Mai Zetterling's career as a filmmaker stemmed from her disillusionment with acting. Trained at Stockholm's Royal Dramatic Theatre, Zetterling debuted on stage and screen in 1941. She considered the film *Torment* her best acting achievement. She worked in British theater, enacting roles in Chekhov, Anouilh, and Ibsen plays, and in British films. After one part in a Hollywood film, *Knock on Wood* with Danny Kaye, she spurned contract offers and returned home.

With her husband, David Hughes, she made several documentaries in the 1960s dealing with political issues. Zetterling's feature films depict the social status and psyche of women, reflecting her feminist concerns. The uncompromising honesty of perception and technical virtuosity in her films correspond to the pervasive and dominant themes of loneliness and obsession. Zetterling says: "I want very strongly to do things I believe in. I can't do jobs for the money. I just can't do it."

In 1960 Roger Moorfoot of the BBC financed her idea for a film on the immigration of Swedes to Lapland, *The Polite Invasion.* Three more followed: *Lords of Little Egypt* depicted the gypsies at Saintes-Maries-de-la-Mer; her view of Swedish affluence in *The Prosperity Race* was not appreciated in Stockholm; and *The Do-It-Yourself Democracy* commented on Icelandic society and government. Her first independent effort was the fifteen-minute antiwar film *The War Game,* in which two boys tussle for possession of a toy gun.

Zetterling's first feature film, *Loving Couples,* was based on the fifth volume of Swedish author Agnes von Krusenstjerna's seven-volume novel, *The Misses von Pahlen.* Zetterling wrote the script in one year, with sketches of each shot to indicate camera positions. In it, three expectant mothers in a Stockholm hospital recall their lives in the moment of, and then beyond, the births of their babies. Critic Derek Elley suggests that Zetterling developed her theories and themes of film in *Loving Couples* and rarely deviated from them in later works. She employed elaborate timelines as well as flashbacks, which she used often and well, intertwining them one within another. Her films peak emotionally in scenes of parties and social gatherings. Her films are cohesive compositions, with a literary base, filmed in the stark contrasts of black to white, with a range of grays intervening. Zetterling's scenes of sexual behavior are integral to her themes of loneliness and obsession. *Loving Couples* exemplifies these characteristics.

Night Games, derived from Zetterling's novel with the same title, was banned from the Venice Film Festival. The critics who saw it were angered by the Marxist and Freudian elements in it; shocked by scenes of vomiting, masturbation, and childbirth. Based on Hjalmar Soderberg's 1905 novel, her next film, *Doktor Glas,* records the haunted love of a young physician for a pastor's wife. Even though the wife does not respond to the physician's erotic overtures, he administers a lethal drug to the pastor. It is Zetterling's grimmest study of loneliness, as Derek Elley observes, and her most pessimistic film, told in one extended flashback, "a far cry from *Night Games.*"

She returned to a strongly feminist story in *Flickorna* and, as in *Loving Couples,* it contains three female roles of equal weight. In *Flickorna* three actresses perform *Lysistrata* on tour, acting out the views of the play in their private lives. Some critics reacted negatively, finding it self-indulgent, a mix of Greek comedy and soap opera, with heavy symbolism and confusing time structures. Other critics liked the various forms of humor effectively employed, and the arresting imagery.

In 1971 Zetterling filmed a documentary in color about Vincent Van Gogh. Titled *Vincent the Dutchman,* it was shown on American and British television. David Wolper then asked her to film any phase of the 1972 Olympics she chose; she filmed the weight-lifting sequence, "The Strongest," for *Visions of Eight.*

In the 1970s Zetterling published three novels, pursuing creative directions other than filmmaking. She also continued making documentaries (one on tennis champion Stan Smith, one dealing with Stockholm, another on marriage customs), along with a seven-hour adaptation for French television of Simone de Beauvoir's *The Second Sex*. Zetterling asserted that whatever she filmed, it would be "something I believe in."

—Louise Heck-Rabi

ZHANG Nuanxin
Chinese director and writer

Born: Hohhot, Inner Mongolia, October 1940; her father was a doctor who immersed himself in Chinese literature and art. **Education:** Studied directing at the Beijing Film Academy, 1958-62. **Family:** Married the Beijing writer/critic Li Tuo. **Career:** After graduation, stayed on to teach in the directing department of the Beijing Film Academy, where she helped train members of China's "Fifth Generation" filmmakers; assigned to the Beijing Film Academy's Youth Film Studio as director; in her early career, she assisted prominent directors Sang Hu and Xie Jin, before progressing to directing her own films; 1985—invited to Paris for a year-long stay as a visiting researcher; upon her return, she served as primary consultant to the Sino-French production of *Tears of Huajiao*. **Awards:** PRC Special Prize, for *Sha'ou's Seagull*, 1981; PRC Best Picture, and Hong Kong Best Chinese Language Film, for *Good Morning, Beijing*, 1991. **Died:** In Beijing, of cancer, 28 May 1995.

Films as Director and Co-Writer

1981   *Sha Ou* (*Sha'ou's Seagull*; *The Seagull*; *The Drive to Win*)
1985   **Qingchunji** (*Sacrificed Youth*)

Films as Director

1991   *Beijing Nin Zao* (*Good Morning, Beijing*)
1994   *Yunnan Qiu Shi* (*The Story of Yunnan*)

Other Films

1979   *Li Siguang* (Ling Zingfeng) (co-sc)
c. 1986   *Huajiao Lei* (*Tears of Huajiao*) (consultant)

Publications by Zhang

Articles

With Li Tuo, "On the Modernization of the Language of Film," in *Dianying Yishu* [Film art] (Beijing), 1979; translated by Hou Jianping in *Chinese Film Theory: A Guide to the New Era,* edited by George S. Semsel, and others, New York, 1990.
With Li Tuo, "Exploration of the New Concept of Film," in *Explorations of Film Directing,* Beijing, 1982.
Interview in *Dianying Yishu Cankao Ziliao* [Reference materials on the film art], Beijing, 1985.
Interview in *Dianying Xinzuo* [New cinema] (Beijing), 1987.

Interview with George Semsel, in *Chinese Film: The State of the Art in the People's Republic,* edited by George S. Semsel, New York, 1987.
Interview with Chris Berry, in *Camera Obscura* (Berkeley), September 1988.
"The Director's Thematic Exposition of *Good Morning, Beijing,*" in *Dangdai Dianying* [Contemporary cinema] (Beijing), 1990.

Publications on Zhang

Books

Quart, Barbara, *Women Directors: The Emergence of a New Cinema,* New York, 1988.
Foster, Gwendolyn Audrey, *Women Film Directors: An International Bio-Critical Dictionary,* Westport, Connecticut, 1995.

Articles

Zhang, Zhenqin, "Cong 'zijue' xiang 'ziyou' de qiusuo: lun Zhang Nuanxin he ta de dianying chuangzuo [Moving the search from 'self-consciousness' to 'freedom': on Zhang Nuanxin and her work in film]," in *Dangdai Dianying* [Contemporary cinema] (Beijing), 1987.
Zhang, Wei, "The Position of the Woman and Historical Transformation: An Allegorical Interpretation of *Good Morning, Beijing,*" in *Dangdai Dianying* [Contemporary cinema] (Beijing), 1990.
Kou, Liguang, and Li Yuzhi, in *Zhongguo Dangdai Youxiu Dianying Xinshang* [Outstanding Chinese contemporary films], Shanxi, China, 1991.
Tang, Xiaobing, "Configuring the Modern Space," in *East-West Film Journal* (Honolulu), 1994.

*   *   *

Zhang Nuanxin declared that Chinese cinema at the end of the Great Proletariat Cultural Revolution (1966-76) was 20 years behind world filmmaking. Influenced first by the Italian neorealists and then by the French new wave, she and husband Li Tuo co-wrote the controversial essay "On the Modernization of the Language of Film" in 1979, in which she argued against the prevailing focus on content over form.

Although the ideas in the article were initially widely criticized, as she began to put them into practice in directing her films, critics began to concede that her approach was both fresh and palatable. It featured the director as auteur, utilizing cinematic realism as a tool to achieve a lyrical effect. The feature film, she urged, should retreat from its over reliance on theatricality and spectacle, and need not always revolve, as it usually does, around a core conflict and its resolution.

Zhang held that cinema could be better if it were closer to real life, but at the same time she sought to go beyond merely capturing an external reality on screen—her goal was to express her subjectivity by capturing dominant features of her own inner landscape in her work. The form of the film, she felt, could and should be used to express the filmmaker's deepest feelings and emotions.

—Cynthia Y. Ning

NATIONALITY INDEX

American

Zoë Akins
Dede Allen
Jay Presson Allen
Allison Anders
Maya Angelou
Dorothy Arzner
Beth B
Anne Bauchens
Kathryn Bigelow
Margaret Booth
Lizzie Borden
Leigh Brackett
Mary Ellen Bute
Ayoka Chenzira
Abigail Child
Joyce Chopra
Christine Choy
Michelle Citron
Shirley Clarke
Lenore J. Coffee
Betty Comden
Martha Coolidge
Julie Dash
Zeinabu irene Davis
Storm De Hirsch
Donna Deitch
Maya Deren
Nora Ephron
Verna Fields
Jodie Foster
Su Friedrich
Lillian Gish
Jill Godmilow
Frances Goodrich
Bette Gordon
Helen Grayson
Maggie Greenwald
Barbara Hammer
Leslie Harris
Edith Head
Amy Heckerling
Faith Elliott Hubley
Irene
Dorothy Jeakins
Ruth Prawer Jhabvala
Barbara Kopple
Alile Sharon Larkin
Caroline Leaf
Isobel Lennart
Sonya Levien
Carol Littleton
Jennie Livingston
Anita Loos
Ida Lupino
Jeanie Macpherson
Cleo Madison
Frances Marion
Penny Marshall
June Mathis
Elaine May

Marie Menken
Bess Meredyth
Jane Murfin
Brianne Murphy
Gunvor Nelson
Claire Parker
Eleanor Perry
Mary Pickford
Yvonne Rainer
Helen Rose
Nancy Savoca
Greta Schiller
Carolee Schneemann
Thelma Schoonmaker
Susan Seidelman
Irene Sharaff
Joan Micklin Silver
Dorothy Spencer
Penelope Spheeris
Barbra Streisand
Trinh T. Minh-Ha
Theadora Van Runkle
Virginia Van Upp
Patrizia von Brandenstein
Lois Weber
Claudia Weill
Mae West

Argentinean

María Luisa Bemberg
Nelly Kaplan
Jeanine Meerapfel

Australian

Gillian Armstrong
Corinne Cantrill
Lottie Lyell
Isobel McDonagh
Paulette McDonagh
Phyllis McDonagh

Austrian

Valie Export
Leontine Sagan

Belgian

Chantal Akerman
Marion Hänsel
Agnès Varda

Brazilian

Gilda de Abreu
Suzana Amaral
Ana Carolina
Tizuka Yamasaki

British

Joy Batchelor
Antonia Bird
Betty E. Box
Muriel Box

Jill Craigie
Carmen Dillon
Elinor Glyn
Joan Harrison
Beeban Kidron
Brianne Murphy
Pratibha Parmar
Sally Potter
Lotte Reiniger
Alma Reville
Shirley Russell
Wendy Toye

Canadian
Janis Cole
Holly Dale
Caroline Leaf
Alison Maclean
Deepa Mehta
Alanis Obomsawin
Mary Pickford
Anne-Claire Poirier
Léa Pool
Nell Shipman
Joyce Wieland

Chilean
Marilú Mallet
Valeria Sarmiento

Chinese
Clara Law
Peng Xiaolian
Zhang Nuanxin

Chinese/Hong Kong
Ann Hui

Cuban
Sara Gómez

Czech
Vera Chytilová
Ester Krumbachová
Vera Šimková-Plívová

Danish
Astrid Henning-Jensen

Dutch
Annette Apon
Marleen Gorris
Helen van Dongen

French
Jacqueline Audry
Colette
Claire Denis
Germaine Dulac
Marguerite Duras
Marie Epstein

Agnès Guillemot
Alice Guy
Marion Hänsel
Danièle Huillet
Nelly Kaplan
Diane Kurys
Sarah Maldoror
Musidora
Euzhan Palcy
Christine Pascal
Coline Serreau
Nadine Trintignant

German
Jutta Brückner
Doris Dörrie
Birgit Hein
Ulrike Ottinger
Leni Riefenstahl
Helke Sander
Helma Sanders-Brahms
Monika Treut
Thea von Harbou
Margarethe von Trotta

Hungarian
Judit Elek
Márta Mészáros

Indian
Deepa Mehta
Mira Nair

Iranian
Rakhshan Bani-Etemad

Italian
Liliana Cavani
Suso Cecchi d'Amico
Elvira Notari
Lina Wertmüller

Japanese
Yoko Ono
Kinuyo Tanaka

Mexican
Marcela Fernández Violante
Matilde Soto Landeta
María Novaro

New Zealander
Jane Campion
Alison Maclean

Norwegian
Anja Breien
Liv Ullmann

Polish
Agnieszka Holland
Wanda Jakubowska

Russian
Kira Muratova
Olga Preobrazhenskaya
Yulia Solntseva

Senegalese
Safi Faye

Spanish
Pilar Miró

Soviet Ukrainian
Larissa Shepitko
Esther Shub

Swedish
Marianne Ahrne
Gunvor Nelson
Mai Zetterling

Swiss
Léa Pool

Ukrainian
Kira Muratova

West Indian
Euzhan Palcy

OCCUPATION INDEX

Actors

Gilda de Abreu
Colette
Jodie Foster
Lillian Gish
Ida Lupino
Lottie Lyell
Jeanie Macpherson
Cleo Madison
Penny Marshall
Elaine May
Isobel McDonagh
Bess Meredyth
Musidora
Yoko Ono
Christine Pascal
Mary Pickford
Olga Preobrazhenskaya
Coline Serreau
Nell Shipman
Yulia Solntseva
Barbra Streisand
Kinuyo Tanaka
Liv Ullmann
Margarethe von Trotta
Mae West
Mai Zetterling

Art directors

Carmen Dillon
Phyllis McDonagh

Abstract filmmakers

Mary Ellen Bute

Animators

Joy Batchelor
Mary Ellen Bute
Ayoka Chenzira
Faith Elliott Hubley
Caroline Leaf
Claire Parker
Lotte Reiniger

Costume designers

Edith Head
Irene
Dorothy Jeakins
Ester Krumbachová
Helen Rose
Shirley Russell
Irene Sharaff
Theadora Van Runkle

Cinematographers

Christine Choy
Brianne Murphy

Composers

Yoko Ono

Directors

Gilda de Abreu
Marianne Ahrne
Chantal Akerman
Suzana Amaral
Allison Anders
Annette Apon
Gillian Armstrong
Dorothy Arzner
Jacqueline Audry
Beth B
Rakhshan Bani-Etemad
María Luisa Bemberg
Kathryn Bigelow
Antonia Bird
Lizzie Borden
Muriel Box
Anja Breien
Jutta Brückner
Jane Campion
Corinne Cantrill
Ana Carolina
Liliana Cavani
Ayoka Chenzira
Abigail Child
Joyce Chopra
Christine Choy
Vera Chytilová
Michelle Citron
Shirley Clarke
Janis Cole
Martha Coolidge
Jill Craigie
Holly Dale
Julie Dash
Zeinabu irene Davis
Storm De Hirsch
Donna Deitch
Claire Denis
Maya Deren
Doris Dörrie
Germaine Dulac
Marguerite Duras
Judit Elek
Nora Ephron
Marie Epstein
Valie Export
Safi Faye
Marcela Fernández Violante
Jodie Foster
Su Friedrich
Lillian Gish
Elinor Glyn
Jill Godmilow
Sara Gómez
Bette Gordon
Marleen Gorris
Helen Grayson
Maggie Greenwald
Alice Guy
Barbara Hammer

Marion Hänsel
Leslie Harris
Amy Heckerling
Birgit Hein
Astrid Henning-Jensen
Agnieszka Holland
Faith Elliott Hubley
Ann Hui
Danièle Huillet
Wanda Jakubowska
Nelly Kaplan
Beeban Kidron
Barbara Kopple
Ester Krumbachová
Diane Kurys
Matilde Soto Landeta
Alile Sharon Larkin
Clara Law
Caroline Leaf
Jennie Livingston
Ida Lupino
Lottie Lyell
Alison Maclean
Jeanie Macpherson
Cleo Madison
Sarah Maldoror
Marilú Mallet
Penny Marshall
Elaine May
Paulette McDonagh
Jeanine Meerapfel
Deepa Mehta
Marie Menken
Márta Mészáros
Pilar Miró
Kira Muratova
Brianne Murphy
Musidora
Mira Nair
Gunvor Nelson
Elvira Notari
María Novaro
Alanis Obomsawin
Yoko Ono
Ulrike Ottinger
Euzhan Palcy
Claire Parker
Pratibha Parmar
Christine Pascal
Peng Xiaolian
Anne-Claire Poirier
Léa Pool
Sally Potter
Olga Preobrazhenskaya
Yvonne Rainer
Leni Riefenstahl
Leontine Sagan
Helke Sander
Helma Sanders-Brahms
Valeria Sarmiento
Nancy Savoca

Greta Schiller
Carolee Schneemann
Susan Seidelman
Coline Serreau
Larissa Shepitko
Nell Shipman
Esther Shub
Joan Micklin Silver
Vera Šimková-Plívová
Yulia Solntseva
Penelope Spheeris
Barbra Streisand
Kinuyo Tanaka
Wendy Toye
Monika Treut
Trinh T. Minh-Ha
Nadine Trintignant
Liv Ullmann
Helen van Dongen
Agnès Varda
Margarethe von Trotta
Lois Weber
Claudia Weill
Lina Wertmüller
Joyce Wieland
Tizuka Yamasaki
Mai Zetterling
Zhang Nuanxin

Editors
Dede Allen
Anne Bauchens
Margaret Booth
Janis Cole
Holly Dale
Marie Epstein
Verna Fields
Agnès Guillemot
Carol Littleton
Valeria Sarmiento
Thelma Schoonmaker
Dorothy Spencer
Helen van Dongen

Lyricists
Betty Comden

Production designers
Patrizia von Brandenstein

Producers
Maya Angelou
Betty E. Box
Ayoka Chenzira
Janis Cole
Holly Dale
Zeinabu irene Davis
Nora Ephron
Joan Harrison
Faith Elliott Hubley
Anita Loos

Phyllis McDonagh
Euzhan Palcy
Mary Pickford
Barbra Streisand
Virginia Van Upp

Writers
Gilda de Abreu
Zoë Akins
Jay Presson Allen
Maya Angelou
María Luisa Bemberg
Kathryn Bigelow
Muriel Box
Leigh Brackett
Ana Carolina
Liliana Cavani
Suso Cecchi d'Amico
Ayoka Chenzira
Lenore J. Coffee
Janis Cole
Colette
Betty Comden
Jill Craigie
Holly Dale
Julie Dash
Claire Denis
Doris Dörrie
Marguerite Duras
Nora Ephron
Marie Epstein
Safi Faye
Marcela Fernández Violante
Elinor Glyn
Frances Goodrich
Marleen Gorris
Maggie Greenwald
Alice Guy
Barbara Hammer
Marion Hänsel
Joan Harrison
Agnieszka Holland
Ruth Prawer Jhabvala

Nelly Kaplan
Ester Krumbachová
Diane Kurys
Matilde Soto Landeta
Isobel Lennart
Sonya Levien
Anita Loos
Jeanie Macpherson
Marilú Mallet
Frances Marion
June Mathis
Elaine May
Paulette McDonagh
Phyllis McDonagh
Jeanine Meerapfel
Bess Meredyth
Pilar Miró
Kira Muratova
Jane Murfin
Musidora
Elvira Notari
María Novaro
Euzhan Palcy
Christine Pascal
Eleanor Perry
Anne-Claire Poirier
Alma Reville
Helke Sander
Helma Sanders-Brahms
Valeria Sarmiento
Nancy Savoca
Coline Serreau
Larissa Shepitko
Vera Šimková-Plívová
Barbra Streisand
Nadine Trintignant
Liv Ullmann
Virginia Van Upp
Thea von Harbou
Margarethe von Trotta
Lina Wertmüller
Mae West
Zhang Nuanxin

AWARDS INDEX

The following index contains a selected list of the awards appearing in *Women Filmmakers & Their Films*. Awards are arranged alphabetically by either the name of the honor or the bestowing organization or festival, whichever was deemed most widely known.

Academy Award, Best Actress
Jodie Foster, 1988, *The Accused*
Jodie Foster, 1991, *The Silence of the Lambs*
Mary Pickford, 1929, *Coquette*
Barbra Streisand, 1968, *Funny Girl*

Academy Award, Best Art Direction—Set Decoration
Carmen Dillon, 1948, *Hamlet*
Patrizia von Brandenstein, 1984, *Amadeus*

Academy Award, Best Costume Design
Dorothy Jeakins, 1948, *Joan of Arc*
Edith Head, 1949, *The Heiress*
Edith Head, 1949, *Samson and Delilah*
Edith Head, 1950, *All about Eve*
Dorothy Jeakins, 1950, *Samson and Delilah*
Edith Head, 1951, *A Place in the Sun*
Irene Sharaff, 1951, *An American in Paris*
Helen Rose, 1952, *The Bad and the Beautiful*
Edith Head, 1953, *Roman Holiday*
Edith Head, 1954, *Sabrina*
Helen Rose, 1955, *I'll Cry Tomorrow*
Irene Sharaff, 1956, *The King and I*
Edith Head, 1960, *The Facts of Life*
Irene Sharaff, 1961, *West Side Story*
Irene Sharaff, 1963, *Cleopatra*
Dorothy Jeakins, 1964, *The Night of the Iguana*
Irene Sharaff, 1966, *Who's Afraid of Virginia Woolf?*
Edith Head, 1973, *The Sting*

Academy Award, Best Feature Documentary
Barbara Kopple, 1976, *Harlan County, U.S.A.*
Barbara Kopple, 1991, *American Dream*

Academy Award, Best Film Editing
Anne Bauchens, 1940, *Northwest Mounted Police*
Verna Fields, 1975, *Jaws*
Thelma Schoonmaker, 1980, *Raging Bull*

Academy Award, Best Foreign Language Film
Marleen Gorris, 1995, *Antonia's Line*

Academy Award, Best Short Subjects—Cwartoons
Faith Elliott Hubley (with John Hubley), 1962, *The Hole*
Faith Elliott Hubley (with John Hubley), 1966, *Herb Alpert and the Tijuana Brass Double Feature*

Academy Award, Best Song
Barbra Streisand, 1976, "Evergreen" from *A Star Is Born*

Academy Award, Best Writing—Achievement
Frances Marion, 1929-30, *The Big House*

Academy Award, Best Writing—Original Story
Frances Marion, 1931-32, *The Champ*

Academy Award, Best Writing—Screenplay Based on Material from Another Medium
Ruth Prawer Jhabvala, 1986, *A Room with a View*
Ruth Prawer Jhabvala, 1992, *Howards End*

Academy Award, Best Writing—Screenplay Written Directly for the Screen
Muriel Box (With Sydney Box), 1946, *The Seventh Veil*
Jane Campion, 1993, *The Piano*

Academy Award, Honorary Career Award
Lillian Gish, 1970
Mary Pickford, 1975
Margaret Booth, 1977

Academy Award, Scientific or Technical Achievement
Brianne Murphy, 1982, for design of the MISI camera insert safety car and trailer

ACE (American Cinema Editors) Achievement Award
Anne Bauchens, 1952, *The Greatest Show on Earth*

ACE (American Cinema Editors) Award, Best Documentary Special
Christine Choy, 1989, *Best Hotel on Skid Row*

American Film and Video Festival, Blue Ribbon
Greta Schiller, 1986, *International Sweethearts of Rhythm*
Trinh T. Minh-Ha, 1991, *Surname Viet, Given Name Nam*

American Film Festival, Emily Award
Jill Godmilow, 1973, *Antonia: A Portrait of the Woman*

American Film Festival, Red Ribbon
Jill Godmilow, 1976, *Nevelson in Process*

American Film Institute, Life Achievement Award
Lillian Gish, 1984

American Indian Film Festival (San Francisco), Best Documentary
Alanis Obomsawin, 1977, *Mother of Many Children*
Alanis Obomsawin, 1986, *Richard Cardinal*
Alanis Obomsawin, 1988, *No Address*

American International Film Festival, Blue Ribbon Award, Best Experimental Feature
1985 Trinh T. Minh-Ha, *Naked Spaces*

American Society of Cinematographers, Governors Award
Jodie Foster, 1996

Ann Arbor Film Festival, Best Subject Matter
Christine Choy, 1980, *To Love, Honor, and Obey*

Ann Arbor Film Festival, Isabel Liddell Art Award
Barbara Hammer, 1995, *Tender Fictions*

Ann Arbor Film Festival, Lawrence Kasdan Award—Best Narrative
Zeinabu irene Davis, 1991, *A Powerful Thang*

Ariel, Best Director, Mexican Academy of Motion Picture Arts and Science
Marcela Fernández Violante, 1979, *Mystery*

Ariel, Best Documentary Short, Mexican Academy of Motion Picture Arts and Science
Marcela Fernández Violante, 1971, *Frida Kahlo*

Ariel, Best Feature Debut, Mexican Academy of Motion Picture Arts and Science
María Novaro, 1989, *Lola*

Ariel, Best Feature Film, Mexican Academy of Motion Picture Arts and Science
Marcela Fernández Violante, 1975, *Whatever You Do, You Lose*
Marcela Fernández Violante, 1979, *Mystery*

Ariel, Best Film Script, Mexican Academy of Motion Picture Arts and Science
María Novaro, 1989, *Lola*

Ariel, Best Screenplay, Mexican Academy of Motion Picture Arts and Science
Matilde Soto Landeta, 1956, *Los Caminos de la vida*

Ariel, Best Short Fiction, Mexican Academy of Motion Picture Arts and Science
María Novaro, 1984, *An Island Surrounded by Water*

Asian Pacific Festival, Best Film
Ann Hui, 1990, *Song of the Exile*

Athens International Film Festival, Best Experimental Film Award
Su Friedrich, 1987, *Damned if You Don't*

Athens International Film Festival, Best Narrative Film Award
Su Friedrich, 1996, *Hide and Seek*

Athens International Film Festival, Golden Athena Award—Best Feature Documentary
Trinh T. Minh-Ha, 1985, *Naked Spaces*
Trinh T. Minh-Ha, 1991, *Shoot for the Contents*

Athens International Film Festival, Special Merit Award
Su Friedrich, 1979, *Cool Hands, Warm Heart*

Atlanta Film/Video Festival, Best Experimental Narrative Award
Su Friedrich, 1987, *Damned if You Don't*

Atlanta Film/Video Festival, Women in Film Award
Barbara Hammer, 1989, *Still Point*

Atlantic Film Festival, First Prize
Léa Pool, 1988, *Straight for the Heart*

Australian Film Institute Award, Best Director
Gillian Armstrong, 1979, *My Brilliant Career*
Jane Campion, 1984, *Girl's Own* Story
Jane Campion, 1985, *2 Friends*
Jane Campion, 1993, *The Piano*

Australian Film Institute Award, Best Experimental Film
Jane Campion, 1984, *Passionless Moments*

Australian Film Institute Award, Best Film
My Brilliant Career, 1979

Australian Film Institute Award, Best Screenplay
Jane Campion, 1993, *The Piano*
Jane Campion, 1984, *Girl's Own Story*

Australian Film Institute Award, Best TV Film
Jane Campion, 1985, *2 Friends*

Australian Film Institute, Raymond Longford Award— Significant Contributions to the Australian Film Industry
Isobel, Paulette, and Phyllis McDonagh, 1978

Australian Film Institute, Silver Award
Corinne Cantrill, 1970, *Earth Message*

BAFTA (British Academy of Film and Television Arts) Alexander Korda Award—Best British Film of the Year
Antonia Bird, 1994, *Priest*

BAFTA (British Academy of Film and Television Arts) Award, Best Adapted Screenplay
Ruth Prawer Jhabvala, 1983, *Heat and Dust*

BAFTA (British Academy of Film and Television Arts) Award, Best Editing
Dede Allen, 1975, *Dog Day Afternoon*
Thelma Schoonmaker, 1980, *Raging Bull*

BAFTA (British Academy of Film and Television Arts) Award, Best Supporting Actress
Jodie Foster, 1976, *Taxi Driver*
Jodie Foster, 1976, *Bugsy Malone*

BAFTA (British Academy of Film and Television Arts), Best TV film
Antonia Bird, 1993, *Safe*

BAFTA (British Academy of Film and Television Arts) Award, Most Promising Newcomer
Jodie Foster, 1976

Berlin International Film Festival, Best Actress
Kinuyo Tanaka, 1975, *Sandakan, House No. 8*

Berlin International Film Festival, Best Director
Astrid Henning-Jensen, 1979, *Winter Children*

Berlin International Film Festival, Best Documentary—Audience Prize
Greta Schiller, 1996, *Paris Was a Woman*

Berlin International Film Festival, FIPRESCI (International Federation of Cinema Press) Prize
Safi Faye, 1975, *Kaddu Beykat*
Larissa Shepitko, 1977, *The Ascent*
Antonia Bird, 1994, *Priest*

Berlin International Film Festival, Golden Bear Award
Helke Sander, 1984, *No. 1—From the Reports of Security Guards and Patrol Services*
Larissa Shepitko, 1977, *The Ascent*

Berlin International Film Festival, Interfilm Award
Jeanine Meerapfel, 1985, *Die Kümmeltürkin geht*

Berlin International Film Festival, Otto Dibielius Award
Jeanine Meerapfel, 1985, *Die Kümmeltürkin geht*

Berlin International Film Festival, Polar Bear Award for Lifetime Contribution to Lesbian/Gay Cinema
Barbara Hammer, 1993

Berlin International Film Festival, Silver Bear, Best Director
Agnès Varda, 1965, *Le Bonheur*
Pilar Miró, 1991, *Beltenebros*

Berlin International Film Festival, Silver Bear, Special Jury Prize
Kira Muratova, 1990, *The Asthenic Syndrome*

Bilbao International Film Festival, Special Jury's Prize
Valie Export, 1983, *Syntagma*

Black American Cinema Society, First Prize
Alile Sharon Larkin, 1982, *A Different Image*

Black Filmmakers Hall of Fame, Best Drama
Ayoka Chenzira, 1993, *MOTV*

Black Filmmakers Hall of Fame, Best Film
Julie Dash, 1992, *Daughters of the Dust*

Black Filmmakers Hall of Fame, Best of category—Experimental
Zeinabu irene Davis, 1989, *Cycles*

Black Filmmakers Hall of Fame, Best Overall
Ayoka Chenzira, 1993, *MOTV*

Black Filmmakers Hall of Fame, Community Choice Award
Ayoka Chenzira, 1993, *MOTV*

Black Filmmakers Hall of Fame, First Place for Animation
Ayoka Chenzira, 1990, *Zajota and the Boogie Spirit*

Black Maria Film Festival, First Prize
Barbara Hammer, 1988, *Endangered*

Black Maria Film Festival, Jurors' Award
Barbara Hammer, 1991, *Vital Signs*

Black Maria Film Festival, Juror's Citation
Christine Choy, 1991, *Yellow Tale Blues*

Bombay International Film Festival, Merit Award
Trinh T. Minh-Ha, 1989, *Surname Viet, Given Name Nam*

Brasilia Film Festival, Best Film
Suzana Amaral, 1985, *The Hour of the Star*

British Critics' Award
Gillian Armstrong, 1979, *My Brilliant Career*

British Women in Films Achievement Award
Betty E. Box, 1992

Brussels International Experimental Film Festival, Best Short Film
Mary Ellen Bute, 1953, *Mood Contrasts*

Brussels International Film Festival, Special Jury Prize
Euzhan Palcy, 1993, *Simeon*

Brussels International Film Festival, Prix l'Age d'Or
Helke Sander, 1977, *Redupers*

Cable ACE Award
Beeban Kidron, 1989, *Oranges Are Not the Only Fruit*

Cairo Film Festival, Critics Prize
Sarah Maldoror, 1996, *Léon G. Damas*

Cairo Film Festival, Jury Prize
Sarah Maldoror, 1996, *Léon G. Damas*

Canadian Film Awards, Wendy Michener Award
Caroline Leaf, 1976

Cannes International Film Festival, Best Short Fiction Film
Wendy Toye, 1953, *The Stranger Left No Card*

Cannes International Film Festival, Camera d'Or—Best First Feature
Mira Nair, 1988, *Salaam Bombay!*

Cannes International Film Festival, Catholic Film Office Award
Astrid Henning-Jensen, 1960, *Paw*

Cannes International Film Festival, FIPRESCI (International Federation of Cinema Press) Prize
Jeanine Meerapfel, 1981, *Malou*

Cannes International Film Festival, Palme d'Or
The Piano, 1993

Cannes International Film Festival, Palme d'Or—Best Short Film
Jane Campion, 1982, *Peel*

Cannes International Film Festival, Prix de Publique— Audience Favorite
Mira Nair, 1988, *Salaam Bombay!*

Cannes International Film Festival Prize
Astrid Henning-Jensen, 1949, *Palle Alone in the World*

Cannes International Film Festival, Special Jury Prize
Napló gyermekeimnek, 1982

Cannes International Film Festival, Special Mention
Anja Breien, 1979, *Next of Kin*

Carthage Film Festival, Best Director Award
Sarah Maldoror, 1969, *Monangambée*
Safi Faye, 1979, *Fad'jal*

Carthage Film Festival, Golden Tanis
Sarah Maldoror, 1972, *Sambizanga*

César Award, Best Director
Agnès Varda, 1983, *Ulysse*

César Award, Best Film
Coline Serreau, 1985, *Trois hommes et un couffin*

César, Best First Film
Euzhan Palcy, 1983, *Sugar Cane Alley*

César Award, Best Screenplay
Coline Serreau, 1985, *Trois hommes et un couffin*

Charlotte Film and Video Festival, Director's Choice Award
Barbara Hammer, 1995, *Tender Fictions*

Charlotte Film and Video Festival, Gold Juror's Choice Award
Su Friedrich, 1990, *Sink or Swim*

Chicago International Children's Fest, Best Film and Video, Children's Jury
Zeinabu irene Davis, 1995, *Mother of the River*

Chicago International Film Festival, Best Screenplay
Marleen Gorris, 1995, *Antonia's Line*

Chicago International Film Festival, First Prize
Jeanine Meerapfel, 1981, *Malou*

Chicago International Film Festival, Hugo Award
Beeban Kidron, 1983, *Carry Greenham Home*

Chicago International Film Festival, Silver Hugo
Zeinabu irene Davis, 1995, *Mother of the River*

Chicago International Film Festival, Silver Plaque Award
Greta Schiller, 1989, *Tiny & Ruby: Hell-Divin' Women*

Chinese Children's Film Competition, Best Director
Peng Xiaolian, 1986, *Me and My Classmates*

Chinese Children's Film Competition, Golden Rooster Award—Best Children's Film
Peng Xiaolian, 1986, *Me and My Classmates*

Ciak d'Oro, Migliore Allievo al Centro Sperimentale di Cinematografia
Liliana Cavani

CINE Golden Eagle Awards (14)
Faith Elliott Hubley

Círculo de Escritores Cinematográficos (Screenwriters' Circle) Award, Best New Director
Pilar Miró, 1976, *The Engagement Party*

Columbus International Film Festival, Bronze Plaque
Janis Cole and Holly Dale, 1996, *Dangerous Offender*

Columbus International Film Festival, Chris Award—Best of Category
Zeinabu irene Davis, 1995, *Mother of the River*

Creative Film Foundation, Special Citation
Marie Menken, 1959, *Dwightiana*

Créteil International Women's Film Festival (France), Audience Prize
Greta Schiller, 1986, *International Sweethearts of Rhythm*

Créteil International Women's Film Festival (France), Best Director
Suzana Amaral, 1985, *The Hour of the Star*

Créteil International Women's Film Festival (France), Best Documentary—Audience Prize
Greta Schiller, 1996, *Paris Was a Woman*

Créteil International Women's Film Festival (France), Best Film
Ann Hui, 1994, *Summer Snow*

Créteil International Women's Film Festival (France), Best Feature Film
Deepa Mehta, 1988, *Martha, Ruth & Edie*

Créteil International Women's Film Festival (France), Special Jury Prize
Peng Xiaolian, 1987, *Nüren de Gushi*

D. W. Griffith Award
Lillian Gish, 1987

Daniel Wadsworth Memorial Video Festival, Festival Prize
Valie Export, 1986, *A Perfect Pair, or, Indecency Sheds Its Skin*

David Di Donatello Award, Foreign Actress
Barbra Streisand, 1968, *Funny Girl*
Barbra Streisand, 1973, *The Way We Were*

David Selznick Award
Agnès Varda, 1965, *Le Bonheur*

Dinard Film Festival, First Prize
Sarah Maldoror, 1969, *Monangambée*

Dinard Film Festival, Silver Hitchcock—Special Jury Prize
Antonia Bird, 1993, *Safe*

Diosa de la Plata, Best Documentary Short
Marcela Fernández Violante, 1971, *Frida Kahlo*

Diosa de la Plata, Critics' Award—Best Experimental Short
Marcela Fernández Violante, 1966, *Blue*

Directors Guild of America, Best Feature Documentary
Barbara Kopple, 1991, *American Dream*

Director's Guild of America, Honors
Dorothy Arzner, 1975

Directors Guild of America, Outstanding Directorial Achievement
Barbara Kopple, 1993, *Fallen Champ*

Dorothy Arzner Award, Women in Film
Julie Dash, 1992
Barbara Kopple, 1993

Dutch Film Days, Best Feature
Marleen Gorris, 1981, *A Question of Silence*

Edinburgh International Film Festival, Charles Chaplin Prize—Best First Feature
Antonia Bird, 1993, *Safe*

Edinburgh International Film Festival, Michael Powell Award—Best British Feature
Antonia Bird, 1994, *Priest*

Emmy Award, Best Afterschool Special
Claudia Weill, 1984, *The Great Love Experiment*

Emmy Award, Best Cinematography
Brianne Murphy, 1978, *Five Finger Discount*

Emmy Award, Best Cultural or Historical Program
Greta Schiller, 1985, *Before Stonewall*

Emmy Award, Best Research
Greta Schiller, 1985, *Before Stonewall*

ETA Creative Arts Foundation (Chicago), Best Experimental Narrative
Zeinabu irene Davis, 1991, *A Powerful Thang*

Etrog Award, Best Documentary
Deepa Mehta, 1975, *At 99: A Portrait of Louise Tandy Murch*

Exposition Internationale des Arts et des Techniques (Paris), Diplome de Grand Prix
Leni Riefenstahl, 1935, *Triumph des Willens*

Fajr International Film Festival (Tehran), Crystal Simorgh Award, Best Director
Rakhshan Bani-Etemad, 1992, *Nargess*

Fajr International Film Festival (Tehran), Crystal Simorgh Award, Best Script
Rakhshan Bani-Etemad, 1995, *The Blue-Veiled*

Festival du Cinema International, Grand Prix Hydro-Quebec
Anne-Claire Poirier, 1988, *Salut Victor!*

Festival International du Film de l'Ensemble Francophone (Geneva), Georges Sadoul Prize
Safi Faye, 1975, *Kaddu Beykat*

Filmband in Gold, West German Film Prize
Helke Sander, 1984, *No. 1—From the Reports of Security Guards and Patrol Services*

Filmband in Gold, West German Film Prize, Artistic Realization
Ulrike Ottinger, 1988, *Johanna d'Arc of Mongolia*

Filmband in Gold, West German Film Prize, Service to German cinema
Lotte Reiniger, 1972

French Exposition Grand Prix du Film Français
Marie Epstein, 1937, *La Mort du cygne*

German Film Critics Award
Ulrike Ottinger, 1985, *China—The Arts—The People*

GLAAD Media Awards, Vito Russo Film Award
Jennie Livingston, 1992

Global Village Film Festival (New York), Best Documentary
Mira Nair, 1985, *India Cabaret*

Golden Bauhinia Award, Best Director
Ann Hui, 1994, *Summer Snow*

Golden Bauhinia Award, Best Picture
Ann Hui, 1994, *Summer Snow*

Golden Globe Award, Best Actress
Barbra Streisand, 1968, *Funny Girl*
Liv Ullmann, 1972, *The Emigrants*

Golden Globe Award, Best Director
Barbra Streisand, 1983, *Yentl*

Golden Globe Award, Best Foreign Language Film
Agnieszka Holland, 1990, *Europa, Europa*

Golden Globe Award, Best Song
Barbra Streisand, 1976, "Evergreen," *A Star Is Born*

Golden Senghor, Best Director
Euzhan Palcy, 1993, *Simeon*

Goya Film Award, Best Director
Pilar Miró, 1997, *The Dog in the Manger*

Hampton's International Film Festival, Best Director
Marleen Gorris, 1995, *Antonia's Line*

Havana International Film Festival, Best Film
Suzana Amaral, 1985, *The Hour of the Star*

Havana International Film Festival, Gran Premio Coral
Tizuka Yamasaki, 1980, *Gaijin*

Hawaii International Film Festival, Best Documentary
Christine Choy, 1988, *Who Killed Vincent Chin?*

Hawaii International Film Festival, People's Choice Award
Peng Xiaolian, 1987, *Nüren de Gushi*

HDF Short Film Prize
Ulrike Ottinger, 1987, *Usinimage*

Hessen-Film Award
Jeanine Meerapfel, 1997, *Zwickel auf Bizykel*

Hong Kong Film Award, Best Chinese Language Film
Zhang Nuanxin, 1991, *Good Morning, Beijing*

Hong Kong Film Award, Best Director
Ann Hui, 1982, *T'ou-Pen Nu-Hai*
Ann Hui, 1994, *Summer Snow*

Hong Kong Film Award, Best Picture
Ann Hui, 1982, *T'ou-Pen Nu-Hai*
Ann Hui, 1994, *Summer Snow*

Hong Kong Film Award, Best Screenplay
Ann Hui, 1982, *T'ou-Pen Nu-Hai*

Hong Kong Film Critics Society, Best Picture
Ann Hui, 1994, *Summer Snow*

Hong Kong International Film Festival, Achievement Award
Christine Choy, 1992, *Mississippi Triangle*

Houston International Film Festival, Best Film
Greta Schiller, 1985, *Before Stonewall*

International Black Film Festival, First Prize
Christine Choy, 1972, *Teach Our Children*

International Festival of Arctic Film (Dieppe, France), Grand Prix
Alanis Obomsawin, 1977, *Mother of Many Children*

International Festival of Women's Films (New York), Honors
Dorothy Arzner, 1972

Iranian Film Critics, Best Film of the Year
Rakhshan Bani-Etemad, 1992, *Nargess*

Iranian Society of Filmmakers, Silver Award
Rakhshan Bani-Etemad, 1995, *The Blue-Veiled*

Japan Kinema Jumpo Award, Best Actress
Kinuyo Tanaka, 1958, *Ballad of Narayama*
Kinuyo Tanaka, 1974, *Sandakan, House No. 8*

Japan Mainichi Eiga Concourse
Kinuyo Tanaka, 1947, 1948, 1957, 1960, 1974

Leipzig International Documentary and Animation Festival (Germany), Jury Prize
Greta Schiller, 1986, *International Sweethearts of Rhythm*

Leipzig International Documentary and Animation Festival (Germany), Special Prize
Safi Faye, 1982, *Selbé One among Others*

Locarno International Film Festival, Bronze Leopard
Rakhshan Bani-Etemad, 1995, *The Blue-Veiled*

Locarno International Film Festival, Festival Award
Marilú Mallet, 1975, *There Is No Forgetting*

Locarno International Film Festival, FIPRESCI (International Federation of Cinema Press) Prize
Kira Muratova, 1987, *Long Farewells*

Locarno International Film Festival, Golden Leopard
Clara Law, 1992, *Autumn Moon*
Claire Denis, 1996, *Nénette et Boni*

Locarno International Film Festival, Silver Leopard
Clara Law, 1996, *Floating Life*

London International Film Festival, Outstanding Film
Christine Choy, 1988, *Who Killed Vincent Chin?*

Los Angeles Film Critics Award, Best Actress
Jodie Foster, 1976, *Taxi Driver*

Los Angeles Film Critics Award, Best Documentary
Jennie Livingston, 1990, *Paris Is Burning*

Los Angeles Film Critics Award, Best Film
Raging Bull, 1980

Los Angeles Film Critics Award, Best Foreign Film
Agnès Varda, 1985, *Vagabond*

Los Angeles FILMEX, Best Documentary Feature
Greta Schiller, 1985, *Before Stonewall*

Mannheim International Film Festival, First Place
Christine Choy, 1989, *Best Hotel on Skid Row*

Mannheim International Film Festival, Golden Ducat
Jeanine Meerapfel, 1981, *In the Country of My Parents*

Mannheim International Film Festival, Special Jury Prize
Deepa Mehta

Mar del Plata Film Festival, Best Film
Pilar Miró, 1996, *The Dog in the Manger*

Maya Deren Award, American Film Institute
Gunvor Nelson, 1977
Yvonne Rainer, 1988
Shirley Clarke, 1989
Trinh T. Minh-Ha, 1991
Julie Dash, 1993
Barbara Kopple, 1994

Meilleur Documentaire d'Essai à Création, FIPA
Marilú Mallet, 1989, *Dear America*

Melbourne Film Festival, Grand Prix
Caroline Leaf, 1979, *Interview*
Su Friedrich, 1990, *Sink or Swim*

Mexican Film Institute (IMCINE), Lifetime Achievement Award
Matilde Soto Landeta, 1992

Milan Film Festival, First Prize
Sarah Maldoror, 1996, *Léon G. Damas*

Milan Film Festival, Prix de la Jeunesse
Euzhan Palcy, 1993, *Simeon*

Montreal World Film Festival, Ban Zil Kreol Award
Euzhan Palcy, 1993, *Simeon*

Montreal World Film Festival, Best Script
Christine Pascal, 1992, *The Little Prince Said*

Montreal World Film Festival, Critics Prize
Léa Pool, 1984, *A Woman in Transit*

Montreal World Film Festival, Ecumenical Prize
Judit Elek, 1988, *Memoirs of a River*

Montreal World Film Festival, FIPRESCI (International Federation of Cinema Press) Prize
Léa Pool, 1984, *A Woman in Transit*

Montreal World Film Festival, Louis Delluc Prize—Directing
Christine Pascal, 1992, *The Little Prince Said*

Mostra Internationale de Film d'Autore, Special Jury Prize
Valie Export, 1976, *Invisible Adversaries*

Mystery International Film Festival, Jury's Special Award
Marcela Fernández Violante, 1979, *Mystery*

Namur Film Festival, First Prize
Léa Pool, 1988, *Straight for the Heart*

National Black Programming Consortium, Best Drama
Zeinabu irene Davis, 1989, *Cycles*

National Black Programming Consortium, Best Historical Documentary
Pratibha Parmar, 1991, *A Place of Rage*

National Black Programming Consortium, Best Producer
Ayoka Chenzira, 1990

National Black Programming Consortium, First Place—Cultural Affairs
Ayoka Chenzira, 1984

National Board of Review, Best Foreign Language Film
Agnieszka Holland, 1990, *Europa, Europa*

National Educational Film and Video Festival, First Place
Greta Schiller, 1985, *Before Stonewall*

National Educational Film and Video Festival, Silver Apple
Ayoka Chenzira, 1990

National Film Prize of Germany
Triumph des Willens, 1935

National Film Registry, American Film Classic Award
Barbara Kopple, 1976, *Harlan County, U.S.A.*

National Society of Film Critics Award, Best Documentary
Jennie Livingston, 1990, *Paris Is Burning*

New England Children's Film Festival, Best Short Feature
Zeinabu irene Davis, 1995, *Mother of the River*

New York Film Critics Award, Best Actress
Ida Lupino, 1943, *The Hard Way*
Liv Ullmann, 1972, *Cries and Whispers*
Liv Ullmann, 1972, *The Emigrants*
Liv Ullmann, 1973, *Scenes from a Marriage*
Liv Ullmann, 1976, *Face to Face*

New York Film Critics Award, Best Documentary
Jill Godmilow, 1973, *Antonia: A Portrait of the Woman*
Jennie Livingston, 1990, *Paris Is Burning*

New York Film Critics Award, Best New Director
Allison Anders, 1992, *Gas Food Lodging*

New York Film Festival Award
Ann Hui, 1982, *T'ou-Pen Nu-Hai*
Beth B, 1983, *Vortex*

New York University Student Film Festival, Haig P. Manoogian Award—Overall Excellence
Nancy Savoca, 1984

New York Women in Film and Television, Muse Award—Outstanding Vision and Achievement
Mira Nair, 1997

New Zealand Film and Television Awards, Best Short Film
Alison Maclean, 1987, *Talkback*
Alison Maclean, 1989, *Kitchen Sink*

Nika Award
Kira Muratova, 1990, *The Asthenic Syndrome*

Nika Award, Best Director
Kira Muratova, 1994, *Passions*

Norman McLaren Award, Ottawa
Caroline Leaf, 1994

Norwegian Academy Award (Amanda), Best Film
Anja Breien, 1985, *Wives: 10 Years After*

Oberhausen International Short Film Festival, Best Film
Anja Breien, 1969, *17 May, a Film about Rituals*

Oberhausen International Short Film Festival, First Prize
Agnès Varda, 1968, *Black Panthers*

Oberhausen International Short Film Festival, Prize of the International Jury
Greta Schiller, 1986, *International Sweethearts of Rhythm*

Open Palm, Independent Feature Project Gotham Award
Jennie Livingston, 1990, *Paris Is Burning*
Leslie Harris, 1993, *Just Another Girl on the I.R.T.*

Orson Welles Prize—Special Cinematic Achievement
Euzhan Palcy, 1989, *A Dry White Season*

Ottawa International Animation Festival, Best Story Award
Caroline Leaf, 1990, *Two Sisters*

Ottawa International Animation Festival, Grand Prix
Caroline Leaf, 1976, *The Street*
Caroline Leaf, 1990, *Two Sisters*

Ouagadougou Film Festival (Upper Volta), Golden Keops
Euzhan Palcy, 1993, *Simeon*

Ouagadougou Film Festival (Upper Volta), International Catholic Film Office Award
Sarah Maldoror, 1972, *Sambizanga*

Outfest '97, Outstanding Documentary Feature
Su Friedrich, 1996, *Hide and Seek*

Paul Robeson Award
Ayoka Chenzira, 1984

Polar Prize, Sweden
Leni Riefenstahl, 1938, *Olympia*

People's Republic of China, Best Picture
Zhang Nuanxin, 1991, *Good Morning, Beijing*

People's Republic of China, Special Prize
Zhang Nuanxin, 1981, *Sha'ou's Seagull*

Prix Louis Delluc—Best Picture (France)
Agnès Varda, 1965, *Le Bonheur*
Diane Kurys, 1977, *Diabolo menthe*

Prix Méliès
Agnès Varda, 1961, *Cléo de cinq à sept*
Agnès Varda, 1985, *Vagabond*

Rimini Festival, Best Film
Ann Hui, 1990, *Song of the Exile*

Rome-Florence Film Festival, Special Jury Award
Maggie Greenwald, 1994, *The Ballad of Little Jo*

Salerno Film Festival, Main Prize
Judit Elek, 1994, *Awakening*

Samuel Goldwyn Award, Screenplay
Allison Anders, 1996, *Lost Highway*

San Francisco Film Festival, Audience Award, Best Short Documentary
Pratibha Parmar, 1991, *Khush*

San Francisco Film Festival, Golden Gate Award
Su Friedrich, 1990, *Sink or Swim*
Christine Choy, 1991, *Homes Apart: Korea*

San Francisco International Lesbian and Gay Film Festival, Audience Award, Best Feature
Beeban Kidron, 1989, *Oranges Are Not the Only Fruit*

San Sebastian International Film Festival Award
Valeria Sarmiento, 1984, *Our Marriage*

San Sebastian International Film Festival, Prize for Young Filmmaker
Jeanine Meerapfel, 1981, *Malou*

Seattle International Film Festival, New Directors Showcase, First Prize
Liv Ullmann, 1992, *Sofie*

Shanghai Young People's Cultural Competition, Best Film Script
Peng Xiaolian, 1985, *Come Back in the Summertime*

Silver Ribbon (Italy), Best New Foreign Director
Barbra Streisand, 1983, *Yentl*

Sindicato Nacional de Espectáculo (National entertainment syndicate) Award, Best Screenplay
Pilar Miró, 1976, *The Engagement Party*

Sindicato Nazionale Giornalisti Cinematografici Italiani, Best Script Award
Suso Cecchi d'Amico, 1986, *Let's Hope It's a Girl*

Sinking Creek Film Celebration, Director's Choice Award
Bette Gordon, 1975, *Still Life*

Strasbourg Film Festival, Festival Award
Marilú Mallet, 1975, *There Is No Forgetting*

Sundance Film Festival, Best Documentary Cinematography
Trinh T. Minh-Ha, 1991, *Shoot for the Contents*
Christine Choy, 1996, *My America*

Sundance Film Festival, Grand Jury Prize
Joyce Chopra, 1985, *Smooth Talk*
Jill Godmilow, 1987, *Waiting for the Moon*

Sundance Film Festival, Grand Jury Prize, Best Documentary
Jennie Livingston, 1990, *Paris Is Burning*

Sundance Film Festival, Honorable Mention
Donna Deitch, 1986, *Desert Hearts*

Sundance Film Festival, Special Jury Prize for First Feature
Leslie Harris, 1993, *Just Another Girl on the I.R.T.*

Swedish Film Institute, Swedish Gold Bug, Best Actress
Liv Ullmann, 1968, *Skammen*

Swedish Film Institute, Swedish Gold Bug, Best Director
Marianne Ahrne, 1976, *Near and Far Away*

Sydney Festival, Best Short Fiction Film
Gillian Armstrong, 1976, *The Singer and the Dancer*

Taipei Golden Horse Film Festival, Golden Horse Award
Ann Hui, 1994, *Summer Snow*

Taormina International Film Festival, Grand Prix
Agnès Varda, 1977, *L'Une chante l'autre pas*

Technik Prize
Astrid Henning-Jensen, 1960, *Paw*

Teddy Award for Best Documentary
Jennie Livingston, 1990, *Paris Is Burning*

Third Maraisiade, Most Political Film
Valie Export, 1968, *Ping Pong*

Toronto International Film Festival of Festivals, Best Canadian Film
Léa Pool, 1984, *A Woman in Transit*
Alanis Obomsawin, 1993, *Kanehsatake*

Toronto International Film Festival of Festivals, Best Picture
Marleen Gorris, 1995, *Antonia's Line*

Toronto International Film Festival of Festivals, Best Short Film
Janis Cole and Holly Dale, 1990, *Shaggie*

Toronto International Film Festival of Festivals, People's Choice Award
Antonia Bird, 1994, *Priest*

Toronto Women in Film and Television, Award for Outstanding Achievement in Direction
Alanis Obomsawin, 1994

Turin Film Festival, Best Director Award
Maggie Greenwald, 1989, *The Kill-Off*

U.S. Film Festival Award
Christine Choy, 1988, *Who Killed Vincent Chin?*

U.S. Film Festival, Grand Jury Prize
Nancy Savoca, 1989, *True Love*

U.S. National Film Critics Award
Jodie Foster, 1976, *Taxi Driver*

USSR Festival, Grand Prix
Kira Muratova, 1987, *Long Farewells*

Utah Film Festival, Best Experimental Film
Barbara Hammer, 1991, *Vital Signs*

Vancouver International Film Festival, Most Popular Canadian Film
Deepa Mehta, 1996, *Fire*

Venice Biennale Film Festival, Best Screenplay
Mira Nair, 1991, *Mississippi Masala*

Venice Biennale Film Festival, Bronze Award
Joyce Chopra, 1963, *A Happy Mother's Day*

Venice Biennale Film Festival, Bronze Lion
Agnès Varda, 1963, *Salut les Cubains*

Venice Biennale Film Festival, Ciak Award—Most Popular Film
Mira Nair, 1991, *Mississippi Masala*

Venice Biennale Film Festival, Director Prize
Astrid Henning-Jensen, 1947, *Denmark Grows Up*

Venice Biennale Film Festival, FIPRESCI (International Federation of Cinema Press) Prize
Wanda, 1970

Venice Biennale Film Festival, First Prize
Olympia, 1938

Venice Biennale Film Festival, Gold Medal
Triumph des Willens, 1935

Venice Biennale Film Festival, Golden Lion Award
Mai Zetterling, 1961, *The War Game*
Nelly Kaplan, 1967, *Le Regard Picasso*
Margarethe von Trotta, 1981, *Die Bleierne Zeit*
Agnès Varda, 1985, *Vagabond*

Venice Biennale Film Festival, Italian Critics Prize
Vivre sa vie, 1962

Venice Biennale Film Festival Prize
Carmen Dillon, 1952, *The Importance of Being Earnest*

Venice Biennale Film Festival, Silver Dolphin
Lotte Reiniger, 1955, *Gallant Little Tailor*

Venice Biennale Film Festival, Silver Lion
Euzhan Palcy, 1983, *Sugar Cane Alley*
Marion Hänsel, 1985, *Dust*

Venice Biennale Film Festival, Silver Lion, Best First Feature
Rue cases-nègres, 1983

Venice Biennale Film Festival, Silver Medal
Leni Riefenstahl, 1932, *Das blaue Licht*

Venice Biennale Film Festival, Special Jury Prize
Vivre sa vie, 1962

Venice Biennale Film Festival, Special Mention
Anja Breien, 1981, *The Witch Hunt*

Women's Festival Prize (Sceaux, France)
Marleen Gorris, 1981, *A Question of Silence*

Women's Film Hyères
Helke Sander, 1977, *Redupers*

Writers Guild Award
Frances Goodrich, 1948, *Easter Parade*
Betty Comden, 1949, *On the Town*
Frances Goodrich, 1951, *Father's Little Dividend*
Betty Comden, 1952, *Singin' in the Rain*
Frances Goodrich, 1954, *Seven Brides for Seven Brothers*
Isobel Lennart, 1955, *Love Me or Leave Me*
Frances Goodrich, 1959, *The Diary of Anne Frank*
Betty Comden, 1960, *Bells Are Ringing*
Isobel Lennart, 1968, *Funny Girl*

Writers Guild of Canada, Top Ten Award
Tanis Cole and Holly Dale, 1996, *Dangerous Offender*

Zagreb World Festival of Animated Films, Life Achievement Award
Caroline Leaf, 1996

FILM TITLE INDEX

The following index lists all film titles cited in the filmographies contained in *Women Filmmakers & Their Films,* including cross-references for alternative or English-language titles. The name(s) in parentheses following the title and date refer the reader to the appropriate filmmaker entry or entries. Titles appearing in bold are covered in separate entries in this volume.

1-94, 1974 (Gordon)
2 Friends, 1985 (Campion)
2, Rue de la Memoire, 1995 (Mallet)
3 ans 5 mois, 1983 (Faye)
3 Men Missing *see* Ztracenci, 1956
3 Years Five Months *see* 3 ans 5 mois, 1983
6½ x 11 *see* Six et demi-onze, 1927
7 AM, 1983 (Novaro)
8 and 90 *see* Otto e Novanta, 1924
8½ *see* Otto e mezzo, 1963
10 Modern Commandments, 1927 (Arzner)
10th Avenue Angel, 1947 (Irene)
10:30 P.M. Summer, 1966 (Duras)
13 Minuten vor zwölf in Lima, 1989 (Meerapfel)
13 West Street, 1962 (Brackett)
15 perc 15 évröl, 1965 (Mészáros)
15/8, 1973 (Akerman)
17, maj—en film om ritualer, 1969 (Breien)
17 May, a Film about Rituals *see* 17, maj—en film om ritualer, 1969
20 let sovetskogo kino *see* Kino za XX liet, 1940
24 Hour Woman, 1998 (Savoca)
29 Acacia Avenue, 1945 (Box, M.)
30 Minutes, Mister Plummer, 1963 (Poirier)
39 Steps, 1935 (Reville)
39 Steps, 1953 (Box, B.)
40 Carats, 1973 (Ullmann)
150 km per Hour *see* 150 na godzine, 1971
150 na godzine, 1971 (Jakubowska)
333, 1968 (Export)
400 Million, 1939 (van Dongen)
625, 1969 (Hein)
$1,000 a Touchdown, 1939 (Head)
1776, or The Hessian Renegades, 1909 (Pickford)
1933, 1967 (Wieland)
1941, 1979 (Marshall)
1963 julius 27,szombat, 1963 (Mészáros)
1968 Persian Letters *see* Petit à petit ou Les Lettres persanes 1968, 1972
4000 Frames, an Eye-Opener Film, 1970 (Cantrill)

A & B in Ontario, 1984 (Wieland)
A.E.I., 1972 (Mallet)
À corps perdu, 1988 (Pool)
A "holdudvar", 1968 (Mészáros)
... a pátý jezdec je Strach, 1964 (Krumbachová)
À la folie, 1994 (Kurys)
A la recherche d'un appartement, 1906 (Guy)
À la source, la femme aimée, 1965 (Kaplan)
A labda varásza, 1962 (Mészáros)
'A Legge, 1920 (Notari)
A lörinci fonóban, 1971 (Mészáros)
A Magzat, 1993 (Mészáros)
'A Mala Nova, 1920 (Notari)
A Marechiaro ce sta 'na Fenesta, 1913 (Notari)
A Piedigrotta, 1920 (Notari)
Á qui appartient ce gage?, 1973 (Poirier)

'A Santa notte, 1922 (Notari)
A szár és a gyökér fejlödése, 1961 (Mészáros)
Aaron Slick from Punkin Crick, 1952 (Head)
Abandon Ship!, 1957 (Zetterling)
Abblenden *see* Aufblenden, 1972
Abbott and Costello in Hollywood, 1945 (Irene)
ABC—We Print Anything—In the Cards, 1976-77 (Schneemann)
Abdication, 1974 (Ullmann)
Abel Gance et son Napoléon, 1983 (Kaplan)
Abel Gance, hier et demain, 1963 (Kaplan)
Abenteuer des Prinzen Achmed *see* Geschichte des Prinzen Achmed, 1923-26
Abenteuer: Die Affenbrücke *see* Doktor Dolittle und seine Tiere, 1928
Abenteuer: Die Reise nach Afrika *see* Doktor Dolittle und seine Tiere, 1928
Abortion Problems in France *see* Abortproblem i Frankrike, 1971
Abortproblem i Frankrike, 1971 (Ahrne)
About Mrs. Leslie, 1954 (Head)
About Overtime and Voluntary Labor *see* Sobre horas extras y trabajo voluntario, 1973
Above and Beyond, 1952 (Rose)
Above Suspicion, 1943 (Irene)
Abraham Lincoln, 1924 (Marion)
Abrik Zaur, 1926 (Shub)
Abstand, 1966 (Meerapfel)
Abstract Film No. 1, 1967-68 (Export)
Abstronic, 1952 (Bute)
Abu series, 1943-44 (Batchelor)
Accident, 1967 (Dillon)
Accidental Tourist, 1988 (Littleton)
Accused, 1936 (Akins)
Accused, 1948 (Head)
Accused, 1988 (Foster)
Accusing Finger, 1936 (Head)
Ace Eli and Rodger of the Skies, 1973 (Van Runkle)
Across the Araks *see* Po tu storonu Araksa, 1946
Across the Mexican Line, 1911 (Guy)
Act of Violence, 1949 (Rose)
Acts of Perception, 1973 (Schneemann)
Ada, 1961 (Rose)
Adam's Rib, 1923 (Bauchens; Macpherson)
Addams Family, 1991 (Allen, D.)
Addio Mia Bella Addio, l'Armata se ne va, 1915 (Notari)
Adjoined Dislocations *see* Adjungierte Dislokationen, 1973
Adjungierte Dislokationen, 1973 (Export)
Adoption *see* Örökbefogadás, 1975
Adultere (mode d'emploi), 1995 (Pascal)
Adultery [A User's Manual] *see* Adultere (mode d'emploi), 1995
Adventure, 1945 (Irene)
Adventure for Two *see* Demi-Paradise, 1943
Adventure in Diamonds, 1940 (Head)
Adventure Playground, 1966 (Cantrill)
Adventurer, 1917 (Guy)
Adventures of Dr. Dolittle *see* Doktor Dolittle und seine Tiere, 1928
Adventures of Don Coyote, 1947 (Pickford)
Adventures of Huckleberry Finn, 1986 (Gish)

Adventures of Prince Achmed *see* Geschichte des Prinzen Achmed, 1923-26
Adventures of Sherlock Holmes, 1939 (Lupino)
Aelita: Queen of Mars, 1924 (Solntseva)
Aerograd, 1935 (Solntseva)
Aesop *see* Ezop, 1969
Affair in Berlin *see* Interno Berlinese, 1986
Affair in Trinidad, 1952 (Van Upp)
Affair of Hearts, 1910 (Macpherson)
Affair of the Skin, 1963 (Fields)
Affairs of Anatol, 1921 (Bauchens; Glyn; Macpherson)
Affairs of Cellini, 1934 (Meredyth)
Affairs of Dr. Holl *see* Angelika, 1951
Affairs of Martha, 1943 (Lennart)
Affairs of Susan, 1945 (Head)
Aftab Nechinha, 1980 (Bani-Etemad)
After Hours, 1984 (Campion)
After Hours, 1985 (Schoonmaker)
After the Thin Man, 1936 (Goodrich)
After the Verdict, 1929 (Reville)
After Tomorrow, 1932 (Levien)
After Tonight, 1933 (Murfin)
Against Oblivion *see* Contre l'oubli, 1991
Agatha, 1979 (Russell)
Agatha et les lectures limitées, 1981 (Duras)
Age of Desire, 1923 (Coffee)
Age of Dissent, 1994 (Schiller)
Age of Indiscretion, 1935 (Coffee)
Age of Innocence, 1993 (Schoonmaker)
Age of Stalin *see* L'eta' di Stalin, 1963
Agent 8¾ *see* Hot Enough for June, 1964
Agnes Kempler's Sacrifice, 1915 (Madison)
Agung Gives Ivor a Haircut, 1991 (Cantrill)
Ah Kam, 1996 (Hui)
Ah, Wilderness!, 1935 (Goodrich)
Ai zai biexiang de jijie, 1990 (Law)
Aimé Césaire: A Voice for History, 1994 (Palcy)
Aimé Césaire, le masque des mots, 1986 (Maldoror)
Air City *see* Aerograd, 1935
Airport, 1970 (Head)
Airport '75, 1974 (Head)
Airport '77, 1977 (Head)
Aizen katsura, 1938 (Tanaka)
Akahige, 1965 (Tanaka)
Aktorzy prowincjonalni, 1979 (Holland)
Al di là del bene e del male, 1977 (Cavani)
Aladdin, 1953 (Reiniger)
Aladdin's Other Lamp, 1917 (Mathis)
Alas and Alack, 1915 (Madison)
Alaska Seas, 1954 (Head)
Albertfalvai történet, 1955 (Mészáros)
Alberto Carliski, Sculpteur, 1981 (Maldoror)
Alcool, alternativa para o furturo, 1981 (Yamasaki)
Alex, 1985 (Kidron)
Algiers, 1938 (Irene)
Algorithm, 1977 (Gordon)
Alias Jane Jones, 1916 (Madison)
Alias Jesse James, 1959 (Head)
Alias Ladyfingers *see* Ladyfingers, 1921
Alibi Inn, 1935 (Box, M.)
Alice Adams, 1935 (Murfin)

Alice Doesn't Live Here Anymore, 1974 (Foster)
Alice et Elsa *see* À la folie, 1994
Alice's Restaurant, 1970 (Allen, D.)
Alien Encounter *see* Starship Invasions, 1977
All about Eve, 1950 (Head)
All-Around Reduced Personality *see* Allseitig reduzierte Persönlichkeit, 1977
All Fall Down, 1962 (Jeakins)
All for Mary, 1955 (Toye)
All Good Countrymen ... *see* Všichni dobrí rodáci, 1968
All in a Night's Work, 1961 (Head)
All Lit Up, 1959 (Batchelor)
All Man, 1916 (Marion)
All Men Are Enemies, 1934 (Coffee)
All Night Long, 1981 (Streisand)
All Night Long *see* Toute une nuit, 1982
All on Account of the Milk, 1910 (Pickford)
All Screwed Up *see* Tutto a posto e niente in ordine, 1974
All the Fine Young Cannibals, 1960 (Rose)
All Women Have Secrets, 1939 (Head)
Allseitig reduzierte Persönlichkeit, 1977 (Sander)
Alma's Rainbow, 1993 (Chenzira)
Aloma of the South Seas, 1941 (Head)
Alone in the Pacific *see* Taiheyo hitoribochi, 1963
Alone in the World, 1916 (Weber)
Along Came Jones, 1945 (Fields)
Along Came Youth, 1930 (Head)
Along the Malibu, 1916 (Madison)
Alphaville, 1965 (Guillemot)
Älskande par, 1964 (Zetterling)
Alt werden in der Fremde, 1978 (Dörrie)
Alte Liebe, 1985 (Sanders-Brahms)
Altered Message, 1911 (Guy)
Altes Material
Altitude 3200, 1938 (Epstein)
Altri tempi, 1952 (Cecchi d'Amico)
Am Abend auf der Heide, 1941 (von Harbou)
Am Ama am Amazons, 1969 (Meerapfel)
Amadeus, 1984 (von Brandenstein)
Amanti, 1968 (Van Runkle)
Amarilly of Clothes-Line Alley, 1918 (Marion; Pickford)
Amazing Mrs. Holliday, 1943 (Levien)
Amazonia, 1990 (Hubley)
Amazons, 1917 (Marion)
Ambassades Nourricières, 1984 (Faye)
Ame d'artiste, 1925 (Dulac)
Amelia Lópes O'Neill, 1991 (Sarmiento)
America, America, 1964 (Allen, D.)
American Aristocracy, 1916 (Loos)
American Dream, 1991 (Kopple)
American Graffiti, 1973 (Fields)
American Graffiti, 1982 (Hein)
American I Ching Apple Pie, 1972 (Schneemann)
American in Paris, 1951 (Sharaff)
American Romance, 1944 (Irene)
American Soldier *see* Der amerikanische Soldat, 1970
American Stories *see* Histoires d'Amérique: Food, Family and Philosophy, 1989
American Writer's Congress, 1981 (Choy)
Americano, 1917 (Loos)
America's Dream, 1996 (Angelou)

Ames de fous, 1917 (Dulac)
Âmes au soleil, 1981 (Faye)
Âmes d'enfants, 1927 (Epstein)
Amiche, 1955 (Cecchi d'Amico)
Amiga, 1988 (Holland; Meerapfel; Ullmann)
Amigomío, 1993-95 (Meerapfel)
Amisk, 1977 (Obomsawin)
Amnesia, 1992 (B)
Among Noisy Sheep see Unter Schafen, 1981
Among the Grey Stones see Sredi serykh kamnei, 1983
Among the Living, 1941 (Head)
Amor und das standhafte Liebespaar, 1920 (Reiniger)
Amore amaro, 1974 (Cecchi d'Amico)
Amore e ginnastica, 1973 (Cecchi d'Amico)
Amore e rabbia, 1969 (Guillemot)
Amorosa, 1986 (Zetterling)
Amuhuelai-Mi, 1971 (Mallet)
An-Magritt, 1968 (Ullmann)
Anatolian Smile see America, America, 1964
Anatomía do Espectador, 1979 (Carolina)
Anatomy of Love see Tempi nostri, 1953
Anchors Aweigh, 1945 (Irene; Lennart)
And Now Tomorrow, 1944 (Head)
And the Angels Sing, 1944 (Head)
And the Dogs Kept Silent see Et les Chiens se taisaient, 1977
... and the Fifth Rider Is Fear see ... a pátý jezdec je Strach, 1964
And the Wild, Wild Women see Nella città l'inferno, 1958
And We've Got "Sabor" see Y tenemos sabor, 1967
And You Act Like One, Too, 1976/77 (Seidelman)
Andechser Gefühl, 1975 (von Trotta)
Andy Hardy's Blonde Trouble, 1944 (Irene)
Andy Hardy's Private Secretary, 1941 (Murfin)
Andy Warhol, 1965 (Menken)
Angel at My Table, 1990 (Campion)
Angel of Broadway, 1927 (Coffee; Weber)
Angel of Contention, 1914 (Gish)
Angelika, 1951 (von Harbou)
Angelika Urban, Salesgirl, Engaged see Angelika Urban, Verkäuferin, Verlobt, 1970
Angelika Urban, Verkäuferin, Verlobt, 1970 (Sanders-Brahms)
Angelina see L'onorevole Angelina, 1947
Angie, 1994 (Coolidge)
Angophora and Sandstone, 1979 (Cantrill)
Angry Harvest see Bittere ernte, 1985
Ani imoto, 1952 (Tanaka)
Animal Farm, 1954 (Batchelor)
Animal Kingdom, 1932 (Irene)
Animal Vegetable Mineral, 1955 (Batchelor)
Anitra's Dance, 1936 (Bute)
Ann Vickers, 1933 (Murfin)
Anna, 1987 (Holland)
Anna Christie, 1930 (Marion)
Anna Karenina, 1935 (Levien)
Anne of Green Gables, 1919 (Marion)
Anne Trister, 1986 (Pool)
Années 25, 1966 (Kaplan)
Années 80, 1983 (Akerman)
Annelie, 1941 (von Harbou)
Annie, 1982 (Booth)
Annie, 1989 (Treut)
Annie Get Your Gun, 1950 (Rose)

Annie Laurie, 1927 (Gish)
Año uno, 1972 (Gómez)
Anonyme, 1951-66 (Parker)
Another Thin Man, 1939 (Goodrich)
Another Time, Another Place, 1958 (Coffee)
Another Way of Life see O necem jiném, 1963
Ansikte mot ansikte, 1976 (Ullmann)
Anskiter, 1969 (Breien)
Ansprache Aussprache, 1968 (Export)
Antigone, 1992 (Huillet)
Antoinette Sabrier, 1926 (Dulac)
Antonia, 1995 (Gorris)
Antonia & Jane, 1991 (Kidron)
Antonia: A Portrait of the Woman, 1973 (Godmilow)
Antonia's Line see Antonia, 1995
Any Wednesday, 1966 (Jeakins)
Anya, 1927 (Preobrazhenskaya)
Anya és leánya, 1981 (Mészáros)
Anybody's Woman, 1930 (Akins; Arzner)
Anything Can Happen, 1952 (Head)
Anything Goes, 1936 (Lupino)
Anything Goes, 1956 (Head)
Apaches pas veinards, 1903 (Guy)
Apfelbaume, 1992 (Sanders-Brahms)
Apokalypse, 1918 (Reiniger)
Apotheosis, 1969 (Ono)
Apotheosis No. 2, 1969 (Ono)
Apple Game see Hra o jablko, 1977
Apple Trees see Apfelbaume, 1992
Appointment with Venus, 1951 (Box, B.)
Après l'amour, 1992 (Kurys)
April 3, 1973, 1973 (Citron)
Arabesque for Kenneth Anger, 1961 (Menken)
Arcadian Maid, 1910 (Pickford)
Arch of Triumph, 1948 (Head)
Archa bláznu aneb Vyprávení z konce zivota, 1970 (Krumbachová)
Are Husbands Necessary?, 1942 (Head)
Arequipa, 1981 (Hammer)
Arise, My Love, 1940 (Head; Irene)
Aristotle, 1973-74 (De Hirsch)
Arizona Mahoney, 1937 (Head)
Ark of Fools see Archa bláznu aneb Vyprávení z konce zivota, 1970
Arkansas Traveler, 1938 (Head)
Armed Eye see Bewaffnete Auge, 1982
Army see Rikugun, 1944
Arnelo Affair, 1947 (Irene)
Arrangement, 1969 (Van Runkle)
Arrest of Bulldog Drummond, 1939 (Head)
Arrivederci, 1906-11 (Notari)
Arrowhead, 1953 (Head)
Ars Lucis, 1967-68 (Export)
Arsène Lupin, 1932 (Coffee)
Art for Art's Sake, 1960 (Batchelor)
Art Lovers, 1960 (Batchelor)
Artful Kate, 1911 (Pickford)
Articulações, 1969 (Carolina)
Artists and Models, 1937 (Head; Lupino)
Artists and Models, 1955 (Head)
Artists and Models Abroad, 1938 (Head)
Arvácska, 1976 (Elek)
Arven, 1979 (Breien)

As Fate Ordained *see* Enoch Arden, 1915
As Fiandeiras, 1970 (Carolina)
As Husbands Go, 1934 (Levien; Spencer)
As It Is in Life, 1910 (Pickford)
As Long as There's Still a Europe—Questions on Peace *see* Solange es Europa noch gibt—Fragen an den Freiden, 1983
As Man Made Her, 1917 (Marion)
As Old as the Hills, 1950 (Batchelor)
As Young as You Are, 1958 (Head)
Ascent *see* Voshojdenie, 1977
Aschenputtel, 1922 (Reiniger)
Asemie, 1973 (Export)
Ash Wednesday, 1973 (Head)
Ask Any Girl, 1959 (Rose)
Ass and the Stick, 1974 (Batchelor)
Assassin *see* Venetian Bird, 1952
Assault on a Queen, 1966 (Head)
Assignment in Britanny, 1943 (Irene)
Assistant Lawyer, 1982 (Peng)
Astenicheskii Sindrom, 1989 (Muratova)
Asthenic Syndrome *see* Astenicheskii Sindrom, 1989
Astonished Heart, 1950 (Box, M.)
At 99: A Portrait of Louise Tandy Murch, 1975 (Mehta)
At a Quarter to Two, 1911 (Pickford)
At Black Range, 1984 (Cantrill)
At Eltham, 1974 (Cantrill)
At First Sight *see* Coup de foudre, 1983
At Land, 1944 (Deren)
At Marechiaro There Is a Window *see* A Marechiaro ce sta 'na Fenesta, 1913
At Midnight, 1913 (Meredyth)
At One O'Clock *see* V trinadtsatom chasu, 1968
At Piedigrotta *see* A Piedigrotta, 1920
At the Duke's Command, 1911 (Pickford)
At the Grey House *see* Zur Chronik von Grieshuus, 1925
At the Lörinc Spinnery *see* A lörinci fonóban, 1971
At the Phone, 1912 (Guy)
At zije republika, 1965 (Krumbachová)
Atencion prenatal, 1972 (Gómez)
Athena, 1954 (Rose)
Atlantic Story *see* Opowiesc Atlantycka, 1954
Au Bal de Flore series, 1900 (Guy)
Au bon beurre, 1980 (Pascal)
Au cabaret, 1899/1900 (Guy)
Au Poulailler!, 1905 (Guy)
Au réfectoire, 1897/98 (Guy)
Au Verre de l'amitié, 1974 (Kaplan)
Aucassin et Nicolette, 1976 (Reiniger)
Audience, 1982 (Hammer)
Audre Lord Story, 1987 (Choy)
Audrey Rose, 1977 (Jeakins)
Auf+Zu+Ab+An, 1968 (Export)
Aufblenden, 1972 (Hein)
Augen wollen sich nicht zu jeder Zeit schliessen oder Vielleicht eines Tages wird Rom sich erlauben, seinerseits zu wählen *see* Othon, 1969
Augurali, 1906-11 (Notari)
Auntie Mame, 1958 (Comden)
Aurélia Steiner series, 1978/79 (Duras)
Aus dem Tagebuch einer Frauenärzin *see* Erste Recht des Kindes, 1932

Ausdatiertes Material, 1973 (Hein)
Aussi longue absence, 1961 (Duras)
Austerlitz/Napoleone ad Austerlitz, 1960 (Kaplan)
Australia Calls, 1913 (Lyell)
Australia in the Swim, Early 1930s (McDonagh Sisters)
Australian by Marriage, 1923 (Lyell)
Austreibung, 1923 (von Harbou)
Auszüge aus einer Biographie, 1970 (Hein)
Autobahn. 2 Teile, 1971 (Hein)
Autobiography of a Princess, 1975 (Jhabvala)
Automania 2000, 1963 (Batchelor)
Automation, 1951-66 (Parker)
Automation Blues, 1960 (Batchelor)
Autour de minuit *see* 'Round Midnight, 1986
Autumn *see* Otoñal, 1992
Autumn Moon *see* Qiuyue, 1992
Autumn Sonata *see* Herbstsonate, 1978
Available Space, 1978 (Hammer)
Aventura de Musidora en España, 1922 (Musidora)
Aventures d'un voyageur trop pressé, 1903 (Guy)
Avenue de l'Opéra, 1900 (Guy)
Avocations *see* Uvletschenia, 1994
Awakening *see* Ébredés, 1994
Awakening, 1909 (Pickford)
Awakening, 1928 (Marion)
Awakenings, 1990 (Marshall)
Az eladás müvészete, 1960 (Mészáros)
Az élet megy tovább, 1959 (Mészáros)
Azul, 1966 (Fernández Violante)

B.F.'s Daughter, 1948 (Irene)
Baal, 1970 (von Trotta)
Baby, I Will Make You Sweat, 1995 (Hein)
Baby ryazanskie, 1927 (Preobrazhenskaya)
Baby Snatcher, 1992 (Chopra)
Bach to Bach, 1967 (May)
Bachelor in Paradise, 1961 (Rose)
Bachelor Mother, 1939 (Irene)
Back Door to Heaven, 1939 (Head)
Back Pay, 1922 (Marion)
Back to God's Country, 1919 (Shipman)
Back to the Soil, 1911 (Pickford)
Backtrack, 1969 (Lupino)
Backtrack, 1989 (Foster)
Bad and the Beautiful, 1952 (Rose)
Bad Bascomb, 1946 (Irene)
Bad Lord Byron, 1948 (Zetterling)
Bad Thing about This Country *see* Mal du pays, 1979
Bad Timing, 1983 (Savoca)
Bag of Fleas *see* Pytel blech, 1962
Bagatelle for Willard Maas, 1961 (Menken)
Bagpipes, 1960 (Batchelor)
Bahama Passage, 1941 (Head; Van Upp)
Baignade dans le torrent, 1897 (Guy)
Bain d'X, 1951-66 (Parker)
Baises volés, 1968 (Guillemot)
Bakery, 1974 (Mehta)
Bakti, 1979 (Hänsel)
Balade en ville, 1996 (Trintignant)
Balatrum, 1936-39 (Parker)
Balcony, 1963 (Fields)

Bali Film, 1990 (Cantrill)
Ball of Fire, 1941 (Head)
Ballad of Little Jo, 1993 (Greenwald)
Ballad of Narayama *see* Narayama bushi-ko, 1958
Ballad of Therese *see* Balladen om Therese, 1970
Balladen om Therese, 1970 (Ahrne)
Ballet de Singe *see* Vérité sur l'homme-singe, 1907
Ballet Girl *see* Ballettens börn, 1954
Ballet Japonais series, 1900 (Guy)
Ballet Libella, 1897 (Guy)
Ballettens börn, 1954 (Henning-Jensen)
Bamboo Xerox, 1984 (Hammer)
Band of Outsiders *see* Bande à part, 1964
Band Wagon, 1953 (Comden)
Bande à part, 1964 (Guillemot)
Bannerline, 1951 (Rose)
Baptême, 1988 (Hänsel)
Bar 20 Justice, 1938 (Head)
Barbara Frietchie, 1915 (Guy)
Barbara Ward Will Never Die, 1969 (Hammer)
Barbara's Blindness, 1965 (Wieland)
Barbarian, 1933 (Loos)
Barbra Streisand: The Concert, 1995 (Streisand)
Barcaiuolo d'Amalfi, 1918 (Notari)
Bare Essentials, 1991 (Coolidge)
Baree, Son of Kazan, 1918 (Shipman)
Barefoot Executive, 1995 (Seidelman)
Barefoot in the Park, 1967 (Head)
Barkleys of Broadway, 1948 (Comden; Irene)
Barnaby—Father Dear Father, 1962 (Batchelor)
Barnaby—Overdue Dues Blues, 1962 (Batchelor)
Barndommens gade, 1986 (Henning-Jensen)
Barnum!, 1986 (Toye)
Barretts of Wimpole Street, 1934 (Booth)
Barrier, 1937 (Head)
Barrier, 1960 (Murphy)
Barrière, 1915 (Musidora)
Baryshnia krestianka, 1916 (Preobrazhenskaya)
Basic Fleetwork, 1955 (Batchelor)
Basilique de Saint Denis, 1980 (Maldoror)
Bataille de boules de neige, 1899/1900 (Guy)
Bataille d'oreillers, 1899/1900 (Guy)
Bathing Beauty, 1944 (Irene)
Battle at Elderbush Gulch, 1913 (Gish)
Battle for Our Soviet Ukraine *see* Bytva za nashu Radyansku Ukrayinu, 1943
Battle of Austerlitz *see* Austerlitz/Napoleone ad Austerlitz, 1960
Battle of the Sexes, 1914 (Gish)
Battle of the Villa Fiorita, 1965 (Dillon)
Baule-les-Pins, 1990 (Kurys)
Baxter, Vera Baxter, 1977 (Duras)
Bay Boy, 1985 (Ullmann)
Bay of St. Michel, 1963 (Zetterling)
Beach House *see* Casotto, 1977
Beachcomber, 1939 (Head)
Beachcomber, 1955 (Box, M.)
Bear *see* Medved, 1961
Bear, a Boy and a Dog, 1921 (Shipman)
Beast at Bay, 1912 (Pickford)
Beast of the City, 1932 (Bauchens)
Beasts of the Jungle, 1913 (Guy)

Beat Street, 1984 (von Brandenstein)
Beau Geste, 1939 (Head)
Beau James, 1957 (Head)
Beautiful Swindlers *see* Plus Belles Escroqueries du monde, 1963
Beauty *see* Mossane, 1996
Beauty Treatment, 1960 (Batchelor)
Bébé embarrassant, 1905 (Guy)
Because of Eve *see* Story of Life, 1948
Because You're Mine, 1952 (Rose)
Bed *see* Lit, 1982
Bed and Board *see* Domicile conjugal, 1970
Bed-In, 1969 (Ono)
Bedevilled, 1955 (Rose)
Bedpeace *see* Bed-In, 1969
Bedtime Stories, 1986 (Hammer)
Bedtime Story, 1941 (Irene)
Before and After, 1979 (Murphy)
Before Need, 1979 (Nelson)
Before Need Redressed, 1995 (Nelson)
Before Stonewall: The Making of a Gay and Lesbian Community, 1985 (Schiller)
Before the Curtain Goes Up *see* Nez se rozhrne opona, 1957
Before the Time Comes *see* Temps de l'avant, 1975
BeFreier und Befreite Krieg, Vergewaltigung, Kinder, 1992 (Sander)
Begegnung im Zwielicht *see* Spotkania w mroku, 1960
Beggar's Uproar, 1960 (Batchelor)
Beginning of the End, 1947 (Irene)
Behind that Curtain, 1928 (Levien)
Behind the Makeup, 1930 (Arzner)
Behind the Mask, 1917 (Guy)
Behind the Scenes, 1914 (Pickford)
Behind the Veil, 1914 (Weber)
Behind the Wall *see* Derrière le mur, 1988
Beijing Nin Zao, 1991 (Zhang)
Bell Partout, 1993 (Leaf)
Bella, My Bella, 1995 (Henning-Jensen)
Belladonna, 1989 (B)
Bellboy, 1960 (Head)
Belle affaire, 1977 (Hänsel)
Belle au bois dormant, 1935 (Parker)
Belle dame sans merci, 1920 (Dulac)
Belle of New York, 1952 (Rose)
Belle of the Nineties, 1934 (West)
Belle of the Yukon, 1944 (Fields)
Belle Starr, 1979 (Wertmüller)
Belle verte, 1996 (Serreau)
Belles on Their Toes, 1952 (Jeakins)
Bellissima, 1951 (Cecchi d'Amico)
Bells Are Ringing, 1960 (Comden)
Bells of St. Mary's, 1945 (Head)
Belly Dancing Class, 1972 (Weill)
Beloved Adventuress, 1917 (Marion)
Beloved Child *see* L'Enfant aimé, 1971
Beloved Motherland *see* Patriamada, 1985
Beltenebros, 1991 (Miró)
Bemused Tourist, 1990-97 (Cantrill)
Ben Bolt, 1913 (Guy)
Ben-Hur, 1926 (Mathis; Meredyth)
Beneath the Czar, 1914 (Guy)
Beneath the Prison *see* Sotto il Carcere di San Francisco, 1923
Beneath the Twelve Mile Reef, 1953 (Jeakins)

Benefactors *see* Salvation!, 1987
Denny & Joon, 1993 (Littleton)
Bent Time, 1983 (Hammer)
Bequest to the Nation, 1973 (Dillon)
Berceau de Dieu, 1926 (Musidora)
Berkeley 12 to 1, 1968 (Deitch)
Berkeley Square, 1933 (Levien)
Berlin Affair *see* Interno Berlinese, 1986
Berlin Apartment, 1987 (Cantrill)
Berlin Fever—Wolf Vostell *see* Vostell—Berlin-fieber, 1973
Bernice Bobs Her Hair, 1976 (Silver)
Berthe, 1976 (Hänsel)
Bertoldo, Bertoldino e Cacasenno, 1984 (Cecchi d'Amico)
Berührte, 1981 (Sanders-Brahms)
Bess the Detectress in Tick, Tick, Tick, 1914 (Meredyth)
Bess the Detectress, or The Dog Watch, 1914 (Meredyth)
Bess the Detectress, or The Old Mill at Midnight, 1914 (Meredyth)
Best Foot Forward, 1943 (Irene)
Best Hotel on Skid Row, 1989 (Choy)
Best Little Whorehouse in Texas, 1982 (Van Runkle)
Best Man, 1964 (Jeakins)
Best of Enemies *see* I due nemici, 1961
Best of the Blues *see* St. Louis Blues, 1939
Best Seller, 1958 (Batchelor)
Best Things in Life Are Free, 1956 (Spencer)
Best Way *see* Meilleure façon de marcher, 1976
Best Years of Our Lives, 1946 (Sharaff)
Betörung der blauen Matrosen, 1975 (Ottinger)
Betrayed, 1988 (von Brandenstein)
Betrothal *see* Petición, 1976
Betsy, 1978 (Jeakins)
Better Spirit, 1949 (Batchelor)
Better Way, 1911 (Pickford)
Better Wife, 1919 (Coffee)
Betty in Search of a Thrill, 1915 (Marion)
Between Heaven and Earth *see* Sur la terre comme au ciel, 1993
Between the Devil and the Deep Blue Sea, 1995 (Hänsel)
Between the Lines, 1977 (Silver; von Brandenstein)
Between Two Women, 1944 (Irene)
Between Two Worlds *see* Der müde Tod, 1921
Between Us *see* Coup de foudre, 1983
Beverly Hillbillies, 1993 (Spheeris)
Beverly Hills Cop III, 1994 (Coolidge)
Bewaffnete Auge, 1982 (Export)
Beware, My Lovely, 1952 (Lupino)
Beware of Children *see* No Kidding, 1960
Bewitchment of the Drunken Sailors *see* Betörung der blauen Matrosen, 1975
Beyond Forty *see* Quarantaine, 1982
Beyond Glory, 1948 (Head)
Beyond Good and Evil *see* Al di là del bene e del male, 1977
Beyond JFK: The Question of Conspiracy, 1992 (Kopple)
Beyond the Blue Horizon, 1942 (Head)
Beyond the Door, 1983 (Cavani)
Beyond the Forest, 1949 (Coffee; Head)
Beyond the Rocks, 1921 (Glyn)
Beyond the Shadow Place, 1997 (Hubley)
Beyond the Square *see* Tul a Kálvin-téren, 1955
Beyond the Wall *see* Der müde Tod, 1921
Bez znieczulenia, 1978 (Holland)
Bhowani Junction, 1955 (Levien)

Bialy mazur, 1978 (Jakubowska)
Bicycle Thief *see* Ladri di biciclette, 1948
Bienfaits du cinématographe, 1904 (Guy)
Big, 1988 (Marshall)
Big Bang and Other Creation Myths, 1981 (Hubley)
Big Broadcast of 1932, 1932 (Head)
Big Broadcast of 1936, 1935 (Head)
Big Broadcast of 1937, 1936 (Head)
Big Broadcast of 1938, 1938 (Head)
Big Carnival, 1951 (Head)
Big Chill, 1983 (Littleton)
Big City, 1948 (Rose)
Big-City Vampires *see* Storstadsvampyrer, 1972
Big Clock, 1948 (Head)
Big Deal on Madonna Street *see* I soliti ignoti, 1958
Big Deal on Madonna Street...20 Years Later *see* I soliti ignoti vent'anni dopo, 1986
Big Events and Ordinary People: Elections *see* Grandes événements et des gens ordinaires: les élections, 1979
Big Fix, 1978 (Head)
Big Girls Don't Cry...They Get Even, 1992 (Silver)
Big Hangover, 1950 (Rose)
Big House, 1930 (Marion)
Big Knife, 1955 (Lupino)
Big Race, 1960 (Batchelor)
Big Sky, 1952 (Jeakins)
Big Sleep, 1946 (Brackett)
Bigamist, 1953 (Lupino)
Bildnis Einer Trinkerin—Aller jamais retour, 1979 (Ottinger)
Billion Dollar Brain, 1967 (Russell)
Bill's Hat, 1967 (Wieland)
Billy Bathgate, 1991 (von Brandenstein)
Billy's Rival, 1914 (Loos)
Bimbo, 1978 (Coolidge)
Binding Sentiments *see* A "holdudvar", 1968
Bingo, Bridesmaids and Braces, 1988 (Armstrong)
Bink Runs Away *see* Bink's Vacation, 1913
Bink's Vacation, 1913 (Loos)
Biography of a Bachelor Girl, 1934 (Loos)
Bird of Happiness *see* El pájaro de la felicidad, 1993
Birdcage, 1996 (May)
Birds, 1963 (Head)
Birds and the Bees, 1956 (Head)
Birds at Sunrise, 1972 (Wieland)
Birds at Sunrise, 1985 (Wieland)
Birth of a Nation, 1915 (Gish)
Birth of the Blues, 1941 (Head)
Birthday Cake, 1960 (Batchelor)
Birthday Treat, 1960 (Batchelor)
Biscuit Eater, 1940 (Head)
Bishop Murder Case, 1930 (Coffee)
Bishop's Wife, 1947 (Sharaff)
Bitch *see* Garce, 1984
Bitchband, 1981 (Treut)
Bitter Fruit *see* Fruits amers, 1966
Bittere ernte, 1985 (Holland)
Bittersweet Survival, 1981 (Choy)
Black Angustias *see* Negra Angustias, 1949
Black Bird, 1975 (Booth)
Black Box, 1978 (B)
Black Leotard *see* Maillot noir, 1917

Black Orchid, 1959 (Head)

Black Orchids, 1917 (Madison)

Black Panthers, 1968 (Varda)

Black Roots see Racines noires, 1985

Black Shack Alley see **Rue cases nègres**, 1983

Black Sheep, 1996 (Spheeris)

Black Sins see Schwarze Sunde, 1989

Black South: The Life and Lifework of Zora Neale Hurston, 1998 (Dash)

Black Thursday see Guichets du Louvre, 1973

Black Widow, 1954 (Spencer)

Black Wolf, 1917 (Shipman)

Blackmailed, 1950 (Zetterling)

Blanche, 1992 (Pool)

Blast, 1971 (Cantrill)

Blaubart, 1984 (von Trotta)

Blaue Licht, 1932 (Riefenstahl)

Blaze of Noon, 1947 (Head)

Blé en herbe, 1953 (Colette)

Bleierne Zeit, 1981 (von Trotta)

Blind Cook, 1961 (Shepitko)

Blind Goddess, 1948 (Box, B.; Box, M.)

Blind Princess and the Poet, 1911 (Macpherson)

Blitz on Bugs, 1944 (Batchelor)

Blizzard of Passion see Bufera d'Anime, 1911

Blockade, 1938 (Irene; Spencer)

Blonde Fever, 1944 (Irene)

Blonde Gypsy see Caraque blonde, 1953

Blonde Trouble, 1937 (Head)

Blondie of the Follies, 1932 (Loos; Marion)

Blood & Donuts, 1995 (Cole)

Blood and Sand, 1922 (Arzner; Mathis)

Blood and Water, 1913 (Guy)

Blood Feud see Fatto di sangue fra due uomini per causa di una vedova, 1978

Blood of Others see Sang des autres, 1983

Blood of the Children, 1915 (Meredyth)

Blood of the Man Devil see House of the Black Death, 1965

Blood Sabbath, 1972 (Murphy)

Bloodlust!, 1961 (Murphy)

Bloodstain, 1912 (Guy)

Blossoms in the Dust, 1941 (Loos)

Blossoms on Broadway, 1937 (Head)

Blot, 1921 (Weber)

Blow-Ball see Bóbita, 1964

Blow up My Town see Saute ma ville, 1968

Blue see Azul, 1966

Blue Country see Pays bleu, 1976

Blue Dahlia, 1946 (Head)

Blue Hawaii, 1961 (Head)

Blue Jeans, 1917 (Mathis)

Blue Light see Blaue Licht, 1932

Blue Mountains Mystery, 1921 (Lyell)

Blue or the Gray, 1913 (Gish)

Blue Scar, 1949 (Craigie)

Blue Skies, 1946 (Head)

Blue Steel, 1990 (Bigelow)

Blue-Veiled see Rusariye Abi, 1995

Bluebeard see Blaubart, 1984

Blueberry Hill, 1989 (Hänsel)

Bluebird, 1976 (Head)

Boa Morte, 1988 (Chenzira)

Boarding House for Single Gentlemen see Pension pro svobodné pány, 1967

Boat People see **T'ou-Pen Nu-Hai**, 1982

Boatman of Amalfi see Barcaiuolo d'Amalfi, 1918

Bóbita, 1964 (Mészáros)

Boccaccio '70, 1962 (Cecchi d'Amico)

Body Collage, 1967 (Schneemann)

Body Heat, 1981 (Littleton)

Body Politics, 1974 (Export)

Body Repaired and the World in Reverse see Mensche verstreut und Welt verkehrt, 1975

Body Rotations see Falling Bodies, 1967

Boeing, Boeing, 1965 (Head)

Bohème, 1926 (Gish)

Boiling Electric Jug Film, 1971 (Cantrill)

Bolly, 1968 (Batchelor)

Bombay Talkie, 1970 (Jhabvala)

Bombshell, 1933 (Booth)

Bon Odoni, 1973 (Yamasaki)

Bondage, 1983 (Treut)

Bonheur, 1965 (Varda)

Bonheur des autres, 1918 (Dulac)

Bonne Absinthe, 1899/1900 (Guy)

Bonnie and Clyde, 1967 (Allen, D.; Van Runkle)

Bonus for Irene see Eine Prämie für Irene, 1971

Booloo, 1938 (Head)

Border Flight, 1936 (Head)

Border Radio, 1988 (Anders)

Border Vigilantes, 1941 (Head)

Borderland, 1937 (Head)

Borgne, 1980 (Sarmiento)

Borinage see Misère au Borinage, 1934

Born in Flames, 1983 (Bigelow; Borden)

Born to the West, 1937 (Head)

Borrowed Clothes, 1918 (Weber)

Borrowers, 1973 (Allen, J.)

Borsós Miklós, 1966 (Mészáros)

Dorea, 1935 (van Dongen)

Bostonians, 1984 (Jhabvala)

Both, 1988 (Child)

Both Sides of the Law see Street Corner, 1953

Bottoms see Film No. 4, 1966

Bouddi, 1970 (Cantrill)

Bought and Paid For, 1916 (Marion)

Bouquetière des Catalans, 1915 (Musidora)

Bout de Zan et le poilu, 1915 (Musidora)

Boy and Tarzan Appear in a Clearing, 1981 (Choy)

Boy Friend, 1971 (Russell)

Boy from the Taiga see Paren iz taigi, 1941

Boy Next Door, 1985 (Gordon)

Boy of Two Worlds see Paw, 1959

Boy Trouble, 1939 (Head)

Boy Who Saw Through, 1956 (Bute)

Boys from the West Coast see Vesterhavs drenge, 1950

Boys in the Band, 1970 (Russell)

Boys Next Door, 1985 (Spheeris)

Boys' Ranch, 1946 (Irene)

Boys, Take Your Dancing Partners! see Chlapci, zadejte se!, 1964

Boys Will Be Boys see Páni kluci, 1975

Braconniers, 1903 (Guy)

Brain Battle, 1995 (Leaf)
Branded, 1951 (Head)
Branded Woman, 1920 (Loos)
Brandstifter, 1969 (von Trotta)
Braslet-2, 1967 (Muratova)
Brat, 1919 (Guy; Mathis)
Brat, 1930 (Levien)
Brave Blacksmith see O statecném kovári, 1983
Brave Tin Soldier, 1941 (Batchelor)
Brawn of the North, 1922 (Murfin)
Bread, 1924 (Coffee)
Bread of the Border, 1924 (Arzner)
Breakdown see Loveless, 1982
Breakfast at Tiffany's, 1961 (Head)
Breakfast Club, 1985 (Allen, D.)
Breaking Away, 1979 (von Brandenstein)
Breaking the Silence, 1988 (Dash)
Breath of Scandal, 1960 (Head)
Breaths, 1994 (Dash)
Brecht die Macht der Manipulateure, 1967 (Sander)
Bribe, 1949 (Irene)
Bride, 1985 (Russell)
Bride Goes Wild, 1948 (Rose)
Bride Wore Boots, 1946 (Head)
Bride Wore Red, 1937 (Arzner)
Bridegroom, the Comedienne and the Pimp see Der Bräutigam, die Komödiantin und der Zuhälter, 1968
Bridge see De brug, 1928
Bridge of San Luis Rey, 1929 (Booth)
Bridge Too Far, 1977 (Ullmann)
Bridges at Toko-ri, 1954 (Head)
Bridges-Go-Round, 1959 (Clarke)
Brief Encounters see Korotkiye vstrechi, 1967
Brigadoon, 1954 (Sharaff)
Bright City see Svetlyi gorod, 1928
Brighton Beach Memoirs, 1986 (Littleton)
Bring on the Girls, 1945 (Head)
Bringing Up Father, 1927 (Booth; Marion)
Britain Must Export, 1946 (Batchelor)
British Army at Your Service, 1950 (Batchelor)
Broadway Rhythm, 1943 (Irene)
Broken Blossoms, 1919 (Gish)
Broken Jug see Der zerbrochene Krug, 1937
Broken Lance, 1954 (Spencer)
Broken Locket, 1909 (Pickford)
Broken Mirrors see Gebroken Spiegels, 1984
Brontosaurus, 1979 (Šimková-Plívová)
Brother Sun, Sister Moon see Fratelli sole, sorella luna, 1972
Brothers, 1947 (Box, M.)
Brother's Heart see Core 'e Frata, 1923
Browning Version, 1951 (Dillon)
Bruno aspetta in macchna, 1996 (Cecchi d'Amico)
Brussels "Loops", 1958 (Clarke)
Brute, 1987 (Guillemot)
Bryn Mawr College, 1948 (Grayson)
Buccaneer, 1938 (Bauchens; Head)
Buccaneer, 1938 (Macpherson)
Buccaneer, 1958 (Head)
Buccaneers, 1913 (Madison)
Buck Benny Rides Again, 1940 (Head)
Bucovina-Ukrainian Earth see Bukovyna-Zemlya, 1940

Budujemy nowe wsi, 1946 (Jakubowska)
Bufera d'Anime, 1911 (Notari)
Bugsy Malone, 1976 (Foster)
Building, 1968-73 (Potter)
Buisson ardent, 1951-66 (Parker)
Bukovyna-Zemlya, 1940 (Solntseva)
Bulldog Drummond Comes Back, 1937 (Head)
Bulldog Drummond Escapes, 1937 (Head)
Bulldog Drummond in Africa, 1938 (Bauchens; Head)
Bulldog Drummond's Bride, 1939 (Head)
Bulldog Drummond's Peril, 1938 (Head)
Bulldog Drummond's Revenge, 1937 (Head)
Bulldog Drummond's Secret Police, 1939 (Head)
Bullfight, 1955 (Clarke)
Bullitt, 1968 (Van Runkle)
Bunch of Flowers, 1914 (Loos)
Buon Giorno, elefante!, 1952 (Cecchi d'Amico)
Burglar Catcher, 1960 (Batchelor)
Burglar's Dilemma, 1912 (Gish)
Burning Hearts see Kolberg, 1945
Burning Soil see Der brennende Acker, 1922
Bus, 1964 (Fields)
Bushwackers, 1925 (Lyell)
Buster Keaton Story, 1957 (Head)
But No One, 1982 (Friedrich)
But Not for Me, 1959 (Head)
But What Do Women Want? see Mais qu'est-ce qu'elles veulent?, 1978
Butch Cassidy and the Sundance Kid, 1969 (Head)
Butcher's Wife, 1991 (Van Runkle)
Butley, 1974 (Dillon)
Butterfield 8, 1960 (Rose)
Butterfly Revolution see Summer Camp Nightmare, 1987
Buy Me That Town, 1941 (Head)
By Rocket to the Moon see Frau im Mond, 1929
By the Steep Ravine see U krutogo yara, 1963
Bye-Bye Red Riding Hood see Piroska és a farkas, 1988
Bytva za nashu Radyansku Ukrayinu, 1943 (Solntseva)

Ça n'arrive qu'aux autres, 1971 (Trintignant)
Cabaret, 1972 (Allen, J.)
Cabbage Fairy see Fée aux choux, 1896
Cabin in the Sky, 1943 (Irene)
Cadavres en Vacances, 1961 (Audry)
Caddies, 1960 (Batchelor)
Caddy, 1953 (Head)
Caddy's Dream, 1911 (Pickford)
Cafe Society, 1939 (Head; Van Upp)
Cage of Doom see Terror from the Year 5000, 1958
Cake-Walk de la pendule, 1903 (Guy)
Calamity see Kalamita, 1980
Calcutta, 1947 (Head)
Calendar Girl, 1993 (Marshall)
Calico Vampire, 1916 (Loos)
California, 1947 (Head)
California Suite, 1978 (Booth; May)
Caliph Storch, 1954 (Reiniger)
Call, 1909 (Macpherson)
Call Me Madam, 1953 (Sharaff)
Call of the Rose, 1912 (Guy)
Call of the Song, 1911 (Pickford)

Call to Arms, 1910 (Pickford)
Callahans and the Murphys, 1927 (Marion)
Callaway Went Thataway, 1951 (Rose)
Calling the Shots, 1988 (Cole; Weill; Zetterling)
Calvaire, 1914 (Musidora)
Calypso Heat Wave, 1957 (Angelou)
Camargue, det forlorade landet, 1972 (Ahrne)
Cambrioleur et agent, 1904 (Guy)
Cambrioleurs, 1897/98 (Guy)
Cambrioleurs de Paris, 1904 (Guy)
Camel Xiang Zi, 1980 (Peng)
Camila, 1984 (Bemberg)
Camilla, 1994 (Mehta)
Camille, 1915 (Marion)
Camille, 1921 (Mathis)
Camille, 1937 (Akins; Booth; Marion)
Camille without Camellias see Signora senza camelie, 1953
Camion, 1977 (Duras)
Camorra, 1986 (Wertmüller)
Campbell's Kingdom, 1958 (Box, B.)
Campus Confessions, 1938 (Head)
Can-Can, 1960 (Sharaff)
Canada Vignettes: June in Povungnituk—Quebec Arctic, 1979 (Obomsawin)
Canada Vignettes: Wild Rice Harvest Kenora, 1979 (Obomsawin)
Cananea, 1977 (Fernández Violante)
Canary Yellow see Zard-e Ghanari, 1989
Cançao de Amor, 1977 (Abreu)
Candidate, 1972 (von Brandenstein)
Candlemaker, 1956 (Batchelor)
Candleshoe, 1977 (Foster)
Canned Harmony, 1912 (Guy)
Cannibals see I Cannibali, 1969
Canta for Our Sisters, 1987 (Davis)
Cap Tourmente, 1993 (Pool)
Cape Fear, 1991 (Schoonmaker)
Caper of the Golden Bulls, 1967 (Head)
Capitana Allegria see Pour Don Carlos, 1921
Capri Incantevole, 1909 (Notari)
Capri Pittoresco, 1912 (Notari)
Caprice, 1913 (Pickford)
Caprices of Kitty, 1915 (Marion)
Captain Courtesy, 1915 (Marion)
Captain Kidd, 1913 (Madison)
Captain Kidd, Jr., 1919 (Marion; Pickford)
Captain Macklin, 1915 (Gish)
Captain Midnight, the Bush King, 1911 (Lyell)
Captain Starlight, 1911 (Lyell)
Captive, 1915 (Macpherson)
Capture of a Madman in Bagnoli see Cattura di un Pazzo a Bagnoli, 1912
Car 99, 1935 (Head)
Carabiniers, 1963 (Guillemot)
Caraque blonde, 1953 (Audry)
Caratteristica Guerra Italo-Turca Tra i Nostri Scugnizzi Napoletani, 1912 (Notari)
Cardboard Cavalier, 1949 (Dillon)
Cardinal's Conspiracy, 1909 (Pickford)
Care and Affection see Szeretet, 1963
Career, 1959 (Head)
Career of Waterloo Peterson, 1914 (Weber)

Cari fottutissimi amici, 1993 (Cecchi d'Amico)
Caribbean, 1952 (Head)
Carl Ruggles' Christmas Breakfast, 1963 (Schneemann)
Carmela la Pazza, 1911 (Notari)
Carmela la Sartina di Montesanto, 1916 (Notari)
Carmela the Dressmaker of Montesanto see Carmela la Sartina di Montesanto, 1916
Carmela the Madwoman see Carmela la Pazza, 1911
Carmen, 1900/07 (Guy)
Carmen, 1915 (Macpherson)
Carmen, 1933 (Reiniger)
Carnaby, M.D. see Doctor in Clover, 1966
Carnaval dans le Sahel, 1977 (Maldoror)
Carnaval en Guinée-Bissau, 1971 (Maldoror)
Carnival, 1946 (Dillon)
Carnival in Guinea-Bissau see Carnaval en Guinée-Bissau, 1971
Carnival in Sahel see Carnaval dans le Sahel, 1977
Carnival in the Clothes Cupboard, 1940 (Batchelor)
Carny, 1980 (Foster)
Caro Michele, 1976 (Cecchi d'Amico)
Carpetbaggers, 1964 (Head)
Carriage Going to Vienna see Kocár do Vídne, 1966
Carriage of Death see 'O Cuppe' d'a Morte, 1923
Carrie, 1952 (Head)
Carrot Top see Poil de carotte, 1972
Carry Greenham Home, 1983 (Kidron)
Carry on Constable, 1960 (Dillon)
Carry on Cruising, 1962 (Dillon)
Carry on Milkmaids, 1974 (Batchelor)
Cas je neúprosný, 1978 (Chytilová)
Casa in Italia, 1964 (Cavani)
Casanova, 1976 (Kurys)
Casanova '70, 1965 (Cecchi d'Amico)
Casanova Brown, 1944 (Fields)
Case against Mrs. Ames, 1936 (Spencer)
Cash McCall, 1960 (Coffee)
Cash on Delivery see To Dorothy a Son, 1956
Casino, 1995 (Schoonmaker)
Canotto, 1977 (Foster)
Cass Timberlane, 1947 (Irene; Levien)
Cassidy of Bar 20, 1938 (Head)
Cast and Credits: A Film to Be Read see Vorspann: Ein Lesefilm, 1968
Cat and the Canary, 1939 (Head)
Cat on a Hot Tin Roof, 1958 (Rose)
Catch Me a Spy, 1971 (Dillon)
Catchfire see Backtrack, 1989
Catfood, 1968 (Wieland)
Cat's Cradle, 1959 (Schneemann)
Cattura di un Pazzo a Bagnoli, 1912 (Notari)
Caught in the Draft, 1941 (Head)
Cavalcade, 1933 (Levien)
Cavanaugh of the Forest Rangers, 1918 (Shipman)
Cayuga Run, 1967 (De Hirsch)
Ce fut un bel été , 1982 (Kaplan)
Ceiling see Strop, 1962
Celluloid Closet, 1995 (Allen, J.)
Celui qui reste, 1915 (Musidora)
Cenpa, 1936-39 (Parker)
Cent et une nuits, 1995 (Varda)
Cent pour cent, 1951-66 (Parker)
Center see Hothouse, 1988

Cento anni d'amore, 1953 (Cecchi d'Amico)
Centralization *see* Tamarkoze, 1987
Century of Women, 1994 (Kopple)
Certain Smile, 1958 (Goodrich)
Cesarée, 1978/79 (Duras)
C'est la faute d'Adam, 1957 (Audry)
C'est la vie *see* Baule-les-Pins, 1990
C'est pour les orphelins!, 1917 (Musidora)
Cesta z Prahy do Ceského Krumlova aneb Jak jsem sestavoval novou
     vládu *see* Co delat?, 1996
C'était le 12 du 12 et chili avait les blues, 1993 (Pool)
Cézanne, 1989 (Huillet)
Chacals, 1917 (Musidora)
Chained to Yesterday *see* Limbo, 1972
Chalice of Sorrow, 1916 (Madison)
Chalk Garden, 1964 (Dillon)
Challenge *see* Sfida, 1958
Challenge of a Lifetime, 1985 (Marshall)
Chambre 1, 1972 (Akerman)
Chambre 2, 1972 (Akerman)
Chambre 666, 1982 (Seidelman)
Champ, 1931 (Marion)
Change of Fate *see* Peremena uchasti, 1987
Change of Heart, 1934 (Levien)
Chapter in Her Life, 1923 (Weber)
Chapter Two, 1979 (Booth)
Charité du prestidigitateur, 1905 (Guy)
Charles et Lucie, 1979 (Kaplan)
Charley series, 1946-49 (Batchelor)
Charlie Chan at the Opera, 1935 (Meredyth)
Charlotte Bunch: One Woman's Legacy, 1988 (Schiller)
Charlotte Moorman's Avant-Garde Festival #9, 1973-74 (De Hirsch)
Charmant FrouFrou, 1901 (Guy)
Charming Sinners, 1930 (Arzner)
Chasing Rainbows, 1930 (Meredyth)
Chasse au cambrioleur, 1903/04 (Guy)
Chaussette, 1906 (Guy)
Cheap Detective, 1978 (Booth)
Cheated Love, 1921 (Levien)
Cheaters, 1930 (McDonagh Sisters)
Check to Song, 1951 (Batchelor)
Checkpoint, 1956 (Box, B.; Dillon)
Cheech and Chong's Nice Dreams, 1981 (Murphy)
Chelsea Girls, 1966 (Menken)
Chère Amérique, 1989 (Mallet)
Chéri, 1950 (Colette)
Cherokee Strip, 1940 (Head)
Chevaux du Vercors, 1943 (Audry)
Chez le magnétiseur, 1897/98 (Guy)
Chez le Maréchal-Ferrant, 1899/1900 (Guy)
Chez le photographe, 1900 (Guy)
Chiarina la Modista, 1919 (Notari)
Chiarina the Milliner *see* Chiarina la Modista, 1919
Chibusa yo eien nare, 1955 (Tanaka)
Chicago, 1927 (Bauchens; Coffee)
Chico Viola Não Morreu, 1955 (Abreu)
Chien fou, 1966 (Guillemot)
Chien jouant á la balle, 1905 (Guy)
Chiens savants, 1902 (Guy)
Chiffonier, 1899/1900 (Guy)
Child Lost Forever, 1992 (Weill)

Child of the Andes *see* Mémoires d'un enfant des Andes, 1988
Children *see* Enfants, 1985
Children and Cars, 1971 (Batchelor)
Children Are Not Cattle *see* Kinder sind nicht Rinder, 1969
Children, Books *see* Gyermekek, könyvek, 1962
Children in the Holocaust, 1983 (Ullmann)
Children Making Cartoons, 1973 (Batchelor)
Children of Desired Sex, 1987 (Nair)
Children of Montmartre *see* **Maternelle**, 1933
Children of the Ruins, 1948 (Craigie)
Children of the Sun, 1960 (Hubley)
Children of the Taiga *see* Paren iz taigi, 1941
Children Pay, 1916 (Gish)
Children's Hour, 1961 (Jeakins)
Children's Souls *see* Âmes d'enfants, 1927
Child's Impulse, 1910 (Pickford)
Child's Sacrifice, 1910 (Guy)
Chilly Scenes of Winter, 1979 (Silver)
Chimmie Fadden Out West, 1915 (Macpherson)
China, 1943 (Head)
China—die Künste—der Alltag, 1985 (Ottinger)
China Moon, 1994 (Littleton)
China—The Arts—The People *see* China—die Künste—der Alltag,
     1985
China Today, 1989 (Choy)
China's 400 Million *see* 400 Million, 1939
Chinoise, 1967 (Guillemot)
Chirurgie fin de siècle, 1900 (Guy)
Chivato, 1961 (Murphy)
Chlapci, zadejte se!, 1964 (Šimková-Plívová)
Chocolat, 1988 (Denis)
Chocolate *see* **Chocolat**, 1988
Chorus Line, 1985 (von Brandenstein)
Christian Triumph *see* Trionfo Cristiano, 1930
Christine of the Big Top, 1926 (Levien)
Christmas at Moose Factory, 1971 (Obomsawin)
Christmas Feast, 1974 (Batchelor)
Christmas in Connecticut, 1945 (Head)
Christmas in July, 1940 (Head)
Christmas Visitor, 1958 (Batchelor)
Christmas Wishes, 1944 (Batchelor)
Christopher Columbus, 1949 (Box, M.)
Christopher Strong, 1933 (Akins)
Chronicle of a Woman *see* Cronica de una Señora, 1971
Chronicle of Anna Magdalena Bach *see* Chronik der Anna Magdalena
     Bach, 1968
Chronicle of Flaming Years *see* Povest plamennykh let, 1961
Chronicle of Hope: Nicaragua, 1984 (Choy)
Chronik der Anna Magdalena Bach, 1968 (Huillet)
Chroniques de France, 1973-74 (Denis)
Chuka, 1967 (Head)
Church and the Woman, 1917 (Lyell)
Chuvstvitel'nyi militsioner, 1992 (Muratova)
Chytilová versus Forman, 1981 (Chytilová)
Ciao, Professore! *see* Io speriamo che me la cavo, 1994
Cible humaine, 1904 (Guy)
Ciccio il Pizzaiuolo del Carmine, 1916 (Notari)
Cielo celeste, 1922 (Notari)
Cielo 'e Napule, 1922 (Notari)
Cielo sulla palude, 1948 (Cecchi d'Amico)
Cigarette, 1919 (Dulac)

Cigarette-Girl from Mosselprom *see* Papirosnitsa ot Mosselproma, 1924

Cigarette, That's All, 1915 (Weber)

Cigarettes Davros, 1936-39 (Parker)

Cimetière du Père Lachaise, 1981 (Maldoror)

Cinderella, 1914 (Pickford)

Cinderella, 1963 (Reiniger)

Cinderfella, 1960 (Head)

Cinéma au service de l'histoire, 1927 (Dulac)

Cinema-Child *see* L'enfant-cinéma, 1997

Cinéma: Embaixada do Brasil, 1981 (Yamasaki)

Cinema Murder, 1920 (Marion)

Cinema's Embassy *see* Cinéma: Embaixada do Brasil, 1981

Circle of Danger, 1950 (Harrison)

Circle of Deceit *see* Fälschung, 1981

Circus Star, 1960 (Batchelor)

Circus World, 1964 (Spencer)

Città violenta, 1970 (Wertmüller)

City, 1971 (Cantrill)

City Girl, 1984 (Coolidge)

City of Bad Men, 1953 (Jeakins)

City of Dim Faces, 1918 (Marion)

City of Pirates *see* Ville des pirates, 1983

City Sentinel *see* Beast of the City, 1932

City Vamp, 1915 (Marion)

Civil Rights: The Struggle Continues, 1989 (Kopple)

Clam-Digger's Daughter *see* Story of Mr. Hobbs, 1947

Clarence, 1937 (Head)

Class Relations *see* Klassenverhältnisse, 1985

Classic Fairy Tales Series, 1966 (Batchelor)

Classified, 1925 (Mathis)

Claudine à l'école, 1937 (Colette)

Cléo de cinq à sept, 1961 (Varda)

Cleopatra, 1934 (Bauchens)

Cleopatra, 1963 (Sharaff; Spencer)

Clock, 1945 (Irene)

Clock, 1971 (Ono)

Clockmaker *see* L'Horloger de Saint-Paul, 1974

Clorae & Albie, 1976 (Chopra)

Clouded Yellow, 1950 (Box, B.)

Cloudland, 1993 (Hubley)

Clouds of Glory, 1978 (Russell)

Clown en sac, 1904 (Guy)

Clowns, 1902 (Guy)

Clubman and the Tramp, 1908 (Macpherson)

Clueless , 1995 (Heckerling)

Cluny Brown, 1946 (Spencer)

Co delat?, 1996 (Krumbachová)

Coast at Pearl Beach, 1979 (Cantrill)

Coastal Navigation and Pilotage, 1953 (Batchelor)

Cobweb, 1955 (Gish)

Cocher de fiacre endormi, 1897/98 (Guy)

Cockaboody, 1973 (Hubley)

Cockpit *see* Lost People, 1949

Cocktail, 1937 (Henning-Jensen)

Cocktail Molotov, 1980 (Kurys)

Coconut Grove, 1938 (Head)

Coeur battant, 1962 (Trintignant)

Coeur de Paris, 1931 (Epstein)

Coeur fidèle, 1923 (Epstein)

Coeur fragile, 1916 (Musidora)

Cold Comfort, 1944 (Batchelor)

Cold Sweat *see* L'uomo dalle due ombre, 1974

Cold Turkey, 1969 (Ono)

Coleçao de marfil, 1972 (Amaral)

College Holiday, 1936 (Head)

College Swing, 1938 (Head)

Collegiate, 1936 (Head)

Collier de perles, 1915 (Musidora)

Colloque de chiens, 1977 (Sarmiento)

Colombo Plan, 1967 (Batchelor)

Colonel Bontemps, 1915 (Musidora)

Color of Money, 1986 (Schoonmaker)

Color Rhapsodie, 1948 (Bute)

Colors of Love *see* Kolory kochania, 1988

Colors of Vásárhely *see* Vásárhelyi szinek, 1961

Colossal Love *see* Kolossale Liebe, 1984

Colossus: The Forbin Project, 1970 (Head)

Colour of Britain, 1994 (Parmar)

Come and Get It, 1936 (Murfin)

Come and Work *see* Fad'jal, 1979

Come Back in the Summertime, 1985 (Peng)

Come Back, Little Sheba, 1952 (Head)

Come Blow Your Horn, 1963 (Head)

Come Live with Me, 1941 (Van Upp)

Come-On, 1956 (Head)

Come on In, 1918 (Loos)

Come on, Marines!, 1934 (Lupino)

Come Rain or Shine *see* Ob's stürmt oder schneit, 1976

Come West with Me, 1998 (Gomis)

Comedians, 1967 (Gish)

Comedians in Africa, 1967 (Gish)

Comin' round the Mountain, 1940 (Head)

Coming Out Party, 1934 (Spencer)

Commandos Strike at Dawn, 1942 (Bauchens; Gish)

Comme on fait son lit on se couche, 1903/04 (Guy)

Comment monsieur prend son bain, 1903 (Guy)

Comment on disperse les foules, 1903/04 (Guy)

Comment on dort á Paris!, 1905 (Guy)

Commonplace Story *see* Egyszeru történet, 1975

Commonwealth, 1967 (Batchelor)

Commuters, 1972 (Weill)

Compagnons de voyage encombrants, 1903 (Guy)

Compensation, 1997 (Davis)

Complicato intrigo di donne, vicoli e delitti *see* Camorra, 1986

Complot *see* To Kill a Priest, 1988

Concealing a Burglar, 1908 (Macpherson)

Concierge, 1900 (Guy)

Concierge revient de suite, 1978 (Guillemot)

Concorde—Airport '79, 1979 (Spencer)

Concours de bébés, 1904 (Guy)

Coney Island, 1943 (Rose)

Confessions *see* L.A. Johns, 1997

Confessions of a Suburban Girl, 1992 (Seidelman)

Confidence, 1909 (Macpherson)

Conmigo la pasas muy bien, 1982 (Novaro)

Connection, 1961 (Clarke)

Conquering Power, 1921 (Mathis)

Conquest of Space, 1955 (Head)

Conscience de prêtre, 1906 (Guy)

Conscience of Hassan Bey, 1913 (Gish)

Conspiracy of Hearts, 1960 (Box, B.)

Constance, 1951-66 (Parker)
Constant Nymph, 1928 (Reville)
Consumer Culture *see* Farahang-e-Massraffi, 1984
Contact, 1973 (Batchelor)
Contact, 1997 (Foster)
Contempt *see* Mépris, 1963
Contessa azzurra, 1960 (Cecchi d'Amico)
Contre l'oubli, 1991 (Akerman; Denis; Serreau; Trintignant)
Convictions, 1997 (Chopra)
Convoy Leaving Paradise *see* Transport z ráje, 1962
Cookie, 1989 (Ephron; Seidelman)
Cooking with Apes, 1973 (Schneemann)
Cool Hands, Warm Heart, 1979 (Friedrich)
Cool World, 1963 (Clarke)
Copper Canyon, 1950 (Head)
Copycat, 1995 (Allen, J.)
Coquette, 1929 (Pickford)
Coquille et le clergyman, 1927 (Dulac)
Coração Materno, 1951 (Abreu)
Corazzata San Giorgio, 1911 (Notari)
Core 'e Frata, 1923 (Notari)
Corn Is Green, 1979 (Dillon)
Corner in Cotton, 1916 (Loos)
Corner in Hats, 1914 (Loos)
Corner in Wheat, 1909 (Macpherson)
Corporeal, 1983 (Cantrill)
Corpse Had a Familiar Face, 1994 (Chopra)
Cós za cós, 1977 (Holland)
Cosi Piange Pierrot *see* Piange Pierrot, 1924
Cosmic Eye, 1985 (Hubley)
Cossacks, 1928 (Marion)
Cossacks of the Don *see* Tikhiy Don, 1930
Couch in New York *see* Divan à New York, 1996
Coucher d'une Parisienne, 1900 (Guy)
Coucher d'Yvette, 1897 (Guy)
Couleur chair, 1978 (Ullmann)
Couleur du vent, 1988 (Pascal)
Count Your Blessings, 1959 (Rose)
Countdown, 1990 (Ottinger)
Counterfeit Traitor, 1962 (Head)
Country Boy, 1966 (Fields)
Country Doctor, 1909 (Pickford)
Country Doctor, 1936 (Levien)
Country Girl, 1954 (Head)
Coup de foudre, 1983 (Kurys; Pascal)
Coup de grâce *see* Der Fangschuss, 1976
Coup du fakir, 1915 (Musidora)
Couple Takes a Wife, 1972 (Marshall)
Cour des miracles, 1902 (Guy)
Courage of Lassie, 1946 (Irene)
Course de taureaux à Nîmes, 1906 (Guy)
Court Jester, 1956 (Head)
Courte échelle, 1899/1900 (Guy)
Courtesans of Bombay, 1982 (Jhabvala)
Courting of Mary, 1911 (Pickford)
Courtship of Eddie's Father, 1963 (Rose)
Cousin cousine, 1975 (Guillemot)
Cover Girl, 1944 (Van Upp)
Covered Wagon, 1923 (Arzner)
Covert Action, 1984 (Child)

Cowboy and the Lady, 1938 (Levien)
Cradle Song, 1933 (Bauchens; Head)
Craig's Wife, 1928 (Bauchens)
Craig's Wife, 1936 (Arzner)
Crazy in Love, 1992 (Coolidge)
Cream Soda, 1976 (Cole)
Créatures, 1966 (Varda)
Crème Simon, 1936-39 (Parker)
Creosoot, 1931 (van Dongen)
Cricket on the Hearth, 1914 (Guy)
Cries and Whispers *see* Viskningar och rop, 1972
Crime at Cuenca *see* El crimen de Cuenca, 1981
Crime de la rue du Temple *see* L'Assassinat de la rue du Temple, 1904
Crime Doctor, 1934 (Murfin)
Crime Doctor's Man Hunt, 1946 (Brackett)
Crime Gives Orders *see* Hunted Men, 1938
Crime Nobody Saw, 1937 (Head)
Crime of the Century, 1933 (Head)
Crime Thief *see* Voleur de crimes, 1969
Crimes and Misdemeanors, 1989 (Ephron)
Criminal Passion, 1994 (Deitch)
Crimson Dove, 1917 (Marion)
Crimson Yoke, 1916 (Madison)
Crinoline, 1906 (Guy)
Crise, 1992 (Serreau)
Crisis *see* Crise, 1992
Critical Choices, 1996 (Weill)
Critic's Choice, 1963 (Head)
Crocodile Conspiracy, 1986 (Davis)
Crocodiles in Amsterdam *see* **Krokodillen in Amsterdam**, 1990
Cronica de una Señora, 1971 (Bemberg)
Crooked Hearts, 1972 (Marshall)
Crooks in Clover *see* Penthouse, 1933
Cross My Heart, 1947 (Head)
Cross Purposes, 1913 (Madison)
Crossing Delancey, 1988 (Silver)
Crosswinds, 1951 (Head)
Crucial Test, 1916 (Marion)
Cruel Embrace *see* Noces barbares, 1987
Crusades, 1935 (Bauchens; Head; Macpherson)
Crush, 1992 (Maclean)
Crush the Power of the Manipulators *see* Brecht die Macht der Manipulateure, 1967
Cry for Help, 1912 (Gish)
Cry Havoc, 1943 (Irene)
Cry of Battle, 1963 (Fields)
Cry Wolf, 1947 (Head)
Crystal Ball, 1943 (Van Upp; Head)
Cuba, 1979 (Russell)
Cuban Love Song, 1931 (Booth; Meredyth)
Cuenca Crime *see* El crimen de Cuenca, 1981
Culinary Embassies *see* Ambassades Nourricières, 1984
Culture intensive ou Le Vieux Mari, 1904 (Guy)
Cummington Story, 1945 (Grayson)
Cuore, 1984 (Cecchi d'Amico)
Cure for Suffragettes, 1913 (Loos)
Curtain Pole, 1908 (Macpherson)
Cuts *see* Schnitte, 1976
Cutting, 1967-68 (Export)
Cycles, 1989 (Davis)
Cynara, 1932 (Marion)

Cynthia, 1947 (Irene)
Cyrano et d'Artagnan, 1963 (Kaplan)
Cytherea, 1924 (Marion)
Cziko, the Blinking Boy see Mrkácek iko, 1982
Czlowiek z Zelaza, 1981 (Holland)

Dada, 1936 (Bute)
Daddy Long Legs, 1919 (Pickford)
Daddy Long Legs, 1931 (Levien)
Daddy's Gone A-Hunting, 1969 (Spencer)
Daguerrotypes, 1975 (Varda)
Daigaku wa detakeredo, 1929 (Tanaka)
Daily-Life Racism see Racisme au quotidien, 1983
Daisies see Sedmikrásky, 1966
Daisy Miller, 1974 (Fields)
Dam the Delta, 1958 (Batchelor)
Damned if You Don't, 1987 (Friedrich)
Damon and Pythias, 1914 (Madison)
Dance, Girl, Dance, 1940 (Arzner)
Dance Hall, 1929 (Murfin)
Dance in Chains see Bialy mazur, 1978
Dance in the Sun, 1954 (Clarke)
Dance Little Lady, 1954 (Zetterling)
Dance of Life see Swing High, Swing Low, 1937
Dance Pretty Lady, 1931 (Toye)
Dancer, 1915 (Madison)
Dancing Girl of Izu see Izu no odoriko, 1933
Dancing Lady, 1933 (Booth)
Dancing on a Dime, 1940 (Head)
Dandelion Child see Maskrosbarn, 1989
Dandy in Aspic, 1968 (Dillon)
Danger of Love, 1992 (Chopra)
Dangerous Age, 1922 (Coffee; Madison)
Dangerous Age, 1922 (Meredyth)
Dangerous Business, 1921 (Loos)
Dangerous Minds, 1995 (May)
Dangerous Moves see Diagonale du fou, 1983
Dangerous Offender, 1996 (Cole)
Dangerous Partners, 1945 (Irene)
Dangerous to Know, 1938 (Head)
Dangerous When Wet, 1953 (Rose)
Dangers de l'acoolisme, 1899/1900 (Guy)
Danish Brigade in Sweden see Dansk politi i Sverige, 1945
Danish Girls Show Everything, 1996 (Treut)
Danjuro sandai, 1944 (Tanaka)
Dans les coulisses, 1900 (Guy)
Dans l'ouragan de la vie, 1916 (Dulac)
Danse basque, 1901 (Guy)
Danse de l'ivresse, 1900 (Guy)
Danse des Saisons series, 1900 (Guy)
Danse du papillon, 1900 (Guy)
Danse du pas des foulards par des almées, 1900 (Guy)
Danse du ventre, 1900/01 (Guy)
Danse fleur de lotus, 1897 (Guy)
Danse mauresque, 1902 (Guy)
Danse serpentine, 1900 (Guy)
Danse serpentine par Mme Bob Walter, 1899/1900 (Guy)
Danses series, 1900 (Guy)
Dansk politi i Sverige, 1945 (Henning-Jensen)
Danske piger viser alt, 1996 (Henning-Jensen)
Dante's Inferno, 1967 (Russell)

Danton, 1983 (Holland)
Danulon gyártás, 1961 (Mészáros)
Danulon Production see Danulon gyártás, 1961
Danzón, 1990 (Novaro)
Daphne and the Pirate, 1916 (Gish)
Dark Angel, 1925 (Marion)
Dark City, 1950 (Head)
Dark Delusion, 1947 (Irene)
Dark Eyes see Oci ciornie, 1987
Dark Mirror, 1946 (Sharaff)
Dark Star, 1919 (Marion)
Dark Waters, 1944 (Harrison)
Darkest Russia, 1917 (Marion)
Darling, How Could You?, 1951 (Head)
Date with Judy, 1948 (Rose)
Daughter of Luxury see Five and Ten, 1931
Daughter of Shanghai, 1937 (Head)
Daughter of the Navajos, 1911 (Guy)
Daughter of the Poor, 1916 (Loos)
Daughter of Vesuvius see Figlia del Vesuvio, 1912
Daughter Rite, 1978 (Citron)
Daughters' Inheritance see Erbtöchter, 1982
Daughters of the Dust, 1992 (Dash)
Dauphine Java, 1951-66 (Parker)
David and Lisa, 1962 (Perry)
David Copperfield, 1935 (Coffee)
David: Off and On, 1972 (Coolidge)
David Wheeler: Theater Company of Boston, 1975 (Chopra)
Dawn of Tomorrow, 1915 (Pickford)
Day after Day see Jour apres jour, 1962
Day of Peace see Giorno Della Pace, 1965
Day the Mercedes Became a Hat, 1993 (Nair)
Day the Sun Turned Cold see Tianguo Niezi, 1994
Day to Remember, 1953 (Box, B.)
Daybreak, 1947 (Box, M.)
Daybreak, 1957 (Schneemann)
Daylight Test Section, 1978 (Child)
Days in the Trees see Journées entières dans les arbres, 1976
Days of Betrayal see Dny zrady, 1973
Days to Remember see Verliebten, 1987
Daytime Wives, 1923 (Coffee)
Dazwischen, 1981 (Dörrie)
De blå undulater, 1965 (Henning-Jensen)
De brug, 1928 (van Dongen)
De cierta manera, 1977 (Gómez)
De encaje y azucar, 1981 (Novaro)
De eso no se habla, 1993 (Bemberg)
De guerre lasse, 1976 (Hänsel)
De kalte ham Skarven, 1965 (Ullmann)
De la part des copains see L'uomo dalle due ombre, 1974
De l'amour, 1964 (Guillemot)
De mère en fille, 1968 (Poirier)
De pokkers unger, 1947 (Henning-Jensen)
De Stilte Rond Christine M, 1981 (Gorris)
De todos modos Juan te llamas, 1975 (Fernández Violante)
Deacon's Whiskers, 1915 (Loos)
Dead, 1987 (Jeakins)
Dead Case, 1978 (Holland)
Dead Earth, 1971 (Choy)
Dead Man Who Killed, 1914 (Madison)
Dead Men Don't Wear Plaid, 1982 (Head)

Deadhead Miles, 1972 (Lupino)

Deadlier than the Male, 1966 (Box, B.)

Deadline for Murder: From the Files of Edna Buchanan, 1995 (Chopra)

Deadly Glass of Beer, 1917 (Loos)

Deadly Trap see Maison sous les arbres, 1972

Dear America see Chère Amérique, 1989

Dear Brat, 1951 (Head)

Dear Carmen see Querida Carmen, 1983

Dear Murderer, 1947 (Box, B.; Box, M.)

Dear Ruth, 1947 (Head)

Dear Squirrel, Don't Snivel see Nefnukej, veverko!, 1988

Death Disc, 1909 (Macpherson)

Death of a Champion, 1939 (Head)

Death of Empedocles see Der Tod des Empedokles, 1986

Deathtrap, 1982 (Allen, J.)

Deathwatch, 1966 (Fields)

Débrouille-toi, 1917 (Musidora)

Deceiver, 1914 (Loos)

Decimo clandestino, 1989 (Wertmüller)

Decision before Dawn, 1952 (Spencer)

Déclassée, 1925 (Akins)

Decline of Western Civilization, 1981 (Spheeris)

Decline of Western Civilization Part II: The Metal Years, 1988 (Spheeris)

Decline of Western Civilization Part III, 1998 (Spheeris)

Decree of Destiny, 1911 (Pickford)

Dedictví aneb Kurvahošigutntag, 1992 (Chytilová)

Deep in My Heart, 1955 (Rose)

Deep in the Mirror Embedded, 1973-74 (De Hirsch)

Deep Valley, 1947 (Lupino)

Defense de savoir, 1973 (Trintignant)

Deficit, 1976/77 (Seidelman)

Dein Herz ist meine Heimat, 1953 (von Harbou)

Déjeuner des enfants, 1899/1900 (Guy)

Délibábok országa, 1983 (Mészáros)

Delicate Delinquent, 1957 (Head)

Delicious, 1931 (Levien)

Delitto di Giovanni Episcopo, 1947 (Cecchi d'Amico)

Della nube alla resistenza, 1979 (Huillet)

Delta: Ein Stück, 1977 (Export)

Démanty noci, 1964 (Krumbachová)

Déménagement see Moving In, 1993

Déménagement à la cloche de bois, 1897/98 (Guy)

Demetrius and the Gladiators, 1954 (Spencer)

Demi-Paradise, 1943 (Dillon)

Demoiselle sauvage, 1991 (Pool)

Demoiselles de Rochefort, 1967 (Varda)

Demoiselles ont en 25 ans, 1993 (Varda)

Den Allvarsamma leken, 1977 (Breien)

Den sista riddarvampyren, 1972 (Ahrne)

Denmark Grows Up, 1947 (Henning-Jensen)

Dent récalcitrante, 1902 (Guy)

Denture Adventure, 1960 (Batchelor)

Denver and Rio Grande, 1952 (Head)

Départ pour les vacances, 1904 (Guy)

Depraved see Pervertida, 1985

Der alte und der junge König, 1935 (von Harbou)

Der amerikanische Soldat, 1970 (von Trotta)

Der Angestellte, 1972 (Sanders-Brahms)

Der Augenblick des Friedens, 1965 (Duras)

Der Beginn aller Schrecken ist Liebe, 1983 (Sander)

Der Bräutigam, die Komödiantin und der Zuhälter, 1968 (Huillet)

Der brennende Acker, 1922 (von Harbou)

Der Erste Walzer, 1978 (Dörrie)

Der Fangschuss, 1976 (Brückner; von Trotta)

Der fliegende Koffer, 1921 (Reiniger)

Der Graf von Carabas, 1934 (Reiniger)

Der grosse Sprung, 1927 (Riefenstahl)

Der Hauptdarsteller, 1977 (Dörrie)

Der heilige Berg, 1926 (Riefenstahl)

Der Herrscher, 1937 (von Harbou)

Der Himmel über Berlin, 1987 (Denis)

Der kleine Schornsteinfeger, 1935 (Reiniger)

Der Kuss, 1968 (Export)

Der Läufer von Marathon, 1933 (von Harbou)

Der Leidensweg der Inge Krafft, 1921 (von Harbou)

Der Mann mit der Pranke, 1935 (von Harbou)

Der müde Tod, 1921 (von Harbou)

Der plötzliche Reichtum der armen Leute von Kombach, 1971 (von Trotta)

Der Rattenfänger von Hameln, 1918 (Reiniger)

Der scheintote Chinese, 1928 (Reiniger)

Der Stern von Bethlehem, 1921 (Reiniger)

Der subjektive Faktor, 1981 (Sander; Sanders-Brahms)

Der Tod des Empedokles, 1986 (Huillet)

Der verlorene Schatten, 1920 (Reiniger)

Der weiss Rausch, 1931 (Riefenstahl)

Der zerbrochene Krug, 1937 (von Harbou)

Derrière le mur, 1988 (Sarmiento)

Desaster, 1973 (von Trotta)

Desembarcos, 1989 (Meerapfel)

Desert Flower, 1925 (Mathis)

Desert Fury, 1947 (Head)

Desert Hearts, 1986 (Deitch)

Desert Nights, 1929 (Coffee)

Desert's Sting, 1914 (Macpherson; Meredyth)

Designing Woman, 1957 (Rose)

Desire in Motion see Mouvements du désir, 1994

Desire see Touha, 1958

Desire Me, 1947 (Akins; Irene)

Desperate Hours, 1955 (Head)

Desperate Moment, 1953 (Zetterling)

Desperately Seeking Susan, 1985 (Seidelman)

Dessert pour Constance, 1980 (Maldoror)

Dessins et merveilles, 1966 (Kaplan)

D'est, 1993 (Akerman)

Destined to Live: 100 Roads to Recovery, 1988 (Murphy)

Destroy, She Said see Détruire, dit-elle, 1969

Detective Story, 1951 (Head)

Detective's Dog, 1912 (Guy)

Détruire, dit-elle, 1969 (Duras)

Deutschen und ihre Männer, 1990 (Sander)

Deutschland, bleiche Mutter, 1980 (Sanders-Brahms)

Deux Françaises, 1915 (Musidora)

Deux Rivaux, 1903/04 (Guy)

Development of the Stalk and the Root see A szár és a gyökér fejlödése, 1961

Devil, 1908 (Macpherson)

Devil Stone, 1917 (Macpherson)

Devils, 1971 (Russell)

Devil's Brother see Fra Diavolo, 1933

Devil's Hairpin, 1957 (Head)

Devil's Imposter *see* Pope Joan, 1972

Devil's Rain, 1975 (Lupino)

Devil's Workshop *see* L'atelier du diable, 1982

Devotion, 1946 (Lupino)

Diable dans la ville, 1924 (Dulac)

Diabolique, 1996 (Littleton)

Diabolo menthe, 1977 (Kurys)

Diagonale du fou, 1983 (Guillemot; Ullmann)

Dialectique, 1966 (Guillemot)

Diálogo de exiliados *see* Dialogue d'exilés, 1974

Dialogo di Roma, 1983 (Duras)

Dialogue d'exilés, 1974 (Sarmiento)

Diamonds of the Night *see* Démanty noci, 1964

Diane of the Follies, 1916 (Gish)

Diario Regional, 1964-68 (Meerapfel)

Diary for My Children *see* **Napló gyermekeimnek**, 1982

Diary for My Father and My Mother *see* Napló apámnak, anyámnak, 1990

Diary for My Loves *see* Napló szerelmeimnek, 1987

Diary of a Mad Housewife, 1970 (Perry)

Diary of an African Nun, 1977 (Dash)

Diary of Anne Frank, 1959 (Goodrich)

Diary of Anne Frank, 1980 (Goodrich)

Diavolo nel cervello, 1972 (Cecchi d'Amico)

Dick Whittington and His Cat, 1913 (Guy)

Didn't Do It for Love, 1997 (Treut)

Difendo il mio amore, 1956 (Cecchi d'Amico)

Different Image, 1982 (Larkin)

Different Places *see* Kulonbozo helyek, 1995

Dig: A Journey into the Earth, 1972 (Hubley)

Diga sul Pacifico, 1958 (Duras)

Digging for Victory, 1942 (Batchelor)

Dimmi che fai tutto per mei, 1976 (Cecchi d'Amico)

Dinkum Bloke, 1923 (Lyell)

Dinner at Eight, 1933 (Marion)

Dinner Date, 1960 (Batchelor)

Dirty Like an Angel *see* Sale comme un ange, 1990

Dirty Mary *see* Fiancée du pirate, 1969

Dis-moi, 1980 (Akerman)

Disappearance of Aimee, 1976 (Head)

Disappearance of Nora, 1993 (Chopra)

Disbarred, 1939 (Head)

Discontent, 1916 (Weber)

Discontented Husbands, 1924 (Madison)

Disorderly Orderly, 1964 (Head)

Disputed Passage, 1939 (Head)

Disque 927, 1928 (Dulac)

Distanciamiento, 1964-68 (Meerapfel)

Dites cariatides, 1984 (Varda)

Ditte: Child of Man *see* Ditte Menneskebarn, 1946

Ditte Menneskebarn, 1946 (Henning-Jensen)

Divan à New York, 1996 (Akerman)

Divertissement, 1951-66 (Parker)

Divided Love *see* Geteilte Liebe, 1988

Divinations, 1964-67 (De Hirsch)

Divine, 1935 (Colette)

Divine Horsemen, 1951 (Deren)

Divorce Game, 1917 (Marion)

Divorce His, Divorce Hers, 1973 (Head)

Divorce Problems in Italy *see* Skilsmässoproblem i italien, 1971

Divorcee, 1919 (Guy; Mathis)

Dix heures et demie du soir en été *see* 10:30 P.M. Summer, 1966

Dny zrady, 1973 (Krumbachová)

Do-It-Yourself Democracy, 1963 (Zetterling)

Do Right and Fear No-one *see* Tue recht und scheue niemand, 1975

Doctor and the Woman, 1918 (Weber)

Doctor at Large, 1957 (Box, B.)

Doctor at Sea, 1955 (Box, B.; Dillon)

Doctor Cyclops, 1940 (Head)

Dr. Gillespie's Criminal Case, 1943 (Irene)

Dr. Holl *see* Angelika, 1951

Doctor in Clover, 1966 (Box, B.)

Doctor in Distress, 1963 (Box, B.)

Doctor in Love, 1960 (Box, B.)

Doctor in the House, 1954 (Box, B.; Dillon)

Doctor in Trouble, 1970 (Box, B.)

Dr. Mabuse, der Spieler, 1922 (von Harbou)

Dr. Paglia, 1992 (Treut)

Doctor Rhythm, 1938 (Head)

Dr. Watson's X-Rays, 1991 (Hammer)

Doctors at War, 1943 (Goodrich)

Doctor's Diary, 1937 (Head)

Documental a proposito del transito, 1971 (Gómez)

Documentary about Mass Transit *see* Documental a proposito del transito, 1971

Documenteur: An Emotion Picture, 1981 (Varda)

Does the Pill Liberate? *see* Macht die Pille Frei?, 1972

Dog Catcher *see* L'Accalappiacani, 1909

Dog Day Afternoon, 1975 (Allen, D.)

Dog in the Manger *see* El perro del hortelano, 1995

Dog Pound, 1960 (Batchelor)

Dogfight, 1991 (Savoca)

Dogs and People *see* Psi a lidé, 1971

Dog's Language *see* Colloque de chiens, 1977

Dogs of Sinai *see* Fortini/Cani, 1976

Dog's Tale: A Mexican Parable, 1986 (Leaf)

Doktor Dolittle und seine Tiere, 1928 (Reiniger)

Doktor Glas, 1967 (Zetterling)

Dokumentation, 1972 (Hein)

Dokumente zum Internationalen Aktionismus, 1988 (Export)

Dolgie provody, 1971 (Muratova)

Doll *see* Child's Sacrifice, 1910

Doll House, 1984 (Hammer)

Doll's House, 1973 (Head)

Dolly Put the Kettle On, 1947 (Batchelor)

Domenica, 1993 (Treut)

Domicile conjugal, 1970 (Guillemot)

Don Is Dead, 1973 (Head)

Don Juan, 1926 (Meredyth)

Don Quichotte, 1933 (Reiniger)

Donde voy a encontrar otra Violeta, 1973 (Mallet)

Donna Nella Resistenza, 1965 (Cavani)

Donovan's Reef, 1963 (Head)

Don't Change Your Husband, 1919 (Bauchens; Macpherson)

Don't Cry, Pretty Girls *see* Szép Iányok, ne sirjatok, 1970

Don't Ever Leave Me, 1949 (Box, B.)

Don't Forget You're Going to Die *see* N'oublie pas que tu vas mourir, 1995

Don't Give Up the Ship, 1959 (Head)

Don't Go Near the Water, 1957 (Rose)

Don't Say It *see* Petit Amour, 1988

Don't Tease the Mosquito *see* Non stuzzicate la zanzara, 1967
Doomed Caravan, 1941 (Head)
Doonesbury Special, 1977 (Hubley)
Doppelprojektion I, 1971 (Hein)
Doppelprojektion II-IV, 1972 (Hein)
Dorian Gray in spiegel der Boulevardprsse, 1984 (Ottinger)
Dornröschen, 1922 (Reiniger)
Dorothy Vernon of Haddon Hall, 1924 (Pickford)
Douaniers et contrebandiers, 1905 (Guy)
Double Harness, 1933 (Murfin)
Double Indemnity, 1944 (Head)
Double or Nothing, 1937 (Head)
Double Strength, 1978 (Hammer)
Double the Trouble, Twice the Fun, 1992 (Parmar)
Double Trouble, 1915 (Loos)
Dove siete? Io sono qui, 1993 (Cavani)
Down a Long Way, 1954 (Batchelor)
Down by Law, 1986 (Denis)
Down in the Delta, 1998 (Angelou)
Down to Earth, 1917 (Loos)
Down to the Sea in Ships, 1949 (Spencer)
Downhill Racer, 1969 (Head)
Downstairs, 1932 (Coffee)
Dragnet Girl *see* Hijosen no onna, 1933
Dragon Seed, 1944 (Irene; Murfin)
Dragons de Villars, 1900/07 (Guy)
Dragons, Dreams—and a Girl from Reality *see* Drakar, drümmar och
    en flicka från verkligheten, 1974
Dragonwyck, 1946 (Spencer)
Drakar, drümmar och en flicka från verkligheten, 1974 (Ahrne)
Dranem series, 1900/07 (Guy)
Dream, 1911 (Pickford)
Dream, 1966 (Cantrill)
Dream Age, 1979 (Hammer)
Dream Circus, 1939 (Reiniger)
Dream Girl, 1916 (Macpherson)
Dream Girl, 1948 (Head)
Dream Is What You Wake Up From, 1978 (Choy)
Dream Wife, 1953 (Rose)
Dream Woman, 1914 (Guy)
Dreamplay *see* Drømspel, 1994
Dreams for Sunday *see* Sny na nedeli, 1958
Dripping Water, 1969 (Wieland)
Drips and Strips, 1963 (Menken)
Drive to Win *see* Sha Ou, 1981
Driven from Home *see* Austreibung, 1923
Driver dagg faller Regn, 1946 (Zetterling)
Drømspel, 1994 (Ullmann)
Druides, 1906 (Guy)
Drums along the Mohawk, 1939 (Levien)
Drunkard *see* O Ébrio, 1946
Dry White Season, 1989 (Palcy)
Du Barry Was a Lady, 1943 (Irene)
Du côté de la Côte, 1958 (Varda)
Duality of Nature *see* Zweiheit der Natur, 1986
Dubliners *see* Dead, 1987
Duchess of Idaho, 1950 (Rose)
Duck Soup, 1933 (Head)
Dudes, 1987 (Spheeris)
Due mogli sono troppe, 1951 (Cecchi d'Amico)
Due vite di Mattia Pascal, 1985 (Cecchi d'Amico)

Duel in the Sun, 1946 (Gish)
Duel tragique, 1904 (Guy)
Dueña de casa *see* Femme au foyer, 1975
Duffy's Tavern, 1945 (Head)
Duie Paravise, 1928 (Notari)
Dulcy, 1923 (Loos)
Dumb Girl of Portici, 1916 (Weber)
During the Round Up, 1913 (Gish)
Dust, 1985 (Hänsel)
Dustbin Parade, 1941 (Batchelor)
Dutch Master, 1995 (Seidelman)
Duzlak, 1997 (Sander)
Dwightiana, 1957 (Menken)
Dying for a Smoke, 1966 (Batchelor)
Dying Swan *see* Mort du cygne, 1937
Dyketactics, 1974 (Hammer)
Dynamite, 1929 (Bauchens; Macpherson)
Dynamite Chicken, 1971 (Ono)

E.T.—The Extraterrestrial, 1982 (Littleton)
E' Piccarella, 1922 (Notari)
E più facile che un cammello, 1950 (Cecchi d'Amico)
E primavera, 1950 (Cecchi d'Amico)
E una Domenica sera di novembre, 1981 (Wertmüller)
Eagle's Mate, 1914 (Pickford)
Ear *see* Ucho, 1970
Early Morning at Borobudur, 1995 (Cantrill)
Early Spring *see* Barndommens gade, 1986
Earth *see* Zemlya, 1930
Earth Message, 1970 (Cantrill)
Earthquake, 1974 (Spencer)
Earthquake in Chile *see* Erdbeben in Chile, 1974
East Is West, 1922 (Marion)
East Lynne, 1925 (Coffee)
East of Shanghai *see* Rich and Strange, 1931
East Side, West Side, 1949 (Lennart; Rose)
Easter Parade, 1948 (Goodrich; Irene)
Easy Come, Easy Go, 1947 (Head)
Easy Come, Easy Go, 1967 (Head)
Easy Living, 1937 (Head)
Easy Money, 1948 (Box, M.)
Easy to Love, 1953 (Rose)
Easy to Take, 1936 (Van Upp)
Easy to Wed, 1946 (Irene)
Ebb Tide, 1937 (Head)
Ébredés, 1994 (Elek)
Echoes of a Summer, 1976 (Foster)
Eclipse, 1911 (Guy)
Economic Measures at the Time of War *see* Ta 'dabir Eghtessadi-y-
    Janghi, 1986
Écrire contre l'oubli *see* Contre l'oubli, 1991
Edison Street *see* Ulica Edisona, 1937
Edith és Marlene, 1992 (Mészáros)
Een blandt mange, 1961 (Henning-Jensen)
Een Schijntje Vrijheid, 1976 (Apon)
Een Winter in Zuiderwoude, 1994 (Apon)
Eggs, 1970 (Hubley)
Eggs, 1976 (Hammer)
Egor Bulychov i drugie, 1953 (Solntseva)
Egor Bulytchev and Others *see* Egor Bulychov i drugie, 1953
Egyszeru történet, 1975 (Elek)

Eigen Haard is Goud Waard, 1973 (Apon)
Eighties *see* Années 80, 1983
Eikon, 1969 (Cantrill)
Ein Blick—und die Liebe bricht aus, 1986 (Brückner)
Ein Familienfilm von Waltraut Lehner, 1968 (Export)
Ein ganz und gar verwahrlostes Mädchen, 1977 (Brückner)
Ein idealer Gatte, 1935 (von Harbou)
Ein Liebe en Deutschland, 1984 (Holland)
Ein Perfektes Paar oder die Unzucht wechselt ihre Haut, 1986 (Export)
Eine Frau für drei Tage, 1944 (von Harbou)
Eine Frau mit Verantwortung, 1977 (Brückner)
Eine Frau ohne Bedetung, 1936 (von Harbou)
Eine Prämie für Irene, 1971 (Sander)
Eine Reise ist eine Reise Wert, 1969 (Export)
Einleitung zu Arnold Schoenberg Begleit Musik zu einer Lichtspielscene, 1969 (Huillet)
El Cid, 1961 (Fields)
El crimen de Cuenca, 1981 (Miró)
El cuerpo repartido y el mundo al revés *see* Mensche verstreut und Welt verkehrt, 1975
El Dorado, 1967 (Brackett)
El hombre cuando es hombre, 1982 (Sarmiento)
El jardín del Edén, 1994 (Novaro)
El juego de la oca, 1965 (Miró)
El Mundo de la Mujer, 1972 (Bemberg)
El niño Raramuri *see* En el país de los pies ligeros, 1980
El pájaro de la felicidad, 1993 (Miró)
El perro del hortelano, 1995 (Miró)
Eleanor's Catch, 1916 (Madison)
Electrocutée, 1904 (Guy)
Element of Crime *see* Forbrydelsens Element, 1984
Elephant Walk, 1954 (Head)
Elisabeth und der Narr , 1934 (von Harbou)
Eliza's Horoscope, 1970 (Obomsawin)
Elle, 1995 (Sarmiento)
Elle à passe tant d'heures sous les sunlights, 1985 (Akerman)
Elle court, elle court la banliene, 1972 (Kurys)
Elmer Gantry, 1960 (Jeakins)
Elsa, 1966 (Varda)
Elsa, Elsa, 1985 (Pascal)
Elsie Haas, 1985 (Faye)
Elsie Haas: Femme peintre et cinéaste d'Haiti *see* Elsie Haas, 1985
Eltávozott nap, 1968 (Mészáros)
Emergence, 1986 (Parmar)
Emergency Squad, 1940 (Head)
Emigrants *see* Utvandrarna, 1972
Emma, 1932 (Marion)
Emmanuel Ungaro, Couturier, 1988 (Maldoror)
Emperor Waltz, 1948 (Head)
Empire Strikes Back, 1980 (Brackett)
Employee *see* Der Angestellte, 1972
Employment of the Rural Migrants in Town *see* Mohojereen Roustai, 1985
Empress, 1917 (Guy)
Empty Suitcases, 1980 (Gordon)
En avoir (ou pas), 1995 (Denis)
En classe, 1897/98 (Guy)
En cours de route *see* Utközben, 1979
En el país de los pies ligeros, 1980 (Fernández Violante)
En faction, 1902 (Guy)

En la otra isla, 1968 (Gómez)
En Passant, 1943 (Parker)
En Passion, 1969 (Ullmann)
En Rachachant, 1982 (Huillet)
Enchanted Desna *see* Zacharovannaya Desna, 1965
Enchanting Capri *see* Capri Incantevole, 1909
Enchantment, 1948 (Head)
Enchantment of the Blue Sailors *see* Betörung der blauen Matrosen, 1975
Encounter *see* Találkozás, 1963
Encounters in the Dark *see* Spotkania w mroku, 1960
End of a Clairvoyant *see* Konec jasnovidce, 1958
End of Our World *see* Koniec naszego swiata, 1963
End of the Affair, 1955 (Coffee)
End of the World in Our Usual Bed in a Night Full of Rain, 1978 (Wertmüller)
Endangered, 1988 (Hammer)
Endowing Your Future, 1957 (Allen, D.)
Ene, mene, mink, 1977 (Dörrie)
Enemy, 1927 (Booth; Gish)
Enemy Paths *see* Vrazhi tropi, 1935
Energy Picture, 1959 (Batchelor)
Enfants, 1985 (Duras)
Enfants du miracle, 1903/04 (Guy)
Enfants gâtés, 1977 (Pascal)
Engagement Party *see* Petición, 1976
Englishman and the Girl, 1910 (Pickford)
Enlèvement en automobile et mariage précipite, 1903 (Guy)
Enllsted Man's Honor, 1911 (Guy)
Enoch Arden, 1911 (Macpherson)
Enoch Arden, 1915 (Gish)
Ensemble for Somnambulists, 1951 (Deren)
Ensign Pulver, 1964 (Jeakins)
Enter Laughing, 1966 (May)
Enter Life, 1981 (Hubley)
Entotsu no mieru basho, 1953 (Tanaka)
Entre Deux Soeurs, 1990 (Leaf)
Entre el cielo y la tierre *see* Sur la terre comme au ciel, 1993
Entre nous *see* Coup de foudre, 1983
Entre tinieblas, 1983 (Pascal)
Equal Opportunity, 1982 (Leaf)
Equilibres, 1977 (Hänsel)
Equine Spy, 1912 (Guy)
Equinox Flower *see* Higanbana, 1959
Erbtöchter, 1982 (Brückner; Sanders-Brahms)
Erdbeben in Chile, 1974 (Sanders-Brahms)
Erection, 1970 (Ono)
Eros/ion, 1971 (Export)
Erotique, 1994 (Borden; Law; Treut)
Errand Boy, 1961 (Head)
Erreur de poivrot, 1904 (Guy)
Erreur judiciaire, 1899/1900 (Guy)
Erste Recht des Kindes, 1932 (von Harbou)
Erzieherin gesucht, 1950 (von Harbou)
Es Gibt Kein Vergessen *see* Desembarcos, 1989
Es hilft nicht, wo Gewalt herrscht *see* Nicht versöhnt oder Es hilft nur Gewalt, wo Gewalt herrscht, 1965
Es kommt ein Tag, 1950 (von Harbou)
Es primera vez, 1981 (Novaro)
Escalier C, 1985 (Guillemot)
Escape, 1914 (Gish)

Escape, 1937 (Bute)
Escape from Fort Bravo, 1953 (Rose)
Escape from Zahrain, 1962 (Head)
Escape Me Never, 1947 (Coffee; Lupino)
Escape of the Cat see Fuga del Gatto, 1910
Escape to Glory, 1941 (Irene)
Escape to Life, 1999 (Schiller)
Eskapade, 1936 (von Harbou)
Esmeralda, 1905 (Guy)
Esmerelda, 1915 (Pickford)
Estate violenta, 1959 (Cecchi d'Amico)
Et les Chiens se taisaient, 1977 (Maldoror)
Eternal Breasts see Chibusa yo eien nare, 1955
Eternal Flame, 1922 (Marion)
Eternal Grind, 1916 (Pickford)
Eternally Yours, 1939 (Irene; Spencer)
Étrange aventure de Lemmy Caution see Alphaville, 1965
Etude cinégraphique sur une arabesque, 1929 (Dulac)
Étude sur l'harmonie des lignes, 1935 (Parker)
Europa, Europa, 1990 (Holland)
Europeans, 1979 (Jhabvala)
Eva, 1987 (von Trotta)
Evelyn Prentice, 1934 (Coffee)
Even as You and I, 1917 (Weber)
Evening at Abdon see Wieczór u Abdona, 1974
Evening Star, 1937 (Bute)
Every Day's a Holiday, 1938 (West)
Every Girl Should Be Married, 1948 (Sharaff)
Every Other Weekend see Week-End sur deux, 1990
Every Revolution Is a Throw of the Dice see Toute révolution est un coup de dés, 1977
Everybody Rides the Carousel, 1976 (Hubley)
Everybody's All-American, 1988 (Van Runkle)
Everybody's Cheering see Take Me Out to the Ball Game, 1948
Everyday Stories see Mindennapi történetek, 1955
Everything I Have Is Yours, 1952 (Rose)
Everything's in Order but Nothing Works see Tutto a posto e niente in ordine, 1974
Eve's Secret, 1925 (Akins)
Evil Roy Slade, 1972 (Marshall)
Examination Day at School, 1910 (Pickford)
Ex-Bad Boy, 1931 (Loos)
Except the People, 1970 (Child)
Excess Baggage, 1928 (Marion)
Exchanges, 1979 (Gordon)
Exciters, 1923 (Levien)
Exclusive, 1937 (Head)
Excursion, 1968 (Menken)
Excursion a Vueltabajo, 1965 (Gómez)
Excuse My Dust, 1951 (Rose)
Executive Suite, 1954 (Rose)
Exil Shanghai, 1997 (Ottinger)
Exiles' Dialogue see Dialogue d'exilés, 1974
Experiment in Meditation, 1971 (De Hirsch)
Experiments in Three-Colour Separation, 1980 (Cantrill)
Export! Export! Export!, 1946 (Batchelor)
Export or Die, 1946 (Batchelor)
Expropiación, 1971 (Sarmiento)
Expulsion see Austreibung, 1923
Extravagance, 1915 (Madison)
Eye for an Eye, 1918 (Mathis)

Eye for an Eye see Dead Man Who Killed, 1914
Eye Music in Red Major, 1961 (Menken)
Eye of the Cat, 1969 (Head)
Eye Witness see Your Witness, 1950
Eyeblink, 1966 (Ono)
Eyes Do Not Want to Close at All Times or Perhaps One Day Rome Will Permit Herself to Choose in Her Turn, Othon see Othon, 1969
Eyes of God, 1913 (Weber)
Eyes that Could Not Close, 1913 (Guy)
Eyes That Saw see Glaza, kotorye videli, 1928
Eyewitness, 1956 (Box, M.)
Ezop, 1969 (Krumbachová)

Få mig att skratta, 1971 (Ahrne)
Fabiola, 1948 (Cecchi d'Amico)
Facciamo paradiso, 1995 (Cecchi d'Amico)
Face, 1997 (Bird)
Face at the Window, 1912 (Guy)
Face Between, 1922 (Coffee)
Face in the Rain, 1963 (Fields)
Face of a Stranger, 1991 (Weill)
Face of Hope, 1991 (Chytilová)
Face of the Enemy see Fashizm budet razbit, 1941
Face to Face see Ansikte mot ansikte, 1976
Faces see Anskiter, 1969
Faces in the Dark, 1960 (Zetterling)
Facial Grimaces see Gesichtsgrimassen, 1968
Facing a Family, 1971 (Export)
Facts of Life, 1960 (Head)
Facts of Love see 29 Acacia Avenue, 1945
Faded Lilies, 1909 (Macpherson; Pickford)
Fad'jal, 1979 (Faye)
Fahrt ins Glück, 1948 (von Harbou)
Faim ... L' occasion ... L'herbe tendre, 1904 (Guy)
Fair Dentist, 1911 (Pickford)
Fairy of Borgo Loreto see Fata di Borgo Loreto, 1924
Fait d'hiver, 1981 (Kaplan)
Faith of Her Fathers, 1915 (Madison)
Faithful in My Fashion, 1946 (Irene)
Fall of Eve, 1929 (Loos)
Fall of the Romanov Dynasty see Padenye dinastii romanovykh, 1927
Fallen Champ: The Untold Story of Mike Tyson, 1993 (Kopple)
Fallen Hero, 1913 (Loos)
Falling Bodies, 1967 (Schneemann)
Falling Leaves, 1912 (Guy)
Fälschung, 1981 (von Trotta)
False Colors, 1914 (Marion; Weber)
False Witness see Fälschung, 1981
Famille et Variations, 1977 (Poirier)
Family see Città violenta, 1970
Family Business, 1984 (Akerman)
Family Film by Waltraud Lehner see Ein Familienfilm von Waltraut Lehner, 1968
Family Jewels, 1965 (Head)
Family Plot, 1976 (Head)
Famous Mrs. Fair, 1923 (Marion)
Fanchon, the Cricket, 1915 (Marion; Pickford)
Fancy Pants, 1950 (Head)
Fanny Hill, 1968 (Ahrne)
Fantasia 'e Surdata, 1927 (Notari)
Fantassin Guignard, 1905 (Guy)

Far from Poland, 1981 (Godmilow)
Far from Vietnam *see* Loin du Vietnam, 1967
Far Horizon, 1955 (Head)
Far Paradise, 1928 (McDonagh Sisters)
Far Shore, 1976 (Wieland)
Farahang-e-Massraffi, 1984 (Bani-Etemad)
Farces de cuisinière, 1902 (Guy)
Farces de Jocko, 1897/98 (Guy)
Farewell *see* Proschanie s Matyoroy, 1981
Farewell China *see* Ai zai biexiang de jijie, 1990
Farewell, My Dear, Farewell...the Army Is Going *see* Addio Mia Bella
    Addio, l'Armata se ne va, 1915
Farewell to Arms, 1932 (Head)
Farewell to Matyora *see* Proschanie s Matyoroy, 1981
Farewell to the Devil *see* Pozegnanie z diablem, 1956
Farmer Charley, 1946-49 (Batchelor)
Farmer's Daughter, 1940 (Head)
Fascination of the Fleur de Lis, 1915 (Madison; Meredyth)
Fascism Will Be Destroyed *see* Fashizm budet razbit, 1941
Fashions for Women, 1927 (Arzner)
Fashizm budet razbit, 1941 (Shub)
Fast Times at Ridgemont High, 1982 (Heckerling)
Fat City, 1972 (Booth; Jeakins)
Fata di Borgo Loreto, 1924 (Notari)
Fatal Dress Suit, 1914 (Loos)
Fatal Finger Prints, 1915 (Loos)
Fatal Hour, 1908 (Macpherson)
Fatal Wedding, 1911 (Lyell)
Fate, 1966 (Cecchi d'Amico)
Fate's Inception, 1912 (Pickford)
Father and Son *see* Vater und Sohn, 1983
Father Brown, Detective, 1935 (Head)
Father Gets in the Game, 1908 (Macpherson)
Father of the Bride, 1950 (Goodrich; Rose)
Father's Bride, 1914 (Meredyth)
Father's Little Dividend, 1951 (Goodrich; Rose)
Fatso, 1980 (Murphy)
Fatto di sangue fra due uomini per causa di una vedova, 1978
    (Wertmüller)
Faucets, 1960 (Menken)
Faunovo prilis pozdni odpoledne, 1983 (Chytilová; Krumbachová)
Faust, 1900/07 (Guy)
Faust et Méphistophélès, 1903 (Guy)
Faut vivre dangereusement, 1975 (Kaplan)
Faute des autres, 1953 (Guillemot)
Fear Strikes Out, 1957 (Head)
Feast and the Law *see* 'A Legge, 1920
Feast of Life, 1916 (Marion)
Febbre di vivere, 1953 (Cecchi d'Amico)
Fedka's Truth, 1925 (Preobrazhenskaya)
Fée au printemps, 1906 (Guy)
Fée aux choux, 1896 (Guy)
Feet of Clay, 1924 (Bauchens)
Fei Tien, Goddess in Flight, 1983 (Choy)
Feira, 1968 (Carolina)
Felicité, 1979 (Pascal)
Felix, 1987 (Sander; Sanders-Brahms; von Trotta)
Fem dagar i Falköping, 1973 (Ahrne)
Female Artillery, 1973 (Lupino)
Female Closet, 1997 (Hammer)
Female Misbehavior, 1992 (Treut)

Female of the Species, 1912 (Pickford; Weber)
Femeile zilelor noastre, 1958 (Mészáros)
Feminist and the Fuzz, 1971 (Marshall)
Femme au foyer, 1975 (Sarmiento)
Femme de l'amant, 1991 (Pascal)
Femme de l'hôtel, 1984 (Pool)
Femme du Ganges, 1974 (Duras)
Femme est une femme, 1961 (Guillemot)
Femme mariée, 1964 (Guillemot)
Fenesta che Lucive, 1914 (Notari)
Feng Jie, 1979 (Hui)
Fer à cheval, 1915 (Musidora)
Ferai, 1970 (Ahrne)
Festök városa—Szentendre, 1964 (Mészáros)
Fête espagnole, 1919 (Dulac)
Fetus *see* A Magzat, 1993
Feu de paille, 1939 (Epstein)
Feud, 1914 (Madison)
Feud in the Kentucky Hills, 1912 (Pickford)
Fever *see* Goraczka, 1981
Fever: The Story of the Bomb *see* Goraczka, 1981
Fiançailles d'Agenor, 1916 (Musidora)
Fiancé ensorcelé, 1903 (Guy)
Fiancée du pirate, 1969 (Kaplan)
Fiancés de 1914, 1914 (Musidora)
Fica Comigo, 1997 (Yamasaki)
Fidgety Little Bouton *see* O neposedném knoflícku, 1975
Field Study #2, 1988 (Nelson)
Fiery Introduction, 1915 (Madison)
Fiesta, 1947 (Irene)
Fifi tambour, 1915 (Musidora)
Fifteen Minutes on Fifteen Years *see* 15 perc 15 évröl, 1965
Fifth Horseman Is Fear *see* ... a pátý jezdec je Strach, 1964
Fight for Your Lady, 1937 (Lupino)
Fighting Breed, 1921 (Meredyth)
Fighting Shepherdess, 1920 (Coffee)
Figlia del Vesuvio, 1912 (Notari)
Figlio del Reggimento, 1915 (Notari)
Figure behind the Glass, 1986 (Krumbachová)
Figurehead, 1953 (Batchelor)
File on Thelma Jordan, 1950 (Head)
Fille à la dérive, 1964 (Guillemot)
Fille d'Eve, 1916 (Musidora)
Fille Galante *see* Fugueuses, 1995
Filles c'est pas pareil, 1974 (Poirier)
Filles du Roi, 1974 (Poirier)
Filling the Gap, 1941 (Batchelor)
Film à venir, 1997 (Sarmiento)
Film about a Woman Who..., 1974 (Rainer)
**Film d'amore e d'anarchia, ovvero stamattina alle 10 in Via dei
    fiori nella nota casa di toleranza**, 1973 (Wertmüller)
Film in the Future *see* Film à venir, 1997
Film No. 4, 1966 (Ono)
Film No. 5, 1968 (Ono)
Film No. 6, 1969 (Ono)
Film of Love and Anarchy, or This Morning at Ten in the Via dei fiori
    at the Well-Known House of Tolerance *see* **Film d'amore e
    d'anarchia, ovvero stamattina alle 10 in Via dei fiori nella nota
    casa di toleranza**, 1973
Filmraum: Reproduktionsimmanente Ästhetik, 1970 (Hein)
Filmstatement, 1982 (Davis)

Fils du garde-chasse, 1906 (Guy)

Fin des étés, 1964 (Poirier)

Finanzen des Grossherzogs, 1924 (von Harbou)

Fine Clothes, 1925 (Booth)

Fine del mondo in una notte piena di poggia *see* End of the World in Our Usual Bed in a Night Full of Rain, 1978

Fine e nota, 1993 (Cecchi d'Amico)

Finestra sul Luna Park, 1956 (Cecchi d'Amico)

Finian's Rainbow, 1968 (Jeakins)

Finnegan Begin Again, 1985 (Silver)

Finnegans Wake, 1965 (Bute; Schoonmaker)

Fiole enchantée, 1902 (Guy)

Fire, 1996 (Mehta)

Fire in the Straw *see* Feu de paille, 1939

Firefly, 1937 (Goodrich)

Fires of Conscience, 1916 (Shipman)

Fires Within, 1991 (Armstrong)

First Born, 1928 (Reville)

First Cigarette *see* Première Cigarette, 1904

First Comes Courage, 1943 (Arzner)

First Comes Love, 1991 (Friedrich)

First Line of Defence, 1947 (Batchelor)

First Love, 1921 (Levien)

First Misunderstanding, 1911 (Pickford)

First Ninety-Nine, 1958 (Batchelor)

First of the Few, 1942 (Dillon)

First Voyage *see* Premier voyage, 1980

First Waltz *see* Der Erste Walzer, 1978

First Year, 1926 (Marion)

Fish in the Bathtub, 1998 (Silver)

Fisher Folks, 1911 (Macpherson)

Fisher-maid, 1911 (Pickford)

Fisher's Ghost, 1924 (Lyell)

Fitzwilly, 1967 (Lennart)

Five, 1970 (Batchelor)

Five and Ten, 1931 (Booth)

Five Angles on Murder *see* Woman in Question, 1950

Five Artists: BillBobBillBillBob, 1971 (Nelson)

Five Corners, 1988 (Foster)

Five Days in Falköping *see* Fem dagar i Falköping, 1973

Five Finger Discount, 1979 (Murphy)

Five Finger Exercise, 1962 (Goodrich)

Five Graves to Cairo, 1943 (Head)

Five Out of Five, 1986 (Chenzira)

Five Pennies, 1959 (Head)

Five Pound Man, 1937 (Dillon)

Five Women around Utamaro *see* Utamaro o mehuri go-nin no onna, 1946

Fixer, 1968 (Jeakins)

Fjols til Fjells, 1957 (Ullmann)

Flag Passes By *see* Passa a Bandiera, 1930

Flamboyant Ladies Speak Out, 1982 (Chenzira)

Flame and the Flesh, 1954 (Rose)

Flame of the West, 1918 (Madison)

Flaming Forties, 1925 (Marion)

Flaming Years *see* Povest plamennykh let, 1961

Flamme cachée, 1920 (Colette; Musidora)

Flapper, 1920 (Marion)

Flapper Wives, 1924 (Murfin)

Flash of Light, 1910 (Macpherson)

Fleay's Fauna Centre, 1994 (Leaf)

Fleet's In, 1942 (Head)

Flemish Farm, 1943 (Craigie)

Flesh and Blood, 1912 (Guy)

Flesh and Fantasy, 1943 (Head)

Flesh and Paper, 1990 (Parmar)

Flesh Will Surrender *see* Delitto di Giovanni Episcopo, 1947

Flickor, kvinnor och en och annan drake, 1997 (Ahrne)

Flickorna, 1968 (Zetterling)

Flight for Freedom, 1943 (Murfin)

Flight of a Nightbird, 1915 (Madison)

Flim-Flam Man, 1967 (Jeakins)

Flirt, 1916 (Weber)

Flirting with Fate, 1916 (Gish)

Floating Life, 1996 (Law)

Floterian—Hand Printings from a Film History, 1981 (Cantrill)

Flower Drum Song, 1961 (Sharaff)

Flowing *see* Nagareru, 1956

Flügel und Fesseln, 1984 (Sanders-Brahms)

Flu-ing Squad, 1951 (Batchelor)

Flurina, 1970 (Batchelor)

Flurry in Art, 1914 (Loos)

Fly, 1970 (Ono)

Fly about the House, 1949 (Batchelor)

Flying Blind, 1941 (Head)

Flying Coffer *see* Der fliegende Koffer, 1921

Flying Down to Rio, 1933 (Irene)

Flyktingar finner en hamn, 1945 (Henning-Jensen)

Fog Pumas, 1967 (Nelson)

Fogo, Ile de Feu, 1977 (Maldoror)

Folie des vaillants, 1925 (Dulac)

Folies Bergère, 1935 (Meredyth)

Folies douces, 1978 (Guillemot)

Folies Masquées series, 1901 (Guy)

Folketingsvalg 1945, 1945 (Henning-Jensen)

Follow Me, Boys!, 1966 (Gish)

Follow that Car, 1964 (Batchelor)

Follow the Leader, 1930 (Head)

Folly of Anne, 1914 (Gish)

Fonderies Martin, 1936-39 (Parker)

Fong Sai-Yuk, 1993 (Hui)

Foo-Foo Series, 1960 (Batchelor)

Food of the Gods, 1976 (Lupino)

Fool and His Money, 1914 (Weber)

Fool Killer, 1965 (Jeakins)

Fool's Highway, 1924 (Coffee)

Fools in the Mountains *see* Fjols til Fjells, 1957

Fool's Paradise, 1921 (Bauchens)

Foot Film *see* Volleyball, 1967

Footsteps in the Fog, 1955 (Coffee)

For Alimony Only, 1926 (Coffee)

For Better, for Worse, 1919 (Bauchens; Macpherson)

For Better for Worse, 1959 (Batchelor)

"For George, Love Donna", 1975 (Deitch)

For Her Brother's Sake, 1911 (Pickford)

For Her Father's Sins, 1913 (Loos)

For Husbands Only, 1917 (Weber)

For Pete's Sake, 1974 (Streisand)

For Sasha *see* Pour Sacha, 1992

For the First Time *see* Es primera vez, 1981

For the Queen's Honor, 1911 (Pickford)

For the Soul of Rafael, 1920 (Coffee)

For Whom the Bell Tolls, 1943 (Head)
Forbidden, 1919 (Weber)
Forbidden Country, 1934 (Reville)
Forbidden Fruit, 1921 (Bauchens; Macpherson)
Forbidden Planet, 1956 (Rose)
Forbidden Room, 1914 (Meredyth)
Forbidden to Know see Defense de savoir, 1973
Forbidden Woman, 1920 (Coffee)
Forbrydelsens Element, 1984 (Henning-Jensen)
Forced Landing, 1941 (Head)
Foreign Affair, 1948 (Head)
Foreign Correspondent, 1940 (Harrison; Spencer)
Foreign Currency see Poul-e Khareji, 1990
Forever and a Day, 1943 (Lupino)
Forever Female, 1953 (Head)
Forfølgelscn, 1981 (Breien)
Forgery see Fälschung, 1981
Forget-Me-Not, 1917 (Marion)
Forlorn River, 1937 (Head)
Fortini/Cani, 1976 (Huillet)
Fortuna di essere donna, 1956 (Cecchi d'Amico)
Fortune Cookies: The Myth of the Model Minority, 1989 (Choy)
Fortune Hunters, 1913 (Guy)
Forward, Savoia see Sempre Avanti Savoia, 1915
Foto-Film, 1970 (Hein)
Fou de Mai, 1977 (Serreau)
Foundling, 1916 (Marion; Pickford)
Fountain, 1934 (Murfin)
Four around a Woman see Kämpfende Herzen, 1921
Four Chimneys see Entotsu no mieru basho, 1953
Four Daughters, 1938 (Coffee)
Four Frightened People, 1934 (Bauchens; Coffee)
Four Horsemen of the Apocalypse, 1921 (Mathis)
Four Hours to Kill, 1935 (Head)
Four Men and a Prayer, 1938 (Levien)
Four Rooms, 1995 (Anders)
Four Women, 1975 (Dash)
Fourberies de Pingouin, 1916 (Musidora)
Fourteen Hours, 1951 (Spencer)
Fourteen's Good, Eighteen's Better, 1980 (Armstrong)
Fowl Play, 1950 (Batchelor)
Fox and the Tiger, 1986 (Leaf)
Foxes, 1980 (Foster)
Foxes, Mice and Gallows Hill see Lišáci-myšáci a Šibenicák, 1970
Fra Diavolo, 1912 (Guy)
Fra Diavolo, 1933 (Macpherson)
Fragilité—ton nom est femme, 1965 (Trintignant)
Fragments, 1971 (Cantrill)
Frame Line, 1984 (Nelson)
Francesco, 1988 (Cavani)
Francesco d'Assisi, 1966 (Cavani)
Frank Capra's American Dream, 1997 (Heckerling)
Franz Schubert's Last Three Sonatas see Trois dernières sonatas de Franz Shubert, 1989
Fratelli sole, sorella luna, 1972 (Wertmüller; Cecchi d'Amico)
Frau am Scheidewege, 1938 (von Harbou)
Frau im Mond, 1929 (von Harbou)
Frauen von Gnadenstein, 1921 (von Harbou)
Freak Orlando, 1981 (Ottinger)
Freaky Friday, 1976 (Foster)
Fredaines de Pierrette series, 1900 (Guy)

Free Breathing see Szabad lélegzet, 1973
Freedom, 1971 (Ono)
Freedom Radio, 1940 (Dillon)
French Doll, 1923 (Marion)
French Downstairs, 1916 (Weber)
French Dressing, 1963 (Russell)
French Game see Coeur battant, 1962
French Milliner, 1916 (Loos)
French Postcards, 1979 (Littleton)
French without Tears, 1939 (Dillon; Head)
Frenzy see Hets, 1944
Fresh Seeds in a Big Apple, 1975 (Choy)
Freundin see Amiga, 1988
Frida Kahlo, 1971 (Fernández Violante)
Friday, the 13th, 1916 (Marion)
Frieda, 1947 (Zetterling)
Friendly, 1990 (Coolidge)
Friendly Persuasion, 1956 (Jeakins)
Friends, 1912 (Pickford)
Friends and Husbands see Heller Wahn, 1983
Friends and Lovers, 1931 (Murfin)
Frightened Bride see Tall Headlines, 1952
Frightening Women see Unheimlichen Frauen, 1992
Frihetens murar, 1978 (Ahrne)
Frivolité, 1901 (Guy)
Frog Prince, 1954 (Reiniger)
Frog Prince, 1961 (Reiniger)
From Here to Eternity see Verdammt in alle Ewigkeit, 1978-79
From Rags to Stitches, 1944 (Batchelor)
From Spikes to Spindles, 1976 (Choy)
From the Bottom of the Sea, 1911 (Pickford)
From the Cloud to the Resistance see Della nube alla resistenza, 1979
From the Terrace, 1960 (Spencer)
Frontier see Aerograd, 1935
Frontiersman, 1938 (Head)
Frozen Justice, 1928 (Levien)
Fruit Bowl see Yes! Yi zu, 1990
Fruit of Paradise see Ovoce stromu rajských jíme, 1969
Fruit Punch see Yes! Yi zu, 1990
Fruits amers, 1966 (Audry)
Fruits de saison, 1902 (Guy)
Fud 69, 1969 (Cantrill)
Fuegos, 1987 (Guillemot)
Fuerchten und Liebe see Paura e amore, 1988
Fuga del Gatto, 1910 (Notari)
Fugitive Lovers, 1934 (Goodrich)
Fugitives Find Shelter see Flyktingar finner en hamn, 1945
Fugueuses, 1995 (Trintignant)
Full Rich Life see Cynthia, 1947
Fumées, 1951-66 (Parker)
Fun in Acapulco, 1963 (Head)
Fun with Music see Polka Graph, 1947
Funfair Has Arrived see Prijela k nám pout, 1973
Funny Face, 1957 (Head)
Funny Girl, 1968 (Lennart; Sharaff; Streisand)
Funny Lady, 1975 (Allen, J.; Booth; Streisand)
Furies, 1930 (Akins)
Furies, 1950 (Head)
Fuses, 1967 (Schneemann)
Fusils pour Banta, 1970 (Maldoror)
Fussball, 1972 (Hein)

Fusswaschung, 1986 (Hein)
Future of Emily see Flügel und Fesseln, 1984
Future of Saint Denis see Saint-Denis sur Avenir, 1971
Fuzz, 1972 (Jeakins)

G.I. Blues, 1960 (Head)
G-Man, 1978 (B)
Gable and Lombard, 1976 (Head)
Gabriel Goes to the City, 1979 (Obomsawin)
Gabriele il Lampionaio di Porto, 1919 (Notari)
Gaby, 1956 (Goodrich; Rose)
Gaby: A True Story, 1987 (Ullmann)
Gage d'amour, 1904 (Guy)
Gaiety George, 1946 (Sagan)
Gaijin: Caminhos da Liberdade, 1980 (Yamasaki)
Gaines Roussel, 1936-39 (Parker)
Galathea, 1935 (Reiniger)
Galaxy, 1963 (Cantrill)
Galileo, 1968 (Cavani)
Gallant Little Tailor, 1954 (Reiniger)
Gambling Ship, 1933 (Head)
Game, 1972 (Child)
Game for Six Lovers see L'Eau à la bouche, 1960
Game of Love see Blé en herbe, 1953
Games of Love and Loneliness see Den Allvarsamma leken, 1977
Gangsters of New York, 1914 (Loos)
Garbo Talks, 1984 (Comden)
Garce, 1984 (Pascal)
Garçonne, 1957 (Audry)
Garden of Eden see El jardín del Edén, 1994
Gardener, 1960 (Batchelor)
Gardener's Son, 1977 (von Brandenstein)
Garrison's Finish, 1923 (Pickford)
Gary Cooper que estás en los cielos, 1981 (Miró)
Gas Food Lodging, 1992 (Anders)
Gaslight, 1944 (Irene)
Gasoline Engagement, 1911 (Pickford)
Gates of the Forest, 1980 (Ullmann)
Gathering of Eagles, 1963 (Irene)
Gattin, 1943 (von Harbou)
Gattopardo, 1963 (Cecchi d'Amico)
Gaucho, 1927 (Pickford)
Gauloises bleues, 1968 (Guillemot)
Gaunt Stranger see Ringer, 1952
Gavotte, 1902 (Guy)
Gay Day, 1974 (Hammer)
Gay Deceiver, 1926 (Booth)
Gay Desperado, 1936 (Lupino; Pickford)
Gay Mrs. Trexel see Susan and God, 1940
Gay Sisters, 1942 (Coffee; Head)
Gayosso de descuentos, 1968 (Fernández Violante)
Gaz, 1936-39 (Parker)
Gaz de Lacq, 1960 (Guillemot)
Gazebo, 1960 (Rose)
Gebroken Spiegels, 1984 (Gorris)
Gefährten meines Sommers, 1943 (von Harbou)
Geisha Boy, 1958 (Head)
Geisha in the Old City see Jotai wa kanashiku, 1957
Geld, 1989 (Dörrie)
Gendarmes, 1907 (Guy)
Généalogies d'une crime, 1997 (Sarmiento)

General's Daughter see De todos modos Juan te llamas, 1975
Generation of the Railroad Builder, 1975 (Choy)
Genitalpanik, 1969 (Export)
Gennariello il Figlio del Galeotto, 1921 (Notari)
Gennariello Polizziotto, 1921 (Notari)
Genroku onna, 1924 (Tanaka)
Gens de toutes partes, Gens de nulle parte, 1980 (Sarmiento)
Gente de todas partes ... Gente de ninguna parte see Gens de toutes partes, Gens de nulle parte, 1980
Gentle Arm see Street Corner, 1953
Gentle Sex, 1943 (Dillon)
Gentleman or Thief, 1913 (Loos)
Gentleman's Agreement, 1918 (Shipman)
Gentlemen Boys see Páni kluci, 1975
Gentlemen Marry Brunettes, 1955 (Loos)
Gentlemen Prefer Blondes, 1928 (Loos)
Gentlemen Prefer Blondes, 1953 (Loos)
Gently down the Stream, 1981 (Friedrich)
Genus: The Life of Jitka and Kveta Válovy see Genus: Zivot Jitky a Kvety Válových, 1995
Genus: The Live of Theater Maker Ota Ornest see Genus: Zivot divadelníka Oty Ornesta, 1995
Genus: Zivot divadelníka Oty Ornesta, 1995 (Krumbachová)
Genus: Zivot Jitky a Kvety Válových, 1995 (Krumbachová)
Géo le mystérieux, 1916 (Dulac)
Geography of the Body, 1943 (Menken)
Geole, 1921 (Musidora)
Geometrics of the Kabballah, 1975 (De Hirsch)
Georgia, Georgia, 1972 (Angelou)
Georgina's Gründe, 1974 (von Trotta)
German Sisters see **Bleierne Zeit**, 1981
Germans and Their Men see Deutschen und ihre Männer, 1990
Germany, Pale Mother see **Deutschland, bleiche Mutter**, 1980
Germination d'un haricot, 1928 (Dulac)
Geronimo, 1939 (Head)
Geschichte des Prinzen Achmed, 1923-26 (Reiniger)
Geschichte eines Lebens see Annelie, 1941<
Geschichtsunterricht, 1972 (Huillet)
Gesichtsgrimassen, 1968 (Export)
Gestohlene Herz, 1934 (Reiniger)
Gesu' mio Fratello, 1965 (Cavani)
Get a Lawyer see Mettete l'Avvocato, 1925
Get Shorty, 1995 (Marshall)
Get Your Man, 1927 (Arzner)
Geteilte Liebe, 1988 (Sanders-Brahms)
Getting Away with Murder, 1996 (Marshall)
Getting Even, 1909 (Pickford)
Getting It Over With, 1977 (Heckerling)
Getting Mary Married, 1919 (Loos)
Getting to Know the World see Poznavaya belyi svet, 1979
Getúlio Vargas, 1974 (Carolina)
Gewalt, 1971 (Sanders-Brahms)
Ghost and Mrs. Muir, 1947 (Spencer)
Ghost Breaker, 1914 (Macpherson)
Ghost Breakers, 1940 (Head)
Ghost Camera, 1933 (Lupino)
Gibson Goddess, 1909 (Pickford)
Gift of Green, 1946 (van Dongen)
Giftas, 1956 (Zetterling)
Gigi, 1949 (Audry; Colette)
Gigi, 1958 (Colette)

Gilda, 1946 (Van Upp)
Gilded Cage, 1916 (Marion)
Ginger Mick, 1920 (Lyell)
Ginza Cosmetics *see* Ginza gesho, 1951
Ginza gesho, 1951 (Tanaka)
Giorno Della Pace, 1965 (Cavani)
Giovanni, 1983 (Apon)
Girl *see* Eltávozott nap, 1968
Girl and the Bronco Buster, 1911 (Guy)
Girl Crazy, 1943 (Sharaff)
Girl from Beyond, 1918 (Shipman)
Girl from God's Country, 1921 (Shipman)
Girl from Missouri, 1934 (Loos)
Girl from Nowhere, 1919 (Madison)
Girl from Scotland Yard, 1937 (Head)
Girl in a Million, 1946 (Box, M.)
Girl in Lower 9, 1916 (Madison)
Girl in Mourning *see* Niña de luto, 1964
Girl in Overalls *see* Swing Shift Maisie, 1943
Girl in the Armchair, 1912 (Guy)
Girl in the Painting *see* Portrait from Life, 1948
Girl in the Shack, 1914 (Loos)
Girl in White, 1952 (Rose)
Girl Named Tamiko, 1962 (Head)
Girl Next Door, 1953 (Lennart)
Girl of the Golden West, 1915 (Macpherson)
Girl of Yesterday, 1915 (Marion; Pickford)
Girl Rush, 1955 (Head)
Girl Was Young *see* Young and Innocent, 1937
Girl Who Had Everything, 1953 (Rose)
Girl Who Lost, 1917 (Madison)
Girl with the Green Eyes, 1916 (Guy)
Girlfriends *see* Amiche, 1955
Girlfriends, 1978 (von Brandenstein; Weill)
Girls *see* Flickorna, 1968
Girls about Town, 1931 (Akins)
Girls at 12, 1975 (Chopra)
Girl's Folly, 1917 (Marion)
Girls from Wilko *see* Panny z Wilka, 1979
Girls! Girls! Girls!, 1962 (Head)
Girls in Uniform *see* **Mädchen in Uniform**, 1931
Girls of the Night *see* Onna bakari no yoru, 1961
Girl's Own Story, 1984 (Campion)
Girls, Women—and Once in a While a Dragon *see* Flickor, kvinnor
    och en och annan drake, 1997
Give a Girl a Break, 1953 (Goodrich; Rose)
Give Me a Sailor, 1938 (Head)
Give Peace a Chance *see* Bed-In, 1969
Glamour Boy, 1941 (Head)
Glass Key, 1935 (Head)
Glass Key, 1942 (Head)
Glass Slipper, 1954 (Rose)
Glaza, kotorye videli, 1928 (Solntseva)
Gli indifferenti, 1963 (Cecchi d'Amico)
Glimpse of the Garden, 1957 (Menken)
Global Gamble, 1986 (Kidron)
Gloria ai Caduti, 1916 (Notari)
Glory Alley, 1952 (Rose)
Glory to the Fallen Soldiers *see* Gloria ai Caduti, 1916
Gnesella, 1918 (Notari)
Go-Between, 1971 (Dillon)

Go Between, 1982 (Choy)
Go! Go! Go!, 1963 (Menken)
Go Naked in the World, 1961 (Rose)
Go West, Young Man, 1936 (West)
Goat, 1918 (Marion)
God Bless America, 1973 (Hein)
Godfather, Part II, 1974 (Van Runkle)
Godless Girl, 1929 (Bauchens; Macpherson)
God's Country and the Woman, 1916 (Shipman)
Goin' to Town, 1935 (West)
Going Hollywood, 1933 (Marion)
Going My Way, 1944 (Head)
Gold and Glitter, 1912 (Gish)
Gold Diggers, 1983 (Potter)
Gold Fugue, 1971 (Cantrill)
Gold Madness, 1923 (Madison)
Gold Necklace, 1910 (Pickford)
Gold of the Seven Saints, 1961 (Brackett)
Golden Autumn, 1983 (Peng)
Golden Bed, 1925 (Bauchens; Head; Macpherson)
Golden Chance, 1915 (Macpherson)
Golden Eighties *see* Window Shopping, 1986
Golden Gate *see* Zolotye vorota, 1969
Golden Gloves, 1940 (Head)
Golden Yukon, 1927 (Shipman)
Goldene Gans, 1944 (Reiniger)
Goldie Gets Along, 1933 (Irene)
Golhayeh Davoodi, 1983 (Bani-Etemad)
Golpe de suerte, 1991 (Fernández Violante)
Golven, 1982 (Apon)
Gongola, 1979 (Hänsel)
Goob na nu, 1979 (Faye)
Good Earth, 1937 (Marion)
Good Fellows, 1943 (Head)
Good Girls Go to Paris, 1939 (Coffee)
Good King Wenceslas, 1946 (Batchelor)
Good Little Devil, 1914 (Pickford)
Good Morning, Beijing *see* Beijing Nin Zao, 1991
Good News, 1930 (Marion)
Good News, 1947 (Comden; Rose)
Good Time Girl, 1950 (Box, M.)
Good-bye-Bill, 1918 (Loos)
Goodbye Charlie, 1964 (Rose)
Goodbye Girl, 1977 (Booth)
Goodbye in the Mirror, 1964 (De Hirsch)
Good-bye, Lover, 1997 (Van Runkle)
Goodbye Sadness, 1982 (Ono)
Good-bye Yesterday, 1979 (Peng)
GoodFellas, 1990 (Schoonmaker)
Goodwill to All Dogs, 1960 (Batchelor)
Goraca linia, 1965 (Jakubowska)
Goraczka, 1981 (Holland)
Gossette, 1923 (Dulac)
Gott om pojkar—ont om män?, 1995 (Ahrne)
Götter der Pest, 1969 (von Trotta)
Grace of My Heart, 1996 (Anders; Schoonmaker)
Gracie Allen Murder Case, 1939 (Head)
Grain, 1936 (Preobrazhenskaya)
Grain of the Voice Series: Rock Wallaby and Blackbird, 1980 (Cantrill)
Grand amour de Balzac, 1972 (Audry)
Grand Canyon, 1991 (Littleton)

Grand chemin, 1987 (Pascal)
Grand Concert, 1960 (Batchelor)
Grand Duke's Finances *see* Finanzen des Grossherzogs, 1924
Grand Highway *see* Grand chemin, 1987
Grand Jury Secrets, 1939 (Head)
Grand Larceny, 1922 (Meredyth)
Grand Matin, 1975 (Guillemot)
Grand Souffle, 1915 (Musidora)
Grande espérance, 1953 (Epstein)
Grandes événements et des gens ordinaires: les élections, 1979
    (Sarmiento)
Grandfather's Journey *see* Morfars Resa, 1993
Grand-père raconte *see* Fad'jal, 1979
Grands chemins, 1963 (Trintignant)
Grands Feux, 1936-39 (Parker)
Grasshopper, 1970 (Marshall)
Grasshopper and the Ant, 1954 (Reiniger)
Graustark, 1925 (Coffee; Marion)
Graziella, 1954 (Cecchi d'Amico)
Great Adventure, 1918 (Guy)
Great Big World and Little Children *see* Wielka Wielksza
    Najwielksza, 1962
Great Caruso, 1951 (Levien; Rose)
Great Chase, 1963 (Gish)
Great Divide, 1924 (Coffee)
Great Gambini, 1937 (Head)
Great Gatsby, 1949 (Head)
Great Goddess, 1977 (Hammer)
Great Hospital Mystery, 1937 (Meredyth)
Great Lie, 1941 (Coffee)
Great Love, 1918 (Gish)
Great Love Experiment, 1984 (Weill)
Great Lover, 1949 (Head)
Great Man's Lady, 1942 (Head)
Great McGinty, 1940 (Head)
Great Meadow, 1931 (Bauchens)
Great Moment, 1920 (Glyn)
Great Moment, 1944 (Head)
Great Moments in Aviation, 1993 (Kidron)
Great Parade of the Fleet *see* Rivista Navale Dell' 11 Novembre 1912,
    1912
Great Race, 1965 (Head)
Great Radium Mystery, 1919-20 (Madison)
Great Road *see* Veliky put', 1927
Great Sinner, 1949 (Irene)
Great Victor Herbert, 1939 (Head)
Great Waldo Pepper, 1975 (Head)
Great Wall of Los Angeles, 1978 (Deitch)
Great White Hope, 1970 (Sharaff)
Greater Glory, 1926 (Mathis)
Greater Love Hath No Man, 1915 (Guy)
Greatest Question, 1919 (Gish)
Greatest Show on Earth, 1952 (Bauchens; Head)
Greatest Show on Earth, 1952 (Jeakins)
Greatest Thing in Life, 1918 (Gish)
Greed, 1923 (Mathis)
Greeks Had a Word for Them, 1932 (Akins)
Green Dolphin Street, 1947 (Irene)
Green-Eyed Devil, 1914 (Gish)
Green-Eyed Woman *see* Take a Letter, Darling, 1942
Green Fire, 1954 (Rose)

Green Hell, 1940 (Marion)
Green Mansions, 1959 (Jeakins)
Green Planet *see* Belle verte, 1996
Green Years, 1946 (Irene; Levien)
Greenwich Village, 1944 (Comden)
Greetings from Washington, D.C., 1981 (Schiller)
Greta's Girls, 1977 (Schiller)
Gretel, 1973 (Armstrong)
Greystoke: The Legend of Tarzan, Lord of the Apes, 1984 (Russell)
Grim Comedian, 1921 (Meredyth)
Grip Till It Hurts, 1997 (Dash)
Grosse Tête, 1962 (Guillemot)
Grounds for Marriage, 1950 (Rose)
Grub Stake, 1922 (Shipman)
Grün, 1968 (Hein)
Gruppo di famiglia in un interno, 1974 (Cecchi d'Amico)
Guaglio *see* Prohibito rubare, 1949
Guérité *see* Douaniers et contrebandiers, 1905
Guerra do Paraguai, 1972 (Carolina)
Guest *see* L'Ospite, 1971
Guichets du Louvre, 1973 (Pascal)
Guide for the Married Man, 1967 (Spencer)
Guilt of Janet Ames, 1947 (Coffee)
Guilty Hands, 1931 (Bauchens)
Guilty One, 1916 (Madison)
Gulf Stream, 1936-39 (Parker)
Gulliver's Travels, 1996 (Russell)
Gunfight at the O.K. Corral, 1957 (Head)
Guns, 1980 (Sarmiento)
Guns for Banta *see* Fusils pour Banta, 1970
Guru, 1968 (Jhabvala)
Gustave Moreau, 1961 (Kaplan)
Guy Named Joe, 1944 (Irene)
Guys and Dolls, 1955 (Sharaff)
Gyermekek, könyvek, 1962 (Mészáros)
Gypsy Girl *see* Sky, West, and Crooked, 1966

Hablamos esta noche, 1982 (Miró)
Haiku, 1960 (Deren)
Hail the Conquering Hero, 1944 (Head)
Hair Piece: A Film for Nappyheaded People, 1984 (Chenzira)
Haircut, 1978 (Hammer)
Haitian Corner, 1987 (Choy)
Hakoiri musume, 1935 (Tanaka)
Half Angel, 1936 (Meredyth)
Half-Breed, 1916 (Loos)
Half Marriage, 1929 (Murfin)
Hallelujah Trail, 1965 (Head)
Hambone and Hillie, 1984 (Gish)
Hamilton in the Musical Festival, 1961 (Batchelor)
Hamilton the Musical Elephant, 1961 (Batchelor)
Hamlet, 1948 (Dillon)
Hammer *see* Marteau, 1986
Hammered: The Best of Sledge, 1986 (Coolidge)
Hammersmith Is Out, 1972 (Head)
Hand Movie, 1968 (Rainer)
Hand that Rocks the Cradle, 1917 (Weber)
Hand-tinting, 1967 (Wieland)
Handling Ships, 1944-45 (Batchelor)
Hanging out—Yonkers, 1973 (Akerman)
Hangman, 1959 (Head)

Hanneles Himmelfahrt, 1934 (von Harbou)
Hansel and Gretel, 1955 (Reiniger)
Happiness *see* Bonheur, 1965
Happy Birthday Türke!, 1991 (Dörrie)
Happy Birthday, Wanda June, 1971 (Spencer)
Happy Family, 1952 (Box, M.)
Happy Go Lucky, 1943 (Head)
Happy Land, 1943 (Spencer)
Happy Mother's Day, 1963 (Chopra)
Harangok városa—Veszprém, 1966 (Mészáros)
Hard, Fast, and Beautiful, 1951 (Lupino)
Hard to Handle: Bob Dylan with Tom Petty and the Heartbreakers, 1986 (Armstrong)
Hard Way, 1942 (Lupino)
Hard Way, 1991 (Marshall)
Hardhat and Legs, 1980 (von Brandenstein)
Harlan County, U.S.A., 1976 (Kopple)
Harlekin, 1931 (Reiniger)
Harlem Wednesday, 1957 (Hubley)
Harlow, 1965 (Head)
Harp in Hock, 1927 (Levien)
Harry & Son, 1984 (Allen, D.)
Harry Hooton, 1970 (Cantrill)
Harvest Is In *see* Goob na nu, 1979
Harvey Girls, 1946 (Irene; Rose)
Hassane, 1990 (Palcy)
Hat, 1964 (Hubley)
Hatari!, 1962 (Brackett; Head)
Hate, 1922 (Mathis)
Hatful of Rain, 1957 (Spencer)
Hättest was Gescheites gelernt, 1978 (Dörrie)
Hauchtext: Liebesgedicht (1970), 1973 (Export)
Haunted Hearts, 1915 (Madison)
Having a Go, 1983 (Armstrong)
Hawaii, 1966 (Jeakins; Van Runkle)
He Comes Up Smiling, 1918 (Marion)
He Learned about Women, 1932 (Head)
He Liu, 1996 (Hui)
He Stayed for Breakfast, 1940 (Irene)
Head over Heels *see* Chilly Scenes of Winter, 1979
Hear Me Good, 1957 (Head)
Heart Beats of Long Ago, 1910 (Macpherson)
Heart o' the Hills, 1919 (Pickford)
Heart of a Cracksman, 1913 (Madison)
Heart of a Hero, 1916 (Marion)
Heart of a Painted Woman, 1915 (Guy)
Heart of Arizona, 1938 (Head)
Heart of Nora Flynn, 1916 (Macpherson)
Heart Thief, 1927 (Levien)
Heartbeat *see* Szivdobogás, 1961
Heartbeeps, 1981 (Van Runkle)
Heartbreak Kid, 1972 (May)
Heartburn, 1986 (Ephron)
Heartland, 1981 (von Brandenstein)
Hearts Adrift, 1914 (Pickford)
Hearts and Guts *see* Tripas Coração, 1982
Hearts Are Trumps, 1920 (Mathis)
Heart's Crucible, 1916 (Madison)
Hearts of the World, 1918 (Gish)
Heat *see* Znoy, 1963
Heat and Dust, 1983 (Jhabvala)

Heat Shimmer, 1978 (Cantrill)
Heat's On, 1943 (West)
Heave Away My Johnny, 1948 (Batchelor)
Heaven Can Wait, 1943 (Spencer)
Heaven Can Wait, 1978 (May; Van Runkle)
Heaven over the Marshes *see* Cielo sulla palude, 1948
Heavenly Body, 1943 (Irene)
Heilige Simplizie, 1920 (von Harbou)
Heinrich, 1977 (Sanders-Brahms)
Heiress, 1949 (Head)
Heiresses *see* Örökseg, 1980
Helen la Belle, 1957 (Reiniger)
Hélène, 1936 (Epstein)
Hell Is Sold Out, 1951 (Zetterling)
Heller in Pink Tights, 1960 (Head)
Heller Wahn, 1983 (von Trotta)
Hellfighters, 1969 (Head)
Hello, 1984 (Hubley)
Hello, Dolly!, 1969 (Sharaff; Streisand)
Hello, Elephant! *see* Buon Giorno, elefante!, 1952
Hello, Everybody, 1933 (Head)
Hello Frisco, Hello, 1943 (Rose)
Hell's Highroad, 1925 (Coffee)
Hell's Island, 1955 (Head)
Hen in the Wind *see* Kaze no naka no mendori, 1948
Henri Gaudier-Brzeska, 1968 (Cantrill)
Henri Langlois, 1970 (Gish)
Henry V, 1945 (Dillon)
Henry Aldrich, Editor, 1942 (Head)
Henry Aldrich for President, 1941 (Head)
Henry Aldrich Gets Glamour, 1943 (Head)
Henry Aldrich Haunts a House, 1943 (Head)
Henry Aldrich's Little Secret, 1944 (Head)
Henry and June, 1990 (Allen, D.)
Her Bitter Cup, 1916 (Madison)
Her Brother *see* Ototo, 1960
Her Darkest Hour, 1911 (Pickford)
Her Defiance, 1916 (Madison)
Her First Affaire, 1932 (Lupino)
Her First Biscuits, 1909 (Pickford)
Her Husband Lies, 1937 (Head)
Her Jungle Love, 1938 (Head)
Her Man o' War, 1926 (Macpherson)
Her Private Life, 1929 (Akins)
Her Twelve Men, 1954 (Rose)
Her Twin Brother, 1914 (Meredyth)
Herb Alpert and the Tijuana Brass Double Feature, 1966 (Hubley)
Herbstsonate, 1978 (Ullmann)
Here and There with My Octoscope and Zenscapes, 1962 (Menken)
Here Come the Girls, 1953 (Head)
Here Come the Huggetts, 1948 (Box, M.; Box, B.)
Here Come the Waves, 1944 (Head)
Here Comes Cookie, 1935 (Head)
Here Comes Mr. Jordan, 1941 (Head)
Here Comes the Groom, 1951 (Head; Van Upp)
Here's to Romance, 1935 (Levien)
Heritage of the Desert, 1939 (Head)
Heritiers de la violence, 1977 (Poirier)
Heroism of an Aviator in Tripoli *see* L'Eroismo di un Aviatore a Tripoli, 1912
Hest på sommerferie, 1959 (Henning-Jensen)

Hester Street, 1975 (Silver)
Het Bosplan, 1978 (Apon)
Het dak van de walvis *see* Toit de la Baleine, 1981
Het is de Schraapzucht, Gentlemen, 1996 (Apon)
Hets, 1944 (Zetterling)
Hicksville Epicure, 1913 (Loos)
Hickville's Finest, 1914 (Loos)
Hidden Agenda, 1990 (Zetterling)
Hidden Eye, 1945 (Irene)
Hidden Flame *see* Flamme cachée, 1920
Hidden Gold, 1940 (Head)
Hidden Scar, 1916 (Marion)
Hide and Seek, 1996 (Friedrich)
Hide-Out, 1934 (Goodrich)
Hideaway Girl, 1937 (Head)
Higanbana, 1959 (Tanaka)
High Barbaree, 1947 (Irene)
High Bright Sun, 1965 (Box, B.)
High Commissioner *see* Nobody Runs Forever, 1968
High Cost of Loving, 1958 (Rose)
High Finance, 1933 (Lupino)
High Fury, 1948 (Pickford)
High Heel Nights, 1994 (B)
High Road *see* Lady of Scandal, 1930
High Sierra, 1941 (Lupino)
High Society, 1956 (Rose)
High Tide, 1987 (Armstrong)
Highbrow Love, 1913 (Loos)
Hijosen no onna, 1933 (Tanaka)
Hills of Old Wyoming, 1937 (Head)
Hillside at Chauritchi, 1978 (Cantrill)
Hindenburg, 1975 (Jeakins)
Hiroshima mon amour, 1959 (Duras)
His Awful Vengeance, 1914 (Loos)
His Better Self, 1911 (Guy)
His Brand, 1913 (Weber)
His Country *see* Ship Comes In, 1928
His Double Life, 1933 (Gish)
His Dress Shirt, 1911 (Pickford)
His Hoodoo, 1913 (Loos)
His Hour, 1924 (Glyn)
His Last Twelve Hours *see* Mondo le condanna, 1952
His Lesson, 1914 (Gish)
His Lordship's White Feather, 1912 (Guy)
His Lost Love, 1909 (Pickford)
His Pal's Request, 1913 (Madison)
His Picture in the Papers, 1916 (Loos)
His Return, 1916 (Madison)
His Sister's Sweetheart, 1911 (Guy)
His Supreme Moment, 1925 (Marion)
His Wife's Visitor, 1909 (Pickford)
Histoires d'Amérique: Food, Family and Philosophy, 1989
   (Akerman)
Historia współczesna, 1960 (Jakubowska)
Historias de ciudad, 1988 (Novaro)
History *see* Storia, 1986
History Lessons *see* Geschichtsunterricht, 1972
History of Albertfalva *see* Albertfalvai történet, 1955
History of the Chinese Patriot Movement in the U.S., 1977 (Choy)
History of the Cinema, 1957 (Batchelor)
History of the World According to a Lesbian, 1988 (Hammer)

Hit the Deck, 1955 (Levien; Rose)
Hit-the-Trail Holliday, 1918 (Loos)
Hitch-Hiker, 1953 (Lupino)
Hitler Gang, 1944 (Goodrich; Head)
Hledám dum holubí, 1985 (Šimková-Plívová)
Hobson's Choice, 1983 (Gish)
Hocus Pocus, 1993 (Marshall)
Hodja fra Pjort, 1985 (Henning-Jensen)
Hold back the Dawn, 1941 (Head)
Hold 'em, Navy, 1937 (Head)
Hold 'em, Yale, 1935 (Head)
Hold That Blonde, 1945 (Head)
Hold-Up, 1911 (Guy)
Hold Your Man, 1933 (Loos)
Hole, 1962 (Hubley)
Hole in the Head, 1959 (Head)
Holiday Affair, 1949 (Lennart)
Holiday Camp, 1947 (Box, M.)
Holiday for Sinners, 1952 (Rose)
Holiday in Mexico, 1946 (Irene; Lennart)
Holiday Inn, 1942 (Head)
Hollywood, 1923 (Macpherson)
Hollywood Boulevard, 1936 (Head)
Hollywood Canteen, 1944 (Lupino)
Hollywood or Bust, 1956 (Head)
Hollywood Vice Squad, 1986 (Spheeris)
Holy Night *see* 'A Santa notte, 1922
Home, 1919 (Weber)
Home, 1978 (Hammer)
Home Folks, 1912 (Pickford)
Home for the Holidays, 1995 (Foster)
Home Movie—A Day in the Bush, 1969 (Cantrill)
Home Remedy, 1987 (Greenwald)
Home, Sweet Home, 1914 (Gish)
Home Trail, 1918 (Shipman)
Homecoming, 1948 (Rose)
Homeland of Electricity, 1987 (Shepitko)
Homerunmuse, 1977 (Schneemann)
Homes Apart: Korea, 1991 (Choy)
Homme amoureux *see* Man in Love, 1987
Homme, une Terre, 1977 (Maldoror)
Hommes de la Wahgi, 1963 (Guillemot)
Homometer II, 1976 (Export)
Honest Bread *see* Nash chestnyi khleb, 1964
Honeymoon, 1969 (Ono)
Honeymoon Deferred *see* Due mogli sono troppe, 1951
Honeymoon in Bali, 1939 (Head; Van Upp)
Honeymoon Machine, 1961 (Rose)
Honeymoon Trip *see* Voyage de noces, 1976
Hong Kong, 1951 (Head)
Honor among Lovers, 1931 (Arzner)
Honor of the Family, 1931 (Coffee)
Honor of the Regiment, 1913 (Meredyth)
Honor Thy Father, 1912 (Pickford)
Honorin et la Lorelei, 1992 (Kaplan)
Honorin et l'Enfant prodigue, 1993 (Kaplan)
Honza, Jakub Kosteczka and a Little Paper Window *see* O Honzovi,
   Jakubovi Kosteckovi a papírovém okénku, 1981
Hoodlum, 1919 (Pickford)
Hoodlum Saint, 1946 (Irene)
Hook and Hand, 1914 (Guy)

Hookers, Hustlers, Pimps and Their Johns, 1993 (Kidron)
Hookers on Davie, 1984 (Cole)
Hoop Skirt see Robe à Cerceaux, 1992
Hop, the Devil's Brew, 1916 (Weber)
Hopalong Rides Again, 1937 (Head)
Hope and Glory, 1987 (Russell)
Hora da Estrêla, 1985 (Amaral)
Horoki, 1962 (Tanaka)
Hors d'oeuvres, 1968-73 (Potter)
Horse on Bill, 1913 (Loos)
Horse on Holiday see Hest på sommerferie, 1959
Hospital see L'Ospite, 1971
Hostages, 1943 (Head)
Hot Enough for June, 1964 (Box, B.)
Hot Flash, 1985 (Hammer)
Hot Flash, 1989 (Hammer)
Hot Line see Goraca linia, 1965
Hot Saturday, 1932 (Head)
Hot Spell, 1958 (Head)
Hot Water, 1978 (Friedrich)
Hotel, 1967 (Head)
Hotel Chronicles, 1990 (Pool)
Hotel for Strangers see Hotel pro cizince, 1966
Hotel Haywire, 1937 (Head)
Hotel Honeymoon, 1912 (Guy)
Hotel Imperial, 1939 (Head)
Hotel Monterey, 1972 (Akerman)
Hotel New Hampshire, 1984 (Foster)
Hotel pro cizince, 1966 (Krumbachová)
Hotheads, 1993 (Livingston)
Hothouse, 1988 (Allen, J.)
Houdini, 1953 (Head)
Houpacka, 1990 (Šimková-Plívová)
Hour before the Dawn, 1944 (Head)
Hour of the Star see Hora da Estrêla, 1985
Hour of the Wolf see Vargtimmen, 1968
House across the Bay, 1940 (Irene; Spencer)
House Built upon Sand, 1917 (Gish)
House Divided, 1913 (Guy)
House in Italy see Casa in Italia, 1964
House in Sea Cliff, 1951 (Grayson)
House Is Not a Home, 1964 (Head)
House of Cards, 1916 (Guy)
House of Cards, 1969 (Head)
House of Darkness, 1913 (Gish)
House of Jade see Maison de jade, 1988
House of Spirit see 'O Munaciello, 1921
House of the Black Death, 1965 (Murphy)
Houseboat, 1958 (Head)
Household Saints, 1993 (Savoca)
Householder, 1963 (Jhabvala)
Housekeeper's Daughter, 1939 (Irene)
Housewife see Femme au foyer, 1975
How Beaver Stole Fire, 1972 (Leaf)
How Come Nobody's on Our Side?, 1975 (Marshall)
How Could You, Jean?, 1918 (Marion; Pickford)
How I Play Cricket, Early 1930s (McDonagh Sisters)
How Long Does Man Matter? see Meddig él az ember?, 1967
How Sweet It Is!, 1968 (Marshall; Rose)
How the Day Was Saved, 1913 (Loos)
How the Motor Car Works: The Carburettor, 1977 (Batchelor)

How to Be a Hostess, 1959 (Batchelor)
How to Keep a Husband, 1914 (Loos)
How to Make an American Quilt, 1995 (Angelou)
How to Marry a Millionaire, 1953 (Akins)
Howards End, 1992 (Jhabvala)
Hra o jablko, 1977 (Chytilová)
Hu Yueh Te Ku Shih, 1981 (Hui)
Huajiao Lei, c. 1986 (Zhang)
Hucksters, 1947 (Irene)
Hud, 1963 (Head)
Huey see Black Panthers, 1968
Huggetts Abroad, 1949 (Box, B.)
Huilor, 1936-39 (Parker)
Huis clos, 1954 (Audry)
Hulda from Holland, 1916 (Pickford)
Hullabaloo over Georgie and Bonnie's Pictures, 1978 (Jhabvala)
Human Comedy, 1943 (Irene)
Humoresque, 1920 (Marion)
Hunchback, 1914 (Gish; Loos)
Hunchback of Notre Dame, 1939 (Levien)
Hundred and One Nights see Cent et une nuits, 1995
Hungarian Village see Istenmezején 1972-73, 1974
Hunger see Sult, 1966
Hungerjahre, 1979 (Brückner)
Hungry Dog, 1960 (Batchelor)
Hungry Heart, 1917 (Marion)
Hunted Men, 1938 (Bauchens; Head)
Hunting We Will Go, 1960 (Batchelor)
Hurra! Ich bin Papa!, 1939 (von Harbou)
Hurricane Irene, 1986 (Kopple)
Hurricane Smith, 1952 (Head)
Hurry! Hurry!, 1957 (Menken)
Husbands and Lovers, 1924 (Booth)
Husbands and Wives, 1992 (Ephron)
Hush, 1921 (Coffee)
Hussards et grisettes, 1901 (Guy)
Hustler, 1961 (Allen, D.)
Hustruer, 1975 (Breien)
Hustruer—10 år etter, 1985 (Breien)
Hustruer III, 1996 (Breien)
Huyue de gushi see Hu Yueh Te Ku Shih, 1981
Hydraulip, 1979 (Hänsel)
Hyperbulie, 1973 (Export)
Hypnotist, 1960 (Batchelor)
Hypocrites, 1914 (Marion; Weber)

I Am an Ox—Women in Soviet Cinema, 1988 (Potter)
I basilischi, 1963 (Wertmüller)
I [(Beat) It], 1978 (Export)
I Can Jump over Puddles Again see Uz zase skácu pres kaluze, 1970
I cani del Sinai see Fortini/Cani, 1976
I Cannibali, 1969 (Cavani)
I Can't Sleep see J'ai pas sommeil, 1993
I Confess, 1953 (Reville)
I Could Go On Singing, 1963 (Head)
I Don't Want to Talk about It see De eso no se habla, 1993
I Dood It, 1943 (Sharaff)
I Dream in Color see Sueño como de colores, 1968-69
I due nemici, 1961 (Cecchi d'Amico)
I Fancy You see 'Nfama, 1924
I figli chiedono perche, 1972 (Cecchi d'Amico)

I Flunked, But... see Rakudai wa shitakeredo, 1931
I Graduated, But... see Daigaku wa detakeredo, 1929
I Know Why the Caged Bird Sings, 1979 (Angelou)
I Lived with You, 1933 (Lupino)
I Look for a House of Pigeons see Hledám dum holubí, 1985
I Love a Mystery, 1973 (Lupino)
I Love a Soldier, 1944 (Head)
I Love Melvin, 1953 (Rose)
I Love You, Alice B. Toklas!, 1968 (Van Runkle)
I magliari, 1959 (Cecchi d'Amico)
I Married a Monster from Outer Space, 1958 (Head)
I Married a Witch, 1942 (Head)
I Married an Angel, 1942 (Loos)
I Met a Man, 1991 (Leaf)
I Nomadi, 1912 (Notari)
I nostri figli see I vinti, 1952
I picari, 1987 (Cecchi d'Amico)
I Really Need Communication see Ich Brauche unbedingt
    Kommunikation, 1981
I Remember You see Ya tebya pomnyu, 1985
I Shall Go to Santiago see Iré a Santiago, 1964
I soliti ignoti, 1958 (Cecchi d'Amico)
I soliti ignoti vent'anni dopo, 1986 (Cecchi d'Amico)
I Suggest Mine, 1980 (Friedrich)
I, the Worst of Them All see Yo, la peor de todas, 1990
I vinti, 1952 (Cecchi d'Amico)
I Walk Alone, 1947 (Head)
I Want a Divorce, 1940 (Head)
I Want You to Be Rich, 1971 (Hein)
I Wanted Wings, 1941 (Head)
I Was/I Am, 1973 (Hammer)
I, Your Mother see Man Sa Yay, 1980
Icarus XB 1 see Ikarie XB 1, 1963
Iceman Cometh, 1973 (Jeakins)
Ices Strip Train Skating, 1972 (Schneemann)
Ich Brauche unbedingt Kommunikation, 1981 (Treut)
Ich und Er, 1987 (Dörrie)
Ich war Jack Mortimer, 1935 (von Harbou)
Iconoclast, 1910 (Macpherson)
Idade de Terra, 1978 (Yamasaki)
IDCA—1970, 1971 (Weill)
Idle Rich, 1921 (Mathis)
Idle Wives, 1916 (Weber)
Idylle, 1897 (Guy)
Idylle interrompue, 1897/98 (Guy)
If a Thousand Clarinets ... see Kdyby tisíc klarinetu, 1964
If These Walls Could Talk, 1996 (Savoca)
If Winter Comes, 1947 (Irene)
Igor Bulichov see Egor Bulychov i drugie, 1953
Ikarie XB 1, 1963 (Krumbachová)
Il n'y à pas d'oubli, 1975 (Mallet)
Il y a longtemps que je t'aime, 1979 (Guillemot)
Il y a longtemps que je t'aime, 1989 (Poirier)
I'll Be Seeing You, 1944 (Head)
I'll Be Your Sweetheart, 1945 (Toye)
I'll Cry Tomorrow, 1955 (Rose)
I'll Take Romance, 1937 (Murfin)
Illegal Traffic, 1938 (Head)
Illinois Central, 1968 (Schneemann)
Illinois Central Transposed, 1968 (Schneemann)
Illumination, 1997 (Russell)

Illusionernas Natt, 1970 (Ahrne)
Illusioniste renversant, 1903 (Guy)
Illusions, 1983 (Dash)
I'm from Missouri, 1939 (Head)
Im Glanze dieses Glückes, 1990 (Meerapfel)
Im Innern des Wals, 1985 (Dörrie)
Im Land miener Eltern, 1981 (Meerapfel)
I'm No Angel, 1933 (Head; West)
Image of Dorian Gray in the Yellow Press see Dorian Gray in spiegel
    der Boulevardprsse, 1984
Imaginations, 1958 (Bute)
Imagine, 1971 (Ono)
Imagine: John Lennon, 1988 (Ono)
Imaging Her Erotics: Carolee Schneemann, 1993 (Schneemann)
Immigrant Experience: The Long Long Journey, 1972 (Silver)
Impalement, 1910 (Macpherson)
Impatient Years, 1944 (Van Upp)
Imperfect Lady, 1947 (Head)
Importance of Being Earnest, 1952 (Dillon)
Impressions of April see Stemning i April, 1947
Imprints, 1969 (Cantrill)
In a Full Moon Night see In una notte di chiaro luna, 1989
In Again, Out Again, 1917 (Loos)
In Any Case, Your Name Is Juan see De todos modos Juan te llamas,
    1975
In Between see Dazwischen, 1981
In Enemy Country, 1968 (Head)
In Gay Madrid, 1930 (Meredyth)
In Heaven as on Earth see Sur la terre comme au ciel, 1993
In Hollywood with Potash and Perlmutter, 1924 (Marion)
In Life's Cycle, 1910 (Macpherson)
In Memoriam László Mészáros see Mészáros László emlékére, 1968
In Name Only, 1939 (Irene)
In Old Chicago, 1938 (Levien)
In Old Colorado, 1941 (Head)
In Old Kentucky, 1909 (Pickford)
In Old Kentucky, 1927 (Booth)
In Old Madrid, 1911 (Pickford)
In Old Mexico, 1938 (Head)
In Our Time, 1944 (Lupino)
In Paris Parks, 1954 (Clarke)
In Search of a Sinner, 1920 (Loos)
In Spite Of, 1991 (Henning-Jensen)
In the Aisles of the Wild, 1912 (Gish)
In the Belly of the Whale see Im Innern des Wals, 1985
In the Best Interest of the Child, 1990 (Murphy)
In the Bishop's Carriage, 1913 (Pickford)
In the Cellar, 1960 (Batchelor)
In the Country of Fast Runners see En el país de los pies ligeros, 1980
In the Country of My Parents see Im Land miener Eltern, 1981
In the Event That Anyone Disappears, 1975 (Choy)
In the Good Old Summertime, 1949 (Irene; Goodrich)
In the Jungle, 1960 (Batchelor)
In the Name of the Emperor, 1995 (Choy)
In the Palace of the King, 1923 (Mathis)
In the Presence of Mine Enemies, 1997 (Silver)
In the Rivers of Mercy Angst, 1997 (Chenzira)
In the Season of Buds, 1910 (Pickford)
In the Shadow of Gunung Batur, 1993 (Cantrill)
In the Spirit, 1990 (May)
In the Sultan's Garden, 1911 (Pickford)

In the Watches of the Night, 1909 (Pickford)
In the Year 2000, 1912 (Guy)
In This House of Brede, 1975 (Dillon)
In This Life's Body, 1984 (Cantrill)
In Time of Pestilence, 1951 (Batchelor)
In una notte di chiaro luna, 1989 (Wertmüller)
Incendiary Blonde, 1945 (Head)
Incident at Restigouche, 1984 (Obomsawin)
Incised Image, 1966 (Cantrill)
Incontro notturno, 1961 (Cavani)
Incredible Petrified World, 1960 (Murphy)
India Cabaret, 1985 (Nair)
India Song, 1975 (Duras)
Indian Runner's Romance, 1909 (Pickford)
Indian Summer, 1912 (Pickford)
Indian Tomb see Indische Grabmal, 1921
Indian's Loyalty, 1913 (Gish)
Indians Are Still Far Away see Indiens sont encore loin, 1977
Indiens sont encore loin, 1977 (Pascal)
Indische Grabmal, 1921 (von Harbou)
Indústria, 1969 (Carolina)
Industrial Reserve Army see Industrielle Reservarmee, 1971
Industrial Symphony see Philips-Radio, 1931
Industrielle Reservarmee, 1971 (Sanders-Brahms)
Inexorable Time see Cas je neúprosný, 1978
Inez from Hollywood, 1924 (Arzner)
Infamous Woman see 'Nfama, 1924
Infanzia, vocazione, e prime esperienze di Giacomo Casanova, Veneziano, 1969 (Cecchi d'Amico)
Inferno, 1953 (Jeakins)
Informer, 1912 (Pickford)
Ingrid, 1985 (Ullmann)
Inhabitants of Castles see Kastélyok lakói, 1966
Inheritance see Örökseg, 1980
Inheritance or Fuckoffguysgoodbye see Dedictví aneb Kurvahošigutntag, 1992
Initiation, 1978 (Clarke)
Inn of the Sixth Happiness, 1958 (Lennart)
Inner Circle, 1912 (Pickford)
Innocent see L'innocente, 1976
Innocent Magdalene, 1916 (Gish)
Innocent Maid see Hakoiri musume, 1935
Inserts, 1975 (Russell)
Inside Daisy Clover, 1965 (Head)
Inside Out, 1992 (Borden)
Inside Women Inside, 1978 (Choy)
Instant de la paix see Der Augenblick des Friedens, 1965
Instant Film, 1968 (Export)
Instant Karma, 1968 (Ono)
Insured for Life, 1960 (Batchelor)
Integration, 1974 (Citron)
Intelligence Men, 1965 (Dillon)
Interior/Exterior, 1978 (Cantrill)
Interior Scroll, 1975 (Schneemann)
Interior Scroll - The Cave, 1995 (Schneemann)
Intermezzo, 1939 (Irene)
International Sweethearts of Rhythm, 1986 (Schiller)
Interno Berlinese, 1986 (Cavani)
Interns Can't Take Money, 1937 (Head)
Interrogation see Przesluchanie, 1982
Interrupted Line, 1971-72 (Export)

Interrupted Melody, 1955 (Levien; Rose)
Interview, 1979 (Leaf)
Into the Dark see Entre tinieblas, 1983
Into the Night, 1985 (Heckerling)
Intolerance, 1916 (Gish; Loos)
Introduction to Arnold Schoenberg's Accompaniment for a Cinematographic Scene see Einleitung zu Arnold Schoenberg Begleit Musik zu einer Lichtspielscene, 1969
Invisible Adversaries see Unsichtbare Gegner, 1976
Invisible Exchange, 1956 (Batchelor)
Invitation, 1952 (Rose)
Invitation see Zaproszenie, 1986
Invitation à la chasse, 1974 (von Trotta)
Invitation au voyage, 1982 (Guillemot)
Invitation to Happiness, 1939 (Head)
Invitation to the Waltz, 1935 (Toye)
Io, io, io ... e gli altri, 1966 (Cecchi d'Amico)
Io speriamo che me la cavo, 1994 (Wertmüller)
Iola's Promise, 1912 (Pickford)
Iré a Santiago, 1964 (Gómez)
Irene, 1926 (Mathis)
Iris och Lojtnantshjarta, 1946 (Zetterling)
Irish Hearts, 1927 (Meredyth)
Iron Duke, 1935 (Meredyth)
Iron Maiden, 1963 (Dillon)
Iron Petticoat, 1956 (Box, B.; Dillon)
Ishtar, 1987 (May)
Isla del tesero, 1969 (Gómez)
Isla rodeada de agua, 1984 (Novaro)
Island, 1990 (Pascal)
Island Fuse, 1971 (Cantrill)
Island of Intrigue, 1919 (Mathis)
Island of Lost Men, 1939 (Head)
Island on the Continent see Sziget a szárazföldön, 1968
Island Rescue see Appointment with Venus, 1951
Island Surrounded by Water see Isla rodeada de agua, 1984
Islas Revillagigedo, 1990 (Landeta)
Isle of Conquest, 1919 (Loos)
Isn't It Romantic?, 1948 (Head)
Ispaniya, 1939 (Shub)
Istenmezején 1972-73, 1974 (Elek)
It, 1928 (Glyn)
It Depends on Us Too ... see Rajtunk is mulik, 1960
It Happened in Brooklyn, 1947 (Lennart)
It Only Happens to Others see Ça n'arrive qu'aux autres, 1971
It Started in Naples, 1960 (Cecchi d'Amico; Head)
It Started with a Kiss, 1959 (Rose)
It Was a Wonderful Life, 1993 (Foster)
Italian Barber, 1911 (Pickford)
Italian Flag see Tricolore, 1913
Italo-Turkish War among Our Neapolitan Urchins see Caratteristica Guerra Italo-Turca Tra i Nostri Scugnizzi Napoletani, 1912
Italy Has Risen see L'Italia s'è Desta, 1927
Itch, 1989 (Kidron)
It's a 2' 6" above the Ground World see Love Ban, 1972
It's a Big Country, 1951 (Lennart)
It's a Good Day, 1969 (Fields)
It's a Wise Child, 1931 (Booth)
It's a Wonderful Life, 1946 (Goodrich)
It's Always Fair Weather, 1955 (Comden; Rose)
It's Always Now, 1965 (Allen, D.)

It's Forever Springtime *see* E primavera, 1950
It's in the Bag, 1945 (Reville)
It's My Turn, 1980 (Allen, J.; Weill)
It's No Laughing Matter, 1914 (Marion; Weber)
It's Not the Size that Counts, 1974 (Box, B.)
It's Now or Never, 1991 (Law)
It's Only Money, 1962 (Head)
Itto, 1934 (Epstein)
Ivan, 1932 (Solntseva)
Ives House: Woodstock, 1973-74 (De Hirsch)
Ivor Paints, 1995 (Cantrill)
Ivor's Exhibition, 1995 (Cantrill)
Ivor's Tiger Xmas Card, 1994 (Cantrill)
Ivory Collection *see* Coleçao de marfil, 1972
Izu no odoriko, 1933 (Tanaka)
Izzy and His Rival *see* Billy's Rival, 1914

Jack and the Beanstalk, 1955 (Reiniger)
Jack Smith, 1974 (Hein)
Jacobo Timerman: Prisoner without a Name, Cell without a Number,
    1983 (Ullmann)
Jacques Rivette, Le Veilleur, 1989 (Denis)
Jacquot de Nantes, 1991 (Varda)
Jag drapte, 1943 (Zetterling)
Jag skall bli Sveriges Rembrandt eller dö!, 1990 (Ahrne)
Jagd nach dem Glück, 1929-30 (Reiniger)
J'ai pas sommeil, 1993 (Denis)
J'ai un hanneton dans mon pantalon, 1906 (Guy)
Jak se tocí Rozmarýny, 1977 (Šimková-Plívová)
Jalan Raya, Ubud, 1995 (Cantrill)
Jama Masjid Street Journal, 1979 (Nair)
Jamaica Inn, 1939 (Harrison; Reville)
Jamaica Run, 1953 (Head)
Jane Austen in Manhattan, 1980 (Jhabvala)
Jane B. par Agnès V., 1988 (Varda)
Jane Brakhage, 1975 (Hammer)
János Tornyai *see* Tornyai János, 1962
Japanese Idyll, 1912 (Weber)
Jaune le soleil, 1971 (Duras)
Jaws, 1975 (Fields)
Jayhawkers, 1959 (Head)
Je, tu, il, elle, 1974 (Akerman)
Je vous y prrrends!, 1897/98 (Guy)
Jean de la lune, 1977 (Guillemot)
Jeanne Dielman, 23 Quai du Commerce, 1080 Bruxelles, 1975
    (Akerman)
Jeanne Eagels, 1957 (Levien)
Jefferson in Paris, 1995 (Jhabvala)
Jennie *see* Portrait of Jennie, 1948
Jennifer, 1953 (Lupino)
Jenny, 1984 (Ullmann)
Jenny Lind *see* Lady's Morals, 1930
Jeopardy, 1953 (Rose)
Jerk, 1979 (Van Runkle)
Jérôme Bosch, 1963 (Guillemot)
Jester and the Queen *see* Sasek a kralovna, 1987
Jesus, My Brother *see* Gesu' mio Fratello, 1965
Jet Storm, 1959 (Zetterling)
Jetzt leben - Juden in Berlin, 1995 (Sanders-Brahms)
Jeune fille la plus méritante de France, 1922 (Musidora)
Jeunes Filles d'hier et d'aujourd'hui, 1916 (Musidora)

Jewel, 1915 (Weber)
Jew's Christmas, 1913 (Weber)
Jidao Zhuizhong, 1991 (Hui)
Jimmy Bruiteur, 1930 (Epstein)
Jin de gu shi *see* Ah Kam, 1996
Jinye Xingguang Canlan, 1988 (Hui)
Jivaro, 1954 (Head)
J'me marie, j'me marie pas, 1973 (Poirier)
Joan of Arc, 1948 (Jeakins)
Joan the Woman, 1917 (Macpherson)
Jocko musicien, 1903 (Guy)
Jodie: An Icon, 1996 (Parmar)
Joe, 1924 (McDonagh Sisters)
Johanna d'Arc of Mongolia, 1988 (Ottinger)
Johanna Enlists, 1918 (Marion; Pickford)
Johannès fils de Johannès, 1918 (Musidora)
John Gilpin, 1951 (Batchelor)
John Goldfarb, Please Come Home, 1965 (Head)
John Meade's Woman, 1937 (Head)
John Needham's Double, 1916 (Weber)
Johnny Bull, 1986 (Weill)
Johnny Dangerously, 1984 (Heckerling)
Johnny Got His Gun, 1971 (Van Runkle)
Johnny in the Clouds *see* Way to the Stars, 1945
Joke of Destiny, Lying in Wait around the Corner Like a Street Ban-
    dit *see* Scherzo del destinoin aqquato dietro l'angelo come un
    brigante di strada, 1983
Joker Is Wild, 1957 (Head)
Jonas in the Desert, 1994 (Ono)
Jonque, 1964 (Guillemot)
Josei no shori, 1946 (Tanaka)
Jostedalsrypa, 1967 (Breien)
Jotai wa kanashiku, 1957 (Tanaka)
Jour apres jour, 1962 (Poirier)
Jour du terme, 1904 (Guy)
Jour Pina m'a demandé, 1983 (Akerman)
Journal inachevé, 1986 (Mallet)
Journées entières dans les arbres, 1976 (Duras)
Journey, 1959 (Spencer)
Journey around a Zero, 1963 (De Hirsch)
Journey Is Worth the Trip *see* Eine Reise ist eine Reise Wert, 1969
Journey to the Pacific, 1968 (Fields)
Journeys from Berlin/1971, 1980 (Rainer)
Joy of Sex, 1984 (Coolidge)
Joyce at 34, 1972 (Chopra; Weill)
Joyu Sumako no koi, 1947 (Tanaka)
Judas City *see* Satan's Bed, 1967
Judex, 1916 (Musidora)
Judge and the Assassin *see* Juge et l'assassin, 1976
Judith of Bethulia, 1914 (Gish)
Juge et l'assassin, 1976 (Pascal)
Jugend, 1938 (von Harbou)
Juguetes, 1978 (Bemberg)
Julia, 1977 (Dillon)
Julia Misbehaves, 1948 (Irene)
Julie de Carneilhan, 1950 (Colette)
Jumpin' Jack Flash, 1986 (Marshall)
Jumping Jacks, 1952 (Head)
June Bride, 1948 (Head)
Jungfrauen Maschine, 1988 (Schiller; Treut)
Jungle Princess, 1936 (Head)

Jungle Warfare, 1943 (Batchelor)
Junior Bonner, 1972 (Lupino)
Juno and the Paycock, 1929 (Reville)
Jupiter's Darling, 1955 (Rose)
Just Another Girl on the I.R.T., 1992 (Harris)
Just around the Corner, 1921 (Marion)
Just Cause, 1995 (von Brandenstein)
Just for You, 1952 (Head)
Just Gold, 1913 (Gish)
Just Kids, 1913 (Gish)
Just Like a Woman, 1912 (Pickford)
Just Like at Home see Olyan, mint otthon, 1978
Just Tell Me What You Want, 1980 (Allen, J.)
Justice for Sale see Night Court, 1932
Justine, 1969 (Sharaff)

K-SH-E, 1932 (Shub)
K.Y.T.E.S.: How We Dream Ourselves, 1985 (Mehta)
Kaddu Beykat, 1975 (Faye)
Kaerlighed pa kredit, 1955 (Henning-Jensen)
Kakafonische Notities, 1980 (Apon)
Kalamita, 1980 (Chytilová)
Kali-filme, 1987-88 (Hein)
Kam Parenky, 1993 (Chytilová)
Kama Sutra, 1996 (Nair)
Kamaszváros, 1962 (Mészáros)
Kämpfende Herzen, 1921 (von Harbou)
Kanehsatake: 270 Years of Resistance, 1993 (Obomsawin)
Kansas City Bomber, 1972 (Foster)
Kanzashi, 1941 (Tanaka)
Kashtanka, 1926 (Preobrazhenskaya)
Kastélyok lakói, 1966 (Elek)
Káta a krokodýl, 1965 (Šimková-Plívová)
Kate and Anna McGarrigle, 1981 (Leaf)
Katharina Eiselt, 1980 (Dörrie)
Katia and the Crocodile see Káta a krokodýl, 1965
Katy and the Twins see Nefnukej, veverko!, 1988
Kaze no naka no mendori, 1948 (Tanaka)
Kdyby tisíc klarinetů, 1964 (Krumbachová)
Kean, 1956 (Cecchi d'Amico)
Keep It for Yourself, 1991 (Denis)
Keep Your Powder Dry, 1945 (Irene)
Keeping On, 1983 (Kopple)
Keiner Liebt Mich, 1994 (Dörrie)
Kelly from the Emerald Isle, 1913 (Guy)
Kempy see Wise Girls, 1929
Képi, 1905 (Guy)
Ketu Qiuhen, 1990 (Hui)
Key to the City, 1950 (Irene)
Keys of Heaven, 1946 (Batchelor)
Keys to Happiness see Klyuchi shchastya, 1913
Kharejaz Mahdoudeh, 1988 (Bani-Etemad)
Khush, 1991 (Parmar)
Kiáltó, 1964 (Mészáros)
Kid Blue, 1973 (Van Runkle)
Kid from Left Field, 1953 (Jeakins)
Kidnapped, 1938 (Levien)
Kidnapped, 1960 (Dillon)
Kids Are Alright, 1979 (Schoonmaker)
Kiki, 1931 (Pickford)
Kilenc hónap, 1976 (Mészáros)

Kill-Off, 1989 (Greenwald)
Kinder sind nicht Rinder, 1969 (Sander)
Kindergärtnerin, was nun?, 1969 (Sander)
Kinegraffiti, 1963 (Cantrill)
King and I, 1956 (Sharaff)
King Creole, 1958 (Head)
King Kongs Faust, 1984 (Dörrie)
King Matthew I see Król Macius I, 1957
King Matthias I see Król Macius I, 1957
King of Alcatraz, 1938 (Head)
King of Chinatown, 1939 (Head)
King of Comedy, 1983 (Schoonmaker)
King of Gamblers, 1937 (Head)
King of Kings, 1927 (Bauchens; Macpherson)
King of Kings see Král Králu, 1962
Kingdom for a Guitar see Království za kytaru, 1989
Kino za XX liet, 1940 (Shub)
King's Breakfast, 1936 (Reiniger; Toye)
Kirsa Nicholina, 1969 (Nelson)
Kismet, 1944 (Irene)
Kiss see Der Kuss, 1968
Kiss of Death, 1995 (Van Runkle)
Kiss the Boys Goodbye, 1941 (Head)
Kisses, 1922 (Mathis)
Kissing Bandit, 1948 (Lennart)
Kitchen Sink, 1989 (Maclean)
Kitch's Last Meal, 1973-78 (Schneemann)
Kladivo na carodejnice, 1969 (Krumbachová)
Klassenverhältnisse, 1985 (Huillet)
Klondike Annie, 1936 (West)
Klyuchi shchastya, 1913 (Preobrazhenskaya)
Kneegrays in Russia, 1990 (Davis)
Knight without Armour, 1937 (Marion)
Knights of the Range, 1940 (Head)
Knock on Wood, 1954 (Head; Zetterling)
Knocturne, 1972 (Wieland)
Knowing Men, 1930 (Glyn)
Kobieta samotna, 1982 (Holland)
Kocár do Vídne, 1966 (Krumbachová)
Kodiyettom see Voshojdenie, 1977
Koibumi, 1953 (Tanaka)
Kolberg, 1945 (von Harbou)
Kolory kochania, 1988 (Jakubowska)
Kolossale Liebe, 1984 (Brückner)
Komsomol—Leader of Electrification see K-SH-E, 1932
Konec jasnovidce, 1958 (Chytilová)
Koniec naszego swiata, 1963 (Jakubowska)
Kopytem Sem, Kopytem Tam, 1987 (Chytilová)
Korczak, 1990 (Holland)
Korotkiye vstrechi, 1967 (Muratova)
Kort år sommaren, 1962 (Henning-Jensen; Ullmann)
Krakonoš a lyzníci, 1980 (Šimková-Plívová)
Král Králu, 1962 (Krumbachová)
Král Šumavy, 1959 (Šimková-Plívová)
Království za kytaru, 1989 (Krumbachová)
Krane's Bakery Shop see Kranes Konditori, 1951
Kranes Konditori, 1951 (Henning-Jensen)
Kransen see Kristin Lavransdatter, 1995
Kristin Lavransdatter, 1995 (Ullmann)
Kristina Talking Pictures, 1976 (Rainer)
Kristina's Harbor, 1993 (Nelson)

Kristinus Bergman, 1948 (Henning-Jensen)
Krokodillen in Amsterdam, 1990 (Apon)
Król Macius I, 1957 (Jakubowska)
Krylya, 1966 (Shepitko)
Krylya kholopa, 1926 (Shub)
Kulonbozo helyek, 1995 (Varda)
Kümmeltürkin geht, 1985 (Meerapfel)
Kundun, 1997 (Schoonmaker)
Kung Fu Master see Petit Amour, 1988
Künstlerfilme I, 1974 (Hein)
Künstlerfilme II, 1974 (Hein)
Kurt Kren. Porträt eines experimentellen Fulmmachers, 1978 (Hein)

L.A. Johns, 1997 (Chopra)
Laagland, 1995 (Apon)
Labor of Love see Heller Wahn, 1983
Lac-aux-Dames, 1934 (Colette)
L'Accalappiacani, 1909 (Notari)
Lace of Summer, 1973-74 (De Hirsch)
Ladies in Retirement, 1941 (Lupino)
Ladies Love Brutes, 1930 (Akins)
Ladies' Man, 1961 (Head)
Ladies Must Live, 1921 (Madison)
Ladies Should Listen, 1934 (Head)
Ladri di biciclette, 1948 (Cecchi d'Amico)
Lady, 1925 (Marion)
Lady and the Mob, 1939 (Lupino)
Lady and the Mouse, 1913 (Gish; Loos)
Lady Be Careful, 1936 (Head)
Lady Bodyguard, 1943 (Head)
Lady Caroline Lamb, 1973 (Dillon)
Lady Chatterley's Lover, 1981 (Russell)
Lady Eve, 1941 (Head)
Lady from Constantinople see Sziget a szárazföldön, 1968
Lady from Shanghai, 1948 (Van Upp)
Lady Has Plans, 1942 (Head)
Lady Helen's Escapade, 1909 (Macpherson)
Lady in a Cage, 1964 (Head)
Lady in a Car with Glasses and a Gun, 1970 (Perry)
Lady in Black, 1913 (Loos)
Lady in Shining Armor see Sonho de Valsa, 1987
Lady in the Dark, 1944 (Goodrich; Head)
Lady in the Lake, 1946 (Irene)
Lady Is Willing, 1942 (Irene)
Lady Liberty see Mortadella, 1971
Lady Musashino see Musashino fujin, 1951
Lady of Burlesque, 1943 (Head)
Lady of Chance, 1928 (Booth)
Lady of Scandal, 1930 (Booth)
Lady of Secrets, 1936 (Akins)
Lady of the Boulevards see Nana, 1934
Lady Oscar, 1978 (Varda)
Lady Peasant see Baryshnia krestianka, 1916
Lady Vanishes, 1938 (Reville)
Lady without Camellias see Signora senza camelie, 1953
Ladybug, Ladybug, 1963 (Perry)
Ladyfingers, 1921 (Coffee)
Lady's from Kentucky, 1939 (Head)
Lady's Morals, 1930 (Booth)
L'Affiche, 1925 (Epstein)
L'Africana see Rückkehr, 1990

L'Age tendre, 1974 (Guillemot)
Lagourdette, gentleman cambrioleur, 1916 (Musidora)
L'allegro squadrone, 1954 (Cecchi d'Amico)
L'Amie see Heller Wahn, 1983
Land, 1942 (van Dongen)
Land of Liberty, 1939 (Macpherson)
Land of Liberty, 1941 (Bauchens)
Land of Mirages see Délibábok országa, 1983
Land of the Bulls see Tierra de los toros, 1924
Land of the Soviets see Strana Sovietov, 1937
L'Angélus, 1899/1900 (Guy)
Långt borta och nära, 1976 (Ahrne)
Laocoon and Sons see Laokoon und Söhne, 1972-74
Laokoon und Söhne, 1972-74 (Ottinger)
Laputa, 1986 (Sanders-Brahms)
Largo Desolato, 1990 (Holland)
L'Arroseur arrosé, 1897/98 (Guy)
Larry's Recent Behaviour, 1963 (Wieland)
Las Tres coronas del marinera see Trois Couronnes du matelot, 1982
Las Vegas Nights, 1941 (Head)
L'Assassinat de la rue du Temple, 1904 (Guy)
L'Assassinat du Courrier de Lyon, 1904 (Guy)
Lasse-Maja, 1941 (Zetterling)
Last Attraction see Poslednyi attraktzion, 1929
Last Butterfly see Poslední motýl, 1990
Last Castle see Echoes of a Summer, 1976
Last Days of Chez Nous, 1992 (Armstrong)
Last Days of Gomorrah see Letzten Tage von Gomorrah, 1974
Last Drink of Whiskey, 1914 (Loos)
Last Drop of Water, 1911 (Macpherson)
Last Island, 1991 (Gorris)
Last Knight Vampire see Den sista riddarvampyren, 1972
Last Married Couple in America, 1979 (Head)
Last of Mrs. Cheyney, 1937 (Arzner)
Last of the Secret Agents, 1966 (Head)
Last of Their Race, 1914 (Madison)
Last Outpost, 1935 (Head)
Last Outpost, 1951 (Head)
Last Stage see Ostatni etap, 1947
Last Stop see Ostatni etap, 1947
Last Summer, 1969 (Perry)
Last Tango in Paris, 1971 (Varda)
Last Temptation of Christ, 1988 (Schoonmaker)
Last Tenant, 1978 (von Brandenstein)
Last Time I Saw Paris, 1954 (Rose)
Last Train from Gun Hill, 1959 (Head)
Last Train from Madrid, 1937 (Head)
Last Trial, 1989 (Peng)
Last Visit to Ms. Iran Daftari, 1996 (Bani-Etemad)
L'atelier du diable, 1982 (Palcy)
Latin Lovers, 1953 (Lennart; Rose)
Latin Women, 1992 (Sarmiento)
L'Attaque d'un diligence, 1904 (Guy)
L'Auberge rouge, 1923 (Epstein)
Laufen lernen, 1980 (Brückner)
Laughing Sinners, 1931 (Meredyth)
Laundry Liz, 1916 (Loos)
Laundry Shed see Lavaderos, 1981
Laurent Lamerre, portier, 1978 (Pool)
Lauter Liebe, 1940 (von Harbou)
L'Autre Victoire, 1915 (Musidora)

Lavaderos, 1981 (Novaro)
Lavatory moderne, 1900/01 (Guy)
L'Avenir d'Emilie *see* Flügel und Fesseln, 1984
L'Aveugle, 1897 (Guy)
Lavrador, 1968 (Carolina)
Law *see* 'A Legge, 1920
Law of the Pampas, 1939 (Head)
Law of Their Kind, 1914 (Madison)
Lawful Larceny, 1930 (Murfin)
Lazy Bones, 1925 (Marion)
Leaden Times *see* **Bleierne Zeit**, 1981
League of Their Own, 1992 (Marshall)
Leap of Faith, 1992 (Van Runkle; von Brandenstein)
Learning to Love, 1925 (Loos)
Learning to Run *see* Laufen lernen, 1980
Leather Saint, 1956 (Head)
Leathernecking, 1930 (Murfin)
L'Eau, 1951-66 (Parker)
L'Eau à la bouche, 1960 (Trintignant)
L'Eau d'Evian, 1936-39 (Parker)
Lebens schönste Seiten, 1992 (Sander)
L'École des cocottes, 1958 (Audry)
Leçon de danse, 1897 (Guy)
Leçons de boxe, 1898/99 (Guy)
Leçons de la guerre, 1915 (Musidora)
Lecture quotidienne, 1900/01 (Guy)
Left Hand of God, 1955 (Spencer)
Left-Handed Man, 1913 (Gish)
Legacy, 1977 (Littleton)
Legacy *see* Dedictví aneb Kurvahošigutntag, 1992
Legend of Fong Sai-Yuk *see* Fong Sai-Yuk, 1993
Legend of Naples *see* Leggenda di Napoli, 1928
Legend of the Boy and the Eagle, 1967 (Fields)
Leggenda di Napoli, 1928 (Notari)
Lek pa regnbagen, 1958 (Zetterling)
L'elisir d'amore, 1939 (Reiniger)
Lemon Drop Kid, 1951 (Head)
Lemon Sisters, 1989 (Chopra)
Lemon Sisters, 1990 (von Brandenstein)
Lena and the Geese, 1912 (Pickford)
L'Enfant aimé, 1971 (Akerman)
L'enfant-cinéma, 1997 (Maldoror)
L'enfant de la barricade *see* Sur la barricade, 1907
L'Enfant sauvage, 1969 (Guillemot)
Leningrad Hospital *see* L'hôpital de Leningrad, 1982
Lentement, 1974 (Mallet)
Léon G. Damas, 1996 (Maldoror)
Leon Morin, pretre, 1961 (Trintignant)
Léonor, 1974 (Ullmann)
Leopard *see* Gattopardo, 1963
Leoš Janácek, 1985 (Krumbachová)
Leper's Coat, 1914 (Weber)
L'Equilibriste, 1902 (Guy)
L'Eroismo di un Aviatore a Tripoli, 1912 (Notari)
Lesbian Avengers Eat Fire Too, 1993 (Friedrich)
Lesbos Film, 1981 (Hammer)
L'Escapade de Filoche, 1915 (Musidora)
Less Than Dust, 1916 (Pickford)
Lesson in Mechanics, 1914 (Loos)
Lest We Forget *see* Contre l'oubli, 1991
Let It Be, 1970 (Ono)

Let It Ride, 1989 (Allen, D.)
Let Joy Reign Supreme... *see* Que la fête commence..., 1975
Let Me Go *see* Tu as Crie, 1997
Let Us Be Gay, 1930 (Marion)
L'eta' di Stalin, 1963 (Cavani)
L'Été prochain, 1985 (Trintignant)
Let's Dance, 1950 (Head)
Let's Face It, 1943 (Head)
Let's Get a Divorce, 1918 (Loos)
Let's Get Married, 1937 (Lupino)
Let's Hope It's a Girl *see* Speriamo che sia femmina, 1986
Let's Make a Million, 1937 (Head)
Let's Make Love, 1960 (Jeakins)
Let's Switch, 1975 (Marshall)
Let's Talk Tonight *see* Hablamos esta noche, 1982
Letter from a Filmmaker *see* Lettre d'un cineaste, 1984
Letter from the Village *see* Kaddu Beykat, 1975
Letter to My Daughter, 1996 (Pool)
Letters, 1973 (Lupino)
Letters to Dad, 1979 (B)
Lettre d'un cineaste, 1984 (Akerman)
Lettre paysanne *see* Kaddu Beykat, 1975
Letzten Tage von Gomorrah, 1974 (Sanders-Brahms)
L'évangile à Solentiname, 1979 (Mallet)
L'evento, 1962 (Cavani)
Lèvres closes, 1906 (Guy)
L'Heritage *see* Arven, 1979
L'Homme à la valise, 1984 (Akerman)
L'Honneur du Corse, 1906 (Guy)
L'hôpital de Leningrad, 1982 (Maldoror)
L'Horloger de Saint-Paul, 1974 (Pascal)
Li *see* Between the Devil and the Deep Blue Sea, 1995
Li Siguang, 1979 (Zhang)
Liberation *see* Osvobozhdenie, 1940
Liberators Take Liberties: War, Rape, Children *see* BeFreier und
    Befreite Krieg, Vergewaltigung, Kinder, 1992
Lie, 1914 (Macpherson)
Liebesgrüsse, 1971 (Hein)
Life and Times of Judge Roy Bean, 1972 (Head)
Life Begins at 8:30, 1942 (Lupino)
Life Goes On *see* Az élet megy tovább, 1959
Life in Bloom *see* Michurin, 1948
Life of Her Own, 1950 (Lennart; Rose)
Life of Juanita Castro, 1966 (Menken)
Life of Oharu *see* Saikaku ichidai onna, 1952
Life of Rufus Dawes, 1911 (Lyell)
Life of Vergie Winters, 1934 (Murfin)
Life on the Flipside, 1988 (Heckerling)
Life with Henry, 1941 (Head)
Life without a Guitar *see* Zivot bez kytary, 1962
Lifeboat, 1944 (Spencer)
Lifers Group: World Tour, 1992 (Spheeris)
Life's Most Beautiful Sides *see* Lebens schönste Seiten, 1992
Lighea, 1983 (Cecchi d'Amico)
Light of Heart *see* Life Begins at 8:30, 1942
Light of Western Stars, 1940 (Head)
Light That Came, 1909 (Pickford)
Light That Failed, 1922 (Coffee)
Light That Failed, 1939 (Head; Lupino)
Light Touch, 1951 (Rose)
Light Years, 1987 (Nelson)

Light Years Expanding, 1987 (Nelson)
Lighted Window *see* Fenesta che Lucive, 1914
Lighted Window *see* Fenesta che Lucive, 1925
Lighthouse Keeper, 1911 (Pickford)
Lightnin', 1925 (Marion)
Lightnin', 1930 (Levien)
Lightning Strikes Twice, 1951 (Coffee)
Lights, 1966 (Menken)
Like Mom, Like Me, 1978 (Murphy)
Like Most Wives, 1914 (Marion; Weber)
Liliom, 1930 (Levien)
Lily and the Rose, 1915 (Gish)
Limbo, 1972 (Silver; Spencer)
L'Impot, et tout et tout, 1970 (Poirier)
L'inchiesta, 1987 (Cecchi d'Amico)
Line, 1969 (Rainer)
Linear Accelerator, 1952 (Batchelor)
Lines of White on the Sullen Sea, 1909 (Macpherson)
L'innocente, 1976 (Cecchi d'Amico)
L'Insoumise, 1996 (Trintignant)
L'Invitation au voyage, 1927 (Dulac)
Lion savant, 1902 (Guy)
Lions Love, 1969 (Clarke; Varda)
Liqueur du couvent, 1903 (Guy)
Liquid Dynamite, 1915 (Madison)
Lis de mer, 1971 (Audry)
Lišáci-myšáci a Šibeničák, 1970 (Šimková-Plívová)
Listen Up!: The Lives of Quincy Jones, 1990 (Streisand)
Lisztomania, 1975 (Russell)
Lit, 1982 (Hänsel)
L'Italia s'è Desta, 1927 (Notari)
Litany for Survival: The Life and Work of Audre Lord, 1995 (Choy)
Littérature tunisienne de la Bibliothèque Nationale, 1983 (Maldoror)
Little American, 1917 (Macpherson)
Little Annie Rooney, 1925 (Pickford)
Little Autogomobile, 1914 (Meredyth)
Little Big Man, 1970 (Allen, D.; Jeakins)
Little Boy Lost, 1953 (Head)
Little by Little *see* Petit à petit ou Les Lettres persanes 1968, 1972
Little Chimney Sweep *see* Der kleine Schornsteinfeger, 1935<
Little Darling, 1909 (Pickford)
Little Dramas of the Big Places: Trail of the North Wind, 1923 (Shipman)
Little Dramas of the Big Places: White Water, 1923 (Shipman)
Little Dramas of the Big Places: The Love Tree, 1924 (Shipman)
Little Dramas of the Big Places: The Light on Lookout, 1923 (Shipman)
Little Forethought, 1949 (Batchelor)
Little Girl Who Lives down the Lane, 1977 (Foster)
Little Girl's Wrong *see* E' Piccarella, 1922
Little House: Look Back to Yesterday, 1983 (Murphy)
Little Iodine, 1946 (Pickford)
Little Liar, 1916 (Loos)
Little Life-Opera *see* Yi Sheng Yitai Xi, 1997
Little Lord Fauntleroy, 1921 (Pickford)
Little Lupin's Investigation *see* Prípad Lupínek, 1960
Little Madonna of the Fisherman *see* Madonnina del Pescatore, 1928
Little Man Tate, 1991 (Foster)
Little Mermaid *see* Malá morská víla, 1976
Little Minister, 1934 (Murfin)
Little Miss Marker, 1934 (Head)

Little Mister Jim, 1946 (Irene)
Little Orphan Annie, 1938 (Head)
Little Pal, 1915 (Pickford)
Little Prince, 1974 (Russell)
Little Prince Said *see* Petit prince à dit, 1992
Little Princess, 1917 (Marion; Pickford)
Little Queen *see* Reginella, 1923
Little Rascals, 1994 (Spheeris)
Little Red Riding Hood, 1911 (Pickford)
Little Sex, 1982 (von Brandenstein)
Little Shepherd of Kingdom Come, 1928 (Meredyth)
Little Soldier *see* Petit Soldat, 1963
Little Teacher, 1909 (Pickford)
Little Women, 1933 (Murfin)
Little Women, 1994 (Armstrong)
Live Water *see* O zivej vode, 1987
Lives of a Bengal Lancer, 1935 (Head)
Lives of Performers, 1972 (Rainer)
Living in a Big Way, 1947 (Irene)
Living It Up, 1954 (Head)
Living Water, 1962 (Shepitko)
Livingstone, 1980 (Kaplan)
Lizards *see* I basilischi, 1963
Llano Kid, 1939 (Head)
Lo straniero, 1967 (Cecchi d'Amico)
Local Power, People's Power *see* Poder local, poder popular, 1970
Locked Out: Ravenswood, 1992 (Kopple)
Locksmith and Chancellor *see* Slesar i kantzler, 1923
Lodging for the Night, 1912 (Pickford)
L'Odyssée du Capitaine Steve *see* Walk into Paradise, 1955
Loin du Vietnam, 1967 (Varda)
Lola, 1989 (Novaro)
Lola Casanova, 1948 (Landeta)
London, 1973 (Hein)
London Story, 1979 (Potter)
Lone Wolf Spy Hunt, 1939 (Lupino)
Lone World Sail, 1960 (Batchelor)
Lonely Lane *see* Horoki, 1962
Lonely Man, 1957 (Head)
Lonely Villa, 1909 (Pickford)
Lonely Woman *see* Kobieta samotna, 1982
Lonesome Ladies, 1927 (Coffee)
Long Absence *see* Aussi longue absence, 1961
Long Farewells *see* Dolgie provody, 1971
Long Goodbye, 1973 (Brackett)
Long Live the Republic! *see* At zije republika, 1965
Long, Long Trailer, 1954 (Goodrich; Rose)
Long Shadow, 1992 (Ullmann)
Long Silence *see* Lungo silenzio, 1993
L'onorevole Angelina, 1947 (Cecchi d'Amico)
Look Who's Talking, 1989 (Heckerling)
Look Who's Talking Too, 1990 (Heckerling)
Looking Forward, 1933 (Meredyth)
Loose Pages Bound, 1978 (Choy)
L'Opéra-Mouffe, 1958 (Varda)
Lord Byron of Broadway, 1930 (Bauchens)
Lord Chumley, 1914 (Gish; Loos)
Lord of the Flies, 1990 (Allen, J.)
Lords of Little Egypt, 1961 (Zetterling)
Lorgnon accusateur, 1905 (Guy)
Los Borges, 1978 (Mallet)

Los Caminos de la vida, 1956 (Landeta)
Los Minuteros, 1972 (Sarmiento)
L'Ospite, 1971 (Cavani)
Lost and Found, 1972 (Weill)
Lost Angel, 1943 (Irene; Lennart)
Lost Command, 1966 (Spencer)
Lost Honor of Katharina Blum see **Verlorene Ehre der Katharina Blum**, 1975
Lost Horizon, 1973 (Ullmann)
Lost House, 1915 (Gish; Loos)
Lost in Yonkers, 1993 (Coolidge)
Lost Man, 1969 (Head)
Lost People, 1949 (Box, M.; Zetterling)
Lost Revue see Ztracená revue, 1961
Lost Son, 1974 (Reiniger)
Lost Weekend, 1945 (Head)
Lothringen!, 1994 (Huillet)
Lottery Lover, 1935 (Spencer)
Louis Aragon—Un Masque à Paris, 1988 (Maldoror)
Louisiana Story, 1948 (van Dongen)
Love, 1927 (Marion)
Love, 1982 (Ullmann; Zetterling)
Love after Love see Après l'amour, 1992
Love among the Roses, 1910 (Pickford)
Love among the Ruins, 1975 (Dillon)
Love and Bullets, 1979 (Jeakins)
Love and Fear see Paura e amore, 1988
Love and the Steadfast Sweethearts see Amor und das standhafte Liebespaar, 1920
Love Ban, 1972 (Box, B.)
Love Crimes, 1992 (Borden)
Love Expert, 1920 (Loos)
Love from a Stranger, 1937 (Marion)
Love Happy, 1949 (Pickford)
Love Has Many Faces, 1965 (Head)
Love Heeds Not the Showers, 1911 (Pickford)
Love Hour, 1925 (Meredyth)
Love in a Fallen City see Qing Cheng Zhi Lian, 1984
Love in a Goldfish Bowl, 1961 (Head)
Love in Germany, 1989 (Dörrie)
Love in Germany see Ein Liebe en Deutschland, 1984
Love Is a Dog from Hell, 1987 (Hänsel)
Love Is Better Than Ever, 1951 (Rose)
Love Laughs at Andy Hardy, 1946 (Irene)
Love Letters, 1945 (Bauchens; Head)
Love Letters see Koibumi, 1953
Love Light, 1921 (Marion; Pickford)
Love Mask, 1916 (Macpherson)
Love Master, 1924 (Murfin)
Love Me or Leave Me, 1955 (Lennart; Rose)
Love Me Tonight, 1932 (Head)
Love of Sumako see Joyu Sumako no koi, 1947
Love of Sunya, 1927 (Coffee)
Love on Credit see Kaerlighed pa kredit, 1955
Love on Toast, 1937 (Head)
Love Piker, 1923 (Marion)
Love Poem see Hauchtext: Liebesgedicht (1970), 1973
Love Potion, 1993 (Chenzira)
Love Stinks—Bilder des taeglichen Wahnsinns, 1982 (Hein)
Love Thy Neighbor, 1940 (Head)
Love Thy Neighbor, 1984 (Marshall)

Love Toy, 1926 (Levien)
Love under the Crucifix see O-gin sama, 1962
Love Victorious, 1914 (Madison; Meredyth)
Love with a Song see Ta naše písnicka ceská, 1967
Love with the Proper Stranger, 1963 (Head)
Loveless, 1982 (Bigelow)
Lover, 1992 (Duras)
Lover Come Back, 1961 (Irene)
Loverboy, 1990 (Silver)
Love's Blindness, 1925 (Glyn)
Lovers?, 1927 (Booth)
Lovers Courageous, 1932 (Booth)
Loving, 1957 (Schneemann)
Loving Couples see Älskande par, 1964
Loving You, 1957 (Head)
Low Finance, 1960 (Batchelor)
Lowland see Tiefland, 1944
Lucas, 1993 (Trintignant)
Luciano, 1965 (Miró)
Luciella, 1921 (Notari)
Luckiest Girl in the World, 1936 (Spencer)
Lucky Break see Golpe de suerte, 1991
Lucky Jordan, 1942 (Head)
Lucky Partners, 1940 (Irene)
Lucky Star, 1928 (Levien)
Lucky Street, 1960 (Batchelor)
Lucky to Be a Woman see Fortuna di essere donna, 1956
Lucky Toothache, 1910 (Pickford)
Lucy Gallant, 1955 (Head)
Ludions, 1965 (Poirier)
Ludwig, 1973 (Cecchi d'Amico)
Lullaby, 1924 (Madison)
Lumière and Company see Lumière et compagnie, 1995
Lumière du lac, 1988 (Guillemot)
Lumière et compagnie, 1995 (Sanders-Brahms; Ullmann; Trintignant)
Luminous City see Svetlyi gorod, 1928
Lunch, 1899/1900 (Guy)
L'Une chante l'autre pas, 1977 (Hänsel; Varda)
Lungo silenzio, 1993 (von Trotta)
L'Union sacrée, 1915 (Musidora)
L'universe de Jacques Demy, 1995 (Varda)
L'uomo dalle due ombre, 1974 (Ullmann)
L'uomo, l'orgoglio, la vendetta, 1967 (Cecchi d'Amico)
Lure, 1914 (Guy)
Lure and the Lore, 1989 (Chenzira)
Lure of the Jungle see Paw, 1959
Lure of the Wilderness, 1952 (Jeakins)
Lure of Youth, 1921 (Madison)
Lust for Gold, 1949 (Lupino)
Lutteurs américains, 1903 (Guy)
Luv, 1967 (May)
Luxury Liner, 1948 (Rose)
Lydia Bailey, 1952 (Spencer)

M, 1931 (von Harbou)
Ma Hoggan's New Boarder, 1915 (Lyell)
Macbeth, 1916 (Loos)
Machine see Maschine, 1973
Machine-Bodies/Body-Space/Body-Machines see Maschinenkörper-Körperraum-Körpermaschinen, 1987
Machorka-Muff, 1963 (Huillet)

Macht die Pille Frei?, 1972 (Sander)
Machu Picchu, 1981 (Hammer)
Maçons, 1905 (Guy)
Mad about Men, 1954 (Box, B.)
Mad Doctor, 1941 (Head)
Mad Love, 1995 (Bird)
Madam Satan, 1930 (Bauchens; Macpherson)
Madame and Wife see Madamu to nyobo, 1931
Madame Butterfly, 1915 (Pickford)
Madame Curie, 1943 (Sharaff)
Madame Pompadour, 1927 (Marion)
Madame Satan see Madam Satan, 1930
Madame Sousatska, 1988 (Jhabvala)
Madame X—An Absolute Ruler see **Madame X—eine absolute Herrscherin**, 1977
Madame X—eine absolute Herrscherin, 1977 (Ottinger)
Madamu to nyobo, 1931 (Tanaka)
Mädchen in Uniform, 1931 (Sagan)
Made in Milan, 1990 (Schoonmaker)
Made in Paris, 1966 (Rose)
Made in U.S.A., 1966 (Guillemot)
Mademoiselle, 1965 (Duras)
Mademoiselle France see Reunion in France, 1942
Madigan, 1968 (Head)
Madison/Wis, 1970 (Hein)
Madonna of the Storm, 1913 (Gish)
Madonnina del Pescatore, 1928 (Notari)
Maestro, 1989 (Hänsel)
Maeva, 1961 (Deren)
Mafu Cage, 1978 (Littleton)
Magic Book, 1960 (Batchelor)
Magic Canvas, 1948 (Batchelor)
Magic Christian, 1969 (Ono)
Magic Flame, 1927 (Mathis; Meredyth)
Magic Horse, 1953 (Reiniger)
Magic Tide, 1962 (Murphy)
Magical Eye see Magische Auge, 1969
Magician, 1960 (Batchelor)
Magie noire, 1904 (Guy)
Magique image, 1950 (Musidora)
Magische Auge, 1969 (Export)
Magnet, 1914 (Meredyth)
Magnificent Fraud, 1939 (Head)
Mahler, 1974 (Russell)
Maid or Man, 1911 (Pickford)
Maidens in Uniform see **Mädchen in Uniform**, 1931
Maillot noir, 1917 (Musidora)
Main Attraction, 1962 (Zetterling)
Main du professeur Hamilton ou Le Roi des dollars, 1903 (Guy)
Main Event, 1979 (Streisand)
Mains négatives, 1978/79 (Duras)
Mais où et donc Ornicar, 1978 (Denis)
Mais qu'est-ce qu'elles veulent?, 1978 (Serreau)
Maisie Goes to Reno, 1944 (Irene)
Maison de jade, 1988 (Trintignant)
Maison sous les arbres, 1972 (Perry)
Majd holnap, 1980 (Elek)
Major and the Minor, 1942 (Head)
Make Me Laugh see Få mig att skratta, 1971
Make Mine Mink, 1960 (Dillon)
Make Way for Tomorrow, 1937 (Head)

Make-Up, 1937 (Craigie)
Making Mr. Right, 1987 (Seidelman)
Making of Agnes of God see Quiet on the Set: Filming Agnes of God, 1985
Making of an American Citizen, 1912 (Guy)
Making of the Sun City, 1987 (Choy)
Mal du pays, 1979 (Sarmiento)
Malá morská víla, 1976 (Krumbachová)
Malaya, 1949 (Head; Irene)
Male and Female, 1919 (Bauchens; Macpherson)
Male Bonding see Männerbunde, 1973
Male oscuro, 1990 (Cecchi d'Amico)
Malencontre, 1920 (Dulac)
Malevitch at the Guggenheim, 1973-74 (De Hirsch)
Malheurs du Sophie, 1945 (Audry)
Malou, 1981 (Meerapfel)
Mama Steps Out, 1937 (Loos)
Mama, There's a Man in Your Bed see Romuald et Juliette, 1989
Mama's Affair, 1921 (Loos)
Mame, 1974 (Van Runkle)
Mam'zelle Chiffon, 1919 (Musidora)
Man, a Country see Homme, une Terre, 1977
Man about Town, 1939 (Head)
Man and Maid, 1925 (Glyn)
Man and the Woman, 1917 (Guy)
Man Beast, 1955 (Murphy)
Man Between, 1914 (Madison)
Man from Down Under, 1943 (Irene)
Man from Kangaroo, 1919 (Meredyth)
Man from the First Century see Muz z prvního století, 1961
Man I Love, 1946 (Lupino)
Man in Half Moon Street, 1944 (Head)
Man in Love, 1987 (Kurys)
Man in Polar Regions, 1967 (Clarke)
Man in the Gray Flannel Suit, 1956 (Spencer)
Man No Run, 1989 (Denis)
Man of Conquest, 1939 (Head)
Man of Iron see Czlowiek z Zelaza, 1981
Man of the Family see Top Man, 1943
Man on a Tightrope, 1953 (Spencer)
Man on the Flying Trapeze, 1935 (Head)
Man, Pride and Vengeance see L'uomo, l'orgoglio, la vendetta, 1967
Man Sa Yay, 1980 (Faye)
Man, When He Is a Man see El hombre cuando es hombre, 1982
Man Who Dared God, 1917 (Weber)
Man Who Envied Women, 1985 (Rainer)
Man Who Finally Died, 1962 (Zetterling)
Man Who Knew Too Much, 1956 (Head)
Man Who Loved Cat Dancing, 1973 (Perry)
Man Who Rose in Price see Muz, který stoupl v cene, 1967
Man Who Shot Liberty Valance, 1962 (Head)
Man Who Stayed at Home, 1919 (Mathis)
Man Who Would Be King, 1975 (Head)
Man with a Million see Million Pound Note, 1953
Man with the Suitcase see L'Homme à la valise, 1984
Man Within, 1947 (Box, M.)
Man, Woman and Animal see Mann & Frau & Animal, 1973
Mandolin Music at Sea see Mandolinata a Mare, 1917
Mandolinata a Mare, 1917 (Notari)
Manhandled, 1949 (Head)
Manhattan Cocktail, 1928 (Arzner)

Manhattan Madness, 1916 (Loos)
Manly Man, 1911 (Pickford)
Mann & Frau & Animal, 1973 (Export)
Männer..., 1986 (Dörrie)
Männerbunde, 1973 (Sander)
Manoever *see* Geteilte Liebe, 1988
Man's Enemy, 1914 (Gish)
Manslaughter, 1922 (Bauchens; Macpherson)
Mantrap, 1926 (Head)
Mantrap, 1961 (Head)
Many Happy Returns, 1934 (Head)
Maori Maid's Love, 1916 (Lyell)
Mar de Rosas, 1977 (Carolina)
Maracaibo, 1958 (Head)
Marâtre, 1906 (Guy)
March on Paris 1914—Of General Obrest Alexander von Kluck—
    and His Memory of Jessie Holladay, 1977 (Clarke)
Marchand de ballons, 1902 (Guy)
Marchand de coco, 1899/1900 (Guy)
Marché à la volaille, 1899/1900 (Guy)
Marguerite Volant, 1997 (Pool)
Maria Rosa, 1916 (Macpherson)
Maria Rosa di Santa Flavia, 1911 (Notari)
Maria Rosa of Santa Flavia *see* Maria Rosa di Santa Flavia, 1911
Mária-nap, 1983 (Elek)
Mariage du Hibou, 1974 (Leaf)
Marian, 1996 (Krumbachová)
Marianne and Juliane *see* **Bleierne Zeit**, 1981
Maria's Day *see* Mária-nap, 1983
Marie, Ltd., 1919 (Murfin)
Mariés d'un jour, 1916 (Musidora)
Mariti in città, 1957 (Cecchi d'Amico)
Mark of Zorro, 1940 (Meredyth)
Marnie, 1964 (Allen, J.; Head)
Marriage, 1972 (Weill)
Marriage Clause, 1926 (Weber)
Marriage Is a Private Affair, 1944 (Coffee; Irene)
Married in Hollywood, 1929 (Spencer)
Married Woman *see* Femme mariée, 1964
Marry Me!, 1949 (Box, B.)
Marseillaise, 1937 (Reiniger)
Marteau, 1986 (Akerman)
Martha Clarke Light and Dark: A Dancer's Journal, 1980 (Chopra)
Martha, Ruth & Edie, 1988 (Mehta)
Martinovics, 1980 (Elek)
Martyrs of Love *see* Mucedníci lásky, 1966
Mary Regan, 1919 (Weber)
Mary the Crazy Woman *see* Miracolo Della Madonna di Pompei,
    1922
Mary's Birthday, 1951 (Reiniger)
Maschera del Vizio, 1917 (Notari)
Maschine, 1973 (Sanders-Brahms)
Maschinenkörper-Körperraum-Körpermaschinen, 1987 (Export)
Mascot of Troop "C", 1911 (Guy)
Masculin-féminin, 1966 (Guillemot)
Masculine-Feminine *see* Masculin-féminin, 1966
Masher, 1910 (Pickford)
Mask of Vice *see* Maschera del Vizio, 1917
Masked Woman, 1926 (Mathis)
Maskrosbarn, 1989 (Ahrne)
Masks of the Devil, 1928 (Marion)

Masquerade in Mexico, 1945 (Head)
Masques, 1951-66 (Parker)
Mass Production of Eggs *see* Nagyüzemi tojástermelés, 1962
Master and the Man, 1911 (Pickford)
Master Key, 1914 (Madison)
Match, 1966 (Ono)
Matchmaker, 1958 (Head)
Matelas alcoolique, 1906 (Guy)
Materialfilme I, 1976 (Hein)
Materialfilme II, 1976 (Hein)
Maternelle, 1933 (Epstein)
Maternité, 1929 (Epstein)
Matine Horner—Portrait of a Person, 1974 (Weill)
Matinee Scandal *see* One Rainy Afternoon, 1936
Mating Game, 1959 (Rose)
Matrimaniac, 1916 (Loos)
Matrimony's Speed Limit, 1913 (Guy)
Matter of Life and Death *see* På liv och död, 1986
Mauprat, 1925 (Epstein)
Mauvais coeur puni, 1904 (Guy)
Mauvaise Soupe, 1899/1900 (Guy)
Maverick, 1994 (Foster)
Max, 1992 (Treut)
Maxine Sullivan: Love to Be in Love, 1991 (Schiller)
May and December, 1910 (Pickford)
May Lady, 1998 (Bani-Etemad)
Maybe Tomorrow *see* Majd holnap, 1980
Mayhem, 1987 (Child)
Mayol series, 1900/07 (Guy)
McGuire, Go Home! *see* High Bright Sun, 1965
Me and Him *see* Ich und Er, 1987
Me and My Classmates, 1986 (Peng)
Me and the Colonel, 1958 (Head)
Me and You *see* Mej och dej, 1969
Meal Ticket, 1914 (Loos)
Meat Joy, 1964 (Schneemann)
Medal for Benny, 1945 (Head)
Meddig él az ember?, 1967 (Elek)
Medea di Porta Medina, 1919 (Notari)
Medea of Porta Medina *see* Medea di Porta Medina, 1919
Medicine Bottle, 1909 (Macpherson)
Medien und das Bild. Andy Warhol's Kunst, 1981 (Hein)
Meditation on Violence, 1948 (Deren)
Meditations, 1971 (Cantrill)
Medium Cool, 1969 (Fields)
Medusa, 1949 (Deren)
Medved, 1961 (Krumbachová)
Meet Me in Las Vegas, 1956 (Rose; Lennart)
Meet Me in St. Louis, 1944 (Sharaff)
Meet Me Tonight, 1952 (Dillon)
Meet the People, 1944 (Irene)
Meet the Prince, 1926 (Murfin)
Meilleure façon de marcher, 1976 (Pascal)
Mej och dej, 1969 (Henning-Jensen)
Melek Leaves *see* Kümmeltürkin geht, 1985
Melody of Love, 1916 (Shipman)
Memoires d'un jeune con, 1995 (Guillemot)
Mémoires d'un enfant des Andes, 1988 (Mallet)
Memoirs of a River *see* Tutajosok, 1988
Memorabilia P P 1, 1969 (Deitch)
Memories of Us, 1974 (Fields)

Memory Lane, 1926 (Booth)
Memory Pictures, 1989 (Parmar)
Memsahib Rita, 1997 (Parmar)
Men... *see* **Männer...**, 1986
Men of Tomorrow, 1932 (Sagan)
Men with Wings, 1938 (Head)
Men without Names, 1935 (Head)
Menace, 1934 (Bauchens)
Menace on the Mountain, 1970 (Foster)
Mender of Nets, 1912 (Pickford)
Men's Favorite Sport?, 1964 (Head)
Mensche verstreut und Welt verkehrt, 1975 (Sarmiento)
Menschen im Variete, 1938 (von Harbou)
Menschenfrauen, 1979 (Export)
Menses, 1974 (Hammer)
Menstruation Film *see* Menstruationsfilm, 1967
Menstruationsfilm, 1967 (Export)
Mental Images, Oder der Zugang der Welt, 1987 (Export)
Mental Images, or, the Gateway to the World *see* Mental Images, Oder
    der Zugang der Welt, 1987
Mentour (1re partie)-L'Alcoholisme: la therapie, 1977 (Poirier)
Mentour (2e partie)-L'Alcoholisme: la maladie, 1977 (Poirier)
Mépris, 1963 (Guillemot)
Merchant of Venice, 1914 (Macpherson; Weber)
Mercy, 1989 (Child)
Merrily We Go to Hell, 1932 (Arzner)
Merrily We Live, 1938 (Irene)
Merry Andrew, 1958 (Lennart)
Merry Widow, 1934 (Loos)
Merry Widow, 1952 (Levien; Rose)
Merton of the Movies, 1947 (Irene; Rose)
Mésaventure d'un charbonnier, 1899/1900 (Guy)
Meshes of the Afternoon, 1943 (Deren)
Mesmerized, 1986 (Foster)
Message, 1909 (Macpherson)
Message in the Bottle, 1911 (Pickford)
Messagère, 1974 (Palcy)
Messe de minuit, 1906 (Guy)
Messenger *see* Messagère, 1974
Mestiça, a Escrava Indomavel, 1974 (Abreu)
Mészáros László emlékére, 1968 (Mészáros)
Metal meccanico e parrucchiera in un turbine di sesso e di politica, 1996
    (Wertmüller)
Meta-Morphose, 1989 (Export)
Meta-Morphosis *see* Meta-Morphose, 1989
Metamorphosis of Mr. Samsa, 1977 (Leaf)
Metello, 1969 (Cecchi d'Amico)
Meteor Crater, Gosse Bluff, 1978 (Cantrill)
Metro by Night *see* Moskva stroit metro, 1934
Metropole, 1968 (Weill)
Metropolis, 1927 (von Harbou)
Metropolitan, 1935 (Meredyth)
Mettete l'Avvocato, 1925 (Notari)
Mexican Sweethearts, 1909 (Pickford)
Mexican's Last Raid, 1914 (Madison)
Mi Prazane me Rozùmeji, 1991 (Chytilová)
Mi Vida Loca, 1993 (Anders)
Michael, 1924 (von Harbou)
Michael, 1996 (Ephron)
Michael Strogoff or The Courier to the Czar, 1914 (Guy)
Michigan Avenue, 1973 (Gordon)

Michurin, 1948 (Solntseva)
Mickey's Pal, 1912 (Guy)
Microbe, 1919 (Mathis)
Midnight, 1939 (Head; Irene)
Midnight Adventure, 1909 (Macpherson; Pickford)
Midnight Lace, 1960 (Irene)
Midnight Madonna, 1937 (Head)
Midnight Man, 1917 (Meredyth)
Midnight Mary, 1933 (Loos)
Midnight Romance, 1919 (Weber)
Midnight Songs, 1985 (Peng)
Midnight Wedding, 1912 (Lyell)
Midsummer Nightmare, 1957 (Batchelor)
Mig og dig *see* Mej och dej, 1969
Mighty Barnum, 1934 (Meredyth)
Mighty Conqueror, Early 1930s (McDonagh Sisters)
Mighty McGurk, 1946 (Irene)
Mignon, 1900/07 (Guy)
Mignon or The Child of Fate, 1912 (Guy)
Mikado, 1939 (Dillon)
Mike's Murder, 1984 (Allen, D.)
Mikey and Nicky, 1976 (May)
Miklós Borsós *see* Borsós Miklós, 1966
Milagro Beanfield War, 1988 (Allen, D.)
Milarepa, 1973 (Cavani)
Militaire et nourrice, 1904 (Guy)
Milky Way, 1936 (Head)
Milky Way Special, 1971 (Cantrill)
Million Dollar Bride, 1914 (Loos)
Million Dollar Legs, 1939 (Head)
Million Dollar Mermaid, 1952 (Rose)
Million Dollar Robbery, 1914 (Guy)
Million Pound Note, 1953 (Craigie)
Mimi metallurgio ferito nell'onore, 1972 (Wertmüller)
Mimi the Metalworker *see* Mimi metallurgio ferito nell'onore, 1972
Min and Bill, 1930 (Marion)
Min bedstefar er en stok, 1967 (Henning-Jensen)
Mind Your Own Business, 1937 (Head)
Mindennapi történetek, 1955 (Mészáros)
Mindwalk, 1991 (Ullmann)
Ming-Wei to Singaraja, 1993 (Cantrill)
Minimum Charge No Cover, 1976 (Cole)
Ministry of Fear, 1944 (Head)
Minne, 1916 (Colette; Musidora)
Minne, l'Ingénue libertine, 1950 (Audry; Colette)
Minne, the Innocent Libertine *see* Minne, l'Ingénue libertine, 1950
Minnie, 1922 (Marion)
Minute Hands *see* Los Minuteros, 1972
Mio figlio professore, 1946 (Cecchi d'Amico)
Mir v treh izmerenijah, 1979 (Solntseva)
Miracle in Milan *see* Miracolo a Milano, 1950
Miracle in Soho, 1957 (Dillon)
Miracle of Morgan's Creek, 1944 (Head)
Miracolo a Milano, 1950 (Cecchi d'Amico)
Miracolo Della Madonna di Pompei, 1922 (Notari)
Miranda, 1948 (Box, B.)
Mireille, 1900/07 (Guy)
Miró, 1981 (Maldoror)
Mirror, 1911 (Pickford)
Mirror Has Two Faces, 1996 (Streisand)
Misérables, 1952 (Jeakins)

Misère au Borinage, 1934 (van Dongen)
Misères de l'aiguille, 1913 (Musidora)
Misfits: 30 Years of Fluxus, 1993 (Ono)
Misguided Tour, 1960 (Batchelor)
Mishaps of Seduction and Conquest, 1984 (Campion)
Misleading Widow, 1919 (Marion)
Miss Fluci Moses, 1987 (Larkin)
Miss Lina Esbrard Danseuse Cosmopolite et Serpentine series, 1902 (Guy)
Miss Mary, 1987 (Bemberg)
Miss Oyu see Oyu-sama, 1951
Miss Peasant see Baryshnia krestianka, 1916
Miss Susie Slagle's, 1946 (Head; Gish)
Miss Tatlock's Millions, 1948 (Head)
Mississippi, 1935 (Head)
Mississippi Mah Jong Blues see Mississippi Triangle, 1983
Mississippi Masala, 1991 (Nair)
Mississippi Mermaid see Sirène du Mississippi, 1969
Mississippi Triangle, 1983 (Choy)
Missouri Breaks, 1976 (Allen, D.)
Mistake, 1913 (Loos)
Mr. and Mrs. Bridge, 1990 (Jhabvala)
Mr. and Mrs. Smith, 1941 (Irene)
Mister Buddwing, 1966 (Rose)
Mr. Casanova, 1954 (Head)
Mr. Jones at the Ball, 1908 (Macpherson)
Mr. Jones Has a Card Party, 1909 (Macpherson)
Mr. Lord Says No! see Happy Family, 1952
Mr. Music, 1950 (Head)
Mr. Skitch, 1933 (Levien)
Misterio, 1979 (Fernández Violante)
Mrs. Dalloway, 1997 (Gorris)
Mrs. Jones Entertains, 1908 (Macpherson)
Mistress Nell, 1915 (Pickford)
Mrs. Parkington, 1944 (Irene)
Mrs. Sew and Sew, 1944 (Batchelor)
Mrs. Soffel, 1984 (Armstrong)
Mrs. Wiggs of the Cabbage Patch, 1934 (Bauchens)
Mrs. Wiggs of the Cabbage Patch, 1942 (Bauchens; Head)
Misunderstood Boy, 1913 (Gish)
Mit den Augen einer Frau, 1942 (von Harbou)
Mitsou, 1956 (Audry; Colette)
Mitten ins Herz, 1983 (Dörrie)
Mixed Nuts, 1994 (Ephron)
Mixed Values, 1915 (Loos)
Miyamoto musashi, 1944 (Tanaka)
M'Liss, 1918 (Marion; Pickford)
Modelage express, 1903 (Guy)
Moderato Cantabile, 1960 (Duras)
Modern Guide to Health, 1946 (Batchelor)
Modern Story see Historia współczesna, 1960
Modest Hero, 1913 (Gish)
Moffie Who Drove with Mandela, 1998 (Schiller)
Mogambo, 1953 (Rose)
Mohojereen Roustai, 1985 (Bani-Etemad)
Moi, Fleur Bleue, 1978 (Foster)
Moi, ta mère see Man Sa Yay, 1980
Molly Maguires, 1970 (Jeakins)
Molotov Cocktail see Cocktail Molotov, 1980
Moment see Øjeblikket, 1980
Moment in Love, 1957 (Clarke)

Momentos, 1981 (Bemberg)
Moments see Momentos, 1981
Mommie Dearest, 1981 (Sharaff)
Mon amour, mon amour, 1967 (Trintignant)
Mon Oncle, 1917 (Musidora)
Mon Paris, 1928 (Dulac)
Monangambée, 1969 (Maldoror)
Mondani a mondhatatlant: Elie Wiesel üzenete, 1996 (Elek)
Mondo le condanna, 1952 (Cecchi d'Amico)
Money see Geld, 1989
Money for Speed, 1933 (Lupino)
Money from Home, 1954 (Head)
Money Pit, 1986 (von Brandenstein)
Monkey King Looks West, 1985 (Choy)
Monnaie de lapin, 1899/1900 (Guy)
Monolutteur, 1904 (Guy)
Monsieur Badin, 1977 (Guillemot)
Monsieur Beaucaire, 1946 (Head)
Monster and the Girl, 1941 (Guy; Head)
Monster of Highgate Pond, 1961 (Batchelor)
Monteiro Lobato, 1970 (Carolina)
Montreal Sextet see Montréal vu par, 1991
Montréal vu par, 1991 (Pool)
Mood Contrasts, 1953 (Bute)
Mood Lyric, 1947 (Bute)
Mood Mondrian, 1963 (Menken)
Moon Goddess, 1976 (Hammer)
Moon Has Risen see Tsuki wa noborinu, 1955
Moon over Burma, 1940 (Head)
Moonbird, 1959 (Hubley)
Moonplay, 1962 (Menken)
Moon's Our Home, 1936 (Spencer)
Moons Pool, 1973 (Nelson)
Moonstruck, 1960 (Batchelor)
Moontide, 1942 (Lupino)
Moral der Ruth Halbfass, 1971 (von Trotta)
More than Friends, 1978 (Marshall)
More than a School, 1973 (Coolidge)
Morfars Resa, 1993 (Zetterling)
Morgan's Raiders, 1918 (Meredyth)
Morning After, 1986 (Allen, J.)
Morning Glory, 1933 (Akins)
Mort de Robert Macaire et Bertrand, 1905 (Guy)
Mort du cygne, 1937 (Epstein)
Mort du soleil, 1921 (Dulac)
Mortadella, 1971 (Cecchi d'Amico)
Mortal Danger, 1992
Morze, 1932 (Jakubowska)
Mosca Addio, 1987 (Ullmann)
Moscow Builds the Subway see Moskva stroit metro, 1934
Moscow Goodbye see Mosca Addio, 1987
Moses and Aaron see Moses und Aron, 1975
Moses und Aron, 1975 (Huillet)
Moskva stroit metro, 1934 (Shub)
Mossane, 1996 (Faye)
Motele the Weaver see Glaza, kotorye videli, 1928
Mother see Okasan, 1952
Mother, 1913 (Loos)
Mother and Country, 1927 (Notari)
Mother and Daughter see Anya és leánya, 1981
Mother and Son, 1967 (Krumbachová)

Mother of Many Children, 1977 (Obomsawin)
Mother of the River, 1995 (Davis)
Mother Right, 1983 (Citron)
Mother-to-Be *see* De mère en fille, 1968
Mothering Heart, 1913 (Gish)
Mother's Atonement, 1915 (Madison)
Mother's Cry, 1930 (Coffee)
Mother's Heart *see* Coração Materno, 1951
Mother's Instinct, 1915 (Madison)
Mots pour le dire, 1983 (Cecchi d'Amico)
MOTV, 1993 (Chenzira)
Mouche, 1903/04 (Guy)
Mouettes, 1994 (Kaplan)
Mountain, 1956 (Head)
Mountain Giant and the Skiers *see* Krakonoš a lyzníci, 1980
Mountain Music, 1937 (Head)
Mountaineer's Honor, 1909 (Pickford)
Mourir à tue-tête, 1979 (Poirier)
Mouvements du désir, 1994 (Pool)
Movers & Shakers, 1985 (Marshall)
Moving In, 1993 (Akerman)
Moving Picture Postcards, 1978 (Cantrill)
Moving Spirit, 1951 (Batchelor)
Moyen Montrage *see* Keep It for Yourself, 1991
Mrkácek Ciko, 1982 (Šimková-Plívová)
Mucedníci lásky, 1966 (Krumbachová)
Mud, 1963 (Cantrill)
Muggsy Becomes a Hero, 1910 (Pickford)
Muggsy's First Sweetheart, 1910 (Pickford)
Multiple Orgasm, 1976 (Hammer)
Munekata shimai, 1950 (Tanaka)
Munekata Sisters *see* Munekata shimai, 1950
Munka vagy hivatás?, 1963 (Mészáros)
Mur Murs, 1980 (Varda)
Mura di Malapaga, 1949 (Cecchi d'Amico)
Mural Murals *see* Mur Murs, 1980
Murder, 1930 (Reville)
Murder and Murder, 1996 (Rainer)
Murder by Death, 1976 (Booth)
Murder Goes to College, 1937 (Head)
Murder, He Says, 1945 (Head)
Murder in New Hampshire: The Pamela Wojas Smart Story, 1992 (Chopra)
Murder in Thornton Square *see* Gaslight, 1944
Murder of Mr. Devil *see* Vrazda ing. Certa, 1970
Murder with Pictures, 1936 (Head)
Musashi Miyamoto *see* Miyamoto musashi, 1944
Musashino fujin, 1951 (Tanaka)
Museum of Modern Art Show, 1971 (Ono)
Music for Millions, 1944 (Irene)
Music in Darkness *see* Musik i moerker, 1948
Music Lovers, 1970 (Russell)
Music Man, 1938 (Batchelor)
Music Man, 1962 (Jeakins)
Musica, 1966 (Duras)
Musical May *see* Maestro, 1989
Musidora en Espagne *see* Aventura de Musidora en España, 1922
Musik i moerker, 1948 (Zetterling)
Musique d'Amérique latine, 1979 (Mallet)
Musketeers of Pig Alley, 1912 (Gish; Loos)
Mutiny, 1983 (Child)
Mutiny on the Bounty, 1916 (Lyell)

Mutiny on the Bounty, 1935 (Booth)
Mutterlied, 1937 (von Harbou)
Muz, který stoupl v cene, 1967 (Krumbachová)
Muz z prvního století, 1961 (Krumbachová)
My America ... or Honk if You Love Buddha, 1996 (Choy)
My American Grandson *see* Shanghai Jiaqi, 1992
My American Wife, 1936 (Van Upp)
My Baby, 1912 (Gish; Loos; Pickford)
My Best Girl, 1927 (Pickford)
My Blue Heaven, 1990 (Ephron)
My Boys Are Good Boys, 1978 (Lupino)
My Brilliant Career, 1979 (Armstrong)
My Brother Talks to Horses, 1946 (Irene)
My Cousin Rachel, 1952 (Jeakins)
My Crazy Life *see* Mi Vida Loca, 1993
My Darling Clementine, 1946 (Spencer)
My Dream Is to Marry an African Prince, 1984 (Larkin)
My Enemy the Sea *see* Taiheyo hitoribochi, 1963
My Father Is Coming, 1991 (Treut)
My Favorite Blonde, 1942 (Head)
My Favorite Brunette, 1947 (Head)
My Favorite Spy, 1951 (Head)
My Fighting Gentleman, 1917 (Shipman)
My Filmmaking, My Life: Matilde Landeta, 1990 (Fernández Violante; Novaro)
My Foolish Heart, 1949 (Head)
My Friend Irma, 1949 (Head)
My Friend Irma Goes West, 1950 (Head)
My Geisha, 1962 (Head)
My Heart Belongs to Daddy, 1942 (Head)
My Life to Live *see* **Vivre sa vie**, 1962
My Little Chickadee, 1940 (West)
My Love for Yours *see* Honeymoon in Bali, 1939
My Love Has Been Burning *see* Waga koi wa moenu, 1949
My Love, My Love *see* Mon amour, mon amour, 1967
My Madonna, 1915 (Guy)
My Name Is Kahentiiosta, 1995 (Obomsawin)
My Name Is Oona, 1969 (Nelson)
My Old Man, 1979 (von Brandenstein)
My Own Country, 1997 (Nair)
My Own True Love, 1948 (Head)
My Own TV *see* MOTV, 1993
My Praguers Understand Me *see* Mi Prazane me Rozùmeji, 1991
My Reputation, 1946 (Head)
My Sister, My Love *see* Mafu Cage, 1978
My Six Loves, 1963 (Head)
My Son John, 1952 (Head)
My Son, My Son!, 1940 (Coffee)
My Universe Inside Out, 1996 (Hubley)
My Wife's Best Friend, 1952 (Lennart)
Myra Breckenridge, 1970 (Van Runkle; West; Head)
Myself When Fourteen, 1989 (Cantrill)
Mysterious Lady, 1928 (Booth; Meredyth)
Mysterious Mrs. M, 1917 (Weber)
Mysterious Rider, 1938 (Head)
Mysterium, 1978 (Clarke)
Mystery *see* Misterio, 1979
Mystery of a Hansom Cab, 1924 (McDonagh Sisters)
Mystery of Wickham Hall, 1914 (Madison; Meredyth)
Mystery Sea Raider, 1940 (Head)
Mystery Woman, 1916 (Meredyth; Madison)

Naar man kun er ung, 1943 (Henning-Jensen)
Naarden Vesting, 1993 (Apon)
Nacht der Regisseure, 1995 (Meerapfel; Riefenstahl; Sander; Sanders-Brahms; von Trotta)
Nad Niemnem, 1939 (Jakubowska)
Nagareru, 1956 (Tanaka)
Nagyüzemi tojástermelés, 1962 (Mészáros)
Náhrdelník melancholie, 1968 (Krumbachová)
Nails, 1995 (Kopple)
Naked Edge, 1961 (Dillon)
Naked Jungle, 1954 (Head)
Naked Spaces: Living Is Round, 1985 (Trinh)
Namibia, Independence Now, 1984 (Choy)
Nana, 1934 (Arzner)
Nancy Goes to Rio, 1950 (Rose)
Naniwa ereji, 1940 (Tanaka)
Nano Rosso, 1917 (Notari)
Naples Connection see Camorra, 1986
Naples, Land of Love see Napoli Terra d'Amore, 1928
Naples, Singing Mermaid see Napoli Sirena Della Canzone, 1929
Napló apámnak, anyámnak, 1990 (Mészáros)
Napló gyermekeimnek, 1982 (Henning-Jensen; Mészáros)
Napló szerelmeimnek, 1987 (Mészáros)
Napoleon and Samantha, 1972 (Foster)
Napoli Sirena Della Canzone, 1929 (Notari)
Napoli Terra d'Amore, 1928 (Notari)
Narayama bushi-ko, 1958 (Tanaka)
Nargeso, 1992 (Bani-Ftemad)
Narrow Escape, 1913 (Loos)
Narrow Road, 1912 (Pickford)
Nash chestnyi khleb, 1964 (Muratova)
Nathalie Granger, 1972 (Duras)
Nation Sets Its Course, 1953 (Grayson)
National Barn Dance, 1944 (Head)
National Lampoon's European Vacation, 1985 (Heckerling)
National Velvet, 1944 (Irene)
Native Country see Strana rodnaya, 1942
Nattlek, 1966 (Zetterling)
Natural Features, 1990 (Nelson)
Nature morte, 1966 (Guillemot)
Naughty Arlette see Romantic Age, 1949
Naughty Marietta, 1935 (Goodrich)
Nausicaa, 1970 (Varda)
Navire Night, 1978 (Duras)
Navy Wife, 1935 (Levien)
Ne bougeons plus, 1903 (Guy)
Néa , 1976 (Kaplan)
Near and Far Away see Långt borta och nära, 1976
Near Dark, 1987 (Bigelow)
Near Wilmington, 1978 (Cantrill)
Nearly a Burglar's Bride, 1914 (Loos)
Nearly a Lady, 1915 (Marion)
'Neath Austral Skies, 1913 (Lyell)
Nebulae, 1963 (Cantrill)
Necklace, 1909 (Pickford)
Necklace of Melancholy see Náhrdelník melancholie, 1968
Ned McCobb's Daughter, 1928 (Bauchens; Coffee)
Nefnukej, veverko!, 1988 (Šimková-Plívová)
Negative/Positive on Three Images by Baldwin Spencer, 1901, 1974 (Cantrill)
Negra Angustias, 1949 (Landeta)
Nell, 1994 (Foster)

Nella città l'inferno, 1958 (Cecchi d'Amico)
Nell's Eugenic Wedding, 1914 (Loos)
Nelson Affair see Bequest to the Nation, 1973
Nelson Pereira Dos Santos, 1979 (Carolina)
Nema Kiáltás, 1982 (Mészáros)
Nénette and Boni see Nénette et Boni, 1996
Nénette et Boni, 1996 (Denis)
Neptune's Daughter, 1949 (Irene)
Nest of Noblemen, 1915 (Preobrazhenskaya)
Netherlands America, 1943 (van Dongen)
Neugier immer weiter treiben see Nacht der Regisseure, 1995
Nevada Smith, 1966 (Head)
Nevelson in Process, 1976 (Godmilow)
Never Again!, 1910 (Pickford)
Never Fear, 1950 (Lupino)
Never Say Die, 1939 (Head)
Never So Few, 1960 (Rose)
New Criminal Underworld see 'A Mala Nova, 1920
New Earth see Nieuwe Gronden, 1934
New Kind of Love, 1963 (Head)
New Land see Nybyggarna, 1973
New Leaf, 1971 (May)
New Moon, 1931 (Booth)
New Movements Generate New Thoughts, 1971 (Cantrill)
New Song [Chilean] see Nueva canción (chilena), 1973
New World, 1953 (Grayson)
New York Hat, 1912 (Gish; Loos; Pickford)
New York Loft, 1983 (Hammer)
New York, New York, 1977 (Van Runkle)
New York, New York Bis, 1984 (Akerman)
New York Stories, 1989 (Schoonmaker)
New York Town, 1941 (Head)
Newlyweds, 1910 (Macpherson; Pickford)
News from Home, 1977 (Akerman)
News Review No. 2, 1945 (van Dongen)
Newsreel: Jonas in The Brig, c. 1965 (De Hirsch)
Next of Kin see Arven, 1979
Next Summer see L'Été prochain, 1985
Nez, 1963 (Parker)
Nez se rozhrne opona, 1957 (Šimková-Plívova)
Nezabivaemoe, 1968 (Solntseva)
'Nfumo, 1924 (Notari)
Ni Une, Ni Deux, 1991 (Denis)
Niagara, 1953 (Jeakins)
Nibelungen, 1923 (Reiniger; von Harbou)
Nice, Very Nice, 1995 (Denis)
Nicht versöhnt oder Es hilft nur Gewalt, wo Gewalt herrscht, 1965 (Huillet)
Nickelodeon, 1976 (Van Runkle)
Niedzielne Dzieci, 1976 (Holland)
Nieuwe Gronden, 1934 (van Dongen)
Nieuwe polders, 1931 (van Dongen)
Nigeria, Nigeria One, 1973 (Choy)
Night after Night, 1932 (West)
Night and Day see Nuit et jour, 1991
Night at Earl Carroll's, 1940 (Head)
Night at the Roxbury, 1998 (Heckerling)
Night Club Scandal, 1937 (Head)
Night Court, 1932 (Coffee)
Night Full of Rain see End of the World in Our Usual Bed in a Night Full of Rain, 1978

Night Games *see* Nattlek, 1966
Night Has a Thousand Eyes, 1948 (Head)
Night Is My Future *see* Musik i moerker, 1948
Night Moves, 1975 (Allen, D.)
Night of January 16th, 1941 (Head)
Night of Love, 1927 (Coffee)
Night of Mystery, 1937 (Head)
Night of Nights, 1939 (Head)
Night of the Beast *see* House of the Black Death, 1965
Night of the Filmmakers *see* Nacht der Regisseure, 1995
Night of the Filmmakers, 1995 (Ottinger)
Night of the Hunter, 1955 (Gish)
Night of the Iguana, 1964 (Jeakins)
Night on Bald Mountain *see* **Nuit sur le Mont Chauve**, 1933
Night People, 1954 (Spencer)
Night Plane from Chungking, 1943 (Head)
Night Porter *see* Portiere di notte, 1974
Night Visitor, 1971 (Ullmann)
Night We Never Met, 1993 (Seidelman)
Night Work, 1939 (Head)
Nikdo se nebude smát, 1965 (Krumbachová)
Nille, 1968 (Henning-Jensen)
Niña de luto, 1964 (Miró)
Nine Image Film, 1971 (Cantrill)
Nine Months *see* Kilenc hónap, 1976
Nine till Six, 1932 (Reville)
Ninfa plebea, 1996 (Wertmüller)
Nishijin no shimai, 1952 (Tanaka)
Nitrate Kisses, 1993 (Hammer)
Nix on Dames, 1929 (Spencer)
No Address, 1988 (Obomsawin)
No Exit *see* Huis clos, 1954
No Exit No Panic *see* Berührte, 1981
No Fear, No Die *see* S'en fout la mort, 1990
No-Gun Man, 1924 (Arzner)
No Kidding, 1960 (Dillon)
No Leave No Love, 1946 (Irene)
No Love for Johnnie, 1961 (Box, B.)
No Man of Her Own, 1950 (Head)
No Mercy, 1986 (von Brandenstein)
No Mercy No Future *see* Berührte, 1981
No, My Darling Daughter, 1961 (Box, B.)
No No Nooky TV, 1987 (Hammer)
No Nukes, 1981 (Kopple)
No Questions Asked, 1951 (Rose)
No Time for Love, 1943 (Head; Irene)
No Trace of Romanticism *see* Von Romantik keine Spur, 1980
Nobody Gets the Laugh *see* Nikdo se nebude smát, 1965
Nobody Loves Me *see* Keiner Liebt Mich, 1994
Nobody Runs Forever, 1968 (Box, B.)
Nobody's Woman *see* Señora de Nadie, 1982
Noce au lac Saint-Fargeau, 1905 (Guy)
Noces barbares, 1987 (Hänsel)
Noces d'argent, 1915 (Musidora)
Nocturnal Love That Leaves *see* Nocturno amor que te vas, 1986
Nocturne, 1946 (Harrison)
Nocturne, 1951-66 (Parker)
Nocturne for Rosario *see* Nocturno a Rosario, 1991
Nocturno a Rosario, 1991 (Landeta)
Nocturno amor que te vas, 1986 (Fernández Violante)
Noisy Neighbors, 1929 (Bauchens)

Nomadic People *see* I Nomadi, 1912
Non stuzzicate la zanzara, 1967 (Wertmüller)
North Country Tour, 1977 (Choy)
North Dalls Forty, 1979 (Jeakins)
North of the Rio Grande, 1937 (Head)
North to Alaska, 1960 (Spencer)
Northwest Mounted Police, 1940 (Bauchens; Head; Macpherson)
Nos Bon Etudiants, 1903/04 (Guy)
Nose *see* Nez, 1963
Not a Pretty Picture, 1975 (Coolidge)
Not a Simple Story, 1995 (Choy)
Not Fourteen Again, 1996 (Armstrong)
Not Just a Pretty Face, 1983 (Armstrong)
Not Reconciled *see* Nicht versöhnt oder Es hilft nur Gewalt, wo Gewalt herrscht, 1965
Not Wanted, 1949 (Lupino)
Not with My Wife, You Don't!, 1966 (Head)
Notebook, 1963 (Menken)
Notes on Berlin, the Divided City, 1986 (Cantrill)
Notes on the Passage of Time, 1979 (Cantrill)
Nothing but Lies *see* Rien que des mensonges, 1991
Nothing but the Truth, 1941 (Head)
Nothing but Trouble, 1944 (Irene)
Notorious, 1946 (Head)
Notorious Lady, 1927 (Murfin)
Notorious Sophie Lang, 1934 (Head)
Notre mariage, 1984 (Sarmiento)
Notte d'estate, con profilo Greco, occhi amandorla e odore di basilico, 1986 (Wertmüller)
Notti bianche, 1957 (Cecchi d'Amico)
N'oublie pas que tu vas mourir, 1995 (Guillemot)
Nouvelle orangerie, 1966 (Kaplan)
Novel Affair *see* Passionate Stranger, 1957
Now Let's Talk about Men *see* Questa volta parliamo di uomini, 1965
Nowhere to Run, 1977 (Cole)
Noyes, 1976 (Gordon)
Nr. 1—Aus Berichten der Wach—und Patrouillendienst, 1984 (Sander)
Nr. 8—Aus Berichten der Wach—und Patrouillendienst, 1984 (Sander)
Nth Commandment, 1923 (Marion)
Nu borjar livet, 1948 (Zetterling)
Nueva canción (chilena), 1973 (Sarmiento)
Nueva Vida, 1967 (Godmilow)
Nuit agitée, 1897 (Guy)
Nuit et jour, 1991 (Akerman)
Nuit noire, Calcutta, 1964 (Duras)
Nuit sur le Mont Chauve, 1933 (Parker)
No. 1—From the Reports of Security Guards and Patrol Services *see* Nr. 1—Aus Berichten der Wach—und Patrouillendienst, 1984
No. 8—From the Reports of Security Guards and Patrol Services *see* Nr. 8—Aus Berichten der Wach—und Patrouillendienst, 1984
Number Seventeen, 1932 (Reville)
Nüren de gushi, 1987 (Peng)
Nuren sishi *see* Xiatian de Xue, 1994
Nursery School *see* **Maternelle**, 1933
Nuts, 1987 (Streisand)
Nutty Professor, 1963 (Head)
Nybyggarna, 1973 (Ullmann)

O Amuleto de Ogum, 1973 (Yamasaki)
'O Cuppe' d'a Morte, 1923 (Notari)

O Ébrio, 1946 (Abreu)
'O Festino e 'a Legge see 'A Legge, 1920
O-gin sama, 1962 (Tanaka)
O Honzovi, Jakubovi Kosteckovi a papírovém okénku, 1981 (Krumbachová)
'O Munaciello, 1921 (Notari)
O n necem jiném, 1963 (Chytilová)
O neposedném knoflícku, 1975 (Krumbachová)
O noviço Rebelde, 1997 (Yamasaki)
O Regresso do Homem Que Não Gostava de Sair de Casa, 1996 (Amaral)
O saisons, o châteaux, 1957 (Varda)
O slavnosti a hostech, 1966 (Krumbachová)
O Snehurce, 1972 (Šimková-Plívová)
O Sonho Acabou, 1973 (Carolina)
O statecném kovári, 1983 (Krumbachová)
O zivej vode, 1987 (Krumbachová)
Ob's stürmt oder schneit, 1976 (Dörrie)
Obsessions see Uvletschenia, 1994
Occupants of Manor Houses see Kastélyok lakói, 1966
Ocean, 1978 (Cantrill)
Ocean Waif, 1916 (Guy)
Oci ciornie, 1987 (Cecchi d'Amico)
Odds against Tomorrow, 1959 (Allen, D.)
Odyssey see Odyssey Tapes, 1980
Odyssey Tapes, 1980 (Godmilow)
Of Flesh and Blood see Grands chemins, 1963
Of Human Rights, 1950 (van Dongen)
Of Lace and Sugar see De encaje y azucar, 1981
Of Men and Demons, 1969 (Hubley)
Of Seals and Men, 1980 (Zetterling)
Of Stars and Men, 1961 (Hubley)
Off Beat, 1986 (Allen, D.)
Off Limits, 1953 (Head)
Off the Limits see Kharejaz Mahdoudeh, 1988
Offbeat, 1961 (Zetterling)
Offenders, 1980 (B)
Oh Uncle, 1909 (Pickford)
Oh, You Women!, 1919 (Loos)
O'Hara's Wife, 1983 (Foster)
Ohio, 1997 (Bigelow)
Ohne Titel Nr. 2, 1968 (Export)
Ohne Titel xn, 1968 (Export)
Oil and Water, 1913 (Gish)
Øjeblikket, 1980 (Henning-Jensen)
Ojosan, 1930 (Tanaka)
Ök ketten, 1977 (Mészáros)
Okasan, 1952 (Tanaka)
Oklahoma!, 1955 (Levien)
Okoto and Sasuke see Okoto to Sasuke, 1935
Okoto to Sasuke, 1935 (Tanaka)
Old Acquaintance, 1943 (Coffee)
Old Actor, 1912 (Pickford)
Old Crow, 1979 (Obomsawin)
Old Digs, 1993 (Nelson)
Old-Fashioned Woman, 1974 (Coolidge)
Old Ironsides, 1926 (Arzner)
Old Lady 31, 1920 (Mathis)
Old Love see Alte Liebe, 1985
Old Maid, 1939 (Akins)
Old Man and Dog, 1970 (Armstrong)

Old Wives for New, 1918 (Macpherson)
Old Wives' Tales, 1946 (Batchelor)
Older Brother, Younger Sister see Ani imoto, 1952
Oldest Profession see Plus Vieux Métier du monde, 1967
Ole, 1967 (Hein)
Olivia, 1951 (Audry)
Olivier, Olivier, 1991 (Holland)
Olly Olly Oxen Free, 1978 (Head)
Oltre il Bene e il Male see Al di là del bene e del male, 1977
Oltre la Porta see Beyond the Door, 1983
Olyan, mint otthon, 1978 (Mészáros)
Olympia, 1938 (Riefenstahl)
Olympische Spiele 1936 see **Olympia**, 1938
Ombres du passé, 1926 (Musidora)
Omen, 1976 (Dillon)
On a Clear Day You Can See Forever, 1970 (Streisand)
On an Island with You, 1948 (Irene)
On Becoming a Woman, 1986 (Chenzira)
On Dangerous Ground, 1916 (Marion)
On Dangerous Ground, 1951 (Lupino)
On est poivrot, mais on a du cœur, 1905 (Guy)
On Golden Pond, 1981 (Jeakins)
On Such a Night, 1937 (Head)
On s'est trompé d'histoire d'amour, 1973 (Serreau)
On the Double, 1961 (Head)
On the Move see Utközben, 1979
On the Neman River see Nad Niemnem, 1939
On the Other Island see En la otra isla, 1968
On the Town, 1949 (Comden; Rose)
On the Twelfth Day, 1956 (Toye)
On the Yard, 1979 (Silver)
On Top of the Whale see Toit de la Baleine, 1981
Once a Hero, 1988 (Weill)
Once a Lady, 1931 (Akins)
Once More, My Darling, 1949 (Harrison)
Once upon a Thursday see Affairs of Martha, 1943
One among Many see Een blandt mange, 1961
One and the Same, 1972 (Nelson)
One Clear Call, 1922 (Meredyth)
One Day Pina Asked Me see Jour Pina m'a demandé, 1983
One Glance, and Love Breaks Out see Ein Blick—und die Liebe bricht aus, 1986
One Good Turn, 1954 (Dillon)
One Hour Late, 1934 (Bauchens)
One Hundred a Day, 1973 (Armstrong)
One Hundred Percent American, 1918 (Pickford)
One Hundred Percent Pure see Girl from Missouri, 1934
One Hundred Years of Mormonism, 1913 (Shipman)
One Little Indian, 1973 (Foster)
One Night in Lisbon, 1941 (Head; Van Upp)
One Plus One, 1968 (Guillemot)
One Rainy Afternoon, 1936 (Lupino; Pickford)
One Romantic Night, 1930 (Gish)
One Second in Montreal, 1969 (Wieland)
One She Loved, 1912 (Gish; Pickford)
One Sings, the Other Doesn't see L'Une chante l'autre pas, 1977
One Two Three, 1978 (Clarke)
One Way or Another see **De cierta manera**, 1977
Only the Brave, 1930 (Head)
Only Thing, 1926 (Glyn)
Only Two Can Play, 1962 (Zetterling)

Onna bakari no yoru, 1961 (Tanaka)
Opened by Mistake, 1940 (Head)
Opening in Moscow, 1959 (Clarke)
Opowiesc Atlantycka, 1954 (Jakubowska)
Opposite Sex, 1956 (Rose)
Optic Nerve, 1985 (Hammer)
Oranges Are Not the Only Fruit, 1989 (Kidron)
Oranges de Jaffa, 1936-39 (Parker)
Orders to Kill, 1958 (Gish)
Orfeo, 1972 (Leaf)
Orlando, 1993 (Potter)
Örmens ägg see Serpent's Egg, 1977
Ornament des verliebten Herzens, 1919 (Reiniger)
Ornament of the Loving Heart see Ornament des verliebten Herzens, 1919
Ornamental Hairpin see Kanzashi, 1941
Ornamentals, 1979 (Child)
Ornette, Made in America, 1985 (Clarke)
Ornithopter, 1985 (Apon)
Örökbefogadás, 1975 (Mészáros)
Örökseg, 1980 (Mészáros)
Orphan of Naples see Scugnizza, 1923
Orphans of the Storm, 1921 (Gish)
Országutak vándora, 1956 (Mészáros)
Osaka Elegy see Naniwa ereji, 1940
Oscar, 1966 (Head)
Oscar & Lucinda, 1997 (Armstrong)
Osram, 1951-66 (Parker)
Ostatni etap, 1947 (Jakubowska)
Osvobozhdenie, 1940 (Solntseva)
Other Half and the Other Half see Wo ai tai kung ten, 1988
Other Half of the Sky: A China Memoir, 1974 (Weill)
Other Love, 1947 (Head)
Other Side of Midnight, 1977 (Sharaff)
Othon, 1969 (Huillet)
Otley, 1968 (Dillon)
Otoñal, 1992 (Novaro)
Ototo, 1960 (Tanaka)
Otto e mezzo, 1963 (Wertmüller)
Otto e Novanta, 1924 (Notari)
Our Betters, 1933 (Murfin)
Our Blushing Brides, 1930 (Meredyth)
Our Hearts Were Growing Up, 1946 (Head)
Our Hearts Were Young and Gay, 1944 (Head)
Our Honest Bread see Nash chestnyi khleb, 1964
Our Leading Citizen, 1939 (Head)
Our Marriage see Notre mariage, 1984
Our Neighbors, the Carters, 1939 (Head)
Our São Paolo see São Paolo de todos nos, 1981
Our Trip, 1981 (Hammer)
Our Vines Have Tender Grapes, 1945 (Irene)
Out from the Shadow, 1911 (Macpherson)
Out in Silence, 1995 (Choy)
Out in South Africa, 1994 (Hammer)
Out of Chaos, 1944 (Craigie)
Out of Darkness, 1990 (Kopple)
Out of Sight/Out of Mind, 1995 (B)
Out of the Fog, 1919 (Mathis)
Out of the Fog, 1941 (Lupino)
Out of the Frying Pan see Young and Willing, 1943
Out of this World, 1945 (Head)

Out to Sea, 1997 (Coolidge)
Outcast, 1937 (Head)
Outcast Lady, 1934 (Akins)
Outcasts of Poker Flat, 1952 (Jeakins)
Outing to Vueltabajo see Excursion a Vueltabajo, 1965
Outlaw Reforms, 1914 (Meredyth)
Outrage, 1950 (Lupino)
Outsider, 1931 (Reville)
Outwitted by Billy, 1913 (Shipman)
Over Forty see Quarantaine, 1982
Over the Waves see Sobre las olas, 1981
Overloop is Sloop, 1974 (Apon)
Ovoce stromu rajských jíme, 1969 (Chytilová; Krumbachová)
Owl and the Pussycat, 1952 (Batchelor)
Owl and the Pussycat, 1970 (Booth; Streisand)
Owl and the Pussycat, 1985 (Leaf)
Owl Who Married a Goose see Mariage du Hibou, 1974
Ox, 1991 (Ullmann)
Oxo Parade, 1948 (Batchelor)
Oyu-sama, 1951 (Tanaka)

P4W, 1982 (Cole)
På liv och död, 1986 (Ahrne)
Pa Says, 1913 (Loos)
Pacific Far East Line, 1979 (Child)
Paddy O'Day, 1935 (Levien)
Padenye dinastii romanovykh, 1927 (Shub)
Pagan Love Song, 1950 (Rose)
Page de gloire, 1915 (Musidora)
Pago, 1972 (Murphy)
Paid in Full, 1950 (Head)
Painted Daughters, 1925 (McDonagh Sisters)
Pair of Briefs, 1961 (Box, B.)
Palace of Illusions see Illusionernas Natt, 1970
Palle alene i Verden, 1949 (Henning-Jensen)
Palle Alone in the World see Palle alene i Verden, 1949
Palm Beach Story, 1942 (Head; Irene)
Pan jin lian zhi qian shii jin sheng, 1989 (Law)
Panchito y El Gringo, 1962 (Murphy)
Pan/Colour Separations, 1980 (Cantrill)
Panelstory, 1979 (Chytilová)
Páni kluci, 1975 (Šimková-Plívová)
Panny z Wilka, 1979 (Pascal)
Pantalon coupé, 1905 (Guy)
Pantanal, 1973 (Carolina)
Papa les petits bateaux, 1971 (Kaplan)
Papageno, 1935 (Reiniger)
Papa's Delicate Condition, 1963 (Head)
Paper Bird see Papirfuglen, 1985
Paper Moon, 1973 (Fields)
Papirfuglen, 1985 (Breien)
Papirosnitsa ot Mosselproma, 1924 (Solntseva)
Pappersdraken see Papirfuglen, 1985
Parabola, 1937 (Bute)
Parade des chapeaux, 1936-39 (Parker)
Paradies, 1986 (Dörrie)
Paradine Case, 1947 (Reville)
Paradise see Paradies, 1986
Paradise Found, 1988 (Leaf)
Paradise, Hawaiian Style, 1966 (Head)
Parahyba, a Macho Woman see Parahyba Mulher-macho, 1983

Parahyba Mulher-macho, 1983 (Yamasaki)
Paralytic, 1912 (Guy)
Paramount on Parade, 1930 (Arzner)
Pardners, 1956 (Head)
Pardon My Trunk see Buon Giorno, elefante!, 1952
Paren iz taigi, 1941 (Preobrazhenskaya)
Parenti serpenti, 1992 (Cecchi d'Amico)
Paresse, 1986 (Akerman)
Paris at Midnight, 1926 (Marion)
Paris Honeymoon, 1939 (Head)
Paris in Spring, 1935 (Lupino)
Paris Is Burning, 1990 (Livingston)
Paris la nuit ou Exploits d' apaches à Montmartre, 1904 (Guy)
Paris, Texas, 1984 (Denis)
Paris vu par...20 ans après, 1984 (Akerman)
Paris Was a Woman, 1996 (Schiller)
Parisian Blinds, 1985 (Hammer)
Parlor, Bedroom and Bath, 1920 (Mathis)
Parnell, 1937 (Coffee)
Parole Fixer, 1940 (Head)
Parson of Panamint, 1941 (Head)
Parthenogenesis, 1975 (Citron)
Partners Again, 1926 (Marion)
Partners in Crime, 1937 (Head)
Partners of the Plains, 1937 (Head)
Party and the Guests see O slavnosti a hostech, 1966
Party Crashers, 1958 (Head)
Party Girl, 1958 (Rose)
Pasqualino settebellezze, 1976 (Wertmüller)
Pasqualino: Seven Beauties see Pasqualino settebellezze, 1976
Passa a Bandiera, 1930 (Notari)
Passage, 1983 (Cantrill)
Passager du Tassili, 1985 (Maldoror)
Passages from James Joyce's Finnegans Wake see Finnegans Wake, 1965
Passante, 1972 (Faye)
Passerby see Passante, 1972
Passing of the Third Floor Back, 1935 (Reville)
Passing Quietly Through, 1971 (Coolidge)
Passion see En Passion, 1969
Passion of Anna see En Passion, 1969
Passionate Stranger, 1957 (Box, M.)
Passionate Thief see Risate di gioia, 1960
Passionless Moments, 1984 (Campion)
Passions see Uvletschenia, 1994
Pastorale, 1950 (Bute)
Pathways of Life, 1916 (Gish)
P tissier et ramoneur, 1904 (Guy)
Patriamada, 1985 (Yamasaki)
Patriotes, 1994 (Pascal)
Patriotism, 1964 (Wieland)
Patriots see Patriotes, 1994
Patro Le Prévost 80 Years Later, 1991 (Obomsawin)
Patsy, 1964 (Head)
Pattes de Velours, 1986 (Kaplan)
Patto col diavolo, 1948 (Cecchi d'Amico)
Paula aus Portugal, 1979 (Dörrie)
Paura e amore, 1988 (von Trotta)
Pause between Frames, 1993 (Cantrill)
Pauvre pompier, 1906 (Guy)
Pavé, 1905 (Guy)

Paw, 1959 (Henning-Jensen)
Pay Me, 1917 (Meredyth)
Pay Off, 1930 (Murfin)
Paying Bay, 1964 (Batchelor)
Payment on Demand, 1951 (Head)
Pays bleu, 1976 (Guillemot)
Peach Basket Hat, 1909 (Macpherson; Pickford)
Pearl Diver, 1984 (Hammer)
Pearl Divers, 1960 (Batchelor)
Pearls of the Deep see Perlicky na dne, 1965
Peasant Letter see Kaddu Beykat, 1975
Peasant Women of Ryazan see Baby ryazanskie, 1927
Peau de pêche, 1928 (Epstein)
Peccato che sia una canaglia, 1954 (Cecchi d'Amico)
Pêcheur dans le torrent, 1897 (Guy)
Peel, 1982 (Campion)
Peg o' My Heart, 1933 (Booth; Marion)
Peggy Sue Got Married, 1986 (Van Runkle)
Peggy's Blue Skylight, 1964 (Wieland)
Pègre de Paris, 1906 (Guy)
Peine de talion, 1916 (Musidora)
Peintre et ivrogne, 1905 (Guy)
Peking Express, 1951 (Head)
Pelle, 1981 (Cavani)
Penelope, 1966 (Head)
Pennington's Choice, 1915 (Loos)
Pension pro svobodné pány, 1967 (Krumbachová)
Penthouse, 1933 (Goodrich)
People against O'Hara, 1951 (Rose)
People from Everywhere, People from Nowhere see Gens de toutes partes, Gens de nulle parte, 1980
People of the Pit, 1915 (Madison)
People People People, 1975 (Hubley)
People vs. John Doe, 1916 (Weber)
People vs. Larry Flint, 1996 (von Brandenstein)
People Will Talk, 1935 (Head)
People's Firehouse Number 1, 1979 (Choy)
Peoples of Indonesia, 1943 (van Dongen)
Pepe, 1960 (Head; Levien)
Pepi, Luci, Bom y otras chicas de montón, 1980 (Pascal)
Peppermint Soda see **Diabolo menthe**, 1977
Percussion, Impression & Reality, 1979 (Choy)
Percy, 1970 (Box, B.)
Percy's Progress see It's Not the Size that Counts, 1974
Peremena uchasti, 1987 (Muratova)
Perez Family, 1995 (Nair)
Perfect Gentlemen, 1978 (Ephron)
Perfect Marriage, 1946 (Head)
Perfect Pair, or, Indecency Sheds Its Skin see Ein Perfektes Paar oder die Unzucht wechselt ihre Haut, 1986
Perfect Woman, 1920 (Loos)
Perils, 1986 (Child)
Perils of Pauline, 1947 (Head)
Period of Adjustment, 1962 (Lennart)
Period Piece, 1991 (Davis)
Peripeteia I, 1977 (Child)
Peripeteia II, 1978 (Child)
Perlicky na dne, 1965 (Chytilová)
Permanent Wave, 1986 (Choy)
Persona, 1966 (Ullmann)
Personal Memoir of Hong Kong: As Time Goes By, 1997 (Hui)

Persons in Hiding, 1939 (Head)
Pervertida, 1985 (Novaro)
Pete 'n' Tillie, 1972 (Head)
Pete Roleum and His Cousins, 1939 (van Dongen)
Peter Ibbetson, 1935 (Head; Lupino)
Peter Pan, 1924 (Head)
Peter Vernon's Silence, 1926 (Lyell)
Petersburg Slums see Petersburgskiye trushchobi, 1915
Petersburgskiye trushchobi, 1915 (Preobrazhenskaya)
Petición, 1976 (Miró)
Petit à petit ou Les Lettres persanes 1968, 1972 (Faye)
Petit Amour, 1988 (Varda)
Petit Manuel d'histoire de France, ch. 1 "Des ancêtres les Gaulois à la prise du pouvoir par Louis X1V", 1979 (Sarmiento)
Petit prince à dit, 1992 (Pascal)
Petit Soldat, 1963 (Guillemot; Trintignant)
Petite magicienne, 1900 (Guy)
Petite refugiée, 1915 (Musidora)
Petits Coupeurs de bois vert, 1904 (Guy)
Petits matins, 1961 (Audry)
Peu beaucoup, passionnément, 1970 (Serreau)
Peyote Queen, 1964-67 (De Hirsch)
Phantom, 1922 (von Harbou)
Phantom Lady, 1944 (Harrison)
Phantom of Paris, 1931 (Meredyth)
Philippe Pétain: Processo a Vichy, 1965 (Cavani)
Philippe Petain: Trial at Vichy see Philippe Pétain: Processo a Vichy, 1965
Philips-Radio, 1931 (van Dongen)
Phillis Wheatley, 1989 (Dash)
Piange Pierrot, 1924 (Notari)
Piano, 1993 (Campion)
Picador, 1932 (Dulac)
Piccadilly Incident, 1946 (Toye)
Piccadilly Third Stop, 1960 (Zetterling)
Picture of Dorian Gray, 1945 (Irene)
Pictures at an Exhibition see Tableaux d'une exposition, 1972
Pictures for Barbara, 1981 (Hammer)
Picturesque Capri see Capri Pittoresco, 1912
Pied Piper of Hamelin see Der Rattenfänger von Hameln, 1918
Pied Piper of Hamelin, 1960 (Reiniger)
Pied qui étreint, 1916 (Musidora)
Pierre Vallières, 1972 (Wieland)
Pierrot assassin, 1903/04 (Guy)
Pierrot Cries see Piange Pierrot, 1924
Pies, 1983 (Leaf)
Pigeon That Took Rome, 1962 (Head)
Pillow to Post, 1945 (Lupino)
Pine's Revenge, 1915 (Madison; Shipman)
Ping Pong, 1968 (Export)
Pinguinho de Gente, 1949 (Abreu)
Pink Gods, 1922 (Levien)
Pink Jungle, 1968 (Head)
Pink Metronome, 1971 (Cantrill)
Pinocchio, 1972 (Cecchi d'Amico)
Pioneers, 1926 (Lyell)
Piper's Tune, 1960 (Box, M.)
Piping Hot, 1959 (Batchelor)
Pirate, 1948 (Goodrich)
Pirates on Horseback, 1941 (Head)
Piroska és a farkas, 1988 (Mészáros)

Pit and the Pendulum, 1913 (Guy)
Pit of Loneliness see Olivia, 1951
Place for Lovers see Amanti, 1968
Place in the Sun, 1951 (Head)
Place Mattes, 1987 (Hammer)
Place of Rage, 1991 (Parmar)
Places in the Heart, 1984 (Littleton)
Plague on You, 1987 (Parmar)
Plain Clothes, 1988 (Coolidge)
Plain Song, 1910 (Pickford)
Plainsman, 1936 (Bauchens; Macpherson)
Plaisir d'amour, 1994 (Kaplan)
Planet of Children see Planète des enfants, 1991
Planète des enfants, 1991 (Sarmiento)
Planton du colonel, 1897 (Guy)
Plateau, 1905 (Guy)
Play, 1968-73 (Potter)
Pleasantville, 1976 (Godmilow)
Please Believe Me, 1950 (Irene)
Please Don't Eat the Daisies, 1960 (Lennart)
Please Turn Over, 1960 (Dillon)
Pleasure Island, 1953 (Head)
Pleasure of His Company, 1961 (Head)
Plebei, 1915 (Preobrazhenskaya)
Plebian see Plebei, 1915
Plenty of Boys, Shortage of Men? see Gott om pojkar—ont om män?, 1995
Plumb Line, 1971 (Schneemann)
Plus Belles Escroqueries du monde, 1963 (Guillemot)
Plus Vieux Métier du monde, 1967 (Guillemot)
Po tu storonu Araksa, 1946 (Shub)
Pobeda na pravoberezhnoi Ukraine i izgnanie Nemetskikh zakhvatchikov za predeli Ukrainskikh Sovetskikh zemel, 1945 (Solntseva)
Pocket Cartoon, 1941 (Batchelor)
Pocket Filled with Dreams, 1973 (Murphy)
Pocketful of Miracles, 1961 (Head)
Poder local, poder popular, 1970 (Gómez)
Poem of an Inland Sea see Poema o more, 1958
Poem of the Sea see Poema o more, 1958
Poema o more, 1958 (Solntseva)
Poesia popular: la teoría y la práctica, 1972 (Sarmiento)
Poet and Painter Series, 1951 (Batchelor)
Poète et sa folle amante, 1916 (Musidora)
Poetic Justice, 1993 (Angelou)
Poil de carotte, 1972 (Kurys)
Point Break, 1991 (Bigelow)
Point of Terror, 1971 (Fields)
Pointe courte, 1954 (Varda)
Policewoman see Street Corner, 1953
Polin series, 1900/07 (Guy)
Polite Invasion, 1960 (Zetterling)
Politiewerk, 1979 (Apon)
Polka Graph, 1947 (Bute)
Polly of the Follies, 1922 (Loos)
Polly West est de retour, 1992 (Kaplan)
Polly with a Past, 1920 (Mathis)
Pollyanna, 1920 (Marion; Pickford)
Pommier, 1902 (Guy)
Pommy Arrives in Australia, 1913 (Lyell)
Pompon malencontreux 1, 1903/04 (Guy)

Pond and Waterfall, 1982 (Hammer)

Pony Express, 1953 (Head)

Pools, 1981 (Hammer)

Poor Consumptive! Poor Mother! *see* Povera Tisa, Povera Madre, 1913

Poor Little Peppina, 1916 (Pickford)

Poor Little Rich Girl, 1917 (Marion; Pickford)

Popas in tabara de vara, 1958 (Mészáros)

Pope Joan, 1972 (Ullmann)

Popovich Brothers of South Chicago, 1977 (Godmilow)

Poppy, 1936 (Head; Van Upp)

Popular Poetry: Theory and Practice *see* Poesia popular: la teoría y la práctica, 1972

Porgy and Bess, 1959 (Sharaff)

Portiere di notte, 1974 (Cavani)

Portrait, 1972 (Deitch)

Portrait d'une jeune fille de la fin des années 60 à Bruxelles, 1994 (Akerman)

Portrait from Life, 1948 (Box, M.; Zetterling)

Portrait of a Lady, 1996 (Campion)

Portrait of a Young Girl at the End of the 1960s in Brussels *see* Portrait d'une jeune fille de la fin des années 60 à Bruxelles, 1994

Portrait of Jason, 1967 (Clarke)

Portrait of Jennie, 1948 (Gish)

Porträts, 1972 (Hein)

Porträts I, 1970 (Hein)

Porträts II, 1975 (Hein)

Porträts III, 1977 (Hein)

Porträts. 4. Nina I-III, 1971 (Hein)

Porträts. Kurt Schwitters I, II, III, 1972 (Hein)

Posillipo as Seen from Naples *see* Posillipo da Napoli, 1909

Posillipo da Napoli, 1909 (Notari)

Positive, 1993 (Maclean)

Poslední motýl, 1990 (Krumbachová)

Poslednyi attraktzion, 1929 (Preobrazhenskaya)

Possedes, 1987 (Holland)

Possessed, 1931 (Coffee)

Postcards from the Edge, 1990 (von Brandenstein)

Postman Always Rings Twice, 1946 (Irene)

Postman Always Rings Twice, 1981 (Jeakins)

Potage indigeste, 1903 (Guy)

Potash and Perlmutter, 1923 (Marion)

Poule fantaisiste, 1903 (Guy)

Poul-e Khareji, 1990 (Bani-Etemad)

Poundmaker's Lodge: A Healing Place, 1987 (Obomsawin)

Pour Don Carlos, 1921 (Musidora)

Pour Sacha, 1992 (Kurys)

Pour secourer la salade, 1902 (Guy)

Pourquoi pas?, 1977 (Serreau)

Povera Tisa, Povera Madre, 1913 (Notari)

Povest plamennykh let, 1961 (Solntseva)

Power and the Land, 1940 (van Dongen)

Power and the Prize, 1956 (Rose)

Power Dive, 1941 (Head)

Power of Fascination, 1915 (Madison)

Power of the Camera, 1913 (Loos)

Power of the Press, 1928 (Levien)

Power to Fly, 1953 (Batchelor)

Powerful Thang, 1991 (Davis)

Pozegnanie z diablem, 1956 (Jakubowska)

Poznavaya belyi svet, 1979 (Muratova)

Practice of Love *see* Praxis der Liebe, 1984

Prague, the Restless Heart of Europe *see* Praha, neklidne srace Europy, 1985

Praha, neklidne srace Europy, 1985 (Chytilová)

Prairie Station, 1941 (Preobrazhenskaya)

Praise House, 1992 (Dash)

Pravdivý príbeh Josta Buergiho, 1988-89 (Krumbachová)

Praxis der Liebe, 1984 (Export)

Preacher's Wife, 1996 (Marshall)

Prefab Story *see* Panelstory, 1979

Prefaces, 1981 (Child)

Premier voyage, 1980 (Trintignant)

Première Cigarette, 1904 (Guy)

Première Gamelle, 1902 (Guy)

Prenatal Care in the First Year *see* Atencion prenatal, 1972

Preparativi Guerreschi a Napoli, 1911 (Notari)

Preparing for the War in Naples *see* Preparativi Guerreschi a Napoli, 1911

Prete, fai un miracolo, 1974 (Cecchi d'Amico)

Preventing Cancer, 1989 (Dash)

Price of a Good Time, 1917 (Weber)

Price of Redemption, 1920 (Madison)

Price of Things, 1930 (Glyn)

Pride and Prejudice, 1940 (Murfin)

Pride of the Clan, 1917 (Marion; Pickford)

Pride of the West, 1938 (Head)

Prière, 1900/07 (Guy)

Priest, 1994 (Bird)

Prijela k nàm pout, 1973 (Šimková Plívová)

Prima donna, 1964 (Kaplan)

Primary Colors, 1998 (May)

Prime of Miss Jean Brodie, 1969 (Allen, J.)

Primitive Lover, 1922 (Marion)

Prince and the Showgirl, 1957 (Dillon)

Prince for Cynthia, 1953 (Box, M.)

Prince of Arcadia, 1933 (Lupino)

Prince of Headwaiters, 1927 (Murfin)

Prince of Players, 1955 (Spencer)

Prince of Shadows *see* Beltenebros, 1991

Prince of the City, 1981 (Allen, J.)

Prince of Tides, 1991 (Streisand)

Princess Fragrance *see* Xiang Xiang Gong Zhu, 1987

Princess from Hoboken, 1927 (Levien)

Princesse Mandane, 1928 (Dulac)

Prins Gustaf, 1944 (Zetterling)

Prinzessin Suwarin, 1923 (von Harbou)

Prinzessin Tourandot, 1934 (von Harbou)

Prípad Lupínek, 1960 (Šimková-Plívová)

Priscilla's Prisoner, 1916 (Madison)

Prison Farm, 1938 (Head)

Prison for Women *see* P4W, 1982

Prison Stories: Women on the Inside, 1991 (Deitch; Silver; Spheeris)

Prisoner of the Harem, 1914 (Guy)

Prisoner of Zenda, 1915 (Reville)

Prisoner without a Name, Cell without a Number *see* Jacobo Timerman: Prisoner without a Name, Cell without a Number, 1983

Prisoners of Hope, 1995 (Kopple)

Private Hell 36, 1954 (Lupino)

Private Life of a Cat, 1945 (Deren)

Private Matter, 1992 (Silver)

Private Show, 1985 (Pascal)

Private's Affair, 1959 (Spencer)
Privilege, 1990 (Rainer)
Prize of Gold, 1955 (Zetterling)
Prizefighter and the Lady, 1933 (Marion)
Procès, 1962 (Parker)
Processo alla città, 1952 (Cecchi d'Amico)
Processo Cuocolo, 1909 (Notari)
Proclamation see Kiáltó, 1964
Prodigal see Southerner, 1931
Prodigal, 1931 (Meredyth)
Professor Beware, 1938 (Head)
Professor My Son see Mio figlio professore, 1946
Prohibito rubare, 1949 (Cecchi d'Amico)
Proibito, 1954 (Cecchi d'Amico)
Project for Thought and Speech see Projeto pensamiento e linguajen, 1980
Projected Light, 1988 (Cantrill)
Projekties, 1984 (Apon)
Projeto pensamiento e linguajen, 1980 (Amaral)
Promenad i de gamlas land, 1974 (Ahrne)
Promenade in the Land of the Aged see Promenad i de gamlas land, 1974
Promis...Jure!, 1989 (Pascal)
Promise see Versprechen, 1994
Proschanie s Matyoroy, 1981 (Shepitko)
Proselyt, 1969 (Export)
Proselyte see Proselyt, 1969
Prosperity Race, 1962 (Zetterling)
Proud and the Profane, 1956 (Head)
Provincial Actors see Aktorzy prowincjonalni, 1979
Przesluchanie, 1982 (Holland)
Psi a lidé, 1971 (Krumbachová)
Psychosynthesis, 1975 (Hammer)
P'tite Violence, 1977 (Poirier)
Publicity Madness, 1927 (Loos)
Pueblo Legend, 1912 (Pickford)
Pull Your Head to the Moon, 1992 (Chenzira)
Pulmonary Function, 1963 (Batchelor)
Pupatella, 1923 (Notari)
Pure beauté, 1951-66 (Parker)
Pursuit of Happiness, 1934 (Head; Van Upp)
Pusilleco Addiruso, 1918 (Notari)
Putney School, 1969 (Weill)
Pytel blech, 1962 (Chytilová)
Pythoness, 1951 (Batchelor)

Qing Cheng Zhi Lian, 1984 (Hui)
Qingchunji, 1985 (Zhang)
Qiuyue, 1992 (Law)
Quadrille réaliste, 1902 (Guy)
Quando de donne avevano la coda, 1970 (Wertmüller)
Quarantaine, 1982 (Poirier)
Quarterback, 1940 (Head)
Quartet, 1949 (Zetterling)
Quartet, 1981 (Jhabvala)
Quatre Temps, 1951-66 (Parker)
Quatre Vérités, 1962 (Cecchi d'Amico)
Que la fête commence..., 1975 (Pascal)
Quebec à vendre, 1977 (Poirier)
Queen of Hearts, 1957 (Batchelor)
Queen of the Mob, 1940 (Head)

Queens see Fate, 1966
Querida Carmen, 1983 (Novaro)
Qu'est-ce qu'on attend pour être heureux!, 1982 (Serreau)
Questa volta parliamo di uomini, 1965 (Wertmüller)
Question of Silence see De Stilte Rond Christine M, 1981
Qui c'est ce garçon, 1987 (Trintignant)
Quick and the Dead, 1995 (von Brandenstein)
Quicksands, 1914 (Gish)
Quiet Don see Tikhiy Don, 1930
Quiet on the Set: Filming Agnes of God, 1985 (Cole)
Quiet Wedding, 1941 (Dillon)
Quille, 1961 (Guillemot)
Quo Vadis, 1951 (Levien)

Rachel and the Stranger, 1948 (Head)
Rachel, Rachel, 1968 (Allen, D.)
Racines noires, 1985 (Faye)
Racisme au quotidien, 1983 (Maldoror)
Radcliffe Blues, 1968 (Weill)
Radio Rock Detente, 1995 (Leaf)
Rafle de chiens, 1904 (Guy)
Raftsmen see Tutajosok, 1988
Rage de dents, 1900 (Guy)
Raging Bull, 1980 (Schoonmaker)
Rags, 1915 (Pickford)
Ragtime, 1981 (von Brandenstein)
Rain see Regen, 1929
Rainbow Island, 1944 (Head)
Rainbows of Hawai'i, 1995 (Hubley)
Rainmaker, 1956 (Head)
Rain's Hat, 1978 (Zetterling)
Rains of Ranchipur, 1955 (Rose; Spencer)
Raising a Riot, 1955 (Toye)
Raising the Wind, 1961 (Dillon)
Raison avant la passion, 1969 (Wieland)
Raison d'être, 1977 (Poirier)
Rajtunk is mulik, 1960 (Mészáros)
Rakudai wa shitakeredo, 1931 (Tanaka)
Ramayana/Legong, 1995 (Cantrill)
Rambling Rose, 1991 (Coolidge)
"Rameau's Nephew" by Diderot (Thanx to Dennis Young) by Wilma Schoen, 1972 (Wieland)
Ramrod, 1947 (Head)
Range War, 1939 (Head)
Rangers of Fortune, 1940 (Head)
Ransom!, 1956 (Rose)
Rape see Film No. 6, 1969
Rape Prevention, 1977 (Schiller)
Rape—The Anders Case see Voldtekt-Tilfellet Anders, 1971
Rapt d'enfant par les romanichels see Erreur de poivrot, 1904
Raramuri Boy see En el país de los pies ligeros, 1980
Rasputin and the Empress, 1932 (Coffee)
Rat Life and Diet in North America, 1968 (Wieland)
Rat Race, 1960 (Head)
Rattle of a Simple Man, 1964 (Box, M.)
Raumsehen und Raumhören, 1974 (Export)
Razor's Edge, 1984 (Russell)
RCA: New Sensations in Sound, 1959 (Bute)
Rè vense jeunesse, 1992 (Trintignant)
Reaching for the Moon, 1917 (Loos)
Reaching for the Sun, 1941 (Head)

Ready for Love, 1934 (Lupino)
Real Genius, 1985 (Coolidge)
Real Life, 1979 (Spheeris)
Reap the Wild Wind, 1942 (Bauchens; Macpherson)
Rear Window, 1954 (Head)
Reason over Passion see Raison avant la passion, 1969
Reassemblage, 1982 (Trinh)
Rebecca, 1940 (Harrison)
Rebecca of Sunnybrook Farm, 1917 (Marion; Pickford)
Rebecca of Sunnybrook Farm, 1932 (Levien)
Rebellion in Cuba see Chivato, 1961
Rebellion of Kitty Belle, 1914 (Gish)
Reckless, 1935 (Booth)
Récolte est finie see Goob na nu, 1979
Recreating Black Women's Media Image, 1983 (Davis)
Recurring Dream, 1973-74 (De Hirsch)
Red Beard see Akahige, 1965
Red Danube, 1949 (Rose)
Red Dice, 1926 (Macpherson)
Red Dwarf see Nano Rosso, 1917
Red Garters, 1954 (Head)
Red Hair, 1928 (Glyn)
Red-Headed Woman, 1932 (Loos)
Red, Hot, and Blue, 1949 (Head)
Red Hot Romance, 1922 (Loos)
Red Hot Wheels see To Please a Lady, 1950
Red Kimono, 1925 (Arzner)
Red Lantern, 1919 (Mathis)
Red Lily, 1924 (Meredyth)
Red Line 7000, 1965 (Head)
Red Margaret, Moonshiner, 1913 (Macpherson)
Red Mill, 1927 (Marion)
Red Mountain, 1952 (Head)
Red News, 1966 (Schneemann)
Red Shift, 1984 (Nelson)
Red Shoe Diaries, 1995 (Borden)
Red Sky at Morning, 1971 (Head)
Red Stone Dancer, 1968 (Cantrill)
Red, White and Blue Blood, 1917 (Mathis)
Redemption, 1930 (Booth)
Reds, 1981 (Allen, D.; Russell)
Redupers see Allseitig reduzierte Persönlichkeit, 1977
Reel Time, 1971-72 (Schneemann)
Referendum—Take 2/Prise deux, 1996 (Obomsawin)
Refinery at Work, 1955 (Batchelor)
Reflections in a Golden Eye, 1967 (Jeakins)
Reflections on Three Images by Baldwin Spencer, 1901, 1974 (Cantrill)
Reformer and the Redhead, 1950 (Rose)
ReFraming AIDs, 1988 (Parmar)
Regard dans le miroir, 1984 (Kaplan)
Regard Picasso, 1967 (Kaplan)
Regarde les hommes tomber, 1994 (Pascal)
Regen, 1929 (van Dongen)
Régiment moderne, 1906 (Guy)
Reginella, 1923 (Notari)
Regionalzeitung, 1967 (Meerapfel)
Regret see Pusilleco Addiruso, 1918
Regrouping, 1976 (Borden)
Regular Girl, 1919 (Marion)
Réhabilitation, 1905 (Guy)

Rehearsal at the Arts Laboratory, 1969 (Cantrill)
Reincarnation of Golden Lotus see Pan jin lian zhi qian shii jin sheng, 1989
Reis Zonder Einde, 1988 (Apon)
Reivers, 1969 (Van Runkle)
Relatives, 1990 (Dash)
Relitto, 1961 (Cecchi d'Amico)
Reluctant Debutante, 1958 (Rose)
Reluctant Inspectors see Revizory ponevole, 1955
Reluctant Widow, 1950 (Dillon)
Remains of the Day, 1993 (Jhabvala)
Remains to Be Seen, 1953 (Rose)
Remarkable Andrew, 1942 (Head)
Remember the Night, 1940 (Head)
Remodeling Her Husband, 1920 (Gish)
... Remote ... Remote ..., 1973 (Export)
Renaissance Man, 1994 (Marshall)
Rendez-vous, 1976 (Serreau)
Rendez-vous d'Anna, 1978 (Akerman)
Rendra's Place, Depok, 1992 (Cantrill)
René Depestre, Poète, 1982 (Maldoror)
Renegade Trail, 1939 (Head)
Renunciation, 1909 (Pickford)
Répétition dans un cirque, 1903 (Guy)
Replay, 1970 (Hein)
Réponses de femmes, 1975 (Varda)
Report of 1993, 1992-94 (Bani-Etemad)
Report on the Chairman of a Farmers' Co-Operative see Riport egy TSZ-elnökröl, 1960
Reportage no. 1 see Reportaz nr 1, 1932
Reportaz nr 1, 1932 (Jakubowska)
Reproductions, 1968 (Hein)
Request see Petición, 1976
Rescuers: Stories of Courage — Two Women, 1997 (Streisand)
Ressac, 1977 (Hänsel)
Restless Sex, 1920 (Marion)
Restoration, 1909 (Pickford)
Restricted Code see Restringierter Code, 1979
Restringierter Code, 1979 (Export)
Reticule of Love, 1973-74 (De Hirsch)
Retour des champs, 1899/1900 (Guy)
Return see Rückkehr, 1990
Return of Sophie Lang, 1936 (Head)
Return of the Soldier, 1982 (Russell)
Return to the Wave see Ritorna all'Onda, 1912
Reunion, 1936 (Levien)
Reunion in France, 1942 (Irene)
Revanche, 1973 (Faye)
Rêve du chasseur, 1904 (Guy)
Réveil du jardinier, 1904 (Guy)
Revenge see Fatto di sangue fra due uomini per causa di una vedova, 1978
Revenge see Revanche, 1973
Revillagigedo Islands see Islas Revillagigedo, 1990
Revizory ponevole, 1955 (Solntseva)
Revolt, 1916 (Marion)
Revolutionary Romance, 1911 (Guy)
Reward, 1960 (Batchelor)
Rhapsody, 1954 (Rose)
Rhapsody in Blue, 1943 (Levien)
Rhinestone, 1984 (Van Runkle)

Rhode Island Red, 1968 (Rainer)
Rhubarb, 1951 (Head)
Rhythm in Light, 1934 (Bute)
Rhythm on the Range, 1936 (Head)
Rhythm on the River, 1940 (Head)
Rich and Strange, 1931 (Reville)
Rich Revenge, 1910 (Pickford)
Rich, Young and Pretty, 1951 (Rose)
Richard Cardinal: Cry from a Diary of a Métis Child, 1986
    (Obomsawin)
Richard III, 1955 (Dillon)
Richard III, 1974 (Kopple)
Richard's Things, 1981 (Ullmann)
Riddance see Szabad lélegzet, 1973
Ride a Crooked Mile, 1938 (Head)
Ride the Pink Horse, 1947 (Harrison)
Riding High, 1943 (Head)
Riding High, 1950 (Head)
Rien que des mensonges, 1991 (Pascal)
Riffraff, 1935 (Loos; Marion)
Right Cross, 1950 (Rose)
Right of Way, 1920 (Mathis)
Right to Lie, 1919 (Murfin)
Right to Love, 1930 (Akins)
Right to Refuse?, 1981 (Leaf)
Rikugun, 1944 (Tanaka)
Rîmes, 1951-66 (Parker)
Rimpianto see Pusilleco Addiruso, 1918
Ring, 1927 (Reville)
Ring a Ring o' Roses see Jak se tocí Rozmarýny, 1977
Ring of Destiny, 1915 (Madison)
Ringer, 1952 (Zetterling)
Rio Bravo, 1959 (Brackett)
Rio Lobo, 1970 (Brackett)
Riport egy TSZ-elnökröl, 1960 (Mészáros)
Riptide, 1934 (Booth)
Risate di gioia, 1960 (Cecchi d'Amico)
Rise and Rise of Michael Rimmer, 1970 (Dillon)
Rise of Helga see Susan Lenox, Her Fall and Rise, 1931
Rise of Susan, 1916 (Marion)
Rita la zanzara, 1966 (Wertmüller)
Rita the Mosquito see Rita la zanzara, 1966
Ritorna all'Onda, 1912 (Notari)
Ritual in Transfigured Time, 1946 (Deren)
Ritzy, 1927 (Glyn)
River see He Liu, 1996
River-Ghost, 1973 (De Hirsch)
Rivista Navale Dell' 11 Novembre 1912, 1912 (Notari)
Roaches' Serenade, 1971 (Weill)
Road House, 1948 (Lupino)
Road Safety, 1946 (Batchelor)
Road Show see Chasing Rainbows, 1930
Road to Bali, 1952 (Head)
Road to Morocco, 1942 (Head)
Road to Plaindale, 1914 (Loos)
Road to Rio, 1947 (Head)
Road to Singapore, 1940 (Head)
Road to Utopia, 1945 (Head)
Road to Yesterday, 1925 (Bauchens; Macpherson)
Road to Zanzibar, 1941 (Head)
Roadie, 1980 (Littleton)

Rob Roy, the Highland Rogue, 1953 (Dillon)
Robe à Cerceaux, 1992 (Denis)
Robert Doisneau, Photographe, 1983 (Maldoror)
Robert Frost: A Lover's Quarrel with the World, 1963 (Clarke)
Robert Klippel Drawings, 1947-1963, 1965 (Cantrill)
Robert Klippel Sculpture Studies, 1964-65 (Cantrill)
Robert Lapoujade, Peintre, 1982 (Maldoror)
Robert Macaire et Bertrand, 1904 (Guy)
Roberta, 1935 (Murfin)
Robinson Charley, 1946-49 (Batchelor)
Rocco and His Brothers see Rocco e i suoi fratelli, 1960
Rocco e i suoi fratelli, 1960 (Cecchi d'Amico)
Rock of Riches, 1916 (Weber)
Rockabye, 1932 (Murfin)
Rock-a-Bye Baby, 1958 (Head)
Rocking-Horse Winner, 1950 (Dillon)
Rockshow, 1980 (Schoonmaker)
Rodina Electrichestva see Homeland of Electricity, 1987
Rodolphe Bresdin 1825-1885, 1961 (Kaplan)
Rogopag, 1962 (Guillemot)
Rogue Cop, 1954 (Rose)
Rogue Song, 1930 (Booth; Marion)
Rogues of Paris, 1913 (Guy)
Rohfilm, 1968 (Hein)
Rollende Rad, 1934 (Reiniger)
Rolling Stones Rock-and-Roll Circus, 1996 (Ono)
Roma città libera, 1946 (Cecchi d'Amico)
Roman de la midinette, 1915 (Musidora)
Roman Holiday, 1953 (Head)
Romance, 1930 (Meredyth)
Romance for Cornet see Romance pro krídlovku, 1966
Romance in Manhattan, 1934 (Murfin)
Romance of a Queen see Three Weeks, 1923
Romance of Book & Sword see Shu Jian En Chou Lu, 1987
Romance of Happy Valley, 1918 (Gish)
Romance of Rosy Ridge, 1947 (Irene)
Romance of Seville, 1929 (Reville)
Romance of Tarzan, 1918 (Madison; Meredyth)
Romance of the Redwoods, 1917 (Macpherson; Pickford)
Romance of the Western Hills, 1910 (Pickford)
Romance pro krídlovku, 1966 (Krumbachová)
Romantic Age, 1949 (Zetterling)
Romantic Story of Margaret Catchpole, 1911 (Lyell)
Romazo d'amore, 1950 (Cecchi d'Amico)
Romeo and Juliet, 1936 (Booth)
Roméo pris au piége, 1905 (Guy)
Romola, 1924 (Gish)
Romona, 1910 (Pickford)
Romuald et Juliette, 1989 (Serreau)
Roof Needs Mowing, 1971 (Armstrong)
Rookie of the Year, 1973 (Foster)
Room, 1971 (Cantrill)
Room with a View, 1986 (Jhabvala)
Roommates see Raising the Wind, 1961
Rooster Cogburn, 1975 (Head)
Roots of Grief see Frihetens murar, 1978
Rope Dancing, 1990 (Coolidge)
Rope of Sand, 1949 (Head)
Rosa Luxemburg, 1986 (von Trotta)
Rose and the Ring, 1979 (Reiniger)
Rose Bowl, 1936 (Head)

Rose Garden, 1989 (Ullmann)
Rose Marie, 1936 (Goodrich)
Rose Marie, 1954 (Rose)
Rose o' the Sea, 1922 (Meredyth)
Rose of Paris, 1924 (Coffee)
Rose of the Circus, 1911 (Guy)
Rose of the Golden West, 1927 (Meredyth)
Rose of the Rancho, 1914 (Macpherson)
Rose Tattoo, 1955 (Head)
Roseland, 1977 (Jhabvala)
Rose's Story, 1911 (Pickford)
Rosita, 1923 (Pickford)
Rossini, Rossini, 1990 (Cecchi d'Amico)
Rossiya Nikolaya II i Lev Tolstoi, 1928 (Shub)
Rough Treatment see Bez znieczulenia, 1978
Roughhouse, 1988 (Coolidge)
Roughneck, 1924 (Madison)
'Round Midnight, 1986 (Pascal)
Roundup, 1941 (Head)
Roustabout, 1964 (Head)
Roy Cohn/Jack Smith, 1995 (Godmilow)
Royal Scandal, 1945 (Spencer)
Rubens, 1936 (Parker)
Rübezahls Hochzeit, 1916 (Reiniger)
Ruby Bridges Story, 1997 (Palcy)
Ruby Gentry, 1952 (Head)
Rückkehr, 1990 (von Trotta)
Ruddigore, 1964 (Batchelor)
Rudd's New Selection, 1921 (Lyell)
Rude Hostess, 1909 (Macpherson)
Rud's Wife, 1985 (Maclean)
Rue cases nègres, 1983 (Palcy)
Rues de Hong Kong, 1964 (Guillemot)
Ruggles of Red Gap, 1935 (Head)
Ruler see Der Herrscher, 1937
Rulers of the Sea, 1939 (Head)
Rules of the Road, 1993 (Friedrich)
Run for Cover, 1955 (Head)
Runaway Bride, 1930 (Murfin)
Runaways see Fugueuses, 1995
Running after Luck see Jagd nach dem Glück, 1929-30
Rusalka, 1962 (Šimková-Plívová)
Rusariye Abi, 1995 (Bani-Etemad)
Russia, 1972 (Muratova)
Russia of Nicholas II and Lev Tolstoy see Rossiya Nikolaya II i Lev Tolstoi, 1928
Russians at War, 1942 (van Dongen)
Rustler's Valley, 1937 (Head)
Ruten no ohi, 1958 (Tanaka)

S.O.B., 1981 (Van Runkle)
S.O.S. Eisberg, 1933 (Riefenstahl)
S.O.S. Kindtand, 1943 (Henning-Jensen)
S.O.S. Molars see S.O.S. Kindtand, 1943
S&W, 1967 (Hein)
SA-I-GU, 1993 (Choy)
Sa zimbeasca toti copiii, 1957 (Mészáros)
Sabotage, 1936 (Reville)
Saboteur, 1942 (Harrison)
Sabrina, 1954 (Head)
Sacrificed Youth see **Qingchunji**, 1985

Sad Sack, 1957 (Head)
Saddle the Wind, 1958 (Rose)
Safari, 1940 (Head)
Safe, 1993 (Bird)
Sage-femme de première classe, 1902 (Guy)
Saigon, 1948 (Head)
Saikaku ichidai onna, 1952 (Tanaka)
Sailboat
Sailor Beware, 1952 (Head)
Sailor from Gibraltar, 1967 (Duras)
Sailor Takes a Wife, 1945 (Irene)
Sailor's Consolation, 1951 (Batchelor)
Sailor's Heart, 1912 (Meredyth)
Sailor's Return, 1978 (Dillon)
Sailors' Wives, 1928 (Meredyth)
Saint-Denis sur Avenir, 1971 (Maldoror)
St. Francis of Assisi see Francesco, 1988
St. Louis Blues, 1939 (Head; Van Upp)
St. Louis Blues, 1958 (Head)
Sainte Odile, 1915 (Musidora)
Sainted Sisters, 1948 (Head)
Salaam Bombay!, 1988 (Nair)
Sale comme un ange, 1990 (Guillemot)
Salesman, 1960 (Batchelor)
Salesmanship see Az eladás müvészete, 1960
Sally, 1925 (Mathis)
Sally in Our Alley, 1931 (Reville)
Salome of the Tenements, 1925 (Levien)
Salt in the Park, 1959 (Wieland)
Salty O'Rourke, 1945 (Head)
Salut les Cubains, 1963 (Varda)
Salut Victor!, 1988 (Poirier)
Salute for Three, 1943 (Head)
Salute to Cuba see Salut les Cubains, 1963
Salute to France, 1943 (Grayson)
Salute to the Theatres, 1955 (Gish)
Salvation!, 1987 (B)
Salvation! Have You Said Your Prayers Today? see Salvation!, 1987
Salvatore Giuiliano, 1961 (Cecchi d'Amico)
Sam & Me, 1991 (Mehta)
Sambizanga, 1972 (Maldoror)
Same Time, Next Year, 1978 (Van Runkle)
Samson, 1914 (Madison)
Samson and Delilah, 1949 (Bauchens; Head; Jeakins)
San Francisco, 1936 (Loos)
Sanctus, 1990 (Hammer)
Sand or Peter and the Wolf, 1969 (Leaf)
Sand under the Pavement see Unter dem Pflaster ist der Strand, 1975
Sandakan hachi-ban shokan: Bokyo, 1974 (Tanaka)
Sandakan, House No. 8 see Sandakan hachi-ban shokan: Bokyo, 1974
Sandpiper, 1965 (Sharaff)
Sandra see Vaghe stelle dell'orsa, 1965
Sang des autres, 1983 (Foster)
Sangaree, 1953 (Head)
Sannu batture, 1979 (Hänsel)
Sans Toit ni loi see Vagabonde, 1985
Sansho dayu, 1954 (Tanaka)
Sansho the Bailiff see Sansho dayu, 1954
Santa Fe Marshal, 1940 (Head)
Santa Fe Trail, 1930 (Head)

São Paolo de todos nos, 1981 (Amaral)
Saphead, 1920 (Mathis)
Sapphire, 1959 (Dillon)
Sappho, 1978 (Hammer)
Sarah and Son, 1930 (Akins; Arzner; Loos)
Sari Red, 1988 (Parmar)
Sasek a kralovna, 1987 (Chytilová)
Satan Junior, 1919 (Mathis)
Satan's Bed, 1967 (Ono)
Satdee Night, 1973 (Armstrong)
Saturday, July 27, 1963 see 1963.julius 27.szombat, 1963
Saturday Night, 1922 (Bauchens; Macpherson)
Saturday Night Fever, 1977 (von Brandenstein)
Saturday Night Kid, 1929 (Head)
Saturday Off see Bear, a Boy and a Dog, 1921
Saturday, Sunday, Monday, 1990 (Wertmüller)
Saut humidifié de M. Plick, 1900 (Guy)
Saute ma ville, 1968 (Akerman)
Savage, 1926 (Murfin)
Savage, 1952 (Head)
Savage Eye, 1960 (Fields)
Savage/Love, 1981 (Clarke)
Savage Messiah, 1972 (Russell)
Savage Seven, 1968 (Marshall)
Savage Woman see Demoiselle sauvage, 1991
Saving Grace, 1914 (Loos)
Saving Pound see Usporená libra, 1963
Saving Presence, 1914 (Loos)
Saving the Family Name, 1916 (Weber)
Savoir-faire s'impose, 1971 (Poirier)
Say It in French, 1938 (Head)
Scandal, 1915 (Weber)
Scandal, 1917 (Meredyth)
Scandal Mongers, 1919 (Weber)
Scandal Sheet, 1938 (Head)
Scapegoat, 1960 (Batchelor)
Scar Tissue, 1979 (Friedrich)
Scared Stiff, 1953 (Head)
Scarlet Hour, 1956 (Head)
Scarlet Lady, 1928 (Meredyth)
Scarlet Letter, 1926 (Gish; Marion)
Scary Time, 1960 (Clarke)
Scene of the Crime, 1949 (Irene)
Scène d'escamotage, 1897/98 (Guy)
Scène en cabinet particulier vue à travers le trou de la serrure, 1902 (Guy)
Scener ur ett äktenskap, 1973 (Ullmann)
Scenes from a Marriage see Scener ur ett äktenskap, 1973
Scenes from the Life of Andy Warhol, 1982 (Ono)
Scènes Directoire series, 1904 (Guy)
Scenic Route, 1978 (Weill)
Scherzo del destinoin aqquato dietro l'angelo come un brigante di strada, 1983 (Wertmüller)
Schimbul de miine, 1959 (Mészáros)
Schiscksal derer von Hapsburg, 1929 (Riefenstahl)
Schizy, 1968 (Hammer)
Schlangenei see Serpent's Egg, 1977
Schmeerguntz, 1965 (Nelson)
Schnitte, 1976 (Export)
Schöne Prinzessin von China, 1916 (Reiniger)
School for Coquettes see L'École des cocottes, 1958

School for Secrets, 1946 (Dillon)
School Teacher and the Waif, 1912 (Pickford)
Schräge Vögel, 1968 (von Trotta)
Schwache Geschlecht muss stärker werden, 1988 (Sander)
Schwarze Sunde, 1989 (Huillet)
Schwestern oder Die Balance des Glücks, 1979 (von Trotta)
Science, 1911 (Pickford)
Scream of Silence see Mourir à tue-tête, 1979
Screaming Woman, 1972 (Head)
Screen Tests see Zdjecia probne, 1977
Scrubbers, 1983 (Zetterling)
Scugnizza, 1923 (Notari)
Sea see Morze, 1932
Sea Bat, 1930 (Meredyth)
Sea Beast, 1926 (Meredyth)
Sea Devils, 1937 (Lupino)
Sea of Roses see Mar de Rosas, 1977
Sea Urchin, 1913 (Macpherson)
Sea Wall see Diga sul Pacifico, 1958
Sea Wolf, 1941 (Lupino)
Seagull see Sha Ou, 1981
Sealed Lips see Lèvres closes, 1906
Sealed Orders, 1914 (Madison)
Sealed Room, 1909 (Pickford)
Sealed Verdict, 1948 (Head)
Search for Beauty, 1934 (Lupino)
Search for Bridey Murphy, 1956 (Head)
Search for Signs of Intelligent Life in the Universe, 1991 (Littleton)
Search for the Evil One, 1967 (Fields)
Seashell and the Clergyman see **Coquille et le clergyman**, 1927
Second Awakening of Christa Klages see Zweite Erwachen der Christa Klages, 1977
Second Chance: Sea, 1976 (Hubley)
Second Journey (To Uluru), 1981 (Cantrill)
Second Sight, 1911 (Pickford)
Second Sight see Trollsyn, 1994
Secours aux naufragés, 1903/04 (Guy)
Secret see Feng Jie, 1979
Secret Agent, 1936 (Reville)
Secret du Chevalier d'Éon, 1960 (Audry)
Secret Garden, 1993 (Holland)
Secret Heart, 1946 (Irene)
Secret Journey see Viaggio clandestino, 1994
Secret Life of Walter Mitty, 1947 (Sharaff)
Secret Mission, 1942 (Dillon)
Secret of Madame Blanche, 1933 (Goodrich)
Secret of the Great Story-Teller see Tajemství velikého vypravece, 1971
Secret of the Incas, 1954 (Head)
Secret of the Wastelands, 1941 (Head)
Secret Six, 1931 (Marion)
Secret Sounds Screaming, 1985 (Chenzira)
Secret War of Harry Frigg, 1968 (Head)
Secrets, 1924 (Marion)
Secrets, 1933 (Marion; Pickford)
Secrets de la prestidigitation dévoilés, 1904 (Guy)
Secrets of the Bermuda Triangle, 1976 (Murphy)
Sedmikrásky, 1966 (Chytilová; Krumbachová)
Seduction of Mimi see Mimi metallurgio ferito nell'onore, 1972
Seduction: The Cruel Woman see Verführung: Die grausame Frau, 1985

See Here, Private Hargrove, 1944 (Irene)
See How They Fall *see* Regarde les hommes tomber, 1994
See What You Hear What You See, 1980 (Hammer)
Seed of Sarah, 1997 (Schiller)
Seeing Space and Hearing Space *see* Raumsehen und Raumhören, 1974
Seems Like Old Times, 1980 (Booth)
Seers & Clowns, 1994 (Hubley)
Seesaw *see* Houpacka, 1990
Segodnya, 1930 (Shub)
Sehtext: Fingergedicht, 1973 (Export)
Seine offizielle Frau *see* Eskapade, 1936
Seishun no yume ima izuko, 1932 (Tanaka)
Selbé et tant d'autres, 1982 (Faye)
Selbé One among Others *see* Selbé et tant d'autres, 1982
Self-Defense, 1973 (Citron)
Self-Portrait, 1969 (Ono)
Semaine en France, 1963 (Guillemot)
Semana de 22, 1971 (Amaral)
Sempre Avanti Savoia, 1915 (Notari)
S'en fout la mort, 1990 (Denis)
Sénégalais en Normandie, 1983 (Maldoror)
Senegalese in Normandy *see* Sénégalais en Normandie, 1983
Sensation Seekers, 1927 (Weber)
Senseless, 1998 (Spheeris)
Senso, 1954 (Cecchi d'Amico)
Sentimental Bloke, 1919 (Lyell)
Sentimental Policeman *see* Chuvstvitel'nyi militsioner, 1992
Sentinel Asleep, 1911 (Pickford)
Sentry at the Gate: The Comedy of Jane Galvin-Lewis, 1995 (Chenzira)
Senza sapere nulla di lei, 1969 (Cecchi d'Amico)
Señora de Nadie, 1982 (Bemberg)
Separate Tables, 1958 (Head)
Sept morts sur ordonnance, 1975 (Serreau)
Sept P., Cuis., S. de B.,... a saisir, 1984 (Varda)
Sept péchés capitaux, 1952 (Colette)
September Affair, 1950 (Head)
September Express, 1973-74 (De Hirsch)
Seraglio, 1958 (Reiniger)
Serious Game *see* Den Allvarsamma leken, 1977
Serpent's Egg, 1977 (Ullmann)
Serpico, 1973 (Allen, D.)
Service De Luxe, 1938 (Irene)
Service: Garage Handling, 1952 (Batchelor)
Service précipité, 1903 (Guy)
Serving in Silence: The Margarethe Cammermeyer Story, 1995 (Streisand)
Set-Up, 1978 (Bigelow)
Sève de la terre, 1951-66 (Parker)
Seven Beauties *see* Pasqualino settebellezze, 1976
Seven Brides for Seven Brothers, 1954 (Goodrich)
Seven Deadly Sins *see* Sept péchés capitaux, 1952
Seven Keys to Baldpate, 1929 (Murfin)
Seven Little Foys, 1955 (Head)
Seven Sinners, 1940 (Irene)
Seven Sisters, 1980 (Cantrill)
Seven Thieves, 1960 (Spencer)
Seven Waves Away *see* Abandon Ship!, 1957
Seven Women—Seven Sins *see* Sieben Frauen—Sieben Sünden, 1986

Seven Women, Seven Sins, 1987 (Akerman; Gordon)
Seventeen, 1940 (Head)
Seventh Cross, 1944 (Irene)
Seventh Day, 1909 (Macpherson; Pickford)
Seventh Sin, 1957 (Rose)
Seventh Veil, 1945 (Box, B.; Box, M.)
Severed Hand, 1914 (Madison)
Severo Torelli, 1914 (Musidora)
Sewer, 1912 (Guy)
Sex and the Married Woman, 1977 (Head)
Sex and the Single Girl, 1964 (Head)
Sextette, 1978 (Head; West)
Sexual Advances, 1992 (Deitch)
Sfida, 1958 (Cecchi d'Amico)
Sha Ou, 1981 (Zhang)
Shades of Fear *see* Great Moments in Aviation, 1993
Shadow of a Doubt, 1943 (Harrison; Reville)
Shadow of Lightning Ridge, 1921 (Meredyth)
Shadow on the Wall, 1949 (Irene)
Shadows and Fog, 1992 (Foster)
Shadows of Life, 1913 (Madison)
Shadows of the Moulin Rouge, 1913 (Guy)
Shaggie, 1990 (Cole)
Shakespeare Wallah, 1965 (Jhabvala)
Shakti—"She Is Vital Energy", 1976 (Poirier)
Shall We Dance, 1937 (Irene)
Shaman: A Tapestry for Sorcerers, 1964-67 (De Hirsch)
Shame *see* Skammen, 1968
Shane, 1953 (Head)
Shanghai Jiaqi, 1992 (Hui)
Shanghai Lil's, 1988 (Choy)
Sha'ou's Seagull *see* Sha Ou, 1981
Shchors, 1939 (Solntseva)
She *see* Elle, 1995
She Asked for It, 1937 (Head)
She-Devil, 1989 (Seidelman)
She Done Him Wrong, 1933 (Head; West)
She Wanted a Millionaire, 1932 (Levien)
She Was a Lady, 1934 (Spencer)
She Was a Visitor, 1970 (Deitch)
She Went to the Races, 1945 (Irene)
She-Wolf *see* U krutogo yara, 1963
She Wouldn't Say Yes, 1945 (Van Upp)
Sheer Madness *see* Heller Wahn, 1983
Shepherd of the Hills, 1941 (Head)
Shepherd of the Southern Cross, 1914 (Shipman)
Sherlock Brown, 1922 (Coffee)
She's No Lady, 1937 (Head)
Shimmy lagarno tarantelle e vino, 1978 (Wertmüller)
Shining Hour, 1938 (Murfin)
Ship Comes In, 1928 (Levien)
Ship San Giorgio *see* Corazzata San Giorgio, 1911
Shirins Hochzeit, 1976 (Sanders-Brahms)
Shirin's Wedding *see* Shirins Hochzeit, 1976
Shocked *see* Mesmerized, 1986
Shoe Show *see* Shoe show aneb Botky mají pré, 1984
Shoe show aneb Botky mají pré, 1984 (Krumbachová)
Shoemaker and the Hatter, 1949 (Batchelor)
Shoes, 1916 (Weber)
Shoot for the Contents, 1991 (Trinh)
Short Cut to Hell, 1957 (Head)

Short History of France, ch. 1 "From the Gaulle Ancestors to the Taking of Power by Louis XIV" *see* Petit Manuel d'histoire de France, ch. 1 "Des ancêtres les Gaulois à la prise du pouvoir par Louis X1V", 1979

Short Is the Summer *see* Kort år sommaren, 1962

Short Tall Story, 1970 (Batchelor)

Shot Heard 'Round the World, 1997 (Choy)

Shout Loud, Louder ... I Don't Understand *see* Spara forte, più forte ... non capisco, 1966

Showdown, 1940 (Head)

Showdown, 1973 (Head)

Showtime *see* Gaiety George, 1946

Shu Jian En Chou Lu, 1987 (Hui)

Shut Up and Suffer, 1991 (B)

Si vous ne m'aimez pas, 1916 (Musidora)

Siamo donne, 1953 (Cecchi d'Amico)

Sichtbarmachung der Wirkungsweise optischer Gesetze am einfachen Beispiel, 1969 (Hein)

Sidewalks, 1966 (Menken)

Sidney's Joujoux series, 1900 (Guy)

Sie Suesse Nummer: Ein Konsumerlebnis, 1968 (Export)

Sieben Frauen—Sieben Sünden, 1986 (Ottinger; Sander)

Sieg des Glaubens, 1933 (Riefenstahl)

Siempre estaré contigo, 1957 (Landeta)

Siesta, 1987 (Foster)

Sight Poem: Finger Poem *see* Sehtext: Fingergedicht, 1973

Sign of the Cross, 1932 (Bauchens; Head)

Signé Charlotte, 1985 (Pascal)

Signed Charlotte *see* Signé Charlotte, 1985

Signora dell'ovest, 1942 (Reiniger)

Signora senza camelie, 1953 (Cecchi d'Amico)

Silence of Dean Maitland, 1914 (Lyell)

Silence of the Lambs, 1991 (Foster)

Silent Call, 1921 (Murfin)

Silent Cry *see* Nema Kiáltás, 1982

Silent Language *see* Stille Sprache, 1971-72

Silent Sandy, 1914 (Gish)

Silent Signal, 1911 (Guy)

Silently, Bearing Totem of a Bird, 1973-74 (De Hirsch)

Silk Stockings, 1957 (Rose)

Silkwood, 1983 (Ephron; von Brandenstein)

Silver City, 1951 (Head)

Silver Cord, 1933 (Murfin)

Silver on the Sage, 1939 (Head)

Silverado, 1985 (Littleton)

Silvio, 1967 (Sander)

Simeon, 1992 (Palcy)

Simon and Laura, 1956 (Box, M.; Dillon)

Simon the Jester, 1925 (Marion)

Simple Charity, 1910 (Pickford)

Simple Observations of a Solar Eclipse, 1976 (Cantrill)

Simple Story *see* Egyszeru történet, 1975

Simple Tailor *see* Glaza, kotorye videli, 1928

Sincerely Charlotte *see* Signé Charlotte, 1985

Sinful Davey, 1969 (Dillon)

Sing Lotus, 1966 (De Hirsch)

Sing, You Sinners, 1938 (Head)

Singer and the Dancer, 1976 (Armstrong)

Singin' in the Rain, 1952 (Comden)

Singing Nun, 1966 (Rose)

Single Room Furnished, 1968 (Murphy)

Sink or Swim, 1990 (Friedrich)

Siódmy pokój, 1995 (Mészáros)

Sirène du Mississippi, 1969 (Guillemot)

Sissi, 1932 (Reiniger)

Sister, Sister, 1982 (Angelou)

Sisters, 1914 (Gish; Loos)

Sisters!, 1974 (Hammer)

Sisters of Darkness *see* Entre tinieblas, 1983

Sisters of Nishijin *see* Nishijin no shimai, 1952

Sisters, or The Balance of Happiness *see* Schwestern oder Die Balance des Glücks, 1979

Sitting Pretty, 1933 (Head)

Siu Ngo Gong Woo *see* Xiao Ao Jiang Hu, 1990

Six Days, Six Nights *see* À la folie, 1994

Six Degrees of Separation, 1993 (von Brandenstein)

Six et demi-onze, 1927 (Epstein)

Six Fifty, 1923 (Coffee)

Six Hours, 1923 (Glyn)

Six Little Jungle Boys, 1945 (Batchelor)

Sixteen Springs, 1997 (Hui)

Skammen, 1968 (Ullmann)

Skating Bug, 1911 (Pickford)

Ski Resort, 1960 (Batchelor)

Skilsmässoproblem i italien, 1971 (Ahrne)

Skin *see* Pelle, 1981

Skin Deep, 1994 (Mehta)

Skin Game, 1931 (Reville)

Skin of Our Teeth, 1964 (Bute)

Skin of Your Eye, 1973 (Cantrill)

Skirts Ahoy!, 1952 (Lennart; Rose)

Skotinins, 1922-25 (Shub)

Skullduggery, 1970 (Head)

Sky Dance, 1980 (Hubley)

Sky Socialist, 1967 (Wieland)

Sky, West, and Crooked, 1966 (Dillon)

Skylark, 1941 (Head; Irene)

Skyscraper, 1958 (Clarke)

Slamený klobouk, 1971 (Krumbachová)

Slap Shot, 1977 (Allen, D.)

Slaughterhouse-Five, 1972 (Allen, D.)

Slave, 1909 (Pickford)

Slave of Fashion, 1925 (Meredyth; Murfin)

Slaves of New York, 1989 (Comden)

Sleep, My Love, 1948 (Pickford)

Sleeping Beauty *see* Belle au bois dormant, 1935

Sleeping Beauty, 1954 (Reiniger)

Sleeping Beauty, 1960 (Batchelor)

Sleepless in Seattle, 1993 (Ephron)

Slender Thread, 1965 (Head)

Slesar i kantzler, 1923 (Preobrazhenskaya)

Slightly Dangerous, 1943 (Irene)

Slightly Honorable, 1940 (Spencer)

Sloth *see* Paresse, 1986

Slowly *see* Lentement, 1974

Slugger's Wife, 1985 (Booth)

Slzy, které svet nevidí, 1962 (Krumbachová)

Small Town Girl, 1936 (Goodrich)

Small Town Girl, 1953 (Rose)

Smart Girl, 1935 (Lupino)

Smile Jenny, You're Dead, 1974 (Foster)

Smile *see* Film No. 5, 1968

Smile *see* Sourire, 1994
Smilin' Through, 1932 (Booth)
Smiling Again *see* Ujra mosolyognak, 1954
Smiling Madame Beudet *see* Souriante Madame Beudet, 1923
Smithereens, 1982 (Seidelman)
Smoker, 1910 (Pickford)
Smokes and Lollies, 1975 (Armstrong)
Smooth Talk, 1985 (Chopra)
Smugglers *see* Man Within, 1947
Smuggler's Daughter, 1914 (Meredyth)
Smugglers of Death *see* Král Šumavy, 1959
Smykketyven, 1990 (Breien)
Snake Pit, 1948 (Spencer)
Snakes and Ladders, 1960 (Batchelor)
Snakes and Ladders *see* El juego de la oca, 1965
Snap and the Beanstalk, 1960 (Batchelor)
Snap Goes East, 1960 (Batchelor)
Sneakers, 1992 (von Brandenstein)
Snip and Snap Series, 1960 (Batchelor)
Snow Bride, 1923 (Levien)
Snow Job: The Media Hysteria of Aids, 1989 (Hammer)
Snow White *see* O Snehurce, 1972
Snow White and Rose Red, 1953 (Reiniger)
Snowfire, 1958 (Fields)
Snowfire, 1994 (Chenzira)
Snows, 1966 (Schneemann)
Sny na nedeli, 1958 (Šimková-Plívová)
So Evil My Love, 1948 (Head)
So Far from India, 1983 (Nair)
So Long at the Fair, 1950 (Box, M.; Box, B.)
So Near, Yet So Far, 1912 (Pickford)
So Runs the Way, 1913 (Gish)
So This Is Hollywood *see* In Hollywood with Potash and Perlmutter, 1924
So This Is London, 1930 (Levien)
Sobre horas extras y trabajo voluntario, 1973 (Gómez)
Sobre las olas, 1981 (Novaro)
Social Exile *see* Déclassée, 1925
Social Highwayman, 1916 (Marion)
Social Leper, 1917 (Marion)
Social Quicksands, 1918 (Mathis)
Social Register, 1934 (Loos)
Social Secretary, 1916 (Loos)
Society Lawyer, 1939 (Goodrich)
Soeurs enemies, 1915 (Dulac)
Sofie, 1992 (Ullmann)
Soil *see* Zemlya, 1930
Sol y sombra *see* Soleil et ombre , 1922
Solange es Europa noch gibt—Fragen an den Freiden, 1983 (Meerapfel)
Sold for Marriage, 1916 (Gish)
Soldier of Fortune, 1955 (Spencer)
Soldier of Victory *see* Zolnierz zwyciestwa, 1953
Soldier's Daughter Never Cries, 1998 (Jhabvala)
Soldier's Fantasy *see* Fantasia 'e Surdata, 1927
Soledad *see* Fruits amers, 1966
Soleil et ombre , 1922 (Musidora)
Solidarity, 1973 (Wieland)
Solo per te, 1937 (von Harbou)
Solstik, 1953 (Henning-Jensen)
Sombre dimanche, 1948 (Audry)

Sombrero, 1953 (Rose)
Some Bull's Daughter, 1914 (Loos)
Some Exterior Presence, 1977 (Child)
Some Girls Do, 1969 (Box, B.)
Some Like It Hot, 1939 (Head)
Somebody Loves Me, 1952 (Head)
Something Different *see* O necem jiném, 1963
Something Else *see* O necem jiném, 1963
Something for Something *see* Cós za cós, 1977
Something New, 1920 (Shipman)
Something of Value, 1957 (Rose)
Something to Live For, 1952 (Head)
Something to Think About, 1920 (Bauchens; Macpherson)
Sometimes a Great Notion, 1971 (Head)
Sommersby, 1993 (Foster)
Son-Daughter, 1932 (Booth)
Son nom de Venises dans Calcutta désert, 1976 (Duras)
Son of Lassie, 1945 (Irene)
Son of Paleface, 1952 (Head)
Son of the Regiment *see* Figlio del Reggimento, 1915
Son of the Sheik, 1926 (Marion)
Song Is Born, 1947 (Sharaff)
Song o' My Heart, 1930 (Levien)
Song of Life, 1922 (Meredyth)
Song of Love, 1924 (Marion)
Song of Love, 1947 (Irene)
Song of Love *see* Cançao de Amor, 1977
Song of Russia, 1943 (Irene)
Song of Surrender, 1949 (Head)
Song of the Clinking Cup, 1972 (Hammer)
Song of the Exile *see* Ketu Qiuhen, 1990
Song of the Thin Man, 1947 (Irene)
Song of the Wildwood Flute, 1910 (Pickford)
Sonho de Valsa, 1987 (Carolina)
Sonny, 1922 (Marion)
Sons of Katie Elder, 1965 (Head)
Sons of the Legion, 1938 (Bauchens; Head)
Son's Return, 1909 (Pickford)
Sophie *see* Sofie, 1992
Sophie Lang Goes West, 1937 (Head)
Sorceress, 1917 (Madison)
Sorrows of the Unfaithful, 1910 (Pickford)
Sorry, Wrong Number, 1948 (Head)
Sosie, 1915 (Musidora)
Sotelo, 1976 (Sarmiento)
Sotto il Carcere di San Francisco, 1923 (Notari)
Sotto, Sotto, 1984 (Wertmüller)
Soul Adrift, 1918 (Guy)
Soul Enslaved, 1916 (Madison)
Soul Kiss *see* Lady's Morals, 1930
Souls at Sea, 1937 (Head)
Souls for Sale, 1923 (Mathis)
Souls in Bondage, 1923 (Madison)
Souls in the Sun *see* Âmes au soleil, 1981
Souls Triumphant, 1915 (Gish)
Sound Film *see* Tonfilm, 1969
Sound of Music, 1965 (Jeakins)
Source, 1900 (Guy)
Souriante Madame Beudet, 1923 (Dulac)
Sourire, 1994 (Pascal)
Souris, tu m'inquiétes, 1973 (Poirier)

South Pacific, 1958 (Jeakins)
South Sea Rose, 1928 (Levien)
Southerner, 1931 (Booth)
Southerner *see* Prodigal, 1931
Space Chaser, 1980 (Treut)
Spain *see* Ispaniya, 1939
Spain in Flames, 1936 (van Dongen)
Spanish Dancer, 1923 (Mathis)
Spanish Earth, 1937 (van Dongen)
Spanish Gypsy, 1911 (Macpherson)
Spara forte, più forte ... non capisco, 1966 (Cecchi d'Amico)
Sparrows, 1926 (Pickford)
Spawn of the North, 1938 (Head)
Speak to, Speak Out *see* Ansprache Aussprache, 1968
Speed the Plough, 1958 (Batchelor)
Spell of the Ball *see* A labda varásza, 1962
Speriamo che sia femmina, 1986 (Cecchi d'Amico; Ullmann)
Spies *see* Spione, 1928
Spione, 1928 (von Harbou)
Spitfire, 1934 (Murfin)
Spitfire *see* First of the Few, 1942
Split Reality, 1970 (Export)
Splitscreen-Solipsismus, 1968 (Export)
Spoiled Children *see* Enfants gâtés, 1977
Spook Sport, 1939 (Bute)
Spooky Bunch *see* Zhuang Dao Zheng, 1980
Sport, Sport, Sport, 1970 (Shepitko)
Spotkania w mroku, 1960 (Jakubowska)
Spring and Winter, 1951 (Batchelor)
Spring Song, 1960 (Batchelor)
Spring to Spring, 1992-94 (Bani-Etemad)
Spudwrench—Kahnawake Man, 1997 (Obomsawin)
Sputum, 1970 (Batchelor)
Spy Train, 1960 (Batchelor)
Spylarks *see* Intelligence Men, 1965
Square Dance, 1969 (Hein)
Square Deal, 1917 (Marion)
Squaw Man, 1931 (Bauchens; Coffee)
Squirrel's Magic Shell *see* Veverka a kouzelná mušle, 1988
Sredi serykh kamnei, 1983 (Muratova)
Stage Fright, 1950 (Reville)
Stage Struck, 1958 (Akins)
Stagecoach, 1939 (Spencer)
Stagecoach War, 1940 (Head)
Stalag 17, 1953 (Head)
Stalking Moon, 1968 (Jeakins)
Stampede, 1911 (Guy; Pickford)
Stand-In, 1937 (Spencer)
Stand Up and Fight, 1939 (Murfin)
Standard Time, 1967 (Wieland)
Standing Room Only, 1944 (Head)
Star Is Born, 1954 (Sharaff)
Star Is Born, 1976 (Streisand)
Star Maker, 1939 (Head)
Star of Bethlehem *see* Der Stern von Bethlehem, 1921
Star of Bethlehem, 1956 (Reiniger)
Star of India, 1913 (Guy)
Star-Spangled Rhythm, 1942 (Head)
Starlore, 1983 (Hubley)
Starry Is the Night *see* Jinye Xingguang Canlan, 1988
Stars and Stripes Forever, 1952 (Jeakins)

Stars Are Singing, 1953 (Head)
Starship Invasions, 1977 (Cole)
Starstruck, 1982 (Armstrong)
Start with What Is under Your Nose, 1949 (Batchelor)
Starting Line, 1947 (Grayson)
State Fair, 1933 (Levien)
State of Grace, 1990 (von Brandenstein)
State of the Union, 1948 (Irene)
Statue, 1905 (Guy)
Steak trop cuit, 1960 (Guillemot)
Stealing Home, 1988 (Foster)
Stella, 1990 (Van Runkle)
Stella Dallas, 1925 (Marion)
Stella Maris, 1918 (Marion; Pickford)
Stemning i April, 1947 (Henning-Jensen)
Step by Step, 1978 (Hubley)
Stepan Razin, 1939 (Preobrazhenskaya)
Stepkids *see* Big Girls Don't Cry...They Get Even, 1992
Stigmata, 1991 (B)
Still Life, 1975 (Gordon)
Still Point, 1989 (Hammer)
Stille Sprache, 1971-72 (Export)
Stills, 1973 (Hein)
Sting, 1973 (Head)
Stockholm, 1977 (Zetterling)
Stolen Bride, 1913 (Gish)
Stolen Harmony, 1935 (Head)
Stolen Heart *see* Gestohlene Herz, 1934
Stolen Heaven, 1938 (Head)
Stolen Kisses *see* Baises volés, 1968
Stolen Masterpiece, 1914 (Loos)
Stolen Paradise, 1917 (Marion)
Stone Circles, 1983 (Hammer)
Stooge, 1951 (Head)
Stop Calling Me Baby! *see* Moi, Fleur Bleue, 1978
Storia, 1986 (Cecchi d'Amico)
Storia del terzo Reich, 1962-63 (Cavani)
Storia di una donna, 1969 (Allen, D.)
Stork Bites Man, 1947 (Pickford)
Stork Club, 1945 (Head)
Storm at Daybreak, 1933 (Booth)
Stormy Weather, 1943 (Rose)
Storstadsvampyrer, 1972 (Ahrne)
Story of a Woman *see* Storia di una donna, 1969
Story of a Woman, 1970 (Head)
Story of Dr. Wassell, 1944 (Bauchens; Macpherson)
Story of Life, 1948 (Allen, D.)
Story of Mr. Hobbs, 1947 (Shipman)
Story of Robin Hood and His Merrie Men, 1952 (Dillon)
Story of the Third Reich *see* Storia del terzo Reich, 1962-63
Story of the Turbulent Years *see* Povest plamennykh let, 1961
Story of Three Loves, 1953 (Rose)
Story of Woo Viet *see* Hu Yueh Te Ku Shih, 1981
Story of Yunnan *see* Yunnan Qiu Shi, 1994
Stowaway, 1960 (Batchelor)
Stradivari, 1989 (Cecchi d'Amico)
Straight for the Heart *see* À corps perdu, 1988
Straight Is the Way, 1921 (Marion)
Straight through the Heart *see* Mitten ins Herz, 1983
Straight to the Heart *see* À corps perdu, 1988
Strana rodnaya, 1942 (Shub)

Strana Sovietov, 1937 (Shub)
Stranded, 1916 (Loos)
Stranded, 1927 (Loos)
Strange Affair of Uncle Harry see Uncle Harry, 1945
Strange Days, 1995 (Bigelow)
Strange Interlude, 1932 (Booth; Meredyth)
Strange Interval see Strange Interlude, 1932
Strange Intruder, 1956 (Lupino)
Strange Love of Martha Ivers, 1946 (Head)
Strange Meeting, 1909 (Pickford)
Stranger see Lo straniero, 1967
Stranger in Town, 1943 (Lennart)
Stranger Left No Card, 1953 (Toye)
Strangers in 7A, 1972 (Lupino)
Strangers of the Night, 1923 (Coffee; Meredyth)
Strass café, 1980 (Pool)
Strasse des Bösen see Via Mala, 1948
Strategic Air Command, 1955 (Head)
Stratton Story, 1949 (Rose)
Strauss's Great Waltz see Waltzes from Vienna, 1934
Straw Fire see Feu de paille, 1939
Straw Hat see Slamený klobouk, 1971
Strawberries and Gold, 1980 (Coolidge)
Street, 1976 (Leaf)
Street Corner, 1953 (Box, M.)
Street Girl, 1929 (Murfin)
Street of Chance, 1930 (Coffee)
Street of My Childhood see Barndommens gade, 1986
Street Photographer see Los Minuteros, 1972
Street Scenes, 1970 (Schoonmaker)
Streetwalker see Trotacalles, 1951
Strenuous Life, 1914 (Madison)
Stress Scars and Pleasure Wrinkles, 1976 (Hammer)
Strictly Dishonorable, 1951 (Rose)
Strictly Personal, 1933 (Head)
Strictly Unconventional, 1930 (Booth)
Strip, 1951 (Rose)
Strohfeuer, 1972 (von Trotta)
Stroke of Luck see Golpe de suerte, 1991
Stronger Love see 'Tween Two Loves, 1911
Stronger than Death, 1915 (Meredyth)
Stronger than Death, 1920 (Guy)
Strop, 1962 (Chytilová)
Struggle, 1931 (Loos)
Struggle see Borza, 1935
Strukturelle Studien, 1974 (Hein)
Student Prince, 1954 (Levien; Rose)
Studies in Image (De)Generation, 1975 (Cantrill)
Studs Lonigan, 1960 (Fields)
Study in Choreography for Camera, 1945 (Deren)
Stunt Woman see Ah Kam, 1996
Stuntwoman Ajin see Ah Kam, 1996
Stürme über dem Montblanc, 1930 (Riefenstahl)
Subjective Factor see Der subjektive Faktor, 1981
Subjectivity see Subjektitüde, 1966
Subjektitüde, 1966 (Sander)
Submarine Command, 1951 (Head)
Submarine Control, 1949 (Batchelor)
Submarine Zone see Escape to Glory, 1941
Suburbia, 1984 (Spheeris)
Subway in the Sky, 1959 (Box, M.)

Such a Little Queen, 1914 (Pickford)
Such Good Friends, 1971 (May)
Such High Mountains see Takie vysokie gory, 1974
Such Women Are Dangerous, 1934 (Coffee)
Sud v Smolenske, 1946 (Shub)
Sudden Fear, 1952 (Coffee)
Sudden Money, 1939 (Head)
Suds, 1920 (Pickford)
Sueño como de colores, 1968-69 (Sarmiento)
Suffering of Susan, 1914 (Loos)
Sugar see With or Without, 1981
Sugar Cane Alley see **Rue cases nègres**, 1983
Sugarland Express, 1974 (Fields)
Suicide Pact, 1913 (Loos)
Sullivan's Travels, 1941 (Head)
Sult, 1966 (Breien)
Summer and Smoke, 1961 (Head)
Summer Camp Nightmare, 1987 (Spheeris)
Summer Girl, 1916 (Marion)
Summer Holiday, 1948 (Goodrich; Irene)
Summer Lightning see Strohfeuer, 1972
Summer Night with Greek Profile, Almond Eyes and Scent of Basil
    see Notte d'estate, con profilo Greco, occhi amandorla e odore di
    basilico, 1986
Summer of My German Soldier, 1978 (von Brandenstein)
Summer Snow see Xiatian de Xue, 1994
Summer Stock, 1950 (Rose)
Sun and Shadow see Soleil et ombre , 1922
Sun Comes Up, 1949 (Irene)
Sunday Children see Niedzielne Dzieci, 1976
Sunday Pursuit, 1990 (Zetterling)
Sundown, 1924 (Marion)
Sundown, 1941 (Irene; Spencer)
Sundowners, 1960 (Lennart)
Sunset Boulevard, 1950 (Head)
Sunset Trail, 1939 (Head)
Sunshine Boys, 1975 (Booth)
Sunshine Christmas, 1977 (Head)
Sunshine Follows Rain see Driver dagg faller Regn, 1946
Sunshine Molly, 1915 (Marion, Weber)
Superbia—Der Stolz, 1986-87 (Ottinger)
Superbia—L'orgueil see Superbia—Der Stolz, 1986 87
Superbia—Pride see Superbia—Der Stolz, 1986-87
Superdyke, 1975 (Hammer)
Superdyke Meets Madame X, 1975 (Hammer)
Superman und Superwoman, 1980 (Hein)
Sur la barricade, 1907 (Guy)
Sur la terre comme au ciel, 1993 (Hänsel)
Surname Viet, Given Name Nam, 1989 (Trinh)
Surprises de l'affichage, 1903/04 (Guy)
Surrender, 1930 (Levien)
Surtout l'hiver, 1976 (Poirier)
Surviving Picasso, 1996 (Jhabvala)
Susan and God, 1940 (Loos)
Susan Lenox, Her Fall and Rise, 1931 (Booth)
Susie Steps Out, 1946 (Pickford)
Suspended Vocation see Vocation suspendue, 1977
Suspense, 1913 (Weber)
Suspicion, 1941 (Harrison; Reville)
Süsse Nummer: Ein Konsumerlebnis, 1973 (Export)
Suzy, 1936 (Coffee)

Svält *see* Sult, 1966
Svengali, 1983 (Foster)
Svenska färger, 1981 (Ahrne)
Svetlyi gorod, 1928 (Preobrazhenskaya)
Swagman's Story, 1914 (Lyell)
Swan, 1925 (Coffee)
Swan, 1956 (Rose)
Swedish Fanny Hill *see* Fanny Hill, 1968
Sweet and Low-Down, 1944 (Spencer)
Sweet and Twenty, 1909 (Pickford)
Sweet Bird of Youth, 1986 (Davis)
Sweet Charity, 1969 (Head)
Sweet Liberty, 1986 (Gish)
Sweet Memories of Yesterday, 1911 (Pickford)
Sweet One: A Consumer Experience *see* Süsse Nummer: Ein
    Konsumerlebnis, 1973
Sweetie, 1989 (Campion)
Swept Away... *see* Travolti da un insolito destino nell'azzurro mare
    d'agosto, 1974
Swept Away...by an Unusual Destiny in the Blue Sea of August *see*
    Travolti da un insolito destino nell'azzurro mare d'agosto, 1974
Swept from the Sea, 1997 (Kidron)
Swimmer, 1968 (Perry)
Swimming to Cambodia, 1987 (Littleton)
Swing High, Swing Low, 1937 (Van Upp)
Swing Shift Maisie, 1943 (Irene)
Swinger, 1966 (Head)
Swingin' Maiden *see* Iron Maiden, 1963
Sword and the Dragon, 1960 (Fields)
Sword and the Rose, 1953 (Dillon)
Swordsman *see* Xiao Ao Jiang Hu, 1990
Sylvia, 1965 (Head)
Sympathy for the Devil *see* One Plus One, 1968
Sympathy Sal, 1915 (Loos)
Sync Touch, 1981 (Hammer)
Synchromy No. 1, 1932 (Bute)
Synchromy No. 2, 1935 (Bute)
Synchromy No. 4 *see* Escape, 1937
Synchromy No. 9 *see* Tarantella, 1940
Synchronization *see* Synchromy No. 1, 1932
Syntagma, 1983 (Export)
Syvilla: They Dance to Her Drum, 1979 (Chenzira)
Szabad lélegzet, 1973 (Mészáros)
Szentendre—Town of Painters *see* Festök városa—Szentendre, 1964
Szép Iányok, ne sirjatok, 1970 (Mészáros)
Szeretet, 1963 (Mészáros)
Sziget a szárazföldön, 1968 (Elek)
Szivdobogás, 1961 (Mészáros)

T.G.M.—Osvoboditel, 1990 (Chytilová)
T.V. Tart, 1989 (Hammer)
Ta 'dabir Eghtessadi-y-Janghi, 1986 (Bani-Etemad)
Ta naše písnicka ceská, 1967 (Krumbachová)
Table Quotes-November 1985 *see* Tischbemerkungen-November
    1985, 1985
Tableaux d'une exposition, 1972 (Parker)
Tag der Freiheit: unsere Wermacht, 1935 (Riefenstahl)
Taiga, 1992 (Ottinger)
Taiheyo hitoribochi, 1963 (Tanaka)
Tailor Made Man, 1922 (Irene)
Tainted Horseplay *see* Kopytem Sem, Kopytem Tam, 1987

Tajemství velikého vypravece, 1971 (Krumbachová)
Take a Letter, Darling, 1942 (Irene)
Take Me Out to the Ball Game, 1949 (Comden; Rose)
Take Off, 1972 (Nelson)
Takie vysokie gory, 1974 (Solntseva)
Taking His Chance, 1914 (Lyell)
Találkozás, 1963 (Elek)
Találkozunk 1972-ben, 1971 (Elek)
Tale of Love, 1995 (Trinh)
Tale of Two Cities, 1958 (Box, B.; Dillon)
Tales, 1969 (Godmilow)
Tales from a Street, 1993 (Gorris)
Tales of Manhattan, 1942 (Irene)
Talk of the Town, 1942 (Irene)
Talkback, 1987 (Maclean)
Tall Headlines, 1952 (Zetterling)
Tall Time Tales, 1992 (Hubley)
Tamarkoze, 1987 (Bani-Etemad)
Taming of the Shrew, 1929 (Pickford)
Taming of the Shrew, 1967 (Cecchi d'Amico; Sharaff)
Tangled Fates, 1916 (Marion)
Tango Lesson, 1997 (Potter)
Tanoureh Deev, 1984 (Bani-Etemad)
Tapp und Tastkino, 1968 (Export)
Tar People, 1975 (Child)
Tarantella, 1940 (Bute)
Tarantelle, 1900 (Guy)
Tarantula, 1912 (Macpherson)
Targets, 1967 (Fields)
Tarnish, 1924 (Marion)
Tarnished Reputations, 1920 (Guy)
Tarzan versus I.B.M. *see* Alphaville, 1965
Tassili Passenger *see* Passager du Tassili, 1985
Tattooed Man, 1969 (De Hirsch)
Taunt, 1982 (Maclean)
Taxi Driver, 1976 (Foster)
Tea and Sympathy, 1956 (Rose)
Tea in the Garden, 1958 (Wieland)
Teach Our Children, 1972 (Choy)
Teacher's Pet, 1958 (Head)
Team Delphin, 1969 (Meerapfel)
Tear on the Page, 1915 (Loos)
Tear that Burned, 1914 (Gish)
Tears Laughter Fear and Rage, 1986 (Potter)
Tears of Huajiao *see* Huajiao Lei, c. 1986
Tears That the World Doesn't See *see* Slzy, které svet nevidí, 1962
Teckman Mystery, 1954 (Toye)
Teenage Zombies, 1958 (Murphy)
Tel est pris qui croyait prendre, 1901 (Guy)
Telephone Girl and the Lady, 1913 (Loos)
Television Spy, 1939 (Bauchens; Head)
Tell Me *see* Dis-moi, 1980
Tell Me a Riddle, 1980 (von Brandenstein)
Tell Them Willie Boy Is Here, 1969 (Head)
Telling the World, 1928 (Booth)
Temperamental Wife, 1919 (Loos)
Tempi nostri, 1953 (Cecchi d'Amico)
Temple of Dusk, 1918 (Marion)
Temps de l'avant, 1975 (Poirier)
Temptation, 1916 (Macpherson)
Temptation, 1923 (Coffee)

Temptation of a Monk *see* You seng, 1993
Ten-Cent Adventure, 1915 (Loos)
Ten Commandments, 1923 (Bauchens; Macpherson)
Ten Commandments, 1956 (Bauchens; Head; Jeakins)
Ten for Survival, 1979 (Batchelor)
Ten Thousand Bedrooms, 1957 (Rose)
Tenants of Castles *see* Kastélyok lakói, 1966
Tenda Dos Milagros, 1977 (Yamasaki)
Tender Comrade, 1943 (Head)
Tender Fictions, 1995 (Hammer)
Tender Game, 1958 (Hubley)
Tender Trap, 1955 (Rose)
Tentation d'Antoine, 1981 (Kaplan)
Tentative d'assassinat en chemin de fer, 1904 (Guy)
Terre des Taureaux *see* Tierra de los toros, 1924
Terrible Lesson, 1912 (Guy)
Terrible Night, 1912 (Guy)
Territoire, 1981 (Sarmiento)
Territory *see* Territoire, 1981
Terror from the Year 5000, 1958 (Allen, D.)
Tesito, 1989 (Faye)
Tess of the Storm Country, 1914 (Pickford)
Tess of the Storm Country, 1922 (Pickford)
Tess of the Storm Country, 1932 (Levien)
Test, 1909 (Pickford)
Test of Friendship, 1908 (Macpherson)
Testament de Pierrot, 1904 (Guy)
Testament des Dr. Mabuse, 1933 (von Harbou)
Testament of Dr. Mabuse *see* Testament des Dr. Mabuse, 1933
Texans, 1938 (Head)
Texas Carnival, 1951 (Rose)
Texas Rangers, 1936 (Head)
Texas Rangers Ride Again, 1940 (Head)
Texas Trail, 1937 (Head)
Thanatopsis, 1991 (B)
Thank You, 1925 (Marion)
Thank Your Lucky Stars, 1943 (Lupino)
Thanks for the Memory, 1938 (Head)
That Certain Feeling, 1956 (Head)
That Kind of Woman, 1959 (Head)
That Lady in Ermine, 1948 (Spencer)
That Midnight Kiss, 1949 (Rose)
That Night in Rio, 1941 (Meredyth)
That Our Children Will Not Die, 1978 (Chopra)
That Uncertain Feeling, 1941 (Irene)
That's Adequate, 1990 (Coolidge)
That's My Boy, 1951 (Head)
Thaumetopoea, 1960 (Guillemot)
Their Hour, 1915 (Madison; Meredyth)
Their Own Desire, 1929 (Marion)
Thèmes et variations, 1928 (Dulac)
Then I'll Come Back to You, 1916 (Marion)
Theodora Goes Wild, 1936 (Arzner)
Theory of Ideas, 1984 (Godmilow)
There Are No Children Here, 1993 (Angelou)
There Goes My Heart, 1938 (Irene)
There Is No Forgetting *see* Il n'y a pas d'oubli, 1975
There Were Times, Dear, 1985 (Murphy)
There's a Magic in the Music, 1941 (Head)
There's No Place Like Home, 1917 (Weber)
These Wilder Years, 1956 (Rose)

They All Kissed the Bride, 1942 (Irene)
They Call Him Skarven *see* De kalte ham Skarven, 1965
They Called Us "Les Filles du Roy" *see* Filles du Roi, 1974
They Drive by Night, 1940 (Lupino)
They Got Me Covered, 1943 (Head)
They Had to See Paris, 1928 (Levien)
They Met in Bombay, 1941 (Loos)
They Say the Moon Is Fuller Here, 1985 (Law)
They Won't Believe Me, 1947 (Harrison)
They Would Elope, 1909 (Pickford)
Thief in Paradise, 1925 (Marion)
Thin Blue Line *see* **Thin Line**, 1977
Thin Ice, 1960 (Batchelor)
Thin Ice, 1981 (Gish)
Thin Line, 1977 (Cole)
Thin Man, 1934 (Goodrich)
Thin Man Goes Home, 1944 (Irene)
Think of the Future, 1956 (Batchelor)
Third Eye Butterfly, 1968 (De Hirsch)
Thirteen Hours by Air, 1936 (Head)
Thirteenth Chamber *see* Trináctá komnata, 1968
Thirty Seconds over Tokyo, 1944 (Irene)
Thirty-Six Hours, 1964 (Head)
This Angry Age *see* Diga sul Pacifico, 1958
This Could Be the Night, 1957 (Lennart; Rose)
This Day and Age, 1933 (Bauchens)
This Gun for Hire, 1942 (Head)
This Is Dynamite, 1952 (Head)
This Is My Life, 1992 (Ephron)
This Is the Air Force, 1947 (Batchelor)
This Is the Home of Mrs. Levant Grahame, 1971 (Weill)
This Love Thing, 1970 (Batchelor)
This Mad World, 1930 (Bauchens)
This Man Is Mine, 1934 (Murfin)
This Man Is News, 1939 (Head)
This Man's Navy, 1945 (Irene)
This Old Man, 1991 (Murphy)
This Other Eden, 1959 (Box, M.)
This Property Is Condemned, 1966 (Head)
This Thing Called Love, 1941 (Irene)
This Time for Keeps, 1947 (Irene)
This Time Let's Talk about Men *see* Questa volta parliamo di uomini, 1965
This Way, Please, 1937 (Bauchens; Head)
Thomas Crown Affair, 1968 (Van Runkle)
Thoroughly Demoralized Girl: A Day in the Life of Rita Rischak *see* Ein ganz und gar verwahrlostes Mädchen, 1977
Those Blasted Kids *see* De pokkers unger, 1947
Those Redheads from Seattle, 1953 (Head)
Those Were the Days, 1940 (Head)
Those Who Love, 1926 (McDonagh Sisters)
Thousands Cheer, 1943 (Irene)
Thread of Destiny, 1910 (Pickford)
Three Broadway Girls *see* Greeks Had a Word for Them, 1932
Three Came Home, 1950 (Spencer)
Three Cases of Murder, 1955 (Toye)
Three Cheers for Love, 1936 (Head)
Three Coins in the Fountain, 1954 (Jeakins)
Three Colors: Blue *see* Trois Coleurs: Bleu, 1993
Three Colors: White *see* Trois Coleurs: Blanc, 1994
Three Colour Separation Studies—Landscapes, 1976 (Cantrill)

Three Colour Separation Studies—Still Lifes, 1976 (Cantrill)
Three Crowns of a Sailor see Trois Couronnes du matelot, 1982
Three Daring Daughters, 1948 (Irene; Levien)
Three Fables of Love see Quatre Vérités, 1962
Three Generations of Danjuro see Danjuro sandai, 1944
Three Guys Named Mike, 1950 (Rose)
Three Hearts for Julia, 1943 (Irene)
Three Little Words, 1950 (Rose)
Three Men and a Baby, 1987 (Serreau)
Three Men and a Cradle see **Trois hommes et un couffin**, 1985
Three Men and a Little Lady, 1990 (Serreau)
Three Men from Texas, 1940 (Head)
Three Men in White, 1944 (Irene)
Three Miles Out, 1924 (Loos)
Three Moods see Trois Thèmes, 1980
Three Mountaineers, 1960 (Batchelor)
Three-Ring Circus, 1954 (Head)
Three Sisters, 1911 (Pickford)
Three Stanzas on the Name Sacher see Trois strophes sur le nom de
     Sacher, 1989
Three Stories see Tri istorii, 1997
Three Violent People, 1956 (Head)
Three Weeks, 1924 (Glyn; Mathis)
Three Wise Fools, 1923 (Mathis)
Three Wise Fools, 1946 (Irene)
Three Wishes, 1954 (Reiniger)
Three Wishes, 1995 (Coolidge)
Three Women of France, 1917 (Meredyth)
Thrill of a Lifetime, 1937 (Head)
Thrill of a Romance, 1945 (Irene)
Thriller, 1979 (Potter)
Through the Back Door, 1921 (Pickford)
Through the Dark, 1924 (Marion)
Through the Wall, 1916 (Shipman)
Thumbelina, 1955 (Reiniger)
Thunder in the East, 1953 (Head)
Thunder Trail, 1937 (Head)
Thundering Dawn, 1923 (Coffee)
Thy Name Is Woman, 1924 (Meredyth)
Ti I Ya, 1971 (Shepitko)
Ti presento un'amica, 1988 (Cecchi d'Amico)
Tianguo Niezi, 1994 (Hui)
Ticket of No Return see Bildnis Einer Trinkerin—Aller jamais retour,
     1979
Tide of Death, 1912 (Lyell)
Tie-Dre, 1976 (Poirier)
Tiefland, 1944 (Riefenstahl)
Tierra de los toros, 1924 (Musidora)
Ties That Bind, 1984 (Friedrich)
Tiger among Us see 13 West Street, 1962
Tiger of the Sea, 1919 (Shipman)
Tigress, 1914 (Guy)
Tikhiy Don, 1930 (Preobrazhenskaya)
Till I Come Back to You, 1918 (Macpherson; Bauchens)
Till the Clouds Roll By, 1946 (Irene; Rose)
Till We Meet Again, 1936 (Head)
Till We Meet Again, 1944 (Coffee; Head)
Tillie, the Little Swede, 1916 (Madison)
Tillie Wakes Up, 1917 (Marion)
Time Being, 1991 (Nelson)
Time/Colour Separations, 1981 (Cantrill)

Time of Indifference see Gli indifferenti, 1963
Time of the Angels, 1987 (Hubley)
Timely Interception, 1913 (Gish)
Times Gone By see Altri tempi, 1952
Timothy's Quest, 1936 (Van Upp)
Tin Star, 1957 (Head)
Tiny & Ruby: Hell-Divin' Women, 1989 (Schiller)
Tiny Tot see Pinguinho de Gente, 1949
Tip-Off Girls, 1938 (Head)
Tip on a Dead Jockey, 1957 (Rose)
Tiroy senet, 1986 (Trintignant)
Tischbemerkungen-November 1985, 1985 (Export)
Tissues, 1981 (Campion)
Titanic, 1953 (Jeakins)
Tivoli Garden Games see Tivoligarden spiller, 1954
Tivoligarden spiller, 1954 (Henning-Jensen)
To Another Woman, 1916 (Madison)
To Be a Woman, 1951 (Craigie)
To Be or Not to Be, 1942 (Irene; Spencer)
To Catch a Thief, 1955 (Head)
To Die, to Sleep, 1992 (Murphy)
To Dorothy a Son, 1956 (Box, M.)
To Each His Own, 1946 (Head)
To Freedom, 1953 (Grayson)
To Have [or Not] see En avoir (ou pas), 1995
To Hell with the Kaiser, 1918 (Mathis)
To Kill a Priest, 1988 (Holland)
To Live in Peace see Vivere in pace, 1946
To Love, Honor, and Obey, 1980 (Choy)
To Please a Lady, 1950 (Rose)
To Please One Woman, 1921 (Weber)
To Save Her Soul, 1909 (Pickford)
To Speak the Unspeakable: The Message of Elie Wiesel see Mondani
     a mondhatatlant: Elie Wiesel üzenete, 1996
To the Limit see À la folie, 1994
To Whom Are You Showing These Films?, 1992-94 (Bani-Etemad)
To Wong Foo, Thanks for Everything! Julie Newmar, 1995 (Kidron)
To Your Health, 1956 (Batchelor)
Toast of New Orleans, 1950 (Rose)
Toccata and Fugue, 1940 (Bute)
Tocher, 1937 (Reiniger)
Today see Segodnya, 1930
Tog Dogs, 1960 (Batchelor)
Together Again, 1944 (Van Upp)
Together for Children: Principle 10 see Ten for Survival, 1979
Tohfehha, 1985 (Bani-Etemad)
Toit de la Baleine, 1981 (Sarmiento)
Tokyo no onna, 1933 (Tanaka)
Tom Sawyer, 1973 (Foster)
Tom Sawyer, Detective, 1938 (Head)
Tomas G. Masaryk—The Liberator see T.G.M.—Osvoboditel, 1990
Tommy, 1974 (Russell)
Tommy's Double Trouble, 1945 (Batchelor)
Tomorrow Is Forever, 1946 (Coffee)
Tomorrow the World, 1944 (Bauchens)
Tondeur de chiens, 1899/1900 (Guy)
Tonfilm, 1969 (Export)
Tongues, 1982 (Clarke)
Tonight Is Ours, 1933 (Bauchens)
Tonight We Sing, 1953 (Spencer)
Tonnelier, 1899/1900 (Guy)

Tony, tobe preskocilo, 1968 (Šimková-Plívová)
Tony, You Have a Bee in Your Bonnet *see* Tony, tobe preskocilo, 1968
Too Bad She's Bad *see* Peccato che sia una canaglia, 1954
Too Early, Too Late *see* Trop tot, trop tard, 1983
Too Late Blues, 1962 (Head)
Too Many Crooks, 1930 (Murfin)
Too Many Husbands, 1940 (Irene)
Too Many Parents, 1936 (Head; Van Upp)
Too Wise Wives, 1921 (Weber)
Too Young for Love, 1959 (Head)
Too Young to Kiss, 1951 (Goodrich; Rose)
Too Young to Love, 1960 (Box, M.)
Tootsie, 1982 (May)
Top Man, 1943 (Gish)
Top of New York, 1922 (Levien)
Topaz, 1969 (Head)
Topper, 1937 (Irene)
Topper Takes a Trip, 1939 (Irene)
Tops Is the Limit *see* Anything Goes, 1936
Torch Singer, 1933 (Coffee)
Torch Song, 1953 (Rose)
Torment *see* Hets, 1944
Torn Curtain, 1966 (Head)
Tornyai János, 1962 (Mészáros)
Torpedo Run, 1958 (Rose)
Toselli *see* Romazo d'amore, 1950
Toss of the Coin, 1911 (Pickford)
Total Eclipse, 1995 (Holland)
Toto Bissainte, Chanteuse, 1982 (Maldoror)
Tou Bun No Hoi *see* **T'ou-Pen Nu-Hai**, 1982
T'ou-Pen Nu-Hai, 1982 (Hui)
Touch Cinema *see* Tapp und Tastkino, 1968
Touch of Larceny, 1960 (Head)
Touch Wood, 1980 (Armstrong)
Touchdown Army, 1938 (Head)
Touched, 1983 (von Brandenstein)
Touching (1970), 1973 (Export)
Touching the Earth Series: Ocean at Point Lookout, near Coober Pedy, at Uluru, Katatjuta, 1977 (Cantrill)
Touha, 1958 (Šimková-Plívová)
Tour de Nèsle, 1954 (Kaplan)
Tourbiers, 1964 (Guillemot)
Tourist, 1985 (Hammer)
Tournage Mossane, 1990 (Faye)
Toute révolution est un coup de dés, 1977 (Huillet)
Toute une nuit, 1982 (Akerman)
Town in the Awkward Age *see* Kamaszváros, 1962
Town on Trial *see* Processo alla città, 1952
Toy, 1982 (Booth)
Toy Wife, 1938 (Akins)
Track of Thunder, 1967 (Fields)
Trade Winds, 1938 (Irene; Spencer)
Tragic Love, 1908 (Macpherson)
Trail of the Arrow, 1920 (Shipman)
Trail of the Lonesome Pine, 1916 (Macpherson)
Train d'enfer, 1984 (Pascal)
Train Trouble, 1940 (Batchelor)
Traitor, 1914 (Marion; Weber)
Trans, 1978 (Clarke)
Transformations, 1899/1900 (Guy)
Transformations, 1904 (Guy)

Transport z ráje, 1962 (Krumbachová)
Trap, 1913 (Madison)
Trap, 1959 (Head)
Trap Dance, 1968 (De Hirsch)
Trap Door, 1981 (B)
Traveling: Marie and Me, 1970 (Hammer)
Travelling Light: The Photojournalism of Dilip Mehta, 1986 (Mehta)
Travels with My Aunt, 1972 (Allen, J.)
Travestie, 1988 (Pascal)
Travolti da un insolito destino nell'azzurro mare d'agosto, 1974 (Wertmüller)
Treasure Hunt, 1960 (Batchelor)
Treasure Island *see* Isla del tesero, 1969
Treasure of Ice Cake Island, 1960 (Batchelor)
Treasure of the Golden Condor, 1952 (Jeakins)
Tree Grows in Brooklyn, 1945 (Spencer)
Trenchcoat in Paradise, 1989 (Coolidge)
Tres Desenhos, 1970 (Carolina)
Trêve, 1968 (Guillemot)
Trey o' Hearts, 1914 (Meredyth; Madison)
Tri istorii, 1997 (Muratova)
Trial *see* Procès, 1962
Trial Cuocolo *see* Processo Cuocolo, 1909
Trial in Smolensk *see* Sud v Smolenske, 1946
Trial Marriage, 1928 (Levien)
Triangulo de Cuatro, 1975 (Bemberg)
Tribe of the "E" Wood *see* Tribu du bois de l'é, 1998
Tribu du bois de l'é, 1998 (Maldoror)
Trick That Failed, 1909 (Pickford)
Tricolore, 1913 (Notari)
Trilogy, 1969 (Perry)
Trináctá komnata, 1968 (Krumbachová)
Trio Film, 1968 (Rainer)
Trionfo Cristiano, 1930 (Notari)
Trip *see* Chelsea Girls, 1966
Trip to Paradise, 1921 (Mathis)
Tripas Coração, 1982 (Carolina)
Triple Entente, 1915 (Musidora)
Triste fin d'un vieux savant, 1904 (Guy)
Triumph, 1924 (Bauchens; Macpherson)
Triumph des Willens, 1935 (Riefenstahl)
Triumph of the Will *see* **Triumph des Willens**, 1935
Triumph of Truth, 1916 (Madison)
Trois Coleurs: Blanc, 1994 (Holland)
Trois Coleurs: Bleu, 1993 (Holland)
Trois Couronnes du matelot, 1982 (Sarmiento)
Trois dernières sonatas de Franz Shubert, 1989 (Akerman)
Trois hommes et un couffin, 1985 (Serreau)
Trois rats, 1915 (Musidora)
Trois strophes sur le nom de Sacher, 1989 (Akerman)
Trois Thèmes, 1980 (Parker)
Troisième Larron, 1916 (Musidora)
Trollstenen, 1973-76 (Nelson)
Trollsyn, 1994 (Breien)
Trompé mais content, 1902 (Guy)
Trône de France, 1936-39 (Parker)
Troop Beverly Hills, 1989 (Van Runkle)
Trooper Campbell, 1914 (Lyell)
Trop tot, trop tard, 1983 (Huillet)
Trophée du zouave, 1915 (Musidora)
Tropic Holiday, 1938 (Head)

Tropic Zone, 1953 (Head)
Tropicana see Heat's On, 1943
Trotacalles, 1951 (Landeta)
Troubadour's Triumph, 1912 (Weber)
Trouble with Angels, 1966 (Lupino)
Trouble with Harry, 1955 (Head)
Trouble with Love see Der Beginn aller Schrecken ist Liebe, 1983
Trouble with Women, 1947 (Head)
Troubleshooters, 1979 (Coolidge)
Truck see Camion, 1977
True as a Turtle, 1957 (Toye)
True as Steel, 1924 (Madison)
True Confession, 1937 (Head)
True Grit, 1969 (Jeakins)
True Heart Susie, 1919 (Gish)
True Love, 1989 (Savoca)
True Story of Jost Buergi see Pravdivý príbeh Josta Buergiho, 1988-
89
True to Life, 1943 (Head)
Trumpetistically, Clora Bryant, 1989 (Davis)
Truth about Women, 1958 (Box, M.; Zetterling)
Trying to Get Arrested, 1909 (Macpherson)
Tsuki wa noborinu, 1955 (Tanaka)
Tu as Crie, 1997 (Poirier)
Tu n'épouseras jamais un avocat, 1914 (Musidora)
Tu nombre envenena mis sueños, 1996 (Miró)
Tue recht und scheue niemand, 1975 (Brückner)
Tul a Kálvin-téren, 1955 (Mészáros)
Tunisian Literature at the National Library see Littérature tunisienne
de la Bibliothèque Nationale, 1983
Tunnel of Love, 1958 (Rose)
Turkey at the Turning Point see Turtsiia na podeme, 1937
Turn Off the Moon, 1937 (Head)
Turn to the Right, 1922 (Mathis)
Turn Your Pony Around see To Die, to Sleep, 1992 (Murphy)
Turning Point, 1952 (Head)
Turtsiia na podeme, 1937 (Shub)
Tutajosok, 1988 (Elek)
Tutto a posto e niente in ordine, 1974 (Wertmüller)
Två kvinnor see Fem dagar i Falköping, 1973
Twa Corbies, 1951 (Batchelor)
'Twas Ever Thus, 1915 (Marion)
'Tween Two Loves, 1911 (Pickford)
Twelve Angry Men, 1957 (Hubley)
Twenty Years of Soviet Cinema see Kino za XX liet, 1940
Twice Blessed, 1945 (Irene)
Twice 'round the Daffodils, 1962 (Dillon)
Twice upon a Time see Smykketyven, 1990
Twilight, 1998 (Littleton)
Twin Beds, 1942 (Irene)
Twin Detectives, 1976 (Gish)
Twisted Trail, 1910 (Pickford)
Two Bad Daughters, 1988 (Hammer)
Two Brothers, 1910 (Pickford)
Two-Colour Separation Studies, 1980 (Cantrill)
Two Daughters of Eve, 1912 (Gish)
Two for the Seesaw, 1962 (Lennart)
Two for Tonight, 1935 (Head)
Two Girls and a Sailor, 1944 (Irene; Irene)
Two Heavens see Duie Paravise, 1928
Two Hours from London, 1994 (Craigie)

Two Kinds of Women, 1932 (Head)
Two Little Rangers, 1912 (Guy)
Two Lives of Mattia Pascal see Due vite di Mattia Pascal, 1985
Two Loves, 1961 (Rose)
Two Minutes Silence, 1933 (McDonagh Sisters)
Two Mrs. Carrolls, 1947 (Head)
Two of Them see Ök ketten, 1977
Two Sisters see Entre Deux Soeurs, 1990
Two Sisters from Boston, 1946 (Rose)
Two Small Bodies, 1993 (B)
Two Smart People, 1946 (Irene)
Two Virgins, 1968 (Ono)
Two Weeks, 1920 (Loos)
Two Weeks with Love, 1950 (Rose)
Two Women see Fem dagar i Falköping, 1973
Two Women see Ök ketten, 1977
Two Women, 1980 (Cantrill)
Type comme moi ne devrait jamais mourir, 1976 (Guillemot)
Typhoon, 1940 (Head)

U.S. Go Home, 1994 (Denis)
U krutogo yara, 1963 (Muratova)
Übernachtung in Tirol, 1973 (von Trotta)
Ucho, 1970 (Krumbachová)
Ugetsu see Ugetsu monogotari, 1953
Ugetsu monogotari, 1953 (Tanaka)
Ujra mosolyognak, 1954 (Mészáros)
Ukjent mann, 1952 (Henning-Jensen)
Ukraine in Flames see Bytva za nashu Radyansku Ukrayinu, 1943
Ukraine in Flames see Nezabivaemoe, 1968
Ulica Edisona, 1937 (Jakubowska)
Ulysse, 1983 (Varda)
Unafraid, 1915 (Macpherson)
Unchanging Sea, 1910 (Pickford)
Uncle Harry, 1945 (Harrison)
Uncle Janco, 1967 (Varda)
Unconquered, 1947 (Bauchens)
Und Sie?, 1967 (Hein)
Under Lock and Key, 1993 (B)
Under My Skin, 1950 (Spencer)
Under the Black Flag, 1913 (Madison)
Under the Clock see Clock, 1945
Under the Crescent, 1915 (Shipman)
Under the Skin of the City, 1997 (Bani-Etemad)
Under the Top, 1919 (Loos)
Under Two Flags, 1936 (Meredyth)
Undercover Doctor, 1939 (Head)
Undercover Maisie, 1947 (Irene)
Undercover Man, 1932 (Head)
Undercurrent, 1946 (Irene; Irene)
Undertow, 1995 (Bigelow)
Unerreichbare Nahe, 1984 (von Trotta)
Unfaithful see Utro, 1966
Unfinished Dance, 1947 (Irene; Rose)
Unfinished Diary see Journal inachevé, 1986
Unforgettable see Nezabivaemoe, 1968
Unforgiven, 1960 (Gish; Jeakins)
Ung flukt, 1959 (Ullmann)
Unguarded Hour, 1936 (Irene)
Unheimlichen Frauen, 1992 (Hein)
Unica, 1988 (Export)

Uninvited, 1944 (Head)
Union City, 1980 (Bigelow)
Union Pacific, 1939 (Bauchens; Head; Macpherson)
United States of America, 1975 (Gordon)
Universal Clip see Dada, 1936
Unjustly Accused, 1914 (Madison)
Unknown Man, 1951 (Rose)
Unknown Man see Ukjent mann, 1952
Unmarried, 1939 (Head)
Unmögliche Frau, 1936 (von Harbou)
Uno scandale per bene, 1984 (Cecchi d'Amico)
Unpublished Story, 1942 (Dillon)
Unseen Enemy, 1912 (Gish)
Unseen Hands, 1924 (Madison)
Unsichtbare Gegner, 1976 (Export)
Unsuspected, 1947 (Meredyth)
Untamed, 1940 (Head)
Unter dem Pflaster ist der Strand, 1975 (Sanders-Brahms)
Unter Schafen, 1981 (Dörrie)
Unthurqua, 1980 (Cantrill)
Untouchables, 1987 (von Brandenstein)
Unusual Tourney, 1983 (Peng)
Unwelcome Guest, 1912 (Pickford; Gish)
Unwilling Inspectors see Revizory ponevole, 1955
Up+Down+On+Off see Auf+Zu+Ab+An, 1968
Up Goes Maisie, 1946 (Irene)
Up She Goes see Up Goes Maisie, 1946
Up the Sandbox, 1972 (Streisand)
Up to and Including Her Limits, 1982 (Schneemann)
Up Your Legs Forever, 1970 (Ono)
Upside Down, 1991 (Hubley)
Upstairs and Downstairs, 1959 (Box, B.)
Urbanissimo, 1966 (Hubley)
Urchins see Pusilleco Addiruso, 1918
Used People, 1992 (Kidron)
Usinimage, 1987 (Ottinger)
Usporená libra, 1963 (Krumbachová)
Utamaro o mehuri go-nin no onna, 1946 (Tanaka)
Utinapló, 1989 (Mészáros)
Utközben, 1979 (Mészáros)
Utro, 1966 (Henning-Jensen)
Utvandrarna, 1972 (Ullmann)
Uvletschenia, 1994 (Muratova)
Uwasa no onna, 1954 (Tanaka)
Uz zase skácu pres kaluze, 1970 (Krumbachová)

V.I.P.s, 1963 (Booth)
V trinadtsatom chasu, 1968 (Shepitko)
Vagabond see Vagabonde, 1918
Vagabond see Vagabonde, 1985
Vagabonde, 1918 (Colette; Musidora)
Vagabonde, 1932 (Colette)
Vagabonde, 1985 (Varda)
Vaghe stelle dell'orsa, 1965 (Cecchi d'Amico)
Vagues, 1901 (Guy)
Valentino, 1977 (Russell)
Valerie a týden divu, 1970 (Krumbachová)
Valerie and a Week of Wonders see Valerie a týden divu, 1970
Valie Export, 1968 (Export)
Valise enchantée, 1903 (Guy)
Valley Girl, 1983 (Coolidge)

Valley of Decision, 1945 (Irene; Levien)
Valley of the Dolls, 1967 (Spencer)
Vampire, 1915 (Guy)
Vampires, 1915-16 (Musidora)
Vampire's Ghost, 1945 (Brackett)
Van Brood Alleen Kan een Mens Niet Leven, 1975 (Apon)
Vanessa: Her Love Story, 1935 (Coffee)
Vangelo '70 see Amore e rabbia, 1969
Vanquished, 1953 (Head)
Vaquero's Vow, 1908 (Macpherson)
Varelserna see Créatures, 1966
Vargtimmen, 1968 (Ullmann)
Variety, 1984 (Gordon)
Variety Girl, 1947 (Head)
Vásárhelyi szinek, 1961 (Mészáros)
Vater und Sohn, 1983 (Sander)
Velia, 1980 (Cecchi d'Amico)
Veliky put', 1927 (Shub)
Venetian Bird, 1952 (Box, B.)
Vénus et Adonis series, 1900 (Guy)
Vénus Victrix, 1916 (Dulac)
Verbotene Bilder, 1984-85 (Hein)
Verdammt in alle Ewigkeit, 1978-79 (Hein)
Verführung: Die grausame Frau, 1985 (Treut)
Vérité sur l'homme-singe, 1907 (Guy)
Verliebten, 1987 (Meerapfel)
Verlorene Ehre der Katharina Blum, 1975 (von Trotta)
Versprechen, 1994 (von Trotta)
Versprich mir nichts!, 1937 (von Harbou)
Vertigo, 1958 (Head)
Verwehte Spuren, 1938 (von Harbou)
Very Curious Girl see Fiancée du pirate, 1969
Very Eye of Night, 1959 (Deren)
Very Late Afternoon of a Faun see Faunovo prilis pozdni odpoledne, 1983
Vesper's Stampede to My Holy Mouth, 1992 (Schneemann)
Vesterhavs drenge, 1950 (Henning-Jensen)
Veszprém—Town of Bells see Harangok városa—Veszprém, 1966
Vêtements Sigrand, 1936-39 (Parker)
Veverka a kouzelná mušle, 1988 (Šimková-Plívová)
Via Mala, 1948 (von Harbou)
Viaggio clandestino, 1994 (Sarmiento)
Vibes, 1988 (Littleton)
Vice Versa, 1948 (Dillon)
Vicenta, 1919 (Musidora)
Vicki, 1953 (Spencer)
Vicoli e delitti see Camorra, 1986
Victim of Jealousy, 1910 (Macpherson; Pickford)
Victoria see Viktoriya, 1917
Victory, 1940 (Head)
Victory in Right-Bank Ukraine and the Expulsion of the Germans from the Boundaries of the Ukrainian Soviet Earth see Pobeda na pravoberezhnoi Ukraine i izgnanie Nemetskikh zakhvatchikov za predeli Ukrainskikh Sovetskikh zemel, 1945
Victory of the Faith see Sieg des Glaubens, 1933
Victory of Women see Josei no shori, 1946
Video Self-Portrait, 1971 (Cantrill)
Videotape I, 1971 (Hein)
Vie de Bohème, 1916 (Marion)
Vie du Christ, 1906 (Guy)
Vie du marin, 1906 (Guy)

Vieilles Estampes series, 1904 (Guy)
Vier um die Frau *see* Kämpfende Herzen, 1921
Vlet-Flakes, 1965 (Schneemann)
View from the Balcony of the Marco Polo Hotel, 1992 (Cantrill)
Vigil, 1980 (Godmilow)
Viktoriya, 1917 (Preobrazhenskaya)
Villa dévalisée, 1905 (Guy)
Village of Sin *see* Baby ryazanskie, 1927
Ville de Madame Tango, 1914 (Musidora)
Ville des pirates, 1983 (Sarmiento)
Vincent the Dutchman, 1971 (Zetterling)
Vindication *see* Fighting Shepherdess, 1920
Vine Bridge, 1965 (Zetterling)
Vinterbørn, 1978 (Henning-Jensen)
Violence *see* Gewalt, 1971
Violence et Passion *see* Gruppo di famiglia in un interno, 1974
Violent City *see* Città violenta, 1970
Violent Journey *see* Fool Killer, 1965
Violent Summer *see* Estate violenta, 1959
Violin Maker of Cremona, 1909 (Pickford)
Violin Maker of Nuremberg, 1911 (Guy)
Violons parfois, 1977 (Guillemot)
Virgin Machine *see* Jungfrauen Maschine, 1988
Virgin President, 1968 (Schoonmaker)
Virginia, 1916 (Madison)
Virginia, 1941 (Head; Van Upp)
Virginian, 1929 (Head)
Virginian, 1946 (Goodrich; Head)
Virgins from Venus, 1957 (Murphy)
Virtuous Vamp, 1919 (Loos)
Visions of Eight, 1973 (Allen, D.; Zetterling)
Visit to a Small Planet, 1960 (Head)
Visiting Desire, 1996 (B)
Viskningar och rop, 1972 (Ullmann)
Visual Variations on Noguchi, 1945 (Menken)
Vital Signs, 1991 (Hammer)
Viva 24 de Maio, 1978 (Yamasaki)
Vivacious Lady, 1938 (Irene)
Vivere in pace, 1946 (Cecchi d'Amico)
Vivre sa vie, 1962 (Guillemot)
Vlady, Peintre, 1988 (Maldoror)
Vlci bouda, 1986 (Chytilová)
Vocation suspendue, 1977 (Sarmiento)
Voglio a Tte *see* 'Nfama, 1924
Vogues, 1937 (Spencer; Irene)
Vogues of 1938 *see* Vogues, 1937
Voice from the Minaret, 1923 (Marion)
Voice in the Night *see* Freedom Radio, 1940
Voices of Experience, Voices for Change, Part 1, 1993 (Obomsawin)
Voiles à Val, 1959 (Guillemot)
Voina i mir, 1915 (Preobrazhenskaya)
Voir Miami, 1963 (Poirier)
Voiture cellulaire, 1906 (Guy)
Voldtekt-Tilfellet Anders, 1971 (Breien)
Volée par les bohémiens, 1904 (Guy)
Voleur de crimes, 1969 (Trintignant)
Voleur sacrilège, 1903 (Guy)
Voleuse, 1966 (Duras)
Volga Boatman, 1926 (Bauchens; Coffee)
Volleyball, 1967 (Rainer)
Von Romantik keine Spur, 1980 (Dörrie)

Von Ryan's Express, 1965 (Spencer)
Vorspann: Ein Lesefilm, 1968 (Export)
Vortex, 1983 (B)
Voshojdenie, 1977 (Shepitko)
Vostell—Berlin-fieber, 1973 (Ottinger)
Vote for Huggett, 1948 (Box, B.)
Vous n'avez rien contre la jeunesse, 1958 (Guillemot)
Voyage around a Hand *see* Voyage autour d'une main, 1985
Voyage autour d'une main, 1985 (Sarmiento)
Voyage de noces, 1976 (Trintignant)
Voyage en Boscavie, 1958 (Guillemot)
Voyage en Espagne series, 1906 (Guy)
Voyage to Next, 1974 (Hubley)
Vrazda ing. Certa, 1970 (Krumbachová)
Vrazhi tropi, 1935 (Preobrazhenskaya)
Vringsveedel Tryptych *see* Vringsveedeler Triptichon, 1980
Vringsveedeler Triptichon, 1980 (Sanders-Brahms)
Vroom, 1988 (Kidron)
Všichni dobrí rodáci, 1968 (Krumbachová)

W. C. Fields and Me, 1976 (Head)
W.O.W., 1975 (Hubley)
Waco, 1966 (Head)
Waga koi wa moenu, 1949 (Tanaka)
Wagner, 1983 (Russell)
Wahine *see* Maeva, 1961
Waikiki Wedding, 1937 (Head)
Waiter No. 5, 1910 (Pickford)
Waiting for the Moon, 1987 (Godmilow)
Wak-Wak, ein Märchenzauber *see* Geschichte des Prinzen Achmed, 1923-26
Wake Island, 1942 (Head)
Wakers and Dreamers *see* Wakers en Dromers, 1994
Wakers en Dromers, 1994 (Apon)
Waking Up: A Lesson in Love, 1989 (Schiller)
Walk into Paradise, 1955 (Guillemot)
Walker, 1992 (Obomsawin)
Walking on Thin Ice, 1981 (Ono)
Walking to Yeh Pelu, 1993 (Cantrill)
Walking Track, 1987 (Cantrill)
Wall Walls *see* Mur Murs, 1980
Walls of Freedom *see* Frihetens murar, 1978
Walls of Malapaga *see* Mura di Malapaga, 1949
Waltzer Dream *see* Pupatella, 1923
Waltzes from Vienna, 1934 (Reville)
Wanderer, 1925 (Head)
Wandering Daughters, 1923 (Coffee)
Wandering Image *see* Wandernde Bild, 1920
Wandering Life *see* Horoki, 1962
Wandering on Highways *see* Országutak vándora, 1956
Wandering Princess *see* Ruten no ohi, 1958
Wandernde Bild, 1920 (von Harbou)
Wandernder Held *see* Wandernde Bild, 1920
Wann ist der Mensch eine Frau?, 1976 (Export)
Wann—Wenn Nicht Jetzt?, 1987 (Dörrie)
Wanted—a Home, 1916 (Weber)
Wanton Contessa *see* Senso, 1954
War and Peace *see* Voina i mir, 1915
War Game, 1961 (Zetterling)
War of Paraguay *see* Guerra do Paraguai, 1972
War of the Worlds, 1953 (Head)

War Series, 1983 (Leaf)
Warning Shot, 1967 (Gish; Head)
Warrah, 1980 (Cantrill)
Warrior Marks, 1993 (Parmar)
Warrior's Husband, 1933 (Levien)
Was bin ich ohne Dich?, 1934 (von Harbou)
Washington Square, 1997 (Holland)
Washington Story, 1952 (Rose)
Wastrel see Relitto, 1961
Watch Your Stern, 1960 (Dillon)
Water for Firefighting, 1948 (Batchelor)
Water Gipsies, 1932 (Reville)
Water Light/Water Needle, 1965 (Schneemann)
Water Nymph see Rusalka, 1962
Waterfall, 1984 (Cantrill)
Watersark, 1965 (Wieland)
Watts with Eggs, 1967 (Menken)
Wavelength, 1967 (Wieland)
Waves see Golven, 1982
Waves and Washes, 1961 (Schneemann)
Way Back Home, 1932 (Murfin)
Way Down East, 1920 (Gish)
Way of All Flesh, 1940 (Coffee; Head)
Way of Learning, 1988 (Obomsawin)
Way of Man, 1909 (Pickford)
Way of the World, 1910 (Macpherson)
Way to the Stars, 1945 (Dillon)
Way We Live, 1946 (Craigie)
Way We Were, 1973 (Booth; Jeakins; Sharaff; Streisand)
Wayne's World, 1992 (Spheeris)
Ways of a Man, 1915 (Madison)
Wayward, 1932 (Head)
We Are Building see Budujemy, 1934
We Are Building see Wy brouwen, 1929
We Are Building New Villages see Budujemy nowe wsi, 1946
We Are in the Navy Now, 1962 (Toye)
We Can't Have Everything, 1918 (Bauchens)
We Eat the Fruit of the Trees of Paradise see Ovoce stromu rajských jíme, 1969
We har manje namn, 1976 (Zetterling)
We Have Many Names see We har manje namn, 1976
We Joined the Navy see We Are in the Navy Now, 1962
We Moderns, 1925 (Mathis)
We the Women see Siamo donne, 1953
We Were Dancing, 1942 (Coffee)
Weaker Sex Must Become Stronger see Schwache Geschlecht muss stärker werden, 1988
Weakness Syndrome see Astenicheskii Sindrom, 1989
Web, 1917 (Madison)
Web of Desire, 1917 (Marion)
Wedding, 1978 (Gish)
Wedding Band, 1990 (Spheeris)
Wedding Gown, 1913 (Loos)
Wedding Present, 1936 (Head)
Wee Sandy, 1962 (Reiniger)
Week of 1922 see Semana de 22, 1971
Weekend, 1967 (Guillemot)
Weekend at the Waldorf, 1945 (Irene)
Week-End sur deux, 1990 (Guillemot)
Weisses Hölle vom Piz Palü see Schischsal derer von Hapsburg, 1929
Welcome, Foreigner see Sannu batture, 1979

Welcome Stranger, 1947 (Head)
Well-Groomed Bride, 1946 (Head)
Well Kept Machine, 1949 (Batchelor)
Well, We Are Alive, 1979 (Schiller)
Wells Fargo, 1937 (Head)
Wendy and Joyce, 1985 (Wieland)
Werbefilm Nr. 1: Bamberg, 1968 (Hein)
Werther, 1922 (Dulac)
Werther, 1986 (Miró)
West of Broadway, 1932 (Meredyth)
West Point Widow, 1941 (Head)
West Side Story, 1961 (Sharaff)
Western Love, 1913 (Guy)
We'll Meet in 1972 see Találkozunk 1972-ben, 1971
We'll Take Her Children in Amongst Our Own, 1915 (Lyell)
Wet Parade, 1932 (Bauchens)
We've Come a Long Way, 1952 (Batchelor)
Whales of August, 1987 (Gish)
Whale's Roof see Toit de la Baleine, 1981
Wharf Rat, 1916 (Loos)
What a Life, 1939 (Head)
What a Way to Go!, 1964 (Comden; Head)
What Are You Waiting for to Be Happy! see Qu'est-ce qu'on attend pour être heureux!, 1982
What Can It Be, 1993 (Dörrie)
What Color Is God?, 1986 (Larkin)
What Do Men Want?, 1921 (Weber)
What Farocki Taught, 1997 (Godmilow)
What Is It, Zach, 1983 (Gordon)
What Next Corporal Hargrove?, 1945 (Irene)
What Now, Nursery Workers see Kindergärtnerin, was nun?, 1969
What Price Glory?, 1952 (Spencer)
What Price Hollywood?, 1932 (Murfin)
What the Daisy Said, 1910 (Pickford)
What to Do? see Co delat?, 1996
What Will People Say?, 1916 (Guy)
What You Take for Granted, 1983 (Citron)
Whatever You Do, You Lose see De todos modos Juan te llamas, 1975
What's Cooking?, 1947 (Batchelor)
What's So Bad about Feeling Good?, 1968 (Head)
What's the Weather Like Up There, 1975 (Mehta)
What's Underground about Marshmallows, 1996 (Godmilow)
What's Up, Doc?, 1972 (Fields; Streisand)
What's Worth While?, 1921 (Weber)
What's Your Hurry, 1909 (Pickford)
When a Girl Loves, 1919 (Weber)
When a Man Loves, 1911 (Pickford)
When a Man Loves, 1927 (Meredyth)
When a Woman Guides, 1914 (Loos)
When Bess Got in Wrong, 1914 (Meredyth)
When Harry Met Sally ..., 1989 (Ephron)
When Husbands Flirt, 1925 (Arzner)
When Is a Human Being a Woman? see Wann ist der Mensch eine Frau?, 1976
When Ladies Meet, 1941 (Loos)
When Memory Speaks see Desembarcos, 1989
When the Bough Breaks, 1947 (Box, M.; Box, B.)
When the Road Parts, 1915 (Loos)
When the Wolf Howls, 1916 (Madison)
When We Were in Our Teens, 1910 (Pickford)

When Women Had Tails *see* Quando de donne avevano la coda, 1970
When Worlds Collide, 1951 (Head)
When You and I Were Young, 1917 (Guy)
Where Am I Going to Find Another Violeta *see* Donde voy a encontrar otra Violeta, 1973
Where Are My Children?, 1916 (Weber)
Where Are You? I'm Here *see* Dove siete? Io sono qui, 1993
Where Have All the Mentally Ill Gone?, 1974 (Godmilow)
Where Love Has Gone, 1964 (Head)
Where Now Are the Dreams of Youth? *see* Seishun no yume ima izuko, 1932
Where There's Life, 1947 (Head)
While Still Young *see* Naar man kun er ung, 1943
While the Cat's Away, 1911 (Pickford)
While the City Sleeps, 1956 (Fields; Lupino)
Whispering Chorus, 1918 (Macpherson)
Whispering Smith, 1948 (Head)
Whistling in Brooklyn, 1943 (Irene)
White Banners, 1938 (Coffee)
White Christmas, 1954 (Head)
White Cliffs of Dover, 1944 (Irene)
White Cradle Inn, 1947 (Dillon; Pickford)
White Dwarf, 1995 (Van Runkle)
White Fang, 1925 (Murfin)
White Flower Passing, 1981 (Choy)
White Heat, 1934 (Weber)
White Hell of Piz Palü *see* Schiscksal derer von Hapsburg, 1929
White Man *see* Squaw Man, 1931
White Mazurka *see* Bialy mazur, 1978
White Nights *see* Notti bianche, 1957
White-Orange-Green, 1969 (Cantrill)
White Palace, 1990 (Littleton)
White Parade, 1934 (Levien)
White Roses, 1911 (Pickford)
White Shoulders, 1931 (Murfin)
White Sister, 1923 (Gish)
White Sister, 1933 (Booth)
White Slave Catchers, 1914 (Loos)
White Witch Doctor, 1953 (Jeakins)
White Woman, 1933 (Head)
Whiteye, 1957 (Schneemann)
Whither Weather, 1977 (Hubley)
Who Am I, 1989 (Hubley)
Who Goes Next?, 1938 (Dillon)
Who Has Seen the Wind?, 1965 (Head)
Who Killed Vincent Chin?, 1988 (Choy)
Who Will Marry Me?, 1919 (Levien)
Who's Afraid of Virginia Woolf?, 1966 (Sharaff)
Who's Been Sleeping in My Bed?, 1963 (Head)
Who's Got the Action?, 1962 (Head)
Who's Minding the Store?, 1963 (Head)
Who's That Knocking at My Door?, 1968 (Schoonmaker)
Whole Town's Talking, 1926 (Loos)
Why Change Your Wife?, 1920 (Bauchens)
Why Men Leave Home, 1924 (Booth)
Why Not? *see* Pourquoi pas?, 1977
Wide-Open Town, 1941 (Head)
Widow's Kids, 1913 (Loos)
Wie konntest du, Veronika?, 1940 (von Harbou)
Wieczór u Abdona, 1974 (Holland)
Wielka Wielksza Najwielksza, 1962 (Jakubowska)

Wife, 1914 (Gish)
Wife Takes a Flyer, 1942 (Irene)
Wife Who Wasn't Wanted, 1925 (Meredyth)
Wild and the Willing, 1962 (Box, B.)
Wild and Woolly, 1917 (Loos)
Wild Child *see* L'Enfant sauvage, 1969
Wild Duck, 1984 (Ullmann)
Wild Girl from the Hills, 1915 (Marion)
Wild Girl of the Sierras, 1916 (Loos)
Wild Harvest, 1947 (Head)
Wild in the Country, 1961 (Spencer)
Wild Irish Rose, 1915 (Madison)
Wild Is the Wind, 1957 (Head)
Wild Man Blues, 1998 (Kopple)
Wild Money, 1937 (Head)
Wild Party, 1929 (Arzner)
Wild Racers, 1968 (Fields)
Wild Side *see* Suburbia, 1984
Wild Strain, 1918 (Shipman)
Wild Style, 1982 (Schiller)
Wildfire, 1988 (Van Runkle)
Wilful Peggy, 1910 (Pickford)
Williamswood, 1992 (Chenzira)
Willie Walrus and the Awful Confession, 1914 (Meredyth)
Wilpena, 1981 (Cantrill)
Wind, 1928 (Gish; Marion)
Wind Cannot Read, 1958 (Box, B.)
Windom's Way, 1957 (Craigie)
Window Shopping, 1986 (Akerman)
Windy Day, 1968 (Hubley)
Wings, 1927 (Head)
Wings *see* Krylya, 1966
Wings against the Wind, 1998 (Palcy)
Wings in the Dark, 1935 (Head; Shipman)
Wings of a Serf *see* Krylya kholopa, 1926
Wings of Desire *see* Der Himmel über Berlin, 1987
Wings to Hawaii, 1949 (Grayson)
Winner Takes All, 1995 (Krumbachová)
Winning, 1969 (Head)
Winning Back His Love, 1910 (Macpherson)
Winning of Barbara Worth, 1926 (Coffee; Marion)
Winsome but Wise, 1912 (Guy)
Winter Carnival, 1939 (Spencer)
Winter Children *see* Vinterbörn, 1978
Winter Garden, 1951 (Batchelor)
Winter in Zuiderwoude *see* Een Winter in Zuiderwoude, 1994
Winter Soldier, 1972 (Kopple)
Winterborn *see* Vinterbörn, 1978
Wintergarden, 1973 (De Hirsch)
Winterkind, 1997 (von Trotta)
Wise Girls, 1929 (Booth)
Witch Hunt *see* Forfølgelsen, 1981
Witch Hunt *see* Kladivo na carodejnice, 1969
Witches, 1990 (Zetterling)
Witches' Cradle, 1943 (Deren)
Witching Hour, 1934 (Head)
With Grotowski at Nienadowka, 1979 (Godmilow)
With Her Card, 1909 (Macpherson)
With Liberty and Justice for All, 1997 (Kopple)
With Me You Do Very Well *see* Conmigo la pasas muy bien, 1982
With or Without, 1981 (Kidron)

With the Enemy's Help, 1912 (Pickford)
Within the Law, 1923 (Marion)
Without Anesthesia *see* Bez znieczulenia, 1978
Without Apparent Motive, 1998 (Bird)
Without Love, 1945 (Irene)
Without Title No. 2 *see* Ohne Titel Nr. 2, 1968
Without Title xn *see* Ohne Titel xn, 1968
Witness for the Prosecution, 1957 (Head)
Wives *see* Hustruer, 1975
Wives and Lovers, 1963 (Head)
Wives Never Know, 1936 (Head)
Wives: 10 Years After *see* Hustruer—10 år etter, 1985
Wives III *see* Hustruer III, 1996
Wiz, 1978 (Allen, D.)
Wo ai tai kung tcn, 1988 (Law)
Wolf Song, 1929 (Head)
Wolf's Hole *see* Vlci bouda, 1986
Woman, 1981 (Ono)
Woman Alone, 1917 (Marion)
Woman Alone *see* Kobieta samotna, 1982
Woman Alone *see* Sabotage, 1936
Woman from Mellon's, 1910 (Pickford)
Woman God Forgot, 1917 (Macpherson)
Woman Hater, 1948 (Dillon)
Woman He Married, 1922 (Meredyth)
Woman in Hiding, 1949 (Lupino)
Woman in Question, 1950 (Dillon)
Woman in the Moon *see* Frau im Mond, 1929
Woman in the Spinnery *see* A lörinci fonóban, 1971
Woman in the Ultimate, 1913 (Gish)
Woman in the Window, 1944 (Fields)
Woman in Transit *see* Femme de l'hôtel, 1984
Woman Is a Woman *see* Femme est une femme, 1961
Woman of Affairs, 1928 (Meredyth)
Woman of Mystery, 1914 (Guy)
Woman of No Importance *see* Eine Frau ohne Bedetung, 1936
Woman of Rumor *see* Uwasa no onna, 1954
Woman of the Ganges *see* Femme du Ganges, 1974
Woman of the Wolf, 1994 (Schiller)
Woman of Tokyo *see* Tokyo no onna, 1933
Woman Suffers, 1918 (Lyell)
Woman to Woman, 1923 (Reville)
Woman to Woman, 1975 (Deitch)
Woman Trap, 1936 (Head)
Woman Who Would Not Pay, 1917 (Madison)
Woman with Responsibility *see* Eine Frau mit Verantwortung, 1977
Woman without a Face *see* Mister Buddwing, 1966
Woman's Debt, 1915 (Madison)
Woman's Place, 1921 (Loos)
Woman's Way, 1916 (Marion)
Woman's Woman, 1922 (Madison)
Women, 1939 (Loos; Murfin)
Women and Development, 1984 (Nair)
Women I Love, 1976 (Hammer)
Women in Chains, 1972 (Lupino)
Women in Limbo *see* Limbo, 1972
Women in Love, 1969 (Russell)
Women Love Once, 1931 (Akins)
Women of Ryazan *see* Baby ryazanskie, 1927
Women of the Night *see* Yoru no onna tachi, 1948
Women of the Resistance *see* Donna Nella Resistenza, 1965

Women of the World *see* W.O.W., 1975
Women without Names, 1940 (Bauchens; Head)
Women's Prison, 1955 (Lupino)
Women's Rites or Truth Is the Daughter of Time, 1974 (Hammer)
Women's Story *see* **Nüren de gushi**, 1987
Won by a Fish, 1912 (Pickford)
Wonder of Women, 1929 (Meredyth)
Wonder of Wool, 1960 (Batchelor)
Woodstock, 1970 (Schoonmaker)
Words and Music, 1948 (Rose)
Work in Progress Teil A, 1969 (Hein)
Work in Progress Teil B, 1970 (Hein)
Work in Progress Teil C, 1971 (Hein)
Work in Progress Teil D, 1971 (Hein)
Work or Profession? *see* Munka vagy hivatás?, 1963
Working Girl, 1988 (von Brandenstein)
Working Girls, 1931 (Akins; Arzner)
Working Girls, 1986 (Borden)
Working Models of Success, 1973 (Dash)
World and His Wife, 1920 (Marion)
Wor[l]d Cinema: A Festival of Languages *see* Wor(l)d Cinema: Ein Sprachfest, 1968
Wor(l)d Cinema: Ein Sprachfest, 1968 (Export)
World in Flames, 1940 (Head)
World in the Three Dimensions *see* Mir v treh izmerenijah, 1979
World of Jacques Demy *see* L'universe de Jacques Demy, 1995
World of Little Ig, 1956 (Batchelor)
World Premiere, 1941 (Head)
World That Nature Forgot, 1955 (Batchelor)
Wot Dot, 1970 (Batchelor)
Would You Like to Meet Your Neighbor?, 1985 (Hammer)
Wounded in Honour *see* Mimi metallurgio ferito nell'onore, 1972
Wreath in Time, 1908 (Macpherson)
Wreath of Orange Blossoms, 1910 (Macpherson)
Wrestling, 1964 (Menken)
Wu Li Chang, 1930 (Marion)
Wy brouwen, 1929 (van Dongen)
Wyatt Earp, 1994 (Littleton)

X, 1974 (Hammer)
Xiang Xiang Gong Zhu, 1987 (Hui)
Xiao Ao Jiang Hu, 1990 (Hui)
Xiaojie Zhuang Dao Gui *see* Zhuang Dao Zheng, 1980
Xiatian de Xue, 1994 (Hui)

Y tenemos sabor, 1967 (Gómez)
Ya tebya pomnyu, 1985 (Muratova)
Yakuza, 1975 (Jeakins)
Yank at Oxford, 1937 (Booth)
Yank in Dutch *see* Wife Takes a Flyer, 1942
Yanks, 1979 (Russell)
Year of the Gun, 1990 (Allen, J.)
Year of the Horse, 1966 (Hubley)
Year of the Woman, 1973 (Weill)
Yearling, 1946 (Irene)
Yearning Laurel *see* Aizen katsura, 1938
Years Between, 1946 (Box, B.; Box, M.)
Years of Hunger *see* **Hungerjahre**, 1979
Yellow Lily, 1928 (Meredyth)
Yellow Passport, 1916 (Marion)
Yellow Rolls-Royce, 1965 (Head)

Yellow Tale Blues: Two American Families, 1991 (Choy)
Yellow Traffic, 1914 (Guy)
Yentl, 1983 (Streisand)
Yes to Europe, 1971 (Hein)
Yes We Can, 1988 (Hubley)
Yes! Yi zu, 1990 (Law)
Yeux ne veulent pas en tout temps se fermer ou Peut-être qu'un jour
    Rome se permettra de choisir à son tour *see* Othon, 1969
Yi Sheng Yitai Xi, 1997 (Hui)
Yo, la peor de todas, 1990 (Bemberg)
Yoga, 1972 (Weill)
Yolanda and the Thief, 1945 (Sharaff)
Yoru no onna tachi, 1948 (Tanaka)
You and I *see* Ti I Ya, 1971
You and Me, 1938 (Head; Van Upp)
You Belong to Me, 1934 (Head)
You Belong to Me, 1941 (Head)
You Came Along, 1945 (Head)
You Can Draw, 1938 (van Dongen)
You Can't Ration Love, 1944 (Head)
You Can't Take It with You, 1938 (Irene)
You seng, 1993 (Law)
You Were Never Lovelier, 1942 (Irene)
Young and Innocent, 1937 (Harrison; Reville)
Young and Willing, 1942 (Head; Van Upp)
Young and Willing *see* Wild and the Willing, 1962
Young April, 1926 (Macpherson)
Young at Heart, 1955 (Coffee)
Young Bride, 1932 (Murfin)
Young Captives, 1959 (Head)
Young Emmanuelle *see* Néa , 1976
Young Escape *see* Ung flukt, 1959
Young Frankenstein, 1974 (Jeakins)
Young Girls of Rochefort *see* Demoiselles de Rochefort, 1967
Young Girls Turn 25 *see* Demoiselles ont en 25 ans, 1993
Young Lions, 1958 (Spencer)
Young Lovers *see* Never Fear, 1950
Young Miss *see* Ojosan, 1930
Young Rajah, 1922 (Mathis)
Younger Generation, 1928 (Levien)
Youngest Profession, 1943 (Irene)
Your Children Come Back to You, 1979 (Larkin)
Your Name Poisons My Dreams *see* Tu nombre envenena mis sueños, 1996

Your Witness, 1950 (Harrison)
You're Never Too Young, 1955 (Head)
You're the One, 1941 (Head)
Yours for the Asking, 1936 (Lupino)
Yours Truly, Andrea G. Stern, 1976/77 (Seidelman)
Youth in Revolt *see* Altitude 3200, 1938
Youth *see* Jugend, 1938
Yukon Quest, 1986 (Export)
Yunnan Qiu Shi, 1994 (Zhang)

Zacharovannaya Desna, 1965 (Solntseva)
Zajota and the Boogie Spirit, 1990 (Chenzira)
Zander the Great, 1925 (Marion)
Zandy's Bride, 1974 (Ullmann)
Zanzibar, 1988 (Pascal)
Zap, 1971 (Cantrill)
Zaproszenie, 1986 (Jakubowska)
Zard-e Ghanari, 1989 (Bani-Etemad)
Zaza, 1938 (Akins; Head)
Zdjecia probne, 1977 (Holland)
Zehn Minuten Mozart, 1930 (Reiniger)
Zeit des Zorns, 1993 (von Trotta)
Zemlya, 1930 (Solntseva)
Zhuang Dao Zheng, 1980 (Hui)
Ziegfeld Follies, 1946 (Irene; Levien; Rose)
Ziegfeld Girl, 1941 (Levien)
Zivot bez kytary, 1962 (Krumbachová)
Znoy, 1963 (Shepitko)
Zodiac Killer *see* Jidao Zhuizhong, 1991
Zolnierz zwyciestwa, 1953 (Jakubowska)
Zolotye vorota, 1969 (Solntseva)
Zoom—kurze Fassung, 1971 (Hein)
Zorn, 1994 (Ullmann)
Ztracená revue, 1961 (Krumbachová)
Ztracenci, 1956 (Chytilová)
Zu früh, zu spät *see* Trop tot, trop tard, 1983
Zu Lucifer Rising von Kenneth Anger, 1973 (Hein)
Zuiderzee Dike, 1931 (van Dongen)
Zur Chronik von Grieshuus, 1925 (von Harbou)
Zuyderzee, 1933 (van Dongen)
Zweiheit der Natur, 1986 (Export)
Zweite Erwachen der Christa Klages, 1977 (von Trotta)
Zwickel auf Bizykel, 1968-97 (Meerapfel)

SELECTED LIST OF DISTRIBUTORS OF FILMS
BY WOMEN FILMMAKERS

Note: Inclusion in this list does not imply an endorsement on the part of the editor or publisher.

The Canadian Filmmakers Distribution Centre
37 Hanna Avenue, Suite 220
Toronto, ON M6K 1W8
Canada
Phone: (416) 588-0725
Fax: (416) 588-7956
Internet: http://www.cfmdc.org
Canada's oldest artist-run center. Distributes about 1,400 titles from more than 400 member/filmmakers. Sales and public-performance rentals of 16mm films and videos.

Canyon Cinema
2325 Third Street, Suite 338
San Francisco, CA 94107
U.S.A.
Phone/Fax: (415) 626-2255
E-mail: canyon@sj.bigger.net
Internet: http://www.sirius.com/~sstark/org/canyon/canyon.html
Alternative distributor for independent filmmakers. Sales and public-performance rentals of films and videos.

Cine-Pro
Schwere-Reiter-Strasse 35
GB 41/11
80797 Munich
Germany
Phone: (49) 89-3072-9430
Fax: (49) 89-3072-9429

Dangerous to Know
17a Newman Street
London W1P 3HB
England
Phone: (44) (0)171-255-1955
Fax: (44) (0)171-255-1956
E-mail: mail@dtk.co.uk
Internet: http://www.dtk.co.uk
Distributes lesbian and gay films and videos in PAL 625 format.

Electronic Arts Intermix
542 West 22nd Street, 3rd Floor
New York, NY 10011
U.S.A.
Phone: (212) 337-0680
Fax: (212) 337-0679
E-mail: info@eai.org
Internet: http://www.eai.org
Distributes more than 2,000 avant-garde and experimental videos from 175 artists worldwide. Sales and rentals.

Facets Multimedia, Inc.
1517 West Fullerton Avenue
Chicago, IL 60614
U.S.A.
Phone: (773) 281-9075
Toll-Free: (800) 331-6197
Fax: (773) 929-5437
E-mail: sales@facets.org
Internet: http://www.facets.org
Catalog includes more than 20,000 titles, with an emphasis on foreign and independent films. Sales and membership rentals in VHS, laserdisc, DVD, and PAL formats.

Filmakers Library, Inc.
124 East 40th Street
New York, NY 10016
U.S.A.
Phone: (212) 808-4980
Fax: (212) 808-4983
E-mail: info@filmakers.com
Internet: http://www.filmakers.com/index.html
Maintains collection of award-winning documentary films and videos primarily for educational use. Sales and rentals to universities, schools, museums, businesses, and community groups.

Film-Makers' Cooperative
175 Lexington Avenue
New York, NY 10016
U.S.A.
Phone: (212) 889-3820
Fax: (212) 477-2714
E-mail: film6000@aol.com
Internet: http://www.film-makerscoop.com
Maintains archive of more than 5,000 independent and avant-garde films and videos. Sales and public-performance rentals.

Frameline Distribution
346 Ninth Street
San Francisco, CA 94103
U.S.A.
Phone: (415) 703-8650
Fax: (415) 861-1404
E-mail: info@frameline.org
Internet: http://www.frameline.org/distribution
Nonprofit organization offers for rental and sale more than 200 lesbian and gay films and videos, including experimental, narrative, documentary, and short fiction titles.

Freunde der Deutschen Kinemathek
Welser Strasse 25
10777 Berlin
Germany
Phone: (49) 30-213-6039; (49) 30-211-1725
Fax: (49) 30-218-4281
E-mail: fdk@forum-ifb.b.shuttle.de
Internet: http://www.b.shuttle.de/forum-ifb/fdk-home.htm

Glenn Video Vistas, Ltd.
6024 Canby Avenue, Suite 103
Reseda, CA 91335
U.S.A.

Phone: (818) 881-8110
Fax: (818) 981-5506
E-mail. mglass@worldnet.att.net
Sells videos of rare silent titles.

Home Film Festival
Post Office Box 2032
Scranton, PA 18501-2032
U.S.A.
Toll-Free: (800) 258-3456
Fax: (717) 344-3810
E-mail: homefilm@scranton.com
Internet: http://www.homefilmfestival.com
Makes available to its members 3,500 of "the finest movies foreign and domestic." Sales and rentals.

Kino on Video
333 West 39th Street
New York, NY 10018
U.S.A.
Phone: (212) 629-6880
Toll-Free: (800) 562-3330
Fax: (212) 714-0871
E-mail: kinoint@infohouse.com
Internet: http://www.kino.com
Sells "the best in world cinema."

Light Cone
27, rue Louis-Braille
75012 Paris
France
Phone: (33) 1-4628-1121
Fax: (33) 1-4346-6376
Offers for rental more than 1,000 films by historically important, experimental, and avant-garde filmmakers worldwide.

London Filmmakers' Coop
2-4 Hoxton Square
London N1 6NU
England
Phone: (44) (0)171-684-0202
Fax: (44) (0)171-684-2222
Internet: http://www.lfmc.org/lfmc

Movies Unlimited
3015 Darnell Road
Philadelphia, PA 19154
U.S.A.
Phone: (215) 637-4444
Toll-Free: (800) 466-8437
Fax: (215) 637-2350
E-mail: movies@moviesunlimited.com
Internet: http://www.moviesunlimited.com
Catalog of more than 45,000 titles. Specializes in hard-to-find titles. Sells videos, DVDs, and laserdiscs.

National Film Board of Canada
Internet: http://www.nfb.ca

in Canada:
National Film Board of Canada
Post Office Box 6100
Station Centre-Ville
Montreal, PQ H3C 3H5
Canada
Toll-Free: (800) 267-7710

in the United States:
National Film Board of Canada
1251 Avenue of the Americas, 16th Floor
New York, NY 10020
U.S.A.
Phone: (212) 596-1770
Toll-Free: (800) 542-2164
Fax: (212) 596-1779
E-mail: johnnfbc@aol.com

outside Canada and the United States:
National Film Board of Canada
International Program
125 Houde Street
Saint-Laurent, PQ H4N 2J3
Canada
Fax: (514) 496-1895
Operates as "a public agency that produces and distributes films and other audiovisual works which reflect Canada to Canadians and the rest of the world." More than 9,000 titles available for purchase or rental.

PopcornQ Video Shop/TLA Video
TLA Video
1520 Locust Street, #200
Philadelphia, PA 19102
U.S.A.
Phone: (215) 790-1510
Toll-Free: (800) 333-8521
Fax: (215) 790-1502
E-mail: pqvideoshop@planetout.com
Internet: http://www.planetout.com/shop/pqvideo/
PopcornQ, the "ultimate online home for the queer moving image," offers an online catalog from which gay and lesbian videos can be purchased directly from TLA Video.

Tapeworm Video Distributors
27833 Hopkins Avenue, Unit 6
Valencia, CA 91355
U.S.A.
Phone: (805) 257-4904
Fax: (805) 257-4820
E-mail: video@tapeworm.com
Internet: http://www.tapeworm.com
Sells "hard-to-find special interest videos."

Third World Newsreel
545 Eighth Avenue, 10th Floor
New York, NY 10018
U.S.A.
Phone: (212) 947-9277
Fax: (212) 594-6417
E-mail: twn@twn.org
Internet: http://www.twn.org

Distributes nearly 300 films and videos by "People of Color in America and by Third World and Indigenous people throughout the world."

Video Out Distribution
1965 Main Street
Vancouver, BC V5T 3C1
Canada
Phone: (604) 872-8449
Fax: (604) 876-1185
E-mail: video@portal.ca
Internet: http://www.video-in.com/distribution/videoout.html
Serves as "Western Canada's leading distributor of independent video." Features a catalog with more than 450 titles available for purchase or rental.

Women Make Movies, Inc.
462 Broadway, Suite 500
New York, NY 10013
U.S.A.
Phone: (212) 925-0606
Fax: (212) 925-2052
E-mail: distdept@wmm.com
Nonprofit organization distributes about 350 independent films and videos by and about women. Sales and rentals.

PICTURE ACKNOWLEDGEMENTS

We are grateful to the following for supplying photographs, and granting permission to reproduce them in this volume.

L'Alma/Alexandre (courtesy Kobal Collection): *Diabolo menthe*.

Columbia Pictures (courtesy Kobal Collection): Claudia Weill.

Di Novi/Columbia (courtesy Kobal Collection): Gillian Armstrong.

Stephane Fefer (courtesy Kobal Collection): Agnes Varda.

Films de la Pleiade (courtesy Kobal Collection): *Vivre sa vie*.

Filmworld International (courtesy Kobal Collection): Maggie Greenwald.

Fine Line Features (courtesy Kobal Collection): *The Ballad of Little Jo*.

Flach-TFI-Soprofilm/Sam Goldwyn (courtesy Kobal Collection): *Trois hommes et un couffin*.

F-M Entertainment/DEG (courtesy Kobal Collection): *Near Dark*.

Handmade Films (courtesy Kobal Collection): Mai Zetterling.

IRS Media (courtesy Kobal Collection): Penelope Spheeris.

The Kobal Collection: Allison Anders; Dorothy Arzner; Lizzie Borden; Betty Box; Muriel Box; Jane Campion; Liliana Cavani; Vera Chytilová; Shirley Clarke; Betty Comden; Martha Coolidge; Donna Deitch; *Deutschland bleiche Mutter;* Marguerite Duras; Nora Ephron; *Film d'amore e d'anarchia;* Lillian Gish; Elinor Glyn; *Harlan County, U.S.A.;* Edith Head; *Hester Street; Hungerjahre;* Irene; Ruth Prawer Jhabvala; Diane Kurys; Anita Loos; Ida Lupino; Jeanie Macpherson; *Mädchen in Uniform;* Frances Marion; Penny Marshall; *La Maternelle;* June Mathis; Márta Mészáros; *Olympia;* Mary Pickford; *Qingchunji;* Lotte Reiniger; Leni Riefenstahl; Alma Reville; Shirley Russell; Helke Sander; Irene Sharaff; Wendy Toye; Nadine Trintignant; Virginia Van Upp; Margarethe Von Trotta; Lina Wertmuller; Mae West.

Mafilm (courtesy Kobal Collection): *Naplo gyermekeimnek*

MGM (courtesy Kobal Collection): Euzhan Palcy.

MGM/UA Entertainment (courtesy Kobal Collection): Barbra Streisand.

Miraai/Jane Balfour (courtesy Kobal Collection): *Salaam Bombay!*

Miramax (courtesy Kobal Collection): *The Piano*.

New Line Cinema (courtesy Kobal Collection): Nancy Savoca.

Norsk Film A/S (courtesy Kobal Collection): Anja Breien.

NSDAP (courtesy Kobal Collection): *Triumph des Willens*.

NSW Film Corp. (courtesy Kobal Collection): *My Brilliant Career*.

Orion Pictures Corp. (courtesy Kobal Collection): Jodie Foster; Susan Seidelman.

Outlook (courtesy Kobal Collection): Jill Craigie.

Paramount Pictures (courtesy Kobal Collection): Elaine May.

NOTES ON
ADVISERS AND CONTRIBUTORS

BARON, Cynthia. Essayist. Visiting assistant professor, Washington University, St. Louis. Contributor to anthologies such as *Screen Acting;* and to journals such as *Film and Philosophy,* and *Spectator.* Essays: Hammer; Palcy; Ullmann.

BARR, Charles. Essayist. Lecturer in film, University of East Anglia, Norwich, England. Author of *Ealing Studios,* 1977. Essay: B. Box.

BARTONI, Doreen. Essayist. Artist-in-residence, Columbia College, Chicago, 1986-87. Essay: Loos.

BASINGER, Jeanine. Adviser and essayist. Corwin-Fuller Professor of Film Studies, Wesleyan University, Middletown, Connecticut; also chair, film studies program, and curator/founder, Wesleyan Cinema Archives. Trustee, American Film Institute; steering committee, National Center for Film and Video Preservation; and formerly on the board of advisers of the AIVF. Author of *Anthony Mann,* 1979; *The World War II Combat Film: Anatomy of a Genre,* 1986; *The* It's a Wonderful Life *Book,* 1986; *A Woman's View: How Hollywood Spoke to Women, 1930-1960,* 1993; and *American Cinema: 100 Years of Filmmaking,* 1994, and numerous articles. Essays: Harrison; Levien.

BERG, Charles Ramírez. Essayist. Instructor in film, University of Texas, Austin. Author of *Cinema of Solitude: A Critical Study of Mexican Film, 1967-1983,* 1992. Essay: Perry.

BOWERS, Ronald. Essayist. Financial editor, E. F. Hutton and Company. Editor, *Films in Review,* 1979-81. Author of *The Selznick Players,* 1976. Co-author (with James Robert Parrish) of *The MGM Stock Company,* 1973. Essay: Lennart.

BROPHY, Stephen. Essayist. Film critic for *L. A. Times, Washington Post,* and others. Co-author (with Peter Harry Brown) of *Howard Hughes: The Untold Story,* 1996. Essay: Butc.

CLARK, Virginia M. Essayist. Assistant professor, English and film, Frostburg State College, Maryland. Film archivist, Library of Congress, 1985, and researcher/cataloger, American Film Institute Catalog of Feature Films, 1985-86. Author of *Aldous Huxley and Film,* 1987. Editor of *What Women Wrote: Scenarios 1912-1929,* 1987. Essays: Meredyth; Murfin.

COOK, Samantha. Essayist. Freelance editor, researcher, and writer, London. Editor of *1989 Women's Film List;* and contributor to *Neglected Audiences,* 1990. Compiler of *Women and Film Bibliography,* 1992. Essays: Bemberg; *Dance, Girl, Dance; Desperately Seeking Susan.*

DEANE, Pamala S. Essayist. Independent writer, Maryland; instructor of writing for media; producer-writer of educational television programming; screenwriter, author. Essays: Larkin; Van Upp.

DELOREY, Denise. Essayist. Writer and educator. Instructor, history of narrative film, Massachusetts Institute of Technology, 1989 and 1991, and American literature, Emerson College, 1994-95. Author of "Parsing the Female Sentence: The Paradox of Containment in Virginia Woolf's Narratives," in *Ambiguous Discourse: Feminist Narratology and British Women Writers,* 1996. Essay: Sharaff.

DERRY, Charles. Essayist. Head of Motion Picture Studies, Wright State University, Dayton, Ohio, since 1978. Author of *Dark Dreams:*

A Psychological History of the Horror Film, 1977; and *The Suspense Thriller: Films in the Shadow of Alfred Hitchcock,* 1988; co-author (with Jack Ellis and Sharon Kern) of *The Film Book Bibliography: 1940-1975,* 1979. Writer/director of *Cerebral Accident,* 1986, and *Joan Crawford Died for Your Sins,* 1987; fiction published in *Reclaiming the Heartland: Gay & Lesbian Voices from the Midwest,* 1996. Essay: J. Allen.

DiBATTISTA, Maria. Essayist. Professor of English and comparative literature, Princeton University. Author of *First Love: The Affectations of Modern Fiction,* 1991. Co-editor (with Lucy McDiarmid) *High and Low Moderns: Literature and Culture, 1889-1939,* 1996. Essays: Savoca; *La Vie du Christ.*

DIXON, Wheeler Winston. Essayist. Professor, Film Studies Program, University of Nebraska at Lincoln. Filmmaker. Author of *The "B" Directors: A Biographical Directory,* 1985; *The Cinematic Vision of F. Scott Fitzgerald,* 1986; *The Charm of Evil: The Life and Films of Terence Fisher,* 1991; *The Films of Freddie Francis,* 1991; *The Early Film Criticism of François Truffaut,* 1992; *The Films of Reginald LeBorg,* 1992; *Re-viewing British Cinema, 1900-1992,* 1994; *It Looks at You,* 1995; *The Films of Jean-Luc Godard,* 1997; *The Exploding Eye,* 1997; and *The Transparency of Spectacle,* 1998. Contributor to *Films in Review, Velvet Light Trap, Literature/Film Quarterly,* and *Post Script.* Essay: Von Harbou.

DUNBAR, Robert. Essayist. Freelance film critic and historian; held various visiting professorships and lectureships, from 1975. Worked for Gainsborough and Gaumont-British Studios, 1933-38, 1948-49; director of public and cultural relations, British Embassy, Moscow, 1944-47; general manager, Imperadio Pictures, 1949-51; independent producer of feature films and documentaries, 1952-63; chairman, London School of Film Technique, 1963-74. Died 1988. Essay: Shub.

DURGNAT, Raymond. Essayist. Visiting professor of film, Wright State University, Dayton, Ohio, and University of East London. Author of numerous publications on film, including *Durgnat on Film,* 1975; and *Michael Powell and the English Genius,* 1991; co-author (with Scott Simmon) of *King Vidor—American,* 1988. Essay: *Cléo de cinq à sept.*

EDELMAN, Rob. Essayist. Author of *Great Baseball Films,* 1994; and *Baseball on the Web,* 1998; co-author of *Angela Lansbury: A Life on Stage and Screen,* 1996; *The John Travolta Scrapbook,* 1997; and *Meet the Mertzes,* forthcoming. Contributing editor of *Leonard Maltin's Movie and Video Guide* and *Leonard Maltin's Movie Encyclopedia.* Director of programming of Home Film Festival. Contributor to *International Dictionary of Films and Filmmakers, The Political Companion to American Film, Total Baseball, The Total Baseball Catalog, International Film Guide,* and *The Whole Film Sourcebook.* Film critic/columnist, *New Haven Register* and *Gazette Newspapers.* Film critic/commentator, WAMC (Northeast) Public Radio. Former adjunct instructor, The School of Visual Arts, Iona College, Sacred Heart University. Essays: Amaral; Anders; Armstrong; Audry; Beth B; Batchelor; Bauchens; Bemberg; Bird; Breien; *Camila;* Campion; Choy; Dörrie; Elek; Godmilow; Gordon; Hänsel; Harris; Holland; Hui; Huillet; *Jaws;* Jhabvala; Kidron; *Krokodillen en Amsterdam;* Livingston; Maclean; *Manner ...;* Marshall; Mehta; Pascal; Poirier; *Raging Bull;* Riefenstahl; Sagan;

Schiller; Seidelman; Shepitko; Silver; Solntseva; Spheeris; *T'ou-Pen Nu-Hai*; Toye; Treut; Trintignant; Varda; Von Trotta; Wertmüller.

EDMUNDS, Jean. Essayist. Freelance writer. Contributor to encyclopedias. **Essay:** Parmar.

EHRLICH, Jane. Adviser and essayist. Instructor in German and Scandinavian film, Washington University, 1972-74, and University of California, Los Angeles, 1976-77. Author of columns in *Arts Editor, Knave, Forum, Ludus, Active Life, Everywoman,* and *London Traveletter.* Contributor to numerous periodicals, including *Harpers & Queen, She Movie Scene, Spare Rib, Irish Post, Good Housekeeping, Period Living, Relax,* and *For Him.* Founder of freelance company, The Editorial Board. Contributor to *Annual Obituary.* **Essay:** Olympia.

ELSNER-SOMMER, Gretchen. Essayist. Film critic and director of Foreign Images distribution company. Formerly associate editor of *Jump Cut.* **Essays:** *Mädchen in Uniform; Die Verlorene Ehre der Katharina Blum;* Von Trotta.

ERENS, Patricia. Essayist. Associate professor, Rosary College (now Dominican University), River Forest, Illinois. Author of *Akira Kurosawa: A Guide to References and Resources,* 1979; and *The Jew in American Cinema,* 1984. Editor of *Sexual Stratagems: The World of Women in Film,* 1979; and *Issues in Feminist Film Criticism,* 1990. **Essay:** *Film d'Amore e d'Anarchia.*

FALLER, Greg S. Essayist. Associate professor of film, Towson State University, Baltimore, since 1986. Taught at Northwestern University, 1984-86. Assistant/associate editor of *International Dictionary of Films and Filmmakers,* first edition, vols. 3, 4, and 5; and of *Journal of Film and Video,* 1985-87. Editor of *Film Reader 6,* 1985. **Essays:** D. Allen; Guillemot; Schoonmaker.

FALSETTO, Mario. Essayist. Associate professor, Cinema Department, Concordia University, Montreal. Author of *Stanley Kubrick: A Narrative and Stylistic Analysis,* 1994. Editor of *Perspectives on Stanley Kubrick,* 1996. **Essays:** Child; Friedrich; *Fuses; Gently down the Stream;* Greenwald; Menken; Schneemann.

FARNSWORTH, Rodney. Essayist. Associate professor of comparative studies, Indiana University-Purdue University, Fort Wayne. Contributor to scholarly publications, including *Literature/Film Quarterly.* **Essay:** *India Song.*

FELANDO, Cynthia. Essayist. Film and television instructor and freelance writer; coordinator for the Los Angeles International Women's Film Festival. **Essays:** Angelou; Apon; *Big;* Borden; *Born in Flames;* Cantrill; Cavani; *Chocolat;* Chopra; Citron; Cole and Dale; Coolidge; Dash; *The Decline of Western Civilization;* Deitch; Denis; Epstein; Export; *Girlfriends;* Gish; Glyn; Gorris; *Harlan County, U.S.A.;* Heckerling; Hein; *Hester Street; The Hitch-Hiker;* Kaplan; Law; Lupino; Lyell; *Madame X—eine absolute Herrscherin; La Maternelle;* McDonagh Sisters; Musidora; Nair; Notari; Pickford; Pool; *Rambling Rose; Surname Viet, Given Name Nam; Thin Line;* Trinh; *Vital Signs;* Weill; West; *Where Are My Children?; Who Killed Vincent Chin?; Working Girls.*

FELPERIN, Leslie. Essayist. Contributor to *Sight and Sound.* **Essay:** Armstrong.

FERRARA, Patricia. Essayist. Member of the faculty, Georgia State University, Atlanta. Contributor to *New Orleans Review.* **Essay:** Reville.

FERRARI, Lilie. Essayist. Writer and researcher, London. **Essay:** Arzner.

FLYNN, Peter. Essayist. Freelance writer. **Essay:** Spencer.

FOREMAN, Alexa L. Essayist. Account executive, Video Duplications, Atlanta. Formerly theater manager, American Film Institute. Author of *Women in Motion,* 1983. **Essays:** Brackett; Macpherson.

FOSTER, Gwendolyn Audrey. Essayist. Assistant professor, University of Nebraska, Lincoln. Author of *Women Film Directors: An International Bio-Critical Dictionary,* 1995; and *Women Filmmakers of the African and Asian Diaspora,* 1997. Filmmaker, *The Women Who Made the Movies,* 1992. **Essay:** "The Evolution of the Woman Filmmaker."

GATEWARD, Frances K. Essayist. Film scholar and independent film and video maker. Has taught at Indiana University, University of Illinois, Urbana-Champaign, and Howard University. Contributor to *Angles, The Paper Channel,* and *The Television Encyclopedia.* **Essays:** Chenzira; Davis; Faye.

GLAESSNER, Verina. Essayist. Freelance critic and lecturer, London. Contributor to *Economist, Guardian, Monthly Film Bulletin, Sight and Sound,* and *Focus on Film.* **Essays:** Cecchi d'Amico; Chytilová; Potter.

GOLDMAN, Ilene S. Adviser and essayist. Film studies instructor, Chicago. Contributor to *Jump Cut, Independent,* and *Studies in Latin American Popular Culture.* **Essays:** Abreu; Carolina; Fernández Violante; Mallet; Meerapfel; Novaro; *Sambizanga;* Sarmiento; Yamasaki.

GOMERY, Douglas. Essayist. Professor, College of Journalism, University of Maryland. Author of nine books, including *The Hollywood Studio System,* 1986; and *Shared Pleasures,* 1992. Co-editor of *The Future of News,* 1992. Contributor of numerous articles to periodicals including *Village Voice, American Journalism Review,* and *Screen.* **Essays:** Booth; Fields.

HECK-RABI, Louise. Essayist. Teacher and freelance writer. Author of *Women Filmmakers: A Critical Reception,* 1984. Died 1995. **Essays:** Akins; Deren; Guy; *La Coquille et le clergyman;* Mészáros; Riefenstahl; Varda; Zetterling.

HOFFMAN, Judy. Essayist. Acting director of Documentary Film Center, Columbia College. Co-founder of Kartemquin Films and contributor to most of their film productions, including as associate producer of *Golub.* Active in Alternative Media movement of the 1970s; became one of the first women to work professionally as a film technician in Chicago, apprenticing with IATSE Camera Local 666. Camera assistant on numerous independent documentary films, including *Family Business; Seeing Red; American Dream;* and *Daley: The Last Boss.* Researcher for PBS series *On the Waterways.* Associate producer of film *Box of Treasures.* Video instructor and media consultant for Kwakiut'l Indians for ten years. Director and editor of museum video on Kwakiut'l salmon fishing for Chicago's Shedd

Aquarium. Teacher of video with Community Television Network. Producer and editor of student production *Time to Make that Change*. Recipient of VOICE Award from Chicago's Center for Community and Media, 1994. **Essay:** Kopple.

HOLMLUND, Chris. Essayist. Associate professor of French, film, and women's studies, University of Tennessee, Knoxville. Co-editor (with Cynthia Fuchs) of *Between the Sheets, in the Streets: Queer, Lesbian, and Gay Documentary*, 1997. Contributor to *Screening the Male, Retakes on Remakes, Discourse of the Other, Feminism and Documentary, Camera Obscura, Cinema Journal, Discourse, Jump Cut, New Formations, Screen*, and *Social Text*. **Essay:** Nelson.

JACOBS, Katrien. Essayist. Lecturer in media studies at Edith Cowan University, Australia. Contributor to *Wide Angle, Etcetera*, and the webzine *Geekgirl*. Editor for Continuum. **Essay:** "The Status of Contemporary Women Filmmakers."

JOHNSON, Mark. Essayist. Freelance writer. Author of *The Swedish Sexpot Stereotype Anita Ekberg and the American Fifties*, 1993. Associate editor of the *Velvet Light Trap*, 1989-91. **Essay:** J. Allen.

KEMP, Philip. Essayist. Freelance writer and film historian. Author of *Lethal Innocence: The Cinema of Alexander Mackendrick*, 1991. Reviewer for *Sight and Sound*. Contributor to periodicals, including *Variety, Film Comment, Metro* (Melbourne), *Liber* (Paris), and *Kino* (Seoul). **Essays:** Bigelow; Craigie; *Diabolo menthe; Napló gyermekeimnek; Near Dark;* Tanaka, *Wanda*.

KNIGHT, Judson. Essayist. Freelance writer, Atlanta. Ghost writer or co-writer for a number of prominent clients; researcher; editorial consultant for the Knight Agency, a firm specializing in literary representation and marketing. **Essays:** Hubley; Murphy.

KNOBLOCH, Susan. Essayist. Doctoral candidate in film and television critical studies, University of California, Los Angeles. Contributor to several anthologies, including *Feminism and Documentary*, edited by Diane Waldman and Janet Walker. **Essays:** *The Ballad of Little Jo*; Ephron; Ono; *Paris Is Burning*; Streisand; *Two Small Bodies*.

KOSTA, Barbara. Essayist. Assistant professor, University of Arizona, since 1989. Author of *Recasting Autobiography: Women's Counterfictions in Contemporary German Literature and Film*, 1994. Contributor to *Gender and German Cinema, Signs*, and *German Studies Review*. **Essay:** Sander.

KUPFERBERG, Audrey E. Essayist. Film historian, appraiser, and archivist. Co-author of *Angela Lansbury: A Life on Stage and Screen*, 1996; *The John Travolta Scrapbook*, 1997; and *Meet the Mertzes*, forthcoming. Contributor to *International Dictionary of Films and Filmmakers*. Film consultant to the Peary-MacMillan Arctic Museum at Bowdoin College. Former director, Yale University Film Study Center. Former assistant director, the National Center for Film and Video Preservation at the American Film Institute. Former instructor, University of Bridgeport. **Essays:** Bauchens; *Bonnie and Clyde*; Comden; Madison; Sanders-Brahms; Shipman; *Vivre sa vie*.

LEE, Edith C. Essayist. Staff member, Synthesis Concepts, Chicago. Editor, *META Magazine*. Worked in video division, Columbia Pictures, 1981-82. **Essays:** Dillon; Rose; Sharaff.

LIPPE, Richard. Essayist. Lecturer in film at Atkinson College, York University, Ontario. On the editorial board of *CineAction!* **Essay:** Silver.

LÓPEZ, Ana M. Essayist. Associate professor, Department of Communications, Tulane University, New Orleans. Co-editor of *Mediating Two Worlds: Cinematic Encounters in the Americas* (with John King and Manuel Alvarado), 1993; and *The Ethnic Eye: Latino Media Arts* (with Chon A. Noriega), 1996. **Essay:** Landeta.

LORENZ, Janet. Essayist. Associate editor and film critic *Z Channel* magazine, since 1984. Assistant supervisor, University of Southern California Cinema Research Library, Los Angeles, 1979-82, and film critic, *SelecTV Magazine*, 1980-84. **Essay:** Jhabvala.

LUPO, Jon. Essayist. Freelance writer. Film editor and critic, *Massachusetts Daily Collegian*, 1991-96. Editor and publisher, *Cinefile* cinema journal, since 1995. **Essay:** Van Dongen.

MANVELL, Roger. Essayist. Formerly professor of film, Boston University. Director, British Film Academy, London, 1947-59, and governor and head of Department of Film History, London Film School, until 1974; Bingham Professor of the Humanities, University of Louisville, 1973. Editor, *Penguin Film Review*, 1946-49, and the Pelican annual *Cinema*, 1950-52; associate editor, *New Humanist*, 1968-75, and director, Rationalist Press, London, from 1966; editor-in-chief, *International Encyclopaedia of Film*, 1972. Author of *Film*, 1944; *The Animated Film*, 1954; *The Film and the Public*, 1955; *On the Air*, 1955; *The Technique of Film Music*, 1957, 1976; *The Living Screen*, 1961; *What Is a Film?*, 1965; *New Cinema in the U.S.A.*, 1968; *New Cinema in Britain*, 1969; *Art in Movement*, 1970; *Shakespeare and the Film*, 1971; *Films and the Second World War*, 1975; *Love Goddesses of the Movies*, 1975; *Theatre and Film*, 1979; *Art and Animation: Halas and Batchelor, 1940-1980*, 1980; and *Ingmar Bergman*, 1980; co-author of *The Technique of Film Animation* (with John Halas), 1959; *Design in Motion* (with John Halas), 1962; *The German Cinema* (with Heinrich Fraenkel), 1971; and *Images of Madness: The Portrayal of Insanity in the Feature Film* (with Michael Fleming), 1985; also author of novels, biographies of theatrical personalities and of personalities of the Third Reich. Died 1987. **Essay:** Mathis.

MARCHETTI, Gina. Adviser. Associate professor, University of Maryland, College Park. Author of *Romance and the "Yellow Peril": Race, Sex, and Discursive Strategies in Hollywood Fiction*, 1993. Staff editor of *Jump Cut*.

McCAFFREY, Donald W. Essayist. Emeritus professor of English, University of North Dakota. Author of *Four Great Comedians: Chaplin, Lloyd, Keaton, and Langdon*, 1968; *The Golden Age of Sound Comedy: Comic Films and Comedians of the Thirties*, 1973; *Three Classic Silent Film Comedies Starring Harold Lloyd*, 1976; and *Assault on Society: Satirical Literature to Film*, 1992. Editor of *Focus on Chaplin*, 1971. **Essays:** Goodrich; *Sleepless in Seattle*.

McCARTY, John. Essayist. Author and freelance writer. Assistant editor of *Mystery Scene*. Author of *Splatter Movies*, 1984; *The Films of John Huston*, 1987; *The Modern Horror Film*, 1990; *Hollywood Gangland*, 1993; *Movie Psychos and Madmen*, 1993; *The Fearmakers*, 1994; *The Sleaze Merchants*, 1995; *The Films of Mel*

Gibson, 1997, and other books on film and television history. **Essay:** Reville.

MERZ, Caroline. Essayist. Freelance journalist and television researcher, Norwich, England. **Essay:** M. Box.

MILICIA, Joseph. Essayist. Professor of English, University of Wisconsin, Sheboygan Center. Contributor to *Multicultural Review, New York Review of Science Fiction, Contemporary Literature,* and others. Author of articles on science-fiction films for Gregg Press. **Essays:** Kurys; *La Rue cases nègres;* Serreau; *Trois hommes et un couffin.*

MITCHELL, John E. Essayist. Humor writer/comic book writer, and publisher. Author of *Very Vicky* comic books, 1993-95; *That Skinny Bastard: Frank Sinatra,* 1995; *Calling All Hillbillies* comic books, 1995; and *Very Vicky Junior Hepcat Funbook,* 1996. **Essay:** Irene.

MONTY, Ib. Essayist. Director of Det Danske Filmmuseum, Copenhagen, since 1960. Literary and film critic for the newspaper *Morgenavisen Jyllands-Posten,* since 1958. Editor-in-chief of the film periodical *Kosmorama,* 1960-67. Author of *Leonardo da Vinci,* 1953. Co-editor (with Morten Piil) of *Se-det-er film I-iii* (anthology of articles on film), 1964-66; editor of *TV Broadcasts on Films and Filmmakers,* 1972. **Essay:** Henning-Jensen.

MORRISON, James. Essayist. Assistant professor, English Department, North Carolina State University, Raleigh. Contributor to *New Orleans Review, Centennial Review,* and *Film Criticism.* **Essay:** Russell.

MRAZ, John. Essayist. Researcher, Center for the Study of Contemporary History, University of Puebla, Mexico, since 1984. Distinguished visiting professor, Mexican-American studies, San Diego State University, 1991; visiting professor, art and Latin American studies, University of Connecticut, 1990, and history, University of California, Santa Cruz, 1988. Coordinator of Graphic History, Center for the Historical Study of the Mexican Labor Movement, 1981-83. Contributor to *Jump Cut.* **Essays:** *De cierta manera;* Gómez.

NING, Cynthia. Essayist. Associate director, Center for Chinese Studies, University of Hawaii. Instructor on Chinese cinema, literature, and language. Consultant to the Hawaii International Film Festival. Author of *Communicating in Chinese* (3 vols.), 1993, 1994. **Essays:** *Qingchunji;* Zhang.

PALMER, R. Barton. Essayist. Chair and professor of English, Clemson University; formerly professor of English, Georgia State University. Author of *Hollywood's Dark Cinema: The American Film Noir,* 1994; and *Perspectives on Film Noir,* 1996. Editor of *Studies in the Literary Imagination.* **Essay:** Foster.

PARDI, Robert. Essayist. Staff writer for *The Motion Picture Guide.* Managing editor/chief reviewer of *Movies on TV* for six editions. Author of *Cable and TV;* co-author of *Movie Blockbusters;* and *The Complete Guide to Videocassette Movies.* Contributor to *International Dictionary of Films and Filmmakers.* Contributor to *Baseline, Delphi Internet, Billboard, Cinemax, Film Journal, Video Business,* and *Cineaste.* **Essay:** May.

PASKIN, Sylvia. Essayist. Freelance film critic, London. Contributor to *Monthly Film Bulletin.* **Essay:** *My Brilliant Career.*

PETLEY, Julian. Essayist. Freelance writer and critic, London. Contributor to *Sight and Sound, Monthly Film Bulletin,* and *Broadcast.* **Essay:** *Die Bleierne Zeit.*

PILLAI, A. Essayist. Screenwriter and journalist. **Essays:** *The Piano; Triumph des Willens.*

PRICHARD, Susan Perez. Essayist. Freelance writer. Author of *Film Costume: An Annotated Bibliography,* 1981. **Essay:** Jeakins.

PROVENCHER, Ken. Essayist. Arts and entertainment staff writer and editor, *Lowell Connector,* 1991-94. **Essay:** von Brandenstein.

RABINOVITZ, Lauren. Essayist. Associate professor of American studies and communication studies, University of Iowa, since 1986. Author of *Points of Resistance: Women, Power and Politics in the New York Avant-Garde Cinema, 1943-71,* 1991; and *For the Love of Pleasure: Women, Movies, and Culture in Turn-of-the-Century Chicago,* 1998; co-author (with Greg Easley) of *The Rebecca Project,* 1995. Co-editor (with Susan Jeffords) of *Seeing through the Media: The Persian Gulf War,* 1994. **Essays:** Clarke; *Meshes of the Afternoon;* Wieland.

REYNAUD, Bérénice. Essayist. Member of staff of permanent faculty, California Institute of Arts. U.S. correspondent for *Cahiers du Cinéma.* Co-editor of *Vingt ans de theories feministes sur le cinéma,* 1993. Contributor to *Sight and Sound, Film Comment, Cinemaya,* and *Afterimage.* **Essays:** Bani Etemad; Maldoror; Peng.

RICHARDS, Allen Grant. Essayist. Freelance writer. **Essay:** Littleton.

ROBSON, Arthur G. Essayist. Professor and chairman, Department of Classics, and professor of comparative literature, Beloit College, Wisconsin, since 1966. Author of *Euripides' Electra: An Interpretive Commentary.* Editor of *Latin: Our Living Heritage, Book III,* 1964. **Essays:** *Deutschland, bleiche Mutter;* Leaf; *Une Nuit sur le Mont Chauve; Nüren de Gushi.*

SALAMIE, David E. Essayist. Contributing editor, *Women Filmmakers and Their Films.* Contributing editor and contributor, third edition of *International Dictionary of Films and Filmmakers: Actors and Actresses.* Freelance writer and editor. Co-owner of InfoWorks Development Group, a reference publication development and editorial services company. **Essays:** Ahrne; Miró; Muratova; Obomsawin; Preobrazhenskaya.

SCHIFF, Lillian. Essayist. Freelance film critic and consultant, New York. Author of *Getting Started in Film-making,* 1978. **Essay:** Akerman.

SITNEY, P. Adams. Essayist. Lecturer, Princeton University. Formerly director of library and publications, Anthology Film Archives. Author of *Film Culture Reader,* 1970; *Visionary Film,* 1974; *The Avant-Garde Film,* 1978; *Modernist Montage: The Obscurity of Vision in Cinema and Literature,* 1990; and *Visual Crises in Italian Cinema,* 1995. **Essay:** *Jeanne Dielman, 23 Quai du Commerce, 1080 Bruxelles.*

SKVORECKÝ, Josef. Essayist. Professor of English and film, University of Toronto, Canada, since 1969. Author of *All the Bright Young Men and Women: A Personal History of the Czech Cinema*, 1972; and *Jiri Menzel and the History of* Closely Watched Trains, 1982. Works as novelist include *Miss Silver's Past*, 1975; *The Bass Saxophone*, 1977; *The Engineer of Human Souls*, 1984; and *The Miracle Game*, 1990. **Essay:** Chytilová.

SLIDE, Anthony. Essayist. Author and editor of more than 50 books on the history of popular entertainment, including *The Films of D. W. Griffith*, 1975; *The American Film Industry: A Historical Dictionary*, 1986; *Nitrate Won't Wait: A History of Film Preservation in the United States*, 1992; *The Encyclopedia of Vaudeville*, 1994; and *Paramount in Paris*, 1998. Also editor of the Scarecrow Press "Filmmakers Series," and a documentary filmmaker. **Essay:** Weber.

STARR, Cecile. Essayist. Freelance writer, lecturer, and filmmaker. Film reviewer (16mm) for *Saturday Review*, New York, 1949-59. Author of *Ideas on Film*, 1951; and *Discovering the Movies*, 1977; co-author (with Robert Russett) of *Experimental Animation*, 1976, 1988. Director of the Women's Independent Film Exchange, since 1977. **Essays:** De Hirsch; Dulac; Grayson; Marion; Parker; Reiniger.

THOMPSON, Frank. Essayist. Author of *William A. Wellman*, 1983; *Alamo Movies*, 1991; *Robert Wise: A Bio-Bibliography*, 1995; *Lost Films: Important Movies that Disappeared*, 1996; and *The Star Film Ranch*, 1996. Editor of *Between Action and Cut: Five American Directors*, 1985. **Essay:** *Christopher Strong.*

TOMLINSON, Doug. Essayist. Associate professor of film studies, Montclair State College, New Jersey. Principal researcher for *Voices of Film Experience*, edited by Jay Leyda, 1977; editor of *Actors on Acting for the Screen*, 1994. Died 1992. **Essay:** Van Runkle.

URGOŠÍKOVÁ, Blazena. Adviser and essayist. Film historian. Head of Department of Film History and Cataloguing, Národní filmovýarchiv Praha. Author of *A Famous Era of the Swedish Cinema*, 1969; *Rudolph Valentino*, 1970; *History of Science Fiction Films*, 1973, 1982; *Remakes*, 1977; and *Czech Fiction Films*, 1995. **Essays:** Jakubowska; Krumbachová; Šimková-Plívová.

VALENTINE, Fiona. Essayist. Member of faculty, School of Speech, Northwestern University, Evanston, Illinois. **Essay:** Head.

VASUDEVAN, Ravi. Essayist. Freelance film critic. Former film critic of *Sunday Observer*, Delhi. **Essay:** *Salaam Bombay!*

WHITE, M. B. Essayist. Assistant professor, Department of Radio-TV-Film, Northwestern University, Evanston, Illinois, since 1982. Contributor to *Enclitic, Purdue Film Studies Annual,* and other periodicals. **Essay:** Duras.

WOLFF, Jessica. Essayist. Freelance researcher, writer, and editor. **Essay:** Rainer.

YECK, Joanne L. Essayist. Lecturer on humanities and film, Art Center College of Design, Pasadena. Co-author (with Tom McGreevey) of *Movie Westerns*, 1994; and *Our Movie Heritage*, 1997. **Essay:** Coffee.

ZANTS, Emily. Essayist. Professor of French, University of Hawaii. Author of *Creative Encounters with French Films*, 1993; and *Chaos Theory, Complexity, Cinema, and the Evolution of the French Novel*, 1996. **Essay:** Colette.

ZUCKER, Carole. Essayist. Associate professor, Department of Cinema, Concordia University, Montreal. Author of *The Idea of Image: Josef von Sternberg's Dietrich Films*, 1988; and *Figures of Light: Actors and Directors Illuminate the Art of Film Acting*, 1995. Editor of *Making Visible the Invisible: An Anthology of Original Essays on Film Acting*, 1990. **Essays:** Brückner; *Hungerjahre*; Ottinger.